AF691457

Designing Software Synthesizer Plug-Ins in C++

Designing Software Synthesizer Plug-Ins in C++

For RackAFX, VST3, and Audio Units

Will Pirkle

Focal Press
Taylor & Francis Group
NEW YORK AND LONDON

First published 2015
by Focal Press
70 Blanchard Road, Suite 402, Burlington, MA 01803

and by Focal Press
2 Park Square, Milton Park, Abingdon, Oxon OX14 4RN

Focal Press is an imprint of the Taylor & Francis Group, an informa business

© 2015 Taylor & Francis

The right of Will Pirkle to be identified as author of this work has been asserted by him in accordance with sections 77 and 78 of the Copyright, Designs and Patents Act 1988.

All rights reserved. No part of this book may be reprinted or reproduced or utilised in any form or by any electronic, mechanical, or other means, now known or hereafter invented, including photocopying and recording, or in any information storage or retrieval system, without permission in writing from the publishers.

Notices
Knowledge and best practice in this field are constantly changing. As new research and experience broaden our understanding, changes in research methods, professional practices, or medical treatment may become necessary.

Practitioners and researchers must always rely on their own experience and knowledge in evaluating and using any information, methods, compounds, or experiments described herein. In using such information or methods they should be mindful of their own safety and the safety of others, including parties for whom they have a professional responsibility.

Product or corporate names may be trademarks or registered trademarks, and are used only for identification and explanation without intent to infringe.

Library of Congress Cataloging in Publication Data

Pirkle, William C., author.
Designing software synthesizer plug-ins in C++ : for RackAFX, VST3, and Audio Units / Will Pirkle.
pages cm
1. Software synthesizers. 2. Plug-ins (Computer programs)
3. C++ (Computer program language) I. Title.
MT723.P572 2015
005.3'76—dc23
2014027976

ISBN: 978-1-138-78707-0 (pbk)
ISBN: 978-1-315-76685-0 (ebk)

Typeset in MinionPro
By Apex CoVantage, LLC

MIX
Paper from responsible sources
FSC® C014174

Printed and bound in the United States of America by Sheridan Books, Inc. (a Sheridan Group Company).

Dedicated to

my brother
James Robert Pirkle

Contents

Preface

Many times during the course of the book development, I asked myself what in the world was I thinking. I should write a book with three different plug-in APIs and platforms? Really? In reality, I have very legitimate ulterior motives: to show the three APIs side-by-side in order to demonstrate just how similar they really are despite all the differences in implementation details. This was one of the points in my first book *Designing Audio Effect Plug-Ins in C++*, which uses RackAFX exclusively as both a teaching tool and a quick and easy way to get real-time signal processing code up and running with a minimum of effort. In the last two years, I've received correspondence from all over the world regarding that book and the RackAFX software and fortunately it has been mostly very positive. A goal of that book is to get novice programmers with little or no experience in Digital Signal Processing (DSP) into plug-in programming in one semester's worth of class time. And since you can compile your RackAFX plug-in as a VST2 product, you can export it and run it in other digital audio workstations. The idea is that after you've trained on RackAFX, you are ready to take on the more complex Application Programming Interfaces (APIs) like VST and Audio Units. It is up to you to filter through the documentation and sample code to figure out which functions correspond to *processAudioFrame()*, *userInterfaceChange()*, etc. (those are RackAFX plug-in functions). But for many people, this was either very difficult or impossible, especially when the person had never looked at a commercial API before.

I thought back to my first API—the Windows 3.1 API from the Software Development Kit (SDK). I think I paid about $600 for it in 1990. My goal was to learn Windows programming and write an FFT application—I was in graduate school. I received a ton of floppy disks and a huge set of beautifully bound paperback manuals. It seemed like I really got my money's worth from the Microsoft Corporation. I eagerly dug into the manuals only to find that there was not one iota of information on how to actually write a Windows application. Nada. Zip. Zero. Of course all the functions were completely documented in detail—back then, you used the C programming language to write Windows applications. It was absolutely overwhelming. I was amazed that there was not a chapter called "How to Write a Windows Application" where they just said "Step 1: Open Microsoft C. Step 2: Start a new Project …". If you read my first book, then you have seen many step-by-step lists on plug-in implementation—my experience with the Windows 3.1 API is the reason for that. Nevertheless, I managed to get my FFT application running but was never able to plot anything on the screen. By then I had graduated and was moving to California.

So this book takes a new approach by showing you complete synthesizer projects in all three APIs, side-by-side. You may use whichever one you wish. And I really encourage you to implement at least one of the six synth projects in all three APIs so you can really get a feel for the strengths and weaknesses of each one. I am confident that once you've implemented a synth on all three platforms, you will understand why I wrote the RackAFX software and plug-in API. But this book isn't just a set of synth projects; it teaches how to write plug-ins on each platform and includes chapters on signal processing and synthesis theory. And there is some math involved including a bit of calculus. Just as in *Designing Audio Effect Plug-Ins in C++*, I do try to keep the heavy math to a minimum, but there's just no way to get around it in some places. Another similarity is that this book does not teach C++; you need to have these skills prior to starting the projects. Likewise it is not a book about trick code, optimization, unit testing, or other software theory.

The projects you will write run on the following APIs/platforms:

RackAFX:	Windows
VST3:	Windows
Audio Units (AU):	MacOS

I chose not to implement the VST3/MacOS versions due to space limitations. Fortunately, the code is very nearly identical to the Windows version and the VST3 SDK contains sample code on both platforms. You may also notice that Avid's AAX API is missing. You must be a registered Avid plug-in developer to receive the SDK. This is not a simple process, as you must first prove that you can write and sell plug-ins. In this way, the AAX API is closed and not openly documented like RackAFX, VST3 and AU so I cannot write about the SDK implementation details.

If you read my first book, then you know that RackAFX packages itself as a VST2 plug-in by using a C++ wrapper. This obscures the actual implementation details. This book does not work that way—each plug-in is implemented in its native language on the native compiler using the SDK tools only; there are no third-party libraries, frameworks or other helpers. You see all the gory details with nothing obscured. This has the most impact on the Audio Units plug-ins. Their GUIs must be implemented with Cocoa, which is written in Objective C. If you are targeting AU, then you need to know Objective C to understand the GUI programming. While we are on that subject, you should be happy to know that all the VST3 and AU plug-ins come with complete pre-built GUIs in the sample code. In RackAFX, you can use the simple drag-and-drop editor to create a GUI with no code, but VST3 and AU are different. In VST3 you use the VSTGUI design objects. These ship with the SDK. In this book, you use the drag-and-drop editor feature that VSTGUI allows but there is still code to write for setting up and maintaining the GUI. In the AU plug-ins, you use InterfaceBuilder (IB) that is built into XCode. I have created several new custom controls for Cocoa so you can create some impressive user interfaces. Of course you may always use the stock IB objects as well.

Another area of improvement in this book came as a suggestion from several of the first book readers. They requested homework assignments. These appear in the form of "Challenges" at the end of most, but not all, chapters. This idea is directly taken from Joe Conway and Aaron Hillegass in their excellent *iOS Programming—The Big Nerd Ranch Guide* book, which is the text I use for my iOS programming class at the University of Miami. The "Challenges" are usually programming assignments and are categorized as Bronze, Silver, Gold, Platinum and Diamond from the least to most challenging. Solutions are not given, but they should show up at my website's forum as students and readers implement them and show their variations (most are open-ended and a few are very difficult).

In the early phases of preparing a book proposal, I needed to make a decision about the synth projects themselves. They could be really simple with plenty of room for expansion or grossly complex with every type of synthesis algorithm and modulation routing possible. The very first thing I decided was not to feature physical modeling algorithms. The reason is that this could easily turn into a whole other book unto itself and would likely be much more of a theory book than a programming book. I decided to feature six complete polyphonic synthesizers using a variety of synthesis techniques. The synths respond to common MIDI continuous controller messages and use a modulation matrix that allows you to spin off countless variations on their architectures. I also needed to make sure that there was not much overlap of theory with the first book and this book features all new algorithms for oscillator and filter designs. The theory sections are also different with slightly more emphasis on analog systems.

Chapter 1 is a brief introduction to synthesizer components and basic signal processing in both the analog and digital domains. Chapter 2 is the most lengthy in the book; it details how to write plug-ins in all three APIs as well as comparing them side-by-side and showing the pros and cons of each. The fun really starts in Chapter 3, where you begin your first "training synth" called NanoSynth and trap MIDI messages on your platform. With the MIDI code in place, we can move on to the theoretical meat of the book in Chapters 4–8. Chapter 4 includes the basic analog and digital signal processing theory you need to understand the filters and oscillators. Chapter 5 explains the oscillator objects, and you add them to your NanoSynth project. Next you add the Envelope Generator (EG) and Digitally Controlled Amplifier (DCA) in Chapter 6. Chapter 7 details the virtual analog filter models (you wind up with five different filter objects); here you add the Moog Ladder Filter model to NanoSynth for testing, then you are on your own to test the other filters. NanoSynth is completed in Chapter 8, where you add the modulation matrix and finally make it polyphonic.

Chapter 9 is a turning point in the book because all of the underlying synthesizer C++ objects are set in code and will not change. Here you design MiniSynth, the Analog Modeling synthesizer. You can deviate from the book at this point, implementing your own synth voice objects and your own module wiring code if you wish. In Chapter 10, you learn how to use audio sample files to implement DigiSynth, a stereo sample playback synthesizer. Chapter 11 on Vector Synthesis reuses the sample-based oscillators in the VectorSynth project and includes a bonus project named AniSynth, which is my interpretation of the Moog AniMoog Anisotropic Synthesizer iPad app. In Chapter 12, you design a clone of the Yamaha DX100 FM synthesizer. Chapter 13 is the audio effects chapter that shows you how to add a suite of delay effects to MiniSynth. In fact, you can jump from any of the synth design chapters directly to Chapter 13 to add the delay effects, which greatly extend your synth's capabilities. A brief Appendix shows you how to convert my VST3 and AU Template Code into the basis code for your projects (this isn't needed with RackAFX since it creates your project for you).

There are two people who greatly influenced the book early on—Bill Jenkins and Andy Leary, both Senior Engineers at Korg Research and Development, were reviewers for the original book proposal. Bill's comments and suggestions shaped the way the C++ code is presented and interleaved as much as possible with descriptive text. In fact, his input is the reason that the different API code is contained in separate sections rather than mixed together as it was in the proposal. There is no word in the English language that describes my gratitude for Andy Leary's input on the theory chapters (4–7). He is an expert on many of the algorithms in these chapters so having his input was invaluable. Andy also proofread these chapters repeatedly, offering a continuous stream of suggestions and ideas. The analog modeling MiniSynth sounds fantastic to me, and much of this is due to Andy's input. Bill and Andy—thank you!

My fellow professors and students were also enthusiastic about the effort and I received full support from my colleagues Dean Shelly Berg, Serona Elton, Rey Sanchez, Colby Leider, Joe Abbati and Chris Bennett, including some much needed leeway in my poor attendance record in Music Engineering Forum class. Although I began teaching synthesis classes in the 1990s, it was only four years ago that the students started using RackAFX. The last few generations of Music Engineering students have also shaped the content of the book and RackAFX software, whether they know it or not. Last year, Colin Francis and Mark Gill improved the stability and performance of several synth components. Rob Rehrig designed many new RackAFX GUI elements. I also need to thank the following students for their input and help in last year's synth class (alphabetically): Daniel Avissar, Andy Ayers, Daniel Bennett, Garrett Clausen, Sammy Falcon, Michael Intendola, Connor McCullough, Tad Nicol, Crispin Odom, Andrew O'neil-Smith, Ross Penniman, Michael Tonry and Francisco Valencia Otalvaro.

You can stay in touch with my by joining the Forum at my website http://www.willpirkle.com/synthbook/, which also contains information and resources that are not included in the book. As usual, I encourage you to send me your plug-in creations or post links and audio samples at the forum. As with my last book, I can't wait to hear what you cook up in your own plug-in development lab!

All the best,
Will Pirkle
June 1, 2014

Foreword

Here are some notes about the book projects, code and conventions.

Skills

For RackAFX and VST, you only need basic C++ programming skills. These are both written in straight ANSI C++. If you have taken a university class or two on the subject, then you should have no problem. In both APIs, you need to be fully competent with the Visual Studio compiler, and you need to know how to add files to your projects, use filters to rearrange the source files, and use the debugger. AU is not written in pure C++. It requires knowledge of MacOS frameworks like AppKit and CoreAudio. In addition, if you want to design a GUI, you need to know Objective C to use Cocoa in InterfaceBuilder, so you need to be competent with the XCode compiler; likewise you need to know how to add files to your projects, use filters to rearrange the source files, and use the debugger.

Hungarian Notation

Nearly 100% of the RackAFX and VST3 code is written using Hungarian notation. Much of the AU code uses it as well (some straight from Apple, Inc.). Here is Microsoft's description of Hungarian notation:

> Long, long ago in the early days of DOS, Microsoft's Chief Architect Dr. Charles Simonyi introduced an identifier naming convention that adds a prefix to the identifier name to indicate the functional type of the identifier. This system became widely used inside Microsoft. It came to be known as "Hungarian notation" because the prefixes make the variable names look a bit as though they're written in some non-English language and because Simonyi is originally from Hungary.
>
> As it turns out, the Hungarian naming convention is quite useful—it's one technique among many that helps programmers produce better code faster. Since most of the headers and documentation Microsoft has published over the last 15 years have used Hungarian notation names for identifiers, many programmers outside of Microsoft have adopted one variation or another of this scheme for naming their identifiers. Perhaps the most important publication that encouraged the use of Hungarian notation was the first book read by almost every Windows programmer: Charles Petzold's *Programming Windows.* It used a dialect of Hungarian notation throughout and briefly described the notation in its first chapter. (Simonyi, 1999)

Synth Projects

During the course of the book, you develop six synthesizer projects from any of the three APIs. The code is split out into sections for each API. The chapters follow the same sequence of presentation of ideas and then coding. You can read the theory first, then skip ahead to the section that contains your target platform and go through the code. The projects are designed so that you may spin off many variations of your own. Here is a list of the synth projects and the components they contain:

NanoSynth

Oscillators: two analog modeling (BLEP) oscillators

Filters: Moog Ladder Filter Model

LFOs: one general purpose LFO

EGs: one combination Amp-EG, Filter-EG and Pitch-EG

MiniSynth

Oscillators: four analog modeling (BLEP) oscillators

Filters: Moog Ladder Filter Model

LFOs: one general purpose LFO

EGs: one combination Amp-EG, Filter-EG and Pitch-EG

DigiSynth

Oscillators: two sample-playback oscillators

Filters: Oberheim SEM SVF Filter Model

LFOs: one general purpose LFO

EGs: one combination Amp-EG, Filter-EG and Pitch-EG

VectorSynth

Oscillators: four sample-playback oscillators

Filters: Korg35 Lowpass Filter Model

LFOs: one general purpose LFO

EGs: one combination Amp-EG, Filter-EG and Pitch-EG and one multi-segment Vector EG

AniSynth

Oscillators: four sample-playback oscillators driven from a bank of 36 wavetables

Filters: Diode Ladder Filter Model

LFOs: one general purpose LFO

EGs: one combination Amp-EG, Filter-EG and Pitch-EG and one multi-segment Vector EG

DXSynth

Oscillators: four wavetable oscillators arranged in 8 FM Algorithms

Filters: None

LFOs: one general purpose LFO

EGs: four FM Operator EGs

Delay FX

The suite of delay effects in Chapter 13 is added to MiniSynth as an example, but it may just as easily be added to any of the synths, and you are encouraged to implement FX in all your synths.

Bibliography

Simonyi, Charles. 1999. "Hungarian Notation." Accessed August 2014. http://msdn.microsoft.com/en-us/library/aa260976(v=vs.60).aspx

CHAPTER 1

Synthesizer Fundamentals

The synthesizer is usually defined vaguely as an electronic musical instrument that produces and controls sounds. When discussing this with some colleagues, we agreed that the electronic dependency of this definition might be constraining. Why couldn't the didgeridoo or the Jew's harp be considered synthesizers? In fact, might not any instrument other than the human voice be a synthesizer? Most consider the American inventor Thaddeus Cahill to be the inventor of the modern synthesizer. In 1897, he applied for a patent for his Telharmonium or Dynamophone, a 200-ton instrument that used steam powered electric generators to synthesize sinusoids—it was even polyphonic (capable of playing more than one note at a time). Leon Theramin invented the Theremin in 1919, which included a touchless interface that controlled the amplitude and pitch of a sinusoid. Unlike the Telharmonium, the Theremin used electronic audio amplifiers to reproduce the sound rather than acoustic horns. For the next 30 years, inventors created more unique instruments including the Ondes Martenot, Trautonium, and Mixturtrautonium, to name a few. The first use of the word synthesizer is in the Couplex-Givelet Synthesizer of 1929. In 1956, RCA marketed the RCA Electronic Music Synthesizer that used 12 tuning forks to render the oscillations. Max Mathews is generally credited as the first to experiment with computers for rendering and controlling an audio signal in 1957, while Robert Moog popularized the hardware synthesizer and is credited with inventing the first voltage-controlled synth in 1963. His synths included many of his own improvements and inventions such as the Moog ladder filter, which we will study in Chapter 7. In 1967, he marketed electronic modules that could be combined together in systems to produce various sounds—he called these systems synthesizers. The driving force for the need of these synthesizers was not electronic dance music but rather neoclassical composers of the 20th century. It is not uncommon to read about associations between composers and electrical engineers, for example Moog worked with composer Herbert Deutsch and Donald Buchla teamed up with two composers Morton Subotnik and Ramon Sender to produce avant-garde compositions. Sergio Franco and Ken Pohlmann worked with composer Salvatore Martirano and the SAL-MAR Construction synth shown in Figure 1.1 in the 1970s.

Moog's synthesizer modules consist of various components, each with its own circuit board, knobs, lights, and input/output jacks. Each module is a complete unit, though generally not very interesting on its own. The oscillator module generates a few primitive waveforms—sinusoid, sawtooth, and square waves. The amplifier module uses a voltage-controlled amplifier to modify the amplitude of a signal. The filter module implements various basic filtering functions such as low-pass and high-pass types. The envelope generator module creates a varying output value that is used to control the amplitude or filtering characteristics of other modules. Combining the modules together in various ways produces the most interesting sounds; the result is somehow greater than the sum of the parts. Each of Moog's modules had its own input, output, and control jacks and were connected together using audio cables called patch cables, which were already in widespread use in recording studios. This is the origin of the term patch, which we use often. A patch is a recipe for both connecting and setting up the parameters of each module to form a specific sound. You hear the terms flute patch or string patch all the time when talking about synthesizers. Moog's earliest synths were fully modular since each module (including the keyboard) existed on its own, disconnected from the others until someone physically connected them. Modular synths are the most generalized in this respect—they have the most number of combinations of modules (patches), but they require that you physically connect each component. Changing a sound means pulling out bunch of cables and rewiring the new sound. Electronic musicians typically use visual charts and diagrams for saving and recalling their patches in fully modular synths.

Later on, it became evident that there were sets of very often used combinations of components that formed the basis for many patches. This led to the semi-modular synthesizer where certain components are hard-wired together and can not be changed. Other components can be routed and connected to a limited degree. The synths we design in this book are semi-modular. You will have all the tools you need to vastly extend the capabilities of the synths. All synth projects are based on features from existing synthesizers.

1.1 Synth Components

Synthesizers are designed with three types of components:

- sources: things that render an audio signal, such as oscillators and noise generators
- modifiers: things that alter the audio signal that the sources generate, such as filters and effects
- controllers: things that control parameters of the sources and/or modifiers; these might be fixed controls such as a knob on a MIDI controller or continuously variable controllers such as envelope generators

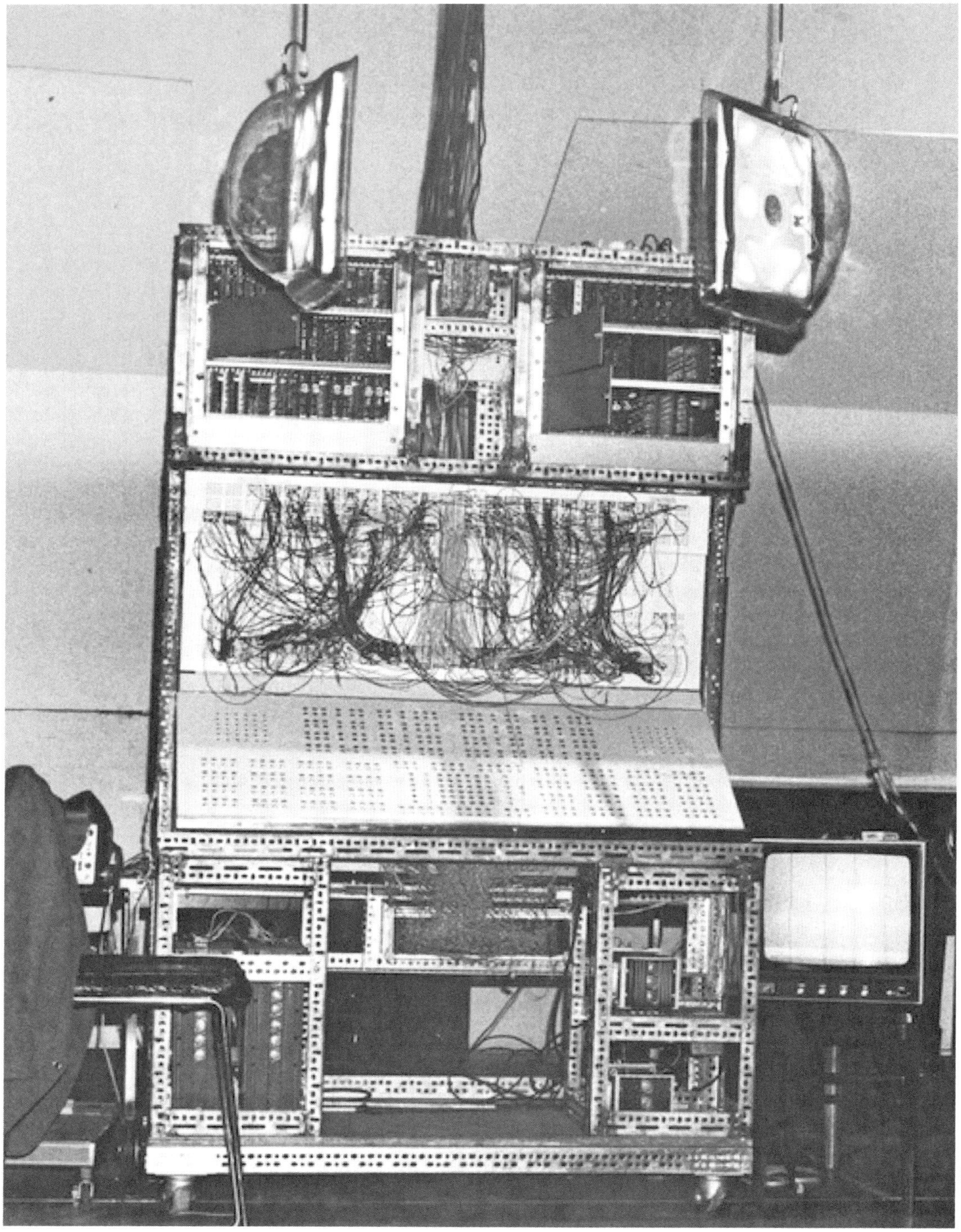

Ken Pohlmann

Figure 1.1: The SAL_MAR Construction Synth in 1978.

The most basic synthesizer patch is shown in Figure 1.2. It consists of one of each of the fundamental building blocks. Notice how the audio signal flows from left to right and the control signal from bottom to top. This is the paradigm we will use throughout the book (and that most synth manufacturers use).

You can also see that the control signal uses an arrow pointing upward while the audio signal is implied to move from left to right; its path does not use arrows. If you do see an arrow in a signal path, it is because the signal is being mixed with something else as shown in Figure 1.3. This shows the outputs of the two sources entering a summer. Here we have added two more controllers to show that controllers can operate on sources, modifiers and even other controllers.

When a controller operates on something, it alters one or more of its parameters. For example a controller might alter the frequency and amplitude of an oscillator. Altering a parameter is called modulation, a term used throughout the book. The controller modulates its target parameter. The controller is also called a modulator. A connection from a controller to a single parameter is called a modulation

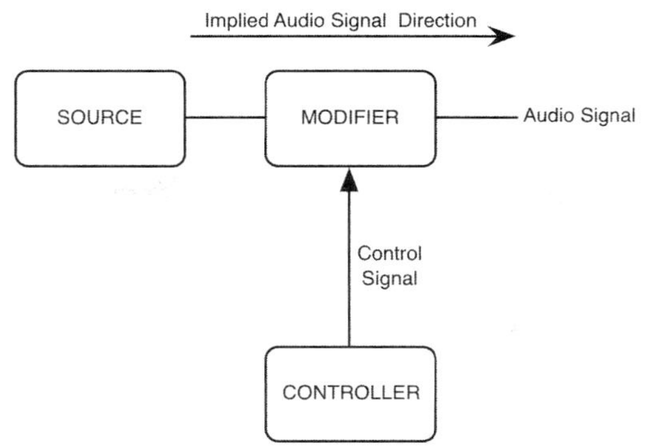

Figure 1.2: A generic synth patch consisting of source, modifier and controller; notice the direction of signal flow.

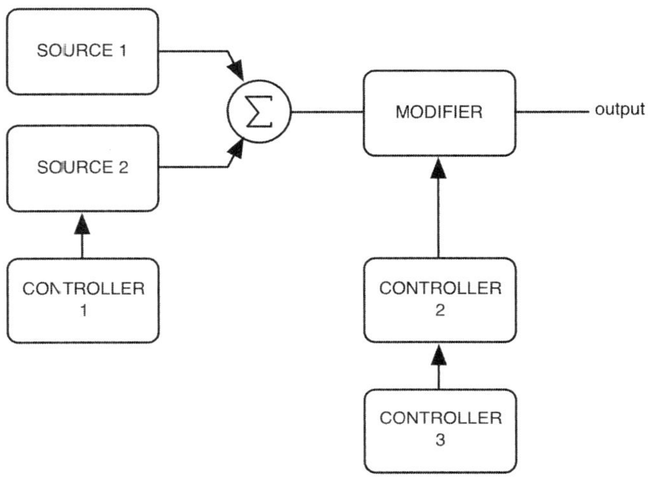

Figure 1.3: A generic synth patch consisting of two sources, a modifier, and three controllers.

routing or routing. The connection has a source (an output on the controller) and a destination (the target parameter to be modulated). Each synth includes a table that contains all the source/destination pairs called a modulation matrix. You can also allow the user to rearrange the modulation routings for more flexibility. A general rule is that a large modulation matrix with a rich supply of sources and destinations produces a highly programmable synth, but it may have a steep learning curve. A synth with a simple modulation matrix is easier to program but has more limited capabilities. We will start by designing simple synths, but they will include a modulation matrix that is very easy to expand and reprogram. In this way, you can spin off countless variations on the basic designs with only a bit of extra programming. As the synths progress, we will add more modulation routings.

1.2 Oscillators

Oscillators render audio without an input. We are going to design and use several types of oscillators that synthesize waveforms in various ways:

- mathematically
- using lookup tables called *wavetables*
- by extracting audio samples contained in WAV files
- Frequency Modulation (FM) and Phase Modulation (PM)

Oscillators can be used as both sources and controllers. We are going to divide oscillators into two groups: pitched oscillators and Low-Frequency Oscillators (or LFOs). In most cases we will call pitched oscillators simply oscillators. In this book, each synth will have two block diagrams—a simple block diagram and a detailed connection graph. The simple block diagram uses easy to read symbols and shows the basic architecture but does not show every connection, while the detailed connection graph shows all connections and Graphical User Interface (GUI) controls. We will discuss these detailed connection graphs as the chapters progress. Oscillators and LFOs will be shown with the two symbols in Figure 1.4 for the simple block diagrams. In Figure 1.4 (a) an LFO modulates a single oscillator. The exact type of modulation is not indicated, but in our synth block diagrams, this is an implied connection to modulate the oscillator's pitch (frequency). This oscillator is shown with a pair of ramp or sawtooth waves in the circle. For our synths, this means

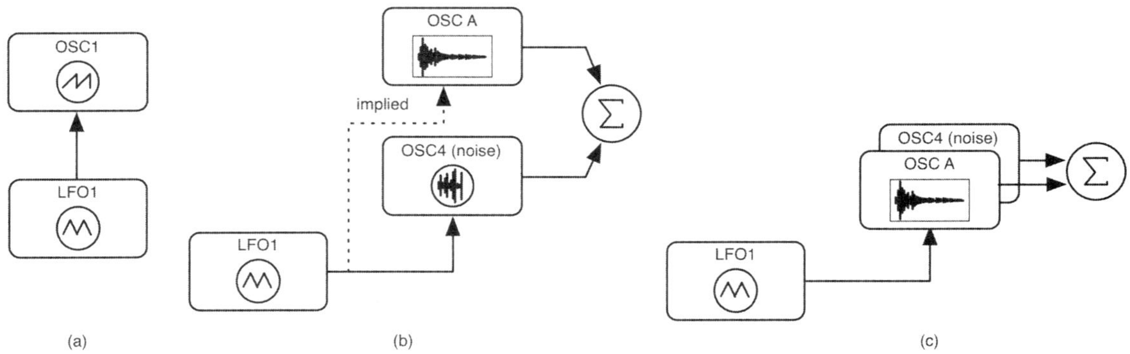

Figure 1.4: (a) An LFO modulates a pitched oscillator. (b) An LFO modulates two oscillators, one is sample-based and the other is a noise generator. (c) An alternate form of (b).

one of the mathematically or wavetable generated waveforms. The FM synth called DXSynth will use sinusoidal oscillators, so in that special case, you will see sinusoids instead of ramps.

The LFO is shown with a pair of triangle waves only because this is a common waveform for modulation, and it distinguishes the LFO from the pitched oscillator visually. In Figure 1.4 (b) you can see two other types: OSC A depicts an audio sample loaded from a WAV file, while OSC4 (noise) is a noise generator. The LFO is placed to the left, but the control arrow is still upward since it is a controller. It is also implied in this diagram that the controller modulates all the oscillators in the stack above the control arrow.

1.3 Filters

Filters modify the frequency content of an audio signal—thus they are modifiers. There are several basic filter types that we will design in Chapter 7. These include:

- lowpass: attenuates high frequencies, may be resonant
- highpass: attenuates low frequencies, may be resonant
- bandpass: allows a band of frequencies to pass through by attenuating both low and high frequencies, may be resonant but usually is not
- bandstop: attenuates a band of frequencies by allowing both low and high frequencies to pass through, may be resonant but usually is not

Although we will get into the details in Chapter 7, you can see the lowpass and highpass varieties may be resonant—this means they produce a resonant peak near the edge of the band of frequencies they are attenuating. The resonant peak may be soft and low or high and sharply peaked. The bandpass and bandstop filters may technically become resonant, though this is uncommon (we will produce an interesting kind of resonant bandstop filter in Chapter 7). Figure 1.5 shows the symbol for filters in the book. It depicts a lowpass filter that is resonant—notice the hump in the curve. Even though it depicts a lowpass filter, it is implied that it might be any kind of filter or a filter that can be changed from one type to another. In Figure 1.5(a) you see a single LFO modulating a filter. The implied modulation is the cutoff frequency of the filter which is the special frequency that the filter operates around. We will design both monophonic and stereo synthesizers; in the later case we need two filters, one for each channel. In Figure 1.5(b) the LFO modulates both left and right filters and once again the implied modulation is cutoff frequency.

1.4 Amplifiers

Amplifiers amplify or attenuate a signal so they are also modifiers. Early analog types are called Voltage Controlled Amplifiers or VCAs. We will be implementing Digitally Controlled Amplifiers or DCAs. Our DCA module controls the output amplitude on the synth as well as handling panning functions. It can be mono or stereo in but will always be stereo out. A controller can be connected to modulate the amplitude and/or panning. Figure 1.6 shows a DCA connected to the output of a filter. The two oscillators feed the filter. One LFO modulates the oscillators, while another modulates the filter and DCA simultaneously. For the DCA, the modulation is implied to be amplitude modulation. We will implement both amplitude and panning modulation in our synths.

1.5 Envelope Generators

Envelope Generators (EGs) create an envelope that can be applied to any kind of modulation destination, such as oscillator pitch (called a Pitch EG), filter cutoff frequency (called a Filter EG) or DCA amplitude (called an Amp EG). The envelope generator creates an amplitude curve that is broken into segments called attack, decay, sustain and release (though there may be more than just those four). We will get into the details of the EG in Chapter 6. Figure 1.7 (a) shows three different EGs acting on three destinations, while

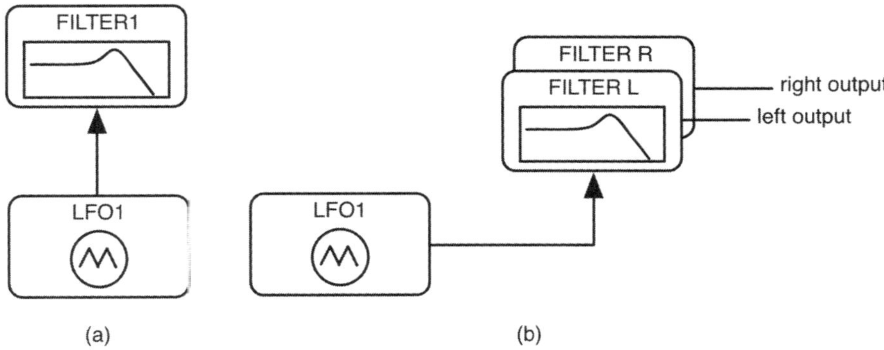

Figure 1.5: (a) An LFO modulates a filter. (b) An LFO modulates both left and right filters.

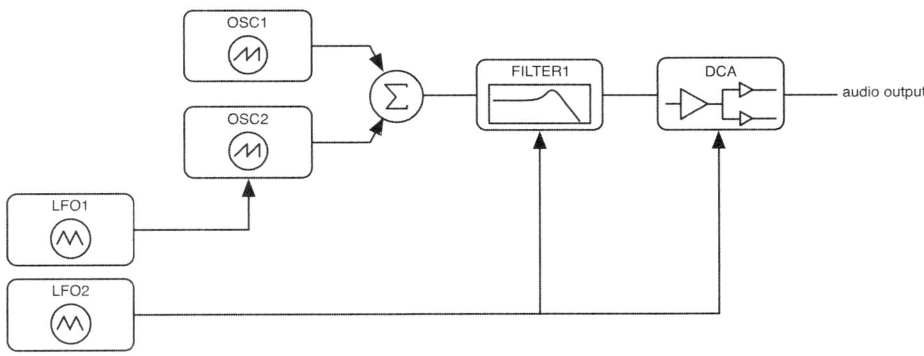

Figure 1.6: A more complicated block diagram with oscillators, LFOs and one filter and DCA.

(b) shows one EG operating on all three. In the first case, you have ultimate control over each modulated component, but there will be many GUI controls. In the second case, having one EG is limiting, but oftentimes the desired pitch, filter and DCA curves are basically the same, if not identical; in addition there will be fewer GUI controls. This also follows the general rule that the more modulators, the more difficult the patch programming.

1.6 Basic Synth Architecture

All of the synths with the exception of DXSynth will have a similar kind of architecture to those in Figure 1.6. The MIDI Manufacturers Association (MMA) divides this kind of architecture into three blocks, shown in Figure 1.8.

- digital audio engine
- articulation
- control

The digital audio engine contains the components that are in the audio signal path, while the articulation block contains the components that act as controllers. On occasion, there can be some overlap. For example you might allow a pitched oscillator to be a controller and modify the filter cutoff frequency. However, our synths will generally follow this same paradigm. The control block consists of the MIDI keyboard, GUI and other signals that are used for controlling the digital audio engine and articulation blocks. Figure 1.8 shows this block diagram format for the synth in Figure 1.7 (b).

1.7 Fundamental Goals of Synth Patch Design

Musical taste is subjective. What constitutes a good or bad musical sound, note or event is likewise subjective. Notwithstanding the various musical tastes and preferences, from studying both traditional musical instruments and the human ear/brain connection, we can learn to fashion a fundamental statement about musical expression objectives—keep the listener engaged to the note events that occur. This really means keep the ears engaged. Our ears are transient-selective transducers. Transient sounds pique our ear/brain's curiosity, whereas steady state sounds quickly fade away into the background. Perhaps this is evolutionary—a hunter walking through the woods freezes in place when he hears the crack of a nearby branch indicating the potential for food collection or the possibility of becoming something else's food. But the same hunter automatically ignores the steady stream of bird chirping or the sound of wind

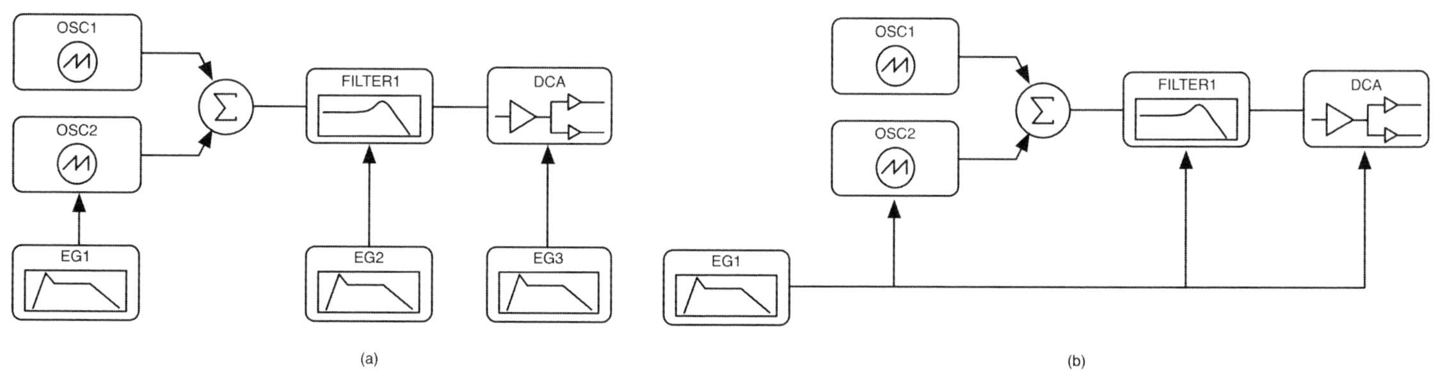

Figure 1.7: (a) A design with pitch, filter and amp EGs. (b) A single EG can modulate all three destinations.

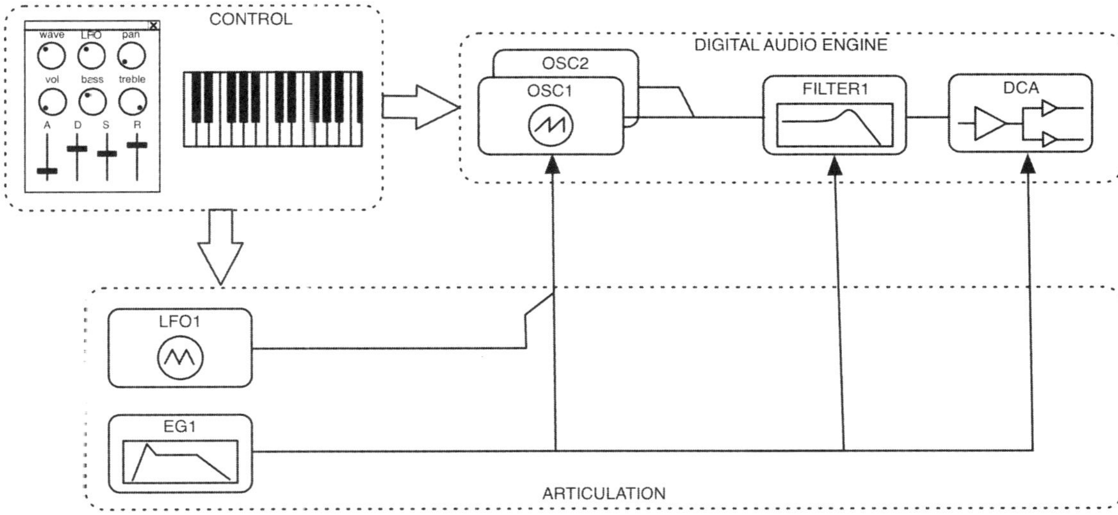

Figure 1.8: The MMA block diagram of a typical synth with digital audio engine, articulation and control blocks.

rustling the leaves, unless the chirping suddenly stops—a transient event that signals something out of the ordinary. So, our ear/brain connection is more sensitive to things that change, not things that stay the same. In this case, it's the time domain amplitude that is changing—the sound of the broken branch or the sudden stop in bird chirping. Our ears are interested in sounds with a changing time domain amplitude envelope. Think about other traditional musical instruments like piano, guitar or cello—these all produce sounds with specific amplitude envelopes. All three can be made to have a fast transient edge at the note onset (called the transient attack). The piano and guitar produce notes that fade away relatively quickly whereas the cello can sustain a note for as long as the musician desires.

But our ears are also designed to track things that have a changing frequency content too—even if the overall amplitude remains relatively constant. Speech and song are both types of communication in which frequency content changes or evolves over time. For example, a singer might steadily glissando a note up an octave while remaining at a constant amplitude—this is an event our ears will track and respond to. But as soon as the singer hits the final pitch and holds it, the ear/brain looses interest. What does the singer do to try to regain your interest? One answer is to add pitch vibrato as the note is sustaining. Vibrato is a form of musical expression in which the pitch of the note fluctuates up and down around the true note pitch. Non-piano and non-percussion musicians commonly use vibrato in their playing styles and it is a generally held notion that vibrato is more effective if it's added after the note has sustained for a while rather than right from the beginning. Why? Because you are adding it just at the time the ear starts to loose interest. Listen to a great saxophonist playing a sweet musical line from a ballad, and you'll certainly hear that vibrato being applied after the fact, and not right at the onset of the note.

You might be saying "alright, but what about ambient synth sounds?" In this case, the goal is to design a sound that is suited as background material; think about the ambient, ominous sound of your favorite computer game. If you listen to just the background part, you might be surprised to hear that the frequency content goes through extreme changes in time—the changes happen very slowly, so you don't really notice during gameplay. In these patches, the sound's frequency content slowly evolves, often in a scary or deliberately unsettling manner. So, even though there are no transient edges or quickly changing frequency components, there is an evolution of frequency content going on, albeit very slowly. If the game composer used a simple sinusoid as the background music for your games, you would just ignore it, and the creepy or disturbing effect would be lost. So, our ears are also interested in the frequency domain envelope of the sound—or how the different frequency components change in time.

All of this leads to a generalization about what we'd like to have in a synthesizer patch, and that ultimately dictates which modules we need for a system.

In general, we seek to create sounds that evolve, morph or change in both time and frequency in order to create sonically interesting events. The time domain envelope dictates changes to the amplitude of the signal during the event in time, while the frequency domain envelope controls the way the frequency components change over the course of the event.

Some patches like a percussion sound might lean more towards the amplitude envelope as the distinguishing feature, whereas others (such as the ambient background loop in a game) might be biased towards the frequency evolution. However, if you examine the large body of existing acoustic musical instruments, you find that they tend to feature significant changes in both time and frequency envelopes. Examine Figure 1.9 which shows a single piano note event played fortissimo (the note is A1) with the release portion of the event removed. This Energy Decay Relief (EDR) shows amplitude, time and frequency all in one plot, sometimes called a waterfall plot.

In these plots, amplitude (dB) is on the y-axis, time is on the x-axis and frequency is on the z-axis. Notice that low frequencies are toward the back, and high frequencies are near the front. Moving along the frequency axis, you can see how the frequency response changes from the onset of the note at the back to the end of the note event at the front, as shown in Figure 1.10. You can

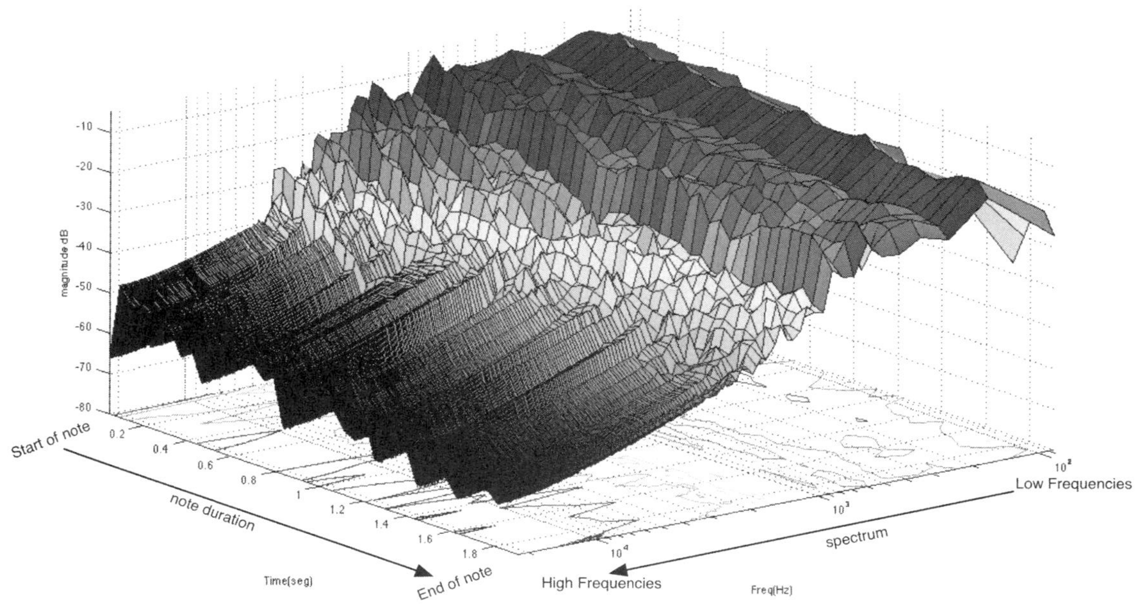

Figure 1.9: EDR for a grand piano sample playing the note A1 fortissimo.

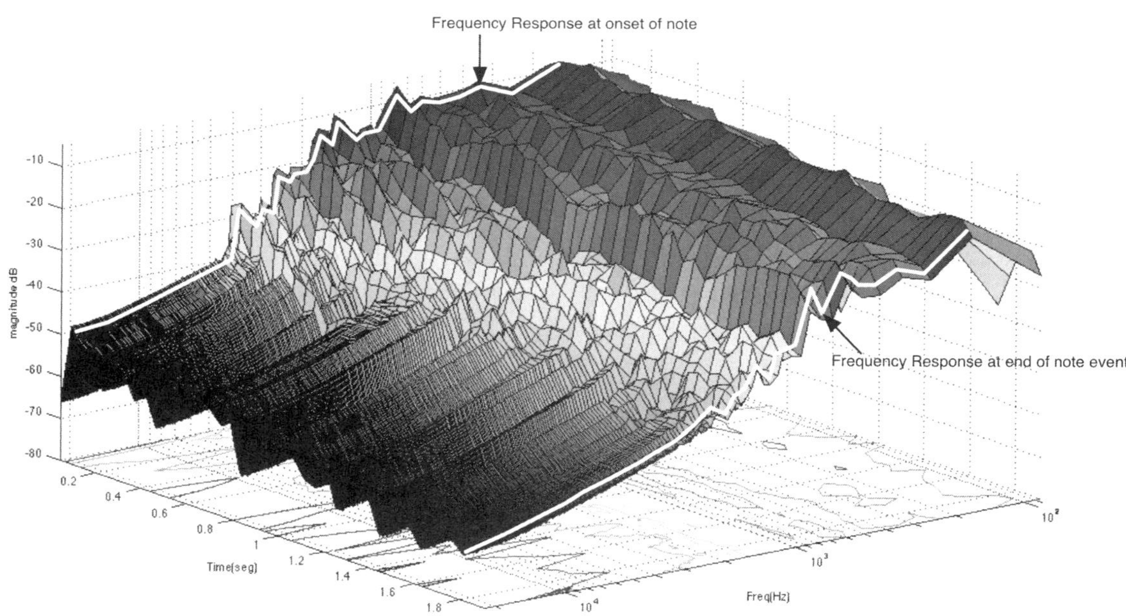

Figure 1.10: In this piano sample, you can see how the overall frequency response changes from the onset of the note to the end of the event; we observe that the main resonant peaks linger, but some of the early mid-frequencies have collapsed.

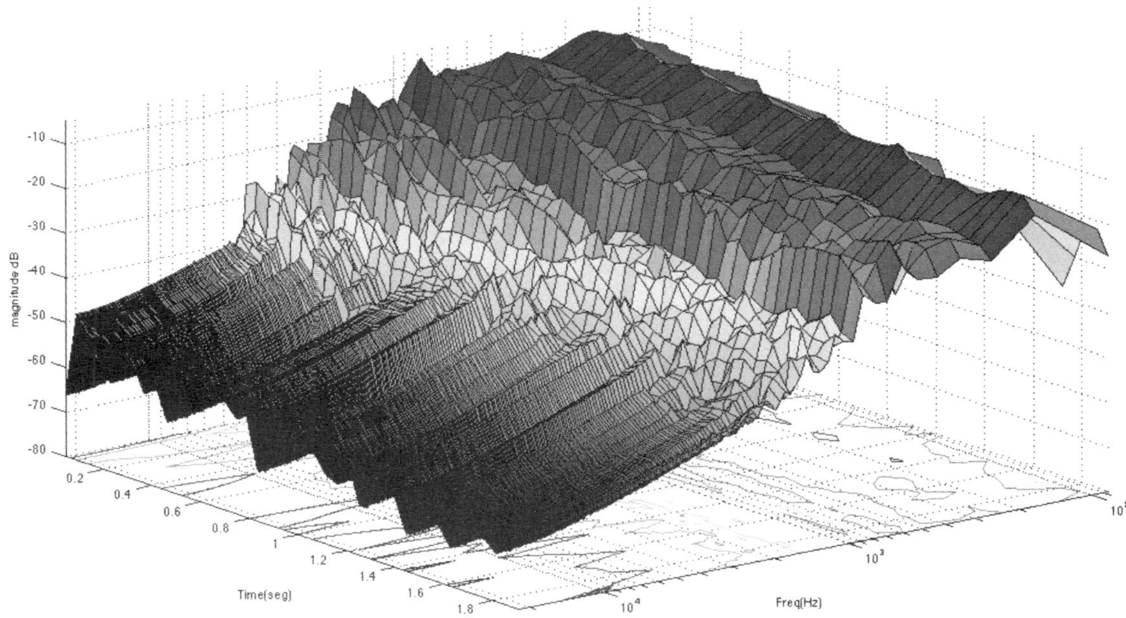

Figure 1.11: Following the time axis, you can see how the low frequencies start at a higher amplitude and remain at almost the same amplitude, while high frequency components start at lower amplitudes and decay much faster and less smoothly.

see how the main resonant peaks are preserved—they last the lifetime of the note event, but other early resonances disappear by the end of the event. You can also observe that all of the high frequencies roll off together and that more high frequencies roll off as time moves on.

On the time axis, you can see how each frequency component changes over time in an undulating manner as shown in Figure 1.11. You can see that the low frequencies have an overall higher amplitude during the entire note event and that they decay slowly and smoothly, whereas the high frequencies start off at a low amplitude and decay away faster and less smoothly than the low frequencies.

Figure 1.12 shows a collection of EDRs of acoustic instruments, applause and rain. Take some time to study the differences in these plots. Even if you have no desire to mimic traditional instruments, they have survived and in some cases thrived for centuries or more, so we can learn something from them—these are instruments with a track record of keeping the ear engaged. The instruments are:

- acoustic bass (F#1)
- bowed cello (C#2)
- bassoon (D4)
- English horn (D4)
- celeste (F#2)
- bell (C#3)
- tinshaw (a type of Tibetan bell, Eb5)
- snare drum
- applause
- rain

In the pitched instruments, we observe evolution in both frequency and time. In the non-bell pitched instruments, you can see there is a pattern across a band of high frequencies—they all ripple together. However, in the bell sounds—especially the celeste—you can see that the higher frequency components undulate against each other rather than as a group as shown in Figure 1.13. These sounds were difficult to realistically synthesize until the Yamaha DX7 FM synth arrived. It specializes in this kind of high frequency behavior.

Notice how the applause and rain are very different from the rest—these are sounds our brains tend to ignore quickly; they have little change in time and frequency over the course of the sound. The applause does have a more pronounced frequency contour, but it remains constant. The bassoon and English horn is an interesting pair to observe—they are playing the same note and have similar overall contours, but clearly the harmonics close to the fundamental are very different. The snare drum also exhibits a visible evolution in time and frequency. In each of the instrument samples except the snare, there is a 0.25 second fade-out applied, visible as the surface falling over the leading edge of the plot.

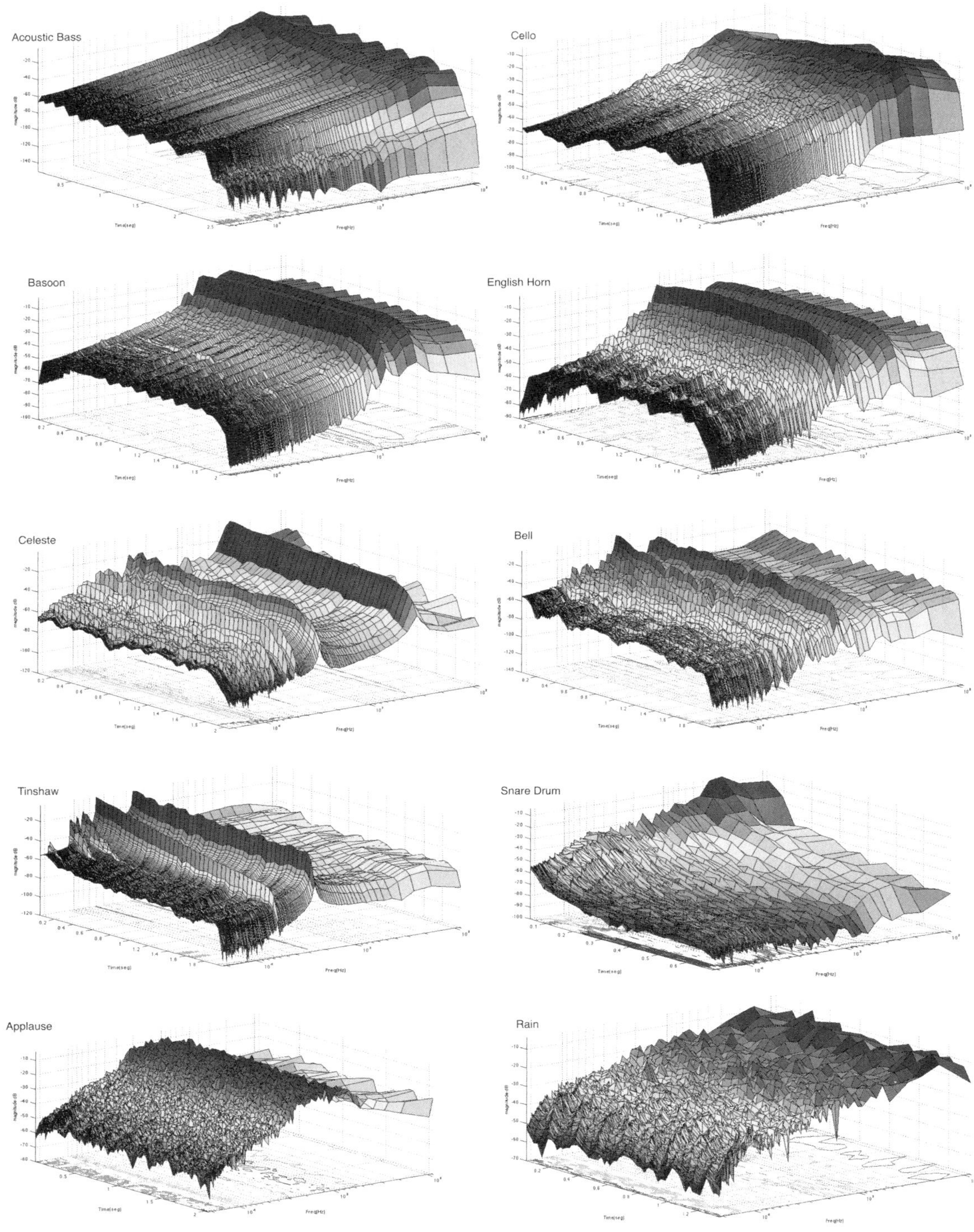

Figure 1.12: EDR plots for various acoustic instruments, bells, snare drum, applause and rain.

Generally speaking, we would like to design our synths to facilitate the creation of patches that have this kind of evolution. We need to easily shape both the time and frequency contours in a way that evolves after the note event is initiated. The synth will be easier to program if the controls are intuitive. In the VectorSynth/AniSynth we'll use a joystick control to drastically alter time contour and timbre of the patch. You will also see that some synths are more difficult to program than others—the DXSynth takes more time to learn because of the way frequencies tend to evolve in its algorithms.

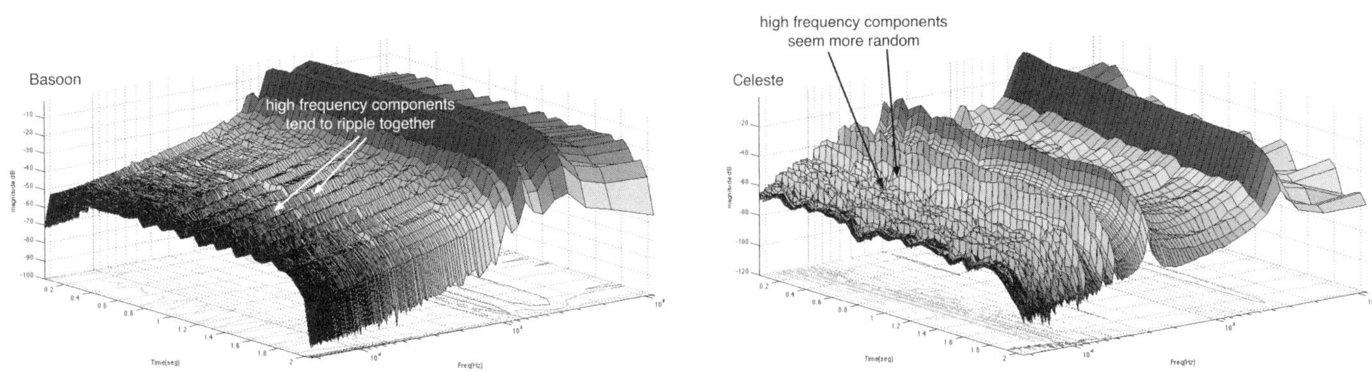

Figure 1.13: The high frequencies in the celeste sample are not organized as they are in the bassoon.

1.8 Audio Data Formats for Plug-Ins

Fortunately, all three of our plug-in formats—RackAFX, VST3 and AU—use the same data format for all audio outputs. Effects plug-ins have both inputs and outputs, whereas synthesizer plug-ins are output-only devices. Audio samples can be represented in a variety of formats. In the earliest analog to digital converters, the data was usually in the unsigned integer format with the most negative value represented as 000000..0 and the most positive value as 111111..1, which worked well in some control circuits and display readouts. In digital audio samples, we would like to represent both positive and negative values and most importantly the value 0.0. Using Pulse Code Modulation (PCM) a signal can be encoded so that it contains both polarities as well as the 0.0 value. Your audio input hardware does this and converts the incoming audio data into PCM-based audio samples. These samples are integers whose range depends on the bit depth of the analog to digital convertor. The ranges for a few different bit-depths are shown in Table 1.1. You can see that the table is skewed in the negative direction. This is because there are an even number of quantization levels for a given bit depth:

$$\text{number of quantization} = 2^N$$
$$N = \text{bit depth}$$

We have assigned one of these levels to the value 0, so we have an odd number of levels to split across the range. The reason the negative side gets the extra value has to do with the way PCM is encoded in two's complement fashion. See *Designing Audio Effects Plug-Ins in C++* for a detailed discussion.

In order to allow Digital Audio Workstations (DAWs) and their plug-ins to operate on any bit-depth of incoming data, the audio is converted to a floating point or double floating point number on the range of −1.0 to +1.0, which is accomplished by simply scaling the PCM value by the absolute value of the negative limit. This actually produces a range of values from −1.0 to +0.9999999 for 24 bit audio. We are going to just round this to the range of −1.0 to +1.0. In this book that range would be denoted as [−1..+1] in this bracket format. This means that the outputs of our synthesizer plug-ins must always lie inside the range of [−1..+1] or else clipping of the signal will occur which introduces distortion. Usually this is easy to detect. However, as shown in Figure 1.14, the signals inside our synths do not necessarily need to fall on this range.

The audio output data formats that are currently supported are:

RackAFX: 32-bit floating point (*float*)
VST3: 32-bit floating point (*float*) and 64-bit double precision (*double*)
AU: 32-bit floating point (*float*)

Table 1.1: The ranges of some different digital audio bit-depths.

Bit Depth	Negative Limit (−)	Positive Limit (+)
16	−32,768	+32,767
24	−8,388,608	+8,388,607
32	−2,147,483,648	+2,147,483,647

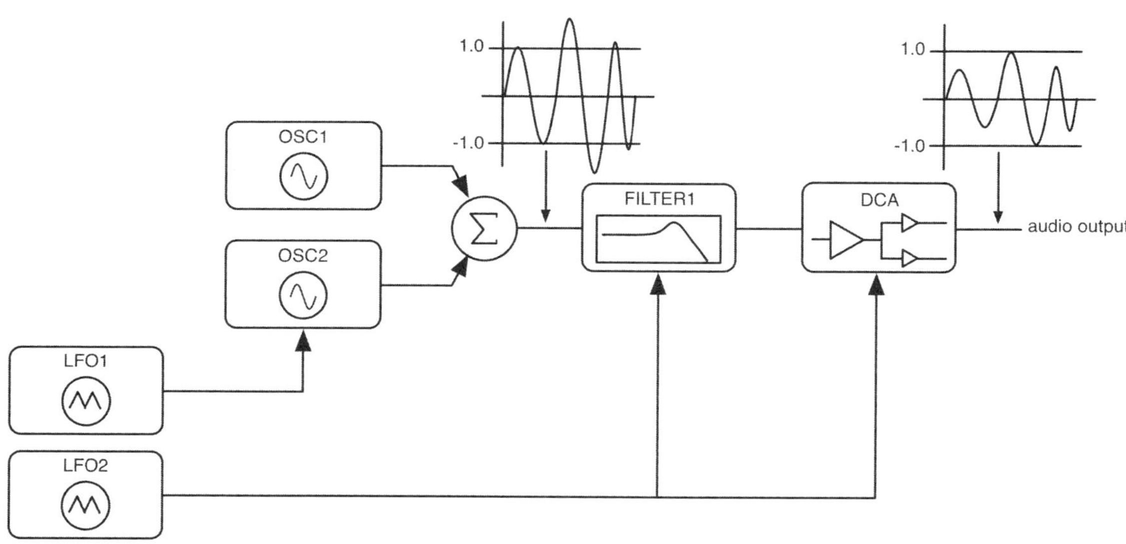

Figure 1.14: The audio signal amplitude inside the synth may exceed the [−1..+1] range, but the output must fall within this range for distortionless audio.

All of our synths will default to produce a 32-bit floating point output for the most compatibility and ease of comparison. If you are targeting VST3, you may additionally add the capability to produce 64-bit outputs. All of our synth outputs are going to be floating point values; however, that does not mean that we need to render and process our data internal to the synth as floating point numbers. Our synths are actually going to be written to render and process double precision data, then output floating point data. Processing in double precision gives us more headroom (if needed) and obviously more precision. It is apparent that computing is moving to 64-bit processing even though some DAWs on the market are still 32-bit in nature. During testing, we built the same synth with all float versus all double variables for processing with little difference in observable CPU usage, though you may experience issues on very old machines.

> All of our synths will default to produce a 32-bit floating point outputs. The internal processing will be done with double precision variables.

1.9 Signal Processing Review

If the preceding time/frequency plots look familiar to you, and you understand the relationships between the time and frequency domain, z^{-1} and the basics of Digital Signal Processing (DSP), then feel free to skip to the next chapter. If you are new to DSP, what follows is a concise primer on the topic but is by no means a complete treatise. If you do not understand how $e^{j\omega t}$ represents a complex sinusoid, you might want to check out *Designing Audio Effects Plug-Ins in C++* or *A DSP Primer* (Stieglitz, 1996) as these books reveal the concepts without excess math. See the Simonyi for other very approachable texts on the topic.

1.10 Continuous Signals

We usually depict an analog signal as a function of time $f(t)$ that follows a continuous curve like that shown in Figure 1.15(a). When we process this kind of signal, we use analog components such as capacitors and inductors. We store it on a continuous media such as magnetic tape. When we sample the signal, we discretize it—that is, we chop it into slices in time and only process and store the value at the discrete slice locations as shown in Figure 1.15(b). Typically, we use the line-with-circle-on-top to denote the individual sample values. We call the signal $f(n)$ where n is the sample number (engineers may also further denote the discretized signal by using brackets as in $f[n]$). The most general form is $f(nT)$ where n is the sample number and T is the sample interval. We often simply let T = 1 and just show $f(n)$ instead.

Nyquist found that no loss of information occurs when sampling the signal as long as it is bandlimited (lowpass filtered) to 1/2 the sample rate, also known as $f_s/2$ or the Nyquist frequency or simply Nyquist. Mathematicians Fourier and Laplace showed that continuous analog signals such as that in Figure 1.15 (a) can be described as linear combinations of simple sinusoids. The Fourier series decomposes a signal into a set of sine and cosine waveforms, each scaled by a coefficient. There may be an infinite number of these components, but they are harmonically related to the base frequency called the fundamental frequency or fundamental. The fundamental is usually, but not always, the lowest frequency component in the group. Figure 1.16 shows the Fourier decomposition of a simple waveform (sketch, not mathematically accurate) while Equation 1.1 shows the Fourier series equation.

$$f(t) = a_0 + \sum_{n=1}^{\infty} a_n \sin(n\omega t) + \sum_{n=1}^{\infty} b_n \cos(n\omega t) \tag{1.1}$$

The equation states that the signal $f(t)$ may be decomposed or reconstructed as a linear combination of *sine* waves scaled by a_n coefficients and *cosine* waves scaled by b_n coefficients plus a constant DC offset a_0. Notice that the relative starting points of the sine and cosine waveforms don't always start at 0 (or a phase of 0 degrees) but rather may start anywhere. There is no general rule about the

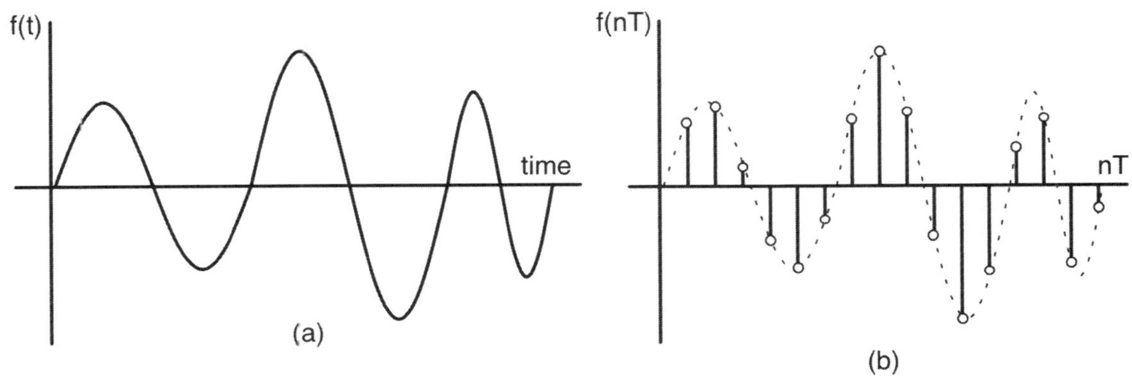

Figure 1.15: (a) An analog signal and (b) the discrete time representation of it.

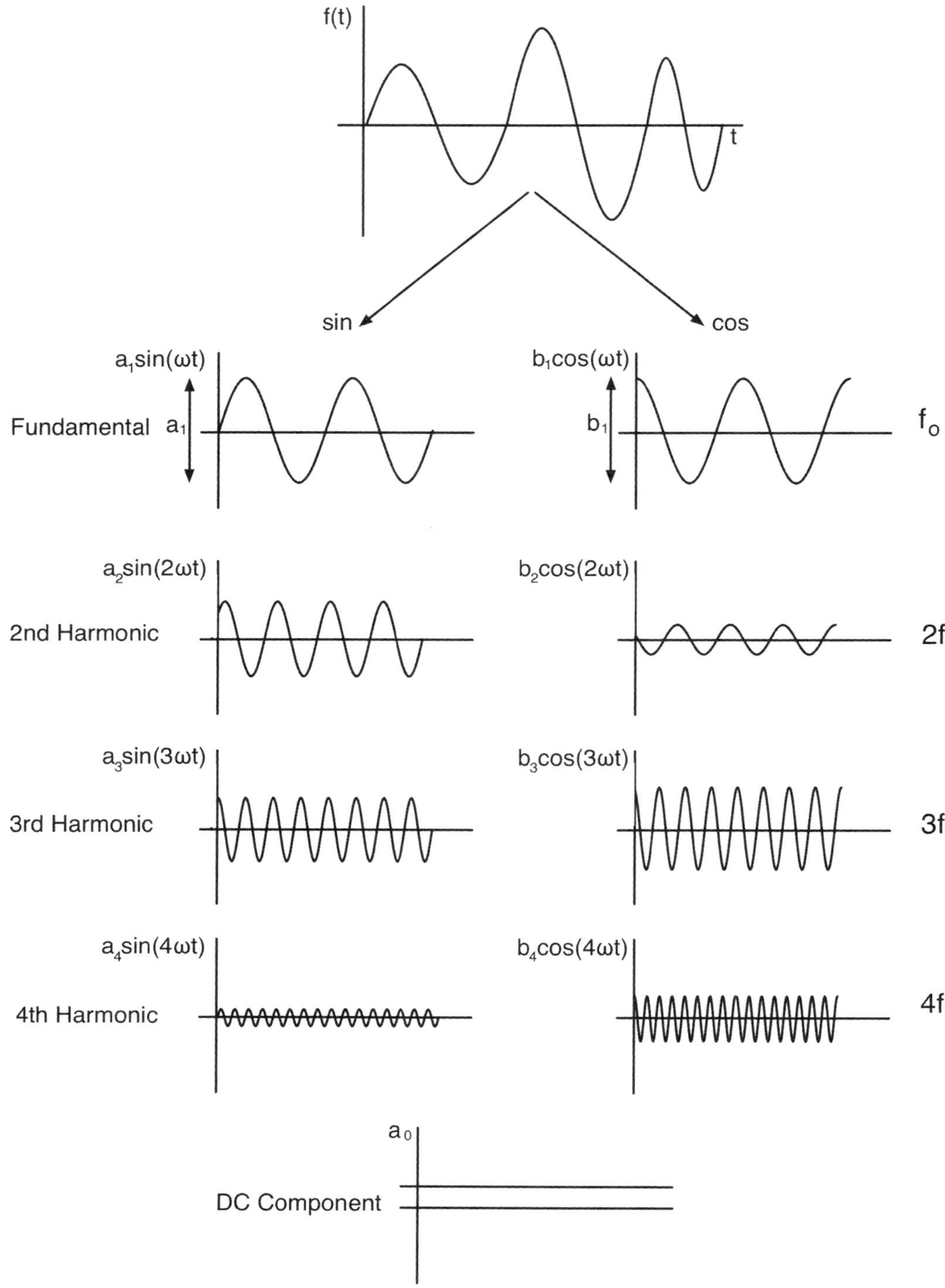

Figure 1.16: The Fourier decomposition of an analog waveform via the Fourier series. Note: the *sine* and *cosine* components exist forever in both directions, they are cut off at the y-axis to show their differences in phase.

amplitudes of the harmonics (whether they get larger or smaller as the frequency increases) nor the phase offset. Since sine and cosine are related by a 90 degree offset, we can rewrite Equation 1.2 in a slightly more compact fashion:

$$
\begin{aligned}
f(t) &= \sum_{n=0}^{\infty} c_n \cos(n\omega t + \phi_n) \\
c_n &= \sqrt{a_n^2 + b_n^2} \\
\phi_n &= \tan^{-1}\left(\frac{-b_n}{a_n}\right)
\end{aligned}
\tag{1.2}
$$

The a and b coefficients represent the same sine and cosine harmonic amplitudes as before. The c terms represent the magnitude of each frequency component while the φ terms represent the phase offset of each component. Referring back to Figure 1.16 you can see that each harmonic component, including the fundamental, has a magnitude and phase that dictate its height and time offset.

Taking this one step further, we can use Euler's identity (pronounced "Oiler"), which further locks the sine and cosine into an orthogonal relationship as:

$$e^{j\omega t} = \cos(\omega t) + j\sin(\omega t) \tag{1.3}$$

Orthogonal is usually defined as "related by 90 degrees," but perhaps a more intuitive definition might be "having absolutely nothing to do with each other, unrelated in the purest sense." Euler's identity is useful because it combines both sine and cosine into one equation, preserving their 90 degree relationship. More importantly, $e^{j\omega t}$ is simple to deal with mathematically since it behaves like a polynomial and calculus with it is simple. The fact that the derivative and integral of e^{at} consist of a constant value (either a or $1/a$) multiplied by the original function is the reason we use them in the Fourier series. It greatly simplifies the solutions for the frequency domain transfer functions that we will observe in Chapter 4.

$$\begin{aligned} &e^a e^b = e^{a+b} && \frac{e^a}{e^b} = e^{a-b} \\ &\frac{d(e^{at})}{dt} = ae^{at} && \int e^{at}dt = \frac{1}{a}e^{at} \end{aligned} \tag{1.4}$$

So we can compact the Fourier series even more by using the complex sinusoid $e^{j\omega t}$ rather than sine, cosine, or phase shifted versions.

$$f(t) = \sum_{n=-\infty}^{\infty} F_n e^{jn\omega t} \tag{1.5}$$

Equation 1.5 describes a set (sum) of complex harmonics of amplitude F_n. Since the harmonics are complex, F_n actually contains both the magnitude and phase at the same time, coded as the real and imaginary parts of the complex sinusoid. This is why the summation term n includes negative values. The magnitude and phase are still extracted with the same equations:

$$\begin{aligned} |F_n| &= \sqrt{\mathrm{Re}(F_n)^2 + \mathrm{Im}(F_n)^2} \\ \phi(F_n) &= \arg(F_n) = \tan^{-1}\left(\frac{\mathrm{Im}(F_n)}{\mathrm{Re}(F_n)}\right) \end{aligned} \tag{1.6}$$

The real and imaginary components come directly from Euler's identity; the real components are the cosine amplitudes and the imaginary components are the sine amplitudes. The phase portion is also called the argument or *arg* of the equation. If all of this real and imaginary stuff is freaking you out, check out *Designing Audio Effects Plug-ins in C++*—it explains all of this (including *e*) in a friendly and easy to understand way.

There are several rules that must be obeyed for the Fourier series to hold true. The signal to be decomposed must:

- be continuous: no discontinuities or glitches
- be periodic
- have been in existence for all time up to now
- remain in existence for all time—forever

The first limitation is not an issue for sampled signals that have been low pass filtered; the filtering would remove discontinuities. However, when rendering signals, discontinuities are to be avoided. The second limitation is a big one—must be periodic. What if the signal is quasi-periodic or not periodic at all, like noise? Fourier answers that with the Fourier integral. It states that a quasi or non-periodic signal can still be represented as a sum of harmonics; however, the harmonics may not necessarily be mathematically related. As before, there might be an infinite number of mathematically related harmonics, but there also might be an infinite number of harmonics in between the ordinary ones. Fourier replaced the summation with an integral—the mathematical way of describing this uncountable number of harmonics:

$$f(t) = \frac{1}{2\pi}\int_{-\infty}^{\infty} F(j\omega)e^{j\omega t}d\omega \tag{1.7}$$

You can safely ignore the $1/2\pi$ constant. Here, the $F(j\omega)$ term represents the harmonic amplitude for any frequency ω. There are no subscripts since $F(j\omega)$ is continuous—that is, it exists for all complex frequencies ($j\omega$) from negative to positive infinity. Each component $F(j\omega)$ has a magnitude and phase. The whole signal $F(j\omega)$ is called the *spectrum*. Figure 1.17(b) shows the magnitude plot of the Fourier integral that represents some arbitrary signal $f(t)$ in Figure 1.17(a) (again, this is a sketch and not mathematically exact). You can see that the spectrum can have both positive and negative amplitudes. We often plot the magnitude or absolute value of the spectrum instead as in Figure 1.17 (c). The dots at the end points of the spectra indicate that these curves theoretically extend out to negative and positive infinity.

When you see plots of spectra in this book, you will always be looking at the magnitude plotted in decibels (dB). You can also see that the spectrum and the magnitude are symmetrical about the y-axis. This is because the input signal *f(t)* is real (has no imaginary components)—this will be the case with all our audio signals. You may also be disturbed at the fact that there are indeed negative frequencies in the spectra—in fact, for our signals each frequency component will have an identical twin frequency over on the negative side of the plot. Figure 1.17 is intentionally drawn that way to show how the magnitude produces the same basic picture, only all positive. It also shows peaks (resonances) and notches (anti-resonances) because these are common in music signals. Most books will show a much more generalized spectrum, usually bell shaped as shown in Figure 1.18 (a). Lowpass filtering this signal to adhere to the Nyquist criteria produces a clipped version shown in Figure 1.18 (b), also common in DSP textbooks. The clipped spectrum is said to be bandlimited.

Equation 1.7 shows a relationship between a continuous time domain signal and its continuous frequency domain spectrum. We can also go in the other direction and represent a spectrum as an infinite sum of time functions with Equation 1.8.

$$F(j\omega) = \int_{-\infty}^{\infty} f(t)e^{-j\omega t}\,dt \tag{1.8}$$

Equation 1.7 is called the Fourier transform and it converts a function in time *f(t)* into a spectrum *F(jω)*. Notably, Equation 1.8 is called the inverse Fourier transform since it performs the opposite function. The Short Time Fourier Transform (STFT) performs the integration over a finite time period between t_1 and t_2.

$$F(j\omega) = \int_{t_1}^{t_2} f(t)e^{-j\omega t}\,dt \tag{1.9}$$

> The Fourier Transform converts a signal or function whose dependent variable is time *t* into a signal or function whose dependent variable is complex frequency *jω*.

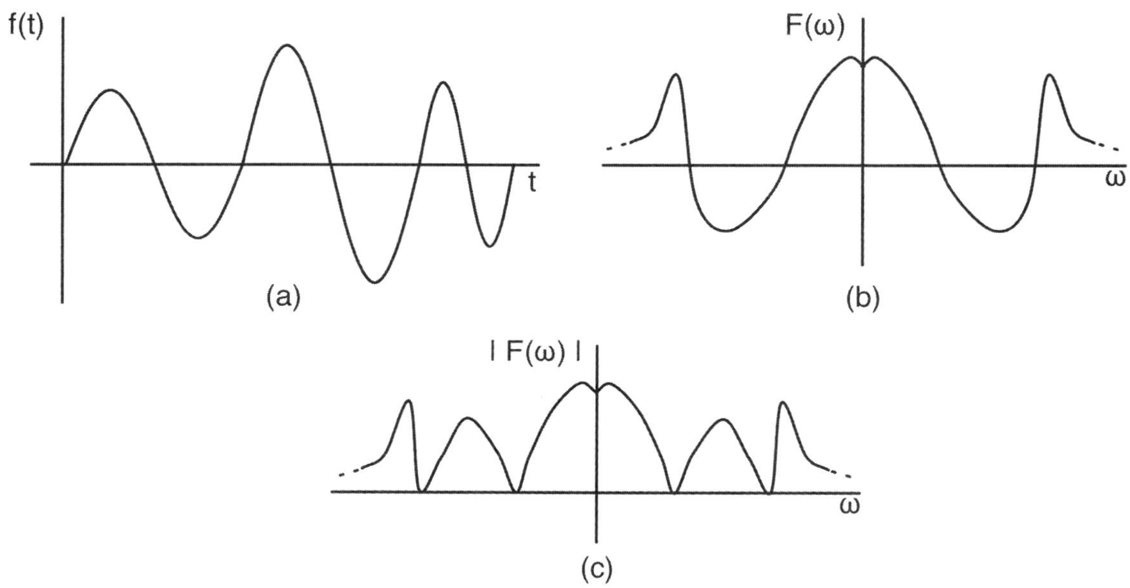

Figure 1.17: (a) Some arbitrary signal *f(t)* and (b) its spectrum and (c) magnitude plot of spectrum.

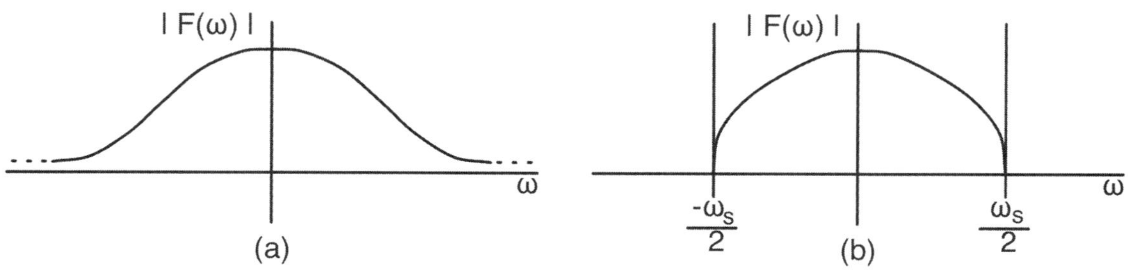

Figure 1.18: (a) The "textbook" generalized spectrum of a continuous analog signal and (b) the spectrum of the same signal that has been lowpass filtered with an analog filter at the Nyquist frequency.

For quasi-periodic waveforms such as audio the STFT is almost always going to have errors in it since we aren't integrating over the complete interval of all time forever in both directions. You can get more information on how to mitigate this error with windowing in most advanced DSP books. In RackAFX and in other spectrum analyzer plug-ins, you are looking at a STFT when you view a spectrum.

1.11 Discretized Signals

If we discretize or sample the input, then we will also be discretizing the spectrum. That is, we will likewise chop it into slivers. The Discrete Fourier Transform (DFT) or the Discrete Time Fourier Transform (DTFT) is the result of taking the Fourier transform of a sampled signal f_s. The sampled signal in Figure 1.19 (b) can be described mathematically as:

$$f_s(t) = f(t)U_o(t - nT) \tag{1.10}$$

The second term $U_0(t - nT)$ represents a train of unit pulses of width T. Figure 1.19 (b)'s infinitely skinny line-with-circle-on-top represented an ideal situation where the sample rate was infinitely fast. In reality, each sample has some finite duration—for f_s = 44.1 kHz the period is about 23 microseconds. So Equation 1.10 is really describing what you see in Figure 1.19(b) where we multiply the pulse train by $f(t)$. A given pulse height is the value of $f(t)$ at the center of the pulse.

Plugging Equation 1.10 into Equation 1.9 yields the DFT (DTFT) or sampled spectrum $F_s(j\omega)$:

$$F_s(j\omega) = \sum_{n=-\infty}^{\infty} f(nT)e^{-jn\omega T} \tag{1.11}$$

Equation 1.11 says that the discrete spectrum is a set of pulses that approximate the original continuous analog curve. In fact, you might have seen something like Figure 1.19(b) in a calculus book where you approximate the area under a curve with a set of rectangular pulses. The DFT can also be thought of as a zero order hold approximation of the original signal. As the sample period T becomes smaller, the approximation becomes more accurate. Plotting the spectral components rather than simply summing them yields more information. Figure 1.20 shows two real world signals and their spectra. The first is a simple sawtooth wave which has been bandlimited to the Nyquist rate. The second is a clip of music (Blink-182's "Feeling This"), also bandlimited. Both are STFT's over a frame of 1024 samples. The sawtooth DFT is shown in the linear frequency domain to show the simple harmonic relationships and amplitudes. You will notice some humps and notches in what should be a smooth contour; this comes from the fact that the signal is bandlimited. This signal obeys the original Fourier series rules, so you can see defined pulses or spikes at the harmonic intervals with empty spaces between them. The short clip of music is only quasi periodic and contains a rich set of harmonics—there are no gaps and the pulses are all smashed together; in this case it is more meaningful to draw the DFT as a curve and understand that the complete spectrum is the area under the curve. The music DFT is plotted in the log frequency domain, an alternate view of the spectrum that coincides with our perception of frequency. Notice that in both cases, only the positive frequency domain is shown. This is because we know that the negative frequency domain contains mirror image of the same data.

In Chapter's 4, 5 and 7 we will be referring to signals in both the time and frequency domains, so it is good to be familiar with the basic concepts. Our synthesizers will be rendering and manipulating signals based on both time and frequency criteria. In addition, Chapter 7's filter derivations and designs will require a basic understanding of this time/frequency exchange. Now if you go back and look at Figures 1.9–1.13, you can see that they are really stacks and stacks of DFT's lined up in the z-dimension.

> The discrete Fourier transform converts a sampled signal or function *f(nT)* into a signal or function whose dependent variable is complex frequency $j\omega$.

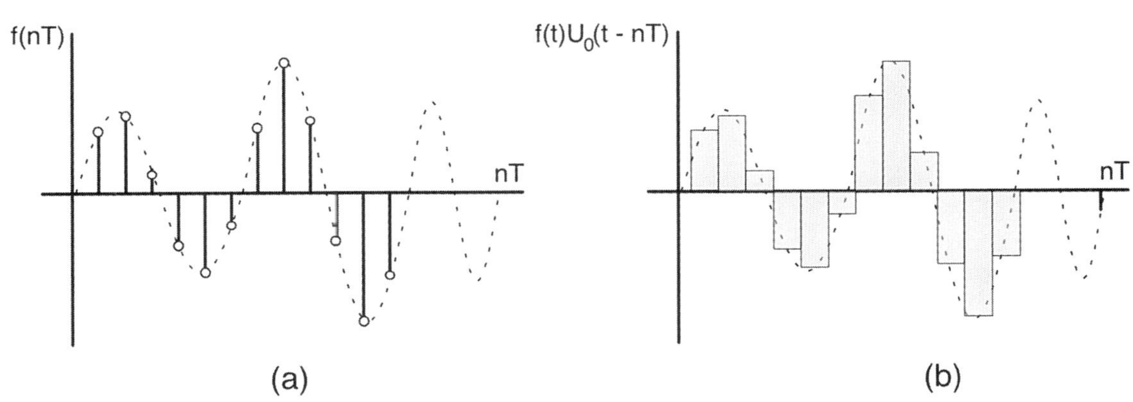

Figure 1.19: (a) An ideally sampled signal with the sample interval T = 0 and (b) the same set of samples with a finite sample period.

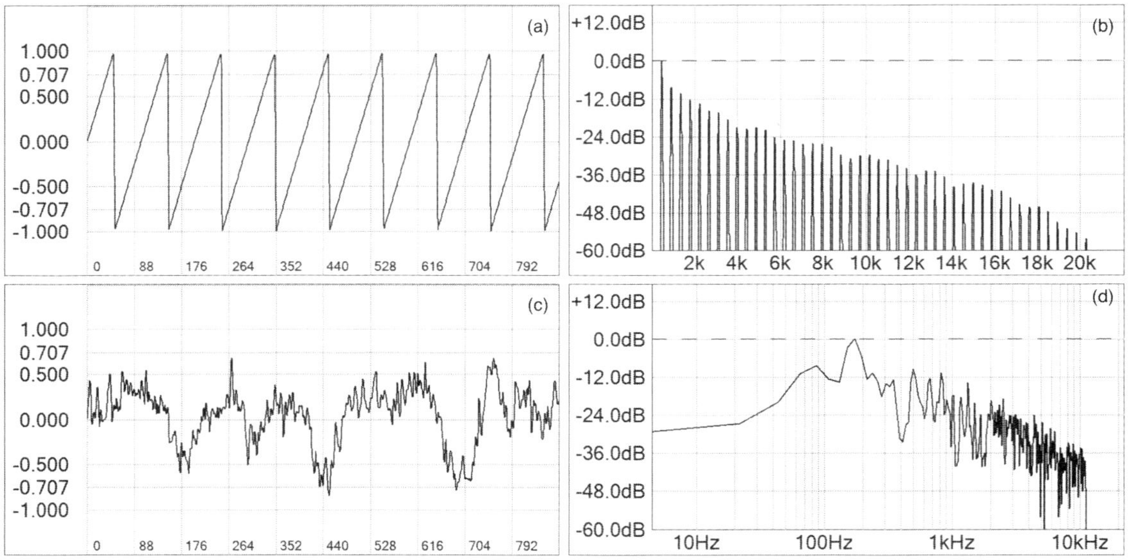

Figure 1.20: (a) A sawtooth or ramp wave at 440 Hz and (b) its spectrum in the linear frequency domain, (c) a short clip of music and (d) its spectrum in the log frequency domain.

The Fast Fourier Transform (FFT) is identical to the DFT in output. The difference is in the way it is computed. Mathematicians J. W. Cooley and John Tukey derived the FFT in 1965 as a way to compute the DFT more efficiently. It takes advantage of similarities in the factors that are used in the calculation to form a recursive solution. In some books, DFT and FFT are used almost interchangeably.

1.12 The Laplace and z-Transforms

Referring back to the Fourier series rules, there are two that might bother you. The signal to be decomposed must:

- have been in existence for all time up to now
- remain in existence for all time—forever

If you remember from Figure 1.16, the sinusoidal components also exist forever in both directions and at the same amplitude. It turns out that the Fourier transform is a specialized case of the Laplace transform. Laplace removed the restrictions regarding the constant amplitudes of the sinusoidal components, which allows for many more input types. In theory, the input signal could have a definite beginning, middle and end, and its frequency components could come and go over time. The Laplace transform replaces the Fourier kernel $e^{-j\omega t}$ with a more general version $e^{-(\sigma+j\omega)t}$ that allows the sinusoidal components to exponentially increase, remain flat (as in Fourier) or exponentially decay in time. The real coefficient σ governs the behavior of the sinusoid's shape in time.

The Laplace transform is:

$$F(s) = \int_{-\infty}^{\infty} f(t)e^{-st}dt \qquad s = \sigma + j\omega \tag{1.12}$$

The discrete version of the Laplace transform is the z-Transform. In the z-Transform, you let $z = e^{sT}$ where T is the sample period; we need to do this to get out of the continuous time domain t and into the discrete time domain nT. This yields:

$$\begin{aligned} F(z) &= \int_{-\infty}^{\infty} f_s(t)e^{-st}dt\Big|_{z=e^{sT}} \\ &= \sum_{n=-\infty}^{\infty} f(nT)z^{-n} \end{aligned} \tag{1.13}$$

The z-Transform is a kind of place-keeping or substitution transform that is clever—by making the simple substitution of $z = e^{sT}$ we arrive at a sum involving a rational function in z instead of the irrational e^{sT}. This means the z-Transform produces a simple polynomial or ratio of polynomials in z that obeys all the laws of polynomial math, making it much easier to work with. It can also operate over a fixed duration rather than an infinite period.

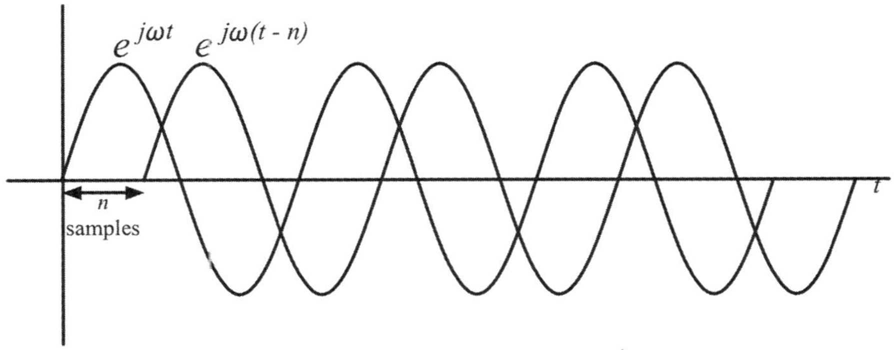

Figure 1.21: Two sinusoids with one delayed by *n* samples.

Consider the z^{-n} terms—what do they mean? Using polynomial math:

$$
\begin{aligned}
(x^m)^n &= x^{mn} \\
z^{-1} &= (e^{sT})^{-1} = e^{-sT} \\
z^{-2} &= (e^{sT})^{-2} = e^{-s2T} \\
z^{-3} &= (e^{sT})^{-3} = e^{-s3T} \\
&etc...
\end{aligned}
\tag{1.14}
$$

The T, 2T and 3T values represent 1, 2 and 3 sample intervals. The negative sign denotes them as past sample intervals; a positive sign indicates future sample intervals that are not realizable in real-time, so you won't see them in this book. When we use the z-Transform to design and evaluate filters in Chapter 4, we will let the real part $\sigma = 0$. This allows us to evaluate the frequency response on our real frequency axis. In this case, the z^{-n} term represents n-samples of delay, and multiplying a signal against it will delay that signal by n-samples. This is astonishing because it turns the operation of delaying a signal by some number of samples into multiplication by a simple term. To understand this, consider the two sinusoids in Figure 1.21. One of them is delayed by n samples.

If we can describe the first sinusoid as $e^{j\omega t}$ then the delayed version would be $e^{j\omega(t-n)}$. Why? Because at time t = 0, the first sinusoid starts, and its complex value is e^{j0}. Then at time $t = n$ samples later, the second sinusoid starts. Its complex value must be the same as the first at this starting point, e^{j0}. The only way this will happen is if we modify the exponent as $e^{j\omega(t-n)}$, so when $t = n$, the result is e^{j0}. Looking at the $e^{j\omega(t-n)}$ term and remembering the polynomial behavior of the exponential, we can write the following:

$$e^{j\omega(t-n)} = e^{j\omega t}e^{-j\omega n}$$

The delayed signal equals the original signal $e^{j\omega t}$ multiplied by $e^{-j\omega n}$—this is really interesting. The operation of delay has been reduced to the simple operation of multiplication. Even more amazing is that the multiplication term is devoid of the dependent variable t. So you can see that when we let the real part of s equal 0 (that is, $\sigma = 0$) then e^{-snT} becomes $e^{-j\omega nT}$ where n is the number of samples delayed and T is the sample interval. Normalizing so that $T = 1$ (meaning a 1 Hz sample rate), the two terms are synonymous; e^{-sn} becomes $e^{-j\omega n}$. Therefore, multiplying a signal by z^{-n} delays it by n samples.

> The z-Transform converts a sampled signal or function whose dependent variable is samples-in-time, nT into a signal or function whose dependent variable is the complex variable $z = a + jb$.

it might look daunting at first, but you can learn to take the Laplace and z-transform of block diagrams by inspection using just a few rules. We will discuss these further in Chapter 4.

1.13 Aliasing

In our oscillator (and some filter) designs, we will be forever fighting against aliasing. In a digital audio system with input and output, aliasing occurs if you do not properly band limit the input signal. A consequence of sampling a signal is that its spectrum is replicated up and down the frequency axis. This is shown in Figure 1.22 where a properly bandlimited signal is sampled at some rate f_s.

Figure 1.23 shows what happens if the sampled signal is not bandlimited to $f_s/2$. In this case, it was improperly bandlimited to a higher frequency. The skirts of the spectra overlap.

The term alias is used since the aliased frequencies are "in disguise." For example, suppose the sample rate is 44,100 Hz and Nyquist is 22,050 Hz and the input signal contains 22,100 Hz. This frequency is 50 Hz *above* Nyquist. The resulting aliased frequency that spills

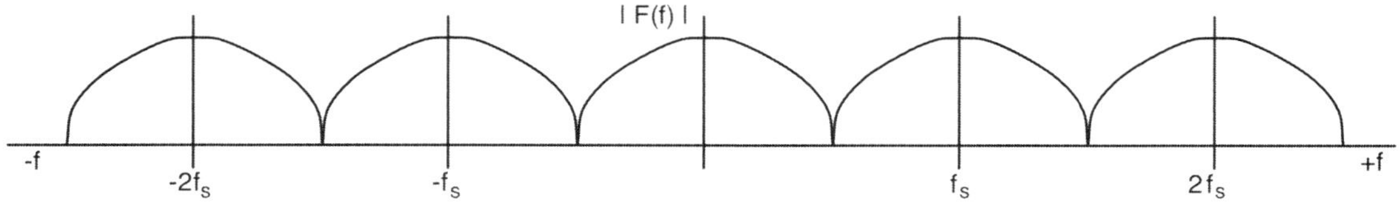

Figure 1.22: A sampled signal produces a set of spectral images replicated around multiples of the sample frequency.

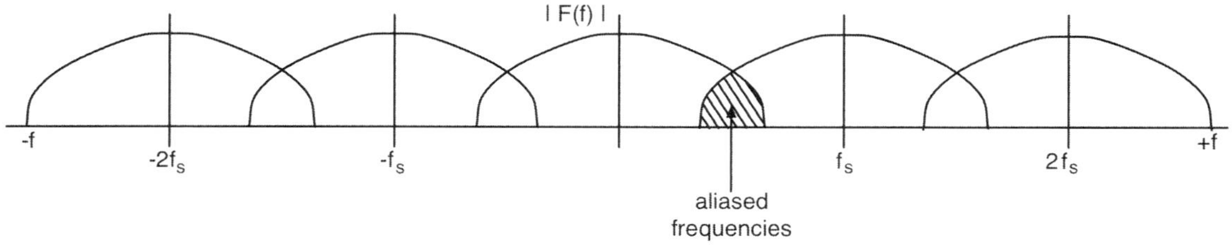

Figure 1.23: An improperly bandlimited signal's spectral replicas overlap; this overlap produces aliasing.

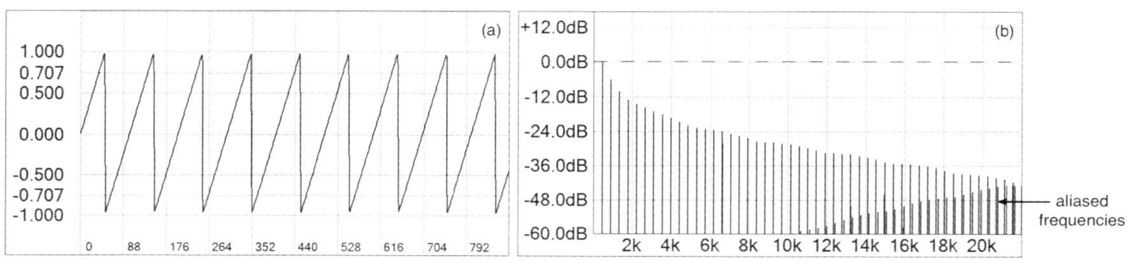

Figure 1.24: (a) A quasi bandlimited sawtooth waveform and (b) its spectrum.

down into our normal spectrum is 22050–50 = 22,000 Hz. The original frequency is now disguised as 22,000 Hz. You can see how part of the first replica's negative frequencies are folded over into the positive frequency portion of the normal spectrum centered around 0 Hz.

So far, this aliasing has been blamed on improper band limiting on the input signal. But we are designing synthesizers and have no input so why should we care? The answer is that we are completely able to mathematically create waveforms that alias. In other words, we can create waveforms that could never have made it past the input lowpass filter on a normal digital system with both input and output. One of the types of oscillators we'll design is called a quasi bandlimited oscillator. The idea is that we will allow a bit of aliasing as long as the aliased frequency components are far away from the fundamental and low in amplitude. Figure 1.24 shows the time domain response and spectrum of a quasi bandlimited sawtooth waveform. You can clearly see the aliased frequencies that have spilled down into our spectrum. If you examine Figure 1.20(a–b) with the bandlimited wavetable, you can see that, although the time domain plots are indistinguishable, the frequency domain plots tell a different story. In this particular case the fundamental is at 440 Hz, and we see the last aliased component above −60 dB at about 10 kHz.

In the preceding sections, we've barely scratched the surface of DSP theory, as a complete treatise on the subject is outside the scope of the book and covered in scores of other texts. This book has been designed to try to minimize the math required to understand the operation of the functional components in our synths. In fact, when we get into Virtual Analog (VA) filters, you will find the math to be refreshingly simple—there is no calculus involved!

Bibliography

Apple, Inc. "Logic 9 Express Instruments." Accessed June 2014, http://manuals.info.apple.com/MANUALS/1000/MA1214/en_US/Logic_Express_9_Instruments.pdf

Moore, Richard. 1990. *Elements of Computer Music*, Chap. 3. Eaglewood Cliffs: Prentice-Hall.

Roads, Curtis. 1996. *The Computer Music Tutorial*, Chap. 2. Cambridge: The MIT Press.

Sound on Sound Magazine. "Synth Secrets." Accessed June 2014, http://www.soundonsound.com/sos/allsynthsecrets.htm

synthmuseum.com. "Thaddeus Cahill's Teleharmonium." Accessed June 2014, http://www.synthmuseum.com/magazine/0102jw.html

Very Approachable DSP Books

Ifeachor, Emmanuel C. and Jervis, Barrie W. 1993. *Digital Signal Processing, A Practical Approach*. Menlo Park: Addison Wesley.

Pirkle, Will. 2012. *Designing Audio Effects Plug-Ins in C++*, Chap. 8. Burlington: Focal Press.

Steiglitz, Ken. 1996. *A DSP Primer with Applications to Digital Audio and Computer Music*. Menlo Park: Addison Wesley.

CHAPTER 2

Writing Plug-ins

A plug-in is a software component that interfaces with another piece of software called the client in order to extend the client's capabilities in some way. In order to start writing plug-ins, you need to know how the plug-in connects to and communicates with the client. Windows plug-ins are packaged as Dynamic-Link Libraries, or DLL files. Apple plug-ins are packaged in a bundle, which is configured as a component. The plug-ins in this book are designed for three different platforms: RackAFX (Windows), VST3 (Windows) and Audio Units (MacOS). The synthesizer core objects that you design in Chapters 4–8 are virtually identical across the three platforms with only minor differences in the file opening and reading operations for the sample-based synths DigiSynth, VectorSynth and AniSynth. However, the base plug-in core is vastly different. This book does not use any C++ wrappers to convert one plug-in to another. All plug-ins are written natively, using only the tools and components that come with each platform's Software Development Kit (SDK). No third party tools or libraries are used, even for opening and reading files. In this way, you are learning the direct implementation of each plug-in on the platform that you choose. Nothing is hidden or obscured behind libraries or frameworks.

The plug-in core is the code you need to implement that deals with the details of communicating with the client, setting up a rendering system and handling a Graphical User Interface (GUI or UI). While the implementation details are very different, the fundamental theory of operation is the same for all three (and practically any other plug-in format out there). When you learn to fly, you find that the fundamentals of pitch, drag, yaw and roll are identical for the tiniest trainer to a jet fighter; however, the interfaces you deal with are very different. In this chapter, we start with the similarities and introduce the RackAFX plug-in API and philosophy. Next we describe the VST3 and AU platforms in depth. If you have never written a plug-in we strongly suggest starting with RackAFX—in fact we still start every project in RackAFX and then port them out to VST3 and AU after debugging the core.

2.1 Dynamic-Link Libraries

C++ compilers include sets of pre-compiled libraries of functions for you to use in your projects. Perhaps the most common of these is the math library. If you try to use the *sin()* method you will typically get an error when you compile stating that "sin() is not defined." In order to use this function, you need to link to the library that contains it. The way you do this is by placing *#include <math.h>* at the top of your file. When you do this, you are statically linking to the *math.h* library, a pre-compiled set of math functions packaged in a special file called a Library (.lib) in Windows or a *Framework* in MacOS. Static linking is also called implicit linking. When the compiler comes across a math function, it replaces the function call with the precompiled code from the library. In this way, the extra code is compiled into your executable. You cannot un-compile the math functions.

To build a component that extends the application's functionality after that application has been compiled and sold to the customer requires a different strategy. The solution is to link to the functions at run-time. This means that these precompiled functions will exist in a separate file that the client will know about and communicate with but only after it starts running. This kind of linking is called dynamic linking or explicit linking. The file that contains the new functions is called a Dynamic-Link Library or DLL. In Windows, the file typically uses the extension *.dll* however in VST3, you rename the extension *.vst3*. In AU, the DLL extension is *.component*.

In order to use the code in a DLL the client must perform two activities:

1. load the DLL into the process address space
2. establish the communication mechanism for functions to be called from the DLL

We won't worry about these client-side details, but it is important to understand how C++ and base classes play a role in plug-in development today.

2.2 C and C++ Style DLLs

A DLL written in the C programming language consists of a set of stand-alone functions. There is no *main*() function. The functions can be defined and implemented in one file or can be broken into an interface file (*.h*) and implementation file (*.c*)—either way, the

DLL performs a set of isolated functions. A problem with using the C programming language to write a DLL is the persistence of data. In C (and C++) the curly brackets ("{}") define the scope of a function. Any variable declared inside a function, after the first open curly bracket ("}") is only defined for the duration of the function. After the closing curly bracket ("}") is encountered, the variable ceases to exist.

A fundamental problem is that the data declared inside a function cannot persist from one call to the next. One solution involves using global variables, which is generally frowned upon. Another solution is for the DLL to dynamically declare a data structure that will hold all the persistent variables and then pass a pointer to this data structure back to the client to maintain. This is very similar to the way that callback functions work. During subsequent calls to the DLL, the client passes the pointer back to the DLL as a function argument so that it may operate on the persistent data. When the DLL is no longer needed, it clears the memory by deleting the structure.

In the C++ programming language, the *class* data-type defines an object that is a collection of member variables and member functions that can operate on those variables or other data. By packaging a plug-in as a C++ class, you get several advantages; first, all of the benefits of C++ (inheritance, encapsulation, polymorphism, etc...) are available during the coding process. Second, rather than allocating a data structure and returning a pointer to that, the DLL can create a new instance of the plug-in object and pass a pointer to the object to the client. The function that the client calls is the creation function. With a plug-in pointer, the client can simply call functions on the object—it does not have to communicate with the DLL again until it is time to either unload the DLL, or better yet, create another instance of the plug-in object. This leads to a third advantage over the C-based DLL: the client can create multiple plug-ins easily. The DLL can serve-up multiple instances of the object. Sometimes, the plug-in is referred to as a server and this becomes another kind of client-server system.

2.3 The Application Programming Interface (API)

In order for the client-server scheme to work, both the client and DLL/plug-in must agree on the naming of the functions. This includes the creation function and all of the functions that the client will be able to call on the plug-in object. The plug-in might implement other functions that the client doesn't know about, but they must agree on a basic set of them. Additionally, rules must be set up to define the sequence of function calls; the plug-in's author (that's you) will need to understand how the client intends on using the object. The client must make sure that once it establishes these rules, it adheres to them in future versions to avoid breaking the plug-in. On the other hand, the plug-in must also promise to implement the basic required functions properly to make the plug-in work and not crash the client. So, you can see that there is an implied *contract* between the client and DLL server. This contract is the Application Programming Interface or API. It is a definition of the functions an object must implement to be considered a proper plug-in, as well as any additional functions that may be called or overridden. It defines the function prototypes and describes how the functions will be called and used. The client manufacturer writes the API and makes it available to programmers who want to create plug-ins for that target client.

C++ is especially useful here. Since the plug-in is an instance of a C++ object, the client manufacturer can specify that the plug-in is a derived class of a special base class that the manufacturer defines. The base class is made to be abstract, containing virtual functions that the derived class overrides. These virtual functions provide the common functionality of the plug-in. There are two options here:

- the manufacturer defines the base class as abstract then provides default implementations of the virtual functions. Typically, the default implementations do nothing but return a success code. The plug-in authors then override whichever methods they need. For example, the plug-in might not care about responding to MIDI messages, so the default implementation of the MIDI function will suffice.
- the manufacturer defines the base class as a pure abstract base class by making one or more of the virtual functions pure virtual functions. A pure abstract base class cannot be instantiated; only derived classes which implement all the pure virtual functions may be instantiated. This forms a binding contract between the plug-in developer and the client manufacturer since the derived class won't work properly unless it implements the pure abstract functions that the client specifies.

RackAFX, VST3 and AU all use the first method, supplying default implementations for all virtual functions. As the plug-in author, you only override the functions you need. But what are the typical required functions and were do they come from?

2.4 API Function Comparisons

Although the various plug-in APIs are different in their implementations, they share a common set of basic operations for making a synthesizer plug-in. Table 2.1 lists the common functionality while Tables 2.2–2.4 detail the responsibility for each function.

You can see that each platform is different in implementation details and complexity; VST3 certainly wins the prize for most number of supporting files, but you can see that only two functions (*setActive()* and *process()*) handle most of the core functionality. In fact, the *process()* function becomes so large that we split it out into three functions. In RackAFX and VST3, there is no GUI code to write since we can use simple drag-and-drop editors, but you will have to write your own GUI in AU (and it's in the Objective-C programming language). The MIDI message handling is simple in RackAFX and AU but complicated in VST3.

Table 2.1: The typical core operations that all plug-in APIs share.

Function	Description
Construction/Dynamic Memory Allocation	called once when the plug-in is instantiated, this function implements any one-time-only initialization, usually consisting of initializing the plug-in variables, GUI and allocating memory buffers dynamically
Destruction	called when the plug-in is to be destroyed, this function de-allocates any memory declared in the One-Time-Initialization and/or in other functions that allocate memory; if there are any owned child-windows, the plug-in destroys them here
Per-run initialization	called once before an audio session starts; this function is usually used to flush buffers containing old data or initialize any variables such as counters that operate on a per-play basis
Render Audio	the function which synthesizes the audio and delivers it to the client
MIDI Event Handling	functions that handle MIDI messages including note on and off, pitch bend, continuous controllers and sustain pedal
GUI Control Changes	functions to deal with changes to the GUI controls
GUI Setup/Instantiation	functions to deal with the lifecycle of the GUI

Table 2.2: Core files and functions for RackAFX, VST3 and AU.

Plug-In Core Files and Functions			
Detail	**RackAFX**	**VST3**	**AU**
Base Class	*CPlugIn*	*AudioEffect*	*AUInstrumentBase*
Supporting files, not including base class	*RackAFXDLL.h RackAFXDLL.cpp*	127 additional files	68 additional files
Dynamic Allocation	constructor	*SetActive()*	constructor
Dynamic Destruction	destructor	*SetActive()*	destructor and *CleanUp()*
Per-run initialization	*prepareForPlay()*	*SetActive()*	*Initialize()*
Render Audio	*processAudioFrame()*	*process()*	*Render()*
GUI Control Changes	*userInterfaceChange()*	*process()*	*Render()*

Table 2.3: MIDI functions for RackAFX, VST3 and AU.

MIDI Functions			
MIDI Message	**RackAFX**	**VST3**	**AU**
Note On	*midiNoteOn()*	*process()*	*StartNote()*
Note Off	*midiNoteOff()*	*process()*	*StopNote()*
Pitch Bend	*midiPitchBend()*	*process()*	*HandlePitchWheel()*
Mod Wheel	*midiModWheel()*	*process()*	*HandleControlChange()*
All other MIDI Messages	*midiMessage()*	*process()*	*HandleControlChange()* *HandleMidiEvent()*

Table 2.4: GUI functions for RackAFX, VST3 and AU.

GUI Setup and Maintenance			
Detail	**RackAFX**	**VST3**	**AU**
Declare/Describe Controls, set limits and defaults	done with an easy to use *Control Designer*—you fill in a parameter form that synthesizes the code for you	you must write the code yourself	you must write the code yourself
Initialize Controls	automatically written for you	you must write the code in *initialize()*	you must write the code in *Initialize()* *GetParameterInfo()* *GetParameterValue String()*
Write control values to file (presets)	automatically written for you	you must write the code in *getState()*	automatically written for you
Read control values from file (presets)	automatically written for you	you must write the code in *setState()*	automatically written for you
Declare/Create GUI	automatically written for you	you must write the code in *createView()*	GUI Class Factory that you design and write
Graphical Design of GUI	Drag-and-Drop GUI editor built into RackAFX	Drag-and-Drop GUI editor via the VST3 Host	InterfaceBuilder in XCode

Table 2.5: Comparison of the three platforms in this book.

Platform	Pros	Cons
RackAFX	• simplest API with very few files and no GUI programming • RackAFX writes some of the code for you • supports multiple Visual Studio compilers including the free *Express* versions • runs with very little system overhead for good polyphony count • highly portable projects that do not require a specific folder hierarchy • debug through RackAFX itself • Vector Joystick programmer is built-in	• only runs in Windows • for ported projects you must write and maintain your own GUI; can't use drag-and-drop editor • GUI controls are limited in appearance (fixed number of bitmap options, can not add your own graphics files)
VST3	• virtually identical code for Windows and MacOS versions (**though this book only covers the Windows version**) • can use VSTGUI library and editor for reasonably simple GUI design • VSTGUI library allows you to customize your own GUI controls with skins/bitmaps • VSTGUI library includes many types of controls • highly flexible and safe thanks to COM implementation	• most complicated API • requires knowledge of Microsoft's Common Object Model (COM) • large number of supporting files to maintain • SDK creates a directory hierarchy that is difficult to modify • must have a Professional version of Visual Studio • has moderate system overhead, reducing polyphony a bit • debug via a VST3 Client that you must also purchase • a few DAWs do not support VST3 (yet) • Visual Studio projects are complex; difficult to copy and rename a project • no built-in Vector Joystick programmer; you write the code for it
AU	• clean and relatively easy API • uses XCode (free from Apple) • runs with very little system overhead for good polyphony count • currently the de facto standard for Apple Logic software but also supported in other clients like Ableton Live • has similarities with iOS for iPhone/iPad development • highly portable projects that do not require a specific folder hierarchy • easy to copy and rename projects	• only runs in MacOS • is slightly different for OS 10.6 and earlier (**this book only supports OS 10.7 and later but the plug-ins are backward compatible**) • requires that you write your own GUI code in Objective- C (for native coding) • flat Cocoa namespace requires renaming of GUI objects for each project • build rules are quirky and require precise settings that are easy to forget/mess up • debug via an AU host that you must also purchase • no built-in Vector Joystick programmer; you write the code for it

In the sections that follow, many of the deeper implementation details of the functions are left out. The details change as the book progresses and are fully explained on a chapter-by-chapter basis starting with Chapter 5, where you begin your first training-synth called NanoSynth. We will also go more in depth on making changes to the GUIs in later chapters.

As with any programming book, you need to implement the projects before you really start to understand the API. This chapter will show you the underlying architecture and some of the code while future chapters will reveal the lower level details.

2.5 The RackAFX Philosophy and API

The fundamental idea behind the RackAFX software is to provide a platform for rapidly developing real-time audio signal processing plug-ins with a minimum of coding, especially with regard to the User Interface. In fact, most of the details of the connection between the RackAFX plug-in and the RackAFX UI screen are hidden from the developer so that he or she may concentrate more on the audio signal processing part and less on the UI details.

The RackAFX API specifies that the plug-in must be written in the C++ language and therefore takes advantage of the Base Class/ Derived Class paradigm. The RackAFX API specifies a base class called *CPlugIn* from which all plug-ins are derived.

- RackAFX will automatically write C++ code for you that creates a blank plug-in by creating a derived class of *CPlugIn*
- as you add and remove controls from the control surface, the RackAFX client will automatically update your C++ code accordingly
- this lets you focus on the signal processing and not the UI, making it a great tool for both rapid plug-in development and for teaching how to write plug-ins
- after learning RackAFX, you will be able to understand other companies' APIs and learn to write plug-ins in their formats quickly and easily

- because the plug-in objects you create are written in C++, you can easily move them around between other APIs or computer platforms. You can wrap them to work easily in other systems too

You only need to implement ten functions in RackAFX to create a synthesizer plug-in:

- constructor
- destructor
- *prepareForPlay()*
- *processAudioFrame()*
- *userInterfaceChange()*
- *midiNoteOn()*
- *midiNoteOff()*
- *midiPitchBend()*
- *midiModWheel()*
- *midiMessage()*

2.6 Writing RackAFX Plug-ins

Simply stated, RackAFX is the simplest, leanest, easiest way to write a real-time processing plug-in in Windows. One of my grad students once said "you write five functions and suddenly you feel like a DSP god." This is also useful for experimenting with an algorithm you find in a book or on the internet—you can have a working prototype up and running in the same amount of time it would take just to create the VST3 or AU skeleton code. Unlike VST3 and AU, RackAFX is not only your plug-in client, but it also helps you setup your projects and writes a lot of tedious code for you. In fact, you don't have to write a single line of GUI code. In VST3 and AU, you start a new project in the Visual Studio or XCode compiler. However, in RackAFX, you start your project directly in the RackAFX software, which then launches and to some extent controls Visual Studio for you. RackAFX runs in tandem with Visual Studio.

Requirements:

- Windows OS (WindowsXP, Vista, Windows7, Windows8)
- RackAFX—free from http://www.willpirkle.com/synthbook/
- Visual Studio 2008, 2010, 2012 and 2013 Professional or Express versions (there is no benefit to the Professional version unless you want to design a GUI outside of RackAFX)

Each of your synthesizer plug-ins will become a C++ object named *CNanoSynth*, *CMiniSynth*, *CDigiSynth*, *CVectorSynth*, *CAniSynth* and *CDXSynth*. These are all derived from the *CPlugIn* base class. The RackAFX plug-in designer will help you write your plug-in. When you create a new RackAFX project, it will set up a new Visual C++ Project folder for you and populate your project with all the files you will need. It will automatically create a new derived class based on the name of your project. When you setup GUI controls like sliders and buttons, it will write and maintain the code for you. You will be switching back and forth between RackAFX and your C++ compiler. There are buttons on the RackAFX GUI that will let you jump to the compiler as well as launch compiler functions like rebuilding and debugging. You use RackAFX to maintain your GUI and your compiler to write the signal processing code. RackAFX also handles MIDI messages and is actually very MIDI-ized. It delivers MIDI messages to your plug-in and interfaces with your MIDI controllers; if you don't have a MIDI controller, there is a built-in piano-control; however, you really need a hardware MIDI controller to exercise all the controller options like continuous controllers and sustain pedal.

Building the DLL

RackAFX sets up your compiler to deliver your freshly built DLL to the /PlugIns folder in the RackAFX Application Directory. If you ever want to see, move or delete a DLL, you can find this folder by using the menu item *PlugIn->Open PlugIns Folder* or *Start Menu->All Programs->RackAFX->PlugIns Folder*. After a successful build, you use RackAFX to test and debug the plug-in. You tell RackAFX to load the DLL and create your plug-in. The client needs to handle four basic operations during the lifecycle of your component:

- creation of the plug-in
- maintaining the UI
- rendering audio from the plug-in
- sending MIDI messages to the plug-in
- destruction of the plug-in

Creation

When you load a plug-in in RackAFX, you are actually passing the system a path to the DLL you've created. RackAFX uses an OS function call to load the DLL into its process space. Once the DLL is loaded, RackAFX first runs a compatibility test, then requests a pointer to the creation method called *createObject()*. It uses this pointer to call the method, and the DLL returns a newly created instance of your plug-in cast as the *CPlugIn** base class type. From that point on, the RackAFX client can call any of the base class methods on your object. Figure 2.1 shows the flow of operation during the creation phase.

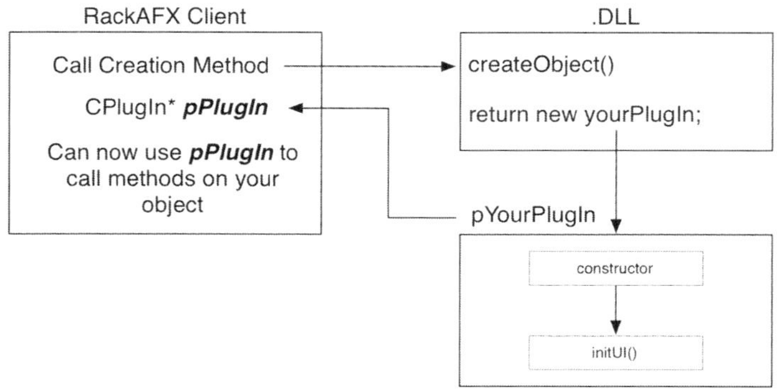

Figure 2.1: The *new* operator in *createObject()* dynamically creates your plug-in, which calls your constructor; the constructor in turn calls *initUI()* to create and initialize the user controls.

Your constructor is where all your variables are initialized. The very first line of code in the constructor has been written for you; it calls *initUI()* which is a method that handles the creation and setup of your GUI controls. You never modify the *initUI()* method; RackAFX maintains this code for you.

Destruction

When the user unloads the DLL either manually or by loading another plug-in, the client first deletes the plug-in object from memory, which calls the destructor. Any dynamically declared variables or buffers need to be deleted here. After destruction, the client unloads the DLL from the process space.

The GUI

RackAFX uses a two-phase approach to GUI design. The first phase is prototyping—here, you create a set of user controls using the main interface consisting of slider controls, buttons and a cool LCD control (more on that in a moment). You don't really need to be overly careful about the ordering of the controls. The user-interface is not flashy; it's a set of rows of sliders and buttons, but it allows you to rapidly prototype your plug-in. When you set up GUI elements on the Prototype Panel, RackAFX adds member variables to the *.h* file of your derived plug-in class. Each slider or button-group controls one variable in your code. You setup each control with minimum, maximum and initial values as well as the variable name and data type. As the user moves a control, RackAFX calculates the new variable's value and delivers it to your plug-in, automatically updating it in real-time. In some cases, this is all you will need and there is nothing left to write. In other cases, you will need to perform more calculations or logic processing in addition to just changing the control variable.

After your plug-in is completed and tested, you move to the second phase by switching to the GUI Designer Panel. Here, you drag and drop controls onto a blank GUI surface, and you link them to the various variables that you set up in the prototyping phase. You can also customize the controls to a reasonable extent, changing the sizes, bitmaps, colors, fonts and other GUI attributes. You can re-arrange the controls however you wish. It is not uncommon to provide the user with a more limited final GUI than you implemented in the prototyping phase—you may decide you do not want the user to have control over some voicing aspects of your plug-in. Many companies go out of their way to prevent the user from making really horrible sounds by limiting the controls and the ranges on them.

Building and Testing

Finally, you will build the DLL then find and fix any issues. After the build succeeds, you can load it into the RackAFX client. You can use the built-in MIDI piano control (limited) or any Windows compatible MIDI input device (recommended) to generate the MIDI messages needed to test the plug-in.

Creating and Saving Presets

The presets are created and maintained on the main RackAFX UI. After you load your plug-in you can move the controls as you like and then save them as a preset. You use the *Save Preset* button on the toolbar. The presets will be saved inside a file until the next time you compile your plug-in; after that, the presets will be built into the DLL. You can add, modify or delete the presets any time the plug-in is loaded.

2.7 Setting Up RackAFX

Start the RackAFX software. You will start in Prototype View where you will see a blank control surface shown in Figure 2.2. Your GUI may look slightly different or have different background images.

The control surface is what you use to create your user interface. It is full of assignable controls you can connect to your plug-in's variables. The surface consists of:

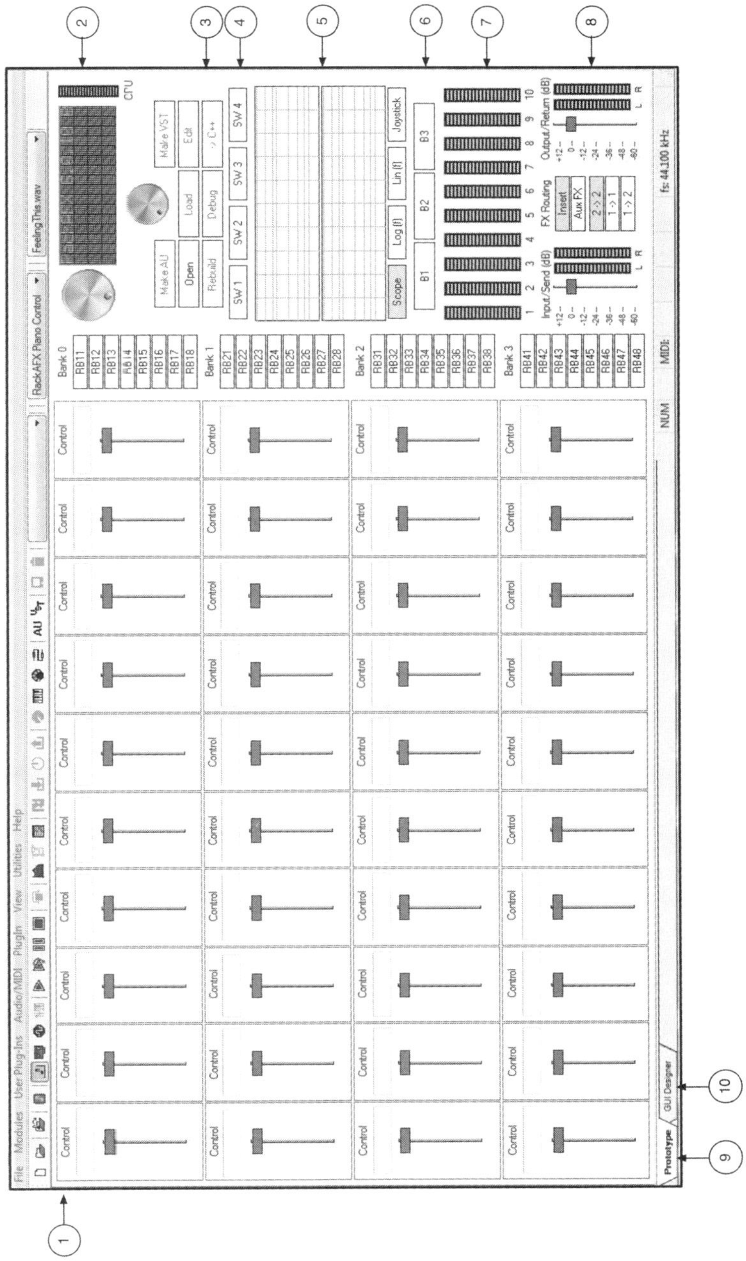

Figure 2.2: When you start RackAFX, it opens in Prototype View. It features the control surface and plug-in routing controls.

1. 40 assignable sliders (continuous controls)
2. universal LCD control with 1024 more continuous controls inside
3. project controls (open, load, edit, rebuild, debug, jump-to-C++)
4. 4 on-off 2-state switches
5. mini-analyzer with scope and spectrum analyzer and joystick control (for vector synths)
6. assignable buttons
7. 10 assignable LED meters
8. input/output controls
9. prototype tab: the main GUI
10. GUI Designer tab: opens the designer for editing; you must have GUI controls declared first

The menu and toolbar consist of two parts; the left and right side. The left side implements the majority of the software functionality while the right side maintains lists.

Menu Items

- **File**: manage projects by creating, editing or clearing the project
- **Modules**: built-in plug-ins that you can use for analysis and testing

- **User plug-ins**: each new plug-in you design gets loaded into this menu; you can audition or show off your plug-in in a stand alone fashion
- **Audio**: manage all audio commands
- **Plug-in**: tools for loading/unloading and presets
- **View**: access the different windows
- **Utilities**: AU and VST template generators
- **Help**: help information

Toolbar Items

1. **New project**: open project folder, open audio file
2. **Setup low-level audio**
3. **Audio input mode**: file, analog audio input, oscillator, user oscillator/synth
4. **Transport controls**: play, loop, pause, stop, bypass
5. **Additional windows**: analyzer, block diagram, status window
6. **Plug-in tools**: synchronize code, load, reset, unload
7. **GUI windows**: custom GUI, RackAFX MIDI piano
8. **Rescan midi and audio ports**
9. **AU and VST template generators**
10. **Presets**: save, delete

On the right are the drop-down boxes that let you select presets, MIDI input devices and files to play. When developing audio effect plug-ins, you use audio files to play through and test them. For our synth projects, we won't need to play audio files, but the capability is there if you need it.

Finally, there is a bank of buttons that allow you to manipulate your projects as well as control the C++ compiler shown in Figure 2.5. The buttons are set up as follows:

- **Open**: open an existing Project
- **Load**: load/unload the DLL from process space
- **Edit**: change an existing project's settings
- **Rebuild**: rebuild the project
- **Debug**: launch the debugger
- **->C++**: jump to the C++ compiler and restore if minimized
- **Make AU**: port the project out to an AU XCode project
- **Make VST**: port the project out to a VST Visual Studio project

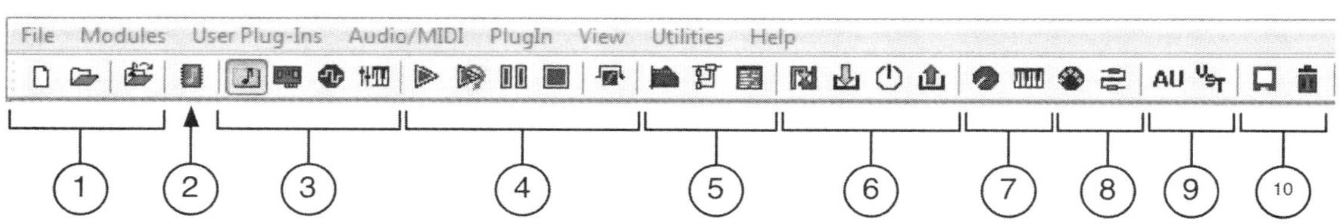

Figure 2.3: The Menu and Toolbar on the left handle most of your plug-in development.

Figure 2.4: The drop-down boxes on the right let you store and recall Presets, choose a MIDI input Controller, and keep track of the audio files you have been using.

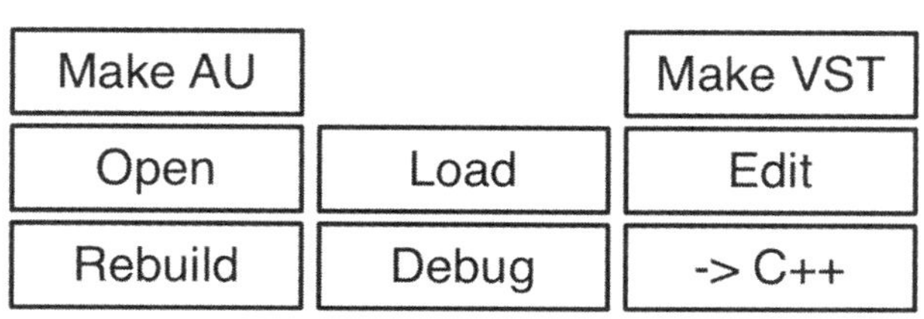

Figure 2.5: The project/compiler buttons make it easy to work with projects and control your compiler.

Setup Preferences

Before you start working on projects, take some time to configure your preferences. This is where you will choose your C++ compiler and set your default directories. Choose View->Preferences to get the interface.

In the preferences you need to:

1. Choose your default folders for projects, WAV files and default WAV file. You can use whatever directory you want for your project folder, and you can also open projects from any other folder at any time; the default is simply for conveniently grouping all your projects together. You can also set the default folders for porting your projects to AU and VST.
2. Choose a Visual C++ compiler.
3. Set the C++ options—Enable C++ Control/Switching should be left on for all but the most advanced users. C++ Control/Switching allows RackAFX to control Visual Studio, save files, launch the debugger, etc.
4. Setup the edit options when entering information in the GUI slider/button dialogs.

Notice the last checkbox in area (3) that automatically names your object with a "C" to match the Hungarian notation in this book as explained in the Forward—see http://www.willpirkle.com/synthbook/ for an explanation of Hungarian notation.

Starting a New Project

For RackAFX you have two options for starting a new project: download one of my sample projects or start a new project from scratch and develop it yourself. Unlike VST3 and AU, starting a new project is simple and takes less than 30 seconds. I suggest starting each project from scratch, but the projects are available if you prefer starting with code. There are a set of downloadable projects for each synth:

- GUI only—the GUI is already done for you and variables declared, but you have to do the rest, including adding the additional files for each project
- Full—the whole project inclusive; we don't recommend simply compiling someone else's code as a learning method, however having the full code allows you to not only check your own work but also step through the code in debug mode so you can see how the client interacts—in short, the full projects are excellent for helping you debug and understand your own projects-in-progress

Unlike VST3 and AU, RackAFX will create your compiler project for you. Use the *File->New Project* or *<Ctrl> N* to start a new project. A form appears for you to enter the project name.

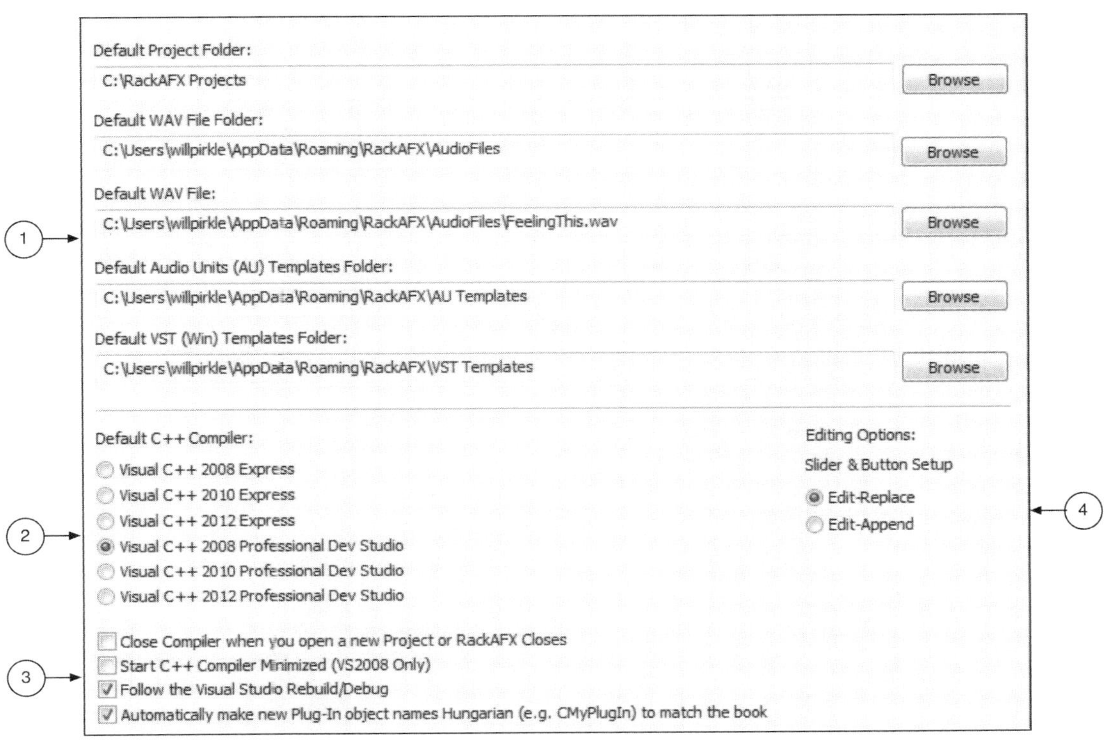

Figure 2.6: The preferences interface.

For the MiniSynth, you would start out with the New Project dialog in Figure 2.7.

In this case, you name the project MiniSynth and check the Hungarian notation box in *View->Preferences*. RackAFX creates the Visual Studio project for you and copies all the core files you need. The Visual Studio project files will be packaged in a folder with your <Project Name>, in this case MiniSynth. The C++ object will be packaged in the files *MiniSynth.h* and *MiniSynth.cpp*. The object will be named *CMiniSynth*. Make sure you check the "Output Only Synthesizer plug-in" and if you forget, you can always come back and change it using *File->Edit Project* or the *<Edit>* button.

> The Project Name will become the name of your C++ class. So, you need to be careful about using a name that is a legal C++ object name. Also, if you check the Hungarian notation box in preferences, a "C" will be added to the name of your object.

The synth projects in this book all require additional files—a few that we provide and a bunch that you will write in the next few chapters. You will always need the file *synthfunctions.h*, which you can get from the website. The other files are your C++ synth objects that implement oscillators, filters and envelope generators. To add the extra files, you need to copy them into your project folder (here it is MiniSynth) then right click on the solution and choose *Add->Existing Items* and browse and select all the new files. You can then use Filters in Visual Studio to organize the files.

So to recap, when you work on a synth project you will create a new project and then manually add the extra files you need to Visual Studio. In each of the project chapters you will get a list of these additional files.

2.8 Designing the User Interface in the Prototype Phase

Each project starts out with a GUI table that lists all the user interface controls and underlying parameters that they control. In RackAFX, each control is automatically connected to a variable that you define. RackAFX writes the code for you. In VST3 and AU, you must manually define each of your controls programmatically. In RackAFX, you use the control designer instead. When you create a new project or open an existing one and the compiler has started and is active, you will then be able to add user controls. The paradigm is to right-click on a control to set it up or alter it. All the synth projects will contain three basic types of controls:

- continuous controls—values that are continuously adjustable generating *float*, *double* or *int* data types
- enumerated UINTs—these controls present the user with a set of strings; they select one of these strings at a time
- on/off switches—a special case of the enumerated UINT where the enumeration is fixed and pre-set to only two values, OFF and ON

An example of a continuous control is a volume control in dB. A slider continuously adjusts a floating point variable that controls the signal amplitude or volume. An example of an enumerated UINT control is a GUI element that lets the user select the filter type from a list of strings like "HPF," "LPF," and "BPF." The reason we call these enumerated is that the string list is formed with an enumeration such as:

```
enum {LPF,HPF,BPF};
```

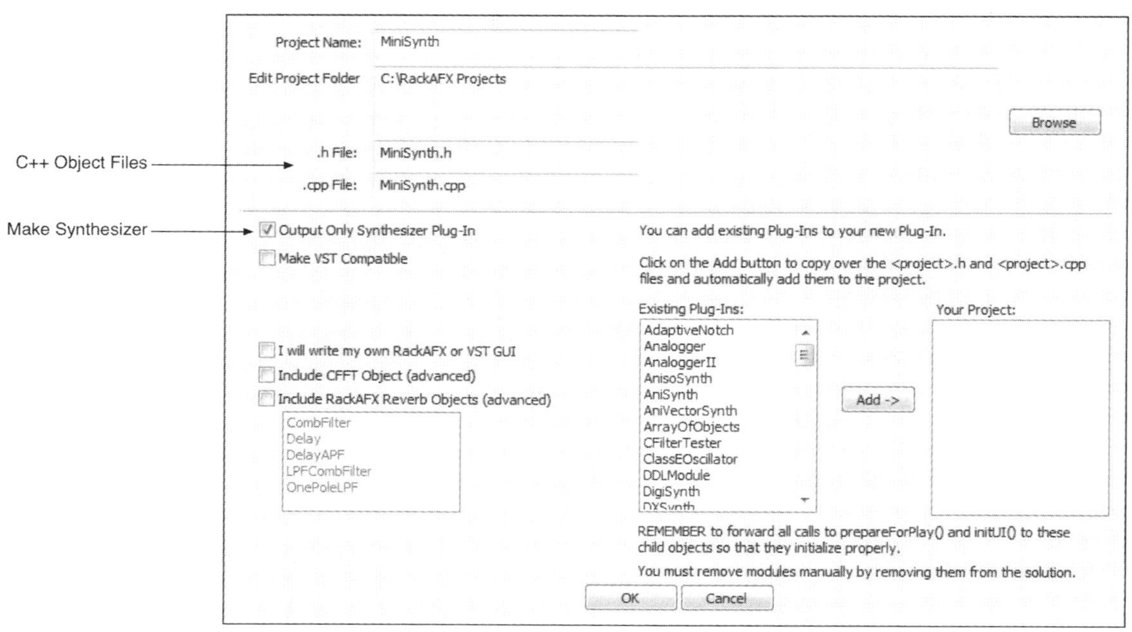

Figure 2.7: The New Project dialog is where you setup your C++ object that will become your project.

In the enumeration, LPF is assigned the value 0, HPF is 1, etc. In VST3 and AU, you create a "string list" or "indexed" parameter—the same thing applies; you provide a set of strings that the control identifies with a zero-based index value. UINT is the Windows *#define* of the standard datatype *unsigned integer*. For AU users, we have also *#defined* this so you can match the book code (Apple uses *UInt32* instead). In RackAFX, the 40 slider controls plus the 1024 LCD controls may be either continuous or enumerated types. The enumerated types support up to 256 sub-strings, though it is unlikely you will ever need that many. In addition there are four sets of radio buttons, each of which can hold an enumeration of up to eight sub-strings.

For each project, you will be given a table like Table 2.6. For RackAFX projects, you can ignore the last column that lists the index value, which only pertains to AU sand VST3. This table has all the GUI controls, limits, defaults, units and variable names and datatypes that you will attach to the controls. In this table you can see two columns Variable Type and Variable Name. The four fundamental types are *float*, *double*, *int* and *enumerated* UINT. The Volume and Octave controls ultimately generate numerical values that the user sees on the GUI and they have minimum or Lo Limit, maximum or Hi Limit and default (Def) values. A control may also have no units ("" or empty string). The Fc (Filter Cutoff) control has the note "volt/octave" which means that this control is logarithmic. Note the Octave control delivers *int* values since the octaves are selected this way.

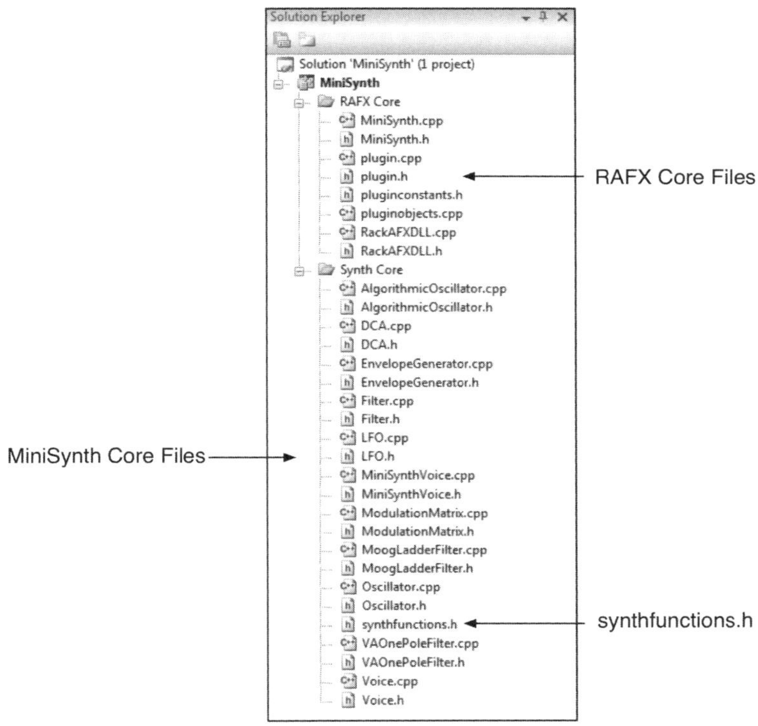

Figure 2.8: Example of Visual Studio files for the MiniSynth project.

Table 2.6: Example of some GUI controls.

***ExampleSynth* Continuous Parameters**				
Control Name (units)	**Type**	**Variable Name (VST3, RAFX)**	**Low/Hi/Default***	**VST3/AU Index**
Volume (dB)	double	m_dVolume_dB	-96 / 24/ 0.0	OUTPUT_AMPLITUDE_DB
Octave	int	m_nOctave	-4 / 4 / 0	OCTAVE
Fc (Hz)(volt/octave)	double	m_dFilterFc	80 / 18000 / 10000	FILTER_FC

*low, high and default values are #defined for VST3 and AU in *SynthParamLimits.h* for each project

Enumerated String Parameters (UINT)			
Control Name	**Variable Name**	**enum String**	**VST3/AU Index**
Filter Type	m_uFilterType	LPF,HPF,BPF	FILTER_TYPE
FX Filter	m_uFXFilter	LPF,HPF,BPF	FX_FILTER
Patches	m_uPatches	Heavy_Lead, Lush_Pad, Space_Cadet	PATCHES

Table 2.7: The RAFX pre-assigned control index values.

Control	Index Range
40 Sliders on main Panel	0–39
1024 Controls in LCD	100–1123
8 Radio Buttons	41–44
4 two-state Switches	45–48

The Filter Type control displays strings that define the current setting. An unsigned integer (UINT) keeps track of the current setting. The *enum* String gives you the comma-separated values that will map to the UINT variable. In this example the mapping is:

LPF: 0
HPF: 1
BPF: 2

For the enumerated UINT type, the default value is always the first value in the *enum* string-list or LPF here.

In the prototype phase, you assign the controls in any order you wish, meaning that you can pick the sliders, buttons or LCD controls as you choose. The main thing to understand is that the RackAFX controls are already indexed for you (which is why you can ignore the last column in Table 2.6). Once your plug-in is complete, you can then use the GUI Designer to craft the final GUI and just as in the prototype phase, the controls do not have to follow any specific ordering. RackAFX indexes the controls as shown in Table 2.7.

One of the fundamental differences between RackAFX and VST3/AU is that in the later two APIs, it is up to you to define and maintain proper indexing of your controls. This is done with a giant enumeration. In RackAFX the indexing is pre-set. You do not need to define or maintain a list and the ordering can be arbitrary. However, you do have to know what the index is for a given control, so RackAFX automatically creates a comment-block identifying the index/control pairs whenever you add or remove controls. We will look at this shortly.

2.9 Setting up Continuous Controls

Your first job for each new synth project will be converting the GUI control table into a set of controls on the RackAFX interface. To practice this, create a new throw-away project in RackAFX (named ThrowAway). After the compiler launches and is alive and awake, you may start adding controls. Let's start with the first control named Volume. To set up this kind of continuous control, right click inside one of the bounding boxes for a slider control. The bounding box is a thin grey frame around each slider cluster as shown in Figure 2.2. Right-clicking starts the Slider Designer, a simple to use form that you fill in to create the control. As an example, right-click on the first slider in the upper left. This produces the following form shown in Figure 2.9.

You need to fill out the Slider Properties with the proper values. You will notice that the *uControlID* value is 0 for this slider. This is the ID number that will link the slider to a variable in the object. You cannot edit this cell. Start with the Control Name and enter "Volume" (no quotes). Hit *<Enter>* to advance to the next cell, then set the Units to *"dB."* The next cell is one of the most important—it is the data type for the variable that the slider will be linked with; the choices are available from a drop-down list. You can select the data type with the mouse, or you can just type the first letter (e.g. "d" for double) while the box is highlighted. Compare this figure with the first row of Table 2.6, and you can see how to transplant table rows into control configurations. You can ignore the MIDI stuff for now—see my website on how to connect MIDI controllers to any of the GUI components to use this option. However, on the left is an important set of options:

- Linear Slider
- Log Slider
- One volt/octave Slider

The linear and log (arithmic) sliders move with these taper offsets, and you could use a log control for a volume control if needed. However, for some synth frequency controls such as the cutoff frequency for a filter, you want to choose the volt/octave option. This will make the control move in a 2^N fashion (i.e. in octaves), which is how synth controls work when using this taper. (NOTE: in VST3/AU this same volt/octave taper is called "Logarithmic Scale"). If you realize you've made a mistake or left something out, just right-click in the slider box and fix the problem. You can also remove the slider by clicking the *<Remove Ctrl>* button on the Properties Window, and you can copy the settings of another slider with the Copy Existing Slider Control drop-down list.

As you add, edit or remove controls from the main UI, you will notice that RackAFX will flash to the compiler and back as it writes the code for you. You might use this flashing as a signal that the code update is synchronized. If you don't like it, minimize the compiler and the flashing will not occur. There is a special check-box in *View->Preferences* to start the compiler minimized for this very reason (Visual Studio 2008 only; Microsoft removed the ability from later versions).

Your plug-in code will use the index value 0 (*uControlID* in the Properties dialog) to map to the Slider named Volume on the UI to the *m_dVolume_dB* variable. After setting up the Volume control, switch to the Visual Studio compiler (hint: use the -> C++ button)

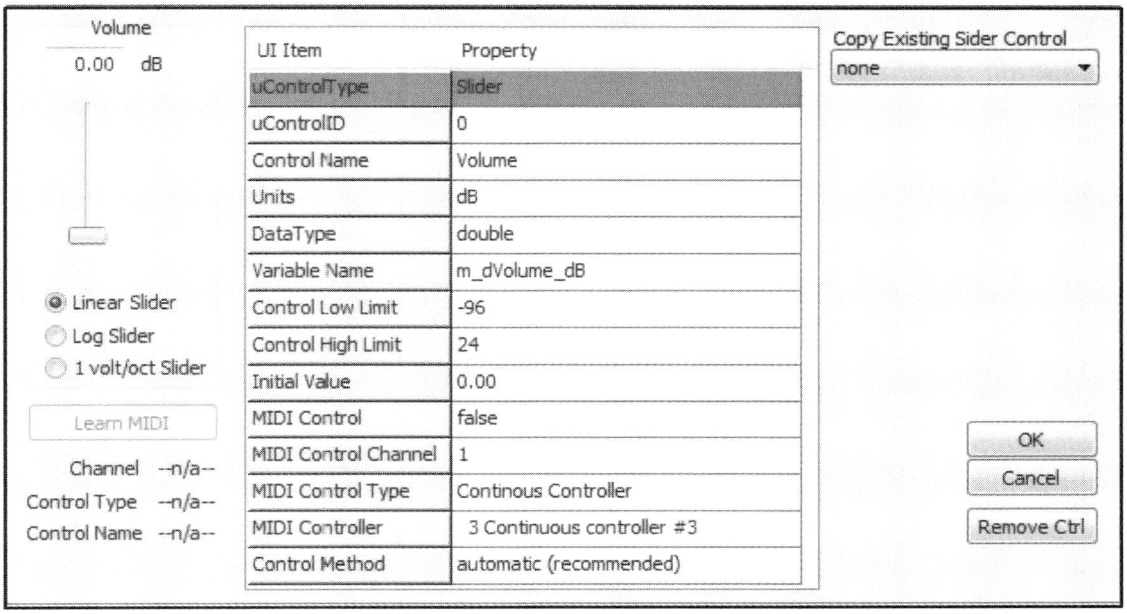

Figure 2.9: The Slider Designer makes it simple to define your control and link it to an underlying variable.

(if prompted to save the *.sln* file, always say YES and see my website for information on getting rid of most of these pop-ups) and open your project's *.h* file. Near the bottom you will see the new variable declaration that RackAFX wrote for you:

```
class CThrowAway : public CPlugIn
{
public:

	<SNIP SNIP SNIP>

	// ADDED BY RACKAFX -- DO NOT EDIT THIS CODE!!! ----------------- //
	//  **--0x07FD--**

	double m_dVolume_dB;

	// **--0x1A7F--**
	// -------------------------------------------------------------- //
};
```

You will see the notation **<SNIP SNIP SNIP>** frequently in the printed code as a reminder that code has been cut out for easier reading.

Aside from the main plug-in functions we discussed in Chapter 2, you will see some more commented areas of code. In the first part marked // **Add your code here:** you can add more variables or function definitions just like you would in any *.h* file. Try to keep your code in the denoted area to make it easier to find and read. The area below that says:

// ADDED BY RACKAFX -- DO NOT EDIT THIS CODE!!!

This is very important—you will see your member variable *m_dVolume* declared in this area. This is the portion of the *.h* file that RackAFX modifies when you add, edit, or delete controls from your control surface. It is imperative that you let RackAFX maintain this part of the C++ code. There are several other portions of code in the *.cpp* file that have similar warnings and interesting hex symbols (0x1A7F, etc.…)—do not edit the code contained between the hex codes or commented areas. RackAFX writes C++ code for you. You have to be careful not to alter the RackAFX C++ code in any way.

Now practice setting up the Octave control—choose the *integer* datatype and use the table to fill in the Slider Designer form. Continuing through the table we find two enumerated index controls. Let's practice setting up a radio button group first.

2.10 Setting up Indexed Controls: Radio Buttons

Right click anywhere on the first radio button group that is on the same row as the first ten sliders and a similar Radio Button Designer appears. You populate this form in the same way, using the *<Enter>* button to quickly advance through the rows. However, this control has the Data Type fixed at *enum*. After entering the control name and UINT variable to link it with (*m_uFilterType*), move to the box labeled "This enum list:" and enter the strings separated by commas. Since this will be a C++ enumeration, you must be careful to make sure you use legal values for the sub-strings; for example your sub-string can not start with a number, contain reserved characters like & and *, etc. If you compile and get an error that refers to the enumeration, check your legality with the string names. If you need to change the *enum* string, do so in RackAFX.

On the left side of Figure 2.10 you can see a mock-up of the three enumerated strings turned into button text. This is so that you can make sure your strings do not flow outside the control (hint: use short meaningful strings). You can also see that this control has an index of 41.

2.11 Setting up Indexed Controls: Sliders

Continuing through Table 2.6 we find another filter selection type named *FX Filter*. This control uses the same three strings as the first filter type control, LPF, HPF, BPF. You can set up a slider control to act as an enumerated index control too. Right click on another slider control group and choose *enum* from the data type list. The dialog box opens up to reveal the string entry box and anther list box populated with the current enumerated string lists. You can share these lists between controls by double-clicking on the string in the lower box, which transfers the string into "This enum list:" box. Figure 2.11 shows the new Slider Designer. In enum mode, the high and low limits and default are not editable or used.

2.12 Placing Controls Inside the LCD Control

In the upper right of the main RackAFX UI is a control that represents an alpha wheel, LCD matrix view, and control knob. During the course of designing your project, you've noticed that the LCD is used to give you feedback about the state of your project and compiler. However, it can also be used as a GUI control just like the other sliders. The LCD Control allows you to store up to 1024 continuous slider controls inside it. Anything you can setup with a normal slider control will work as one of the LCD embedded controls, and the GUI Designer lets you place one of these controls on your own custom GUI. There are several uses for the control:

- it's a different way to store the continuous controls
- if you run out of sliders, you can always put 1024 more of them in the LCD

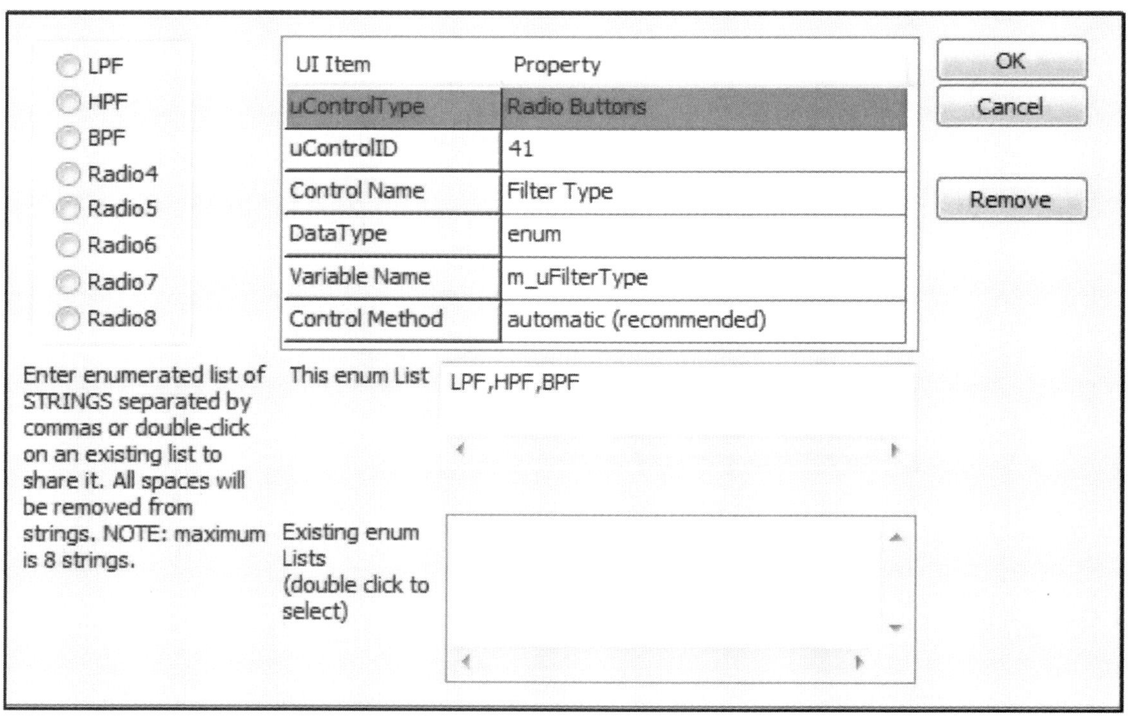

Figure 2.10: Configuring the radio button group is as simple as the slider control.

- you can use enumerated controls to create a set of presets or other global functions or configurations—we will use this extensively for global parameters in the synths such as pitch bend range, and it will also tidy up the GUI by packaging the controls in a small footprint

Figure 2.12 shows an example of the LCD control with two controls embedded inside. The alpha wheel is used to select the control; here it selects either Filter Fc or Patches. The value knob is used to adjust the control's parameter value. An indicator on the right shows which control you are using.

Let's add the *Filter Fc* control from Table 2.6. first. To setup the LCD control, right- click on it when you are in development mode (not with a plug-in loaded). A box pops up as shown in Figure 2.13. Click on <*New*> to open the very familiar Slider Properties dialog. Use Table 2.6 to fill out the form, noticing that the volt/octave taper is used.

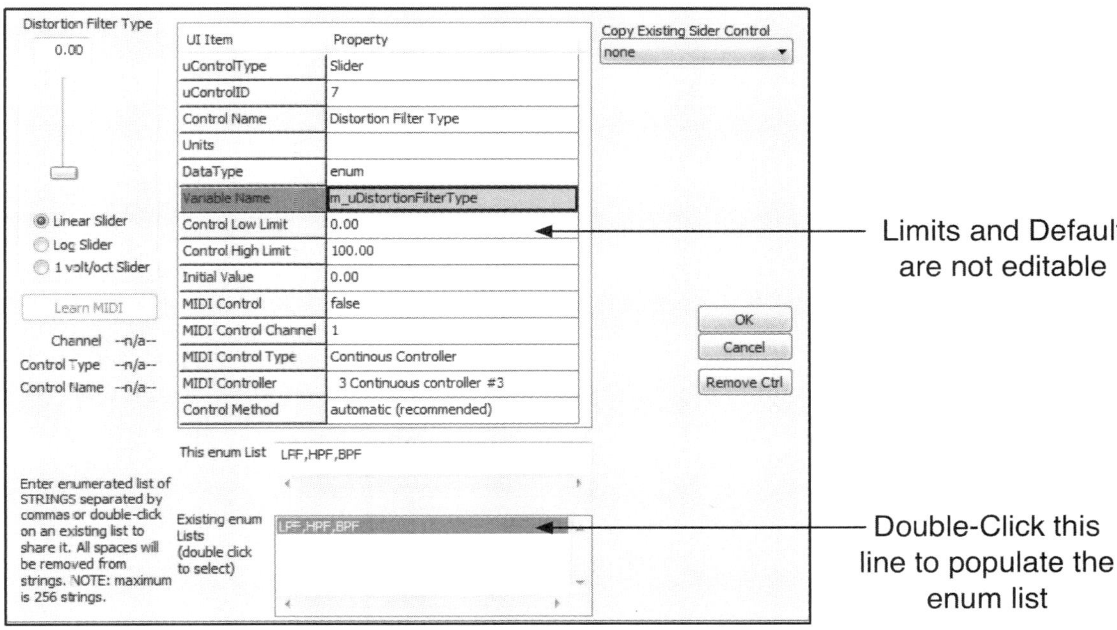

Figure 2.11: You can use a slider as an indexed control too.

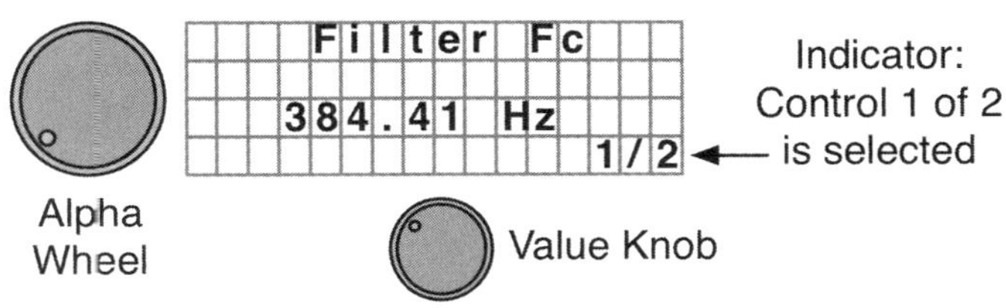

Figure 2.12: The RackAFX LCD control with the Filter Fc control selected.

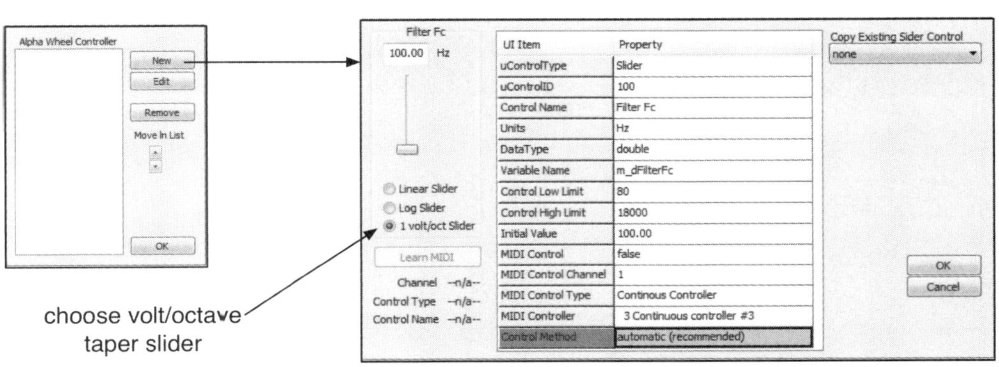

Figure 2.13: Adding controls to the LCD is easy using the *New*, *Edit* and *Remove* buttons; here we are setting up the Filter Fc control which uses the volt/octave taper.

You can add, edit or remove controls with the buttons. You can also change the order of the controls in the list with the *Move In List* nudge-buttons. The order in the list is the order the controls will appear in the compiled plug-in's LCD control. Next, setup the Patch control using the enumerated index data type. Here you can take advantage of a feature of the LCD Control: You can use the underscore (_) to separate strings in your list (you can't have spaces in an enumerated name). When the LCD Control uses them, it replaces the underscores with single white-spaces. This allows you much more flexibility than the radio buttons or normal sliders provide. So, when you enter the enumerated string, use underscores between the words Heavy_Lead, Lush_Pad, and Space_Cadet. After setting up this control, rebuild your project either in Visual Studio directly or in RackAFX with the *Rebuild* button. After compiling, use the *Load* button to load the DLL. Play with the different controls and notice how the LCD control with Patch selected has spaces between the words as shown in Figure 2.14.

If you download the sample projects, you will see that the LCD control has multiple controls embedded inside.

2.13 Using the RackAFX GUI Designer

RackAFX has a powerful GUI Designer that lets you arrange visually appealing GUIs in a matter of just a few minutes. The GUI Designer is always being updated with more features so always check the latest additions at the website. Depending on which version you have, your GUI Designer will look more or less like that shown in Figure 2.15. The flow of operations is as follows:

- In prototype view (the main RackAFX View) you assemble your plug-in. You create controls, give them min, max and initial values, connect them to variables, etc. Because this is development mode, you will probably change some controls, add or remove them and so on. Also, because we are prototyping, we can setup a bunch of controls we really would not want the user to be able to adjust in the final plug-in.
- After your plug-in is complete, debugged and ready to go, you click on the GUI Designer tab to reveal Figure 2.15's blank GUI surface.
- You drag and drop controls from the palette on the left side and arrange them however you like on the surface. Because they have transparent backgrounds, they can be overlapped.
- for the slider, radio buttons and knob controls, you must connect the control with the variable in your plug-in that it will control.
- The vector joystick control doesn't need any additional setup.

Use the Background Pattern box to select a background image or color; here we selected the white color. The global buttons at the top allow you to change the font, clear all the controls from the design area and update the code (more on that later). When you drag a

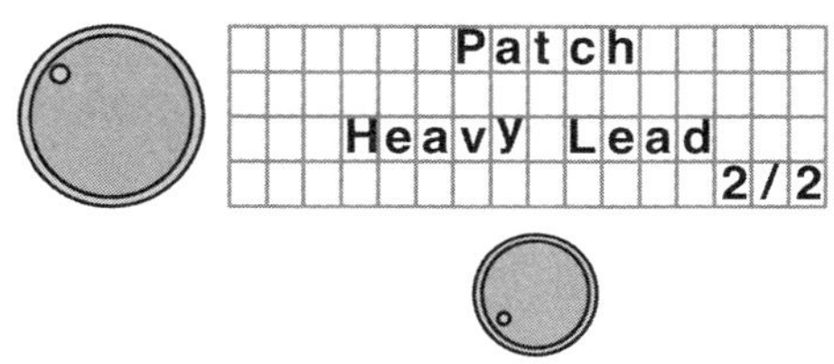

Figure 2.14: The enumerated strings can use blank spaces by inserting underscores in the designer form.

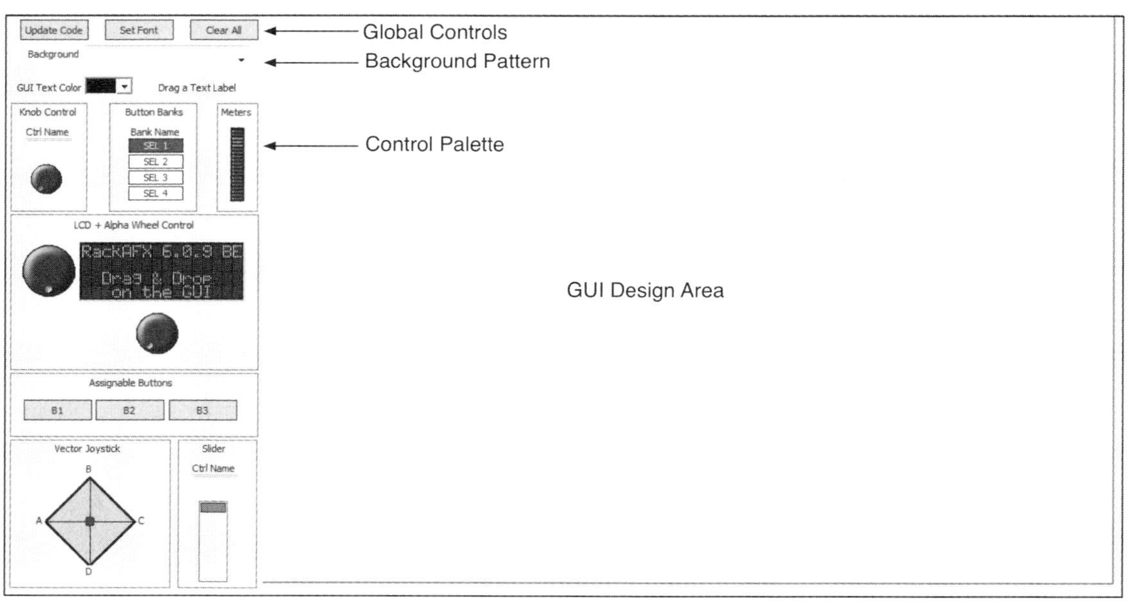

Figure 2.15: The GUI Designer consists primarily of a control palette on the left and a large GUI design area on the right.

control, click on the operative portion. For example, to drag a knob, click right on the knob itself; for a radio button, click on any of the buttons; and for the slider, click on the slider control. After you drop it in the design area you can move it around and customize it. You right-click on the control to bring up the variable linkage and customization box.

> NOTE: When you add controls to the design area, always arrange them starting from the upper left corner so that the controls will be cropped correctly in the final GUI.

Any of the prototype's sliders can be dragged and dropped either as knobs or sliders using the palette on the left. Figure 2.16 shows the GUI Designer after the first knob control has been placed, and after right-clicking on the placed knob to set it up.

In the GUI control group setup, you can:

- connect the knob to a variable via the drop list
- change the appearance of the knob and dot combination
- change the edit box behavior; hide it or change its colors
- set all the other knobs to match this one

Now, do the same thing but drag a slider instead. It connects to the Filter FX control, so select it form the control drop-down box and play with the customization options for the slider. To remove a slider or knob, select "none" from the variable drop down list. Drag a radio button group and likewise set it up by right-clicking. The GUI Designer automatically assigns the radio button groups for you starting with the first bank and working down. If you try to drag a radio button group and it won't let you, it means that you have run out of these controls. Finally, drag the LCD control into the design area and right-click to set it up. You should have something similar to Figure 2.17.

In the LCD setup, you add or remove controls and set up the color scheme. You can change the ordering of the controls. The GUI LCD control is slightly different than the one on the prototype UI in that any of the continuous controls can be placed inside, not just the ones you assigned when prototyping. This means that you could have a GUI consisting of just the LCD control and radio buttons. You add and remove controls with the *Add-->* and *<--Remove* buttons. You can re-arrange the order in the control with the *Move In List* nudge buttons. After adding the LCD controls, close the setup dialog. At this point, the GUI is finished. However, you have one last step before it is ready—you need to go back and re-compile your plug-in code to embed the GUI information inside the DLL. This is identical to the way the VSTGUI Designer works for VST3 as well as Interface Builder in AU. You always need to rebuild the project to embed the GUI. In RackAFX, this means you need to update the Visual Studio code. There are two ways to do this: either switch back to the Prototype panel or use the *Update Code* button at the top left of the form. If you do not update the code in this way the GUI design will not be saved. Switch back to Prototype view to save the GUI and hit the *Rebuild* button to rebuild the project. Now use the *Load* button to load the DLL. You will notice that the *Custom GUI* item on the toolbar is now active—it looks like a blue knob. Click on this button (or use *View->Custom Plugin GUI*) and your GUI will appear in its own child window. It will be cropped so that it just holds all your controls as shown in Figure 2.18.

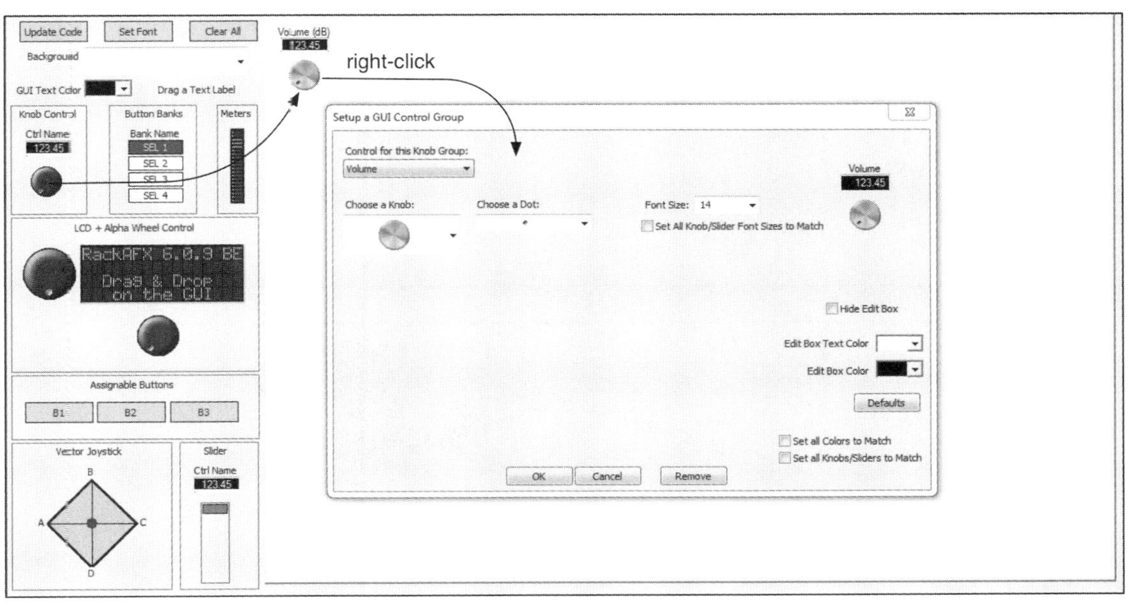

Figure 2.16: The first control has been added and assigned to the Volume control; then I customized the knob appearance and text colors.

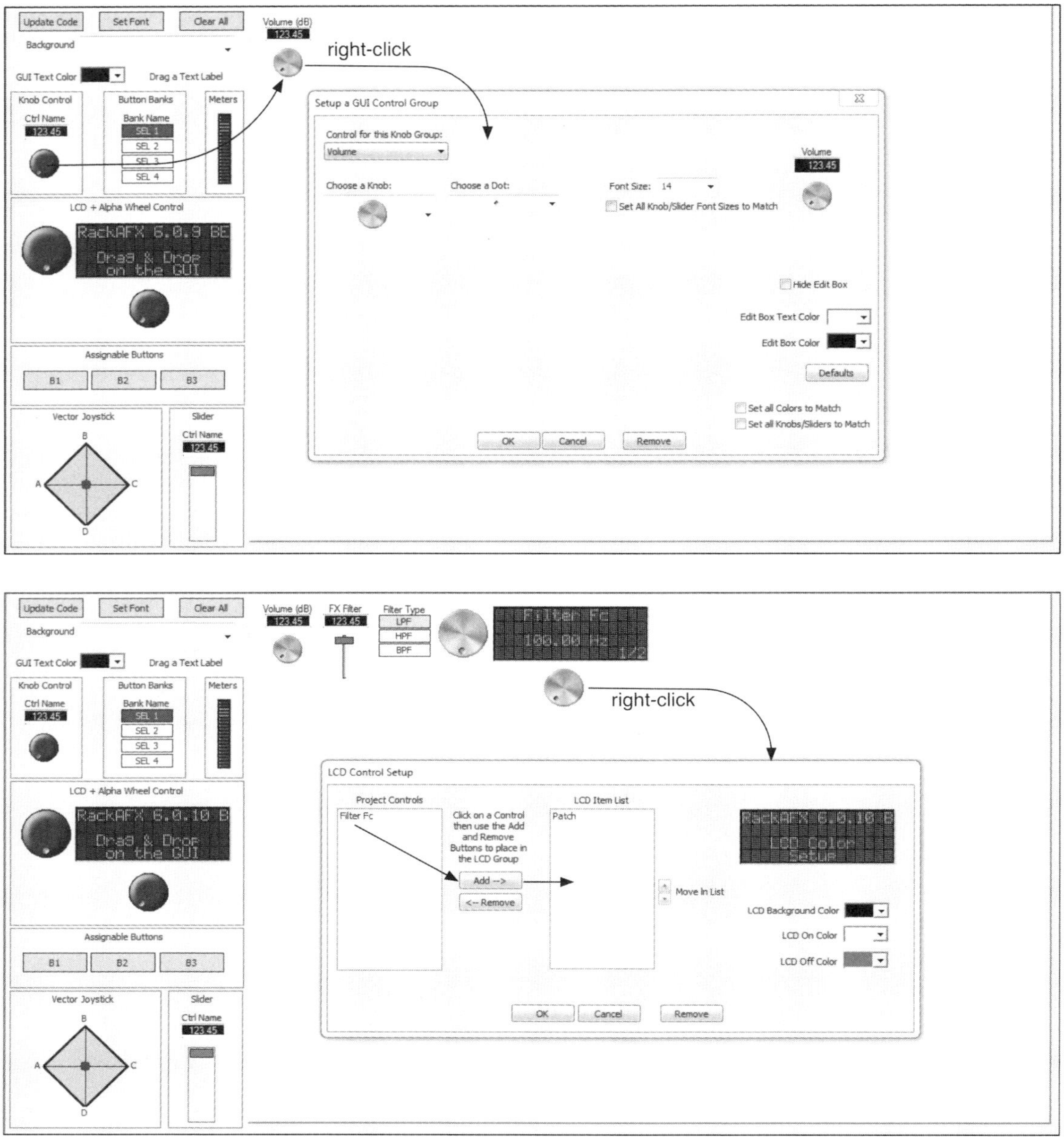

Figure 2.17: The completed GUI with LCD Setup.

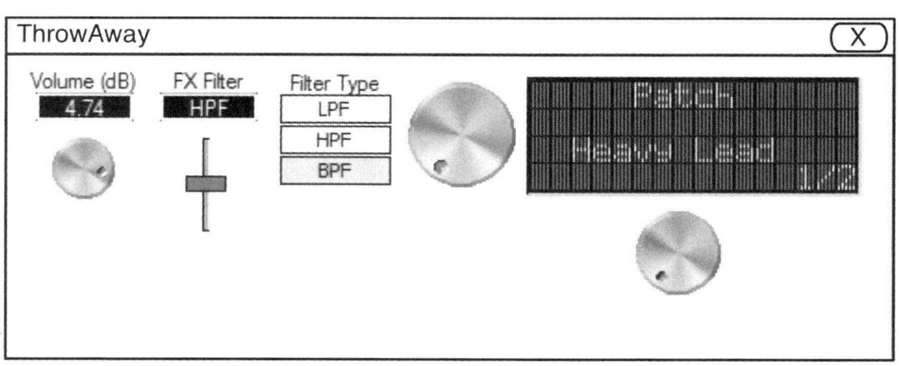

Figure 2.18: The finished GUI in RackAFX.

GUI Designer Rules and Paradigms

- when you run out of continuous controls (sliders) you can't drag any more knobs/slider controls
- each time you drag a knob or slider you must set it up before dragging any other knobs or sliders
- the joystick can have its colors altered, and you can set the program button to look like the assignable buttons—there can be only one joystick
- you can add any continuous control (slider) to the GUI LCD group; it is a separate entity from the one on your main RackAFX GUI
- when you add radio button controls, RackAFX starts with the topmost button bank on the main GUI and automatically links your control variable for you. It then moves from top to bottom as you drag the radio buttons. If you need to skip button banks, add all of them at first, then remove the ones you don't want. The buttons banks are highly customizable.
- the RackAFX GUI Designer is constantly being updated so the control images and options are steadily improved which means that your version of the software may not exactly resemble the figures here. Be sure to check the website http://www.willpirkle.com/synthbook/ for updates and instructions on how to use the most recent version of the GUI Designer.

> For the synth projects in this book, we will not be using the meter or assignable button controls. If you want to learn how to use these, see *Designing Audio Effects Flug-Ins in C++*, which has several projects that feature these controls.

Compiling as a VST2/VST3 Plug-in

Once your plug-in is completed, and you've added a GUI with the GUI Designer, you can go back to the project setup dialog using either *File->Edit Project* or the *Edit* button on the right. Here you can select "Make VST2/3 Compatible" and "Use RackAFX Custom GUI." When you say OK, it will take some time, as RackAFX copies over some files and re-configures your Visual Studio Project files. Once complete, rebuild the project. The DLL can be found by using the menu item *Plug-In->Open PlugIns Folder*. This DLL can be placed in the VST folder of any VST2 client and used as any other plug-in. You can also copy this DLL and change the extension to *.vst3* and place it in the VST3 folder of any VST3 client to use the same DLL as a VST3 plug-in. The GUI you designed will appear as the custom GUI in both the VST2 and VST3 clients.

__stdcall

> In the RackAFX code you will see the qualifier ***__stdcall*** preceding each function prototype as well as implementation. The ***__stdcall*** calling convention is there for future compatibility with other compilers as well as other 3rd party software. The ***__stdcall*** is a directive that lets the compiler know how the stack will be cleaned up after method calls; it has no effect on the math or audio processing whatsoever.

2.14 The RackAFX Plug-in Object

Now that you know how to set up a GUI and use the GUI Designer, let's focus on the synth plug-in object itself. We need to look at an example that shows you how the functions in Tables 2.2 and 2.3 are implemented. After setting up the prototype GUI, your next job will be filling in the various functions that will implement the plug-in according to Tables 2.2 and 2.3. Remember, you need to fill in ten functions plus any others you add to make a completed plug-in, so let's look at those functions. Also remember that since RackAFX project names are actually the plug-in C++ object name, each synth project will be implemented as a different plug-in object.

- download the MiniSynth project and open it in RackAFX by using the *File->Open* menu or the *Open* button on the right.
- place the MiniSynth folder in the RackAFX Projects folder that you selected in *View->Preferences* (you can always change it). RackAFX projects can be located in any folder except the desktop or a virtual drive but RackAFX will first default to the directory you chose in preferences.
- browse to find the *MiniSynth.prj* file and open it; the compiler will start.

In Visual Studio, select the *MiniSynth.h* file and scroll to the bottom to see all the variables that were added when we set up the GUI. Notice the combination of *doubles*, *ints*, *UINTs* and *enums*. For example, the *UINT m_uVoiceMode* uses the *enum* list just below it to show the user the possible Voice settings.

```
class CMiniSynth : public CPlugIn
{
public:
      // RackAFX plug-in API Member Methods:

      <SNIP SNIP SNIP>
```

```
// ADDED BY RACKAFX -- DO NOT EDIT THIS CODE!!! -------------------- //
//   **--0x07FD--**

UINT m_uVoiceMode;
enum{Saw3,Sqr3,Saw2Sqr,Tri2Saw,Tri2Sqr};
double m_dDetune_cents;
double m_dFcControl;
double m_dLFO1Rate;
etc...

// **--0x1A7F--**
// ------------------------------------------------------------ //
```

Now, focus on the member functions at the top of the file. We will be overriding and/or implementing the following *CPlugIn* functions for our synth projects:

Standard plug-in Functions:

Here you see the constructor and destructor, which we use to initialize variables and destroy objects.

```
CMiniSynth();
```

- allocate dynamic memory
- initialize variables

```
virtual ~CMiniSynth(void);
```

- deallocate any allocated memory

```
virtual bool __stdcall prepareForPlay();
```

- the per-run initialization function
- always set the sample rate on sub-components
- always update the synth objects

```
virtual bool __stdcall processAudioFrame(float* pInputBuffer,
                                         float* pOutputBuffer,
                                         UINT uNumInputChannels,
                                         UINT uNumOutputChannels);
```

- this is where you render the synthesized audio output

```
virtual bool __stdcall userInterfaceChange(int nControlIndex);
```

- this is called after the user moves a control on the GUI; you may optionally do more processing here; in all cases we will call the synth updating function

MIDI and Joystick Control Functions

Table 2.3 lists the MIDI functions we will implement, and you can find their prototypes in the area marked “Advanced Functions.” In the VectorSynth and AniSynth, we will use the vector joystick, which issues location and mixing information. That method is also in this group of functions:

```
virtual bool __stdcall joystickControlChange(float fControlA,
                                             float fControlB,
                                             float fControlC,
                                             float fControlD,
                                             float fACMix,
                                             float fBDMix);
```

- indicates the user has moved the built-in vector joystick which we use in VectorSynth and AniSynth

```
<SNIP SNIP SNIP> -- you can skip functions 8 and 9
virtual bool __stdcall midiNoteOn(UINT uChannel,
                                  UINT uMIDINote,
                                  UINT uVelocity);
```

- called for each MIDI note off event delivering channel, note number and velocity

```
virtual bool __stdcall midiNoteOff(UINT uChannel, UINT uMIDINote,
                                   UINT uVelocity, bool bAllNotesOff);
```

- called for each MIDI note-of event
- also called for an all notes off panic message

```
virtual bool __stdcall midiModWheel(UINT uChannel, UINT uModValue);
```

- function to handle changes to the Mod Wheel (found on most synth controllers)

```
virtual bool __stdcall midiPitchBend(UINT uChannel,
                                     int nActualPitchBendValue,
                                     float fNormalizedPitchBendValue);
```

- specialized function for the pitch bend wheel/joystick

```
<SNIP SNIP SNIP> -- we won't be implementing MIDI clock in the book projects
virtual bool __stdcall midiMessage(unsigned char cChannel,
                                   unsigned char cStatus,
                                   unsigned char cData1,
                                   unsigned char cData2);
```

- all the rest of the MIDI messages including continuous controllers, program change, after-touch, etc. . .

The last part of the *MiniSynth.h* file consist of a few member variables. For the MiniSynth these are:

```
CMiniSynthVoice* m_pVoiceArray[MAX_VOICES];
void incrementVoiceTimestamps;
CMiniSynthVoice* getOldestVoice();
CMiniSynthVoice* getOldestVoiceWithNote(UINT uMIDINote);

// --- updates all voices at once
void update();

// --- for portamento
double m_dLastNoteFrequency;

// --- our receive channel
UINT m_uMidiRxChannel;
```

The synthesizer's polyphony is accomplished by maintaining an array of voice object pointers. This array is named *m_pVoiceArray* for all the synths. The difference is in the kind of pointers they hold; in this case the array holds *CMiniSynthVoice* pointers. The three functions below its definition are for handling the time ordering of the voices. The *update()* function is for updating all of the synth variables at once. We will get into the details of these as well as the few remaining variables as Chapters 3–12 progress.

Now, let's look at each function implementation one by one. The synth projects are actually all very similar from the plug-in object's point of view. Most of the work that differentiates the synths is done in the *CVoice* objects that we will design. So, once you understand one synth, the others are very easy to grasp. Open the *MiniSynth.cpp* file, and let's start at the top and work our way down through the implementation.

constructor

The constructor in each RackAFX plug-in does the following:

- call *initUI()* on the very first line to instantiate and initialize your GUI control objects
- initialize derived class variables
- set *m_bWantAllMIDIMessages = true* so we can get all MIDI messages
- initialize our custom variables
- create the voice objects and load them into the array

Much of the constructor was written for you when you created the project; these variables do not need to be altered, so you can safely ignore them here. Perhaps the most important part is at the end where the voices are allocated.

```
CMiniSynth::CMiniSynth()
{
      // Added by RackAFX - DO NOT REMOVE
      //
      // initUI() for GUI controls
      initUI();
      // END initUI()

      // built in initialization
      m_PlugInName = "MiniSynth";

      <SNIP SNIP SNIP>

      // we want all messages
      m_bWantAllMIDIMessages = true;

      // Finish initializations here
      m_dLastNoteFrequency = -1.0;

      // receive on all channels
      m_uMidiRxChannel = MIDI_CH_ALL;

      // load up voices
      // detailed in future chapters
}
```

destructor

The destructor simply deletes all dynamically declared objects and variables.

prepareForPlay()

In *prepareForPlay()*, you initialize the sample rate of the voice objects and call each one's *prepareForPlay()*, which initializes them. The voice objects are NOT derived from *CPlugIn*—we just named the one-time-init function the same to make it easy to remember. After this, you call the *update()* method to update each voice's internal variables and reset the last note frequency that we will use for portamento/glide effects.

```
bool __stdcall CMiniSynth::prepareForPlay()
{
      // Add your code here:
      for(int i=0; i<MAX_VOICES; i++)
      {
              CMiniSynthVoice* pVoice = m_pVoiceArray[i];
```

```
            pVoice->setSampleRate((double)m_nSampleRate);
            pVoice->prepareForPlay();
        }

        // mass update
        update();

        // clear
        m_dLastNoteFrequency = -1.0;

        return true;
    }
```

update()

The update method does a brute-force update of each voice's variables. We will get into the details of this function in Chapter 8.

```
    void CMiniSynth::update()
    {
        // detailed in future chapters
    }
```

processAudioFrame()

The default mechanism for processing or rendering synthesized audio is to process in frames. In RackAFX, a frame is a single sample period's worth of values. For a mono plug-in, this represents a single sample. For a stereo plug-in, a frame is a left-right pair of samples. The VST3 and AU synths process in buffers of frames rather than single frames. You can do this in RackAFX as well by using the *processVSTBuffers()* function. See my website for more information about this. Processing by buffers has advantages and disadvantages. Processing by individual frames is not only easier conceptually, but it also allows GUI control changes to be virtually sample accurate. When you process in buffers, handling control changes can get tricky since they may be distributed as events in time relative to the individual samples in the buffers.

RackAFX can be used to make both audio effect and synthesizer plug-ins, so the arguments to *processAudioFrame()* reflect this. The arguments are:

- *float* pInputBuffer*: a pointer to a buffer of one (mono) or two (stereo) samples; ignore for synth plug-ins
- *float* pOutputBuffer*: a pointer to a buffer of one (mono) or two (stereo) locations for us to render out audio—this is our synth output buffer
- *UINT uNumInputChannels*: for effects processor, this is the number of inputs; ignore for synth plug-ins
- *UINT uNumOutputChannels*: the number of outputs, either 1 (mono) or 2 (stereo)

If you compare the MiniSynth *processAudioFrame()* function to the equivalent functions in the VST3 and AU versions, you will see that the actual synth rendering is identical across all three formats. The only difference is in the processing buffers rather than frames. In each case, we loop through the voices, accumulating each voice's output and then write that to the output buffer. The left channel is *pOutputBuffer[0]* and the right channel is *pOutputBuffer[1]*. The voice objects do all the rendering. We simply accumulate and write. We will get into more details of this loop in Chapter 8.

```
    bool __stdcall CMiniSynth::processAudioFrame(float* pInputBuffer,
                                                 float* pOutputBuffer,
                                                 UINT uNumInputChannels,
                                                 UINT uNumOutputChannels)
    {
        // Do LEFT (MONO) Channel
        double dLeftAccum = 0.0;
        double dRightAccum = 0.0;

        // --- 12dB headroom
        float fMix = 0.25;
        double dLeft = 0.0;
```

```
        double dRight = 0.0;

        // --- loop and accumulate voices
        for(int i=0; i<MAX_VOICES; i++)
        {
                // detailed in future chapters
        }

        pOutputBuffer[0] = dLeftAccum;

        // Mono-In, Stereo-Out (AUX Effect)
        if(uNumInputChannels == 1 && uNumOutputChannels == 2)
                pOutputBuffer[1] = dLeftAccum;

        // Stereo-In, Stereo-Out (INSERT Effect)
        if(uNumInputChannels == 2 && uNumOutputChannels == 2)
                pOutputBuffer[1] = dRightAccum;

        return true;
}
```

userInterfaceChange()

In *userInterfaceChange()* you normally first decode the control's index (passed via the *nControlIndex* argument) and then call the appropriate updating function or calculation based on that. In our RackAFX synth projects (as well as the VST3 and AU versions), we will be doing a brute-force update of all variables even if only one of them has changed. This is mainly done to greatly simplify the code. After characterization testing, we found that the added overhead of the full update did not appreciably add to the CPU load; the updating function turns out to be quite inexpensive compared to the actual audio synthesis itself. However, you are encouraged to change this paradigm and decode each control individually after you get the completed synth up and running. To facilitate decoding, RackAFX leaves a comment block above the *userInterfaceChange()* function to remind you of the index mapping.

```
/* ADDED BY RACKAFX -- DO NOT EDIT THIS CODE!!! -------------------------- //
        **--0x2983--**

        Variable Name                                   Index
-----------------------------------------------------------
        m_uVoiceMode                                      0
        m_dDetune_cents                                   1
        m_dFcControl                                      2
        m_dLFO1Rate                                       3

        etc...

        **--0xFFDD--**
// ----------------------------------------------------------------------- */
// Add your UI Handler code here ----------------------------------------- //
//
bool __stdcall CMiniSynth::userInterfaceChange(int nControlIndex)
{
        // --- just update all, ignoring the index value
        update();
        return true;
}
```

MIDI Message Functions and Helpers

The last block of functions all concern MIDI messages. The nice thing is that with the exception of the type of voice pointer our array holds, all the MIDI functions for all the synth projects are identical, so once you've grasped it for the first synth, you can just copy and paste for the rest.

MIDI Note Timestamp Functions

There are three functions to help with polyphony.

```
void CMiniSynth::incrementVoiceTimestamps()
CMiniSynthVoice* CMiniSynth::getOldestVoice()
CMiniSynthVoice* CMiniSynth::getOldestVoiceWithNote(UINT uMIDINote)
```

We will discuss these in detail in Chapter 8. They are used to implement dynamic voice allocation or voice-stealing. For now you can skip over them.

MIDI Note On and Off

These are clearly the two most important MIDI messages we will deal with. We will get into the exact details of these methods in Chapter 8; however, you need to know about how RackAFX simplifies some of the work for you, depending on the MIDI message. For the note on messages, RackAFX converts the MIDI *byte* data into more manageable UINT types. The three arguments are:

UINT uChannel: 0–15 for 16 total channels
UINT uMIDINote: the MIDI note number 0->127 for the note event
UINT uMIDIVelocity: the note ON velocity 0->127 for the note event

The first step is to check the MIDI channel and bail out if it is not a channel we are playing or support. More details will surface in the next chapter when we look more closely at the MIDI messages. After checking, we do the necessary event stuff.

```
bool __stdcall CMiniSynth::midiNoteOn(UINT uChannel, UINT uMIDINote,
                                       UINT uVelocity)
```

For note off messages, RackAFX converts the MIDI *byte* data into more manageable UINT types. The three arguments are:

UINT uChannel: 0–15 for 16 total channels
UINT uMIDINote: the MIDI note number 0->127 for the note event
UINT uMIDIVelocity: the note off velocity 0->127 for the note event (most MIDI keyboards do not transmit this value)
bool bAllNotesOff: a MIDI panic message to turn every note off

```
bool __stdcall CMiniSynth::midiNoteOff(UINT uChannel, UINT uMIDINote,
                                        UINT uVelocity, bool bAllNotesOff)
```

MIDI Mod Wheel

The mod wheel is standard on most MIDI keyboard controllers. It is typically mapped to the LFO depth. Unlike VST3 and AU, RackAFX decodes and sends this message separately from the other continuous controller (CC) messages simply because it is so common on synth products. The mod wheel value is 0 to 127. As with note on and off, RackAFX converts the *bytes* into UINTs for you.

UINT uChannel: 0–15 for 16 total channels
UINT uModValue: the wheel position from 0->127

```
bool __stdcall CMiniSynth::midiModWheel(UINT uChannel, UINT uModValue)
```

MIDI Pitch Bend

Pitch bend is a special MIDI message because it uses a 14-bit value to indicate the pitch bend amount to make the bends smoother. With a range of 0 to 127 only (seven bits), you would hear pitch transitions that would not sound smooth. For this message RackAFX sends you two versions of the pitch bend value, once as a signed integer (−8192 to + 8191) and again as a floating point value (−1.0 to +1.0). In both cases, 0 represents the center position of the control or no pitch bend.

```
// nActualPitchBendValue        = -8192 -> +8191, 0 at center
// fNormalizedPitchBendValue    = -1.0  -> +1.0,  0 at center
```

```
bool __stdcall CMiniSynth::midiPitchBend(UINT uChannel,
                                          int nActualPitchBendValue,
                                          float fNormalizedPitchBendValue)
```

All Other MIDI Messages

To tell the host that you want all the MIDI messages, you set the *m_bWantAllMIDIMessages* flag to *true* in the constructor. All of our synths (on all platforms) support the following additional MIDI messages:

- volume (cc 7)
- pan (cc 10)
- expression (cc 11)
- sustain pedal
- program change
- polyphonic aftertouch
- channel aftertouch

We will discuss the meaning of "CC 7" and the like in the next chapter. Right now it is important to understand that this message sends MIDI *bytes* as arguments (an *unsigned char* is a *byte*). After testing the MIDI channel, we next decode the status byte. If it is a control change message, we then decode the type of message in data byte 1 and forward the information to the voice objects. The value is encoded in data byte 2. This is detailed in the next chapter.

```
bool __stdcall CMiniSynth::midiMessage(unsigned char cChannel,
                                        unsigned char cStatus,
                                        unsigned char cData1,
                                        unsigned char cData2)
```

This wraps up our basic discussion of RackAFX plug-ins. You will learn more and more about RackAFX programming as you go through the chapters on developing the synth objects and handling MIDI messages (Chapters 3–8). Chapter Challenges will require you to do more and more of your own programming. By the time we get to the synth design chapters (Chapters 9–13) you will be quite proficient and won't need any more hand-holding—you'll be able to start your own synth projects from scratch.

2.15 Writing VST3 Plug-ins

Steinberg, GmbH originally developed the VST plug-in API in 1996 to provide a simple cross-platform compatible plug-in solution. The API for versions 1 and 2 was very lean in comparison with Microsoft's Direct-X, a competing format at the time, and VST was met with success: nearly every audio recording and editing software package eventually adhered to the VST client specification. VST2.4 represents the most mature version of that branch of the VST tree. It is likely that there are more plug-ins available, both commercial and free, in the VST2 format than any other plug-in format to date. VST2 plug-ins are packaged in a Dynamic-Link Library with the *.dll* file extension.

VST3 was introduced in 2008, not as an update but rather a complete overhaul and redo from scratch, so VST3 and VST2 are not directly compatible. Like VST2, the plug-in is packaged in a dynamic-link library, however the extension is renamed from *.dll* to *.vst3*. In September 2013, Steinberg officially stopped support for VST2 and removed the VST2 Software Developer's Kit (SDK) from its website. Steinberg's removal of the SDK and obsoleting of the API means that eventually just about all major VST clients will support VST3. Due to the large number of VST2 plug-ins available, it is unlikely that clients will stop support for VST2 any time soon. In addition, VST3 provides a wrapper mechanism, similar to the one in *Designing Audio Effects Plug-Ins in C++*, to wrap a VST3 plug-in so that it appears as a VST2.

> VST2 and VST3 provide two mechanisms for implementing a GUI. The VST client provides a default GUI in case the plug-in does not implement one. There is also an option for a custom GUI. We will implement both. We need to define the default GUI first and then connect the custom GUI to its parameters. You can alternate back and forth between the two GUIs in the VST Client.

This book covers VST3 only. If you want to get into VST2 for Windows, you might want to check out RackAFX since it can compile directly as a VST2 plug-in and also has VST2 plug-in template generators. The first thing you need to do is download the Steinberg VST3 SDK. You will need a developer's account (free) and a version of Microsoft Visual Studio Professional (the Express versions won't work here). The SDK contains examples for both VS2008 and VS2010.

You can get the SDK at http://www.steinberg.net/en/company/developer.html, and the projects in this book were written with the newest version at the time, 3.6.0. When you unzip the SDK, you will find a fairly massive hierarchy of folders and sub-folders containing all the base class object files, VSTGUI editor files and sample code. You may install this set of folders just about anywhere on a local drive, but we suggest simply placing it in your root directory.

The documentation is in HTML in the main directory as *index.html*—you should open that in your browser and bookmark it; you will be referring to it often. A fundamental issue with the SDK lies in the hierarchical nature of the folders, which manifests itself as *#include* statements in the files in various folders In other words, the files are pre-set to reference each other in this specific directory hierarchy. If you modify the folder hierarchy, try to move files around, or consolidate or flatten out directories, bad things will happen when you try to compile either the Steinberg sample projects or any of the projects in this book.

> Do not under any circumstances alter the hierarchy of the SDK folders. In some cases you may get away with re-naming folders, but in general you should avoid modifying the directories, except in the manner revealed in this chapter.

Setting up the Directory Hierarchy

It is critical that you create your projects in the correct folder hierarchy, otherwise the compiler won't be able to find all the files to build and link with. When you install the SDK, you will need to find the folder containing the sample code for a Windows plug-in; here we are going to use the project named *note_expression_synth*, but any sample code folder will do. This folder is located at:

```
<Root>
- VST3SDK
        - public.sdk
                - samples
                        - vst
                                - note_expression_synth
                                        - win
```

The *win* folder contains the Visual Studio project files. The important thing to notice here is that *win* project folder is four layers deep inside of *public.sdk*. You have two options here: either keep all your synth project folders in the *vst* folder and declare a subfolder under each project folder (you can name it *win* if you like, but the actual name is unimportant), or build your own hierarchy that mimics the four-layers-from-public.sdk. This is what we did so that we could keep our synth projects in one main folder. We created the following hierarchy:

```
<Root>
- VST3 SDK
        - public.sdk
                - MyProjects
                        - SynthProjects
                                - Windows
                                        - NanoSynth
                                        - MiniSynth
                                        - DigiSynth
                                        - VectorSynth
                                        - AniSynth
                                        - DXSynth
```

Each synth project folder is inside the *Windows* folder, and each one is four layers deep inside *public.sdk*. Make sure you get this sorted out at the beginning else your code won't compile at all.

Starting a New Project

Starting a new VST3 project from scratch is arduous at best and downright frustrating at worst. Our strongest advice is to download the sample projects and use them as a basis. We have multiple versions you may download, a set for each synth project:

- empty—you write everything and you design the GUI—if you are already an advanced VST3 programmer, this might be a good option
- GUI only—the GUI code and UI is already done so you can focus on the synth components and processing; in each chapter you'll have the chance to go in and modify the GUI a bit at a time, and after a few projects, you might want to take on the complete GUI design NOTE: this is the recommended option!
- full—the whole project inclusive; we don't recommend simply compiling someone else's code as a learning method, however having the full code allows you to not only check your own work but also step through the code in debug mode so you can see how the client interacts—in short, the full projects are excellent for helping you debug and understand your own projects-in-progress

Another method is to start with one of the sample projects, copy the project folder to a new project name, then modify the files and Visual Studio as described in Appendix A. It shows you step-by-step how to modify the project to convert it anew. This is especially useful since the progression of MiniSynth, DigiSynth, VectorSynth, AniSynth all build upon one another. If you really want to start a complete project from scratch, you can get that information from the website too, but beware: it is not for the faint of heart.

Once you have the SDK installed and a supported version of Visual Studio running, you are ready to start developing VST3 plug-ins. However, you will need a way to test your plug-in functionality. Remember that a DLL is an incomplete entity and requires a client to load it, instantiate its objects and use it. You will need to install a Windows VST3 host; we prefer Cubase since it is a Steinberg product, and we expect the tightest and most robust integration. Remember to make sure the client specifically supports VST3. In the chapters that follow, you will get specific instructions on building the VST3 synths. They will often refer back to this chapter so bookmark it for later. Let's get started.

Project Details

Each VST3 project is packaged in a Visual Studio Solution. Its name will vary depending on your Visual Studio version. VS2008 users need to open projects using the solution *(.sln)* file named *<project>.sln* while VS2010 and later users will open the *<project>_vc10.sln*. The solution has two projects inside; the first is a base library project. The second project is your actual synth. The base project differs according to the Visual Studio version while the synth project is identical for both. The solution for the MiniSynth project is shown in Figure 2.19. We used Visual Studio Filters to group the sets of files accordingly. The SynthCore filter contains all the object files for the synth—this will be different for each project. The plug-in files are located in the VSTSource filter.

When you compile the solution, it first compiles the base project into a static library. Then, it compiles your synth project and statically links it to the previously built base. The resulting file is a DLL with its suffix changed to *.vst3*. The only real major issue here is that all these added files (127 in total) can be difficult to maintain. The sheer number of files makes starting these projects from scratch quite tedious. In any event, one thing you must do for yourself is decide where the output folder is going to be located. This is the folder that will receive the final *.vst3* plug-in file. You then copy this file into your client's VST3 folder and have the client re-scan it to pick up the changes. It may be tempting to set the file destination folder to the client's VST3 folder, saving you the hassle of manually copying the file. However, do this at your own risk. An issue is that this folder must also be the output destination for the static base library that gets compiled first. The compiler creates and writes a slew of intermediate files to this folder that are not deleted upon successful compilation. This pollutes the folder with a bunch of non-VST3 files.

To set up your output folders, open the project properties for both the base library and synth. In the *Configuration Properties -> General*, browse and find your output destination folder. Make this the intermediate directory also (it will do this by default). Make sure to set these folders in both the release and debug configurations (easy to forget).

Additional Files

We have set up the VST projects to be as similar as possible. The main difference will be in the SynthCore—the set of C++ objects that make up each individual synth. You will get a list of these files for each synth project, however there are three files that are necessary for each one and are identical:

- *synthfunctions.h*: a collection of the structures and functions that are used throughout the synth objects; you can add more of your own here too
- *pluginconstants.h*: another collection of structures, functions and objects that are used in the synth projects
- *pluginobjects.cpp*: the implementations of objects declared in *pluginconstants.h*

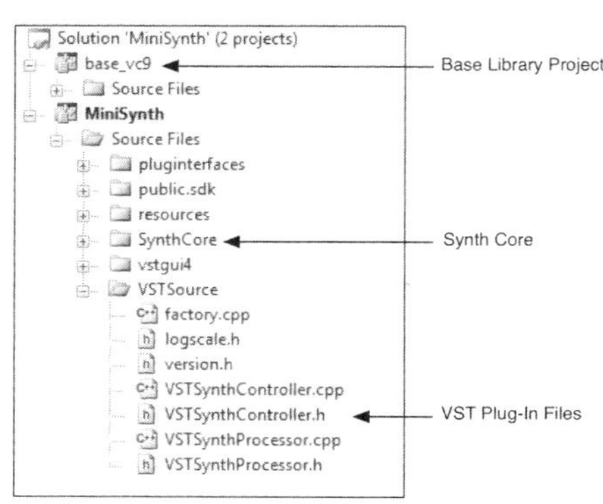

Figure 2.19: The MiniSynth VST3 solution contains two projects.

2.16 VST3: Processor and Controller

You learned how plug-ins are packaged inside of dynamic-link libraries or DLLs in the beginning of this chapter and how C++ is useful because we can define an abstract base class that the plug-in developer users in his or her own derived classes. For example in RackAFX the base class is called *CPlugIn*, and it defines and implements methods for handling the processing and user interaction with the GUI.

VST2 is similar in that it defines a single base class that handles both the audio processing and the user interaction with the GUI controls. The base class is called *AudioEffectX*, and it inherits from an earlier base class named *AudioEffect*. One of the ways that VST3 is different (make that very different) is that it uses two separate C++ objects to handle the two main tasks of audio processing and user interaction. These are named the *Processor* and *Controller* objects. You will be spending most of your coding time inside these two objects. Figure 2.20 shows a very simplistic block diagram—the Processor handles audio input/output processing while the Controller maintains the user interface. VST3 plug-ins may have any number of audio inputs and outputs and may also be side-chained.

Your Processor object will inherit from a base class called *AudioEffect* (no relation to VST2's base class of the same name), and this object will handle the job of audio processing or in our case, synthesis also called rendering. It will also receive control change information when the user adjusts a control, and it will modify the processing as needed. The Processor object will answer queries from the client regarding the audio bussing capabilities and audio format capabilities. It will also receive, decode and handle MIDI note on and note off messages. The Processor also implements the task of serialization, which means the loading and storing of the state of the plug-in at any given time to and from a serialized binary file. The term serialize is used because the parameters will be stored in series, one after another in the file. This allows the client to initialize your plug-in the same way it was left when the project was last saved/closed, as well as providing very basic user-preset loading and storing capabilities.

Your Controller object will inherit from a base class called *EditController*. In VST parlance, the terms "edit" and "editor" refer to the GUI or its associated objects and not a text or audio editor. If the Processor is already receiving control change information, why do you need a separate Controller object? The answer is that your Controller object will handle initialization and setup of the GUI control parameters and implement the communication mechanism that sends and receives information to and from the GUI. This is a separate job from dealing with the control change messages that alter the rendering of the audio. The Controller also handles the automation of your controls if the user wishes to record and playback control movements. The Controller must also handle serialization (again) but only on the read-side. Finally, your Controller object will also deal with the setup of MIDI controllers.

To recap, the two main VST3 objects implement the following:

Processor:

- initialization and queries from host about channel count and audio formats
- handling GUI control changes
- responding to MIDI note on and note off events
- processing (rendering) the audio stream
- serialization of the plug-in's parameters to and from a file (read/write)

Controller:

- declaration and initialization of the GUI control parameters
- implementation of sending and receiving parameter changes
- MIDI controller setup
- read-side serialization
- creation and maintenance of a custom GUI (optional)

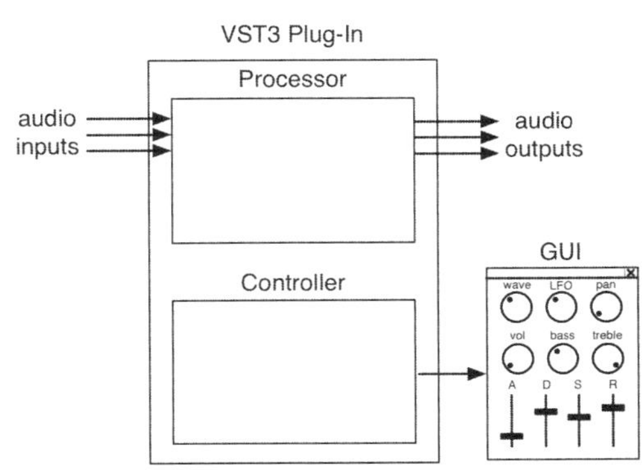

Figure 2.20: A VST3 plug-in consists of Processor and Controller sub-components.

There are a few details of the Processor/Controller model to consider. First, the Processor should be able to run completely on its own without the Controller and should not need to know about the Controller's existence. You can see that it is already setup for this since it deals with control information, processing and serialization—all the basic operations of the plug-in. Next, the desirable configuration is to implement two completely separate objects, which could not only run without knowledge of each other, but could also run on different processors or even separate computers in different locations. Our synths will be implemented in this configuration, though as the documentation points out, some plug-ins might require resources that do not allow the Processor and Controller to run on separate processors or in different processor contexts. Lastly, it is possible to combine the two objects into one, but Steinberg highly discourages this, so we won't pursue that option.

2.17 The Common Object Model: COM

VST3 is developed using the Common Object Model or COM. COM programming is a Microsoft invention. Simply stated, COM programming is a way of writing software components. It is neither a separate language nor an extension to a language. In fact, it is language independent, though of course here we will be using C++. COM is a programming paradigm that evolved from a Microsoft technology of the 1980s called Object Linking and Embedding (OLE), where the idea was to allow you to edit multiple things in one document. It effectively allowed one piece of software to run—or at least appear to run—inside another (you can see there is a relationship to plug-ins here, where the DLL "runs" inside the client). OLE was ambitious but often glitchy and sometimes crash-y. COM helped fix some of the issues there. Microsoft then used COM again in the Direct-X plug-in API in the 1990s, parts of which still survive today.

The good news is that you won't need to do any COM programming if you are using the projects in this book since that code is already written for you. In fact, much of the low level COM stuff is buried deep inside of base classes, and we won't need to go there. However, you will see COM programming paradigms in the VST3 documentation and in our code. If you want to go deeper into it and implement things like Steinberg's note expression or give your plug-in the ability to load and store banks of presets or other extended functionality, you will have to do some COM programming work.

One of the most important things that COM does is that it completely separates the client and plug-in from one another in a safe way. It does this by using the concepts of components and interfaces. A long time ago, software was written in a monolithic way with a set of variable declarations and a run-loop all packaged inside of one executable. As the applications got larger, software engineers began to break up the monolithic application into a set of functional component blocks. In this way, separate teams of programmers could work on separate components. A special problem with this approach involves making sure that the components all fit together and communicate properly, and most importantly that they do not ultimately break the application—also known as a crash. This is where the interface concept comes into play.

Suppose that for some reason, you are determined to put a big-block Chevy V8 engine in your Honda automobile. You rip out the tiny Honda motor and drop in the V8. But the V8 expects to be connected to a Chevy transmission. The Honda transmission mounting plate is the wrong size and the mounting holes are all metric! What you need is an interface that lets you connect the two in a robust and safe way. With this Chevy-Honda interface in place, the Honda transmission doesn't know it's connected to a Chevy—as far as it is concerned, it's connected to a Honda engine. Likewise, the V8 thinks it's connected to a Chevy transmission. Interfaces are portable, so you could take the Chevy-Honda interface and connect it to the side of your house so that now a Chevy motor can be attached to it on one side and a Honda transmission on the other. With the interface established, the two do not need to know about each other, nor do they care about each other's implementation details. They also don't care about the language used to design each other.

This makes a lot of sense for our client/plug-in design paradigm. The client software doesn't need to know about the details of the implementation of the plug-in and vice-versa. And, as long as the plug-in implements the required set of functions, it is guaranteed to be seen as a proper plug-in and loaded into the client's address space. If you've used RackAFX to make a VST2/3 compatible DLL, then you have already seen this. The single RackAFX DLL file works as both a RackAFX plug-in, VST2 plug-in, and a VST3 plug-in. This is because it implements three sets of interfaces—it can "dock" to either platform.

Broadly speaking, a COM interface is a set of functions whose function pointers are laid out in memory in a specific way. Since we are writing in C++, a COM interface will consist of member functions on a C++ base class object. Interestingly, this COM base class is actually known as an interface too. These COM C++ classes (interfaces) are pure abstract. When we want to implement a COM interface in one of our plug-in objects, we will derive our plug-in object from that COM object. In other words, we will inherit from the abstract base class and implement the functions that will define the interface. By making the COM class pure abstract, it forces the derived class to implement specific functions. This forms a kind of contract between the two.

Once the derived class has properly implemented the required functions, it is now considered to possess the interface and the client can safely use it. If we want to implement another COM interface that lets us add some new functionality, we will add that COM interface to our class declaration and inherit from it—thus multiple inheritance is key for implementing multiple COM interfaces on your objects. In COM jargon, when you derive your class from a COM base class (interface), and you implement the base class functions, you are "exposing the interface." Microsoft packages the fundamental COM interfaces in a COM Library. The 32-bit Microsoft version of COM is packaged in OLE32.LIB. VST3 uses its own version of COM, and these files are compiled directly into your VST3 plug-in. The names of the interfaces and functions are nearly identical to the Microsoft version. Remember that COM is a way of programming, so manufacturer variations can exist.

COM objects connect together and communicate via the interfaces. If you have done any serious C++ programming, you have already used a similar concept perhaps many times. Suppose object A needs to call a function on object B—they need to be connected and communication needs to occur. One way to handle this is to give object A a pointer to object B (let's name the pointer pObjectB). Object A then uses that pointer to call an object B method:

```
float fCoefficient = pObjectB->calculateCoefficient();
```

There is a safety issue here. Suppose this is part of a large project where one team is working on this component. A junior engineer, thinking he's cleaning up properly, then writes:

```
float fCoefficient = pObjectB->calculateCoefficient();
delete pObjectB;
```

Poof! Object B is destroyed. But, object B is used later on in another component module that another team is designing. Because the project is component-ized, this bug may not appear until months later when a senior software engineer finally connects the components together. Someone is going to have some explaining to do.

COM gets around this problem. The client can't get a pointer to a COM-derived object. It can only get a pointer to an interface on that object. With this interface pointer, the client can use the COM object by calling its methods to do work. It can even use this interface pointer to query the object and ask it which other interfaces it exposes. But how can the client get an interface pointer from an object without having a pointer to the object—doesn't the object need to be created before the client can ask it for an interface pointer? The answer is that when the client creates the COM object, it does not use the *new* operator. Instead, it uses a COM creation function—in VST3 it is named *createInstance()*; Microsoft's version is called *CoCreateInstance()*. This function creates the object (with the *new* operator) but does not return a pointer to the derived class object. It returns a pointer to the base class COM interface instead. But if the client calls the *createInstance()* method, it must have some way of specifying the component it wants to instantiate such as the Will Pirkle MiniSynth object. We will see how this is handled shortly and don't worry—we're almost done with the COM stuff.

All COM objects must expose a common interface that the client uses to connect to the other interfaces. All communication from the client to the plug-in is done via interfaces. If you use Hungarian notation like we do, then you have become accustomed to naming your C++ classes with a capital "C," for example *CSynth* or *CReverb*. The capital letter "*I*" indicates that a C++ object is really a COM interface. Your VST3 Processor object ultimately inherits from *IAudioProcessor*, and your Controller object inherits from *IEditController*. You are going to see these "*I*" terms all over the VST3 plug-in code. Since all objects must expose a common interface that the client uses to connect to other interfaces, what should that interface be named? Microsoft chose to call it *IUnknown*. Steinberg's version is called *FUnknown*. Funky, eh? Either way, the notion of an "unknown" interface is something that has probably turned off more than a few programmers from exploring COM; it does seem confusing. We don't have a better name for it either.

Let's wrap up this section on COM by learning how the creation function knows what kind of COM object to instantiate. This is done by uniquely identifying each COM object. Your Processor needs one of these unique identifiers and so does your Controller. Every COM object requires one. When the VST client creates a VST3 plug-in, it will use one of these unique identifiers to specify which plug-in it wants. Therefore it is important that every VST3 plug-in component we write has a unique identifier. Two developers might accidentally name their plug-in the same way—GoldenFlanger. But as long as they have unique identifiers, the VST3 host can instantiate both GoldenFlangers without conflicts. If you accidentally create a new VST3 plug-in that has the same unique identifier as one that is already loaded in the client, the client will either ignore its existence or instantiate the wrong object when asked.

Microsoft calls these unique identifiers Globally Unique IDentifiers or GUIDs (pronounced "goo-idz"). Steinberg's COM version names them FUIDs—"foo-idz." A GUID or FUID is a 128-bit value. The easiest way to generate one is with Microsoft's GUID generator, which is called *guidgen.exe*. You can find it in your Microsoft Visual Studio compiler folder. Launch this executable, and a window will pop up with a button that says "New GUID"—hit that button and then hit the Copy button below it to copy it to the clipboard. Then, you can paste it into your VST3 code with just a bit of formatting manipulation. The *guidgen.exe* program generates a GUID from a unique timestamp based on the number of 100 nanosecond intervals that have elapsed since midnight of 15 October 1582. This guarantees that no duplicate GUIDs will be generated until around 3400A.D. Microsoft GUIDs have the format:

```
[Guid("846EB93F-3247-487F-A901-10E8ED4ACC34")]
```

Steinberg FUIDs are declared like this (here it's the FUID for a Controller object):

```
FUID Controller::cid(0xB561D747, 0xBA004597, 0xA3BF911A, 0x5DA2AFA4);
```

Both Microsoft and Steinberg's GUIDs are 128-bits, you just have to format the numbers properly. For example, to use the above Microsoft GUID as a VST3 FUID for this Controller you would just manipulate the digits as follows, removing the dashes and consolidating:

```
[Guid("846EB93F-3247-487F-A901-10E8ED4ACC34")]
```

becomes:

```
FUID Controller::cid(0x846EB93F, 0x3247487F, 0xA90110E8, 0xED4ACC34);
```

2.18 VST3 Synth Plug-in Architecture

Now that you understand some of the basics of COM, let's re-examine the VST3 plug-in architecture, focusing specifically on synth plug-ins. Figure 2.21 shows a more COM-centric view of the VST3 synth plug-in; the Processor and Controllers are really COM components with interfaces, represented by the circle-and-line, which somewhat resemble gear-shift controls. You might think of the VST3 client as a multi-armed entity with hands on each of the interface controls jumping back and forth between the interfaces.

On the Processor, the *IAudioProcessor* interface exposes many more interfaces that we will use to receive MIDI events, control information, and audio I/O, though our synth plug-ins will be output-only. On the Controller, *IEditController* maintains the GUI parameters, *IMIDIMapping* deals with mapping the MIDI CC's to GUI parameters, and *IPlugView* is used to instantiate our GUI.

One of the responsibilities of the Processor is to declare the plug-in's input and output capabilities. There are three different kinds of I/O for the Processor: audio, MIDI events and parameters. Figure 2.22 shows the block diagram of a generic Processor component. The audio and MIDI Events move though busses, which are zero-indexed and named bus 0, bus 1, etc. A plug-in may have any combination of input and output busses. In the most generic version here, the Processor may receive and transmit MIDI events and control change information.

Audio busses may have any number of channels so do not confuse bus with channel. Our synth plug-ins are going to implement a single audio output bus named bus 0 but that bus is stereo with two channels. MIDI event busses support some number of MIDI channels, which we decide upon. There is only one parameter bus that the processor does not have to declare. Our synth plug-ins will only accept input parameters and will not transmit any, though template code is in place if you want to experiment with passing parameters and MIDI information out of the plug-in.

The Controller component shown in Figure 2.23 depicts how the GUI communicates with the Parameters in its container. In this case the GUI might be the default version or a custom design. MIDI CC information may be mapped to the GUI controls as a kind of external control mechanism. Also, we may use sub-controllers as helpers for some of the more complicated GUI controls; we will use this for the vector joystick control in Chapter 11. The Controller object does not have to declare any busses, and the underlying interfaces do most of the work for you, so you really only need to setup the Controller and optionally a custom GUI. After everything is properly set up, it will essentially handle its own operation. This is a nice feature of VST3.

Figure 2.24 shows a complete diagram of our VST3 synth architecture. A MIDI controller sends note events to the Processor and control events to the Controller. The Processor has only one input bus, the event bus 0 and only one output bus, the stereo audio output bus 0. Although the Controller maintains the user interface, the Processor will also receive control change information. This figure is very revealing. First, notice the roundabout way that MIDI controller messages are routed through the parameter container and then

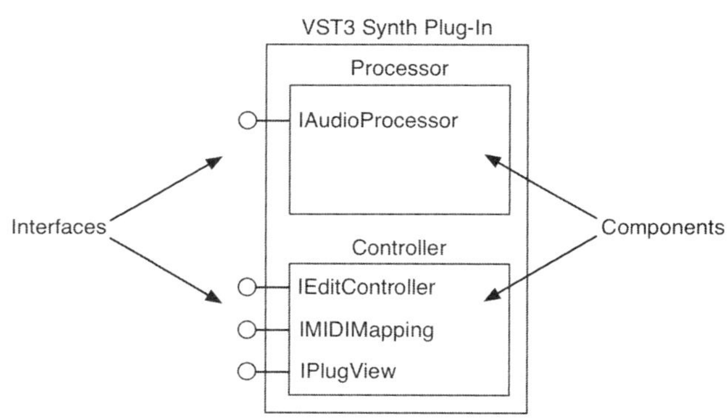

Figure 2.21: A more complete view of the VST3 plug-in architecture shows its COM components and interfaces.

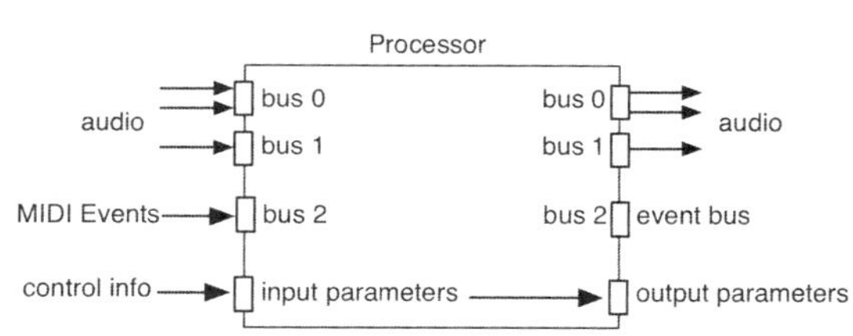

Figure 2.22: A generic plug-in Processor component includes busses for dealing with I/O.

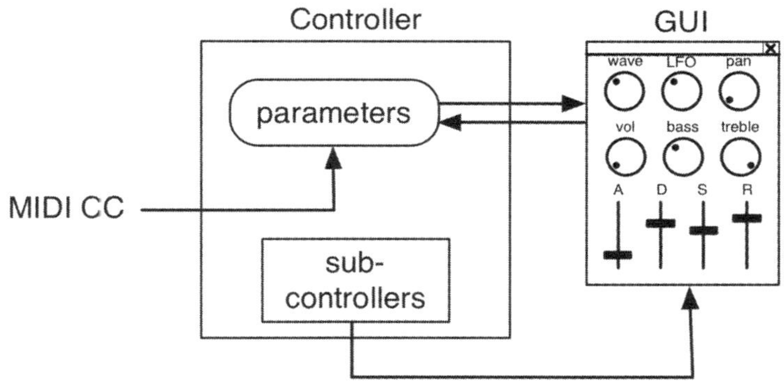

Figure 2.23: A Controller stores the parameters, communicates with the GUI, handles MIDI CC mapping and optionally creates sub-controllers for finer control of the GUI.

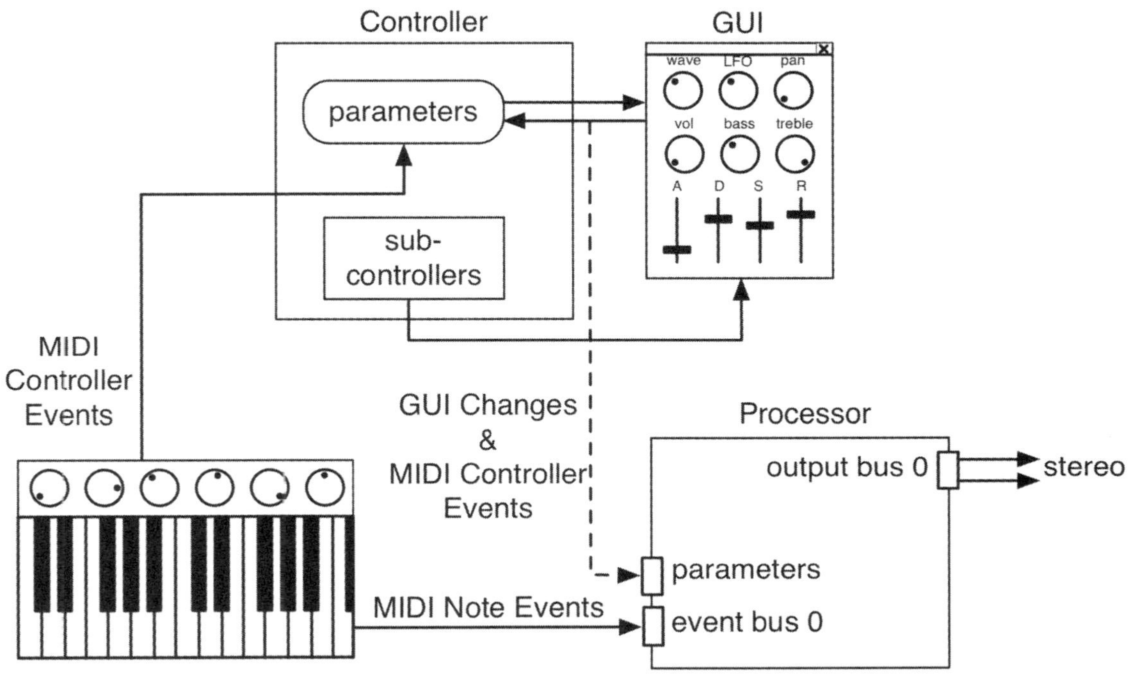

Figure 2.24: Our VST3 Synth Architecture.

into the Processor. The dotted line shows the parameters that the VST3 framework delivers to the Processor, consisting of GUI control changes and MIDI controller events. This is by design, so that we may re-route MIDI controllers on-the-fly. We will discuss the MIDI controller details in Section 2.25. Next, you might be wondering why we need the VST3 framework to deliver the parameters. Why can't you just query the Controller object directly in a similar fashion to the way you query the AU parameter cloud when you need to access its GUI data. The separation of the Controller and Processor objects is a critical part of the design paradigm in VST3, and great care is taken to try to keep these objects apart. While it is possible to set up a communication path between the two objects via the host, you cannot use that signal path during real-time processing; it is excessively slow and would bog down the system. See the VST3 documentation for more details. Part of writing VST3 plug-ins involves declaring variables for each GUI control; we would not have to do that if the Processor could directly access the Controller's parameters. This is the case in AU plug-ins where the processing function can directly access the GUI control variables.

2.19 Processor and Controller Declarations

Before looking at the COM creation mechanism, let's look at simple examples of a Processor and Controller. This is taken from the MiniSynth project, so you can open it in Visual Studio and trace through the base classes and interfaces. With a little poking around you can even find the declaration of the *FUnknown* interface.

The Processor object we are going to use in all the synths in the book will have the same name—*Processor*. The Controller will be named *Controller* and these two objects will be packaged in the files:

VSTSynthProcessor.h
VSTSynthProcessor.cpp
VSTSynthController.h
VSTSynthController.cpp

These files are in every synth project, and you will be spending the majority of your plug-in programming time working in them. The *Processor* object for the MiniSynth project is declared here:

```
class Processor : public AudioEffect
{
public:
     // --- constructor
     Processor();

     <SNIP SNIP SNIP>

};
```

If you look into the *AudioEffect* object (right-click on *AudioEffect* and choose "Go To Declaration"), you will find:

```
class AudioEffect: public Component,
                   public IAudioProcessor
{
public:
     /** constructor */
     AudioEffect ();

     <SNIP SNIP SNIP>

};
```

Drilling down into the *Component* object, we get:

```
class Component: public ComponentBase,
                 public IComponent
{
public:
     /** constructor */
     Component ();

     <SNIP SNIP SNIP>

};
```

If you keep descending through the *ComponentBase*, you will ultimately terminate at an interface derived from *FUnknown*—everything ultimately derives from this interface. So your controller has many sets of interfaces on it. You don't really have to get too deep in this, but you need to know what's down there. Back in the *VSTProcessor.h* file, you can find the following two COM declarations, which all COM objects must implement:

```
     // --- our COM creation method
     static FUnknown* createInstance(void*) { return (IAudioProcessor*)new
                                              Processor(); }
     // --- our Globally Unique ID
     static FUID cid;
```

The *createInstance()* method creates and returns a pointer to the *IAudioProcessor* interface; since *IAudioProcessor* ultimately derives from *FUnknown*, the function returns the *FUnknown* pointer as we expect—the *FUnknown* pointer is always the return value from creation functions. Below that is the declaration for the FUID. At the top of the *VSTProcesssor.cpp* file you can find the definition of the FUID named "cid:"

```
FUID Processor::cid(0x91F037DC, 0xA35343AB, 0x852C37B1, 0x3774DC90);
```

In the *VSTController.h* file you can find the declaration for the Controller:

```
class Controller: public EditController, public IMidiMapping, public
                  ST3EditorDelegate
{
public:

    <SNIP SNIP SNIP>

}
```

IMIDIMapping is a "direct" interface as it inherits only from *FUnknown*, while *EditController* (like *AudioEffect*) is a set of interfaces many layers deep. When you see the "I," you know that there is a bit more to do than just the *createInstance()* and FUID declarations. The *VST3EditorDelegate* is an object that deals with the certain kind of GUI we will implement. We need to override a few of its functions later. As before, we can find these two declarations:

```
    // --- Our COM Creating Method
    static FUnknown* createInstance(void*) {return (IEditController*)new
                                                Controller();}
    // --- our globally unique ID value
    static FUID cid;
```

createInstance() returns a pointer to the *IEditController* interface (as an *FUnknown* pointer). When we specify the direct interface *IMIDIMapping* in the class declaration, we need to override all of its pure abstract functions. Looking into that file (*ivsteditcontroller.h*), you will see that it only has one pure abstract function, denoted by the " = 0;" below:

```
virtual tresult PLUGIN_API getMidiControllerAssignment(int32 busIndex,
                                        int16 channel,
                                        CtrlNumber midiControllerNumber,
                                ParamID& id/*out*/) = 0;
```

PLUGIN_API

- is defined as __stdcall, the same as RackAFX uses and described in the RackAFX section

tresult

is defined as **int32** which is just a normal *int* datatype and is a return code that usually is either true (*kResultTrue*) or false (*kResultFalse*) and you can find the others in *funknown.h*

So, we need to implement this method to expose the *IMIDIMapping* interface. You will also see a line of code near the bottom of the *Controller* declaration that says

```
    DEF_INTERFACE (IMidiMapping)
```

This is our declaration of an interface. If you go deeper into VST3 programming and want to add more interfaces, you will need to remember to implement the required pure abstract methods and declare the interface. Note that some interface methods will be optional and will already have a base class implementation. You choose the additional methods you want to override in that case. It has a "use only what you need" quality to it.

2.20 The Class Factory

We only have one more file to discuss and then we'll be finished with the basics of VST3 and we can move on to implementation strategy. We still have the detail of construction of the Processor and Controller objects. COM uses the class factory approach, where the class factory is a COM component whose sole job is to create new components. You can dig down and find the class factory files if you want to, but we only need to deal with one short file to declare and identify our two VST3 objects for the factory. This file is called *factory.cpp* and it declares our objects. You will need to modify this file each time you create a new VST3 plug-in. At the top of the file you will find (for the MiniSynth project):

```
#define stringPluginName "MiniSynth"
BEGIN_FACTORY_DEF ("Will Pirkle",
                   http://www.willpirkle.com/synthbook/",
                   mailto:will@willpirkle.com")
```

If you are using this as a template you will need to change the plugin name string from MiniSynth to whatever your new plug-in name is and of course change the manufacturer from Will Pirkle and website, etc. Below this you find the two massive declarations starting with the Processor:

```
DEF_CLASS2 (INLINE_UID_FROM_FUID(Steinberg::Vst::MiniSynth::
                                 Processor::cid),
                                 PClassInfo::kManyInstances,
                                 kVstAudioEffectClass,
                                 stringPluginName,
                                 Vst::kDistributable,
                                 Vst::PlugType::kInstrumentSynth,
                                 FULL_VERSION_STR,
                                 kVstVersionString,
                                 Steinberg::Vst::MiniSynth::
                                 Processor::createInstance)
```

The important variables are identified in bold—at the top is the cid or FUID that uniquely identifies this component. *PClassInfo::kManyInstances* states that the host may instantiate the same plug-in object multiple times. Unless you have a really compelling reason to limit your plug-in to one instance—perhaps it is a demo version—then leave this alone. *kAudioEffectClass* tells the client we are an audio effect, while *kDistributable* identifies that we implement two separate and distinct components that may be run on different processors or processor contexts or computers. The *PlugType* is a synth (*kInstrumentSynth*) and the last argument is our creation function.

The Controller's declaration is similar with a FUID (cid) and other flags. In the Controller declaration, the *kDistributable* and *PlugType* are not used, thus the 0 and "" in the argument list.

```
DEF_CLASS2 (INLINE_UID_FROM_FUID(Steinberg::Vst::MiniSynth::
                                     Controller::cid),
                                     PClassInfo::kManyInstances,
                                     kVstComponentControllerClass,
                                     stringPluginName, 0, "",
                                     FULL_VERSION_STR,
                                     kVstVersionString,
                            Steinberg::Vst::MiniSynth::
                                     Controller::createInstance)
```

So, ultimately every one of your synth plug-in projects is going to contain the following files. Each time you start a new project, you will be working mainly in these files.

factory.cpp
VSTSynthProcessor.h
VSTSynthProcessor.cpp
VSTSynthController.h
VSTSynthController.cpp

Back in the MiniSynth project in Visual Studio, you can see that the Solution contains two Projects. One is named *base_vcX* where X is either 9 or 10 depending on your Visual Studio version. This project is compiled first, and it creates a static library packaged in a *.lib* file. The second Project contains several file groups:

- plugininterfaces
- public.sdk
- vstgui4

These first three groups contain scores of support files that are needed for everything from base class management and interfaces to the GUI controls. You will never need to alter any of these files.

The SynthCore group contains all the synthesizer C++ object files that you will develop first. These files will vary from project to project but will generally be about 90% similar. After you have properly designed and debugged these objects in the early chapters, you should not need to alter them again when designing the synthesizers unless you want to add stuff that isn't in the stock projects.

The Resources group contains the knob and background images and *.uidesc* files that are needed to build the GUI.

The VSTSource filter is where you spend most of your time. It has the five object files we discussed in the previous section as well as a couple of helper files named *logscale.h* and *version.h*, neither of which you will need to modify.

2.21 VST3 Conventions

There are some conventions you will see in VST3 that you need to be aware of.

Use of namespaces

VST3 makes use of namespaces to avoid name collisions. The Processor, Controller and classfactory files all enclose their contents with three namespaces. For each synth, you need to change the third namespace to the synth name; here is how the namespaces look for MiniSynth.

```
namespace Steinberg {
namespace Vst {
namespace MiniSynth {

<--- interface or implementation --->

}}} // namespaces
```

You will see these in use in the *factory.cpp* file in the class definitions, for example:

```
INLINE_UID_FROM_FUID(Steinberg::Vst::MiniSynth::Processor::cid)
and
Steinberg::Vst::MiniSynth::Processor::createInstance
```

You can also see how the different namespace scopes are used (again from *factory.cpp*):

```
Vst::kDistributable
```

If you need more information on namespaces, visit www.cplusplus.com.

Constant Values Start with the Letter 'k'

In the VST3 API, you will see a mixed use of Hungarian notation. When Steinberg declares constant values, they add the Hungarian notation hint "k" to the beginning of the constant, for example *kResultTrue* and *kResultFalse*. Perhaps this is because the German word for "constant" is konstante?

Methods Return a tresult

Almost all VST methods (other than COM) return a success code of type *tresult*, which is simply defined as a 32-bit integer. *kResultTrue* and *kResultFalse* are the common return values for success or failure.

Methods are Declared as PLUGIN_API

PLUGIN_API is simply defined as *__stdcall* which is discussed in the RackAX section.

Multi-Byte-Characters and UString

VST3 is designed to use the multi-byte-character set (or wide strings). Whereas ASCII characters are encoded with 8-bit bytes, multi-byte-characters use 16 bits, allowing for more characters. Steinberg provides an object called *UString* to handle these strings and even convert back and forth from ASCII. The only time this really manifests itself in our projects is when we want to pass a string-literal as a function argument. For example with ASCII string-literals you might call a method like this:

```
setPluginName("Awesome Synth");
```

There is macro called USTRING() in *ustring.h* that lets us simply write:

```
setPluginName(USTRING("Awesome Synth"));
```

and converts the string-literal to a wide string on the fly.

Class Templates

Much of the VST3 API is written using class templates that allow flexibility in dealing with parameter types (*float*, *double*, *int*, etc.). This is especially useful if you want to support 32 and 64 bit processing—your 64 bit code will need to replace *floats* with *doubles*, though much of the ancillary code would remain the same. Using class templates helps reduce the amount of code you would need to write. If you are new to class templates, visit www.cplusplus.com.

Redeclaration of Datatypes

VST3 also redeclares datatypes such as *int32*, *uint32*, *int16*, *int64*, etc., so just be aware of this. You can always use your familiar datatypes *int*, *float*, *double*, etc.; however, on occasion you can get burned if you try to override a base class function that uses the redeclared type, but you substitute a standard type. The compiler will not recognize your function as an override.

2.22 Implementing a VST3 Plug-in: Controller

The Controller component implements the COM creation, plug-in initialization, file serialization, audio processing, handles MIDI note events and receives control change information. In the *VSTSynthController.h* file, you can find the function prototypes that will handle these chores. We'll discuss each of these except the custom view portion, which is reserved for later in the chapter. Remember, you can implement a VST3 plug-in without a custom interface if you wish. Either way, you need to provide the same initialization information.

COM Creation:

- *createInstance()*
- FUID cid

Initialization:

- *initialize()*
- *terminate()*

Serialization:

- *setComponentState()*
- *setState()*

Setup MIDI controller assignments

- *getMIDIControllerAssignment()*

Creating a custom view

- *createView()*
- *createSubController()* (optional, used for VectorSynth joysticks)

You can identify the prototypes here in the *.h* file. At the end you can see the interface declarations. Note the base classes:

- *EditController*: handles core GUI and parameter functionality

- *IMidiMapping*: the MIDI mapping interface
- *VST3EditorDelegate*: handles the custom view creation and interfacing for joystick and other more complicated controls

```
tresult PLUGIN_API initialize(FUnknown* context);
```

- setup the GUI controls, define min, max, defaults
- setup log control template

```
tresult PLUGIN_API setComponentState(IBStream* fileStream);
```

- serialize (read) to set the GUI state for startup and preset loads

```
tresult PLUGIN_API setParamNormalizedFromFile(ParamID tag,
                                              ParamValue value);
```

- helper function for serialization (custom, not Steinberg)

```
virtual tresult PLUGIN_API setParamNormalized(ParamID tag,
                                              ParamValue value);
```

- set a normalized [0..+1] parameter

```
virtual ParamValue PLUGIN_API getParamNormalized(ParamID tag);
```

- get a normalized [0..+1] parameter

```
virtual IPlugView* PLUGIN_API createView(FIDString name);
```

- create the view object (GUI or custom GUI)

```
virtual tresult PLUGIN_API getMidiControllerAssignment(int32 busIndex,
                                                       int16 channel,
                                                       CtrlNumber
                                                              midiControllerNumber,
                                                       aramID& id/*out*/);
```

- link MIDI controllers to underlying GUI controls
- the MIDI controller messages will be routed into the Processor object via the dummy variables we will set up

```
IController* createSubController(UTF8StringPtr name,
                                 IUIDescription* description,
                                 VST3Editor* editor)
                                 VSTGUI_OVERRIDE_VMETHOD;
```

- we will use this when we need to create the joystick controller in VectorSynth and AniSynth

```
static FUnknown* createInstance(void*) {return (IEditController*)new
                                  Controller();}
```

- COM creation function

```
static FUID cid;
```

- the globally unique identifier value for this object

When you implement the synths you will get instructions on how to place various chunks of code into these files. The process is going to be the same for every synth, though the variable names and some code will be slightly different. You may want to refer back to this chapter, as it will explain what's going on in the plug-in without getting into details of each synth. You are going to modify the Controller when you want to add, remove or change any of the user GUI control underpinnings. There is a simple four step process for setting up the controls for use; as long as you follow this sequence properly, your GUI should work just fine.

The Controller object is going to define your plug-in's default GUI controls, and our custom GUI will depend on this as well. Objects called *Parameters* represent the GUI controls, and the Controller stores a set of these *Parameter* objects inside a *Container*. You can access the container and get *Parameters* out of it if needed. The Controller sends and receives values from the GUI. Each control on the GUI is identified by a zero-based index. When the user moves a control, the GUI sends a normalized value from 0.0 to 1.0 called

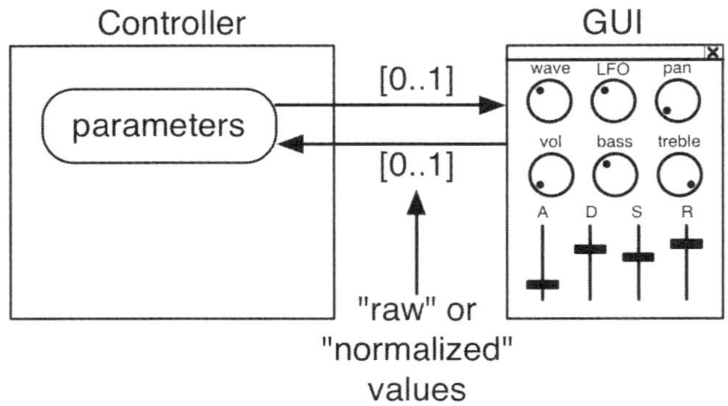

Figure 2.25: The Controller sends and receives normalized values from the controls; a container named *parameters* stores the set of *Parameter* objects.

a *value*, and an index or ID called a *tag*, which identifies the control. When the Controller wants to change the position of the controls during start-up or control automation, it sends indexed, normalized values out to the GUI. So it is important to understand that each Parameter (GUI control) has an index. Controls may share the same index, in which case they will move together, but we will not have any shared controls—each of our index values must be unique.

On the Processor side, each GUI control will ultimately be used to control an underlying variable. That variable will change when the user moves a control, and the audio rendering will be modified accordingly. All of the synth projects in this book will use these three types of variables:

double
int
enumerated UINT aka enum

Controls that connect to a *double* variable will ultimately generate continuous double floating point values. The *int* controls will generate integer-based values. The *enumerated UINT* controls will generate unsigned integer values (UINTs) that will map to strings in an enumerated list. In VST3 you don't have to implement the enumerations like you do in RackAFX, but you will be responsible for knowing which strings map to which values.

2.23 VST3 Controller Initialization

Initialization of the Controller involves declaring all the parameters for your UI, whether you are using a custom or built-in version. In each synth project chapter you will get a table that defines the GUI control list like the one in Table 2.8. You will need to translate the rows of this table into your controls. For VST3, you will use this table in both the Controller and the Processor implementation. Here is a list of which parts of the row the two objects will use (both components will use the same index when referencing the various *Parameters*, and it is not included in this table; it is up to you to establish the index list):

Controller:

- control name
- units
- lo limit
- high limit
- default
- enum string
- variable type (for serialization only)

Processor:

- variable type (for both serialization and controlling the synth)
- lo limit
- high limit
- default

The "Variable Name" below represents variables that are defined on your Processor object. The Controller object will not reference the controls with this variable name, and this separation is important. We will re-visit this table again when we discuss implementing the Processor object. Suppose we look at four particular controls in one of the tables:

Table 2.8: Example of some GUI controls.

***ExampleSynth* Continuous Parameters**				
Control Name(units)	**Type**	**Variable Name(VST3, RAFX)**	**Low/Hi/Default ***	**VST3/AU Index**
Volume (dB)	double	m_dVolume_dB	−96 / 24/ 0.0	OUTPUT_ AMPLITUDE_DB
Octave	int	m_nOctave	−4 / 4 / 0	OCTAVE
Fc (Hz)(volt/octave)	double	m_dFilterFc	80 / 18000 / 10000	FILTER_FC
* low, high and default values are #defined for VST3 and AU in *SynthParamLimits.h* for each project				

Enumerated String Parameters (UINT)			
Control Name	**Variable Name**	**enum String**	**VST3/AU Index**
Filter Type	m_uFilterType	LPF,HPF,BPF	FILTER_TYPE

The four fundamental variable types are *float, double, int* and *enumerated* UINT. The Volume and Octave controls ultimately generate numerical values that the user sees on the GUI, and they have minimum or Lo Limit, maximum or Hi Limit and default (Def) values. The control may also have no units ("" or empty string). The Fc (Filter cutoff) control has the note "volt/octave" which means that this control is logarithmic.

The Filter Type control displays strings that define the current value. An unsigned integer (UINT) keeps track of the current setting. The enum String column gives you the comma-separated values that will map to the UINT variable. In this example the mapping is:

LPF: 0
HPF: 1
BPF: 2

For the enumerated UINT type, the default value is always the first value in the enum string-list or LPF here.

> Each control is called a "parameter," and there is a *Parameter* object that handles the details. The controls or parameters are referenced with an index value. It is up to you to keep track of and maintain this indexing system. If you change the index values, your controls might not map correctly. The easiest way to keep track of the index values is with an enumeration.
> The VST3 limits, default values, and parameter enumerations are all contained in the file *SynthParamLimits.h*, which is different for each synth.

There are three fundamental types of parameter objects we will use in our code plus a container object to hold them.

RangeParameter

The *RangeParameter* represents a continuous control that has a minimum, maximum and default value. An easy example is a volume control in dB where the minimum is −96, maximum is +24 and default is 0 dB. The control moves smoothly across this range.

StringListParameter

The *StringListParameter* defines a control with a fixed set of states defined by strings. An example might be a "Filter Type" control where the user chooses from a list of strings like LPF, HPF, BPF etc. We will also use this as an on/off switch control by limiting the two strings to ON and OFF

LogScaleParameter

The *LogScaleParameter* is similar to the *RangeParameter* but the control moves logarithmically. We will use this exclusively for the filter cutoff frequency control, which we want to move in a logarithmic manner.

Parameter Container

The *EditController* base class declares a *Container* to hold all your controls. This *Container* is essentially a linked list. You declare your Parameters and then add them to the *Container*. You can also get parameters from the *Container* and evaluate the control's current value if needed. The *Container's* name is *parameters*, and it is declared in the *vsteditcontroller.h* file.

```
ParameterContainer parameters;
```

Normalized and Plain Parameters

An important concept in VST is that the GUI controls transmit values to your plug-in that are always on the range of 0.0 to 1.0. Steinberg calls these "normalized" parameters. In my previous book (and in earlier versions of VST), they are called "raw" values. Sometimes a parameter may actually have a range of 0.0 to 1.0, but most of the time the controls will not. For example the filter cutoff frequency control for all our filters will have a range of 80.0 Hz to 18 kHz—on the UI you will see these values, but when the user moves a control, the GUI always transmits the normalized or raw value. It is up to you to write the code to figure out what the mapped value will be. VST3 calls the mapped value the "plain" value, whereas in VST2 and RackAFX it is called the "cooked" value, and the function that converts the normalized/raw value to the plain/cooked value is the "cooking function." We have already supplied you with functions that will cook and un-cook your variables in *synthfunctions.h*; you supply the minimum, maximum and raw/cooked values. For all our synth projects, the Controller will handle the job of making sure the UI has the proper cooked values as the user moves the controls. It does this by making a linear (or logarithmic if you use a *LogScaleParameter*) mapping to and from the normalized value. This poses a slight issue in the case of control automation where the user wants to record his or her control movements in real-time, along with the song information. If your control does not map in a linear or logarithmic way, you will need to provide some translation code that converts from plain to normalized and back. We won't need this in our projects since we will provide all the cooking functions and keep track of our own variables and their raw and cooked mappings.

In order to implement your Controller object, follow these steps:

- every control will need an index so lay those out as an enumeration in the *SynthParamLimits.h* file
- decide on a UI and establish min, max and default values for each control
- write the code that declares the UI parameters in the *VSTSynthController.cpp* file and add them to the *parameters* container; this will also setup the default UI
- write the code that performs the read-side serialization
- implement the MIDI Control Mapping (the controller exposes *IMIDIMapping*)

Let's start with the parameters. Pretend we are implementing the four controls above in the Controller. Make sure you understand this so that you can add your own controls and variable later as part of the Chapter Challenges.

Step One: Enumerate Some Constants for Indexing the Controls

You can really choose whatever order you want here. The order that you add the parameters to the control list will ultimately dictate their order in the default GUI, but in the custom GUI you can place them anywhere. Even though this is an arbitrary assignment, it is important not to re-arrange these later, otherwise you may need to change some connections in the custom GUI. In each synth, this enumeration is listed at the top of the *SynthParamLimits.h* file:

```
enum {
        VOLUME_DB,          /* 0 */
        OCTAVE,             /* 1 */
        FILTER_CUTOFF,      /* 2 */
        FILTER_TYPE,        /* 3 */

        etc...

        NUMBER_OF_SYNTH_PARAMETERS};// always last, here it would be 4
```

The enumeration automatically creates the UINT list of values. The last value in the list will always be the count of parameters. You will be modifying this list a lot as you add or remove your own controls.

Step Two: Decide on the Control Min, Max and Default Values

These are all *#defined* in the file *SynthParamLimits.h* that is included with each synth project. Please see this file for the definitions.

Step Three: Create the Parameters and Add Them to the Container in the Initialize() Method

This is a fairly straightforward process best explained by example working in the *VSTSynthController.cpp* file. We'll create and add these four controls as follows; first call the base class, passing it the *FUnknown* pointer, then create and add the parameters:

```
tresult PLUGIN_API Controller::initialize(FUnknown* context)
{
      // --- base class does its thing
```

```
tresult result = EditController::initialize(context);

// --- now define the controls
if (result == kResultTrue)
{
        // Init parameters
        Parameter* param;

        // create a volume parameter
        param = new RangeParameter(USTRING("Volume"),       /* Ctrl Name */
                                   VOLUME_DB,               /* index */
                                   USTRING("dB"),    /* units */
                                   MIN_OUTPUT_AMPLITUDE_DB, /* LOW */
                                   MAX_OUTPUT_AMPLITUDE_DB, /* HIGH */
                                   DEFAULT_OUTPUT_AMPLITUDE_DB);/* DEF */
        // set the sig digits for the UI
        param->setPrecision(1);

        // add it to the container
        parameters.addParameter(param);
```

The *RangeParameter* constructor takes values from the control table as well as the index value we setup in the enumeration. It should be easy to see how this constructor is related to the table and enumeration. Note that the min, max and default values are from the *SynthParamLimits.h* file.

```
#define MIN_OUTPUT_AMPLITUDE_DB -96.0
#define MAX_OUTPUT_AMPLITUDE_DB 24.0
#define DEFAULT_OUTPUT_AMPLITUDE_DB 0.0
```

After creating the control, the *setPrecision()* method tells the UI how many significant digits to display after the decimal place, so here it would display one e.g. –21.6. Finally, use the *addParameter()* method to add the new object to the container. Now look at the Octave control:

```
        param = new RangeParameter(USTRING("Octave"),       /* Ctrl Name */
                                  OCTAVE,                   /* index */
                                  USTRING(""),              /* units */
                                  MIN_OCTAVE,               /* LOW */
                                  MAX_OCTAVE,               /* HIGH */
                                  DEFAULT_OCTAVE);          /* DEF */
        // integer, no sig digits
        param->setPrecision(0); // <--- this is an Integer (int)

        // add to container
        parameters.addParameter(param);
```

So far this is fairly straightforward; here we set the precision to 0 which indicates an integer display—note that the control will still transmit a raw value from 0.0 to 1.0. The log-scale parameter takes a bit more work to setup. First, outside of the object methods at the top of the *.cpp* file you declare the scaling:

```
// --- these are defined in SynthParamLimits.h
#define MIN_UNIPOLAR 0.0
#define MAX_UNIPOLAR 1.0
#define DEFAULT_UNIPOLAR 0.0
```

```
#define MIN_FILTER_FC 80.0
#define MAX_FILTER_FC 18000.0
#define DEFAULT_FILTER_FC 10000.0
#define FILTER_RAW_MAP 0.5
#define FILTER_COOKED_MAP 1800.0

// this defines a logarithmic scaling for the filter Fc control
LogScale<ParamValue> filterLogScale(MIN_UNIPOLAR,  /* GUI MIN */
                                    MAX_UNIPOLAR,       /* GUI MAX */
                                    MIN_FILTER_FC,      /* LO */
                                    MAX_FILTER_FC,      /* HI*/
                                    FILTER_RAW_MAP,     /* 0.5 */
                                    FILTER_COOKED_MAP); /* 1800 */
            // set the normalized value
            param->setNormalized(param->toNormalized(DEFAULT_FILTER_FC));

            // sig digits
            param->setPrecision(1);

            // add to container
            parameters.addParameter(param);
```

The first four parameters show the range mapping of the control where 0.0 to 1.0 will map from 80.0 to 18000.0 and the last two arguments show the center-anchor point—you could read these arguments as "when the raw control value is 0.5 the control will display 1800." The last two arguments allow you to create quasi-logarithmic controls that have expanded or compressed upper or lower ranges.

For the *LogScaleParameter*, you have to set the default value in a separate function call, and you may only set the normalized (raw) value. To do this, you use a helper method called *toNormalized()*, which converts the value for you. This is especially important here where the control is logarithmic and the mapping is not linear. In this case, we set the control to the default value, DEFAULT_FILTER_FC.

Lastly, we can use the *StringListParameter* to define the Filter Type control. First, you create the *Parameter* then you load up the strings:

```
StringListParameter* enumStringParam =
                  new StringListParameter(
                        USTRING("Filter Type"), /* name */
                        FILTER_TYPE);           /* index */

// now add the strings for the list IN THE SAME ORDER AS DECLARED
// IN THE enum in Synth Project
enumStringParam->appendString(USTRING("LPF"));      // <- 0
enumStringParam->appendString(USTRING("HPF"));      // <- 1
enumStringParam->appendString(USTRING("BPF"));      // <- 2

// add to the container
parameters.addParameter (enumStringParam);
```

Notice that the string indexing—remember that in VST3 it is up to you to reconcile the integer values (0,1,2. . .) with the strings (LPF,HPF,BPF. . .).

2.24 VST3 Controller Serialization

Step Four: Implement the Serialize-Read Code in the setComponentState() Method

For the Controller, the *setComponentState()* method is the serialize-read method. The Processor uses slightly different function names, which we will get to shortly. In both objects, the argument that is passed to the function is an *IBStream* interface pointer. This interface allows reading and writing to a binary serialized file. We will be storing and loading our synth variables, which will be of the types listed above, *double*, *int* and UINT. The *IBStream* interface provides relatively easy methods for writing and reading values to and from the file. In this case, we will be reading values. The most important thing to remember with this code is that the order of variable reading and writing must be exactly identical, or your variables will not be read or written properly. Since our datatypes are a mixture of *double*, *int* and UINT, we need to be very careful about the order of the serialization. Serialization code can be tedious—you have to write code for every variable, and our synths will generally have 30 to 50 parameters to load and store.

The storing (writing) code in the Processor dictates the order that we read values out. The Processor stores the cooked parameter values rather than the normalized values; this simplifies the coding in the Processor, but it means that when the Controller object reads the file, it must convert the cooked (plain) parameters into raw (normalized) ones. The Parameter object that is used to store each parameter features conversion methods that let you convert back and forth from raw to cooked. We can take advantage of this and make the coding a little less tedious by writing a helper function that is declared in the *Controller.h* file:

```
    // --- helper function for serialization
    tresult PLUGIN_API setParamNormalizedFromFile(ParamID tag,
                                                  ParamValue value);
```

The *ParamID* is an unsigned integer that is the control index. *ParamValue* is a *double* datatype. The function is implemented in the *Controller.cpp* file:

```
tresult PLUGIN_API Controller::setParamNormalizedFromFile(ParamID tag,
                                                          ParamValue value)
{
    // --- get the parameter
    Parameter* pParam = EditController::getParameterObject(tag);

    // --- verify pointer
    if(!pParam) return kResultFalse;

    //  --- convert serialized value to normalized (raw)
    return setParamNormalized(tag, pParam->toNormalized(value));
}
```

It gets the *Parameter* object from the container, then uses the *toNormalized()* method to convert the cooked data back into raw and calls its own *setParamNormalized()* method to actually set the value on the object. You might want to check out the other *Parameter* methods in the file *vstparameters.h*. You give the *toNormalized()* function the *ParamValue* (e.g. 1000.0 for the filter Fc) and it uses the limits you setup in the *initialize()* method above to calculate the normalized value. The calculation is simple and is also included in *synthfunctions.h* as *convertToVSTGUIVariable()*.

The *IBStream* interface provides a multitude of read and write methods. Since our variables are limited to *double*, *int* and UINT, we will use six of these methods:

```
    bool writeDouble(double);
    bool readDouble(double&);

    bool writeInt32(int32);
    bool readInt32(int32&);

    bool writeInt32u(uint32);
    bool readInt32u(uint32&);
```

Reading and converting the *double* values from the file poses no problem for us since the *ParamValue* datatype is simply defined as a *double*. However the *int* and UINT versions will need to be cast as *ParamValues* before sending to the helper function. So, we will read them into dummy variables called *data* and *udata*, then cast them during the method call.

An issue with serialization is versioning—if you release your plug-in to the public and then later revise it to add more parameters, you will need to update the serialization code and implement it in a way that doesn't crash since the new file structure will be different. This is usually done by writing a version number as the very first value in the file. Then, when you read the file you can use that version number to figure out the sequence of variables in the file. The version number is a 64-bit integer and it is defined in the *Processor.cpp* file. We will read this value first, then use it if we need to—you don't really need to worry about versioning until you release your plug-in to the public. You will see an example of versioning in Chapter 13. The first part of the function is:

```
tresult PLUGIN_API Controller::setComponentState(IBStream* fileStream)

{
    // --- make a streamer interface using the
    //     IBStream* fileStream; this is for PC so
    //     data is LittleEndian
    IBStreamer s(fileStream, kLittleEndian);

    // --- variables for reading
    uint64 version = 0;
    double dDoubleParam = 0;

    // --- needed to convert to our UINT reads
    uint32 udata = 0;
    int32 data = 0;

    // --- read the version
    if(!s.readInt64u(version)) return kResultFalse;
```

You use the *IBStream* pointer to make an *IBStreamer* interface that you use to perform the read operations. The first read is for the 64 bit unsigned integer *version*. If any read operation fails, we stop and return the *kResultFalse* error code. What follows is a set of read operations in the same sequence as the write version in the *Processor.cpp* file. You use the helper method to convert the cooked value and adjust the control's position. Here are the next few read operations from the MiniSynth plug-in—notice the cast to *ParamValue* in the first read:

```
    // --- then read Version 0 params
    if(!s.readInt32u(udata)) return kResultFalse;
    else
        setParamNormalizedFromFile(VOICE_MODE, (ParamValue)udata);

    if(!s.readDouble(dDoubleParam)) return kResultFalse;
    else
        setParamNormalizedFromFile(DETUNE_CENTS, dDoubleParam);

    if(!s.readDouble(dDoubleParam)) return kResultFalse;
    else
        setParamNormalizedFromFile(PULSE_WIDTH_PCT, dDoubleParam);
```

In this case, the index values show what we are reading (VOICE_MODE, DETUNE_CENTS, etc.). After performing the read operations and setting our controls, we return the *kResultTrue* code. Depending on the VST client, returning a *kResultFalse* value from this method may prohibit the UI from being shown or cause other issues, so it is very important to make sure this method works properly. This wraps up the basic Controller component implementation; we will discuss the MIDI mapping in the next chapter and custom GUI creation after the next section on the Processor component.

2.25 VST3 Controller MIDI Mapping

Step Five: MIDI Mapping

VST3 implements an interesting and somewhat confusing strategy for dealing with MIDI messages. The note on and note off messages are handled in the Processor. MIDI controller messages, such as those sent from the pitch-bend, joystick or knob/slider continuous controllers, are handled in the Controller. Specifically, each MIDI controller must control a *Parameter* object stored in your container. When the user moves a controller such as the pitch bend wheel, it changes the value of the underlying *Parameter* object and alters the appearance of the control on the GUI. In some cases this makes sense; for example you might map MIDI Continuous Controller (CC) Message 0x07 (volume) to the master volume control on your synth. When the user turns this controller on a MIDI device, the volume control automatically moves on the GUI. Note that the Processor will actually deal with the MIDI control value and apply it to the synth rendering. However, we want to design synths that are configurable during operation that might change the mapping. For example, in our synths the mod wheel control (CC 0x01) will be mapped to the LFO Depth parameter by default. But we want to make sure our synths will allow the user to change this mapping to some other destination. You will get into the details of this when you learn about the modulation matrix—a component that greatly extends the flexibility of our synths.

Ultimately, the Processor will receive the MIDI controller events disguised as synth parameters and issue changes to the underlying synth objects. Therefore, we have chosen to simply map each MIDI Controller to a dummy *Parameter* object on the Controller. These *Parameters* will appear as controls in the default GUI only; our custom GUI will hide them. In this way, we can re-map MIDI Controllers on-the-fly.

The Controller exposes the *IMIDIMapping* interface and must implement its one and only pure abstract method *getMIDIControllerAssignment()*. At startup, the host will query the plug-in, asking it how to map a given controller message. There are 130 controller messages. They are enumerated in the *ControllerNumbers* structure in the *ivstmidicontrollers.h* file. All of our synths are going to respond to a basic set of control change messages, but you are encouraged to explore the possibilities of supporting other controllers, and you should check out that *.h* file for the other controller constants available. Our basic set of MIDI controllers consists of:

- pitch bend
- mod wheel
- volume
- pan
- expression
- sustain pedal
- channel pressure (aftertouch)
- all notes off

As we discussed before, the plan is to make each of these map to a dummy *Parameter*. These are enumerated along with the others from step one, above. In the next section where we implement the Processor, you will see how to use these index values.

```
enum {
      VOLUME_DB,      /* 0 */
      OCTAVE,         /* 1 */
      FILTER_CUTOFF,  /* 2 */
      FILTER_TYPE,    /* 3 */

      etc...

      // now the MIDI params
      MIDI_PITCHBEND,
      MIDI_MODWHEEL,
      MIDI_VOLUME_CC7,
      MIDI_PAN_CC10,
      MIDI_EXPRESSION_CC11,
      MIDI_SUSTAIN_PEDAL,
      MIDI_CHANNEL_PRESSURE,
      MIDI_ALL_NOTES_OFF,

      NUMBER_OF_SYNTH_PARAMETERS // always last
};
```

Next, a set of these dummy parameters is added to the container in step three, above. Each of these parameters will be normalized by default where MIN_UNIPOLAR and MAX_UNIPOLAR are defined as 0.0 and 1.0, respectively. Here are the first few of them.

```
// MIDI Params - these have to appear in default GUI so we can rx them
param = new RangeParameter(USTRING("PitchBend"), MIDI_PITCHBEND,
                           USTRING(""),
                           MIN_UNIPOLAR, MAX_UNIPOLAR,
                           DEFAULT_UNIPOLAR);
param->setPrecision(1); // fractional sig digits
parameters.addParameter(param);
```

```
param = new RangeParameter(USTRING("MIDI Vol"), MIDI_VOLUME_CC7,
                           USTRING(""),
                           MIN_UNIPOLAR, MAX_UNIPOLAR,
                           DEFAULT_UNIPOLAR);
param->setPrecision(1); // fractional sig digits
parameters.addParameter(param);


etc...
```

With the dummy parameters created and placed in the container, we can now implement the *getMIDIControllerAssignment()* method. It is a simple case of decoding the MIDI control number and mapping it to one of our parameters. Here is the prototype of this *IMIDIMapping* interface method:

```
tresult PLUGIN_API Controller::getMidiControllerAssignment(int32 busIndex,
                                          int16 channel,
                                          CtrlNumber midiControllerNumber,
                                          ParamID& id);
```

The client will query us, sequentially passing values from 0 to 129 for the *midiControllerNumber* using the constants defined in *ivstmidicontrollers.h*. If we want to map this controller to one of our parameters, we send that parameter index (ID) back in the last argument and return *kResultTrue*. If not, we set the ID to 0 and return *kResultFalse*. The *busIndex* and *channel* arguments define the MIDI event bus number and MIDI channel respectively. Both are zero-indexed values. Since we have only one event bus 0, we first check that parameter, then implement the decision tree as a switch/case statement:

```
// NOTE: we only have one EventBus (0)
if (busIndex == 0)
{
        id = 0;
        switch (midiControllerNumber)
        {
                // these are handled in the Processor::process() method
                case kPitchBend:
                        id = MIDI_PITCHBEND;
                        break;
                case kCtrlModWheel:
                        id = MIDI_MODWHEEL;
                        break;
                case kCtrlVolume:
                        id = MIDI_VOLUME_CC7;
                        break;
                case kCtrlPan:
                        id = MIDI_PAN_CC10;
                        break;
                case kCtrlExpression:
                        id = MIDI_EXPRESSION_CC11;
                        break;
                case kAfterTouch:
                        id = MIDI_CHANNEL_PRESSURE;
                        break;
                case kCtrlSustainOnOff:
                        id = MIDI_SUSTAIN_PEDAL;
                        break;
```

```
                    case kCtrlAllNotesOff:
                            id = MIDI_ALL_NOTES_OFF;
                            break;
            }
            return id != 0 ? kResultTrue : kResultFalse;
    }
    return kResultFalse;
}
```

2.26 Implementing a VST3 Plug-in: Processor

The Processor component implements the COM creation, plug-in initialization, file serialization, audio processing, handles MIDI note events, and receives control change information. In the *VSTSynthProcessor.h* file, you can find the function prototypes that will handle these chores.

COM Creation:

- *createInstance()*
- FUID cid

Initialization:

- *Processor()* (constructor)
- *initialize()*
- *setBusArrangements()*
- *canProcessSampleSize()*
- *setActive()*

Serialization:

- *getState()*
- *setState()*

MIDI Events, Control changes and Processing (rendering):

- *process()*

Interestingly, the *process()* method handles MIDI and control changes, in addition to processing. It is the most complicated of the methods and we will handle it last. We are going to use a few helper functions to break down the complexity of this function.

Core Plug-in Functions:

```
Processor();
```

- initialize all parameters
- initialize all MIDI controller dummy variables

```
tresult PLUGIN_API initialize(FUnknown* context);
```

- declare our input and output ports (audio and MIDI)

```
tresult PLUGIN_API setBusArrangements(SpeakerArrangement* inputs,
                                      int32 numIns,
                                      SpeakerArrangement* outputs,
                                      int32 numOuts);
```

- define which output arrangement we support (stereo output for all synths)

```
tresult PLUGIN_API canProcessSampleSize(int32 symbolicSampleSize);
```

- declare the audio word-length(s) we support; currently this is 32-bit only

```
tresult PLUGIN_API setActive(TBool state);
```

- this is the on/off function and acts as the per-run initialization function
- set the sample rate on all sub-components
- clear out any per-run variables

```
tresult PLUGIN_API setState(IBStream* fileStream);
```

- serialize (read) to load the synth state from a preset file or startup file

```
tresult PLUGIN_API getState(IBStream* fileStream);
```

- serialize (write) the current synth state into a file

```
tresult PLUGIN_API process(ProcessData& data);
```

- the audio rendering function
- also processes MIDI events and control changes

```
static FUnknown* createInstance(void*) { return (IAudioProcessor*)new
                                               Processor (); }
```

- the COM creation function

```
static FUID cid;
```

- the globally unique identifier for this object

In addition to these methods, we will also be declaring variables for each control on the GUI that will alter the synth's output. When we handle control changes, we will change the values of these variables accordingly, and then call an update method to set the variables in the synth object. If you look in the MiniSynth project's *VSTSynthProcessor.h* file, you can see the additional declarations. Don't worry about the first part involving the voice array; we will get to that in Chapter 8 when we discuss polyphony. We will discuss the *doControlUpdate()* and *doProcessEvent()* functions when we discuss the *process()* function.

The important part of the code for this section is the list of variables known as synth parameters or just parameters. These are the variables that will directly affect the synth operation.

> You need to declare a variable for each parameter you setup in in the Controller's *initialize()* method. These variables are named and listed in the GUI design table for each synth. You add those variables to your Processor object's *.h* file for each project. For VST3 only, you also add variables that correspond to the dummy MIDI controls you set up in the Controller's *initialize()* method.

After these, you see the set of the dummy MIDI controller variables. The log filter control is going to require some conversion when we are decoding control changes during the *process()* function. For this, we will create a special helper object, a *Parameter** that is setup the same way as the filter parameter you setup in the Controller. It is named *m_pFilterLogParam*.

Other Functions and Variables

The following functions are used to aid in polyphony. We will discuss these in detail in Chapter 8. They are used to implement dynamic voice allocation or voice-stealing. For now you can skip over them.

```
void incrementVoiceTimestamps()
CMiniSynthVoice* getOldestVoice()
CMiniSynthVoice* getOldestVoiceWithNote(UINT uMIDINote)
bool doControlUpdate(ProcessData& data);
```

- helper function for dealing with GUI control changes

```
bool doProcessEvent(Event& vstEvent);
```

- helper function for processing MIDI note and aftertouch events

```
void update();
```

- function to update the synth parameters

We will discuss these variables in detail in Chapters 3 and 8.

```
// --- for portamento
double m_dLastNoteFrequency;

// --- our recieve channel (optional)
UINT m_uMidiRxChannel;

// --- for converting the log filter control value
Parameter* m_pFilterLogParam;
```

Last are the synth parameters that you declare using the table of GUI controls that come with each synth design chapter.

```
// --- synth parameters; initialized in constructor! WP
double m_dNoiseOsc_dB;
double m_dPulseWidth_Pct;
double m_dEG1OscIntensity;
double m_dFcControl;
etc...
```

And, the MIDI dummy variables for trapping the MIDI controller changes.

```
// these are VST3 specific variables for non-note MIDI messages!
double m_dMIDIPitchBend; // -1 to +1
UINT m_uMIDIModWheel;
UINT m_uMIDIVolumeCC7;
UINT m_uMIDIPanCC10;
UINT m_uMIDIExpressionCC11;
etc...
```

2.27 VST3 Processor Initialization

In the *VSTSynthProcessor.cpp* file you handle the initialization of the plug-in, beginning with the constructor. For VST3 plug-ins, the first line of the constructor calls the method *setControllerClass()* and passes the Controller's FUID as the argument declaring the Controller it is paired with. This is part of the underlying COM component and you don't need to worry about it, just make sure your Processor components always call this in the constructor. Following this are the defaults for all the synth parameters, declared in the *SynthParamLimits.h* file. Open the MiniSynth's *VSTController.cpp* file and compare the parameter declarations in the *initialize()* method with the initialization in the Processor's constructor. You will see a match between them—one variable for each control. Notice also that they share the same default values—the string parameters always default to the first string in the list. The following code shows the setup for the log parameter helper (an identical *LogScale* object as the Controller's) and then the constructor.

```
// this defines a logarithmic scaling for the filter Fc control
LogScale<ParamValue>  filterLogScale2(0.0,/* VST GUI Variable MIN */
                                      1.0,/* VST GUI Variable MAX */
                                      80.0,/* filter fc LOW */
                                      18000.0,   /* filter fc HIGH */
                                      0.5, /* at position 0.5 will be:*/
                                      1800.0);   /* 1800 Hz */

Processor::Processor()
{
      // --- we are a Processor
      setControllerClass(Controller::cid);

      // --- our inits
      m_dNoiseOsc_dB = DEFAULT_NOISE_OSC_AMP_DB;
      m_dPulseWidth_Pct = DEFAULT_PULSE_WIDTH_PCT;
      m_dEG1OscIntensity = DEFAULT_BIPOLAR;
```

```
        m_dFcControl = DEFAULT_FILTER_FC;
        etc...

        // MIDI VST3 specific
        m_dMIDIPitchBend = DEFAULT_MIDI_PITCHBEND; // -1 to +1
        m_uMIDIModWheel = DEFAULT_MIDI_MODWHEEL;
        m_uMIDIVolumeCC7 = DEFAULT_MIDI_VOLUME;  // note defaults to 127
        m_uMIDIPanCC10 = DEFAULT_MIDI_PAN;      // 64 = center pan
        m_uMIDIExpressionCC11 = DEFAULT_MIDI_EXPRESSION;
        etc...

        // Finish initializations here
        m_dLastNoteFrequency = -1.0;

        // receive on all channels
        m_uMidiRxChannel = MIDI_CH_ALL;

        // this is created/destroyed in SetActive()
        m_pFilterLogParam = NULL;
    }
```

Now that the constructor has initialized the variables, we can move on to the other methods.

initialize()

This method is identical for all synth projects in the book. It receives the *FUnknown* interface pointer from the host and implements the following:

- call the base class's *initialize()* method passing the FUnknown pointer
- declare one output bus of type stereo (Steinberg calls this the "Speaker Arrangement")
- declare 16 MIDI event bus inputs so you can receive on all 16 channels

The declarations of our I/O are done with *addAudioOutput()* and *addEventInput()*. There are also methods named *addAudioInput()* for effects plug-ins that need an input and optionally an *addEventOutput()* if we want to send MIDI events out of the Processor.

```
    tresult PLUGIN_API Processor::initialize(FUnknown* context)
    {
        tresult result = AudioEffect::initialize(context);
        if(result == kResultTrue)
        {
                // stereo output bus
                addAudioOutput(STR16 ("Audio Output"), SpeakerArr::kStereo);
                // MIDI event input bus, 16 channels
                addEventInput(STR16 ("Event Input"), 16);
        }
        return result;
    }
```

setBusArrangements()

This method is identical for all synth projects in the book. The host will query the object repeatedly for different speaker arrangements based on the audio capabilities of the host computer. Since we have one stereo output on our synths, we decode the query arguments and call the base class implementation for the case of a single stereo output on bus 0. The arguments consist of *SpeakerArrangement* pointers that the host set up for us after it called the *initialize()* method and integers with the number of input and output channels. Our synths have no input, one output, and a *SpeakerArrangement* of *kStereo*.

```
tresult PLUGIN_API Processor::setBusArrangements(SpeakerArrangement* inputs,
                                                  int32 numIns,
                                                  SpeakerArrangement* outputs,
                                                  int32 numOuts)
{
    // we only support one stereo output bus
    if(numIns == 0 && numOuts == 1 && outputs[0] == SpeakerArr::kStereo)
    {
            return AudioEffect::setBusArrangements(inputs, numIns, outputs,
                                                    numOuts);
    }
    // --- we don't support other arrangements
    return kResultFalse;
}
```

canProcessSampleSize()

This method is identical for all synth projects in the book. The host will query the object to see if it supports 32-bit or 64-bit processing. Our synths are all 32-bit processing only. If you want to support 64-bit, uncomment the *if()* code that I have left here (NOTE: this is not trivial because you will also have to modify your *process()* method to accommodate the different sample size). The input argument is an integer, either 32 or 64 and *kSample32* simply defines 32.

```
tresult PLUGIN_API Processor::canProcessSampleSize(int32 symbolicSampleSize)
{
    // --- here is where you can support 64-bit processing
//  if (symbolicSampleSize == kSample32 || symbolicSampleSize == kSample64)
    // --- currently 32-bit only
    if (symbolicSampleSize == kSample32)
    {
            return kResultTrue;
    }
    return kResultFalse;
}
```

setActive()

This method will vary slightly for different synths. The host calls this method to turn the synth on and off. Steinberg recommends doing dynamic memory allocations here when activated, then destroying or releasing the assets when de-activated. Each synth in the book will create and destroy its array of voices here. The sample-based synth projects will also initialize dynamically created sample arrays here. When the host calls this method, the sample rate will have been set (or changed) for the project. All of our synths require the sample rate for proper operation, so this is where we will initialize them. Details will follow in the next chapters. The Processor object inherits from the base class *AudioEffect*, which declares a member variable called *processSetup*:

```
protected:
    ProcessSetup processSetup;
```

ProcessSetup is a structure that holds the following variables:

```
    int32 processMode;          //< ProcessModes
    int32 symbolicSampleSize;   //< SymbolicSampleSizes
    int32 maxSamplesPerBlock;   //< max number of samples per audio block
    SampleRate sampleRate;      //< sample rate
```

We will be using the *sampleRate* variable (*SampleRate* is of type *double*) to set the sample rate on our voice objects after they are added to the stack.

In this example, we show the method for MiniSynth. If the state argument is *true*, we create a load up of our voice objects into the array, set the sample rate on our voice objects, call the *update()* method to initialize the synth parameters and reset the last note frequency variable. Then, we create the log parameter helper object. The *prepareForPlay()* method will be discussed in Chapter 8. In the code below, the functionality is split into two *for()* loops that could easily be combined into one. The reason for keeping the two loops is for comparison with the other APIs, where these two operations are split and not in the same function.

```
tresult PLUGIN_API Processor::setActive(TBool state)
{
        if(state)
        {
                // --- load up voices
                for(int i=0; i<MAX_VOICES; i++)
                {
                        CMiniSynthVoice* pVoice = new CMiniSynthVoice;
                        if(!pVoice)
                                return kInvalidArgument;

                        m_pVoiceArray[i] = pVoice;
                }
                for(int i=0; i<MAX_VOICES; i++)
                {
                        m_pVoiceArray[i]->setSampleRate(
                                                (double)processSetup.sampleRate);
                        pVoice->prepareForPlay();
                }
                // mass update
                update();

                // clear
                m_dLastNoteFrequency = -1.0;

                // helper
                m_pFilterLogParam = new LogScaleParameter<ParamValue> (USTRING
                                        ("Filter fc"),
                                        FILTER_FC,
                                        filterLogScale2,
                                        (USTRING("Hz")));
}
```

If the argument to *setActive()* is *false*, we unload the voice stack and delete the pointers. MAX_VOICES defines the maximum polyphony for the particular synth. Finally, the base class is called to do its setup work.

```
        else
        {
                // --- delete voices
                for(int i=0; i<MAX_VOICES; i++)
                {
                        delete m_pVoiceArray[i];
                }
```

```
            if(m_pFilterLogParam)
                    delete m_pFilterLogParam;
        }

        // base class method call is last
        return AudioEffect::setActive(state);
}
```

2.28 VST3 Processor Serialization

Serialization is handled with the *getState()* and *setState()* methods.

getState()

This method will vary slightly for different synths. The host calls this method when the user saves their project or saves a preset. The host passes a file-stream pointer that you use to write your synth parameter variables. The Controller's *setComponentState()* method (which reads from a file to setup the GUI) follows the ordering we set in this method and great care must be taken to ensure the exact same sequence of operations. Here is part of the method from MiniSynth. As with the Controller example from the previous sections, we create an *IBStreamer* interface and use its methods to write our variables:

```
tresult PLUGIN_API Processor::getState(IBStream* fileStream)
{
        // get a stream I/F
        IBStreamer s(fileStream, kLittleEndian);

        // --- MiniSynthVersion - place this at top so versioning can be used
        //      during the READ operation
        if(!s.writeInt64u(MiniSynthVersion)) return kResultFalse;

        // --- these follow the same order as the enum
        if(!s.writeDouble(m_dNoiseOsc_dB)) return kResultFalse;
        if(!s.writeDouble(m_dPulseWidth_Pct)) return kResultFalse;
        if(!s.writeDouble(m_dEG1OscIntensity)) return kResultFalse;

        etc...

        return kResultTrue;
}
```

setState()

This method will vary slightly for different synths. The host calls this method to setup the synth from a preset-file. This is very similar to what you saw in the Controller's *setComponentState()* method. The difference is that in this function you load your variables directly from the file without having to convert them to normalized values. The sequence of read operations must exactly match that in the *getState()* method. Here is part of the method for MiniSynth, and you can see the same use of the *udata* and *data* dummy variables needed for reading *UINT* and *int* data that you saw in the Controller example. You can also see the use of versioning for adding additional parameters after your product has been released and rev-ed.

```
tresult PLUGIN_API Processor::setState(IBStream* fileStream)
{
        IBStreamer s(fileStream, kLittleEndian);
        uint64 version = 0;
```

```
        // --- needed to convert to our int/UINT reads
        uint32 udata = 0;
        int32 data = 0;

        // read the version
        if(!s.readInt64u(version)) return kResultFalse;

        if(!s.readDouble(m_dNoiseOsc_dB)) return kResultFalse;
        if(!s.readDouble(m_dPulseWidth_Pct)) return kResultFalse;
        if(!s.readDouble(m_dEG1OscIntensity)) return kResultFalse;
        etc...

        // --- do next version...
        if (version >= 1)
        {
                // add v1 stuff here
        }

        return kResultTrue;
    }
```

update()

This method will vary slightly for different synths. This is not a Steinberg function, but rather one that we declare to update the synth voice array. We will get into the details of this method in Chapters 3–8. This method will be called from the *process()* method whenever we detect that the user controls have been altered.

2.29 VST3 Note Events, Control Changes and Rendering

The rest of the Processor functionality is contained in the *process()* method. VST3 processes data in blocks. For an audio effect, you receive a buffer of audio input samples, process them and then write them out to an output buffer; the input and output buffers are the same size. For synthesizers, you only write to the output buffer—there is no input. The size of the output buffer is not guaranteed to remain constant, so you cannot hard-code some aspects of the *process()* method. Cubase tends to use buffers that are 1/100 the sample rate or 10mSec in length. The important thing to note is that the MIDI event and control information is time-aligned with the buffer so that the events and control changes that happened during that time-slice are delivered to the *process()* method along with the buffers. The *process()* method has only one argument called *ProcessData*:

```
tresult PLUGIN_API Processor::process(ProcessData& data);
```

The *ProcessData* struct contains everything you need to process a block of data:

- audio input and output buffer pointers
- MIDI event input and output interfaces
- parameter change input and output interfaces
- integers telling us the number of inputs, outputs, and samples-per-block

For our VST3 synth projects, we will be using three of these components:

- output buffer pointers
- MIDI event inputs
- parameter change inputs

Figure 2.26 diagrams this information; control changes are packaged in queues, which are arrays of values. There is one queue per control and our synths all have 30–40+ controls. The control changes that happened during this processing block are delivered in these arrays. MIDI events are packaged in an *event list*. In the diagram, each black diamond is a MIDI note on event. Note off events are also contained in the same list (not shown for simplicity). The audio output buffer holds our rendered output. Be aware that the control changes and MIDI events are time-stamped with sample offsets from the top of the buffer, so Figure 2.26 is a simplification in how it shows the alignment of control, MIDI and audio data.

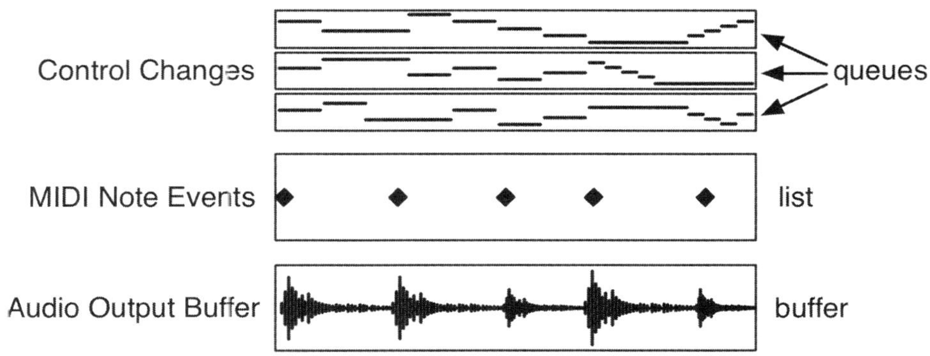

Figure 2.26: Control change information is packaged into queues, one for each control while MIDI events arrive in a list, and the audio data is written into a buffer.

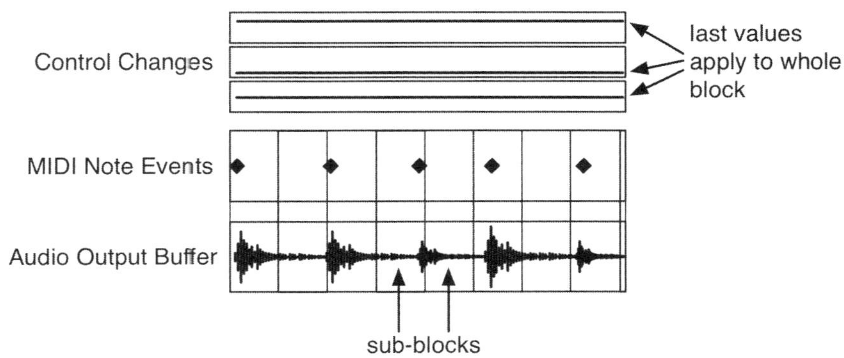

Figure 2.27: Our MIDI event processing and synth rendering occurs in sub-blocks and we apply the last control value to the entire block.

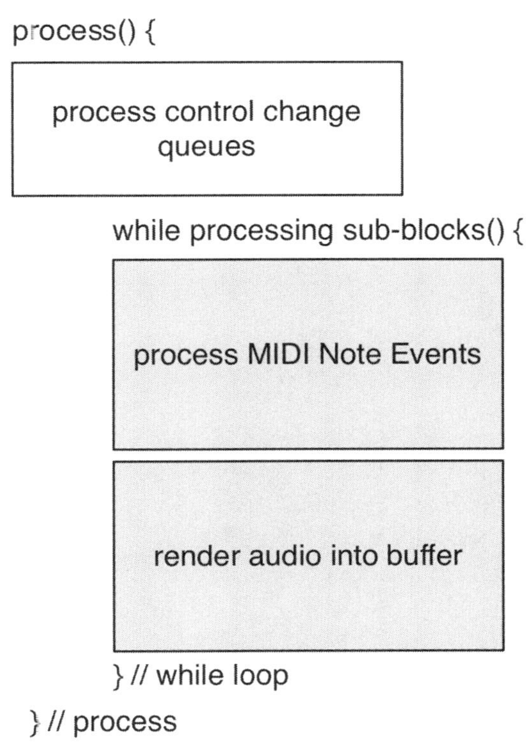

Figure 2.28: Diagram of the *process()* method shows processing of the three blocks: parameters, MIDI and audio; the shaded blocks are essentially identical for all of our synths.

The strategy we follow for dealing with these three components exactly follows the Steinberg sample code for the note expression synth: to simplify coding, only the last control change value from each queue is processed. The processing of the MIDI events and output rendering occur in sub-blocks of 32 samples, as defined by our own SYNTH_PROC_BLOCKSIZE at the top of the *.cpp* file. Feel free to change this value for experimentation. We can now re-draw Figure 2.26 as Figure 2.27 showing how all but the last control change data is ignored and the MIDI and audio rendering is broken into sub-blocks. Notice that there is a partial block at the end which occurs when the audio buffer size is not a multiple of SYNTH_PROC_BLOCKSIZE; it will be handled automatically in our process loop.

Figure 2.28 shows the structure of the *process()* method as code blocks. The shaded blocks will have essentially identical code for all the synths.

Accessing the Control Queues

To make the *process()* function shorter, we created two helper functions to handle control queues and MIDI events. The control queue handler is called *doControlUpdate()*, which accepts a *ProcessData* reference that is passed into the *process()* function.

```
bool Processor::doControlUpdate(ProcessData& data)
```

We first get the control change count from the *IParameterChanges* interface packaged inside the *processData* struct then loop through the queues. If the user has not changed any controls, there is nothing to process. The *IParamValueQueue* interface is used to access each queue. The *getPoint()* method is called, passing the value *queue->getPointCount()-1* as the parameter for the point in question; this represents the last point in the queue. In Cubase, this means the controls are updated every 10mSec. The other arguments are return values: a *sampleOffset* value that we ignore for simplicity since we only parse the last control value and the normalized (raw) value of the control on the range of [0..1]. In order to convert this value into meaningful information for our synth, we need to cook it. This is done with a helper function we have written in *synthfunctions.h* called *cookVSTGUIVariable()*, and the arguments are the minimum and maximum values of the control along with the normalized value. It returns the cooked data as a *float* based on the arguments. That value may then be cast to *int*, UINT or other datatypes such as a *bool*. In this example, you can see the OCTAVE control change being processed. So, these control ID values are all identical to the ones you setup in the Controller's *initialize()* method. For each synth you will need to write a long switch/case statement to decode and handle each individual control change, saving it to our Processor's control variables. At the end of the statement, you call the *update()* method to set the new variables on the synth voice objects after checking that the count is greater than zero. This code is extracted from the *doControlUpdate()* function.

```
// loop through the parameters
int32 count = data.inputParameterChanges->getParameterCount();
for (int32 i = 0; i < count; i++)
{
      // get the message queue for ith parameter
      IParamValueQueue* queue =
                        data.inputParameterChanges->getParameterData(i);
      if(queue)
      {
               int32 sampleOffset;
               ParamValue value;

               // we are taking the last value in the queue:
               // queue->getPointCount()-1

               if(queue->getPoint(queue->getPointCount()-1,     /* last point */
                                 sampleOffset,                  /* sample offset */
                                 value) == kResultTrue)         /* value = [0..1] */
               {
                        // do something with value
                        ParamID pid = queue->getParameterId();
                        switch (pid) // same as RAFX uControlID
                        {

                        case OCTAVE:
```

```
            {
                    m_nOctave = (int)(cookVSTGUIVariable(MIN_OCTAVE,
                                       MAX_OCTAVE, value));
                    break;
            }

            etc...

    }
    if(count > 0)
            // now do a mass VOICE update
            update();
```

Accessing the MIDI Events

The MIDI event helper function is called *doProcessEvent()*, and it accepts an *Event* structure reference for input.

```
bool Processor::doProcessEvent(Event& vstEvent)
```

The *IEventList* interface us used to access the MIDI events. The code below only shows the accessing of events for simplicity; this will be embedded inside a *while()* loop that processes the sub-blocks in the next section. The *processData's inputEvent* interface is used for MIDI input events We will examine *Events* in more depth in the next chapter.

```
// --- get our list of events
IEventList* inputEvents = data.inputEvents;
Event e = {0}; // clear
Event* eventPtr = 0;

// --- count of events
int32 numEvents = inputEvents ? inputEvents->getEventCount () : 0;

// get the first event
if(numEvents)
{
     inputEvents->getEvent (0, e);
     eventPtr = &e;
}

switch(e.type)
{
     case Event::kNoteOnEvent:
     {
             // do note on stuff
             break;
     }
     case Event::kNoteOffEvent:
     {
             // do note off stuff
             break;
     }
     case Event::kPolyPressureEvent:
     {
```

```
                // do polyphonic aftertouch stuff
                break;
        }
}
```

Accessing the Audio Buffers

Remember that the audio travels through busses. In our case, we have declared one stereo output bus. The *processData* structure has a member named *outputs* that is of the *AudioBusBuffers** type. We use this variable to write to the output buffers. Each channel has its own output buffer; they are not interleaved. And there are separate buffers for 32 and 64 bit audio samples since they are different data-types. So we have one bus (0) with two 32-bit output channel buffers. The 32-bit buffers are referenced by pointers inside the output's *channelBuffers32* array. Therefore the *channelBuffer32* represents a buffer of pointers to audio buffers. In our case, *channelBuffer32[0]* contains a pointer to the left channel buffer and *channelBuffer32[1]* contains a pointer to the right channel buffer. The following chunk of code shows how we access and then flush the buffer with zeros. In this code, OUTPUT_CHANNELS is defined as 2.

In the first line, we declare a static buffer with two slots in it. Each of these will hold a pointer to the actual audio buffer

```
// if doing a 64-bit version, you need to replace float* with double*
float* buffers[OUTPUT_CHANNELS];
```

Next, setup a loop to access the channel buffer pointers and flush them with *memset()*. You need to do this in case no note events occur in the process block. The buffers are not guaranteed to be empty. We can break down the essential line of code:

```
buffers[i] = (float*)data.outputs[0].channelBuffers32[i];
```

as follows:

```
(float*) = cast the resulting pointer as float since we are 32-bit processing
data.outputs[0] = output bus 0
channelBuffers.32[i] = a pointer to the ith channel buffer

for(int i = 0; i < OUTPUT_CHANNELS; i++)
{
        // data.outputs[0] = BUS 0
        // note cast to float*, if 64-bit you cast to double
        buffers[i] = (float*)data.outputs[0].channelBuffers32[i];
        // sizeof uses float, change to double for 64-bit version
        memset(buffers[i], 0, data.numSamples*sizeof(float));
}
```

At this point the *buffers* array holds two pointers, one for the left buffer of data and one for the right. You can access the first sample of the left and right buffer like this:

```
buffers[0] [0]  = first sample in left buffer (0)
buffers[1] [0]  = first sample in right buffer (1)
```

Or you could access the jth sample in a loop:

```
buffers[0] [j]  = jth sample in left buffer (0)
buffers[1] [j]  = jth sample in right buffer (1)
```

Processing the Sub-blocks

All we really need to process the sub-blocks are a *while()* loop and some sample counters. This is pretty much straight-up C/C++ programming and should be easy to understand. We use the following counters to keep track of samples; this is directly from the sample code in the SDK:

```
numSamples = samples left to process, used in while() loop
```

```
while(numSamples > 0)
{
     // do processing here
}

samplesProcessed = count of samples we've rendered
samplesToProcess = number of samples remaining
```

The *process()* method for the MiniSynth is shown here though the details of the parameter changes, MIDI events and rendering are omitted and will be covered in Chapters 3–8; after the control information is updated you can see how the counters and *while()* loop render the audio in chunks. If it is not clear, use the Visual Studio debugger and step through one processing loop to watch the counters update. The loop counters are highlighted along with the snipped code. Here you can also see the code that uses the MIDI event's *sampleOffset* value to move the event into the next sub-block if needed. This ensures that MIDI events line up in time with the rendered audio.

```
tresult PLUGIN_API Processor::process(ProcessData& data)
{
```

First, you call the control update function to process the control changes that occurred during the block; we only process the last control event in the queue. If you want to process control events in a sample-accurate way, you need move this function call into the processing loop and alter the function itself to extract control change points that line up with the block's sample offsets.

```
     // --- check for control changes and update synth if needed
     doControlUpdate(data);

     // --- we process 32 samples at a time
     const int32 kBlockSize = SYNTH_PROC_BLOCKSIZE;
```

Next, access the audio buffers and clear them, storing each pointer in the *buffers* array.

```
     // initialize audio output buffers
     float* buffers[OUTPUT_CHANNELS];

     // clear the buffers 32-bit is float
     for(int i = 0; i < OUTPUT_CHANNELS; i++)
     {
          // data.outputs[0] = BUS 0
          buffers[i] = (float*)data.outputs[0].channelBuffers32[i];
          memset (buffers[i], 0, data.numSamples * sizeof(float));
     }
```

This code initializes the counter and total number of samples for the process loop.

```
     // --- total number of samples in the input Buffer
     int32 numSamples = data.numSamples;

     // --- this is used when we need to shove an event into the       //      next  block
     int32 samplesProcessed = 0;
```

This code deals with the MIDI events that arrived in the *data.inputEvents* interface. Before entering the main processing loop, you setup an *Event* pointer and initialize it with the first event.

```
     // --- get our list of events
     IEventList* inputEvents = data.inputEvents;
     Event e = {0};
     Event* eventPtr = 0;
     int32 eventIndex = 0;
```

```
// --- count of events
int32 numEvents = inputEvents ? inputEvents->getEventCount() : 0;

// get the first event
if(numEvents)
{
        inputEvents->getEvent (0, e);
        eventPtr = &e;
}
```

The main *while()* loop processes both MIDI events (first) then audio rendering. We need to keep this order so that we pick up note on and note off events prior to calling the voice object's rendering function.

```
// the loop
while(numSamples > 0)
{
        // bound the samples to process to BLOCK SIZE (32)
        int32 samplesToProcess = std::min<int32> (kBlockSize,
                                                  numSamples);
        while(eventPtr != 0)
        {
                // if the event is not in the current processing
                // block then adapt offset for next block
                if(e.sampleOffset > samplesToProcess)
                {
                        e.sampleOffset -= samplesToProcess;
                        break;
                }

                // --- find MIDI note on/off and broadcast
                doProcessEvent(e);

                // get next event
                eventIndex++;
                if(eventIndex < numEvents)
                {
                        if(inputEvents->getEvent(eventIndex, e) ==
                           kResultTrue)
                {
                                e.sampleOffset -= samplesProcessed;
                        }
                        else
                        {
                                eventPtr = 0;
                        }
                }
                else
                {
                        eventPtr = 0;
                }
        }       // end while (event != 0)
```

This is the main audio rendering loop. You accumulate voices and then write them out to the output buffers and set the *samplesToProcess* for the next trip through the main loop. We will discuss the details of the rendering in depth in Chapters 5–13.

```
            // the loop - samplesToProcess is more like framesToProcess
            // since we will to a pair of samples at a time
            for(int32 j = 0; j < samplesToProcess; j++)
            {
                   double dLeftAccum = 0.0;
                   double dRightAccum = 0.0;

                   <SNIP SNIP SNIP - render and accumulate voices>

                   // write out to buffer
                   buffers[0][j] = dLeftAccum;  // left
                   buffers[1][j] = dRightAccum; // right
            }

            // --- update the counter
            for(int i = 0; i < OUTPUT_CHANNELS; i++)
                  buffers[i] += samplesToProcess;

            // --- update the samples processed/to process
            numSamples -= samplesToProcess;
            samplesProcessed += samplesToProcess;

     } // end while (numSamples > 0)
```

If you want to experiment with outputting parameter changes back to the GUI, for example outputting a value to a signal meter, then you can do it here. The synths in the book do not output any parameters. You can find examples of outputting data at the website.

```
     // can write OUT to the GUI; see documentation
     if(data.outputParameterChanges)
     {
            // write to GUI or Parameters
     }
```

If you know the synth is silent during this processing block, you should set the silence flag on the data output structure. This notifies the client to ignore (mute) the buffers from this block. The *getNoteOnCount()* function is a simple helper function we use and will be discussed in Chapter 8 when we implement polyphony.

```
     // --- set silence flags if no notes playing
     if(getNoteOnCount() == 0 && data.numOutputs > 0)
     {
            data.outputs[0].silenceFlags = 0x11; // L/R channel are silent
     }

     return kResultTrue;
}
```

2.30 Implementing a VST3 Plug-in: GUI Design

You don't really need to design a custom GUI if you don't want to since it is only window-dressing for your plug-in. GUI design is the subject of many other textbooks and outside the scope of this book, but most of us know the difference between a cluttered, confusing GUI and a clean one. VST is very flexible when it comes to custom GUI design and there are many options. We decided to use the GUI designer called VSTGUI that is packaged with the VST3 SDK. This tool is maintained by a third party and can be used to design GUIs for a variety of plug-in APIs. In fact, the most recent version of RackAFX uses VSTGUI for its custom GUI controls as well. Details about VSTGUI are found at http://sourceforge.net/projects/vstgui/, and if you decide to really dig into this product, join the mailing list there. VSTGUI is powerful and can be used on any platform and any plug-in API including Apple's AU and Avid's AAX.

VSTGUI is a set of C++ objects that encapsulate and implement GUI control behavior. Most controls also have associated graphic resources like a bitmap, JPEG or PNG files that are used to skin them and change their look and feel. All of our resources will be PNG files. You can implement a VSTGUI in two ways: programmatically or using the drag-and-drop editor. When you implement your GUI programmatically, you usually start out with a piece of graph-paper and you decide on the types and locations of the controls within an outer container (or window). You use a GUI coordinate system to codify your control's size and position in the container, identify the graphics resources for skinning, and you instantiate the objects in code. Many seasoned programmers actually prefer this method, and once you practice for a while, it isn't that intimidating.

However, we live in a drag-and-drop world and we have chosen to use that route for the VST3 plug-ins in this book. The VSTGUI drag-and-drop editor has its advantages and disadvantages, but we are going to keep things as simple as possible in our GUI designs. And by using this editor, you don't have to write a single line of GUI code. On the downside, the drag-and-drop interface can be sluggish at times. But with a little practice and use of templates and coordinates, you can assemble a flashy GUI fairly quickly using a combination of dragging/dropping and then manually setting the final location by typing in the coordinates. The only bit of code we will need to write is in implementing the vector joystick in Chapter 11.

Before we get into the GUI design, you need to understand the concept of view containers and the VSTGUI coordinate system—both are very similar to the way Windows and MacOS GUIs work. Let's start with the coordinate system in the context of the outer container for the GUI. Figure 2.29 shows a mock-up of the MiniSynth GUI. Look at the outer container; the origin is located at the upper left corner. Like our familiar cartesian coordinate system, the x-value increases as you move to the right. However, the y-value increases as you move down. This is the opposite of what you normally use in your math classes but is standard for GUI programming. After you get used to it, the discrepancy with the y-value will not be a problem.

The outer container is called a view container. VSTGUI uses a C++ object named *CViewContainer* to represent it. The *CViewContainer* object has an attribute that allows you to skin it with a background. If you use PNG files, your skins can be transparent or partially transparent. Inside of the outer container, you can see some blocks labeled Osc, Filter, etc. These contain groupings of controls. If you look at the screenshots of the actual GUIs, you will see that the blocks also have a skin, with rounded corners and a dark area at the top for a label. In fact, these too are *CViewContainers* with a PNG file resource used for the skin. They are referenced by the location of their origins (upper left corners) relative to their outer container. Figure 2.30 shows the corner-coordinates these columns. They all have the same y-coordinate of 5 units down (positive). Their x-coordinates reveal that the columnar view containers must be 85 units wide, thus the progression 5, 90, 175, 260, etc. There are two (or three for DXSynth) rows of controls on the right, which always have the same coordinate locations. The rows are 110 pixels in height thus the progression of 5, 115, etc. for the *y*-coordinate.

This layout of *CViewContainers* in Figure 2.29 is the same for five of the six synth projects: NanoSynth, MiniSynth, DigiSynth, VectorSynth and AniSynth all use this same format, making it easy to copy the project files.

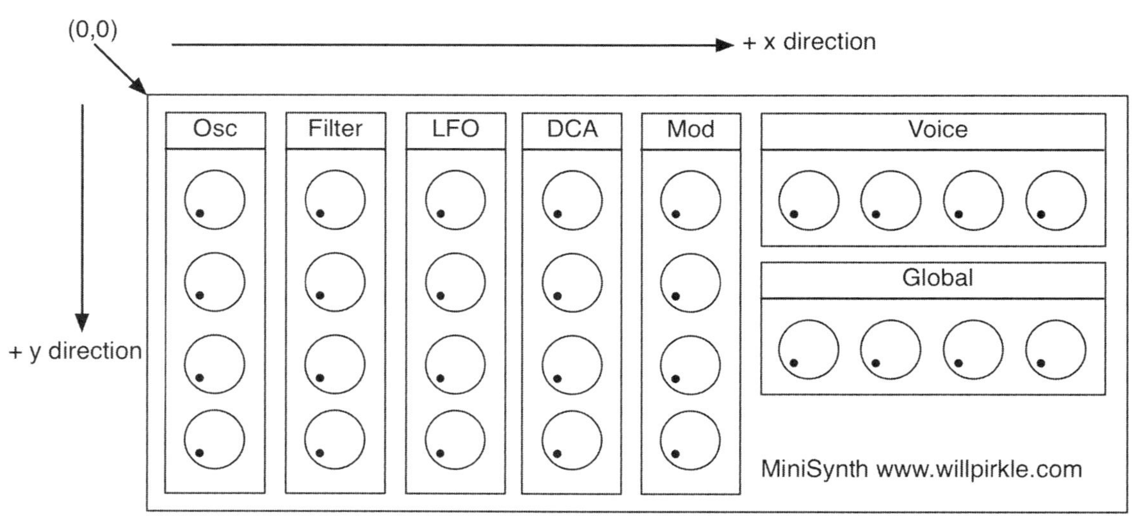

Figure 2.29: In GUI coordinate systems, the origin is a the upper left, positive x moves to the right and positive y moves down.

At the top of each column is a *CTextLabel* that represents text. It is positioned by setting its origin relative to its container, the columnar view container. So you can see an important concept here—all sub-views are referenced by their positions relative to their containers. This means that the text label at the top of each column will always be positioned at the same location (5,3) regardless of its actual location within the giant outer container. Ultimately this makes positioning the controls easy if you are making duplicated sets of them as we have here.

Examining one of the columnar view containers in detail, you can see that the controls are laid out in groups as shown in Figure 2.32. These groups are inside the dotted boxes. In each synth project we have left some room for you to add your own controls as part of the Challenges at the end of each chapter.

These groups of controls are called templates. Using templates makes creating and assembling the GUI easy. The knob group templates we have designed for you are designated "KG" (Knob Group). The knob groups will handle all the parameters that are continuous controllers, linked to *float*, *double* or *int* types. You can break the knob group down into its fundamental components as shown in Figure 2.33.

- *CViewContainer*: a transparent container with no PNG file associated with it
- *CTextLabel*: this label has a transparent background
- *CAnimKnob*: an animated knob that rotates
- *CTextEdit*: a text edit box that the user can click on and change the value to an exact one; the knob will rotate in response
- all of the knob group templates are 75x85 (width x height in pixels)

And, it should be no surprise that the text label, knob and edit box are all positioned relative to their output *CViewContainer*. When you set up a Template, it is like making a mini-GUI, and everything is relatively positioned.

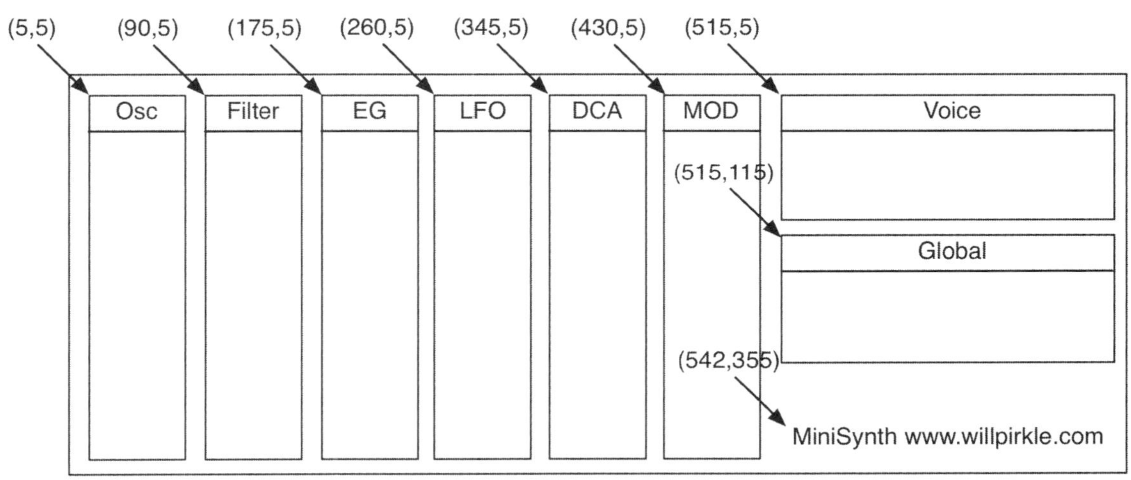

Figure 2.30: The columnar view containers are positioned inside the outer view container using their origin coordinates relative to the outer container.

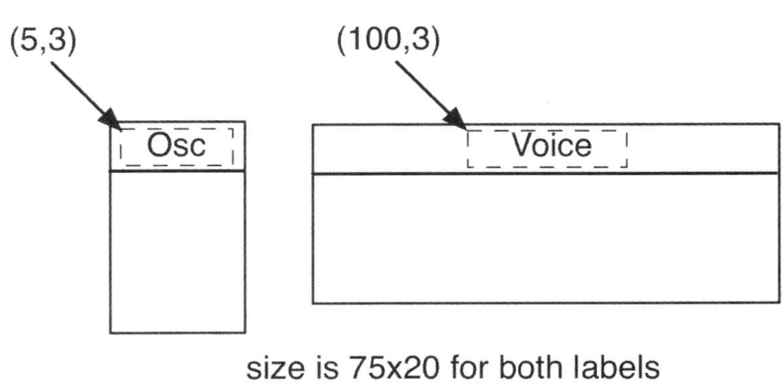

Figure 2.31: The text label at the top of the vertical container is located 5 units over and 3 units down relative to that container; the label in the horizontal containers is positioned at the origin (100,3) and both have the same dimensions 75x20 pixels.

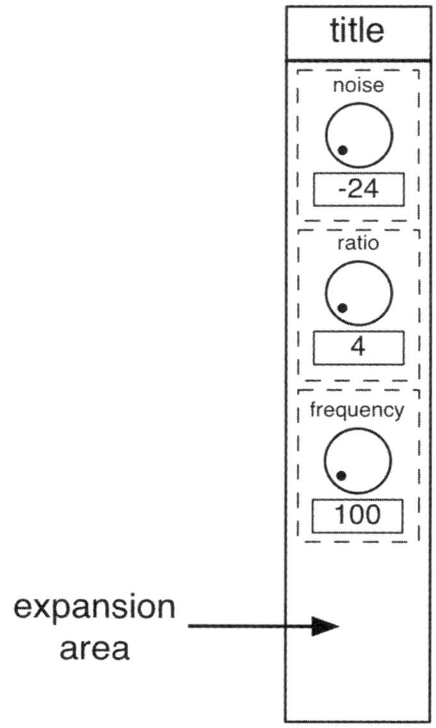

Figure 2.32: A column of control groups.

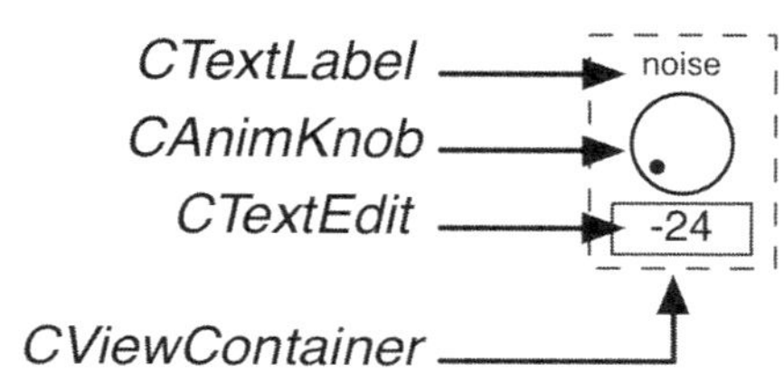

Figure 2.33: A KG (knob-group) consists of an outer *CViewContainer*, a *CTextLabel*, *CAnimKnob* and *CTextEdit* control.

When you INSERT these knob group Templates into a *CViewContainer*, you position them using the Template view container origins relative to the columnar view container. For all the synths, these are located at the corner-coordinates shown in Figure 2.34, and since they are relative, they are the same for all the columns. We have placed the knob groups 5 pixels apart; since they are 85 pixels in height, each group's y-coordinate is 90 pixels greater than the group above it. In Figure 2.34 you can see that the y-coordinates progress this way; (20,110,200,290). However, for vertically placed controls, the 5 pixel padding is not required, so the x-coordinates progress in increments of the width of 75 pixels (5,80,155,230).

For the MinSynth, DigiSynth, VectorSynth, and AniSynth, these control containers all have the same sizes:

- columns: (85,380)
- rows: (310,110)

The second kind of control you need to implement will provide the user with a list of items from which they will select only one. For example, you might have a control where the user picks a filter type from a list of {LPF,HPF,BPF} as you saw in Table 2.8. You saw how to declare these in the Controller's *initialize()* function where you load strings into the Parameter object. The VSTGUI component that handles these kinds of string-based parameters is called *COptionMenu*. We provide you with a set of templates that combine a text label and an option menu into one cluster; these are designated "OMG" (Option Menu Group) and consist of:

- *CViewContainer*: a transparent container with no PNG file associated with it
- *CTextLabel*: this label has a transparent background
- *COptionMenu*: the drop-down list of items
- All of the option menu groups are 75x42 (width x height in pixels) so you can stack two together in the same space as one knob group

Figure 2.35 shows the option menu group components.

We have also designed a third template that you may use that combines a text label, option menu, tiny knob and a second text label for the knob value in the same half-sized space as the option menu group. This template is used once per synth GUI to give you an idea of how it looks; for some GUIs with high knob counts, the mini-knob/option menu can save layout space. These templates are designated "SWG" (SWitch Group) since they are used for on/off switches that need a buddy knob control. This template is shown in Figure 2.36.

The Global and Voice rows of MiniSynth, DigiSynth, VectorSynth and AniSynth use combinations of the full and half-sized templates, and the corner coordinates are shown in Figure 2.37. These coordinates are given so you can quickly position the templates on the GUI.

The VectorSynth and AniSynth projects include an additional column of knobs for the Rotor controls. The DXSynth is laid out differently using rows instead of columns. The locations of the *CViewContainers* for these synths are shown in Figures 2.38 and 2.39. Since the template locations are relative to the *CViewContainer* that holds them, the knob and option menu group corner coordinates are the same as Figure 2.37.

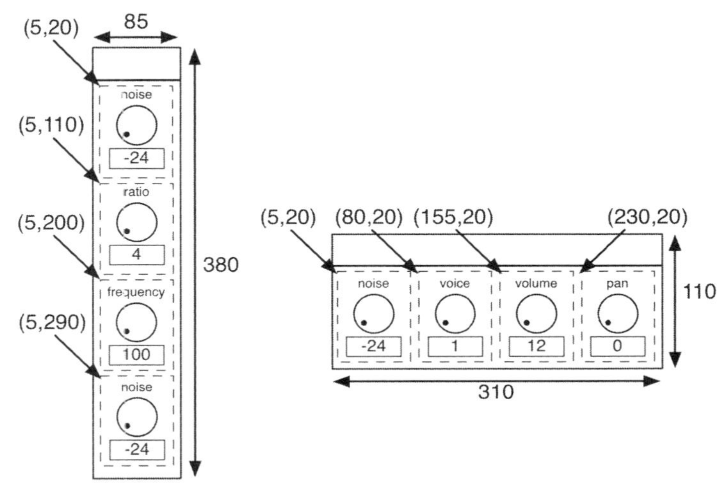

Figure 2.34: The locations of the vertical and horizontal ViewContainer sub-view templates.

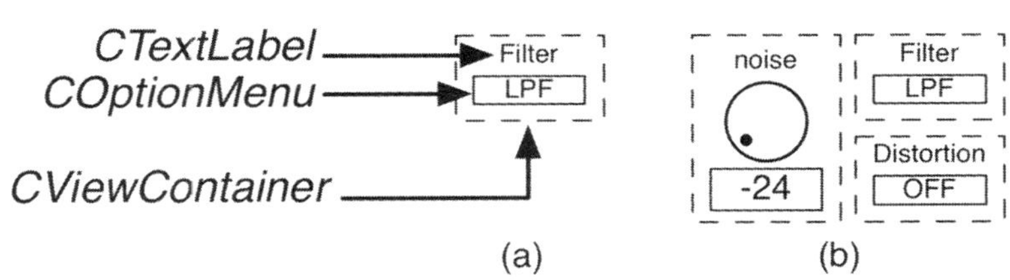

Figure 2.35: (a) The Option Menu Group (OMG) consists of a view container with a text label and option menu (b) two option menu groups occupy the same area as one knob group with one pixel of padding between them.

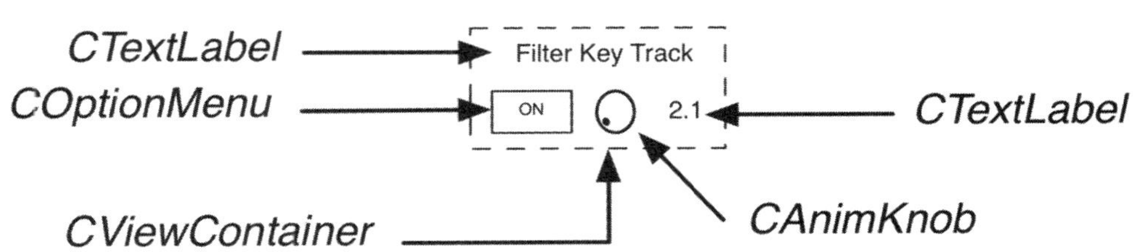

Figure 2.36: The switch group combines an option menu and tiny knob in the same half-sized template.

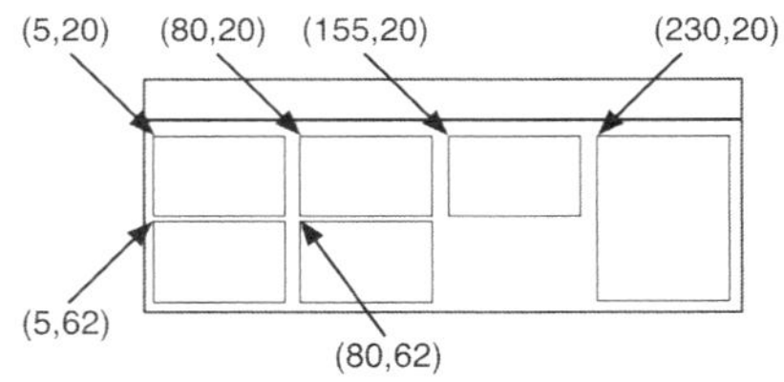

Figure 2.37: The corner coordinates for the controls embedded in the rows are always the same since they are always relative to the outer container.

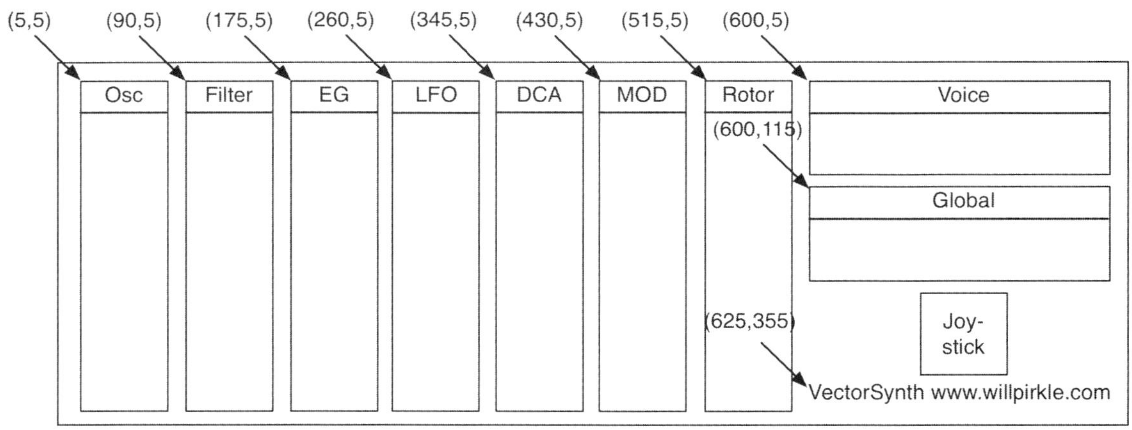

Figure 2.38: Corner coordinates for the VectorSynth and AniSynth projects; the joystick control will be covered in Chapter 10.

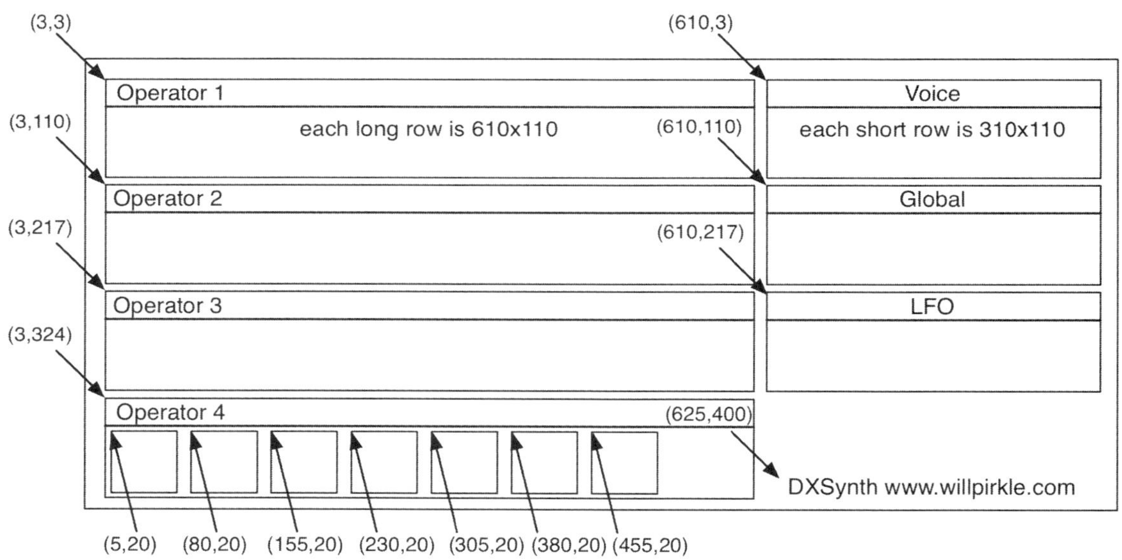

Figure 2.39: Layout and corner coordinates for the DXSynth; the locations of the controls for the Operator 1, 2 and 3 are the same as the fourth row while the locations of controls in the Voice, Global and LFO containers are the same as in Figures 2.37—notice also there is ample room for adding your own controls to each row.

2.31 Using the VSTGUI Drag-and-Drop Interface

To open the VSTGUI editor, you first compile your synth in debug mode in Visual Studio. Then, copy the *.vst3* file into the client's VST3 folder and open the client. Create a new track with your synth plug-in and open the GUI (this varies from client to client). If you are using the GUI-less template, you will see a black box for the GUI, otherwise you will see the stock GUI that ships with the projects. Right-click on the GUI and choose "Open UIDescription Editor" from the menu. This opens the VSTGUI editor. You can get much more information and help from the VST SDK documentation, the VSTGUI website and http://www.willpirkle.com/synthbook/

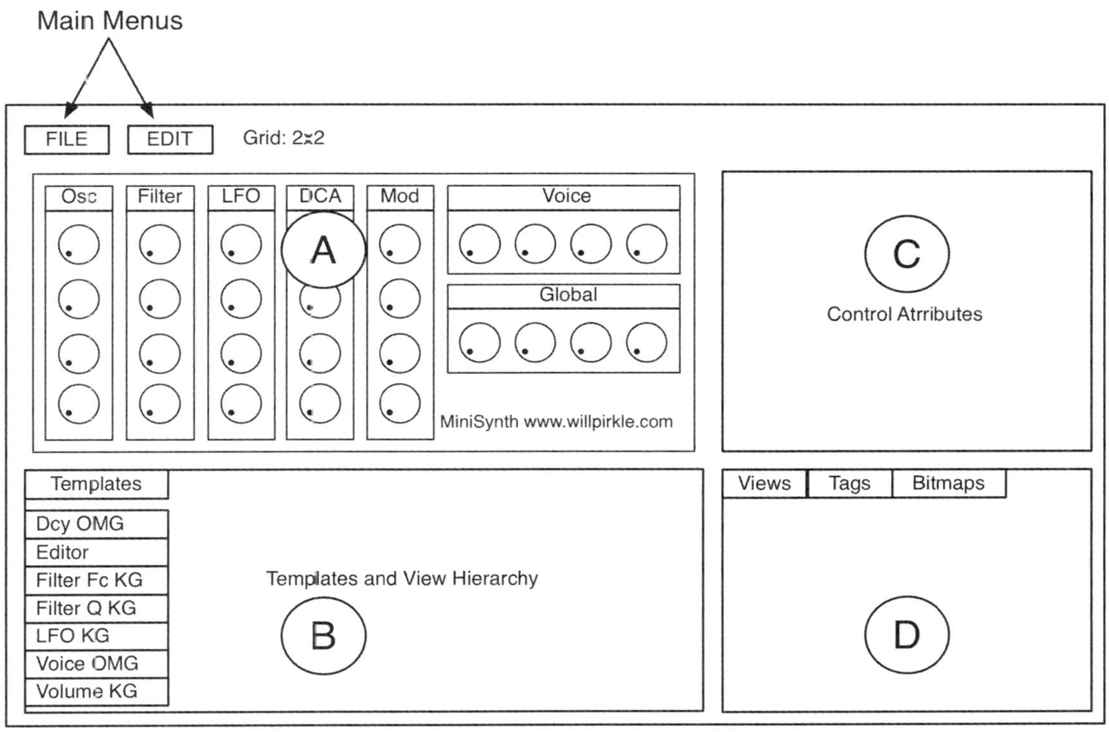

Figure 2.40: The layout of the VSTGUI editor.

The editor layout is shown in Figure 2.40. Note: this shows the version of the VSTGUI editor at the time of this writing; your version may look different in the future, so please consult the documentation for additional information.

The most important thing to understand about this editor is that the main controls are all accessed from the *FILE* and *EDIT* boxes at the upper left which each open menus. The *FILE* menu includes Save and Close functionality while the *EDIT* menu contains all the controls for manipulating the templates. You will spend most of the time in the *EDIT* menu, copying, inserting and creating templates. We will refer back to this chapter for creating the custom GUIs, so take some time and practice the operations described here.

The editor's areas are labeled A, B, C and D. These areas are used for the following functions.

A: The Design Area

This is where you visually assemble your GUI as well as design and build your templates. You can click on the main outer *CViewContainer* to change its size to accommodate more or less controls. However, if you change the size you must also use *EDIT->Template Settings* and choose "Use Current" for the Minimum and Maximum size areas. If you forget this step, your outer container will be the wrong size. When working with templates in the design area, you don't have to worry about changing the sizes for template settings—these sub-templates will automatically have their sizes stored properly.

B: Templates and View Hierarchy

The templates are all organized alphabetically and the template labeled "Editor" is the main completed GUI that you see in the design area. The templates we have supplied will also show up in this list. You can click on a template to see it in the design area. Clicking on "Editor" will bring you back to the main GUI. Remember, your GUI is really a collection of templates rather than a bunch of individual controls; this makes copying and placing the control-clusters easier. NOTE: do not change the name of the main GUI from "Editor" or you will need to alter some of your C++ code to match.

C: Control Attributes

This area is where you set the attributes of the controls that are embedded in the templates. The controls include knobs, option menus and edit boxes. The attributes you set are:

- *origin*: the (x,y) coordinates of the upper left corner of a control
- *size*: the width and height of the control
- *bitmap*: for the knob controls, you select the "knob" bitmap here

- *control-tag*: the control tag is a zero-based index that links the control to an underlying variable; although they can be any string, it makes sense to match them with the enumerations you made in the *SynthParamLimits.h* file
- *transparent*: all templates feature controls with transparent backgrounds; you may change this by un-checking the "transparent" check-box
- *title*: for text-based controls, this is where you set the default text
- *font*: for text-based controls, this is where you set the font (and size)
- *font color*: for the text fields, you may want to modify the font color

D: Views/Tags/Bitmaps

This is an important area in the editor because it shows you the C++ objects (Views), the control ID values (Tags) and graphical elements (Bitmaps).

Views

The Views tab reveals a list of the C++ objects you can drag and drop into the GUI. You click on a view such as *CViewContainer* then hold, drag and drop into the GUI. Once it is added to the interface, the control attributes area will change to reflect this new GUI control. At that point, you usually manually adjust the origin and size to move the control to an exact position in the GUI with an exact size. The columns you see in the MiniSynth GUI are *CViewContainers* with the bitmap set to "groupframe"—VSTGUI automatically stretches the image to fit the container size for some control types.

Tags

Tags are a list of the indexed control ID values you set up in the enumeration step in the GUI design. You use the + and – buttons at the bottom to add or remove Tags. You double click on the Tag value in the second column to change it. The Tags are alphabetized, so they probably won't be listed in numerical order. The Tags can be any text string, but it makes sense to use the same strings as the enumeration (e.g. OCTAVE) so everything matches up. If you make mistakes with the Tags, your controls won't work properly. If you duplicate the Tag values, then any controls with the same index will move each other and move together if automated.

Bitmaps

Bitmaps are the graphical elements in your GUI. They do not have to strictly be in the .BMP format; you can use JPEG, PNG or other types that Visual Studio supports. The bitmaps are resources you add to Visual Studio. You will see them in the Resources folder in the Visual Studio projects. The files we will use for all of the projects are:

- *background.png*: the grey background image for the main outer *CViewContainer*
- *groupframe.png*: the transparent grey frames that are the background image for the columnar and row-shaped control groups
- *knob.png*: the medium sized blue rotary knob used for most of the knob controls
- *knob2.png*: the tiny sized blue knob used in the switch group templates

If you want to add your own graphics to change the look and feel or to experiment with the numerous other controls provided in the VSTGUI library, you need to be careful about the path locations when you import the resources into Visual Studio. The graphics in our synthesizers are stock objects included with the SDK but you may find many more knob and button graphics files at http://www.willpirkle.com/synthbook/ After importing and compiling your project, then re-opening the VSTGUI editor, you use the + and – buttons at the bottom of the Bitmaps tab to add and remove these resources. After adding an item, click the button labeled "more," and you should get a preview of your image file. If the preview is blank, that means there is a problem with your file path. Check with the VSTGUI website http://sourceforge.net/projects/vstgui/ for more information.

2.32 VSTGUI Design Example

To demonstrate the paradigm that we used for all the projects in the book, download the VST3 "MiniSynth—Empty" project. Compile the template, move the VST3 file into the client and create a new track in your DAW to instantiate the plug-in, then open the UIDescription editor. Figure 2.41 shows the progression we will follow not only for creating main GUIs but also templates.

In the design area, you will see a black rectangle that is the empty outer view container. Click on the empty container, and a red outline appears around it. Then, the control attributes area will change to reflect the attributes of this *CViewContainer*. In the attributes area, click on bitmap and a list will appear; select "background" and the container will fill with the grey background image. Alternatively, you can set a background color in the background-color field.

Next, click the Views tab in the Views/Tags/Bitmaps area. Click on *CViewContainer* and drag and drop it into the outer container. It will appear as a black box and will be automatically selected into the attributes area. At this point, you can use the mouse to move and resize the container object (this can be sluggish on some machines), or you can set its exact position and size quickly in the attributes

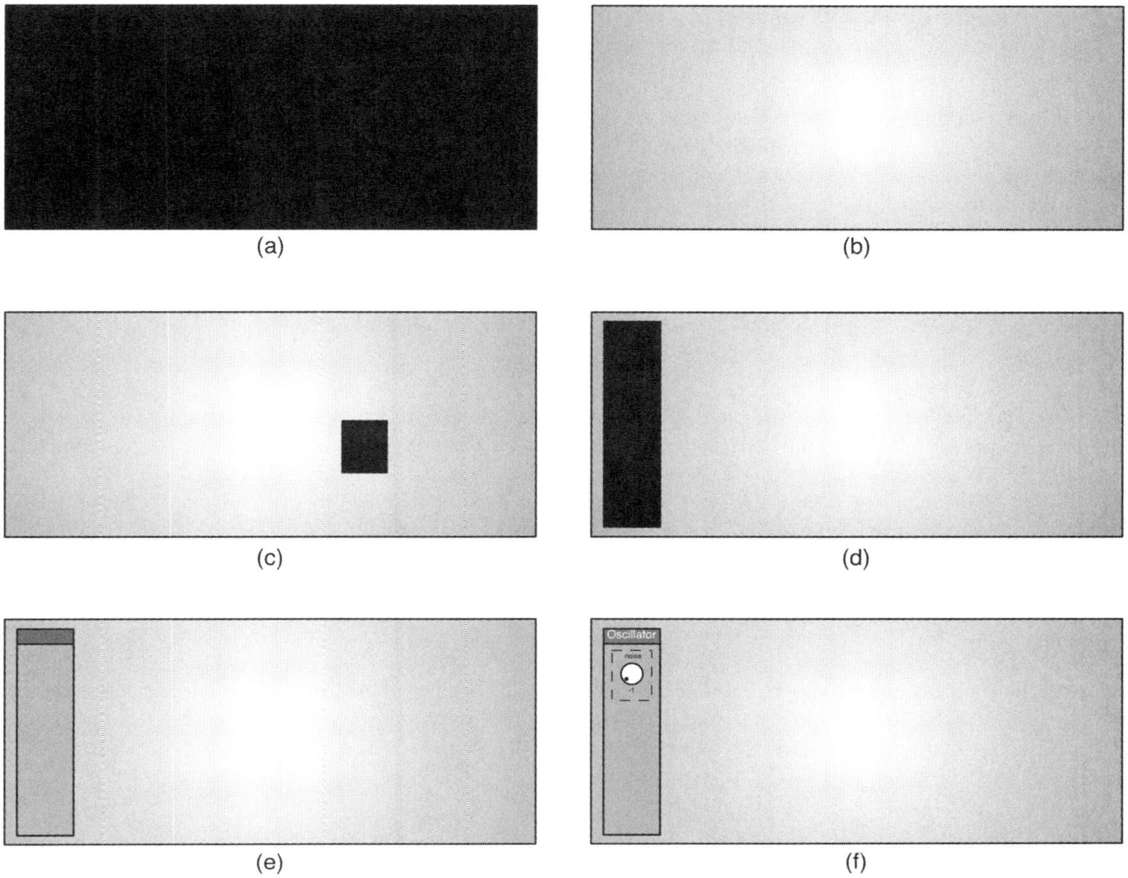

Figure 2.41: (a) Blank container, (b) with background image, (c) addition of new *CViewContainer*, (d) repositioning and sizing the new container, (e) addition of groupframe background bitmap and (f) addition of Oscillator text label in white at top of column and insertion of NoiseOsc KG.

area. Referring back to Figure 2.38, you can see that the columnar view container has the size of 85 x 380 pixels or (85,380). And in Figure 2.38 you find the corner location of the first column to be (5,5). So, in the attributes area, set the following:

origin: 5,5
size: 85,380

The container will jump to the correct location and resize itself to your new measurements. Add the graphic component by clicking on bitmap and choosing groupframe. The container will change to show the new graphic.

Make sure the container is still selected and has the red outline—it is easy to loose selection of the container by clicking in other areas of the GUI. With the container selected, click, drag and drop a *CTextLabel* object form the Views tab into the container. Referring back to Figure 2.31, go to the attributes area and position it at the location:

origin: 5,3
size: 75,20

Now change the text attributes:

title: Oscillators
font: ~ System Font
font-color: ~ WhiteCColor
back-color: ~ BlackCColor

At this point we have the columnar container with a white title, and we are ready to add control groups to it. Once again, ensure that the container is selected and then click on the main *EDIT* box and choose *INSERT Template*. From the list, select NoiseOsc KG, and the template will appear inside the container but positioned with its origin at 0,0. Now, click on the newly added template so that it has a red outline (do not click on a sub-control in the template or you will have the wrong attributes). Referring back to Figure 2.34, set the origin to 5,20 and the control group will snap into the position at the top of the column. This is the basic operation—create rows and columns of *CViewContainers* and INSERT templates into them. If you re-position a row or column's *CViewContainer*, all the inserted templates will move as well, so the row or column behaves as one graphical block.

Let's examine the template you just added. In the templates and view hierarchy area, click on the template named NoiseOsc KG. The template appears in the design area with the outer container selected. So a template is also contained inside a *CViewContainer*, and you build them just the same way. Click on the text label Noise Osc (dB) and examine the attributes, such as position within the container, font color and transparency. Next, click on the knob. In the Attributes area, find control-tag, and you will see that it is set to NOISE_OSC_AMP_DB. In the Tags area, you can see that NOISE_OSC_AMP_DB is linked to the index value 0. Click on the *CTextEdit* box just under the knob and examine its attributes. Notice that its control-tag is identical to the knob's tag. When the user moves the knob, the text in the edit box will automatically change, and if the user selects and changes the text in the box, the knob will automatically change its position. Finally, examine the bitmap for this control—it is set to knob.

Copy a Template

In this example we'll create a bogus knob group solely as an example of copying another group—something you will get used to doing as you build your own GUIs. From the *EDIT* menu, choose *Duplicate Template*, but beware: this menu item is right next to *Delete Template* in the list; if you accidentally delete a template, immediately use *EDIT->Undo Delete Template* to fix it. From the list choose NoiseOsc KG. In the templates area, a new row will be added, but won't be selected yet. The template will be named NoiseOsc KG 1. Find it and double click on the name to change it to Test KG. The newly named template will disappear and move to its alphabetic location in the list. Find it and click on it. Now play with the three embedded controls. Click on the text label and change its text attributes to whatever you want—play with the options. Click on the knob and set its control-tag to something else. Likewise, experiment with the edit box attributes, especially the transparency and color; some may prefer a black background with bright green or yellow text color.

Click on Editor in the templates area to re-open the main GUI container. Click somewhere in the first column to select the column's *CViewContainer*. Choose *EDIT->INSERT Template* and select your new Test KG, and it will be added into the container in the wrong spot, overlapping the first knob group. Referring to Figure 2.34, change the origin to 5,110 and the new cluster of controls will snap into place below the first one.

Create a Template

Although you won't need to create any new templates if you use our projects (the Empty versions still include all the templates), you may still want to play around with building your own. The process is essentially identical to building that first column—you start with an empty view container and add controls to it. That new container of controls can be inserted and moved as a group. If you want to experiment, go back to the Test KG template and write down the locations of the controls and their attributes including the size of the outer view container. Then use *EDIT->Add New Template* and choose *CViewContainer* from the list. Now, try to duplicate the Test KG controls; you'll need to drag and drop the three objects *CTextLabel*, *CAnimKnob* and *CTextEdit* from the Views to the GUI. You will need to set up the bitmap for the knob; try both knob and knob2. Try making your own variations in sizes and colors. Then you can experiment with placing them into other view containers. Incidentally, all the bitmaps that come with the projects are stock items that come with the VST3 SDK, except the backgrounds for the vector joystick in Chapter 11. The drag and drop VST3 GUI editor actually writes an XML file named *vstgui.uidesc,* which is included inside your Visual Studio project and compiled as a resource. If you are adventurous (or you get tired of using the drag and drop editor) you can edit this file directly. You can find much more information about directly editing this file at the VSTGUI website and http://www.willpirkle.com/synthbook/.

2.33 Implementing a VST3 Plug-in: Debugging

Debugging your synth plug-in is critical for your success. As soon as you start experimenting with your own code and the Chapter Challenges, you will likely have problems as we all do when implementing new code or ideas. To debug and test your plug-in, you will need a VST3 client as discussed earlier. To debug with it, you need to tell Visual Studio where it is located. Open the Project Properties and select *Configuration Properties -> Debugging*. In the Command field, browse to find the executable for the client. Then, in the Attach field, choose Yes. Place your VST3 file in the proper folder for your client and launch the client. You can't start the debugger until the client is running. With the client running, start the Visual Studio debugger and set breakpoints. When you instantiate your plug-in, the breakpoints will become active and you can step through the code and debug as usual. You will be flipping back and forth between Visual Studio and the plug-in client—this is normal for plug-in development on just about any platform.

2.34 Writing Audio Unit (AU) Plug-ins

Apple's Audio Unit (AU) plug-in format is different from both RackAFX and VST3, which are both written in "straight" C++ and require no additional libraries outside of ANSI C++. AU plug-ins are written in C++ using Apple's XCode compiler. However there are many MacOS-specific concepts that require the programmer to know more than just C++. To write AU plug-ins, you need to already be familiar with MacOS programming, specifically the CoreServices and AppKit frameworks (an XCode framework is a statically linked library). Additionally, the Apple-preferred way of creating a GUI for your plug-in is with the Cocoa framework, which is done in another programming language: Objective-C. The AU plug-ins in this book all use Cocoa, so you will need to understand the Objective-C language as well as concepts like *IBActions*, *IBOutlets*, target-action pairs, and referencing outlets. We developed our own custom controls for the Cocoa GUI, all in Objective-C, and while you don't need to understand how they work on the inside to do the projects in this book, you will if you want to modify the look and feel or behavior. And that means you will need to be competent in Objective-C. If you don't know Objective-C but you are already good with C++ then the good news is that you can learn it fairly easily.

> AU provides two mechanisms for implementing a GUI. The AU client provides a default GUI in case the plug-in does not implement one. There is also an option for a custom GUI. We will implement both: we need to define the default GUI first and then connect the custom GUI to its parameters. You can alternate back and forth between the two GUIs in the AU Client.

Even with all these differences, the AU API follows the same pattern as discussed in the beginning of the chapter and the same paradigm that RackAFX and VST3 follow—in this respect it is just as ordinary as the others. The plug-ins are derived from a special base class. You override and implement the necessary functions to handle GUI control changes and audio signal processing/rendering. If you make a custom GUI, then you need to add the code for that as well. If you have the basic MacOS and Objective-C skills, AU is easier and more straightforward than VST3. For synthesizer plug-ins, AU closely resembles RackAFX in how it handles incoming MIDI messages, so going from RackAFX to AU is actually conceptually easier than going to VST3.

In order to develop the AU plug-ins in this book, you will need the following:

- a Mac with MacOS 10.7 or greater
- the XCode version that is best/most recent for your OS
- the AU project files from the website
- an AU client like Logic or Ableton Live

There is no AU SDK per se. The additional support files you need are usually included with XCode, or as an additional download. As of this writing, the latest update to these files was done in November 2013, and you can get the latest updates at developer.apple.com by searching for the following string: "Audio Unit Examples (AudioUnit Effect, Generator, Instrument, and Offline)." In addition to the support files, you will find the latest sample code. These files are all contained in a set of folders in a specific hierarchy. If you want to play with the Apple sample code, it will be accessing files in other folders in that hierarchy, much like VST3.

However, unlike VST3, the additional files do not reference each other in specific locations. So, to make the projects easier to manage and stand-alone like RackAFX, we created self-contained project folders that have all the necessary files included. So if you download the sample projects, you won't really need the stuff from Apple, unless they make an update to the core files. And, each of your synth projects files is independent of the others. With the projects self-contained, this means that you can put them in any folder you wish, so there are no restrictions like you have with VST3.

An AU plug-in is also a dynamically linked library. The file extension is *.component* in MacOS, so you will ultimately be building a component project. The Cocoa GUI is packaged in a resource file with the extension *.bundle*. The *.component* file must be placed in the folder:

~/Library/Audio/Plug-Ins/Components

The *.bundle* file must be placed in a Resources folder relative to the project. To facilitate this, we set up Build Phases in XCode to copy the two files to their destinations.

Figure 2.42 shows a generalized block diagram for an AU with a Cocoa view. The two components are separate entities and even reside in different folders, but you can think of them as a pair. Like VST3, AU plug-ins have some number of input and output busses. These

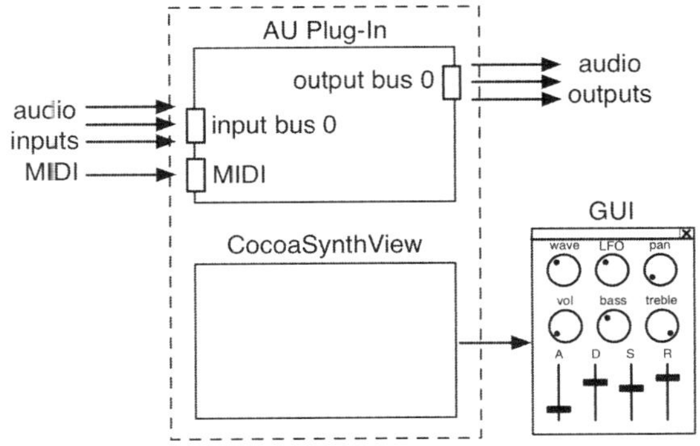

Figure 2.42: An AU plug-in with a Cocoa View.

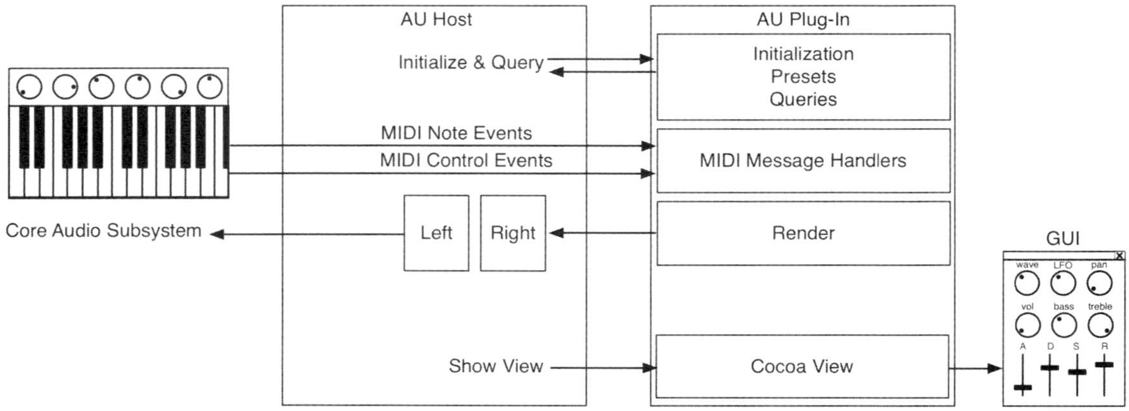

Figure 2.43: The plug-in implements functions that the host uses to transmit MIDI and render audio.

I/O busses may be mono or multi-channeled. For a synth plug-in, there is no input bus and one output bus. AU plug-ins can also accept MIDI messages either as synth plug-ins or as MIDI controlled effects.

In Figure 2.43 you can see the grand scheme of operation between the AU plug-in and the host. The host initializes the plug-in and then queries it for special behaviors. MIDI is routed through the host to the plug-in via MIDI message handlers. Audio is rendered into buffers that are shipped out to the *Core Audio* subsystem. The Cocoa view maintains the GUI.

2.35 AU XCode Projects

The XCode projects we have created for you all follow the same paradigms for file naming, GUI object naming, and file groups. All six synths have a Cocoa GUI included, though you may choose to use the projects marked "Empty" if you want to design your own GUI. The "NO GUI" versions have empty Cocoa files and an Interface Builder .NIB file that has no controls. So each XCode Project consists of two targets, one for the synth and one for the UI. The UI target is always named the same (CocoaUI), while the synth target's name changes for each project. The synth target will be the same name as the Project: NanoSynth, MiniSynth, DigiSynth, VectorSynth, AniSunth and DXSynth.

Starting a New Project

You have two options for starting a new AU project: start from scratch or modify an existing project. Modifying an existing project is far and away the simpler option. An existing project can be converted to a new one in less than ten minutes in ten easy steps (see the Appendix).

There are multiple project versions you may download, a set for each synth project:

- Empty—you write everything and you design the GUI—if you are already an advanced AU programmer, this might be a good option
- GUI only—the GUI code and UI is already done so you can focus on the synth components and processing; in each Chapter you'll have the chance to go in and modify the GUI a bit at a time, and after a few projects, you might want to take on the complete GUI design. NOTE: this is the recommended option!
- Full—the whole project inclusive; we don't recommend simply compiling someone else's code as a learning method, however having the full code allows you to not only check your own work but also step through the code in debug mode, so you can see how the client interacts—in short, the full projects are excellent for helping you debug and understand your own projects-in-progress

Additional Files

The AU projects are designed to be as similar as possible. The main difference will be in the SynthCore—the set of C++ objects that make up each individual synth. You will get a list of these files for each synth project, however there are three files that are necessary for each one and are identical. These are included in each synth project sample code:

- *synthfunctions.h*: a collection of structures and functions that are used throughout the synth objects; you can add more of your own here, too
- *pluginconstants.h*: another collection of structures, functions and objects that are used in the synth projects
- *pluginobjects.cpp*: the implementations of objects declared in *pluginconstants.h*

Download the MiniSynth project and open it in XCode to see the contents. Let's first examine the file groups:

- *AU Source*: this contains the files for the plug-in object itself as well as a few necessary ancillary files
- *MiniSynth*: all the synth core files; these include the oscillators, filters, and envelope generators you develop first as well as specialized Voice objects
- *CoreAudio*: the base class files and their supporting files
- *CocoaUI*: the GUI files including custom controls
- *Resources*: images for custom controls and backgrounds, the *.NIB* file and the *.plist* files for the project
- External Frameworks:
    - o AppKit
    - o QuartzCore
    - o CoreMIDI
    - o Cocoa
    - o CoreServices
    - o AudioToolbox
    - o AudioUnit
    - o CoreAudio
- *Products*: contains file references for the two target output files, the *.component* and *.bundle*; you can right click on either and choose "Show in Finder" to locate them

Of these folders, you will be spending the majority if time in the AU Source group. Its files include:

- *AUSynth.h* and *AUSynth.cpp*: your plug-in object named *AUSynth*; the name of this object does NOT change from one project to the next
- *AUSynthStructures.h* and *AUSynthVersion.h*: helper files to split out struct definitions and version information
- *AUSynth.r*: the project Rez file (this is only needed for backwards compatibility with Logic 9); it is now replaced by a Dictionary in your *Info.plist* file
- *AUSynth.exp*: the exported symbols file (more on this shortly)
- *AUSynth_Prefix.pch*: the pre-compiled header file that you can safely ignore

In the CocoaUI group, you can see the Objective-C files (*.h* and *.m*) for the GUI as well as the custom controls all prefixed with WP. Inspection of the objects here reveals something different than we saw in the AU Synth group: objects are all named according to the Synth project, either directly with MiniSynth or with MS:

- *MiniSynthViewFactory*: the .NIB File's Owner that loads the View
- *MiniSynthView*: the custom view that the factory loads
- *WPRotaryKnobMS*: a custom rotary knob control cluster
- *WPEditBoxMS*: a custom edit control
- *WPOptionMenuGroupMS*: a custom option menu group control (aka pop up button control)
- *WPPopUpButtonCellMS*: a custom pop up button cell

> The reason these files are named according to the synth project is that Cocoa has a flat namespace and therefore each object must have a unique *name*. For example, if all the synths used WPRotaryKnob as the name of these controls, and you customized the knob in one project to look different from the others, the names would collide, and you would loose the uniqueness of the object. For example, if you load the plug-in with the unique knob first, all subsequent plug-ins you load will show the same knob, even though they were compiled with different resources.
>
> RULE: rename all GUI objects in a potentially unique way—Apple recommends using your initials as the first three letters of any GUI object

In XCode, select the MiniSynth target and examine its Build Phases. Let's go over each one:

- *Target Dependencies*: the synth projects all require that their GUIs also be built without errors, so you see CocoaUI listed here
- *Copy Headers*: all of the *.h* files that are required to support the plug-in
- *Copy Bundle Resources*: the *info.plist* file
- *Compile Sources*: all of the *.cpp* files that are required to support the plug-in
- *Link Binaries with Libraries*: the five frameworks required for the synth portion of the plug-in
- *Build Carbon Resources*: *AUSynth.r*; this is only for compatibility with Logic 9
- *Copy Files (1 Item)*: copies your *CocoaSynthView.bundle* to the /Resources folder
- *Copy Files (1 Item)*: copies your synth's *.component* file to the /Components folder

Select the CocoaUI target and examine its Build Phases and you will see basically the same thing, though there is no copying of files. When you select and build the MiniSynth project, it will first build the CocoaUI, then build the Synth component, and then copy the two files to their destinations.

Re-select the MiniSynth target and examine its Build Settings. The most important things to note are:

- uses an exported symbol file with the *.exp* extension
- Info.plist file is named Info.plist
- product name is MiniSynth
- wrapper extension is component

The *.exp* file contains the exported symbols that define the entry points into the component. These entry points do not change from one project to the next so you don't need to worry about that. The two symbols are named as follows and should never be changed for our projects:

_AUSynthEntry
_AUSynthFactory

2.36 The Info.plist File

The *Info.plist* file contains some items that are critical in declaring your plug-in to the client. You must ensure that this file is correct, or your plug-in may not appear in the client. The *Info.plist* file contains information about your *.component* that the client needs to properly recognize and load your GUI.

- Your plug-in is ultimately and uniquely identified by two four-character values. One four-character value represents your company name ("WILL" for mine). The other represents the product. MiniSynth uses "MS0x" as its four-character code where "x" is a revision number (currently it is three, so the code is "MS03").
- The name that will be displayed in a client is based on a string consisting of <Manufacturer>:<Synth name>, so for example "Will Pirkle: MiniSynth" would cause Logic to create a new AU Instrument Menu Item named "Will Pirkle" and a new menu sub-item named "MiniSynth," whereas Ableton Live 9 would create a Folder named "Will Pirkle" with a content item "MiniSynth."
- AU plug-ins are differentiated by a special four character code: music synthesizers use the code "aumu".
- Your AU plug-in is part of a bundle and has a bundle identifier. This identifier is needed to access your Cocoa GUI as well as other stuff such as finding your synth folder (we do this when using samples in WAV files that must be in specific locations relative to the *.components*). Each synth has its own bundle identifier. The projects are set up with the default identifier:
  developer.audiounit.yourname.synthname
  So for the MiniSynth, we would specify our identifier as:
  developer.audiounit.willpirkle.MiniSynth

Open the *Info.plist* file in the MiniSynth's Resources group. You will need to modify this file each time you make a new synth plug-in. First, open the Dictionary:

- Information Property List
- AudioComponents
- Item0

You need to set the following dictionary key values for your own company/synth name:

- *manufacturer*: the four character company code, WILL for me
- *subtype*: the four character product code; currently it is MS03
- *name*: the company/product concatenation, here it is WILL: MiniSynth
- *type*: aumu—do not change this!

In the main *info.plist* table, choose your bundle identifier or

developer.audiounit.willpirkle.MiniSynth

for me.

After this, go back and select the synth target and examine its Info. You should see the changes to the dictionary and bundle identifier. Make sure the info here matches the *Info.plist* file (note on older versions of XCode you have to manually synchronize the bundle identifier).

Logic 9 Backwards Compatibility

Apple added the dictionary you found in the *Info.plist* file when OS 10.7 arrived. Prior to that, the company and product codes and company/product concatenation were declared in the Rez file. For backward compatibility, we have included a *.r* file that you can modify. Open this file and you will see the declarations at the bottom:

```
#define RES_ID                kAudioUnitResID_AUSynth
#define COMP_TYPE             'aumu'
#define COMP_SUBTYPE          'MS03'
#define COMP_MANUF            'WILL'
#define VERSION               kAUSynthVersion
#define NAME                  "WILL: MiniSynth"
#define DESCRIPTION           "MiniSynth AudioUnit"
#define ENTRY_POINT           "AUSynthEntry"

#include "AUResources.r"
```

You can see where to alter these values. The constant (k) values are declared either at the top of the file or in the *AUSynthVersion.h* file. You don't need to start rev-ing these numbers until you release product to customers. Also notice the *AUResouces.r* file is *#included*. This is necessary; however, if you click on the file and examine its Target Membership, you will see that it is not a member of either target—don't change that or the product will not build properly.

2.37 Managing AU Parameters

In RackAFX and VST3, when you declare a GUI control you also link it to an underlying variable. In RackAFX, when the GUI control changes, this underlying variable is automatically updated for you. You are then notified with a call to *userInterfaceChange()* in case there is any secondary processing you need to do. Your controls will have minimum, maximum and default values, and for each project you will be given a table of GUI controls like Table 2.9.

> In AU, you do not have to declare these control variables as you do with RackAFX and VST3—you can if you want but it doesn't really make things easier. AU names your controls "parameters," and it provides you with a kind of *cloud* where your parameters are stored. When the user moves a control, the variable in the cloud is updated for you. All variables are floating point types even if they represent integer or a string-selection. It is up to you to figure that out and cast the data types accordingly.

In this table you can see two columns Type and Variable Name. The four fundamental variable types are *float*, *double*, *int* and *enumerated* UINT. The Volume and Octave controls ultimately generate numerical values that the user sees on the GUI, and they have minimum or Lo Limit, maximum or Hi Limit and default (Def) values. The control may also have no Units ("" or empty string). The Fc (Filter Cutoff) control has the note "volt/octave" which means that this control is logarithmic.

The Filter Type control displays strings that define the current value. An unsigned integer (UINT) keeps track of the current setting. The enum String column gives you the comma-separated values that will map to the UINT variable. In this example the mapping is:

LPF: 0
HPF: 1
BPF: 2

Table 2.9: Example of some GUI controls.

***ExampleSynth* Continuous Parameters**				
Control Name(units)	**Type**	**Variable Name(VST3, RAFX)**	**Low/Hi/Default ***	**VST3/AU Index**
Volume (dB)	double	m_dVolume_dB	-96 / 24/ 0.0	OUTPUT_AMPLITUDE_DB
Octave	int	m_nOctave	-4 / 4 / 0	OCTAVE
Fc (Hz)	double	m_dFilterFc	80 / 18000 / 10000	FILTER_FC
* low, high and default values are #defined for VST3 and AU in *SynthParamLimits.h* for each project				

Enumerated String Parameters (UINT)			
Control Name	**Variable Name**	**enum String**	**VST3/AU Index**
Filter Type	m_uFilterType	LPF,HPF,BPF	FILTER_TYPE

For the enumerated UINT type, the default value is always the first value in the enum string-list or LPF here.

Your parameters stored in the container are all zero-indexed. It is up to you to devise the indexing system. This is done easily with an enumeration the same way you do for VST3. The enumerations are declared in your synth project's *SynthParamLimits.h* file. For example, the first few of these for MiniSynth are:

```
enum {
        NOISE_OSC_AMP_DB,
        PULSE_WIDTH_PCT,
        EG1_TO_OSC_INTENSITY,
        FILTER_FC,
        etc...
        NUMEBER_OF_SYNTH_PARAMETERS}
```

You use these enumerated values when declaring, initializing or accessing your parameters on the AU container. By placing the enumeration NUMBER_OF_SYNTH_PARAMETERS last in the list, it always represents your count of parameters.

Figure 2.44 shows the conceptual container (or cloud) storage arrangement. You get a pointer to the container with:

```
Globals()
```

and then get and set the parameter values with :

```
GetParameter(AudioUnitParameterID paramID)
SetParameter(AudioUnitParameterID paramID, AudioUnitParameterValue inValue)
```

The *paramID* is the zero-based index (*AudioUnitParameterID* is *#defined* as a *UInt32* and *AudioUnitParameterValue* is a *Float32*).

To declare a parameter, you just call *SetParameter()* with an index and default value once. Subsequent calls will then set that parameter. There is no need to destroy parameters when your plug-in is unloaded. We will look at the setup of the parameters in detail in the Section 2.40.

2.38 AU Conventions

Function Return Types:

Most of the AU functions return an error code of type *OSStatus* or *ComponentResult*. These are essentially the same thing (both are unsigned integers). The return code for success is *noErr* for both types. There are many error codes but the most common are:

```
kAudioUnitErr_InvalidProperty
kAudioUnitErr_InvalidParameter
```

Redeclaration of Datatypes

Like VST3, AU also redeclares datatypes such as *Int32, UInt32, Float32* etc., so just be aware of this. You can always use your familiar datatypes *int, float, double,* etc.; however, on occasion you can get burned if you try to override a base class function that uses the redeclared type but you substitute a standard type. The compiler will not recognize your function as an override.

Scopes and Elements

You will see the argument datatypes *AudioUnitScope* and *AudioUnitElement* in several of the AU functions we override. Scopes are used to identify a "major attribute" of an audio unit. Typically you will see *input, output* and *global* (both input and output). For example, output bus #2 would use Scope = *output* and Element = *2* while input bus #1 would use Scope = *input* and Element = *1*.

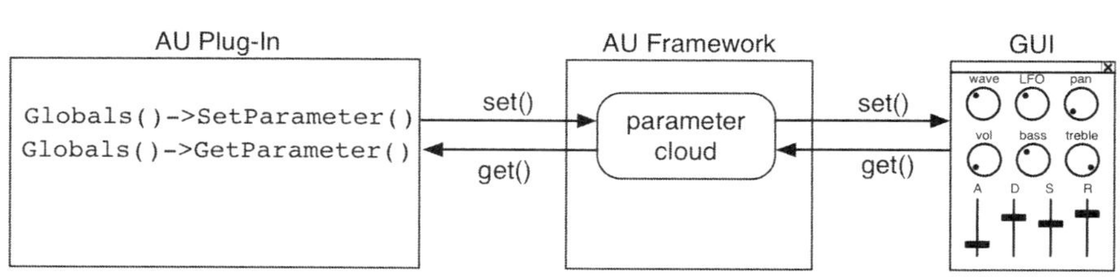

Figure 2.44: The AU framework stores your variables for you.

2.39 AUSynth and the AUInstrumentBase Class

The base class for AU synth plug-ins is named *AUInstrumentBase*. It is derived from another object called *MusicDeviceBase*, which is derived from both *AUBase* and *AUMIDIBase*. If you look in the Apple documentation, you may run across references to *AUMonotimbralInstrumentBase* and *AUMultitimbralInstrumentBase*, which are also derived from *AUInstrumentBase*. These objects were added later in the development of the Audio Units API and are supposed to be there to make your life easier; we do not find this to be the case and were equally perplexed that the definition for *AUMultitimbralInstrumentBase* in the *AUInstrumentBase.h* file says "this is a work in progress."

We decided to bypass these objects and design a straight-up synth plug-in template that you can easily modify. As a bonus, the operation of the synth voices very much parallels the way that RackAFX and VST3 operate, making it easy to move from one API to the next. Additionally, you can easily modify your voice stealing heuristic (Chapter 8), which is not so straightforward using the *AUXXXtimbralInstrumentBase* classes.

The *AUInstrumentBase* functions we need to override and implement can be loosely categorized as follows:

- standard plug-in functions initialization and destruction
- function for rendering/processing audio
- functions to declare user interface controls (called "Parameters")
- functions to handle presets and saved states
- functions to declare custom GUI and MIDI capabilities
- functions to handle MIDI events

We will implement all of these on our single synth object *AUSynth*; remember, all projects use the same *AUSynth* object name. The *AUInstrument* base class and its base classes handle the rest of the AU instrument functionality (and there is a lot of it). You don't really have to worry about the implementation details, but it wouldn't hurt for you to examine the *AUInstrumentBase* object definition in the CoreAudio group's *AUInstrumentBase.h* file.

Download the MiniSynth project, open the *AUSynth.h* file and look at the functions.

Standard Plug-in Functions:

Here you see the constructor and destructor, which we use to initialize variables and destroy objects.

```
AUSynth(AudioUnit inComponentInstance);
virtual ~AUSynth();
```

- the constructor's argument is the instance of an Audio Unit object
- you will allocate memory in the constructor and destroy these objects in the destructor
- you will declare the parameters for the first time here also

```
virtual OSStatus Initialize();
```

- this is where you declare your user interface and initialize our synth object
- you also initialize your base class by calling its initialize function

```
virtual void Cleanup();
```

- called after user has unloaded the plug-in but before the destructor

```
virtual OSStatus Reset();
```

- similar to *prepareForPlay()* in RackAFX, this is called when the plug-in is first opened and again if the user makes any changes to the project's global settings, such as sample rate or bit depth

Audio Rendering:

The audio is synthesized in the *Render()* function and done on a buffer-basis. We will support mono or stereo busses, and each channel has its own buffer.

```
virtual OSStatus Render(AudioUnitRenderActionFlags& ioActionFlags,
                        const AudioTimeStamp& inTimeStamp,
                        UInt32 inNumberFrames);
```

You can ignore the action flags and time stamp for now. The *inNumberFrames* argument is the number of audio frames to process, where a frame represents a single sample for mono and a left/right pair for stereo. Since our left and right channels each have their own buffers, *inNumberFrames* represents the length of these buffers.

Functions to Declare User Interface Controls:

In the constructor we will declare the user interface controls by first defining the number of controls, then calling *SetParameter()* once for each control to set the initial value, but the parameter is not yet completely initialized. This happens in another pair of functions:

```
virtual OSStatus GetParameterInfo()
virtual OSStatus GetParameterValueStrings()
```

For each parameter we declare in the constructor, the AU framework will subsequently call *GetParameterInfo()* and pass it the index of the parameter in question. This happens in a loop after construction occurs. In *GetParameterInfo()* you decode the index and setup the control by declaring:

- control name
- control units
- minimum control value
- maximum control value
- default control value
- if your control is an indexed list of strings (as in Filter Type from Table 2.9)

When you are working on a synth project from this book, you use the GUI control table to help with the set up—it contains all this information (remember you can ignore the variable declarations).

After AU loops through your parameter setup, for each parameter you declared as an indexed list of strings in *GetParameterInfo()*, the framework will call *GetParameterValueStrings()*, passing the zero-based index of the string-list parameter. You decode this value and then pass back a string consisting of substrings separated with commas, for example "LPF,HPF,BPF" from Table 2.9. When you declared that your parameter was indexed, you also set a minimum (0), maximum (string count–1) and default value. If your string count does not match the number of substrings in the comma-separated string, you will get a validation error. So, you need to be careful with parameter setup.

Functions to Handle Presets and Saved States:

Fortunately, presets are fairly simple to deal with in AU and RackAFX, unlike VST3 where you must serialize them yourself. The functions you need to implement are:

```
virtual ComponentResult    GetPresets()
virtual OSStatus NewFactoryPresetSet()
OSStatus RestoreState()
```

The AU framework will query your plug-in for a list of names of presets you have compiled into the instrument by calling *GetPresets()*. You pass it back an array of strings that are your preset names. It is OK if you have no presets; our synths will have one preset as an example, and you are urged to add more of your own.

The framework calls *NewFactoryPresetSet()* when the user recalls one of your factory presets. It gives you a zero-based index value for the preset and you respond by decoding the value and updating your synth parameters using the preset values. One way of handling presets is with a simple array that is the same length as the number of parameters in your cloud. This is declared in the *.h* file as:

```
double factoryPreset[NUMBER_OF_SYNTH_PARAMETERS]
```

The array is declared as a *double* because all of our non-integer synth parameters are *doubles* internally. You could also declare this as a *float* or *Float32* array.

RestoreState() is an optional function that is called to restore the plug-ins internal state. If you need to do more processing after a preset is loaded, you can implement that here. None of the book projects uses this function, they simply forward the call to the base class.

Functions to Declare Custom GUI and MIDI Capabilities

The AU host will query your plug-in at start-up to find out if it has capabilities beyond the stock Audio Unit. There are three functions that are implemented:

```
virtual OSStatus GetPropertyInfo()
virtual OSStatus GetProperty()
virtual OSStatus SetProperty()
```

The host first calls your *GetPropertyInfo()* function to see what extra properties you support. We are going to respond by replying *noErr* for the following property:

```
kAudioUnitProperty_CocoaUI
```

Since we support a Cocoa GUI we need to answer *noErr* to this query.

After *GetPropertyInfo()*, the host will call *GetProperty()* for the items we replied with *noErr*. In this function you must reply with information the host can use to retrieve your GUI and show/maintain it. It is critical to implement this function perfectly or else your GUI will not appear, even if your code compiles fine.

Functions to Handle MIDI Events:

Like RackAFX's *CPlugIn* base class, *AUInstrumentBase* is set up to automatically call a set of MIDI message functions for the most common messages. We will implement each of these, as we will be interested in all of them. These are all overrides of either *AUInstrumentBase* or one of its base classes, *AUMIDIBase*.

```
virtual OSStatus StartNote()
virtual OSStatus StopNote()
virtual OSStatus HandlePitchWheel()
virtual OSStatus HandleControlChange()
OSStatus HandleMidiEvent()
```

The first four are reasonably self-explanatory; these handle the MIDI note on, note off, pitch bend and continuous controller change messages. The fifth function is where you handle anything else. We will use it for handling program change and aftertouch messages.

The last part of the *AUSynth.h* file consists of a few private member variables. We will discuss these in detail in Chapters 3–12. For the MiniSynth these are:

```
CMiniSynthVoice* m_pVoiceArray[MAX_VOICES];
void incrementVoiceTimestamps;
CMiniSynthVoice* getOldestVoice();
CMiniSynthVoice* getOldestVoiceWithNote(UINT uMIDINote);

// --- updates all voices at once
void update();

// --- for portamento
double m_dLastNoteFrequency;

// --- our receive channel
UINT m_uMidiRxChannel;
```

The synthesizer's polyphony is accomplished by maintaining an array of voice object pointers. This array is named *m_pVoiceArray* for all the synths. The difference is in the kind of pointers they hold; in this case the array holds *CMiniSynthVoice* pointers. The three functions below its definition are for handling the time ordering of the voices. The *update()* function is for updating all of the synth variables at once. We will get into the details of the remaining variables as the Chapters progress.

2.40 Implementing the AUSynth Object

Open the *AUSynth.cpp* file and examine its contents. This file is nearly identical for each synth. At the very top of the file, you see the definition of the preset names. We will use this to tell the host about our preset names during the function call *GetPresets()*.

```
static const int numPresets = 1;
static AUPreset presetNames[numPresets] =
{
    // --- {index, Preset Name}
    //      add more with commas
```

```
        // {0, CFSTR("Factory Preset")},
        // {1, CFSTR("Another Preset")} //<-- no comma
        {0, CFSTR("Factory Preset")}
};
```

The code that follows is crucial to the plug-in's operation:

```
AUDIOCOMPONENT_ENTRY(AUMusicDeviceFactory, AUSynth)
```

This is the entry-point into the dynamic-linked library. This line of code is the same for all synths. The syntax is:

```
AUDIOCOMPONENT_ENTRY(AUMusicDeviceFactory, <Your Synth Object Name>).
```

constructor:

The constructor initializes the plug-in and preset(s):

- create the input and output ports with a call to the base class *CreateElements()*
- initialize our one and only preset
- setup our global parameters (controls) for the GUI
- create the voice objects and load the voice pointer array

In the *AUInstrumentBase* part of the constructor, the two arguments at the end are the number of inputs and outputs; we have no inputs and one output. The output may be multi-channel and we will support mono and stereo. The call to *UseIndexedParameters()* with our parameter count as the argument sets up our cloud storage. Then, the calls to *SetParameter()* create the skeleton of parameters.

```
AUSynth::AUSynth(AudioUnit inComponentInstance)
        : AUInstrumentBase(inComponentInstance, 0, 1)
{
        // --- create input, output ports, groups and parts
        CreateElements();

        // --- setup default factory preset (as example)
        factoryPreset[NOISE_OSC_AMP_DB] = -12.0;
        factoryPreset[PULSE_WIDTH_PCT] = 25;
        factoryPreset[EG1_TO_OSC_INTENSITY] = 0;
        factoryPreset[FILTER_FC] = 750.0;
        factoryPreset[FILTER_Q] = 8.9;
        etc ...

        // --- define number of params (controls)
        Globals()->UseIndexedParameters(NUMBER_OF_SYNTH_PARAMETERS);

        // --- initialize the controls here!
        // --- these are defined in SynthParamLimits.h
        Globals()->SetParameter(NOISE_OSC_AMP_DB, DEFAULT_NOISE_OSC_AMP_DB);
        Globals()->SetParameter(PULSE_WIDTH_PCT, DEFAULT_PULSE_WIDTH_PCT);
        Globals()->SetParameter(EG1_TO_OSC_INTENSITY, DEFAULT_BIPOLAR);
        Globals()->SetParameter(FILTER_FC, DEFAULT_FILTER_FC);
        Globals()->SetParameter(FILTER_Q, DEFAULT_FILTER_Q);
        etc ...

        // Finish initializations here
        m_dLastNoteFrequency = -1.0;
```

```
        // receive on all channels
        m_uMidiRxChannel = MIDI_CH_ALL;

        // load up voices
        // details in future chapters
}
```

destructor:

In the destructor, we just delete all the voices. The *CleanUp()* function is called just before destruction if there is any pre-processing to do. The base class versions of this function are also empty.

Reset()

In the *Reset()* function, you call the base class function then optionally kill any notes that may be playing. You also use this to set the sample rate and call *prepareForPlay()* since AULab initializes the instrument this way, which is different from Logic. In this function, you pass the Scope and Element to the base class call, but otherwise they are unused.

```
ComponentResult AUSynth::Reset(AudioUnitScope inScope,
                               AudioUnitElement inElement)
{
        AUBase::Reset(inScope, inElement);
        // --- all notes off
        for(int i=0; i<MAX_VOICES; i++)
        {
                CMiniSynthVoice* pVoice = m_pVoiceArray[i];

                if(pVoice)
                {
                        // --- turn off
                        pVoice->noteOff(pVoice->m_uMIDINoteNumber);

                        // --- reset (AULab works differently from Logic)
                        pVoice->setSampleRate(GetOutput(0)->GetStreamFormat()
                                                          .mSampleRate);
                        pVoice->prepareForPlay();
                }
        }
        return noErr;
}
```

Initialize()

In the *Initialize()* function, you call the base class function then initialize your sub-components. This involves looping through the voice objects and calling initialization functions. We will discuss the specifics of these functions as well as the *update()* function in Chapter 8 when we complete the NanoSynth project. Notice that we set the sample rate (again) here. Logic and AULab behave differently when instantiating your plug-in and this covers both cases.

```
ComponentResult AUSynth::Initialize()
{
        // --- init the base class
        AUInstrumentBase::Initialize();
```

```
        // clear
        m_dLastNoteFrequency = -1.0;

        // --- inits
        // --- NOTE: very important to set the sample rate and call
        //           prepareForPlay()!
        for(int i=0; i<MAX_VOICES; i++)
        {
                m_pVoiceArray[i]->setSampleRate(GetOutput(0)->
                                                GetStreamFormat().mSampleRate);
                pVoice->prepareForPlay();

                // --- update voice
                pVoice->update();
        }
        //--- update the synth
        update();

        return noErr;
}
```

SetParameterInfo()

In order to reduce the code, we created a helper function called *SetParameterInfo()* that sets up the parameter's name, units, minimum, maximum and default values. It also identifies the parameter as logarithmic (which we use for filter cutoff controls) or string-list-control. A string list uses a comma separated string list to show the user a set of choices. The *AudioUnitParameterInfo* struct contains the attributes for a given parameter. Our parameters may all be read or written to, so we set those flags. A base class call fills in the name (you can ignore the *false* argument which is for releasing the name string). Then we set the units. For a string list control, the units are *kAudioUnitParameterUnit_Indexed*. AU includes many other built-in unit types such as Hertz, Percent, etc., but to make the synths as similar as possible, we choose to use the *kAudioUnitParameterUnit_CustomUnit* flag, which just means "I will set the unit string myself." Finally, we identify a log control and set the limits and default value.

```
void AUSynth::setAUParameterInfo(AudioUnitParameterInfo& outParameterInfo,
                                 CFStringRef paramName,
                                 CFStringRef paramUnits,
                                 Float32 fMinValue,
                                 Float32 fMaxValue,
                                 Float32 fDefaultValue,
                                 bool bLogControl,
                                 bool bStringListControl)
{
        // --- set flags
        outParameterInfo.flags = kAudioUnitParameterFlag_IsWritable;
        outParameterInfo.flags += kAudioUnitParameterFlag_IsReadable;

        // --- set Name
        AUBase::FillInParameterName(outParameterInfo, paramName, false);

        // --- set units
        if(bStringListControl)
                outParameterInfo.unit = kAudioUnitParameterUnit_Indexed;
```

```
	else
	{
		outParameterInfo.unit = kAudioUnitParameterUnit_CustomUnit;
		outParameterInfo.unitName = paramUnits;
	}

	// --- is log control?
	if(bLogControl)
		outParameterInfo.flags +=
				kAudioUnitParameterFlag_DisplayLogarithmic;
	// --- set min, max, default
	outParameterInfo.minValue = fMinValue;
	outParameterInfo.maxValue = fMaxValue;
	outParameterInfo.defaultValue = fDefaultValue;
}
```

GetParameterInfo()

GetParameterInfo() is called once for each parameter, and here is where the aforementioned helper function comes into play. After checking to make sure you are initializing Global parameters, you decode the *ParameterID* (index) and call the helper function to complete the operation. If the index is not found, you return an error code.

```
ComponentResult AUSynth::GetParameterInfo(AudioUnitScope inScope,
					AudioUnitParameterID inParameterID,
					AudioUnitParameterInfo&
					outParameterInfo)
{
	// --- we only handle Global params
	if (inScope != kAudioUnitScope_Global)
	return kAudioUnitErr_InvalidScope;

	// --- decode the parameters
	// --- use our built-in helper function setAUParameterInfo()
	switch(inParameterID)
	{
		case NOISE_OSC_AMP_DB:
		{
			setAUParameterInfo(outParameterInfo, CFSTR("Noise Osc"),
					CFSTR("dB"), MIN_NOISE_OSC_AMP_DB,
					MAX_NOISE_OSC_AMP_DB,
					DEFAULT_NOISE_OSC_AMP_DB);
			return noErr;
			break;
		}
		case PULSE_WIDTH_PCT:
		{
			setAUParameterInfo(outParameterInfo, CFSTR("Pulse Width"),
					CFSTR("%"), MIN_PULSE_WIDTH_PCT,
					MAX_PULSE_WIDTH_PCT,
					DEFAULT_PULSE_WIDTH_PCT);
			return noErr;
```

```
                break;
            }
            etc...
        }
        return kAudioUnitErr_InvalidParameter;
}
```

SetAUParameterStringList()

Another helper function is used to facilitate setting up the string list controls. This function is called *SetAUParameterStringList()* and simply creates an array from a comma-delimited string.

```
void AUSynth::setAUParameterStringList(CFStringRef stringList,
                                       CFArrayRef* outStrings)
{
    // --- create array from comma-delimited string
    CFArrayRef strings = CFStringCreateArrayBySeparatingStrings(NULL,
                                                                stringList,
                                                                CFSTR(","));
    // --- set in outStrings with copy function
    *outStrings = CFArrayCreateCopy(NULL, strings);
}
```

GetParameterValueStrings()

In *GetParameterValueStrings()*, you declare the sets of strings that will populate the control using the helper function. After checking the scope, you decode the *ParameterID* and set the string list. Notice the last cluster of parameters, which are all ON/OFF 2-state switch variables,

```
ComponentResult AUSynth::GetParameterValueStrings(AudioUnitScope inScope,
                                                  AudioUnitParameterID
                                                  inParameterID,
                                                  CFArrayRef* outStrings)
{
    if(inScope == kAudioUnitScope_Global)
    {
        if (outStrings == NULL)
            return noErr;
        // --- decode the ID value and set the string list;
        switch(inParameterID)
        {
            case VOICE_MODE:
            {
                setAUParameterStringList(CFSTR("3Saw,3Sqr,2SawSqr,
                            2TriSaw,2TriSqr"), outStrings);
                return noErr;
                break;
            }
        }

        etc...
            // --- all are OFF,ON 2-state switches
```

```
                    case RESET_TO_ZERO:
                    case FILTER_KEYTRACK:
                    case VELOCITY_TO_ATTACK:
                    case NOTE_NUM_TO_DECAY:
                    {
                        setAUParameterStringList(CFSTR("OFF,ON"),
                                                 outStrings);
                    return noErr;
                    break;
                    }
            }
        }
        return kAudioUnitErr_InvalidParameter;
}
```

update()

In the *update()* function, we loop through the voices and update all their parameters at once. Unless we override more *SetParameter()* functions, we won't know which control (if any) changed from one buffer to the next, so a brute force update is done; this also matches the other synths. The updates require surprisingly little overhead, but you can always make this more efficient if you like. Notice how you retrieve your parameter using *Globals()->GetParameter()* passing the index as argument.

Render()

The all-important *Render()* function does three main things:

1. broadcasts received MIDI events
2. updates the synth voices
3. synthesizes the audio

The MIDI events are updated using a base class function *PerformEvents()*, and then an update of the synth voices follows. AU uses buffer processing. In the render operation here, you follow a similar strategy as VST3, which is to update the synth voices only once during the whole processing block. As a Challenge, you may try to interleave control changes into the buffer processing. You retrieve your buffers by accessing the output bus of the plug-in (Scope = output, Element = 0) and getting its buffer-list. This is an array of pointers to buffers. The first pointer is for the left channel and the second is for the right. We only support mono or stereo, so we first check the number of buffers. The pointers to your buffers are found at:

```
bufferList.mBuffers[0].mData
```

However, the *mData* member is actually a *void**, so you have to cast it to a *float** to use it. The rest of the operation is straightforward: you loop through the number of frames (samples in each buffer) and accumulate the voices. Then, you write the resulting value into the output buffers. We will discuss the *doVoice()* loop in Chapter 8.

```
OSStatus AUSynth::Render(AudioUnitRenderActionFlags& ioActionFlags,
                         const AudioTimeStamp& inTimeStamp,
                         UInt32 inNumberFrames)
{
```

First, broadcast MIDI events and then do a synth voice update.

```
    // --- broadcast MIDI events
    PerformEvents(inTimeStamp);

    // --- do the mass update for this frame
    update();
```

Next, get pointers to the buffers and setup the processing loop.

```
        // --- get the number of channels
        AudioBufferList& bufferList = GetOutput(0)->GetBufferList();
        UInt32 numChans = bufferList.mNumberBuffers;

        // --- we only support mono/stereo
        if(numChans > 2) return kAudioUnitErr_FormatNotSupported;

        // --- get pointers for buffer lists
        float* left = (float*)bufferList.mBuffers[0].mData;
        float* right = numChans == 2 ? (float*)bufferList.mBuffers[1].mData :
                       NULL;
```

This is the processing loop where you accumulate voices and write to the output buffers.

```
        double dLeftAccum = 0.0;
        double dRightAccum = 0.0;

        float fMix = 0.25; // -12dB HR per note

        // --- the frame processing loop
        for(UInt32 frame=0; frame<inNumberFrames; ++frame)
        {
                // --- zero out for each trip through loop
                dLeftAccum = 0.0;
                dRightAccum = 0.0;
                double dLeft = 0.0;
                double dRight = 0.0;

                // --- synthesize and accumulate each note's sample
                // detailed in future chapters

                // --- accumulate in output buffers
                // --- mono
                left[frame] = dLeftAccum;

                // --- stereo
                if(right) right[frame] = dRightAccum;
        }
        return noErr;
}
```

The next three functions are to help with polyphony.

```
void AUSynth::incrementVoiceTimestamps()
CMiniSynthVoice* AUSynth::getOldestVoice()
CMiniSynthVoice* AUSynth::getOldestVoiceWithNote(UINT uMIDINote)
```

We will discuss these in detail in Chapter 8. They are used to implement dynamic voice allocation or voice-stealing.

MIDI Note on and off

The MIDI event functions follow. In these functions you decode the MIDI event and modify the voices accordingly. We will discuss the MIDI messages in the next chapter and polyphony in Chapter 8.

```
OSStatus AUSynth::StartNote(MusicDeviceInstrumentID inInstrument,
                            MusicDeviceGroupID inGroupID,
                            NoteInstanceID *outNoteInstanceID,
                            UInt32 inOffsetSampleFrame,
                            const MusicDeviceNoteParams &inParams)
```

StartNote() is the MIDI note on message handler. The *MusicDeviceNoteParams* argument is a structure that holds the MIDI note number and velocity of the note event.

```
MIDI Note Number   = inParams.mPitch
MIDI Note On Velocity = inParams.mVelocity
```

The *mPitch* variable is a floating-point number. Normally it will be integer in nature. If it has a fractional portion, this will represent a global tuning offset, so mPitch = 60.75 would be MIDI note 60 (middle C) + 75 cents of pitch offset. In the synths in this book we will be ignoring global tuning, so we simply cast this as an unsigned integer. As a challenge, you can implement global tuning in your own synths.

```
OSStatus AUSynth::StopNote(MusicDeviceGroupID inGroupID,
                           NoteInstanceID inNoteInstanceID,
                           UInt32 inOffsetSampleFrame)
```

StopNote() is the MIDI note off message handler. The MIDI note number of the released note is in the *NoteInstanceID* variable, which is an unsigned integer. We use that note number to help find the voice to turn off.

MIDI Pitch Bend

The MIDI Pitch Bend messages arrive via the *HandlePitchWheel()* function. We just decode the value and set it in the synth's voices.

```
OSStatus AUSynth::HandlePitchWheel(Int8 inChannel,
                                   UInt8 inPitch1,
                                   UInt8 inPitch2,
                                   UInt32 inStartFrame)
```

MIDI Controller Messages

MIDI Continuous Controller (CC) messages arrive via *HandleControlChange()* and our synths support many of these including volume, pan, expression, mod wheel and sustain pedal.

```
OSStatus AUSynth::HandleControlChange(UInt8 inChannel,
                                      UInt8 inController,
                                      UInt8 inValue,
                                      UInt32 inStartFrame)
```

Other MIDI Messages

HandleMIDIEvent() allows you to receive all the other MIDI messages. We will trap program change, polyphonic and channel aftertouch messages in the synths in this book, but you are encouraged to experiment with other MIDI functionality, such as master tuning and MIDI clock synchronization.

```
OSStatus AUSynth::HandleMidiEvent(UInt8 status,
                                  UInt8 channel,
                                  UInt8 data1,
                                  UInt8 data2,
                                  UInt32 inStartFrame)
```

GetPropertyInfo()

GetPropertyInfo() is where we answer queries from the host about other non-standard properties we handle. This involves us setting the size of the output variable and then calling the base class. For the most part, you can ignore this function unless you want to implement more advanced property handling, such as latency or reverb tail time. However, you can not ignore the following function:

GetProperty(). The host will query us again for each property we acknowledged in the previous function. When queried about our Cocoa interface, it is critical to get every little piece correct, or your GUI may not be visible or may even crash the host. In the first part of the *if()* statement, you find the bundle using the Bundle Identifier you setup in the *Info.Plist* file. You need to make sure these strings exactly match. Next, a bundle URL is parsed using the bundle and the name of your GUI's view. In all our synths, this will be the same name *CocoaSynthView*. Lastly, you need to declare the name of the view factory that will load the *CocoaSynthView* and this must be unique for each synth. The factory for MiniSynth is named *MiniSynthViewFactory*. The final statements setup an info structure to hold all the information needed for the host to instantiate our GUI from the bundle. This struct is returned through the *outData* argument.

```
OSStatus AUSynth::GetProperty(AudioUnitPropertyID inID,
                              AudioUnitScope inScope,
                              AudioUnitElement inElement,
                              void* outData)
{
    if (inScope == kAudioUnitScope_Global)
    {
        if(inID == kAudioUnitProperty_CocoaUI)
        {
            // Look for a resource in the main bundle by name and type.
            CFBundleRef bundle = CFBundleGetBundleWithIdentifier(
                    CFSTR("developer.audiounit.yourname.MiniSynth"));

            if(bundle == NULL) return fnfErr;

            CFURLRef bundleURL = CFBundleCopyResourceURL(bundle,
                                     CFSTR("CocoaSynthView"),
                                     CFSTR("bundle"), NULL);

            if(bundleURL == NULL) return fnfErr;

            CFStringRef className =
                                 CFSTR("MiniSynthViewFactory");

            AudioUnitCocoaViewInfo cocoaInfo;
            cocoaInfo.mCocoaAUViewBundleLocation = bundleURL;
            cocoaInfo.mCocoaAUViewClass[0] = className;
            *((AudioUnitCocoaViewInfo *)outData) = cocoaInfo;

            return noErr;
        }
    }
    // --- call base class to do its thing
    return AUBase::GetProperty (inID, inScope, inElement, outData);
}
```

Presets and State Changes

The remaining functions handle presets and state-changes. *RestoreState()* is called when someone opens a project in the host and has saved its state at some point. The host will take care of setting your parameters and restoring the GUI. This function is called in case you have any extra stuff to take care of after the parameters are updated. We don't need to do anything except call the base class implementation.

```
ComponentResult AUSynth::RestoreState(CFPropertyListRef plist)
{
    return AUInstrumentBase::RestoreState(plist);
}
```

GetPresets() is called at start-up time and we fill in an array of strings representing our preset names. The host then uses that array to populate its preset menu. The order of strings in the list must match your presets. In our case, we only have one preset so it is simple.

```
OSStatus AUSynth::GetPresets(CFArrayRef *outData) const
{
      // --- this is used to determine if presets are supported
      //     which in this unit they are so we implement this method!
      if (outData == NULL) return noErr;

      // --- make the array
      CFMutableArrayRef theArray = CFArrayCreateMutable (NULL, numPresets,
                                                          NULL);
      // --- copy our preset names
      for (int i = 0; i < numPresets; ++i)
      {
             CFArrayAppendValue (theArray, &presetNames[i]);
      }

      // --- set
      *outData = (CFArrayRef)theArray;

      return noErr;
}
```

NewFactoryPresetSet() is called when the user loads a factory preset. We respond by updating our Global Parameters using the array of preset variables.

```
OSStatus AUSynth::NewFactoryPresetSet(const AUPreset& inNewFactoryPreset)
{
      // --- parse the preset
      SInt32 chosenPreset = inNewFactoryPreset.presetNumber;

      if (chosenPreset < 0 || chosenPreset >= numPresets)
                return kAudioUnitErr_InvalidPropertyValue;

      // --- only have one preset, could have array of them as challenge
      for(int i=0; i<NUMBER_OF_SYNTH_PARAMETERS; i++)
      {
             Globals()->SetParameter(i, factoryPreset[i]);
      }

      return noErr;
}
```

That takes care of the synth object so now we can turn our attention to the Cocoa GUI.

2.41 Implementing the Cocoa View Objects

The GUIs for the synth projects are all implemented as Cocoa classes. To use Cocoa, you create two sets of files, a view factory and the main GUI view. In the synth projects, the factory is always named *<Synth>ViewFactory* (e.g. *MiniSynthViewFactory*) and the view is named *<Synth>View* (e.g. *MiniSynthView*). The two objects are packaged in the standard *.h* and *.m* files. When you tell the host that you support a Cocoa interface, you reply with the name of the view factory. When the framework initializes your factory object, it passes in a pointer to the Audio Unit plug-in. The factory loads the view object and passes it this AU pointer. The view can then establish communication with the Audio Unit so that control change information can be transferred. The relationship between the factory and view is set up in Interface Builder. The NIB file is named *CocoaView.NIB* for all the synths in the book. Figure 2.45 shows how the two are connected in InterfaceBuilder (IB).

Notice that the NIB File's Owner is set to the *<Synth>ViewFactory*, and the *<Synth>View* is connected via a Referencing Outlet. Since they are connected in IB this way, the View is loaded when the NIB is unarchived, so the factory does not explicitly need to alloc/init and then load the sub-view. All of the controls on the view are connected to it using Referencing Outlets (*IBOutlets*) and Sent Actions (*IBActions*). The controls are not connected to the factory, only the view.

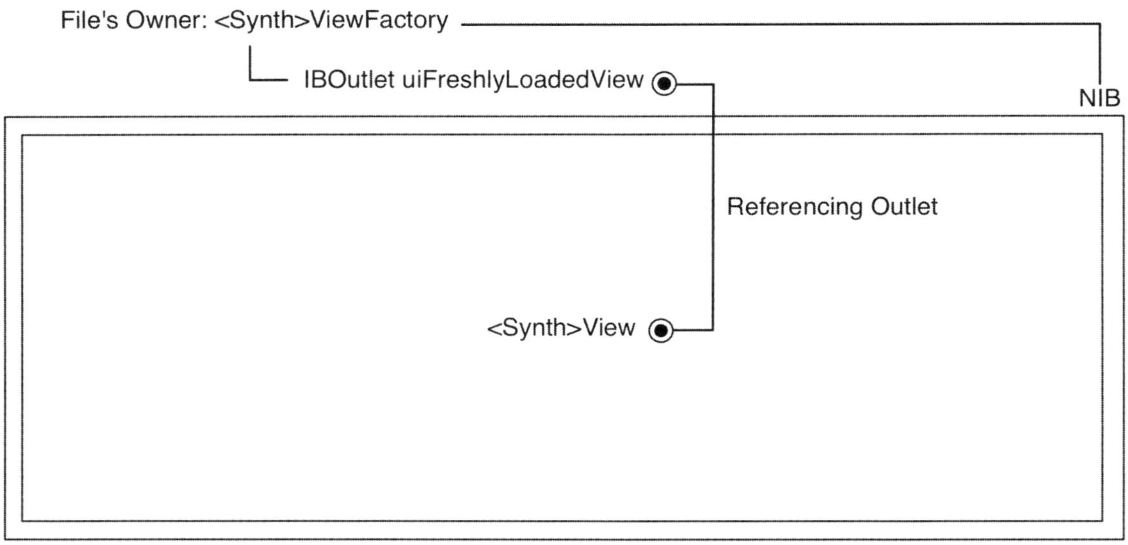

Figure 2.45: The View's Referencing Outlet is the Factory's IBOutlet called *uiFreshlyLoadedView*.

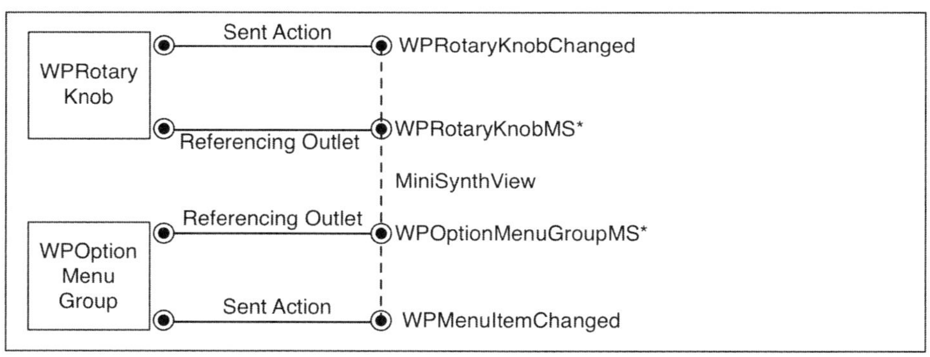

Figure 2.46: The knob and menu controls are connected to the View with Referencing Outlets and Sent Actions; since this is the MiniSynth (MS), the objects are named accordingly.

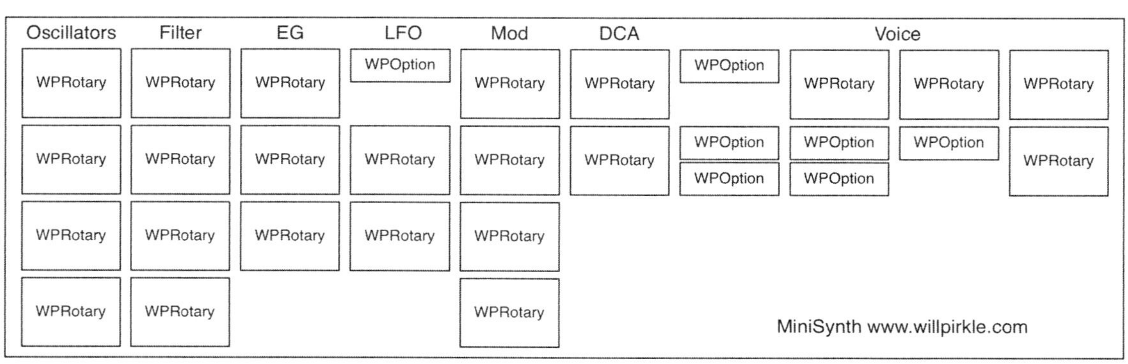

Figure 2.47: The MiniSynth Cocoa View in I.B.

Every synth in this book uses jut two kinds of controls: one that shows continuous control like a knob or slider and another that shows a menu or list of strings that are indexed. We have custom-designed two control groups; a rotary knob and option menu group. The rotary knob controls are of type *WPRotaryKnobXY*, and the option menu groups are *WPOptionMenuGroupXY* objects where XY is a two-letter abbreviation for the synth (MS = MiniSynth, DX = DXSynth, etc.). As we discussed, Cocoa has a flat namespace so you need to rename your view objects including the factory, view and any custom views and controls. If you make your GUI using stock IB objects like *NSSlider* or *NSButton*, then you don't have to worry about renaming them—only the custom made stuff gets renamed. In IB, you drag and drop a Custom View object from the palette into the View and then assign its Custom Class to be either the *WPKnob* or *WPOptionMenu* objects. Then, you connect an *IBOutlet* and *IBAction* to use the control. This is depicted in Figure 2.46 for the MiniSynth.

If you open the *CocoaView.NIB* file in the MiniSynth project, you will see something like Figure 2.47. There are a few stock *NSTextFields* for the column headings and blurb. The column headings are in white because the background image is dark.

Right-clicking on any of the custom views will show the outlet and action connections. The deeper details of the controls themselves are beyond the scope of the book, but you can get more information about them at http://www.willpirkle.com/synthbook/. The knobs are particularly interesting—you will notice that the bumpy shadows also move.

2.42 WPRotaryKnob

The *WPRotaryKnob* object consists of three controls: a static text label that is the control name, a knob that rotates as the user drags the mouse over it and an edit box that displays the current value. This is depicted in Figure 2.48.

The user can also type a value into the box and hit <*enter*>, and the knob will rotate to the updated position. In this way, precise values may be entered. The edit box is also a custom control of type *WPEditBox*. The *WPRotaryKnob* object is derived from *NSControl*, and the *WPEditBox* is derived from *NSTextField*.

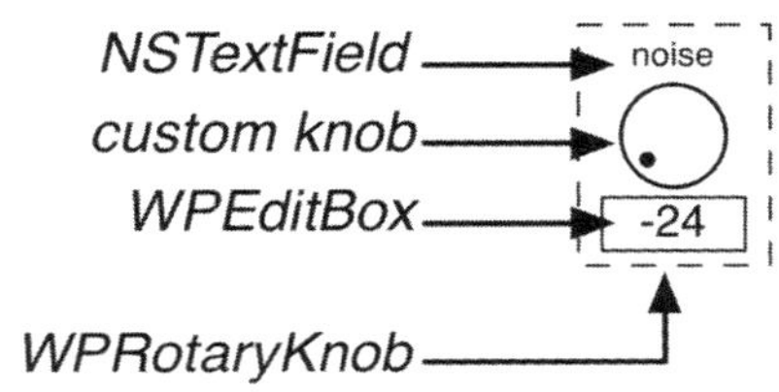

Figure 2.48 The *WPRotaryKnob* is actually a cluster of controls.

Initialization

Since IB is used to connect the Referencing Outlet, you don't have to explicitly alloc/init the controls. Initialization is done in the View's *awakeFromNib* method by calling a special function that initializes the stock control.

```
(void)initControlWithName:(NSString*)name
                controlIndex:(int)index
                         min:(float)minV
                         max:(float)maxV
                         def:(float)defaultV
                 voltOctave:(bool)vpo
              integerControl:(bool)intControl;
```

In this function, you set the control's name, index min, max and default values along with two flags, one for a volt/octave (logarithmic) control, and the other to specify an integer display. By default, the background of the edit box is transparent, and the edit box is visible. You can alter this by using two methods and passing a boolean to toggle on and off:

```
- (void)hideEditBox:(bool)hide;
- (void)setTransparentEditBoxBackground:(bool)transparent;
```

The knob also has a drawing option—you can make a mini-knob that is about 1/4 the size of the regular one by calling the method:

```
- (void)setMiniKnob:(bool)mini;
```

Setting and Getting the Position of the Knob

You set the position of the knob (and text that is entered into the edit box) using the method:

```
- (void)setControlValue:(float)userValue;
```

The value you pass in is a "user value," meaning it is not normalized as in VST3. This is the regular cooked value you use for your calculations.

A very important aspect of the control is that it stores the zero-based index of the global parameter to which it is ultimately connected. This is set when you initialize the control. There are two accessor methods that the View will use to retrieve the index and control value when the knob is moved:

```
- (int)controlID;
- (float)controlValue;
```

The action handler for knob movements is *WPRotaryKnobChanged* and the knob passes its *id* as the argument. The handler then uses the methods *controlID* and *controlValue* to alter the global parameter. In this way, one handler can be used for all the knobs, and there is no *id* decoding required since the control stores its GUI parameter index.

```
- (IBAction)WPRotaryKnobChanged:(id)sender
{
      if(![sender respondsToSelector:@selector(controlID)] ||
              ![sender respondsToSelector:@selector(controlValue)])
              return;
      if([sender controlID] >= 0)
      {
              // --- get the knob's user-value
              Float32 floatValue = [sender controlValue];

              // --- use the value to create a Parameter
              AudioUnitParameter param = {buddyAU, [sender controlID],
                                           kAudioUnitScope_Global, 0};

              // --- alter the Global parameter (explained below)
              <SNIP SNIP SNIP>
      }
}
```

If you want to modify the control, look at the initializer method *initWithFrame* in the *.m* file. Here you can see how to change the background and text color of the edit box as well as a few other customizations. The knob images are stored in an array; there are 128 images depicting the knob in 128 different rotational positions. As you drag the mouse, a new image is selected thereby animating the movement. Because discrete images are used, the shadows will also move properly. This can not be accomplished by simple image rotation. If you want to try your own images, you can change the count of them with the *#define* statement at the top of the *.m* file:

```
#define KNOB_COUNT 128
```

The images are loaded into the array in the initializer. For our images, the file names are sequentially numbered so you use that scheme to get the file paths. Make sure you understand how to add resources to XCode before you start modifying the images.

2.43 WPOptionMenuGroup

The *WPOptionMenuGroup* object consists of two controls: a static text label that is the control name and a *NSPopUpButton* which shows a list of strings in a menu. This is depicted in Figure 2.49. This control is half the height of the knob control and the same width.

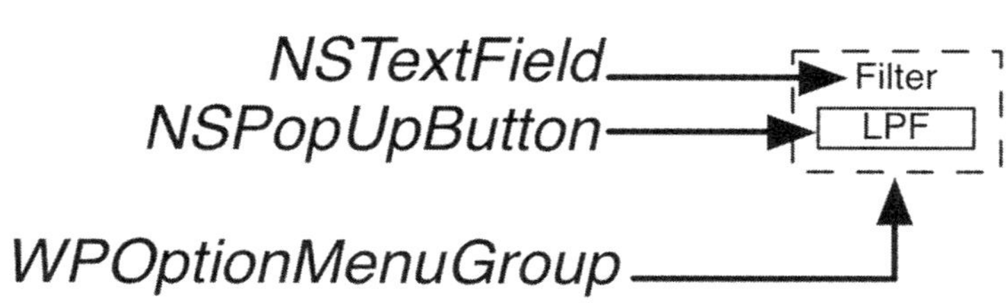

Figure 2.49: The *WPOptionMenuGroup* is also a cluster of controls.

The string list is zero-indexed and when the user selects a new string, an action handler is triggered. This control transmits an integer value representing the index of the string that is currently selected. As with the *WPRotaryKnob*, this control also stores the index of the global parameter to which it is connected.

Initialization

Since IB is used to connect the Referencing Outlet, you don't have to explicitly alloc/init the controls. Initialization is done in the view's *awakeFromNib* method by calling a special function that initializes the control.

```
- (void)initControlWithName:(NSString*)name
               controlIndex:(int)index
                enumString:(NSString*)enumStr
                        def:(float)defaultV
              verySmallFont:(bool)smallFont;
```

You set the name and index with the first two arguments. The third is the "enumString," which is a comma-separated set of substrings such as "LPF,HPF,BPF" that will populate the menu. The substrings are enumerated so that LPF is 0, HPF is 1, etc. in this example. The default value is a *float* but represents the integer index of the default string, which will always be the first one for our synths. The default value is a *float* for compatibility with some other control clusters that we use (not part of the book projects). You can also specify a very small font flag, but we do not use this in any of the book projects.

Setting and Getting the Index of the Selected Menu Item

You set the index value of the control using a method with the same name as that for the *WPRotaryKnob*:

```
- (void)setControlValue:(float)userValue;
```

We did this on purpose—it makes synchronizing the UI with the global parameters simple (it is explained shortly). There are two accessor methods that the view will use to retrieve the control index (ID) and selected string index when the control is updated:

```
- (int)controlID;
- (float)getSelectedIndex;
```

The action handler for knob movements is *WPOptionMenuGroupChanged*, and the knob passes its *id* as the argument. The handler then uses the methods *controlID* and *getSelectedIndex* to alter the global parameter.

```
- (IBAction)WPOptionMenuItemChanged:(id)sender
{
     if(![sender respondsToSelector:@selector(controlID)] ||
            ![sender respondsToSelector:@selector(getSelectedIndex)])
            return;

     if([sender controlID] >= 0)
     {
            // --- get the OMG selection index
            Float32 floatValue = [sender getSelectedIndex];

            // --- make an AudioUnitParameter to set in our AU buddy
            AudioUnitParameter param = {buddyAU, [sender controlID],
                                        kAudioUnitScope_Global, 0 };

            // --- set the AU Parameter
            <SNIP SNIP SNIP
     }
}
```

You can customize this control by altering the initializer *initWithFrame*, where colors and backgrounds are set up.

2.44 The View Factory and CocoaSynthView.plist

The View Factory is a very simple object whose only real job is to load the view and pass it the AU pointer. However, you must get the naming correctly tied to the *GetProperty()* function for it to work. In addition, you need to setup the factory in a *.plist* file. The class definition for the *MiniSynthViewFactory* is:

```
@class MiniSynthView;
@interface MiniSynthViewFactory : NSObject <AUCocoaUIBase>
{
      IBOutlet MiniSynthView *uiFreshlyLoadedView;
}
- (NSString*)description;   // string description of the view
@end
```

The sole member variable is the *IBOutlet* connected to the View in IB. A get-function returns a description string that you may or may not use see depending on the host. The implementation is also simple. Notice that the factory is a delegate of *<AUCocoaUIBase>*. It implements a delegate method that initializes the view called *uiViewForAudioUnit:withSize*. In this method, you load the NIB file named CocoaView. If all goes well, you will have a freshly created view. The factory nils out the pointer after it is finished, effectively releasing it after creation.

```
#import "MiniSynthViewFactory.h"
#import "MiniSynthView.h"

@implementation MiniSynthViewFactory

// version 0
- (unsigned) interfaceVersion {
      return 0;
}
// string description of the Cocoa UI
- (NSString *) description {
      return @"Your Name: CocoaGUI";
}

// this class is simply a view-factory,
// returning a new autoreleased view each time it's called.
(NSView *)uiViewForAudioUnit:(AudioUnit)inAU
                    withSize:(NSSize)inPreferredSize
{
      if(![NSBundle loadNibNamed: @"CocoaView" owner:self])
      {
             NSLog (@"Unable to load nib for view.");
                    return nil;
      }

      // This particular nib has a fixed size,
      // so we don't do anything with the inPreferredSize argument.
      // It's up to the host application to handle.

      // pass the AU pointer to the view
      [uiFreshlyLoadedView setAU:inAU];

      NSView *returnView = uiFreshlyLoadedView;
      // zero out pointer.  This is a view factory.
```

```
        // Once a view's been created
        // and handed off, the factory keeps no record of it.
        uiFreshlyLoadedView = nil;
        return [returnView autorelease];
    }
    @end
```

You also need to make sure the *CocoaSynthView.plist* file contains the proper information. It is used to identify attributes of the factory that tie in with the *GetProperty* method we override to notify the host that we support a Cocoa GUI. Open the *CocoaSynthView.plist* file and make sure the fields are set properly; the fields in bold will vary from synth to synth while the others remain the same. This one is from the MiniSynth

CFBundleExecutable	CocoaFilterView
CFBundleIdentifier	**developer.audiounit.yourname.MiniSynth**
CFBundlePackageType	BNDL
NSMainNibFile	CocoaView
NSPricipleClass	**MiniSynthViewFactory**

That last field is crucial—this is where you set the view factory. If it does not match the factory you expose in the *GetProperty* method, your GUI will not appear or may crash the host.

2.45 The View Event Listeners

The view object is more complicated, but mainly because our synths have so many controls (most are 30–40 or so) and we need to conform to an event callback scheme. First, we will need *IBOutlets* for each control group. Next, we need *IBActions* to act as action handlers. Rather than write a separate handler for each control, we only implement two, one for the knob and one for the option menu controls. We also set the controls up so that they store the index of the parameter they control. With this, we can make the handlers very short.

We also need some way of communicating with our "buddy" Audio Unit plug-in. The communication will need to go both ways—when the user moves controls, we need to notify the plug-in, and when a user loads a preset or changes the state of the plug-in, we need to update our controls accordingly. These are done with an Event Listener Callback scheme.

To set up the Event Listening system, you need to implement some methods and call some AU functions. First we need to implement a method that the host will query to ask what kinds of events we want to support. The events consist of:

- parameter changes: the user moves a control and changes a parameter
- gestures: these consist of mouse clicks and movements
- property changes: a property such as reverb tail time or your support of a Cocoa GUI has changed

For our synths, we only care about the parameter changes, so we set the event type using a constant and then call *AUEventListenerAddEventType* to register it.

```
void addParamListener(AUEventListenerRef listener,
                      void* refCon, AudioUnitEvent *inEvent)
{
    // set the event type to kAudioUnitEvent_ParameterValueChange
    inEvent->mEventType = kAudioUnitEvent_ParameterValueChange;

    // register it
    verify_noerr(AUEventListenerAddEventType(listener, refCon,
                                             inEvent));
}
```

The next step is to create the *AUEventListener* and pass it a selector to a callback function that you implement. You then tell the *AUEventListener* about all your parameters, and it sets up a private Listener for each one. You also define a private Event Listener function that responds by telling the controls to update their positions. The Event Listener callback is named *EventListenerDispatcher* but you may name it whatever you wish. Look at the function call that creates the *AUEventListener*:

```
verify_noerr(AUEventListenerCreate(EventListenerDispatcher,
                                   self,
                                   CFRunLoopGetCurrent(),
```

```
                                        kCFRunLoopDefaultMode, 0.05, 0.05,
                                        &AUEventListener));
```

The two arguments you need to understand are the first one that names the callback method and the second one that is a pointer to our *self*. This pointer will be passed to the callback function cloaked as a *void**, which is a standard trick in callback functions since the function stands alone, outside any other object definition. If this is new to you, see the website for more information about callbacks. The callback function is declared at the top of the *<Synth>View.cpp* file, outside the object implementation:

```
void EventListenerDispatcher(void *inRefCon,
                             void *inObject,
                             const AudioUnitEvent *inEvent,
                             UInt64 inHostTime,
                             Float32 inValue)
{
    MiniSynthView* SELF = (MiniSynthView*)inRefCon;
    [SELF eventListener:inObject
                  event:inEvent
                  value:inValue];
}
```

The *inRefCon* is our *self* pointer cloaked as a void*, so we uncloak it and use it to call our own method named *eventListnener:event:value*. It seems convoluted but needs to be done like this since the callback is all alone, outside the object definition. Calling the *eventListener:event:value* method tells the control to update and redraw itself. Remember that the factory will call our *setAU* method. Look at its implementation:

```
- (void)setAU:(AudioUnit)inAU
{
    // remove previous listeners
    if(buddyAU)
        [self removeListeners];

    // our buddy
    buddyAU = inAU;

    // add new listeners
    [self addListeners];

    // initial setup
    [self synchronizeUIWithParameterValues];
}
```

The AU pointer is named *buddyAU* and you will use it to call Parameter functions on the AU. After saving it, the View first calls *addListeners*, then *synchronizeUIWithParameterValues*, which initializes the GUI with the very first parameter value. Let's look at all of these methods.

In *addListners* you create the *AUEventListener* as described above, giving it your callback function name and a *self* pointer to store. You need to add a Listener for each of your parameters. This is done in a somewhat convoluted manner:

- create an *AUEvent*
- create an *AudioUnitParameter* for our *first* parameter with index 0
- set the parameter on the *AUEvent*
- add the event
- loop through the rest of the parameters setting the *AUEvent's mParameterID* variable to the parameter index
- add the event

```
- (void)addListeners
{
    if (buddyAU)
```

```
    {
        // --- create the event listener
        // and tell it the name of our Dispatcher function
        // EventListenerDispatcher
        verify_noerr(AUEventListenerCreate(EventListenerDispatcher, self,
                                           CFRunLoopGetCurrent(),
                                           kCFRunLoopDefaultMode, 0.05,
                                           0.05,
                                           &AUEventListener));

        // --- start with first control 0
        AudioUnitEvent auEvent;
        // --- parameter 0
        AudioUnitParameter parameter = {buddyAU, 0,
                                        kAudioUnitScope_Global, 0};

        // --- set param & add it
        auEvent.mArgument.mParameter = parameter;
        addParamListener(AUEventListener, self, &auEvent);

        // --- parameters 1 -> NUMBER_OF_SYNTH_PARAMETERS-1
        //     notice the way additional params are added using
        //     mParameterID
        for(int i=1; i<NUMBER_OF_SYNTH_PARAMETERS; i++)
        {
            auEvent.mArgument.mParameter.mParameterID = i;
            addParamListener(AUEventListener, self, &auEvent);
        }
    }
}
```

The *removeListener* method simply disposes of the *EventListener.*

```
- (void)removeListeners
{
    if(AUEventListener)
        verify_noerr(AUListenerDispose(AUEventListener));

    // clear our pointers
    AUEventListener = NULL;
    buddyAU = NULL;
}
```

You call your own method *synchronizeUIWithParameterValues* to sync up the GUI with the parameters in the *setAU* method above. It operates in a similar manner, declaring the first parameter, then looping through the rest of the parameters. We call *GetAudioUnitParameter()* to fetch the current parameter value using the pass-by-pointer mechanism into *paramValue*. Then, we lookup the control (either a knob or option menu group) in the master array of controls and call the method *setControlValue* on it. We set up both of the custom objects to implement the same method to simplify this operation. For the knob, *setControlValue* changes the image and updates the edit control text. For the option menu group, this method selects a string from the list.

```
- (void)synchronizeUIWithParameterValues
{
    // get the parameter values
    Float32 paramValue;
```

```
        // make an AudioUnitParameter get from our AU buddy
        AudioUnitParameter parameter = {buddyAU, 0, kAudioUnitScope_Global, 0};

        // --- parameters 0 -> NUMBER_OF_SYNTH_PARAMETERS-1
        //     notice the way additional params are added using mParameterID
        for(int i=0; i<NUMBER_OF_SYNTH_PARAMETERS; i++)
        {
                // --- change the parameterID for subsequent controls
                parameter.mParameterID = i;
                if(AudioUnitGetParameter(buddyAU, i, kAudioUnitScope_Global, 0,
                                         &paramValue) != noErr)
                        return;

        // --- update controls
        id control = [self getControlWithIndex:i];
        if(control && [control respondsToSelector:
                                         @selector(setControlValue:)])
                [control setControlValue:paramValue];
        }
    }
```

The last method to implement is named *eventListener* and is called from the callback function described above. This method uses the *inEvent's mArgument.mParameter.mParameterID* to decode the parameter index, get it from the array (*controlWithIndex*) and call the same *setControlValue* methods as above.

```
    (void)eventListener:(void*)inObject
                event:(const AudioUnitEvent*)inEvent
                value:(Float32)inValue
    {
        switch (inEvent->mEventType)
        {
                // --- for presets this gets called for each parameter
                case kAudioUnitEvent_ParameterValueChange:
                {
                        // --- get the control from our array
                        id control = [self getControlWithIndex:
                                inEvent->mArgument.mParameter.mParameterID];

                        // --- all of MY (WP) controls use the same method,
                        //     setControlValue: so there is nothing else to do
                        if(control && [control respondsToSelector:
                                                 @selector(setControlValue:)])
                        [control setControlValue:inValue];
                }
        }
    }
```

Before wrapping up Event Listening, take a look at the two action handlers, one for the knob and the other for the option menu group. Action handlers are usually in the form *<name>:(id)sender*, so the control passes its *id* as an argument. When we set up the knobs and menus, we give each one the index of the parameter it will control—these index values are called "*controlIDs*." So, we can just retrieve this index and use it to call *AUParameterSet()* with the new value. These two methods are essentially identical except that the knob value is accessed with *controlValue* and the menu's with *getSelectedIndex*. The important thing to understand is that a user control change results in a call to *AUParameterSet()*.

```
- (IBAction)WPRotaryKnobChanged:(id)sender
{
      if(![sender respondsToSelector:@selector(controlID)] ||
         ![sender respondsToSelector:@selector(controlValue)])
         return;

      // controlID is the index of the parameter
      if([sender controlID] >= 0)
      {
              // --- get the knob's user-value
              Float32 floatValue = [sender controlValue];

              // --- make an AudioUnitParameter set in our AU buddy
              AudioUnitParameter param = {buddyAU, [sender controlID],
                                          kAudioUnitScope_Global, 0 };

              // --- set the AU Parameter; this calls SetParameter() in the au
              AUParameterSet(AUEventListener, sender, &param,
                             (Float32)floatValue, 0);
      }
}

- (IBAction)WPOptionMenuItemChanged:(id)sender
{
      if(![sender respondsToSelector:@selector(controlID)] ||
         ![sender respondsToSelector:@selector(getSelectedIndex)])
          return;

      if([sender controlID] >= 0)
      {
              // --- get the CMG selection index
              Float32 floatValue = [sender getSelectedIndex];

              // --- make an AudioUnitParameter set in our AU buddy
              AudioUnitParameter param = {buddyAU, [sender controlID],
                        kAudioUnitScope_Global, 0 };

              // --- set the AU Parameter; this calls SetParameter() in the au
              AUParameterSet(AUEventListener, sender, &param,
                            Float32)floatValue, 0);
      }
}
```

To put this in perspective, here is the sequence of operations that occur when the user moves a knob:

- user moves the knob
- the *IBAction WPRotaryKnobChanged* is triggered
- this calls *AUParameterSet()*
- the new parameter value is set in the Audio Unit's "cloud" (parameter container)
- the Audio Unit then notifies any listeners of this control that it has changed by using the callback function *EventListenerDispatcher*
- the callback function calls *eventListener*, which then calls *setControlValue*, which tells the control to update itself, including any re-painting that needs to be done

We designed these controls for more than just use in AU, so they have methods that will update the controls automatically without using the Event Listener scheme. In other words, when you move a control, it repaints and updates itself without needing the AU plug-in to tell it to do so. There are a few lines of code that you un-comment to enable this functionality. You can un-comment the code now without any issues, except that the controls will get repainted twice.

2.46 The View Interface and Initialization

Now we can put the last pieces of the puzzle in place by looking at the view interface (*.h* file) and initialization. We've already covered all the other functions in the view. Open the *MiniSynthView.h* file and check out the interface definition. First are the *IBOutlets*, one for each control. These are arranged by column since the final MiniSynth GUI is arranged that way. After these declarations are two arrays; one for holding the knob images, and the other for holding all the controls on the view. For efficiency, we only create one array of knob images that all the knob controls share.

```
@interface MiniSynthView : NSView
{
            // --- rotary knob groups
            //
            // --- column 1
            IBOutlet WPRotaryKnobMS* wpRotaryKnob_0;
            IBOutlet WPRotaryKnobMS* wpRotaryKnob_1;
      etc...

            // --- voice row
            IBOutlet WPOptionMenuGroupMS* wpOMG_1;
            IBOutlet WPOptionMenuGroupMS* wpOMG_2;
            IBOutlet WPRotaryKnobMS* wpRotaryKnob_24; // unused
            IBOutlet WPRotaryKnobMS* wpRotaryKnob_25; // unused
            etc...

            // --- array for controls
            NSMutableArray* controlArray;
            NSMutableArray* knobImages;

            // --- AU members
            AudioUnit buddyAU; // the AU we connect to
            AUEventListenerRef AUEventListener;

            // --- a background color
            NSColor* backgroundColor;     // the background color (pattern)*2*
            NSImage* backImage;           // background image
}

// --- find a control in our array
- (id)getControlWithIndex:(int)index;

// --- set our buddy AU and init
- (void)setAU:(AudioUnit)inAU;

// --- action handlers
- (IBAction)WPRotaryKnobChanged:(id)sender;
- (IBAction)WPOptionMenuItemChanged:(id)sender;
```

```
// --- event listener stuff
- (void)synchronizeUIWithParameterValues;
- (void)addListeners;
- (void)removeListeners;

- (void)eventListener:(void *) inObject event:(const AudioUnitEvent *)inEvent
   value:(Float32)inValue;
@end
```

After the arrays, you can see the Event Listener objects—the buddy AU and the *AUEventListener* and the background image objects. Finally, the *getControlWithIndex* method searches the control array for an object with a specific control index (the global parameter index).

Open the *MiniSynthView.m* file and look at the initializer *awakeFromNib*. In the first part, you create the knob array and load it with images. After this are the knob and option menu group initializers, which set the names, index values, min, max and default values. The control limits and defaults are defined in *SynthParamLimits.h*. For the option menu group, you also pass the enum string. After setting up the controls, they are added to the control array. You set the knob image array on each knob control *after* the initialize method is called using the method *setKnobImageArray*.

```
@implementation MiniSynthView


-(void) awakeFromNib
{
     // --- initialize the knobs
     //
     NSBundle* bundle = [NSBundle bundleForClass:[self class]];
```

Create an array of the knob images.

```
     // --- create image array
     knobImages = [[NSMutableArray alloc] initWithCapacity:KNOB_COUNT];
     for(int i=0; i<KNOB_COUNT; i++)
     {
          NSImage* image = nil;
          NSString* file = [NSString stringWithFormat:@"knob%04d", i];
          NSString* path = [[bundle pathForResource:file ofType: @"png"]
                                   autorelease];

          if(path)
               image = [[NSImage alloc] initWithContentsOfURL:
                                        [NSURL fileURLWithPath:path]];
          if(image)
               [knobImages addObject:image];
     }
```

Create each of the controls and add to the *controlArray*.

```
     // --- initialize the knobs
     //
     controlArray = [[NSMutableArray alloc] init];

     // --- column 1
     [wpRotaryKnob_0 initControlWithName:@"Noise Osc (dB)"
                              controlIndex:NOISE_OSC_AMP_DB
```

```
                                        min:MIN_NOISE_OSC_AMP_DB
                                        max:MAX_NOISE_OSC_AMP_DB
                                        def:DEFAULT_NOISE_OSC_AMP_DB
                                  voltOctave:NO
                              integerControl:NO];
        [controlArray addObject:wpRotaryKnob_0];
        [wpRotaryKnob_0 setKnobImageArray:knobImages];

        [wpRotaryKnob_1 initControlWithName:@"Pulse Width"
                                controlIndex:PULSE_WIDTH_PCT
                                        min:MIN_PULSE_WIDTH_PCT
                                        max:MAX_PULSE_WIDTH_PCT
                                        def:DEFAULT_PULSE_WIDTH_PCT
                                  voltOctave:NO
                              integerControl:NO];
        [controlArray addObject:wpRotaryKnob_1];
        [wpRotaryKnob_1 setKnobImageArray:knobImages];
        etc...

        [wpOMG_0 initControlWithName:@"LFO Waveform"
                        controlIndex:LFO1_WAVEFORM
                               enumString:@"sine,usaw,dsaw,tri,square,expo,rsh,qrsh"
                                     def:DEFAULT_LFO_WAVEFORM
                               verySmallFont:NO];
        [controlArray addObject:wpOMG_0];

        etc...

        [wpRotaryKnob_27 initControlWithName:@"PBRange"
                                controlIndex:PITCHBEND_RANGE
                                        min:MIN_PITCHBEND_RANGE
                                        max:MAX_PITCHBEND_RANGE
                                        def:DEFAULT_PITCHBEND_RANGE
                                  voltOctave:NO
                              integerControl:YES];
        [controlArray addObject:wpRotaryKnob_27];
        [wpRotaryKnob_27 setKnobImageArray:knobImages];

        --- parse background image
        NSString* path = [[[NSBundle bundleForClass:[MiniSynthView class]] pathForResource:@"medGrey-
        Brushed" ofType: @"bmp"] autorelease];

        backImage = [[NSImage alloc] initWithContentsOfURL:
                                          [NSURL fileURLWithPath:path]];
    }
```

The last part of the initializer finds, opens and stores the background image. For this synth, it is a brushed metal Bitmap file. You can change the background image here, so feel free to experiment. The image will be tiled. The *dealloc* method releases the resources we've retained; notice that it also removes the Event Listeners that we set up.

```
- (void)dealloc
{
        [self removeListeners];

        [backImage release];
        [backgroundColor release];
        [controlArray dealloc];
        [knobImages dealloc];

        [super dealloc];
}
```

Lastly, the *drawRect* method tiles the background image and then sets up the group frames for each row or column. The image for the frame is taken from the VSTGUI library and is stretched to fit. Simple graphics calculations are used to place the row and column frames, and the method *drawInRect* is used to place the group frame image.

```
- (void)drawRect:(NSRect)rect
{
        // --- make the tiled background pattern as a NSColor
        NSColor *backgroundPattern = [NSColor colorWithPatternImage:backImage];

        // --- fill it
        [backgroundPattern setFill];
        NSRectFill(rect);

        // --- do group frame background images
        float x, y, w, h;
        float yOffset = -7;

        // --- column 1
        //
        // --- bottom knob
        NSRect knob3Rect = [wpRotaryKnob_3 frame];
        x = NSMinX(knob3Rect);
        w = NSWidth(knob3Rect);

        // --- top knob
        NSRect knob0Rect = [wpRotaryKnob_0 frame];
        y = NSMinY(knob0Rect);

        // --- height of col
        h = y + NSHeight(knob0Rect) + 50;

        // --- group frame rect
        NSRect groupRect1 = NSMakeRect(x, yOffset, w, h);

        // --- get the image
        NSString* path = [[[NSBundle bundleForClass:[MiniSynthView class]]
                    pathForResource:@"groupframe" ofType: @"png"] autorelease];

        NSImage* image = [[NSImage alloc] initWithContentsOfURL:
                    [NSURL fileURLWithPath:path]];
```

```
        float alpha = 1.0;

        // --- paint it
        if(image)
                [image drawInRect:groupRect1 fromRect:NSZeroRect
                          operation:NSCompositeSourceOver fraction:alpha];

        // --- column 2
        etc...

        // --- we call super to draw all other controls after we have filled
                the background
        [super drawRect: rect];
}
```

2.47 Implementing an AU Plug-in: Debugging

Before you try to load your plug-in into a client, it is vital that you validate it using Apple's AU validation tool. AU clients typically validate each new plug-in they find. If the plug-in fails validation, the client may refuse to ever load it again. If this happens, you need to correct your errors and then change the four-character product code to a new value. Apple's Logic stores a list of product codes that failed validation once and will never load them again.

Validate your plug-in by opening Terminal and using the AU validation:

```
auval -v aumu <PLUG> <COMP>
```

Where <PLUG> is your 4-character plug-in code and <COMP> is your four-character company name. For my MiniSynth that would be:

```
auval -v aumu MS03 WILL
```

If your validation does not succeed, go back and check your code. Once it does succeed, you are ready to debug the synth.

Debugging your synth plug-in is critical for your success. As soon as you start experimenting with your own code and the Chapter Challenges, you will likely have problems as we all do when implementing new code or ideas. To debug and test your plug-in, you will need an AU host (client); we have tested with AULab, Logic 9, Logic Pro X and Ableton Live 9. There are two ways to debug. The easiest is to edit the Scheme for your project and choose an executable in the Run panel (described in the Appendix)—the executable is the AU host. Then, you can set your breakpoints, do a rebuild and launch the host for debugging in one step by clicking on the triangular <*Run*> button. This method allows you to log strings to the console window.

You can also start the debugger after the client is running (you have to start the client manually). With the client running, choose *Debug->Attach To Process* and choose the client from the process list, then set breakpoints. When you instantiate your plug-in, the breakpoints will become active and you can step through the code and debug as usual. The difference is that when you use the Attach To Process mechanism, you can't log information to the console window with *printf* statements. Debug logging is very useful, and we will use it in the next Chapter to log MIDI events. You will be flipping back and forth between your compiler and the plug-in client—this is normal for plug-in development on just about any platform.

Bibliography

Apple, Inc. "The Audio Unit Programing Guide." Accessed June 2014, https://developer.apple.com/library/mac/documentation/MusicAudio/Conceptual/AudioUnitProgrammingGuide/Introduction/Introduction.html

Pirkle, Will. 2012. *Designing Audio Effects Plug-Ins in C++*, Chap. 2. Burlington: Focal Press.

Rogerson, Dale. 1997. *Inside COM*, Chap. 1–7. Redmond: Microsoft Press.

Steinberg GmbH. "VST3 SDK." Accessed June 2014, http://www.steinberg.net/nc/en/company/developers/sdk_download_portal.html

CHAPTER 3

MIDI

The Musical Instrument Digital Interface or MIDI dates to 1981 when Dave Smith and Chet Wood presented a paper at the 70th Audio Engineering Society Convention in New York. Their paper was entitled *The 'USI' or Universal Synthesizer Interface* and discussed the implementation of a communication system for synthesizers, sequencers, personal computers and controllers. The communications included information about timing, configuration, note and control events, however no actual audio data was transmitted. Ikutaru Kakehashi from the Roland Corporation is also given credit for the original USI idea, as he and Smith had previously held meetings together regarding the standardization of synth connections. After a meeting between the major synthesizer corporations in 1982, the MIDI specification was born. MIDI used the core concepts of USI, but the implementation was very different. The final MIDI spec used a rate of 3.125k bits/second. A note-on message takes slightly less than one millisecond to transmit. The MIDI Manufacturers Association (MMA) publishes the spec. You are encouraged to get the MIDI 1.0 spec for your files.

In this chapter we will start a synth project called NanoSynth. This is going to be an important project because we are going to use it to build up a synth architecture that will be used in all the rest of the projects. Additionally, when you design the C++ objects that will become the synth guts in Chapters 4–8, you will test them in NanoSynth. The MIDI message decoding we set up in NanoSynth will be used throughout the rest of the book. To save space, it won't be reprinted for every project, so even if you know MIDI, it is still important to understand how NanoSynth works.

3.1 MIDI Messages

MIDI is a messaging system. There is a sender and a receiver for each message. The messages are designed to codify as much information as possible in the shortest message possible. The messages also need to convey vastly different types of information. Some messages require extra data to fully transmit the information. The MIDI inventors first broke down the types of messages their synthesizers would need to send and receive. They also implemented a system to handle future messages and data that would likely be invented as time progressed. Figure 3.1 shows the different kinds of MIDI messages in the specification. The Voice Message is where you will spend the majority of your time in the book projects.

The Channel Messages have a particular destination on a device in the system whereas System Messages are global and are broadcast to all devices. The rest of the messages are as follows:

Channel:

Voice: performance information and note events and manipulation
Channel Mode: configuration changes

System:

System Common: information for all the devices in the system
System Real Time: timing (clock) information
System Exclusive: any and everything else (open ended)

The synth projects in this book only deal with Channel Voice messages, the most common and certainly most important for note synthesis. These not only include note messages, but all the Continuous Controller Messages (CCs) for the knobs and sliders on your MIDI controllers.

MIDI messages are transmitted serially in bytes. Figure 3.2 shows the structure of a MIDI byte. MIDI bytes encode two basic types of information: status—the kind of message being sent and data—information about the message. The status/data bit is the Most Significant Bit (MSB), which is the left-most bit of a MIDI byte.

The status byte is broken into two four-bit nibbles. The lower nibble encodes the MIDI channel where 0–15 represents MIDI channel 1–16. The upper nibble is the message whose upper bit is always 1. For data bytes, the lower seven bits encode the data information. This provides 128 different values encoded as 0 to 127. A MIDI message consists of at least one status byte and zero or more data bytes. The status byte is always the first in the message. It determines the number of data bytes that will follow. This way, the receiving device knows how to interpret future data bytes.

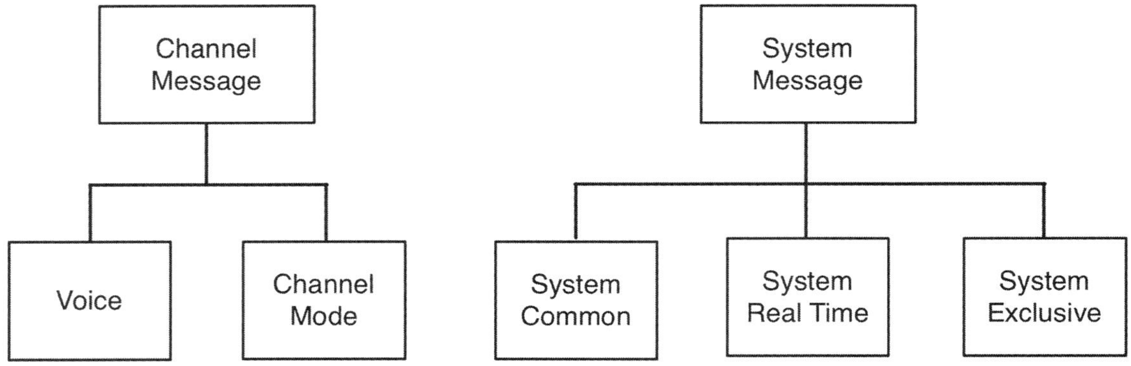

Figure 3.1: The MIDI Message hierarchy.

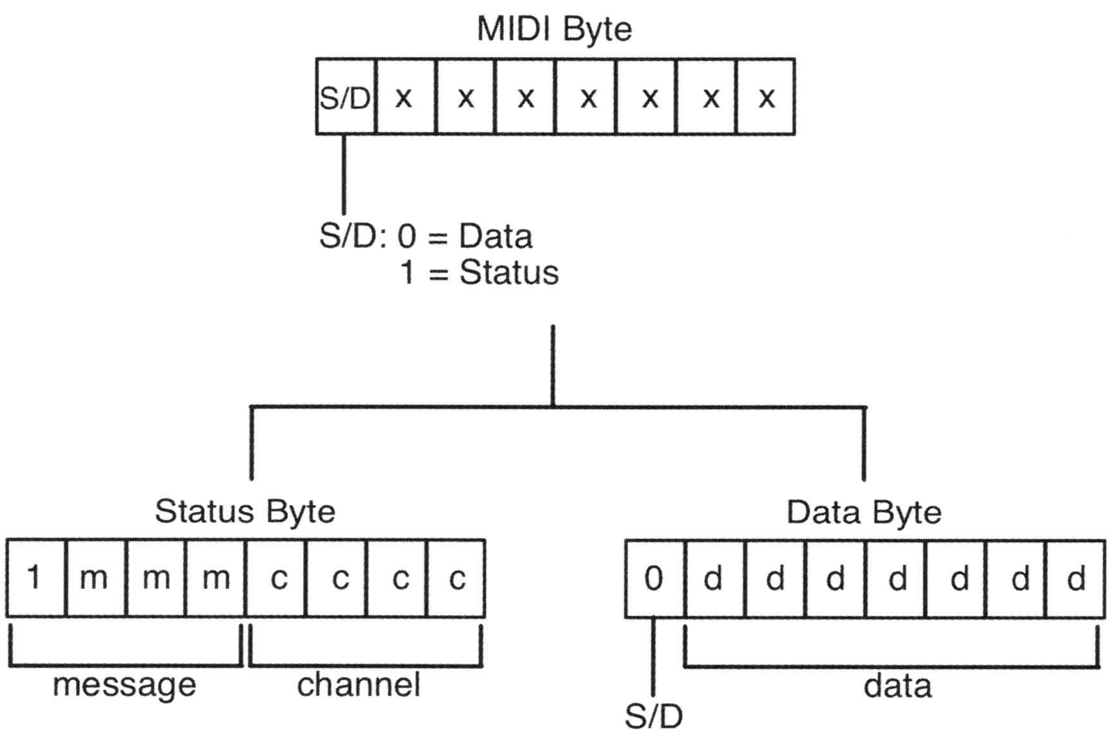

Figure 3.2: The MIDI byte uses a status/data MSB to identify the type of message component.

3.2 Channel Voice Messages

The Channel Voice messages contain the most important information that we need. These are listed in Table 3.1.

Let's examine each message.

0x8n—Note Off

The note off message encodes the MIDI note number and the velocity with which the key was released, though most keyboards do not offer this release-velocity option. The note number and velocity are interpreted the same way as for note on messages below. Interestingly you can also transmit a note off message by sending a note on message with a velocity of 0. This is common because it is part of another scheme called running status, which is a way of compressing data when the status bytes are the same.

0x9n—Note On

The note on message encodes the MIDI note number and the velocity with which the key was struck. For controllers that do not respond to velocity such as vintage synths or inexpensive USB controllers, a value of 64 is often transmitted. There are 128 MIDI

Table 3.1: MIDI messages.

Message Byte n = channel	Message	Data Byte 1	Data Byte 2
1000n = 0x8n	Note Off	MIDI Note #	Velocity
1001n = 0x9n	Note On	MIDI Note #	Velocity
1010n = 0xAn	Aftertouch	MIDI Note #	Pressure
1011n = 0xBn	Control Change	Type	Value
1100n = 0xCn	Program Change	Program #	-------
1101n = 0xDn	Channel Pressure	Pressure	-------
1110n = 0xEn	Pitch Bend	LSB	MSB
1111n = 0xFn	unused	unused	unused

notes, indexed from 0 to 127. The MIDI 1.0 spec places middle C at note number 60 and the entire set of notes spans the range of 128 semitones (or 12800 cents) or frequencies from note 0 (a C at ~8.18 Hz) to note 127 (a G at ~12.5 kHz).

Velocity is specified as follows: 0 is silence, 1 is *ppp*, 64 is between *mp* and *mf*, and 127 is *fff*. Using the musical conventions, *ppp* is pianissimo, *mp* and *mf* are mezzo-piano and mezzo-forte, and *fff* is fortissimo. Several schemes exist for converting the velocity value 0–127 into this musical loudness range, which is essentially exponential in nature. We will use the MMA's convex transform for this when the time comes for implementation, but you are encouraged to seek out and try different mapping schemes.

OxAn—Aftertouch

Some keyboards can sense pressure after the key has been struck and has bottomed out. You strike the key and then press down after the note sounds. Force sensing components convert that pressure into a voltage that is converted into a pressure value. If the keyboard can do this for individual notes—that is, sense different pressures on different keys that have been pressed—then it supports Aftertouch (also known as Key Aftertouch, Polyphonic Key Pressure, and Polyphonic Aftertouch).

OxBn—Control Change

Most MIDI controllers feature an abundance of assignable controller knobs, sliders, ribbons and switches, in addition to a pitch bend control (joystick or wheel) and a modulation control (usually a wheel or slider labeled Mod or Modulation). All of these controls, including sustain and sostenuto pedals, are types of Continuous Controllers. There are 128 continuous controllers indexed from 0 to 127. The MIDI spec only implements some of them; many are designated as "Undefined." All of our synths are going to respond to a core set of CCs. These are shown in Table 3.2.

Table 3.2: Control Change messages that all your synths will support.

Control Number	Controller Message
1 = 0x01	Mod Wheel
7 = 0x07	Channel Volume
10 = 0x0A	Pan
11 = 0x0B	Expression
64 = 0x40	Sustain Pedal
123 = 0x7B	All Notes Off (Panic/Reset)

OxCn—Program Change

The Program Change Message transmits a single data value between 0 and 127, which selects a patch usually numbered 1 to 128 on a synth. We will trap and identify this message in our synths but will not use it until you forge ahead and build your own multi-program synth.

OxDn—Channel Aftertouch

Channel Aftertouch is similar to Aftertouch but is not transmitted separately for each note. Instead, it is transmitted globally and applied to all notes on a particular channel. Since it is a less expensive option, many more controllers implement it instead of Polyphonic Key Pressure.

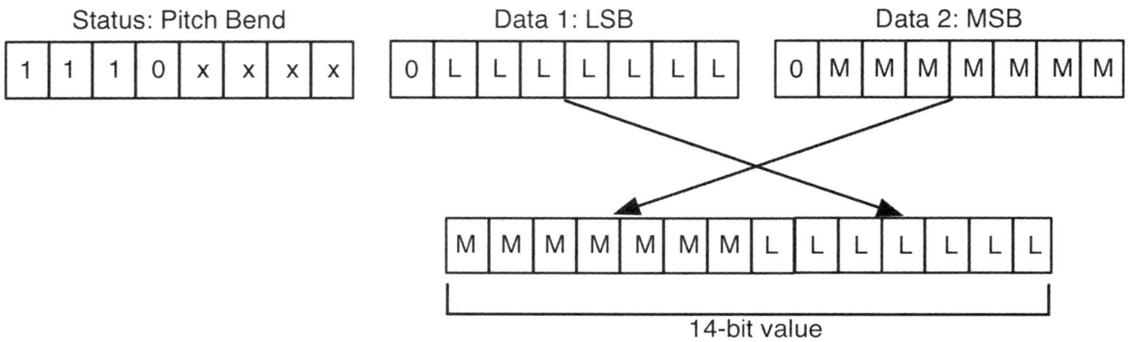

Figure 3.3: The Pitch Bend message has two data bytes, each contributing 7 bits to a 14-bit word.

OxEn—Pitch Bend

The Pitch Bend Message is a special kind of Voice Message because of the way it is decoded. It is usually generated with a joystick or wheel. Pitch bend applies to all notes on a channel. It uses two data bytes to encode a bipolar value with 0 in the center (no pitch bend). Positive pitch bend values indicate an increase in pitch (sharp) while negative values indicate a drop in pitch (flat). Most synthesizers feature a pitch bend range of at least an octave while some allow +/– 4 octaves or more. If only one data byte was used to transmit the value, your ear would hear the bend as a series of discrete bumps in pitch rather than a smooth and continuous change. Smooth transitions are accomplished using two data bytes, each contributing 7 bits to a 14-bit value resulting in 16,384 discrete values—enough to produce smooth bends. The first data byte encodes the LSB and the second the MSB of this 14-bit word as shown in Figure 3.3.

MIDI 1.0 specifies pitch bend as a unipolar range of values with:

0x00 00 = most negative (flat) pitch bend
0x00 64 = center (0)
0x7F 7F = most positive (sharp) pitch bend

For calculations it is easier to convert this into a bipolar value, such that 0 applies no pitch change. The 16,384 values are then spread across a bipolar range of –8192 to +8191 or –1.0 to +0.999.

3.3 Project: NanoSynth

NanoSynth is going to provide the basis for the MIDI portion of every other synth project, as well as act as a test bed for your C++ objects. You will build NanoSynth up over the next five chapters. In this chapter you will learn how your platform deals with MIDI messages and configure the fundamental messaging system. There are no user controls to deal with, so this is a simple project that you should get running quickly. You will need a MIDI controller that can provide as many of the controller messages listed in Section 3.2 as possible. You will trap MIDI events and log them to an output window to make a basic MIDI monitor. In the next chapter, you will use the note on and note off events to turn your oscillators on and off for testing. So this plug-in won't make any noise yet, but it will ease you into coding on the platform you choose. Take a look at Table 3.3 from the last chapter showing the differences in the MIDI function implementation for each API. In this project, we'll be working in those functions.

Table 3.3: MIDI functions for RackAFX, VST3 and AU.

MIDI Functions			
MIDI Message(s)	**RackAFX**	**VST3***	**AU**
Note On	*midiNoteOn()*	*process()*	*StartNote()*
Note Off	*midiNoteOff()*	*process()*	*StopNote()*
Pitch Bend	*midiPitchBend()*	*process()*	*HandlePitchWheel()*
Mod Wheel	*midiModWheel()*	*process()*	*HandleControlChange()*
All other MIDI Messages	*midiMessage()*	*process()*	*HandleControlChange()HandleMidiEvent()*

*for VST3, we will create a sub-function *doProcessEvents()* to handle the actual decoding, but the information arrives during the *process()* function; we will call *doProcessEvents()* from *process()*

Common Files

All three platforms will use some common files that are identical and included in every synth project:

- *synthfunctions.h*—a collection of constants, structures and functions used widely in each project
- *pluginconstants.h*—originally a RackAFX file, this includes more constants, functions, and objects such as the *CWaveData* object that opens and reads wave files
- *pluginobjects.cpp*—the implementation file for objects declared in *pluginconstants.h*

VST3 and AU plug-ins will need one additional file. Note that this file is slightly different for each synth since it is based on the synth's parameters—the GUI controls. This file is not needed in RackAFX because of the way the controls are declared and created—with a properties form rather than in code.

- *synthparamlimits.h*—enumerations and *#defines* for the zero-based parameter index values, as well as the parameter limits (min, max, default) that will match your GUI tables

3.4 NanoSynth: RackAFX

In RackAFX, start a new Project named NanoSynth and remember to check the *Output Only Synthesizer Plug-In* box. Next, copy the file *synthfunctions.h* from the Core Object Files folder that you download from http://www.willpirkle.com/synthbook/ into your NanoSynth project folder. In Visual Studio, add the new file using the technique in Chapter 2 (right-click on the project in the Solution Explorer and choose *Add->Existing*). If you are using filters in Visual Studio to organize your files, place the RackAFX core files in RAFX Core and *synthfunctions.h* in Synth Core. Of course you can name the filters however you like; these names are what you will find in the sample code.

When the compiler becomes active, first remember to *#include synthfunctions.h* at the top of the *NanoSynth.h* file:

```
// base class
#include "plugin.h"
#include "synthfunctions.h"

class CNanoSynth : public CPlugIn
{
      etc...
```

Next, you need to add a variable that keeps track of the MIDI channel. You want to be able to discern the MIDI channel, especially for multi-timbral projects. In our synths, we will receive messages on all channels by default. You can then change this later as your projects get more advanced, and you want to allow the user to control the MIDI receive channel. In the *.h* file near the bottom where it says "// Add your code here:," add the following UINT variable:

```
// Add your code here: ------------------------------------------ //
UINT m_uMidiRxChannel;
```

Now initialize it in the constructor in *NanoSynth.cpp*. There is an enumeration in *synthfunctions.h* that accommodates the 16 MIDI channels plus an omni-mode (all MIDI channels):

```
enum midiChannels{MIDI_CH_1 = 0, MIDI_CH_2, MIDI_CH_3, MIDI_CH_4, MIDI_CH_5,
                  MIDI_CH_6, MIDI_CH_7, MIDI_CH_8, MIDI_CH_9, MIDI_CH_10,
                  MIDI_CH_11, MIDI_CH_12, MIDI_CH_13, MIDI_CH_14, MIDI_CH_15,
                  MIDI_CH_16, MIDI_CH_ALL};
```

Initialize the MIDI receive variable with MIDI_CH_ALL:

```
CNanoSynth::CNanoSynth()
{
      <SNIP SNIP SNIP>

      // Finish initializations here

      // receive on all channels
      m_uMidiRxChannel = MIDI_CH_ALL;
}
```

Then find the core MIDI messages in the lower part of the *NanoSynth.cpp* file:

```
midiNoteOn()
midiNoteOff()
midiModWheel()
midiPitchBend()
midiMessage()
```

The first thing you do in each of these functions is to test the MIDI channel to make sure you are capable of receiving messages on it. This code is essentially identical for all functions.

```
    // test channel/ignore
    if(m_uMidiRxChannel != MIDI_CH_ALL && uChannel != m_uMidiRxChannel)
            return false;
```

You will be using the TRACE macro to log messages to the Visual Studio Output Window (make sure it is open in Visual Studio). The TRACE macro is already defined if you have a Professional version of Visual Studio. For Express versions, you can use the *TRACE()* function defined in *trace.h*, which you can find in the NanoSynth project folder. The TRACE macro and function use the same arguments as *printf*, so make sure you understand how that function works with the specifiers %d, %f, etc. You also want to be able to easily enable or disable logging. Make a *#define* to enable logging. At the top of the *NanoSynth.cpp* file, add the *#define*:

```
#include "trace.h"
#define LOG_MIDI 1
```

When a MIDI note is turned on, we want to log the event, note number and velocity, so that it shows up like this:

```
-- Note On: Ch:1 Note:60 Vel:96
```

which would indicate a note on event on MIDI Channel 1 with MIDI note number 60 (middle C) and velocity 96. Of course you can format this string how you like, but the above is short and simple. Find the Note On Message. The arguments have been converted from bytes to UINTs to make manipulation easier on your end. The easiest way to understand the string functions and logging is by examination. Here is the implementation for midiNoteOn:

```
bool __stdcall CNanoSynth::midiNoteOn(UINT uChannel,
                                      UINT uMIDINote,
                                      UINT uVelocity)
{
    // test channel/ignore
    if(m_uMidiRxChannel != MIDI_CH_ALL && uChannel != m_uMidiRxChannel)
            return false;

    #ifdef LOG_MIDI
            TRACE("-- Note On Ch:%d Note:%d Vel:%d \n", uChannel, uMIDINote,
                  uVelocity);
    #endif

    return true;
}
```

Build the plug-in and load it into RackAFX. You can use either the built-in RackAFX piano controller with *Audio/MIDI->RackAFX MIDI Piano Control* or your own controller. I strongly recommend using your own controller since the piano control is very limited. If you connect your MIDI controller after RackAFX has been launched, use the *Re-scan MIDI* button (looks like a MIDI port) or *Audio/MIDI->Re-scan MIDI Devices* to hook your new controller into RackAFX. Logging will only work when debugging, so launch the VS debugger or use the *Debug* button on RackAFX. Play some notes and make sure you see the events logged in the output window.

Once you get this first message logging properly, implement the note off and mod wheel functions. The *midiNoteOff()* function has an extra argument *bAllNotesOff* that is actually a continuous controller message. RackAFX decodes it and calls *midiNoteOff()* with this flag set instead of making you decode it.

```
bool __stdcall CNanoSynth::midiNoteOff(UINT uChannel,
                                        UINT uMIDINote,
                                        UINT uVelocity,
                                        bool bAllNotesOff)
{   // test channel/ignore
    if(m_uMidiRxChannel != MIDI_CH_ALL && uChannel != m_uMidiRxChannel)
            return false;

    #ifdef LOG_MIDI
            if(bAllNotesOff)
                    TRACE("-- All Notes OFF Ch:%d \n", uChannel);
            else
                    TRACE("-- Note Off Ch:%d Note:%d Vel:%d \n",
                        uChannel, uMIDINote, uVelocity);
    #endif
    return true;
}
bool __stdcall CNanoSynth::midiModWheel(UINT uChannel, UINT uModValue)
{
    // test channel/ignore
    if(m_uMidiRxChannel != MIDI_CH_ALL && uChannel != m_uMidiRxChannel)
            return false;

    #ifdef LOG_MIDI
            TRACE("-- Mod Wheel Ch:%d Value:%d \n", uChannel, uModValue);
    #endif
    return true;
}
```

Build and test the MIDI logging to make sure you are properly trapping the messages. Now add the code for the Pitch Bend Message. RackAFX automatically calculates the pitch bend value from the 14-bit concatenated word and delivers it to you in two forms: the actual value is a bipolar *integer*, while the normalized value is a *float*. This message will be logged in the format:

```
-- Pitch Benc Ch:1 int:2048 float:0.2500
```

where the first term is the bipolar integer value (+2048), and the second is the normalized version (0.25). Build and test your plug-in again, noticing the pitch bend values that will pour through the status window as you move the pitch bend controls around.

```
// nActualPitchBendValue          = -8192 -> +8191, 0 at center
// fNormalizedPitchBendValue      = -1.0 -> +1.0, 0 at center
bool __stdcall CNanoSynth::midiPitchBend(UINT uChannel,
                                         int nActualPitchBendValue,
                                         float fNormalizedPitchBendValue)
{
    // test channel/ignore
    if(m_uMidiRxChannel != MIDI_CH_ALL && uChannel != m_uMidiRxChannel)
            return false;

    #ifdef LOG_MIDI
            TRACE("-- Pitch Bend Ch:%d int:%d float:%f \n", uChannel,
                    nActualPitchBendValue, fNormalizedPitchBendValue);
    #endif
    return true;
}
```

All of the remaining messages will get processed in the catch-all function *midiMessage()*, however it is not enabled by default. To enable it, you need to set a flag in your constructor (you will do this for all synths) to let RackAFX know you will handle all messages. Go back to the constructor and add the following line of code at the end in the area indicated:

```
CNanoSynth::CNanoSynth()
{
      // Added by RackAFX - DO NOT REMOVE
      //
      // initUI() for GUI controls

      < SNIP SNIP SNIP>

      // Finish initializations here

      // receive on all channels
      m_uMidiRxChannel = MIDI_CH_ALL;

      // set flag for all MIDI
      m_bWantAllMIDIMessages = true;
}
```

Now we need to decode the rest of the messages (ten in total):

Voice Messages:

Aftertouch
Control Change
- *Volume CC7*
- *Pan CC10*
- *Expression CC11*
- *Sustain Pedal CC64*
- *All Notes Off (handled in midiNoteOff())*

Program Change
Channel Pressure

You can use the constant definitions in the *synthfunctions.h* file to make the code more readable. Find the *midiMessage()* function in the *NanoSynth.cpp* file. Notice that the arguments are bytes (*unsigned char = byte*). To decode the message, decode the *cStatus* byte first. Then, if it is a CC, decode the *cData1* byte for the control number. This is all done with switch/case statements. A default in the CC logic handles anything not trapped with your supported list. The MIDI channel test code is slightly different because the channel must be cast to a UINT. Also notice the logic for the sustain pedal.

```
bool __stdcall CNanoSynth::midiMessage(unsigned char cChannel,
                                       unsigned char cStatus,
                                       unsigned char cData1,
                                       unsigned char cData2)
{
      // test channel/ignore
      if(m_uMidiRxChannel != MIDI_CH_ALL &&
              (UINT)cChannel != m_uMidiRxChannel)
                      return false;

      switch(cStatus)
      {
              case POLY_PRESSURE:
              {
```

```
                #ifdef LOG_MIDI
                        TRACE("-- Poly Pressure Ch:%d Note:%d Value:%d \n", (UINT)cChannel,
                        (UINT)cData1, (UINT)cData2);
                #endif

                break;
        }
        case CONTROL_CHANGE:
        {
                switch(cData1)
                {
                        case VOLUME_CC07:
                        {
                                #ifdef LOG_MIDI
                                        TRACE("-- Volume Ch:%d Value:%d \n",
                                              (UINT)cChannel, (UINT)cData2);
                                #endif

                                break;
                        }
                        case PAN_CC10:
                        {
                                #ifdef LOG_MIDI
                                        TRACE("-- Pan Ch:%d Value:%d \n",
                                               (UINT)cChannel, (UINT)cData2);
                                #endif

                                break;
                        }
                        case EXPRESSION_CC11:
                        {
                                #ifdef LOG_MIDI
                                        TRACE("-- Expression Ch:%d Value:%d \n",
                                               (UINT)cChannel,(UINT) cData2);
                                #endif

                                break;
                        }
                        case SUSTAIN_PEDAL:
                        {
                                // --- 64 or greater = ON for switch messages
                                bool sus = (UINT)cData2 > 63 ? true : false;

                                #ifdef LOG_MIDI
                                        if(sus)
                                                TRACE("-- Sustain Pedal ON");
                                        else
                                                TRACE("-- Sustain Pedal OFF");
```

```
                        #endif
                        break;
                    }
                    case ALL_NOTES_OFF:
                    {
                        // handled in midiNoteOff() for RackAFX
                        break;
                    }
                    case MOD_WHEEL:
                    {
                        // handled separately
                        break;
                    }
                    // --- all other controllers
                    default:
                    {
                        #ifdef LOG_MIDI
                        if((UINT)cData1 != RESET_ALL_CONTROLLERS)
                        TRACE("-- CC Ch:%d Num:%d Value:%d \n",
                                (UINT)cChannel, (UINT)cData1,
                                (UINT)cData2);
                    #endif

                    break;
                }
            }
            break;
        }
        case PROGRAM_CHANGE:
            {
            #ifdef LOG_MIDI
                    TRACE("-- Program Change Ch:%d Num:%d \n",
                        (UINT)cChannel, (UINT)cData1);
            #endif

            break;
        }
        case CHANNEL_PRESSURE:
        {
            #ifdef LOG_MIDI
                TRACE("-- Channel Pressure Ch:%d Value:%d \n",
                    (UINT)cChannel, (UINT)cData1);
            #endif

            break;
            }
            default:
                break;
        }
        return true;
}
```

Build and test the plug-in. Your controller may not support all the messages your synth can decode, particularly Polyphonic Aftertouch and Channel Pressure. You may have to program your controllers for the pan and expression controls; most have the main slider mapped to Volume. You should now wind up with a Status Window like that in Figure 3.4—lots of MIDI messages flowing and trapped. Notice that the Channel is reported as 0—this is what the user will call MIDI Channel 1.

```
-- Pitch Bend Ch:0 int:0 float:0.000000
-- Volume Ch:0 Value:72
-- Volume Ch:0 Value:69
-- Volume Ch:0 Value:68
-- Pan Ch:0 Value:60
-- Pan Ch:0 Value:58
-- Pan Ch:0 Value:56
-- Pan Ch:0 Value:54
-- Pan Ch:0 Value:53
-- Expression Ch:0 Value:75
-- Expression Ch:0 Value:76
-- Expression Ch:0 Value:77
-- Expression Ch:0 Value:78
-- Note On Ch:0 Note:38 Vel:76
-- Note Off Ch:0 Note:38 Vel:0
-- Mod Wheel Ch:0 Value:123
-- Mod Wheel Ch:0 Value:121
-- Mod Wheel Ch:0 Value:120
-- Mod Wheel Ch:0 Value:119
-- Mod Wheel Ch:0 Value:118
-- Mod Wheel Ch:0 Value:117
-- Mod Wheel Ch:0 Value:115
-- Mod Wheel Ch:0 Value:113
-- Mod Wheel Ch:0 Value:112
-- Mod Wheel Ch:0 Value:111
-- Mod Wheel Ch:0 Value:110
-- Volume Ch:0 Value:71
-- Volume Ch:0 Value:72
-- Volume Ch:0 Value:73
-- Volume Ch:0 Value:74
-- Volume Ch:0 Value:75
-- Pan Ch:0 Value:56
-- Pan Ch:0 Value:57
-- Pan Ch:0 Value:58
-- Pan Ch:0 Value:59
```

Figure 3.4: The completed MIDI Monitor in the VS Output Window.

3.5 RackAFX Status Window

An alternative to the TRACE macro is the RackAFX Status Window. The primary difference is that you can log information to the Status Window without being in active debug mode in Visual Studio. It is a bit of a chore to set up the strings, but it is straightforward. You can find the Status Window in *View -> Status Window* or with the toolbar button (hover your mouse over buttons for tool tips). To log messages, you use the built-in function:

```
void CPlugIn::sendStatusWndText(char* pText)
```

The argument is a *char** and can be as simple as a string-literal like "MIDI Note On." However, to make our message log more meaningful, we will need to use some more built-in functions for converting numbers to strings and concatenating strings. So, when a MIDI note is turned on, we want to log the event and note number and velocity so that it shows up like this:

MIDI Note On: 60 96

which would indicate a Note On Message with MIDI note number 60 (middle C) and velocity 96. Of course you can format this string how you like, but the above is short and simple. Find the note on message. The arguments have been converted from bytes to UINTs to make manipulation easier on your end. The easiest way to understand the string functions and logging is by examination. Here is the implementation for *midiNoteOn*:

```
bool __stdcall CNanoSynth::midiNoteOn(UINT uChannel,
                                      UINT uMIDINote,
                                      UINT uVelocity)
{
      // test channel/ignore
      if(m_uMidiRxChannel != MIDI_CH_ALL && uChannel != m_uMidiRxChannel)
             return false;
```

```
    // --- convert NOTE to char*
    char* note = uintToString(uMIDINote);

    // --- add a blank space
    char* note_ = addStrings(note, " ");

    // --- convert VEL to char*
    char* vel = uintToString(uVelocity);

    // --- create sub-string
    char* noteVel = addStrings(note_, vel);

    // --- final message
    char* message = addStrings("MIDI Note On: ", noteVel);

    // --- log it!
    sendStatusWndText(message);

    // --- clean up
    delete [] note;
    delete [] note_;
    delete [] vel;
    delete [] noteVel;
    delete [] message;

    return true;
}
```

The first step is to convert the note number to a string with *uintToString()* (there are also *floatToString()*, *doubleToString()* and *intToString()* functions). Then, the blank space that will separate it and the velocity is inserted with *addStrings()*. Similarly, the velocity is converted into a string and concatenated with the note number in another call to *addStrings()*. The final message is created by adding the string-literal "MIDI Note On:" to the note/velocity combination. The status logging message is called and then all *char**s are deleted. The reason for this is that all of the number-to-string conversion functions as well as *addStrings()* will allocate the return string from memory. It is up to the caller to delete these strings when done. We chose to use *char**s in RackAFX to try to maximize compatibility with MacOS, as well as other C++ compilers that we previously supported.

Build the plug-in and load it into RackAFX. Now, open the status window and play a few notes on your controller. You can see a few other events logged at the top of the window—this is because RackAFX uses the status window to provide information to the user. You can tell the difference between message sources because messages coming from a plug-in are always indented. If you want to use the Status Window, get this first message logging properly, then implement the rest of the MIDI message logging.

3.6 NanoSynth: VST3

Use the TemplateSynth or TemplateSynth with MIDI project as a basis and follow the instructions in Appendix A to change it to NanoSynth. It comes pre-loaded with the helper files you will need and your first example of a file named *SynthParamLimits.h*, which you will modify for every synth. If you want to practice by coding the simple MIDI logger in this chapter use the TemplateSynth; the other version TemplateSynth with MIDI has the MIDI logging code from this chapter, but nothing else.

VST3 handles MIDI in an unusual and somewhat confusing manner. Right from the start, VST3 does not support the Voice Program Change Message (0xCn where n = channel), so we will omit it from the VST3 versions of our synths. The mechanism for handling Continuous Controller Messages is limited; in an effort to make your life easier by mapping MIDI controllers directly to your controls, it is more difficult to create a rich modulation matrix where a controller may have multiple destinations and is able to be configured on the fly. Some events such as note on and off are handled in a typical manner, but others are not. VST3 does also offer its own kind of MIDI control called Note Expression, though we will not use it in any of the book projects.

3.7 MIDI Events in VST3

VST3 breaks up the MIDI messaging into two parts: events and control changes. Events consist of note on, note off, polyphonic pressure (aftertouch), system exclusive and two musical types: chord and scale. The different events are delivered as structures—a different structure for each event. All but chord and scale events contain the standard MIDI information of channel, note number, velocity, etc.

Events are packaged in the VST3 *Event* structure, which contains an event type index, as well as a set of member structures packaged as a union. The event type index is named *type*. We will trap the following event types:

```
kNoteOnEvent
kNoteOffEvent
kPolyPressureEvent
```

Each type corresponds to one of the union's structs:

```
NoteOnEvent noteOn
NoteOffEvent noteOff
PolyPressureEvent polyPressure
```

Placing the structs in a union makes it easy to access the various event specific attributes. The Event that is delivered to the *doProcessEvent()* is named *vstEvent*. For note on and note off, you retrieve the *channel*, *note* and *velocity* in ordinary MIDI range (0–127) like this:

note on:

```
UINT uMIDIChannel = (UINT)vstEvent.noteOn.channel;
UINT uMIDINote = (UINT)vstEvent.noteOn.pitch;
UINT uMIDIVelocity = (UINT)(127.0*vstEvent.noteOn.velocity);
```

note off:

```
UINT uMIDIChannel = (UINT)vstEvent.noteOff.channel;
UINT uMIDINote = (UINT)vstEvent.noteOff.pitch;
UINT uMIDIVelocity = (UINT)(127.0*vstEvent.noteOff.velocity);
```

With polyphonic pressure, you retrieve the note and pressure like this:

```
UINT uMIDINote = (UINT)vstEvent.polyPressure.pitch;
float pressure = vstEvent.polyPressure.pressure;
```

We will only trap these three events. Everything else will be done through CCs. We created a special function called *doProcessEvent()* to handle these messages as described in Chapter 2. It gets called in the *process()* function, which receives the events in its input argument. In the TemplateSynth, *doProcessEvents()* is partly blank, so you need to fill in the code to log the MIDI messages.

Next, find or declare the variable that keeps track of the MIDI channel. You want to be able to discern the MIDI channel, especially for multi-timbral projects. In our synths, we will be receiving on all channels by default. You can then change this later as your projects get more advanced, and you want to allow the user to control the MIDI receive channel. In the *.h* file near add the following UINT variable:

```
class Processor : public AudioEffect
{
     <SNIP SNIP SNIP>

protected:
     // --- functions to reduce size of process()
     bool doControlUpdate(ProcessData& data);

     // --- for MIDI note-on/off
     bool doProcessEvent(Event& vstEvent);

     // updates all voices at once
     void update();
```

```
    // --- our MIDI receive channel
    UINT m_uMidiRxChannel;
};
```

Now initialize it in the constructor in *VSTSynthProcessor.h*. There is an enumeration in *synthfunctions.h* that accommodates the 16 MIDI channels plus an omni-mode (all MIDI channels):

```
enum midiChannels{MIDI_CH_1 = 0, MIDI_CH_2, MIDI_CH_3, MIDI_CH_4, MIDI_CH_5,
                  MIDI_CH_6, MIDI_CH_7, MIDI_CH_8, MIDI_CH_9, MIDI_CH_10,
                  MIDI_CH_11, MIDI_CH_12, MIDI_CH_13, MIDI_CH_14, MIDI_CH_15,
                  MIDI_CH_16, MIDI_CH_ALL};
```

Initialize the MIDI receive variable with MIDI_CH_ALL in the constructor, along with the other two variables:

```
Processor::Processor()
{
    // --- we are a Processor
    setControllerClass(Controller::cid);

    // --- our inits
    // receive on all channels
    m_uMidiRxChannel = MIDI_CH_ALL;
}
```

You will be using the *FDebugPrint* macro to log messages to the Visual Studio Output Window (make sure it is open in Visual Studio). Steinberg defines this macro; it is essentially the same as *OutputDebugString()*. The *FDebugPrint* macro uses the same arguments as *printf*, so make sure you understand how that function works with the specifiers %d, %f, etc. You also want to be able to easily enable or disable logging. Make a *#define* to enable logging. At the top of the *NanoSynthProcessor.cpp* file, add the *#define*:

```
#define LOG_MIDI 1
```

When a MIDI note is turned on, we want to log the event, note number and velocity so that it shows up like this:

```
-- Note On: Ch: 1 Note:60 Vel:96
```

which would indicate a note on event on MIDI Channel 1 with MIDI note number 60 (middle C) and velocity 96. Of course you can format this string how you like, but the above is short and simple. Find the *doProcessEvents()* function and find the note on, note off and polyphonic pressure *case* statements. Fill them in with the appropriate *FDebugPrint* statement. Notice the *doProcessEvent()* returns true if an event was processed. For now you can safely ignore the first lines of the note on and note off portions involving *noteID*. The first thing you do in each of these functions is test the MIDI channel to make sure you are capable of receiving messages on it. This code is essentially identical for all functions. The *FDebugPrint* macro is only available in the debug version of your project, so this is why you see the added term _DEBUG in the #if statements:

```
#if(LOG_MIDI && _DEBUG)

#endif

// test channel/ignore
if(m_uMidiRxChannel != MIDI_CH_ALL && uChannel != m_uMidiRxChannel)
    return false;

bool Processor::doProcessEvent(Event& vstEvent)
{
    bool noteEvent = false;

    // --- process Note On or Note Off messages here
    switch(vstEvent.type)
    {
                // --- NOTE ON
```

```
case Event::kNoteOnEvent:
{
// --- get the channel/note/vel
UINT uMIDIChannel = (UINT)vstEvent.noteOn.channel;
UINT uMIDINote = (UINT)vstEvent.noteOn.pitch;
UINT uMIDIVelocity = (UINT)
        (127.0*vstEvent.noteOn.velocity);

// --- test channel/ignore
if(m_uMidiRxChannel != MIDI_CH_ALL && uMIDIChannel !=
        m_uMidiRxChannel)
                return false;

// --- event occurred
noteEvent = true;

// --- fix noteID as per SDK
if(vstEvent.noteOn.noteId == -1)
        vstEvent.noteOn.noteId = uMIDINote;

#if(LOG_MIDI && _DEBUG)
        FDebugPrint("-- Note On Ch:%d Note:%d Vel:%d \n",
                uMIDIChannel, uMIDINote, uMIDIVelocity);
#endif

break;
}
// --- NOTE OFF
case Event::kNoteOffEvent:
{
        // --- get the channel/note/vel
        UINT uMIDIChannel = (UINT)vstEvent.noteOff.channel;
        UINT uMIDINote = (UINT)vstEvent.noteOff.pitch;
        UINT uMIDIVelocity = (UINT)
                    (127.0*vstEvent.noteOff.velocity); // not used

        // --- test channel/ignore
        if(m_uMidiRxChannel != MIDI_CH_ALL && uMIDIChannel !=
                        m_uMidiRxChannel)
                    return false;

        // --- event occurred
        noteEvent = true;

        // --- fix noteID as per SDK
        if(vstEvent.noteOff.noteId == -1)
                vstEvent.noteOff.noteId = uMIDINote;

        #if(LOG_MIDI && _DEBUG)
        FDebugPrint("-- Note Off Ch:%d Note:%d Vel:%d \n",
```

```
                        uMIDIChannel, uMIDINote, uMIDIVelocity);
                #endif

                break;
            }
            // --- polyphonic aftertouch 0xAn
            case Event::kPolyPressureEvent:
            {
                // --- get the channel
                UINT uMIDIChannel = (UINT)vstEvent.polyPressure.channel;
                UINT uMIDINote = (UINT)vstEvent.polyPressure.pitch;
                float fPressure = vstEvent.polyPressure.pressure;

                // --- test channel/ignore
                if(m_uMidiRxChannel != MIDI_CH_ALL && uMIDIChannel !=
                   m_uMidiRxChannel)
                        return false;

                //--- note event did not occurr
                noteEvent = false;

                #if(LOG_MIDI && _DEBUG)
                    FDebugPrint("-- Poly Pressure Ch:%d Note:%d Value:%d
                                \n", uMIDIChannel, uMIDINote, fPressure);
                #endif

                break;
            }
        }
        // -- note event occurred?
        return noteEvent;
}
```

We will add the additional code to start and stop oscillators and control the synth in the next few chapters. In the meantime, this is all you need to do for MIDI events.

3.8 MIDI Controllers in VST3

Interestingly (and confusingly), a VST3 host will not deliver MIDI control changes directly to your plug-in. Steinberg tries to justify this by noting that delivering MIDI data directly to a plug-in that uses the data to alter its parameters and GUI can interfere with the host's automation of parameters. To make things even more interesting, VST3 groups the Channel Pressure and Pitch Bend Messages with the control change index values. These are MIDI messages, not controller indexes! And it creates a condition that requires controller index values greater than 127, which may confuse existing MIDI data verification routines. We want to have access to many of these controllers in our synths. Each synth will support the CC sources listed in Table 3.2.

If you want to receive these messages, VST3 requires the use of a MIDI Map, via the interface *IMIDIMap*. The idea is that you typically create a GUI with controls for parameters, and you map a CC—say, Expression—to one of your parameters, such as Filter Cutoff Frequency. The mod wheel control is almost always mapped to LFO amplitude by default. And the volume control is usually mapped to the output level. The *IMIDIMap* interface consists of only one function that you override, *getMidiControllerAssignment()*. The host queries you at startup to find out which MIDI control messages to map to your GUI controls, which in turn changes underlying parameters in the synth. It queries you with controller index values 0 to 129, and you reply by setting the index of the GUI parameter you want to control. A controller may only be linked to one parameter—this sets up a problem for any kind of advanced synth plug-in; you can't map a controller (source) to more than one destination. In addition, you can't re-wire the MIDI map on the fly.

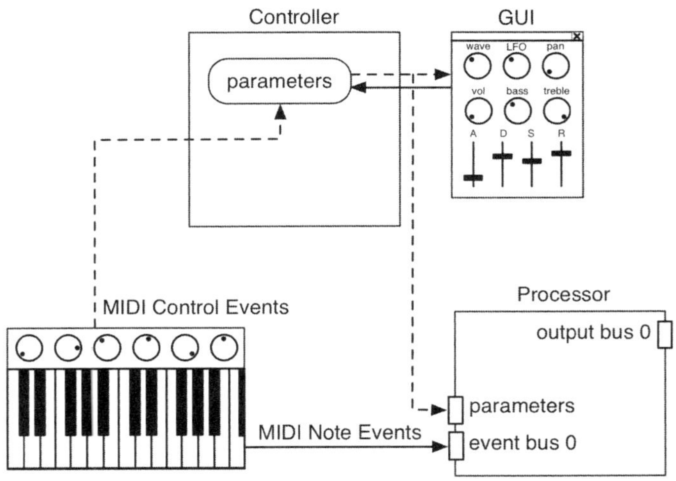

Figure 3.5: The dotted line shows the flow of MIDI control change information from the controller to the dummy variables in the parameter list and then eventually into the Processor.

A simple solution is to create dummy GUI parameters for the MIDI messages you want to receive. You normally don't intend for the user to see them on the final GUI. Then, you map these MIDI controller messages to your dummy parameters. During the *process()* function call, these parameters are extracted as if they were coming from the GUI itself. Having trapped the messages as parameter changes, you may now route them as you please. Figure 3.5 shows the flow of information. You can see the roundabout manner in which the CC messages finally get delivered to the Processor as *Parameter* changes. A fundamental drawback here is that the *Parameter* value is normalized between 0 and 1. The MIDI channel information is lost, so you can't know the original CC channel. The channel information is also lost using the default Stienberg method as well.

A helper function called *doControlUpdate()* handles parameter changes. It gets called in the *process()* function, which receives the events in its input argument. The MIDI control changes will arrive along with the GUI control changes for processing.

Defining Parameter Index Values

As with all GUI parameters, these dummy MIDI parameters are identified with an index value. We use the same index value to initialize the parameter as well as decode it later during the *doControlUpdate()* function. For all the VST3 synths, these parameter index values are implemented with an enumeration found at the top of the *SynthParamLimits.h* file:

```
enum {
      MIDI_PITCHBEND,
      MIDI_MODWHEEL,
      MIDI_VOLUME_CC7,
      MIDI_PAN_CC10,
      MIDI_EXPRESSION_CC11,
      MIDI_SUSTAIN_PEDAL,
      MIDI_CHANNEL_PRESSURE,
      MIDI_ALL_NOTES_OFF,

      NUMBER_OF_SYNTH_PARAMETERS // always last
};
```

Initializing the MIDI Parameters

The GUI parameters are always created and initialized in the *Controller::Initialize()* function. Initializing the *Parameter* objects involves linking them to the enumerated parameter indexes, as well as establishing the min, max and default values. Our parameter values will get delivered to the Processor as a normalized value anyway, so the simplest thing is to set them up as unipolar. The *SynthParamLimits.h* file has constant declarations for the min, max and default values of all parameters in all the synths and includes unipolar and bipolar limits as well. Open the *VSTSynthController.cpp* file and set up the dummy variables (refer to Chapter 2 if you need to), using the indexes and limits in the *SynthParamLimits.h* file:

```
tresult PLUGIN_API Controller::initialize(FUnknown* context)
{
    // --- base class does its thing
    tresult result = EditController::initialize(context);

    // --- now define the controls
    if(result == kResultTrue)
    {
        // --- Init parameters
        Parameter* param;

        // MIDI Params - these have no knobs in custom GUI but do have to
        //              appear in default
        // NOTE: this is for VST3 ONLY! Not needed in AU or RAFX
        param = new RangeParameter(USTRING("PitchBend"), MIDI_PITCHBEND,
                                   USTRING(""), MIN_UNIPOLAR,
                                   MAX_UNIPOLAR, DEFAULT_UNIPOLAR);
        param->setPrecision(1);
        parameters.addParameter(param);

        param = new RangeParameter(USTRING("MIDI Vol"), MIDI_VOLUME_CC7,
                                   USTRING(""), MIN_UNIPOLAR,
                                   MAX_UNIPOLAR, DEFAULT_UNIPOLAR);
        param->setPrecision(1);
        parameters.addParameter(param);

        param = new RangeParameter(USTRING("MIDI Pan"), MIDI_PAN_CC10,
                                   USTRING(""), MIN_UNIPOLAR,
                                   MAX_UNIPOLAR, DEFAULT_UNIPOLAR);
        param->setPrecision(1);
        parameters.addParameter(param);

        param = new RangeParameter(USTRING("MIDI Mod Wheel"),
                                   MIDI_MODWHEEL, USTRING(""),
                                   MIN_UNIPOLAR, MAX_UNIPOLAR,
                                   DEFAULT_UNIPOLAR);
        param->setPrecision(1);
        parameters.addParameter(param);

        param = new RangeParameter(USTRING("MIDI Expression"),
                                   MIDI_EXPRESSION_CC11, USTRING(""),
                                   MIN_UNIPOLAR, MAX_UNIPOLAR,
                                   DEFAULT_UNIPOLAR);
        param->setPrecision(1);
        parameters.addParameter(param);

        param = new RangeParameter(USTRING("MIDI Channel Pressure"),
                                   MIDI_CHANNEL_PRESSURE, USTRING(""),
                                   MIN_UNIPOLAR, MAX_UNIPOLAR,
                                   DEFAULT_UNIPOLAR);
```

```
            param->setPrecision(1);
            parameters.addParameter(param);

            param = new RangeParameter(USTRING("MIDI Sustain Pedal"),
                                       MIDI_SUSTAIN_PEDAL, USTRING(""),
                                       MIN_UNIPOLAR, MAX_UNIPOLAR,
                                       DEFAULT_UNIPOLAR);
            param->setPrecision(1);
            parameters.addParameter(param);

            param = new RangeParameter(USTRING("All Notes Off"),
                                       MIDI_ALL_NOTES_OFF, USTRING(""),
                                       MIN_UNIPOLAR, MAX_UNIPOLAR,
                                       DEFAULT_UNIPOLAR);
            param->setPrecision(1);
            parameters.addParameter(param);
        }

        return kResultTrue;
    }
```

The next step is to override and implement the *IMidiMapping* interface function *getMidiControllerAssignment()* and map the MIDI controllers to your dummy parameters. This is a matter of decoding the *midiControlNumber* and setting the parameter ID value to your associated parameter index.

```
tresult PLUGIN_API Controller::getMidiControllerAssignment(
                              int32 busIndex,
                              int16 channel,
                              CtrlNumber midiControllerNumber,
                              ParamID& id /*out*/ )
{
    // NOTE: we only have one EventBus(0)
    //       but it has 16 channels on it
    if(busIndex == 0)
    {
        id = -1;
        switch (midiControllerNumber)
        {
            // see Processor::process() method for handling
            case kPitchBend:
                id = MIDI_PITCHBEND;
                break;
            case kCtrlModWheel:
                id = MIDI_MODWHEEL;
                break;
            case kCtrlVolume:
                id = MIDI_VOLUME_CC7;
                break;
            case kCtrlPan:
                id = MIDI_PAN_CC10;
                break;
```

```
                case kCtrlExpression:
                        id = MIDI_EXPRESSION_CC11;
                        break;
                case kAfterTouch:
                        id = MIDI_CHANNEL_PRESSURE;
                        break;
                case kCtrlSustainOnOff:
                        id = MIDI_SUSTAIN_PEDAL;
                        break;
                case kCtrlAllNotesOff:
                        id = MIDI_ALL_NOTES_OFF;
                        break;
            }
            return id >= 0 ? kResultTrue : kResultFalse;
        }

        return kResultFalse;
    }
```

Now that the dummy variables are set up in the controller, you need to create a new parallel set of variables on the Processor object and initialize them in the constructor. You only need to create variables for things your synth supports; you will still trap the messages though. Open the *VSTSynthProcessor.h* file and add the variables:

```
class Processor : public AudioEffect
{
        <SNIP SNIP SNIP>

protected:
        // --- functions to reduce size of process()
        bool doControlUpdate(ProcessData& data);

        // --- for MIDI note-on/off
        bool doProcessEvent(Event& vstEvent);

        // --- our MIDI receive channel
        UINT m_uMidiRxChannel;

        // these are VST3 specific variables for non-note MIDI messages!
        double m_dMIDIPitchBend;
        UINT m_uMIDIModWheel;
        UINT m_uMIDIVolumeCC7;
        UINT m_uMIDIPanCC10;
        UINT m_uMIDIExpressionCC11;
};
```

Now initialize them in the Processor's constructor using the defaults from the *SynthParamLimits.h* file. The only thing to note is that the default MIDI volume is 127, to avoid a synth with no output upon opening.

```
Processor::Processor()
{
        // --- we are a Processor
        setControllerClass(Controller::cid);
```

```
    // --- MIDI RX
    m_uMidiRxChannel = MIDI_CH_ALL;

    // --- VST3 specific
    m_dMIDIPitchBend = DEFAULT_MIDI_PITCHBEND;
    m_uMIDIModWheel = DEFAULT_MIDI_MODWHEEL;
    m_uMIDIVolumeCC7 = DEFAULT_MIDI_VOLUME;  // note defaults to 127
    m_uMIDIPanCC10 = DEFAULT_MIDI_PAN;      // 64 = center pan
    m_uMIDIExpressionCC11 = DEFAULT_MIDI_EXPRESSION;
}
```

Now, implement the *doControlUpdate()* function to access the Parameter changes and log them to the Output window (see Chapter 2 for details about the queue). Notice the conversion functions that are used to convert the normalized value to a meaningful one for the synth. This function returns true if a parameter change was processed:

```
bool Processor::doControlUpdate(ProcessData& data)
{
    bool paramChange = false;

    <SNIP SNIP SNIP See Chapter 2>

// --- loop (indent removed for printing)
for(int32 i=0; i<count; i++)
{
    // get the message queue for ith parameter
    IParamValueQueue* queue = data.
                        inputParameterChanges->getParameterData(i);

    if(queue)
    {
        // --- check for control points
        if(queue->getPointCount() <= 0) return false;

        int32 sampleOffset = 0.0;
        ParamValue value = 0.0;
        ParamID pid = queue->getParameterId();

        // --- get the last point in queue
        if(queue->getPoint(queue->getPointCount()-1,
                           sampleOffset,
                           value) == kResultTrue)
        {
            // --- at least one param changed
            paramChange = true;

            switch(pid) // same as RAFX uControlID
            {
                // --- MIDI messages
                case MIDI_PITCHBEND: // want -1 to +1
```

```
{
        m_dMIDIPitchBend = unipolarToBipolar
                                            (value);
        #if(LOG_MIDI && _DEBUG)
                FDebugPrint("-- Pitch Bend: %f\n",
                        m_dMIDIPitchBend);
        #endif
        break;
}
case MIDI_MODWHEEL: // want 0 to 127
{
        m_uMIDIModWheel = unipolarToMIDI(value);
        #if(LOG_MIDI && _DEBUG)
                FDebugPrint("-- Mod Wheel: %d\n",
                             m_uMIDIModWheel);
        #endif
        break;
}
case MIDI_VOLUME_CC7: // want 0 to 127
{
        m_uMIDIVolumeCC7 = unipolarToMIDI(value);
        #if(LOG_MIDI && _DEBUG)
            FDebugPrint("-- Volume: %d\n",
                        m_uMIDIVolumeCC7);
        #endif
        break;
        }
case MIDI_PAN_CC10: // want 0 to 127
{
        m_uMIDIPanCC10 = unipolarToMIDI(value);
        #if(LOG_MIDI && _DEBUG)
                FDebugPrint("-- Pan: %d\n",
                             m_uMIDIPanCC10);
        #endif
        break;
        }
        case MIDI_EXPRESSION_CC11: // want 0 to 127
        {
        m_uMIDIExpressionCC11 = unipolarToMIDI
                                            (value);
        #if(LOG_MIDI && _DEBUG)
        FDebugPrint("-- Expression: %d\n",
                m_uMIDIExpressionCC11);
        #endif
        break;
        }
        case MIDI_CHANNEL_PRESSURE:
        {
                #if(LOG_MIDI && _DEBUG)
```

```
                    FDebugPrint("-- Channel Pressure:
                                %f\n", value);
                    #endif
                break;
                }
                case MIDI_SUSTAIN_PEDAL: // want 0 to 1
                {
                m_bSustainPedal = value > 0.5 ? true : false;
                    #if(LOG_MIDI && _DEBUG)
                    if(m_bSustainPedal)
                        FDebugPrint("-- Sustain Pedal ON\n");
                else
                    FDebugPrint("-- Sustain Pedal OFF\n");
                    #endif
                break;
                }
                case MIDI_ALL_NOTES_OFF:
                {
                    #if(LOG_MIDI && _DEBUG)
                    if(AllNotesOff)
                         FDebugPrint("-- All Notes OFF\n");
                #endif
                break;
            }
        }
    }
    }
    return paramChange;
}
```

Build and test the plug-in. Your controller may not support all the messages your synth can decode, particularly Polyphonic Aftertouch and Channel Pressure. You may have to program your controllers for the pan and expression controls; most have the main slider mapped to the volume CC. You should now wind up with an Output Window like that in Figure 3.4 (the same as for RackAFX)—lots of MIDI messages flowing and trapped. Notice that the MIDI channel is reported as 0—this is what the user will call "MIDI channel 1."

3.9 NanoSynth: AU

Use the TemplateSynth or TemplateSynth with MIDI project as a basis and follow the instructions in Appendix A to change it to NanoSynth. It comes pre-loaded with the helper files you will need and your first example of a file named *SynthParamLimits.h*, which you will modify for every synth. If you want to practice by coding the simple MIDI logger in this chapter use the *TemplateSynth*; the other version *TemplateSynth with MIDI* has the MIDI logging code from this chapter but nothing else. For AU projects, the majority of work is done in *AUSynth.h* and *AUSynth.cpp*. The template already has all the overridden MIDI functions that you need to implement.

Next, find the variable that keeps track of the MIDI channel—open the *AUSynth.h* file and notice the variable at the bottom. You want to be able to discern the MIDI channel, especially for multi-timbral projects. In our synths, we will be receiving on all channels by default. You can then change this later as your projects get more advanced, and you want to allow the user to control the MIDI receive channel. In the *.h* file near the end of the class declaration add the following UINT variable:

```
class AUSynth : public AUInstrumentBase
{
public:
    // --- const/dest
    AUSynth(AudioUnit inComponentInstance);
    virtual ~AUSynth();
```

```
    <SNIP SNIP SNIP>
private:
    // --- updates all voices at once
    void update();

    // --- our receive channel
    UINT m_uMidiRxChannel;
};
```

Now initialize it in the constructor in *VSTSynthProcessor.h*, along with the other two variables. There is an enumeration in *synthfunctions.h* that accommodates the 16 MIDI channels plus an omni-mode (all MIDI channels):

```
enum midiChannels{MIDI_CH_1 = 0, MIDI_CH_2, MIDI_CH_3, MIDI_CH_4, MIDI_CH_5,
                  MIDI_CH_6, MIDI_CH_7, MIDI_CH_8, MIDI_CH_9, MIDI_CH_10,
                  MIDI_CH_11, MIDI_CH_12, MIDI_CH_13, MIDI_CH_14, MIDI_CH_15,
                  MIDI_CH_16, MIDI_CH_ALL};
Initialize the MIDI receive variable with MIDI_CH_ALL in the constructor:
AUSynth::AUSynth(AudioUnit inComponentInstance)
       :AUInstrumentBase(inComponentInstance, 0, 1)
{
    // --- create input, output ports, groups and parts
    CreateElements();

    <SNIP SNIP SNIP>

    // receive on all channels
    m_uMidiRxChannel = MIDI_CH_ALL;
}
```

You will be using the *printf* macro to log messages to the XCode Console (output) Window. Make sure you understand how that function works with the specifiers %d, %u, etc. You also want to be able to easily enable or disable logging. Make a *#define* to enable logging. At the top of the *AUSynth.cpp* file add the *#define*:

```
#define LOG_MIDI 1
```

When a MIDI note is turned on, you want to log the event, note number and velocity so that it shows up like this:

```
-- Note On: Ch:1 Note:60  Vel:96
```

which would indicate a Note On Message on MIDI channel 1 with MIDI note number 60 (middle C) and velocity 96. Of course you can format this string how you like, but the above is short and simple. The MIDI note messages are handled in the functions *StartNote()* and *StopNote()*. Interestingly, these have very different arguments.

```
OSStatus AUSynth::StartNote(MusicDeviceInstrumentID    inInstrument,
                            MusicDeviceGroupID         inGroupID,
                            NoteInstanceID             *outNoteInstanceID,
                            UInt32                     inOffsetSampleFrame,
                            const MusicDeviceNoteParams &inParams)
```

You can safely ignore three of these arguments—all your information is contained in the *MusicDeviceGroupID* and *MusicDeviceNoteParams* arguments. The *inGroupID* is the MIDI channel. The note and velocity information is in the *inParams*. This structure contains the two variables:

- *mPitch*: fractional note number, for example 60.5 would be MIDI note 60 with +50 cents offset that would come from master tuning changes; we will ignore this offset in our projects, but you are encouraged to investigate this on your own
- *mVelocity*: the MIDI velocity value 0 to 127

The Note Off Message is:

```
OSStatus AUSynth::StopNote(MusicDeviceGroupID     inGroupID,
                           NoteInstanceID         inNoteInstanceID,
                           UInt32                 inOffsetSampleFrame)
```

The MIDI channel is *inGroupID*, and the note number is *inNoteInstanceID*.

The first thing you do in all of the MIDI functions is to test the MIDI channel to make sure you are capable of receiving messages on it. This code is essentially identical for all functions.

```
// test channel/ignore
if(m_uMidiRxChannel != MIDI_CH_ALL && uChannel != m_uMidiRxChannel)
    return false;
```

Fill in the note on and off handlers and use *printf* to log the information to the console.

```
// --- Note On Event handler
OSStatus AUSynth::StartNote(MusicDeviceInstrumentID     inInstrument,
                            MusicDeviceGroupID          inGroupID,
                            NoteInstanceID              *outNoteInstanceID,
                            UInt32                      inOffsetSampleFrame,
                            const MusicDeviceNoteParams &inParams)
{
    UINT uMIDINote = (UINT)inParams.mPitch;
    UINT uVelocity = (UINT)inParams.mVelocity;
    UINT uChannel = (UINT)inGroupID;

      // --- test channel/ignore; inGroupID = MIDI ch 0->15
      if(m_uMidiRxChannel != MIDI_CH_ALL && uChannel != m_uMidiRxChannel)
           return noErr;

#ifdef LOG_MIDI
    printf("-- Note On Ch:%d Note:%d Vel:%d \n", uChannel, uMIDINote, uVelocity);
#endif

    return noErr;
}
// --- Note Off handler
OSStatus AUSynth::StopNote(MusicDeviceGroupID     inGroupID,
                           NoteInstanceID         inNoteInstanceID,
                           UInt32                 inOffsetSampleFrame)
{
    UINT uMIDINote = (UINT)inNoteInstanceID;
    UINT uChannel = (UINT)inGroupID;

    // --- test channel/ignore; inGroupID = MIDI ch 0->15
           if(m_uMidiRxChannel != MIDI_CH_ALL && uChannel != m_uMidiRxChannel)
                  return noErr;

#ifdef LOG_MIDI
    // --- NOTE: AU does not transmit note off velocity!
    printf("-- Note Off Ch:%d Note:%d \n", uChannel, uMIDINote);
#endif

    return noErr;
}
```

Next, implement the pitch bend handler, which has a different set of arguments:

- *inChannel*: MIDI receive Channel
- *inPitch1* and *inPitch2*: the LSB and MSB of the pitch bend message

First convert the LSB and MSB into a 14-bit word and decode.

```
// -- Pitch Bend handler
OSStatus AUSynth::HandlePitchWheel(UInt8 inChannel,
                                   UInt8 inPitch1,
                                   UInt8 inPitch2,
                                   UInt32 inStartFrame)
{
     UINT uChannel = (UINT)inChannel;

     // --- test channel/ignore
            if(m_uMidiRxChannel != MIDI_CH_ALL && uChannel != m_uMidiRxChannel)
                   return noErr;

     // --- convert 14-bit concatenation of inPitch1, inPitch2
     int nActualPitchBendValue = (int) ((inPitch1 & 0x7F) |
                                 ((inPitch2 & 0x7F) << 7));
     float fNormalizedPitchBendValue = (float)(nActualPitchBendValue -
                                      0x2000) / (float) (0x2000);
#ifdef LOG_MIDI

printf("-- Pitch Bend Ch:%d int:%d (float:%f \n", uChannel,
       nActualPitchBendValue, fNormalizedPitchBendValue);
#endif

     return noErr;
}
```

The Control Change Messages are handled in *HandleControlChange()* with the arguments:

- *inChannel*: the MIDI channel
- *inController*: the MIDI CC index
- *inValue*: the CC value 0 to 127

All our synths respond to a default set of CCs:

- *Mod Wheel*
- *Volume CC7*
- *Pan CC10*
- *Expression CC11*

Sustain Pedal CC64
All Notes Off

You will trap and log these messages as well as a catch-all for other CC messages in *HandleControlChange()*. Decode the controller index and log the information. Notice that the sustain pedal is on when the CC value is 64 or greater. The CC indexes (e.g. MOD_WHEEL) are defined in *synthfunctions.h*.

```
OSStatus AUSynth::HandleControlChange(UInt8         inChannel,
                                      UInt8         inController,
                                      UInt8         inValue,
                                      UInt32        inStartFrame)
```

```
{
    UINT uChannel = (UINT)inChannel;

    // --- test channel/ignore
    if(m_uMidiRxChannel != MIDI_CH_ALL && uChannel != m_uMidiRxChannel)
        return noErr;

    switch(inController)
    {
        case MOD_WHEEL:
        {
            #ifdef LOG_MIDI
            printf("-- Mod Wheel Ch:%d Value:%d \n", uChannel, inValue);
            #endif

            break;
        }
        case VOLUME_CC07:
        {
            // --- NOTE: LOGIC 9 CAPTURES VOLUME FOR ITSELF ---
            #ifdef LOG_MIDI
            printf("-- Volume Ch:%d Value:%d \n", uChannel, inValue);
            #endif

            break;
        }
        case PAN_CC10:
        {
            // --- NOTE: LOGIC 9 CAPTURES PAN FOR ITSELF ---
            #ifdef LOG_MIDI
            printf("-- Pan Ch:%d Value:%d \n", uChannel, inValue);
            #endif

            break;
        }
        case EXPRESSION_CC11:
        {

            #ifdef LOG_MIDI
            printf("-- Expression Ch:%d Value:%d \n", uChannel, inValue);
            #endif

            break;
        }
        case SUSTAIN_PEDAL:
        {
            // --- 64 or greater = ON for all switch messages
            bool m_bSustainPedal = (UINT)inValue > 63 ? true : false;
            #ifdef LOG_MIDI
            if(m_bSustainPedal)
```

```
                printf("-- Sustain Pedal ON");
                else
                        printf("-- Sustain Pedal OFF");
                #endif
                break;
            }
            case ALL_NOTES_OFF:
            {
                #ifdef LOG_MIDI
                printf("-- All Notes Off!");
                #endif
                break;
            }
            // --- all other controllers
            default:
            {
                #ifdef LOG_MIDI
                if(inController != RESET_ALL_CONTROLLERS) // ignore these
                printf("-- CC Ch:%d Num:%d Value:%d \n", uChannel,
                        inController, inValue);
                #endif
                break;
            }
        }

        return true;
    }
```

You catch the rest of the MIDI messages in *HandleMIDIEvent()*, the arguments of which are MIDI bytes of a MIDI event:

- status
- channel (extracted from status)
- data1
- data2

You handle Polyphonic Pressure, Program Change and Channel Pressure Messages in this function.

```
OSStatus AUSynth::HandleMidiEvent(UInt8 status,
                                  UInt8 channel,
                                  UInt8 data1,
                                  UInt8 data2,
                                  UInt32 inStartFrame)
{
    UINT uChannel = (UINT)channel;

    // test channel/ignore
    if(m_uMidiRxChannel != MIDI_CH_ALL && uChannel != m_uMidiRxChannel)
        return false;

    switch(status)
    {
        case POLY_PRESSURE:
        {
                #ifdef LOG_MIDI
```

```
            printf("-- Poly Pressure Ch:%d Note:%d Value:%d \n", uChannel, (UINT)data1,
            (UINT)data2);
                  #endif

            break;
        }

        case PROGRAM_CHANGE:
        {
            #ifdef LOG_MIDI
            printf("-- Program Change Num Ch:%d Value:%d \n", uChannel, (UINT)data1);
            #endif

            break;
        }
        case CHANNEL_PRESSURE:
        {
            #ifdef LOG_MIDI
            printf("-- Channel Pressure Value Ch:%d Value:%d \n", uChannel, (UINT)data1);
            #endif

            break;
        }
    }

    // --- call base class to do its thing
    return AUMIDIBase::HandleMidiEvent(status, channel, data1, data2,
                                        inStartFrame);
}
```

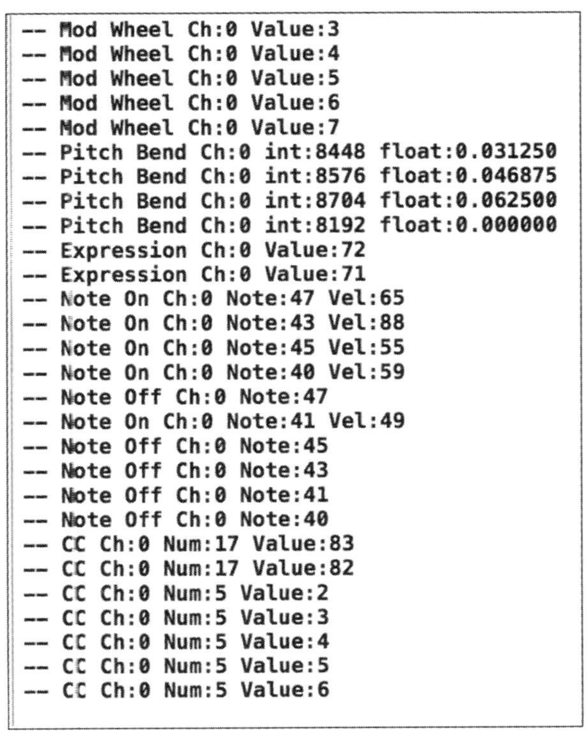

Figure 3.6: The Console Window in XCode shows the MIDI events we logged.

Build and test the plug-in. Your controller may not support all the messages your synth can decode, particularly Polyphonic Aftertouch and Channel Pressure Messages. You may have to program your controllers for the pan and expression controls; most have the main slider mapped to the volume CC. You should now wind up with a Console Window like that in Figure 3.6—lots of MIDI messages flowing and trapped. Notice that the channel is reported as 0—this is what the user will call MIDI channel 1.

Bibliography

Braut, Christian. 1994. *The Musician's Guide to MIDI*, Chaps. 3–4. Alameda: SYBEX.
Messick, Paul. 1998. *Maximum MIDI*, Chap. 2. Greenwich: Manning.
MIDI Manufacturers Association. 1995. *The Complete MIDI 1.0 Detailed Specification.*
MIDI Manufacturers Association. 2004. *Downloadable Sounds Level 1*. v1.1b.
MIDI Manufacturers Association. 1999. *Downloadable Sounds Level 2*. v1.0.
MIDI Manufacturers Association. 2006. *Downloadable Sounds Level 2. Amendment 2.*
MIDI Manufacturers Association. "Tutorial: History of MIDI." Accessed June 2014, http://www.midi.org/aboutmidi/tut_history.php
Smith, Dave and Wood, Chet. 1981. *The 'USI' or Universal Synthesizer Interface*. 70th Audio Engineering Society Convention, Preprint 1845.

CHAPTER 4

Analog and Digital Signal Processing

Since we are designing synthesizers, an obvious place to start working on the modules would be the analog world since the original modules were analog. We would like to make analog equivalents in the digital domain. In this chapter we discuss two ways to do this, with the majority of time spent on the latter method named Virtual Analog. In Chapter 7, we will be implementing the synth filters from Chapter 1 (lowpass, highpass, bandpass and bandstop), so we need to get the signal processing theory out of the way. In Chapter 5, a few of our oscillator designs will also use some signal processing blocks from this chapter.

4.1 Analog and Digital Building Blocks

Analog and digital signal processing algorithms either process an input x into an output y, such as a lowpass filter, or render an output y, such as an oscillator. In analog signal processing, the input and output signals are usually labeled $x(t)$ and $y(t)$ where t is the continuous time variable. Analog algorithms can often be described in a block diagram format rather than a circuit. In doing so, the details of the circuit are removed so that you can focus on the details of the algorithm to understand it better and figure out different ways of implementing or improving it. The block diagrams use analog building blocks that consist of three components:

- scalar coefficient multipliers
- summers
- integrators

A scalar coefficient multiplier simply multiplies the signal by a value called a coefficient, while a summer adds or subtracts two signals. An integrator performs the mathematical operation of time integration on the signal. Integration is required because analog circuits that include capacitors and/or inductors can be described mathematically using a differential equation (or set of them). Solving these equations often requires one or more integrations.

In digital signal processing, the input and output signals are usually labeled $x(n)$ and $y(n)$ or $x[n]$ and $y[n]$ where n is the discrete time variable. Some engineers specifically reserve the bracketed version such as $x[n]$ for digital signals and the other version $x(t)$ for analog signals, though we do not apply this paradigm here. Digital algorithms can usually be described in a block diagram format rather than a flowchart. The block diagrams use digital building blocks that consist of three components:

- scalar coefficient multipliers
- summers
- delay elements

The scalar coefficient multipliers and summers behave the same way as their analog counterparts. A delay element performs the mathematical operation of time delay on the signal. Time delay is used to create the digital equivalent of phase shift in the signal. Digital algorithms often produce block diagrams that add or subtract feed-forward and feedback sub-branches of scaled and delayed signals. Figure 4.1 shows the analog and digital building blocks. The input/output relationships are shown. In the digital time delay, the z^{-1} term represents one sample of delay. The delay is indicated with the (–) sign, the number of samples by the exponent. The output is $y(n) = x(n - 1)$ where the delay is indicated with the (–) sign and the number of samples by the value after it. As you saw in Chapter 1, multiplying a signal by z^{-1} effectively delays it by one sample interval.

4.2 Analog and Digital Transfer Functions

It is often convenient to describe the input/output relationship of the signals in analog and digital algorithms in frequency rather than time. The resulting equations explain how the algorithm affects the frequency components of the signal rather than the time domain response. For analog algorithms, this is done with the Laplace transform, while digital algorithms use the z-Transform. Recalling Chapter 1, the Laplace transform converts a signal or function whose dependent variable is time t into a signal or function whose dependent variable is s. The variable s represents a complex frequency, which means that it can be described with real and imaginary components indicated as $s = \sigma + j\omega$ where ω is frequency in radians/second. The need for a complex number arises from the fact that the Laplace transform's kernel is e^{st}, which represents a complex sinusoid that may be a steady state signal, an exponentially decaying signal or an exponentially increasing signal, depending on the value of σ in the s-term. The input and output signals $x(t)$ and $y(t)$ are transformed into $X(s)$ and $Y(s)$, the Laplace spectra of the input and output. The transfer function of an algorithm is its output divided by its input and denoted as H. The time domain version of H is h and represents the impulse response of the system. The impulse response is the output of the system when a single impulse is applied at the input. For analog signals, the impulse is infinitely

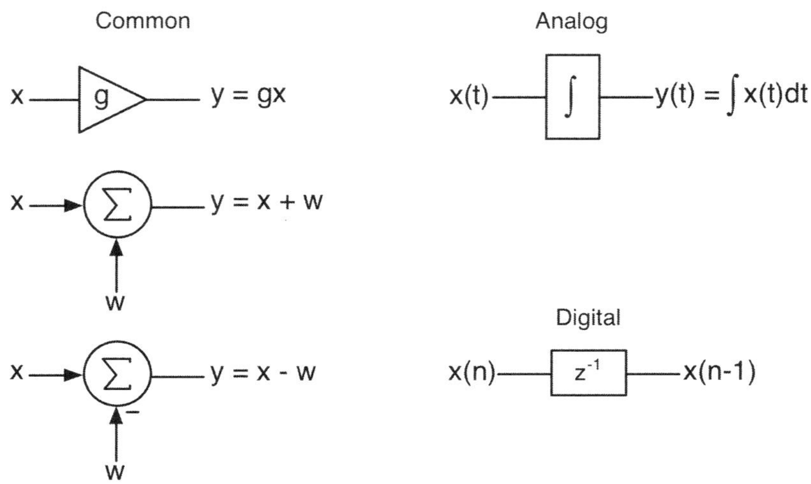

Figure 4.1: Analog and digital signal building blocks.

narrow and is called the Dirac function. The Laplace transform might look daunting, but you can learn a few rules and use the Laplace transform without doing any calculus. In fact, for this book's projects, you can analyze block diagrams and apply the transform essentially by inspection. The first Laplace transform relationships to learn are fairly easy.

$$\begin{aligned} x(t) &\rightarrow X(s) \\ ax(t) &\rightarrow aX(s) \\ \\ y(t) &\rightarrow Y(s) \\ by(t) &\rightarrow bY(s) \end{aligned} \tag{4.1}$$

These first rules state that instances of $x(t)$ will become instances of $X(s)$, and likewise $y(t)$ becomes $Y(s)$. The scalar property also translates through the transform so that multiplying by a scalar a or b in time turns into multiplication in the Laplace spectrum. Figure 4.2 shows a simple example block diagram of an amplifier that amplifies the input by a factor of K.

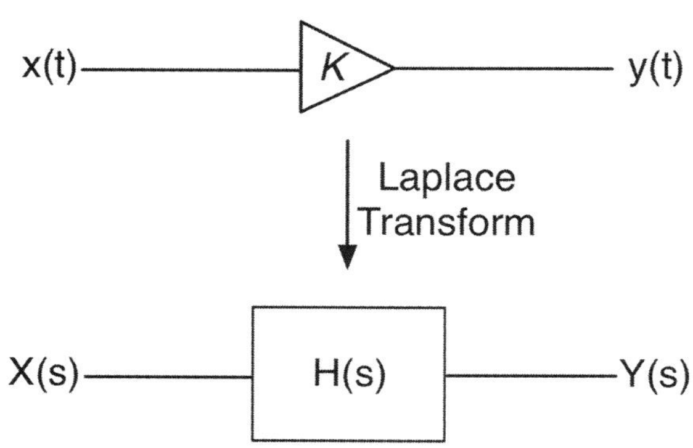

Figure 4.2: The Laplace transform of a simple block diagram.

You can see that the input and output $x(t)$ and $y(t)$ have been transformed into $X(s)$ and $Y(s)$ by inspection. Let's look at how we form the transfer function $H(s)$:

$$y(t) = Kx(t) \rightarrow Y(s) = KX(s)$$

$$\begin{aligned} H(s) &= \frac{Y(s)}{X(s)} = K \\ Y(s) &= X(s)H(s) = KX(s) \end{aligned} \tag{4.2}$$

Multiplying the input by $H(s)$ yields $Y(s)$. So in the block diagram in Figure 4.2, when an input is applied to a transfer function block $H(s)$, the output is simply the input multiplied by the transfer function.

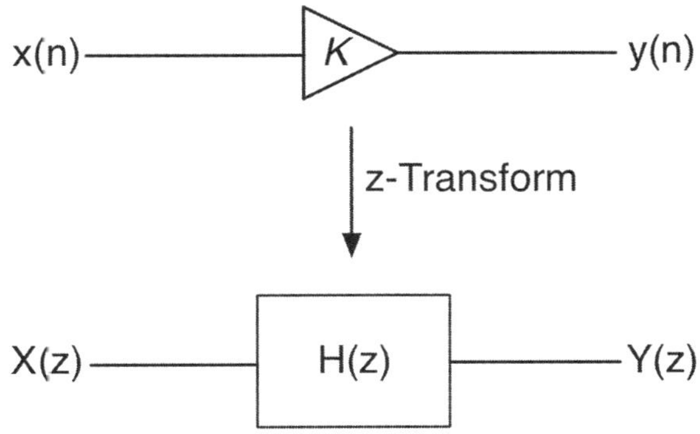

Figure 4.3: The z-Transform of a simple block diagram.

Referring back to Chapter 1, the z-Transform is the discrete version of the Laplace transform, and it converts a signal or function whose dependent variable is discrete time n into a signal or function whose dependent variable is z. The variable z represents a complex frequency, which means that it can be described with real and imaginary components; this is indicated as $z = a + jb$ or $z = re + im$. The input and output signals $x(n)$ and $y(n)$ are transformed into $X(z)$ and $Y(z)$. The transfer function is likewise denoted as $H(z)$. The time domain version of $H(z)$ is $h(n)$ and represents the impulse response of the system. The impulse response is the output of the system when a single impulse is applied at the input. For digital signals, the impulse is a single sample with value 1.0 in a stream of samples with value 0.0. Figure 4.3 shows the digital equivalent of the simple amplifier in Figure 4.1 and the z-Transform operation.

You can see that the input and output $x(n)$ and $y(n)$ have been transformed into $X(z)$ and $Y(z)$ by inspection. Let's look at how we form the transfer function $H(z)$:

$$y(n) = Kx(n) \rightarrow Y(z) = KX(z)$$

$$\begin{aligned} H(z) &= \frac{Y(z)}{X(z)} = K \\ Y(z) &= X(z)H(z) = KX(z) \end{aligned} \tag{4.3}$$

This is fundamentally identical to the Laplace version—the only thing that really changes is the dependent variable from s to z. So far, the two transforms seem to operate directly in parallel. The only real difference, which turns out to be a major difference mathematically, is that analog circuit filtering equations are based on the mathematical operation of integration. Digital filtering algorithms are almost always based on the concept of delaying samples in time, rather than integration.

4.3 Digital Delay

The scalar multiplication and addition (or subtraction) operations are simple mathematical operations. As you saw in Chapter 1, time delay is also treated as a mathematical operation. Consider the M-sample delay line in Figure 4.4 (a). Applying a discrete complex sinusoid $e^{j\omega nT}$ (where n is the sample number, and T is the sampling period) at the input produces a M-sample delayed version at the output, $e^{j\omega(nT-M)}$. Using the polynomial behavior of e ($e^a e^b = e^{a+b}$), we can split the output term as:

$$e^{j\omega(nT-M)} = e^{j\omega nT} e^{-j\omega M} \tag{4.4}$$

This means we can treat time delay as a mathematical operation of multiplying by $e^{-j\omega M}$ where M is the number of samples of delay.

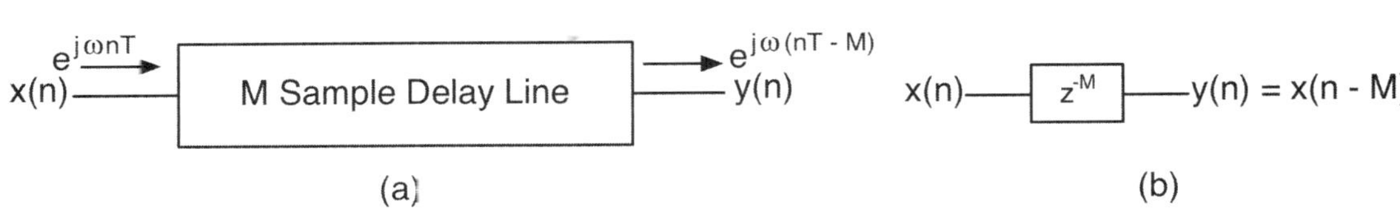

Figure 4.4: (a) An M-sample delay line with complex sinusoid applied and (b) the digital block diagram.

Now we can let $z = e^{j\omega}$ and rename the M-sample delay z^{-M} giving us the difference equation:

$$y(n) = x(n - M) \tag{4.5}$$

The last z-Transform rule you need to learn (yes, there are only three) has to do with delaying the signal by some number of samples M. We already know that this results in multiplication by z^{-M} or $e^{-j\omega M}$. In this case:

$$\begin{aligned}
&x(n-M) \rightarrow X(z)z^{-M}\\
&so\\
&x(n\text{-}1) \rightarrow X(z)z^{-1}\\
&x(n-2) \rightarrow X(z)z^{-2}\\
&y(n-1) \rightarrow Y(z)z^{-1}\\
&etc...
\end{aligned} \tag{4.6}$$

To form the transfer function $H(z)$, take the z-Transform of Equation 4.5 by inspection:

$$\begin{aligned}
&y(n) = x(n\text{ - }M)\\
&apply\ z\text{ - }Transform\\
&y(n) \rightarrow Y(z)\\
&x(n-M) \rightarrow X(z)z^{-M}\\
&so\\
&Y(z)\ = X(z)z^{-M}\\
&H(z) = \frac{Y(z)}{X(z)} = z^{-M}
\end{aligned} \tag{4.7}$$

4.4 Digital Differentiation

We will see a few oscillator algorithms with digital differentiators in them. The differentiator takes the time derivative of the signal. Since the derivative represents the rate of change, the differentiator's output is the current (or instantaneous) slope of the signal. This is easy to find since the slope m is:

$$m = \frac{\Delta y}{\Delta x} \tag{4.8}$$

For our digitized signal, the change in x is constant between point pairs, so the digital differentiator will be providing:

$$m = \frac{\Delta y}{sample} \tag{4.9}$$

Since the change in y is the difference between the current and last input values, we can fashion the differentiator easily as shown in Figure 4.5.

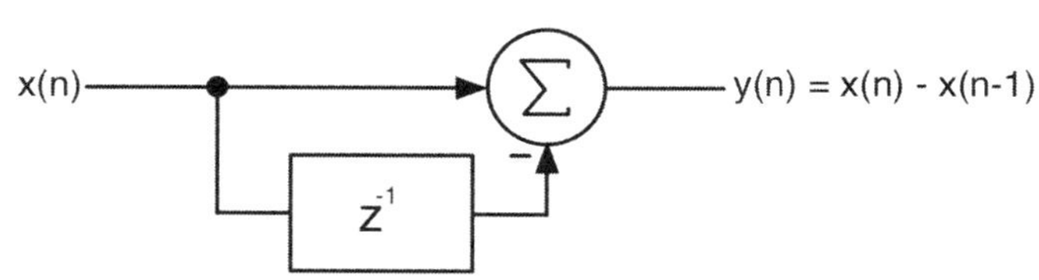

Figure 4.5: A simple digital differentiator outputs the slope between the current and last inputs.

4.5 Analog and Digital Integration

Analog integrators integrate over continuous time; they calculate the area under the signal's curve. The traditional analog integrator circuit consists of an op-amp with a capacitor in the feedback path (if you don't know what that means, don't worry—we won't be analyzing it). You can think of the charge on a capacitor as the integrating component. The transfer function of an analog integrator shown in the block diagram in Figure 4.6 is found by applying $x(t)$ as a complex sinusoid to form an output $y(t)$ then taking the Laplace transform.

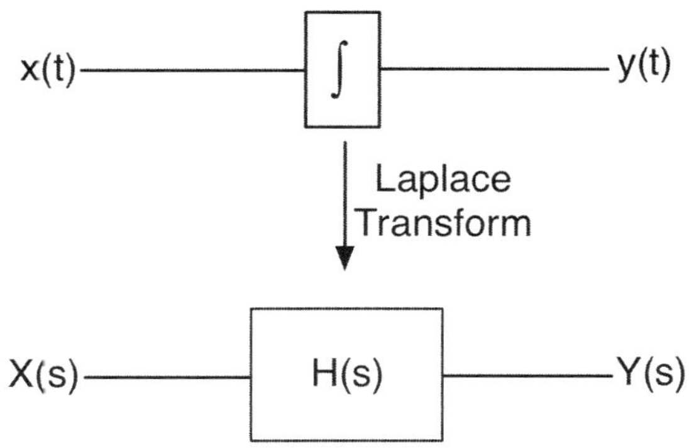

Figure 4.6: An analog integrator and its Laplace transform block diagram.

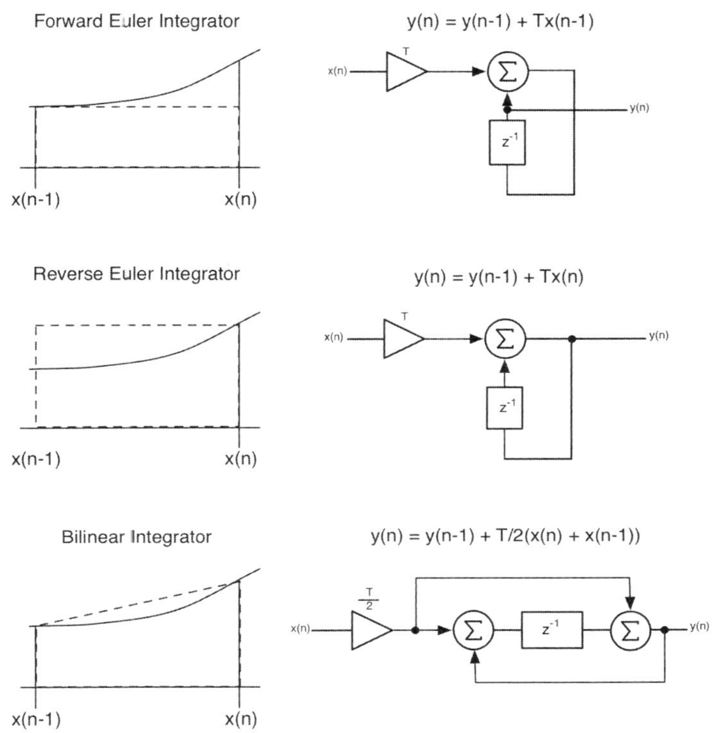

Figure 4.7: Three simple digital integrators (Lindquist, 1989) showing the vintegration approximation over one sample interval.

To find the transfer function, let the input to the analog system be e^{sT}, integrate, and apply Laplace by inspection:

$$
\begin{array}{ll}
\text{analog equation:} & \text{applying Laplace:} \\
y(t) = \int x(t)dt & y(t) \rightarrow Y(s) \\
let\ x(t) = e^{st} & \frac{1}{s}x(t) \rightarrow \frac{1}{s}X(s) \\
y(t) = \int e^{st}(t)dt & so \\
y(t) = \frac{1}{s}e^{st} & Y(s) = \frac{1}{s}X(s) \\
y(t) = \frac{1}{s}x(t) & H(s) = \frac{Y(s)}{X(s)} = \frac{1}{s}
\end{array}
\tag{4.10}
$$

So, the integrator's transfer function is $H(s) = 1/s$, and it is evaluated by letting $s = j\omega$. As ω increases, $H(s)$ decreases. When ω = 0, $H(s)$ is infinite. A digital integrator seeks to perform this same function, calculating the area under a discrete "curve" (think stair-steps). The closer the integrator's output is to the actual area, the better it performs. Digital integrators must approximate this area since they only have discrete data points to deal with.

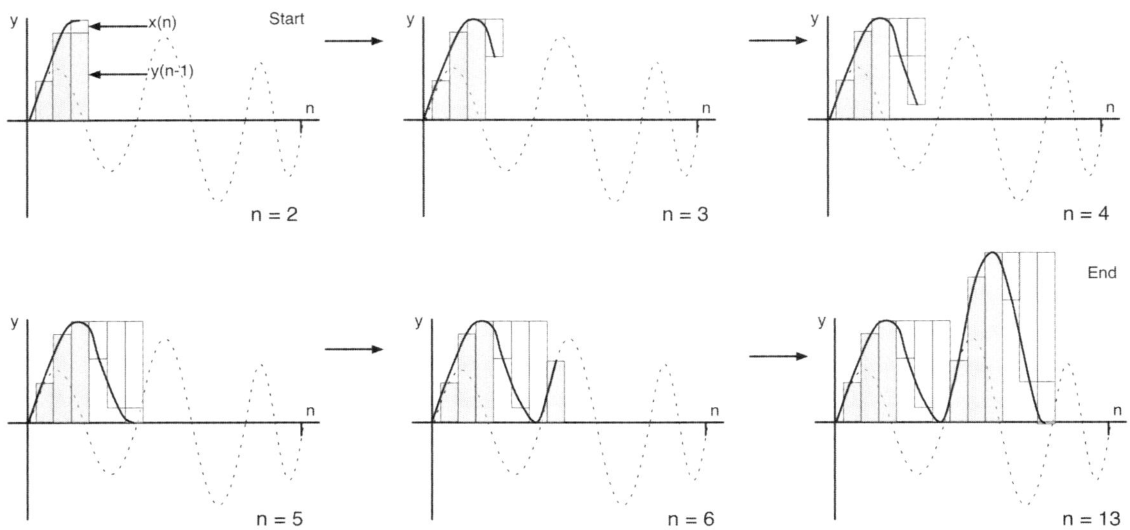

Figure 4.8: The output of the forward Euler integrator (solid dark line) over several sample periods; the positive (grey) blocks add to the running total while the negative (white) blocks subtract from it.

There are three common digital integrators: the forward Euler, backwards or reverse Euler, and bilinear integrators. The forward and backwards Euler integrators are simple to implement but do a poor job of approximating the area under the curve, as they are zero-order hold functions. This is shown in Figure 4.7. In these equations, T is the sample period. For simplicity, we often normalize the equations so that $T = 1$.

Figure 4.8 shows a digital approximation of an analog curve and a step-by-step visual demonstration of the forward Euler integrator; those rectangles summed together produce the area under the curve, or the integration of the signal. In Figure 4.8, the positive rectangles are shaded grey and the negative ones are white. The positive chunks add together and the negative chunks subtract off the running sum. On the very first sample interval $n = 0$, we let $x(n - 1) = 0$ here. Each successive output is the sum of the previous output chunks plus (or minus if negative) the current input. Figure 4.8 is revealing; some people think an integrator is a smoother, but this is technically only the case when it is combined in a certain kind of analog block diagram that we'll discuss shortly. If you look at the complete plot, you see that it covers two of the "cycles" of the input signal. At the point we stop, the instantaneous integration value is 0.0, which makes sense; those two cycles were constructed with two perfect sinusoids with the second cycle larger in amplitude. Since sinusoids have the same positive area as negative area, we expect the total area to be 0.0 over the period of one cycle. This happens twice in the plots, at the end of each of these cycles where the instantaneous area is 0.0.

In Figure 4.7 the bilinear integrator approximates the area under the curve using a trapezoid and produces the most accurate result of the three. It will be our digital integrator of choice. We will still find the reverse Euler integrator in a few algorithms. The bilinear integrator is also known as the Tustin integrator or the trapezoidal integrator. It is called bilinear because it is composed of two linear equations, one in the numerator and the other in the denominator.

4.6 The Bilinear z-Transform

There are two approaches to converting analog filtering algorithms and their associated transfer functions into digital ones. The first approach (classical) makes use of the bilinear integrator as the basis for transform called the bilinear transform. The second approach (Virtual Analog) makes use of the bilinear integrator by directly substituting it for each analog integrator in an analog block diagram. Both methods result in filters that technically have identical frequency responses, but the benefits of using the virtual analog method will become apparent later. The filters in this book all use this newer virtual analog technique. For completeness, the classical approach is discussed first. There is an abundant collection of analog to digital filter conversions using the bilinear transform, so you should not discount it. There are some algorithms for which no virtual analog model exists yet, so you want to be able to use these kinds of filters when necessary. An example bilinear transformed filter algorithm is shown to compare later with the virtual analog version.

To find the transfer function of the bilinear integrator, use the rules you have amassed and apply them to the difference equation in Figure 4.7.

$$\begin{aligned}
&y(n) = y(n-1) + \frac{T}{2}\left[x(n) + x(n-1)\right] \rightarrow Y(z) = Y(z)z^{-1} + \frac{T}{2}\left[X(z) + X(z)z^{-1}\right] \\
&\text{then:} \\
&Y(z) - Y(z)z^{-1} = \frac{T}{2}\left[X(z) + X(z)z^{-1}\right] \\
&Y(z)\left[1 - z^{-1}\right] = \frac{T}{2}X(z)\left[1 + z^{-1}\right] \\
&H(z) = \frac{Y(z)}{X(z)} = \frac{T}{2}\frac{1+z^{-1}}{1-z^{-1}}
\end{aligned} \tag{4.11}$$

The idea behind the Bilinear Z-Transform (BZT) is that if a digital integrator $H(z)$ is approximating the analog $H(s) = 1/s$, then we have a solid relationship between z and s.

$$\begin{aligned} &H(z) \rightarrow \frac{1}{s} \\ &s \rightarrow \frac{1}{H(z)} = \frac{2}{T}\frac{1-z^{-1}}{1+z^{-1}} = \frac{2}{T}\frac{z-1}{z+1} \end{aligned} \tag{4.12}$$

This means we could take an analog transfer function $H(s)$ and replace the instances of s with $2/T(z-1)/(z+1)$. This should produce a transfer function $H(z)$ in the digital domain that corresponds to $H(s)$ in the analog domain.

It would appear that this is a done deal, but the transform is not perfect in two respects. First, it does not linearly transform the analog domain to the digital domain. At low frequencies, the mapping is very close, but as the frequency increases, an error in the mapping increases. The mapping is done with the tangent or *tan()* function. Secondly, it has to map an infinite number of analog frequencies to a finite number of digital ones, and it does this in a fractal manner, smashing and folding all the analog frequencies outside of Nyquist into a tiny area very near Nyquist. Moreover, it maps frequencies at infinity directly to Nyquist. See *Designing Audio Effects Plug-Ins in C++* for a detailed discussion.

The consequence of the first issue is that we need to pre-warp the analog frequency domain first so that after the transformation, the correct digital frequency response is obtained. The mapping equation is:

$$\begin{aligned} &\omega_a = \frac{2}{T}\tan\left[\frac{\omega_d T}{2}\right] \\ &\omega_a = \text{the prewarped analog frequency} \\ &\omega_d = \text{the desired digital frequency} \\ &T = \text{the sample period} \end{aligned} \tag{4.13}$$

Suppose you want to implement a bilinear-transformed lowpass filter with a cutoff frequency f_c. Before doing any calculations, you would need to pre-warp f_c. The code for doing this is:

```
double wd = 2*pi*fc;
double T  = 1/sampleRate;
double wa = (2/T)*tan(wd*T/2);
```

In this code, *wd* (omega d) is the desired digital frequency and *wa* (omega a) is the warped analog frequency.

The consequence of the second issue is that for some filter types (notably the lowpass and bandpass), there will be an error in the very high frequency response, and the filter's output will go all the way to zero at the Nyquist frequency rather than taking on a finite value. See the Bibliography for more information on this issue.

Once the bilinear transform is applied to an arbitrary $H(s)$, the resulting polynomial numerator and denominator are grouped into first order and second order sections. A simple example shows the transformation of an analog RC lowpass filter in Figure 4.9 into the bilinear equivalent. The complete derivation is done in *Designing Audio Effects Plug-Ins in C++*.

The transfer function of this filter is:

$$\begin{aligned} &H(s) = \frac{1}{s/\omega_c + 1} \\ &\omega_c = \frac{1}{RC} \\ &\text{or} \\ &H(s) = \frac{1}{b_1 s + 1} \\ &b_1 = RC \end{aligned} \tag{4.14}$$

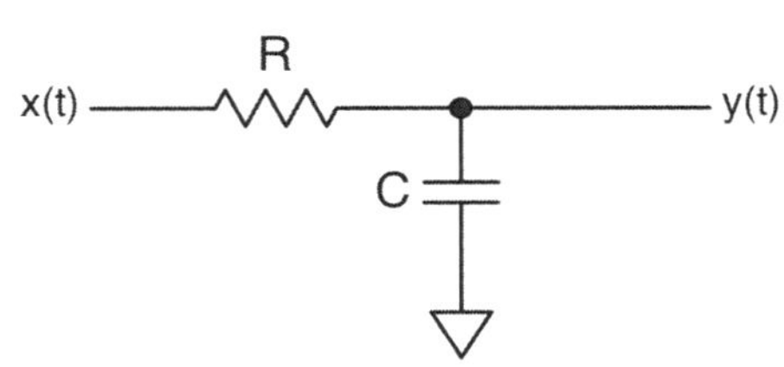

Figure 4.9: A simple analog RC lowpass filter.

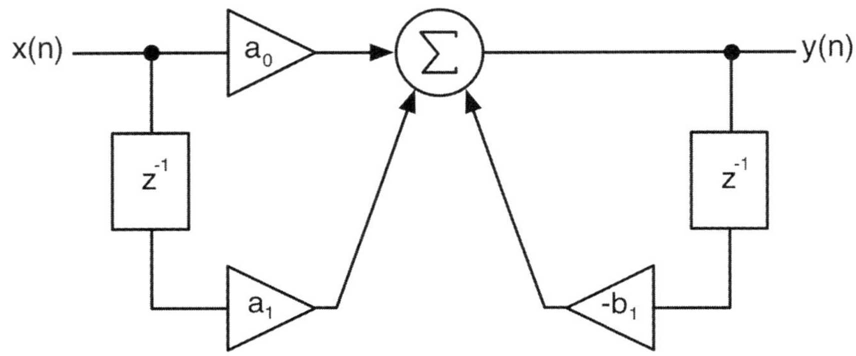

Figure 4.10: The digital block diagram of the first order analog lowpass filter.

The term b_1 is called a coefficient, and the denominator is a first order polynomial in *s*.

Applying the bilinear transform by replacing *s* with $(z-1)/(z+1)$ results in a transfer function $H(z)$:

$$H(z)=\frac{a_0+a_1z^{-1}}{1+b_1z^{-1}} \tag{4.15}$$

The $2/T$ term in the bilinear transform equation washes out mathematically. The terms a_0, a_1, and b_1 are called the coefficients of the new transfer function and are intimately related to the cutoff frequency f_c. You may see a very vague resemblance to the analog transfer function, but the b_1 coefficient is not simply equal to RC as it is in the analog version. This results in the digital block diagram shown in Figure 4.10.

The equations for the coefficients are:

$$\begin{aligned}&\theta_c=2\pi f_c/f_s\\&\gamma=\frac{\cos\theta_c}{1+\sin\theta_c}\\&a_0=\frac{1-\gamma}{2}\qquad a_1=\frac{1-\gamma}{2}\qquad b_1=-\gamma\end{aligned} \tag{4.16}$$

When the user changes the f_c control of the filter, these coefficients must be recalculated. This requires two trigonometric functions. Additionally, two memory locations are used to implement the two delay blocks. Interestingly, this transform took a transfer function that had a first order denominator and turned it into another one with both first order numerator and denominator; however, the transfer function is still first order.

Higher order analog filters will result in higher order digital transfer functions. A second order lowpass filter $H(s)$ will result in a second order $H(z)$ that is described as:

$$H(z)=\frac{a_0+a_1z^{-1}+a_2z^{-2}}{1+b_1z^{-1}+b_2z^{-2}} \tag{4.17}$$

Since both the numerator and denominator are quadratic equations, this is called a bi-quadratic transfer function or simply a "biquad." The block diagram for the biquad is shown in Figure 4.11. You can see that this structure adds two more coefficients and two more storage locations to the first order version. The calculation of coefficients again will involve trig functions and algebra.

Because the resulting higher order bilinear z-transformed filters are sectioned into bi-quadratic pieces, we call this the "BZT-to-biquad" method. The BZT is covered in detail in just about every DSP book on the market, so there is plenty of information out there if you are interested.

4.7 Virtual Analog Filters

The term "Virtual Analog" has varied meanings; some take it to mean a filter that has been designed using digital components that mimic one and two-port networks (part of analog filter theory) and implement analog circuits in a direct fashion called Wave Digital Filtering. For others it might mean a filter whose frequency response is virtually identical to an analog filter's response. Some engineers restrict Virtual Analog to mean the design of filters based on non-linear analog circuits. In this book, Virtual Analog (VA) filtering refers to the algorithms designed using a two-part technique: analog to digital integrator replacement and resolution of delay-free loops.

In the traditional BZT-to-biquad approach, you start with the analog transfer function and apply the BZT to get a digital transfer function directly. In VA, you start with the analog block diagram and replace the analog integrators with digital bilinear integrators. The result is a filter that has a frequency response that is identical to that of a BZT-to-biquad version, but typically with fewer

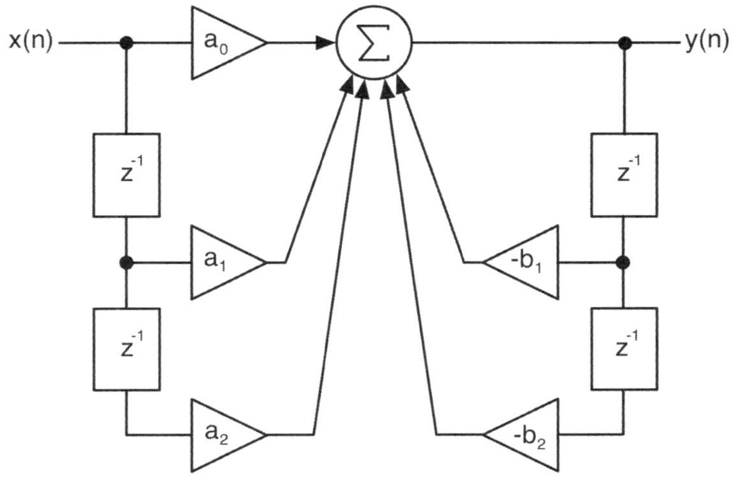

Figure 4.11: The digital biquad block diagram.

coefficients, lower memory requirements, and the ability to go directly from an analog block diagram to a digital filter without the BZT or any of the ensuing algebra. This integrator replacement technique is not new. Fettweis (1971), Bruton (1975), El-Masry (1979), and others experimented with analog to digital integrator replacement using analog block diagrams and signal flow graphs (which are discussed in Section 4.15). In 1989, Lindquist repackaged El-Masry's technique, which he called the Analog Filter Simulation Design Method. In this method, passive analog filters are converted directly to digital form by extracting the analog block diagram (or signal flow graph) and replacing the analog integrators with digital integrators (Lindquist, 1989). In all of these cases, the resulting delay-free loops presented fundamental design problems, typically overcome with signal flow manipulation or modification of the digital replacement integrators. Resolving and implementing these delay-free loops is the second part of the VA technique.

Implementing delay-less loops in discrete algorithms is not a trivial problem and has been approached in several different ways over the last few decades. In 1975, Szczupak and Mitra published "Detection, Location, and Removal of Delay-Free Loops in Digital Filter Configurations," in which they describe a method for detecting and removing any zero-delay loop by manipulating signal flow graphs. Härmä (1998) provides a technique for resolving delay-less loops in any generalized recursive (feedback) filter with any number of delay-less loops in "Implementation of Recursive Filters Having Delay Free Loops." Another technique is described in Borin, De Poli and Rocchesso (2000), involving delay-less loops in non-linear waveguide (physical modeling) algorithms. Vadim Zavalishin described a delay-free resolution method in a self-published paper in 2008, then again in the self-published book "The Art of VA Filter Design" in 2012. This method uses an instantaneous response technique to remove the delay-free loop in an algebraic manner. In this chapter we will introduce another design technique that we call the Modified Härmä method (Pirkle, 2014). This method is explained in more detail, with examples, both here and in Chapter 7. Both Zavalishin's and our Modified Härmä methods produce identical results, and we will do examples with each of them. Zavalishin's work is centered on the preservation of the original analog signal flow through the filtering elements: coefficient multipliers, summers, and integrators. He names this method the Topology-Preserving Transform or TPT. He theorizes that preservation of the analog topology also preserves the way that the corresponding digital filter will respond under time-varying conditions in which the filter's cutoff frequency is modulated. The VA filters in this book follow this topology preservation as well, and we choose to use Zavalishin's notation for the filtering blocks even when using the Modified Härmä method to resolve the delay-free loops.

4.8 Analog Block Diagrams

In this approach, you start with the analog circuit's differential equation, produce a block diagram and take the Laplace transform of its equation to get the transfer function *H(s)*. Start with the same simple RC lowpass filter, shown in Figure 4.9. A simple way to approach this circuit that many electronics books use is based on the voltage divider equation and the impedances of the elements to produce a transfer function.

$$y(t) = x(t)\frac{Z_C}{Z_R + Z_C}$$

$$\frac{y(t)}{x(t)} = \frac{\frac{1}{j\omega C}}{R + \frac{1}{j\omega C}}$$

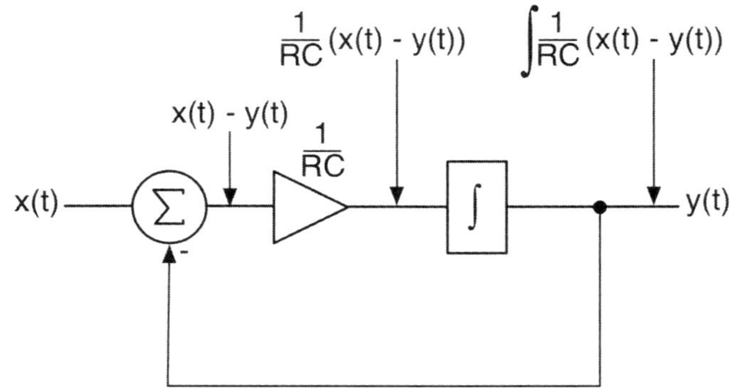

Figure 4.12: The block diagram for the analog RC filter.

$$H(s)=\frac{Y(s)}{X(s)}=\frac{\frac{1}{sC}}{R+\frac{1}{sC}}$$
$$=\frac{1}{sRC+1}$$
or
$$H(s)=\frac{1}{s/\omega_c+1}$$
$$\omega_c=\frac{1}{RC} \tag{4.18}$$

By letting RC = 1, f_c = 1, we get the normalized transfer function:

$$H(s)=\frac{1}{s+1} \tag{4.19}$$

Normalizing the transfer function makes the math easier since the filter is scalable in frequency. This approach yields the transfer function in a relatively simple manner but it hides the analog signal flow that is occurring in the filter. We want to use that signal flow to directly produce digital equivalents. Next we look at the differential equation of the circuit. The differential equation that relates the output signal voltage y to the input signal voltage x is shown in Equation 4.20; if you are curious, you can get two different derivations of this equation at http://www.willpirkle.com/synthbook/.

$$\frac{dy}{dt}=\frac{1}{RC}(x(t)-y(t)) \tag{4.20}$$

Taking the integral of both sides solves this equation. The result can then be simplified as:

$$y(t)=\int\frac{1}{RC}(x(t)-y(t))dt \tag{4.21}$$

A block diagram can be constructed from Equation 4.21 and is shown in Figure 4.12.

Now we can take the Laplace transform of the entire block diagram. All the familiar rules apply. In Section 4.5 we saw that the transfer function of the analog integrator is $H(s) = 1/s$, so the integrator can be replaced with a $1/s$ block as shown in Figure 4.13. We can also make the substitution $f_c = 1/RC$ that we found from the voltage divider approach. To form the virtual analog equivalent, you replace the analog integrator with a digital one. This effectively digitizes the analog filter.

4.9 First Order VA Lowpass Filter

The VA approach replaces the analog integrator $H(s) = 1/s$ with a digital version. And we choose to use the bilinear integrator, as it is superior to the other two. For the curious, there are many more analog to digital transforms that could be used; however, only the bilinear transform preserves the magnitude characteristics of the frequency response, albeit with the response compression/warping in Equation 4.13. In some cases, such as systems that only operate on very low frequencies, other transforms could work, but for full frequency systems (0 Hz to Nyquist), the bilinear transform rules. An alternate form of the bilinear integrator is shown in Figure 4.14. It produces the same input/output relationship as the bilinear integrator in Figure 4.13. It should be noted that technically any bilinear

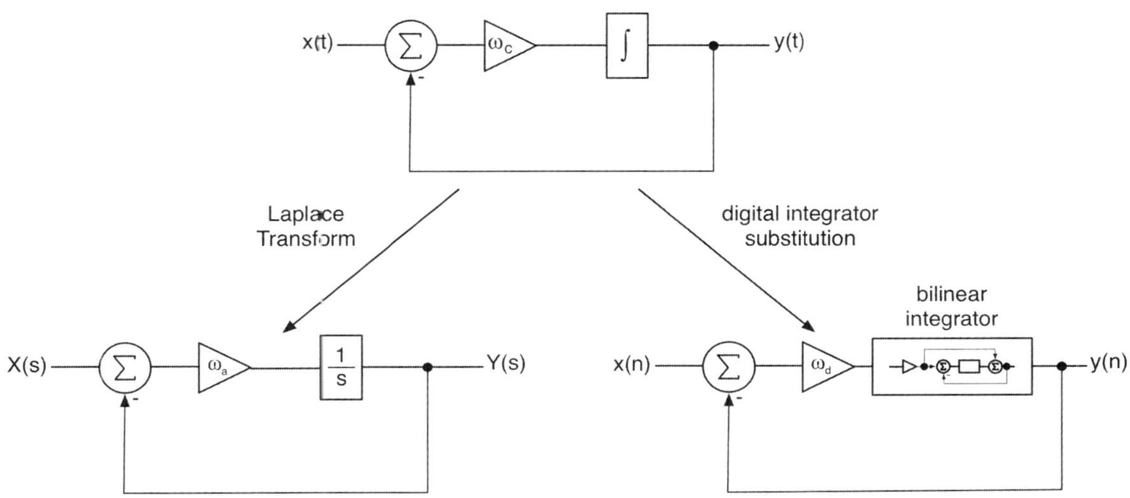

Figure 4.13: Using the Laplace transform, the integrator is replaced by the analog filter equivalent 1/s, while the digital integ-ator substation replaces it with a bilinear integrator.

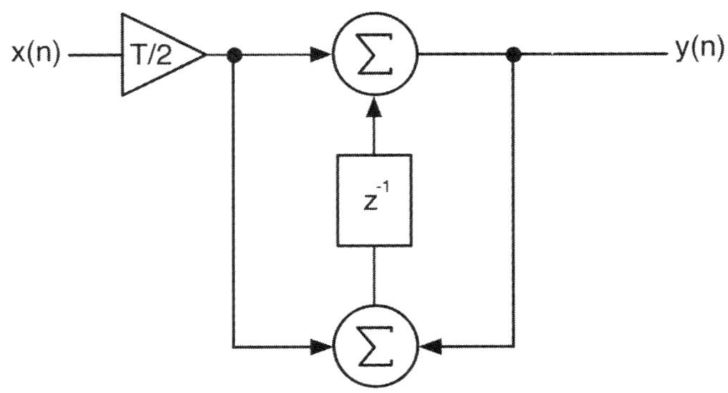

Figure 4.14: An alternate form of the bilinear integrator or trapezoidal integrator.

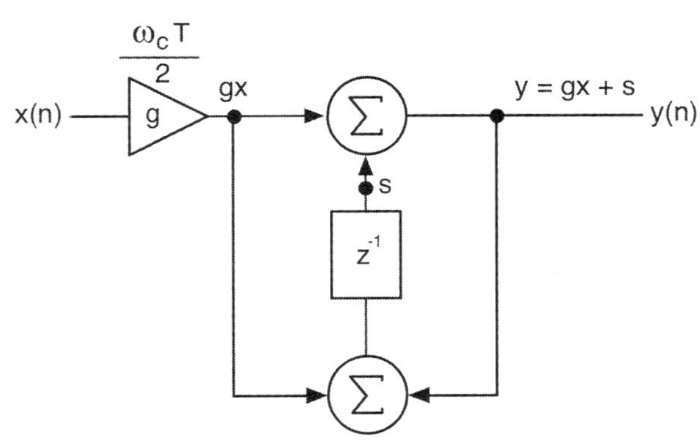

Figure 4.15: The un-normalized version of the bilinear integrator.

integrator structure may be used in these fi.ters; the form in Figure 4.14 is a desirable version since it requires only one memory element. Other versions require one or two memory locations. You can find derivations using these alternate bilinear structure forms at http://www.willpirkle.com/synthbook/—they all produce the same frequency response.

The un-normalized version of the bilinear integrator is shown in Figure 4.15, where the normalized T/2 multiplier is replaced by f_c *T/2*.

The output of the z^{-1} delay block is labeled *s* and the f_c T/2 multiplier is labeled *g*. The output of the integrator is then a linear equation

$$y(n) = gx(n) + s(n)$$

This is Zavalishin's notation: the *g* corresponds to gain and *s* corresponds to storage. Both Zavalishin's and the Modified Härmä methods rely on this ability to express the input/output relationship of the system as a linear equation or set of linear equations. In this case, the

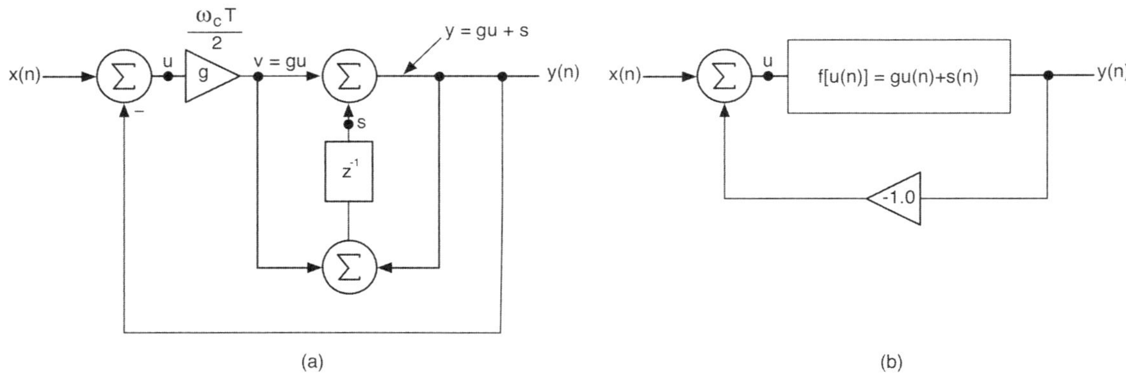

Figure 4.16: (a) The digitized version of the analog block diagram with the bilinear integrator shown inside the feedback loop; *u* is the input to the integrator and (b) replacing the integrator with a simple function *f(u)* and using a positive feedback gain of −1.0 instead of subtracting.

system is a single integrator. By building VA "circuits" with this component, the overall systems will still have a similar input/output relationship. The un-normalized version is shown in Figure 4.16, where the normalized T/2 multiplier is replaced by f_c T/2.

In this circuit, the output of the integrator *y* is ultimately the output of the lowpass filter. The input into the integrator is $u(n) = (x(n) - y(n))$, so the equation becomes:

$$\begin{aligned} y(n) &= gu(n) + s(n) \\ &= g(x(n) - y(n)) + s(n) \\ &= gx(n) - gy(n) + s(n) \end{aligned} \tag{4.22}$$

This appears problematic as *y(n)* appears on both sides of the equation since we have a delay-less loop between input and output. Zavalishin's algebraic solution involves ignoring the fact that the discrete time output *y(n)* appears on both sides of the equation and asserting that the loop can be resolved since the *g* and *s* terms are fixed at any instance in time, *n*. Therefore, Equation 4.22 could be thought of as an instantaneous response equation. Dropping the discrete time variable *n* (for convenience) and separating variables results in Equation 4.23.

$$y = g(x - y) + s \tag{4.23}$$

Then, apply some algebra:

$$\begin{aligned} y &= g(x - y) + s \\ y + gy &= gx + s \\ y &= \frac{gx + s}{1 + g} \end{aligned} \tag{4.24}$$

This equation is once again another version of $y = gx + s$ and can be found by separating the terms in the numerator and factoring as:

$$y = \frac{g}{1+g}x + \frac{s}{1+g} \tag{4.25}$$

Replacing the two quotients with *G* and *S* yields:

$$\begin{aligned} & y = \frac{g}{1+g}x + \frac{s}{1+g} \\ & let: \\ & G = \frac{g}{1+g} \\ & S = \frac{s}{1+g} \\ & then: \\ & y = Gx + S \end{aligned} \tag{4.26}$$

It was the linear relationship $y = gx + s$ that allowed the delay-less loop to be resolved in the input/output equation, so now we need to alter the block diagram to remove that delay-less path. Evaluating the input *v* to the summing node of the integrator reveals the new modified structure. It is relatively easy to show that (Zavalishin, 2012):

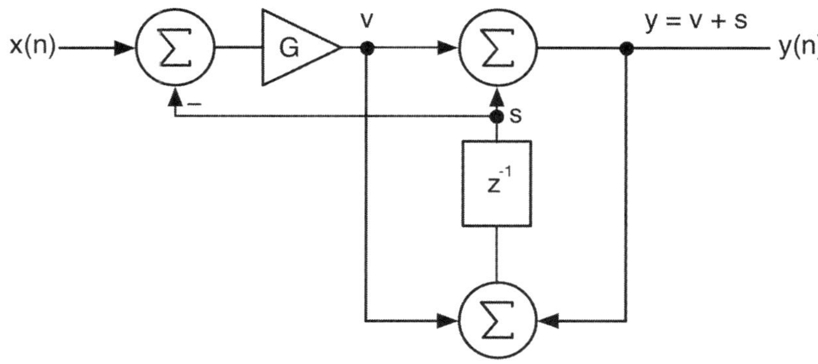

Figure 4.17: The completed VA first order LPF.

$$
\begin{aligned}
v &= g(x-y) = g(x-Gx-S) = g\frac{x-s}{1+g} \\
&= (x-s)\frac{g}{1+g} \\
&= G(x-s)
\end{aligned}
\tag{4.27}
$$

With this, the final form of the first order VA lowpass filter is synthesized and shown in Figure 4.17, and you can see that $v = G(x - s)$. This is accomplished by relocating the feedback path from the output of the filter to the output of the delay element *s(n)*.

The importance of the linear $y = Gx + S$ relationship can't be stressed enough. Think about this: we took an integrator with output $y = gx + s$, stuck it inside a delay-less loop and got an output that can be expressed as $y = Gx + S$. What do you suppose would happen if we took this lowpass filter and stuck it inside another delay-less feedback loop, or if we took a series of these and stuck that cascade into a delay-less feedback loop? Would it surprise you that the output always winds up being in the form $y = \Gamma x + \Sigma$ (here, Γ and Σ represent some generic *G* and *S* values)?

The effect of choosing the bilinear integrator is that the resulting filter behaves identically to the classical BZT-to-biquad approach—it is also a bilinear transform filter, but without applying the BZT to the analog transfer function. It also requires the pre-warping of the filter cutoff frequency. The complete calculation of the single coefficient G is:

```
double wd  = 2*pi*Fc;
double T   = 1/SampleRate;
double wa  = (2/T)*tan(wd*T/2);
double g   = wa*T/2;

double G = g/(1.0 + g);
```

Look at the difference between the VA LPF in Figure 4.17 and the direct form (half biquad) filter in Figure 4.10. The VA version only has one coefficient to calculate using only one trig function, *tan()*, and it only requires one memory location. This is a significant advantage for speed of implementation. There are other advantages, too, regarding sensitivity of the filter to rounding errors in the coefficients.

4.10 First Order VA Highpass Filter

The first order VA highpass filter is derived in the same manner from the equivalent analog RC highpass filter. The resulting filter has an output y_{HP} that is mathematically related to the output of the lowpass filter y_{LP}. The relationship is:

$$
y(n)_{HP} = x(n) - y(n)_{LP} \tag{4.28}
$$

We can simply reuse the VA lowpass filter and subtract the input from the lowpass output. This is shown in Figure 4.18.

Because the two filters share the same lowpass component, we can implement a single filter that produces both outputs. Ultimately, our C++ object in Chapter 7 will provide both versions with very little extra code.

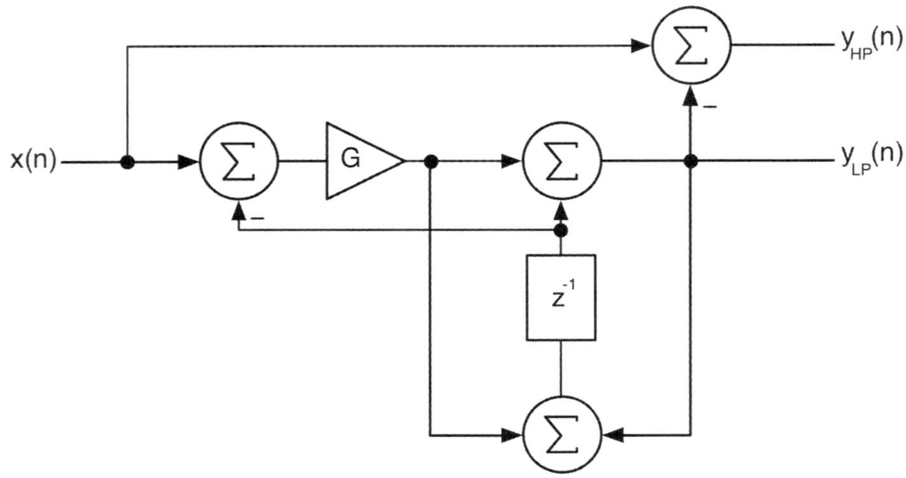

Figure 4.18: The VA highpass filter uses an altered version of the lowpass filter.

If the lowpass filter can be described as $y_{LP} = Gx + S$, then the highpass filter would be:

$$\begin{aligned} y_{HP} &= x - (Gx + S) \\ &= x - Gx - S \\ &= (1 - G)x - S \\ &= G_H x + S_H \\ G_H &= 1 - G \\ S_H &= -S \end{aligned} \tag{4.29}$$

This means that yet again, the filter has the form y = Gx + S. All but one of the filters in Chapter 7 use just these two simple first order building blocks to implement their structures.

4.11 Second Order VA Filters

Second order analog transfer functions result in a generalized transfer function:

$$H(s) = H_0 \frac{num}{s^2 / \omega_c^2 + 2\zeta s / \omega_c + 1} \tag{4.30}$$

The *num* or numerator term varies with filter type, but the denominator is the same. H_o represents the overall filter gain and is a constant scalar that is pulled out of the transfer function. The term ζ refers to a "damping factor" in classical analog filter theory, but in musical applications we prefer to replace it with the term Q, which stands for "qualvity factor" where:

$$Q = \frac{1}{2\zeta} \tag{4.31}$$

Second order VA filters can be synthesized from any second order block diagram containing scalar multipliers, summers and integrators. Interestingly, there are many analog block diagrams that produce the same transfer function. Historically, analog filtering theory books categorize and list the pros and cons of using the different structures. Lindquist's "Active Network Design with Signal Filtering Applications" tabulates scores of different filter structures, differential equations and block diagrams. Some of the algorithms are more sensitive to errors in the filter components (the real world, non-ideal values of the R's, L's or C's). Others allow the cutoff frequency or the Q of the filter to be controlled by a single gain factor. In analog filter design, choosing the proper structure usually depends on the application at hand, so there isn't necessarily a universal algorithm that everyone agrees on. However, there is a structure that is especially popular with audio designers called the State Variable Filter or SVF. It is also known as the Kerwin-Huelsman-Newcomb (KHN) filter, after its inventors. One of the interesting features of this filter topology is that it directly implements three of the four mother-filters, the second order LPF, HPF and BPF. The BSF can be calculated by summing the LPF and HPF outputs. Figure 4.19 shows the analog block diagram for the SVF filter that you can find in just about any analog filter theory book. The derivation of the transfer function from input to y_{LP} is done later in the Chapter and produces the standard second order LPF function; you could also start with this function and work your way backwards to this block diagram.

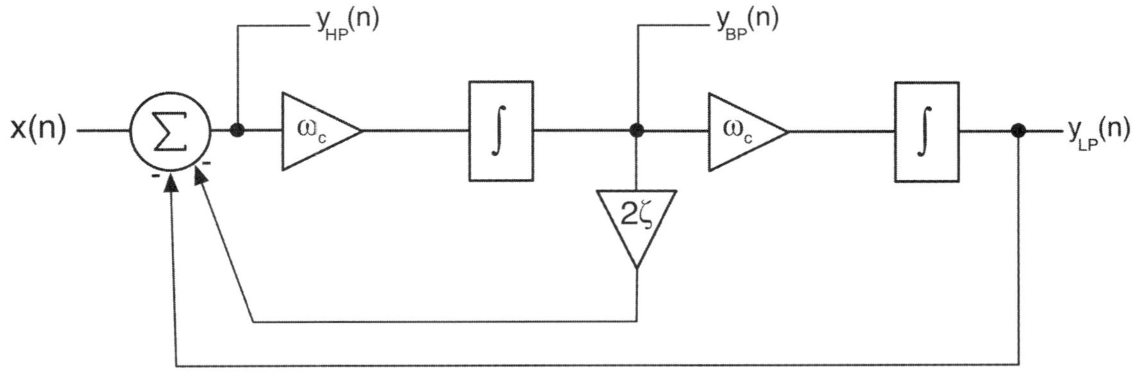

Figure 4.19: Block diagram of the SVF (or KHN filter) with the three outputs labeled.

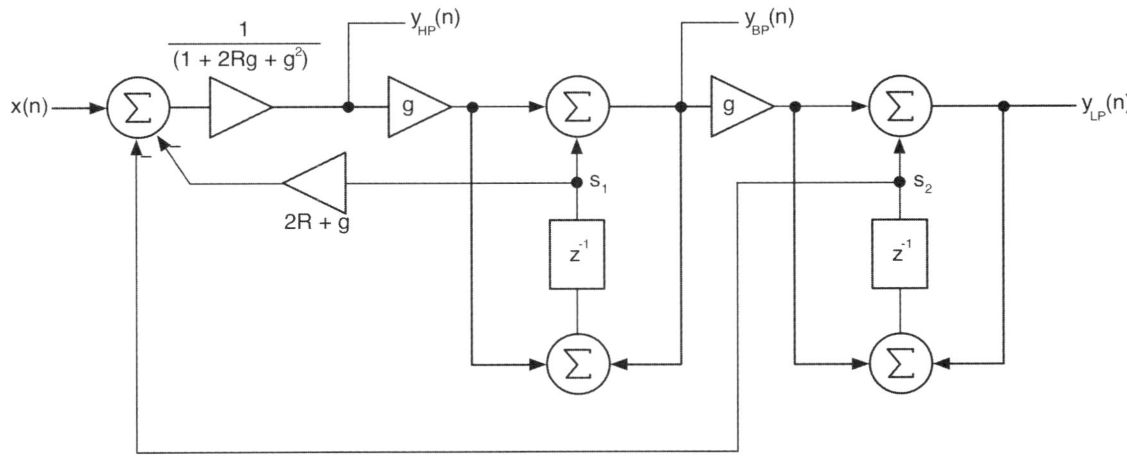

Figure 4.20: The VA SVF.

Zavalishin converts this to virtual analog using the same method as before, replacing the analog integrators with digital trapezoidal versions and resolving the delay-less feedback loops. This results in the VA SVF in Figure 4.20; the loops have been relocated to the outputs of each delay element s_i, and the coefficient c_i for the first delay element is $\rho = 2R+g$, while the coefficient for the second delay output is 1.0.

The input coefficient:

$$\alpha_0 = \frac{1}{1+2Rg+g^2} \tag{4.32}$$

is the result of resolving the loop. The method involves first finding the output y_{HP} that feeds the rest of the structure. The complete derivation is described in Zavalishin (2012). The block diagram in Figure 4.20 makes use of a convention we use in Chapter 7 where the feed-forward coefficient (*G* in the first order LPF and HPF) is replaced by ζ. The design equations are:

$$\begin{aligned}
\omega_d &= 2\pi f_c \\
T &= 1/f_s \\
\omega_a &= \frac{2}{T}\tan\left(\frac{\omega_d T}{2}\right) \\
g &= \frac{\omega_a T}{2} \qquad R = \frac{1}{2Q} \\
\alpha_0 &= \frac{1}{1+2Rg+g^2} \qquad \alpha_1 = \alpha_2 = g \qquad \rho = 2R+g
\end{aligned} \tag{4.32}$$

In this implementation, you first calculate $y_{HP}(n)$ as:

$$y_{HP}(n) = \alpha_0(x(n) - \rho s_1(n) - s_2(n)) \tag{4.33}$$

and use it to feed the rest of the structure. This method of finding the input that feeds the inner loop is one of the ways you can derive the implementation of these VA filters, although you can approach it differently and calculate other outputs or inputs to the sections. For any given structure, there are usually several different implementation approaches, all of which produce the same result. We prefer to use the approach that yields the simplest block diagram with the least number of coefficients and equations.

The bandpass and lowpass outputs are:

$$\begin{aligned} y_{BP}(n) &= \alpha_1 y_{HP}(n) + s_1(n) \\ y_{LP}(n) &= \alpha_1 y_{BP}(n) + s_2(n) \end{aligned} \tag{4.34}$$

We can also generate the missing bandstop filter output by using another filtering shortcut:

$$y_{BS}(n) = x(n) - 2Ry_{BP}(n) \tag{4.35}$$

Each output of this filter produces another VA filter with the instantaneous response equation

$y = Gx + S$. For the highpass output y_{HP}, we can expand the equation out to see this.

$$\begin{aligned} y_{HP}(n) &= \alpha_0\left(x(n) - \rho s_1(n) - s_2(n)\right) \\ &= \frac{x - (2R+g)s_1 - s_2}{1 + 2Rg + g^2} \\ &= Gx + S \\ & \textit{where} \\ G &= \frac{1}{1 + 2Rg + g^2} \\ S &= \frac{-(2R+g)s_1 - s_2}{1 + 2Rg + g^2} \end{aligned} \tag{4.36}$$

The derivations for the LP and BP outputs are left as an exercise for the reader. The answers are:

$$\begin{aligned} y_{LP} &= Gx + S & \qquad y_{BP} &= Gx + S \\ G &= \frac{g^2}{1 + 2Rg + g^2} & G &= \frac{g}{1 + 2Rg + g^2} \\ S &= \frac{-g^2\rho s_1 - g^2 s_2}{1 + 2Rg + g^2} + gs_1 + s_2 & S &= \frac{-g\rho s_1 - gs_2}{1 + 2Rg + g^2} + s_1 \end{aligned} \tag{4.37}$$

Zavalishin's version of the SVF is not the only solution. Simper (2011, 2013) details a completely different derivation and implementation of the SVF using analog circuit analysis with equivalent capacitor current calculations and nodal analysis. Simper also shows optimized solutions for calculating the filter coefficients. See the Bibliography for more details.

4.12 Series and Parallel VA Filters

It is easy to derive the filter equations for the series and parallel VA filters shown in Figure 4.21, and they both end up as $y = Gx + S$ type filters. Once again we only require simple algebra and zero calculus to create the necessary filter equations. In the case of series filters, an intermediate node u is inserted between them and used to calculate the output.

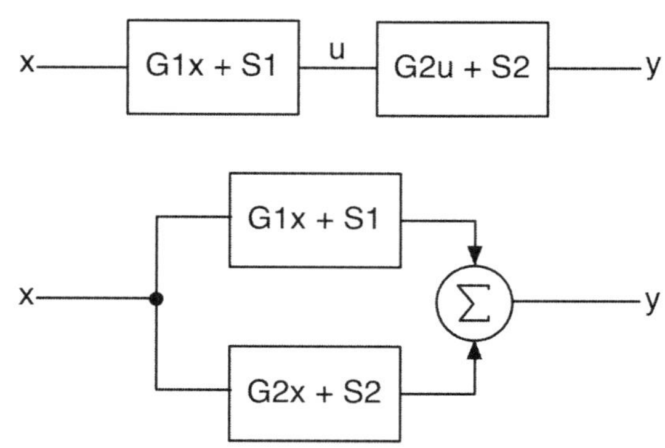

Figure 4.21: Series (top) and parallel (bottom) connections of VA filters.

$$\begin{aligned} &\text{series} & &\text{parallel} \\ u &= G1x + S1 & y &= G1x + S1 + G2x + S2 \\ y &= G2u + S2 & &= (G1 + G2)x + S1 + S2 \\ &= G2(G1x + S1) + S2 & &= Gx + S \\ &= G1G2x + G2S1 + S2 & G &= G1 + G2 \\ &= Gx + S & S &= S1 + S2 \\ G &= G1G2 \\ S &= G2S1 + S2 \end{aligned} \tag{4.38}$$

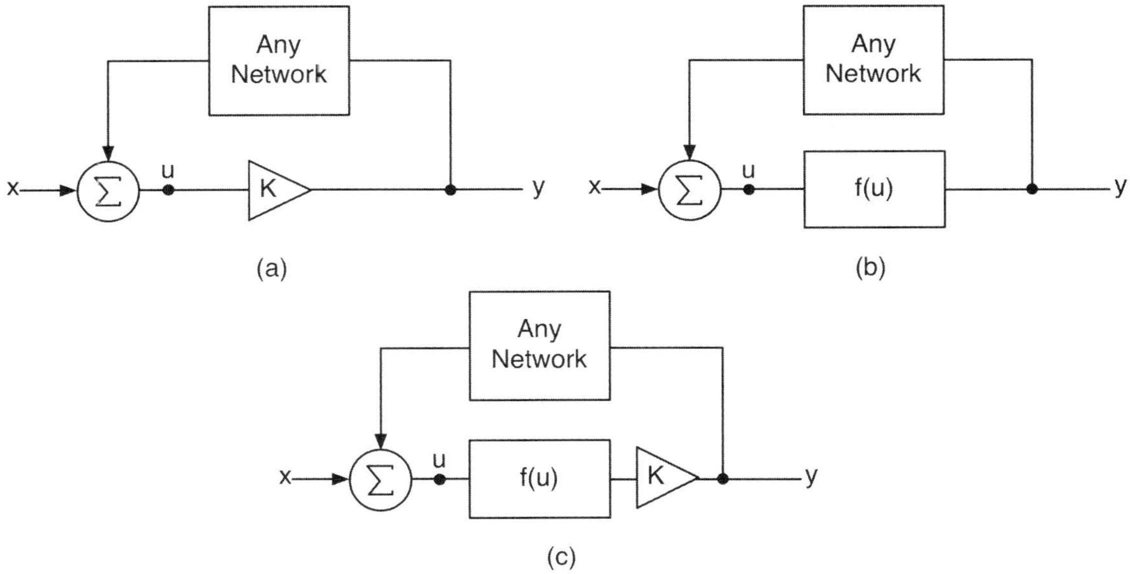

Figure 4.22: Three delay-less feedback networks; (a) the feed-forward path contains a simple multiplier (b) the feed-forward path is processed through some function *f(u)* and (c) the feed-forward path contains both a multiplier and a function block; the block marked Any Network can contain anything that includes at least one (or more) delay-less path.

4.13 Resolving Delay-less Loops: Modified Härmä Method

Next, let's look at some generic examples involving delay-less loops to see how more complex structures can be realized using the Modified Härmä method. With it, you can easily find the filter structure that resolves the delay-less loop. For a single loop filter, the process can be applied swiftly. Recursive filters will take on one of the three forms shown in Figure 4.22. The box marked "Any Network" can be anything from a short, to a simple multiplier, to a complex network that includes at least one delay-less path; it can also contain more than one delay-less path. If there is a processing function in the feed-forward path, it is shown as a generic function of the loop input $f(u)$. Notice that in these generic examples, the variables labeled G and S are likewise generic—they represent any coefficient multiplier.

Härmä describes the technique for the block diagram in Figure 4.22 (a) and with K = 1 so that the feed-forward path is a short circuit. We modify the technique (Pirkle, 2014) to accommodate the other situations where there is something meaningful in the feed-forward path, either a constant gain factor or some function of the loop input u, $f(u)$. You can find the full derivation at http://www.willpirkle.com/synthbook/. This modified method can be applied to any filter in this book and is named the Modified Härmä method. Both the Modified Härmä and Zavalishin methods produce the same results and structures. We often find the Modified Härmä method produces results quicker and with fewer equations than Zavalishin's. Härmä's basic idea is to split the algorithm/block diagram into two parts—one that depends only on previous samples and not the passing value of the current output y, and the other that depends on the input summed with something that does depend on the current output y. These are combined together in an equation that runs the delay-less loop an infinite number of times in a single sample period. With a bit of power series algebra, it reduces down to a very manageable and simple difference equation. The structure is synthesized by inspection of the equation or the value of u the loop input.

For a single loop system, the five-step process is:

1. Disconnect the loop by severing the loop input point at the node u so that the output of the summer and input to the loop are open; then insert 0.0 into the feed-forward path, around the feedback loop, and into the summer, forming a temporary input $u_o(n)$. This includes any processing that occurred in the loop.
2. This step is modified to accommodate processing in the feed-forward path. If there is nothing except a short in the feed-forward path, then $y_o(n) = u_o(n)$ and the normal Härmä method is used. If there is only a gain constant K in the forward path, then $y_o(n) = Ku_o(n)$. However, if there is processing that includes past samples in the forward path, then you form the temporary output $y_p(n)$ by processing $u_o(n)$ through the filter (or series or parallel filters). If the filters use only the linear difference equations, then $y_p(n)$ will have two components: $y_o(n)$ is the part that depends only on the loop input $u_o(n)$ and $y_s(n)$ is the part that depends only on the past samples so $y_p(n) = y_o(n) + y_s(n)$.
3. Find the overall loop gain coefficient X by creating a delay-free structure that is the original filter structure with all delay elements removed/disconnected and apply an input of 1.0 into the loop with the filter input disconnected; the gain elements are then multiplied together.

4. The final difference equation is found with Equation 4.39, and it reveals the modified structure by inspection; remember that each delay-less loop will always be relocated to the output of one or more delay elements in the overall filter structure.

$$y(n) = \frac{y_o(n)}{1-X} + y_s(n) \tag{4.39}$$

5. When implementing the filter, we would like to also solve for $u(n)$, the loop input value. We can then push that value through the processing blocks. This value will also help derive the final structure.

The best way to explain this method is by example. After just a bit of practice, you will be impressed at the speed with which you can synthesize these structures. Figure 4.23 shows the first example.

Step 1:

Break the feedback loop at node u and drive it with 0.0 input as shown in Figure 4.24 (a), then find the temporary value u_o. The output of the loop is S after injecting the 0.0 value though it. So the temporary input u_o is:

$$u_o(n) = x(n) + S(n) \tag{4.40}$$

Step 2:

Process u_o through the feed-forward path to find the temporary output y_o and y_s as shown in Figure 4.24 (b); here $y_s = 0$ as there is no storage component in the feed-forward path.

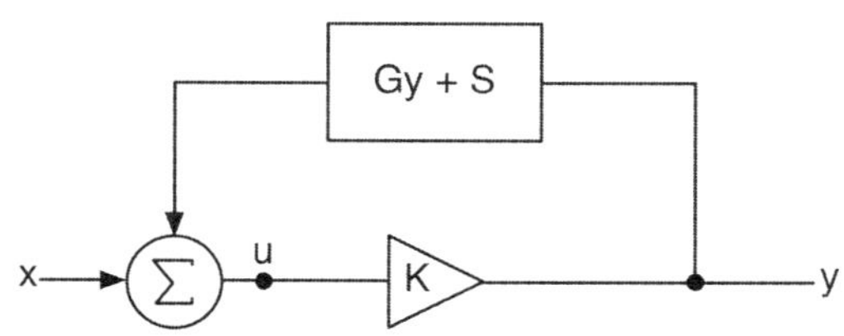

Figure 4.23: Generic structure with a filter in the feedback path of a delay-less loop.

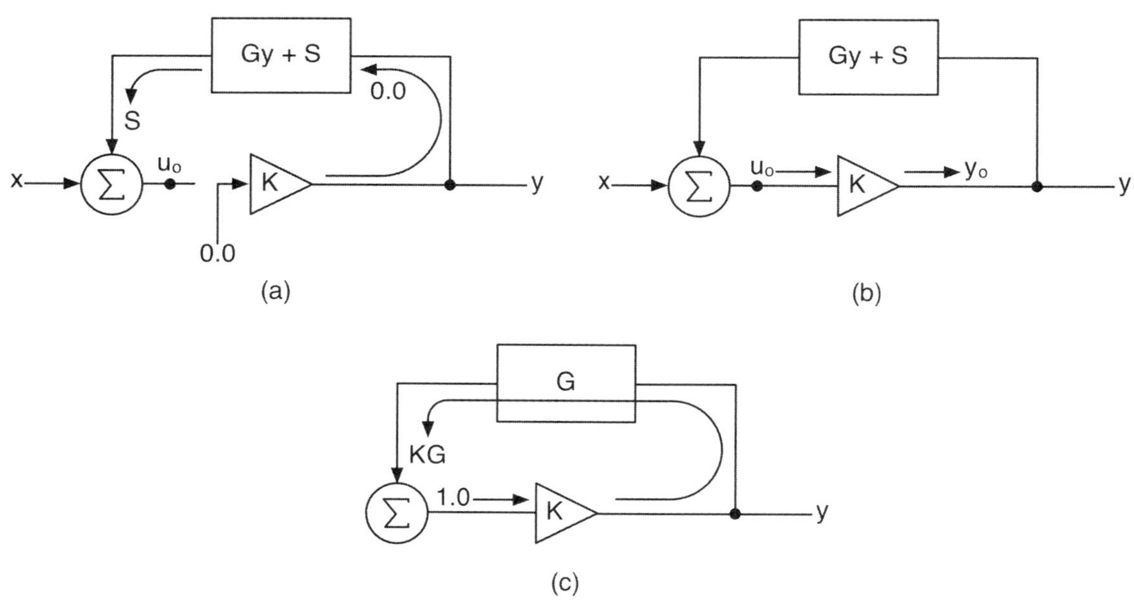

Figure 4.24: (a) Break the loop and find the disconnected loop output. (b) Apply the temporary (disconnected) input u_o through the feed-forward path to form the output y_o. (c) Find the loop gain by removing all delay elements from the structure and applying 1.0 into the loop with input disconnected. Note: The discrete time variable n has been removed for ease of reading.

$$\begin{aligned} y_P(n) &= y_o(n) + y_s(n) \\ y_o(n) &= Ku_o(n) \\ y_s(n) &= 0 \end{aligned} \tag{4.41}$$

Step 3:

Find the overall loop gain by removing the delay elements from the filter and applying a value of 1.0 to the input of the loop. If we remove the delay element from our filter, there will be no *S* component since it's output depends on the output of the delay. The filter will still have a gain *G*, however. So, the overall loop gain as shown in Figure 4.24 (c) is:

$$X = KG \tag{4.42}$$

Step 4:

Find the difference equation using Equation 4.39, and from that you can synthesize the block diagram by inspection. Since it is a set of products, the components will commute and can be reordered as shown in Equation 4.43.

$$\begin{aligned} y(n) &= \frac{y_o(n)}{1-X} + y_s(n) \\ &= \frac{K(x(n)+S(n))}{1-KG} + 0 \\ &\textit{reordering:} \\ y(n) &= K\left[\frac{x(n)+S(n)}{1-KG}\right] \end{aligned} \tag{4.43}$$

Step 5:

Find *u(n)* for filter implementation. Referring to the block diagram, you can see that the loop input value *u(n)* is the sum of the input *x(n)* and $y_P(n)$ processed through the feedback filter.

$$\begin{aligned} & u(n) = x(n) + Gy_P(n) + S(n) \\ & \textit{and} \\ & y_P(n) = Ku(n) \\ & \textit{so} \\ & u(n) = x(n) + GKu(n) + S \\ & u(n) = \frac{x(n)+S}{1-KG} \end{aligned} \tag{4.44}$$

Trace through the Figure 4.25 to prove to yourself that it implements the difference equation correctly. During implementation, we would combine the two coefficients in the feed-forward path as *K/(1 – KG)*; they are separated here only to show how the original structure is modified.

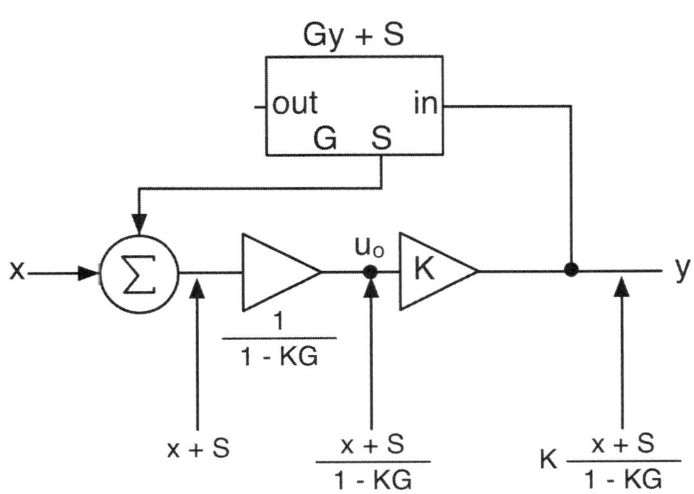

Figure 4.25: The modified filter structure that resolves the delay-less loop.

Let's try another generic feedback filter shown in Figure 4.26 (a). In this case, the filtering component is in the feed-forward path, and we only have a constant value K in the feedback path (note this could be a value of $K = -1$ to indicate subtraction via the summer). We will move more quickly this time.

Step 1:

Disconnecting the loop and injecting 0.0 into the feed-forward path produces a feedback output value of $KS(n)$ as shown in Figure 4.26(b) and a temporary loop input value:

$$u_0(n) = x(n) + KS(n) \tag{4.45}$$

Step 2:

Find the temporary output by processing the temporary input through the filter in the feed-forward path:

$$\begin{aligned} y_P(n) &= Gu_o(n) + S(n) \\ &= y_o(n) + y_s(n) \\ y_o(n) &= Gu_o(n) \\ y_s(n) &= S(n) \end{aligned} \tag{4.46}$$

Step 3:

Find the loop gain by removing all delay elements from the original structure and tracing through the loop shown in Figure 4.26(c):

$$X = KG \tag{4.47}$$

Step 4:

Find the final difference equation and block diagram using Equation 4.39. Figure 4.26(d) shows the modified structure with delay-less loops resolved. Trace through the block diagram to show that it does indeed implement Equation 4.48.

$$\begin{aligned} y(n) &= \frac{y_o(n)}{1-X} + y_s(n) \\ &= \frac{G(x(n) + KS(n))}{1-KG} + S(n) \end{aligned} \tag{4.48}$$

Step 5:

Find $u(n)$ for filter implementation. Referring to the block diagram, you can see that the loop input value $u(n)$ is the sum of the input $x(n)$ and $y_P(n)$.

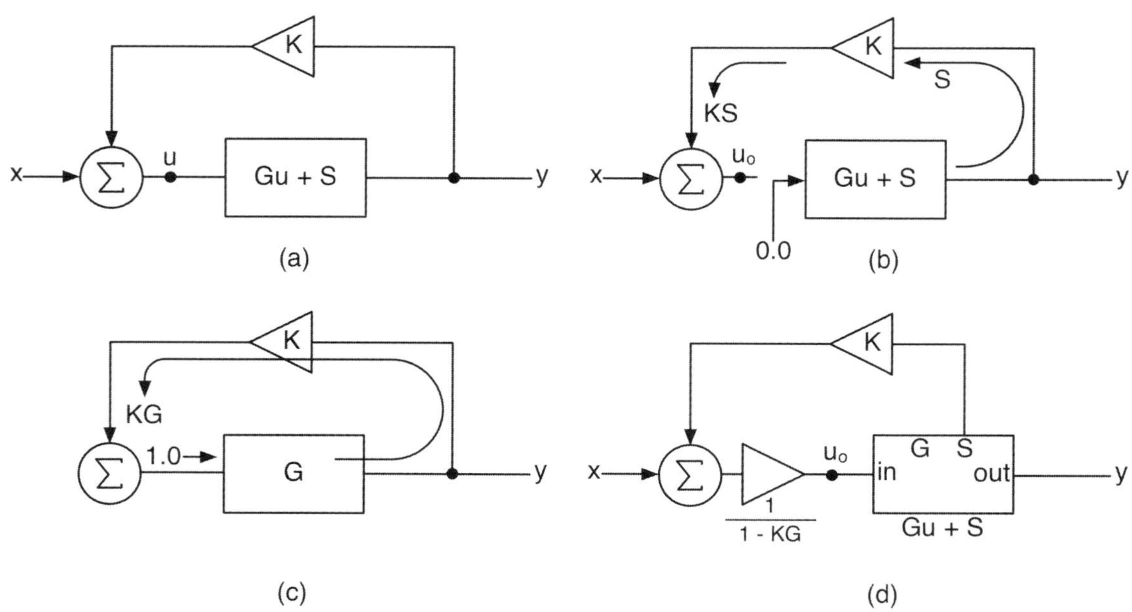

Figure 4.26: (a) Generic structure with a filter in the feed-forward path of a delay-less loop. (b) Breaking the loop to extract the temporary feedback value and calculate u_o. (c) Finding the loop gain X by removing the delay elements. (d) The final algorithm with delay-less loop resolved.

$$\begin{aligned}
&u(n) = x(n) + Ky_P(n)\\
&and\\
&y_P(n) = Gu(n) + S(n)\\
&so\\
&u(n) = x(n) + K(Gu(n) + S(n))\\
&u(n) = \frac{x(n) + KS(n)}{1 - KG}
\end{aligned} \tag{4.49}$$

As a final example, let's use the Modified Härmä method to resolve the delay-less loop in the original VA lowpass filter in Figure 4.27(a). The feedback loop has been modified to be additive but with a constant scalar of −1.0 to implement the subtraction. This forces it to match the topology in Figure 4.22.

Step 1:

Disconnecting the loop and injecting 0.0 into the feed-forward path (i.e. $u = 0$) produces a feedback output value of $-s(n)$ as shown in Figure 4.27(b) and a temporary loop input value:

$$u_0(n) = x(n) - s(n) \tag{4.50}$$

Step 2:

Find the temporary output by processing the temporary input through the filter in the feed-forward path:

$$\begin{aligned}
y_P(n) &= gu_o(n) + s(n)\\
&= y_o(n) + y_s(n)\\
y_o(n) &= gu_o(n)\\
y_s(n) &= s(n)
\end{aligned} \tag{4.51}$$

Step 3:

Find the loop gain by removing all delay elements from the original structure, disconnecting the input x and tracing through the loop shown in Figure 4.27(c):

$$X = -g \tag{4.52}$$

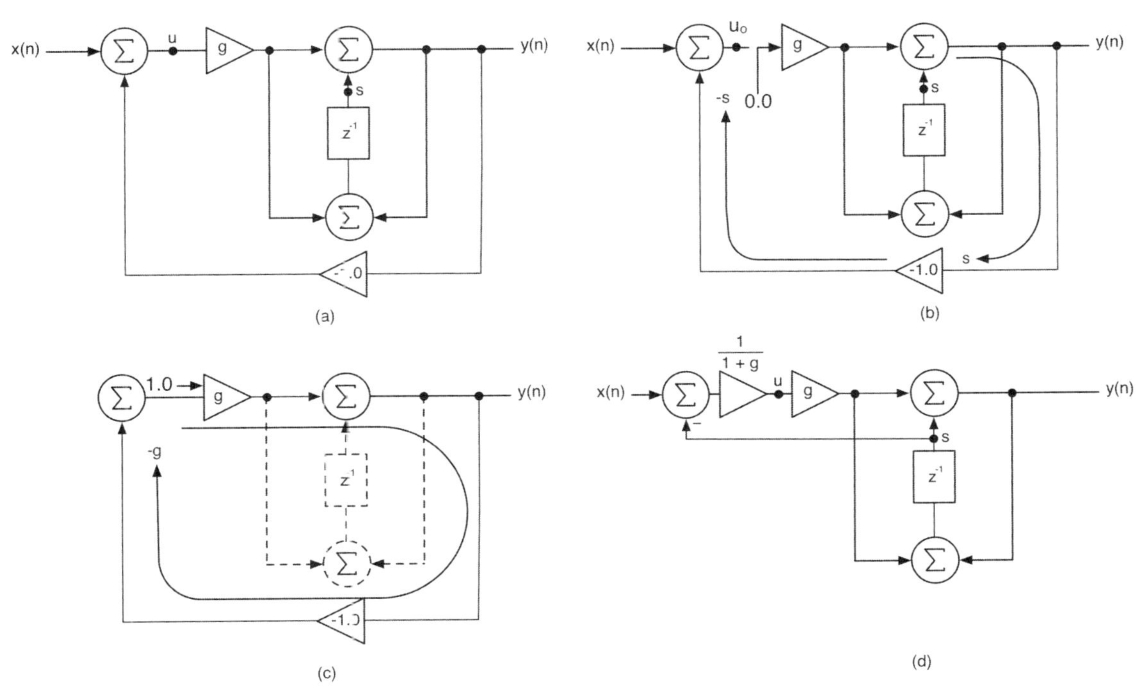

Figure 4.27: (a) The original VA lowpass filter structure. (b) Breaking the loop to extract the temporary feedback value ($-s(n)$) and calculate u_o. (c) Finding the loop gain X. (d) The final algorithm with delay-less loop resolved.

Step 4:

Find the final difference equation and block diagram using Equation 4.39. Figure 4.27(d) shows the modified structure with delay-less loops resolved. Trace through the block diagram to show that it does indeed implement Equation 4.53.

$$\begin{aligned} y(n) &= \frac{y_o(n)}{1-X} + y_s(n) \\ &= \frac{g(x(n)-s(n))}{1+g} + s(n) \end{aligned} \tag{4.53}$$

Step 5:

Find $u(n)$ for filter implementation. Referring to the block diagram you can see that the loop input value $u(n)$ is the sum of the input $x(n)$ and $y_P(n)$. The result in Figure 4.27(d) shows the two gain blocks separated so you can see the location of $u(n)$; in practice the two blocks are combined as g/(1 + g).

$$\begin{aligned} &u(n) = x(n) + y_P(n) \\ &\textit{and} \\ &y_P(n) = gu(n) + s(n) \\ &\textit{so} \\ &u(n) = \frac{x(n)+s(n)}{1+g} \end{aligned} \tag{4.54}$$

4.14 Resolving Delay-Less Loops: Zavalishin's Method

When working with Zavalishin's method, you can either solve for the output y directly or solve for u, the input to the loop. In either case, you synthesize the filter structure by examining the resulting equations in exactly the same manner as in the Modified Härmä method—by inspection. Zavalishin's method is more of an algebraic approach. You may or may not find it easier than the Modified Härmä method.

> In this first example it is trivial to solve for u, but as the filters become more complex, solving for u usually leads to a less complicated realization than solving for the output y. For the rest of the filters in the book, we'll be solving for this input value not only to synthesize the block diagram but also to facilitate the coding. You can also cross-check your work using the Modified Härmä method to find both loop input u and output y.

Figure 4.28 shows a VA filter in the same loop configuration as the first example, this time with internal node y_1 identified. In Zavalishin's method, you can drop the discrete time variable n using instead the instantaneous equations.

First, let's solve for the output y directly. This equation shows that this filter-in-a-loop is yet another $y = Gx + S$ filter (we won't use these G_1 and S_1 variables directly here; they just show the recurring $y = Gx + S$ theme).

$$\begin{aligned} y_1 &= Gy + S \\ y &= K(x + y_1) \\ &= Kx + KGy + KS \\ y - KGy &= Kx + KS \\ y &= \frac{Kx+KS}{1-KG} \\ &\textit{or}: \\ y &= G_1x + S_1 \qquad G_1 = \frac{K}{1-KG} \qquad S_1 = \frac{KS}{1-KG} \\ &\textit{Note}: \text{Modified Härmä Method produces the same result (discrete time variable included)} \\ y(n) &= \frac{K(x(n)+S(n))}{1-KG} \end{aligned} \tag{4.55}$$

Now let's solve for u and reveal the structure in Figure 4.29. Like the difference equation above, it is identical to the one we derived with the Modified Härmä method. Again, make sure you can trace through the filter and prove that the structure implements the equations.

$$\begin{aligned} y = Ku \quad y_1 &= Gy + S \quad u = x + y_1 \\ u &= x + Gy + S \\ &= x + KGu + S \\ &= \frac{x+S}{1-KG} \end{aligned} \tag{4.56}$$

This example uses positive feedback (yes, we will also use positive feedback in a couple of designs). For Negative FeedBack (NFB), it is easy to show that the signs simply swap in the numerator and denominator:

$$u_{NFB} = \frac{x - S}{1 + KG} \tag{4.57}$$

Next, examine the structure with a filter in the feed-forward path and gain K in the feedback path, shown in Figure 4.30.

Using the same process, you can easily find that the Positive FeedBack (PFB) and NFB versions yield:

$$u_{PFB} = \frac{x + KS}{1 - KG} \qquad u_{NFB} = \frac{x - KS}{1 + KG} \tag{4.58}$$

The PFB version is shown diagrammatically in Figure 4.31, which also reveals how the loop delay is operating.

The last case involves filters and gain components in both the feed-forward and feedback paths shown in Figure 4.32. The equations for both PFB and NFB versions are:

$$u_{PFF} = \frac{x + K_1K_2G_2S_1 + K_2S_2}{1 - K_1K_2G_1G_2} \qquad u_{NFB} = \frac{x - K_1K_2G_2S_1 - K_2S_2}{1 + K_1K_2G_1G_2} \tag{4.59}$$

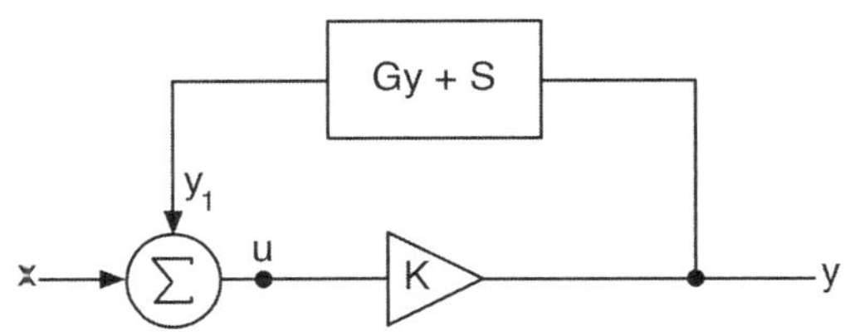

Figure 4.28: A VA filter in the delay-less loop.

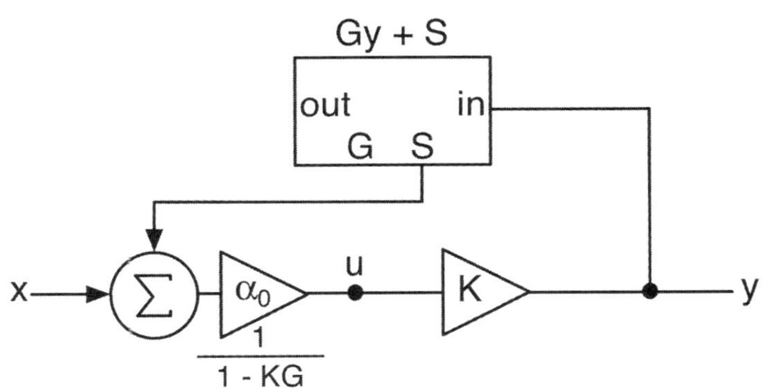

Figure 4.29: Solving for *u* reveals this structure.

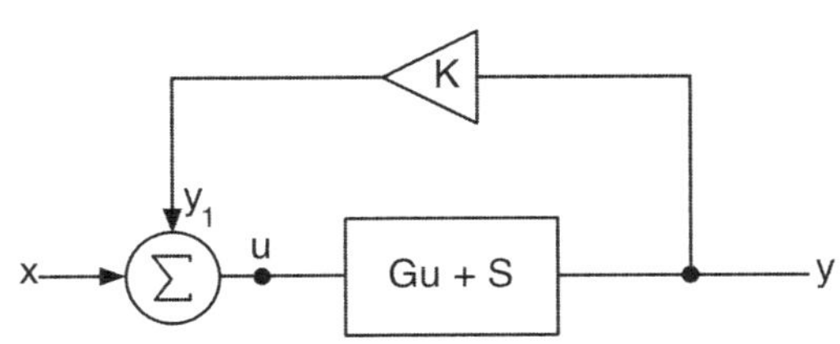

Figure 4.30: Another delay-less loop example with feed-forward filter and feedback gain.

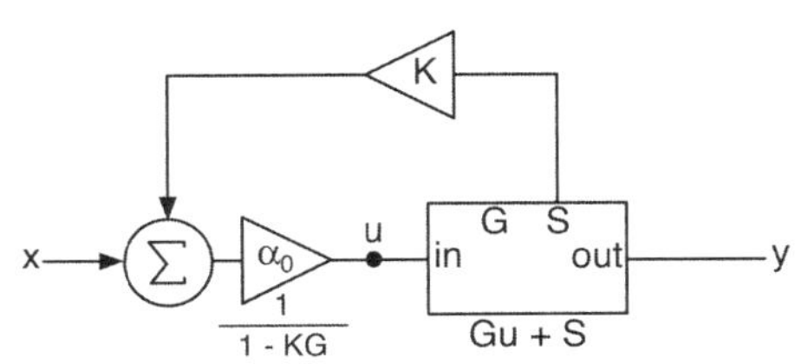

Figure 4.31: The PFB feed-forward filter with loop gain K.

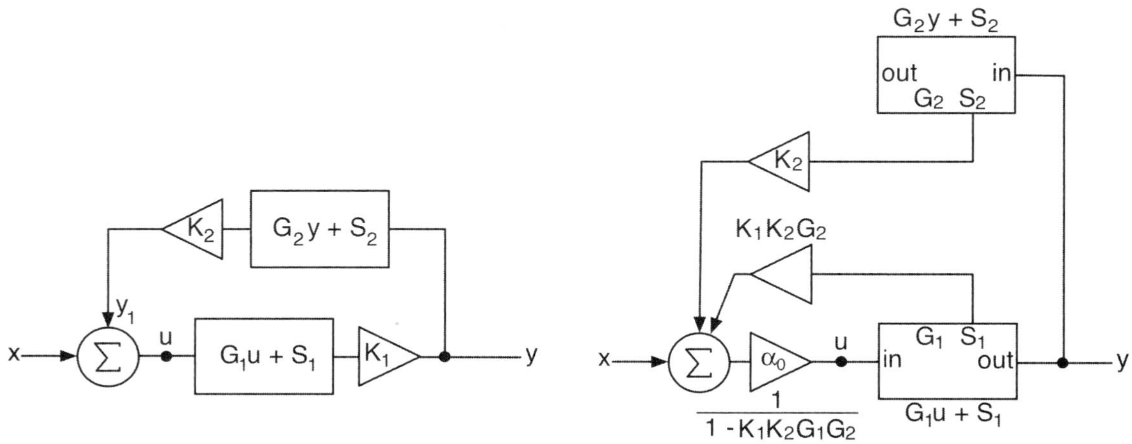

Figure 4.32: Filters and gain factors all around for this PFB filter.

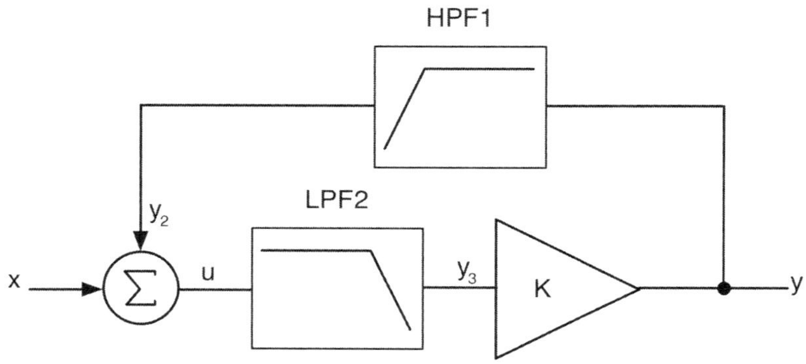

Figure 4.33: A piece of a more complex filter to examine.

In Chapter 7, we will implement a filter that has a PFB delay-less loop with filters in both feed-forward and feedback paths shown in Figure 4.33. The gain factor K_2 is 1.0. There is a LPF in the forward branch and a HPF in the reverse branch. Both filters are first order. In this filter, the LPF and HPF have the same cutoff frequency f_c; therefore they have the same G value, which is based solely on cutoff frequency. In the equations, they will share the same G but will each have their own S values, *S3* for LPF2 and *S2* for HPF1. The reason for indexing them as such will become evident in Chapter 7, where there are other filtering blocks in the complete structure.

Let's derive the equation for u, the input to LPF2. You can see that the final output of the filter y is:

$$y = Ky_3 \tag{4.60}$$

First, define the filter equations for each component:

$$\begin{aligned} &\text{HPF1} && \text{LPF2} \\ y_2 &= y-(Gy+S2) & y_3 &= Gu+S3 \\ &= y-Gy-S2 & S3 &= \frac{s_3}{1+g} \\ S2 &= \frac{s_2}{1+g} \end{aligned} \tag{4.61}$$

Now form u:

$$\begin{aligned} y &= K(Gu+S3) \\ y_2 &= y-Gy-S2 \\ u &= x+y_2 \\ &= x+y-Gy-S2 \\ &= x+KGu+KS3-G(KGu+KS3)-S2 \\ &= \frac{x-S2+S3(K-KG)}{1-KG+KG^2} \end{aligned} \tag{4.62}$$

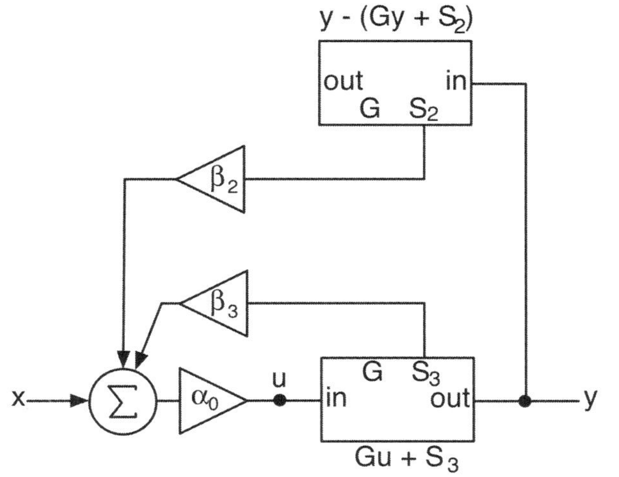

Figure 4.34: The realization of the filter in Figure 4.33 with delay-less loops resolved.

Let α_0 be a scaling factor:

$$\begin{aligned}
&\alpha_0 = \frac{1}{1 - KG + KG^2} \\
&\text{then:} \\
&u = \alpha_0 (x - S2 + S3(K - KG)) \\
&\text{define:} \\
&\qquad S2 = \beta_2 s_2 \qquad S3 = \beta_3 s_3 \qquad \beta_2 = \frac{-1}{1+g} \qquad \beta_3 = \frac{K - KG}{1+g} \\
&\text{then:} \\
&u = a_0 (x + \beta_2 s_2 + \beta_3 s_3)
\end{aligned} \tag{4.63}$$

By using these β coefficients, we can alter the structure of the VA filter to incorporate a feedback output port that will simplify processing in the filter. This is covered in Chapter 7. The final structure is shown in Figure 4.34. Once again, verify that the value of the input *u* is correct by tracing through the filter. Use the Modified Härmä method and Equation 4.39 to verify the results.

4.15 Analog Signal Flow Graphs

We saw examples of analog signal flow diagrams in the beginning of the chapter. Another kind of signal flow diagram exists called a signal flow graph. It graphically describes filters in feed-forward and feedback paths connected together with nodes. The transfer functions of each filter component are labeled T_{NM}, where N is the input node and M is the output, so T_{13} would be the transmission from node 1 to node 3. In our last example shown in Figure 4.33, we had a LPF in the feed-forward path and an HPF in the feedback path. The signal flow graph for this filter is shown in Figure 4.35. Notice the way the nodes are numbered; the input is always node 1, the output is node 2 and the rest of the nodes are serialized in the loop starting with node 3.

Typically, the labels LPF1 and HPF1 (which stand for first order LPF and HPF) are left out of the diagram; it is up to the reader to recognize the T values; after some practice this is relatively easy. Mason's gain equation lets you write the analog transfer function of the system straight off the graph.

For this simple graph:

$$H(s) = \frac{KT_{34}}{1 - KT_{34}T_{53}} \tag{4.64}$$

For this kind of simple block diagram/signal flow, Mason's gain equation rules are:

- the numerator is the product of all feed-forward transmissions (a.k.a. feed-forward gains)
- the denominator is [1 – (sum of all loop transmissions (a.k.a. loop gains) taken one at a time)], which is done by tracing through each loop and multiplying the transmissions. This is similar but not identical to step three of the Modified Härmä method

Notice that the loop gains include any forward transmission in the loop, thus the loop gain of the single feedback loop in Figure 4.35 is T_{34} (forward) times T_{53} (reverse). In more complex Signal Flow Graphs, both numerator and denominator are augmented with more factors. A complete analysis is beyond the scope of this book but may be found in any good analog filtering book such as (Lindquist,

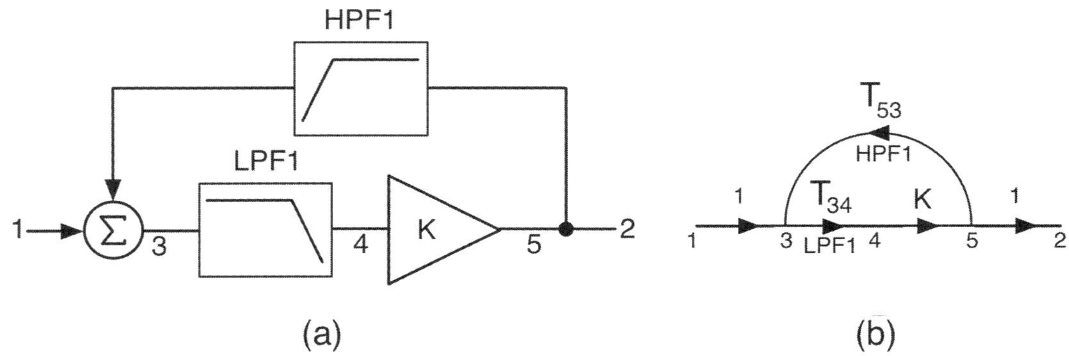

Figure 4.35: (a) The filter in Figure 4.33 with nodes renumbered and (b) the resulting signal flow graph.

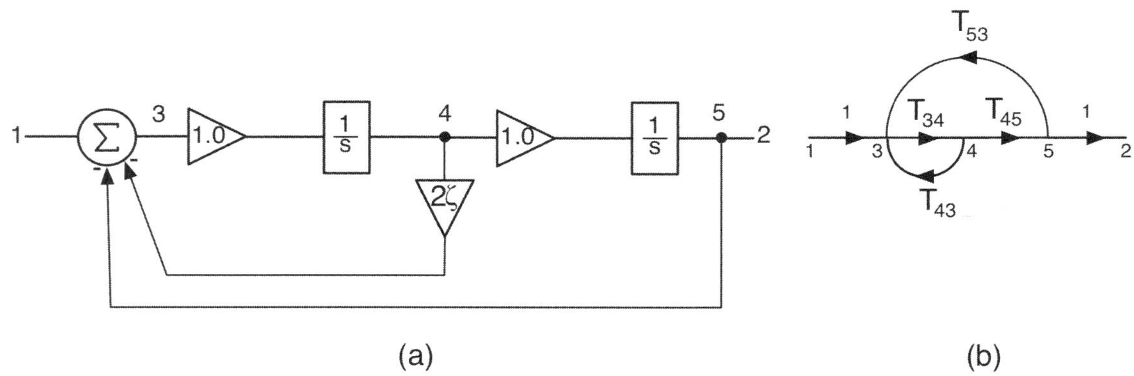

Figure 4.36: (a) The state variable filter with nodes renumbered and (b) the resulting Signal Flow Graph.

1977). We will use these Signal Flow Graph as a visual aid when discussing block diagrams in Chapter 7, but you won't need to solve any of these equations; they are here only to show that analog filters may be described and solved in this manner rather than using the analog block diagrams. In fact, you can convert any analog signal flow graph directly into a virtual analog filter using this method. As an example, let's analyze another simple signal flow graph from the analog state variable filter shown in Figure 4.36(a). The signal flow graph is shown in Figure 4.36(b). For simplicity, we will let $\omega_c = 1$ and get the normalized transfer function.

From the state variable filter figure, you can read directly that the normalized transmissions (or transfer functions) between nodes are:

$$\begin{aligned} T_{34} &= T_{45} = \frac{1}{s} \\ T_{43} &= -2\zeta \\ T_{53} &= -1 \end{aligned} \tag{4.65}$$

Then using Mason's Equation we can derive the transfer function as:

$$\begin{aligned} H(s) &= \frac{T_{34}T_{45}}{1-(T_{34}T_{43}+T_{34}T_{45}T_{53})} \\ &= \frac{\frac{1}{s^2}}{1-\left(\frac{-2\zeta}{s}-\frac{1}{s^2}\right)} \\ &= \frac{1}{s^2+2\zeta s+1} \end{aligned} \tag{4.66}$$

4.16 Wave Shaping

Wave shaping uses a non-linear function to process and purposefully distort an input signal. We will use it in Chapter 5 to change the shape of an oscillator's output. All of the filters in Chapter 7 have a NonLinear Processing (NLP) block that may be enabled. This saturates the signal with a soft clipping function. In several of the filter models, the clipping comes from diodes found in the original analog circuits. In others, it is built into the analog circuit equations, specifically as the hyperbolic tangent function, *tanh()*. There are

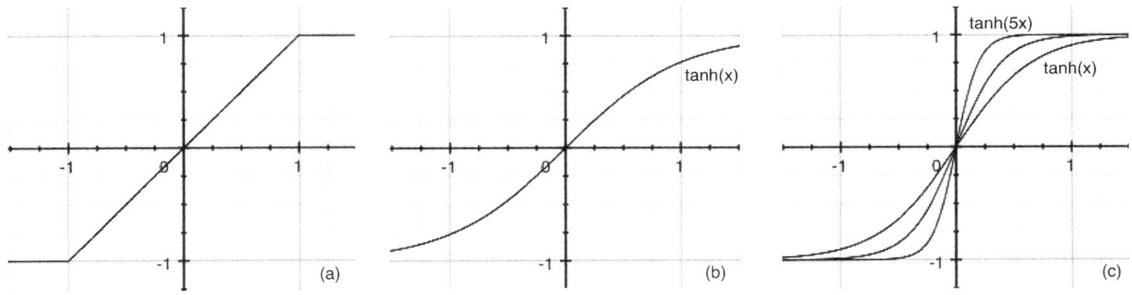

Figure 4.37: (a) Perfectly linear and (b) *tanh()* amplitude transfer functions and (c) *tanh(kx)* with k = 1, 2.5 and 5.

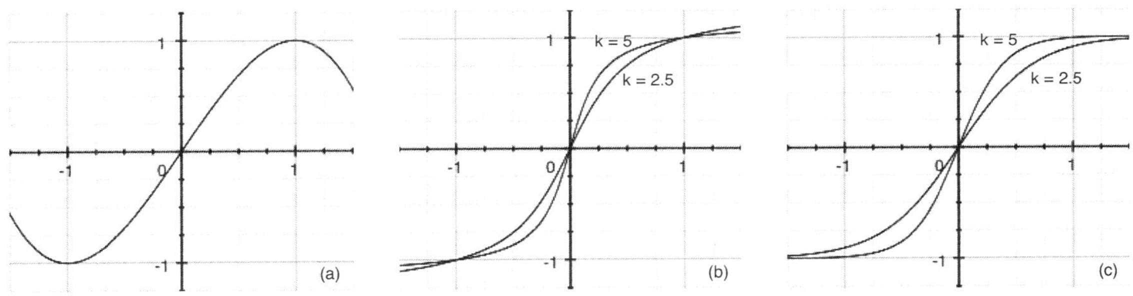

Figure 4.38: (a) Arraya and Suyama (b) *arctan()* and (c) sigmoid-exponential wave shaping functions with various values of the saturation variable *k*.

many wave shaping functions to choose from. Some produce more harmonic distortion than others. We will be specifically focusing on soft-clipping wave shapers, which produce less distortion and attempt to limit the signal in a way that is still pleasing to the ear. Figure 4.37(a) shows a perfectly linear amplitude transfer function (ATF) and the ATF of the hyperbolic tangent function. In these graphs, the x-axis represents the input signal and the y-axis is the output signal. The range of values we can use is -1 to $+1$ on both axes. In the perfectly linear function, the output always equals the input from -1 to $+1$ and is then clamped at these extremes outside these bounds. The *tanh()* function in Figure 4.37(b) saturates the signal, clipping it at about $+/-0.8$ for an input signal from -1 to $+1$.

The limiting of the signal to about $+/-0.8$ only roughly corresponds to the way diode clippers work. They saturate (or limit) the signal to a smaller range than the actual total operating range of the circuit, but the shape of the transfer function curve depends on the diode's material construction. In Figure 4.38(c) you can see that amplifying the input x prior to the *tanh()* function can produce outputs that are on the range of -1 to $+1$ and also adds gain and thus more harmonic distortion. In the projects that use NLP, we refer to this amplifying value as the saturation control. You can experiment with a more efficient numerical approximation to *tanh()* called *fasttanh()*, available in *synthfunctions.h*.

> The problem with nonlinear wave shaping is that it will always cause aliasing in the signal. If the nonlinearity is small, this might not be a problem. However if the saturation variable is increased, or a more nonlinear function is used, the aliasing components will begin to stand out. The way to mitigate this aliasing is with oversampling techniques.

Figure 4.38 shows some more wave shaping functions you can experiment with. Figure 4.38(a) is an algorithm that Yamaha's Araya and Suyama patented in 1996 for the purposes of generating tube-like distortion algorithms. On the range of -1 to $+1$ it produces a very soft clip. Figure 4.38(b) shows a normalized *arctan()* wave shaper while (c) shows an exponential sigmoid function. The equations for these NLP functions are:

$$\text{Arraya} \quad y=\frac{3x}{2}\left(1-\frac{x^2}{3}\right) \qquad \text{arctan} \quad y=\frac{\arctan(kx)}{\arctan(k)} \qquad \text{sigmoid} \quad y=2\frac{1}{1+e^{-kx}}-1 \tag{4.67}$$

> For simplicity's sake, all of the non-linear processing blocks in our synthesizers use the *tanh()* function. In some cases, this is warranted as the nonlinearity results from a hyperbolic tangent function in the filter equations. In other cases involving diode-based distortion, other wave shapers may yield more accurate results. Of course you are encouraged to experiment with all of the wave shapers in your projects.

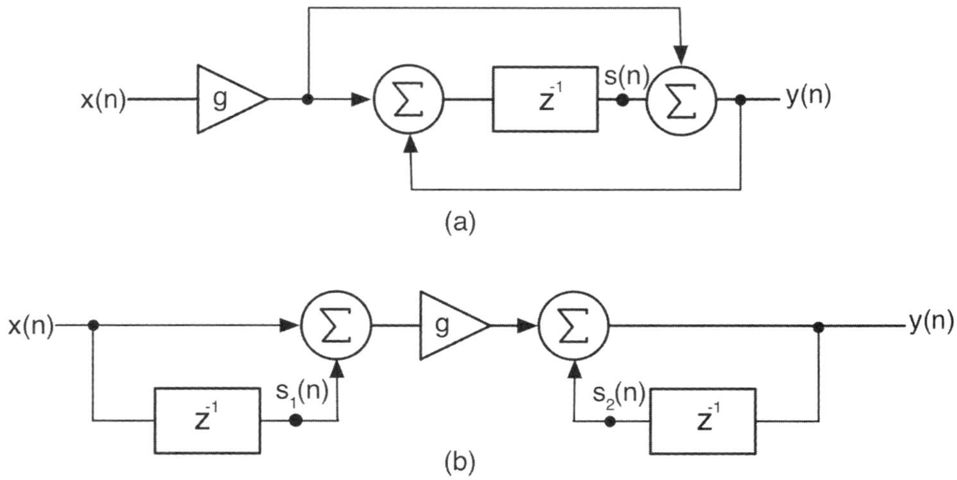

Figure 4.39: (a) and (b) two alternate versions of the bilinear integrator.

4.17 Challenges

Bronze

Derive the equation for y_{HP} for the VA state variable filter.

Sliver

Derive the equations for y_{LP} and y_{BP} for the VA state variable filter.

Gold

Use signal flow graphing and Mason's Gain Equation to verify that the input/output relationship of the three filters-in-feedback-loops (Figures 4.29, 4.31 and 4.33) all produce the relationship $y = Gx + S$.

Platinum

Use the Modified Härmä method to resolve the delay-free loop in Figure 4.33.

Diamond

Two alternate versions of the bilinear integrator are shown in Figure 4.39. Replace the bilinear integrator in the VA lowpass filter with each of these and use the Modified Härmä method to derive the resulting modified structures with delay-less loops resolved. Hint: formulate the difference equations of the integrators using the s node values.

Bibliography

Avanzini, Frederico, Fontana, Frederico and Rocchesso, Davide. 2000. "Computation of Nonlinear Filter Networks Containing Delay Free Paths." *Proceedings from the Seventh International Conference on Digital Audio Effects.*

Borin, Gianpaolo, De Poli, Giovanni and Rocchesso, Davide. 2000. "Estimation of Delay Free Loops in Discrete-Time Models of Nonlinear Acoustic Systems." *IEEE Transactions on Speech and Signal Processing*, vol. 23, pp. 558–562.

Bruton, Len. 1975. "Low-Sensitivity Digital Ladder Filters." *IEEE Transactions on Circuits and Systems*, vol. CAS-22, no. 3, pp. 168–176.

Dodge, Charles and Jerse, Thomas. 1997. *Computer Music Synthesis: Composition and Performance*, Chap. 6. New York: Schirmer.

El-Masry, Ezz. 1979. "Low-Sensitivity Digital Ladder Networks," *Proceedings from the 13th Asilomar Conference on Circuits, Systems, and Computers*, pp. 273–278. Pacific Grove, California.

Fettweis, Alfred. 1971. "Some Principles on Designing Digital Filters Imitating Classical Filter Networks." *IEEE Transactions on Circuit Theory*, vol. CT-18, pp. 314–316.

Härmä, Aki. 1998. "Implementation of Recursive Filters Having Delay Free Loops." *Proceedings from the 1998 IEEE International Conference on Acoustics, Speech and Signal Processing*, vol. 3, pp. 1261–1264.

Lindquist, Claude. 1977. *Active Network Design with Signal Filtering Applications*, pp. 61–69. Long Beach: Steward and Sons.

Lindquist, Claude. 1989. *Adaptive and Digital Signal Processing*, pp. 804–808. Long Beach: Steward and Sons.

Pakarinen, Jyri, and Yeh, David. 2009. "A Review of Digital Techniques for Modeling Vacuum-Tube Guitar Amplifiers." *The Computer Music Journal*, vol. 33, no. 2, pp. 85–100. Cambridge: MIT Press.

Pirkle, Will. 2014. "Resolving Delay-Free Loops in Recursive Filters Using the Modified Härmä Method." Presented at the 136th Audio Engineering Society Convention. Los Angeles.

Simper, Andrew. 2011. "Linear Trapezoid Integrated State Variable Filter with Low Noise Optimization." Accessed June 2014, http://cytomic.com/files/dsp/SvfLinearTrapOptimised.pdf

Simper, Andrew. 2013. "Solving the Continuous SVF Equations using Trapezoidal Integration and Equivalent Currents." Accessed June 2014, http://cytomic.com/files/dsp/SvfLinearTrapOptimised2.pdf

Szczupak, Jaques and Mitra, Sanjit. 1975. "Detection, Location, and Removal of Delay-Free Loops in Digital Filter Configurations." *IEEE Transactions on Acoustics, Speech and Signal Processing*, vol. 23, pp. 558–562.

Välimäki, Vesa and Huovilainen, Antti. 2006. "Oscillator and Filter Algorithms for Virtual Analog Synthesis." *Computer Music Journal*, vol. 30, no. 2, pp 19–31. Cambridge: MIT Press.

Wanhammar, Lars. 2009. *Analog Filters Using MATLAB*. Heidelberg: Springer.

Zavalishin, Vadim. 2008. *Preserving the LTI System Topology in s- to z-Plane Transforms*. Accessed June 2014, http://www.native-instruments.com/fileadmin/ni_media/downloads/pdf/KeepTopology.pdf

Zavalishin, Vadim. 2012. *The Art of VA Filter Design*. Accessed June 2014, http://www.native-instruments.com/fileadmin/ni_media/downloads/pdf/VAFilterDesign_1.0.3.pdf

CHAPTER 5

Synthesizer Oscillator Design

Oscillators are the components that will render pitched notes or act as controllers. In this chapter we will discuss and design the oscillator objects we will use in the synthesizers in Chapters 8–12. We need a variety of oscillators to build the synth plug-ins. There are two basic types of oscillators in a synthesizer: Low-Frequency Oscillators (LFOs) and pitched oscillators. The LFOs potentially produce mathematically perfect waveforms since they are only used as modulators (controllers). These trivial oscillators produce massive amounts of aliasing due to the discontinuities in their signals.

The pitched oscillators will be used for the synthesis of the notes and therefore cannot be mathematically perfect. We need to mitigate the aliasing that can occur with pitched oscillator designs. The oscillators we will design in this chapter consist of:

- sawtooth or ramp*
- square with adjustable pulse width
- triangle
- modified sawtooth (pitched oscillator only)
- sinusoid

*Note: some categorize *ramp* and *sawtooth* as being two different waveforms where the ramp waveform has a perfectly linear ramp edge as shown in Figure 5.1 while the sawtooth edge is curved outward as in Figure 5.19(a) and (d). In this book, *sawtooth* refers to the same waveform as *ramp*, both having a linear edge.

5.1 Trivial Oscillator Algorithms

The trivial oscillators are simple to design and calculate. We will use them again inside of pitched oscillators by modifying their discontinuities, so it is important to examine the modulo counter concept. Every oscillator in the chapter will use the modulo counter as its inner clock. A modulo counter is a counter that starts at zero, counts upward to a specified value, then rolls over and back to zero where it begins counting up again. Our modulo counters are unipolar and count from zero up to 1.0. Once the counter hits or exceeds 1.0, it rolls over back to zero, plus the amount it exceeds the 1.0 value. The counter is reset to zero when the oscillator is triggered and counts upwards with a constant increment called *inc*. The *inc* value represents the current phase of the oscillator and is also commonly called the phase increment. The *inc* value determines the frequency of the oscillator. The output of the modulo counter is a ramp or sawtooth waveform. Therefore, it directly implements the trivial sawtooth oscillator. The modulo counter is shown in Figure 5.1.

The modulo counter has two variables: f_o (frequency of oscillation) and f_s (sampling frequency). The value of *inc* is calculated as the ratio:

$$inc = \frac{f_0}{f_s} \tag{5.1}$$

The *inc* value is actually the slope of the sawtooth waveform.

5.2 Trivial Sawtooth Oscillator

The code for adding the increment and rolling over to the new location is simple.

```
// check for modulo wrap test
if(modulo >= 1.0)
      modulo -= 1.0; // wrap
```

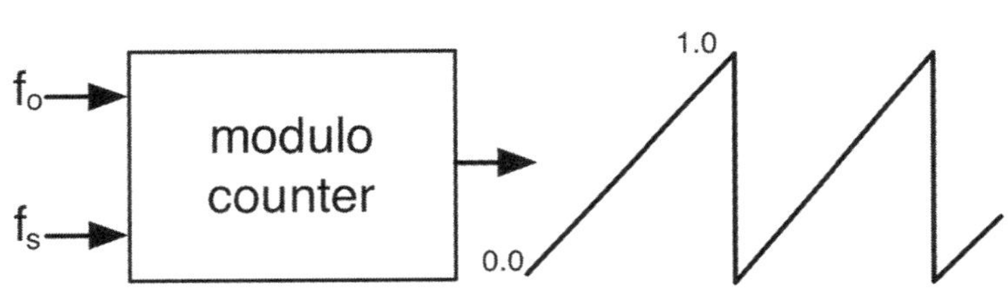

Figure 5.1: The modulo counter produces a ramp or sawtooth waveform.

```
// increment the counter
modulo += m_Inc;
```

This produces a unipolar sawtooth waveform, but we are going to want a bipolar output. Multiplying the modulo value by 2.0 and subtracting 1.0 creates a bipolar output.

```
// modulo wrap test
if(modulo >= 1.0)
      modulo -= 1.0;

// unipolar to bipolar
double trivial_saw = 2.0*modulo -1.0;

// increment the counter
modulo += m_Inc;

// output the bipolar sawtooth
return trivial_saw;
```

5.3 Trivial Square Wave Oscillator

A square wave jumps back and forth between its most negative and positive values. A bipolar square wave would alternate its output between −1 and +1. The pulse width (or duty cycle) of the waveform is the location within the period that the alternation occurs, such that a 50% pulse width indicates the transition occurs 50% of the way into the period. The convention is to let the pulse width dictate the positive value, so a 20% pulse width would produce the high value (+1) for only 20% of the period and produce the low value (−1) for the other 80%. Figure 5.2 shows some various pulse widths.

The trivial square wave oscillator will produce these kinds of outputs because it will only be used as a LFO to control something. If you look at the waveforms, you can see that unless the pulse width is 50%, there will be a DC offset in the signal. Our pitched square wave oscillators will need to remove this offset.

The code for converting the modulo counter sawtooth into a square wave is also simple. In this code snippet, PW is a value between 0% and 100%, and the ternary operator is used as a fast if-then-else statement.

```
// modulo wrap test
if(modulo >= 1.0)
      modulo -= 1.0;

// unipolar to bipolar
double trivial_square = modulo > PW/100.0 ? -1.0 : +1.0;

// increment the counter
modulo += m_Inc;

// output the bipolar sawtooth
return trivial_square;
```

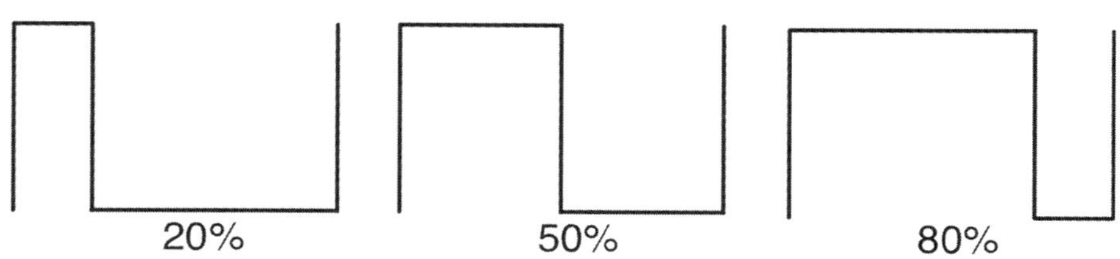

Figure 5.2: Square waves with 20%, 50% and 80% pulse widths.

5.4 Trivial Triangle Wave Oscillator

A triangle wave is shaped exactly as the name implies and can also be generated from the modulo counter. The equation is:

$$triangle = 2 * abs(trivialsaw) - 1.0 \tag{5.2}$$

The code for the triangle wave is also simple:

```
// modulo wrap test
if (modulo >= 1.0)
        modulo -= 1.0;

// (2*modulo - 1) = trivial saw
double trivial_tri = 2.0*fabs(2.0*modulo - 1.0) - 1.0;

// increment the counter
modulo += m_Inc;

// output the bipolar triangle
return trivial_tri;
```

Aliasing in the Trivial Oscillators

The sawtooth and square wave trivial oscillators alias wildly. Their spectrums are littered with aliasing components. However, the trivial triangle wave, which does not feature a discontinuity, has almost no aliasing. It can be used as a pitched oscillator directly, although we will also implement another algorithm that produces a nearly clean output. You can decide for yourself if there is an audible difference. Figure 5.3 shows the waveforms and spectra of the three trivial oscillators. The oscillator frequency is 440.0 Hz. The sawtooth spectrum

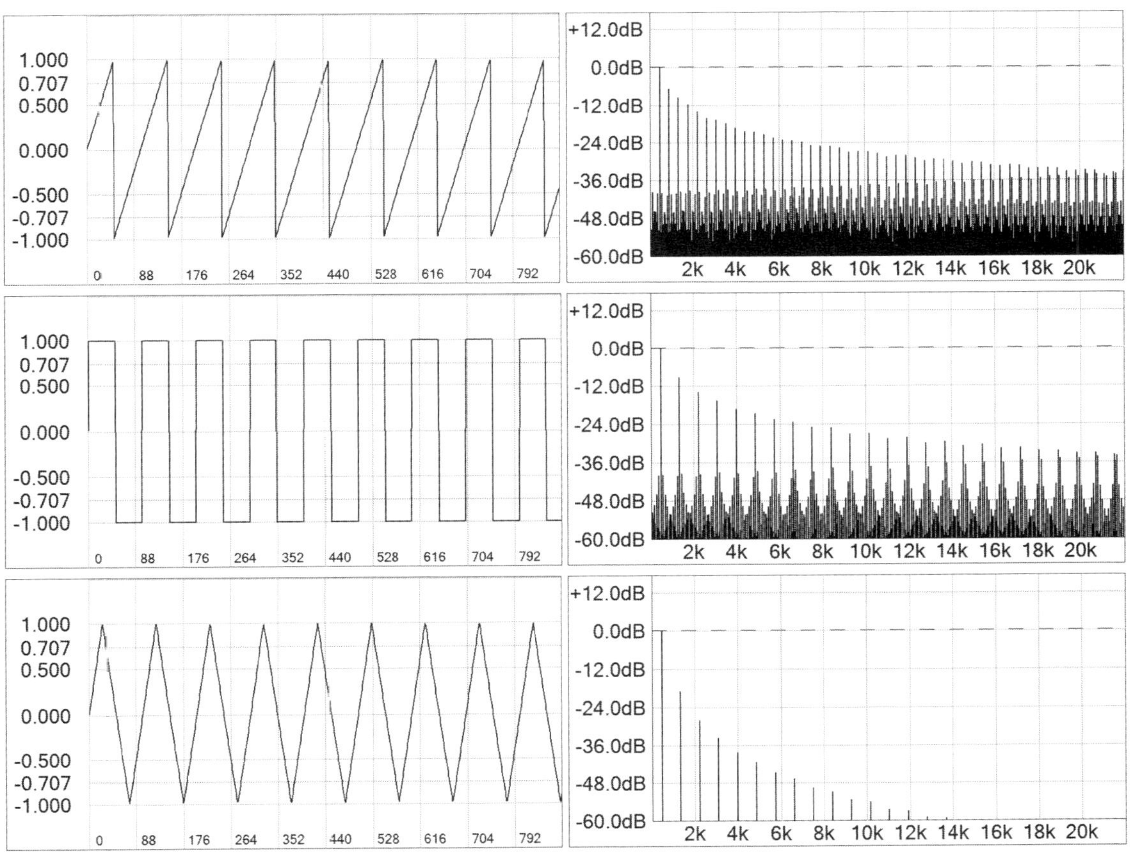

Figure 5.3: The waveforms and spectra of (top) trivial sawtooth, (middle) trivial square and (bottom) trivial triangle waves for *fo*= 440 Hz; the sawtooth and square wave spectra demonstrate massive aliasing components while the triangle spectrum is clean.

should feature spikes at each multiple of the fundamental (440 Hz, 880 Hz, 1320 Hz, etc.), while the square and triangle should include only the odd harmonics (440 Hz, 1320 Hz, 2200 Hz, etc.) You can see that all the other spikes and filled in areas there are aliasing components. For the FFT plots in this chapter, the length is 131,072 points with Blackman-Harris windowing.

5.5 Quasi Bandlimited Oscillator Algorithms

Now we can focus on the pitched oscillator design. There are two directions we can take with regards to aliasing: eliminate it altogether or allow it to happen if the aliasing components are sufficiently low in level (especially near Nyquist) and relatively far away from the fundamental frequency. To eliminate aliasing completely requires additive synthesis, where you add sinusoids of proper harmonic frequencies and amplitudes to create the desired waveform. This could be done in real-time as note events occur, or we could store the waveforms in a table and use wavetable synthesis, which is covered later in the chapter. The problem with pure additive synthesis is that it is computationally expensive. Even though the trigonometric functions like *sin()*, *cos()* and *tan()* are very efficient on modern desktop and laptop systems, a low pitched note like A0 (the lowest note on a piano) is 27.5 Hz and includes the fundamental plus 800 harmonics before reaching Nyquist. This would result in 801 calls to a *sin()* method or 801 lookups from a single-sinusoid wavetable. Bandlimited wavetable synthesis, a de-facto standard in synthesizer design for decades, has its own issues. The table uses a different *inc* value (also called a phase increment) to look up and interpolate values. If the phase increment is greater than one sample, the table is not guaranteed to be bandlimited for non-sinusoidal waveforms. We will cover this later in the chapter.

The idea for quasi bandlimited designs is relatively new. These designs seek to create alias-suppressed oscillators in which we tolerate some aliasing. The idea is especially attractive when the quasi bandlimited algorithm is simple and requires no trigonometric functions, table lookups, look ahead or other expenses. The different algorithms focus on the discontinuities in the edges in the waveform.

5.6 Bandlimited Impulse Trains (BLIT)

Stilson and Smith proposed a method for creating alias-free waveforms using a BandLimited Impulse Train or BLIT. The idea is to generate a softened or rounded discontinuity that would have resulted in lowpass filtering an impulse, and then produce a stream of these filtered impulses. This produces a stream of *sinc()* functions as shown in Figure 5.4.

The idea is to take this impulse train and filter it to produce sawtooth and square waves. For example, integrating the unipolar BLIT results in a sawtooth wave with a rounded discontinuity. Integrating a bipolar BLIT produces a square wave, while doubly integrating it produces a triangle wave. The outputs of these oscillators feature a bit of ringing on the band edges. The three block diagrams are shown in Figure 5.5, and the integrators are simple backwards Euler types. The aliasing is reduced but not eliminated with these simple BLIT algorithms.

More complex versions of BLIT can produce very good results sonically but not as good as pure additive synthesis. BLIT has problems that make it one of the more difficult algorithms to implement. First is generation of the BLIT sequence itself. Using the *sinc()* function would require two calls to the *sin()* function. The BLIT sequences in Figure 5.4 are generated with:

$$\begin{aligned} \text{sinc}(x) @ \frac{\sin(\pi x)}{M \sin(\pi x / M)} \\ M = \text{number of harmonics} \end{aligned} \tag{5.3}$$

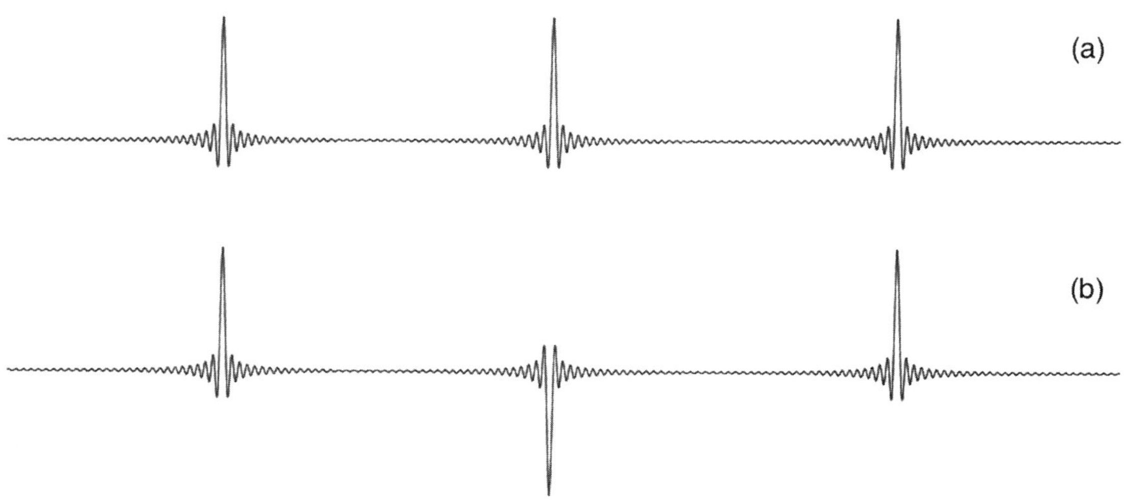

Figure 5.4: An equally spaced train of bandlimited impulses (a) unipolar and (b) bipolar.

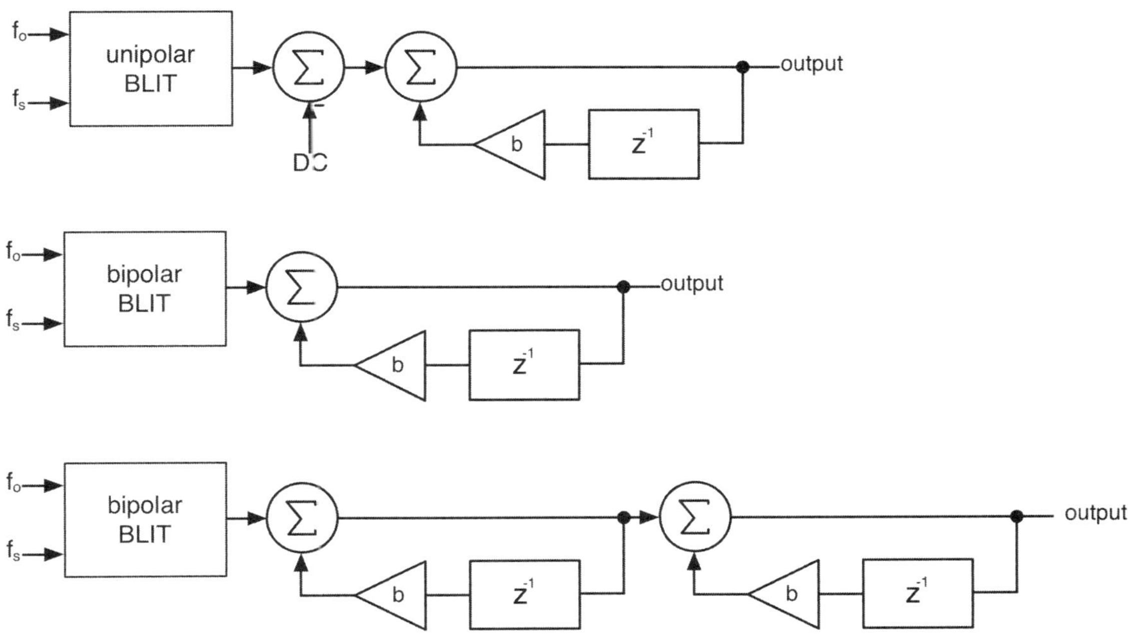

Figure 5.5: Simple BLIT algorithms for producing (a) sawtooth, (b) square and (c) triangle waves.

Another idea is to sample a sum of windowed *sinc()* functions and store them in a set of tables corresponding to different fractional shifts of the impulse. This is necessary because the period of the desired waveform may not be an integer multiple of the sample rate. Thus the tables would need to be interpolated at runtime. This is known as BLIT-SWS.

A larger issue is that the bandlimited impulses overlap, and the tail of one must be mixed with the head of the next. This requires knowing when the next discontinuity is going to occur and requires a look-ahead delay. This can be problematic because we would like to have zero delay in synthesizing the waveform. The bandlimited impulse has to be generated for each discontinuity, so as the frequency becomes higher, the CPU usage increases. As Andy Leary points out, another issue with these methods is that the integration steps in BLIT and BLIT-SWS introduce an unwanted and undesirable DC offset into the signal when the oscillator starts.

5.7 Bandlimited Step Functions (BLEP)

Brandt improved on the idea by starting with a single bandlimited impulse and integrating it beforehand, then storing that pre-integrated waveform. This removes the requirement for integration on-the-fly and produces a single band edge shown in Figure 5.6. This is called a BandLimited stEP function or BLEP.

The idea behind BLEP is to start with a trivial waveform containing discontinuities, then merge this BLEP edge into the trivial waveform edges to soften or smooth the discontinuities. This means that you will modify some number of samples on each side of the discontinuity. The number of samples you choose to modify may depend on resources (memory, CPU usage, etc.) In practice, you only need to modify a few sample values to experience a drastic reduction in aliasing. The sound quality of BLEP is considered to be excellent—better than BLIT-SWS. Brandt also experimented with filtering the BLIT signal with a minimum phase lowpass filter before integrating it to create the BLEP. He calls this MinBLEP. It effectively eliminates most of the lookahead requirement but has its

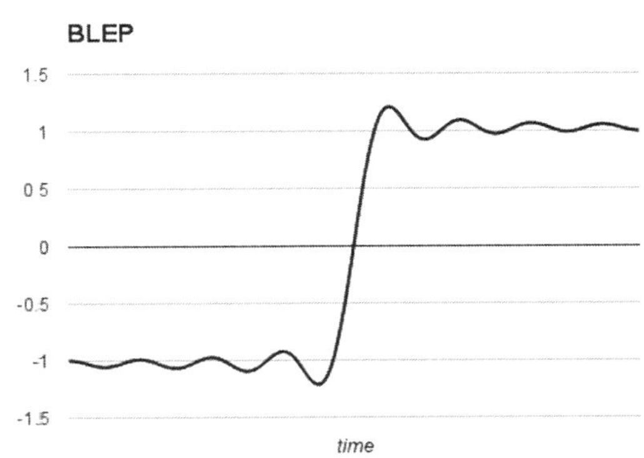

Figure 5.6: The band edge produced by integrating the bandlimited impulse signal.

own problems. Andy Leary explains that MinBLEP introduces a frequency dependent DC offset into the signal and requires precise knowledge of the phase and amplitude of the discontinuity prior to application. In practice, we are only going to alter a few samples around the discontinuity, and so the lookahead issue really isn't very much of a problem.

In 2009, Andy Leary and Charlie Bright of Korg Research and Development were awarded US Patent 7,589,272 for Bandlimited Digital Synthesis of Analog Waveforms. It describes both a method for generating the bandlimited signals, as well as hard-syncing two oscillators with discontinuous waveforms. This patent describes a system that is the basis for our quasi bandlimited oscillator for use in the analog modeling synth called MiniSynth. The patent uses bandlimited step functions (BLEPs) for alias reduction. The bandlimited step function starts out as a lowpass-filter impulse response. An ideal lowpass filter with a cutoff at Nyquist has an impulse response *h(t)*, described with the *sinc()* function in Equation 5.4 and shown in Figure 5.7(a). The zero crossings occur at one-sample-period intervals. Integrating this signal and converting to bipolar form produces the step signal in Figure 5.7(b).

$$h(t) = \frac{\sin(\pi f_s t)}{\pi f_s t} \tag{5.4}$$

The BLEP is merged with the trivial waveform mathematically by using a residual. The residual is the signal that remains after an ideal unit step has been subtracted from the BLEP. For a rising edge, the residual is added, while for a falling edge, it is subtracted. This may be implemented with an inverted residual as shown in Figures 5.8(a) and (b).

BLEP is somewhat open-ended when it comes to generating these signals (as well as the final implementation details). For example, we choose an obvious and simple lowpass filter impulse response using the ideal *sinc()* function. The Leary/Bright patent also uses the windowed *sinc()* function as a theoretical basis for the patent's BLEP design. However, you do not necessarily need to use a *sinc()* function. You may use any lowpass filter impulse response you want. You may also decide to make trade-offs in the filter design to reduce aliasing in some parts of the spectrum while allowing it in others. A common goal is to try to eliminate aliasing that is close to the Nyquist frequency. Andy Leary states that a linear phase DC balanced BLEP provides excellent results and that the Korg Kronos and OASYS both use this approach; however, the exact functions used in those instruments are a trade secret. If you have the RackAFX software, you may use its FIR design tools to generate impulse responses—RackAFX designs linear phase FIR filters, and you can easily extract the impulse response data points as a text file with the data pre-formatted as a C/C++ array. See http://www.willpirkle.com/synthbook/ for more information on the RackAFX FIR designer.

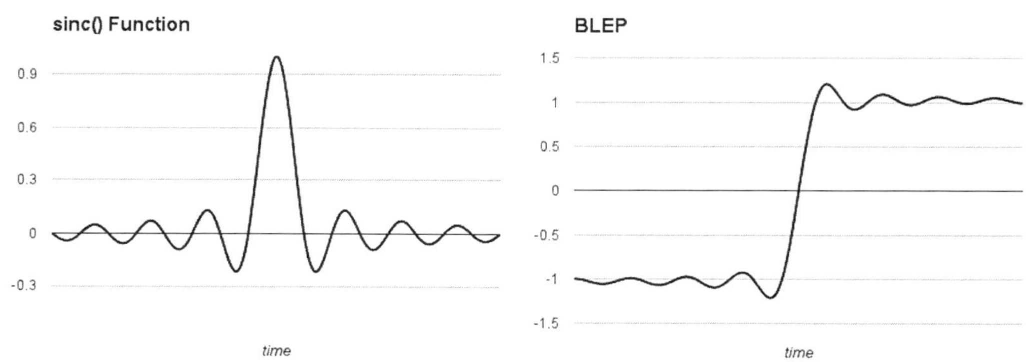

Figure 5.7: (a) The impulse response of an ideal lowpass filter. (b) The step signal resulting from integrating the impulse response and converting to bipolar.

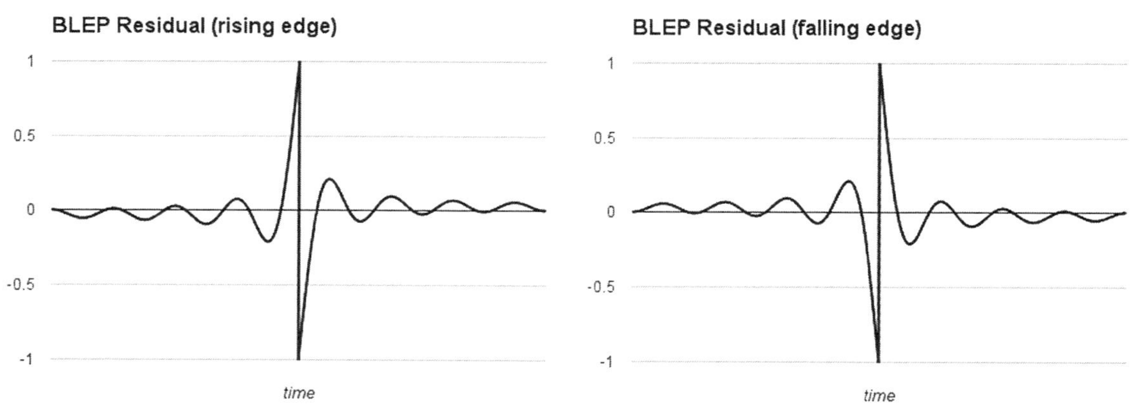

Figure 5.8: (a) The BLEP residual after subtracting the unit step from Figure 5.7(b) and (b) the inverted version used for falling edges.

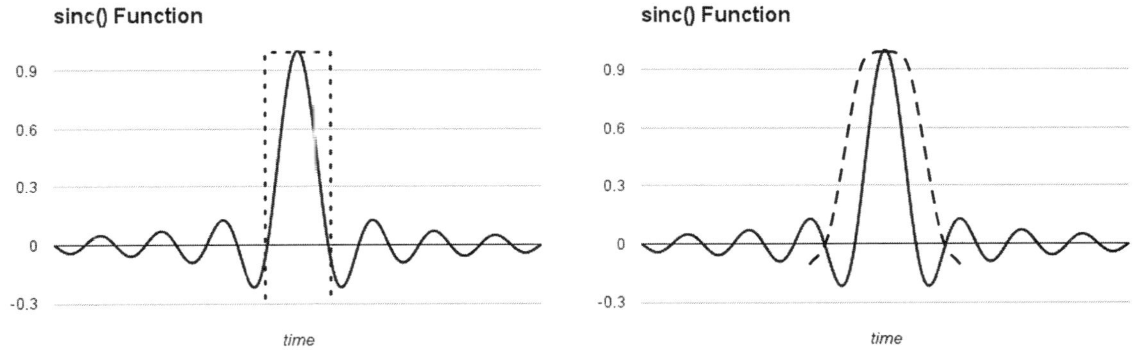

Figure 5.9: (a) A rectangular window (dotted line) selects the central pulse of the *sinc()* function, and (b) a wider, non-rectangular window over a larger piece of the function.

After deciding on the impulse response, the next step is to choose how much of the edge you want to adjust. In general, the more points you adjust, the better the aliasing rejection, however it comes at the cost of processing time and storage. You usually select the points symmetrically around the discontinuity. In our simplest BLEP oscillators, we will apply correction to just one point on each side of the discontinuity, for a total of two points. We also implement a four-point-per-side correction in the next section. The reduction in aliasing is dramatic, though not 100% complete. This is definitely an area for experimentation in your own designs. Since we will also implement completely alias-free wavetable versions as well, you have something to compare with. Do some of your own listening tests between the quasi bandlimited and wavetable oscillators and judge for yourself.

Knowing the width of the adjustment zone, you can then window the selected impulse response (that is, select only a portion of it). This is another area for experimentation—you may choose different windowing functions such as Hann, Hamming, Blackman, etc.

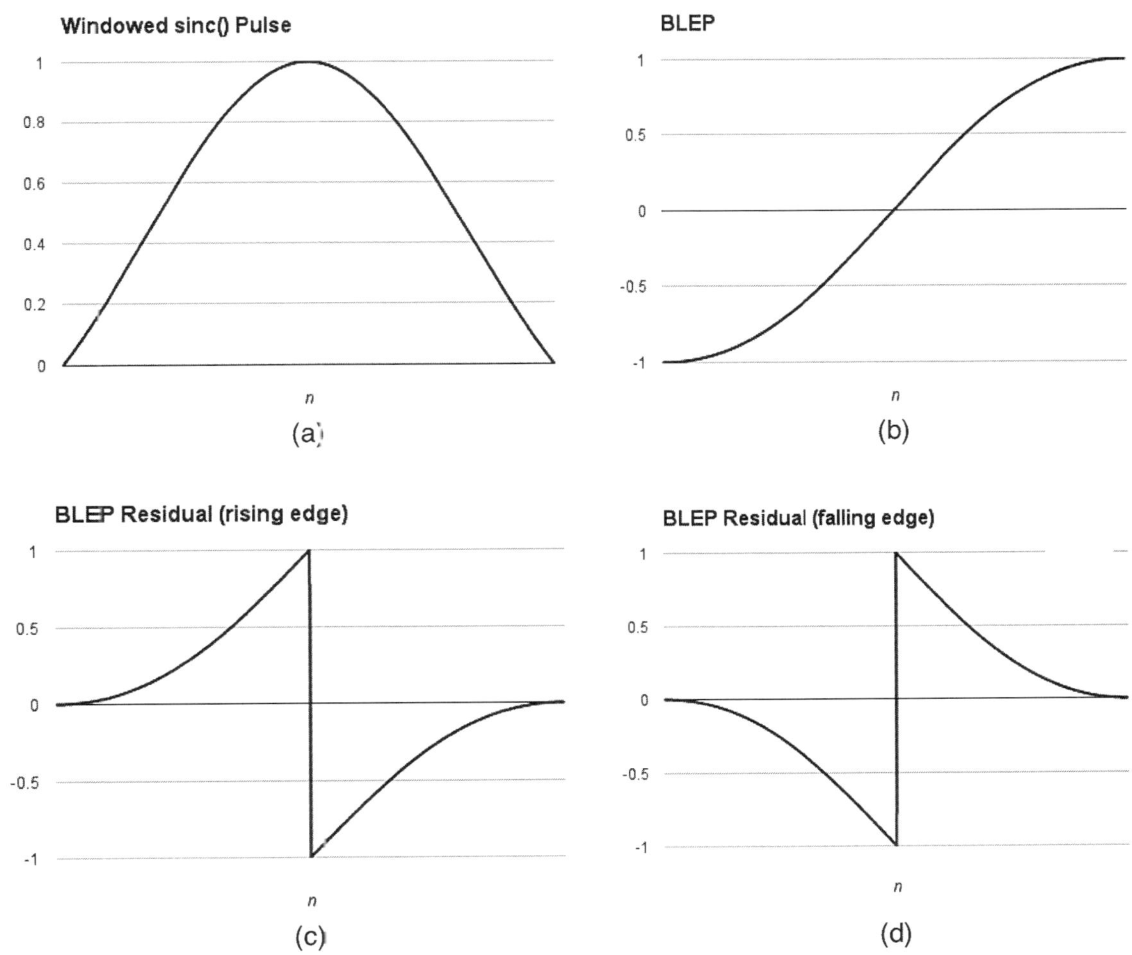

Figure 5.10: (a) The windowed *sinc()* function selects only the central pulse (b) the resulting BLEP edge after integration and bipolar conversion (c) the BLEP residual for the rising edge and (d) falling edge case.

that scale the impulse response values. The selection of the window size and window function alter the way the aliasing is reduced, so many variations exist. In our simplest BLEP oscillators, we use a rectangular window on the original *sinc()* function to limit the pulse width to its first zero crossings, as shown in Figure 5.9(a), which gives a correction width of two samples. This is also the choice used to demonstrate the Leary/Bright patent if you are following along in that document. However, the Korg Kronos and other Korg instruments may use different correction widths and windowing; this is another trade secret. Figure 5.9(b) shows the use of a non-rectangular window around a wider piece of the impulse.

With the window size and type selected, we can generate the BLEP residual. This BLEP residual is pre-calculated and contained in a 4096 element array in *synthfunctions.h* for you to use called *dBLEPTable[4096]*. You may download the C/C++ code we used to generate the residuals in this chapter from http://www.willpirkle.com/synthbook/ for your own experiments. You may also use MATLAB or other tools to generate and window an impulse response. The residual is stored in this relatively large 4096-point finely sampled array. We can then use lookup techniques to find the residual value to apply to a given waveform sample.

There are a multitude of ways of implementing a BLEP oscillator. The residual is stored in a relatively large, finely sampled array. We can then use lookup techniques to find the residual value to apply to a given waveform sample. Other manifestations are less memory intensive, and there are different table lookup techniques that may be applied. For example, if you knew you were going to alter eight points in the discontinuity (four on each side), then you might instead create many eight-point tables corresponding to different phase increment values from the modulo counter and interpolate between them. Our realization is less hardware-like; BLEP is implemented in a function that returns the residual correction value or 0.0 if we are outside the discontinuity window called the transition region. It uses simple lookup table techniques to fetch the proper residual value according to the current phase of the oscillator. You may enable or disable linear interpolation of the BLEP table (it is disabled by default to save processing time), and of course you are encouraged to experiment with other forms of interpolation.

Figures 5.10(a)–(d) show the results of our BLEP residual generation. For implementation, we won't keep a separate falling edge version; instead we can just subtract rather than add the rising edge version. We will use the left half of the residual in Figure 5.10(c) to process the sample on the left of the discontinuity and the right half to process the other side. Figure 5.11 (adapted from Figure 4 in the Leary/Bright patent) shows how the residual is applied to offset the samples around the discontinuity. Figure 5.11(b) shows the output of our BLEP function; notice it is a falling edge type since the sawtooth contains only falling edges, and it is usually zero where no correction is needed. The grey samples are the targets for correction. The BLEP residual shifts the trivial waveform samples up or down as indicated. You can also see that the closer the point is to the discontinuity, the more alteration it gets. Notice how the BLEP pulses are centered around the original waveform discontinuities. After adjustment, in Figure 5.11(d) you can see how altering just two points around the discontinuity visibly smooths the waveform. The softer edges now resemble the smooth and curvy BLEP edge in Figure 5.7(b). Figure 5.12(a) shows

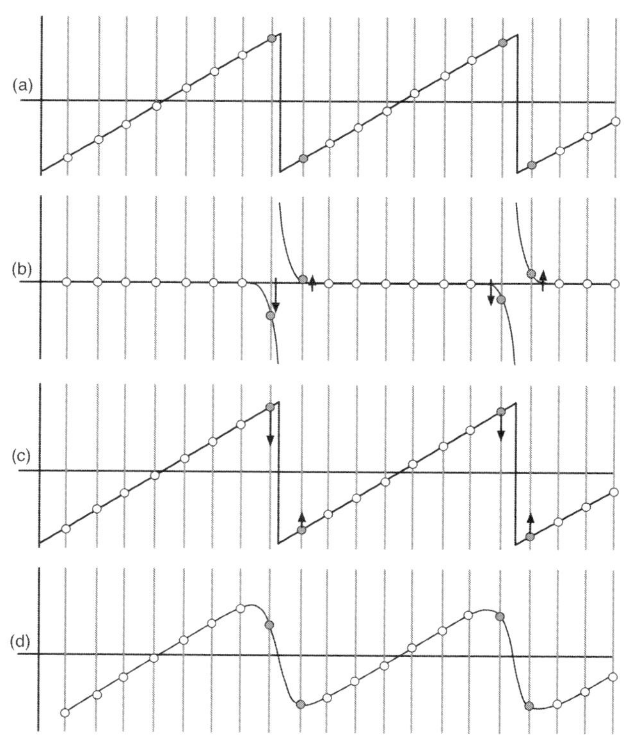

Figure 5.11: Adapted from Leary and Bright (2009) (a) the trivial sawtooth waveform; one sample (shown in grey) on each side of the discontinuity will be altered (b) the BLEP residual signal (falling edge) contains the offset values that will be applied to the samples (arrows show the magnitude and direction) (c) applying the offsets results in (d) the smoothed waveform.

the spectrum of the trivial sawtooth and 5.12(b) shows the extreme reduction in aliasing components after applying the two-point BLEP correction. We choose −60 dB as a threshold for the aliasing components; if they are below this value, we consider them absent. However, you can use the RackAFX spectrum analyzer's control settings to alter this (say to −96 dB) to view the shape of the aliased components.

5.8 Wider Window BLEP

We get very good results in alias suppression with the two-point BLEP, so let's increase the width of the windowed *sinc()* function and correct more points to reduce aliasing further. The tradeoff will be computational time. The windowed *sinc()* function is altered to include the next lobe zero-crossings. This produces a residual for correcting four samples on each side of the discontinuity (by doubling the window size but keeping the same table length, the zero crossings are now on two-sample-interval boundaries). Figure 5.13(a) shows a rectangularly windowed *sinc()* pulse, while Figure 5.13(b) shows the resulting BLEP edge, and Figure 5.13(c) shows the resulting residual.

We can now experiment with this widened window and generate a set of BLEP tables with various windowing applied to see how the windowing affects the alias suppression as well as distorts the desired sawtooth spectrum. Figures 5.14(a)–(e) show the resulting spectra when a variety of window functions are applied. If you are not using RackAFX, then you will need to use a third party FFT analyzer in your DAW to test the oscillators we implement in this chapter. In Figure 5.14(a) the rectangular shaped windowing introduces aliasing

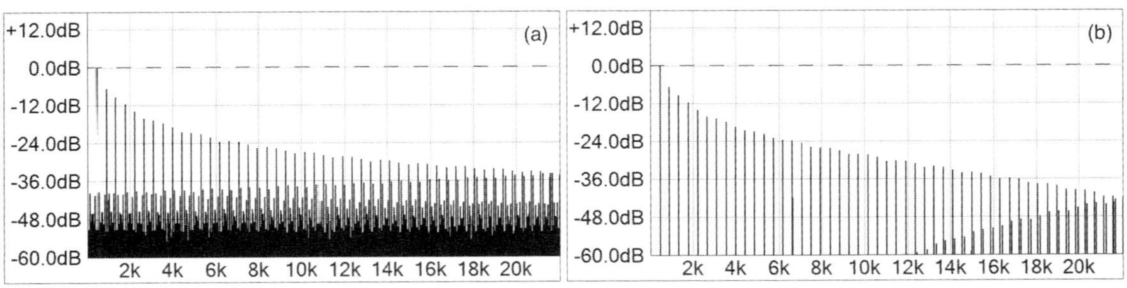

Figure 5.12: (a) The trivial sawtooth spectrum reveals massive aliasing while (b) the two-point BLEP corrected spectrum suppresses most of the aliasing, pushing the components below −60 dB and off the plot; *fo* = 440 Hz.

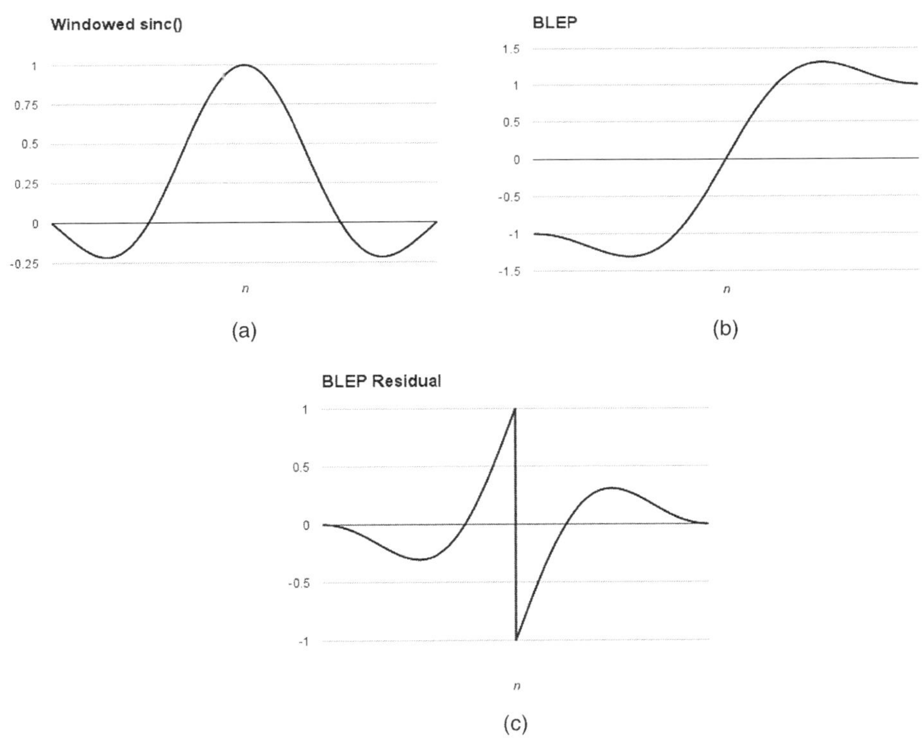

Figure 5.13: (a) A wider rectangular window extracts the central pulse and next pair of lobes (b) the resulting BLEP edge after integrating and (c) the BLEP residual.

components that are wider but lower in amplitude than the two-point version in Figure 5.12; aliasing components near Nyquist are much more suppressed.

These windowed *sinc()* versions of the BLEP residuals are also prepackaged for you in *synthfunctions.h* as the following arrays (all are 4096 points):

- *dBLEPTable_8_RECT*
- *dBLEPTable_8_TRI*
- *dBLEPTable_8_HANN*
- *dBLEPTable_8_HAMM*
- *dBLEPTable_8_BLKHAR*
- *dBLEPTable_8_WELCH*

> Our BLEP oscillators will default to the original two-point version without interpolation between lookup points. You may easily alter this in the BLEP function described later in the chapter; you may also generate and then test your own BLEP tables using the BLEP function. In the rest of the chapter, "two-point BLEP" refers to the one-point-per-side BLEP correction from the last section. "Eight-point BLEP" refers to the widened transition region version with four points per side that are corrected.

Even though Figures 5.14(b)–(d) have clean spectra, notice how the spectral components are shaped relative to one another—as the windowing gets more severe, the sawtooth spectral envelope becomes less and less sawtooth-like (compare with the wavetable spectrum in Figure 5.34(a)). This should help you understand just how important the window length, window type and original impulse response are to the success of the BLEP algorithm.

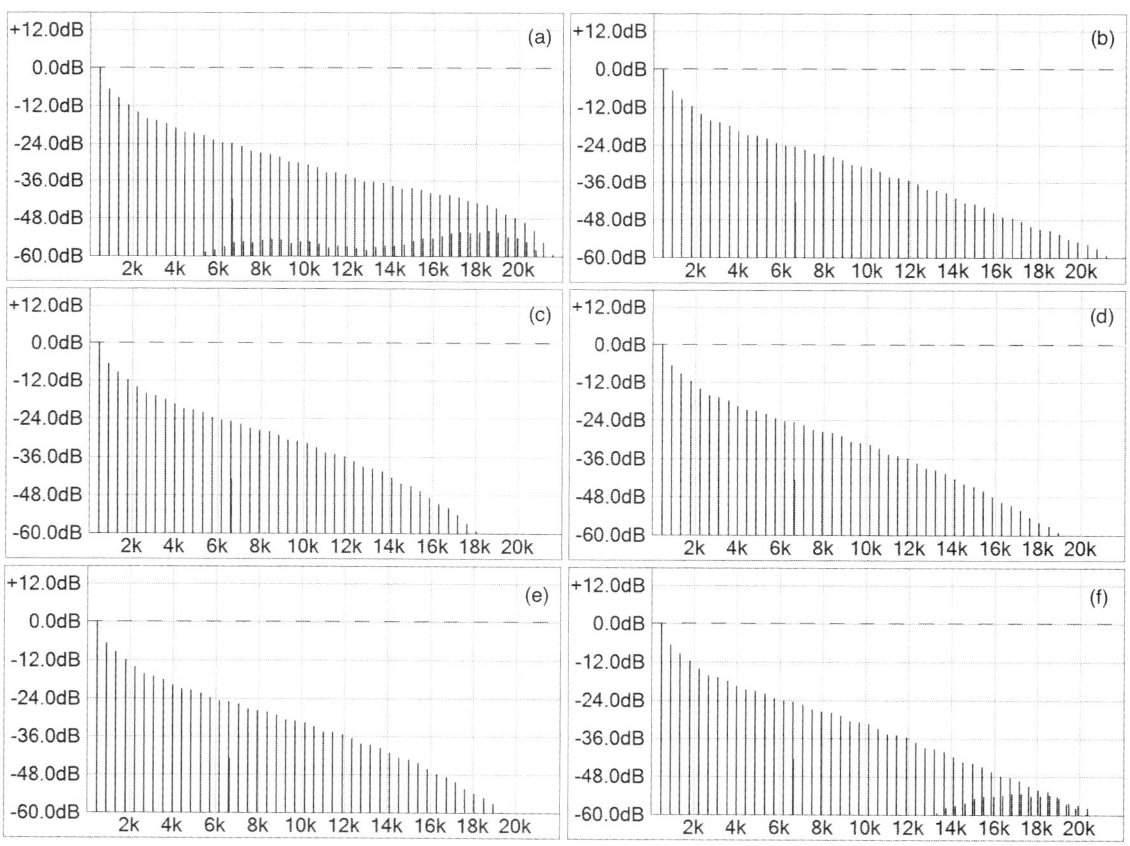

Figure 5.14: Spectra of BLEP sawtooth oscillators with four-point-per-side correction and the following windowing applied to the *sinc()* pulse pre-integration (a) rectangular, (b) triangular, (c) Hann, (d) Hamming, (e) Blackman-Harris, and (f) Welch windows; *fo* = 440 Hz.

5.9 Polynomial BLEP (PolyBLEP)

Välimäki proposes implementing the BLEP residual by approximating the original *sinc()* function with a polynomial. Different polynomials of different orders may be chosen, but a simple solution is to use a unipolar triangular pulse shown in Figure 5.15(a)—it is the linear approximation of the windowed *sinc()* pulse in Figure 5.10(a). Integrating it produces the curve in Figure 5.15(b) that can be expressed in closed form and thus requires no table. The integrated triangle pulse is:

$$s_{tri}(t) = \begin{cases} 0 & t < -1 \\ t^2/2 + t + 1/2 & -1 \le t \le 0 \\ t - t^2/2 + 1/2 & 0 < t \le 1 \\ 1 & t > 1 \end{cases} \tag{5.5}$$

In this equation, the time t is the distance from the discontinuity which is centered at $t = 0.0$. Subtracting out the perfect step and then converting to bipolar results in the following two part residual, shown in Figure 5.15(c). The polynomials compute each of the curves in Figure 5.15(c).

$$\text{PolyBLEP}(t) = \begin{cases} t^2 + 2t + 1 & -1 \le t \le 0 \\ 2t - t^2 - 1 & 0 < t \le 1 \end{cases} \tag{5.6}$$

Figure 5.15(d) compares the PolyBLEP and normal BLEP residuals we've generated so far. You can see that they almost line up perfectly. The error in the PolyBLEP version manifests itself as slightly more aliasing in the final signal. The DC component for the PolyBLEP residual measures a respectable 6.05×10^{-10}.

PolyBLEP removes the need for a table and produces its offset values with simple second order equations, one for the left side and the other for the right side of the discontinuity. For memory challenged devices, such as mobile phones and tablets, PolyBLEP might make

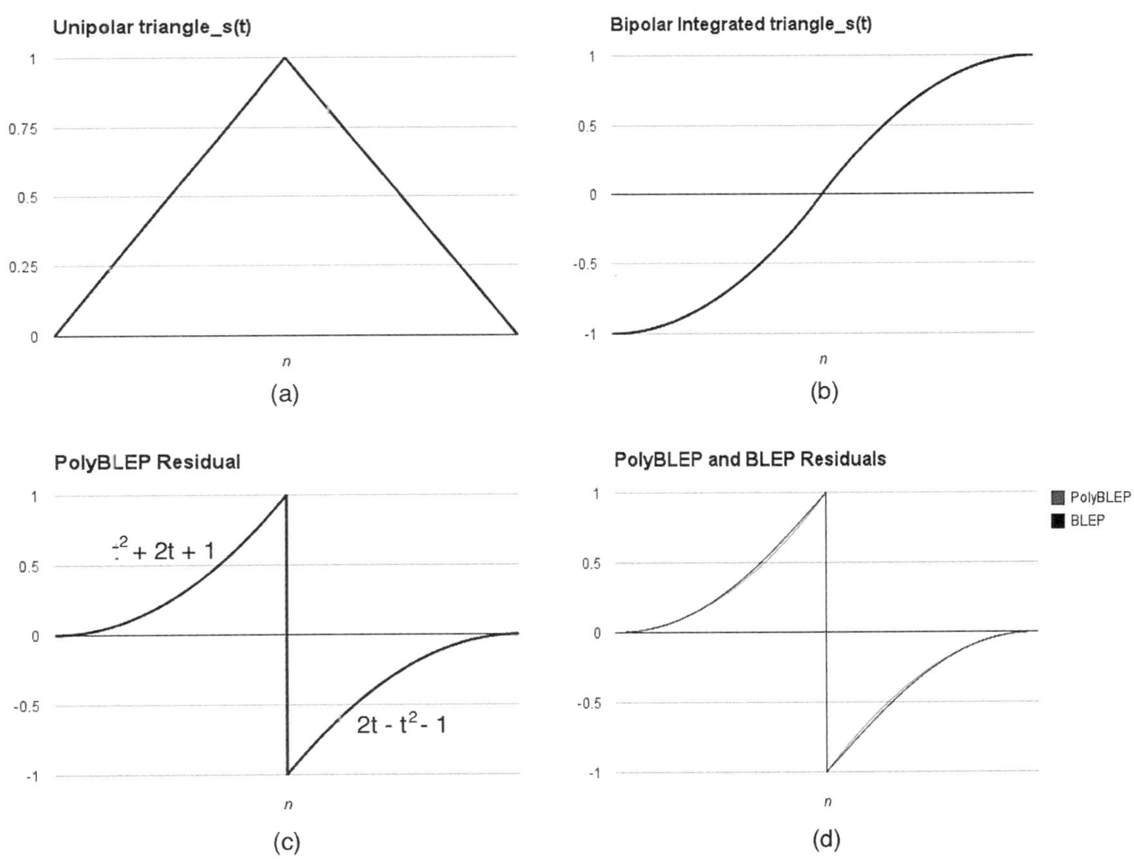

Figure 5.15: (a) A unipolar triangle pulse replaces the windowed *sinc()*, while (b) integrating it and converting to bipolar produces a similar bandlimited edge, (c) the resulting PolyBLEP residual, and (d) a comparison with the normal BLEP residual.

a nice alternative, as it requires no lookup tables at the expense of a bit more aliasing. Our bandlimited oscillators default to normal BLEP, but we've implemented both BLEP and PolyBLEP functions for your experiments. You can also generate your own polynomials; once you have a good BLEP residual table, you might enter some of its data points into a polynomial curve-fitting algorithm and come up with your own polynomial equations that approximate the residual curves. This way, you could experiment with a wider transition band around the discontinuity. Figures 5.16(a) and (b) show the difference between the normal two-point BLEP and PolyBLEP spectra. The PolyBLEP approximation error results in slightly more aliasing.

5.10 Coding the BLEP and PolyBLEP Algorithms

The BLEP and PolyBLEP functions are quite similar. They both need to do the following:

- identify when a trivial sawtooth point is in the transition region around the discontinuity
- identify whether the point is on the left or right side of the discontinuity
- measure the distance from the point to the discontinuity
- use this distance to:
    - lookup the residual offset value from a table (BLEP)
    - calculate the residual offset value from polynomial equations (PolyBLEP)

> Our BLEP and PolyBLEP functions will be used solely for sawtooth waveforms, so the location of the edge is where the modulo counter crosses over the value 1.0. For a sawtooth, the edges are always falling, for an inverted sawtooth they are always rising. Their amplitude is always 1.0. If you want to use the BLEP or PolyBLEP functions to process discontinuities that are at some other location than the modulo crossing 1.0, you will need to make some minor alterations to these functions. You can get more information at http://www.willpirkle.com/synthbook/.

Let's consider the simple case where the number of points per side of the discontinuity is one, so we can use either BLEP or PolyBLEP. Figure 5.17 shows how the logic works for both identifying when the point is in the transition region but also its distance from the discontinuity. The identification and distances are found as:

Identification:

- left side: modulo > (1 − *inc*)
- right side: modulo < *inc*

Distance:

- t(−) = (modulo − 1) / *inc*
- t(+) = modulo/*inc*

The PolyBLEP function is named *doPolyBLEP_2()* and is hard coded to process only one point on each side of the discontinuity using the previous logic. The arguments are:

double dModulo:	the current modulo counter value
double dInc:	the current phase increment value
double dHeight:	the height of the discontinuity between 0.0 and 1.0
bool bRisingEdge:	true for rising edge, false for falling edge

The point location and distance *t* are found easily from the logic; if outside the region, the function returns 0.0.

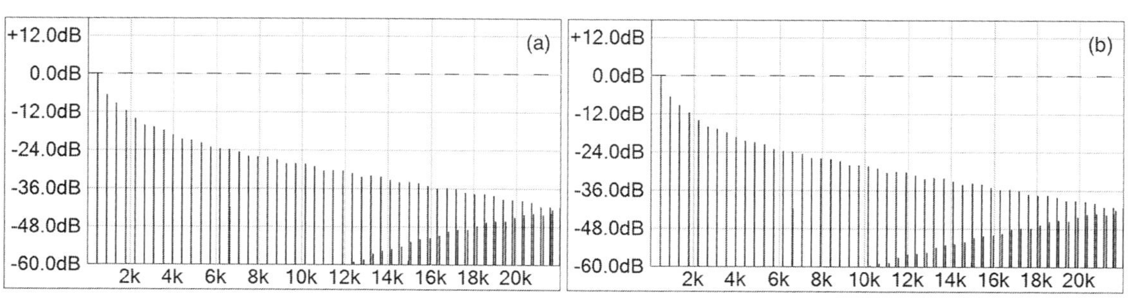

Figure 5.16: Aliasing in (a) the normal two-point BLEP oscillator and (b) the PolyBLEP version; *fo* = 440 Hz.

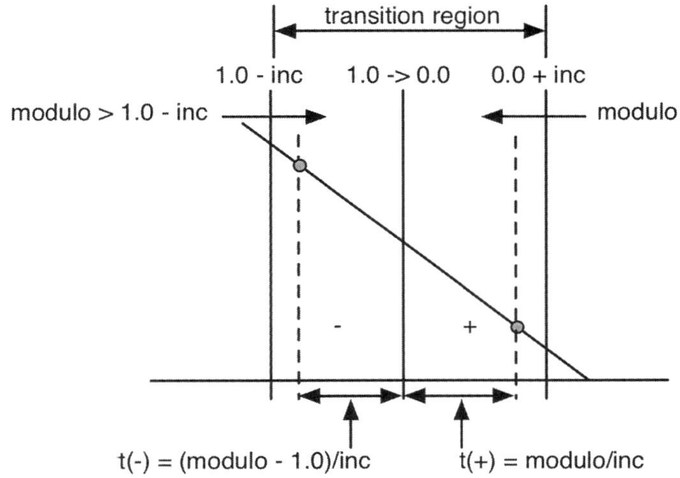

Figure 5.17: The discontinuity edge is shown as a dark line where the modulo counter crosses from 1.0 to 0.0; identifying the location and calculating the distances are shown in the equations.

```
inline double doPolyBLEP_2(double dModulo, double dInc,
                           double dHeight, bool bRisingEdge)
{
    // --- return value
    double dPolyBLEP = 0.0;

    // --- LEFT side of discontinuity
    //       -1 < t < 0
    if(dModulo > 1.0 - dInc)
    {
        // --- calculate distance
        double t = (dModulo - 1.0)/dInc;

        // --- calculate residual
        dPolyBLEP = dHeight*(t*t + 2.0*t + 1.0);

    }
    // --- RIGHT side of discontinuity
    //     0 <= t < 1
    else if(dModulo < dInc)
    {
        // --- calculate distance
        double t = dModulo/dInc;

        // --- calculate residual
        dPolyBLEP = dHeight*(2.0*t - t*t - 1.0);
    }

    // --- subtract for falling, add for rising edge
    if(!bRisingEdge)
        dPolyBLEP *= -1.0;

    return dPolyBLEP;
}
```

The normal BLEP function processing just two points is identical, except for the calculation of the return residual value. The BLEP function looks up the value from a BLEP table using interpolation if it is enabled. Each BLEP table is 4096 points in length. The first half from index 0 to 2047 contains the BLEP residual for the points on the left of the discontinuity, while the right half from index 2048 to 4095 contains the BLEP residual for the points on the right of the discontinuity. The discontinuity itself is located between the index values 2047 and 2048.

For the point on the left side of the discontinuity and using simple truncation of the index to find the value, we might write the function as follows (*dTableCenter* is location 2047):

```
// --- LEFT side of discontinuity
//       -1 < t < 0
if(dModulo > 1.0 - dInc)
{
        // --- calculate distance
        double t = (dModulo - 1.0)/dInc;

        // --- calculate residual index location
        float fIndex = (1.0 + t)*dTableCenter;

        // --- truncated:
        dBLEP = pBLEPTable[(int)fIndex];
}
```

We find the index of the point in question by adding *t*, which will always be negative in this case, to 1.0 and multiplying this by the table center index value. It will then produce the offset from the center to the left side of the table. Truncating the index is accomplished by casting the location as in integer. We might do linear interpolation as follows. This uses the built-in linear interpolation function *linterp()*, which we will cover shortly.

```
// --- interpolated:
float fIndex = (1.0 + t)*dTableCenter;
float frac = fIndex - int(fIndex);
dBLEP = dLinTerp(0, 1, pBLEPTable[(int)fIndex], pBLEPTable[(int)fIndex+1],
                   frac);
```

For the point on the right side of the discontinuity and using simple truncation of the index to find the value, we might write the function as follows:

```
// --- RIGHT side of discontinuity
//   0 <= t < 1
else if(dModulo < dInc)
{
        // --- calculate distance
        double t = dModulo/dInc;

        // --- calculate residual index location
        float fIndex = t*dTableCenter + (dTableCenter + 1.0);

        // --- truncate:
        dBLEP = pBLEPTable[(int)fIndex];
}
```

In this case, we change the lookup equation to advance to the right half of the table. For interpolation, we have a bit more work to do, checking to see if we are interpolating across the last and first entries in the table:

```
// --- interpolated:
float fIndex = t*dTableCenter + (dTableCenter + 1.0);
float frac = fIndex - int(fIndex);
```

```
if((int)fIndex+1 >= dTableLen)
   dBLEP = dLinTerp(0, 1, pBLEPTable[(int)fIndex], pBLEPTable[0], frac);
else
    dBLEP = dLinTerp(0, 1, pBLEPTable[(int)fIndex], pBLEPTable[(int)fIndex+1],
                     frac);
```

The BLEP function is called *doBLEP_N()* and processes *N* points on each side of the discontinuity. This function is more complex since it also allows you to specify a BLEP table of some length *dTableLen*. It's almost the same as the previous function, except it calculates the distances based on the total number of points per side, which is the total number of increment distances on each side. The arguments are:

double pBLEPTable:*	pointer to the BLEP table of choice
double dTableLen:	length of BLEP table
double dPointsPerSide:	number of points per side of the discontinuity (*N*) to correct
bool bInterpolate:	flag for enabling interpolation; default is *false* (disabled)

```
inline double doBLEP_N(const double* pBLEPTable, double dTableLen,
                        double dModulo, double dInc, double dHeight,
                        bool bRisingEdge, double dPointsPerSide,
                        bool bInterpolate = false)
{
     // return value
     double dBLEP = 0.0;

     // t = the distance from the discontinuity
     double t = 0.0;

     // --- find the center of table (discontinuity location)
     double dTableCenter = dTableLen/2.0 - 1;

     // LEFT side of edge
     // -1 < t < 0
     for(int i = 1; i <= (UINT)dPointsPerSide; i++)
     {
            if(dModulo > 1.0 - (double)i*dInc)
            {
                   // --- calculate distance
                   t = (dModulo - 1.0)/(dPointsPerSide*dInc);

                   // --- calculate residual index location
                   float fIndex = (1.0 + t)*dTableCenter;

                   // --- truncation
                   if(!bInterpolate)
                          dBLEP = pBLEPTable[(int)fIndex];
                   else
                   {
                          float frac = fIndex - int(fIndex);
                          dBLEP = dLinTerp(0, 1, pBLEPTable[(int)fIndex],
                                           pBLEPTable[(int)fIndex+1], frac);
                   }

                   // --- subtract for falling, add for rising edge
                   if(!bRisingEdge)
```

```
                        dBLEP *= -1.0;
                    return dBLEP*dHeight;
                }
            }

            // RIGHT side of discontinuity
            // 0 <= t < 1
            for(int i = 1; i <= (UINT)dPointsPerSide; i++)
            {
                if(dModulo < (double)i*dInc)
                {
                    // calculate distance
                    t = dModulo/(dPointsPerSide*dInc);

                    // --- calculate residual index location
                    float fIndex = t*dTableCenter + (dTableCenter + 1.0);

                    // truncation
                    if(!bInterpolate)
                        dBLEP = pBLEPTable[(int)fIndex];
                    else
                    {
                        float frac = fIndex - int(fIndex);
                        if((int)fIndex+1 >= dTableLen)
                            dBLEP = dLinTerp(0, 1, pBLEPTable[(int)fIndex],
                                             pBLEPTable[0], frac);
                        else
                            dBLEP = dLinTerp(0, 1, pBLEPTable[(int)fIndex],
                                            pBLEPTable[(int)fIndex+1],
                                            frac);
                    }

                    // subtract for falling, add for rising edge
                    if(!bRisingEdge)
                        dBLEP *= -1.0;

                    return dBLEP*dHeight;
                }
            }

            // --- no BLEP residual
            return 0.0;
        }
```

Using either the BLEP or PolyBLEP function is easy—you create the trivial waveform data point then add the residual value afterwards.

5.11 Wave Shaped BLEP Sawtooth Oscillator

Välimäki observed that the sawtooth waveform from an analog Moog synthesizer did not look like a mathematically perfect sawtooth. The ramp portion was not linear but rather had an "S" or sigmoid shape. We also observe similar waveforms in the analog Korg Volca Keys and MS-20 Mini, whose sawtooth waveforms and spectra are shown in Figures 5.19(g)–(j). This S-shaped sawtooth is not unlike the imperfect sawtooth created with phase distortion synthesis that Casio used on the CZ line of synths in the 1980s. The Roland

TB-303 features a clipped S-shaped sawtooth waveform. Andy Leary notes that the Moog oscillators were actually quite linear and that the distortion came from the amplifier. If you are interested in exactly modeling these synths, you will need to add these nonlinearities to the DCA in Chapter 6. This is because the filters in those synths also introduced nonlinearities. The sequence of nonlinearities from filter to amplifier must be preserved for accurate modeling of these synths. We will discuss the nonlinear filter models in Chapter 7.

However, an inexpensive and flexible way to generate many different sawtooth waveforms is to alter the shape of the trivial sawtooth ramp using a nonlinear processing function with the waveshaping you saw in Chapter 4 and then let BLEP/PolyBLEP handle the discontinuity. By altering the waveshaper's gain, we can change the shape significantly. The hyperbolic tangent or *tanh()* is a common sigmoid waveshaping function and was introduced in Chapter 4. By using the normalized version with saturation control, we can create a sigmoid-sawtooth that approaches a square wave as the saturation is increased. This is shown in Figure 5.18(d). The equation for the wave shaper is:

$$y = \frac{\tanh(sat * x)}{\tanh(sat)} \tag{5.7}$$

In this equation, *sat* is a saturation variable that can take on any value but 0.0. Typically, we start at 1.0 as the minimum value. This is implemented in code after the unipolar to bipolar conversion:

```
// unipolar to bipolar
trivial_saw = 2.0*SawModulo - 1.0;

// saturation through wave shaper
trivial_saw = tanh(sat*trivial_saw)/tanh(sat);
```

Another option is to perform one-sided saturation on the modulo value prior to or during the conversion to bipolar. This produces another set of waveforms including the "fat sawtooth," which also resembles the imperfect analog sawtooth waveforms found on some synths shown in Figure 5.18(a). This is done with the following code:

```
// wave shape the modulo, then convert to bipolar
trivial_saw = 2.0*(tanh(sat*SawModulo)/tanh(sat)) - 1.0;
```

Figures 5.19(g–j) show the sawtooth waveforms from the Korg Volca Keys and MS-20 Mini analog synths. They both resemble the unipolar waveshaped sawtooth in both time and frequency. Please note that the oscillator outputs are hard-wired to the filters in these synths. In these synths, the filter cutoffs are at their most extreme positions (lowpass cutoff is at the maximum, while highpass is at the minimum). For example, in Figure 5.19(j) you can clearly see the lowpass filter with cutoff at 15 kHz rolling off the upper end of the spectrum. The MS-20 version is inverted but otherwise has a similar sawtooth spectrum. You can also see a tradeoff in the BLEP designs; the simple two-point PolyBLEP (and normal BLEP) produce higher amplitude harmonics in the region close to Nyquist that more closely resembles the analog oscillators but produces more aliasing components, especially close to Nyquist. The eight-point Blackman-Harris *sinc()* windowed BLEP produces an alias-free spectrum down to about -76 dB but rolls off the very high frequency harmonics. Compare Figure 5.19(c), the eight-point BLEP, and (h), the Korg Volca Keys oscillator outputs—they are very similar. You need to conduct some listening test of your own and compare all the different BLEP implementations.

The synthesized unipolar waveshaped version does have issues: it will alias at very high frequencies and very high saturation settings. You need to be aware that BLEP and PolyBLEP may only be used to correct a certain kind of discontinuity called a C1 continuity. This means that the magnitude and direction of the tangent vectors of the top and bottom of the point of the discontinuity are identical; this occurs in the pure sawtooth, square, and bipolar waveshaped sawtooth, but not for the unipolar waveshaped sawtooth. We observe only slightly more aliasing in the unipolar waveshaped sawtooth with low saturation values than the normal sawtooth.

In addition unipolar waveshaped version produces significant DC offset that may produce problems when many unfiltered waveforms are summed together; the higher the saturation value, the higher the DC offset. This is may be remedied with a tight highpass filter with a cutoff of <5 Hz or so. Since a bilinear highpass filter preserves its zeros at DC, it will completely remove the DC component but will alter the wave shape somewhat. We find the waveshaped sawtooth waveforms to be fun and interesting for experimentation. You might experiment with modulating the saturation value in time to produce dynamic spectra. In particular, adjusting the saturation in the bipolar waveshaped sawtooth moves the shape from saw to square and back, producing a very nice modulation.

5.12 BLEP Square Wave Oscillator

Using BLEP/PolyBLEP to make a square wave oscillator is more complicated because we also wish to alter the square wave's pulse width. This is known as Pulse Width Modulation or PWM and is a standard feature on analog synths. PWM on digital synths has generally been somewhat problematic. Some early digital synths left out PWM altogether. Using BLEP to smooth the discontinuities in a square would involve:

- keeping track of the rising and falling edges to apply the BLEP correction properly
- adjusting the pulse width edge value on-the-fly, as it may be in constant flux

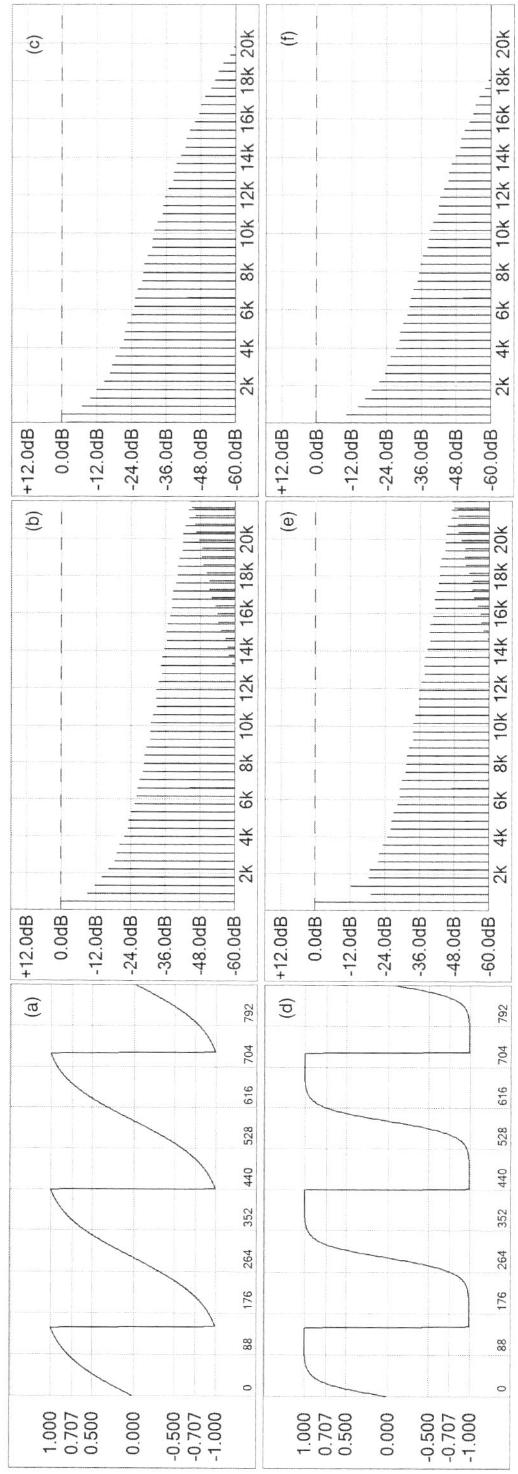

Figure 5.18: The output of the bipolar wave shaped 440 Hz sawtooth for (a) sat = 1.5, (b) its spectrum using two-point BLEP and (c) eight-point BLEP with Blackman-Harris *sinc()* windowing, (d) the output of the bipolar wave shaped 440 Hz sawtooth for sat = 5, (e) its spectrum using two-point BLEP, and (f) eight-point BLEP with Blackman-Harris *sinc()* windowing.

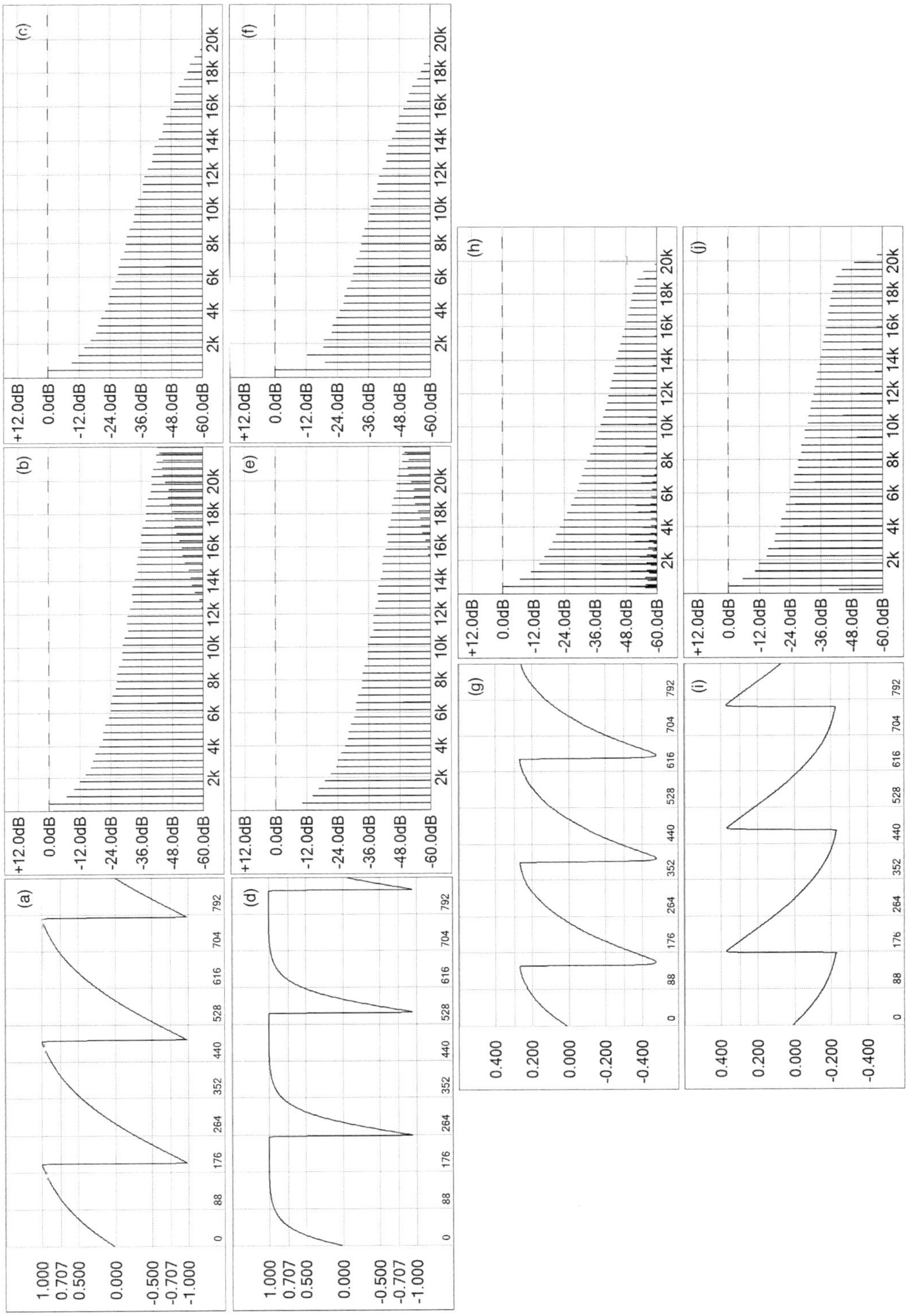

Figure 5.19: The output of the unipolar wave shaped 440 Hz sawtooth for (a) sat = 1.5, (b) its spectrum using two-point BLEP and (c) eight-point BLEP with Blackman-Harris *sinc()* windowing, (d) the output of the unipolar wave shaped 440 Hz sawtooth for sat = 5, (e) its spectrum using two-point BLEP, and (f) eight-point BLEP with Blackman-Harris *sinc()* windowing—for comparison the sawtooth waveform and spectra for (g,h) Korg Volca Keys and (i,j) Korg MS-20 Mini analog synths; notice the similarity in the spectral envelopes of (c) and (h).

These are not difficult issues to deal with and can be implemented using a modified BLEP or PolyBLEP function (you can find the code for this kind of oscillator at http://www.willpirkle.com/synthbook/). The spectra of the trivial square wave and PolyBLEP version are shown in Figure 5.20. The pulse width is 50% and the reduction in aliasing is as dramatic as for the sawtooth waveform.

However, there is an important issue that makes this a less desirable implementation. When the pulse-width is at an extreme value close to 1% or 99%, the edges will be very close together at one end of the waveform. If the frequency of oscillation rises high enough, the edges come within a sample interval of each other. At a 1% pulse width, this occurs at about 2 kHz for a 44.1 kHz sample rate, which is actually a relatively low frequency. This would require using BLEP at least twice since we have overlapping BLEP transition regions. For BLEP with a wider transition region, this becomes tricky since there are more points to overlap.

An alternate way of generating pulse width modulate-able square waves is by summing two sawtooth waves where one has been inverted and phase shifted. Changing the phase shift of the inverted ramp alters the PWM. This is shown graphically in Figure 5.21. A 50% phase shift results in a pulse width of 50%, while a 20% shift results in an 80% pulse width.

This method of generating PWM is a synth programming trick that was used on older digital synths that did not offer a PWM square wave oscillator. On the down side, it uses up two oscillators to create one output. Figure 5.22 shows a block diagram of this algorithm. Phase shifting the second oscillator relative to the first is easily done by altering its modulo counter. You add or subtract up to 1.0 from the modulo to implement the phase shift. With an offset of 0.5, you get 50% pulse width, so the pulse width in percent is directly related to the shift in the modulo counter.

Figure 5.23 shows the output of BLEP based square wave oscillators using this sum-of-saws method. These use both the simple two-point and wider eight-point BLEP sawtooth oscillators; the wider transition BLEP versions have slight ringing at the edges but

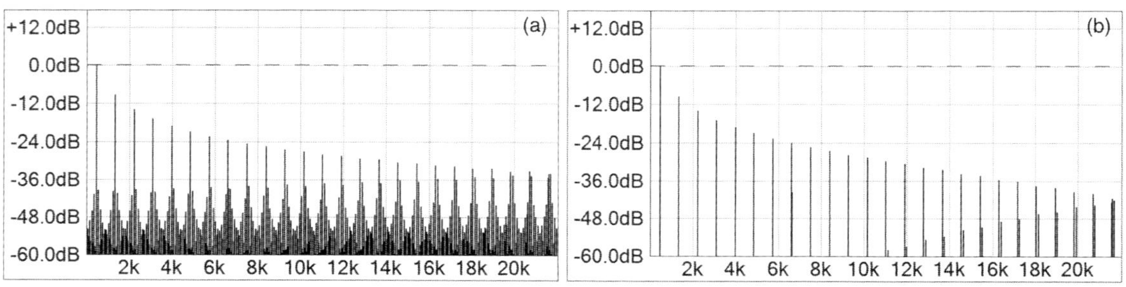

Figure 5.20: A 440 Hz (a) trivial square wave and (b) two-point PolyBLEP square wave.

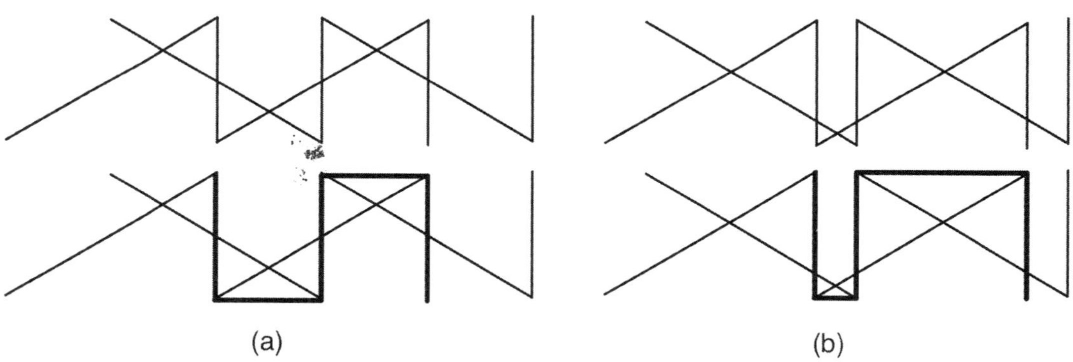

Figure 5.21: Summing sawtooth waves (a) the inverted sawtooth is 50% out of phase and (b) the inverted sawtooth is 20% out of phase.

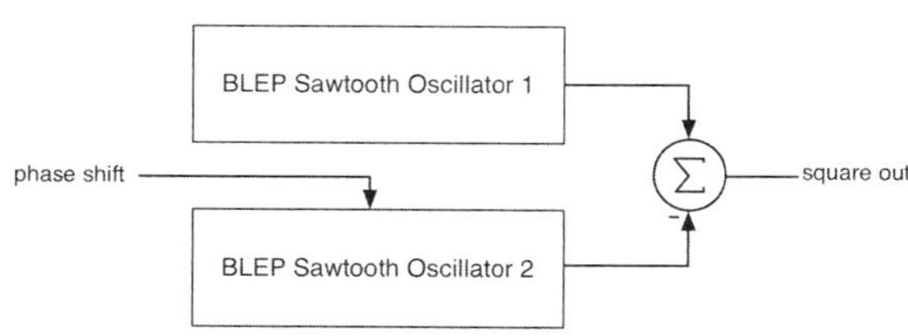

Figure 5.22: BLEP sawtooth oscillators are combined together to create the square wave oscillator; the phase offset between the two determines the resulting pulse width.

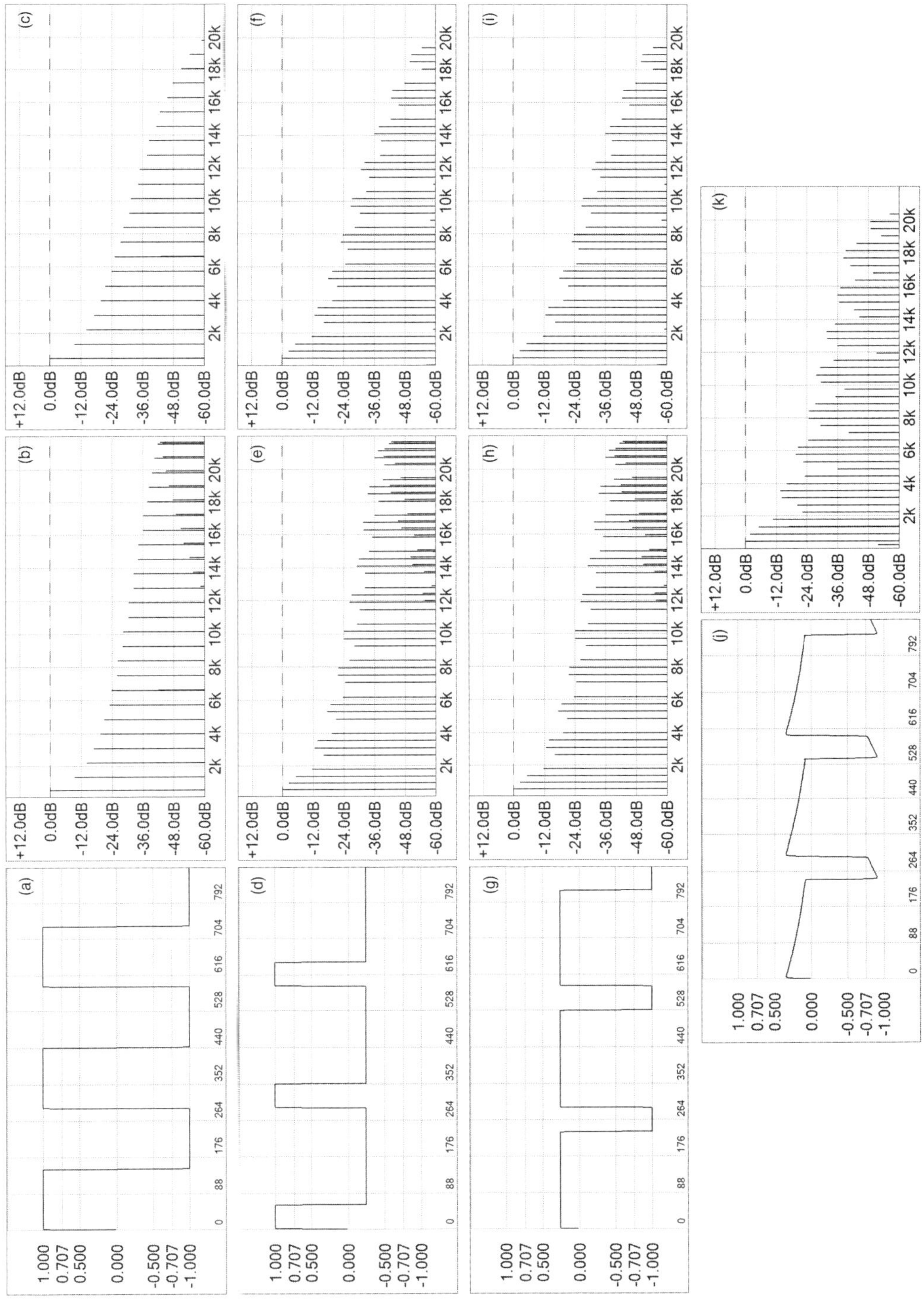

Figure 5.23: The BLEP square wave oscillator output and spectra and pulse width of 50% (a) waveform, (b) two-point PolyBLEP, (c) eight-point BLEP with Blackman-Harris *sinc()* windowing, and pulse width of 20%, (d) waveform, (e) two-point PolyBLEP, (f) eight-point BLEP with Blackman-Harris *sinc()* windowing, and pulse width of 80% (g) waveform, (h) two-point PolyBLEP, (i) eight-point BLEP with Blackman-Harris *sinc()* windowing along with the output of the Korg MS-20 Mini, pulse width of 80%, (j) waveform, and (k) spectrum; as with the MS-20 sawtooth, the oscillators are hardwired to the filters; all spectra have *fo* = 440 Hz.

lower amplitude aliased components. Again, you can see the aliasing components as the non-harmonic spikes above about 12 kHz, and the eight-point BLEP oscillator is alias-free but also rolls off the very high frequency harmonics. The same tradeoff in aliasing versus harmonic envelope between the two-point and eight-point BLEP outputs also occurs. The humpy envelopes and missing spectral components in the 20% and 80% pulse width waveforms are correct; the aliased components are the error. The 20% and 80% spectral envelopes look identical, as they should. For a general comparison, the 80% pulse width output of a Korg MS-20 Mini analog synth is included in (j) and (k).

As the pulse width changes, so does the DC offset of the waveform—at 50% pulse width the DC offset is zero. In Figure 5.23(d) and (g) you can see what the output should look like. When the pulse width is less than 50%, the waveform is shifted up to remove the DC offset. It is also scaled in amplitude. Likewise, it is shifted down and similarly scaled when the width is greater than 50%. Failure to do this will result in a potentially massive DC offset in your signal. Fortunately, the code for this scaling is simple. Equation 5.8 shows the DC correction values for the pulse width *pw* given in percent. After summing the sawtooth waveforms at 50% levels each, you calculate the correction factor and multiply it with the output.

$$
\begin{aligned}
&square = 0.5saw1 - 0.5saw2 \\
&correction = \begin{cases} \dfrac{1}{pw/100} & pw \geq 50\% \\ \dfrac{1}{1-(pw/100)} & pw < 50\% \end{cases} \\
&square = square * correction
\end{aligned}
\tag{5.8}
$$

5.13 Differentiated Parabolic Waveform Oscillators

Välimäki (2005) observed that differentiating a parabolic waveform produced an output that was similar in shape to a trivial sawtooth but with greatly reduced aliasing. A parabolic waveform can be generated by squaring a bi-polar ramp or sawtooth waveform. The resulting parabolic waveform is differentiated with a simple digital differentiator shown in Figure 5.24.

The block diagram for the Differentiated Parabolic Waveform (DPW) sawtooth oscillator is shown in Figure 5.25. The output of the differentiator is modified with the *c* coefficient where:

$$c = \frac{f_s}{4f_o(1 - f_o / f_s)} \tag{5.9}$$

Figure 5.26 compares the output of the PolyBLEP and DPW sawtooth oscillator's spectra, revealing slightly more aliasing in the DPW output. Also, the harmonic amplitudes are not exactly the same since the DPW sawtooth isn't a perfect ramp shape. Even with the aliasing components, the DPW output is still cleaner than the trivial sawtooth.

The code for the DPW sawtooth uses the same trivial sawtooth generator as all our oscillators then performs the DPW operation on that.

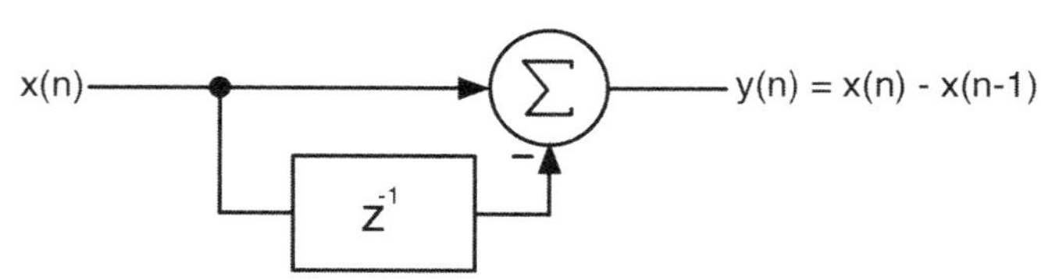

Figure 5.24: A simple digital differentiator.

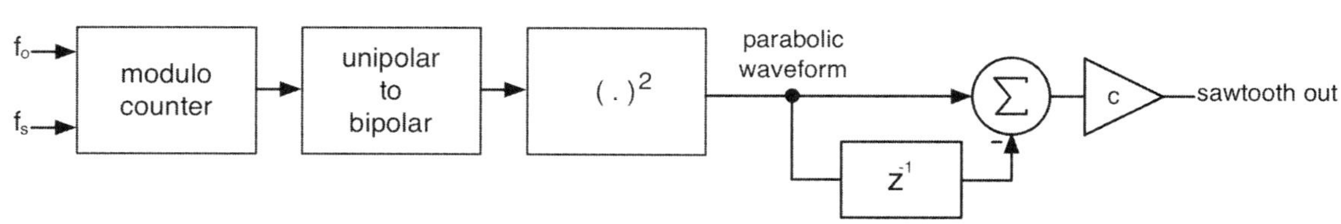

Figure 5.25: The DPW sawtooth block diagram.

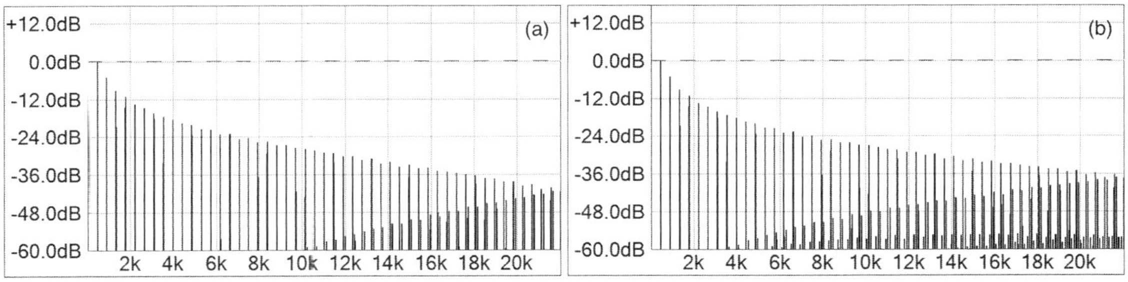

Figure 5.26: (a) The PolyBLEP sawtooth and (b) DPW sawtooth spectra with *fo* = 440 Hz.

5.14 DPW Triangle Wave Oscillator

PolyBLEP outperforms DPW for sawtooth and square wave generation, but it cannot be used to create triangle waves. Remember that the trivial triangle wave generator produces low aliasing components. The DPW triangle oscillator produces very slightly less aliasing components. The DPW algorithm is shown in Figure 5.27.

In this algorithm, the bipolar modulo counter runs at twice the oscillator frequency. A trivial square wave also running at $2f_o$ modulates the bipolar converted counter value. Then it is differentiated and scaled by the same *c* coefficient as the sawtooth generator but with the $2f_o$ value. Figure 5.28 compares the spectrum of the trivial triangle wave oscillator with the DPW version and reveals only a slight difference in harmonic amplitudes.

5.15 Other Non-Sinusoidal Oscillators

There are a few more non-sinusoidal waveforms that are commonly used for both pitched and low frequency oscillators. These include:

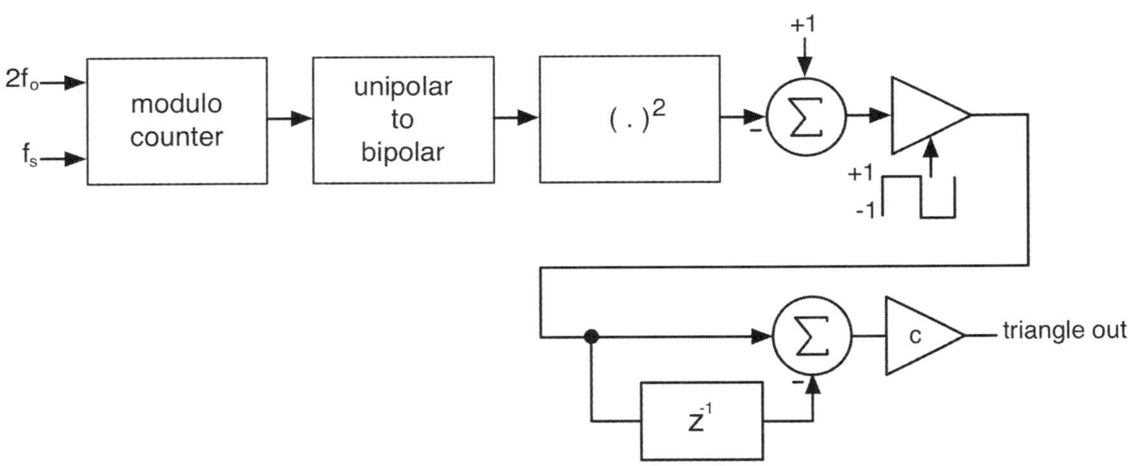

Figure 5.27: The DPW triangle wave oscillator block diagram.

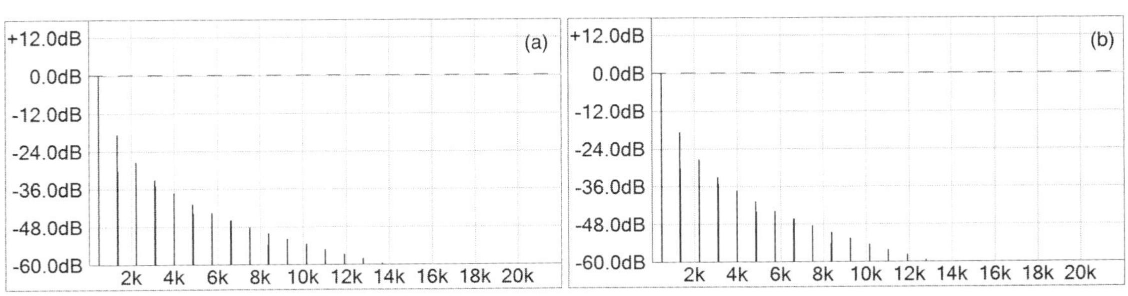

Figure 5.28: The spectra of (a) trivial triangle wave and (b) DPW triangle wave oscillators with *fo* = 440 Hz.

Pitched and LFO:

- white noise
- pseudo-random noise

LFO only:

- random sample and hold
- exponential decay

5.16 White Noise Oscillator

White noise is technically a purely random waveform. Its spectrum is flat and it contains all harmonics up to Nyquist. The C function *rand()* will generate random integers between 0 and 32767. Prior to use, the random number generator should be seeded with a value that changes on each run of the oscillator or plug-in. This is done with the *srand()* function. The *srand()* function takes an argument that is the seed value. Typically, the *time()* function is used (which is in *time.h*). This function returns the number of seconds that have elapsed since midnight, January 1, 1970 (UTC).

The random noise generation function is available for you in *synthfunctions.h* and is named *doWhiteNoise()*. You must first seed the random number generator (*prepareForPlay()* would be a good location).

```
srand(time(NULL));
```

Then you can use the *doWhiteNoise()* function in *synthfunctions.h* to produce a random value.

```
inline double doWhiteNoise()
{
        // fNoise is 0 -> 32767.0
        float fNoise = (float)rand();

        // normalize and make bipolar
        fNoise = 2.0*(fNoise/32767.0) - 1.0;

        return fNoise;
}
```

5.17 Pseudo Random Noise (PN Sequence) Oscillator

Pseudo random Noise (PN) generators create a noise-like output that is not purely flat in spectral content but which possesses a pleasing sound. The spectral content is neither white, nor exactly pink (roll off of –3 dB/octave from DC to Nyquist). It has a roll off that resembles a shallow lowpass or shelving filter. The noise sequence eventually repeats so it can be used analytically. For example, a recording of a room could be made with the noise stimulus, then the signal could be de-convolved and the impulse response of the room recovered. The de-convolution can be carried out since the signal is deterministic and known a priori. There are several ways to create a PN Sequence. The version here is from D'Attorro (2002) and we will use a 32-bit unsigned integer (UINT) to perform the operations.

The PN Sequence is generated by first pre-loading a 32-bit register with an initial non-zero value (any non-zero value may be used). During each sample interval, two or more selected bits are XOR-ed together and stored. The XOR (Exclusive-Or) operation outputs a binary 1 only when the two input bits are different (0 and 1 or 1 and 0). Then, the entire register is bit-shifted to the right by one. The stored XOR value is inserted into the MSB of the register. The resulting register is the value for that sample period. The bit locations that are XOR-ed during the operation are pre-determined by PN algorithms. Different register sizes, and therefore output word widths, have different sets of acceptable bits for the XOR-ing process.

For a 32-bit register, the bits to XOR together are bits b0, b1, b27, and b28. The algorithm then becomes:

- start with a 32-bit register initialized to any value
- on each sample period form the result:

$$b_{31} = b_0 \otimes b_1 \otimes b_{27} \otimes b_{28} \tag{5.10}$$

- shift the register to the right by one bit
- load the MSB (b31) with the calculated value
- convert the UINT register to a floating point number and scale

Here is a table of commonly used word lengths and the XOR-ing formulas for each:

Word Length	Formula
8	$b_7 = b_0 \otimes b_1 \otimes b_5 \otimes b_6$
16	$b_{15} = b_0 \otimes b_2 \otimes b_3 \otimes b_5$
24	$b_{23} = b_0 \otimes b_1 \otimes b_3 \otimes b_4$
32	$b_{31} = b_0 \otimes b_1 \otimes b_{27} \otimes b_{28}$
64	$b_{63} = b_0 \otimes b_1 \otimes b_3 \otimes b_4$

(5.11)

The C++ code for this generator is already implemented for you in *synthfunctions.h* and it requires a macro definition to extract the bits from the 32-bit unsigned integer register, which is the argument to the main function.

```
#define EXTRACT_BITS(the_val, bits_start, bits_len) ((the_val >> (bits_start
                                                 -1)) & ((1 << bits_len)
                                                 -1))

inline double doPNSequence(UINT& uPNRegister)
{
     // get the bits
     UINT b0 = EXTRACT_BITS(uPNRegister, 1, 1); // 1 = b0
     UINT b1 = EXTRACT_BITS(uPNRegister, 2, 1); // 2 = b1
     UINT b27 = EXTRACT_BITS(uPNRegister, 28, 1); // 28 = b27
     UINT b28 = EXTRACT_BITS(uPNRegister, 29, 1); // 29 = b28

     // form the XOR
     UINT b31 = b0^b1^b27^b28;

     // form the mask to OR with the register to load b31
     if(b31 == 1)
            b31 = 0x10000000;

     // shift one bit to right
     uPNRegister >>= 1;

     // set the b31 bit
     uPNRegister |= b31;

     // convert the output into a floating point number
     // to a range of 0 to +2.0
     float fOut = (float)(uPNRegister)/((pow((float)2.0,(float)32.0))/16.0);

     // shift down to form a result from -1.0 to +1.0
     fOut -= 1.0;

     return fOut;
}
```

Figure 5.29 shows the difference in frequency content between the white and pseudo random sequence oscillators.

5.18 Random Sample and Hold Oscillator

The Random Sample and Hold (RS&H) oscillator samples and then holds random values from a white noise source. The hold-time is the period T of the oscillator frequency f_o, so a 1 Hz RS&H would hold each output value for one second. This produces a random stair step sequence. When used to modulate the pitch of an oscillator, it produces random note values and sounds like a game-show

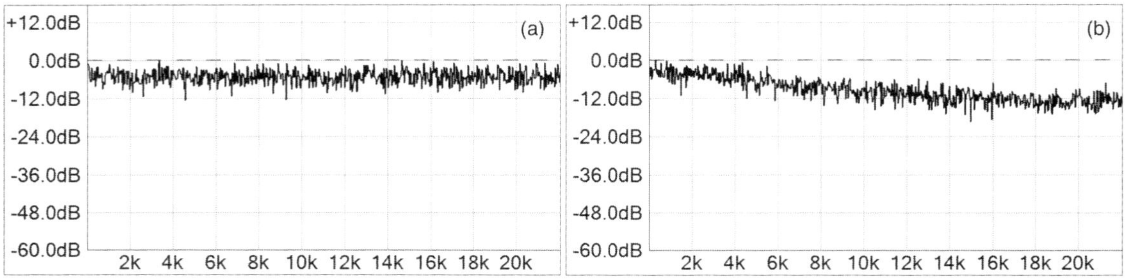

Figure 5.29: The spectra of (a) white noise and (b) the PN sequence generator.

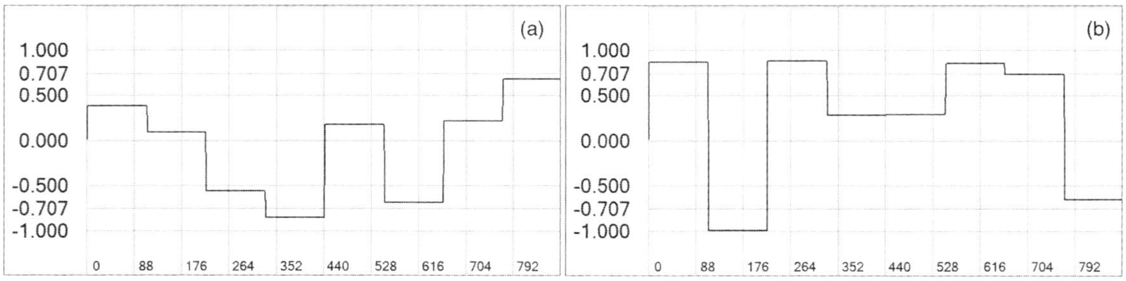

Figure 5.30: The output of the random sample and hold oscillator at two different times.

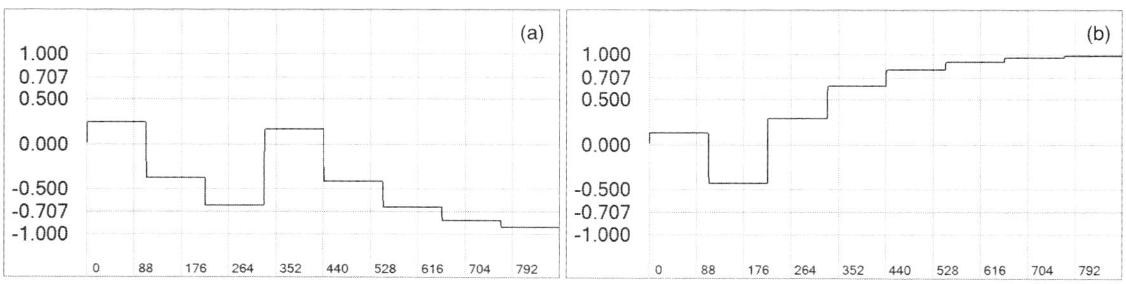

Figure 5.31: The output of the pseudo random sample and hold at two different times; a quasi-periodicity is revealed.

sound effect. When using the PN sequence as the source, the random fluctuations have inner patterns that repeat quasi-randomly and quasi-periodically. Figure 5.30 shows a couple of outputs of the RS&H oscillator taken at different times in the sequence, and you can clearly see the random stair step pattern. Figure 5.31 uses the PN sequence as the noise source and looks quite different.

To make a RS&H oscillator in code, you need a counter to count samples between successive sampling of the noise source. When the counter exceeds f_s/f_o, you wrap the value around, similar to the modulo counter. In the oscillator object's constructor, you would initialize the counter to −1.0, which serves as a flag for the function to know when the very first sample is being generated. You also need a variable to hold the value during times when the counter hasn't expired. You can initialize these variables as follows:

```
rshCounter = -1.0;
rsHoldValue = 0.0;
```

Then, during the oscillator function you can check the timer and resample the noise if needed.

```
// this is the very first run
if(rshCounter < 0)
{
        // sample the noise
        rsHoldValue = doWhiteNoise();

        // or do PN seq
        // rsHoldValue = doPNSequence(m_uPNRegister);
```

```
        rshCounter = 1.0;
        return rsHoldValue;
}

// time exceeded?
if(rshCounter > (double)m_nSampleRate/m_fo)
{
        rshCounter -= (double)m_nSampleRate/m_fo;

        // sample the noise
        rsHoldValue = doWhiteNoise();

        // or do PN seq
        // rsHoldValue = doPNSequence(m_uPNRegister);
}

// inc the counter
rshCounter += 1.0;

return rsHoldValue;
```

5.19 Exponential Decay Oscillator

An exponential decay oscillator outputs pulses of exponentially decaying curves. The time to decay is the period of the waveform. Traditionally, this is a unipolar output oscillator. The output is shown in Figure 5.32. This waveform is useful as a LFO for percussive sounds.

This oscillator is simple to design using the Concave Inverted Transform (CIT). The CIT takes values from 0 to 1 and produces an exponentially decaying output that drops from 1 to 0. We only need a single modulo counter to keep track of the timebase then repeated calls to the function, which is implemented in *synthfunctions.h*.

```
// modulo wrap test
if(m_ExpDecayModulo >= 1.0)
        m_ExpDecayModulo -= 1.0;

// calculate the output directly
double out = concaveInvertedTransform(m_ExpDecayModulo);

// inc the counter
m_ExpDecayModulo += m_Inc;

return out;
```

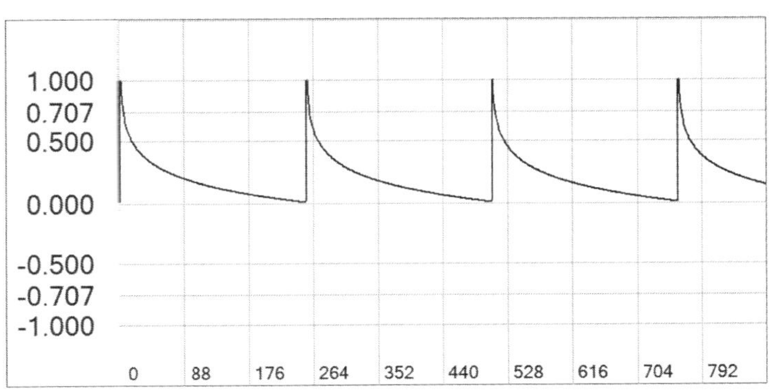

Figure 5.32: The exponential decay oscillator output.

5.20 Wavetable Oscillators

A Wavetable Oscillator is a table-based system for creating periodic signals. A buffer is pre-loaded with one cycle, minus one sample, of a waveform. The waveform may be mathematical (sin, cos, pulse, square, saw, triangle, etc.) or a recorded signal. The idea is that you read through the table and output samples from it. Consider a table of 1024 samples consisting of one cycle of a sinusoid, minus one sample shown in Figure 5.33.

The table is indexed with the value i, which starts at 0; the last entry in the table is at $i = 1023$, the sample just before the waveform starts all over again.

Suppose you start at $i = 0$ and, during each sample period, you read out one value and advance to the next. At the end of the buffer, you wrap around and start all over. You can see now why the table stores almost one cycle but not exactly—this allows the two ends of the waveform to be sewn back together properly during the circular wrap. If you did read out one value per sample period, what would the resulting frequency of the waveform be? The answer is $f_{table} = f_s/L$, when the index increment is exactly 1.0 through the table. For a 1024-point wave table at a 44,100 Hz sample rate, f_{table} is 43.066 Hz. If you happen to need a super precise sinusoid at exactly 43.066 Hz, then this method will produce nearly perfect results. The only factor is the precision of the sinusoid loaded into the table. If you had a saw-tooth waveform stored in the table, it too would have a table frequency of 43.066 Hz.

You can also see how this once again uses a kind of modulo counter that wraps around as a time base, so it also has an increment or *inc* value known as the phase increment. In order to keep this increment separate from our timebase $inc = f_o/f_s$, we call this one *inc*WT. The equation for *inc*WT is:

$$\begin{aligned} inc_{WT} &= L\frac{f_o}{f_s} \\ &= L(inc) \\ inc &= \frac{f_o}{f_s} \end{aligned} \tag{5.12}$$

The phase increment value will be used to skip through the table, moving forward by *inc*WT during each sample interval. Most likely, the *inc*WT value is going to be non-integer and will therefore consist of an integer part and a fractional part. For example, if *inc*WT = 24.9836 then the integer part would be 24 and the fractional part 0.9836. Here, the integer part is called *int* and the fractional part is called *frac.*

There are several options for dealing with the fractional part of the increment value. You could:

- truncate the value, and forget *frac*
- linearly interpolate the table *frac* distance between *int* and *int+1*
- use polynomial interpolation or another interpolation method instead of linear interpolation

If you truncate the inc_{WT} value, then you have multiple problems—the note you synthesize won't be exactly in tune. Additionally, it will be distorted because of the inaccuracy of the value in the table. Linear and polynomial interpolation overcomes these problems, though there is still distortion in the output. A commonly used polynomial method employs fourth order Lagrange interpolation, where the neighboring four points (two to the left and two to the right) of the target value are used. One advantage of wavetables is that when the highest harmonic in the table is far below Nyquist, or the harmonic amplitudes fall rapidly as the frequency increases, then simple linear interpolation of the table will provide excellent results. Both linear and Lagrange interpolation functions are included in *pluginconstants.h*.

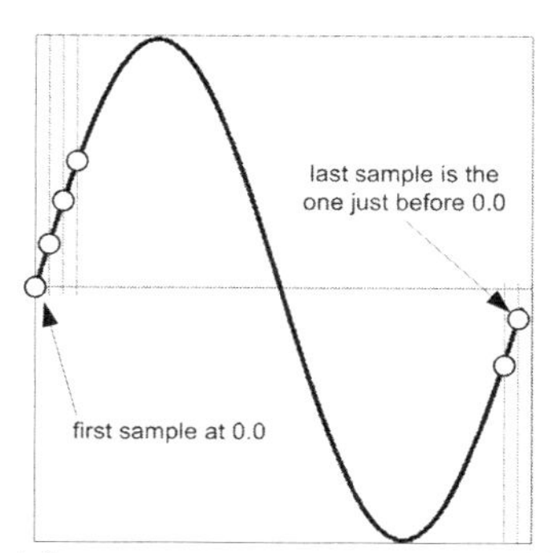

Figure 5.33: One cycle minus one sample of a sinusoid in a 1024-point wavetable.

A potential problem with a wave table is that the cycle of data stored inside might be full of aliasing components. In other words, you can create a table of data that could have never made it past the input LPF if it were an analog signal being sampled. There are other issues as well. If the table contains a non-sinusoidal waveform, it can still cause aliasing even if the waveform is already bandlimited and alias-free. This happens when the phase increment is greater than one, which would occur for any frequency above 43.066 Hz in this 1024-point system. The waveform is effectively decimated by the factor of *inc*WT as you go skipping through the table. This places an upper limit on the phase increment related to the highest harmonic component in the table. A simple way to limit the effect of this is to make the tables shorter as the frequencies get higher.

$$inc_{WT}(\max) = \frac{Lf_o}{f_s n_h} \qquad (5.13)$$

$$n_h = \text{highest harmonic number in table}$$

Negative Frequencies

For Frequency Modulation (FM) synthesis, the oscillators will need to generate negative frequencies as well as positive ones. This means they will need to run forward or backwards. We only need this for pitched oscillators, not LFOs. We will pre-design all pitched oscillators except the *CSampleOscillator* in Chapter 10 to run in either direction in time. It is not required for noise oscillators.

5.21 Bandlimited Wavetable Oscillators

To produce non-sinusoidal waveforms that are alias-free, you need to preload the tables with bandlimited versions of the waveforms. For the classical waveforms like sawtooth, triangle and square, you use Fourier synthesis—the summing of individual harmonic components.

Here are the three Fourier synthesis formulas for these waveforms. The saw tooth waveform has both even and odd harmonics scaled according to $(1/k)$:

$$\begin{aligned} y(n)_{SAW} &= \sum_{k=1}^{\infty}(-1)^{k+1}\frac{1}{k}\sin(k\omega nT) \\ &= [\sin(\omega nT) - \frac{1}{2}\sin(2\omega nT) + \frac{1}{3}\sin(3\omega nT) - \frac{1}{4}\sin(4\omega nT) + \ldots] \end{aligned} \qquad (5.14)$$

The triangle waveform has only odd harmonics. The $(-1)^k$ term alternates the signs of the harmonics. The harmonic amplitudes drop off at a rate given by $1/(2k+1)^2$, which is exponential in nature.

$$\begin{aligned} y(n)_{TRI} &= \sum_{k=0}^{\infty}(-1)^{k}\frac{1}{(2k+1)^2}\sin((2k+1)\omega nT) \\ &= [\sin(\omega nT) - \frac{1}{9}\sin(3\omega nT) + \frac{1}{25}\sin(5\omega nT) - \frac{1}{49}\sin(7\omega nT) + \ldots] \end{aligned} \qquad (5.15)$$

The square wave is also composed of odd harmonics like the triangle wave. The harmonic amplitudes drop off at a rate of $1/(2k+1)$, which is not as severe as the triangle wave. Therefore, the square wave has higher sounding harmonics and a more gritty texture.

$$\begin{aligned} y(n)_{SQUARE} &= \sum_{k=0}^{\infty}\frac{1}{2k+1}\sin((2k+1)\omega nT) \\ &= [\sin(\omega nT) + \frac{1}{3}\sin(3\omega nT) + \frac{1}{5}\sin(5\omega nT) + \frac{1}{7}\sin(7\omega nT) + \ldots] \end{aligned} \qquad (5.16)$$

Using these Fourier series equations, you can implement Fourier synthesis to build up a waveform that is band limited to Nyquist. One issue is the number of tables that are needed. The lowest note on a piano is A0 at 27.5 Hz, and there are 800 harmonics of this frequency before the Nyquist limit is reached using the h_{lim} equation.

$$h_{\lim} = \frac{f_o}{f_s/2} - 1 \qquad (5.17)$$

The upper note on the piano is C8 at 4816 0 Hz, which has five harmonics before Nyquist. We often use these piano limits even though the MIDI spec allows for 128 notes, with MIDI note 0 at 8.175 Hz and MIDI note 127 at 12543.85 Hz. So we see that we have a wide range of harmonic components, from five to 800. For the highest resolution, you could store a separate table for each note-range of harmonics. You would need a table for each waveform (saw, triangle, square) as well. This would produce a large number of tables to manage. It would also use a lot of memory, which would really only be an issue if the target platform is a mobile or other resource-limited device. Another possibility is to store one set of tables for each octave from A0 to C8, or for all ten octaves of sound from 20 Hz to 20480 Hz. Another is to store a set of tables for each minor third interval from A0 to C8. This would produce a reasonably smooth transition, as the notes are played through the intervals whereas octave-based table sets might produce an audible change in timbre as the octave boundary is crossed.

Figure 5.34(a) is the spectrum of a perfectly bandlimited sawtooth wavetable at 440 Hz containing the fundamental plus 50 harmonics, while Figure 5.34(b) shows the waveform of a 150 Hz sawtooth using the same wavetable. The ripples you see are exaggerated because the table lacks the upper harmonics; a 150 Hz bandlimited table should contain 147 harmonics. Adding more harmonics will smooth out the ripples. Multiplying each harmonic by the Lanczos sigma factor will further smooth the ripples, but this is sometimes ignored for pitched oscillators where a perfect frequency domain response is more desirable than a time domain response. The Lanczos sigma factor is:

$$\sigma_N = \frac{n\pi}{M} \qquad \sigma_n = \frac{\sin(\sigma_N)}{\sigma_N}$$

$$M = \text{number of harmonics} \tag{5.18}$$

$$n = \text{harmonic number}$$

$$\sigma_n = \text{Lanczos sigma for harmonic n}$$

Pulse width modulation of a square wave presents a problem in wave table synthesis since the harmonic content of the square wave changes with pulse width. An option might be to pre-calculate several different tables of various pulse width and interpolate between them. A simpler option is to use the sum-of-saws method from Section 5.12.

Figure 5.35 shows the difference in the waveform shape with and without applying the Lanczos sigma factor. The spectrum of the Lanczos smoothed waveform is not the same as the un-smoothed one; however, in the case of the sawtooth, we want to apply it so that the square waves we generate with the sum-of-saws method will have their pulse widths modulated properly, which is more dependent on the shape of the waveform than its spectrum.

You should also know that the Lanczos sigma correction does alter the spectrum a bit—in fact both the waveform and spectrum resemble the results we got with the eight-point BLEP oscillator using non-rectangular windowing. Figure 5.36 shows the spectra of a 440 Hz sawtooth with and without the sigma correction. Compare these with the BLEP oscillator spectra including the waveshaped sawtooth. You should also do some listening tests to see if you can hear a difference in the normal and corrected versions.

The code below implements a wavetable lookup using a read index and increment value.

- the two samples that surround the target index value are found
- the output is interpolated between them
- the read index is incremented by the *inc* value

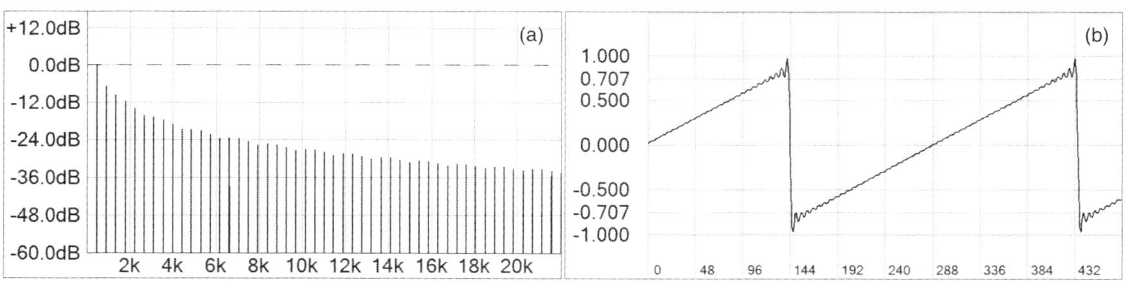

Figure 5.34: (a) The spectrum of a 440 Hz sawtooth wave using a bandlimited wavetable and (b) the waveform shape of a 150 Hz sawtooth using the same wavetable as (a).

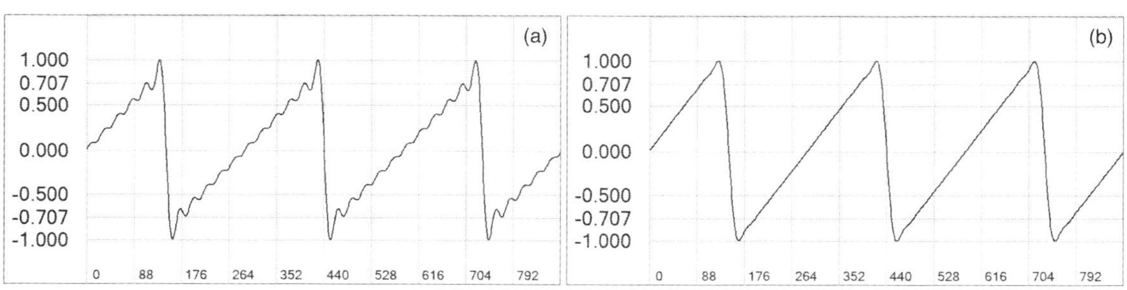

Figure 5.35: A 150 Hz wavetable sawtooth (a) without and (b) with Lanczos sigma correction.

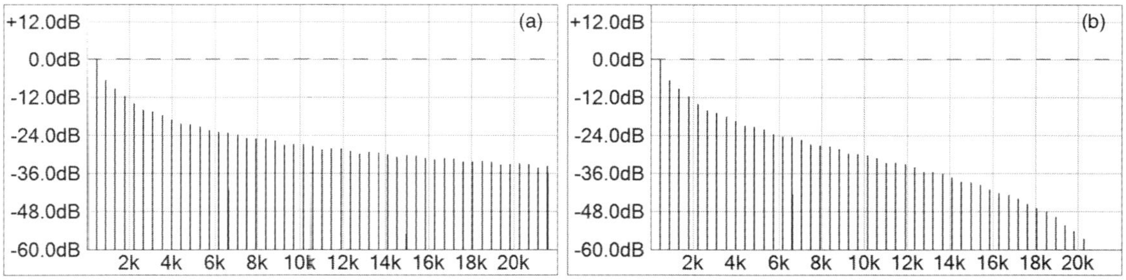

Figure 5.36: Spectra for (a) the 440 Hz wavetable without Lanczos sigma correction (b) 440 Hz wavetable with Lanczos sigma correction.

- check for wrap, both forward and reverse (for negative frequencies in FM/PM)
- bound the read index to the table boundaries (for FM/PM)
- *m_pCurrentTable* is a pointer to the table being used

```
double doWaveTable(double& dReadIndex, double dWT_inc)
{
     double dOut = 0;

     // get INT part
     int nReadIndex = abs((int)dReadIndex);

     // get FRAC part
     float fFrac = dReadIndex - nReadIndex;

     // setup second index for interpolation; wrap the buffer if needed
     int nReadIndexNext = nReadIndex + 1 > WT_LENGTH-1 ? 0 : nReadIndex + 1;

     // interpolate the output
     dOut = dLinTerp(0, 1, m_pCurrentTable[nReadIndex],
                    m_pCurrentTable[nReadIndexNext], fFrac);

     // add the increment for next time
     dReadIndex += dWT_inc;

     // check for wrap
     if(dWT_inc >= 0) // forward
     {
          if(dReadIndex >= WT_LENGTH)
               dReadIndex = dReadIndex - WT_LENGTH;
     }
     else
     {
          if(dReadIndex < 0) // reverse
               dReadIndex = WT_LENGTH + dReadIndex;
     }

     // clamp the index to table bounds for FM
     dReadIndex = min(dReadIndex, WT_LENGTH);
```

```
        dReadIndex = max(dReadIndex, 0);

        return dOut;
    }
```

With the Fourier equations, we can create bandlimited triangle and square waves. The triangle waves work perfectly. However, the square waves are static and cannot have their pulse width changed. A simple solution is to use the same sum-of-saws method we used in the BLEP square wave oscillator. The same block diagram applies. The coding details are discussed later, but you should compare the wavetable versions with the BLEP oscillators as shown in Figure 5.37. Once again, aliasing is improved using wider transition regions in the BLEP correction.

5.22 Sinusoidal Oscillators by Approximation

Wavetables with linear or Lagrange interpolation can produce very clean sinusoids even at high frequencies, and you only need one sinusoid wavetable. However, there are other methods for creating sinusoidal oscillators, such as the direct form and Gordon/Smith and Smith/Cook topologies. These three all implement the oscillator as a feedback structure without an input. Instead of inputs, oscillator algorithms have initial conditions. An issue with all three involves changing the frequency of oscillation after the oscillator has started since the initial conditions for the new oscillation frequency must be recalculated. The Gordon/Smith oscillator requires a call to the *sin*() function, the Smith/Cook oscillator requires a *cos*() and two *tan*() function calls, while the direct form oscillator requires an *arcsin*() function call. This renders them less efficient than simply calling the trigonometric functions themselves if the goal is continuous frequency control.

Approximating the sine and cosine functions has been an ongoing mathematical topic. There are several approximations to choose from, but two that are simple and produce low error are the parabolic and Bhāskara I approximations. The parabolic approximation uses a 2nd order parabola constructed for a best fit to a sinusoid half. The parabola is flipped to produce the other half wave. The equation for the parabolic approximation for one half the waveform is:

$$y = \frac{4x}{\pi} - \frac{4x^2}{\pi^2} \qquad 0 \leq x \leq \pi \tag{5.19}$$

The error in the output can be further minimized by averaging in a squared version of the parabola and finding the optimum weighting factor. Interestingly, after correction, this parabola is nearly identical to the parabola calculated for DPW oscillators. Combining these together in code results in the *sine*() function available in *synthfunctions.h*. The *bHighPrecision* flag adds the squared parabola correction.

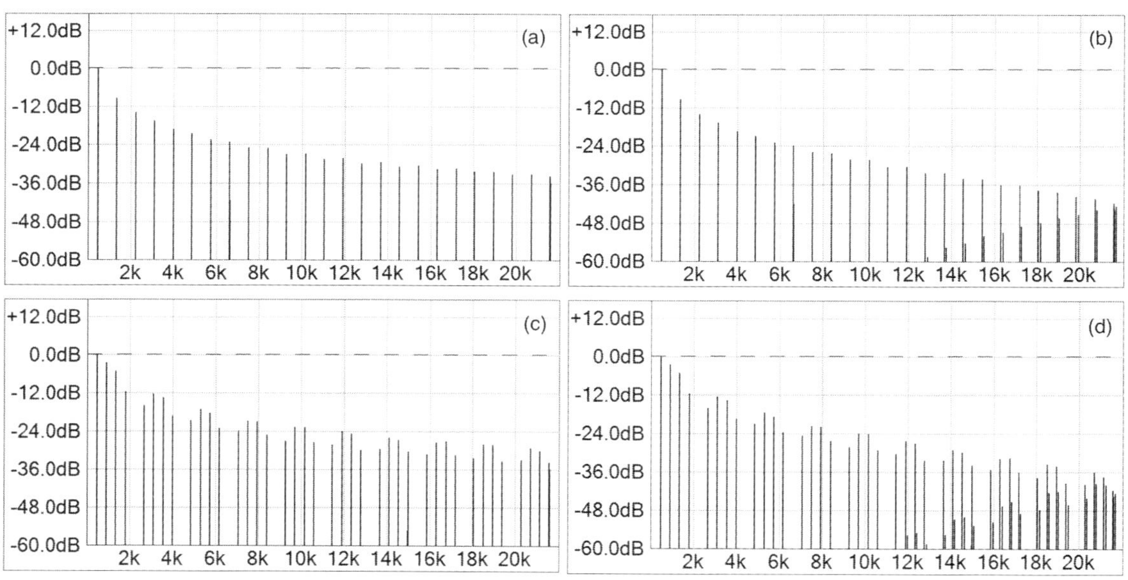

Figure 5.37: (a) The sum-of-saws wavetable (no Lanczos correction) and (b) two-point BLEP square wave with 50% pulse width, and (c) the sum-of-saws wavetable (no Lanczos correction) and (d) two-point BLEP square wave with 20% pulse width.

```
const double B = 4/pi;
const double C = -4/(pi*pi);
const double P = 0.225;

// http://devmaster.net/posts/9648/fast-and-accurate-sine-cosine
// input is -pi to +pi
inline double sine(double x, bool bHighPrecision = true)
{
     double y = B * x + C * x * abs(x);

     if(bHighPrecision)
            y = P * (y * abs(y) - y) + y;

     return y;
}
```

Another simple and interesting sinusoid approximation is Bhāskara I's approximation. Bhāskara I was an Indian mathematician in the seventh century ad. Although he did not include a proof with the approximation, many scholars have second-guessed his method, which also uses a parabola. The approximation only works as written from 0 to pi radians. The other half cycle is calculated by flipping the signs in equation. For the first half cycle, the approximation in radians/second is:

$$\sin(x)B\frac{16x(\pi - x)}{5\pi - 4x(\pi - x)} \tag{5.20}$$

The function *BhaskaraISine() in synthfunctions.h* is:

```
const double D = 5.0*pi*pi;
inline double BhaskaraISine(double x)
{
     double sgn = x/abs(x);
     return 16.0*x*(pi - sgn*x)/(D - sgn*4.0*x*(pi - sgn*x));
}
```

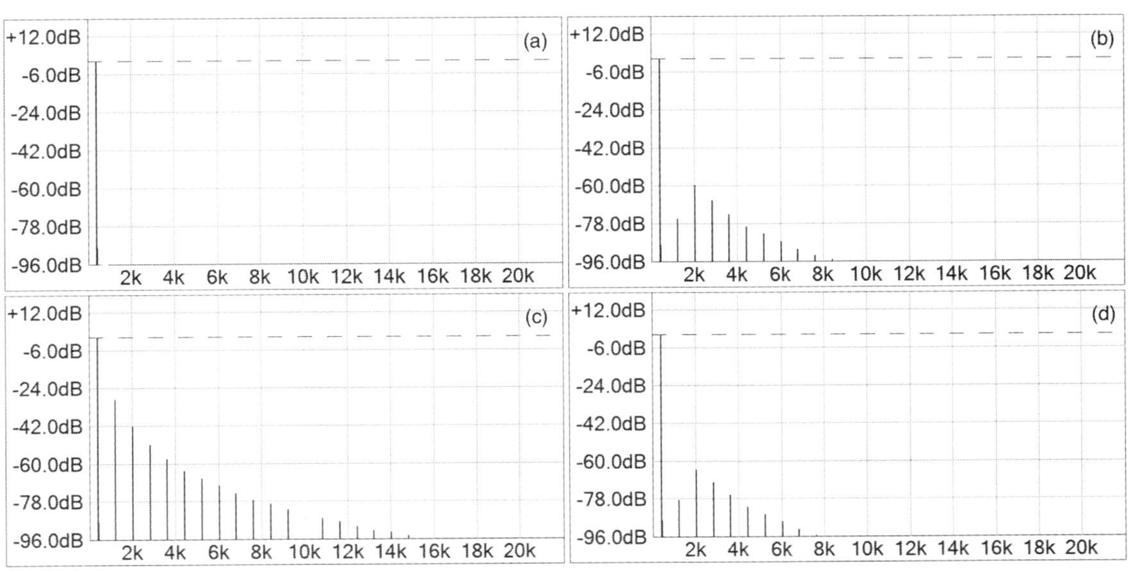

Figure 5.38: The spectra of (a) linearly interpolated wavetable, (b) Bh skara I, (c) low and (d) high accuracy parabolic approximations at fo = 400 Hz.

Figure 5.38 compares the spectra of wavetable, Bhāskara I, low and high accuracy parabolic approximation. The extra frequency components in the non-wavetable versions represent the error in the signal or harmonic distortion. Both the Bhāskara I and high accuracy parabolic approximation have harmonic distortion components at or below −60 dB. The matching spectral envelopes of Bhāskara I and high accuracy parabolic reveal the parabolic nature of Bhāskara I's algorithm. Visually, there is no difference in any of the waveforms. For an LFO, the low accuracy parabolic approximation may be fine. For a pitched oscillator, any of the other three could be chosen, though purists may prefer the wavetable.

5.23 Pitched Oscillator Calculations

The fundamental frequency of a pitched oscillator comes from the MIDI note pitch value, unlike the LFO where the user adjusts a control manually. For our synths, we can use a pre-calculated array of pitches, where the array index is the MIDI note number. This array is already declared in *synthfunctions.h* as *midiFreqTable[128]*, and you used it in Chapter 3 for the MIDI logging; the code to calculate the pitches is (from the Steinberg VST 2.4 API):

```
double k = 1.059463094359; // 12th root of 2
double a = 6.875;   // a
a *= k;      // b
a *= k;      // bb
a *= k;      // c, frequency of midi note 0
for (int i = 0; i < 128; i++)      // 128 midi notes
{
      // Hz Table
      midiFreqTable[i] = (float)a;

      // update for loop…
      a *= k;
}
```

Many oscillators feature additional tweaks to this fundamental pitch. Typically, the oscillator's pitch may be varied by allowing a change in its octave, semitone or cents. This is easily accomplished with a pitch shift multiplier where:

$$\begin{aligned} Mp &= 2^{N/12} \\ N &= \text{pitch shift in semitones} \end{aligned} \tag{5.21}$$

We have supplied a function to do this in *synthfunctions.h* called *pitchShiftMultiplier()*.

```
/* pitchShiftMultiplier()

      returns a multiplier for a given pitch shift in semitones
      to shift octaves,    call pitchShiftMultiplier(octaveValue*12.0);
      to shift semitones,  call pitchShiftMultiplier(semitonesValue);
      to shift cents,      call pitchShiftMultiplier(centsValue/100.0);
*/
double pitchShiftMultiplier(double dPitchShiftSemitones)
{
      // 2^(N/12)
      return pow2(dPitchShiftSemitones/12.0);
}
```

Suppose you have an oscillator running at 440 Hz that allows the tweaking of all three values, and the user has modified the controls such that:

- octave = +2
- semitones = −7
- cents = +50

The final calculation for the pitch is the product of the fundamental multiplied by each frequency shift multiplier.

```
double octave = pitchShiftMultiplier(2.0*12.0);
double semi = pitchShiftMultiplier(-7.0);
double cents = pitchShiftMultiplier(50.0/100.0);

// put it all together
double finalOscFreq = m_dFrequency_Hz*octave*semi*cents;
```

However, there is another implementation that produces identical results with only one call to the pitch shift multiplier function, and it is a simple mathematical rule with the exponents—instead of calculating each multiplier individually, you can simply sum the modulation values prior to calling the pitch shift function:

```
double finalOscFreq = m_dFrequency_Hz*pitchShiftMultiplier(2.0*12.0 +
                                                          -7.0 +
                                                          (50.0/100.0));
```

5.24 Sources of Modulation

Modulating the pitch of an oscillator is a commonly used synthesis technique. Interesting sounds feature both time and frequency domain evolution, and modulating pitch is a fundamental component of frequency domain evolution. Musicians use the vibrato effect to modulate the pitch of their instruments or voices. Modulating the pitch of an oscillator with a LFO produces the vibrato effect. Most synths also contain a dedicated pitch-bend control in the form of a wheel or joystick. The control centers itself when released and sends pitch bend messages when moving. An envelope generator (EG) is often used to modulate the pitch over the duration of a note event. For LFO, EG and pitch-bend, the pitch modulation is exponential and is expressed in pitch-cents. If you apply vibrato with a depth of one octave to the note 440 Hz, then the upper extreme would be 880 Hz while the lower would be 220 Hz—this is not linearly centered around 440 Hz. However, with FM synthesis, the modulation is linear around the oscillator pitch. This means that we have more pitch multipliers to implement. For our oscillators, we will need three pitch modulation inputs:

- pitch bend
- exponential modulation
- linear modulation

The pitch bend and exponential modulation inputs will use the same pitch multiplier function to calculate their shift. Linear modulation will add or subtract an offset that represents the modulation amount at any given time. For pitch bend, the user chooses the minimum and maximum value for the shift. For the exponential modulations, either hard-coded or user-defined limits are employed. For linear modulation in FM synthesis, the limits become +/− Nyquist as described in Chapter 13 (note that we will actually use phase modulation in Chapter 13, but we will discuss that later).

Bipolar Modulation

We will allow the pulse width to be modulated if the waveform is a square wave. The oscillator's PWM modulation input will accept values from [−1..+1]. It is worth examining the pulse width calculation in detail since you will see other modulation calculations done the same way. The pulse width control variable acts as the center of modulation. The current modulation value *dPWMod* ranges from [−1..+1], so multiplying this by the difference in the limits divided by the minimum limit produces the proper modulation offset value. For any kind of linear bipolar modulation, the function will be:

$$finalValue = center + modValue\left[\frac{highLimit - lowLimit}{lowLimit}\right] \tag{5.22}$$

In the case of unipolar modulation, we will almost always simply convert the unipolar value to a bipolar one first. As the next few chapters unfold, you will see the rare exceptions to this rule.

Finally, we also note that any oscillator should be allowed to modulate any other oscillator. For example, a LFO could modulate the frequency of another LFO. Figure 5.39(a) shows the detailed block diagram for a pitched oscillator, while Figure 5.39(b) shows the simplified version. The oscillator may be mono or stereo out. Our first few synths will use mono oscillators, so we can focus on that for now. The inputs to the oscillator block consist of two types: modulation and control. Typically (but not always) the control inputs will connect to GUI controls on the user interface, while modulation inputs will connect to other synth objects. Figure 5.39(a) shows all possible control and modulation inputs, but in our detailed block diagrams, we may exclude some of the inputs if we are not using them (for example, the Phase Modulation input is only used in our FM synth). In Figure 5.39(b) notice how the modulation input at the bottom is implied to be exponential frequency modulation.

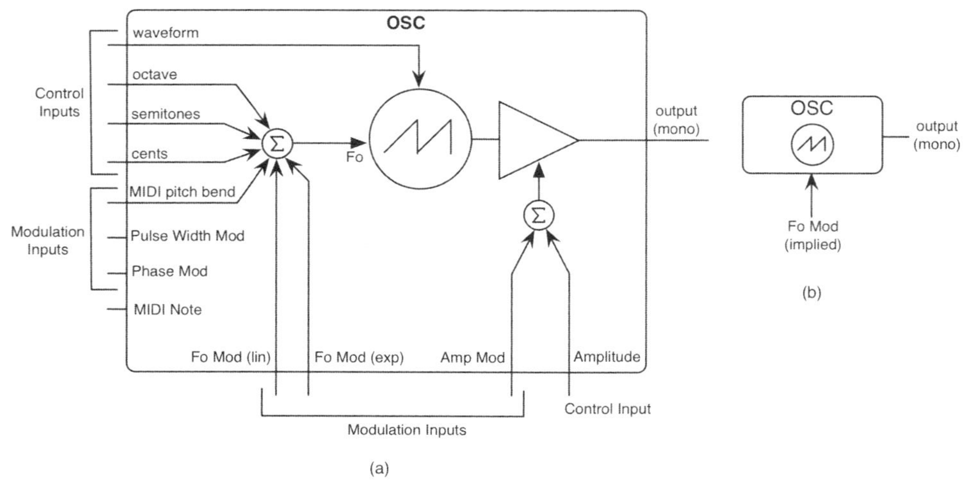

Figure 5.39: Two pitched oscillator symbols: (a) the generic, detailed block diagram and (b) the simplified version.

5.25 Pitched Oscillator Starting Phase Considerations

For pitched quasi bandlimited oscillators, it is important that the phases of the oscillators line up properly with a sinusoid. This means that the zero crossings at the half-way point would line up, assuming 50% duty cycle for the square wave. The square wave already lines up properly with the sinusoid, but the sawtooth and triangle wave do not. Their zero crossing edge is 50% offset from the sinusoid or square. This means their modulo counter's starting point needs to be changed. The sawtooth and triangle waveforms will need to start with the *modulo* = 0.5. This is shown graphically in Figure 5.40. We will not implement this phase line-up for LFOs because we usually desire their intrinsic shapes, especially in one-shot mode. This is also not necessary for the wavetable oscillators, since their table location is based on a read index and not a modulo value and because the bandlimited wavetables are already aligned properly as in Figure 5.40(b).

5.26 LFO Features

For a LFO, the user is always allowed to adjust the waveform rate (frequency) and depth (amplitude) of the oscillator. Additional controls may also include:

- time delay before oscillations start
- fade-in (attack) time
- phase offset

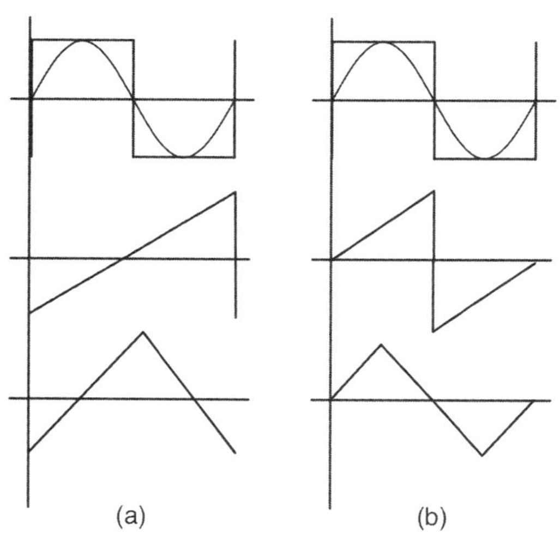

Figure 5.40: (a) The outputs of the modulo generated sawtooth and triangle wave don't line up properly with the square and sinusoid (b) all phases are aligned with the modulo starting point offset to 0.5 for the sawtooth and the triangle.

The time delay before oscillation and fade-in time mimics the way traditional musicians apply vibrato—they usually do not begin applying it at the onset of the note event, but rather wait a while and apply it as the note is decaying or sustaining. Likewise, they often fade-in the vibrato, increasing its intensity over time. A phase offset may also be added so that the oscillator starts at a non-zero value at some other starting point. These are optional, and you are encouraged to implement them as homework in the Chapter Challenges.

An important feature that we will add to our LFO objects is the ability to operate in three different modes:

- free-running
- synchronized
- one-shot

A free-running LFO starts oscillating either at start-up or after the first note event occurs. After that, it free-runs and is applied as-is during subsequent note events. A synchronized LFO restarts from the beginning on each new note event. Its application will be identical each time a note is triggered; this is more useful for vibrato effects. A one-shot LFO outputs one cycle of the waveform and then shuts off. This is an important mode to implement because it is useful for creating drum and other transient sounds. The exponential oscillator is often used in a one-shot LFO to create one exponentially decaying pulse that may be used to modulate pitch, amplitude or cut-off frequency of a filter, or all three at once.

> In one-shot mode, it is important that we end the oscillator sequence with a value of 0.0. If the one-shot LFO does not end on 0.0, then you will hear an abrupt change in the modulated parameter(s). The ramp and triangle waves will need to be adjusted to unipolar.

We also need to address the LFO's quad-phase capabilities. We often find it useful to modulate parameters in-phase, out of phase and in quadrature phase, which means "90 degrees out of phase." We can accomplish phase inversion by simply multiplying the LFO output by -1.0, but quadrature phase must be implemented when we render the LFO output. This is actually rather simple—you just offset the modulo counter by 0.25 (1/4 of a period or 90 degrees) and perform the trivial oscillator calculation again. Figure 5.41(a) shows the detailed block diagram for a pitched oscillator, while Figure 5.41(b) shows the simplified version. As with the pitched oscillators, we may leave out some of the pins if they are not used in the design (for example the quad phase output is only used in a few synths). You can also see that the names of the LFO controls vary slightly; the frequency control is named "rate" and the amplitude is "depth" to match conventions.

5.27 Designing the Oscillator Objects

We can now start designing objects for our synths. These will include oscillators, envelope generators, filters and controlled amplifiers. These objects are all cross-platform compatible, so you can freely move them between projects. In addition, we will design the objects to operate in a stand-alone fashion so that you may incorporate them into other plug-ins that don't necessarily need to be synth devices. For example you may want to use some of the filters in your existing audio effects plug-ins. All objects will be designed using base classes. This way you can extend the functionality of existing objects or spin off your own variations. The base classes will do the majority of the low level work for you so that you can concentrate on the synth topologies instead. Later in Chapter 8, we will introduce the concepts of a modulation matrix and global parameterization. At that time we will need to go back and make some modifications to the objects—these will only make the synth design easier and more flexible, and we will not alter the stand-alone capability of any objects.

The C++ objects that will implement our LFO and pitched oscillators include the following three classes. In Chapter 10 we will add a fourth oscillator that uses audio samples extracted from WAV files called *CSampleOscillator*. Since this object is very different from the others, we will save it for Chapter 10.

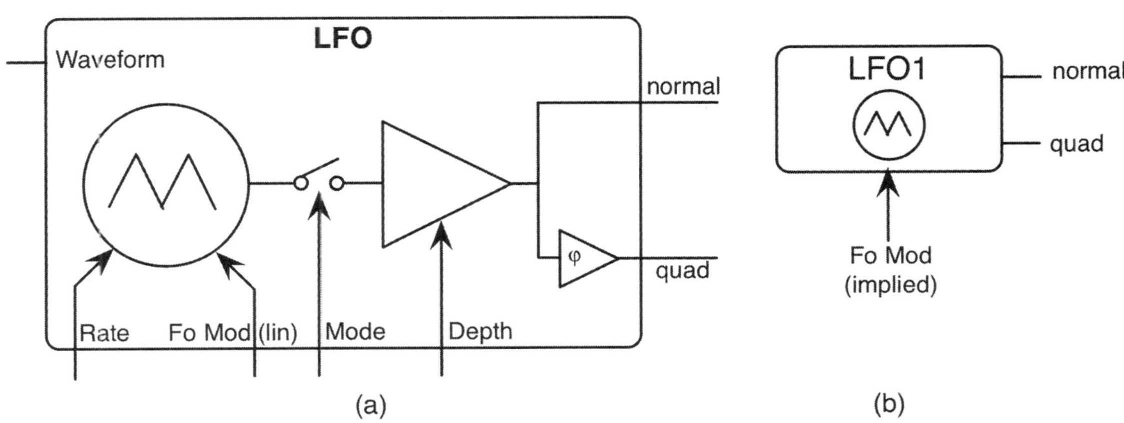

Figure 5.41: Two LFO symbols (a) the generic detailed block diagram and (b) the simplified version.

CLFO: for LFOs only

- trivial saw (both up and down: *usaw* and *dsaw*)
- triangle
- square with PWM
- parabolic sine approximation
- exponential
- random sample/hold
- quasi-random sample/hold

CQBLimitedOscillator: for virtual analog synths

- BLEP saw
- BLEP unipolar waveshaped saw
- BLEP bipolar waveshaped saw
- BLEP sum-of-sawtooth square with PWM
- DPW triangle
- parabolic sine approximation
- white noise
- quasi-random noise

CWTOscillator: for wavetable synths

- wavetable sine
- wavetable saw
- wavetable triangle
- sum-of-sawtooth square with PWM

All oscillators are derived from an abstract base class called *COscillator*. The base class object will also handle updating and calculating all variables, as well as modulating the oscillator's frequency (both linear and exponential), phase shift (for phase modulation), pulse width, and anything else we decide to add at a later time. Since all oscillators are derived from it, this object needs to have attributes and member functions that are common to most of the derived classes. As is typical in C++, if we need some new functionality that is not common to the other oscillators, we'll subclass an existing object and add the functionality. We will do this in Chapter 11.

5.28 The COscillator Base Class

The *COscillator* base class will expose the oscillator interface. It will store all variables that are common to all models, as well as provide *set()* methods to control the modulation inputs. Virtual functions are provided, so a derived class may override them and implement its own special functionality. There are different C++ coding conventions that are common. In one case, you make all member variables private or protected, then implement *get()* and *set()* functions to read or write the values. In this kind of coding, the end user never accesses variables directly with the dot (.) operator. For example these two lines of code:

```
double m_dAmplitude = m_Oscillator.m_dAmplitude;
m_Oscillator.m_dAmplitude = 0.707;
```

use direct access of the variable, so it must be declared as public. Using the "declare all variables as private/protected" paradigm, you would write them as:

```
double m_dAmplitude = m_Oscillator.getAmplitude();
m_Oscillator.setAmplitude(0.707);
```

This kind of coding-with-functions allows the programmer to control read/write access to the variable. However, for variables that require both read and write access all the time, declaring the extra *get()* and *set()* functions can add excess code (please don't flood my inbox with email here . . .). Our objects are coded with the following convention that makes it easy to remember when to use direct access or functions:

- member variables that are *control inputs* are read/write and declared as *public*; you use the dot operator to access them
- member variables that are *modulation inputs* are write-only and declared as *protected*; you use the *set()* function to control them
- member variables that are used internally and are not read or writeable will be declared as *protected* to allow derived classes to access them properly
- variables that specifically connect to a GUI control have the word "control" in them, such as *m_dPulseWidthControl*
- variables which specifically connect to a MIDI variable or control have the word "MIDI" in them
- variables are named using Hungarian Notation
- member functions that will be called during realtime note-rendering are declared as *inline* and implemented in the *.h* file of the class definition

When we wire the objects together, this paradigm will make more sense. Once we add the modulation matrix and global parameters in Chapter 8, we won't need to worry about the dot operator on public variables. The synths will almost always use function calls instead.

Oscillator.h

Download the code for *NanoSynth: Oscillators* from http://www.willpirkle.com/synthbook/. Open the *oscillator.h* file and examine the variable declarations. Tables 5.1(a) and 5.2(b) show the public and protected member variables. These were assembled by taking all

Table 5.1(a): *COscillator* public member variables.

COscillator public Member Variables		
Type	**Variable Name**	**Description**
double	m_dOscFo	the oscillator frequency; for pitched oscillators it is the MIDI note frequency, for LFOs it is the Rate control on the GUI
double	m_dFoRatio	oscillator frequency ratio (FM/PM synth only)
double	m_dAmplitude	the output amplitude [0..+1]
double	m_dPulseWidthControl	the pulse width in % controlled on the GUI
double	m_dModulo	modulo counter value
double	m_dInc	phase increment value
int	m_nOctave	octave pitch offset
int	m_nSemitones	semitone pitch offset
int	m_nCents	cent pitch offset
bool	m_bNoteOn	state variable; true = oscillator is running, false = oscillator is off
UINT	m_uWaveform	the oscillator waveform
UINT	m_uLFOMode	LFO mode
UINT	m_uMIDINoteNumber	MIDI note number of current pitch (not for LFOs)
enum	SINE,SAW1,SAW2,-SAW3,TRI,SQUARE,NOISE,PNOISE	pitched oscillator waveforms
enum	sine,usaw,dsaw,tri,square,expo,rsh,qrsh	LFO waveforms
enum	sync,shot,free	LFO Modes

Table 5.1(b): *COscillator* protected member variables.

COscillator protected Member Variables		
Type	**Variable Name**	**Description**
double	m_dSampleRate	the current sample rate
double	m_dFo	the current oscillator frequency (may change every sample period)
double	m_dPulseWidth	the pulse width in % as used in the calculation (not GUI control)
double	m_dRSHValue	the current random sample and hold output value (needs to be held)
double	m_dDPWSquareModulator	square modulator for DPW triangle oscillator
double	m_dDPW_z1	memory register for DPW
double	m_dFoMod	frequency modulation (exponential)
double	m_dFoModLin	frequency modulation (linear)
double	m_dPitchBendMod	pitch bend modulation [-1..+1]
double	m_dPhaseMod	phase modulation in radians
double	m_dPWMod	pulse width modulation [-1..+1]
double	m_dAmpMod	amplitude modulation [0..+1] (not tremolo)
UINT	m_uPNRegister	register for the quasi random noise generator
int	m_nRSHCounter	counter for holding the random sample and hold output

the algorithms from this chapter and extracting the required variables for operation. As you code and test the synths, they will become more familiar. When required, the variable ranges are shown as [low..high] so that unipolar is [0..+1] and bipolar is [−1..+1].

The member functions either operate on the modulation variables or perform the actions we need for the oscillator object. We keep similarities between all the objects (oscillators, EGs, filters, etc.) For example, all objects have the same functions named *update()* and *reset()* that simplify coding.

Table 5.2(a): *COscillator* non-virtual member functions.

***COscillator* Member Functions (non virtual)**	
Function Name	**Description**
incModulo	add the phase increment value to the modulo counter
checkWrapModulo	check the modulo counter to see if it has crossed the 1.0 value; if so, wrap it around
resetModulo	reset the modulo counter to 0.0
setAmplitudeMod	set the amp modulation value
setFoModExp	set the exponential frequency modulation value
setFoModLin	set the linear frequency modulation value
setPitchBendMod	set the pitch bend modulation value
setPhaseMod	set the phase modulation value
setPWMod	set the pulse width modulation value

Table 5.2(b): *COscillator* virtual member functions.

***COscillator* Member Functions (virtual)**	
Function Name	**Description**
startOscillator	start the oscillator (pure abstract)
stopOscillator	stop the oscillator (pure abstract)
doOscillate	render the oscillator's output(s) (pure abstract)
setSampleRate	set the sample rate (usually not overridden)
reset	reset all oscillator variables
update	update the internal member variables

Limits

Modulating parameters requires knowing the limits of the modulated variable. In each of our synth objects, the modulate-able variable limits are defined at the top of the *.h* file. For the oscillator objects these are:

```
#define OSC_FO_MOD_RANGE 2                //2 semitone default
#define OSC_PITCHBEND_MOD_RANGE 12        //12 semitone default
#define OSC_FO_MIN 20                     //20 Hz
#define OSC_FO_MAX 20480                  //20.480 kHz = 10 octaves up from 20 Hz
#define OSC_FO_DEFAULT 440.0              //A5
#define OSC_PULSEWIDTH_MIN 2              //2%
#define OSC_PULSEWIDTH_MAX 98             //98%
#define OSC_PULSEWIDTH_DEFAULT 50         //50%
```

Waveform Enumerations

We will implement many types of oscillator waveforms. To make coding easier, the waveforms are selected via an enumerated string. The user sees strings in a GUI control but is really selecting an index value (see Chapter 2). For the pitched oscillators, the strings are:

```
enum {SINE,SAW1,SAW2,SAW3,TRI,SQUARE,NOISE,PNOISE};
```

- SINE: sinusoid
- SAW1: normal sawtooth
- SAW2: unipolar waveshaped sawtooth, saturation value = 1.5

- SAW3: bipolar waveshaped sawtooth, saturation value = 1.5
- NOISE: white noise
- PNOISE: pseudorandom noise sequence

For the LFO, the enumeration is similar but in lower case to avoid name conflicts; there is also a different set of waveforms:

```
enum {sine,usaw,dsaw,tri,square,expo,rsh,qrsh};
```

- sine: sinusoid
- usaw: up-sawtooth (rising ramp edges, falling discontinuities)
- dsaw: down-sawtooth (falling ramp edges, rising discontinuities)
- expo: exponential pulses
- rsh: random sample-and-hold
- qrsh: quasi-random sample-and-hold

Member Functions

The member variables in Table 5.1 are based on the trivial, quasi bandlimited and wavetable oscillator requirements. Refer back to those sections to examine the algorithms and code snippets if you need clarification. Examining the member functions will also help you understand the base class functionality. The member functions are split between implementations in the *.h* and *.cpp* files according to the coding convention above.

Constructor

The constructor initializes all the variables. These include:

- modulo and phase increment values
- oscillator defaults for frequency and pulse width
- seeding random number generator for noise oscillators, setting the initial value for the PN noise oscillator in *m_uPNRegister*, and resetting the random sample and hold value to −1, which is a flag for the reset condition
- the amp modulation defaults to 1.0 (rather than 0.0 like the others), so the oscillator will start in an un-muted state

Most importantly notice how the oscillator frequency and pulse width variables seem to be doubled, referring back to Table 5.1:

- *m_dOscFo* is the pitch of the oscillator as set with a MIDI note or GUI control
- *m_dFo* is the actual, current pitch of the oscillator that is a combination of all modulation sources (octave, semitone and cent offsets, frequency modulation, etc.)
- *m_dPulseWidthControl* is the setting from the GUI
- *m_dPulseWidth* is the current pulse width using the pulse width control as the center value; in this way, the modulation will occur around the center value the user has chosen on the GUI

We need to store the user control and current values separately. This is a recurring theme in objects that will have a GUI control and modulation that move around the GUI control as a center position, so make sure you understand why we need to double up these variables.

```
// --- construction
COscillator::COscillator(void)
{
    // --- initialize variables
    m_dSampleRate = 44100;
    m_bNoteOn = false;
    m_uMIDINoteNumber = 0;
    m_dModulo = 0.0;
    m_dInc = 0.0;
    m_dAmplitude = 1.0; // default ON
    m_dOscFo = OSC_FO_DEFAULT; // GUI
    m_dFo = OSC_FO_DEFAULT;
    m_dPulseWidth = OSC_PULSEWIDTH_DEFAULT;
    m_dPulseWidthControl = OSC_PULSEWIDTH_DEFAULT; // GUI
```

```
    // --- seed the random number generator
    srand(time(NULL));
    m_uPNRegister = rand();

    // --- continue inits
    m_nRSHCounter = -1; // flag for reset condition
    m_dRSHValue = 0.0;
    m_dAmpMod = 1.0; // note default to 1 to avoid silent osc
    m_dFoModLin = 0.0;
    m_dPhaseMod = 0.0;
    m_dFoMod = 0.0;
    m_dPitchBendMod = 0.0;
    m_dPWMod = 0.0;
    m_nOctave = 0.0;
    m_nSemitones = 0.0;
    m_nCents = 0.0;
    m_dFoRatio = 1.0;
    m_uLFOMode = 0;

    // --- pitched
    m_uWaveform = SINE;
}
```

reset()

The oscillators are reset for each new note event. The *reset*() function has a base class implementation that handles most of the re-initialization of the variables. It is essentially similar to the constructor, resetting the values that are needed on a per-note basis. However, each derived class will need to implement this function, call the base class first and then reset additional parameters specific to that object.

```
// --- VIRTUAL FUNCTION; base class implementations
void COscillator::reset()
{
    // --- Pitched modulos, wavetables start at 0.0
    m_dModulo = 0.0;

    // --- needed for triangle algorithm, DPW
    m_dDPWSquareModulator = -1.0;

    // --- flush DPW registers
    m_dDPW_z1 = 0.0;

    // --- for random stuff
    srand(time(NULL));
    m_uPNRegister = rand();
    m_nRSHCounter = -1; // flag for reset condition
    m_dRSHValue = 0.0;

    // --- modulation variables
    m_dAmpMod = 1.0; // note default to 1 to avoid silent osc
    m_dPWMod = 0.0;
    m_dPitchBendMod = 0.0;
```

```
        m_dFoMod = 0.0;
        m_dFoModLin = 0.0;
        m_dPhaseMod = 0.0;
    }
```

update()

The oscillator's update function will be called on every sample interval. It is important to keep this code as short and efficient as possible. Do not ever allocate or destroy memory in this function, as these are CPU intensive. The *update()* function may be overridden in a derived class if necessary (we need this only in the wave table oscillator). The *update()* function:

- calculates the pitch shift multiplier for all modulation sources except linear frequency modulation
- calculates the new *fo* value based on the current note/frequency and all exponential modulation sources
- adds the linear frequency modulation value
- sets the current pulse width value
- clamps the oscillator frequency and pulse width to the limit values

For the pitch calculation, we use the method of adding all modulations (in semitones) prior to calling the pitch shift multiplier function. The resulting offset is multiplied by the current oscillator pitch and the ratio value. The ratio value will always be 1.0 except for the *DXSynth*, whose oscillators are designed to operate at multiples of one another. Notice how the pitch is modulated first, then the linear frequency modulation applied after that.

It is worth examining the pulse width calculation since it uses linear bipolar modulation, as shown in Equation 5.22.

```
    // --- update the frequency, amp mod and PWM
    inline virtual void update()
    {
        // --- ignore LFO mode for noise sources
        if(m_uWaveform == rsh || m_uWaveform == qrsh)
          m_uLFOMode = free;

        // --- do the complete frequency mod
        m_dFo = m_dOscFo*m_dFoRatio*pitchShiftMultiplier(m_dFoMod +
                                                        m_dPitchBendMod +
                                                        m_nOctave*12.0 +
                                                        m_nSemitones +
                                                        m_nCents/100.0);

        // --- apply linear FM (not used in book projects)
        m_dFo += m_dFoModLin;

        // --- bound Fo (can go outside for FM/PM mod)
        //   +/- 20480 for FM/PM
        if(m_dFo > OSC_FO_MAX)
               m_dFo = OSC_FO_MAX;
        if(m_dFo < -OSC_FO_MAX)
               m_dFo = -OSC_FO_MAX;

        // --- calculate increment (a.k.a. phase a.k.a. phaseIncrement, etc...)
        m_dInc = m_dFo/m_dSampleRate;

        // --- Pulse Width Modulation --- //
        // --- limits are 2% and 98%
        m_dPulseWidth = m_dPulseWidthControl +
```

```
                    m_dPWMod*(OSC_PULSEWIDTH_MAX - OSC_PULSEWIDTH_MIN)/
                              OSC_PULSEWIDTH_MIN;

        // --- bound the PWM to the range
        m_dPulseWidth = fmin(m_dPulseWidth, OSC_PULSEWIDTH_MAX);
        m_dPulseWidth = fmax(m_dPulseWidth, OSC_PULSEWIDTH_MIN);
    }
```

5.29 NanoSynth: Oscillators

We will continue with our learning-synth that we started in Chapter 3, where we trapped and logged MIDI events. In this chapter we will use the MIDI note on and note off events to trigger our oscillators for testing. This is the first chapter where you will need to be in charge of your GUI design using the strategies from Chapter 2, along with the sample code from http://www.willpirkle.com/synthbook/. You are urged to implement some or all of the Chapter Challenges, as they will help wean you off the sample code and give you lots of practice implementing and maintaining the user interface in your chosen API. Figure 5.42 shows the simplified block diagram for NanoSynth. The dotted lines show the modules we will implement in the next few chapters. Here we are concerned only with the oscillator portion. NanoSynth requires three oscillators; two pitched oscillators that are detuned by 2.5 cents from each other and one LFO to modulate their pitches. This will give you a nice thick sound for any waveform other than sine, and vibrato courtesy of the LFO.

We will first design the NanoSynth GUI, then add the *COscillator* base class and implement the quasi bandlimited and wavetable oscillators after that. You can then use the NanoSynth plug-in to test the functionality of the objects and extend them with the Chapter Challenges. Table 5.3 shows the continuous and enumerated string list GUI controls you need to implement in NanoSynth. You might want to look at the sample code first then try your own implementation. Figure 5.43 shows one incarnation of the NanoSynth GUI in RackAFX (the GUI designer is very open-ended, so you might design a completely different GUI here). Notice that there is plenty of room for expansion—we will add more controls over the next three chapters. Also notice that it uses the LCD control. We will be placing the global synth controls inside it. Figure 5.44 shows the NanoSynth GUI that comes with the VST3 and AU projects; you are encouraged to modify and personalize the GUIs as you wish.

Figure 5.45 shows the detailed connection diagram for this portion of NanoSynth. It shows how the controls from Table 5.3 connect to the underlying synth objects. There are knobs and switches. The legend shows you the difference between continuous control knobs (normal) and switch-knobs (also called chicken-head knobs).

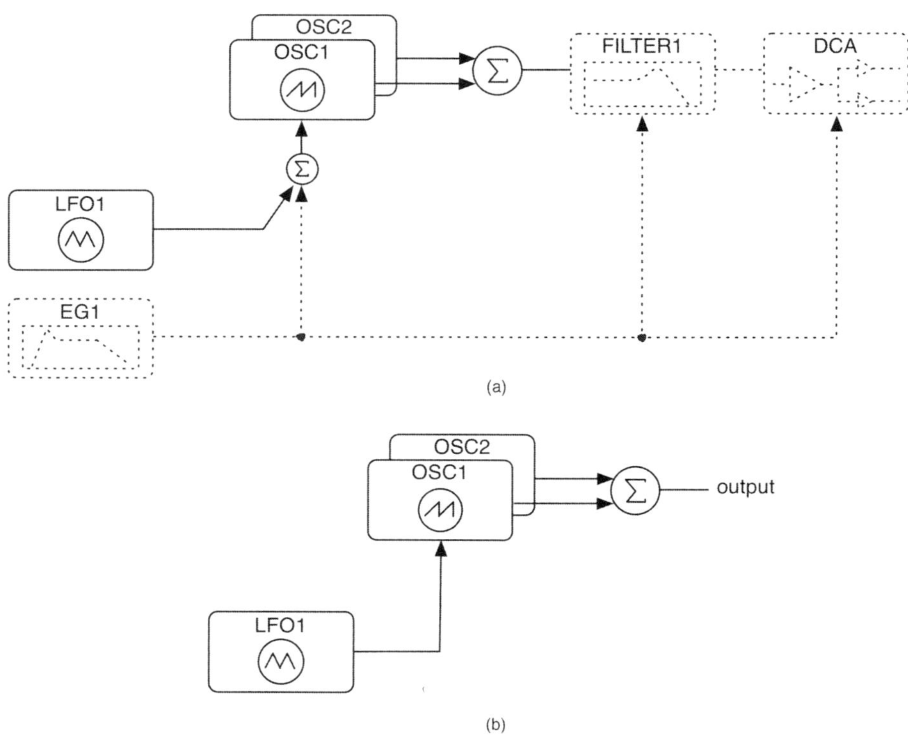

Figure 5.42: (a) The complete NanoSynth block diagram with dotted lines showing future modules (b) the portion we will implement in this chapter; the connection between the LFO and pitched oscillators implies that the LFO will modulate both.

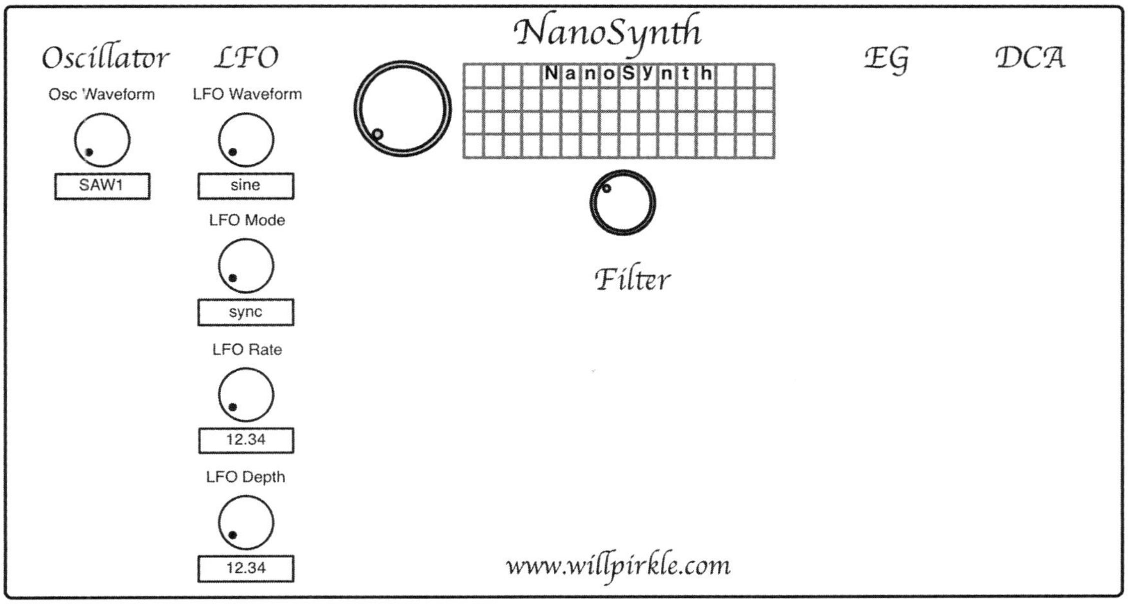

Figure 5.43: One of many versions of the NanoSynth Oscillators GUI that you can assemble in RackAFX's GUI Designer.

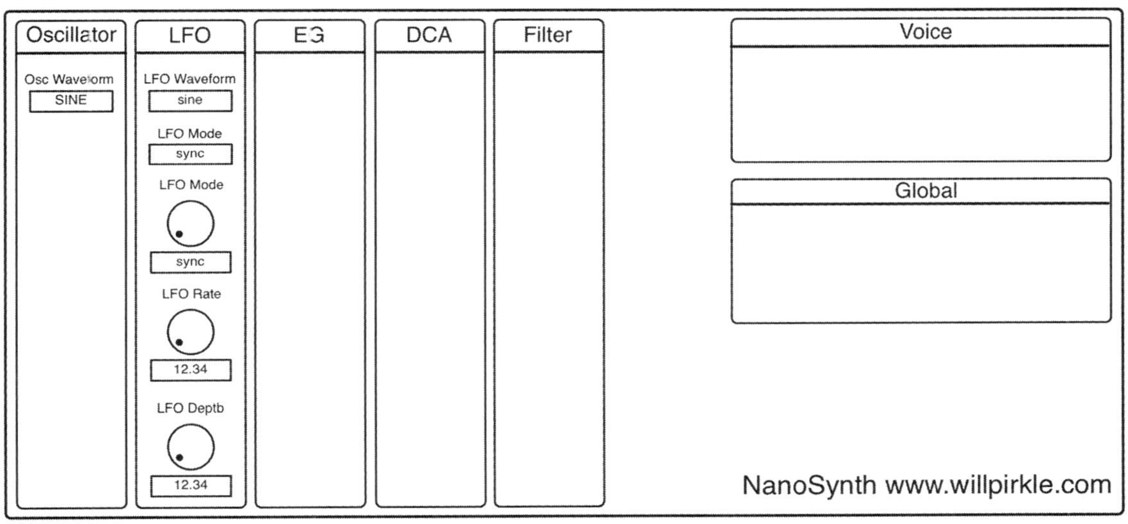

Figure 5.44: The NanoSynth Oscillators GUI that comes with the VST3 and AU versions.

Table 5.3: The continuous and enumerated string parameters for the NanoSynth GUI.

NanoSynth Continuous Parameters				
Control Name(units)	**Type**	**Variable Name(VST3, RAFX)**	**Low/Hi/Default***	**VST3/AU Index**
LFO1 Rate (Hz)	double	m_dLFO1Rate	−0.02 / 20 / 0.5	LFO1_RATE
LFO1 Amplitude	double	LFO1 Amplitude	0 / 1 / 0	LFO1_AMPLITUDE
* low, high and default values are #defined for VST3 and AU in *SynthParamLimits.h* for each project				

NanoSynth Enumerated String Parameters (UINT)			
Control Name	**Variable Name**	**enum String**	**VST3/AU Index**
Osc Waveform	m_uOscWaveform	SINE,SAW1,SAW2,-SAW3,TRI,SQUARE,NOISE,PNOISE	OSC_WAVEFORM
LFO Waveform	m_uLFO1Waveform	sine,usaw,dsaw,tri,square,expo,rsh,qrsh	LFO1_WAVEFORM
LFO Mode	m_uLFO1Mode	synx,shot,free	LFO1_MODE

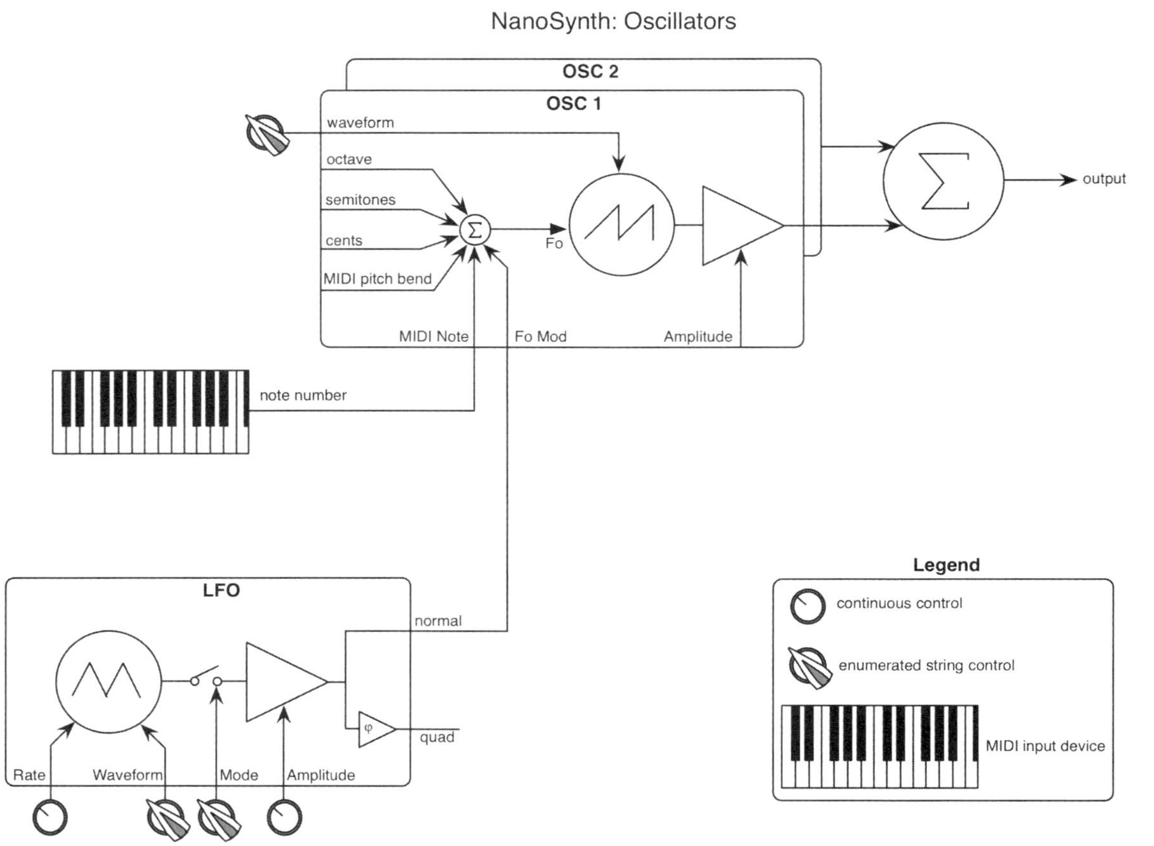

Figure 5.45: The NanoSynth detailed connection graph reveals two continuous controls and three enumerated string parameters; you will need to supply a MIDI controller (if using RackAFX, there is a built-in piano control).

5.30 NanoSynth Oscillators: RackAFX/VST3/AU Add the Base Class Files

Download the files for the NanoSynth: Oscillators project. You need to add the following files if you are creating the synth from scratch:

Oscillator.h
Oscillator.cpp
synthfunctions.h
SynthParamLimits.h (VST3 and AU only)

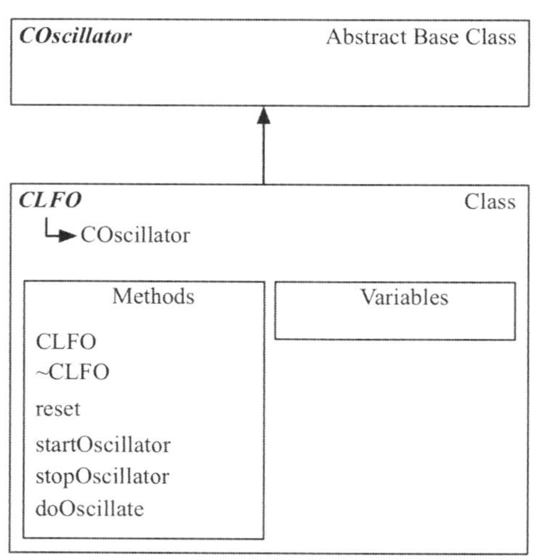

Figure 5.46: Class diagram for the LFO object.

Now we are ready to implement the pitched and LFO oscillators.

5.31 The CLFO Object

Let's start by creating and implementing the LFO object. Add a new class to your project named CLFO and make sure to set its base class to COscillator. Figure 5.46 shows the class diagram. Refer to the code listing for the LFO.h file below and copy it into your file (or, alternatively you can download the sample code). Figure 5.46: class diagram for CLFO.

CLFO Member Variables

There are no members to declare; they are all in the base class.

CLFO Member Methods

We only need to override a few virtual functions because so much functionality is built into the base class.

```
LFO.h

class CLFO : public COscillator
{
public:
	CLFO(void);
	CLFO(void);

	// virtual overrides
	virtual void reset();
	virtual void startOscillator();
	virtual double doOscillate();
	virtual void stopOscillator();
};
```

LFO.cpp

Implement the following methods to fill out the rest of the object.

Constructor

- initialize the LFO mode variable to *sync*; the waveform is initialized to sine in the base class—you may change the default here

```
CLFO::CLFO(void)
{
	m_uLFOMode = sync;
}
```

reset()

- call the base class method for base reset

```
void CLFO::reset()
{
	// --- call base class
	COscillator::reset();
}
```

startOscillator()

- if not in free run mode, call reset
- set the note on flag

stopOscillator()

- clear the note on flag

```
void CLFO::startOscillator()
{
      // --- if one shot or sync'd LFO, reset
      if(m_uLFOMode == sync || m_uLFOMode == shot)
              reset();

      // --- set flag
      m_bNoteOn = true;
}

void CLFO::stopOscillator()
{
      // --- clear flag
      m_bNoteOn = false;
}
```

doOscillate()

This is the most important function on the object. It will use the algorithms and code snippets from Sections 5.x and 5.y to implement the trivial waveforms and noise oscillators. The function *doOscillate()* has the following prototype:

```
inline virtual double doOscillate(double* pQuadPhaseOutput = NULL)
```

The argument is an optional pointer to a variable to receive the quad phase output. If the receiving object does not need this output, the function can be called without the argument. The function implements the following sequences:

- first, check to make sure the oscillator is running by checking the note on flag
- call *checkWrapModulo()* to check and wrap it if needed
- for one-shot LFO, if we just wrapped the modulo, we are done and return 0.0 and turn note off
- create a temporary quad phase modulo counter and add 0.25 to it; check for wrap
- follow the algorithms in the chapter, and if there is a quad phase variable, calculate this secondary output as well
    - sine uses a parabolic approximation
    - saw (up and down) are extracted directly from modulo counter
    - triangle and square are mathematically calculated via modulo counter
    - exponential uses the built-in *convexInvertedTransform()* function
    - the noise oscillators call a function in *synthfunctions.h* and then perform the hold using a counter to count sample periods of hold time
- for ramp and triangle, check the LFO mode and make unipolar for one-shot
- increment the modulo and return the amplitude-scaled output sample
- calculate normal and quad phase outputs by multiplying the output by the amplitude and amp modulation values

```
inline virtual double doOscillate(double* pQuadPhaseOutput = NULL)
{
      if(!m_bNoteOn)
      {
              if(pQuadPhaseOutput)
                      *pQuadPhaseOutput = 0.0;

              return 0.0;
      }
```

```
// output
double dOut = 0.0;
double dQPOut = 0.0;

// always first
bool bWrap = checkWrapModulo();

// one shot LFO?
if(m_uLFOMode == shot && bWrap)
{
        m_bNoteOn = false;

        if(pQuadPhaseOutput)
                *pQuadPhaseOutput = 0.0;

        return 0.0;
}

// for QP output
// advance modulo by 0.25 = 90 degrees
double dQuadModulo = m_dModulo + 0.25;

// check and wrap
if(dQuadModulo >= 1.0)
        dQuadModulo -= 1.0;

// decode and calculate
switch(m_uWaveform)
{
        case sine:
        {
                // calculate angle
                double dAngle = m_dModulo*2.0*pi - pi;

                // call the parabolicSine approximator
                dOut = parabolicSine(-dAngle);

                // use second modulo for quad phase
                dAngle = dQuadModulo*2.0*pi - pi;
                dQPOut = parabolicSine(-dAngle);

                break;
        }

        case usaw:
        case dsaw:
        {
                // --- one shot is unipolar for saw
                if(m_uLFOMode != shot)
                {
                        // unipolar to bipolar
                        dOut = unipolarToBipolar(m_dModulo);
```

```
                dQPOut = unipolarToBipolar(dQuadModulo);
            }
            else
            {
                dOut = m_dModulo - 1.0;
                dQPOut = dQuadModulo - 1.0;
            }

            // invert for down-saw
            if(m_uWaveform == dsaw)
            {
                dOut *= -1.0;
        dQPOut *= -1.0;
            }

            break;
        }

        case square:
        {
            // check pulse width and output either +1 or -1
            dOut = m_dModulo > m_dPulseWidth/100.0 ? -1.0 : +1.0;
            dQPOut = dQuadModulo > m_dPulseWidth/100.0 ? -1.0 : +1.0;

            break;
        }

        case tri:
        {
            // triv saw
            dOut = unipolarToBipolar(m_dModulo);

            // bipolar triagle
            dOut = 2.0*fabs(dOut) - 1.0;

            if(m_uLFOMode == shot)
                // convert to unipolar
                dOut = bipolarToUnipolar(dOut);

            // -- quad phase
            // triv saw
            dQPOut = unipolarToBipolar(dQuadModulo);

            // bipolar triangle
            dQPOut = 2.0*fabs(dQPOut) - 1.0;

            if(m_uLFOMode == shot)
                // convert to unipolar
                dQPOut = bipolarToUnipolar(dQPOut);

            break;
        }
```

```
        // --- expo is unipolar!
        case expo:
        {
                // calculate the output directly
                dOut = concaveInvertedTransform(m_dModulo);
                dQPOut = concaveInvertedTransform(dQuadModulo);

                break;
        }

        case rsh:
        case qrsh:
        {
                // this is the very first run
                if(m_nRSHCounter < 0)
                {
                        if(m_uWaveform == rsh)
                                m_dRSHValue = doWhiteNoise();
                        else
                                m_dRSHValue = doPNSequence(m_uPNRegister);

                        m_nRSHCounter = 1.0;
                }
                // hold time exceeded?
                else if(m_nRSHCounter > m_dSampleRate/m_dFo)
                {
                        m_nRSHCounter -= m_dSampleRate/m_dFo;

                        if(m_uWaveform == rsh)
                                m_dRSHValue = doWhiteNoise();
                        else
                                m_dRSHValue = doPNSequence(m_uPNRegister);
                }

                // inc the counter
                m_nRSHCounter += 1.0;

                // output held value
                dOut = m_dRSHValue;

                // not meaningful for this output
                dQPOut = m_dRSHValue;
                break;
        }

        default:
                break;
}

// --- ok to inc modulo now
incModulo();
```

```
        // --- quad phase output
        if(pQuadPhaseOutput)
                *pQuadPhaseOutput = dQPOut*m_dAmplitude*m_dAmpMod;

        // --- m_dAmplitude & m_dAmpMod is calculated in update() on base class
        return dOut*m_dAmplitude*m_dAmpMod;
}
```

5.32 The CQBLimitedOscillator Object

Add a new class to your project named *CQBLimitedOscillator* and make sure to set its base class to *COscillator*. Refer to the code listing below and copy it into your file (or, alternatively you can download the sample code). Figure 5.47 shows the class diagram for *CQBLimitedOscillator*.

CQBLimitedOscillator Member Variables

There are no extra members to declare; they are all in the base class.

CQBLimitedOscillator Member Methods

Aside from the base class overrides (*reset(), startOscillator()* and *stopOscillator()*) there are sub-functions to handle each of the three oscillator types. The function *doOscillate()* will call these sub-functions for sawtooth, square and triangle waveforms and directly calculate the other noise waveforms.

Constructor

- there is nothing to do here because it is all done in the base class

reset()

- always call the base class method first
- adjust the starting phase of the modulo counter for sawtooth and triangle waves

```
void CQBLimitedOscillator::reset()
{
        COscillator::reset();
```

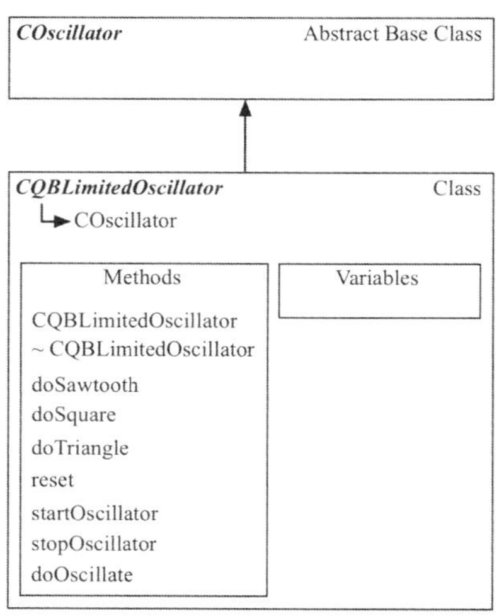

Figure 5.47: Class diagram for the CQBLimitedOscillator object.

```
        // --- saw/tri starts at 0.5
        if(m_uWaveform == SAW1 || m_uWaveform == SAW2 ||
           m_uWaveform == SAW3 || m_uWaveform == TRI)
        {
                m_dModulo = 0.5;
        }
}
```

startOscillator()

- call *reset()*
- set the note on flag

stopOscillator()

- clear the note on flag

```
void CQBLimitedOscillator::startOscillator()
{
        reset();
        m_bNoteOn = true;
}

void CQBLimitedOscillator::stopOscillator()
{
        m_bNoteOn = false;
}
```

doSawtooth()

- use the modulo to create a bipolar trivial sawtooth
- wave shape if a shaped version is selected; note one-sided and two-sided shaping
- call the BLEP (or polyBLEP) method to generate a residual and add that to the output sample; the default is two-point BLEP, but you can un-comment the other portions to implement two-point PolyBLEP or eight-point BLEP

> ***If using eight-point BLEP:***
>
> Notice that eight-point BLEP can only be used easily if the frequency is less than 1/4 Nyquist, where you have more than eight points per cycle (four points per side of the discontinuity); above this value we switch to two-point BLEP in the commented code.
>
> If you want to use the eight-point BLEP algorithm across the spectrum, you will need to deal with overlapping BLEP transition regions, and you will need to do some buffering and mixing in order to perform the proper corrections. You will also need to call the BLEP function more than once per sample period. Failure to do this will result in an output signal that is unacceptable.

```
inline double doSawtooth(double dModulo, double dInc)
{
        double dTrivialSaw = 0.0;
        double dOut = 0.0;

        if(m_uWaveform == SAW1)                  // SAW1 = normal sawtooth (ramp)
                dTrivialSaw = unipolarToBipolar(dModulo);
```

```
    else if(m_uWaveform == SAW2)          // SAW2 = one sided wave shaper
           dTrivialSaw = 2.0*(tanh(1.5*dModulo)/tanh(1.5)) - 1.0;
    else if(m_uWaveform == SAW3)          // SAW3 = double sided wave shaper
    {
           dTrivialSaw = unipolarToBipolar(dModulo);
           dTrivialSaw = tanh(1.5*dTrivialSaw)/tanh(1.5);
    }

    // --- fs/8 = Nyquist/4; uncomment to use 8-point BLEP
    // if(m_dFo <= m_dSampleRate/8.0)
    //     dOut = dTrivialSaw + doBLEP_N(&dBLEPTable_8_BLKHAR[0], 4096,
    //                                  dModulo, fabs(dInc), 1.0, false,
    //                                  4, false);
    //else // --- 2-point BLEP correction
           dOut = dTrivialSaw + doBLEP_N(&dBLEPTable 4096,
                                        dModulo, fabs(dInc), 1.0, false,
                                        1, false);

    // --- or uncomment this to use PolyBLEP correction
    //dOut = dTrivialSaw + doPolyBLEP_2(dModulo,
    //                     abs(dInc),      /* abs(dInc)for negative freqs */
    //                     1.0,            /* sawtooth edge = 1.0 */
    //                     false);         /* falling edge */

    return dOut;
}
```

doSquare()

- use the sum-of-saws method; this requires some trickery—we temporarily set our waveform variable to SAW1 (the pure saw) and call *doSawtooth()* twice
- the first call is normal, then we modify the modulo counter variable by offsetting it based on the pulse width; notice how we check the phase increment value for positive (normal) or negative frequency operation—the wrapping operation also works in both forward and reverse time
- we can call the sawtooth function twice safely since the modulo counter is not incremented until after the square wave function ends (see *doOscillate()*)
- lastly apply the DC correction value to maintain a 0.0 DC offset value

```
inline double doSquare(double dModulo, double dInc)
{
    // --- sum-of-saws method
    // --- pretend to be SAW1 type
    m_uWaveform = SAW1;

    // --- get first sawtooth output
    double dSaw1 = doSawtooth(dModulo, dInc);

    // --- phase shift on second oscillator
    if(dInc > 0)
           dModulo += m_dPulseWidth/100.0;
    else
           dModulo -= m_dPulseWidth/100.0;
```

```
// --- for positive frequencies
if(dInc > 0 && dModulo >= 1.0)
       dModulo -= 1.0;

// --- for negative frequencies
if(dInc < 0 && dModulo <= 0.0)
       dModulo += 1.0;

// --- get second saw output
double dSaw2 = doSawtooth(dModulo, dInc);

// --- subtract = 180 out of phase
double dOut = 0.5*dSaw1 - 0.5*dSaw2;

// --- calculate DC correction
double dCorr = 1.0/(m_dPulseWidth/100.0);

// --- modify for less than 50%
if((m_dPulseWidth/100.0) < 0.5)
       dCorr = 1.0/(1.0-(m_dPulseWidth/100.0));

// --- apply correction
dOut *= dCorr;

// --- reset back to SQUARE
m_uWaveform = SQUARE;

return dOut;
```

doTriangle()

- refer to the DPW block diagram in Figure 5.27 for this algorithm
- create the bipolar sawtooth
- square it to get the parabola
- invert the parabola
- modulate with square modulo
- differentiate it with simple differentiator that finds slope of curve by storing and subtracting the last input
- correct with the *c* correction factor

```
double CQBLimitedOscillator::doTriangle(double dModulo, double dInc,
                                        double dFo,
                                        double dSquareModulator,
                                        double* pZ_register)
{
       double dOut = 0.0;
       bool bDone = false;

       // bipolar conversion and squaring
       double dBipolar = unipolarToBipolar(dModulo);
       double dSq = dBipolar*dBipolar;

       // inversion
       double dInv = 1.0 - dSq;
```

```
        // modulation with square modulo
        double dSqMod = dInv*dSquareModulator;

        // original differentiation
        double dDifferentiatedSqMod = dSqMod - *pZ_register;
        *pZ_register = dSqMod;

        // c = fs/[4fo(1-2fo/fs)]
        double c = m_dSampleRate/(4.0*2.0*dFo*(1-dInc));

        return dDifferentiatedSqMod*c;
}
```

doOscillate()

- Since these oscillators are based on the modulo counter like the LFO, a similar strategy is applied: *checkWrapModulo()*, call the appropriate function, then *inc* the modulo
- for pitched oscillators, we implement the phase modulation in the *doOscillate()* function by adjusting the current modulo counter value based on the phase modulation then checking for wrap—we will discuss this more in Chapter 12
- the sinusoidal approximation is identical to the LFO
- notice pass-by-pointer mechanism for triangle so that the DPW z−1 register is updated (see algorithm)
- the triangle wave needs to have the modulo incremented twice (see algorithm)
- as with the LFO, the output value is based on the current amplitude and amp modulation values
- for *doOscillate()* on pitched oscillators, the prototype is:

```
virtual inline double doOscillate(double* pAuxOutput = NULL)
```

In this case, we rename the secondary output that is optionally passed as an argument. It is now called *pAuxOutput* and will be used for stereo oscillators. The *CQBLimitedOscillators* are all monophonic, so we simply copy the normal output into this aux output variable if needed. Refer back to the LFO *doOscillate()*, as much of the general outline is the same (for example, starting with checking the note on flag).

```
virtual inline double doOscillate(double* pAuxOutput = NULL)
{
        if(!m_bNoteOn)
                return 0.0;

        double dOut = 0.0;

        // always first
        bool bWrap = checkWrapModulo();

        // added for PHASE MODULATION
        double dCalcModulo = m_dModulo + m_dPhaseMod;
                checkWrapIndex(dCalcModulo);

        switch(m_uWaveform)
        {
                case SINE: // same as LFO

                case SAW1:
                case SAW2:
                case SAW3:
                {
                        dOut = doSawtooth(dCalcModulo, m_dInc);
```

```
                break;
            }

            case SQUARE:
            {
                dOut = doSquare(dCalcModulo, m_dInc);
                break;
            }

            case TRI:
            {
                if(bWrap)
                    m_dDPWSquareModulator *= -1.0;

                dOut = coTriangle(dCalcModulo, m_dInc,
                                  m_dFo, m_dDPWSquareModulator,
                                  &m_dDPW_z1);
                break;
            }

            case NOISE:    // same as LFO
            case PNOISE:   // same as LFO

            default:
                break;
        }

        // --- ok to inc modulo now
        incModulo();

        // --- inc twice for Triangle
        if(m_uWaveform == TRI)
            incModulo();

        // --- m_dAmpMod is set in update()
        if(pAuxOutput)
            *pAuxOutput = dOut*m_dAmplitude*m_dAmpMod;

        // --- m_dAmpMod is set in update()
        return dOut*m_dAmplitude*m_dAmpMod;
    }
```

5.33 The CWTOscillator Object

The wavetable oscillator is different from the others. It will feature one sinusoid table and a set of sawtooth and triangle tables of varying harmonic counts. For these non-sinusoidal tables, there is one table per octave starting with the lowest note on the piano, A0 (27.5 Hz), and going up through nine octaves. In the tenth octave, there is only one harmonic before Nyquist, so this is equivalent to a simple sinusoid. We can use the sine table for that octave. The sawtooth and triangle tables are created dynamically depending on the sample rate, so they must be re-created if the sample rate changes; this necessitates overriding the *setSampleRate()* virtual function. A pointer to each table is stored in a nine-slot array of pointers, one array for each waveform as shown in Figure 5.48 for the sawtooth array.

The frequency of the oscillator may be under modulation and constantly changing. We need a function to figure out which table to use at any given time. We also need a pointer to the currently selected table, even if it is the *sine* table, because we will use that pointer to

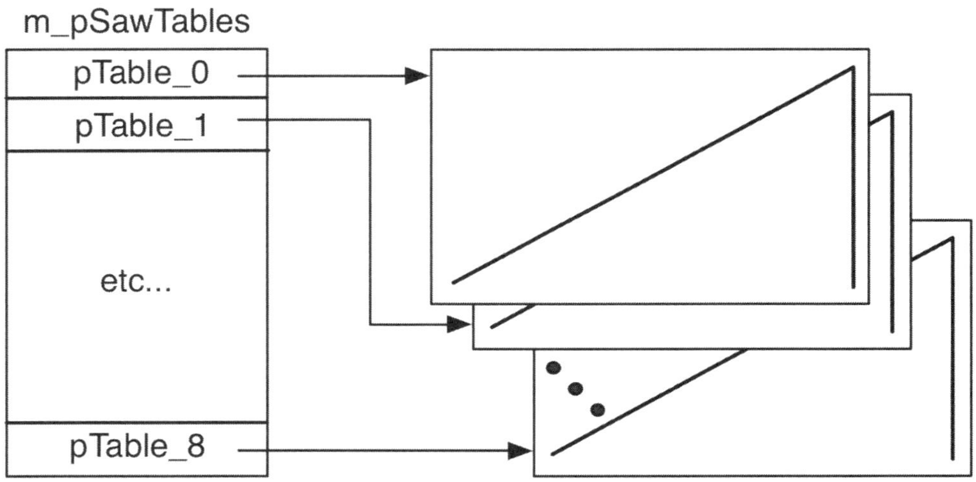

Figure 5.48: Nine different tables are pre-calculated and pointers to each are loaded into an array.

call the functions. Another DC offset issue arises from using the sum-of-sawtooth method to generate square waves with PWM: as the tables become more and more sparse harmonically, they deviate more and more from a true ramp slope, even when using the Lanczos sigma smoothing. This necessitates a per-table correction factor to be applied prior to output scaling. These factors will be stored in a nine-slot array and are found empirically.

The harmonic limits of the nine tables are calculated using the h_{lim} equation. Table 5.4 lists the fundamental frequency and the upper harmonic limit (number of harmonics) for each octave.

Anything above A8 will simply use the sine table, as there will be only one harmonic. Each table is 512 samples in length, and you can control this with a defined constant that is at the top of the wavetable object's *.h* file.

```
#define WT_LENGTH 512
```

Also, remember that one way to help minimize aliasing is to force the tables to become shorter and shorter as the number of harmonics drops off (you can see that they approximately halve on each octave transition), with the last octave covered with 32 or 64 sample tables. You may certainly experiment with this approach, but you will need to keep track of the table length to properly calculate the phase increment variable.

Add a new class to your project named *CWTOscillator* and make sure to set its base class to *COscillator*. Refer to the code listing for the *WTOscillator.h* file below and copy it into your file (or alternatively, you can download the sample code). Figure 5.49 shows the class diagram for *CWTOscillator*. The member variables and functions are described next.

CWTOscillator Member Variables

The wavetable oscillator is distinct and different from the other oscillators since it uses tables and indices to generate the output. Because of this, we need to declare some extra variables that are specific only to the wave table oscillator.

Table 5.4: The fundamental frequency and upper harmonic limit for the nine octaves of wavetables.

Octave Starting Note	Fundamental Frequency	Number of Harmonics before Nyquist
A0	27.500	800
A1	55.000	399
A2	110.000	199
A3	220.000	99
A4	440.000	49
A5	880.000	24
A6	1760.000	11
A7	3520.000	5
A8	7040.000	2

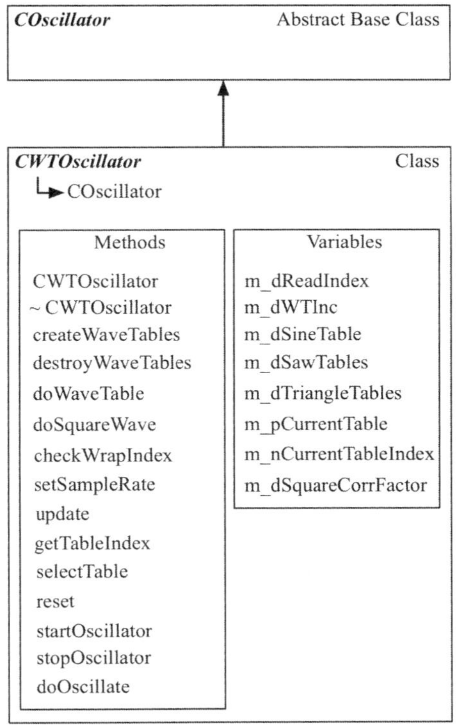

Figure 5.49: Class diagram for the CWTOscillator object.

We need to declare a read index and wavetable increment value. The index is used to fetch samples from the table. The increment value is based on the modulo counter and calculated with Equation 5.12.

```
// oscillator
double m_dReadIndex;
double m_dWT_inc;
```

For the tables, we need one dedicated sine table and arrays of saw and triangle tables.

```
// one single Sine table
double m_dSineTable[WT_LENGTH];

// arrays of pointers to Saw and Tri tables
double* m_pSawTables[NUM_TABLES];
double* m_pTriangleTables[NUM_TABLES];
```

We also need to keep track of the currently selected table and store its index to use for the square wave correction array.

```
// for storing current table
double* m_pCurrentTable;
int m_nCurrentTableIndex; //C - 9

// correction factor table sum-of-sawtooth
double m_dSquareCorrFactor[NUM_TABLES];
```

CWTOscillator Member Methods

Once again, it makes sense to implement sub-functions that will perform the proper oscillator algorithm using the table lookup index and increment values. Pass-by-reference is used to modify these variables inside the sub-functions.

```
// do the selected wavetable
double doWaveTable(double& dReadIndex, double dWT_inc);

// for square wave
double doSquareWave();
```

We also need functions to create and destroy the tables, as well as choose the proper table based on current oscillator frequency.

```
// find the table with the proper number of harmonics for our pitch
int getTableIndex();
void selectTable();

// create an destroy tables
void createWaveTables();
void destroyWaveTables();
```

Lastly, we need to override the typical base class virtual functions plus the one for altering the sample rate, in which case the tables must be re-calculated. We also need to override *update()* to calculate our read locations and select a new table if the frequency has changed.

Constructor

- initialize/clear variables
- initialize the square correction table
- set the sine table as the currently selected table

There are two constant definitions in the *.h* file; this is where you can alter and experiment with different table lengths and granularity. For example, you might try implementing tables on every minor third interval or use shorter tables.

```
#define WT_LENGTH 512
#define NUM_TABLES 9

CWTOscillator::CWTOscillator(void)
{
      // --- clear out arrays
      memset(m_pSawTables, 0, NUM_TABLES*sizeof(double*));
      memset(m_pTriangleTables, 0, NUM_TABLES*sizeof(double*));

      // --- init variables
      m_dReadIndex = 0.0;
      m_dWT_inc = 0.0;
      m_nCurrentTableIndex = 0;

      // --- setup correction factors (empirical)
      m_dSquareCorrFactor[0] = 0.5;
      m_dSquareCorrFactor[1] = 0.5;
      m_dSquareCorrFactor[2] = 0.5;
      m_dSquareCorrFactor[3] = 0.49;
      m_dSquareCorrFactor[4] = 0.48;
```

```
        m_dSquareCorrFactor[5] = 0.468;
        m_dSquareCorrFactor[6] = 0.43;
        m_dSquareCorrFactor[7] = 0.34;
        m_dSquareCorrFactor[8] = 0.25;

        // --- default to SINE
        m_pCurrentTable = &m_dSineTable[0];
}
```

Destructor

- destroy the dynamically created tables

```
CWTOscillator:: CWTOscillator(void)
{
        // --- destroy
        destroyWaveTables();
}
```

reset()

- call the base class method for base reset
- reset read index value to top of buffers

```
void CWTOscillator::reset()
{
        COscillator::reset();

        // back to top of buffer
        m_dReadIndex = 0.0;
}
```

startOscillator()

stopOscillator()

- these are identical to the LFO and quasi bandlimited oscillators

setSampleRate()

- call the base class implementation
- then re-create the tables if the sample rate has changed

```
void CWTOscillator::setSampleRate(double dFs)
{
        // test for change
        bool bNewSR = m_dSampleRate != dFs ? true : false;

        // --- base class first
        COscillator::setSampleRate(dFs);

        // --- recreate the tables only if sample rate has changed
        if(bNewSR)
        {
```

```
            // --- then recreate
            destroyWaveTables();
            createWaveTables();
        }
}
```

update()

- call the base class *update()*
- calculate the table increment value
- call *selectTable()* to make sure we have the proper table for our frequency of oscillation

```
void CWTOscillator::updateOscillator()
{
    // --- base class first
    COscillator::updateOscillator();

    // --- calculate inc
    m_dWT_inc = WT_LENGTH*m_dInc;

    // --- select the table
    selectTable();
}
```

createWaveTables()

- follow the equations in section 5.22 to load up the tables with one cycle minus one sample of the waveform
- apply Lanczos sigma smoothing to sawtooth (triangle is already smooth enough)
- sine has its own table, the others are arrayed in sets
- notice the seed frequency for the one-octave-per-table loop

destroyWaveTables()

- unload the arrays and delete the pointers

```
void CWTOscillator::createWaveTables()
{
    // create the tables
    //
    // SINE: only need one table
    for(int i = 0; i < WT_LENGTH; i++)
    {
            // sample the sinusoid, WT_LENGTH points
            // sin(wnT) = sin(2pi*i/WT_LENGTH)
            m_dSineTable[i] = sin(((double)i/WT_LENGTH)*(2*pi));
    }

    // SAW, TRIANGLE: need 10 tables
    double dSeedFreq = 27.5; // Note A0, bottom of piano
    for(int j = 0; j < NUM_TABLES; j++)
    {
            double* pSawTable = new double[WT_LENGTH];
            memset(pSawTable, 0, WT_LENGTH*sizeof(double));
```

```
double* pTriTable = new double[WT_LENGTH];
memset(pTriTable, 0, WT_LENGTH*sizeof(double));

int nHarms = (int)((m_dSampleRate/2.0/dSeedFreq) - 1.0);
int nHalfHarms = (int)((float)nHarms/2.0);

double dMaxSaw = 0;
double dMaxTri = 0;

for(int i = 0; i < WT_LENGTH; i++)
{
        // sawtooth: += (-1)^g+1(1/g)sin(wnT)
        for(int g = 1; g <= nHarms; g++)
        {
                // Lanczos Sigma Factor
                double x = g*pi/nHarms;
                double sigma = sin(x)/x;

                // only apply to partials above fundamental
                if(g == 1)
                        sigma = 1.0;

                double n = double(g);
                pSawTable[i] += pow((float)-1.0,(float)(g+1))*(1.0/n
                                     *sigma*sin(2.0*pi*i*n/WT_LENGTH);
        }

        // triangle: += (-1)^g(1/(2g+1+^2)sin(w(2n+1)T)
        // NOTE: the limit is nHalfHarms here because of the way
        //       the sum is constructed (look at the (2n+1)
        //       components
        for(int g = 0; g <= nHalfHarms; g++)
        {
                double n = double(g);
                pTriTable[i] += pow((float)-1.0, (float)n)*
                                (1.0/pow((float)
                                 (2*n + 1),(float)2.0))*sin(2.0*pi*
                                2.0*n + 1)*i/WT_LENGTH);
        }

        // store the max values
        if(i == 0)
        {
                dMaxSaw = pSawTable[i];
                dMaxTri = pTriTable[i];
        }
        else
        {
                // test and store
```

```
                    if(pSawTable[i] > dMaxSaw)
                        dMaxSaw = pSawTable[i];

                    if(pTriTable[i] > dMaxTri)
                        dMaxTri = pTriTable[i];
                }
            }
            // normalize
            for(int i = 0; i < WT_LENGTH; i++)
            {
                // normalize it
                pSawTable[i] /= dMaxSaw;
                pTriTable[i] /= dMaxTri;
            }

            // store
            m_pSawTables[j] = pSawTable;
            m_pTriangleTables[j] = pTriTable;

            // --- go to next octave seed
            dSeedFreq *= 2.0;
        }
}

void CWTOscillator::destroyWaveTables()
{
        for(int i = 0; i < NUM_TABLES; i++)
        {
            double* p = m_pSawTables[i];
            if(p)
            {
                delete [] p;
                m_pSawTables[i] = 0;
            }

            p = m_pTriangleTables[i];
            if(p)
            {
                delete [] p;
                m_pTriangleTables[i] = 0;
            }
        }
}
```

getTableIndex()

- get the index of the saw or triangle table for a given frequency
- upper octave returns –1, a flag to use the sine table instead
- uses same seed frequency method as setting up the tables

```
// get table index based on current m_dFo
int CWTOscillator::getTableIndex()
```

```
{
	if(m_uWaveform == SINE)
		return -1;

	double dSeedFreq = 27.5; // Note A0, bottom of piano
	for(int j = 0; j < NUM_TABLES; j++)
	{
		if(m_dFo <= dSeedFreq)
		{
			return j;
		}

		dSeedFreq *= 2.0;
	}

	return -1;
}
```

selectTable()

- get the index of the saw or triangle table for a given frequency
- store index to use if square correction is needed
- select the appropriate table address and set the pointer

```
void CWTOscillator::selectTable()
{
	m_nCurrentTableIndex = getTableIndex();

	// if the frequency is high enough, the sine table will be returned
	// even for non-sinusoidal waves; anything about 10548 Hz is one
	// harmonic only (sine)
	if(m_nCurrentTableIndex < 0)
	{
		m_pCurrentTable = &m_dSineTable[0];
		return;
	}

	// choose table
	if(m_uWaveform == SAW1 || m_uWaveform == SAW2 || m_uWaveform == SAW3 ||
		m_uWaveform == SQUARE)
			m_pCurrentTable = m_pSawTables[m_nCurrentTableIndex];
	else if(m_uWaveform == TRI)
			m_pCurrentTable = m_pTriangleTables[m_nCurrentTableIndex];
}
```

checkWrapIndex()

This function is required for the phase modulation we will use on the *DXSynth*. The phase modulation will shift the phase up to 8π radians, so we have to check for multiple wraps around the table. This is done with *while()* loops.

```
inline void checkWrapIndex(double& dIndex)
{
	while(dIndex < 0.0)
		dIndex += WT_LENGTH;
```

```
        while(dIndex >= WT_LENGTH)
                dIndex -= WT_LENGTH;
}
```

doWaveTable()

- apply phase modulation and check for wrap
- calculate the location of the two samples to interpolate
- interpolate samples for output
- add the WT increment
- check the Read Index in both positive and negative directions

```
double CWTOscillator::doWaveTable(double& dReadIndex, double dWT_inc)
{
     double dOut = 0;

     // apply phase modulation, if any
     double dModReadIndex = dReadIndex + m_dPhaseMod*WT_LENGTH;

     // check for multi-wrapping on new read index
     checkWrapIndex(dModReadIndex);

     // get INT part
     int nReadIndex = abs((int)dModReadIndex);

     // get FRAC part
     float fFrac = dModReadIndex - nReadIndex;

     // setup second index for interpolation; wrap the buffer if needed
     int nReadIndexNext = nReadIndex + 1 > WT_LENGTH-1 ? 0 : nReadIndex + 1;

     // interpolate the output
     dOut = dLinTerp(0, 1, m_pCurrentTable[nReadIndex],
                    m_pCurrentTable[nReadIndexNext], fFrac);

     // add the increment for next time
     dReadIndex += dWT_inc;

     // check for wrap
     checkWrapIndex(dReadIndex);

     return dOut;
}
```

doSquareWave()

- calculate the output of a square wave using sum-of-saws method
- offset the index to create the phase shifted version
- use one index for the normal sawtooth and the other for the inverted/shifted one
- use the square correction factor
- use the normal DC offset correction
- you can see that this function follows the same outline as the *CQBLimitedOscillator*'s square wave but uses the *doWaveTable()* helper function instead of *doSawtooth()*

```
double CWTOscillator::doSquareWave()
{
```

```
    double dPW = m_dPulseWidth/100.0;
    double dPWIndex = m_dReadIndex + dPW*WT_LENGTH;

    // --- render first sawtooth using dReadIndex
    double dSaw1 = doWaveTable(m_dReadIndex, m_dWT_inc);

    // --- find the phase shifted output
    if(m_dWT_inc >= 0)
    {
        if(dPWIndex >= WT_LENGTH)
            dPWIndex = dPWIndex - WT_LENGTH;
    }
    else
    {
        if(dPWIndex < 0)
            dPWIndex = WT_LENGTH + dPWIndex;
    }

    // --- render second sawtooth using dPWIndex (shifted)
    double dSaw2 = doWaveTable(dPWIndex, m_dWT_inc);

    // --- find the correction factor from the table
    double dSqAmp = m_dSquareCorrFactor[m_nCurrentTableIndex];

    // --- then subtract
    double dOut = dSqAmp*(dSaw1 - dSaw2);

    // --- calculate the DC correction factor
    double dCorr = 1.0/dPW;
    if(dPW < 0.5)
        dCorr = 1.0/(1.0-dPW);

    // --- apply correction
    dOut *= dCorr;

    return dOut;
}
```

doOscillate()

- if square wave, call that routine, scale output amplitude
- if others, use *doWaveTable()* method
- output is monophonic so just copy to aux output if needed
- uses same amplitude and amp mod scaling as all other oscillators

```
double CWTOscillator::doOscillate(double* pAuxOutput)
{
    if(!m_bNoteOn)
    {
        if(pAuxOutput)
            *pAuxOutput = 0.0;

        return 0.0;
    }
```

```
        // if square, it has its own routine
        if(m_uWaveform == SQUARE && m_nCurrentTableIndex >= 0)
        {
                double dOut = doSquareWave();
                if(pAuxOutput)
                        *pAuxOutput = dOut;

                return dOut;
        }

        // --- get output
        double dOutSample = doWaveTable(m_dReadIndex, m_dWT_inc);

        // mono oscillator
        if(pAuxOutput)
                *pAuxOutput = dOutSample*m_dAmplitude*m_dAmpMod;

        return dOutSample*m_dAmplitude*m_dAmpMod;
}
```

5.34 NanoSynth Oscillators: Processing Code

The NanoSynth plug-in object will possess member variables and functions to implement the synth processing. All objects will define the following:

```
        // --- two oscillators
        CQBLimitedOscillator m_Osc1;
        CQBLimitedOscillator m_Osc2;

        // --- one LFO
        CLFO m_LFO1;

        // --- update function for synth
        void update();
```

We will test the *CQBLimitedOscillator* first, then you can replace it with the wavetable oscillator and re-test.

The processing code for NanoSynth will render audio. This is an important function to understand since we will keep modifying it in the subsequent chapters, then we will find a way to both simplify and greatly extend the synth's capabilities in Chapter 8. That will be difficult if you have not followed along with the processing code. Regardless of platform, the processing for NanoSynth is going to follow the same pattern. The first part involves checking to see if the oscillator is running by examining its note on flag. In the articulation block, we render the modifier outputs. In this case, it is our single LFO object:

```
if(m_Osc1.m_bNoteOn)
{
        // --- ARTICULATION BLOCK --- //
        //
        // --- render LFO output
        double dLFO1Out = m_LFO1.doOscillate();
```

Next we take that LFO output, which is swinging on the range of [−1..+1], and modulate the pitched oscillators' frequency by calling the *setFoModExp()* function. Notice how the LFO output value is scaled by the modulation range limit (defined in *oscillator.h* and given in semitones) to create a value that now swings between [−OSC_FO_MOD_RANGE.. +OSC_FO_MOD_RANGE]. Understanding how this works will be important later. After the modulation is applied, we call the *update()* function to apply the changes in the oscillator.

```
    // --- apply to the Exp modulation inputs
    m_Osc1.setFoModExp(dLFO1Out*OSC_FO_MOD_RANGE);
    m_Osc2.setFoModExp(dLFO1Out*OSC_FO_MOD_RANGE);

    // --- update
    m_Osc1.update();
    m_Osc2.update();
```

Lastly, the audio engine block is implemented. The two oscillator outputs are mixed at a 50/50 ratio.

```
    // --- DIGITAL AUDIO ENGINE BLOCK --- //
    dOut = 0.5*m_Osc1.doOscillate() + 0.5*m_Osc2.doOscillate();
}
```

We will need to alter the MIDI note on and note off handling. In Chapter 3 we simply logged the MIDI messages. Now we get to use them.

Note On

For the note on event, we need to:

- set the oscillator pitch using the MIDI note number to the frequency lookup table that is declared in *synthfunctions.h*
- update the oscillator to calculate the new oscillator frequency variables
- turn on the LFO and pitched oscillators by using the start function.

```
<< ** Code Listing 5.1: Note on ** >>

// --- set the new oscillator pitch with table
m_Osc1.m_dOscFo = midiFreqTable[uMIDINote];
m_Osc2.m_dOscFo = midiFreqTable[uMIDINote];
m_Osc1.update();
m_Osc2.update();

// --- start all oscillators
m_Osc1.startOscillator();
m_Osc2.startOscillator();
m_LFO1.startOscillator();

<< END ** Code Listing 5.1: Note On ** END >>
```

Note Off

For the note off event, we just need to stop all the oscillators.

```
<< ** Code Listing 5.2: Note off ** >>

// --- stop all oscillators
m_Osc1.stopOscillator();
m_Osc2.stopOscillator();
m_LFO1.stopOscillator();

<< END ** Code Listing 5.2: Note Off ** END >>
```

5.35 NanoSynth Oscillators: RackAFX

Since this is the first project with GUI controls, we'll go over the setup, initialization and message handling for them. Refer back to Chapter 2, since it details the setup of GUI controls. In future projects, it will be up to you to read and decode the GUI control tables and detailed connection graphs to implement the user controls.

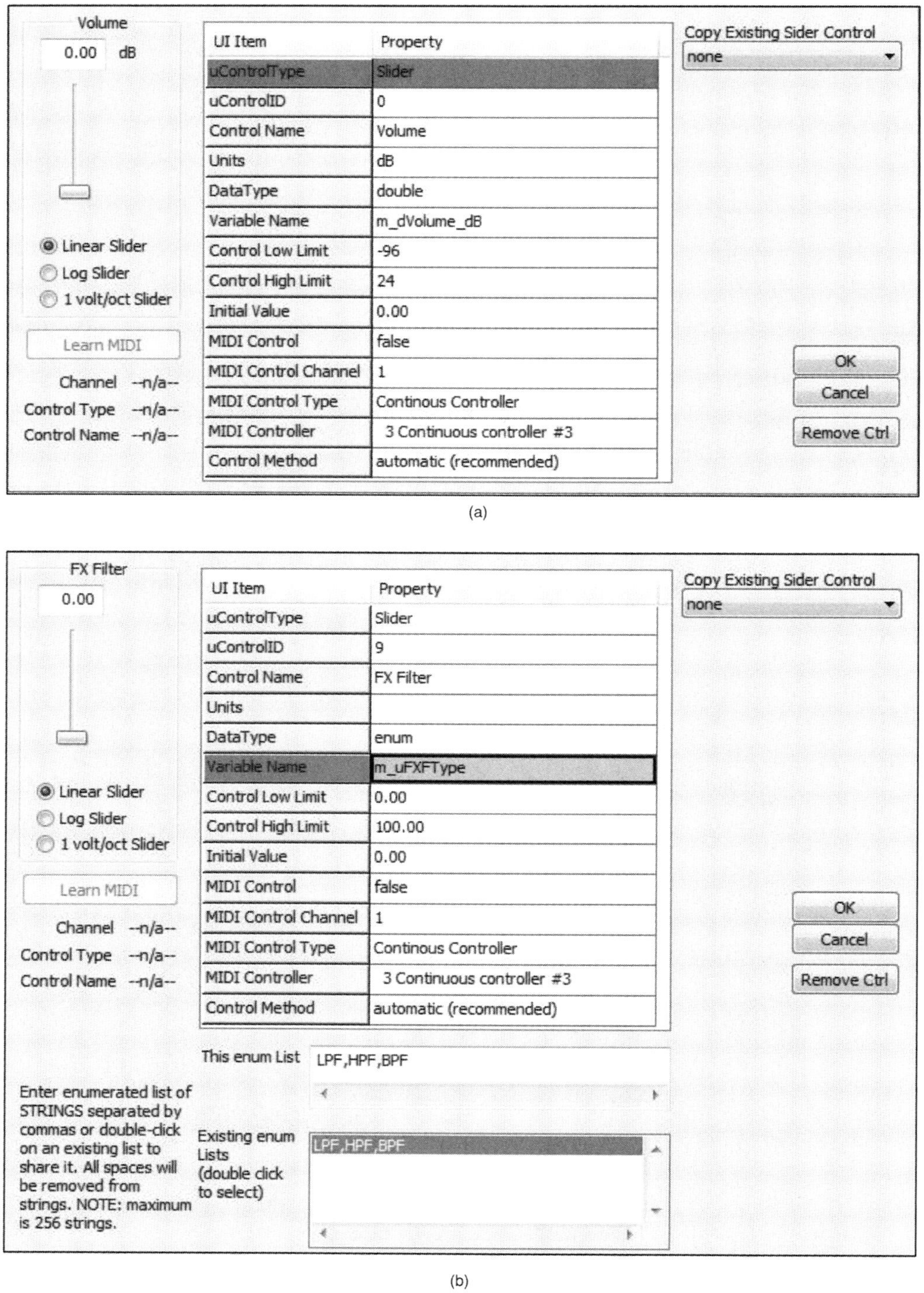

Figure 5.50: Examples of the slider designer forms for (a) continuous controls and (b) enumerated string types.

RackAFX GUI Controls: One Step Only

In RackAFX's main interface, right click on slider controls to reveal the slider designer form. As per the instructions in Chapter 2, you can also use Radio Button banks for enumerated string type variables of eight values or less. You can also embed 1024 more controls in the LCD Control. For NanoSynth, we just use sliders for all the controls. Figure 5.50 shows an example of both a continuous control and enumerated string type. Create a new control for each row in Table 5.3. After filling in the form, hit the <OK> button, and you are done with all the code for that control. All the GUI code is written for you. After testing and debugging, you can then optionally use the RackAFX drag and drop GUI designer to create a more visually appealing GUI that can be used in VST plug-ins as well. See Chapter 2 for details.

Next, open the NanoSynth object files and modify the following to implement the rest of the synth.

NanoSynth.h

In the *.h* file, we need to *#include* the member objects and declare them. We'll start with the *QBLimitedOscillators* first.

```
#include "QBLimitedOscillator.h"
#include "WTOscillator.h"
#include "LFO.h"

// abstract base class for RackAFX filters
class CNanoSynth : public CPlugIn
{
public:
      <SNIP SNIP SNIP>


      // Add your code here: ---------------------------------------- //
      // --- our two oscillators
      CQBLimitedOscillator m_Osc1;
      CQBLimitedOscillator m_Osc2;

      // --- one LFO
      CLFO m_LFO1;

      // --- update function for synth
      void update();

      // --- MIDI receive channel
      UINT m_uMidiRxChannel;
      // END OF USER CODE ----------------------------------------- //
```

NanoSynth.cpp

Start at the top of the file and work your way through the RackAFX functions:

Constructor:

- set the flag to capture all MIDI and set the MIDI receive channel (nothing has changed since the last NanoSynth, so there is nothing to do here)

prepareForPlay()

Implement the one time initialization code to:

- set the sample rate on all oscillators
- detune the second oscillator
- update the synth

```
bool __stdcall CNanoSynth::prepareForPlay()
{
    // --- sample rates
    m_Osc1.setSampleRate((double)m_nSampleRate);
    m_Osc2.setSampleRate((double)m_nSampleRate);
    m_LFO1.setSampleRate((double)m_nSampleRate);

    // --- detune by 2.5 cents
    m_Osc2.m_nCents = 2.5; // +2.5 cents detuned

    // --- update the synth
    update();

    return true;
}
```

update()

Connect the GUI controls to the synth by transferring our GUI control variables over to the synth objects, then call the update functions.

```
void CNanoSynth::update()
{
    // --- oscillators
    m_Osc1.m_uWaveform = m_uOscWaveform;
    m_Osc2.m_uWaveform = m_uOscWaveform;
    m_Osc1.update();
    m_Osc2.update();

    // --- LFO
    m_LFO1.m_uWaveform = m_uLFO1Waveform;
    m_LFO1.m_dAmplitude = m_dLFO1Amplitude;
    m_LFO1.m_dOscFo = m_dLFO1Rate;
    m_LFO1.m_uLFOMode = m_uLFO1Mode;
    m_LFO1.update();
}
```

processAudioFrame()

Implement the audio rendering described previously and write to the RackAFX output variables. This is a mono synth, so we only need to calculate one output.

```
bool __stdcall CNanoSynth::processAudioFrame(args…)
{
    // render
    double dOut = 0.0;
    if(m_Osc1.m_bNoteOn)
    {
            // --- ARTICULATION BLOCK --- //
            //
            // --- render LFO output
            double dLFO1Out = m_LFO1.doOscillate();
```

```
            // --- apply to the Exp modulation inputs
            m_Osc1.setFoModExp(dLFO1Out*OSC_FO_MOD_RANGE);
            m_Osc2.setFoModExp(dLFO1Out*OSC_FO_MOD_RANGE);

            // --- update
            m_Osc1.update();
            m_Osc2.update();

            // --- DIGITAL AUDIO ENGINE BLOCK --- //
            dOut = 0.5*m_Osc1.doOscillate() + 0.5*m_Osc2.doOscillate();
        }

        pOutputBuffer[0] = dOut;

        // Mono-In, Stereo-Out (AUX Effect)
        if(uNumInputChannels == 1 && uNumOutputChannels == 2)
            pOutputBuffer[1] = dOut;

        // Stereo-In, Stereo-Out (INSERT Effect)
        if(uNumInputChannels == 2 && uNumOutputChannels == 2)
            pOutputBuffer[1] = dOut;

        return true;
    }
```

userInterfaceChange()

Just do a brute force update of the whole synth by calling the object's helper function.

```
    bool __stdcall CNanoSynth::userInterfaceChange(int nControlIndex)
    {
        // --- all at once
        update();

        // --- done
        return true;
    }
```

midiNoteOn()

Here we simply implement the note on code from the last section. You can keep or delete the MIDI logging code as you wish.

```
    bool __stdcall CNanoSynth::midiNoteOn(args…)
    {
        // test channel/ignore
        if(m_uMidiRxChannel != MIDI_CH_ALL && uChannel != m_uMidiRxChannel)
            return false;

        #ifdef LOG_MIDI
            TRACE("-- Note On Ch:%d Note:%d Vel:%d \n", uChannel, uMIDINote,
                uVelocity);
        #endif
```

```
        << INSERT ** Code Listing 5.1: Note On ** HERE >>

        return true;
}
```

midiNoteOff()

Once again we simply implement the note off code from the last section. You can keep or delete the MIDI logging code as you wish.

```
bool __stdcall CNanoSynth::midiNoteOff(args…)
{
        // test channel/ignore
        if(m_uMidiRxChannel != MIDI_CH_ALL && uChannel != m_uMidiRxChannel)
                return false;

        #ifdef LOG_MIDI
                if(bAllNotesOff)
                        TRACE("-- All Notes OFF Ch:%d \n", uChannel);
                else
                        TRACE("-- Note Off Ch:%d Note:%d Vel:%d \n", uChannel,
                                uMIDINote, uVelocity);
        #endif

        << INSERT ** Code Listing 5.2: Note Off ** HERE >>

        return true;
}
```

You can now move to the RackAFX GUI designer and use the drag and drop interface to create your knobby/slider/LCD based GUI. See Chapter 2 for details.

5.36 NanoSynth Oscillators: VST3

Open the NanoSynth project. Since this is the first project with GUI controls, we'll go over the setup, initialization and message handling for them. Refer back to Chapter 2 since it details the setup of GUI controls. In future projects, it will be up to you to read and decode the GUI control tables and detailed connection graphs to implement the user controls.

VST3 GUI Controls Step 1: Enumeration and Declaration

For VST3, the first step is to setup the GUI indexing in *SynthParamLimits.h*. The new parameters need to go before the MIDI parameters we implemented in Chapter 3.

```
enum {
        OSC_WAVEFORM,
        LFO1_WAVEFORM,
        LFO1_RATE,
        LFO1_AMPLITUDE,
        LFO1_MODE,

        MIDI_PITCHBEND,
        MIDI_MODWHEEL,
        MIDI_VOLUME_CC7,
        MIDI_PAN_CC10,
        MIDI_EXPRESSION_CC11,
```

```
    MIDI_SUSTAIN_PEDAL,
    MIDI_CHANNEL_PRESSURE,
    MIDI_ALL_NOTES_OFF,

    NUMBER_OF_SYNTH_PARAMETERS // always last
};
```

Then, declare the variables from Table 5.3 in the *VSTProcessor.h* file. Each variable goes along with one of the enumerated index values for bookkeeping later.

```
class Processor : public AudioEffect
{
public:
    <SNIP SNIP SNIP>

    UINT m_uOscWaveform;
    UINT m_uLFO1Waveform;
    double m_dLFO1Rate;
    double m_dLFO1Amplitude;
    UINT m_uLFO1Mode;

    etc...
```

VST3 GUI Controls Step 2: Creation

Now you can setup the default GUI objects in the initialization function. We have both types of controls to deal with—continuous and enumerated string types. There are five GUI controls on NanoSynth so far, so there will be five chunks of code to create the parameters.

VSTController.cpp

Modify the *initialize()* function to add the new controls, as per the instructions in Chapter 2. You already added the parameters for MIDI controls in Chapter 3, so you can add the following code before or after—we like to keep all the MIDI control stuff at the bottom.

```
tresult PLUGIN_API Controller::initialize(FUnknown* context)
{
    // --- base class does its thing
    tresult result = EditController::initialize(context);

    // --- now define the controls
    if (result == kResultTrue)
    {
        // --- Init parameters
        Parameter* param;

        StringListParameter* enumStringParam = new
                    StringListParameter(USTRING("Osc Waveform"),
                                        OSC_WAVEFORM);
        // now add the strings for the list IN THE SAME ORDER AS DECLARED
        // IN THE enum in Synth Project
        enumStringParam->appendString(USTRING("SINE"));
        enumStringParam->appendString(USTRING("SAW1"));
        enumStringParam->appendString(USTRING("SAW2"));
        enumStringParam->appendString(USTRING("SAW3"));
```

```
enumStringParam->appendString(USTRING("TRI"));
enumStringParam->appendString(USTRING("SQUARE"));
enumStringParam->appendString(USTRING("NOISE"));
enumStringParam->appendString(USTRING("PNOISE"));
parameters.addParameter(enumStringParam);

enumStringParam = new StringListParameter(USTRING("LFO
                  Waveform"), LFO1_WAVEFORM);
// now add the strings
enumStringParam->appendString(USTRING("sine"));
enumStringParam->appendString(USTRING("usaw"));
enumStringParam->appendString(USTRING("dsaw"));
enumStringParam->appendString(USTRING("tri"));
enumStringParam->appendString(USTRING("square"));
enumStringParam->appendString(USTRING("expo"));
enumStringParam->appendString(USTRING("rsh"));
enumStringParam->appendString(USTRING("qrsh"));
parameters.addParameter(enumStringParam);

param = new RangeParameter(USTRING("LFO1 Rate"), LFO1_RATE,
                           USTRING("Hz"), MIN_LFO_RATE,
                           MAX_LFO_RATE, DEFAULT_LFO_RATE);
param->setPrecision(2); // fractional sig digits
parameters.addParameter(param);

param = new RangeParameter(USTRING("LFO1 Amplitude"),
                           LFO1_AMPLITUDE, USTRING(""),
                           MIN_UNIPOLAR, MAX_UNIPOLAR,
                           DEFAULT_UNIPOLAR);
param->setPrecision(1); // fractional sig digits
parameters.addParameter(param);

enumStringParam = new StringListParameter(USTRING("LFO1 Mode"),
                                          LFO1_MODE);
// now add the strings
enumStringParam->appendString(USTRING("sync"));
enumStringParam->appendString(USTRING("shot"));
enumStringParam->appendString(USTRING("free"));
parameters.addParameter(enumStringParam);

// MIDI Params - these have no knobs in main GUI but do have to
// appear in default
// NOTE: this is for VST3 ONLY! Not needed in AU or RAFX

etc...
```

VST3 GUI Controls Step 3: Initialization

Now switch over to the Processor object (we will come back to the Controller shortly). We need to initialize the GUI controls in the constructor. The defaults are in *SynthParamLimits.h* for this project.

```
Processor::Processor()
{
    // --- define our controller class FUID
    setControllerClass(Controller::cid);

    // --- initialize
    m_uOscWaveform = DEFAULT_PITCHED_OSC_WAVEFORM;
    m_uLFO1Waveform = DEFAULT_LFO_WAVEFORM;
    m_dLFO1Rate = DEFAULT_LFO_RATE;
    m_dLFO1Amplitude = DEFAULT_UNIPOLAR;
    m_uLFO1Mode = DEFAULT_LFO_MODE;

    // receive on all channels
    m_uMidiRxChannel = MIDI_CH_ALL;

    // VST3 specific
    m_dMIDIPitchBend = DEFAULT_MIDI_PITCHBEND; // -1 to +1

    etc…
}
```

VST3 GUI Controls Step 4: Serialize Write

You need to write the code to save the current GUI controls as discussed in Chapter 2. There are five GUI control variables to write. As always, pay careful attention to the ordering of the writing. The reading code must exactly match it. In the Processor object, the writing is done in *getState()*.

```
tresult PLUGIN_API Processor::getState(IBStream* fileStream)
{
    // --- get a stream I/F
    IBStreamer s(fileStream, kLittleEndian);

    // --- NanoSynthVersion - place this at top so versioning can be used
    //   during the READ operation
    if(!s.writeInt64u(NanoSynthVersion)) return kResultFalse;

    // --- write code
    if(!s.writeInt32u(m_uOscWaveform)) return kResultFalse;
    if(!s.writeInt32u(m_uLFO1Waveform)) return kResultFalse;
    if(!s.writeDouble(m_dLFO1Rate)) return kResultFalse;
    if(!s.writeDouble(m_dLFO1Amplitude)) return kResultFalse;
    if(!s.writeInt32u(m_uLFO1Mode)) return kResultFalse;

    return kResultTrue;
}
```

VST3 GUI Controls Step 5: Serialize Read (Processor)

Next, you need to write the code to read the current GUI parameter values from a file as discussed in Chapter 2. Modify the *setState()* function to perform the read operation in the same order as the writing.

```
tresult PLUGIN_API Processor::setState(IBStream* fileStream)
{
```

```
        IBStreamer s(fileStream, kLittleEndian);
        uint64 version = 0;

        // --- needed to convert to our UINT reads
        uint32 udata = 0;
        int32 data = 0;

        // --- read the version
        if(!s.readInt64u(version)) return kResultFalse;

        // --- read code
        if(!s.readInt32u(udata)) return kResultFalse;
               else m_uOscWaveform = udata;
        if(!s.readInt32u(udata)) return kResultFalse;
               else m_uLFO1Waveform = udata;
        if(!s.readDouble(m_dLFO1Rate)) return kResultFalse;
        if(!s.readDouble(m_dLFO1Amplitude)) return kResultFalse;
        if(!s.readInt32u(udata)) return kResultFalse;
               else m_uLFO1Mode = udata;

        // --- do next version...
        if (version >= 1)
        {
               // add v1 stuff here
        }

        return kResultTrue;
}
```

VST3 GUI Controls Step 6: Serialize Read (Controller)

Switch back to the Controller object and implement the reading code in *setComponentState()*. Make sure to follow the same order as the reading code you just wrote. Remember that you need to use the helper functions we discussed in Chapter 2 for setting the GUI variables.

```
tresult PLUGIN_API Controller::setComponentState(IBStream* fileStream)
{
        // --- make a streamer interface using the
        //    IBStream* fileStream; this is for PC so
        //    data is LittleEndian
        IBStreamer s(fileStream, kLittleEndian);

        // --- variables for reading
        uint64 version = 0;
        double dDoubleParam = 0;

        // --- needed to convert to our UINT reads
        uint32 udata = 0;
        int32 data = 0;

        // --- read the version
        if(!s.readInt64u(version)) return kResultFalse;
```

```
    if(!s.readInt32u(udata)) return kResultFalse;
    else
        setParamNormalizedFromFile(OSC_WAVEFORM, (ParamValue)udata);

    if(!s.readInt32u(udata)) return kResultFalse;
    else
        setParamNormalizedFromFile(LFO1_WAVEFORM, (ParamValue)udata);

    if(!s.readDouble(dDoubleParam)) return kResultFalse;
    else
        setParamNormalizedFromFile(LFO1_RATE, dDoubleParam);

    if(!s.readDouble(dDoubleParam)) return kResultFalse;
    else
        setParamNormalizedFromFile(LFO1_AMPLITUDE, dDoubleParam);

    if(!s.readInt32u(udata)) return kResultFalse;
    else
        setParamNormalizedFromFile(LFO1_MODE, (ParamValue)udata);

    // --- do next version…
    if (version >= 1)
    {
        // add v1 stuff here
    }

    return kResultTrue;
}
```

VST3 GUI Controls Step 7: Parsing GUI Control Values

Lastly, you need to write the code that will pick up the GUI control changes as discussed in Chapter 2. This is done in the Processor object so switch back to that code. You need to modify the *doControlUpdate()* function to add the new control parameters. You already have code there from picking up the MIDI control values in Chapter 3 so add the code just before it.

```
bool Processor::doControlUpdate(ProcessData& data)
{
    bool paramChange = false;
    <SNIP SNIP SNIP and Indents Removed>
if(queue)
{
    // --- check for control points
    if(queue->getPointCount() <= 0) return false;

    int32 sampleOffset = 0.0;
    ParamValue value = 0.0;
    ParamID pid = queue->getParameterId();

    // --- get the last point in queue
    if(queue->getPoint(queue->getPointCount()-1, /* last update point */
        sampleOffset,                            /* sample offset */
        value) == kResultTrue)                   /* value = [0..1] */
```

```
{
        // --- at least one param changed
        paramChange = true;

        switch(pid) // same as RAFX uControlID
        {
                // --- control code
                case OSC_WAVEFORM:
                {
                        m_uOscWaveform = (UINT)cookVSTGUIVariable
                                          (MIN_PITCHED_OSC_WAVEFORM,
                                          MAX_PITCHED_OSC_WAVEFORM, value);
                        break;
                }
                case LFO1_WAVEFORM:
                {
                        m_uLFO1Waveform = (UINT)cookVSTGUIVariable
                                          (MIN_LFO_WAVEFORM,
                                          MAX_LFO_WAVEFORM, value);

                        break;
                }
                case LFO1_RATE:
                {
                        m_dLFO1Rate = cookVSTGUIVariable(MIN_LFO_RATE,
                                                    MAX_LFO_RATE, value);
                        break;
                }
                case LFO1_AMPLITUDE:
                {
                        m_dLFO1Amplitude = cookVSTGUIVariable(MIN_UNIPOLAR,
                                                MAX_UNIPOLAR, value);
                        break;
                }
                case LFO1_MODE:
                {
                        m_uLFO1Mode = cookVSTGUIVariable(MIN_LFO_MODE,
                                          MAX_LFO_MODE, value);
                        break;
                }

                // --- MIDI messages
                case MIDI_PITCHBEND: // want -1 to +1

                etc…
```

Now that the GUI code is done, we can turn our attention to the synth itself. Remember you will need to implement this seven-step GUI coding solution anytime you add new GUI controls.

VSTProcessor.h

In the *.h* file, we need to *#include* the member objects and declare them. We'll start with the *QBLimitedOscillators* first.

```
#include "QBLimitedOscillator.h"
#include "WTOscillator.h"
#include "LFO.h"

// abstract base class for RackAFX filters
class Processor : public AudioEffect
{
public:
     <SNIP SNIP SNIP>

     // --- our two oscillators
     CQBLimitedOscillator m_Osc1;
     CQBLimitedOscillator m_Osc2;

     // --- one LFO
     CLFO m_LFO1;

     // --- update function for synth
     void update();

     etc…
```

VSTProcessor.cpp

Start at the top of the file and work your way through the functions:

Constructor:

- you already setup the GUI controls here

setActive()

This is the one time initialization/destruction code that gets called when the plug-in is activated or deactivated. Add the one time init code here.

```
tresult PLUGIN_API Processor::setActive(TBool state)
{
     if(state)
     {
            // --- do ON stuff;
            // set sample rates
     m_Osc1.setSampleRate((double)processSetup.sampleRate);
     m_Osc2.setSampleRate((double)processSetup.sampleRate);
     m_LFO1.setSampleRate((double)processSetup.sampleRate);

     // --- detune
     m_Osc2.m_nCents = 2.5; // +2.5 cents detuned

     // --- update all
     update();
     }
else
{
```

```
            // --- do OFF stuff; delete stuff allocated above
        }

        // --- base class method call is last
        return AudioEffect::setActive (state);
    }
```

update()

Connect the GUI controls to the synth by transferring our GUI control variables over to the synth objects; then call the update functions.

```
void Processor::update()
{
        // --- oscillators
        m_Osc1.m_uWaveform = m_uOscWaveform;
        m_Osc2.m_uWaveform = m_uOscWaveform;
        m_Osc1.updateOscillator();
        m_Osc2.updateOscillator();

        // --- LFO
        m_LFO1.m_uWaveform = m_uLFO1Waveform;
        m_LFO1.m_dAmplitude = m_dLFO1Amplitude;
        m_LFO1.m_dOscFo = m_dLFO1Rate;
        m_LFO1.m_uLFOMode = m_uLFO1Mode;
        m_LFO1.updateOscillator();
}
```

process()

Implement the audio rendering described previously and write to the VST3 output arrays. This is a mono synth, so we only need to calculate one output per sample period

```
tresult PLUGIN_API Processor::process(ProcessData& data)
{
        // --- check for control changes and update synth if needed
        doControlUpdate(data);

        <SNIP SNIP SNIP and Indents Removed>

                // --- output "accumulator"
                double dOut = 0.0;

                for(int32 j=0; j<samplesToProcess; j++)
                {
                        // --- clear accumulators
                        dOut = 0.0;

                        if(m_Osc1.m_bNoteOn)
                        {
                                // --- ARTICULATION BLOCK --- //
                                //
```

```
                    // --- render LFO output
                    double dLFO1Out = m_LFO1.doOscillate();

                    // --- apply to the Exp modulation inputs
                    m_Osc1.setFoModExp(dLFO1Out*OSC_FO_MOD_RANGE);
                    m_Osc2.setFoModExp(dLFO1Out*OSC_FO_MOD_RANGE);

                    // --- update
                    m_Osc1.update();
                    m_Osc2.update();

                    // --- DIGITAL AUDIO ENGINE BLOCK --- //
                    dOut = 0.5*m_Osc1.doOscillate() +
                           0.5*m_Osc2.doOscillate();
                }
            }

            // write out to buffer
            buffers[0][j] = dOut; // left
            buffers[1][j] = dOut; // right
        }

        // --- update the counter
        for(int i = 0; i < OUTPUT_CHANNELS; i++)
            buffers[i] += samplesToProcess;

        etc…
```

doProcessEvents()

Here we simply implement the note on code from the last section. You can keep or delete the MIDI logging code as you wish.

```
bool Processor::doProcessEvent(Event& vstEvent)
{
    bool noteEvent = false;

    // --- process Note On or Note Off messages here
    switch(vstEvent.type)
    {
        // --- NOTE ON
        case Event::kNoteOnEvent:
        {
            <SNIP SNIP SNIP>

            #if(LOG_MIDI && _DEBUG)
                FDebugPrint("-- Note On Ch:%d Note:%d Vel:%d \n",
                            uMIDIChannel, uMIDINote, uMIDIVelocity);
            #endif
            << INSERT ** Code Listing 5.1: Note On ** HERE >>
            break;
        }
```

```
// --- NOTE OFF
case Event::kNoteOffEvent:
{

        <SNIP SNIP SNIP>
        #if(LOG_MIDI && _DEBUG)
                FDebugPrint("-- Note Off Ch:%d Note:%d Vel:%d \n",
                            uMIDIChannel, uMIDINote, uMIDIVelocity);
        #endif
        << INSERT ** Code Listing 5.2: Note Off ** HERE >>
        break;
}
etc…
```

Design the VST3 GUI by loading your DLL into a VST3 client and using the drag-and-drop method described in Chapter 2. You can always just use the default VST3 GUI if you don't want to perform this step. See the VSTGUI website for more information if needed.

5.37 NanoSynth Oscillators: AU

Open the NanoSynth project. Since this is the first project with GUI controls, we'll go over the setup, initialization and message handling for them. Refer back to Chapter 2 since it details the setup of GUI controls. In future projects, it will be up to you to read and decode the GUI control tables and detailed connection graphs to implement the user controls.

AU GUI Controls Step 1: Enumeration

For AU, the first step is to setup the GUI indexing in *SynthParamLimits.h*. Unlike VST3 and RackAFX, you do not need to declare variables for the controls—they will be stored in your parameter container instead.

```
enum {
    OSC_WAVEFORM,
    LFO1_WAVEFORM,
    LFO1_RATE,
    LFO1_AMPLITUDE,
    LFO1_MODE,

    NUMBER_OF_SYNTH_PARAMETERS // always last
};
```

AU GUI Controls Step 2: Initialization

Declare the number of indexed parameters then initialize the parameters in the AUSynth constructor. The number of parameters matches the enumeration in Step 1.

```
AUSynth::AUSynth(AudioUnit inComponentInstance)
        : AUInstrumentBase(inComponentInstance, 0, 1)
{
    // --- create input, output ports, groups and parts
    CreateElements();

    // --- define number of params (controls)
    Globals()->UseIndexedParameters(NUMBER_OF_SYNTH_PARAMETERS);

    // --- initialize the controls here!
    // --- these are defined in SynthParamLimits.h
```

```
    //
    Globals()->SetParameter(OSC_WAVEFORM, DEFAULT_PITCHED_OSC_WAVEFORM);
    Globals()->SetParameter(LFO1_WAVEFORM, DEFAULT_LFO_WAVEFORM);
    Globals()->SetParameter(LFO1_RATE, DEFAULT_LFO_RATE);
    Globals()->SetParameter(LFO1_AMPLITUDE, DEFAULT_UNIPOLAR);
    Globals()->SetParameter(LFO1_MODE, DEFAULT_LFO_MODE);

    // receive on all channels
    m_uMidiRxChannel = MIDI_CH_ALL;
}
```

AU GUI Controls Step 3: Setup the Parameter Information

The attributes of the GUI parameters are setup in *GetParameterInfo()*. Use Table 5.3 to setup this function. The helper function is called *setAUParameterInfo()*, and the last two arguments are flags for log controls and indexed strings. Setting the indexed string parameter to *true* identifies it as an enumerated string type.

```
ComponentResult AUSynth::GetParameterInfo(args…)
{
    // --- we only handle Global params
    if (inScope != kAudioUnitScope_Global)
        return kAudioUnitErr_InvalidScope;

    // --- decode the parameters, use our built-in helper function
    //      setAUParameterInfo()
    switch(inParameterID)
    {
        case OSC_WAVEFORM:
        {
            setAUParameterInfo(outParameterInfo, CFSTR("Osc Waveform"),
                               CFSTR(""), MIN_PITCHED_OSC_WAVEFORM,
                               MAX_PITCHED_OSC_WAVEFORM,
                               DEFAULT_PITCHED_OSC_WAVEFORM, false,
                               true); // true = indexed strings
            return noErr;
            break;
        }
        case LFO1_WAVEFORM:
        {
            setAUParameterInfo(outParameterInfo, CFSTR("LFO Waveform"),
                               CFSTR(""), MIN_LFO_WAVEFORM,
                               MAX_LFO_WAVEFORM, DEFAULT_LFO_WAVEFORM,
                               false, true);
            return noErr;
            break;
        }
        case LFO1_RATE:
        {
            setAUParameterInfo(outParameterInfo, CFSTR("LFO Rate"),
                               CFSTR("Hz"), MIN_LFO_RATE, MAX_LFO_RATE,
                               DEFAULT_LFO_RATE);
```

```
                return noErr;
                break;
            }
            case LFO1_AMPLITUDE:
            {
                setAUParameterInfo(outParameterInfo, CFSTR("LFO Amp"),
                                   CFSTR(""), MIN_UNIPOLAR, MAX_UNIPOLAR,
                                   DEFAULT_UNIPOLAR);
                return noErr;
                break;
            }
            case LFO1_MODE:
            {
                setAUParameterInfo(outParameterInfo, CFSTR("LFO Mode"),
                CFSTR(""), MIN_LFO_MODE, MAX_LFO_MODE,
                DEFAULT_LFO_MODE, false, true);
            return noErr;
            break;
            }
        }
        return kAudioUnitErr_InvalidParameter;
}
```

Next, for any parameter that you setup as an indexed string type, you need to reply to a query about that enumerated string list. You get these out of Table 5.3 also.

```
ComponentResult AUSynth::GetParameterValueStrings(args…)
{
    if(inScope == kAudioUnitScope_Global)
    {
        if(outStrings == NULL)
            return noErr;

        // --- decode the ID value and set the string list; I do it this
        //   way to match the "enum UINT" described
        //   in the book; take the strings from the GUI tables and
        //   embed here
        switch(inParameterID)
        {
            case OSC_WAVEFORM:
            {
                setAUParameterStringList(CFSTR("SINE,SAW1,
                                         SAW2,SAW3,TRI,
                                         SQUARE,NOISE,PNOISE"),
                                         outStrings);
                return noErr;
                break;
            }
            case LFO1_WAVEFORM:
```

```
                {
                        setAUParameterStringList(CFSTR("sine,usaw,dsaw,
                        tri,square,expo,rsh,qrsh"),
                        outStrings);
                        return noErr;
                        break;
                }
                case LFO1_MODE:
                {
                        setAUParameterStringList(CFSTR("sync,shot,free"),
                        outStrings);
                return noErr;
                break;
                }
        }
    }

return kAudioUnitErr_InvalidParameter;
}
```

Now that the GUI code is done, we can turn our attention to the synth itself. Remember you will need to implement this three-step GUI coding solution anytime you add new GUI controls.

AUSynth.h

In the *.h* file, we need to *#include* the member objects and declare them. We'll start with the *QBLimitedOscillators* first.

```
#include "QBLimitedOscillator.h"
#include "WTOscillator.h"
#include "LFO.h"

// abstract base class for RackAFX filters
class AUSynth : public AUInstrumentBase
{
public:
    <SNIP SNIP SNIP>

    // --- our two oscillators
    CQBLimitedOscillator m_Osc1;
    CQBLimitedOscillator m_Osc2;

    // --- one LFO
    CLFO m_LFO1;

    // --- update function for synth
    void update();

    // --- our receive channel
    UINT m_uMidiRxChannel;

    etc...
```

AUSynth.cpp

Start at the top of the file and work your way through the functions:

Constructor:

- you already setup the GUI controls there

Initialize()

Perform the one-time initialization described in the previous section in the *Initialize()* function. Then call the *update()* function.

```
ComponentResult AUSynth::Initialize()
{
        // --- init the base class
        AUInstrumentBase::Initialize();

        // --- inits
        m_Osc1.setSampleRate(GetOutput(0)->GetStreamFormat().mSampleRate);
        m_Osc2.setSampleRate(GetOutput(0)->GetStreamFormat().mSampleRate);
        m_Osc2.m_nCents = 2.5; // +2.5 cents detuned

        m_LFO1.setSampleRate(GetOutput(0)->GetStreamFormat().mSampleRate);

        // --- init the synth
        update();

        return noErr;
}
```

update()

Update the synth variables in the *update()* function. Retrieve the parameters from the container with *Globals() –>GetParameter()*. Always call the subcomponent's *update()* function after setting the variables to recalculate the parameters.

```
void AUSynth::update()
{
        // --- oscillators
        m_Osc1.m_uWaveform = Globals()->GetParameter(OSC_WAVEFORM);
        m_Osc2.m_uWaveform = Globals()->GetParameter(OSC_WAVEFORM);
        m_Osc1.update();
        m_Osc2.update();

        // --- LFO
        m_LFO1.m_uWaveform = Globals()->GetParameter(LFO1_WAVEFORM);
        m_LFO1.m_dAmplitude = Globals()->GetParameter(LFO1_AMPLITUDE);
        m_LFO1.m_dOscFo = Globals()->GetParameter(LFO1_RATE);
        m_LFO1.m_uLFOMode = Globals()->GetParameter(LFO1_MODE);
        m_LFO1.update();
}
```

Render()

Perform the audio rendering code as described previously. You first call the *update()* function we just wrote. It sets the parameters for the entire block of processing. As with VST3 you may decide to make the parameter updates finer in granularity by calling update periodically during block processing. Note: RackAFX processes in sample frames (mono or stereo pairs), so control changes take effect within one sample period.

```
OSStatus AJSynth::Render(args…)
{
      // --- broadcast MIDI events
      PerformEvents(inTimeStamp);

      // --- do the mass update for this frame
      update();


      <SNIP SNIP SNIP>
      // --- output "accumulator"
      double dOut = 0.0;

      // --- the frame processing loop
      for(UInt32 frame=0; frame<inNumberFrames; ++frame)
      {
            // --- clear accumulators
            dOut = 0.0;

            if(m_Osc1.m_bNoteOn)
            {
                  // --- ARTICULATION BLOCK --- //
                  //
                  // --- render LFO output
                  double dLFO1Out = m_LFO1.doOscillate();

                  // --- apply to the Exp modulation inputs
                  m_Osc1.setFoModExp(dLFO1Out*OSC_FO_MOD_RANGE);
                  m_Osc2.setFoModExp(dLFO1Out*OSC_FO_MOD_RANGE);

                  // --- update
                  m_Osc1.update();
                  m_Osc2.update();

                  // --- DIGITAL AUDIO ENGINE BLOCK --- //
                  dOut = 0.5*m_Osc1.doOscillate() + 0.5*m_Osc2.doOscillate();
            }

            // write out to buffer
            // --- mono
            left[frame] = dOut;

            // --- stereo
            if(right) right[frame] = dOut;
      }
      return noErr;
}
```

StartNote()

Add the note on event code from Section 5.10 after the MIDI logging.

```
OSStatus AUSynth::StartNote(args…)
{
      <SNIP SNIP SNIP>
      #ifdef LOG_MIDI
              printf("-- Note On Ch:%d Note:%d Vel:%d \n", uChannel, uMIDINote,
                      uVelocity);
      #endif
      << INSERT ** Code Listing 5.1: Note On ** HERE >>
      return noErr;
}
```

StopNote()

Add the note off event code from Section 5.10 after the MIDI logging.

```
OSStatus AUSynth::StopNote(args…)
{
      <SNIP SNIP SNIP>
      #ifdef LOG_MIDI
              // --- NOTE: AU does not transmit note of velocity!
              printf("-- Note Off Ch:%d Note:%d \n", uChannel, uMIDINote);
      #endif
      << INSERT ** Code Listing 5.2: Note Off ** HERE >>

      return noErr;
}
```

Design your AU GUI using Interface Builder and the method described in Chapter 2. Remember the flat Cocoa namespace issue when copying projects in XCode.

5.38 NanoSynth: Wavetables

Build and test the plug-in on your platform. If you are using RackAFX, then you can use it as the client and use the Analyzer to make sure you have the oscillators working properly, compare their spectra, etc. Turn on the LFO and pitched oscillators independently then try the modulation. Next, you can swap out the quasi bandlimited oscillators for the wavetable oscillators as a comparison. It is simple and identical on all the platforms. In the plug-in object's *.h* file, substitute the wavetable oscillators for the quasi bandlimited ones:

```
// --- comment out old oscillators
// CQBLimitedOscillator m_Osc1;
// CQBLimitedOscillator m_Osc2;

// --- use wavetable instead
CQBLimitedOscillator m_Osc1;
CQBLimitedOscillator m_Osc2;
```

Now retest the plug-in and make sure everything works as expected. Since the oscillators have the same base class and interface, swapping them is simple.

5.39 Challenges

Bronze

Add/implement start delay and attack time and phase offset as described in Section 5.27 to the LFO object. Add controls to the plug-in to test.

Sliver

Alter the NanoSynth plug-in to allow you to freely switch between the quasi bandlimited and wavetable oscillators. You will need to assign a control to implement the switch (use an enumerated string type with the values OFF, ON or the RackAFX 2-state switches if you like). Perform listening tests on the two oscillator types. The wavetables technically have no aliasing, so you have something to compare with. Can you hear a difference in aliasing components between the two? (Hint: declare a *COscillator* pointer and use it to manipulate/switch the oscillators)

Gold

We will implement and test the pulse width modulation capabilities of the oscillators in Chapter 9. However, you can get a head start by implementing it now. When the user selects the square wave oscillator, use the LFO to modulate the pulse-width instead of the pitch of the oscillator. Then, use the LFO to modulate both. Next, declare a second LFO and use one for pitch modulation and the other for pulse-width modulation. Add the new GUI controls to your interface for practice.

Platinum

Design your own BLEP residual table starting with a lowpass filter impulse response from a linear or minimum phase FIR filter. You might want to use MATLAB or look at the C++ code we used to generate the windowed *sinc()* function. Test various BLEP oscillators designed from different filter impulse responses.

Diamond: Hard Sync Sawtooth Oscillator

Brandt's original paper that produced the MinBLEP method was actually dealing with hard syncing two oscillators. Hard sync is a common synthesis technique to develop rich and different harmonics. In hard sync, one oscillator is designated as the master, and the other is the slave. The two oscillators run at different frequencies with the slave always running at a higher rate. The output is from the slave oscillator. When the master oscillator's modulo rolls over, it re-triggers the slave's modulo counter to start over. This forces the slave oscillator to have the same fundamental frequency as the master, but with a chopped waveform. Figure 5.51 shows the output of two hard-sunk sawtooth waves with the master f_0 = 500 Hz and the slave f_0 = 1200 Hz. The arrows show the point where the slave modulo counter has been reset. The spectrum is rich with harmonics, and modulating the slave oscillator with a LFO produces a commonly used and very interesting output.

So for this case of hard syncing two sawtooth oscillators, we have multiple discontinuities to deal with. This means our two oscillators will need some coupling, and we will need to know whether a reset operation is pending for the next sample period or occurring during the present sample period. If there is no reset pending or occurring, we still have to check our position relative to the ordinary sawtooth discontinuity. The height of the reset discontinuity is found as the fractional component of the ratio of the oscillation frequencies.

$$R = \frac{f_{slave}}{f_{master}} \qquad (5.22)$$
$$Height = R - (\text{int})R$$

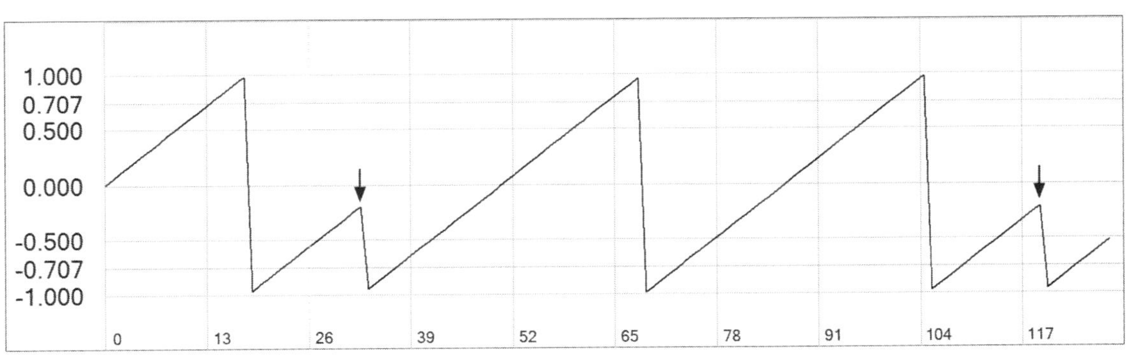

Figure 5.51: Hard syncing two sawtooth waveforms.

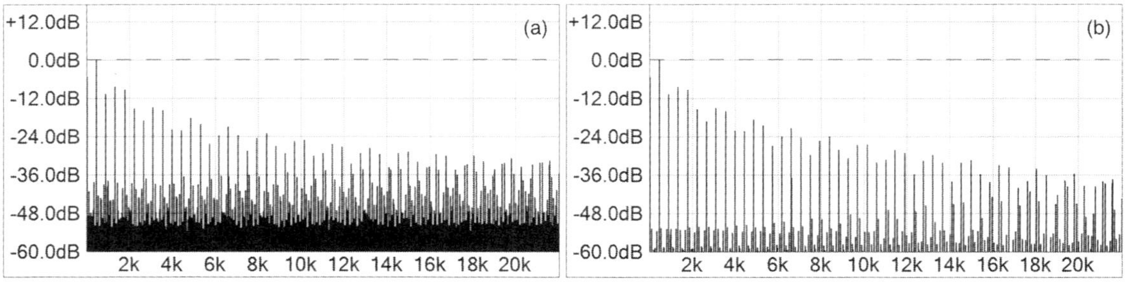

Figure 5.52: The spectrum of two hard sunk sawtooth waveforms (a) before and (b) after application of two-point PolyBLEP with *fo*(master) = 440 Hz and *fo*(slave) = 600 Hz.

BLEP/PolyBLEP can be used to smear over the discontinuities, but there are some major issues to deal with. In fact, the Brandt paper fails to disclose any implementation details or any real or simulated results. In a simple case where the master and slave oscillators operate at relatively low frequencies, semi-decent results can be obtained as shown in Figure 5.52, where two-point PolyBLEP has been applied to the discontinuities. However, as Andy Leary points out, there are problems when the frequencies become high enough and BLEP correction must be applied in overlapping pulses, or when the master and slave both reset during the same sample interval (see the Leary/Bright patent in the Bibliography). This is especially bad when the master and/or slave oscillator frequencies become very high, at which point unacceptable aliasing will occur. The PolyBLEP oscillator used to produce Figure 5.52 suffers from this problem and does not produce acceptable results at higher master/slave frequencies or when the oscillator sync-ratio is modulated at high frequencies.

Obtain the Leary/Bright patent and study how the authors handle the hard-sync situation. Use the block diagrams provided to implement an alias free hard-sync oscillator pair. The BLEP oscillators in this chapter are based on the first part of the patent, and you can certainly start with them as a basis for your work.

Bibliography

Brandt, Eli. 2001. "Hard Sync Without Aliasing." *Proceedings from the International Computer Music Conference.* Havana, Cuba.

Dattorro, Jon. 2003. "Effect Design Part 3 Oscillators: Sinusoidal and Pseudonoise." *Journal of the Audio Engineering Society*, vol. 50, no. 3.

Kleimola, Jari and Välimäki, Vesa. 2012. "Reducing Aliasing from Synthetic Audio Signals Using Polynomial Transition Regions." *IEEE Signal Processing Letters*, vol. 19, no. 2.

Leary, Andrew and Bright, Charles. 2009. "Bandlimited Digital Synthesis of Analog Waveforms." United States Patent 7,589,272.

Moore, Richard. 1990. *Elements of Computer Music.* Eaglewood Cliffs: Prentice-Hall.

Moorer, James. 1976. "The Synthesis of Complex Audio Spectra by Means of Discrete Summation Formulae." *Journal of the Audio Engineering Society*, vol. 24, no. 9, pp. 717–727.

Nam, Juhan; Välimäki, Vesa; Abel, Jonathan; and Smith, Julius O. 2010. "Efficient Antialiasing Oscillator Algorithms Using Low-Order Fractional Delay Filters." *IEEE Transactions on Audio, Speech and Language Processing*, vol. 18, no. 4.

Pekonen, Jussi; Lazzarini, Victor; Timoney, Joseph; Kleimola, Jari; and Välimäki, Vesa. 2011. "Discrete-Time Modeling of the Moog Sawtooth Waveform." *EURADISP Journal on Advances in Signal Processing.*

Stilson, Tim and Smith, Julius O. 1996. "Alias-Free Digital Synthesis of Classic Analog Waveforms." *Proceedings from the 1996 International Computer Music Conference.*

Välimäki, Vesa and Huovilainen, Antti. 2006. "Oscillator and Filter Algorithms for Virtual Analog Synthesis." *Computer Music Journal*, vol. 30, no. 2, pp.19–31. Cambridge: MIT Press.

Välimäki, Vesa. 2005. "Discrete-Time Synthesis of the Sawtooth Waveform With Reduced Aliasing." *IEEE Signal Processing Letters*, vol. 12, no. 3.

Välimäki, Vesa; Nam, Juhan; Abel, Jonathan; and Smith, Julius O. 2010. "Alias-Suppressed Oscillators Based on Differential Polynomial Waveforms." *IEEE Transactions on Audio, Speech and Language Processing*, vol. 18, no. 4.

CHAPTER 6

Envelope Generators and Controlled Amplifiers

Envelope Generators (EGs) are used to shape the amplitude, pitch, and frequency domain content of the synthesized signal. The three applications are usually called Amp-EG, Pitch-EG, and Filter-EG, respectively. In this chapter we will investigate and code an envelope generator that will provide the basic functionality we need for all three applications. An Amp-EG is referred to as a Transient Generator (TG) on older synthesizers. The transient generator shapes the time domain or transient edge of the signal. The Amp-EG is applied to a controlled amplifier. In analog synths, this is a Voltage Controlled Amplifier (VCA) whereas on a digital synth, this is a Digitally Controlled Amplifier (DCA). In this chapter we will design the EG and investigate its application to all amplitude, pitch and frequency shaping. We will design a flexible EG that can provide an analog mode based loosely on the CEM3310 integrated circuit from 1979, and a digital mode that operates linearly-in-dB, similar to the decay and release curves of the Yamaha DX7.

6.1 Analog Envelope Generators

The earliest analog envelope generators were based around the charging and discharging of a capacitor. A capacitor is an electronic component that is designed to store a charge Q. When combined with a series resistor R_{ATT} and shunt resistor R_{DCY}, it charges and discharges exponentially as shown in Figure 6.1. The series resistor R_{ATT} controls the charge (attack) time, while the shunt resistor R_{DCY} controls the discharge (decay) time.

Figure 6.2 shows this concept. In Figure 6.1(a) SW1 is closed, connecting a constant voltage source to the capacitor via R1, which limits the current (charge flow) and therefore controls the charging time. SW2 is open so that the capacitor has no way to discharge. The capacitor charges up quickly at first and then tapers off. In Figure 6.2(b) SW1 is opened, disconnecting the source, and SW2 is closed, providing a discharge path to ground. R2 limits the current flow during the discharge and therefore controls discharging time. The capacitor voltage V_{CAP} therefore moves exponentially up or down.

When combined with some switching logic, the basic circuit of Figure 6.3 can generate multiple attack and/or decay phases, as different resistors may be switched in and out and the control voltage turned on or off. If the decay resistor is connected to a voltage V_{SUS}, the capacitor will decay down to this voltage level as seen in Figure 6.3.

The flattened top of the attack portion of the curve is generally not desirable in the envelope generator application for synthesis. The way to remove it is to prevent the capacitor from fully charging. In the Curtis CEM3310 envelope generator chip used in several older synth designs, the capacitor only charges to about 77% of the asymptote value, giving the attack portion of the curve a more linear contour. This is shown in Figure 6.4.

The CEM3310 is essentially a variation of this controlled charge/discharge circuit, and it produces the time domain graph shown in Figure 6.5, where a note on event triggers switching logic that applies a series attack resistor to charge the capacitor over an attack time, t_{ATT}. Then, a discharge resistor is applied after the discharge switch is closed, and the capacitor discharges down to a fixed sustain level, V_{SUS}. A note off event triggers the logic to apply a different shunt resistor across the capacitor, which then discharges the rest of the way to ground. This creates four phases of operation: attack, decay, sustain, and release, abbreviated as ADSR.

The most important feature of Figure 6.5 is that the A, D and R segments are not linear but rather exponential, following the capacitor charge/discharge curves. When used to control an amplifier, they result in an amplitude contour that sounds correct to our ears which sense amplitude logarithmically. When applied to pitch control of an oscillator or filter cut-off of a filter, this EG would move the corresponding control value around exponentially; fortunately these are also natural-sounding pitch and frequency changes for our ears. For oscillators and filters, the envelope generator will modify the oscillator pitch and filter cutoff frequency in a musical way based on movement in octaves—this is desirable.

You can see that the note on and note off events are the trigger mechanisms for the attack and release segments. The decay and release times shown in Figure 6.5 are what you would see in a synthesizer manual, yet for many synths this is not completely accurate. The synth manufacturers aren't trying to mislead anyone—it's just easier and more intuitive to label the envelope that way. These are actually the times for these segments to decay/release from a full scale value down to 0.0. Therefore, the decay and release controls do not set the absolute decay and release times, but rather the decay and release rates. In Section 6.6 you will see that the Yamaha DX7 synth EG actually refers to all "times" as "rates" instead. The decay and release rates are exponential rates, making them significantly more difficult to deal with than simple linear rates or slopes. More importantly, the sustain level ultimately sets the actual decay and release time durations as shown in Figure 6.6, where the dotted lines are the original full-scale capacitor discharge curves.

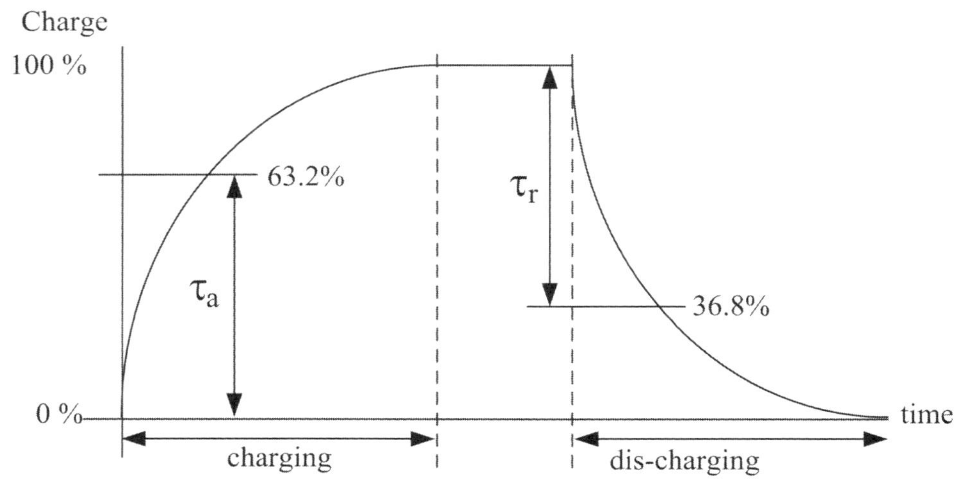

Figure 6.1: Charging and discharging of a capacitor.

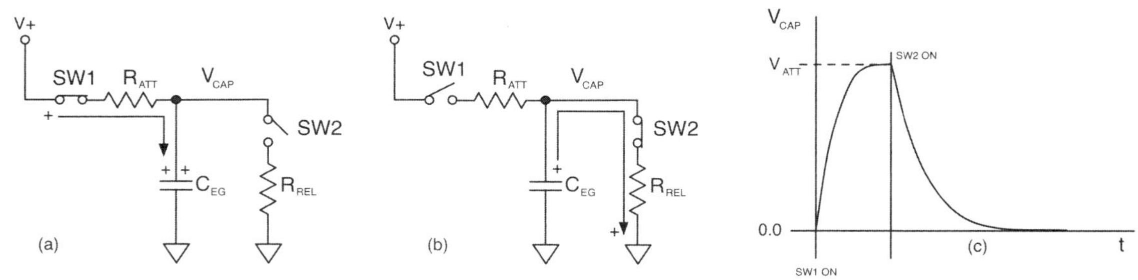

Figure 6.2: (a) The capacitor during the charging phase and (b) during the discharging phase results in (c) the envelope.

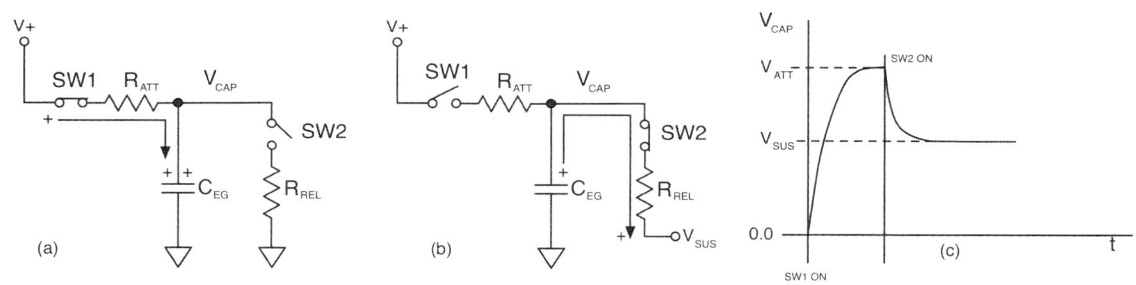

Figure 6.3: (a) Connecting the release resistor to (b) a voltage source creates an envelope (c) with a sustain level.

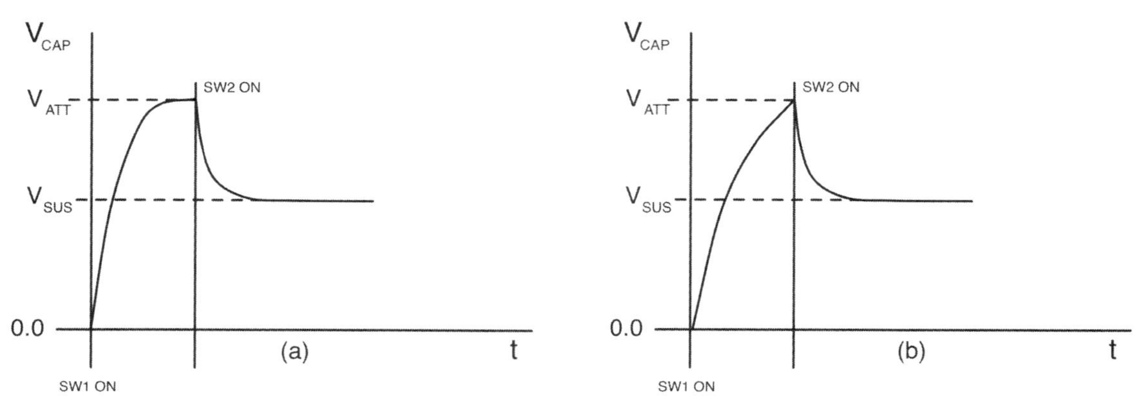

Figure 6.4: By stopping the capacitor charging at about 77%, the flattened top in (a) is removed, and the resulting attack contour in (b) is more linear.

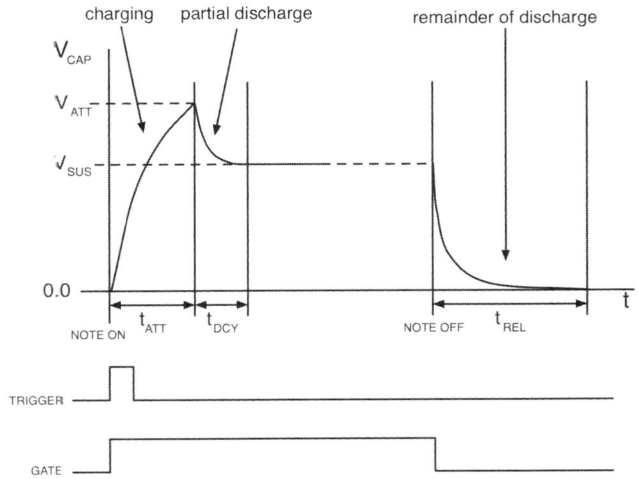

Figure 6.5: A basic analog ADSR envelope generator with attack, decay and release times labeled as you would see in a synthesizer manual.

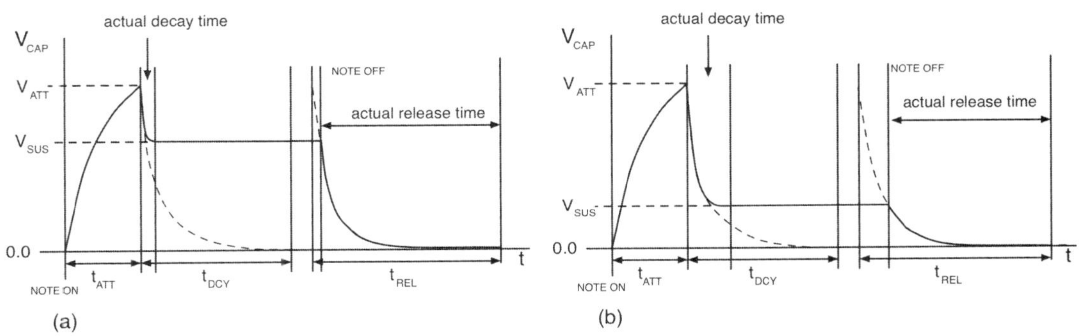

Figure 6.6: (a) The actual decay and release times are the discharge times from full scale value down to 0.0 (b) the effect of lowering the sustain level is to lengthen the decay time and shorten the release time.

A low sustain value would lengthen the decay and shorten the release segments, while a high sustain value would do the opposite. As it turns out, this sounds natural to our ears. For example, if a sound has a very low sustain level, we would expect it to have a shorter release time; we typically observe that soft sounds decay faster. When we implement this kind of EG in software, we will still store the user's time settings but then calculate the actual decay and release time values based on the sustain level. Additionally, we will refer to decay and release rates rather than times. The equations for the charge *Q* and discharge of a capacitor normalized to a unit capacitor voltage and value are:

$$\text{charging} \quad Q = 1 - e^{-t/RC} \qquad \text{discharging} \quad Q = e^{-t/RC} \tag{6.1}$$

The *RC* term is called the time constant or τ. The capacitor's charge/discharge time is related to the time constant. A real-world, non-ideal capacitor charges to about 98% at the time $t = 5\tau$. It takes the same amount of time to discharge to 2%. To model the CEM3310, we'll only let the capacitor charge to 77% and discharge from there as well. It charges to 77% of the total at the approximate time $t = 1.5\tau$. It discharges in about $t = 4.95\tau$. This is shown in Figure 6.6(a). We want to create a normalized graph with the *x* and *y* range both on the range [0..1], where the *x*-axis is normalized time and the *y*-axis is the normalized charge. This allows us to generate these curves scaled by any time duration. Normalizing the R and C values to 1.0, we obtain the equations for a 77% capacitor charge/discharge over a range $x = [0..1]$ and $y = [0..1]$.

$$\text{charging} \quad y = \frac{1}{0.77}(1 - e^{-1.5x}) \qquad \text{discharging} \quad y = e^{-4.95x} \tag{6.2}$$

So Figure 6.7(a) can be split into two components, one for the attack (charging) and the other for the decay and release (discharging) portions.

For controlling an amplifier, it might be desirable to implement an EG output that is linear-in-dB; when you use a fader on a mixing board to control the envelope of a signal, and you move the fader linearly over time, the amplitude changes in a way that is then linear-in-dB. The exponential capacitor voltage movement approximates the linear-in-dB behavior of a logarithmic potentiometer that is found in the mixing board fader. Figure 6.8 shows the exponential capacitor discharge and linear-in-dB curves normalized over the range 0 to 1. For the linear-in-dB curve, the output is normalized over the range from 0 dB to −96 dB (−96 dB is chosen as the lower limit since it is the theoretical noise floor for 16-bit digital audio).

Suppose we use that lower limit of −96 dB, which is a raw value of 0.000016, and solve backwards to find the RC multiplier that would give us the same minimum value at $x = 1$, using the natural log function ln(0.000016) = −RC. The answer is 11.05, and the $e^{-11.05x}$ curve is identical to the linear-in-dB curve normalized over this range; this is not a surprise since e and log_{10} are mathematically related by ln. You can see from Figure 6.8 that the capacitor curve does not make the same abrupt turn as the linear-in-dB curve. For our analog envelope generator model, we will use the 77% capacitor charge/discharge equations. For the digital model, we will use the linear-in-dB

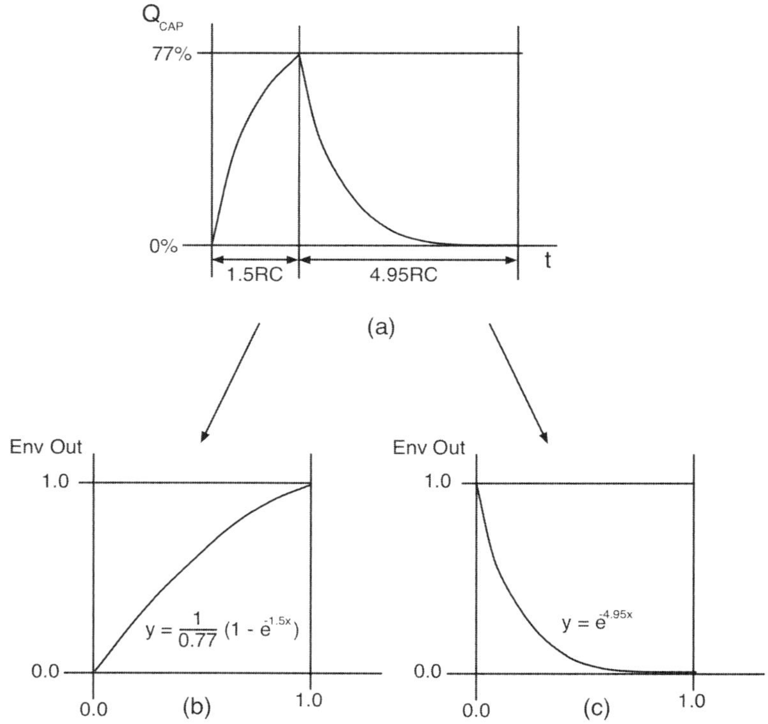

Figure 6.7: (a) The charge and discharge portions may be split into (b) the charging curve and (c) the discharging curve by normalizing RC to 1.

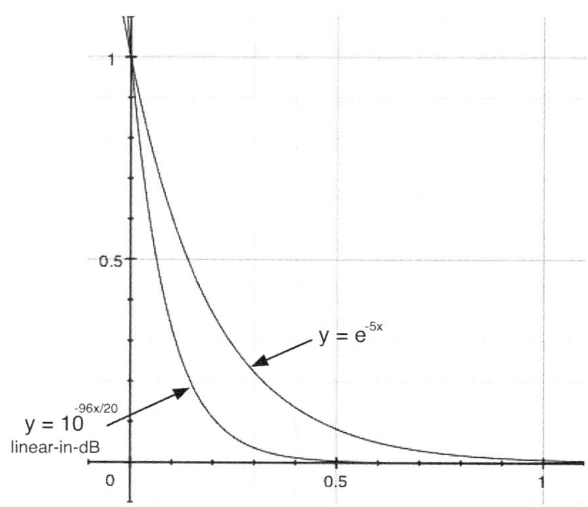

Figure 6.8: The exponential capacitor curve approximates a linear-in-dB curve.

version, which will give us a slightly different and tighter exponential shape. It is important to remember, however, that they are both variations on the same exponential attack and decay functions; the difference is in the time constant multiplier (5.0 versus 11.05). Our EG is very flexible and allows for many variations.

6.2 Triggers, Gates, and Reset to Zero

In Figure 6.8 you can see the trigger and gate signals below the graph. In most early analog synths, there were three signals generated when the user pressed a key on the keyboard: a pitch control voltage (CV) that corresponded to the pitch of the note, and two control signals called the trigger and gate that identified note on and off events. The trigger is a digital pulse representing the start of a note event. The gate changes on the same edge as the trigger but stays on for the duration of the note event. Therefore, in this 1 = ON logic, the trigger's rising edge represents the note on event and the gate's falling edge the note off. In some implementations a reverse (falling edge) logic is used, but the result is the same. Not all manufacturers implemented the same kind of trigger/gate mechanism. Some used a single trigger called an S-trigger, which is essentially a gate only. In this implementation a new note on event will not be triggered if the musician doesn't fully release each key before the next is pressed.

6.3 Note on Modes

To investigate some more, let's start with the case of a user triggering notes in fast succession, starting a new note before the old note has fully decayed away. In this case, the user has lifted his fingers off the keyboard, which generates the note off event on the falling edge of the gate signal. Since the EG operation revolves around a capacitor charge, the new envelope starts its attack at the current capacitor voltage. This causes the envelopes to overlap in a blurry way, as shown in Figure 6.9, and also prevents audible clicks or pops as the new note is applied. This occurs in a monophonic synth with only one Amp-EG or a polyphonic synth in unison (mono) mode.

What would happen if the user pressed a key and then pressed another key without releasing the first note on a monophonic synth? For a synth with the conventional trigger and gate combination, the new key press would generate the trigger signal, which would restart the EG in the attack segment from the current capacitor voltage. The gate would simply remain ON. This is shown in Figure 6.10, where we have another smearing of events. For the musician, the small attack segment provides articulation to the musical line that is played. For many sounds this may be appropriate.

Suppose the same situation occurs with the S-trigger envelope generator. With only the one gate signal, the EG does not know when new note events occur because the signal is already high or ON. This means that subsequent note events are ignored, as shown in Figure 6.11. This kind of articulation often occurs with legato string parts; a cellist may start raking the bow across the string with one finger held on a note (the attack segment), then, while still raking the bow, press a new note on the same string. In this case, the cellist's envelope generator—the bow across the string—does not restart on each note, thus slurring the notes together. This is one of the reasons musicians collect different brands of analog synths—each may be better suited to one kind of sound than the other.

Some synths implement both schemes and allow you to choose either kind of trigger/gate system. The S-trigger variation is usually called legato mode, while the trigger/gate version is sometimes called mono mode, if it is named at all. Some synths simply feature an on/off switch labeled "legato."

Another variation on triggering the envelope generator is called reset-to-zero or simply reset. In this mode, if the EG is re-triggered while still active, it first resets back down to zero by quickly draining the capacitor through a low resistance. This creates a super-fast release before the new note is triggered. In our envelope generator, we will call this short phase of operation shutdown. This fast release is not instantaneous but rather occurs over a few milliseconds. The same fast succession of notes in Figure 6.10 now becomes

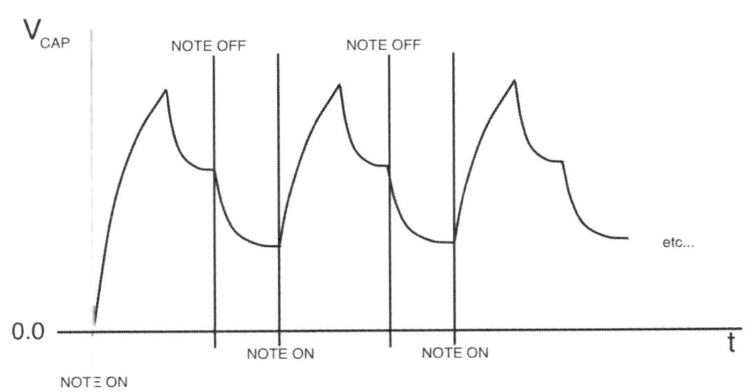

Figure 6.9: A fast succession of note events smears the envelopes together, as the capacitor doesn't have a chance to fully discharge before the next attack segment.

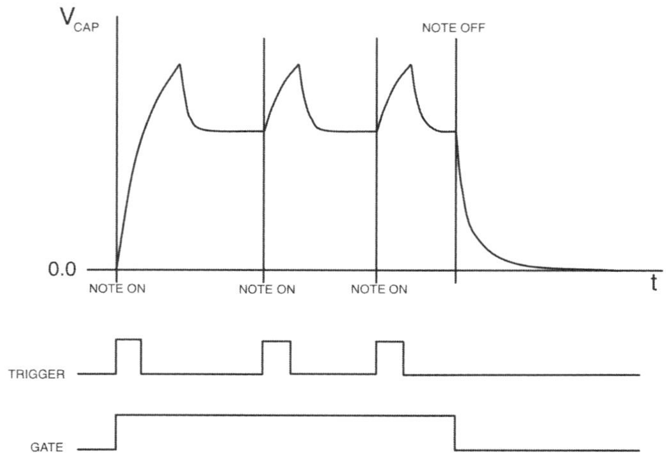

Figure 6.10: Triggering new notes starts the attack segment from the current capacitor voltage in a trigger/gate synth.

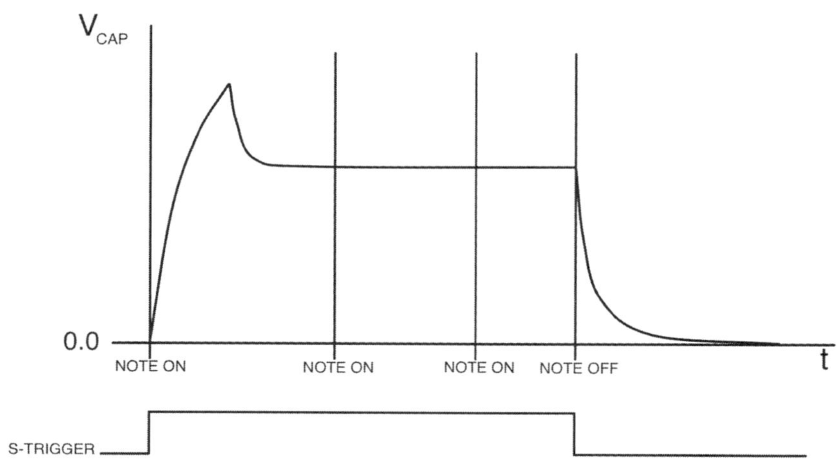

Figure 6.11: In a synth with S-triggering, subsequent note on events are ignored as long as more than one note is held down.

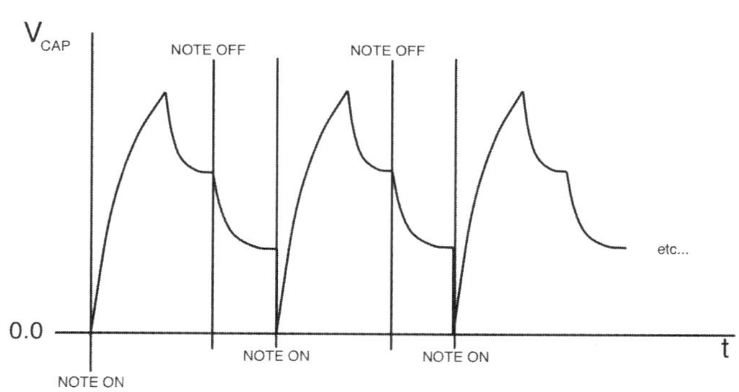

Figure 6.12: An envelope generator with reset-to-zero forces the voltage back to 0.0 when new note events occur while the EG is still active.

the chopped up series of notes in Figure 6.12. As with the other schemes, there may be sounds that require this kind of behavior. Additionally, in polyphonic synthesizers, once the maximum number of voices is playing and a new note event occurs, voice-stealing will require the synth to sacrifice one of its current voices to trigger the new one in its place. We will investigate this further in Chapter 8. During this voice-stealing operation, we will employ the shutdown mode in order to prevent audible clicks or pops as the new note is triggered.

6.4 Note Off Modes

The release or shutdown state may get triggered before the EG has entered the sustain state represented by the "NOTE OFF" arrows in Figure 6.13. In this event, we use the last EG output as the starting point, and then descend the release or shutdown segment from that value. For our analog EG, this means that the release time will be longer if the note is released at a level above the sustain point and shorter if released below the sustain point, as shown in Figures 6.13(c) and (d). This also tends to sound natural for many types of patches. In Figure 6.13(a) you can see the importance of the concept that the release time is the decay time from full scale to 0.0, as the note is above the sustain level.

A few synths such as the Moog MemoryMoog offer another note off mode of operation called unconditional mode. In this case, the note off event does not immediately advance the EG into the release state. Instead the current state continues until it expires and only then does the EG move to the release state. This allows you to create swells that contain the same length segments even after removing your finger from the keyboard. Figure 6.14 shows this kind of release triggering, where the note off occurs in the attack phase. The EG waits until the phase is complete before moving to the release phase. If the EG is in the sustain phase when the note off event occurs, it simply advances to the release phase as normal.

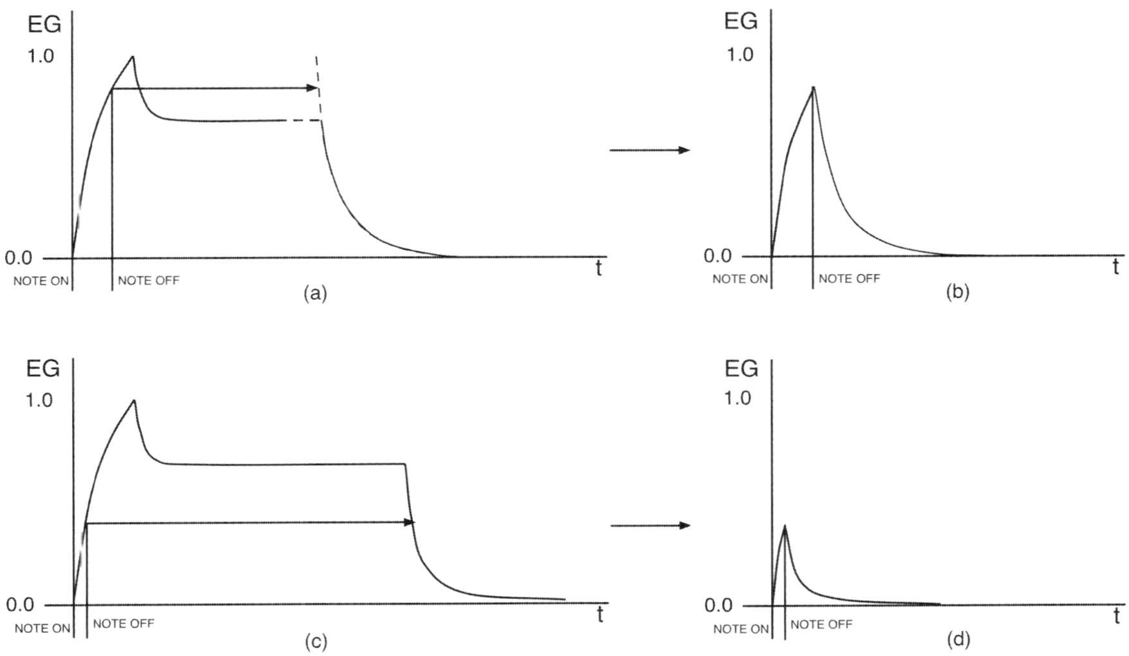

Figure 6.13: The note is released during the attack section (a) above the sustain level, which results in (b) and (c) below the sustain level, resulting in (d).

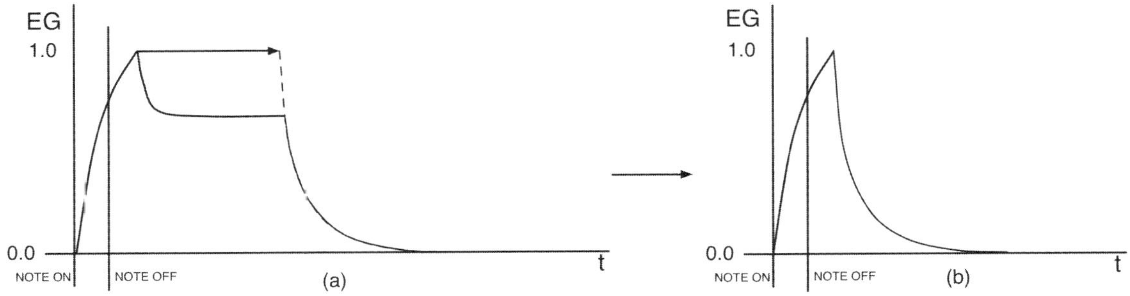

Figure 6.14: An unconditional mode envelope shape only moves into the release phase when the current phase expires.

6.5 Digital Envelope Generators

When digital synths arrived in the 1980s, manufacturers and computer musicians alike realized they were not bound to a capacitor any more and could therefore create envelope generators with any shape and number of segments they wanted. Since the envelope curves are created digitally, we can implement an envelope generator that is linear-in-dB or that follows any curve or equation we like. The Yamaha DX7 envelope generators were implemented digitally using counters that mimicked exponential behavior.

For digital synthesis, we represent the maximum capacitor voltage V_{CAP} with our maximum value 1.0, and therefore the sustain voltage V_{SUS} will be represented with a sustain level L_{SUS} that is less than 1.0. When diagraming an EG, it is often customary to represent the segments as lines rather than curves and plotted on a graph with the y-axis labeled "dB"—linear-in-dB. In addition we are free to use either the analog decay/release rates or the absolute times for the segments. Figure 6.15 shows these digital versions with linear segments and plotted in dB. The attack segment is not linear-in-dB; only the decay and release are.

The linear-in-dB EG is one popular digital EG incarnation, but you are only limited by your imagination here. Quite exotic EGs may be implemented using a variety of curve equations. Whether these EGs are musically useful or not is up for debate, but the sheer power you have to experiment is exciting. Figure 6.16 shows some simple attack and release curves with accompanying equations.

$$\begin{array}{lll} A: y = x^{0.4-0.4x} & B: y = x^{0.6-0.4x} & C: y = x^{0.9-0.4x} \\ D: y = x^{0.3+0.4x} & E: y = x^{0.5+0.4x} & F: y = x^{0.7+0.4x} \\ G: y = 1-x^{0.4-0.4x} & H: y = 1-x^{0.6-0.4x} & I: y = 1-x^{0.9-0.4x} \\ J: y = 1-x^{0.3+0.4x} & K: y = 1-x^{0.5+0.4x} & L: y = 1-x^{0.7+0.4x} \end{array} \tag{6.3}$$

6.6 Envelope Generator Variations

Although the four-segment ADSR is perhaps the most common EG configuration, others that are more or less complicated also exist. Notice that we call the sustain portion a "segment" in this chapter, even though technically it is a level. Figure 6.17 shows four other common incarnations including: (a) attack-release (AR), (b) attack-sustain-release (ASR), (c) attack-decay-sustain-decay (ADSD), and (d) attack-hold-decay-sustain-release (AHDSR) envelope generators. All segments are shown as lines for easier viewing. The Roland TB-303 bass synth is an example that features an AR EG. The EMS VCS3 featured an ASR EG, while the Korg Volca Keys, Moog

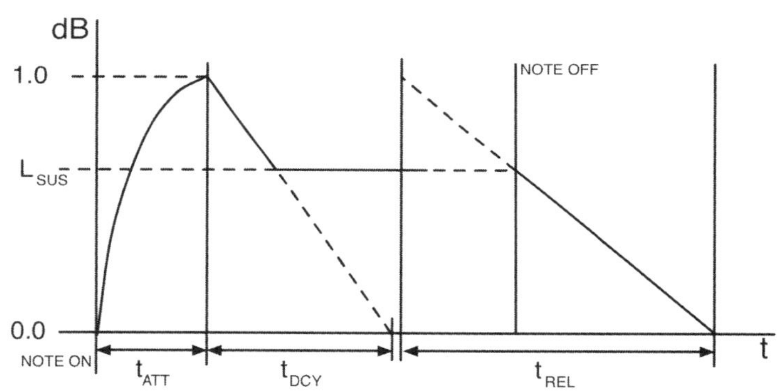

Figure 6.15: An envelope generator with decay and release segments that are linear in dB but still using decay/release times from full-scale (rates).

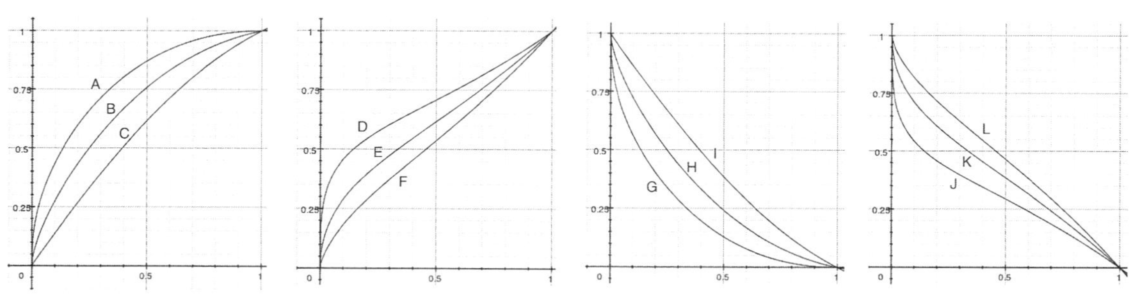

Figure 6.16: A variety of attack and release curves.

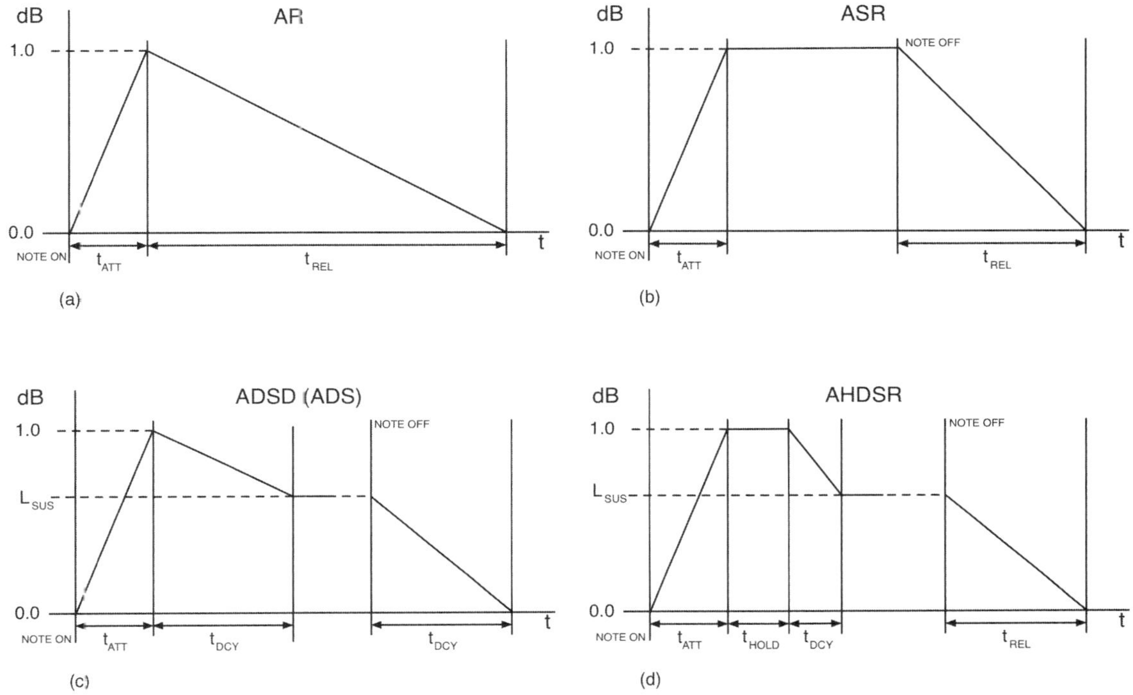

Figure 6.17: (a) Attack-release (AR), (b) attack-sustain-release (ASR), (c) attack-decay-sustain-decay (ADSD), and (d) attack-hold-decay-sustain-release (AHDSR) envelope generators.

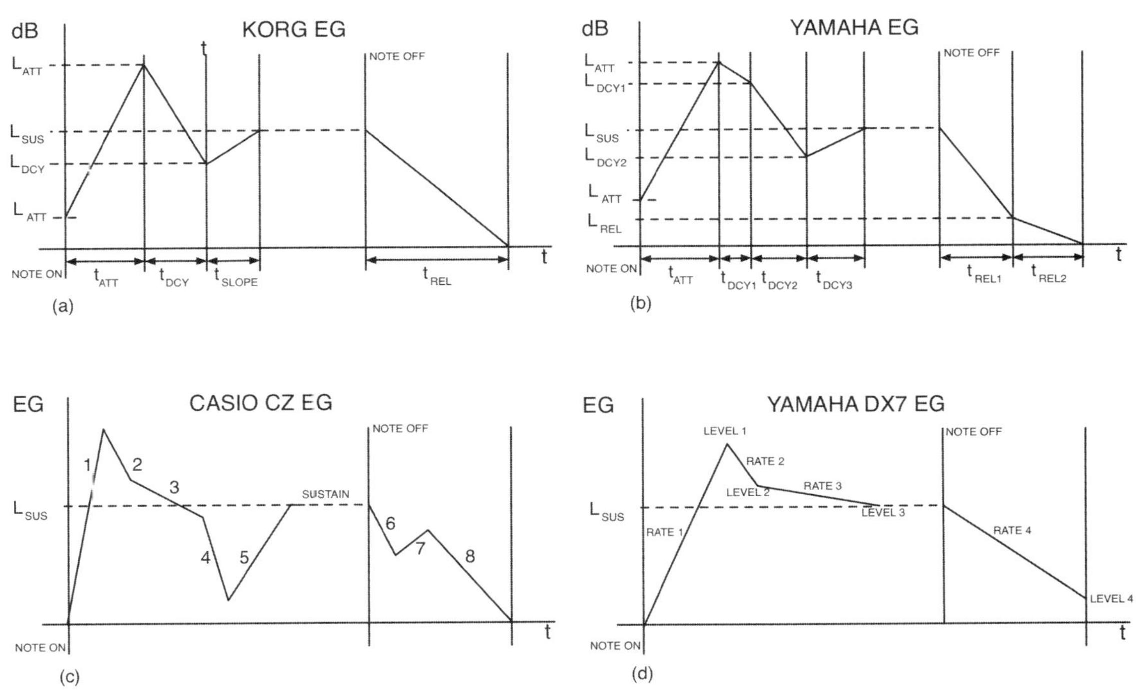

Figure 6.18: (a) Five-segment Korg EG from the Triton/Karma (b) seven-segment Yamaha EG from the EX5/7 (c) Casio CZ series eight-segment + sustain EG and (d) the five-segment Yamaha DX7 EG; notice that this EG labels times as rates.

mini-Moog, and Oberhiem Synth Expander Module (SEM) are examples that feature an ADSD (or ADS). In the ADS EG, the decay and release rates are identical and controlled with one potentiometer. In the AR EG, there is no note off event, as the EG sweeps though its full cycle all at once.

The AHDSR EG is suited for sample-based synthesizers that came online in the 1980s. In these synths, the attack and decay are usually built-in to the transient edge of the sample, and often the EG's attack time is set to 0.0 to let the sample's own attack come through. The hold time allows the complete transient portion of the sample to be passed through unaffected. All four of the EGs in Figure 6.17 have an attack edge that rises to an amplitude of 1.0, and thus all other levels must be lower than the attack level.

Digital EGs may be programmed to start and end at arbitrary levels so that the attack segment might start at a non-zero value and end before full scale is reached. The decay segment could end at a point higher than the attack segment and so on. Figure 6.18 shows four different EGs from Korg, Yamaha and Casio. The Casio CZ-series of synths has impressive eight-segment + sustain EGs, where the segments were simply numbered 1–8. The Yamaha DX7 EG refers to rates rather than times. All of these EGs allow you to program the start and stop levels for each segment except the DX7, which does not allow a non-zero starting point. For this chapter's EG designs, we will stick to the standard four-segment EG, but adding more segments and programmable levels is not much more difficult. These are featured as Challenges if you would like to implement them.

6.7 Iterative Generation of the Exponential Function

To implement an envelope generator with an exponential output, we will need to generate exponential curves based on *e*. Not only will this be computationally expensive, it poses a fundamental problem: exponential functions never decay all the way down to 0.0. Consider the *analog* version using e^{-5x} as the basis for the release curve (we will actually use $e^{-4.95x}$ to mimic the 77% charged cap in our analog version). During the release phase, the imaginary capacitor would discharge to e^{-5} or 0.00673 or about −43 dB. The digital version, which is linear-in-dB or $e^{-11.05x}$, decays down to 0.000016. It would be nice to have them decay all the way to 0.0. We can take care of both issues by generating the exponential curves iteratively. This is conceptually the same as feedback in a digital filter. Imagine a feedback filter with a single coefficient 0.9 that is energized with a single impulse as shown in Figure 6.19. The output of the filter would decay exponentially as the filter keeps multiplying its own output by 0.9 repeatedly. The succession of output values would be {1.0, 0.9, 0.81, 0.73, 0.66, 0.59, 0.53, 0.48, 0.43…} and the output would never actually decay away to zero.

To implement this exponentially decaying output, the only required calculation would be for the filter coefficient *b*, which sets the multiplicative step-size. But we still have the issue of the output never reaching zero. There are several ways to approach this issue, but Nigel Redmon's implementation (see the Bibliography) solves the exponential decay issue and provides flexibility for many different curve shapes. It is also easy to modify. It does, however, require a call to both the exponential and natural log functions when the user alters the segment times. This should not pose a problem unless you intend to modulate the segment durations on every sample period, which is not recommended.

For the time constant multiplier of 5.0, we would only get down to the value 0.00673 at our normalized $x = 1$. But we could setup the filter with a base or offset value x_o that is subtracted from the output on each iteration so that the output decays below zero, down to −0.00637 instead, as shown in Figure 6.20. This way, we get the shape of that particular curve but with a decay all the way to zero. The same thing applies to the attack curve, where iteratively multiplying a coefficient and adding an offset will create an exponentially increasing curve that overshoots 1.0 by some amount instead.

So for each segment (attack, decay and release), we will need three variables; the coefficient, the offset and the TC overshoot variable that sets both the over/undershoot and the curvature; smaller TC overshoot values result in tighter curves. The calculation for the coefficient *b* gives us the "first step" multiplier (TCO is Time Constant Overshoot):

$$b = e^{\frac{-\ln\left(\frac{1+TCO}{TCO}\right)}{time(samples)}} \tag{6.4}$$

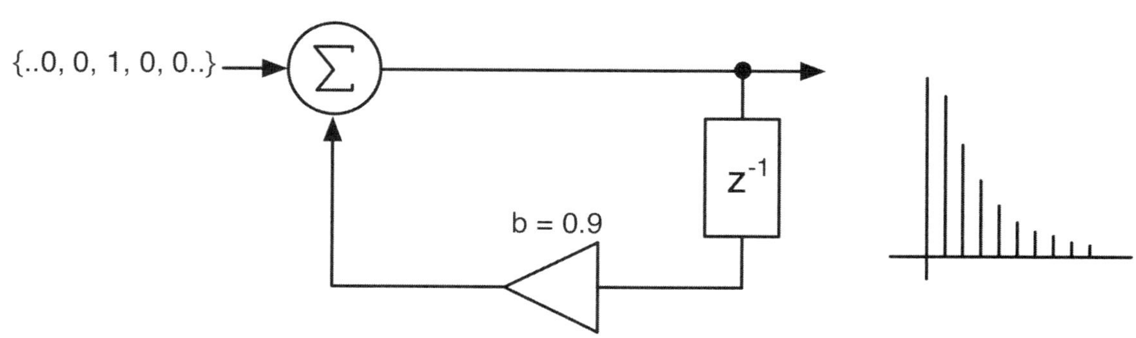

Figure 6.19: Using a feedback filter to generate an exponentially decaying output sequence.

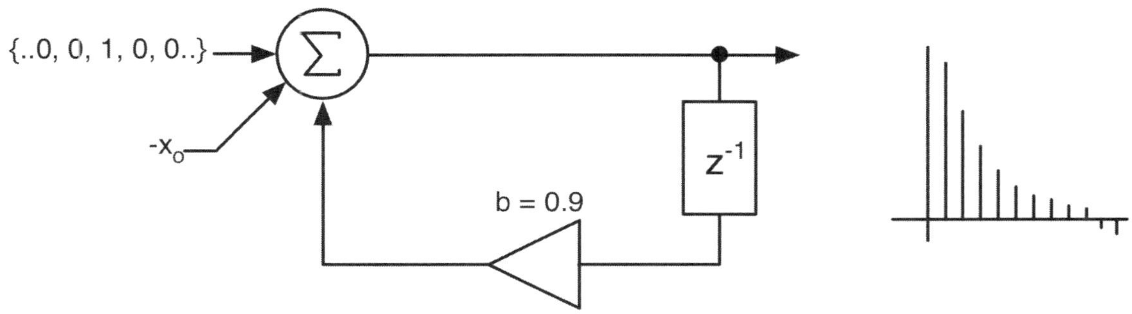

Figure 6.20: When a constant offset x_o is subtracted from each successive output, the signal decays below 0.0.

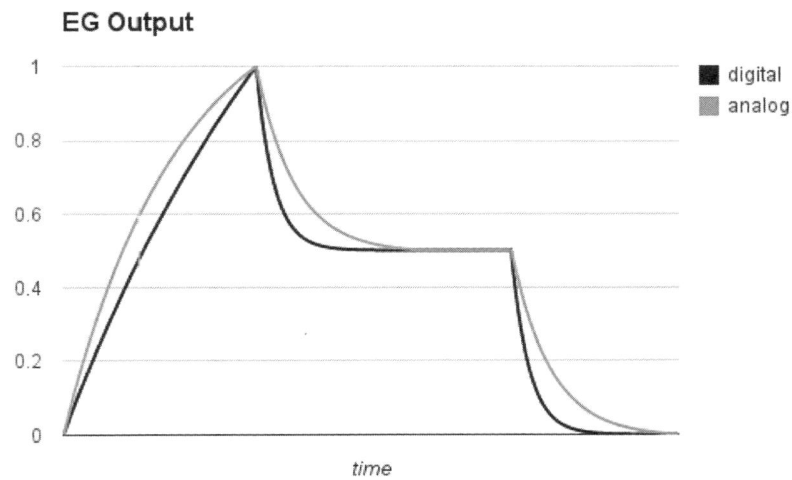

Figure 6.21: The envelope generator output in analog and digital modes; the sustain level is 0.5 for both.

The *time(samples)* is the time in samples for the segment to rise from 0 to 1, or decay from 1 to 0 (i.e. the full range value), and is calculated from the time control on the user interface. We supply the value for the TCO to control the curvature, for example, if we let the TCO = 0.00673 (since e^{-5} = 0.00673) then:

$$-\ln\left(\frac{1+0.00673}{0.00673}\right) = -5.007$$

$$b = e^{\frac{-5.007}{time(samples)}} \tag{6.5}$$

For our analog EG model, we just let the TCO equal the decay exponent (see Equation 6.2). This gives us the proper 77% charge/discharge curves. For the digital version, we can make the attack more linear by setting the TCO to a value close to 1.0 and then use the linear-in-dB exponential. The EG outputs are plotted in Figure 6.21.

$$\begin{array}{ll} \text{analog} & \text{digital} \\ TCO_{attack} = e^{-1.5} & TCO_{attack} = 0.99999 \\ TCO_{decay} = TCO_{release} = e^{-4.95} & TCO_{decay} = TCO_{release} = e^{-11.05} \end{array} \tag{6.6}$$

Calculating the offset x_o is different for each segment. It is the value that is added to or subtracted from the iterative multiplication in the form:

$$\begin{aligned} y(n) &= x_0 + by(n-1) \\ y(n-1) &= \text{the last EG output} \end{aligned} \tag{6.7}$$

The three offset equations are set so that the initial start value is correct for each segment. They are:

$$\begin{aligned} x_0(attack) &= (1 + attackTCO)(1 - b_{attack}) \\ x_0(decay) &= (sustainLevel - decayTCO)(1 - b_{decay}) \\ x_0(release) &= -releaseTCO)(1 - b_{release}) \end{aligned} \tag{6.8}$$

These two values for the coefficient and offset are all that are needed to generate the exponential output. Since the segments will over or under-shoot their target values, we can use this as the trigger mechanism to move through the segments of the envelope generator.

6.8 Biased Envelope Generator Output

The EG outputs in Figure 6.21 will work fine for controlling the time domain amplitude of our notes. The envelope starts and ends at a volume of 0.0. If this EG is used to modulate the pitch of an oscillator or the cutoff frequency of a filter, however, it might not give the desired effect. For example, suppose the EG is used to alter the pitch of an oscillator with a maximum offset of 2 semitones. The EG would start at 0.0, so no pitch alteration is applied. Then the note would go two semitones sharp, as the EG advances through the attack portion. During the decay the pitch would fall to the sustain level and would remain sharp. Only at the end of the release segment would the note's pitch become correct. In this case, the synth would be playing out of tune. It's worth noting that on some very old synths, this was the standard mode of operation. Pitch EGs and Filter EGs often use a biased EG output. The sustain level is subtracted from the output so that during the sustain portion there is no modulation. In the case of a Pitch EG, the note would start flat, then go sharp, then drop to correct pitch during the sustain segment. After release, the pitch would go flat. Setting non-zero start and end values is an option to keep the note in pitch at these time extremes. The biased output EG is shown in Figure 6.22.

6.9 Envelope Generator Intensity Controls and Connections

Many synths feature an additional control placed between the EG and the target value it modulates. The control is usually labeled intensity and usually has a range of [−1..+1]. The intensity control scales and, if negative, inverts the output of the EG. The way this changes the patch depends on how the user controls are set. Suppose the normal un-biased EG output is connected to the filter cutoff frequency input, and the user has the filter control in the center position as shown in Figure 6.23. The intensity control modifies the apparent setting of the user's control—the control does not move, but it sets the center of operation for the EG. In Figure 6.23(a) the intensity is set to +1, and at the top of the attack, the filter cutoff frequency will have moved to the maximum value. With the intensity at +0.5, the filter cutoff moves half the distance between the center and maximum. The opposite polarity settings do the same thing in the opposite direction, causing the cutoff frequency to decrease from center as the attack increases. What if the user had placed the control near the top of the range in Figure 6.23(a)? The answer is that the filter cutoff would eventually try to go above its maximum value and must be clamped to the maximum value. Likewise for negative intensity values, the filter's lower limit acts as the floor, and we clamp the lower end to it.

A biased EG works differently with the intensity control as shown in Figure 6.24. In this case, the filter cutoff value is at the center value when the EG hits the sustain segment. In the other phases, it either over or undershoots the center value depending on the intensity setting.

When connected to the output amplifier which always uses the normal un-biased output, it's easier to think of the intensity control changing the time domain envelope as shown in Figure 6.25. Care must be taken—if the intensity control is at 0.0, the amplifier is shut off. This is one of the controls we will always default to +1.0 to avoid problems.

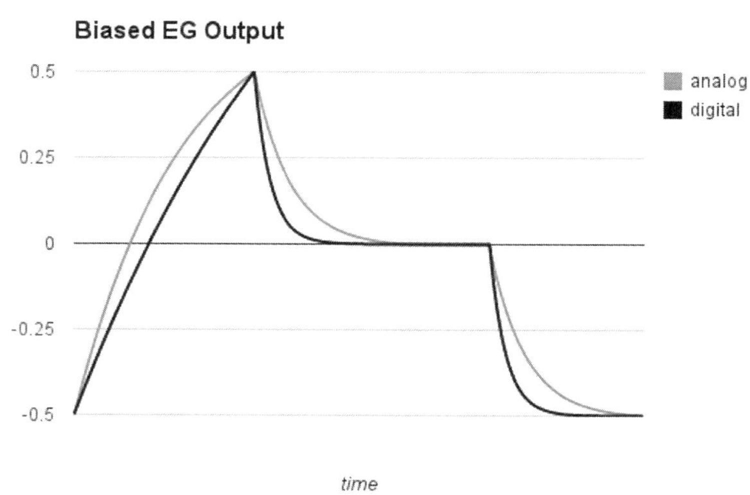

Figure 6.22: The biased EG has a sustain level of zero for certain modulation applications; here the sustain level is set at 0.5 and then subtracted out, thus giving the low and high values of −0.5 to +0.5.

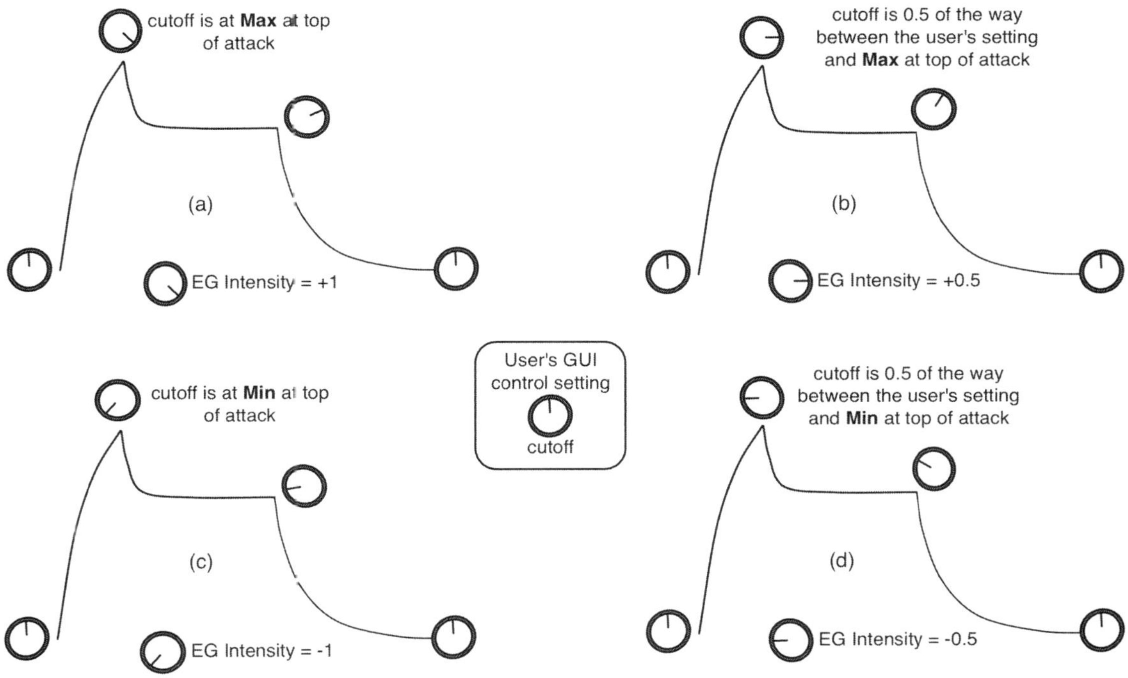

Figure 6.23: The operation of EG intensity on an un-biased EG output with a variety of settings with intensity equal to (a) +1, (b) +0.5, (c) −1, (d) −0.5.

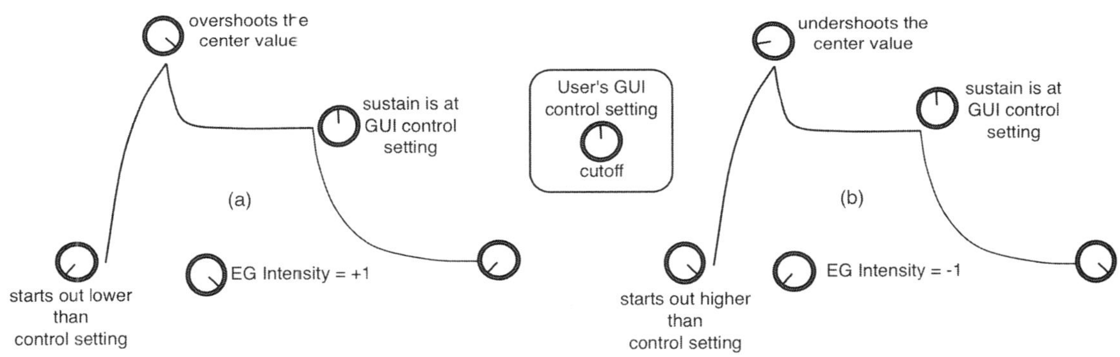

Figure 6.24: The operation of EG intensity on a biased EG output with a variety of settings with intensity equal to (a) +1, (b) −1.

6.10 Envelope Generator Implementation

The EG can be modeled as a Finite State Machine (FSM) with the following states:

- OFF
- ATTACK
- DECAY
- SUSTAIN
- RELEASE
- SHUTDOWN (optional)

The EG starts in the OFF state. A note on event advances the FSM into the ATTACK state, and the output begins increasing. When the output of the EG reaches or crosses 1.0, we move to the DECAY state, where the output begins dropping. When the exponential output reaches or crosses the sustain level, the FSM advances to the SUSTAIN state, where the EG simply outputs the current sustain level that the user sets. A note off event then advances the FSM into the RELEASE state, where the output begins its final descent until it reaches or crosses zero. The FSM moves back into the OFF state. If a note off event occurs in any of the states, the FSM goes into the RELEASE

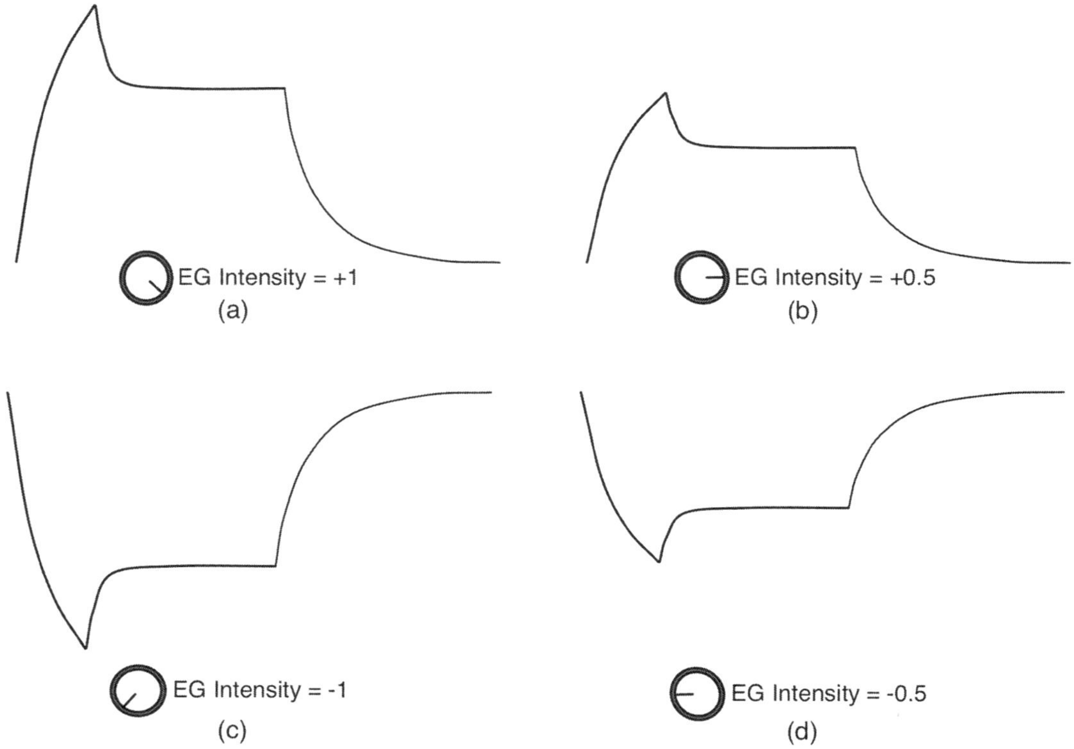

Figure 6.25: The operation of EG intensity on an un-biased EG output connected to an output amplifier in a variety of settings with intensity equal to (a) +1, (b) +0.5, (c) −1, (d) −0.5.

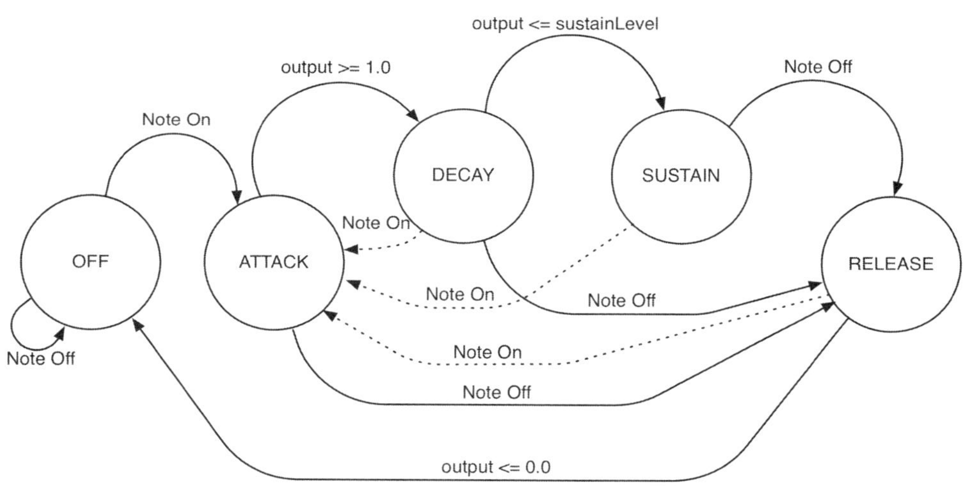

Figure 6.26: Finite state machine for the four-segment envelope generator, no shutdown.

state. If the EG is shut down (reset-to-zero), the FSM moves into the SHUTDOWN state, where a short linear taper is applied to shut off the output.

Figure 6.26 shows this basic five-state FSM for an analog envelope generator. In this version, there is no shutdown state, and the attack state is re-entered at the current output level on its attack curve.

Figure 6.27 shows the six-state version with shutdown or reset-to-zero. The dotted lines are now labeled "Shutdown," and on more complex instruments, this state may be triggered by conditions other than a new note event. When re-triggered, this EG only goes back to the attack state after shutdown first, and then starts back at 0.0 for the next cycle.

The EG shutdown duration is only a few milliseconds, so there is no reason to try to make it exponential. In this case, we just calculate a linear taper value that is subtracted from the current output on each sample interval.

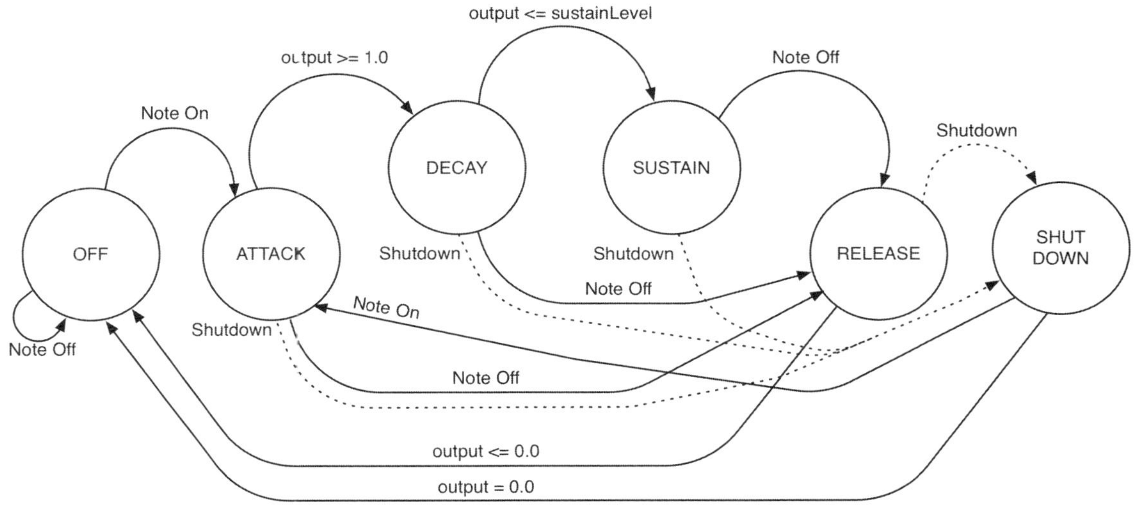

Figure 6.27: The EG FSM with the SHUTDOWN state.

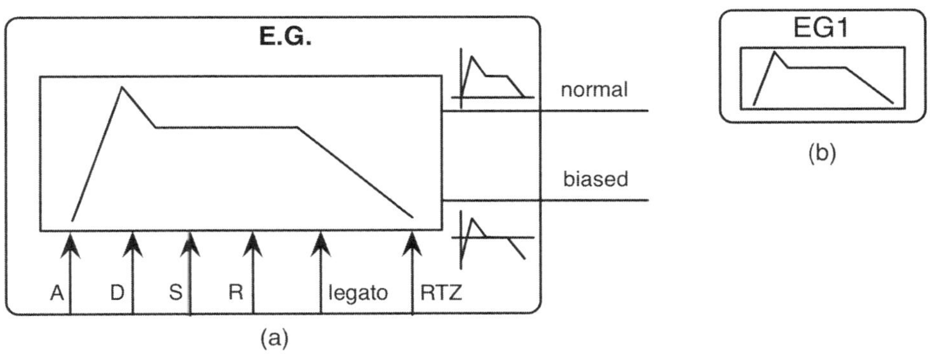

Figure 6.28: (a) Detailed connection graph diagram and (b) simplified block diagram for the *CEnvelopeGenerator* object.

6.11 The CEnvelopeGenerator Object

Download the NanoSynth: EG/DCA project, and we will go through the *CEnvelopeGenerator* object functionality, taking into account options like reset-to-zero and legato mode operations. Table 6.1 lists the member variables and methods for *CEnvelopeGenerator*. There is no base class, but you could certainly use it to derive your own variations. The block diagrams for the EG object are shown in Figure 6.28 using the typical linear segments in the drawing.

Though the operation of the state machine is simple, the object seems to have many variables and methods. One thing you will learn is that the EG's state is very important. We use it to determine if note events have ended, or if the EG is capable of accepting a note off event. So there are a few query functions to handle that. There are also a lot of duplicate type variables; each of the states has a set of variables to use in the calculation. Also notice the member variable *m_bOutputEG*, which is a flag that is set to true if the EG is connected to an output amplifier. When an EG connected to an output amplifier expires and goes into the off state, it is the signal that a note event is completely finished. It will play an important role when we make the synths polyphonic. The easiest way to understand the object is to step through the functions and discuss them. Let's start with the most important function of all, *doEnvelope()*. Open the *EnvelopeGenerator.h* and *.cpp* files and examine the functions.

doEnvelope()

The calculations for the outputs of the EG are simple once we have the exponential coefficients and bases calculated. Although we will discuss the envelope generator code in detail later, it's worth looking at the straightforward and simple implementation. The *doEnvelope()* function will get called once per sample period. The return value is the current EG output value. It can also optionally return the biased output via the function argument, a pointer to a variable to receive the information. Take a moment to study the flow and follow the state machine operation:

Table 6.1: *CEnvelopeGenerator* member variables and methods.

CEnvelopeGenerator public Member Variables		
Type	**Variable Name**	**Description**
bool	m_bResetToZero	RTZ mode flag
bool	m_bLegatoMode	legato mode flag
bool	m_bOutputEG	true if this EG is connected to the output amplifier of the patch
UINT	m_uEGMode	mode flag
enum	analog,digital	mode strings

CEnvelopeGenerator protected Member Variables		
Type	**Variable Name**	**Description**
double	m_dSampleRate	the sample rate
double	m_dEnvelopeOutput	the current envelope output value
double	m_dAttackCoeff	coeff b for attack
double	m_dAttackOffset	the attack offset x_o
double	m_dAttackTCO	the attack time constant overshoot
double	m_dDecayCoeff	coeff b for decay
double	m_dDecayOffset	the decay offset x_o
double	m_dDecayTCO	the decay time constant overshoot
double	m_dReleaseCoeff	coeff b for release
double	m_dReleaseOffset	the release offset x_o
double	m_dReleaseTCO	the release time constant overshoot
double	m_dAttackTime_mSec	attack time in milliseconds
double	m_dDecayTime_mSec	decay time in milliseconds
double	m_dReleaseTime_mSec	release time in milliseconds
double	m_dShutdownTime_mSec	shutdown time in milliseconds
double	m_dSustainLevel	sustain level [0..+1]
double	m_dIncShutdown	increment value for shutdown mode
UINT	m_uState	state variable
enum	off,attack,decay,sustain,release,shutdown	possible states

CEnvelopeGenerator Member Functions (non virtual)	
Function Name	**Description**
getState	returns the current state variable
isActive	true if EG is running
canNoteOff	true if EG can accept a Note Off message
reset	reset
setEGMode	set the mode; analog or digital
calculateAttackTime	calculate the attack variables based on attack time in mSec
calculateDecayTime	calculate the decay variables based on decay time in mSec
calculateReleaseTime	calculate the release variables based on release time in mSec
setAttackTime_mSec	set the attack time in mSec
setDecayTime_mSec	set the decay time in mSec
setReleaseTime_mSec	set the release time in mSec
setSustainLevel	set the sustain level
setSampleRate	set the sample rate
update	update variables (not used yet)
startEG	start the EG's finite state machine
stopEG	stop the EG's finite state machine
doEnvelope	render the envelope output values (normal and biased)

- the function is one big switch/case statement
- in the non-off states, the output is rendered first then state-change condition is evaluated (for attack this means crossing past 1.0, etc.)
- the sustain segment simply holds a constant output value
- the shutdown state implements the reset-to-zero operation from Section 6.3; if it is not enabled, it simply moves to the off state, holding the current capacitor "charge" as the last output value in *m_dEnvelopeOutput*
- the off state sets the envelope to 0.0 only if reset-to-zero is enabled
- the biased output is simple to calculate—just subtract out the sustain level

```
inline double doEnvelope(double* pBiasedOutput = NULL)
{
      // --- decode the state
      switch(m_uState)
      {
              case off:
              {
                      // --- output is OFF
                      if(m_bResetToZero)
                              m_dEnvelopeOutput = 0.0;
                      break;
              }
              case attack:
              {
                      // --- render value
                      m_dEnvelopeOutput = m_dAttackOffset +
                                              m_dEnvelopeOutput*m_dAttackCoeff;
                      // --- check go to next state
                      if(m_dEnvelopeOutput >= 1.0 || m_dAttackTime_mSec <= 0.0)
                      {
                              m_dEnvelopeOutput = 1.0;
                              m_uState = decay; // go to next state
                              break;
                      }
                      break;
              }
              case decay:
              {
                      // --- render value
                      m_dEnvelopeOutput = m_dDecayOffset +
                                              m_dEnvelopeOutput*m_dDecayCoeff;
                      // --- check go to next state
                      if(m_dEnvelopeOutput <= m_dSustainLevel ||
                         m_dDecayTime_mSec <= 0.0)
                      {
                              m_dEnvelopeOutput = m_dSustainLevel;
                              m_uState = sustain;    // go to next state
                              break;
                      }
                      break;
              }
```

```
            case sustain:
            {
                // --- render value
                m_dEnvelopeOutput = m_dSustainLevel;
                break;
            }
            case release:
            {
                // --- render value
                m_dEnvelopeOutput = m_dReleaseOffset +
                                    m_dEnvelopeOutput*m_dReleaseCoeff;
                // --- check go to next state
                if(m_dEnvelopeOutput <= 0.0 || m_dReleaseTime_mSec <= 0.0)
                {
                    m_dEnvelopeOutput = 0.0;
                    m_uState = off;           // go to next state
                    break;
                }
                break;
            }
            case shutdown:
            {
                if(m_bResetToZero)
                {
                    // --- the shutdown state is just a linear taper
                    m_dEnvelopeOutput += m_dIncShutdown;
                    // --- check go to next state
                    if(m_dEnvelopeOutput <= 0)
                    {
                        m_uState = off;           // go to next state
                        m_dEnvelopeOutput = 0.0; // reset envelope
                        break;
                    }
                }
                else
                {
                    // --- we are guaranteed to be re-triggered
                    //     just go to off state
                    m_uState = off;
                }
                break;
            }
        }
        // --- set the biased (pitchEG) output if there is one
        if(pBiasedOutput)
            *pBiasedOutput = m_dEnvelopeOutput - m_dSustainLevel;
        // --- set the normal
        return m_dEnvelopeOutput;
    }
```

Next, step through the rest of the methods

Constructor

- initialize all variables
- set default shutdown time
- analog mode is default
- legato and reset to zero are off
- EG_DEFAULT_STATE_TIME is defined as 1000 (milliseconds) in the *.h* file

```
CEnvelopeGenerator::CEnvelopeGenerator(void)
{
	// defaults
	m_dSampleRate = 44100;
	m_dAttackTime_mSec = EG_DEFAULT_STATE_TIME;
	m_dDecayTime_mSec = EG_DEFAULT_STATE_TIME;
	m_dReleaseTime_mSec = EG_DEFAULT_STATE_TIME;
	m_dSustainLevel = 1.0;
	m_dEnvelopeOutput = 0.0;
	m_dIncShutdown = 0.0;

	// --- user normally not allowed to set the time
	m_dShutdownTime_mSec = 10.0; // mSec

	// --- states and flags
	m_uState = off;
	m_bOutputEG = false;
	m_uEGMode = analog;
	setEGMode(m_uEGMode);
	m_bResetToZero = false;
	m_bLegatoMode = false;
}
```

Destructor

- there is nothing to do here because there are no dynamically created variables in this object

setEGMode()

- saves the mode (not used, but you may need it in your own designs)
- sets the exponential TCO values depending on mode
- when the mode changes, we must recalculate the coefficients and offsets

```
void CEnvelopeGenerator::setEGMode(UINT u)
{
	// --- save it
	m_uEGMode = u;
	// --- analog - use e^-1.5x, e^-4.95x
	if(m_uEGMode == analog)
	{
		m_dAttackTCO = exp(-1.5);  // fast attack
		m_dDecayTCO = exp(-4.95);
		m_dReleaseTCO = m_dDecayTCO;
	}
	else
	{
```

```
            // digital is linear-in-dB so use
            m_dAttackTCO = 0.99999;
            m_dDecayTCO = m_dDecayTCO = exp(-11.05);
            m_dReleaseTCO = m_dDecayTCO;
        }

        // --- recalc these
        calculateAttackTime();
        calculateDecayTime();
        calculateReleaseTime();
    }
```

reset()

- reset state to off
- reset mode
- recalculate release time (explained in Chapter 8)
- if reset to zero is enabled, clear the output variable

```
void CEnvelopeGenerator::reset()
{
        // --- state
        m_uState = off;

        // --- reset
        setEGMode(m_uEGMode);

        // --- may be modified in noteOff()
        calculateReleaseTime();
        // --- if reset to zero, clear
        //     else let it stay frozen
        if(m_bResetToZero)
        {
                m_dEnvelopeOutput = 0.0;
        }
}
```

calculateAttackTime()

- calculate the iterative exponential variables for exponential attack output

```
void CEnvelopeGenerator::calculateAttackTime()
{
        // --- samples for the exponential rate
        double dSamples = m_dSampleRate*((m_dAttackTime_mSec)/1000.0);

        // --- coeff and base for iterative exponential calculation
        m_dAttackCoeff = exp(-log((1.0 + m_dAttackTCO)/m_dAttackTCO)/
                                dSamples);
        m_dAttackOffset = (1.0 + m_dAttackTCO)*(1.0 - m_dAttackCoeff);
}
```

calculateDecayTime()

- calculate the iterative exponential variables for exponential decay output

```
void CEnvelopeGenerator::calculateDecayTime()
{
    // --- samples for the exponential rate
    double dSamples = m_dSampleRate*((m_dDecayTime_mSec)/1000.0);

    // --- coeff and base for iterative exponential calculation
    m_dDecayCoeff = exp(-log((1.0 + m_dDecayTCO)/m_dDecayTCO)/dSamples);
    m_dDecayOffset = (m_dSustainLevel - m_dDecayTCO)*(1.0 - m_dDecayCoeff);
}
```

calculateReleaseTime()

- calculate the iterative exponential variables for exponential release output

```
void CEnvelopeGenerator::calculateReleaseTime()
{
    // --- samples for the exponential rate
    double dSamples = m_dSampleRate*(m_dReleaseTime_mSec/1000.0);

    // --- coeff and base for iterative exponential calculation
    m_dReleaseCoeff = exp(-log((1.0 + m_dReleaseTCO)/m_dReleaseTCO)/
                          dSamples);
    m_dReleaseOffset = -m_dReleaseTCO*(1.0 - m_dReleaseCoeff);
}
```

noteOff()

- MIDI note off events will trigger the output EGs to go into note off mode; this means jumping directly to the release state as per Figure 6.27
- if the sustain level was set to 0.0 and had reached that point, just go to off state

```
void CEnvelopeGenerator::noteOff()
{
    // --- go directly to release state
    if(m_dEnvelopeOutput > 0)
        m_uState = release;
    else // sustain was already at zero
        m_uState = off;
}
```

shutDown()

- ignore in legato mode; we want the EG to stay in its state
- calculate linear shutdown increment value (the 1000 converts the millisecond shutdown time)
- go to shutdown state

```
void CEnvelopeGenerator::shutDown()
{
    // --- legato mode - ignore
    if(m_bLegatoMode)
        return;
```

```
        // --- calculate the linear inc values based on current output
        m_dIncShutdown = -(1000.0*m_dEnvelopeOutput)/m_dShutdownTime_mSec/
                              m_dSampleRate;

        // --- set state and reset counter
        m_uState = shutdown;
    }
```

startEG(), stopEG() & Legato Mode

In legato mode on a mono synth, if you hold a key then presses another key, you will get a shutdown signal since the synth has run out of notes. In the shutdown function above, we simply ignore the request and return without shutting down. Likewise, we ignore start messages and simply return without leaving the current state. Shutting off the EG just pushes it into the off state (you may need to modify this for more exotic EGs).

```
    inline void startEG()
    {
        // ignore
        if(m_bLegatoMode && m_uState != off && m_uState != release)
                return;

        // reset and go to attack state
        reset();
        m_uState = attack;
    }

    // --- go to off state
    inline void stopEG(){m_uState = off;}
```

isActive() & canNoteOff() state queries

We will need to answer some questions from the outer object that owns the EG. We define these states as:

- *active*: if we are not in the release or off states
- *can note off*: we can accept a note off event if we are not in the release, shutdown or off states

```
    inline bool isActive()
    {
        if(m_uState != release && m_uState != off)
                return true;
        return false;
    }
    inline bool canNoteOff()
    {
        if(m_uState != release && m_uState != shutdown && m_uState != off)
                return true;
        return false;
    }
```

set ADSR values

The user will see an interface that is usually (but not necessarily) labeled in time units. We have discussed the time versus rate issue for decay and release segments. This EG follows the same rules and calculates its parameters using rates. The following functions store the current GUI control value and update the segment variables. Notice that the sustain level affects the decay and release calculations. If already in the release state, we do not recalculate anything to avoid possible glitches that this would generate.

```
// --- called during updates
inline void setAttackTime_mSec(double d)
{
      m_dAttackTime_mSec = d;
      calculateAttackTime();
}
inline void setDecayTime_mSec(double d)
{
      m_dDecayTime_mSec = d;
      calculateDecayTime();
}
inline void setReleaseTime_mSec(double d)
{
      m_dReleaseTime_mSec = d;
      calculateReleaseTime();
}
inline void setSustainLevel(double d)
{
      m_dSustainLevel = d;

      // --- sustain level affects decay
      calculateDecayTime();

      // --- and release, if not in release state
      if(m_uState != release)
             calculateReleaseTime();
}
```

We will add an EG to the NanoSynth and connect it to the output amplifier to setup a time domain envelope.

6.12 Digitally Controlled Amplifier (DCA)

In this chapter we will also investigate and implement a digitally controlled amp or DCA. The DCA will be connected to the amp EG. It will apply all gain control values to the final output of each synthesizer's voice or patch. It will also implement a pan (left/right balance), control and the pan value may be modulated. Figure 6.29 shows the detailed connection graph and simple block diagram versions of the DCA component. The DCA may be mono or stereo input but is always stereo output.

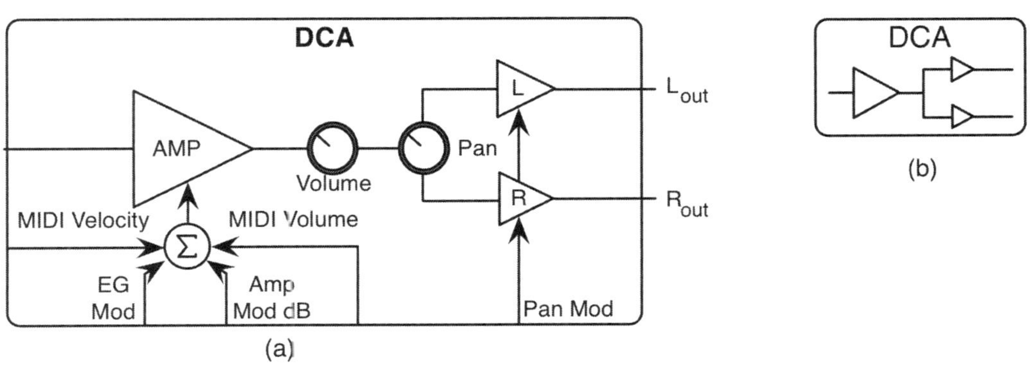

Figure 6.29: The DCA and Pan controls are grouped together into one DCA object.

In Figure 6.29, the volume and pan knob controls you see are usually on the GUI. The amplitude modulation control is unipolar so that it can only attenuate the output and not amplify it. The DCA has multiple inputs for controlling gain and pan:

- Amplitude: the GUI control for output volume
- MIDI Velocity: the DCA will convert MIDI velocity values from note on events into a gain multiplier
- MIDI Volume: the MIDI volume control is (continuous controller) CC7
- MIDI Pan: the MIDI pan control is CC10
- Amplitude Modulation: this is connected to a unipolar modulation source for amp modulation (not tremolo)
- Pan: the GUI control for panning
- Pan Modulation: this connects to a bipolar modulation source for pan modulation
- Amp Mod (dB): for tremolo

The DCA will calculate a final gain value after taking all gain inputs into consideration. It will then calculate a pan value based on the pan control (that may or may not be on the GUI). The Pan value is calculated using equal power curves based off the first quadrant of a sine and cosine wave. The MIDI Pan control delivers values between 0 and 127 and therefore has no true center value—it is asymmetrical. To handle this, the MMA specifies the following calculation:

MIDI CC10 = 0 or 1; the Pan control is fully LEFT
MIDI CC10 = 64; the Pan control CENTER
MIDI CC10 = 127; the Pan control is fully RIGHT

The Pan calculation is:

$$\begin{aligned} p &= \frac{\pi}{4}(bipolarControl + 1) \\ L_{OUT} &= \cos(p) \\ R_{OUT} &= \sin(p) \end{aligned} \tag{6.9}$$

The coding for the DCA update method ultimately calculates a gain value based on all the amp inputs. For use as an attenuator, the MMA defines the convex transform to produce an attenuation value based on the MIDI velocity or volume value (0 to 127) as:

$$attenuation_{dB} = \begin{cases} -96 & x = 0 \\ 20\log\left(\dfrac{x^2}{127^2}\right) & 0 < x \leq 127 \end{cases} \tag{6.10}$$

Therefore, this is simply an exponential squaring control. Other schemes may also be implemented in case you'd like to experiment.

6.13 The CDCA Object

The DCA functionality is encapsulated in the *CDCA* object. This object implements the gain and panning functionality and allows modulation of these values. In Chapter 8 we will modify it to accept inputs from MIDI continuous controllers 7 (volume) and 10 (pan). Table 6.2 lists the member variables and methods.

The easiest way to understand the object is to step through the functions and discuss them. Open the *DCA.h* and *.cpp* files and examine the functions.

Constructor

- initialize all variables; notice that many of this object's variables default to 1.0 to avoid the DCA starting in an off state—these include the amplitude controls, gain and EG modulation values
- the MIDI velocity also defaults to the maximum value to avoid a muted condition if you are not using MIDI velocity

```
CDCA::CDCA(void)
{
	// --- initialize variables
	m_dAmplitudeControl = 1.0;
	m_dAmpMod_dB = 0.0;
	m_dGain = 1.0;
	m_dAmplitude_dB = 0.0;
	m_dEGMod = 1.0;
	m_dPanControl = 0.0;
	m_dPanMod = 0.0;
	m_uMIDIVelocity = 127;
}
```

Table 6.2: *CDCA* member variables and methods.

CDCA protected Member Variables		
Type	**Variable Name**	**Description**
double	m_dGain	the total gain value during a given sample period
double	m_dAmplitude_dB	the amplitude in dB (GUI control)
double	m_dAmplitudeControl	the amplitude in raw multiplier form
double	m_dPanControl	the GUI pan control on the range [−1..+1], where −1 is hard left and +1 is hard right
double	m_dAmpMod_dB	amp modulation in dB for tremolo
double	m_dEGMod	input for EG connection
double	m_dPanMod	input for pan modulation

CDCA Member Functions (non virtual)	
Function Name	**Description**
setMIDIVelocity	sets the MIDI velocity of the current note (for output EGs)
setPanControl	sets the GUI pan control on the range [−1..+1], where −1 is hard left and +1 is hard right
reset	Reset
setAmplitude_dB	sets the GUI amplitude in dB (volume) control
setAmpMod_dB	modulation input for amp (dB)—tremolo
setEGMod	sets the EG input modulation value [0..+1]
setPanMod	sets the pan modulation [−1..+1]
update	updates the gain and pan values
doDCA	render the DCA, mono or stereo

Destructor

- there is nothing to do here because there are no dynamically created variables in this object

setMIDIVelocity(), setPanControl(), setPanMod(), setEGMod()

These are simple set functions that just set the values of the member variables *m_uMIDIVelocity, m_dPanControl, m_dPanMod* and *m_dEGMod.*

setAmpMod_dB()

The connection is ordinarily a bipolar output such as LFO for tremolo; we need to convert this to unipolar before saving.

```
inline void setAmpMod_dB(double d){m_dAmpMod_dB = bipolarToUnipolar(d);}
```

setAmplitude_dB()

This function connects the GUI volume control to the amplitude control variable.

```
inline void setAmplitude_dB(double d)
{
      m_dAmplitude_dB = d;
      m_dAmplitudeControl = pow((double)10.0, m_dAmplitude_dB/(double)20.0);
}
```

reset()

- clear the modulation variables

```
inline void reset()
{
    m_dEGMod = 0.0;
    m_dAmpMod = 0.0;
}
```

update()

- recalculates the gain variable
- notice it is a combination of all modulation inputs and MIDI control values
- uses the *midiToAtten()* function supplied in *synthfunctions.h* to use the convex transform, though you can feel free to change this to any kind of amplitude curve you wish

```
inline void update()
{
    // --- check polarity
    if(m_dEGMod >= 0)
            m_dGain = m_dEGMod;
    else
            m_dGain = m_dEGMod + 1.0;

    // --- amp mod is attenuation only, in dB
    m_dGain *= pow(10.0, m_dAmpMod_dB/(double)20.0);

    // --- use MMA MIDI->Atten (convex) transform
    m_dGain *= mmaMIDItoAtten(m_uMIDIVelocity);
}
```

doDCA()

- calculate total pan value as a sum of controls and modulation
- limit the pan values to [−1 .. +1] in case there is a bias due to user's control setting
- calculate equal power pan values
- form left and right outputs from a combination of gain and panning variables
- use pass-by-reference to pass output values; always acts in stereo, even if no right input exists

```
inline void doDCA(double dLeftInput, double dRightInput,
                  double& dLeftOutput, double& dRightOutput)
{
    // total pan value
    double dPanTotal = m_dPanControl + m_dPanMod;

    // limit in case pan control is biased
    dPanTotal = fmin(dPanTotal, 1.0);
    dPanTotal = fmax(dPanTotal, -1.0);

    double dPanLeft = 0.707;
    double dPanRight = 0.707;

    // equal power calculation in synthfunction.h
    calculatePanValues(dPanTotal, dPanLeft, dPanRight);

    // form left and right outputs
    dLeftOutput =  dPanLeft*m_dAmplitudeControl*dLeftInput*m_dGain;
    dRightOutput =  dPanRight*m_dAmplitudeControl*dRightInput*m_dGain;
}
```

6.14 NanoSynth: EG/DCA

We will continue with our learning-synth that we modified in the last chapter. In this chapter, we will add an envelope generator and DCA. Figure 6.30 shows the simplified block diagram for NanoSynth with the EG and DCA added. For this chapter we will only use the EG as an output EG on the DCA. In subsequent chapters we will use it to modulate the oscillators and filters.

You can use the NanoSynth plug-in to test the functionality of the objects and extend them with the Chapter Challenges. Table 6.3 shows the continuous and enumerated string list GUI controls you need to add to the existing NanoSynth project. You might want to look at the sample code first, then try your own implementation. Remember, it is up to you to design, code and maintain your GUI on your platform of choice. Refer back to Chapter 2 or the video tutorials at http://www.willpirkle.com/synthbook/ for assistance. Figures 6.31 and 6.32 show the NanoSynth GUI in RackAFX, VS3 and AU after this chapter is complete. In subsequent chapters we will continue to fill in the rest of the controls. For RackAFX, several of the controls have been embedded in the LCD control—make sure you understand how to do this from Chapter 2 since we will add more and more controls inside the LCD. These will almost always consist of global synth parameters and not individual component controls.

Figure 6.33 shows the detailed connection diagram of NanoSynth. It shows how the controls from Table 6.3 connect to the underlying synth objects. You can see the addition of the intensity control as well.

You should be getting into the flow of how the projects progress now. For all platforms, the first thing is to implement the GUI controls. Refer back to Chapters 2 and 5 if you need help. Once you have the GUI control code in place, you are ready to start adding the code for the new modules and connections. You will also need to add four new files (or create them manually) for the new objects:

- *EnvelopeGenerator.h* and *.cpp*
- *DCA.h* and *.cpp*

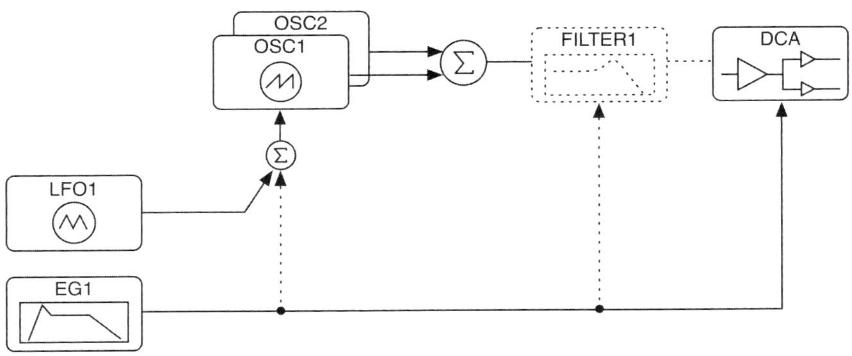

Figure 6.30: The NanoSynth project gets two new additions; EG and DCA modules.

Table 6.3: The new additions of continuous and enumerated string parameters for the NanoSynth GUI.

***NanoSynth* Continuous Parameters**				
Control Name (units)	**Type**	**Variable Name (VST3, RAFX)**	**Low/Hi/Default ***	**VST3/AU Index**
Attack (mS)	double	m_dAttackTime_mSec	0.0 / 5000 / 100	EG1_ATTACK_MSEC
Decay (mS)	double	m_dDecayTime_mSec	0.0 / 5000 / 100	EG1_DECAY_MSEC
Sustain	double	m_dSustainLevel	0.0 / 1.0 / 0.707	EG1_SUSTAIN_LEVEL
Release (mS)	double	m_dReleaseTime_mSec	0.0 / 10000 / 2000	EG1_RELEASE_MSEC
Pan	double	m_dPanControl	−1.0 / +1.0 / 0.0	OUTPUT_PAN
Volume	double	m_dVolume_dB	−96.0 / +24.0 / 0.0	OUTPUT_AMPLITUDE_DB
EG1 DCA Int	double	m_dEG1DCAIntensity	−1.0 / +1.0 / 0.0	EG1_TO_DCA_INTENSITY
* low, high and default values are #defined for VST3 and AU in *SynthParamLimits.h* for each project				

***NanoSynth* Enumerated String Parameters (UINT)**			
Control Name	**Variable Name**	**enum String**	**VST3/AU Index**
Legato Mode	m_uLegatoMode	mono,legato	LEGATO_MODE
Reset To Zero	m_uResetToZero	OFF,ON	RESET_TO_ZERO

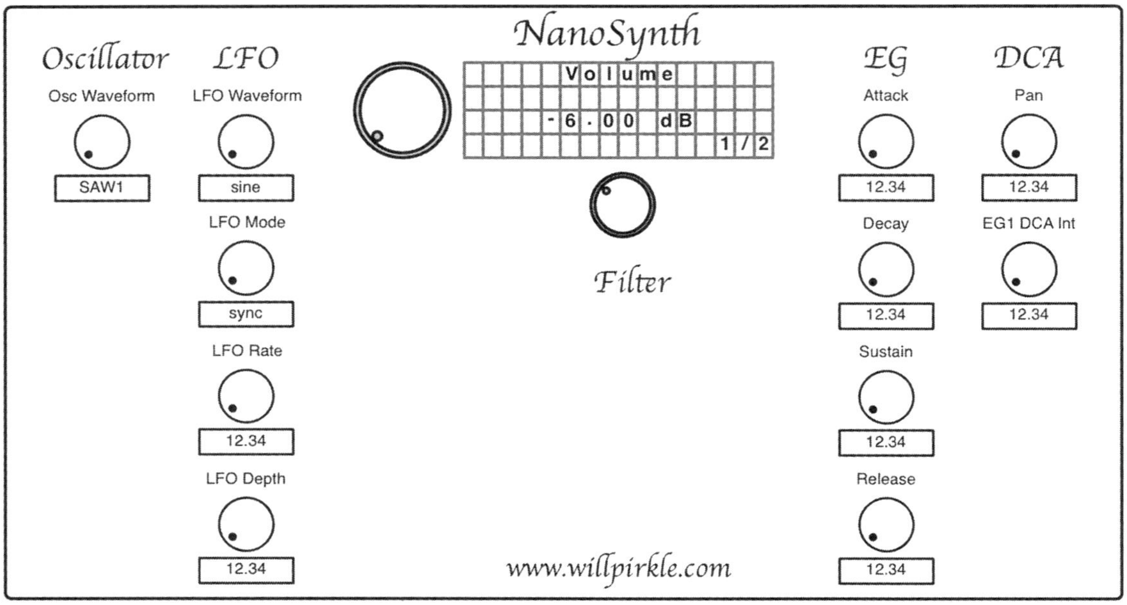

Figure 6.31: One possible NanoSynth GUI in RackAFX; notice that several controls are embedded in the LCD control.

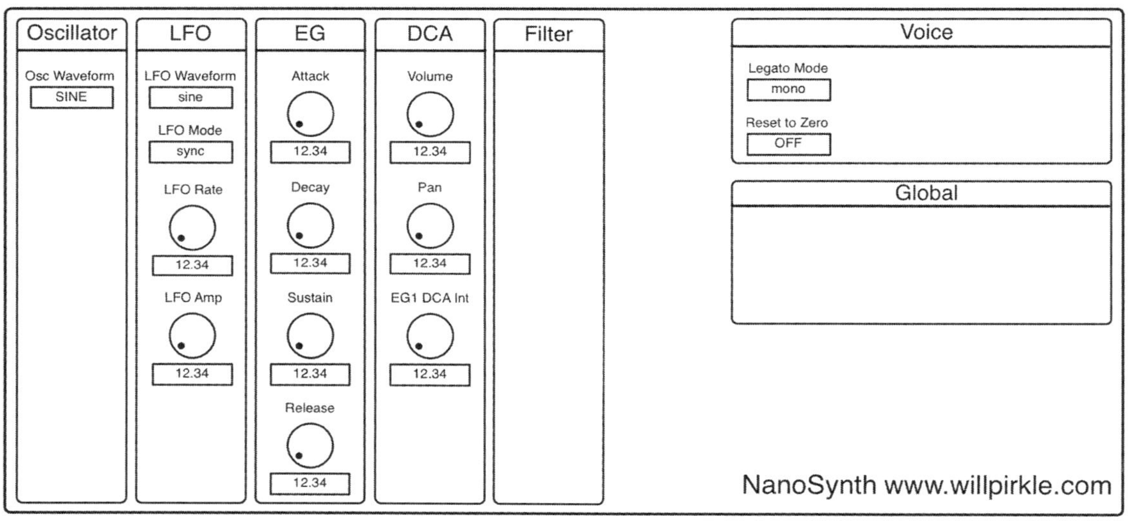

Figure 6.32: The NanoSynth GUI for the VST3 and AU projects.

6.15 NanoSynth: EG/DCA Audio Rendering

For all platforms, the core audio rendering code is the same. Compare with the code in the last chapter (here only new code is **bold**).

- the EG is part of the articulation block, so we need to render its output in the same chunk of code
- the EG output is multiplied by the intensity control variable
- after rendering the output, we check to see if the EG has moved into the off state, which indicates that the note event is finished, and we can stop the oscillators

```
if(m_Osc1.m_bNoteOn)
{
     << ** Code Listing 6.1: Rendering Audio ** >>

     // --- ARTICULATION BLOCK --- //
```

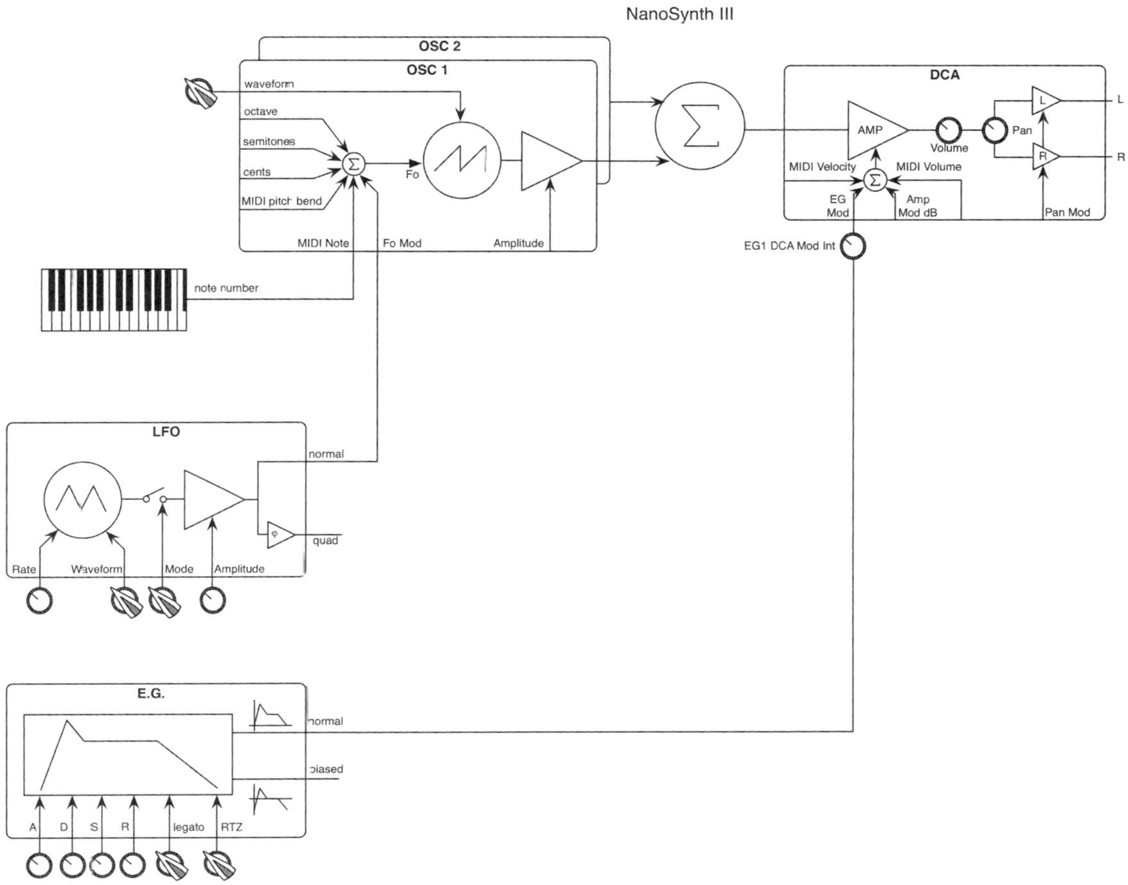

Figure 6.33: The NanoSynth detailed connection graph reveals the new controls from Table 6.3; the Pan and Volume controls are inside the DCA block.

```
double dLFO1Out = m_LFO1.doOscillate();
double dEGOut = m_EG1.dcEnvelope();

m_Osc1.setFoModExp(dLFO1Out*OSC_FO_MOD_RANGE);
m_Osc2.setFoModExp(dLFO1Out*OSC_FO_MOD_RANGE);
m_Osc1.update();
m_Osc2.update();

m_DCA.setEGMod(dEGOut*m_dEG1DCAIntensity);
        m_DCA.update();

// --- DIGITAL AUDIO ENGINE BLOCK --- //
// (OSC1 + OSC2) --> DCA
double dOscOut = 0.5*m_Osc1.doOscillate() + 0.5*m_Osc2.doOscillate();

// --- now process through DCA
m_DCA.dcDCA(dOscOut, dOscOut, dOutL, dOutR);

// now check for note off
if(m_EG1.getState() == 0) // 0 = off
{
```

```
            m_Osc1.stopOscillator();
            m_Osc2.stopOscillator();
            m_LFO1.stopOscillator();
            m_EG1.stopEG();
        }
        << END ** Code Listing 6.1: Rendering Audio ** END >>
    }
```

6.16 NanoSynth EG/DCA: RackAFX

Use Table 6.3 to add the new controls to the GUI. Then, open the *NanoSynth.h* and *.cpp* files for editing.

NanoSynth.h

Add new *#include* statements for the two new objects and then add member variables for each of them.

```
// --- synth objects
#include "QBLimitedOscillator.h"
#include "WTOscillator.h"
#include "LFO.h"
#include "EnvelopeGenerator.h"
#include "DCA.h"

// abstract base class for RackAFX filters
class CNanoSynth : public CPlugIn
{
public:

    <SNIP SNIP SNIP>

    // Add your code here: ----------------------------------------- //
    CQBLimitedOscillator m_Osc1;
    CQBLimitedOscillator m_Osc2;
    CLFO m_LFO1;

    // --- one EG
            CEnvelopeGenerator m_EG1;

    // --- one DCA
            CDCA m_DCA;

    void update();
    etc...
```

NanoSynth.cpp

Work through the *.cpp* file and alter the functions as needed. We are mainly just adding new lines of code, as we did not declare any new functions.

Constructor:

- there is nothing to add since member constructors will initialize the objects

prepareForPlay()

- set the sample rate on the EG
- set the EG's *m_bOutputEG* flag to *true* since this EG will be connected to the DCA

```
bool __stdcall CNanoSynth::prepareForPlay()
{
	// init:
	m_Osc1.setSampleRate((double)m_nSampleRate);
	m_Osc2.setSampleRate((double)m_nSampleRate);
	m_Osc2.m_nCents = 2.5; // +2.5 cents detuned
	m_LFO1.setSampleRate((double)m_nSampleRate);
	m_EG1.setSampleRate((double)m_nSampleRate);
	m_EG1.m_bOutputEG = true;

	// --- mass update
	update();
	return true;
}
```

update()

- update the EG and DCA with the GUI control variables
- there is no reason yet to call the update function on the EG; we will add this in Chapter 8

```
void CNanoSynth::update()
{
	<SNIP SNIP SNIP>

	// --- EG controls
	m_EG1.setAttackTime_mSec(m_dAttackTime_mSec);
	m_EG1.setDecayTime_mSec(m_dDecayTime_mSec);
	m_EG1.setSustainLevel(m_dSustainLevel);
	m_EG1.setReleaseTime_mSec(m_dReleaseTime_mSec);
	m_EG1.m_bResetToZero = (bool)m_uResetToZero;
	m_EG1.m_bLegatoMode = (bool)m_uLegatoMode;

	// --- DCA controls
	m_DCA.setPanControl(m_dPanControl);
	m_DCA.setAmplitude_dB(m_dVolume_dB);
	m_DCA.update();
}
```

processAudioFrame()

- modify the audio rendering code

```
bool __stdcall CNanoSynth::processAudioFrame(args…)
{
	double dOutL = 0.0;
	double dOutR = 0.0;
	if(m_Osc1.m_bNoteOn)
	{
```

```
            << INSERT ** Code Listing 5.1: Audio Rendering ** HERE >>
        }
        pOutputBuffer[0] = dOutL;
        etc...
```

midiNoteOn()

- we need to modify this to start up the EG, otherwise it is the same as before

```
    bool __stdcall CNanoSynth::midiNoteOn(args...)
    {
        <SNIP SNIP SNIP>

        if(!m_Osc1.m_bNoteOn)
        {
            m_Osc1.startOscillator();
            m_Osc2.startOscillator();
        }
        m_LFO1.startOscillator();
        m_EG1.startEG();

        return true;
    }
```

midiNoteOff()

- remove (comment out) the original code that stopped the oscillators; this is now done only after the output EG has decayed into the off state
- only call the EG's *noteOff()* function if the oscillator is playing the designated MIDI pitch

```
    bool __stdcall CNanoSynth::midiNoteOff(args...)
    {
        <SNIP SNIP SNIP>

        // --- NO NOT WITH EG!!
        // m_Osc1.stopOscillator();
        // m_Osc2.stopOscillator();
        // m_LFO1.stopOscillator();

        // --- turn off IF this is the proper note (last note played)
        if(uMIDINote == m_Osc1.m_uMIDINoteNumber || bAllNotesOff)
            m_EG1.noteOff();

        return true;
    }
```

You can now move to the RackAFX GUI designer and use the drag and drop interface to create your knobby/slider/LCD based GUI. See Chapter 2 for details.

6.17 NanoSynth EG/DCA: VST3

Use Table 6.3 to add the new controls to the GUI. Then, open the *VSTSynthProcessor.h* and *.cpp* files for editing.

VSTSynthProcessor.h

Add new *#include* statements for the two new objects and then add member variables for each of them.

```
// --- synth objects
#include "QBLimitedOscillator.h"
#include "WTOscillator.h"
#include "LFO.h"
#include "EnvelopeGenerator.h"
#include "DCA.h"

// abstract base class for RackAFX filters
class Processor : public AudioEffect
{
public:

	<SNIP SNIP SNIP>

	// Add your code here: ----------------------------------------- //
	CQBLimitedOscillator m_Osc1;
	CQBLimitedOscillator m_Osc2;
	CLFO m_LFO1;

	// --- one EG
	CEnvelopeGenerator m_EG1;

	// --- one DCA
	CDCA m_DCA;

	void update();

	etc...
```

VSTSynthProcessor.cpp

Work through the .cpp file and alter the functions as needed. We are mainly just adding new lines of code, as we did not declare any new functions.

Constructor:

- there is nothing to add since member constructors will initialize the objects (though you do need to initialize your GUI controls here)

setActive()

- set the sample rate on the EG
- set the EG's *m_bOutputEG* flag to *true* since this EG will be connected to the DCA

```
tresult PLUGIN_API Processor::setActive(TBool state)
{
	if(state)
	{
		// --- do ON stuff; dynamic allocations
		m_Osc1.setSampleRate((double)processSetup.sampleRate);
		m_Osc2.setSampleRate((double)processSetup.sampleRate);
		m_Osc2.m_nCents = 2.5; // +2.5 cents detuned
```

```
        m_LFO1.setSampleRate((double)processSetup.sampleRate);

        m_EG1.setSampleRate((double)processSetup.sampleRate);
        m_EG1.m_bOutputEG = true;

        update();
    }
    etc…
```

update()

- update the EG and DCA with the GUI control variables
- there is no reason yet to call the update function on the EG; we will add this in Chapter 8

```
void Processor::update()
{
    <SNIP SNIP SNIP>

    // --- EG controls
    m_EG1.setAttackTime_mSec(m_dAttackTime_mSec);
    m_EG1.setDecayTime_mSec(m_dDecayTime_mSec);
    m_EG1.setSustainLevel(m_dSustainLevel);
    m_EG1.setReleaseTime_mSec(m_dReleaseTime_mSec);
    m_EG1.m_bResetToZero = (bool)m_uResetToZero;
    m_EG1.m_bLegatoMode = (bool)m_uLegatoMode;

    // --- DCA controls
    m_DCA.setPanControl(m_dPanControl);
    m_DCA.setAmplitude_dB(m_dVolume_dB);
    m_DCA.update();
}
```

process()

- modify the audio rendering code

```
bool __stdcall Processor::process(args…)
{
    <SNIP SNIP SNIP and Indents Removed>
    for(int32 j=0; j<samplesToProcess; j++)
    {
        // --- clear accumulators
        dOutL = 0.0;
        dOutR = 0.0;
        if(m_Osc1.m_bNoteOn)
        {
            << INSERT ** Code Listing 5.1: Audio Rendering ** HERE >>
        }

        // write out to buffer
        buffers[0][j] = dOutL;  // left
        buffers[1][j] = dOutR; // right

        etc…
```

doProcessEvent()

- for MIDI note on events, we need to modify this to start up the EG
- for MIDI note off events, remove (comment out) the original code that stopped the oscillators; this is now done only after the output EG has decayed into the off state
- only call the EG's *noteOff()* function if the oscillator is playing the designated MIDI pitch

```
bool Processor::doProcessEvent(Event& vstEvent)
{
      bool noteEvent = false;

      // --- process Note On or Note Off messages here
      switch(vstEvent.type)
      {
            // --- NOTE ON
            case Event::kNoteOnEvent:
            {
                  <SNIP SNIP SNIP>
                  m_LFO1.startOscillator();
                  m_EG1.startEG();
                  break;
            }

            // --- NOTE OFF
            case Event::kNoteOffEvent:
            {
                  <SNIP SNIP SNIP>
                  // --- turn off IF this is the proper note
                  //      (last note played)
                  if(uMIDINote == m_Osc1.m_uMIDINoteNumber)
                        m_EG1.noteOff();
                  break;
            }

            etc...
```

Design the VST3 GUI by loading your DLL into a VST3 client and using the drag-and-drop method described in Chapter 2. You can always just use the default VST3 GUI if you don't want to perform this step. See the VSTGUI website for more information if needed.

6.18 NanoSynth EG/DCA: AU

Use Table 6.3 to add the new controls to the GUI. Then, open the *AUSynth.h* and *.cpp* files for editing.

AUSynth.h

Add new *#include* statements for the two new objects and then add member variables for each of them.

```
// --- synth objects
#include "QBLimitedOscillator.h"
#include "WTOscillator.h"
#include "LFO.h"
#include "EnvelopeGenerator.h"
#include "DCA.h"
```

```
// --- AU Synth
class AUSynth : public AUInstrumentBase
{
public:

      <SNIP SNIP SNIP>

      // Add your code here: ----------------------------------------- //
      CQBLimitedOscillator m_Osc1;
      CQBLimitedOscillator m_Osc2;
      CLFO m_LFO1;

      // --- one EG
      CEnvelopeGenerator m_EG1;

      // --- one DCA
      CDCA m_DCA;

      void update();

      etc...
```

AUSynth.cpp

Work through the *.cpp* file and alter the functions as needed. We are mainly just adding new lines of code, as we did not declare any new functions.

Constructor:

- there is nothing to add since member constructors will initialize the objects (though you do need to initialize your GUI controls here)

Initialize()

- set the sample rate on the EG
- set the EG's *m_bOutputEG* flag to *true* since this EG will be connected to the DCA

```
ComponentResult AUSynth::Initialize()
{
      // --- init the base class
      AUInstrumentBase::Initialize();

      // --- inits
      m_Osc1.setSampleRate(GetOutput(0)->GetStreamFormat().mSampleRate);
      m_Osc2.setSampleRate(GetOutput(0)->GetStreamFormat().mSampleRate);
      m_Osc2.m_nCents = 2.5;

      m_LFO1.setSampleRate(GetOutput(0)->GetStreamFormat().mSampleRate);
      m_EG1.setSampleRate(GetOutput(0)->GetStreamFormat().mSampleRate);

      // --- big update
      update();

      return noErr;
}
```

update()

- update the EG and DCA with the GUI control variables
- there is no reason yet to call the update function on the EG; we will add this in Chapter 8

```
void AUSynth::update()
{
     <SNIP SNIP SNIP>

     // --- update EG
     m_EG1.setAttackTime_mSec(Globals()->GetParameter(EG1_ATTACK_MSEC));
     m_EG1.setDecayTime_mSec(Globals()->GetParameter(EG1_DECAY_MSEC));
     m_EG1.setSustainLevel(Globals()->GetParameter(EG1_SUSTAIN_LEVEL));
     m_EG1.setReleaseTime_mSec(Globals()->GetParameter(EG1_RELEASE_MSEC));
     m_EG1.m_bResetToZero = Globals()->GetParameter(RESET_TO_ZERO);
     m_EG1.m_bLegatoMode = Globals()->GetParameter(LEGATO_MODE);

     // --- update DCA
     m_DCA.setPanControl(Globals()->GetParameter(OUTPUT_PAN));
     m_DCA.setAmplitude_dB(Globals()->GetParameter(OUTPUT_AMPLITUDE_DB));
     m_DCA.update();
}
```

Render()

- modify the audio rendering code

```
OSStatus AUSynth::Render(args…)
{
     // --- broadcast MIDI events
     PerformEvents(inTimeStamp);

     <SNIP SNIP SNIP>
      // --- the frame processing loop
     for(UInt32 frame=0; frame<inNumberFrames; ++frame)
     {
            // --- clear accumulators
            dOutL = 0.0;
            dOutR = 0.0;
            if(m_Osc1.m_bNoteOn)
            {
                   << INSERT ** Code Listing 5.1: Audio Rendering ** HERE >>
            }
            // write out to buffer
            // --- mono
            left[frame] = dOutL;

            etc…
```

StartNote()

- for MIDI note on events, we need to modify this to start up the EG

```
OSStatus AUSynth::StartNote(args…)
{
    <SNIP SNIP SNIP>
    m_LFO1.startOscillator();
    m_EG1.startEG();
    return noErr;
}
```

StopNote()

- for MIDI note off events, remove (comment out) the original code that stopped the oscillators; this is now done only after the output EG has decayed into the off state
- only call the EG's *noteOff()* function if the oscillator is playing the designated MIDI pitch

```
OSStatus AUSynth::StopNote(args…)
{
            <SNIP SNIP SNIP>

            // --- turn off IF this is the proper note (last note played)
            if(uMIDINote == m_Osc1.m_uMIDINoteNumber)
                m_EG1.noteOff();
    return noErr;
}
```

Design your AU GUI using Interface Builder and the method described in Chapter 2. Remember the flat Cocoa namespace issue when copying projects in XCode.

Build and test the plug-in on your platform. Play with the new EG and DCA controls. Be sure to try the legato and reset to zero modes as well as the EG1 DCA Intensity control. In the next chapter, we will add the final component to NanoSynth's core—a lowpass filter.

6.19 Challenges

Bronze

Add another mode to the EG to implement the simple but very useful AR (attack-release) EG.

Sliver

Modify the AR EG in the Bronze challenge to operate in unconditional mode as described in Section 6.4.

Gold

Implement the AHDSR EG with the extra hold segment between attack and decay. This kind of EG is useful when working with sampled sounds that already have interesting attack envelopes. You can then use it in the sample-based synth DigiSynth in Chapter 10.

Platinum

Add the ability to start the EG from a non-zero value. Note that this will require some work in the function to calculate the attack parameters. This is especially useful for the *DXSynth* project.

Diamond

See the website https://code.google.com/p/music-synthesizer-for-android/wiki/Dx7Envelope for a complete description of the Yamaha DX7 envelope generator implementation. The EG has an extra segment and uses rates rather than absolute times to program itself. It also allows you to start or end the EG on non-zero values. The description at this site is extremely detailed, showing how counters and offsets are used to produce the linear-in-dB release and decay segments. There is also in interactive applet to generate EG curves. Use this information to make an accurate DX7 EG—you can then use it in our *DXSynth* project.

Bibliography

Google. "DX7 Envelope." Accessed June 2014, https://code.google.com/p/music-synthesizer-for-android/wiki/Dx7Envelope
Hurtig, Brent (Ed.). 1984. *Synthesizer Basics*, pp. 29–35. Winona: Hal Leonard Corporation.
Korg, Inc. 1997. *Triton Music Workstation Basic Guide*. Tokyo: Korg, Inc.
Korg, Inc. 1997. *Karma Music Workstation Parameter Guide*. Tokyo: Korg, Inc.
Redmon, Nigel. "Envelope Generators." Accessed June 2014, http://www.earlevel.com/main/2013/06/02/envelope-generators-adsr-part-2
Sound on Sound Magazine. "Synth Secrets." Accessed June 2014, http://www.soundonsound.com/sos/allsynthsecrets.htm
synthtech.com. "CEM3310 Voltage Controlled Envelope Generator Datasheet." Accessed June 2014, http://www.synthtech.com/cem/c3310pdf.pdf
Yamaha, Inc. 1983. *DX7 User's Manual*. Tokyo: Yamaha, Inc.
Yamaha, Inc. 1998. *EX5/EX7 User's Manual*. Tokyo: Yamaha, Inc.

CHAPTER 7

Synthesizer Filter Design

Filters are a crucial component for most synthesis algorithms. They are used to sculpt the harmonic content of the oscillator outputs. Filters may also be used in the effects section of a synthesizer. In Chapter 4 we investigated DSP Theory and basic filter types. as well as the biquad and virtual analog variations for several first and second order filters. In this chapter we are going to combine the virtual analog building blocks into filters and implement them in code. The goal is to create a set of C++ objects that represent various filter designs. The fundamental filter types we will implement in our designs consist of:

- first order Lowpass and Highpass Filters (LPF and HPF)
- second order Resonant LPF and HPF
- second order Bandpass and Bandstop Filters (BPF and BSF)
- fourth order ladder filters in several variations

In this chapter we will often refer to the manufacturers of the synths that incorporate various versions of these filters, with an emphasis on modeling the analog resonant lowpass and highpass types. The filters can be used as starting points for your own designs; these filters are modeled on the block diagrams and signal flow charts of specific designs, though different manufacturers may model the same filter with their own subtle or not-so-subtle variations. There are some desirable qualities we would like in our filter algorithms:

- ease of calculations
- simplicity of filter structures
- decoupling of controls from the underlying coefficients
- self-oscillation for some resonant versions
- ways to prevent, lessen, or at least limit the distortion that high resonance values can cause

7.1 Virtual Analog Filters

In Chapter 4 we studied Zavalishin's Virtual Analog (VA) Filters. We looked at the trapezoidal integrator and learned that it can preserve the topology of the original analog block diagram. We also saw that the filter equations for the first order sections were simple and linear. For our synthesizer filters, we can make use of these virtual analog designs. In some cases there may be more coefficients to calculate, but the calculations may be mathematically simpler than other designs. Additionally, the filter parameters are less coupled to each other, which can also reduce overall processing loads. VA filters will allow us to implement all of the filters we need using easy to calculate equations and fewer memory or z^{-1} locations than the BZT-to-biquad versions. It should be noted, however, that these filters are also considered bilinear designs because they are based on the trapezoidal (or bilinear) integrator, and so the frequency responses are going to be essentially identical to the BZT-to-biquad versions, including the error at very high frequencies in the LPF and BPF cases. We will synthesize filters using the three VA building blocks: first order LPF and HPF and second order State Variable Filter (SVF). We will implement these in two C++ objects, one for the first order pair and the other for the SVF. Figure 7.1 shows the frequency response for the first order LPF and HPF. The LPF has a noticeable plummet to zero at Nyquist—this is due to the bilinear transform which relocates analog zeros at infinity to Nyquist. All filters based on the bilinear transform will suffer from this problem.

Figure 7.2 shows the VA LPF while Figure 7.3 shows the VA HPF output added to the block diagram. Both filters use the same equation and coefficients for setting the cutoff frequency. We can then use one structure to realize both filters. The only difference is in how the outputs are formed. The coefficient and instantaneous difference equations are shown in Equations 7.1 and 7.2.

$$\begin{aligned}
\omega_d &= 2\pi f_c \\
T &= 1/f_s \\
\omega_a &= \frac{2}{T}\tan\left(\frac{\omega_d T}{2}\right) \\
g &= \frac{\omega_a T}{2} \\
\alpha &= \frac{g}{1+g}
\end{aligned} \tag{7.1}$$

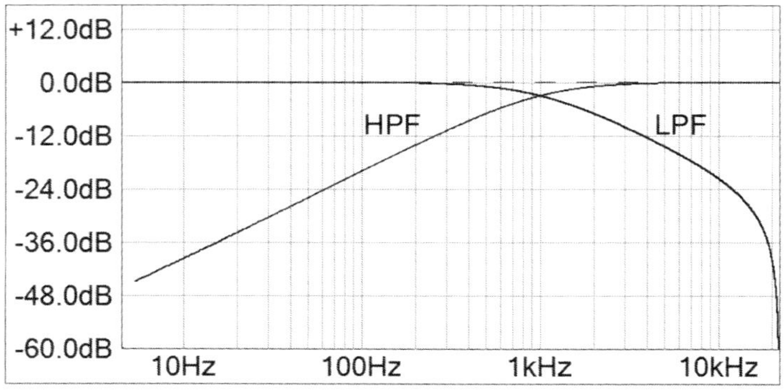

Figure 7.1: The first order VA LPF and HPF frequency response.

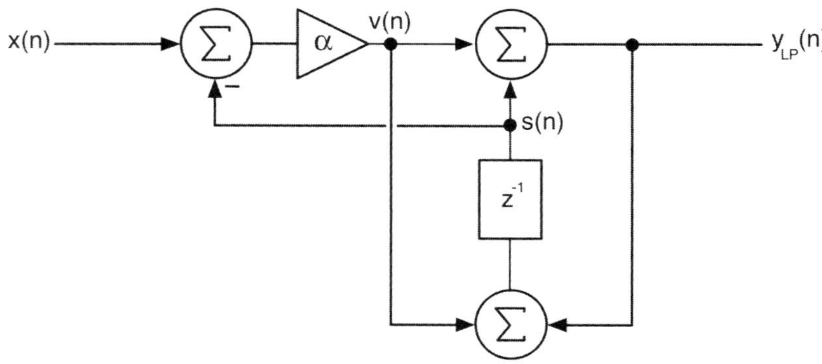

Figure 7.2: The VA implementation of the first order analog lowpass filter.

$$\begin{aligned}
&\text{For the LPF}\\
&y_{LP} = Gx + S\\
&G = \frac{g}{1+g} \qquad S = \frac{s}{1+g}\\
&\text{For the HPF}\\
&y_{HP} = x - (Gx + S)\\
&G = \frac{g}{1+g} \qquad S = \frac{s}{1+g}
\end{aligned} \tag{7.2}$$

The variables x, y and s in the instantaneous response equations refer to the nodes $x(n)$, $y(n)$ and $s(n)$ in the block diagrams, and $v(n)$ is the intermediate node you need to calculate first.

The VA SVF is shown in Figure 7.4 and has the three outputs y_{LP}, y_{HP}, and y_{BP}.

$$\begin{aligned}
\omega_d &= 2\pi f_c\\
T &= 1/f_s\\
\omega_a &= \frac{2}{T}\tan\left(\frac{\omega_d T}{2}\right)\\
g &= \frac{\omega_a T}{2} \qquad R = \frac{1}{2Q}\\
\alpha_0 &= \frac{1}{1+2Rg+g^2} \qquad \alpha_1 = \alpha_2 = g \qquad \rho = 2R + g
\end{aligned} \tag{7.3}$$

In this design, you first calculate $y_{HP}(n)$ as:

$$y_{HP}(n) = \alpha_0 (x(n) - \rho s_1(n) - s_2(n)) \tag{7.4}$$

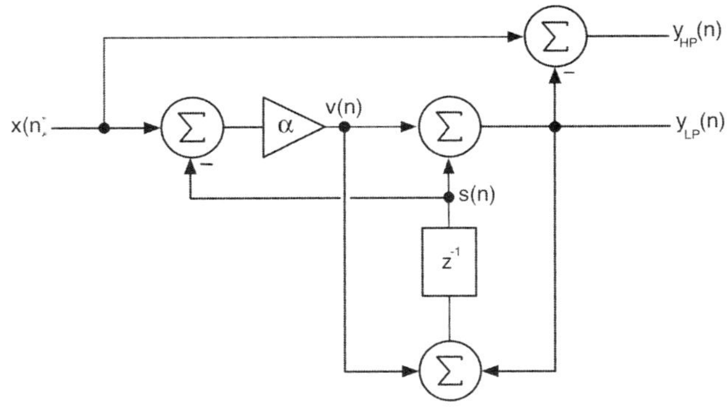

Figure 7.3: The multi-mode filter produces both LPF and HPF outputs.

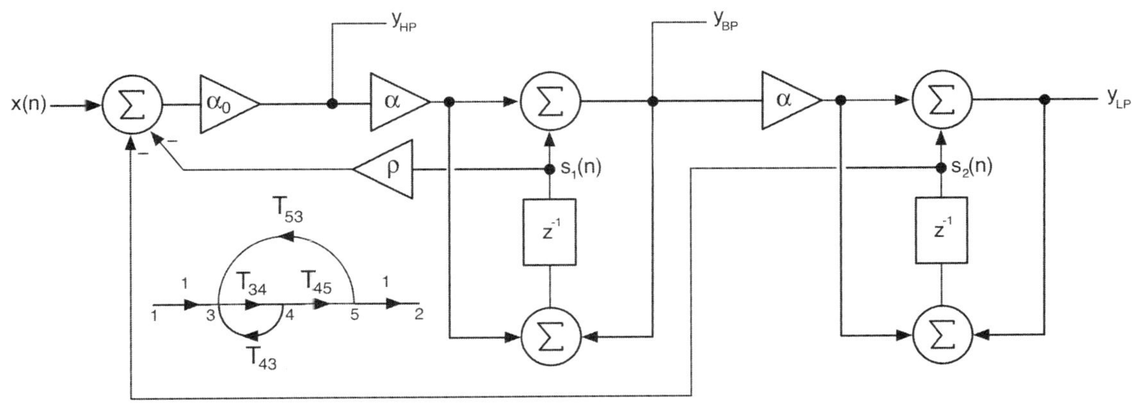

Figure 7.4: The VA implementation of the SVF with three outputs; the signal flow graph is shown at the left.

The bandpass and lowpass outputs are:

$$
\begin{aligned}
y_{BP}(n) &= \alpha_1 y_{HP}(n) + s_1(n) \\
y_{LP}(n) &= \alpha_1 y_{BP}(n) + s_2(n)
\end{aligned}
\tag{7.5}
$$

We can also generate the missing bandstop filter output by using another shortcut:

$$
y_{BS}(n) = x(n) - 2Ry_{BP}(n) \tag{7.6}
$$

7.2 Oberheim SEM State Variable Filter Model

Oberheim's Synthesizer Expander Module (SEM) introduced in 1974 featured a modified state variable design. It allowed for the three standard outputs for LPF, HPF and BPF, plus a variable BSF that could produce asymmetrical resonant bandstop responses in addition to a perfect notch. More importantly, it featured a limiter mechanism in the inner feedback path that controlled the Q of the filter. Examining the block diagram, you can see the inner feedback path connects the output of the BP section to the input in a negative feedback loop. In the analog design, the feedback level is controlled with a potentiometer (variable resistor). Therefore, as this feedback signal increases, the overall resonance or Q will decrease. An issue with the SVF design is that when the resonance increases, the gain at resonance also increases. This can lead to clipping and distortion, especially at low frequencies. With the resonance control at a very high setting, only a small amount of feedback is applied, and the output of the cascade of sections is greatly amplified. The SEM filter has a kind of switch that turns on when the output of the BP section becomes large enough and bypasses around the resonance potentiometer. Figure 7.5(a) shows a simplified analog circuit version of the SEM filter. The Operational Transconductance Amplifier (OTA) and companion capacitor in each of the dotted boxes implements a voltage controlled filter approximating the tuned integration sections. You can see the familiar succession of HPF, BPF and LPF outputs. The BSF output is formed by summing the HPF and LPF outputs. Resistor R_5 provides the global negative feedback path from the LPF output back to the input, which is designed around an inverting summer circuit with an input impedance approximately the same as R_5. We are particularly interested in the circuitry that forms the inner feedback path from the BPF output back to the input.

Figure 7.5(b) shows a hybrid block diagram with ideal integrators replacing the OTA versions. The feedback limiter consists of the pair of diodes D1 and D2, along with an attenuator a that is formed by voltage divider R1/R2. When the output at y_{BP} is small, it is fed back via the Q potentiometer. When the signal becomes large enough, the switch made of the two diodes turns on and bypasses part of the signal around the feedback control. Resistors R3 and R4 control the mix of the bypassed and straight signals. The threshold is adjusted with the

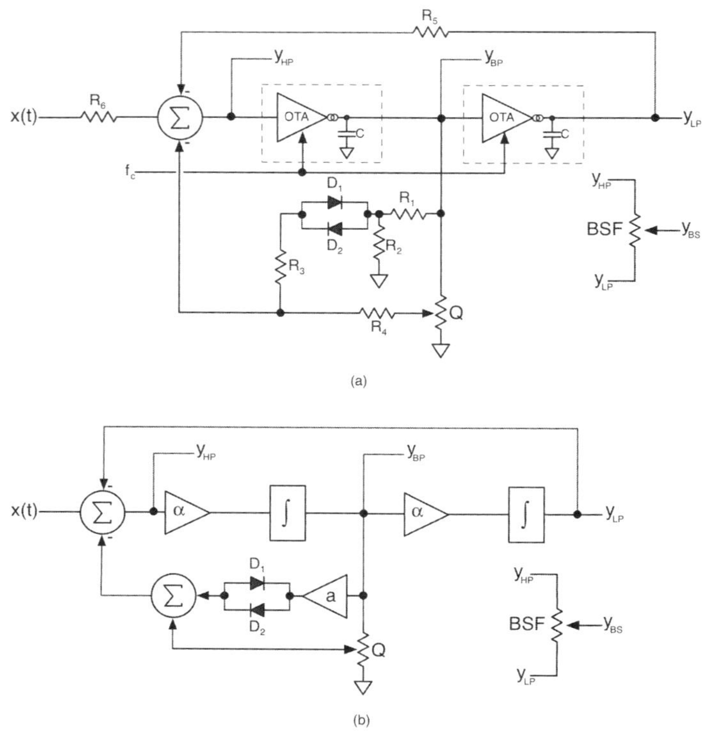

Figure 7.5: (a) The simplified analog circuit and (b) a hybrid block diagram of the Oberheim SEM filter.

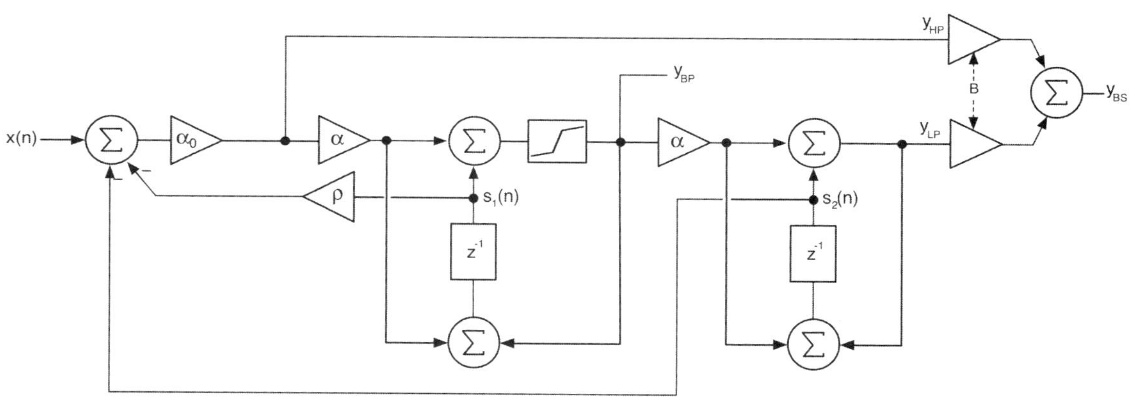

Figure 7.6: The completed Oberheim SEM Filter Block Diagram; the nonlinear saturator is in the loop of the first integrator and shown as the zig-zag "S" block.

attenuator *a*. This circuit results in a nonlinearity since the diodes do not turn on and off like a perfect switch. In addition, each diode is separately engaged for the negative portion (D1) and the positive portion (D2) of the feedback waveform. While we can use any number of wave shapers to try to emulate the diodes and splitter variables to route portions of the signal around them, a larger problem arises in that the nonlinearity this creates will cause a problem with the design equations of the filter. Experimentation with several schemes yielded filters with horrible tuning stability and often resonant frequency instability. Zavalishin proposes a simple solution by placing the nonlinearity inside of the first integrator. This produces a filter that has good tuning stability but is very much an approximation, so the term "SEM Model" should be taken lightly. You are certainly encouraged to experiment with this design issue. The block diagram for our SEM emulation is shown in Figure 7.6. A value *B* is used to mix the HPF and LPF outputs to create the BSF variations.

> With any nonlinear waveshaping, aliasing can and will occur; the extent of the damage will depend on the saturation function and settings you choose. This can be mitigated with oversampling. Any of the other filters in the chapter with nonlinear processing blocks may have the same issue with aliasing. Because the oversampling will require some extra CPU processing, you may decide to leave out the nonlinear processing or just live with the aliasing.

To illustrate the importance of the NLP or saturation, the peak gain at the resonant frequency is:

$$gain_{dB} = 20\log\left(\frac{Q^2}{\sqrt{Q^2 - 0.25}}\right) \quad Q \geq 0.707 \tag{7.7}$$

So for Q = 20, the peak gain is 26 dB, or an amplification factor of about 20, so any input sample greater than 0.05 will clip at the output. Figure 7.7(a) shows the output of the SEM LPF with a full scale input, Q = 2.5 and NLP turned off—the input is already starting to clip. Figure 7.7(b) shows the output with NLP engaged using the *tanh()* saturator. The triangle shape is due to the lowpass filtering. Increasing the *tanh()* saturation to 1.15 restores a nearly full-scale signal as shown in Figure 7.7(c). Figure 7.8(a) shows the familiar family of curves for a resonant LPF that this structure produces. Since it is still a SVF, the other outputs will resemble the response plots from Chapter 4. Figure 7.8(b) shows the bandpass output and Figures 7.8(c–d) show the BSF output with different settings for the *B* and Q controls. The output varies from a perfect BSF to asymmetrical versions emphasizing either the high band or low band. You can see

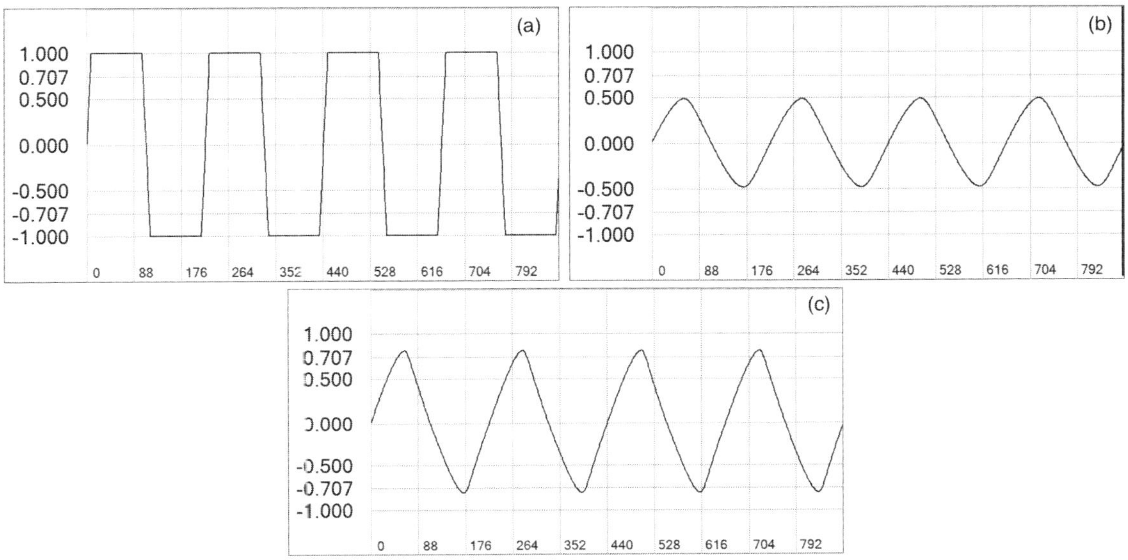

Figure 7.7: The SEM LPF with Q = 2.5, f_c = 200 Hz and the input signal also is 200 Hz, and various settings of NLP and saturation(a) without NLP (b) with NLP and saturation = 1.0 and (c) with NLP and saturation = 1.15.

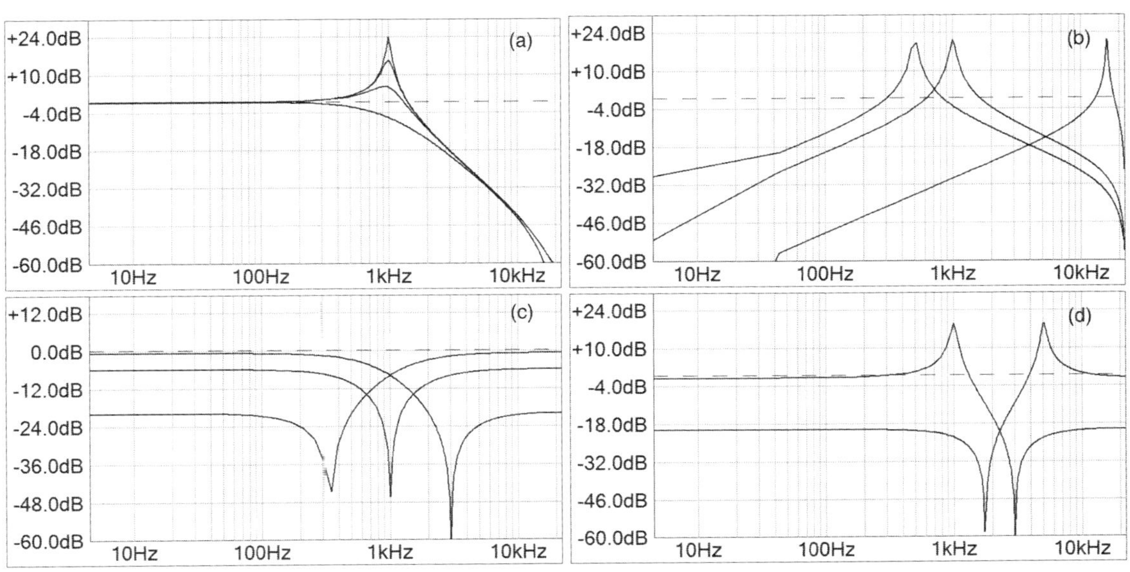

Figure 7.8: (a) The SEM LPF with f_c = 1 kHz and Q = 0.5, 2, 5 and 25 (b) SEM BPF with Q = 5 and a variety of center frequencies (c) SEM BSF with various settings of the mix control *B*; the BSF becomes biased at low or high frequencies depending on the value of *B*, and with Q > 0.707 (d) resonant peaks appear along with the notches.

that the notch frequency changes and that the emphasized band will have gain. You can also make a resonant notch filter by increasing Q above 0.707.

7.3 Korg35 Sallen-Key Filter Model

Korg used several different filter architectures in its early synthesizer designs, but the Korg35 filter used in the MS-10 and early MS-20 synths stands out as an interesting and useful design. It has reappeared in several Korg products, including the more modern Monotribe synths. The term "Korg35" actually refers to a sub-circuit where a Control Voltage (CV) modifies the cutoff frequency of the main filtering circuit. Here we are using the term to include the larger LPF or HPF circuit as well. The Korg35 LPF and HPF are voltage controlled versions of the Sallen-Key filter topology. This is one the many early filter designs that includes the SVF; some analog filtering books refer to it as "Class 2A" (Lindquist) and "PF1" (Wanhammer) Sallen-Key filters have a positive feedback path in addition to a negative feedback path, and this allows the filter to self-oscillate. Korg took advantage of this to produce a simple but effective highly resonant filter. Both LPF and HPF are second order types and will self-oscillate, but the Korg35 HPF has an interesting quirk; its roll-off slope is 6 dB/octave instead of the normal 12 dB/octave. This produces a HPF with more bass response.

7.4 Korg35 LPF Model

Figure 7.9 shows the block diagram of the two amplifier Sallen-Key LPF. Two LPF blocks are formed by the cascade of R1/C1 and R2/C2. K = K1K2 is the strength of the amplifier blocks together, and you can see the output is fed back into the filter via capacitor C1.

The reason for choosing the two-amplifier version is that the amps buffer the two LPF stages to prevent loading. Our digital filters do not suffer from impedance loading, so we use this version. The original Korg analog version uses the single amplifier circuit. The difference in the two designs ultimately boils down to the self-oscillation gain value; the lossy loading effects of the single amplifier circuit raise the gain before oscillation value. You can find a complete derivation and implementation of the lossy single-amplifier Korg35 design at http://www.willpirkle.com/synthbook/. Its frequency response is identical to this version but requires slightly more complex design equations to emulate the lossy sections. Using signal flow graphing, we can derive the block diagram and signal flow graph of the filter shown in Figure 7.11. In the signal flow graph, "LPF1 and HPF1" mean first order filters. In this design, we let $K1$ = 1.0, neglect the effects of loading and use an ideal version of the original single amplifier design that Korg implemented.

Using Mason's Gain Equation, we can form the transfer function.

$$\begin{aligned} H(s) &= \frac{KT_{13}T_{45}}{1-KT_{45}T_{63}} \\ &= \frac{K}{s^2R_1C_1R_2C_2 + s(R_1C_1(1-K)+R_2C_2)+1} \\ K &= K1K2 \end{aligned} \tag{7.8}$$

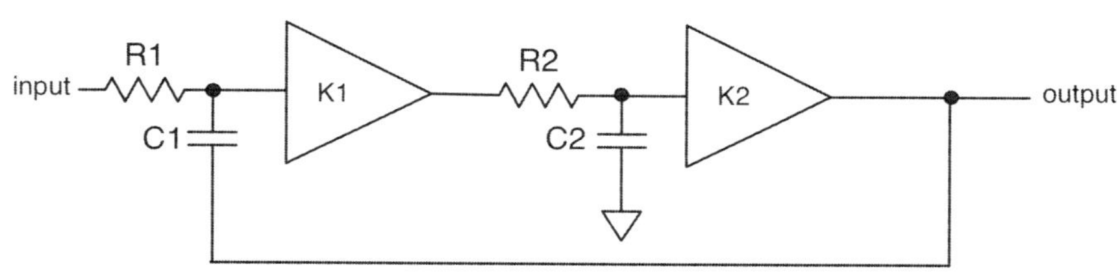

Figure 7.9: The Sallen-Key LPF topology employs a positive feedback path through C1.

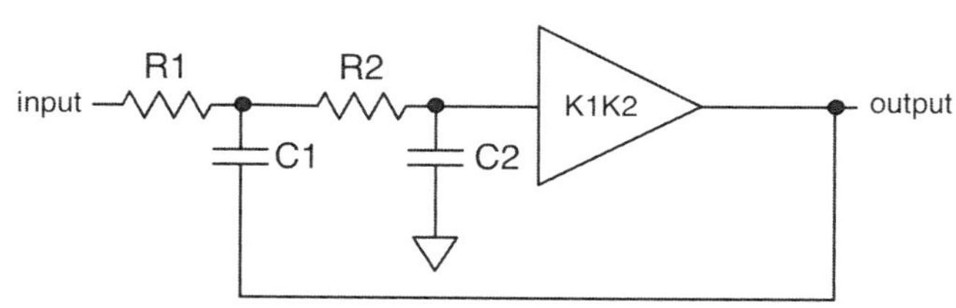

Figure 7.10: The single amplifier version of the Sallen-Key lowpass filter used in the Korg35 design.

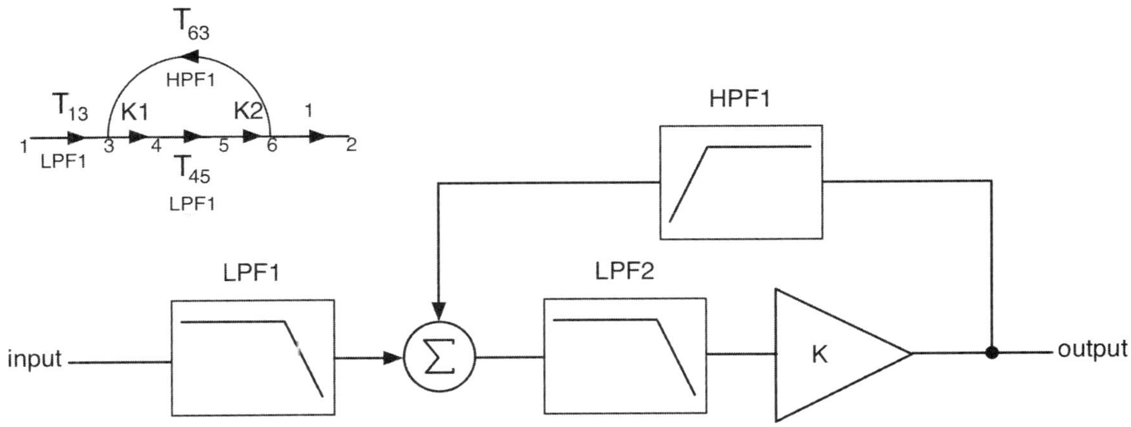

Figure 7.11: The signal flow graph and block diagram of the Sallen-Key LPF.

The term $T_{13}T_{45}$ in the numerator is a cascade of two first order LPFs (LPF1 and LPF2) and represents the feed-forward branch. The term $T_{45}T_{63}$ in the denominator represents a second order BPF in the feedback path consisting of LPF2 and HPF1. All filters have the same cutoff frequency f_c and are said to be synchronously tuned. This results in a BPF with a Q of 0.5 in the feedback branch. By adding this signal back with the input cascade of LPFs, the Q is either emphasized (high feedback) or de-emphasized (low feedback), and the value of K determines this amount of feedback and thus the Q of the filter. This conceptual block diagram is shown in Figure 7.12.

We can extract the gain, cutoff frequency and Q from the transfer function as:

$$H_0 = K = K1K2$$
$$\omega_c = \sqrt{\frac{1}{R_1C_1R_2C_2}} \tag{7.9}$$
$$Q = \frac{\sqrt{R_1C_1R_2C_2}}{(1-K1K2)R_1C_2 + R_2C_2}$$

For a normalized filter with $R_1C_1 = R_2C_2 = 1$

$$Q = \frac{1}{2-K1K2} \tag{7.10}$$

Letting $K1 = 1.0$, self-oscillation occurs when $K2 = 2.0$ and Q goes to infinity, which is the value for our model. Also notice that since $H_0 = K$, we will need to normalize the output at $1/K$ to keep the overall filter gain at 1.0. In the original filter, the feedback into C2 can be set to 0.0, resulting in a critically damped LPF with Q = 0.5. The problem is that when $K = 0$ there is no forward gain through our model. So, we can let K assume a very small, non-zero minimum value to emulate the zero feedback condition. In our emulation K varies from 0.01 to 2.0.

Like the Oberheim SEM filter, high resonance settings can cause the filter to clip and distort. As the resonance approaches self-oscillation, the gain at resonance becomes excessive and in excess of 60 dB (a factor of 1000). To mitigate this, Korg engineers placed a diode clipping circuit in the feedback loop. The circuit is similar to the diode clipping circuits found in many distortion circuits used in effects boxes and processors. This clipping circuit produces the limiting function but also adds its own soft clipping distortion, and so the Korg35 filters are known for their distorted outputs at high resonance settings. In our Virtual Analog model of the Korg35, we use VA blocks as the LPF and HPF components in a delay-less feedback loop. The addition of the nonlinear processing (NLP) of the feedback loop causes a very slight tuning drift, however it is negligible as long as you use a soft clipping function. Figure 7.13 shows the nonlinear model. Notice that the NLP block is placed before LPF2; this is required because of the way the conceptual bandpass filter works in the feedback loop. LPF2 forms half of this bandpass filter, and the signal needs to be saturated prior to the loop and thus prior to this filter.

The synthesis of the VA Korg35 LPF begins with labeling the input and output nodes of all the filters. Next, the VA equations can be extracted for the series cascades of filters. Then, the delay-less feedback path through the BPF block can be resolved, and we can get a single VA equation to describe the complete filter. An example of this technique was shown in Chapter 4; if you intend on understanding the filter synthesis, please review this example. Figure 7.14 shows the block diagram with the filter inputs and outputs labeled for establishing the instantaneous response (we ignore the NLP and output scaling blocks; they will be inserted into the model later). We will also use the same variable naming scheme in the filter design.

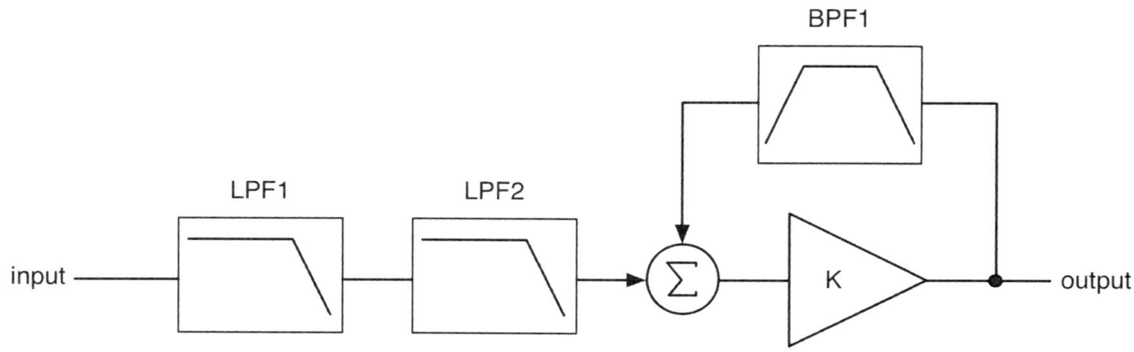

Figure 7.12: Conceptual block diagram of the Sallen-Key LPF.

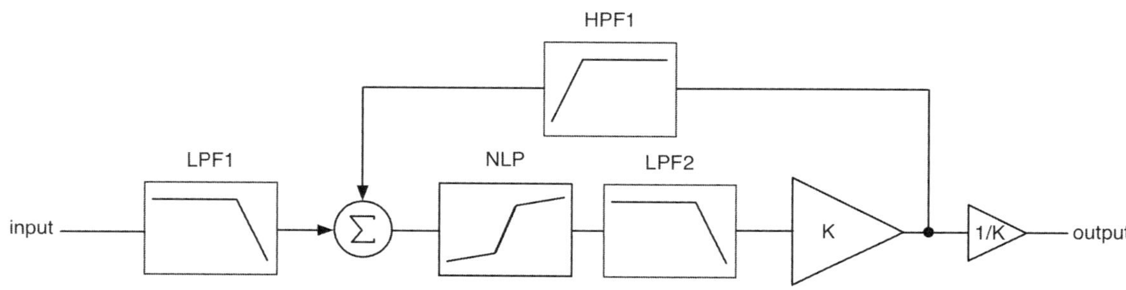

Figure 7.13: The Korg35 LPF nonlinear model with NLP in the feedback loop.

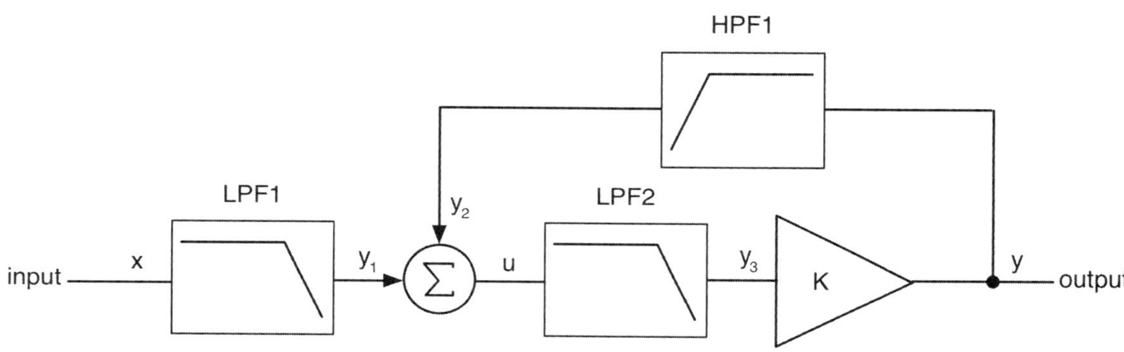

Figure 7.14: The Korg35 LPF model with all nodes labeled.

The design equations for each output are found by using the same VA technique over and over; the output of one filter becomes the input of the next, and so on. In Chapter 4 we derived the loop portion of the filter and solved for the input u in Section 4.14 using Zavalishin's method (go back and review it if you need to).

$$u = \frac{y_1 - S2 + S3(K - KG)}{1 - KG + KG^2}$$

let

$$\alpha_0 = \frac{1}{1 - KG + KG^2}$$

then

$$u = \alpha_0(y_1 - S2 + S3(K - KG)) \tag{7.11}$$

define

$$S2 = \beta_2 s_2 \qquad S3 = \beta_3 s_3 \qquad \beta_2 = \frac{-1}{(1+g)} \qquad \beta_3 = \frac{(K - KG)}{(1+g)}$$

then

$$u = \alpha_0(y_1 + \beta_2 s_2 + \beta_3 s_3)$$

We need to extract and scale the values from each s_n node of each filter to form the S terms above (e.g., $S2 = \beta_2 s_2$). This can be accomplished by modifying the block diagram of our first order LPF and HPF to include a feedback output path labeled *fb_out*. Figure 7.15 shows LPF1 with the new feedback coefficient labeled.

This lets us synthesize the final block diagram for the filter (including the NLP and output scaling) as shown in Figure 7.16. Figure 7.17 shows the same filter in abbreviated form using the notation from Chapter 4.

Look at the node u and verify that it is indeed:

$$u = \alpha_0 (y_1 + \beta_2 s_2 + \beta_3 s_3) \tag{7.12}$$

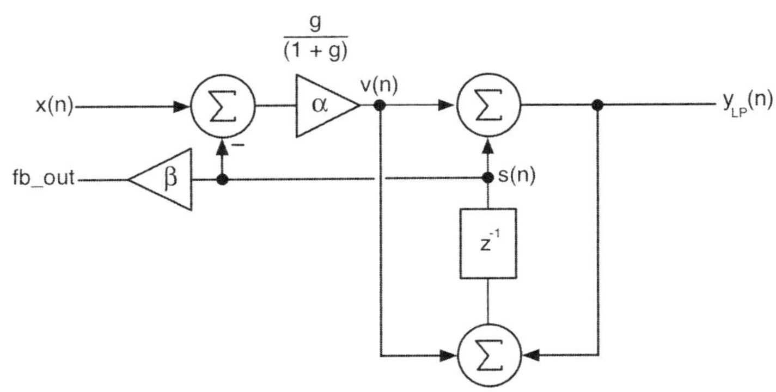

Figure 7.15: The modified LPF structure now includes a feedback output path.

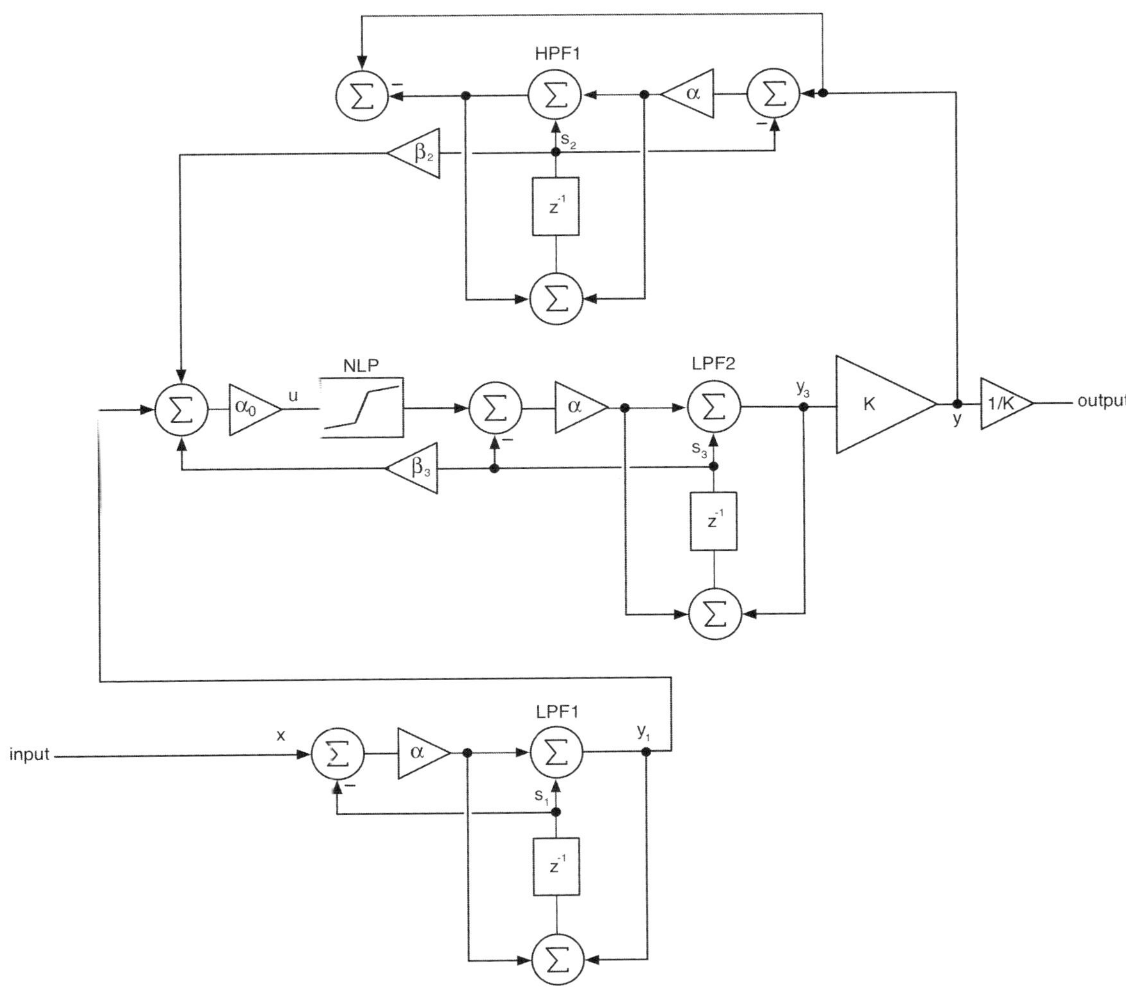

Figure 7.16: The completed Korg35 LPF model.

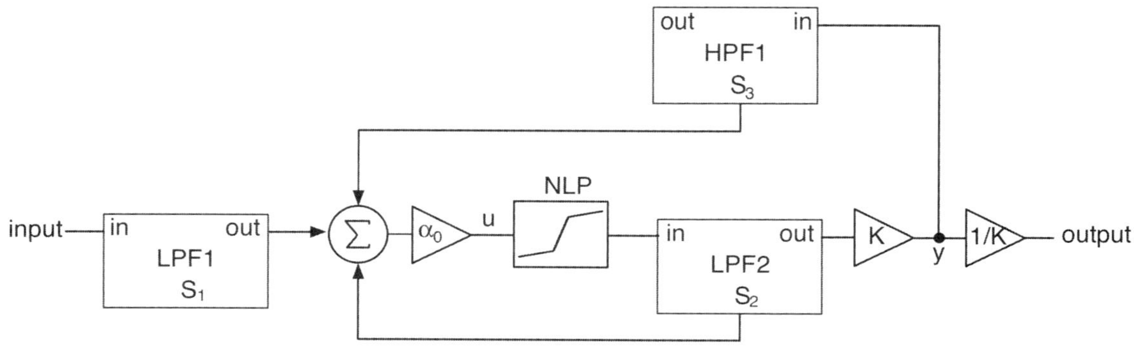

Figure 7.17: The Korg35 LPF abbreviated block diagram using the notation from Chapter 4.

The sequence for processing the filter is:

- process x through LPF1 to get y_1
- form $u = alpha0*(y1 + feedback\ S2\ and\ S3)$
- add nonlinear processing to u if desired
- process u through LPF2 to get y_3
- calculate $y = Ky_3$
- process y through HPF1 (whose output appears to go nowhere)

7.5 Korg35 HPF Model

The Korg35 HPF circuit results from an analog method of converting a LPF to HPF by grounding the input and driving the ground (Lindquist, 1977). When this is applied to the Sallen-Key topology, the resulting HPF has only 6 dB/octave of rolloff instead of 12 dB. Stinchcombe (2006) derived the resulting analog transfer function that revealed a BPF in parallel with the second order HPF, which caused the first order rolloff phenomenon. By starting with the Sallen-Key HPF topology and then adding a parallel BPF in the HPF input section, we can achieve the same result. Figure 7.18 shows the block diagram of the Sallen-Key HPF with the parallel BPF added to the input path and the NLP block in the feedback loop. However, we can greatly simplify this model by creating another hybrid signal flow graph with a first order HPF in the feedforward path and a second order BPF in the feedback loop, resulting in the signal flow graph and block diagram shown in Figure 7.19. Not bound to the analog circuit domain, we can synthesize a hybrid version easily in code. We can also derive the resulting transfer function and show that it is identical to the conceptual model (Pirkle, 2013a).

Like the LPF, the HPF analog filter equations can be derived from the signal flow graph. This reveals the bandpass filter (first term) in parallel with the second order highpass filter (second term) and the gain, cutoff and Q values.

$$\begin{aligned}
H(s) &= \frac{KT_{13}}{1-KT_{63}} \\
&= K\left[\frac{sR_1C_1}{s^2R_1C_1R_1C_1 + s(R_1C_1(1-K)+R_2C_2)+1} + \frac{s^2R_1C_1R_2C_2}{s^2R_1C_1R_1C_1 + s(R_1C_1(1-K)+R_2C_2)+1}\right] \\
K &= K1K2 \\
H_0 &= K \\
\omega &= \frac{1}{\sqrt{R_1C_1R_1C_1}} \\
Q &= \frac{\sqrt{R_1C_1R_1C_1}}{(1-K1K2)R_1C_1 + R_2C_2}
\end{aligned} \tag{7.13}$$

For a normalized filter with $R_1C_1 = R_2C_2 = 1$

$$Q = \frac{1}{2-K1K2} \tag{7.14}$$

Letting K1 = 1.0, self-oscillation occurs when K2 = 2.0, which is the value for our model. Since $H_0 = K$ we will need to normalize the output to $1/K$ to keep the overall filter gain at 1.0. Like the LPF version, the feedback value K can be set to 0.0 so that none of the bandpass signal is added to the input filter. Again, with $K = 0$ there is no forward gain through the filter. So, we can let K take on a very small non-zero minimum value. In our emulation, K varies from 0.01 to 2.0.

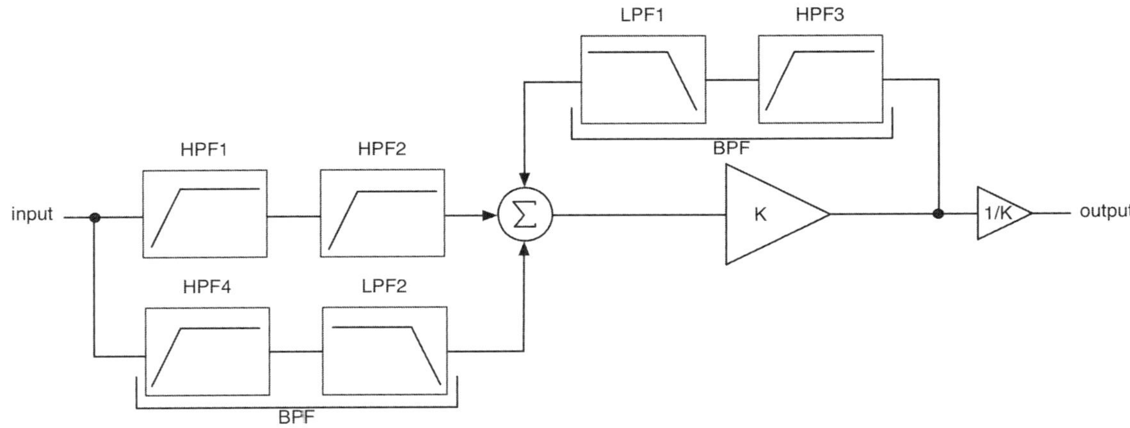

Figure 7.18: The Korg35 HPF conceptual model.

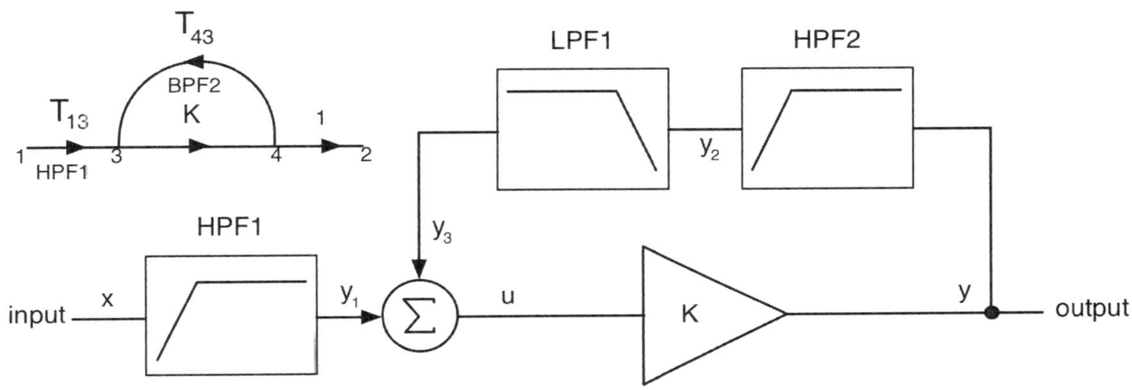

Figure 7.19: The simplified hybrid filter signal flow graph and block diagram producing the same frequency response and transfer function as the more complex version.

The derivation for the HPF uses the same strategy of finding the input u to the amplifier K and follows the same logic as for the LPF, but is actually simpler than the LPF version because it lacks one filtering block. The resulting filter equations are shown in Equation 7.15. This produces the final block diagram in Figure 7.20 and the abbreviated version in Figure 7.21.

$$
\begin{array}{lll}
\text{HPF1} & HPF2 & \text{LPF1} \\
y_1 = x - (Gx + S1) & y_2 = y - (Gy + S2) & y_3 = Gy_2 + S3 \\
\quad = x - Gx - S1 & \quad = y - Gy - S2 & \quad = G(y - Gy - S2) + S3 \\
G = \dfrac{g}{1+g} & S2 = \dfrac{s_2}{1+g} & \quad = Gy - G^2 y - GS2 + S3 \\
S1 = \dfrac{s_1}{1+g} & & S3 = \dfrac{s_3}{1+g}
\end{array}
\tag{7.15}
$$

Now find u:

$$
\begin{aligned}
& u = y_1 + y_3 = y_1 + Gy - G^2 \\
& \quad\quad \textit{and} \\
& y = Ku \\
& u = y_1 + GKu - G^2 Ku - GS2 + S3 \\
& \quad = \frac{y_1 - GS2 + S3}{1 - KG + KG^2} \\
& \quad\quad \text{let}
\end{aligned}
$$

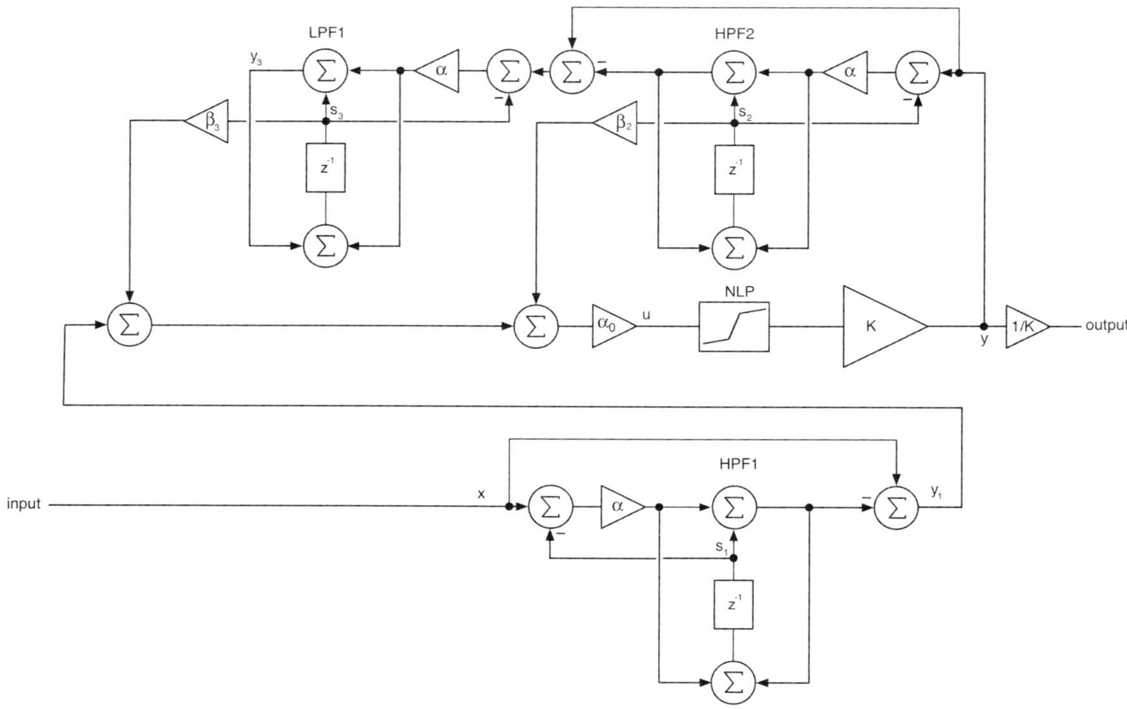

Figure 7.20: The Korg35 HPF model with NLP block.

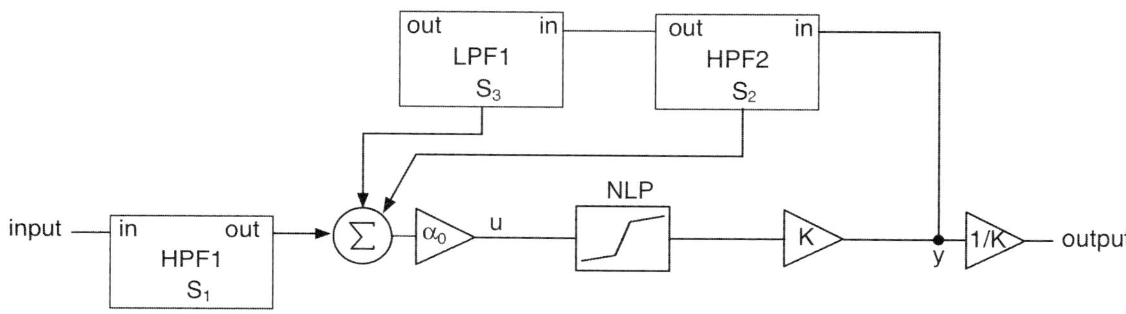

Figure 7.21: The Korg35 HPF in abbreviated form.

$$\alpha_0 = \frac{1}{1-KG+KG^2}$$

then

$$u = \alpha_0(y_1 - GS2 + S3)$$

define

$$S2 = \beta_2 s_2 \qquad S3 = \beta_3 s_3 \qquad \beta_2 = \frac{-G}{(1+g)} \qquad \beta_3 = \frac{1}{(1+g)} \tag{7.16}$$

then

$$u = \alpha_0(y_1 + \beta_2 s_2 + \beta_3 s_3)$$

Look at the node u and see that it is indeed:

$$u = \alpha_0(y_1 + \beta_2 s_2 + \beta_3 s_3) \tag{7.17}$$

The sequence for processing the filter is:

- process x through HPF1 to get y_1
- form $u = y_1$ + feedback values S2 + S3
- calculate $y = Ku$
- add nonlinear processing if desired
- process y through HPF2 to get y_2
- process y_2 through LPF1 (whose output appears to go nowhere)

Figure 7.22 shows the LPF and HPF responses for a variety of values of feedback *K*. You can see the different rolloff slopes of the two filters. The slight difference in peaking (for similar values of *K*) is due to the fact that the HPF version has the added BPF reinforcing Q. Figure 7.20 shows the output of the Korg35 LPF model with a 0 dBFS sinusoidal input signal at f_o =250 Hz, filter f_c = 250 Hz, with K = 1.6. In Figure 7.23(a), the filter is clipping. In Figure 7.23(b) you can see the soft-clipping action of the NLP using the *tanh()* saturator and how it reduces the loop gain. In Figure 7.23(c) the saturation control is 2.0, increasing loop gain and adding more distortion. Overall amplitude is reduced, but the apparent loudness is nearly the same. You can further increase gain by allowing the *K* value to go slightly above 2.0 in order to restore the full whistling, ringing oscillations. Finally, Figure 7.24 shows the wide range of stability and self oscillation capability.

We can take advantage of the flexibility of the Sallen-Key topology and generate the other two filters: a hybrid second order LPF with 6 dB/octave rolloff and a true second order HPF with 12 dB/octave rolloff.

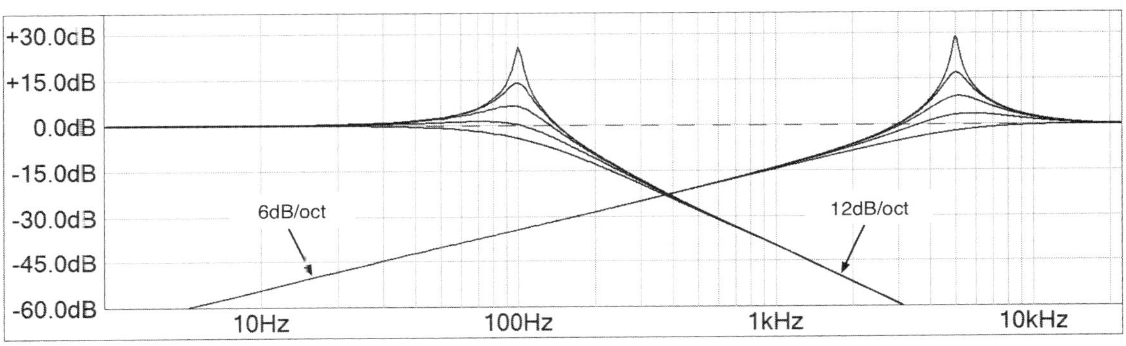

Figure 7.22: The Korg35 LPF and HPF responses; for the LPF, *fc* = 100 Hz and Q varies from 0.15 to 1.95, while the HPF has *fc* = 5 kHz and Q varies from 0.264 to 1.95.

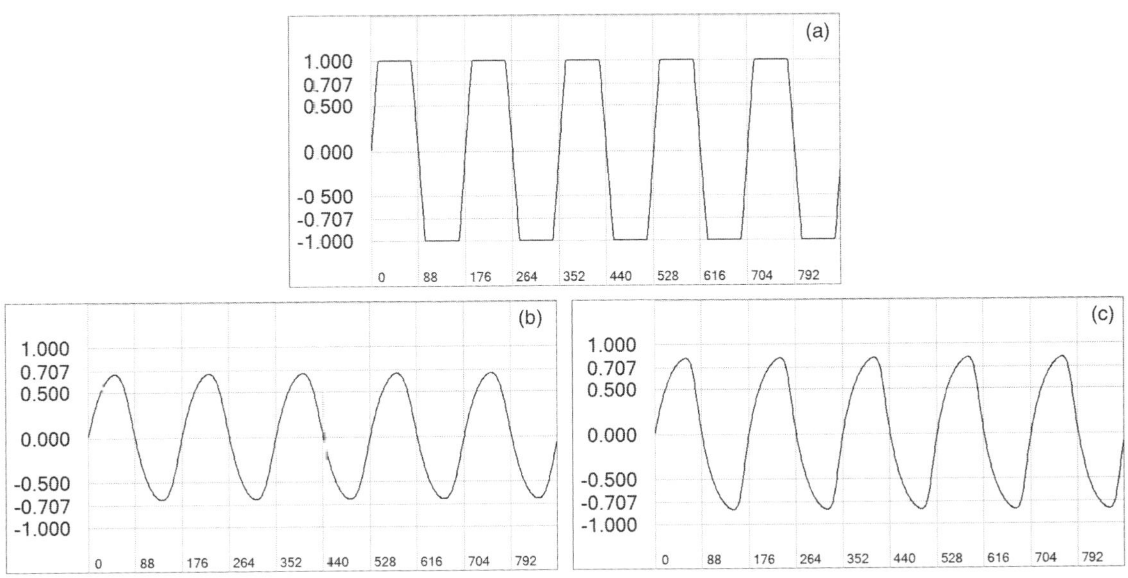

Figure 7.23: The Korg35 LPF model (a) without NLP the Korg35 LPF model clips and distorts while (b) shows a reduced and soft-clipped output; increasing the saturation to 2.0 results in (c) a more distorted and ringing waveform (0dBFS sinusoidal input signal at *fo* =250 Hz, filter *fc* = 250 Hz, and K = 1.6).

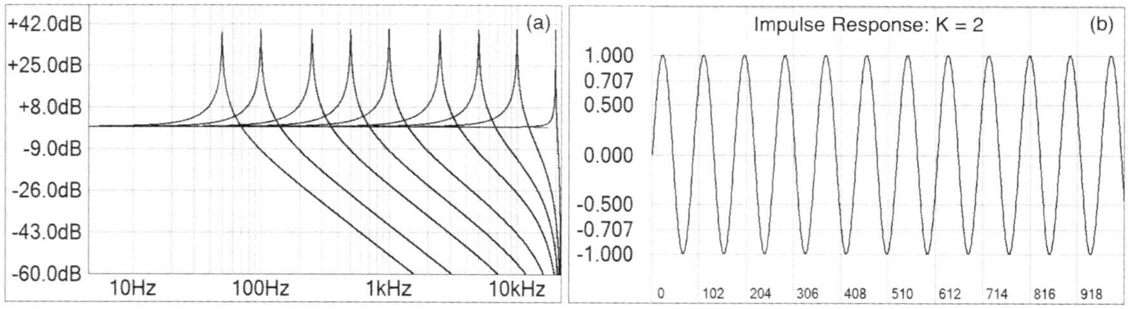

Figure 7.24: The frequency response (a) with K = 1.99 and a sweep across a variety of frequencies reveals stability across the ten octave range; the impulse response (b) with K = 2 shows the filter in self-oscillation.

7.6 Moog Ladder Filter Model

The analog filtering term "ladder filter" generally refers to a structure of passive components—resistors and/or inductors and/or capacitors—connected together with series (forward) and shunt (to ground) paths, forming a circuit that typically resembles a ladder. Robert Moog invented a filter that became known as a ladder filter; however, it appears to have gotten the name from a ladder shaped arrangement of transistors and capacitors. From this point on, referring to a ladder filter means the Moog version (as well as the diode ladder filter which follows). This filter might be the most celebrated, copied and tweaked of any designer's filters. Several Integrated Circuit (IC) companies made variations on this circuit including the Curtis CEM3328, CEM3372 and Precision Monolithics PMI SSM2044. They optimized, modified, tweaked and extended the design. The devices were used in countless synthesizers from nearly every company in the 1970s and 1980s. A unique feature of this filter is that changes in resonance create changes in the overall filter gain; as the Q increases, the filter gain drops as shown in Figure 7.25. In addition you can see that the resonant frequency moves slightly as the Q increases. The rolloff slope is 24dB/octave as a fourth order filter.

In the Sallen-Key filter, resonance is formed with a positive feedback loop through a bandpass filter that reinforces the resonant frequency of the filter. The Moog ladder filter also creates a positive feedback path for frequencies at and very near the resonant frequency. It can also self-oscillate at the resonant frequency. The Moog ladder filter consists of a cascade of four first order synchronously tuned LPF stages in a global negative feedback loop as shown in Figure 7.26.

Putting four first order LPFs in series does make a fourth order filter, but it is not yet resonant. The way this filter becomes resonant has to do with the phase response of each first order section. The phase shift at the cutoff frequency is −45 degrees for a first order

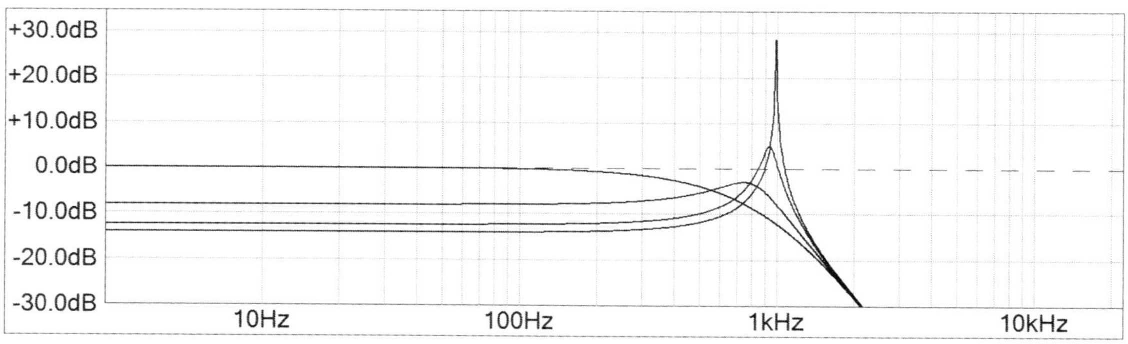

Figure 7.25: The Moog ladder filter at a variety of Q settings.

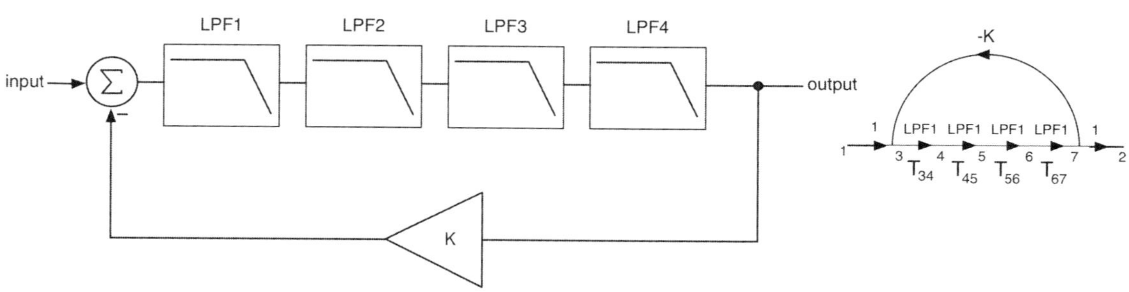

Figure 7.26: The Moog ladder filter topology and analog signal flow graph.

LPF stage. Each stage then adds another −45 degrees of phase shift. After going through four of these filters, the phase shift at the cut-off frequency will be −180 degrees. The output is exactly out of phase with the input. The output is fed back into the input through a negative scalar $-K$, which flips the phase at the cut-off so it is in phase with the input. This amplifies the cutoff frequency and frequencies that are very close to it, resulting in a resonant peak. If $K = 0$ there is no feedback and no resonance. As soon as K becomes non-zero, the Q increases and peaking occurs. When $K = 4$ we achieve 100% feedback through the loop; K needs to be 4 (rather than 1) because the feedback energy is spread across the four first order filters. When $K = 4$ the filter self-oscillates.

7.7 Moog Ladder Filter Gain Compensation

The loss of gain as the Q is increased is sometimes considered problematic, especially if the filter is being used on a bass instrument. However, the reduction in gain also prevents the filter from overloading. Like the Oberhiem SEM and Korg35, there is a built-in mechanism to alleviate clipping. Curtis Electromusic Specialists showed how to control the loss of gain. The filter in the ARP2600 is also a Moog ladder filter derivative that incorporates passband gain compensation. Zavalishin proposes simply boosting the input x by a factor of $1 + K$. By making the boost factor $1 + a$K, a variable version is implemented as shown in Figure 7.27.

7.8 Oberheim Xpander Variations

In 1984, Tom Oberheim modified the ladder filter design for the Xpander synth. He realized that by taking outputs from each of the four LPFs and combining them in various ratios, many new filters could be obtained. The following are some of the variations available (other than the normal fourth order LPF):

- second order LPF
- second order BPF
- fourth order BPF
- second order HPF
- fourth order HPF

Details of how this was accomplished in analog as well as even more filter combinations are in (Oberheim, 1984). The Xpander used a CEM3372 IC, which labels the four LPFs as A, B, C, D. We can label the gain coefficients in the same manner and produce the model in Figure 7.28.

The values of the *A, B, C, D,* and *E* coefficients are listed in Table 7.1 (Välimäki and Huovilainen, 2006), and the frequency responses are plotted in Figure 7.29. You can see that the bandpass filters are of the peaking variety and do not have unity gain passbands. The highpass filter is also not the usual shape but features a dip after resonance. Experimentation shows these are musically useful and will all whistle or self-oscillate under the proper conditions.

7.9 Nonlinear Moog Ladder Filter Models

The analog Moog filter is nonlinear in nature due to the way the transistor ladder differential pairs conduct current. The differential voltage and current relationship uses the *tanh()* function. Huovilainen (2006) proposed a nonlinear model that inserted a *tanh()* block in each first order LPF stage (which was based on a biquad structure) and another in the feedback path. Zavalishin (2012) proposed an "advanced nonlinear model" by inserting two *tanh()* blocks in each trapezoidal integrator, one at the input and another in the feedback path. Välimäki and Huovilainen (2006) and Zavalishin (2012) both proposed "cheap" versions with only one *tanh()* block; for Välimäki it is at the input $x(n)$, while for Zavalishin it is just inside the feedback loop as shown in Figure 7.30. We have also experimented with the same saturating integrator used in the Oberheim SEM model in one or more of the LPF stages. You are urged to experiment with these as well as your own nonlinear variations. Remember that for true self-oscillation, the loop gain must be 4.0 including nonlinear saturation gain. This is why the waveshapers from Chapter 4 feature a saturation control that brings their gain up to, and beyond, unity.

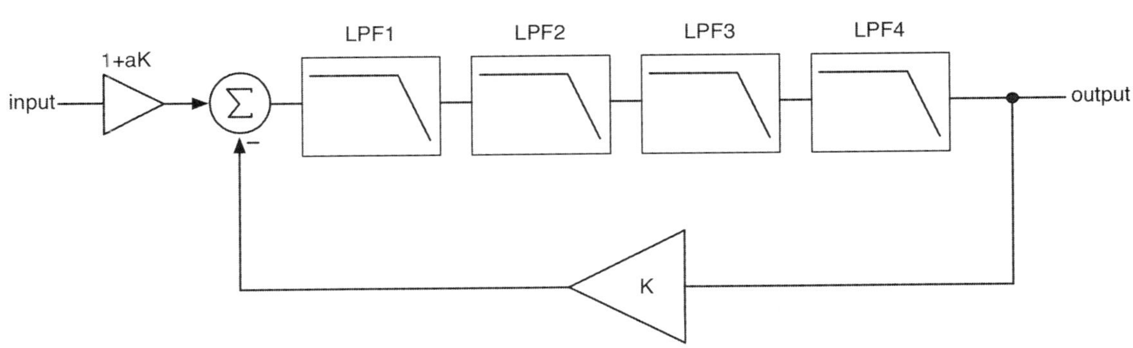

Figure 7.27: Moog ladder filter with passband gain compensation.

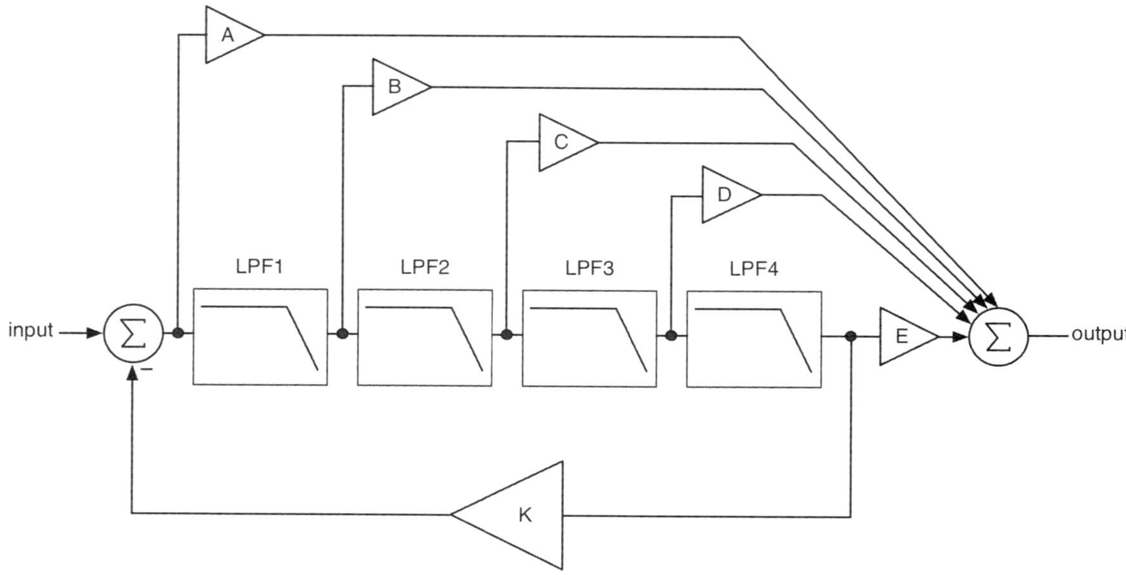

Figure 7.28: The Oberheim ladder filter variations.

Table 7.1: The A, B, C, D and E values for the various filters.

Filter	A	B	C	D	E
Second order LPF	0	0	1	0	0
Fourth order LPF	0	0	0	0	1
Second order BPF	0	2	−2	0	0
Fourth order BPF	0	0	4	−8	4
Second order HPF	1	−2	1	0	0
Fourth order HPF	1	−4	6	−4	1

In 1996 Stilson and Smith implemented a digital version of the Moog ladder filter. Their version features four first order lowpass filters in cascade designed with a modified version of the bilinear to biquad transformation. To deal with the zero delay feedback loop, a unit delay was inserted into the feedback path, which added an extra pole and threw off the tuning of the filter. Välimäki and Huovilainen (2006) proposed a correction factor for bringing the tuning inline using a polynomial curve fit; however, the delay in the feedback path remained and the filter seemed to be over-corrected. Interestingly, the Stilson and Smith Moog Ladder filter is realizable without needing the delay in the feedback path using the Modified Härmä method and bilinear transform filter stages, using the simple first order lowpass biquad design equations in Section 4.6. The tuning of this repaired filter is stable across the full ten octaves of audio. Zavalishin's version simply replaces the first order half-biquad structures with the equivalent first order VA structures and also leaves out the delay in the feedback path.

The Härmä-repaired Silson and Smith filter has an identical frequency response to Zavalishin's version and can likewise self-oscillate. On the downside, it uses twice the memory registers and coefficients as the Zavalishin version and can suffer from coefficient rounding errors. It also performs differently when the cutoff frequency is modulated. In our tests involving modulating the cutoff frequency of each model with a sawtooth LFO, we found differences of −48 dB (~0.4%) in the test residuals, with extreme differences in the way the filter behaves when the cutoff frequency makes a sudden jump at the sawtooth discontinuity. The two filters clearly perform differently under time-varying operation, which Zavalishin (2012) predicts. If you are interested in implementing and comparing the filters, you can get the full Modified Härmä derivation and sample code at http://www.willpirkle.com/synthbook/. We will be implementing our ladder filter using first order VA sections. Its tuning is accurate, it is stable up to Nyquist, and it uses a minimum of memory registers and coefficients. It can also self-oscillate.

The block diagram is fundamentally different from that of the Korg35 model; the multiplier K is in the feedback path, while the filters are in the feed forward branch. Synthesizing the block diagram requires first relating the input to the cascaded filters u to the output y for the filter as shown in Figure 7.31 to resolve the delay less loop.

This time let's use our Modified Härmä method to resolve the delay-less loop and derive the block diagram. We will be using the simple VA One Pole filters in the model, and they have the input/output equations $y = Gx + S$.

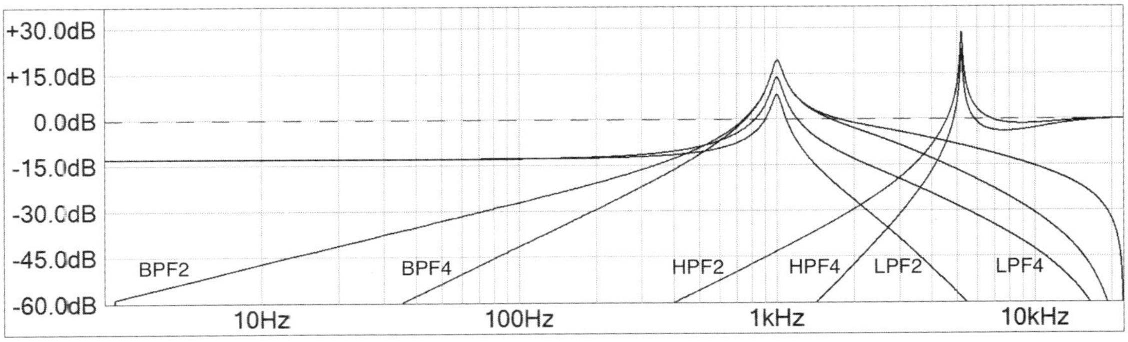

Figure 7.29: The Oberheim Xpander variations; the HPFs have f_c = 5 kHz while all others are f_c = 1 kHz; all filters have K = 3.2.

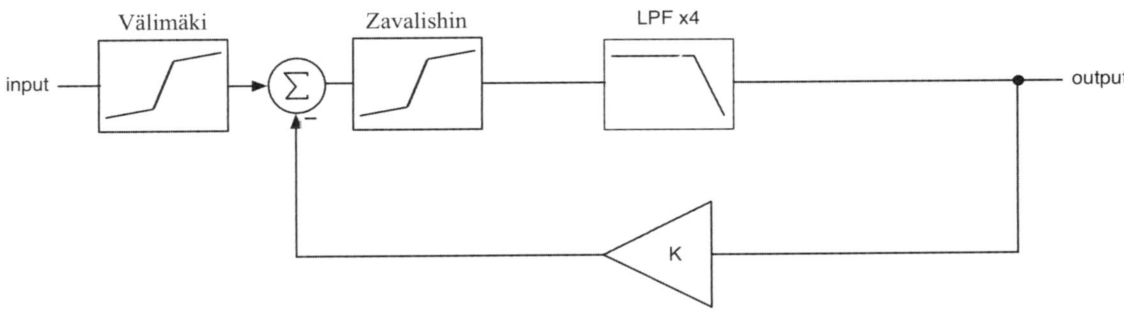

Figure 7.30: Locations of NLPs in Välimäki and Zavalishin's "cheap" nonlinear versions.

Refer to Figure 7.32, which shows the Modified Härmä sequence:

Step 1:

Disconnecting the loop in Figure 7.32(b) and injecting 0.0 into the feedforward path produces a feedback output value of:

$$\begin{aligned} loop\_fb &= -K\left(G^3S1(n) + G^2S2(n) + GS3(n) + S4(n)\right) \\ &= -K\sum(n) \\ \sum(n) &= G^3S1(n) + G^2S2(n) + GS3(n) + S4(n) \end{aligned} \tag{7.18}$$

and a temporary loop input value:

$$u_0(n) = x(n) - K\sum(n) \tag{7.19}$$

Step 2:

Find the temporary output by processing the temporary input through the filter in the feed-forward path:

$$\begin{aligned} y_P(n) &= G^4u_0(n) + G^3S1(n) + G^2S2(n) + GS3(n) + S4(n) \\ &= y_o(n) + y_s(n) \\ y_o(n) &= G^4u_o(n) \\ y_s(n) &= G^3S1(n) + G^2S2(n) + GS3(n) + S4(\text{n}) \\ &let: \\ \Gamma &= G^4 \\ y_P(n) &= \Gamma u_o(n) + \sum(n) \end{aligned} \tag{7.20}$$

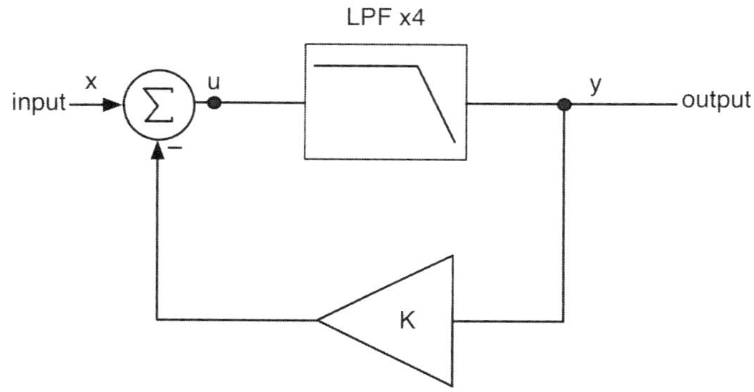

Figure 7.31: The three nodes of the VA ladder filter.

Step 3:

Find the loop gain by removing all delay elements from the original structure, disconnecting the input x and tracing through the loop shown in Figure 7.32(c):

$$\begin{aligned} X &= -KG^4 \\ &= -KT \end{aligned} \tag{7.21}$$

Step 4:

Find the final difference equation and block diagram using Equation 4.39. Figure 7.32 (d) shows the modified structure with delay-less loop resolved. Trace through the block diagram to show that it does indeed implement Equation 4.39.

$$\begin{aligned} y(n) &= \frac{y_o(n)}{1-X} + y_s(n) \\ &= \frac{G^4(x(n) - K\sum(n))}{1+KT} + G^3S1(n) + G^2S2(n) + GS3(n) + S4(n) \end{aligned} \tag{7.22}$$

Step 5:

Find $u(n)$ for filter implementation. Referring to the block diagram, you can see that the loop input value $u(n)$ is the sum of the input $x(n)$ and $y_P(n)$. The result in Figure 7.32(d) shows the abbreviated block diagram for the modified structure that resolves the loop.

$$\begin{aligned} &u(n) = x(n) - Ky_p(n) \\ &\quad and \\ &y_P(n) = \Gamma u(n) + \sum(n) \\ &\quad so \\ &u(n) = \frac{x(n) - K\sum(n)}{1+KT} \end{aligned} \tag{7.23}$$

Figure 7.33 shows the detailed block diagram using the following coefficients:

$$\begin{aligned} &G = \frac{g}{1+g} = \alpha \\ &\quad S1 = \frac{s_1}{1+g} \quad S2 = \frac{s_2}{1+g} \quad S3 = \frac{s_3}{1+g} \quad S4 = \frac{s_4}{1+g} \\ &\quad \text{and} \\ &\sum = \beta_1 s_1 + \beta_2 s_2 + \beta_3 s_3 + \beta_4 s_4 \\ &\quad \beta_1 = \frac{G^3}{1+g} \quad \beta_2 = \frac{G^2}{1+g} \quad \beta_3 = \frac{G}{1+g} \quad \beta_4 = \frac{1}{1+g} \\ &\quad \text{and} \\ &\alpha_0 = \frac{1}{1+KT} \end{aligned} \tag{7.24}$$

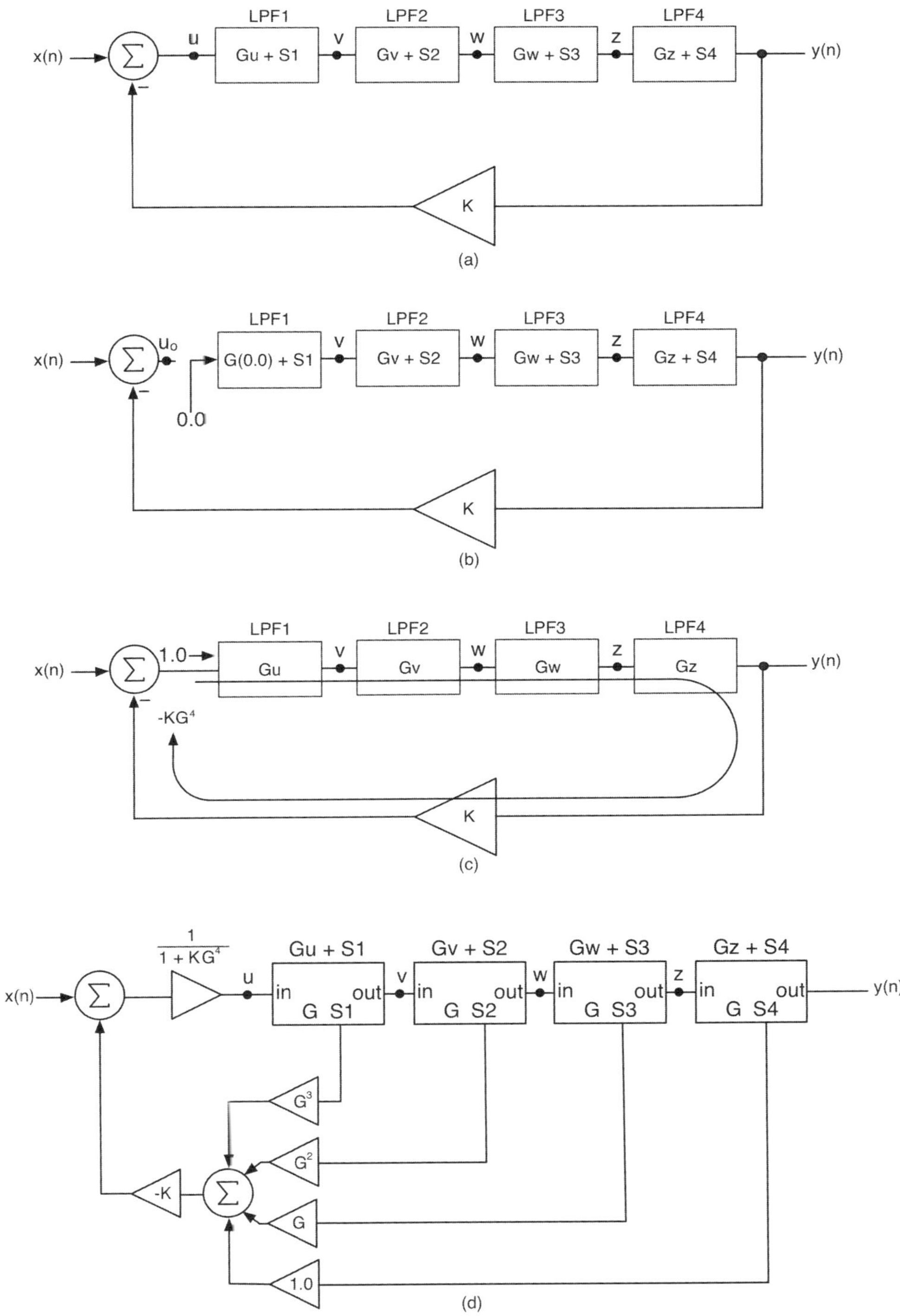

Figure 7.32: The Modified Härmä method: (a) the original filter structure with nodes relabeled (b) breaking the loop to extract the temporary feedback value and calculate u_o and y_o (c) finding the loop gain X and (d) synthesizing the final block diagram with delay-less loop resolved; once again the loops have been relocated to the outputs of the *S* registers.

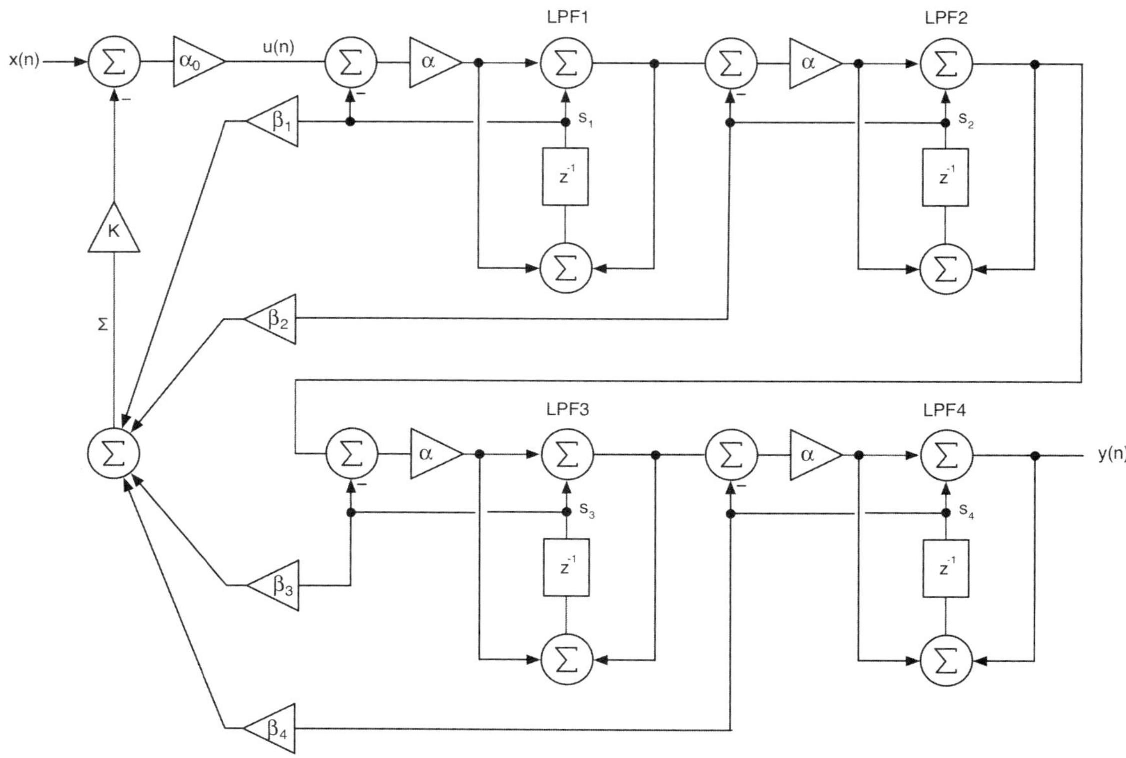

Figure 7.33: Detailed block diagram of the VA Moog ladder filter.

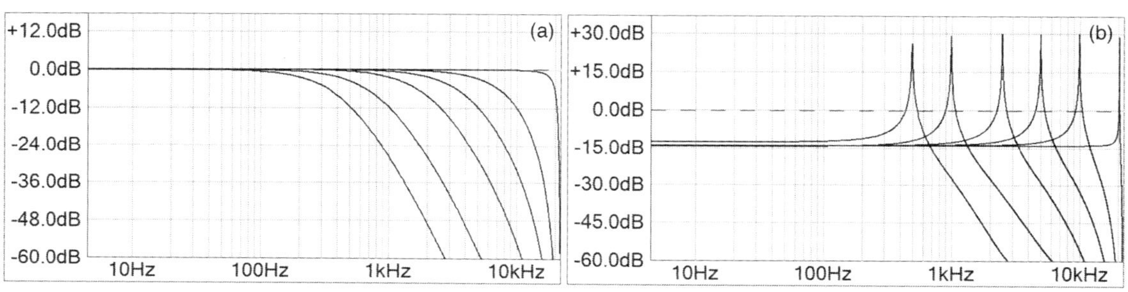

Figure 7.34: Frequency response of the VA Moog ladder filter for (a) K = 0 and (b) K = 3.99 with f_c = 500 Hz, 1 kHz, 2.5 kHz, 5 kHz, 10 kHz and 20,480 Hz.

Look at the block diagram and locate the node marked *u(n)*. It is $\alpha 0x(n)-K\,\Sigma(n)$ or:

$$u(n)=\frac{x(n)-K\sum(n)}{1+KT} \tag{7.25}$$

Figure 7.34 shows the output of the filter at various settings for f_c, with $K = 0$ and $K = 3.99$.

For the nonlinear model, you can choose one of several options; the Välimäki simplification places the NLP at the input prior to the summer, while the Zavalishin cheap version places it after the node *u* and before the first LPF, or you can try using the saturated integrators as in the SEM model.

7.10 The Second Order Moog Half-Ladder Filter

This interesting filter started out as a homework project for students in the University of Miami's music engineering technology program. the name half-ladder is our own invention and not found in the literature. The idea is to use the same Moog ladder loop to create a second order version of the filter. In addition to the second order −12 dB/octave roll off, this filter also looses less bass response as the Q is increased. Figure 7.35 shows the difference between the (a) ordinary and (b) half-ladder filters.

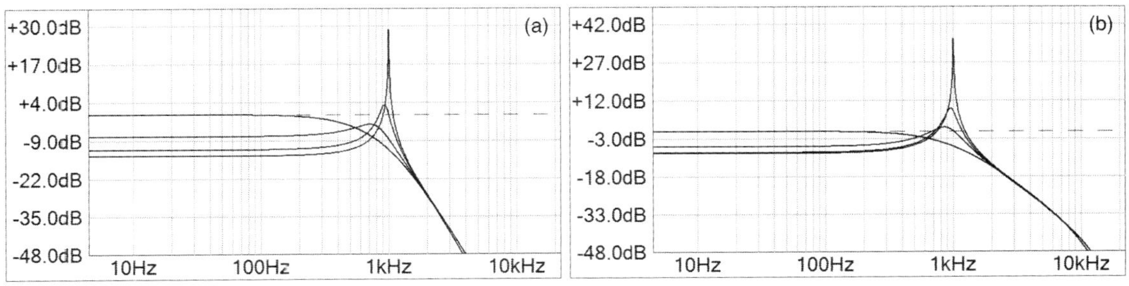

Figure 7.35: Frequency response with f_c = 1 kHz of the (a) ordinary fourth order and K = 0, 2.0, 3.2 and 3.99, and (b) second order half-ladder filter with K = 0, 1.0, 1.6 and 2.0.

In order to use the same topology but reduce the filter order, a first order All Pass Filter (APF) is used to replace two of the LPF blocks. The APF provides the missing −90 degrees of phase shift but does not alter the frequency response and therefore passband gain. Figure 7.36 shows the block diagram of the new second order Moog ladder-based filter. The filter has the typical 12 dB/octave roll-off but with only about −9 dB of passband attenuation. Because there are only two LPFs absorbing energy from the loop, the K value is reduced from −4 to −2 for self-oscillation.

The Virtual Analog APF is shown in Figure 7.37. It is the one-pole VA filter with the outputs subtracted $y_{AP} = y_{LP} - y_{HP}$. As with the other VA implementations, we modify the original structure with a feedback coefficient β to produce the output $\beta s(n)$, which allows simplification of the block diagram and implementation. This single building block is used to implement the three filters in the design.

First, let's look at the VA equation for the APF:

$$
\begin{aligned}
y_{LP} &= Gx + S \\
y_{HP} &= x - Gx - S \\
y_{AP} &= (2G-1)x + 2S \\
&= G_A x + S_A \\
G_A &= 2G - 1 \\
S_A &= 2S
\end{aligned}
\tag{7.26}
$$

Solving for u, the input to the first LPF in the feedback loop (and ignoring the NLP *tanh()* block), we start with the equation for the output y:

$$
\begin{aligned}
y_{LP1} &= Gx + S1 \\
y_{LP2} &= Gx + S2 \\
y_{AP1} &= G_A x + S_A \\
G = \frac{g}{1+g} \quad S1 &= \frac{s_1}{1+g} \quad S2 = \frac{s_2}{1+g} \\
y &= G_A G^2 u + G_A G S1 + G_A S2 + S_A \\
&= G_M u + S_M \\
G_M &= G_A G^2 \\
S_M &= G_A G S1 + G_A S2 + S_A
\end{aligned}
\tag{7.27}
$$

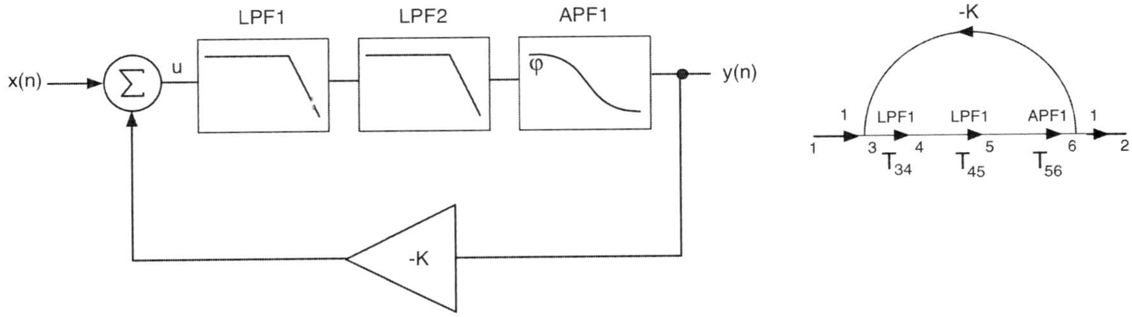

Figure 7.36: The block diagram and signal flow graph for the Moog Half-Ladder Filter.

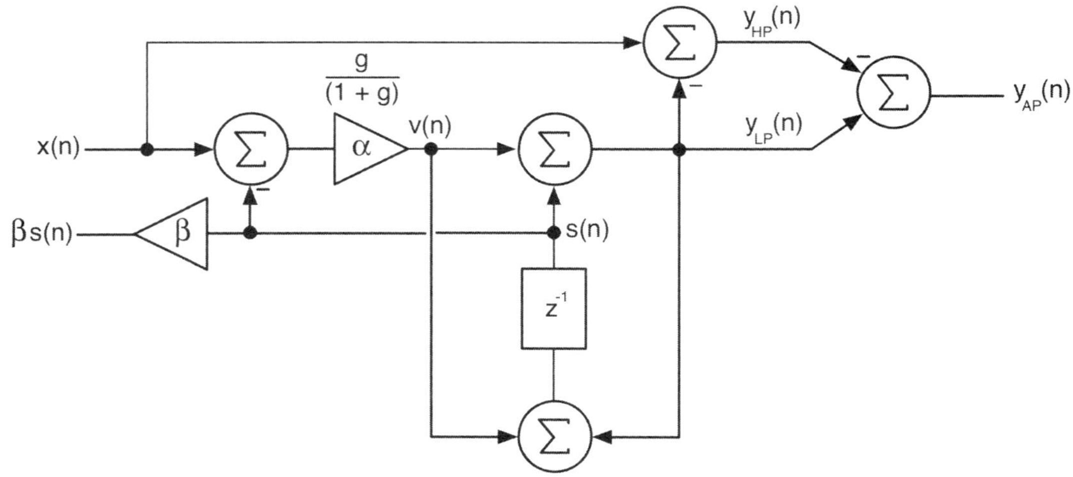

Figure 7.37: APF building block in virtual analog form.

Now rearrange and find u:

$$
\begin{aligned}
u &= \frac{x - KS_M}{1 + KG_M} \\
&\textit{let} \\
&\alpha_0 = \frac{1}{1 + KG_M} \quad \beta_1 = \frac{G_A G}{1+g} \quad \beta_2 = \frac{G_A}{1+g} \quad \beta_3 = \frac{2}{1+g} \\
&\textit{then} \\
u &= \alpha_0 (x - KS_M) \\
&= \alpha_0 (x - K(\beta_1 s_1 + \beta_2 s_2 + \beta_3 s_3))
\end{aligned}
\tag{7.28}
$$

Using the result for u, we can construct a block diagram of the filter, shown in Figure 7.38. The nonlinear processing may also be added in the same potential locations as the previous filter.

7.11 The Diode Ladder Filter Model

The Diode Ladder Filter first appeared in the EMS VCS3 Monophonic Synth designed by David Cockerell in 1969. It is more famously incorporated in the Roland TB-303 BassLine monophonic bass synth from 1982. In 1974, Steiner presented another resonant lowpass filter using diodes, but it implemented the Sallen-Key topology. In 1977, Yamaha patented the ring-diode method of implementing a voltage controlled filter in another Sallen-Key topology, and Korg used yet another Sallen-Key ring-diode variation in numerous synths including the S700. In all cases, the diodes performed the variable-resistance function, and these Sallen-Key versions are unrelated to the diode ladder filter in this section.

This diode ladder filter is based on the Moog ladder filter topology, but uses diodes as voltage controlled resistors rather than transistors, and incorporates multiple feedback paths between sections. The effect of the feedback paths on the signal is two-fold: first, like the Moog Ladder, it reduces overall filter gain as the resonance increases, but the reduction is more extreme (by about 12 dB); and secondly, as the resonance increases, the resonant frequency migrates upwards, but never makes it to the cutoff frequency, which does not occur in the Moog ladder. Like the Moog Ladder, it also self-oscillates. At the point of self-oscillation, the poles (and therefore the resonant peak) will have drifted up to $0.707f_c$. Figure 7.39 shows how the filter's gain changes more drastically than the Moog ladder filter as the loop gain K is varied. In this filter, K ranges from 0 to 17, at which point self-oscillation occurs.

Like the Moog Ladder Filter, the Diode Ladder incorporates four synchronously tuned first order LPFs in series, embedded in a global feedback loop. The negative feedback loop has a gain K, which creates positive feedback only at the cutoff frequency as with the Moog ladder filter. The output is fed back into the input through a negative scalar $-K$, which results in flipping the phase at the cut-off so it is in phase with the input. This amplifies the cutoff frequency and frequencies that are very close to it, resulting in a resonant peak.
If $K = 0$ there is no feedback and no resonance. As soon as K becomes non-zero, the Q increases and peaking occurs. When $K = 17$ we have 100% feedback through the loop. When $K = 17$ the filter self-oscillates.

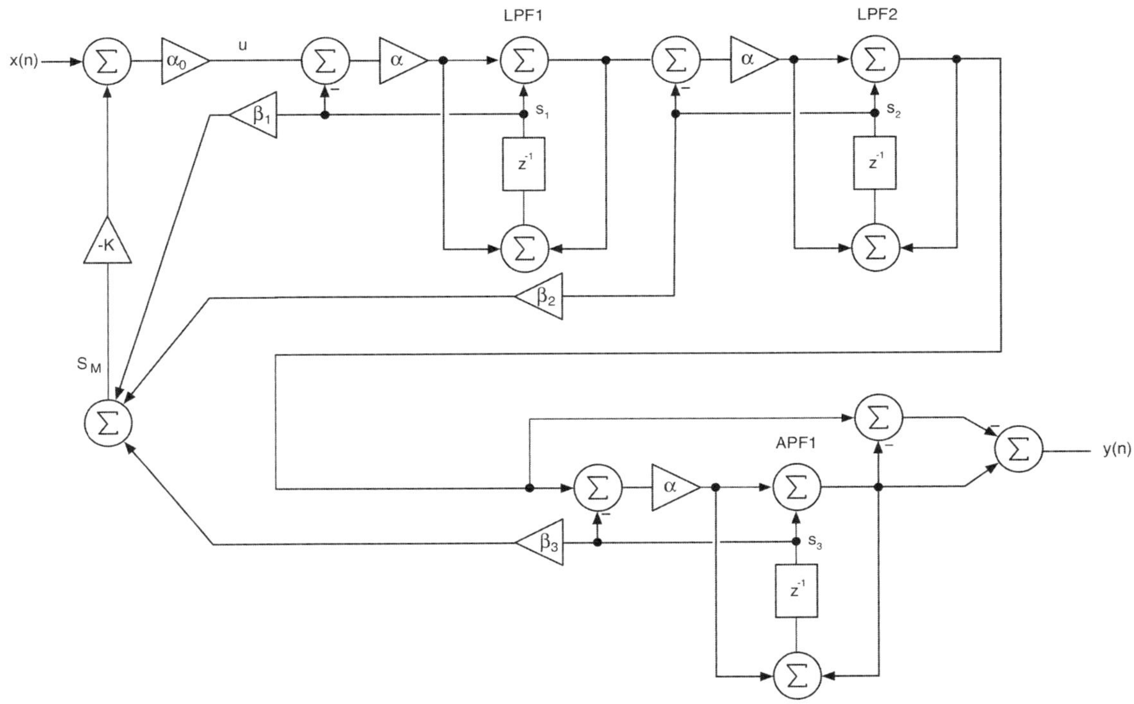

Figure 7.38: The block diagram for the second order Moog Half-Ladder Filter.

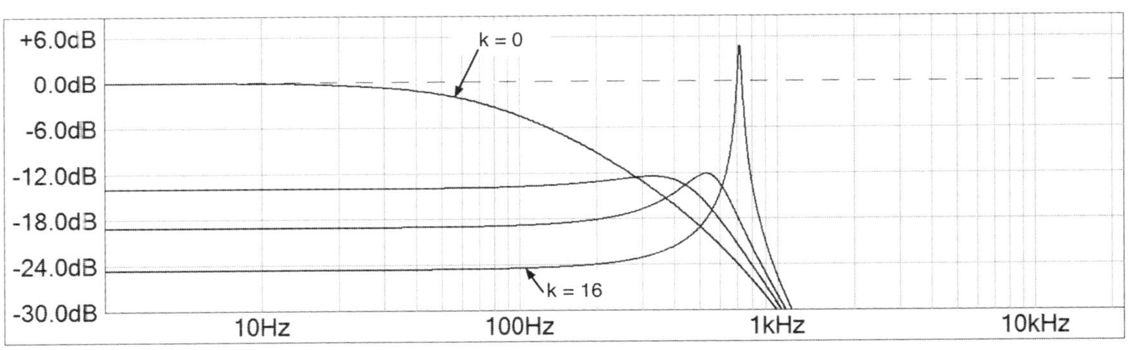

Figure 7.39: The relationship between filter gain and resonance in the Diode ladder filter; f_c = 1 kHz with K = 0, 4, 8, and 16; at K = 16 the filter is approaching self oscillation, and the peak is close to $0.707f_c$.

However, unlike the Moog ladder, the diode ladder structure creates multiple feedback loops around each section (LPF2 feeds back into LPF1, LPF3 feeds back into LPF2, LPF4 feeds back into LPF3) as shown in Figure 7.40 (Zavalishin, 2012). This is a topology known as leap-frog-form (LFF). In addition to the feedback paths, there are also attenuators on the inputs to the last three LPFs.

As with the Moog ladder filter, we can eliminate some or all of the passband gain loss simply by boosting the input x by a factor of $1 + K$. A variable version can then be implemented by making the boost factor $1 + aK$, where a is on the range of 0.0 to 1.0 in the same manner as shown in Figure 7.27. Depending on your taste and the application, you may find that some kind of compensation is needed.

The diode ladder filter is full of nonlinearities. Zavalishin's advanced model places *tanh()* saturators in the input and in local feedback paths around each integrator. As before we can attempt simpler solutions using the same schemes of placing the nonlinear block at the input, just inside the loop after u but before the first LPF or inside each LPF. Because of the massive gain reduction with resonance, placing the nonlinearity at the input seems to preserve the self-oscillatory nature of the filter best while not being technically superior to the others; they are all approximations.

Due to the complex interactions of the multiple feedback paths, the filter analysis and synthesis of the block diagram is much more difficult than any of the filters in this chapter. The full derivation is at http://www.willpirkle.com/synthbook/. Examination of the block

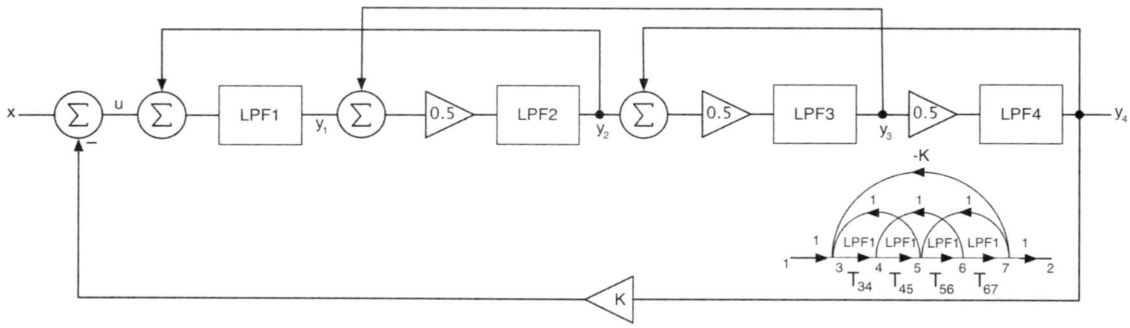

Figure 7.40: Block diagram and analog signal flow graph of the diode ladder filter with intermediate nodes labeled x (input), u, y_1, y_2, y_3 and y_4 (output).

diagram in Figure 7.40 reveals that there are feedback paths cascading backwards; LPF4 feeds back into LPF3, etc., so the block diagram for each LPF section will need to be modified to allow not only feedback outputs to the $N-1$ stage but also feedback inputs from the $N + 1$ stage. The VA design equations for each filter are:

$$\begin{aligned}
&y_4 = G4y_3 + S4 \qquad && G4 = \frac{0.5g}{1+g} \qquad && S4 = \frac{s_4}{1+g}\\
&y_3 = G3y_2 + S3 && G3 = \frac{0.5g}{1+g-0.5gG4} && S3 = \frac{0.5gS4 + s_3}{1+g-0.5gG4}\\
&y_2 = G3y_1 + S2 && G2 = \frac{0.5g}{1+g-0.5gG3} && S2 = \frac{0.5gS3 + s_2}{1+g-0.5gG3}\\
&y_1 = G1x + S1 && G1 = \frac{g}{1+g-gG2} && S1 = \frac{gS2 + s_1}{1+g-gG2}
\end{aligned} \tag{7.29}$$

What we need to do is find x_N for LPF N, where x_N is the input into the filter (or filter with attenuator $a0$) after the feedback summer. Since three of the four LPFs have the 0.5 attenuator, we can roll that coefficient into the filter block diagram (and C++ object). Look at Figure 7.24 and think about the input to LPF3. Solving for this input x_3:

$$\begin{aligned}
x_3 &= y_2 + y_4\\
&= y_2 + G4y_3 + S4\\
&= y_2 + G4(G3y_2 + S3) + S4\\
&= y_2 + G3(G4y_2 + G4S3) + S4\\
&= y_2(1 + G3G4) + G4S3 + S4
\end{aligned} \tag{7.30}$$

The G4 and S4 values represent the feedback components. We need to realize this structure in a block diagram. Isolating just this portion, we could implement it as in Figure 7.41.

The feedback loops and attenuators make for a complex block diagram synthesis. Figure 7.42 shows a modified LPF stage with multiple coefficients to handle the synthesis equations and feedback input and output ports.

There is an implied connection between feedback input and output ports with the same label. Figure 7.43 shows the connection between the last two filters, LPF3 and LPF4. The dotted line shows the implied connection between S4 from LPF4 into LPF3. The

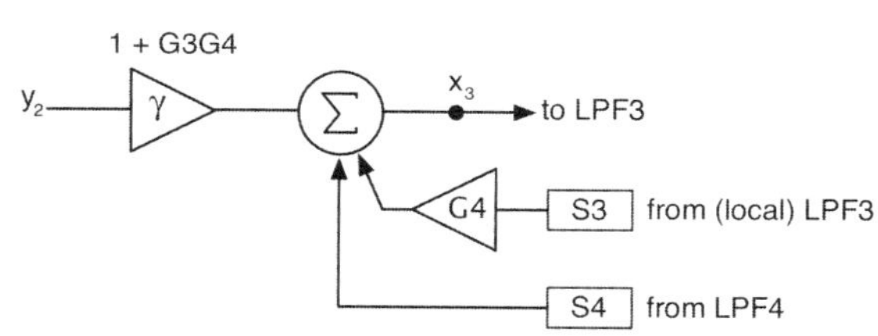

Figure 7.41: Forming the input x_3 for LPF3 by applying the equations directly.

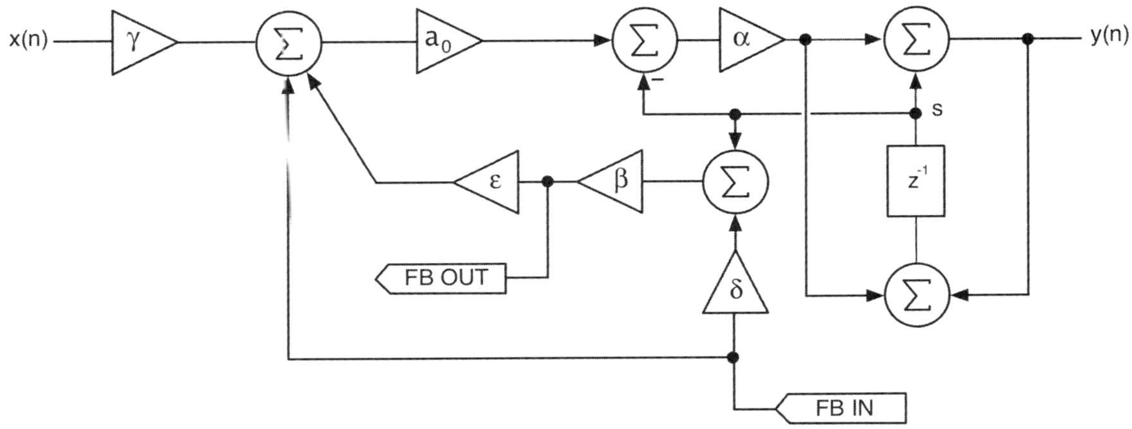

Figure 7.42: A modified one-pole filter stage with feedback input and output ports for the VA diode ladder filter.

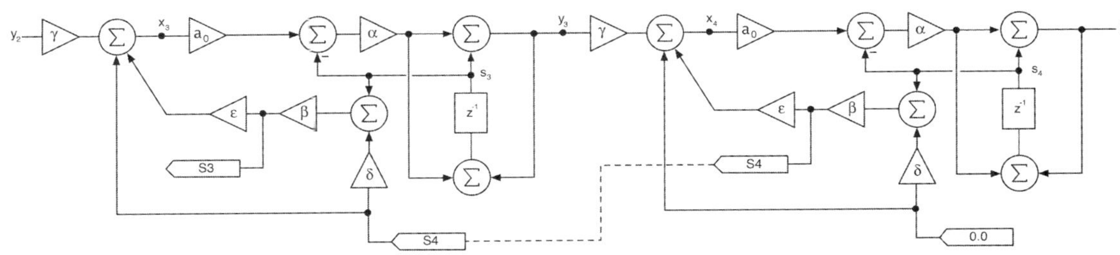

Figure 7.43: The connection between LPF3 and LPF4 shows the implied connection between ports with the same label.

port labeled S3 will connect back into LPF2, whose port S2 will connect back into LPF1. Figure 7.44 shows the compete block diagram for the diode ladder filter. The overall feedback loop uses the same method of calculating the value u that feeds the bank of filters. To insert this series of LPFs into the feedback loop, we use the same method as before and shown in Chapter 4 to find the value of u.

To find the final output y_4 of the series connection, you solve Equations 7.29–7.30 by substituting one into the other. This is not a trivial operation, so see the website for a full derivation.

$$y_4 = G4y_3 + S4 = G4(G3y_2 + S3) + S4 = G4(G3(G2y_1 + S2) + S3) + S4 ... etc$$

$$\begin{aligned} y_4 &= G4G3G2G1x + G4G3G2S1 + G4G3S2 + G4S3 + S4 \\ &= \Gamma x + \sum \\ \Gamma &= G4G3G2G1 \\ \sum &= G4G3G2S1 + G4G3S2 + G4S3 + S4 \\ & and \\ u &= \frac{x - K\sum}{1 + KT} \end{aligned} \tag{7.31}$$

We changed the notation to capital Greek letters to avoid confusion with all the other G and S terms. We can implement u by observing that $1/1 + K\Gamma$ is a scalar value, so the input will be the difference of x and $K\Sigma$ multiplied by $1/1 + k\Gamma$, where Σ is the sum of S's.

In Figure 7.44 we have labeled the nodes G4, G3 and G2 in each filter stage. These contribute to the global feedback path around the entire structure eventually being summed and multiplied by the loop gain K. The a_0 coefficients in each block represent the attenuators of 0.5 for the last three LPFs, and it is set to 1.0 for the first LPF as per Figure 7.24. Figure 7.45 shows the frequency response for the filter with various values for f_c with K = 16.0 and no NLP.

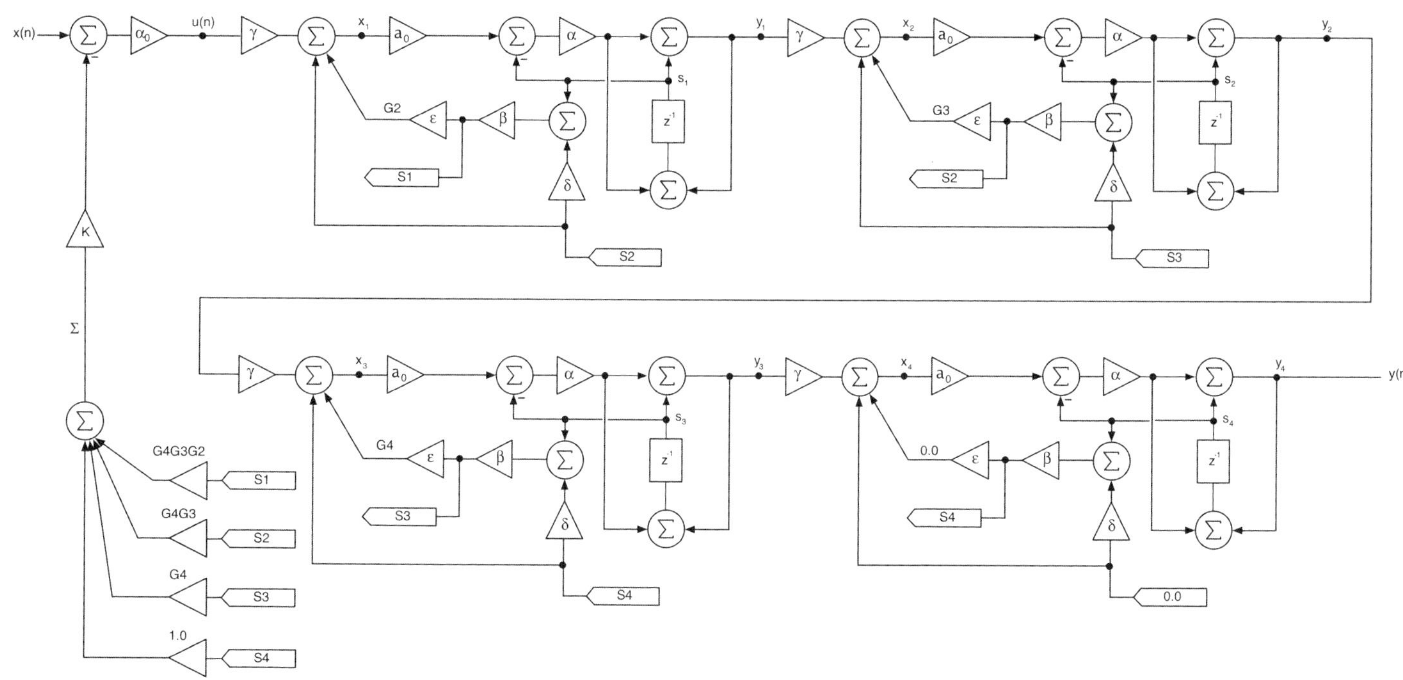

Figure 7.44: The complete diode ladder filter block diagram.

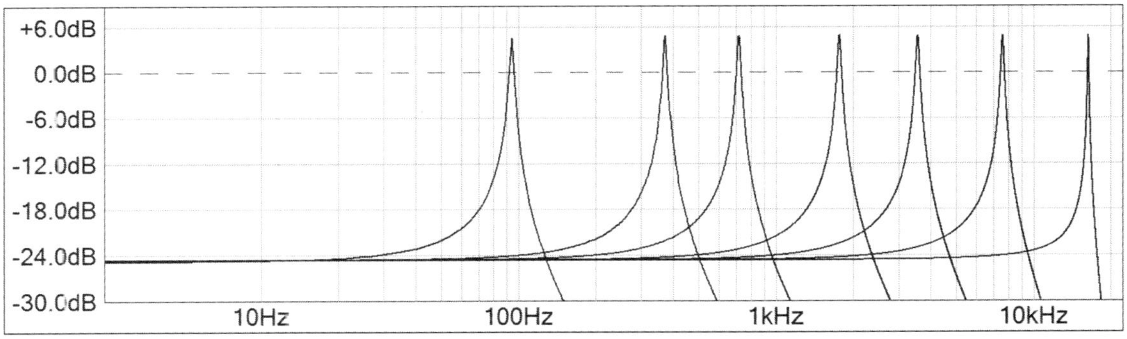

Figure 7.45: The filter's response is consistent across the spectrum; here K = 16 and f_c is 100 Hz, 500 Hz, 1 kHz, 2.5 kHz, 5 kHz, 10 kHz and 20,480 Hz.

7.12 Designing the Filter Objects

It's time to design our C++ objects that will handle the filtering duties of our synth projects. We are going to design a separate C++ object for each of the five categories of filters in the chapter. This will result in a total of 15 filters for you to choose from in your own projects.

- *CVAOnePoleFlter*: the first order VA LPF and HPF
- *CSEMFilter*: the Oberheim SEM LPF, HPF, BPF and variable BSF
- *CKThreeFiveFilter*: the Korg35 second order LPF and HPF
- *CMoogLadderFilter*: the Moog ladder fourth order LPF, plus all the Oberheim variations (LPF2, HPF2, HPF4, BPF2, BPF4)
- *CDiodeLadderFilter*: the diode ladder fourth order LPF

All filters are derived from an abstract base class called *CFilter*. The base class object will handle modulating the cutoff frequency since it is the same for all filters. All filters except the first order LPF and HPF can optionally feature nonlinear processing. The *CFilter* object will define the user interface variables and controls. An *Aux Control* will be assigned to the variable BSF control in the SEM filter and to passband gain compensation in the ladder filters. You may optionally use it for whatever you wish in the other models. We will design and code all the filters first. Then we will add the Moog ladder filter to NanoSynth. You can then test all the other filters. This is simplified since all filters are derived from the same object and have the same core functions.

As with most synths, our filters will use an exponential cutoff frequency GUI control, known as a "volt/octave" control. As the user moves the control, the cutoff frequency varies by the octave, producing a more musically useful control. In addition, modulating the cutoff frequency will also be exponential in nature. The file *synthfunctions.h* has the necessary functions to assist in the exponential control and modulation. All filters are stable over a full ten octave range of cutoff frequencies from 20 Hz to 20,480 Hz. In our synth designs, however, we limit the range of operation to 80 Hz to 18 kHz, though you may certainly change this if you like. As with many synths, the Q control will be labeled simply from 1 to 10, and we will map this according to the filter type. For the SEM filter, this will become a value for Q between 0.5 (critically damped) and 25 (highly resonant), while for the others it will be converted to a value for the filter feedback gain K. All filters will use the same nonlinear processing block consisting of the *tanh()* function and a saturation control. The saturation control will range from 1 (none) to 2 (+6 dB) providing ample distortion.

7.13 The CFilter Base Class

The *CFilter* base class exposes the filter interface. It stores all variables that are common to all models as well as provides mutators (*set()* methods) for modulation inputs. Virtual functions are provided so the derived class filters may override them and implement their own special functionality. Table 7.2 lists the *CFilter* member variables and methods. Figure 7.46 shows the detailed and simplified block diagram for a filter. Things to note about the block diagrams:

- the filter is always shown as a lowpass type but of course may be any type or switchable between types (for example, the Moog ladder with Oberheim variations)
- in the detailed block diagram, the NLP block is shown inline after the filter; this is not accurate since the NLP block exists within the filter structure in different locations depending on filter model

The easiest way to understand the object is to step through the functions and discuss them. Open the *Filter.h* and *.cpp* files and examine the functions. At the top of the *Filter.h* file, you will find the default and constant declarations used for setting limits, clamping values and calculating the modulation variable. Here is where you may adjust the range of the filter's cutoff frequency

Table 7.2: The *CFilter* member variables and methods.

CFilter public Member Variables		
Type	**Variable Name**	**Description**
double	m_dFcControl	the GUI cutoff frequency [80 Hz..18 kHz]
double	m_dQControl	the GUI Q value [1..10]
double	m_dAuxControl	a spare control; used in SEM and ladder filters
double	m_dSaturation	saturation control for NLP
UINT	m_uFilterType	selected filter type
UINT	m_uNLP	NLP on/off switch
enum	LPF1,HPF1,LPF2,HPF2, BPF2,BSF2,LPF4,HPF4,BPF4	various filter types
enum	OFF, ON	on/off for NLP

CFilter protected Member Variables		
Type	**Variable Name**	**Description**
double	m_dSampleRate	the sample rate
double	m_dFc	the current cutoff frequency value
double	m_dQ	the current Q value
double	m_dFcMod	the cutoff frequency modulation input

CFilter Member Functions (non virtual)	
Function Name	**Description**
setFcMod	sets the modulation value for cutoff frequency

CFilter Member Functions (virtual)	
Function Name	**Description**
doFilter (pure abstract)	performs the filtering operation on an input to produce an output; all filters are monophonic
setSampleRate	set the sample rate
reset	reset the filter
setQControl	calculate the Q control; must be overridden by any filter with Q
Update	recalculate the filter variables

if you wish. You must calculate the number of semitones between the lower and upper cutoff limit and divide this value by two. The *semitonesBetweenFrequencies()* function is provided for you in *synthfunctions.h*, and we will use it in other places later on.

```
// 46.881879936465680 = semitonesBetweenFrequencies(80, 18000.0)/2.0
#define FILTER_FC_MOD_RANGE 46.881879936465680
#define FILTER_FC_MIN 80            // 80 Hz
#define FILTER_FC_MAX 18000         // 18 kHz
#define FILTER_FC_DEFAULT 10000     // 10 kHz
#define FILTER_Q_DEFAULT 0.707      // Butterworth
```

Now let's get to the methods themselves in the *Filter.h* and *Filter.cpp* files.

Constructor:

- initialize all variables
- NLP is OFF by default (you can change that here)

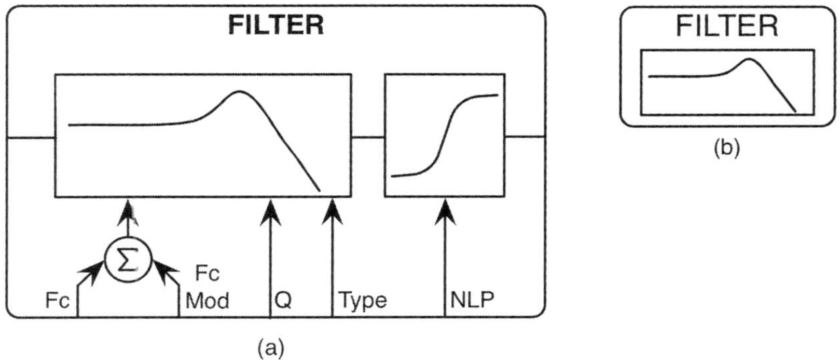

Figure 7.46: (a) Detailed and (b) simple filter block diagrams.

```
CFilter::CFilter(void)
{
	// --- defaults
	m_dSampleRate = 44100;
	m_dQControl = 1.0; // Q is 1 to 10 on GUI
	m_dFc = FILTER_FC_DEFAULT;
	m_dQ = FILTER_Q_DEFAULT;
	m_dFcControl = FILTER_FC_DEFAULT;

	// --- clear
	m_dFcMod = 0.0;
	m_dAuxControl = 0.0;
	m_uNLP = OFF;
	m_dSaturation = 1.0;
}
```

setFcMod() and setSampleRate()

These simple mutators just set the underlying variables. You can override them if needed.

```
inline void setFcMod(double d){m_dFcMod = d;}
inline virtual void setSampleRate(double d){m_dSampleRate = d;}
```

reset() and setQControl()

These functions must be overridden in the derived class. They have empty (blank) implementations in the base class. They are coded in case you need to add anything later.

doFilter()

This is the only pure virtual function on the object. This has two ramifications: derived classes must override this method, and the *CFilter* object is pure abstract, so it can not be instantiated on its own. The function takes an input *xn* and produces the filtered output.

```
virtual double doFilter(double xn) = 0;
```

update()

The *update()* function will be called once per sample period. It performs the calculation for cutoff frequency modulation in exponential form using the *pitchShiftMultiplier()* function that we also use when modulating oscillator pitch. The *setQControl()* function is called in case you are modulating the Q value (this is a Chapter Challenge) since it too would need to be re-calculated on each sample interval.

```
inline virtual void update()
{
      // --- update Q (filter-dependent)
      setQControl(m_dQControl);

      // --- do the modulation freq shift
      m_dFc = m_dFcControl*pitchShiftMultiplier(m_dFcMod);

      // --- bound the final frequency
      if(m_dFc &;g FILTER_FC_MAX)
            m_dFc = FILTER_FC_MAX;
      if(m_dFc < FILTER_FC_MIN)
            m_dFc = FILTER_FC_MIN;
}
```

The *CFilter* object is fairly short and simple. Now let's use it as a base class and design all the rest of the filters in the chapter starting with the VA one-pole filters.

7.14 The CVAOnePoleFilter Object

The *CVAOnePoleFilter* object is required for all of the filters except the SEM model. The others all contain multiple instances of lowpass and highpass versions of the VA one-pole filter. Fortunately, this is a simple structure. However, we need to prepare ahead and make sure it will function properly in all filters. Figure 7.47(a) shows the most simple form of the one-pole filter that implements both first order lowpass and highpass functions. Figure 7.47(b) shows the modified lowpass structure for the diode ladder filter. Figure 7.47(b) turns into Figure 7.47(a) under the following conditions:

$$\gamma = 1.0 \qquad a_0 = 1.0 \qquad \beta = 0.0 \qquad \varepsilon = 0.0 \qquad \delta = 0.0 \tag{7.32}$$

So if we default to these values, then the structure is immediately useful in its simple first order lowpass/highpass configuration.

We need to implement the storage register and all filter parameters as member variables. We will also provide functions to get or set the feedback input on the structure. Figure 7.48 shows the class diagram for the *CVAOnePoleFilter* object. The member variables are straightforward—they represent all of the values and coefficients in the structure. Let's step through the functions.

Constructor:

- initialize the member variables
- set our default filter type (LPF1)
- call *reset()* to flush the register

```
CVAOnePoleFilter::CVAOnePoleFilter(void)
{
      // --- init defaults to simple
      //     LPF/HPF structure
      m_dAlpha = 1.0;
      m_dBeta = 0.0;
      m_dZ1 = 0.0;
      m_dGamma = 1.0;
      m_dDelta = 0.0;
      m_dEpsilon = 0.0;
      m_da0 = 1.0;
      m_dFeedback = 0.0;

      // --- always set the default!
      m_uFilterType = LPF1;

      // --- flush storage
      reset();
}
```

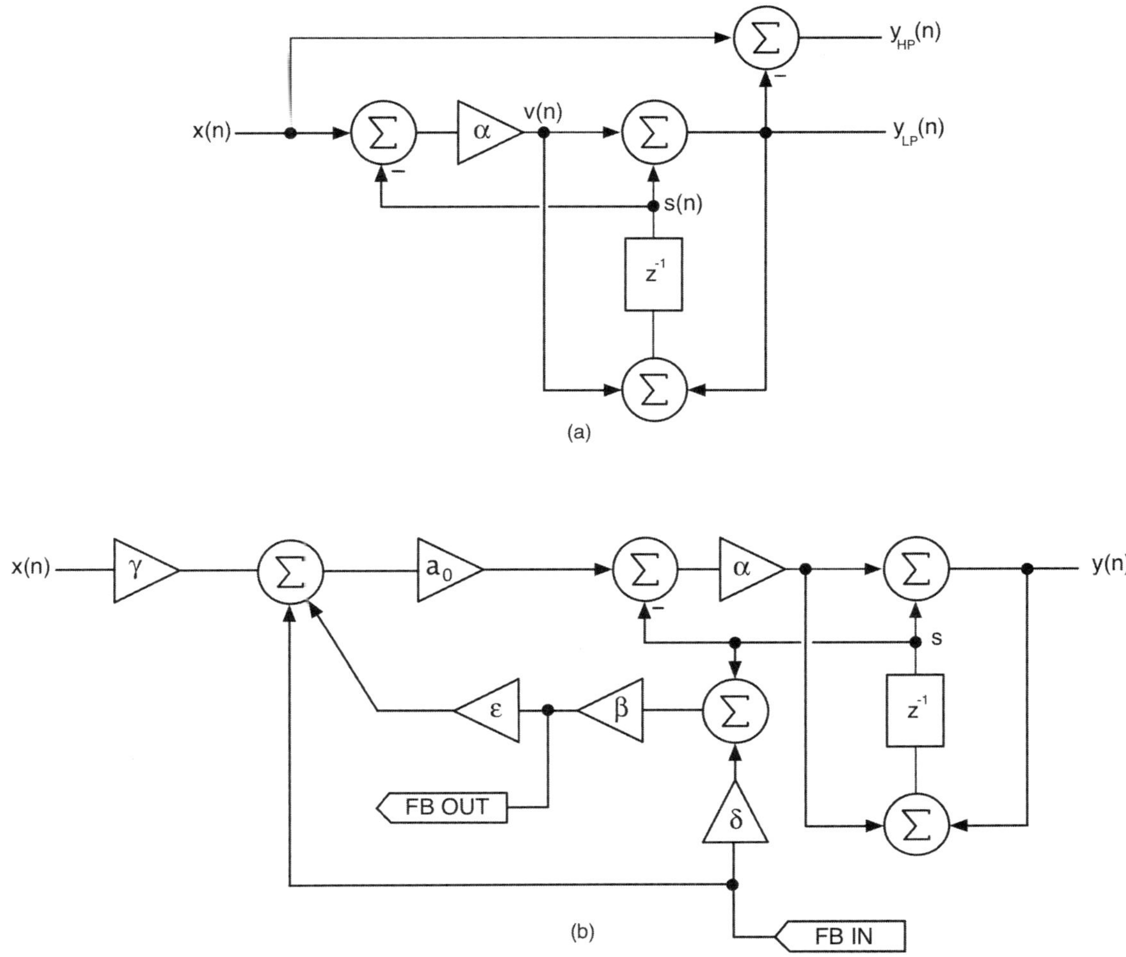

Figure 7.47: (a) The simple first order lowpass/highpass structure and (b) the more complex structure required for the diode ladder filter.

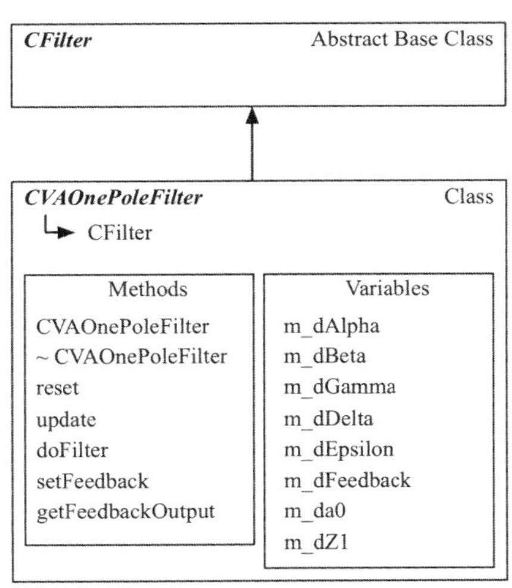

Figure 7.48: The class diagram for the CVAOnePoleFilter.

update()

- call the base class to modulate the filter f_c
- as with all bilinear filters, we need to pre-warp the cutoff frequency
- apply warped cutoff to the alpha coefficient
- you can experiment with both the *tan()* and *tan()* functions

```
void CVAOnePoleFilter::update()
{
	// base class does modulation, changes m_fFc
	CFilter::update();

	double wd = 2*pi*m_dFc;
	double T  = 1/m_dSampleRate;
	double wa = (2/T)*tan(wd*T/2);
	double g  = wa*T/2;

	m_dAlpha  = g/(1.0 + g);
}
```

setFeedback(), getFeedbackOutput and reset()

These are all simple functions that get, set and clear values. Refer back to Figure 7.47(b) to understand the *getFeedbackOutput()* function. The variable *m_dZ1* is the storage register value, the output of which is node *s(n)* in our structures.

```
// set feedback
void setFeedback(double fb) {m_dFeedback = fb;}

// provide access to our feedback output
// m_dFeedback & m_dDelta = 0 for non-Diode filters
double getFeedbackOutput() {return m_dBeta*(m_dZ1 + m_dFeedback*m_dDelta);}

// flush storage and clear feedback
virtual void reset() {m_dZ1 = 0; m_dFeedback = 0;}
```

doFilter()

The sequence of calculations for the trapezoidal integrator LPF and HPF consist of:

- calculate the intermediate variable *v(n)*
- form the output by adding the storage value
- update the storage location with new value
- form the HPF output
- return the proper output

This function also implements the added code for the diode ladder structure.

```
double CVAOnePoleFilter::doFilter(double xn)
{
	// --- return xn if filter not supported
	if(m_uFilterType != LPF1 && m_uFilterType != HPF1)
		return xn;

	// --- see diode filter structure
	xn = xn*m_dGamma + m_dFeedback + m_dEpsilon*getFeedbackOutput();
```

```
    // --- calculate v(n)
    double vn = (m_da0*xn - m_dZ1)*m_dAlpha;

    // --- form LP output
    double lpf = vn + m_dZ1;

    // --- update memory
    m_dZ1 = vn + lpf;

    // --- do the HPF
    double hpf = xn - lpf;

    // --- select output
    if(m_uFilterType == LPF1)
          return lpf;
    else if(m_uFilterType == HPF1)
          return hpf;

    return xn; // should never get here
}
```

7.15 The CSEM Filter Object

The SEM based model is the only one that does not use the VA one-pole filters we just coded; it has its own architecture. We will be implementing the block diagram from Figure 7.6, so you need to be familiar with it. Figure 7.49 shows the class diagram for the object.

Like the *CVAOnePoleFilter*, this object's member variables are self-explanatory when referring to the block diagram and equations. The methods are all base class overrides, so let's step through them.

Constructor:

- initivalize all variables
- initialize filter type to LPF2
- set the Aux Control to 0.5, which centers the control for the BSF output
- call *reset()* to flush storage registers

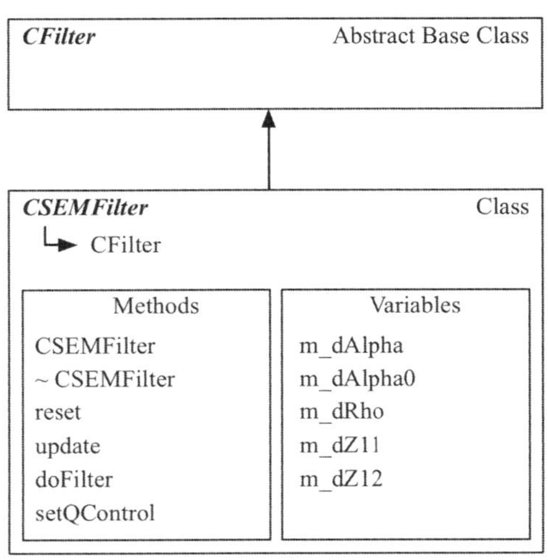

Figure 7.49: The CSEMFilter class diagram.

```
CSEMFilter::CSEMFilter(void)
{
	// --- init
	m_dAlpha0 = 1.0;
	m_dAlpha = 1.0;
	m_dRho = 1.0;
	m_dAuxControl = 0.5; // for BSF

	//--- our default filter type
	m_uFilterType = LPF2;

	// --- flush registers
	reset();
}
```

resetv()

This simple function just clears the storage registers.

```
virtual void reset() {m_dZ11 = 0; m_dZ12 = 0.0;}
```

setQControl()

The Q control on the GUI is always labeled 1 to 10 or a range of [1..10], and this needs to be remapped to a meaningful value for each filter. We will let the filter's actual Q vary from 0.5 to 25 over this range. The mapping function is straightforward.

```
void CSEMFilter::setQControl(double dQControl)
{
	// this maps dQControl = 1->10 to Q = 0.5->25
	m_dQ = (25.0 - 0.5)*(dQControl - 1.0)/(10.0 - 1.0) + 0.5;
}
```

update()

This function recalculates the filter parameters from the current cutoff and Q values. It uses the equations in Section 7.2 for the parameter calculations.

- always call base class first in the update method
- as with all bilinear filters we need to pre-warp the cutoff frequency

```
void CSEMFilter::update()
{
	// base class does modulation
	CFilter::update();

	// pre-warp the cutoff- these are bilinear-transform filters
	double wd = 2*pi*m_dFc;
	double T = 1/m_dSampleRate;
	double wa = (2/T)*tan(wd*T/2);
	double g = wa*T/2;

	// note R is the traditional analog damping factor
	double R = 1.0/(2.0*m_dQ);
```

```
        // set the coeffs
        m_dAlpha0 = 1.0/(1.0 + 2.0*R*g + g*g);
        m_dAlpha = g;
        m_dRho = 2.0*R + g;
}
```

doFilter()

The *doFilter()* function performs the processing. Its code is extracted directly from the filter block diagram. It calculates all outputs and then returns the appropriate output. As with all other filters, you must first check to make sure the filter is supported (this makes it easier to implement multiple filter selection in your plug-in).

- check to make sure filter is supported, otherwise return the input value
- calculate the HPF output (which is *u*, the input to the first block)
- process to get the BPF
- saturate the integrator, if NLP is ON
- process the BSF with the Aux Control
- update the filter
- decide on what to output

```
double CSEMFilter::doFilter(double xn)
{
        // return xn if filter not supported
        if(m_uFilterType != LPF2 && m_uFilterType != HPF2 &&
        m_uFilterType != BPF2 && m_uFilterType != BSF2)
                return xn;

        // form the HP output first
        double hpf = m_dAlpha0*(xn - m_dRho*m_dZ11 - m_dZ12);

        // BPF Out
        double bpf = m_dAlpha*hpf + m_dZ11;

        // for nonlinear proc
        if(m_uNLP == ON)
                bpf = tanh(m_dSaturation*bpf);

        // LPF Out
        double lpf = m_dAlpha*bpf + m_dZ12;

        // note R is the traditional analog damping factor
        double R = 1.0/(2.0*m_dQ);

        // BSF Out
        double bsf = xn - 2.0*R*bpf;

        // SEM BPF Output
        // using m_dAuxControl for this one-off control
        double semBSF = m_dAuxControl*hpf + (1.0 - m_dAuxControl)*lpf;

        // update memory
        m_dZ11 = m_dAlpha*hpf + bpf;
        m_dZ12 = m_dAlpha*bpf + lpf;
```

```
        // return our selected type
        if(m_uFilterType == LPF2)
              return lpf;
        else if(m_uFilterType == HPF2)
              return hpf;
        else if(m_uFilterType == BPF2)
              return bpf;
        else if(m_uFilterType == BSF2)
              return semBSF;

        // return input if filter not supported
        return xn;
}
```

7.16 The CKThreeFiveFilter Object

The object we will design will implement both the lowpass and highpass varieties of the Korg35 Sallen-Key filter. The Korg35 model uses the VA one-pole filter objects we already designed. They do the processing, so the filter object needs to handle the calculating and updating of these blocks and the final processing. The same four *CFilter* overrides will also be implemented. Figure 7.50 shows the class diagram for the *CKThreeFiveFilter*.

CKThreeFiveFilter Member Variables

Refer to Figure 7.19 to see that there are three sub-filters: LPF1, LPF2 and HPF1, as well as two coefficients, the *K* value and f_0. These will make up the member variables of the object. To make the LPF, we need two first order LPFs and one first order HPF. To make the HPF, we need two first order HPFs and one first order LPF. Therefore, we need two of each type for the implementation. These are declared as member objects of type *CVAOnePoleFilter* and named *m_LPF1*, *m_LPF2*, *m_HPF1* and *m_HPF2*.

CKThreeFiveFilter Member Methods

Constructor:

- initialize the member variables
- set default type to second order LPF
- reset to flush storage registers

```
CKThreeFiveFilter::CKThreeFiveFilter(void)
{
        // --- init
        m_dK = 0.01;
        m_dAlpha0 = 0;

        // --- set filter types
        m_LPF1.setFilterType(LPF1);
        m_LPF2.setFilterType(LPF1);
        m_HPF1.setFilterType(HPF1);
        m_HPF2.setFilterType(HPF1);

        // --- default filter type
        m_uFilterType = LPF2;

        // --- flush everything
        reset();
}
```

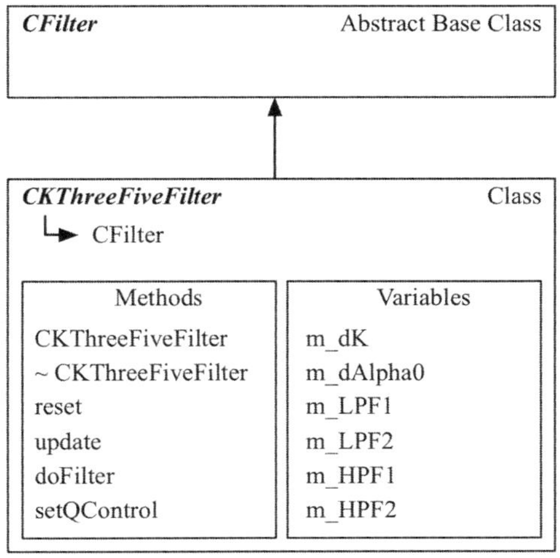

Figure 7.50: The class diagram for the CKThreeFiveFilter.

reset()

- call *reset()* on the member objects; nothing for us to reset in the main outer object

```
void CKThreeFiveFilter::reset()
{
      // flush everything
      m_LPF1.reset();
      m_LPF2.reset();
      m_HPF1.reset();
      m_HPF2.reset();
}
```

setQControl()

- map the Q control on the GUI (1 to 10) to a range of K values 0.01 to 2 (self-oscillation)
- use the same simple equation to map ranges

```
void CKThreeFiveFilter::setQControl(double dQControl)
{
      // this maps dQControl = 1->10 to K = 0.01 -> 2
      m_dK = (2.0 - 0.01)*(dQControl - 1.0)/(10.0 - 1.0) + 0.01;
}
```

update()

- always call the base class method first
- pre-warp the cutoff and set the α value on each member object
- calculate the β feedback values
- set coefficients according to the equations

```
void CKThreeFiveFilter::update()
{
      // do any modulation first
      CFilter::update();
```

```
        // pre-warp for BZT
        double wd = 2*pi*m_dFc;
        double T  = 1/m_dSampleRate;
        double wa = (2/T)*tan(wd*T/2);
        double g  = wa*T/2;

        // G - the feedforward coeff in the VA One Pole
        //     same for LPF, HPF
        double G = g/(1.0 + g);

        // set alphas; same for LPF, HPF
        m_LPF1.m_dAlpha = G;
        m_LPF2.m_dAlpha = G;
        m_HPF1.m_dAlpha = G;
        m_HPF2.m_dAlpha = G;

        // set m_dAlpha0 variable; same for LPF, HPF
        m_dAlpha0 = 1.0/(1.0 - m_dK*G + m_dK*G*G);

        if(m_uFilterType == LPF2)
        {
                m_LPF2.m_dBeta = (m_dK - m_dK*G)/(1.0 + g);
                m_HPF1.m_dBeta = -1.0/(1.0 + g);
        }
        else // HPF
        {
                m_HPF2.m_dBeta = -1.0*G/(1.0 + g);
                m_LPF1.m_dBeta = 1.0/(1.0 + g);
        }
}
```

doFilter()

- check to make sure filter is supported, otherwise return the input value
- both filters follow the same basic sequences (refer to text above)
- process input through the input filter (LPF or HPF)
- form the feedback term named S35 here
- calculate u, the input to the next filter
- add NLP if desired
- calculate the output $y = \alpha0(y1 + S35)$ and multiply it by K
- feed the output to the filter in the feedback loop (HPF or BPF depending on type)
- normalize the output by $1/K$

```
double CKThreeFiveFilter::doFilter(double xn)
{
        // return xn if filter not supported
        if(m_uFilterType != LPF2 && m_uFilterType != HPF2)
                return xn;

        double y = 0.0;
```

```
        // two filters to implement
        if(m_uFilterType == LPF2)
        {
                // process input through LPF1
                double y1 = m_LPF1.doFilter(xn);

                // form S35
                double S35 = m_HPF1.getFeedbackOutput() +
                             m_LPF2.getFeedbackOutput();

                // calculate u
                double u = m_dAlpha0*(y1 + S35);
                // NLP
                if(m_uNLP == ON)
                        u = tanh(m_dSaturation*u);

                // feed it to LPF2, then add gain K
                y = m_dK*m_LPF2.doFilter(u);

                // feed y to HPF
                m_HPF1.doFilter(y);
        }
        else // HPF
        {
                // process input through HPF1
                double y1 = m_HPF1.doFilter(xn);

                // form S35
                double S35 = m_HPF2.getFeedbackOutput() +
                             m_LPF1.getFeedbackOutput();

                // calculate u
                double u = m_dAlpha0*y1 + S35;

                // form output
                y = m_dK*u;

                // NLP
                if(m_uNLP == ON)
                        y = tanh(m_dSaturation*y);

                // process y through feedback BPF
                m_LPF1.doFilter(m_HPF2.doFilter(y));
        }

        // auto-normalize
        if(m_dK > 0)
                y *= 1/m_dK;

        return y;
}
```

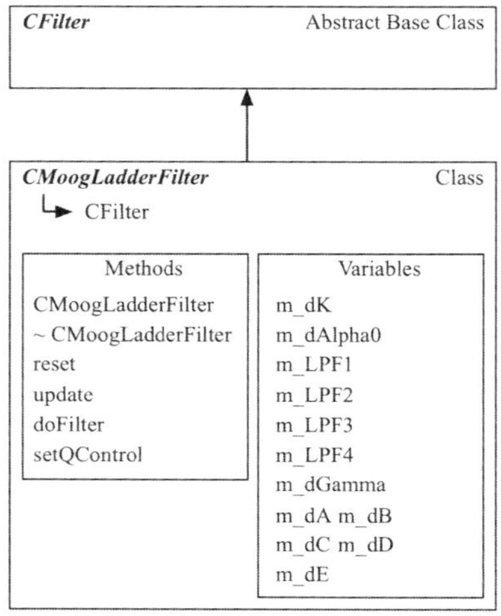

Figure 7.51: The class diagram for the CMoogLadderFilter.

7.17 The CMoogLadderFilter Object

This object implements the normal fourth order Moog LPF plus all the Oberheim variations in Table 7.1. The model uses four VA one-pole filter objects to implement the four filtering stages. The same four *CFilter* overrides will also be implemented. Figure 7.51 shows the class diagram for the *CMoogLadderFilter.*

CMoogLadderFilter Member Variables

Refer to Figures 7.27 and 7.28 to see that there are four sub-filters (LPF1, LPF2, LPF3, LPF4) several coefficients, the K and f_0 values and all the Oberheim variation coefficients. These will make up the member variables of the object. The filters are declared as member objects of type CVAOnePoleFilter and named *m_LPF1*, *m_LPF2*, *m_LPF3* and *m_LPF4*.

CMoogLadderFilter Member Methods

Aside from the constructor and destructor, the member methods are the same four overrides we implemented in the SEM and Korg35 filters from the base class.

Constructor

- initialize the member variables
- set default type to fourth order LPF
- reset filter

```
CMoogLadderFilter::CMoogLadderFilter(void)
{
    // --- init
    m_dK = 0.0;
    m_dAlpha_0 = 1.0;

    // --- Oberheim variables
    m_dA = 0.0; m_dB = 0.0; m_dC = 0.0;
    m_dD = 0.0; m_dE = 0.0;

    // --- set all as LPF types
    m_LPF1.m_uFilterType = LPF1; m_LPF2.m_uFilterType = LPF1;
    m_LPF3.m_uFilterType = LPF1; m_LPF4.m_uFilterType = LPF1;
```

```
        // --- set default filter type
        m_uFilterType = LPF4;

        // --- flush everything
        reset();
    }
```

reset()

- call *reset()* on the member objects; nothing for us to reset in the main outer object

```
    void CMoogLadderFilter::reset()
    {
        // flush everything
        m_LPF1.reset();
        m_LPF2.reset();
        m_LPF3.reset();
        m_LPF4.reset();
    }
```

setQControl()

- map the Q control on the GUI (1 to 10) to a range of *K* values 0 to 4 (self oscillation)
- use the same simple equation to map ranges

```
    void CMoogLadderFilter::setQControl(double dQControl)
    {
        // this maps dQControl = 1->10 to K = 0 -> 4
        m_dK = (4.0)*(dQControl – 1.0)/(10.0 - 1.0);
    }
```

update()

- always call the base class method first
- pre-warp the cutoff and set the α value on each member object
- calculate the β feedback values
- set coefficients according to the equations

See Figures 7.25 and 7.27 and the filter equations; it is all implemented in this method.

```
    inline virtual void update()
    {
        // do any modulation first
        CFilter::update();

        // pre-warp for BZT
        double wd = 2*pi*m_dFc;
        double T  = 1/m_dSampleRate;
        double wa = (2/T)*tan(wd*T/2);
        double g  = wa*T/2;

        // G - the feedforward coeff in the VA One Pole
        //     same for LPF, HPF
        double G = g/(1.0 + g);
```

```
    // set alphas
    m_LPF1.m_dAlpha = G; m_LPF2.m_dAlpha = G;
    m_LPF3.m_dAlpha = G; m_LPF4.m_dAlpha = G;

    // set betas
    m_LPF1.m_dBeta = G*G*G/(1.0 + g);
    m_LPF2.m_dBeta = G*G/(1.0 + g);
    m_LPF3.m_dBeta = G/(1.0 + g);
    m_LPF4.m_dBeta = 1.0/(1.0 + g);

    m_dGamma = G*G*G*G; // G^4

    m_dAlpha_0 = 1.0/(1.0 + m_dK*m_dGamma);

    // Oberheim variation
    switch(m_uFilterType)
    {
        case LPF4:
            m_dA = 0.0; m_dB = 0.0; m_dC = 0.0; m_dD = 0.0; m_dE = 1.0;
            break;

        case LPF2:
            m_dA = 0.0; m_dB = 0.0; m_dC = 1.0; m_dD = 0.0; m_dE = 0.0;
            break;

        case BPF4:
            m_dA = 0.0; m_dB = 0.0; m_dC = 4.0; m_dD = -8.0;
            m_dE = 4.0;
            break;

        case BPF2:
            m_dA = 0.0; m_dB = 2.0; m_dC = -2.0; m_dD = 0.0;
            m_dE = 0.0;
            break;

        case HPF4:
            m_dA = 1.0; m_dB = -4.0; m_dC = 6.0; m_dD = -4.0;
            m_dE = 1.0;
            break;

        case HPF2:
            m_dA = 1.0; m_dB = -2.0; m_dC = 1.0; m_dD = 0.0;
            m_dE = 0.0;
            break;

        default: // LPF4
            m_dA = 0.0; m_dB = 0.0; m_dC = 0.0; m_dD = 0.0; m_dE = 1.0;
            break;
    }
}
```

doFilter()

- check to make sure filter is supported, otherwise return the input value
- calculate the main feedback sum Σ
- optionally add passband gain compensation with the *Aux Control* (uncomment the code below)
- formulate *u*, the input to the filters
- add NLP if desired
- cascade the filters and calculate the individual outputs
- scale according to the Oberheim variation table

```
double CMoogLadderFilter::doFilter(double xn)
{
      // return xn if filter not supported
      if(m_uFilterType == BSF2 || m_uFilterType == LPF1 ||
         m_uFilterType == HPF1)
              return xn;

      double dSigma = m_LPF1.getFeedbackOutput() +
                      m_LPF2.getFeedbackOutput() +
                      m_LPF3.getFeedbackOutput() +
                      m_LPF4.getFeedbackOutput();

      // for passband gain compensation!
      // xn *= 1.0 + m_dAuxControl*m_dK;

      // calculate input to first filter
      double dU = (xn - m_dK*dSigma)*m_dAlpha_0;

      if(m_uNLP == ON)
              dU = tanh(m_dSaturation*dU);

      // cascade of 4 filters
      double dLP1 = m_LPF1.doFilter(dU);
      double dLP2 = m_LPF2.doFilter(dLP1);
      double dLP3 = m_LPF3.doFilter(dLP2);
      double dLP4 = m_LPF4.doFilter(dLP3);

      // Oberheim variation
      return m_dA*dU + m_dB*dLP1 + m_dC*dLP2 + m_dD*dLP3 +  m_dE*dLP4;
}
```

7.18 The CDiodeLadderFilter Object

The Diode Ladder filter is the most complex of the group. The multiple feedback paths complicate the design and increase the complexity of the block diagram, as well as the VA one-pole filter object that will implement each stage. Therefore this model is optional; feel free to skip over it, as it only adds one more filter—another fourth order LPF. This model uses four VA one-pole filter objects to implement the four filtering stages. The same four *CFilter* overrides will also be implemented. Figure 7.52 shows the class diagram for the *CDiodeLadderFilter*.

CDiodeLadderFilter Member Variables

Refer to Figures 7.40 and 7.44 to see that there are four sub-filters: LPF1, LPF2, LPF3 and LPF4, as well as coefficients SG1, SG2, SG3, SG4, and *K*. These will make up the member variables of the object. The filters are declared as member objects of type CVAOnePoleFilter and named *m_LPF1*, *m_LPF2*, *m_LPF3* and *m_LPF4*.

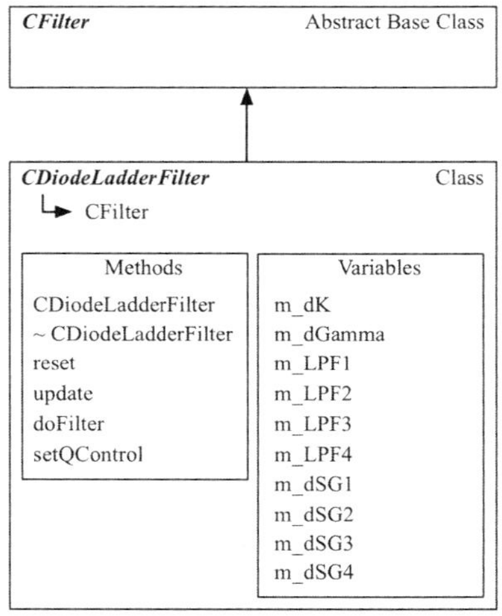

Figure 7.52: The class diagram for the CDiodeLadderFilter.

CDiodeLadderFilter Member Methods

Aside from the constructor and destructor, the member methods are the same four overrides we implemented in the SEM filter from the base class.

Constructor

- initialize the member variables
- set default type to fourth order LPF
- reset filter

```
CDiodeLadderFilter::CDiodeLadderFilter(void)
{
	// --- init
	m_dK = 0;
	m_dGamma = 0.0;

	// --- feedback scalars
	m_dSG1 = 0.0; m_dSG2 = 0.0; m_dSG3 = 0.0; m_dSG4 = 0.0;

	// --- set all as LPF types
	m_LPF1.setFilterType(LPF1);
	m_LPF2.setFilterType(LPF1);
	m_LPF3.setFilterType(LPF1);
	m_LPF4.setFilterType(LPF1);

	// --- set default filter type
	m_uFilterType = LPF4;

	// --- flush everything
	reset();
}
```

reset()

- call *reset()* on the member objects; nothing for us to reset in the main outer object

```
void CDiodeLadderFilter::reset()
{
    // flush everything
    m_LPF1.reset();
    m_LPF2.reset();
    m_LPF3.reset();
    m_LPF4.reset();
}
```

setQControl()

- map the Q control on the GUI (1 to 10) to a range of K values 0 to 17 (self-oscillation)
- use the same simple equation to map ranges

```
void CDiodeLadderFilter::setQControl(double dQControl)
{
    // this maps dQControl = 1->10 to K = 0 -> 17
    m_dK = (17.0)*(dQControl - 1.0)/(10.0 - 1.0);
}
```

update()

- always call the base class method first
- pre-warp the cutoff and set the α value on each member object
- main filter coefficients γ and SG values
- set the VA one-pole coefficients according to the equations
- you can get the full derivation of these equations from http://www.willpirkle.com/synthbook/

```
void CDiodeLadderFilter::update()
{
    // base class does modulation
    CFilter::update();

    // calculate alphas
    double wd = 2*pi*m_dFc;
    double T  = 1/m_dSampleRate;
    double wa = (2/T)*tan(wd*T/2);
    double g = wa*T/2;

    // Big G's
    double G4 = 0.5*g/(1.0 + g);
    double G3 = 0.5*g/(1.0 + g - 0.5*g*G4);
    double G2 = 0.5*g/(1.0 + g - 0.5*g*G3);
    double G1 = g/(1.0 + g - g*G2);
    m_dGamma = G4*G3*G2*G1;

    m_dSG1 =  G4*G3*G2;
    m_dSG2 =  G4*G3;
    m_dSG3 =  G4;
    m_dSG4 =  1.0;

    // set alphas
    double G = g/(1.0 + g);

    m_LPF1.m_dAlpha = G; m_LPF2.m_dAlpha = G;
    m_LPF3.m_dAlpha = G; m_LPF4.m_dAlpha = G;
```

```
        // set betas
        m_LPF1.m_dBeta = 1.0/(1.0 + g - g*G2);
        m_LPF2.m_dBeta = 1.0/(1.0 + g - 0.5*g*G3);
        m_LPF3.m_dBeta = 1.0/(1.0 + g - 0.5*g*G4);
        m_LPF4.m_dBeta = 1.0/(1.0 + g);

        // set deltas
        m_LPF1.m_dDelta = g;   m_LPF2.m_dDelta = 0.5*g;
        m_LPF3.m_dDelta = 0.5*g;m_LPF4.m_dDelta = 0.0;

        m_LPF1.m_dGamma = 1.0 + G1*G2; m_LPF2.m_dGamma = 1.0 + G2*G3;
        m_LPF3.m_dGamma = 1.0 + G3*G4; m_LPF4.m_dGamma = 1.0;

        // set epsilons
        m_LPF1.m_dEpsilon = G2; m_LPF2.m_dEpsilon = G3;
        m_LPF3.m_dEpsilon = G4; m_LPF4.m_dEpsilon = 0.0;

        // set a0s
        m_LPF1.m_da0 = 1.0; m_LPF2.m_da0 = 0.5;
        m_LPF3.m_da0 = 0.5; m_LPF4.m_da0 = 0.5;
    }
```

doFilter()

- check to make sure filter is supported, otherwise return the input value
- this filter has local feedback paths around the LPF pairs, so we need to get the feedback values backwards starting with LPF4 and feeding back each successive value into the upstream filter
- calculate Σ, the global feedback loop sum of contributions from each filter
- optionally add passband gain compensation—this filter obliterates the passband gain, so you might want to un-comment this
- form the input *u*
- add NLP if desired
- feed *u* into the cascade of filters

```
double CDiodeLadderFilter::doFilter(double xn)
{
        // return xn if filter not supported
        if(m_uFilterType != LPF4)
                return xn;

        m_LPF4.setFeedback(0.0);
        m_LPF3.setFeedback(m_LPF4.getFeedbackOutput());
        m_LPF2.setFeedback(m_LPF3.getFeedbackOutput());
        m_LPF1.setFeedback(m_LPF2.getFeedbackOutput());

        // form input
        double dSigma = m_dSG1*m_LPF1.getFeedbackOutput() +
                        m_dSG2*m_LPF2.getFeedbackOutput() +
                        m_dSG3*m_LPF3.getFeedbackOutput() +
                        m_dSG4*m_LPF4.getFeedbackOutput();

        // for passband gain compensation!
        // xn *= 1.0 + m_dAuxControl*m_dK;
```

```
    // form input
    double dU = (xn - m_dK*dSigma)/(1 + m_dK*m_dGamma);

    // add NLP if wanted
    if(m_uNLP == ON)
          dU = tanh(m_dSaturation*dU);

    // cascade of four filters
    return m_LPF4.doFilter(m_LPF3.doFilter(m_LPF2.doFilter(m_LPF1.doFilter(dU))));
}
```

7.19 Filter Key Tracking Modulation

Before we give NanoSynth a filter upgrade, we need to discuss a type of modulation that we will incorporate into it and all future synths as well. It is called filter key-tracking or filter key-follow, and is one of several key-tracking modulations. In key-tracking, the MIDI note number is used to modify some synth parameter. In filter key-tracking, the MIDI note number adjusts the cutoff frequency of the filter. This can yield some interesting and exceptional sounds. The idea is that when the user plays a new note, the frequency of that pitch is used to set the cutoff frequency of the filter. If the filter Q is very high, this will greatly reinforce the fundamental pitch of the note, and works well in self-oscillating conditions since the filter oscillates at the same pitch as the note. Filter key-tracking is an ON/OFF option that is global to the synth. An adjustment can be made as to how the tracking works with the Filter Key-Track Intensity control. This control has a range of 0.5 to 2.0, though you can feel free to change it for experimenting. The intensity control is a pitch multiplier; when set to 0.5, the filter's cutoff frequency is one octave below the note pitch, while it is one octave above when set to 2.0. In intermediate ranges, the cutoff frequency leads or lags the MIDI note pitch by some amount. To implement the modulation, we will need two variables to keep track of it—an on/off switch and a continuous intensity control. Note that there are many variations on key-tracking. In some cases the key-tracking modulation varies based on a line or curve rather than a constant offset, as we are applying here.

7.20 NanoSynth: Filters

NanoSynth is going to get a nice upgrade with the addition of the filter and its key-tracking modulation capability. We will also connect the EG to modulate both oscillator pitch and filter cutoff frequency with its biased output. Figure 7.53 shows the simplified block diagram. In this version we are going to add and connect the *CMoogLadderFilter*. After that you can test all the other filters from the chapter in a similar manner; these are also part of the Chapter Challenges.

Remember, it is up to you to design, code and maintain your GUI on your platform of choice. Refer back to Chapter 2 or the video tutorials at http://www.willpirkle.com/synthbook/ for assistance. Figures 7.54 and 7.55 show the NanoSynth GUI after this chapter is complete for RackAFX and VST3/AU. In subsequent chapters, we will continue to fill in the rest of the controls. For RackAFX, the filter key-tracking and key-tracking intensity controls are embedded in the LCD control—make sure you understand how to do this from Chapter 2. For VST3 and AU users, you can now use the mini knob control for key-track enabling and intensity. See Chapter 2 for details and use the sample code as a guide.

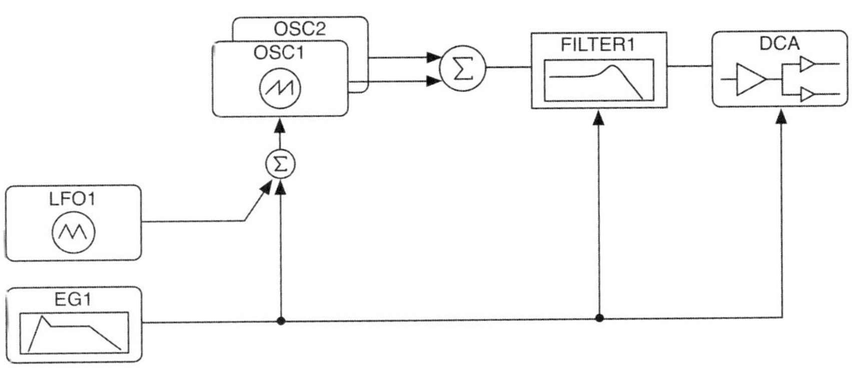

Figure 7.53: The NanoSynth project gets a filter upgrade, along with more EG modulation routings.

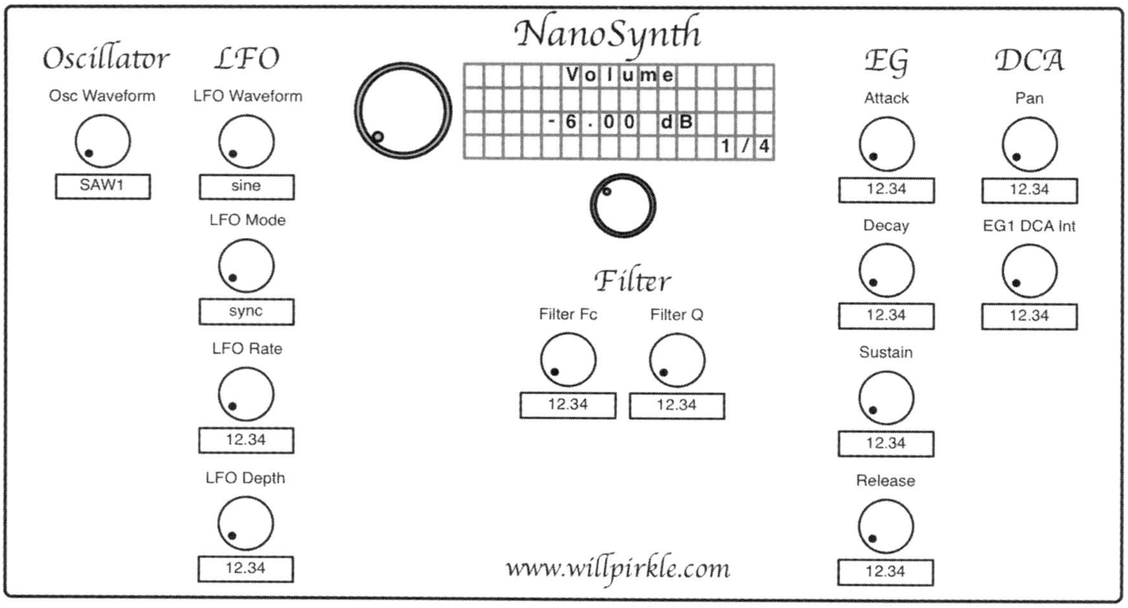

Figure 7.54: One possible NanoSynth GUI in RackAFX; notice that several controls are embedded in the LCD control.

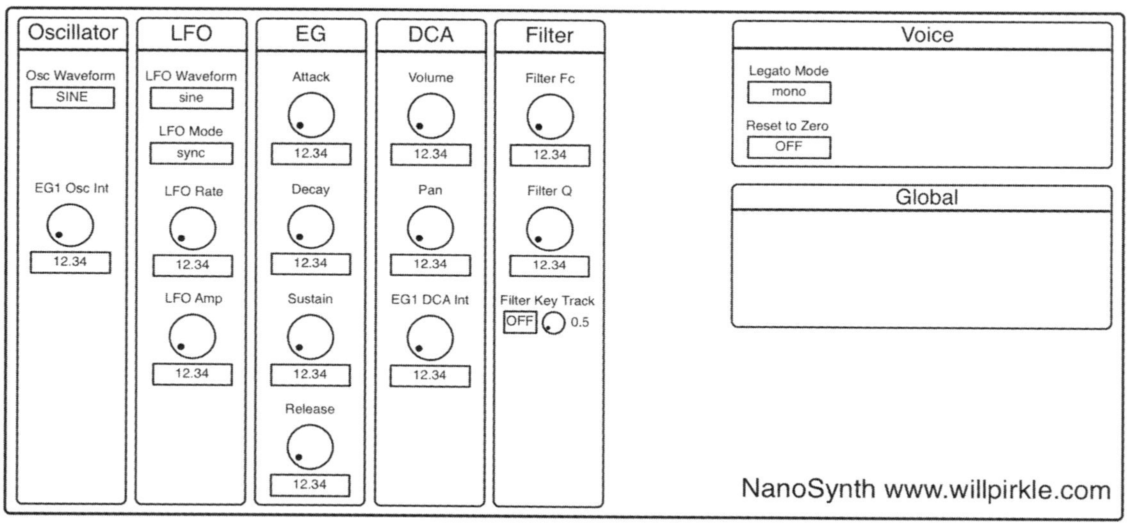

Figure 7.55: The NanoSynth GUI for the VST3 and AU projects.

Table 7.3: The new additions of continuous and enumerated string parameters for the NanoSynth GUI.

***NanoSynth* Continuous Parameters**				
Control Name (units)	**Type**	**Variable Name (VST3, RAFX)**	**Low/Hi/Default ***	**VST3/AU Index**
Filter Fc (Hz)	double	m_dFcControl	80 / 18000 / 10000	FILTER_FC
Filter Q	double	m_dQControl	1 / 10 / 1	FILTER_Q
Filter Keytrack Int	double	m_dFilterKeyTrackIntensity	0.5 / 2.0 / 1.0	FILTER_KEYTRACK_INTENSITY
EG1 Osc Int	double	m_dEG1OscIntensity	−1.0 / 1.0 / 0.0	EG1_TO_OSC_INTENSITY

* low, high and default values are #defined for VST3 and AU in *SynthParamLimits.h* for each project

***NanoSynth* Enumerated String Parameters (UINT)**			
Control Name	**Variable Name**	**enum String**	**VST3/AU Index**
Filter Keytrack	m_uFilterKeyTrack	OFF,ON	FILTER_KEYTRACK

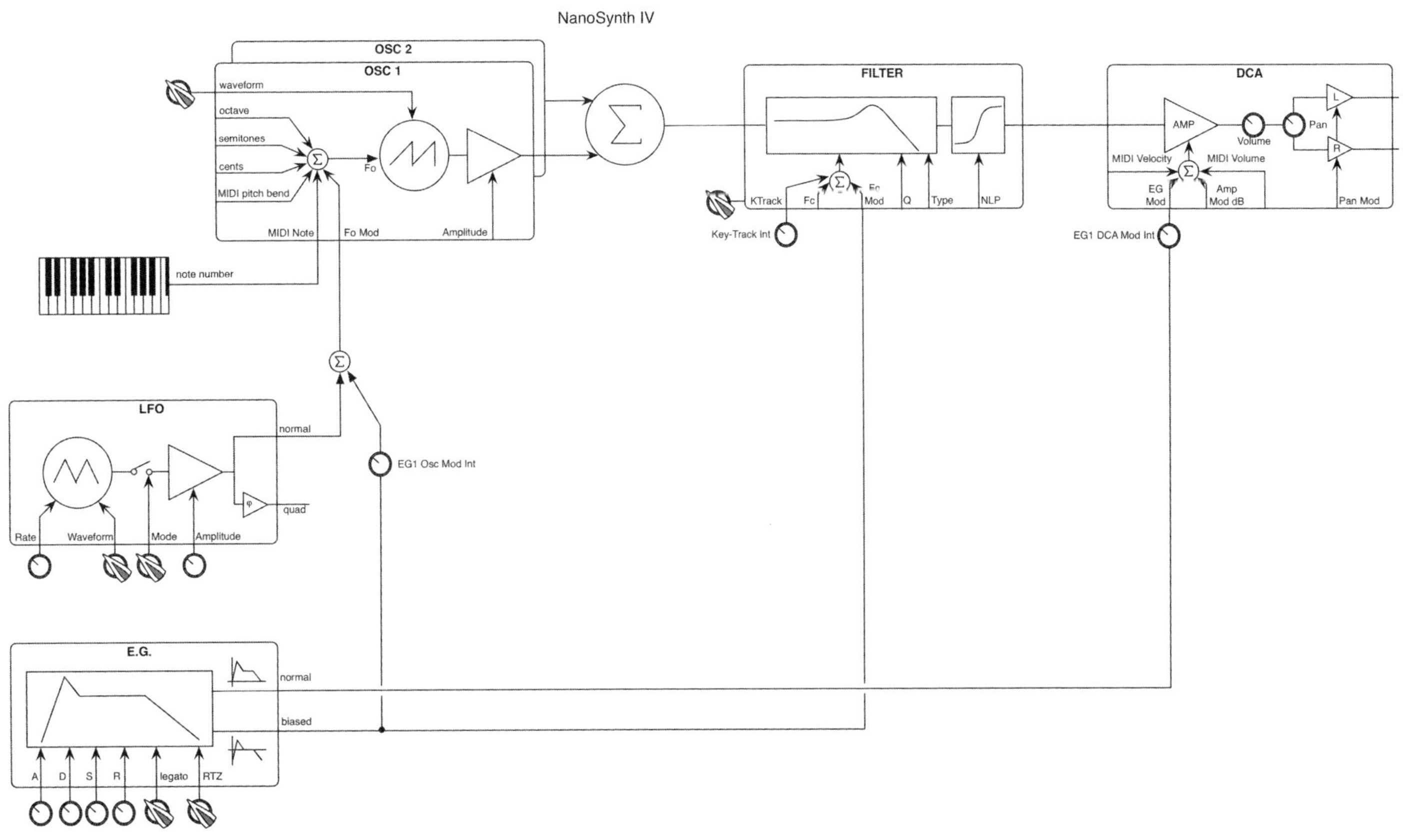

Figure 7.56: The NanoSynth detailed connection graph reveals the new controls from Table 6.x.

Figure 7.56 shows the detailed connection diagram for NanoSynth. It shows how the controls from Table 7.3 connect to the underlying synth objects. Notice how the EG and LFO outputs are summed before application to the oscillator pitch modulation. You will need to remember this when we approach the Modulation Matrix in Chapter 8.

For all platforms, you first implement the GUI controls. Refer back to Chapters 2 and 5 if you need help. Once you have the GUI control code in place, you are ready to start adding the code for the new modules and connections. You will also need to add all of the new filter files (or create them manually) for the new objects.

- *CVAOnePoleFilter.h* and *.cpp*
- *CSEMFilter.h* and *.cpp*
- *CKThreeFiveFilter.h* and *.cpp*
- *CMoogLadderFilter.h* and *.cpp*
- *CDiodeLadderFilter.h* and *.cpp* (optional)

7.21 NanoSynth: Filters Audio Rendering

For all platforms, the core audio rendering code is the same. Compare with the code in the last chapter (here only new code is **bold**).

- the EG's biased output is now connected to both the filter cutoff and the oscillator pitch modulation inputs
- the EG to filter modulation is direct; there is no intensity control
- the EG to oscillator modulation includes an intensity control
- we need to check for filter key-tracking and force the filter's cutoff to that modulated value if needed
- the filter processing happens between the oscillator and DCA blocks

It is important to notice how the modulation calculations work. In every case, the equation comes down to:

```
mod = (intensity)(range)(modulator output)
```

In some cases the intensity and/or range might be 1.0, but the above equation is universal. We will exploit it when we design the modulation matrix in the next Chapter.

```
if(m_Osc1.m_bNoteOn)
{

    << ** Code Listing 7.1: Rendering Audio ** >>

    // --- ARTICULATION BLOCK --- //
    double dLFO1Out = m_LFO1.doOscillate();
    double dBiasedEG = 0.0;
    double dEGOut = m_EG1.doEnvelope(&dBiasedEG);

    // --- calculate the EG --> Osc modulation (intensity)(range)(output)
    double dEGOscMod = m_dEG1OscIntensity*OSC_FO_MOD_RANGE*dBiasedEG;

    // --- sum the EG modulation with the LFO modulation
    //     (intensity = 1.0)(range)(output) and apply to oscillator pitch
    m_Osc1.setFoModExp(OSC_FO_MOD_RANGE*dLFO1Out + dEGOscMod);
    m_Osc2.setFoModExp(OSC_FO_MOD_RANGE*dLFO1Out + dEGOscMod);
    m_Osc1.update();
    m_Osc2.update();

    // --- check for keytrack
    if(m_uFilterKeyTrack == ON)
            // --- set to match the oscillator's pitch
            //     scaled by the intensity
            m_Filter1.m_dFcControl =
                        m_Osc1.m_dOscFo*m_dFilterKeyTrackIntensity;
```

```
	// --- set the EG->Filter modulation ((intensity = 1.0)(range)(output)
	m_Filter1.setFcMod(FILTER_FC_MOD_RANGE*dEGOut);
	m_Filter1.update();

	// --- set the EG->DCA modulation (intensity)(1.0)(output)
	m_DCA.setEGMod(m_dEG1DCAIntensity*dEGOut);
	m_DCA.update();

	// --- DIGITAL AUDIO ENGINE BLOCK --- //
	// (OSC1 + OSC2) --> FILTER --> DCA
	double dOscOut = 0.5*m_Osc1.doOscillate() + 0.5*m_Osc2.doOscillate();

	// --- filter
	double dFilterOut = m_Filter1.doFilter(dOscOut);

	// --- DCA
	m_DCA.doDCA(dFilterOut, dFilterOut, dOutL, dOutR);

	// now check for note off
	if(m_EG1.getState() == 0) // 0 = off
	{
		m_Osc1.stopOscillator();
		m_Osc2.stopOscillator();
		m_LFO1.stopOscillator();
		m_EG1.stopEG();
	}

	<< END ** Code Listing 7.1: Rendering Audio ** END >>
}
```

7.22 NanoSynth Filters: RackAFX

Start with your existing NanoSynth project (the NanoSynth: Filters project is available for download if you want to go straight to the code). Use Table 7.3 to add the new controls to the GUI. Then, open the *NanoSynth.h* and *.cpp* files for editing.

NanoSynth.h

Add a new *#include* statement for the Moog ladder filter object and add a member variable instance of it. After testing, you can come back and add the others.

```
// --- synth objects
#include "QBLimitedOscillator.h"
#include "WTOscillator.h"
#include "LFO.h"
#include "EnvelopeGenerator.h"
#include "DCA.h"
#include "MoogLadderFilter.h"

class CNanoSynth : public CPlugIn
{
public:
```

```
<SNIP SNIP SNIP>

// Add your code here: ---------------------------------------- //
CQBLimitedOscillator m_Osc1;
CQBLimitedOscillator m_Osc2;
CLFO m_LFO1;
CEnvelopeGenerator m_EG1;
CDCA m_DCA;

// --- Moog LPF
CMoogLadderFilter m_Filter1;

void update();

etc...
```

NanoSynth.cpp

Work through the *.cpp* file and alter the functions as needed. We are mainly just adding new lines of code, as we did not declare any new functions.

Constructor:

- there is nothing to add since member constructors will initialize the objects

prepareForPlay()

- set the sample rate on the filter

```
bool __stdcall CNanoSynth::prepareForPlay()
{
    // init:
    m_Osc1.setSampleRate((double)m_nSampleRate);
    m_Osc2.setSampleRate((double)m_nSampleRate);
    m_Osc2.m_nCents = 2.5; // +2.5 cents detuned
    m_LFO1.setSampleRate((double)m_nSampleRate);
    m_EG1.setSampleRate((double)m_nSampleRate);
    m_EG1.m_bOutputEG = true;

    m_Filter1.setSampleRate((double)m_nSampleRate);

    // --- mass update
    update();
    return true;
}
```

update()

- update the filter f_c control directly
- call the *setQControl()* function to set the Q value accordingly; it is different for each synth and never simply 1 to 10 as on the GUI
- call the filter *update()* function to apply the changes

```
void CNanoSynth::update()
{
```

```
        <SNIP SNIP SNIP>

        // --- DCA controls
        m_DCA.setPanControl(m_dPanControl);
        m_DCA.setAmplitude_dB(m_dVolume_dB);
        m_DCA.update();

        // --- filter controls
        m_Filter1.m_dFcControl = m_dFcControl;
        m_Filter1.setQControl(m_dQControl);
        m_Filter1.update();
}
```

processAudioFrame()

- modify the audio rendering code

```
bool __stdcall CNanoSynth::processAudioFrame(args…)
{
        double dOutL = 0.0;
        double dOutR = 0.0;
        if(m_Osc1.m_bNoteOn)
        {
                << INSERT ** Code Listing 7.1: Audio Rendering ** HERE >>
        }

        pOutputBuffer[0] = dOutL;

        etc...
```

You can now move to the RackAFX GUI designer and use the drag-and-drop interface to create your knobby/slider/LCD based GUI. See Chapter 2 for details.

7.23 NanoSynth Filters: VST3

Start with your existing NanoSynth project (the NanoSynth: Filters project is available for download if you want to go straight to the code). Use Table 7.3 to add the new controls to the GUI. Then, open the *VSTSynthProcessor.h* and *.cpp* files for editing.

VSTSynthProcessor.h

Add a new *#include* statement for the Moog ladder filter object and add a member variable instance of it. After testing, you can come back and add the others.

```
// --- synth objects
#include "QELimitedOscillator.h"
#include "WTOscillator.h"
#include "LFO.h"
#include "EnvelopeGenerator.h"
#include "DCA.h"
#include "MoogLadderFilter.h"

class Processor : public AudioEffect
{
public:
```

```
<SNIP SNIP SNIP>

// Add your code here: ---------------------------------------- //
CQBLimitedOscillator m_Osc1;
CQBLimitedOscillator m_Osc2;
CLFO m_LFO1;
CEnvelopeGenerator m_EG1;
CDCA m_DCA;

// --- Moog LPF
CMoogLadderFilter m_Filter1;

void update();

etc...
```

VSTSynthProcessor.cpp

Work through the *.cpp* file and alter the functions as needed. We are mainly just adding new lines of code, as we did not declare any new functions.

Constructor:

- there is nothing to add since member constructors will initialize the objects (though you do need to initialize your GUI controls here)

setActive()

- set the sample rate on the filter

```
tresult PLUGIN_API Processor::setActive(TBool state)
{
    if(state)
    {
        // --- do ON stuff; dynamic allocations
        m_Osc1.setSampleRate((double)processSetup.sampleRate);
        m_Osc2.setSampleRate((double)processSetup.sampleRate);
        m_Osc2.m_nCents = 2.5; // +2.5 cents detuned
        m_LFO1.setSampleRate((double)processSetup.sampleRate);
        m_EG1.setSampleRate((double)processSetup.sampleRate);
        m_EG1.m_bOutputEG = true;

        m_Filter1.setSampleRate((double)processSetup.sampleRate);

        update();
    }

    etc...
```

update()

- update the filter f_c control directly
- call the *setQControl()* function to set the Q value accordingly; it is different for each synth and never simply 1 to 10 as on the GUI
- call the filter *update()* function to apply the changes

```
void Processor::update()
{
     <SNIP SNIP SNIP>

     // --- DCA controls
     m_DCA.setPanControl(m_dPanControl);
     m_DCA.setAmplitude_dB(m_dVolume_dB);
     m_DCA.update();

     // --- filter controls
     m_Filter1.m_dFcControl = m_dFcControl;
     m_Filter1.setQControl(m_dQControl);
     m_Filter1.update();
}
```

process()

- modify the audio rendering code

```
bool __stdcall Processor::process(args…)
{
     <SNIP SNIP SNIP and Indents Removed>

     for(int32 j=0; j<samplesToProcess; j++)
     {
          // --- clear accumulators
          dOutL = 0.0;
          dOutR = 0.0;
          if(m_Osc1.m_bNoteOn)
          {
               << INSERT ** Code Listing 7.1: Audio Rendering ** HERE >>
          }
          // write out to buffer
          buffers[0][j] = dOutL;  // left
          buffers[1][j] = dOutR; // right

          etc...
```

Design the VST3 GUI by loading your DLL into a VST3 client and using the drag-and-drop method described in Chapter 2. You can always just use the default VST3 GUI if you don't want to perform this step. See the VSTGUI website for more information if needed.

7.24 NanoSynth Filters: AU

Start with your existing NanoSynth project (the NanoSynth: Filters project is available for download if you want to go straight to the code). Use Table 7.3 to add the new controls to the GUI. Then, open the *AUSynth.h* and *.cpp* files for editing.

AUSynth.h

Add a new *#include* statement for the Moog ladder filter object and add a member variable instance of it. After testing, you can come back and add the others.

```
// --- synth objects
#include "QBLimitedOscillator.h"
#include "WTOscillator.h"
```

```
#include "LFO.h"
#include "EnvelopeGenerator.h"
#include "DCA.h"
#include "MoogLadderFilter.h"

// --- AU Synth
class AUSynth : public AUInstrumentBase
{
public:

    <SNIP SNIP SNIP>

    // Add your code here: --------------------------------------- //
    CQBLimitedOscillator m_Osc1;
    CQBLimitedOscillator m_Osc2;
    CLFO m_LFO1;
    CEnvelopeGenerator m_EG1;
    CDCA m_DCA;

    // --- Moog LPF
    CMoogLadderFilter m_Filter1;

    void update();
    etc...
```

AUSynth.cpp

Work through the *.cpp* file and alter the functions as needed. We are mainly just adding new lines of code, as we did not declare any new functions.

Constructor:

- there is nothing to add since member constructors will initialize the objects (though you do need to initialize your GUI controls here)

Initialize()

- set the sample rate on the filter

```
ComponentResult AUSynth::Initialize()
{
    // --- init the base class
    AUInstrumentBase::Initialize();

    // --- inits
    m_Osc1.setSampleRate(GetOutput(0)->GetStreamFormat().mSampleRate);
    m_Osc2.setSampleRate(GetOutput(0)->GetStreamFormat().mSampleRate);
    m_Osc2.m_nCents = 2.5;
    m_LFO1.setSampleRate(GetOutput(0)->GetStreamFormat().mSampleRate);
    m_EG1.setSampleRate(GetOutput(0)->GetStreamFormat().mSampleRate);

    m_Filter1.setSampleRate(GetOutput(0)-
    >GetStreamFormat().mSampleRate);
```

```
        // --- big update
        update();

        return noErr;
}
```

update()

- update the filter f_c control directly
- call the *setQControl()* function to set the Q value accordingly; it is different for each synth and never simply 1 to 10 as on the GUI
- call the filter *update()* function to apply the changes

```
void AUSynth::update()
{
        <SNIP SNIP SNIP>
        // --- update DCA
        m_DCA.setPanControl(Globals()->GetParameter(OUTPUT_PAN));
        m_DCA.setAmplitude_dB(Globals()->GetParameter(OUTPUT_AMPLITUDE_DB));
        m_DCA.update();

        // --- update filter
        m_Filter1.m_dFcControl = Globals()->GetParameter(FILTER_FC);
        m_Filter1.setQControl(Globals()->GetParameter(FILTER_Q));
        m_Filter1.update();
}
```

Render()

- modify the audio rendering code

```
OSStatus AUSynth::Render(args…)
{
        // --- broadcast MIDI events
        PerformEvents(inTimeStamp);

        <SNIP SNIP SNIP>
         // --- the frame processing loop
        for(UInt32 frame=0; frame<inNumberFrames; ++frame)
        {
                // --- clear accumulators
                dOutL = 0.0;
                dOutR = 0.0;
                if(m_Osc1.m_bNoteOn)
                {
                        << INSERT ** Code Listing 7.1: Audio Rendering ** HERE >>
                }
                // write out to buffer
                // --- mono
                left[frame] = dOutL;

                etc...
```

Design your AU GUI using Interface Builder and the method described in Chapter 2. Remember the flat Cocoa namespace issue when copying projects in XCode.

7.25 Build and Test

Build and test on your platform. Although it is a simple synth, you can already get some nice, fat sounds thanks to the BLEP oscillators and virtual analog filters. Be sure to play with the filter key-track and intensity controls to get a feel for how much the patch changes with this modulation routing engaged. Test the filters in self-oscillation mode when Q is maxed out and definitely try it with NLP engaged to hear the difference. Once you are satisfied with the results, go back and test all the rest of the filters. Since they are derived from the same class, all you need to do is:

- *#include* the proper *.h* file
- change the filter member object declaration to the new filter
- add any controls to the GUI that are required for that filter; for example the SEM filter requires an *Aux Control* if you want to use the BSF; likewise the Moog and diode ladder filters require it if you want to experiment with passband gain compensation

In the next chapter, we will take a step back and examine the code. We will then modify NanoSynth again to:

- make the synths more flexible in modulation routings and programmability
- add polyphony
- reduce redundant coding with global parameterization

7.26 Challenges

Bronze

The SEM filter's Q control adjusts from 0.5 to 25 but does not self-oscillate at the maximum value. Add the capability for self-oscillation when Q reaches this maximum limit of 25. Hint: look at the equation for the *R* variable in the filter *update()* function and take the limit as Q goes to infinity. What value of *R* causes self-oscillation? Once you have it oscillating, enable the NLP and adjust the saturation control until it rings the way you like.

Sliver

Modify the *CFilter* base class and any or all of the derived filters to implement a modulate-able Q control. You will be copying the same ideas for the cutoff frequency control except that the Q modulates in a linear manner, so there is no volt/octave conversion needed. For this challenge, implement only a single modulation input such as *setModQ()* and make sure to properly calculate the modulated Q value in *updateFilter*().

Gold

Give NanoSynth the ability to feature multiple filter models and types. For example, you could use the Moog ladder filter with Oberheim variations to create a multi-filter. Create the controls to allow the user to select the filter type then update the filter by modifying its *m_uFilterType* variable. Once in place, try it with the other filters as well. Then design a single C++ object that implements all the filter types. You can then use that object in future projects to greatly increase your synthesizers' flexibility and feature sets.

Platinum

Derive the Korg35 LPF and HPF block diagrams using the Modified Härmä method. Hint: Zavalishin's method produces identical results, so you have the solution if needed.

Diamond

Derive the Moog Half-Ladder Filter block diagram using the Modified Härmä method. Implement the filter in code (it is optional and not part of the book projects, but if you need help you can get the derivation and sample code at http://www.willpirkle.com/synthbook/). Next, relocate the all pass filter into the feedback path and derive the new equations and block diagram using whatever method you like. What are the differences between the designs? Do you expect the frequency responses to be identical? What about filter phase response (identical or not)?

Bibliography

D'Angelo, Stefano and Välimäki, Vesa. 2013. "An Improved Virtual Analog Model of the Moog Ladder Filter," *Proceedings from the 2013 International Conference on Acoustics, Speech and Signal Processing*, pp. 729–733.

Fontana, Fredrico and Civolani, Marco. 2010. "Modeling of the EMS VCS3 Voltage-Controlled Filter as a Nonlinear Filter Network." *IEEE Transactions on Audio, Speech and Language Processing*, vol. 18, no. 4.

Huovilainen, Antti. 2006. "Nonlinear Digital Implementation of the Moog Ladder Filter." *Proceedings from the International Conference on Digital Audio Effects*. Naples.

Lindquist, Claude. 1977. *Active Network Design with Signal Filtering Applications*. Long Beach: Steward and Sons.

Nagahama, Yasuo. 1977. "Voltage Controlled Filter." United States Patent 4,039,980.

Oberheim, Tom. 1984. *Oberheim XPander Service Manual*. Los Angeles: ECC Development Corp.

Pirkle, Will. 2013a. "Modeling the Korg35 Highpass and Lowpass Filters." Presented at the 135th Audio Engineering Society Convention. New York.

Pirkle, Will. 2013b. "Virtual Analog (VA) Diode Ladder Filter." Accessed June 2014, http://www.willpirkle.com/synthbook/Downloads/AN-6DiodeLadderFilter.pdf

Pirkle, Will. 2013c. "Virtual Analog (VA) 2nd Order Moog Half-Ladder Filter." Accessed June 2014, http://www.willpirkle.com/synthbook/Downloads/AN-8MoogHalfLadderFilter.pdf

Pirkle, Will. 2014. "Novel Hybrid Virtual Analog Filters Based on the Sallen-Key Architecture." Presented at the 136th Audio Engineering Society Convention. Los Angeles.

Stilson, Tim and Smith, Julius O. 1996. "Analyzing the Moog VCF with Considerations for Digital Implementation." *Proceedings from the 1996 International Computer Music Conference*. San Francisco.

Stinchcombe, Tim. 2006. "A Study of the Korg MS10 and MS20 Filters." Accessed June 2014, http://www.timstinchcombe.co.uk/synth/MS20_study.pdf

synthfool.com. n.d. "Oberheim SEM Schematics." Accessed June 2014, http://www.synthfool.com/docs/Oberheim/Oberheim_SEM1A/Oberheim_SEM_1A_Schematics.pdf

synthtech.com. n.d. "CEM3328 Four Pole Low-Pass VCF Datasheet." Accessed June 2014, http://www.synthtech.com/cem/c3328pdf.pdf

synthtech.com. n.d. "CEM3372 uP Controllable Signal Processor Datasheet." Accessed June 2014, http://www.synthtech.com/cem/c3372pdf.pdf

synthtech.com. n.d. "SSM2044 Four Pole Voltage Controlled Filter Datasheet." Accessed June 2014, http://www.synthtech.com/cem/ssm2044.pdf

Välimäki, Vesa and Huovilainen, Antti. 2006. "Oscillator and Filter Algorithms for Virtual Analog Synthesis." *Computer Music Journal*, vol. 30, no. 2, pp. 19–31. Massachusetts: MIT Press.

Zavalishin, Vadim. 2012. *The Art of VA Filter Design*. Accessed June 2014, http://www.native-instruments.com/fileadmin/ni_media/downloads/pdf/VAFilterDesign_1.0.3.pdf

CHAPTER 8

Modulation Matrix, Polyphony, and Global Parameterization

The NanoSynth project is taking shape but there are some problems that need to be fixed and flexibility that needs to be added. First, NanoSynth is hard-wired into a specific configuration or patch. For example, the user can't re-route the LFO away from the oscillators and to some other destination such as the filter cutoff frequency. And, each time we design a new synth architecture, we will have to manually connect the components by writing the wiring code. Second, it is monophonic, and we would like to make polyphonic synthesizers (or at least understand how). In this chapter, we will address the first issue with a modulation matrix that is programmed with a patch configuration as a series of rows in the matrix. This will allow the user more control over modulation routings as well as simplify the coding for the render function. The modulation matrix also simplifies architecture changes as you design your own synths. Next, we will add the standard MIDI controller modulations that all the book projects will contain. Then, we will add another note of polyphony to the synth and experiment with voice-stealing in the two-note NanoSynth Poly. Finally, we will use global parameterization to streamline the synth updating process. We are going to try to add these new features to NanoSynth in the most easy-to-understand manner as possible. In the next chapter, however, we will address some of the issues that arise and modify the paradigm slightly—NanoSynth is our "learning synth," and we will be using that experience to help mold the future projects. This is an important chapter—since the rest of the synth projects use the same core MIDI functionality, modulation matrix concepts and global parameterization, this is the last time we will print the details of several of the plug-in functions.

> You are strongly urged to obtain the MIDI Manufacturers Association *DLS Level II Specification*. It is the spec for a software synth that uses audio samples in its oscillators. More importantly, it describes the modulation matrix concept on which this chapter is based. It also includes a set of GUI and object min, max and default values, an alternate and interesting resonant filter design, and copious information on the sample-based synthesis. Finally, it is an actual specification intended for major synth manufactures to use. So unless you work at a synth company, this is the closest you will come to seeing an actual professional synth specification.

8.1 Modulation Routings

Figure 8.1 shows the block diagram for NanoSynth so far. The modulation routings are in dotted lines. You can make some observations:

- the EG1 to Oscillator and EG1 to DCA routings have intensity controls that alter their modulation amounts
- the LFO to Oscillator and EG1 to Filter routings do not have these controls
- the LFO intensity is globally controlled with its amplitude variable
- the EG and LFO outputs are summed before applying to the Oscillator f_0 modulation
- there is no control between EG1 and the filter cutoff
- there are no switches that let you re-route modulator outputs
- there are no switches that enable or disable routings

In this chapter, you will learn how to set up a modulation matrix both with and without the intensity controls in which multiple modulation sources can feed multiple modulation destinations in a highly flexible way. It will also be easy for you to add your own custom sources and destinations. You will also learn how to enable or disable routings in the matrix. Figure 8.1 shows the detailed connection graph for NanoSynth so far. The dotted lines show the modulation routings.

Let's list the modulation sources and destinations in Figure 8.1 by tracing the dotted line connections.

Sources:

- EG1 output
- EG1 biased output
- LFO1 output
- MIDI Note Number (for filter key-track modulation)

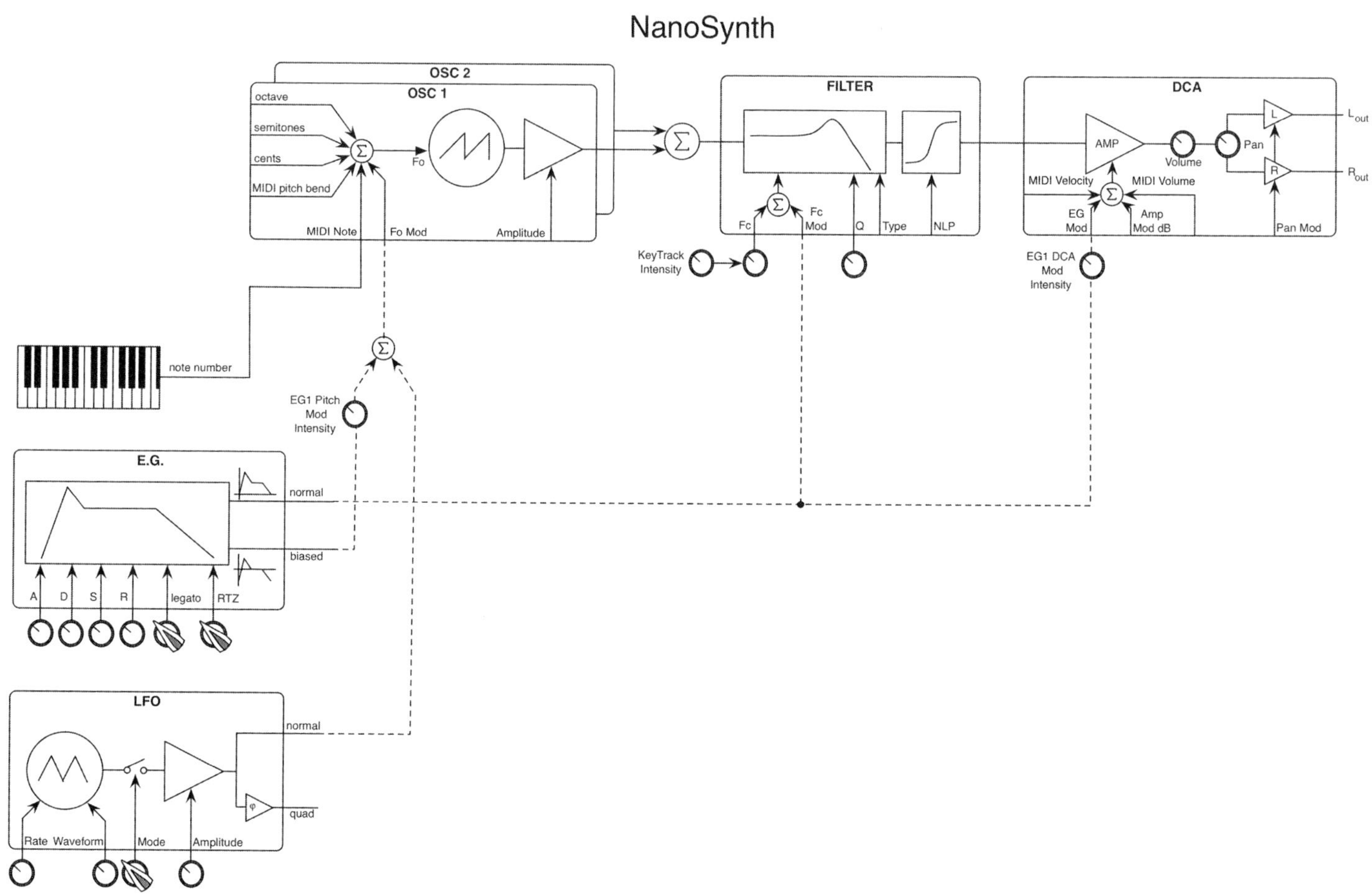

Figure 8.1: The detailed NanoSynth block diagram.

Destinations:

- Osc1 f_o Mod
- Osc2 f_o Mod
- Filter f_c Mod
- DCA EG Mod

There are more possible sources and destinations, and in this chapter we will add several of them. Figure 8.2 shows a conceptual diagram of the modulation routings in the current version of NanoSynth. The sources are lined up on the left and the destinations on the right. You can see instances where one source feeds multiple destinations and where one destination's input is the sum of multiple sources. We want to design the modulation matrix with this kind of flexibility built-in and no limit to the number of routings.

Now, think about how the code looked when rendering the audio. For the EG to Oscillator Fo routing, the final modulation value is the product of the intensity, range and modulator output:

```
double dEGOscMod = m_dEG1OscIntensity*OSC_FO_MOD_RANGE*dBiasedEG;
```

Next, the LFO1 scaled output is added directly to the EG's modulation value. In this case, the LFO1 intensity is fixed at 1.0 and the range is also OSC_FO_MOD_RANGE.

```
m_Osc1.setFoModExp(dLFO1Out*OSC_FO_MOD_RANGE + dEGOscMod);
```

The EG1 to filter cutoff has the intensity fixed at 1.0 and uses the filter cutoff range FILTER_FC_MOD_RANGE.

```
m_Filter1.setFcMod(dEGOut*FILTER_FC_MOD_RANGE);
```

When the filter key track is enabled, the filter's control is forced to match the oscillator's frequency, which is derived from the MIDI note number, so that is the Note Number to Filter Fc Mod connection you see in Figure 8.1. Here, the intensity (0.5 to 2.0) controls the range as well. Remember that the MIDI note number had to be transformed into a frequency before being multiplied with the intensity value.

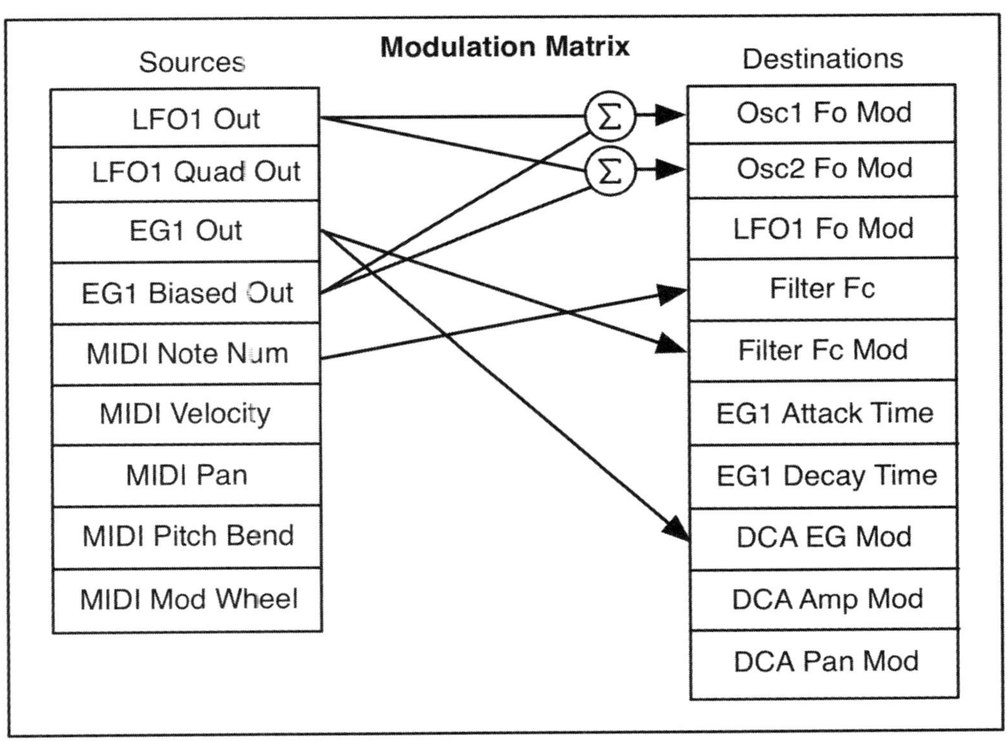

Figure 8.2: The modulation routings in the NanoSynth modulation matrix.

Table 8.1: Modulation matrix routings: each row in the table is a source->destination pair complete with intensity, range and transform.

Source	Transform	Intensity	Range	Destination
LFO1 Output	none	1.0	OSC_FO_MOD_RANGE	OSC1 f_o
LFO1 Output	none	1.0	OSC_FO_MOD_RANGE	OSC2 f_o
EG1 Biased Output	none	1.0	FILTER_FC_ MOD_RANGE	Filter f_c
EG1 Output	none	DCA Intensity	1.0	DCA EG In
EG1 Biased Output	none	EG1 Osc Intensity	OSC_FO_MOD_RANGE	OSC1 f_o
EG1 Biased Output	none	EG1 Osc Intensity	OSC_FO_MOD_RANGE	OSC2 f_o
MIDI Note Num	Note Number to Frequency	Filter Key Track Intensity	1.0	Filter f_c

```
m_Filter1.m_dFcControl = midiFreqTable[m_Osc1.m_uMIDINoteNumber]*
                         m_dFilterKeyTrackIntensity;
```

The EG1 to DCA modulation uses the intensity control with a range of 1.0

```
m_DCA.setEGMod(dEGOut*m_dEG1DCAIntensity);
```

So you can see that the modulation values use *intensities* (controlled or fixed at 1.0) and ranges (which may or may not be 1.0). There is also a transform built into the modulation matrix. For MIDI Note Number to Filter Key Track, we convert the MIDI Note Number to a frequency before applying the intensity. The modulation matrix is also going to handle this for us, so the Filter Key Track modulation routing will include an additional transform operation. We can expand the modulation matrix in Figure 8.2 to include all the variables and the transform shown in Table 8.1. Each of the individual routings occupies one row. You can see that multiple sources are feeding multiple destinations. The source and destination enumerations are found in *synthfunctions.h*.

8.2 The Modulation Matrix Object

Here is the idea behind the modulation matrix: currently, you have to write the code that takes the modulation outputs from the LFO, EG and the MIDI Note Number, scale them by range and intensity, optionally transform them, and then accumulate them. You also must write the code that sets the final modulation values on the destination objects (the oscillators, filter and DCA) before calling the *update()* functions.

Instead of having to write this code, you setup a system where the modulators write their outputs to pre-defined locations. The destination objects have been told where to pick up these modulation values, and they do this automatically when you update them. The articulation and processing code can be written without all those intermediate variables. Let's look at the code for the current NanoSynth articulation code. The lines in **bold** show how we generate the intermediate articulation variables, scale them and then apply them to the target objects.

```
// --- ARTICULATION BLOCK --- //
double dLFO1Out = m_LFO1.doOscillate();
double dBiasedEG = 0.0;
double dEGOut = m_EG1.doEnvelope(&dBiasedEG);

// --- calculate the EG->Osc modulation (intensity)(range)(output)
double dEGOscMod = m_dEG1OscIntensity*OSC_FO_MOD_RANGE*dBiasedEG;

// --- sum the EG modulation with the LFO modulation (intensity)(1.0)(output)
//     and apply to oscillator pitch
m_Osc1.setFoModExp(dLFO1Out*OSC_FO_MOD_RANGE + dEGOscMod);
```

```
m_Osc2.setFoModExp(dLFO1Out*OSC_FO_MOD_RANGE + dEGOscMod);
m_Osc1.update();
m_Osc2.update();

// --- check for keytrack
if(m_uFilterKeyTrack == ON)
      // --- set to match the oscillator's ptich scaled by the intensity
      m_Filter1.m_dFcControl = m_Osc1.m_dOscFo*m_dFilterKeyTrackIntensity;

// --- set the EG->Filter modulation (1.0)(range)(output)
m_Filter1.setFcMod(dEGOut*FILTER_FC_MOD_RANGE);
m_Filter1.update();

// --- set the EG->DCA modulation (intensity)(1.0)(output)
m_DCA.setEGMod(dEGOut*m_dEG1DCAIntensity);
m_DCA.update();
```

The modulation matrix replaces much of this. The pseudocode looks like this:

```
// --- modulators render their outputs
m_LFO1.doOscillate();
m_EG1.doEnvelope();

// --- let mod matrix handle connections and scaling
m_ModMatrix.doModulationMatrix();

// --- then update the targets
m_Osc1.update();
m_Osc2.update();
m_Filter1.update();
m_DCA.update();

// --- now do the digital audio rendering
etc...
```

Notice how the clutter is removed; there are no intermediate variables or variables to pass between objects. In fact, there are no more arguments on the functions! It is very clean and streamlined. In addition, the same code can be used repeatedly for many different patches since the patching information is coded inside the modulation matrix. Our rendering functions no longer need to know or handle the details of the patch routing.

The modulation matrix is implemented as a C++ object. The matrix actually consists of three components:

- an array of *Source* registers
- an array of *Destination* registers
- an array of pointers to *modMatrixRow* structures called the matrix core

The source and destination registers are *double* values, so the sources and destinations are simply arrays of *doubles*. The modulation sources will write their outputs into predefined locations in the source array. The modulation destinations will read their values from predefined locations in the destination array.

The job of the modulation matrix is to take values from the source array, optionally transform them, scale them by their range and intensity variables, then accumulate the values into locations in the destination array.

The matrix core is the array of pointers to the matrix rows that define each modulation routing. The core is created dynamically and there are get/set functions so that a single core may be shared with multiple matrixes.

Figure 8.3 shows the matrix core; it is a fixed array full of *modMatrixRow* pointers or NULL pointers indicating that no row exists. The size of the matrix core is equal to the number of non-NULL rows.

Figures 8.4–8.6 show the sequence of operations for modulation via the modulation matrix. The operations can be broken into three phases:

- Phase 1: the modulators write their outputs into the *Sources* array (MIDI modulations will arrive via MIDI messages that we apply)
- Phase 2: the modulation matrix loops through its array, extracting values form the *Sources* array, transforming, scaling, and accumulating them into the *Destinations* array
- Phase 3: the synth components read their modulation values from the *Destinations* array

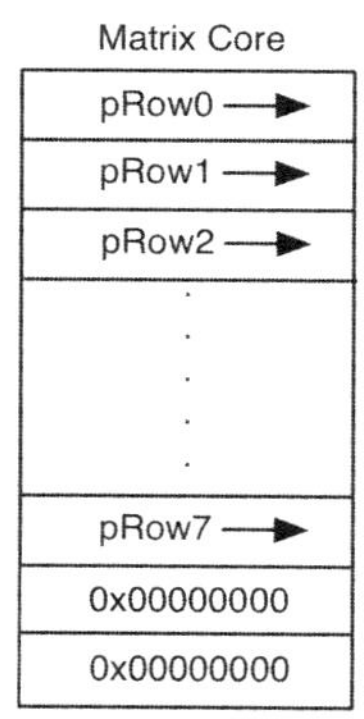

Figure 8.3: The matrix core contains either matrix row pointers or NULL; this matrix would have a size of eight (8) since it has eight non-NULL rows.

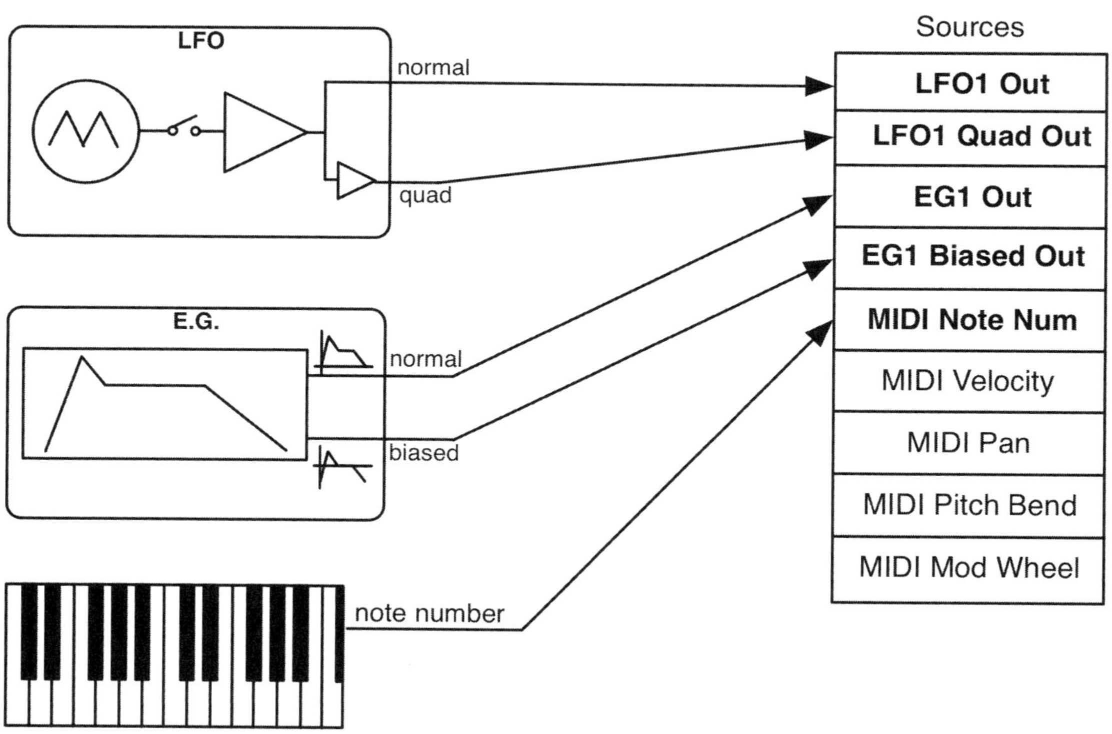

Figure 8.4: Phase 1: the modulators write their outputs into the *Sources* array at pre-determined locations.

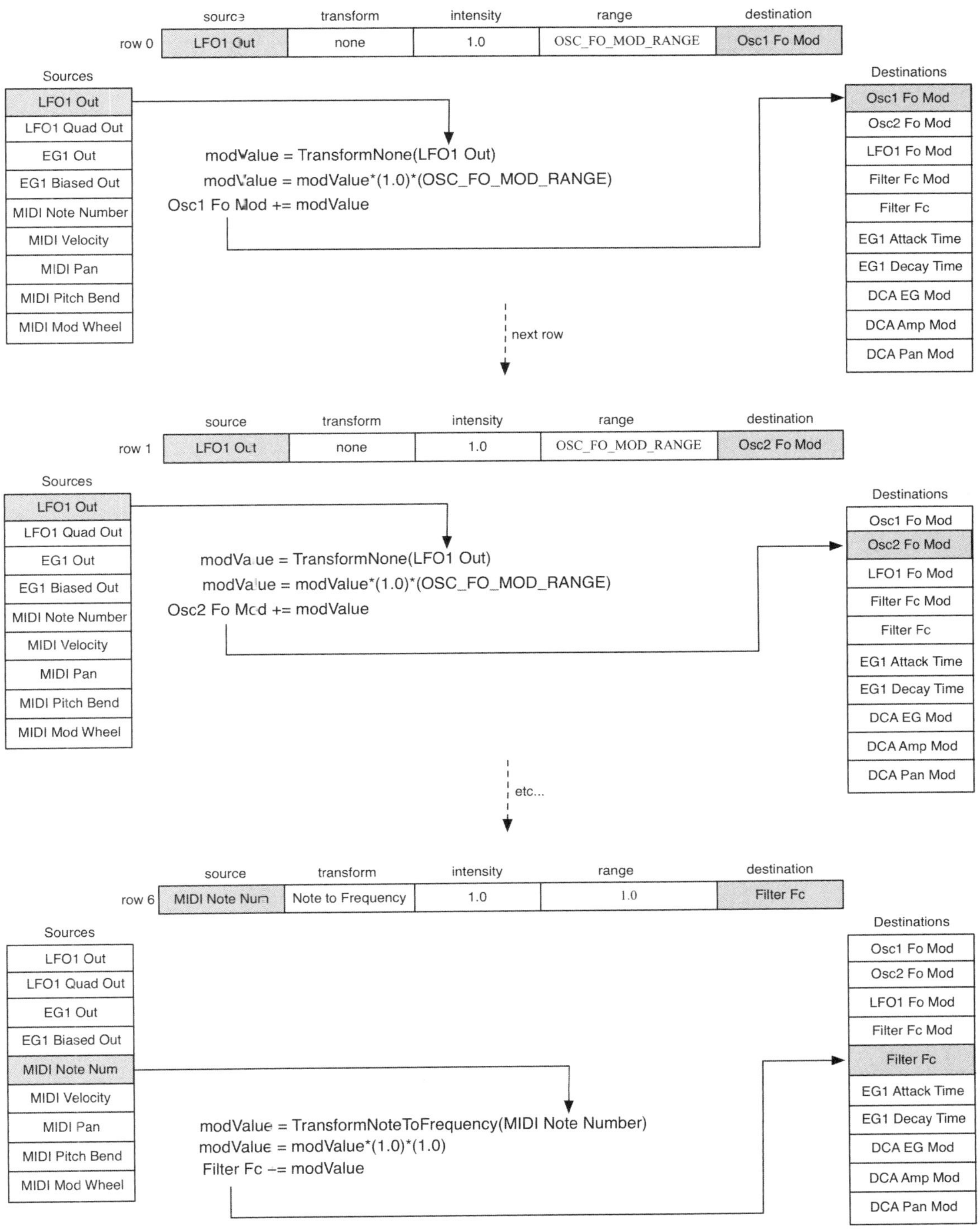

Figure 8.5: Phase 2: the modulation matrix steps through each row, transforming, scaling and accumulating the sources into destinations.

We will need a way to index the source and destination arrays for both the modulation matrix and the objects that will be reading and writing to the arrays. The index values are defined in two enumerations in *synthfunctions.h*. You can see that we have defined many more sources and destinations that exist in NanoSynth—we will use these in the more advanced projects to come. It is important to note the way the *destinations* enumeration is set up—the Layer 0 destinations are first, followed by the Layer 1 destinations; layers are described below.

```
enum sources{
    SOURCE_NONE = 0,
```

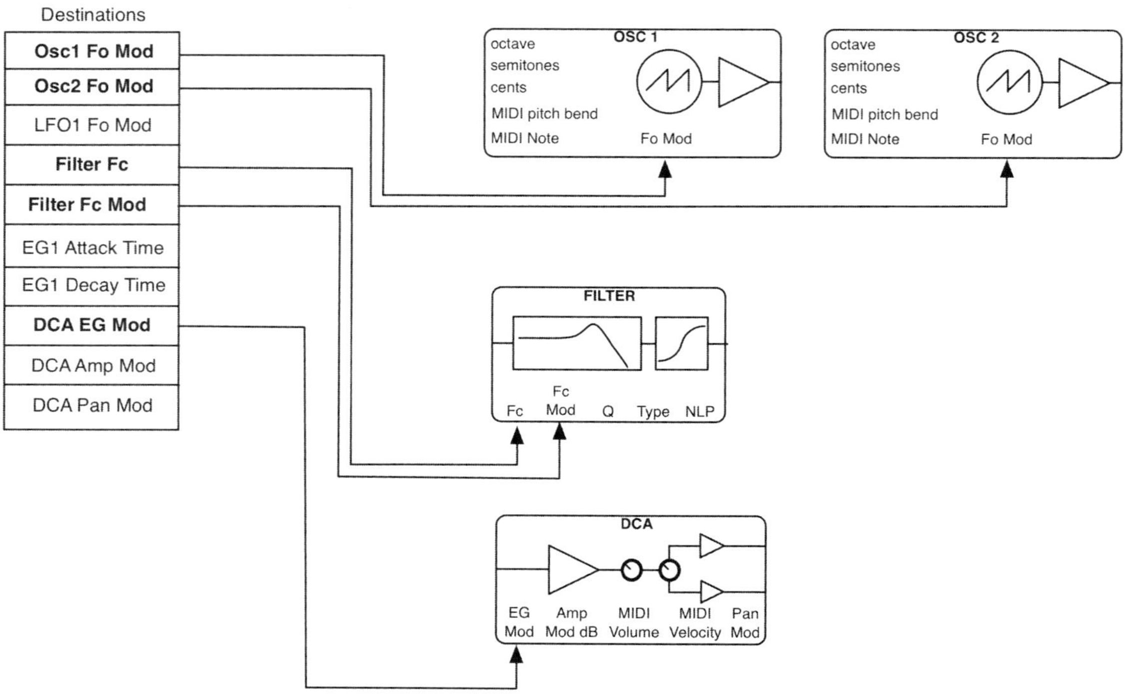

Figure 8.6: Phase 3: the synth components read their modulation values from the *Destinations* array from predefined locations.

```
    SOURCE_LFO1,
    SOURCE_LFO2,

    <SNIP SNIP SNIP>

    SOURCE_MIDI_JS_X,
    SOURCE_MIDI_JS_Y,
    MAX_SOURCES
};

enum destinations{
    DEST_NONE = 0,

    // --- LAYER 0 DESTINATIONS
    //     add more L0 destinations in this chunk
    //     see CModulationMatrix::checkDestinationLayer())
    DEST_LFO1_FO, // <- keep this first
    DEST_LFO2_FO,
    DEST_ALL_LFO_FO,

    <SNIP SNIP SNIP>

    DEST_EG4_SUSTAIN_OVERRIDE,
    DEST_ALL_EG_SUSTAIN_OVERRIDE, // <- keep this last
    // --- END OF LAYER 0 DESTINATIONS

    // --- LAYER 1 DESTINATIONS
```

```
DEST_OSC1_FO,
DEST_OSC2_FO,
DEST_OSC3_FO,

etc...
```

Notice the following "universal" destinations:

```
DEST_ALL_OSC_FO
DEST_ALL_OSC_PULSEWIDTH
DEST_ALL_OSC_FO_RATIO
DEST_ALL_OSC_OUTPUT_AMP
DEST_ALL_LFO_FO
DEST_ALL_LFO_OUTPUT_AMP
DEST_ALL_FILTER_FC
DEST_ALL_FILTER_KEYTRACK
DEST_ALL_FILTER_Q
DEST_ALL_EG_ATTACK_SCALING
DEST_ALL_EG_DECAY_SCALING
```

These make it easier to apply a single source to multiple destinations that all share the same intensity, range and transform attributes, which reduces the number of rows in the matrix.

The *modMatrixRow* structure has member variables for each of the items in Table 8.1. It is defined in *synthfunctions.h* as:

```
struct modMatrixRow
{
    // --- index of source
    UINT uSourceIndex;

    // --- index of destination
    UINT uDestinationIndex;

    // --- needs to default to 1.0 in case no GUI control
    double* pModIntensity; // <- "ucControl" in MMA DLS
    double* pModRange;     // <- "lScale" in MMA DLS

    // --- transform on Source
    UINT uSourceTransform;

    // --- to easily turn on/off a modulation routing
    bool bEnable;
};
```

This structure includes index values for a source and a destination. Notice that the intensity and range values are pointers; this is so you can control them directly from your plug-in's control variables. For example, when the user moves the EG1 to DCA Intensity control, they will be directly modifying this variable in the modulation matrix. A *boolean* variable enables or disables a row.

The transforms are indexed with another enumeration in *synthfuncions.h*. You can see the TRANSFORM_NOTE_NUMBER_TO_FREQUENCY index, which we need for the Filter Key Track modulation. We will discuss the other transforms as we need them, though their names are fairly self-explanatory.

```
enum transform{
      TRANSFORM_NONE = 0,
      TRANSFORM_UNIPOLAR_TO_BIPOLAR,
      TRANSFORM_BIPOLAR_TO_UNIPOLAR,
      TRANSFORM_MIDI_NORMALIZE,
      TRANSFORM_INVERT_MIDI_NORMALIZE,
      TRANSFORM_MIDI_TO_BIPOLAR,
      TRANSFORM_MIDI_TO_PAN,
      TRANSFORM_MIDI_SWITCH,
      TRANSFORM_MIDI_TO_ATTENUATION,
      TRANSFORM_NOTE_NUMBER_TO_FREQUENCY,
      MAX_TRANSFORMS
};
```

Creating Rows

In the modulation matrix, you create all the rows dynamically at startup time; you add a row for every possible modulation routing you support even if some modulations are turned off by default. Another option is to create a matrix that can dynamically grow and shrink as you add and remove rows on the fly. But this opens up many potential traps and pitfalls, especially since both the processing and GUI threads would need to access it. By creating a fixed matrix, we don't have those problems. You only need to set the *bEnable* flag for each row when you create the rows; default modulation routings are enabled while optional routings are disabled. In Section 8.11 we will experiment with turning rows on and off to let the user configure the patch from the GUI. Although you can create the rows yourself, we added a helper function in *synthfunctions.h* to create rows for you. This function is straightforward and self-explanatory.

```
inline modMatrixRow* createModMatrixRow(UINT uSource,
                                        UINT uDestination,
                                        double* pIntensity,
                                        double* pRange,
                                        UINT uTransform,
                                        bool bEnable = true)
{
      modMatrixRow* pRow = new modMatrixRow;
      pRow->uSourceIndex = uSource;
      pRow->uDestinationIndex = uDestination;
      pRow->pModIntensity = pIntensity;
      pRow->pModRange = pRange;
      pRow->uSourceTransform = uTransform;
      pRow->bEnable = bEnable; // on/off

      return pRow;
}
```

Modulation Layers

Before looking at the modulation matrix object, we need to think about the modulation layers. For NanoSynth, it's very simple; the LFO and EG modulate the oscillators, filter and DCA. There is only one layer of modulation. But what if we added another LFO called LFO2 to NanoSynth so that it modulated LFO1's frequency as shown in Figure 8.7? Then we would have two layers and would need to use the modulation matrix twice. The important thing to keep in mind is that the destinations define the layer number.

The modulation matrix is designed to use two layers at the most; however, you can easily modify it to use as many layers as you want. We will start by implementing the Layer 1 modulation in the NanoSynth. Later in the chapter, we will add some advanced MIDI modulations that will occur in Layer 0.

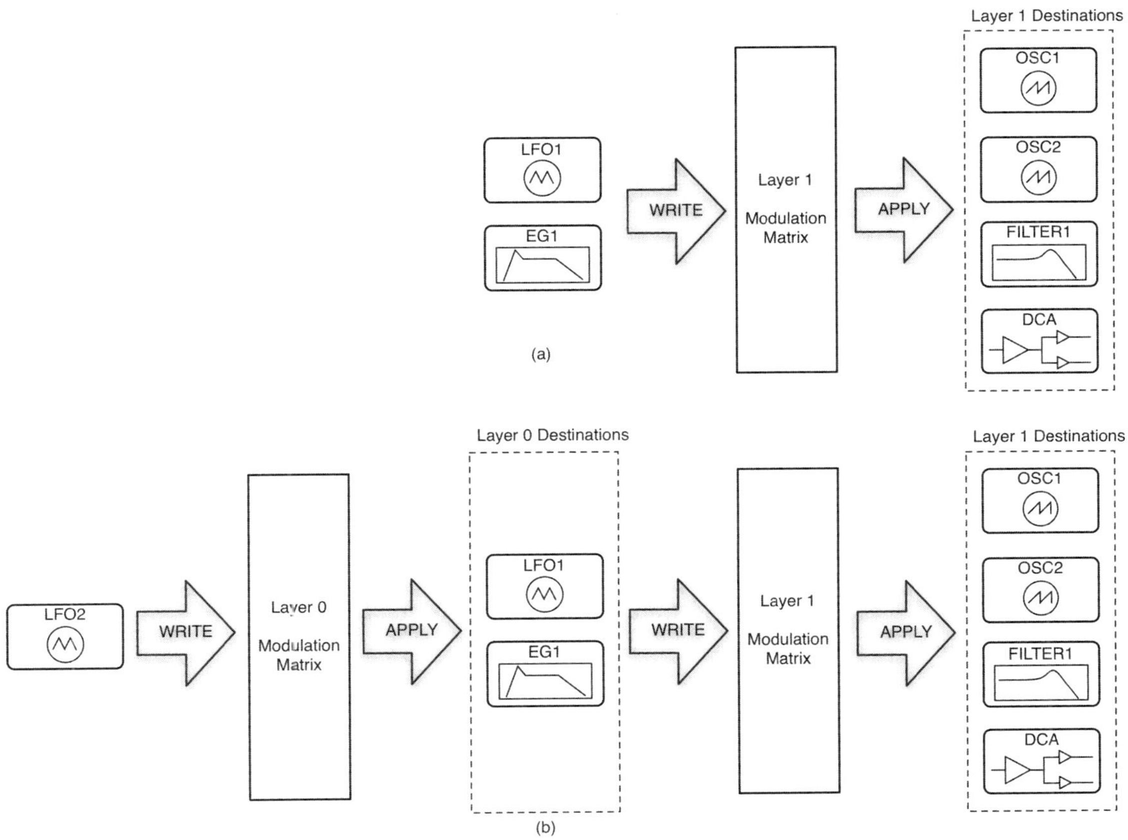

Figure 8.7: (a) The Layer 1 destinations are the synth engine components. (b) The Layer 0 destinations are the Sources for Layer 1.

A conceptual *CModulationMatrix* class diagram is shown in Figure 8.8 while Table 8.2 lists the member variables and functions. The object is fairly simple; the member variables consist of arrays for the sources and destinations, followed by a pointer to the modulation matrix, and a size variable indicating the number of rows in the matrix. The member functions are named in a straightforward manner; the two most important functions are:

- *addModMatrixRow()*—adds a newly created row to the matrix after checking to make sure the row doesn't already exist
- *doModMatrix()*—performs the operation of looping through rows and accumulating sources into destinations

The majority of the object's functionality is implemented in the *ModulationMatrix.h* file, so have a look at that. The first part consists of the member declarations. Notice that the matrix is statically declared and is of the maximum worst-case size in which every source modulated every destination. This is why there is no *removeModMatrixRow()* function—you can't. When you design the synth, you fill up only the rows that you need for your routings. The unused rows are not processed.

```
class CModulationMatrix{
public:
    CModulationMatrix(void);
    ~CModulationMatrix(void);
protected:
    // --- the matrix of mod-rows with the worst-case size (every source
    //     modulates every destination
    //     This is a double-pointer because it is allocated dynamically (*)
    //     and points to an array of pointers(**)
    modMatrixRow** m_ppMatrixCore;
```

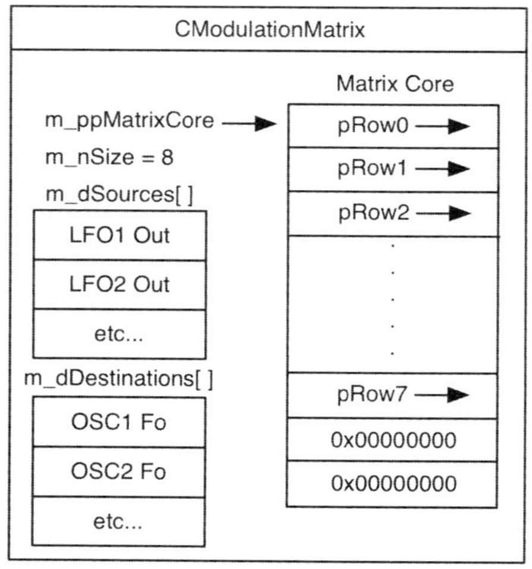

Figure 8.8: A conceptual class diagram for *CModulationMatrix* showing its member attributes; in this example the matrix size is eight.

Table 8.2: *CModulationMatrix* member variables and functions.

***CModulationMatrix* Member Variables**		
Type	**Variable Name**	**Description**
modMatrixRow**	m_ppMatrixCore	pointer to array of matrix row pointers—the core
int	m_nSize	number of non-NULL rows in core
double [ ]	m_dSources	array of source registers
double [ ]	m_dDestinations	array of destination registers

***CModulationMatrix* Member Functions**	
Function Name	**Description**
getModMatrixCore	returns the pointer to the matrix core
setModMatrixCore	sets the matrix core pointer
getMatrixSize	returns the number of non-NULL rows
clearMatrix	clears core matrix, does not delete pointers
clearSources	clears source array
clearDestinations	clears destination array
addModMatrixRow	adds a new row, checks to see if row exists before adding
matrixRowExists	checks to see if a row exists
createMatrixCore	creates a new matrix core; deletes existing core first
deleteModMatrix	deletes row pointers then deletes matrix array
enableModMatrixRow	enables or disables an existing row for flexible routing
checkDestinationLayer	checks to see if a destination is in a certain Layer N group
doModulationMatrix	do the matrix operation

```
	// --- current size depending on number of rows added
	int m_nSize;

public:
	// sources: where each source (LFO, EG, ETC) writes its output value
	double m_dSources[MAX_SOURCES];

	// destinations: where the newly calculated mod values are read from
	double m_dDestinations[MAX_DESTINATIONS];
```

getModMatrixCore() *and* setModMatrixCore()

The *getModMatrixCore()* and *setModMatrixCore()* simply get and set the pointer; during the *set* operation, the matrix is deleted if it already exists. The matrix core is dynamically allocated during construction. *getMatrixSize()* just iterates through the rows and calculates the size.

```
// --- get the matrix core
modMatrixRow** getModMatrixCore(){return m_ppMatrixCore;}

// --- set the matrix core
void setModMatrixCore(modMatrixRow** pModMatrix)
{
      if(m_ppMatrixCore)
      {
              for(int i=0; i<m_nSize; i++)
              {
                      // delete pointer
                      modMatrixRow* pRow = m_ppMatrixCore[i];
                      delete pRow;
                      m_nSize--;
              }
              m_nSize = 0;
              delete [] m_ppMatrixCore;
      }

      m_ppMatrixCore = pModMatrix;
      m_nSize = getMatrixSize();
}
```

clearSources() *and* clearDestinations()

This is followed with simple clearing methods for the source and destination arrays and the matrix core. The *clearDestinations()* function is called every time the modulation matrix runs since it accumulates values into the *Destinations* array.

```
// called once at init
inline void clearSources()
{
      memset(m_dSources,0,sizeof(m_dSources));
}

// called on each pass through the matrix
inline void clearDestinations()
{
      memset(m_dDestinations,0,sizeof(m_dDestinations));
}
```

addModMatrixRow() *and others*

The *addModMatrixRow()* function adds a row but checks to make sure it doesn't exist using the *modMatrixRowExists()* function. A matrix row exists if the source and destination array index values are the same, indicating the same modulation routing. Rows are never duplicated. The *deleteModMatrix()* function destroys all pointers and the array. The *enableModMatrixRow()* function enables or disables matrix rows using the *boolean bEnable* flag in the *modMatrixRow* structure. The rows are identified in the same manner as *modMatrixRowExists*, based on the source/destination index pairing.

```
inline void addModMatrixRow(modMatrixRow* pRow)
{
      if(!m_ppMatrixCore)
             createMatrixCore();

      // add if not already existing
      if(!matrixRowExists(pRow->uSourceIndex, pRow->uDestinationIndex))
      {
             m_ppMatrixCore[m_nSize] = pRow;
             m_nSize++;
      }
      else
        delete pRow;
}
inline bool matrixRowExists(UINT uSourceIndex, UINT uDestinationIndex)
{
      if(!m_ppMatrixCore) return false;

      for(int i=0; i<m_nSize; i++)
      {
             modMatrixRow* pRow = m_ppMatrixCore[i];

             // find matching source/destination pairs
             if(pRow->uSourceIndex == uSourceIndex &&
                pRow->uDestinationIndex == uDestinationIndex)
             {
                    return true;
             }
      }
      return false;
}
inline void deleteModMatrix()
{
      if(!m_ppMatrixCore) return;

      for(int i=0; i<m_nSize; i++)
      {
             // delete pointer
             modMatrixRow* pRow = m_ppMatrixCore[i];
             delete pRow;
             m_nSize--;
      }
      m_nSize = 0;
      delete [] m_ppMatrixCore;
      m_ppMatrixCore = NULL;
}
inline bool enableModMatrixRow(UINT uSourceIndex, UINT uDestinationIndex,
                               bool bEnable)
```

```
{
    if(!m_ppMatrixCore) return false;

    for(int i=0; i<m_nSize; i++)
    {
        modMatrixRow* pRow = m_ppMatrixCore[i];

        // find matching source/destination pairs
        if(pRow->uSourceIndex == uSourceIndex &&
           pRow->uDestinationIndex == uDestinationIndex)
        {
            pRow->bEnable = bEnable;
            return true; // found it
        }
    }
    return false;
}
```

checkDestinationLayer()

The *checkDestinationLayer()* function checks the destination index to decide if it is a Layer 0 or Layer 1 destination. This is where you can define more layers if you wish. You can now see why the *destinations* enumeration has the Layer 0 destinations first—you just check to see if the target destination is within the bounds of the first and last enumeration in the group.

```
inline bool checkDestinationLayer(UINT uLayer, modMatrixRow* pRow)
{
    bool bLayer0 = false;
    if(pRow->uDestinationIndex >= DEST_LFO1_FO &&
          pRow->uDestinationIndex <= DEST_ALL_EG_SUSTAIN_OVERRIDE)
          bLayer0 = true;

    if(uLayer == 0)
          return bLayer0;

    if(uLayer == 1)
          return !bLayer0;

    return false;
}
```

Finally, the meat of the object is in the *doModulationMatrix()* function. The argument is the destination layer. Refer back to the *modMatrixRow* structure; each row is a pointer to one of these structs, and each row contains all the necessary information to process one source into one destination.

The operations are:

- clear the destinations
- loop through the matrix rows and:
    - get the matrix row pointer
    - check to see if row is enabled
    - check to make sure this is the proper destination to process (layer)
    - get the source value from the array
    - apply a transform if there is one
    - check the destination; if one of the Universal "ALL" types, process into all of them (notice that it also writes the value into the ALL slot as well), or just do a single source->destination if not

Notice that the processing function is identical for all rows accumulating the scaled sources into the destinations:

```
destination += source*intensity*range

inline void doModulationMatrix(UINT uModLayer)
{
     if(!m_ppMatrixCore) return;

     // clear dest registers
     clearDestinations();

     for(int i=0; i<m_nSize; i++)
     {
          // get the row
          modMatrixRow* pRow = m_pModMatrix[i];

          // --- this should never happen!
          if(!p) continue;

          // --- if disabled, skip row
          if(! pRow->bEnable) continue;

          // --- check the mod layer
          if(!checkDestinationLayer(uModLayer, pRow)) continue;

          // get the source value
          double dSource = m_dSources[pRow->uSourceIndex];

          switch(pRow->uSourceTransform)
          {
               case TRANSFORM_UNIPOLAR_TO_BIPOLAR:
                    dSource = unipolarToBipolar(dSource);
                    break;

               case TRANSFORM_BIPOLAR_TO_UNIPOLAR:
                    dSource = bipolarToUnipolar(dSource);
                    break;

               <SNIP SNIP SNIP>

               default:
                    break;
          }

          // destination += source*intensity*range
          //
          double dModValue = dSource*(*pRow->pModIntensity)*
                                        (*pRow->pModRange);

          // first check DEST_ALL types
          switch(pRow->uDestinationIndex)
```

```
            {
                case DEST_ALL_OSC_FO:
                    m_dDestinations[DEST_OSC1_FO] += dModValue;
                    m_dDestinations[DEST_OSC2_FO] += dModValue;
                    m_dDestinations[DEST_OSC3_FO] += dModValue;
                    m_dDestinations[DEST_OSC4_FO] += dModValue;
                    m_dDestinations[DEST_ALL_OSC_FO] += dModValue;
                    break;

                <SNIP SNIP SNIP>

                // for all "single" source/dest, this is the modulation
                default:
                    m_dDestinations[pRow->uDestinationIndex]
                                                        += dModValue;
            }
        }
}
```

The *ModulationMatrix.cpp* file houses the very simple constructor and destructor. Notice that the constructor allocates the matrix core, and the destructor does nothing—since the core will be shared it will be up to the global owner to delete the core.

```
CModulationMatrix::CModulationMatrix(void)
{
    // --- dynamic allocation of matrix core
    m_ppMatrixCore = new modMatrixRow*[MAX_SOURCES*MAX_DESTINATIONS];
    memset(m_ppMatrixCore, 0, MAX_SOURCES*MAX_DESTINATIONS*
                                        sizeof(modMatrixRow*));

    m_nSize = 0;
    clearMatrix(); // fill with NULL
    clearSources();
    clearDestinations();
}

CModulationMatrix::~CModulationMatrix(void)
{
}
```

8.3 Using and Programming the Modulation Matrix

In all of our synths, the modulation matrix is a shared object; there is only one matrix per device. In NanoSynth, the plug-in object owns the master modulation matrix, programs it by creating and filling its rows, then gives a pointer to the mod matrix object to each of the synth components in the design. This will change slightly when we introduce polyphony. Figure 8.9 shows a simplified connection diagram for NanoSynth, and a conceptual diagram showing the single modulation matrix and each component owning a pointer to it.

The matrix is programmed in two steps; first, each object must be told where in the *Sources* or *Destinations* array to read or write its modulation values. Then, the matrix rows are dynamically allocated and added to the matrix, which then sets the modulation routing. Note that the order of this two-step sequence is not important. In order to add the modulation matrix, you need to add the following Synth Core files to your NanoSynth Project:

- *ModulationMatrix.h*
- *ModulationMatrix.cpp*

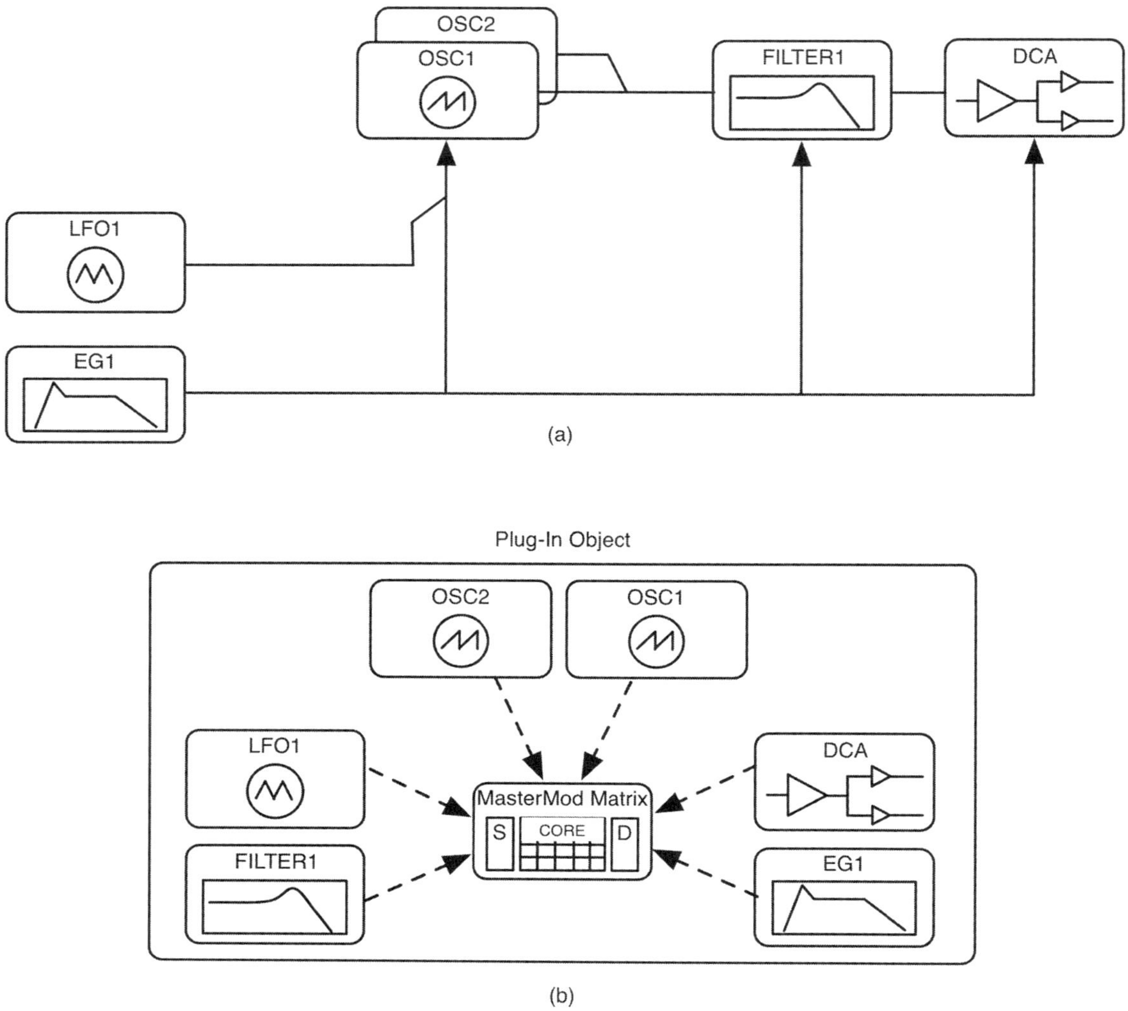

Figure 8.9: (a) Simplified connection diagram for NanoSynth. (b) Each component holds a pointer to a common master modulation matrix.

You then need to either modify the existing NanoSynth files or download the *NanoSynth MM1* project.

- *Oscillator.h*
- *Oscillator.cpp*
- *Filter.h*
- *Filter.cpp*
- *EnvelopeGenerator.h*
- *EnvelopeGenerator.cpp*
- *DCA.h*
- *DCA.cpp*

The base class objects are going to handle the modulation matrix, so you don't need to alter any derived objects. The additions to the objects are simple:

- a pointer to the common modulation matrix
- index values in the Sources array for modulation sources
- index values in the Destinations array for modulation destinations

Some objects will only have modulation sources, others destinations, and a few will have both. You will need to alter the *update()* function on objects that are modulated, and you will need to modify the *doOutput()* functions of the derived objects so they write their values to the proper matrix locations.

Oscillator.h

In the *Oscillator.h* file, you first *#include* the modulation matrix's *.h* file, then make declarations for the modulation matrix pointer, sources and destinations. For the oscillator we have:

Sources (where we read our modulation input values):

- oscillator f_o
- pulse width (for square wave only)
- amplitude (for Amplitude Modulation or AM)

Destinations (where we write our outputs):

- output 1 (for LFO this is the normal output; for pitched oscillators, it is the left output)
- output 2 (for LFO this is the quad phase output; for pitched oscillators, it is the right output)

```
#include "ModulationMatrix.h"

#define OSC_FO_MOD_RANGE 2                //2 semitone default
#define OSC_HARD_SYNC_RATIO_RANGE 4       //4
#define OSC_PITCHBEND_MOD_RANGE 12        //12 semitone default
#define OSC_FC_MIN 20                     //20 Hz
#define OSC_FC_MAX 20480                  //20.480 kHz = 10 octaves up from 20 Hz
#define OSC_PULSEWIDTH_MIN 2              //2%
#define OSC_PULSEWIDTH_MAX 98             //98%

class COscillator
{
public:
     COscillator(void);
     virtual ~COscillator(void);

     // --- Modulation Matrix --------------------
     //
     // --- the shared modulation matrix
     CModulationMatrix* m_pModulationMatrix;     // the matrix

     // --- sources that we read from
     //       indexes in m_pModulationMatrix->Sources[]
     UINT m_uModSourceFo;
     UINT m_uModSourcePulseWidth;
     UINT m_uModSourceAmp;

     // --- destinations that we write to
     //       indexes in m_pModulationMatrix->Destinations[]
     UINT m_uModDestOutput1;
     UINT m_uModDestOutput2;
     // -----------------------------------------

     // --- oscillator run flag
     bool m_bNoteOn;

     etc...
```

Next, you modify the *update()* function so that it picks up the modulation values from the matrix. Notice how the Amp Mod value is inverted:

```
inline virtual void updateOscillator()
{
     // --- ignore LFO mode for noise sources
```

```
    if(m_uWaveform == rsh || m_uWaveform == qrsh)
            m_uLFOMode = free;

    // --- Modulation Matrix
    //
    // --- get from matrix Sources
    if(m_pModulationMatrix)
    {
            // --- zero is norm for these
            m_dFoMod = m_pModulationMatrix->
                                    m_dDestinations[m_uModSourceFo];
            m_dPWMod = m_pModulationMatrix->
                                    m_dDestinations[m_uModSourcePulseWidth];

            // --- amp mod is 0->1
            // --- invert for oscillator output mod
            m_dAmpMod = m_pModulationMatrix->m_dDestinations
                                                 [m_uModSourceAmp];
            m_dAmpMod = 1.0 - m_dAmpMod;
    }

    // --- do the  complete frequency mod
    m_dFo = m_dOscFo*m_dFoRatio*pitchShiftMultiplier(m_dFoMod +
                                                m_dPitchBendMod +
                                                m_nOctave*12.0 +
                                                m_nSemitones +
                                                m_nCents/100.0);

    etc...
```

Oscillator.cpp

You initialize the variables in the constructor. The modulation matrix pointer is NULL and is always optional in our objects. We know the matrix is in use if this pointer is non-NULL. The default sources and destinations are all of the NONE variety, indicating that nothing is connected.

```
COscillator::COscillator(void)
{
    // --- initialize variables
    m_dSampleRate = 44100;

    <SNIP SNIP SNIP>

    // --- for hard sync
    m_pBuddyOscillator = NULL;
    m_bMasterOsc = false;

    // --- default modulation matrix inits
    m_pModulationMatrix = NULL;

    // --- everything is disconnected unless you use mod matrix
    m_uModSourceFo = DEST_NONE;
```

```
        m_uModSourcePulseWidth = DEST_NONE;
        m_uModSourceAmp = DEST_NONE;
        m_uModDestOutput1 = SOURCE_NONE;
        m_uModDestOutput2 = SOURCE_NONE;
}
```

COscillator Derived Classes

Modify the *doOscillate()* function of the derived classes to add the matrix functionality. For the LFO, the destination outputs are normal and quad phase while the pitched oscillators write their outputs as left and right pairs.

LFO.h

Modify the *doOscillate()* function to write outputs to the matrix Sources array:

```
inline virtual double doOscillate(double* pQuadPhaseOutput = NULL)
{
        if(!m_bNoteOn)
        {
                if(pQuadPhaseOutput)
                        *pQuadPhaseOutput = 0.0;

                return 0.0;
        }

        // output
        double dOut = 0.0;
        double dQPOut = 0.0;

        <SNIP SNIP SNIP>

        // ok to inc modulo now
        incModulo();

        if(m_pModulationMatrix)
        {
                // write our outputs into their destinations
                m_pModulationMatrix->m_dSources[m_uModDestOutput1] =
                                                dOut*m_dAmplitude*m_dAmpMod;

                // add quad phase/stereo output
                m_pModulationMatrix->m_dSources[m_uModDestOutput2] =
                                                dQPOut*m_dAmplitude*m_dAmpMod;
        }

                etc...
}
```

QBLimitedOscillator.h

Modify the *doOscillate()* function to write outputs to the matrix *Sources* array. This is a monophonic oscillator, so you just copy the final output to both left and right slots in the array.

```
virtual inline double doOscillate(double* pAuxOutput = NULL)
{
      if(!m_bNoteOn)
            return 0.0;

      <SNIP SNIP SNIP>


      // ok to inc modulo now
      incModulo();
      if(m_uWaveform == TRI)
            incModulo();

      if(m_pModulationMatrix)
      {
            // write our outputs into their destinations
            m_pModulationMatrix->m_dSources[m_uModDestOutput1] =
                                                      dOut*m_dAmplitude*m_dAmpMod;

            // add quad phase/stereo output (QBL is mono)
            m_pModulationMatrix->m_dSources[m_uModDestOutput2] =
                                                dOut*m_dAmplitude*m_dAmpMod;
      }

      // m_dAmpMod is set in updateOscillator()
      if(pAuxOutput)
            *pAuxOutput = dOut*m_dAmplitude*m_dAmpMod;;

      // m_dAmpMod is set in updateOscillator()
      return dOut*m_dAmplitude*m_dAmpMod;
}
```

WTOscillator.cpp

Modify the *doOscillate()* function to write outputs to the matrix *Sources* array. This is a monophonic oscillator, so you just copy the final output to both left and right slots in the array.

```
double CWTOscillator::doOscillate(double* pAuxOutput)
{
      if(!m_bNoteOn)
      {
            if(pAuxOutput)
                  *pAuxOutput = 0.0;

            return 0.0;
      }
      <SNIP SNIP SNIP>

      // get first output
      double dOutSample = doWaveTable(m_dReadIndex, m_dWT_inc);
```

```
        if(m_pModulationMatrix)
        {
                // write our outputs into their destinations
                m_pModulationMatrix->m_dSources[m_uModDestOutput1] =
                                                dOutSample*m_dAmplitude*m_dAmpMod;

                // add quad phase/stereo output (QBL is mono)
                m_pModulationMatrix->m_dSources[m_uModDestOutput2] =
                                                dOutSample*m_dAmplitude*m_dAmpMod;
        }

        // mono oscillator
        if(pAuxOutput)
                *pAuxOutput = dOutSample*m_dAmplitude*m_dAmpMod;

        return dOutSample*m_dAmplitude*m_dAmpMod;
}
```

Filter.h

In the *Filter.h* file, you first *#include* the modulation matrix's *.h* file, then make declarations for the modulation matrix pointer, sources and destinations. For the filter we have:

Sources:

- filter f_c
- filter *fc* control (for Filter Key Track, where the *fc* control value is overwritten with the MIDI note pitch)

Destinations:

- none

```
#include "ModulationMatrix.h"

// 46.881879936 semitones = semitonesBetweenFrequencies(80, 18000.0)/2.0
#define FILTER_FC_MOD_RANGE 46.881879936465680
#define FILTER_FC_MIN 80            // 80 Hz
#define FILTER_FC_MAX 18000         // 18 kHz

class CFilter
{
public:
        CFilter(void);
        ~CFilter(void);

        // --- Modulation Matrix --------------------
        //
        // --- the shared modulation matrix
        CModulationMatrix* m_pModulationMatrix;

        // --- sources that we read from
        //          indexes in m_pModulationMatrix->Sources[]
        UINT m_uModSourceFc;
```

```
    UINT m_uSourceFcControl; // direct control over Fc, for key-track mod
    // ----------------------------------------

    // --- the user's cutoff frequency control position
    double m_dFcControl;

    etc...
```

Filter.cpp

Like the oscillator, you just initialize the variables in the constructor. The modulation matrix pointer is NULL and is always optional in our objects. The default connections are DEST_NONE.

```
CFilter::CFilter(void)
{
    // defaults
    m_dSampleRate = 44100;
    m_dFc = 10000.0;
    m_dQ = 0.707;
    m_dFcControl = 10000.0;

    m_dFcMod = 0.0;
    m_dAuxControl = 0.5;
    m_uNLP = OFF;
    m_dSaturation = 1.0;

    // --- default modulation matrix inits
    m_pModulationMatrix = NULL;

    // --- everything is disconnected unless you use mod matrix
    m_uModSourceFc = DEST_NONE;
    m_uSourceFcControl = DEST_NONE;
}
```

EnvelopeGenerator.h

In the *EnvelopeGenerator.h* file, you first *#include* the modulation matrix's *.h* file, then make declarations for the modulation matrix pointer, sources and destinations. For the EG we have:

Sources:

- EG attack scaling
- EG decay scaling

Destinations:

- normal EG output
- biased EG output

We are going to discuss the EG attack and decay scaling shortly. The destinations are simply the two outputs of the object.

```
#include "ModulationMatrix.h"

class CEnvelopeGenerator
{
public:
```

```
CEnvelopeGenerator(void);
~CEnvelopeGenerator(void);

// --- Modulation Matrix --------------------
//
// --- the shared modulation matrix
CModulationMatrix* m_pModulationMatrix;

// --- sources that we read from
//        indexes in m_pModulationMatrix->Sources[]
UINT m_uModSourceEGAttackScaling;
UINT m_uModSourceEGDecayScaling;

// --- destinations that we write to
//        indexes in m_pModulationMatrix->Destinations[]
UINT m_uModDestEGOutput;
UINT m_uModDestBiasedEGOutput;
// -----------------------------------------

etc...
```

EnvelopeGenerator.cpp

Like the oscillator, you just initialize the variables in the constructor. The modulation matrix pointer is NULL and is always optional in our objects. The default connections are the NONE types.

```
CEnvelopeGenerator::CEnvelopeGenerator(void)
{
    m_dSampleRate = 44100;

    <SNIP SNIP SNIP>

    m_bResetToZero = false;
    m_bLegatoMode = false;

    // --- default modulation matrix inits
    m_pModulationMatrix = NULL;

    // --- everything is disconnected unless you use mod matrix
    m_uModSourceEGAttackScaling = DEST_NONE;
    m_uModSourceEGDecayScaling = DEST_NONE;
    m_uModDestEGOutput = SOURCE_NONE;
    m_uModDestBiasedEGOutput = SOURCE_NONE;
}
```

DCA.h

In the *DCA.h* file, you first *#include* the modulation matrix's *.h* file, then make declarations for the modulation matrix pointer, sources and destinations. For the EG we have:

Sources:

- EG Mod
- Amp Mod (dB) for vibrato
- Velocity
- Pan

Destinations:

- none

```
#include "ModulationMatrix.h"

#define AMP_MOD_RANGE -96    // -96 dB

class CDCA
{
public:
     CDCA(void);
     ~CDCA(void);

     // --- ATTRIBUTES
     // --- PUBLIC: these variables may be get/set
     //             you may make get/set functions for them
     //             if you like, but will add function call layer
     //
     // --- Modulation Matrix --------------------
     //
     // --- the shared modulation matrix
     CModulationMatrix* m_pModulationMatrix;

     // --- sources that we read from
     //         indexes in m_pModulationMatrix->Sources[]
     UINT m_uModSourceEG;
     UINT m_uModSourceAmp_dB;
     UINT m_uModSourceVelocity;
     UINT m_uModSourcePan;

     // --- we have no destinations
     // ----------------------------------------

protected:

     etc...
```

DCA.cpp

Like the oscillator, you just initialize the variables in the constructor. The modulation matrix pointer is NULL and is always optional in our objects. The default connections are the NONE variety.

```
CDCA::CDCA(void)
{
     // --- initialize variables
     m_dAmplitudeControl = 1.0;
     m_dAmpMod_dB = 0.0;

     <SNIP SNIP SNIP>
```

```
        // --- default modulation matrix inits
        m_pModulationMatrix = NULL;

        // --- everything is disconnected unless you use mod matrix
        m_uModSourceEG = DEST_NONE;
        m_uModSourceAmp_dB = DEST_NONE;
        m_uModSourceVelocity = DEST_NONE;
        m_uModSourcePan = DEST_NONE;
}
```

There is another detail to handle—the modulation intensity and range values are pointers in the *modMatrixRow* structure. This is so that you can directly control these values with parameters from your GUI. We need to declare a couple of variables to connect to these pointers. We need default intensity and range values of 1.0, and we also need filter and oscillator frequency ranges (the same ones we used in the processing for NanoSynth). In the plug-in's *.h* file, you need to add:

```
        // need these for mod matrix
        double m_dDefaultModIntensity;// 1.0
        double m_dDefaultModRange;    // 1.0
        double m_dOscFoModRange;      // variable
        double m_dFilterModRange;     // variable
```

These are initialized in the constructor. Notice that the ranges are initialized with constants defined in the objects' *.h* files, but you could also connect these to GUI parameters and make them variable or user-programmable.

Programming the Master Modulation Matrix

Table 8.1 is somewhat simplified in that it does not list the exact intensity variable names and does not use the enumerations that set the source/destination pairs, transform, intensity and enabled/disabled status. Each synth in the book features a more complete modulation matrix table. For NanoSynth, Table 8.1 is rewritten as Table 8.2. In this table, each pair of rows makes a complete mod matrix row. For example, the first row-pair is decoded as:

Source:	LFO1
Destination:	all OSC f_o
Intensity:	m_dDefaultModIntensity
Range:	m_dOscFoModRange
Transform:	none
Enabled by default:	Yes

Examining Table 8.1, you can see the LFO1 output modulates both the oscillator f_o values. Table 8.3 shows information for this row in the modulation matrix. Notice the use of the DEST_ALL_OSC_FO value. We try to use these when possible to minimize the number of matrix rows and simplify coding.

The plug-in object will own the master modulation matrix and share it with the synth components. In this version of NanoSynth, it shares the object in its entirety—the core, source and destination arrays. In the polyphonic synths, the plug-in will only share the matrix core. In all plug-ins, the master modulation matrix is declared and named the same way in the object's *.h* file:

```
        // --- the Modulation Matrix
        CModulationMatrix m_GlobalModMatrix;
```

You program the matrix by creating *modMatrixRows* and adding them to the core array. You need to create one row for every source/destination pair your synth will feature; there is enough room in the matrix for every possible connection combination (about 4,000 bytes in total). You decode the rows in the modulation matrix table and convert each one into two lines of C++ code that create the row, then add it to the matrix. Examine Table 8.3 and the code below to make sure you understand how the rows are converted to code.

```
        << ** Code Listing 8.1: Mod Matrix Routings I ** >>
```

Table 8.3: The NanoSynth mod matrix table

NanoSynth Modulation Matrix			
Source	**Destination/Intensity**	**Transform/Range**	**enabled**
SOURCE_LFO1	DEST_ALL_OSC_FO	TRANSFORM_NONE	TRUE
	m_dDefaultModIntensity	m_dOscFoModRange	
SOURCE_BIASED_EG1	DEST_ALL_OSC_FO	TRANSFORM_NONE	TRUE
	m_dEG1OscIntensity	m_dOscFoModRange	
SOURCE_BIASED_EG1	DEST_ALL_FILTER_FC	TRANSFORM_NONE	TRUE
	m_dDefaultModIntensity	m_dFilterModRange	
SOURCE_EG1	DEST_DCA_EG	TRANSFORM_NONE	TRUE
	m_dEG1DCAIntensity	m_dDefaultModRange	
SOURCE_MIDI_NOTE_NUM	DEST_ALL_FILTER_KEYTRACK	TRANSFORM_NOTE_ NUMBER_TO_FREQUENCY	TRUE
	m_dFilterKeyTrackIntensity	m_dDefaultModRange	

```
// --- The Mod matrix "wiring" for DEFAULTS for all synths
// create a row for each source/destination pair
modMatrixRow* pRow = NULL;

// LFO1 -> ALL OSC1 FC
pRow = createModMatrixRow(SOURCE_LFO1,
                          DEST_ALL_OSC_FO,
                          &m_dDefaultModIntensity,
                          &m_dOscFoModRange,
                          TRANSFORM_NONE,
                          true); // enabled!
m_GlobalModMatrix.addModMatrixRow(pRow);

// EG1 -> ALL OSC1 FC
pRow = createModMatrixRow(SOURCE_BIASED_EG1,
                          DEST_ALL_OSC_FO,
                          &m_dEG1OscIntensity,
                          &m_dOscFoModRange,
                          TRANSFORM_NONE,
                          true); // enabled!
m_GlobalModMatrix.addModMatrixRow(pRow);

// EG1 -> FILTER1 FC
pRow = createModMatrixRow(SOURCE_BIASED_EG1,
                          DEST_ALL_FILTER_FC,
                          &m_dDefaultModIntensity,
                          &m_dFilterModRange,
                          TRANSFORM_NONE,
                          true); // enabled!
m_GlobalModMatrix.addModMatrixRow(pRow);

// EG1 -> DCA EG
pRow = createModMatrixRow(SOURCE_EG1,
                          DEST_DCA_EG,
                          &m_dEG1DCAIntensity,
```

```
                            &m_dDefaultModRange,
                            TRANSFORM_NONE,
                            true); // enabled!
m_GlobalModMatrix.addModMatrixRow(pRow);

// NOTE NUMBER -> FILTER Fc CONTROL
pRow = createModMatrixRow(SOURCE_MIDI_NOTE_NUM,
                            DEST_ALL_FILTER_KEYTRACK,
                            &m_dFilterKeyTrackIntensity,
                            &m_dDefaultModRange,
                            TRANSFORM_NOTE_NUMBER_TO_FREQUENCY,
                            true); // enabled!
m_GlobalModMatrix.addModMatrixRow(pRow);

<< END ** Code Listing 8.1: Mod Matrix Routings I ** END >>
```

After loading the matrix core with the matrix routing rows, you then initialize the range variables and set up the individual synth components with a pointer to the master modulation matrix. Examine Code Listing 8.2 carefully and notice the initialization of the components' *m_pModulationMatrix* variable. Then, look at the default source and destinations for each component; these are going to be the same for all synths in the book, so we will only examine it in detail here. For this version of NanoSynth, the DCA has only one source connection to the EG and nothing else. That will change as we develop NanoSynth further in the chapter.

```
<< ** Code Listing 8.2: Mod Matrix Connections I ** >>

// --- initialize intensities
m_dDefaultModIntensity = 1.0;
m_dDefaultModRange = 1.0;

// --- initialize mod ranges
// OSC_FO_MOD_RANGE defined in oscillator.h
m_dOscFoModRange = OSC_FO_MOD_RANGE;

// FILTER_FC_MOD_RANGE defined in filter.h
m_dFilterModRange = FILTER_FC_MOD_RANGE;

// --- this sets up the DEFAULT CONNECTIONS!
m_Osc1.m_pModulationMatrix = &m_ModulationMatrix;

// --- NOTE: Oscillator Source is a Destination of a modulator
m_Osc1.m_uModSourceFo = DEST_OSC1_FO;
m_Osc1.m_uModSourceAmp = DEST_OSC1_OUTPUT_AMP;

// --- do same for Osc2
m_Osc2.m_pModulationMatrix = &m_ModulationMatrix;
m_Osc2.m_uModSourceFo = DEST_OSC2_FO;
m_Osc2.m_uModSourceAmp = DEST_OSC2_OUTPUT_AMP;

// --- now the filter
m_Filter1.m_pModulationMatrix = &m_ModulationMatrix;
m_Filter1.m_uModSourceFc = DEST_FILTER1_FC;
m_Filter1.m_uSourceFcControl = DEST_ALL_FILTER_KEYTRACK;
```

```
// --- these are modulators: they write their outputs into
//     what will be a Source for something else
m_LFO1.m_pModulationMatrix = &m_ModulationMatrix;
m_LFO1.m_uModDestOutput1 = SOURCE_LFO1;
m_LFO1.m_uModDestOutput2 = SOURCE_LFO1Q;

m_EG1.m_pModulationMatrix = &m_ModulationMatrix;
m_EG1.m_uModDestEGOutput = SOURCE_EG1;
m_EG1.m_uModDestBiasedEGOutput = SOURCE_BIASED_EG1;

// --- DCA Setup:
m_DCA.m_pModulationMatrix = &m_ModulationMatrix;
m_DCA.m_uModSourceEG = DEST_DCA_EG;
m_DCA.m_uModSourceAmp_dB = DEST_NONE; // not connected (yet)
m_DCA.m_uModSourceVelocity = DEST_NONE; // not connected (yet)
m_DCA.m_uModSourcePan = DEST_NONE; // not connected (yet)

<< END ** Code Listing 8.2: Mod Matrix Connections I ** END >>
```

Study these initializations carefully, and you will see a potentially confusing paradigm here: the modulators write their outputs into the *Sources* array location. Thus their output "destinations" are going into a "source array." This leads to statements like this:

```
m_LFO1.m_uModDestOutput1 = SOURCE_LFO1;
```

This says that LFO1's modulation destination (output) will be written into the *Sources* array at location SOURCE_LFO1. The same thing happens for modulation destination; they read their modulation sources from the *Destinations* array:

```
m_Filter1.m_uModSourceFc = DEST_FILTER1_FC;
```

Enabling and Disabling Rows

This first version of NanoSynth has only one modulation routing that may be enabled or disabled—filter key-track. Enabling and disabling a routing is easy; just call the function on the object. The logic will look like this (notice the way the rows are identified by source and destination index values; these must match identically to the way you set up the matrix core):

```
// --- mod matrix stuff
if(m_uFilterKeyTrack == 1)
     m_GlobalModMatrix.enableModMatrixRow(SOURCE_MIDI_NOTE_NUM,
                                          DEST_ALL_FILTER_KEYTRACK, true);
else
     m_GlobalModMatrix.enableModMatrixRow(SOURCE_MIDI_NOTE_NUM,
                                          DEST_ALL_FILTER_KEYTRACK, false);
```

Calling the doModulationMatrix() *Function*

The argument for the *doModulationMatrix()* function is the layer index. Even though we have no Layer 0 modulators yet, we will be using this same code repeatedly, so it's worth implementing here. First, you do the Layer 0 modulation matrix, then update the Layer 0 modulators, which are EG1 and LFO1 here. Then, you do the Layer 1 modulation matrix and update the components that were modulated. Then, the digital audio engine processing can happen.

The code for rendering the audio is in Code Listing 8.3—this identical block of code is used on all three platforms.

```
<< ** Code Listing 8.3: Mod Matrix Render I ** >>
```

```
// --- ARTICULATION BLOCK --- //
// --- DO layer 0 modulators
m_GlobalModMatrix.doModulationMatrix(0);

// --- update layer 1 modulators
m_EG1.update();
m_LFO1.update();

// --- DO layer 1 modulators
m_EG1.doEnvelope();
m_LFO1.doOscillate();

// --- modulation matrix Layer 1
m_GlobalModMatrix.doModulationMatrix(1);

// --- update Layer 1 targets
m_DCA.update();
m_Filter1.update();
m_Osc1.update();
m_Osc2.update();

// --- DIGITAL AUDIO ENGINE BLOCK --- //
// (OSC1 + OSC2) --> FILTER --> DCA
double dOscOut = 0.5*m_Osc1.doOscillate() +
                 0.5*m_Osc2.doOscillate();

// --- filter the mix
double dFilterOut = m_Filter1.doFilter(dOscOut);

// --- apply DCA to output
m_DCA.doDCA(dFilterOut, dFilterOut, dOutL, dOutR);

<< END ** Code Listing 8.3: Mod Matrix Render I ** END >>
```

Now, let's complete the rest of the new NanoSynth MM1 (Mod Matrix 1) project—you can start a new project or just keep modifying your existing NanoSynth. You can also download the NanoSynth MM1 project.

8.4 NanoSynth MM Part One: RackAFX

Copy the *ModulationMatrix.h* and *.cpp* files into your project folder and add them into the Visual Studio project.

NanoSynth.h

Open the *NanoSynth.h* file and add the following:

```
#include "ModulationMatrix.h"
```

In the variable declarations, add the matrix and its intensity and range variables.

```
class CNanoSynth : public CPlugIn
{
public:
```

```
<SNIP SNIP SNIP>

// Add your code here: ------------------------------------------ //
// --- synth components
CQBLimitedOscillator m_Osc1;

<SNIP SNIP SNIP>

// --- synth update function
void update();

// --- RX channel
UINT m_uMidiRxChannel;

// --- the Modulation Matrix
CModulationMatrix m_GlobalModMatrix;

// need these for mod matrix
double m_dDefaultModIntensity;       // 1.0
double m_dDefaultModRange;           // 1.0
double m_dOscFoModRange;
double m_dFilterModRange;

// END OF USER CODE ---------------------------------------------- //
```

NanoSynth.cpp

In the Constructor, add the initializations for the modulation ranges, then create and add the matrix rows. After that, you initialize the sub-components by setting the source and/or destination index values and setting their modulation matrix pointers to our global matrix. Make sure you understand how the matrix rows are setup according to Table 8.1, so that you can easily add more modulation routings as the projects progress.

```
CNanoSynth::CNanoSynth()
{
    // Added by RackAFX - DO NOT REMOVE
    //
    initUI();
    // END initUI()

    <SNIP SNIP SNIP>

    // receive on all channels
    m_uMidiRxChannel = MIDI_CH_ALL;

    // --- initialize mod ranges
    m_dDefaultModIntensity = 1.0;
    m_dDefaultModRange = 1.0;

    // --- initialize mod ranges
    m_dOscFoModRange = OSC_FO_MOD_RANGE;
    m_dFilterModRange = FILTER_FC_MOD_RANGE;
```

```
        // --- create the Mod Matrix Rows
        << INSERT ** Code Listing 8.1: Mod Matrix Routings I ** HERE >>

        // --- set the source and destination indexes on the components
        << INSERT ** Code Listing 8.2: Mod Matrix Connections I ** HERE >>
}
```

In the Destructor, destroy the rows that we created.

```
CNanoSynth::~CNanoSynth(void)
{
        // --- delete on master ONLY
        m_GlobalModMatrix.deleteModMatrix();
}
```

In *processAudioFrame()* alter the function to use the new modulation matrix:

```
bool __stdcall CNanoSynth::processAudioFrame(float* pInputBuffer,
                                             float* pOutputBuffer,
                                             UINT uNumInputChannels,
                                             UINT uNumOutputChannels)
{
        double dOutL = 0.0;
        double dOutR = 0.0;

        if(m_Osc1.m_bNoteOn)
        {
                << INSERT ** Code Listing 8.3: Mod Matrix Render I ** HERE >>

                // now check for note off
                if(m_EG1.getState() == 0) // 0 = off
                {
                        m_Osc1.stopOscillator();
                        m_Osc2.stopOscillator();
                        m_LFO1.stopOscillator();
                        m_EG1.stopEG();
                }
        }

        pOutputBuffer[0] = dOutL;

        <SNIP SNIP SNIP>

        return true;
}
```

In *midiNoteOn()* add a single line of code to write the new note number into the modulation matrix *Sources* array:

```
bool __stdcall CNanoSynth::midiNoteOn(UINT uChannel, UINT uMIDINote,
                                      UINT uVelocity)
```

```
{
        // test channel/ignore
        if(m_uMidiRxChannel != MIDI_CH_ALL && uChannel != m_uMidiRxChannel)
                return false;

        <SNIP SNIP SNIP>

        // not playing, reset and do updateOscillator()
        if(!m_Osc1.m_bNoteOn)
        {
                m_Osc1.startOscillator(); // this does updateOscillator()
                m_Osc2.startOscillator();
        }
        else // if note is playing, just change the pitch
        {
                m_Osc1.updateOscillator();
                m_Osc2.updateOscillator();
        }

        // --- KT routing
        // --- set the note number in the mod matrix for filter key track
        m_GlobalModMatrix.m_dSources[SOURCE_MIDI_NOTE_NUM] = uMIDINote;

        return true;
}
```

Build and test the synth—it should sound and behave exactly as before, but using the modulation matrix instead. If something doesn't work, go back and check your code carefully.

8.5 NanoSynth MM Part One: VST3

Copy the *ModulationMatrix.h* and *.cpp* files into your project folder and add them into the Visual Studio project.

VSTSynthProcessor.h

Open the *VSTSynthProcessor.h* file and add the following:

```
#include "ModulationMatrix.h"
```

In the variable declarations, add the matrix and its intensity and range variables.

```
class Processor : public AudioEffect
{
public:

        <SNIP SNIP SNIP>

        CMoogLadderFilter m_Filter1;

        // --- the Modulation Matrix
        CModulationMatrix m_GlobalModMatrix;
```

```
// need these for mod matrix
double m_dDefaultModIntensity;      // 1.0
double m_dDefaultModRange;          // 1.0
double m_dOscFoModRange;
double m_dFilterModRange;

etc...
```

VSTSynthProcessor.cpp

In the Constructor, add the initializations for the modulation ranges. Make sure you understand how the matrix rows are setup according to Table 8.1, so that you can easily add more modulation routings as the projects progress.

```
Processor::Processor()
{
    <SNIP SNIP SNIP>

    m_dFilterKeyTrackIntensity = DEFAULT_FILTER_KEYTRACK_INTENSITY;
    m_dEG1OscIntensity = DEFAULT_BIPOLAR;

    // --- initialize intensities
    m_dDefaultModIntensity = 1.0;
    m_dDefaultModRange = 1.0;
    m_dOscFoModRange = OSC_FO_MOD_RANGE;
    m_dFilterModRange = FILTER_FC_MOD_RANGE;

    // VST3 specific
    m_dMIDIPitchBend = DEFAULT_MIDI_PITCHBEND; // -1 to +1

    etc...
```

In *setActive()*, add the initializations for the objects then dynamically allocate the matrix rows and initialize the sub-components by setting the source and/or destination index values and their modulation matrix pointers to our global matrix when activated, and destroy the global matrix when deactivated.

```
tresult PLUGIN_API Processor::setActive(TBool state)
{
    if(state)
    {
        <SNIP SNIP SNIP>

        // clear
        m_dLastNoteFrequency = 0.0;

        // --- create the Mod Matrix Rows
        << INSERT ** Code Listing 8.1: Mod Matrix Routings I ** HERE >>

        // --- set the source and destination indexes on the components
        << INSERT ** Code Listing 8.2: Mod Matrix Connections I ** HERE >>

        etc...
    }
```

```
        else
        {
                // --- do OFF stuff; delete stuff allocated above
                if(m_pFilterLogParam)
                        delete m_pFilterLogParam;

                // --- delete on master ONLY
                m_GlobalModMatrix.deleteModMatrix();
        }

        // --- base class method call is last
        return AudioEffect::setActive (state);
}
```

In *update()* add code to enable and disable the filter key track row in the matrix.

```
void Processor::update()
{
        <SNIP SNIP SNIP>

        // --- DCA
        m_DCA.setPanControl(m_dPanControl);
        m_DCA.setAmplitude_dB(m_dVolume_dB);

        // --- mod matrix stuff
        if(m_uFilterKeyTrack == 1)
                m_GlobalModMatrix.enableModMatrixRow(SOURCE_MIDI_NOTE_NUM,
                                                DEST_ALL_FILTER_KEYTRACK, true);
        else
                m_GlobalModMatrix.enableModMatrixRow(SOURCE_MIDI_NOTE_NUM,
                                                DEST_ALL_FILTER_KEYTRACK, false);
}
```

In *process()* remove the old hard-wired code and replace it with the streamlined version using the modulation matrix.

```
tresult PLUGIN_API Processor::process(ProcessData& data)
{
                        <SNIP SNIP SNIP Indents Removed>

                        // --- output "accumulator"
                        double dOutL = 0.0;
                        double dOutR = 0.0;

                        for(int32 j=0; j<samplesToProcess; j++)
                        {
                                // --- clear accumulators
                                dOutL = 0.0;
                                dOutR = 0.0;

                                if(m_Osc1.m_bNoteOn)
                                {
                                        << INSERT ** Code Listing 8.3: Mod Matrix Render ** HERE >>
```

```
                        // now check for note off
                        if(m_EG1.getState() == 0) // 0 = off
                        {
                                m_Osc1.stopOscillator();
                                m_Osc2.stopOscillator();
                                m_LFO1.stopOscillator();
                                m_EG1.stopEG();
                        }
                }

                etc...
```

In *doProcessEvent()* modify the note on logic to write the note number into the matrix:

```
bool Processor::doProcessEvent(Event& vstEvent)
{
        <SNIP SNIP SNIP>

                // --- NOTE ON
                case Event::kNoteOnEvent:
                {
                        <SNIP SNIP SNIP>

                        m_LFO1.startOscillator();
                        m_EG1.startEG();

                        // --- note number in the mod matrix for filter key track
                        m_GlobalModMatrix.m_dSources[SOURCE_MIDI_NOTE_NUM] =
                                uMIDINote;
                        break;
                }

                etc...
```

Build and test the synth—it should sound and behave exactly as before, but using the modulation matrix instead. If something doesn't work, go back and check your code carefully.

8.6 NanoSynth MM Part One: AU

Add the *ModulationMatrix.h* and *.cpp* files into your XCode Project. Then modify the AUSynth object:

AUSynth.h

Open the *VSTSynthProcessor.h* file and add the following:

```
#include "ModulationMatrix.h"
```

In the variable declarations, add the matrix and its intensity and range variables. For AU, you must also specifically add three new variables for the EG to OSC and DCA intensities, and the filter key-track intensity. The variables are stored in the AU parameter container, but we need to link them to actual variables. This is because the *modMatrixRow* structure uses pass-by-pointer for these variables so your GUI can directly control them.

```
class AUSynth : public AUInstrumentBase
{
```

```
public:

    <SNIP SNIP SNIP>

    CMoogLadderFilter m_Filter1;

    // --- the Modulation Matrix
    CModulationMatrix m_GlobalModMatrix;

    // need these for mod matrix
    double m_dDefaultModIntensity;       // 1.0
    double m_dDefaultModRange;           // 1.0
    double m_dOscFoModRange;
    double m_dFilterModRange;

    // AU ONLY
    double m_dEG1OscIntensity;
    double m_dEG1DCAIntensity;
    double m_dFilterKeyTrackIntensity;

    // --- updates all voices at once
    void update();

    etc...
```

AUSynth.cpp

In the Constructor, add the initializations for the objects and matrix as we discussed previously. Make sure you understand how the matrix rows are set up according to Table 8.1, so that you can easily add more modulation routings as the projects progress.

```
AUSynth::AUSynth(AudioUnit inComponentInstance)
    : AUInstrumentBase(inComponentInstance, 0, 1)
{
    // --- create input, output ports, groups and parts
    CreateElements();

    <SNIP SNIP SNIP>

    // receive on all channels
    m_uMidiRxChannel = MIDI_CH_ALL;

    // --- AU must declare these for pointer passing
    m_dEG1OscIntensity = 0.0;
    m_dEG1DCAIntensity = 1.0;
    m_dFilterKeyTrackIntensity = 1.0;

    // --- initialize intensities
    m_dDefaultModIntensity = 1.0;
    m_dDefaultModRange = 1.0;

    // --- initialize mod ranges
```

```
        m_dOscFoModRange = OSC_FO_MOD_RANGE;
        m_dFilterModRange = FILTER_FC_MOD_RANGE;

        // --- create the Mod Matrix Rows
        << INSERT ** Code Listing 8.1: Mod Matrix Routings I ** HERE >>

        you will// --- set the source and destination indexes on the components
        << INSERT ** Code Listing 8.2: Mod Matrix Connections I ** HERE >>
    }
```

In *update()* add the code to enable/disable the filter key track modulation.

```
    void AUSynth::update()
    {
        <SNIP SNIP SNIP>

        // --- mod matrix stuff
        if(Globals()->GetParameter(FILTER_KEYTRACK))
                m_GlobalModMatrix.enableModMatrixRow(SOURCE_MIDI_NOTE_NUM,
                                                DEST_ALL_FILTER_KEYTRACK, true);
        else
                m_GlobalModMatrix.enableModMatrixRow(SOURCE_MIDI_NOTE_NUM,
                                                DEST_ALL_FILTER_KEYTRACK, false);
    }
```

In *Render()* alter the function to use the new modulation matrix. First, pick up the latest updated values for the new intensity variables you had to declare, then use the code described previously to render the audio.

```
    OSStatus AUSynth::Render(AudioUnitRenderActionFlags& ioActionFlags,
                             const AudioTimeStamp& inTimeStamp,
                             UInt32 inNumberFrames)
    {
        // --- broadcast MIDI events
        PerformEvents(inTimeStamp);

        // --- do the mass update for this frame
        update();

        // --- NanoSynth/AU variable delivery
        m_dEG1OscIntensity = Globals()->GetParameter(EG1_TO_OSC_INTENSITY);
        m_dEG1DCAIntensity = Globals()->GetParameter(EG1_TO_DCA_INTENSITY);
        m_dFilterKeyTrackIntensity = Globals()->GetParameter
                                         (FILTER_KEYTRACK_INTENSITY);

        // --- get the number of channels
        AudioBufferList& bufferList = GetOutput(0)->GetBufferList();
        UInt32 numChans = bufferList.mNumberBuffers;

        <SNIP SNIP SNIP>

        // --- the frame processing loop
        for(UInt32 frame=0; frame<inNumberFrames; ++frame)
```

```
{
        // --- clear accumulators
        dOutL = 0.0;
        dOutR = 0.0;
        if(m_Osc1.m_bNoteOn)
        {
        << INSERT ** Code Listing 8.3: Mod Matrix Render I ** HERE >>

                // now check for note off
                if(m_EG1.getState() == 0) // 0 = off
                {
                        m_Osc1.stopOscillator();
                        m_Osc2.stopOscillator();
                        m_LFO1.stopOscillator();
                        m_EG1.stopEG();
                }
        }

        etc...
```

In *StartNote()* modify the note on logic to write the note number into the matrix:

```
OSStatus AUSynth::StartNote(MusicDeviceInstrumentID inInstrument,
                            MusicDeviceGroupID inGroupID,
                            NoteInstanceID *outNoteInstanceID,
                            UInt32 inOffsetSampleFrame,
                            const MusicDeviceNoteParams &inParams)
{
    <SNIP SNIP SNIP>

    m_LFO1.startOscillator();
    m_EG1.startEG();

    // --- set the note number in the mod matrix for filter key track
    m_GlobalModMatrix.m_dSources[SOURCE_MIDI_NOTE_NUM] = uMIDINote;

    return noErr;
}
```

Build and test the synth—it should sound and behave exactly as before, but using the modulation matrix instead. If something doesn't work, go back and check your code carefully.

8.7 More MIDI Modulation Routings

In this section we will add all the rest of the MIDI modulator routings that each synth will possess. This includes adding a key-velocity to DCA routing so that your synth becomes velocity sensitive. Table 8.4 lists the new modulation routings.

The first four rows are fairly self-explanatory—we want to map Velocity to the DCA velocity input, the Pitch Bend wheel to the oscillator pitch, and MIDI volume and pan controls (CC7 and CC10 respectively) to the DCA volume and pan mod inputs. The sustain pedal transmits a value that is either below 64 (off) or equal to or above 64 (on). The MIDI to On/Off Switch transform handles this simple logic.

These are not the only routings—you can get very clever and very expressive here. For example, you could add a row that lets MIDI Velocity alter the cut-off frequency so that the cutoff moves up with increasing key velocity. Using the MIDI note number as a modulation source is extremely popular as well. The last two routings are more advanced because these are Layer 0 modulations. These modulations need to be applied to the Envelope Generator(s) before the EGs write their outputs.

Table 8.4: Additional MIDI modulation routings for all synths.

NanoSynth Modulation Matrix			
Source	**Destination/Intensity**	**Transform/Range**	**enabled**
SOURCE_VELOCITY	DEST_DCA_VELOCITY	TRANSFORM_NONE	TRUE
	m_dDefaultModIntensity	m_dDefaultModRange	
SOURCE_PITCHBEND	DEST_ALL_OSC_FO	TRANSFORM_NONE	TRUE
	m_dDefaultModIntensity	m_dOscFoPitchBendModRange	
SOURCE_MIDI_VOLUME_CC07	DEST_DCA_AMP	TRANSFORM_INVERT_MIDI_NORMALIZE	TRUE
	m_dDefaultModIntensity	m_dAmpModRange	
SOURCE_MIDI_PAN_CC10	DEST_DCA_PAN	TRANSFORM_MIDI_TO_PAN	TRUE
	m_dDefaultModIntensity	m_dDefaultModRange	
SOURCE_SUSTAIN_PEDAL	DEST_ALL_EG_SUSTAIN_OVERRIDE	TRANSFORM_MIDI_SWITCH	TRUE
	m_dDefaultModRange	m_dDefaultModIntensity	
SOURCE_VELOCITY	DEST_ALL_EG_ATTACK_SCALING	TRANSFORM_MIDI_NORMALIZE	FALSE
	m_dDefaultModRange	m_dDefaultModIntensity	
SOURCE_MIDI_NOTE_NUM	DEST_ALL_EG_DECAY_SCALING	TRANSFORM_MIDI_NORMALIZE	FALSE
	m_dDefaultModRange	m_dDefaultModIntensity	

Sustain Pedal

The MIDI sustain pedal directly affects the EG object; when the sustain pedal is held, the EG stays in the sustain state, even if the note is released. This is called the sustain pedal override. When the sustain pedal override occurs, we set the flag indicating this condition. When the note is released with the sustain pedal held, we will set the release pending flag to indicate that we need to move to the release state when the sustain pedal is released.

Velocity to Attack Scaling

In this modulation, the key velocity controls the attack time; higher velocities shorten the attack while lower velocities do not (or alternatively extend it). In this case, we have hardcoded the scaling range linearly across the velocity, but you could alter this to create exotic attack scaling modulation routings.

Note Number to Decay Scaling

In this modulation, the note number scales the decay time of the envelope. Typically, it is set so that higher note numbers shorten the decay time while lower numbers do not (or alternatively extend it). The scaling may be applied to the decay time only, or both decay and release times.

Both modulations require that the MIDI value [0..127] needs to be normalized [0..1] and then inverted [1..0] because of the direction of modulation (note: you could experiment with the opposite versions too). We need to add four more variables to the EG object for handling the sustain pedal and the two new modulation routings. In the *.h* file, declare them:

```
class CEnvelopeGenerator
{
    <SNIP SNIP SNIP>

    // --- sustain is a level, not a time
    double m_dSustainLevel;

    // --- for modulating attack and decay times
    double m_dAttackTimeScalar;   // for velocity -> attack time mod
    double m_dDecayTimeScalar;    // for note# -> decay time mod

    // special override for sustain pedal
    bool m_bSustainOverride;
    bool m_bReleasePending;

    etc...
```

Next, implement the function to set this override value. If the sustain is released and we have a release pending, call the *noteOff()* method, which transfers the EG into the release state.

```
// --- for sustain pedal
inline void setSustainOverride(bool b)
{
      m_bSustainOverride = b;

      if(m_bReleasePending && !m_bSustainOverride)
      {
             m_bReleasePending = false;
             noteOff();
      }
}
```

Lastly, implement the sustain override in the *doEnvelopeGenerator()* function. The EG stays in the release state for as long as the pedal is held. We will add the rest of the sustain pedal code when we discuss this modulation routing. Modify the release state portion of the function to hold the sustain level in the event of the sustain override.

```
inline double doEnvelope(double* pBiasedOutput = NULL)
{
      // --- decode the state
      switch(m_uState)
      {
             <SNIP SNIP SNIP>

             case release:
             {
                    // --- if sustain pedal is down, override and return
                    if(m_bSustainOverride)
                    {
                           m_dEnvelopeOutput = m_dSustainLevel;
                           break;
                    }
                    else
                    // --- render value
                           m_dEnvelopeOutput = m_dReleaseOffset +
                                        m_dEnvelopeOutput*m_dReleaseCoeff;

                    // --- check go to next state
                    if(m_dEnvelopeOutput <= 0.0 || m_dReleaseTime_mSec <= 0.0)
                    {
                           m_dEnvelopeOutput = 0.0;
                           m_uState = off;              // go to next state
                           break;
                    }
                    break;
             }

             etc...
```

In the *.cpp* file, first initialize the new variables in the constructor.

```
CEnvelopeGenerator::CEnvelopeGenerator(void)
{
      <SNIP SNIP SNIP>
      m_dAttackTimeScalar = 1.0;
      m_dDecayTimeScalar = 1.0;
      m_bSustainOverride = false;
      m_bReleasePending = false;

      etc...
```

Next, alter the functions for calculating the attack and decay times. Optionally, you may alter the function that calculates the release time in a similar manner using the decay time scalar. All you need to do is scale the attack or decay time in milliseconds by the scalar value.

```
void CEnvelopeGenerator::calculateAttackTime()
{
      // --- samples for the exponential rate
      double dSamples = m_dSampleRate*
                  ((m_dAttackTimeScalar*m_dAttackTime_mSec)/1000.0);

      // --- coeff and base for iterative exponential calculation
      m_dAttackCoeff = exp(-log((1.0 + m_dAttackTCO)/m_dAttackTCO)/
                              dSamples);
      m_dAttackOffset = (1.0 + m_dAttackTCO)*(1.0 - m_dAttackCoeff);
}

void CEnvelopeGenerator::calculateDecayTime()
{
      // --- samples for the exponential rate
      double dSamples = m_dSampleRate*
                        ((m_dDecayTimeScalar*m_dDecayTime_mSec)/1000.0);

      // --- coeff and base for iterative exponential calculation
      m_dDecayCoeff = exp(-log((1.0 + m_dDecayTCO)/m_dDecayTCO)/dSamples);
      m_dDecayOffset = (m_dSustainLevel - m_dDecayTCO)*(1.0 - m_dDecayCoeff);
}
```

Back in the *.h* file, alter the *update()* function to rescale the attack and decay times. Up until this point, there was no per-sample update needed for the EG. The calculation of the attack and decay time is intensive, however, so we only want to call this once when the note is struck. Notice how the attack and decay are handled as inversions—this is because a 0 in the destination array means "no modulation," and we need to invert it for these two routings. Add the code to check for the sustain pedal and call the sustain pedal override as needed.

```
inline void update()
{
      if(!m_pModulationMatrix || !m_bOutputEG) return;

      // --- with mod matrix, when value is 0 there is NO modulation,
      //     so here we calc (1.0 - dScale) as a comparison
      if(m_uModSourceEGAttackScaling != DEST_NONE &&
                                    m_dAttackTimeScalar == 1.0)
      {
            double dScale = m_pModulationMatrix->m_dDestinations
                                    [m_uModSourceEGAttackScaling];
```

```
            if(m_dAttackTimeScalar != 1.0 - dScale)
            {
                    m_dAttackTimeScalar = 1.0 - dScale;
                    calculateAttackTime();
            }
    }

    // --- for vel->attack and note#->decay scaling modulation
    //     NOTE: make sure this is only called ONCE during a new note  //      event!
    if(m_uModSourceEGDecayScaling != DEST_NONE &&
                                    m_dDecayTimeScalar == 1.0)
    {
            double dScale = m_pModulationMatrix->m_dDestinations
                                            [m_uModSourceEGDecayScaling];
            if(m_dDecayTimeScalar != 1.0 - dScale)
            {
                    m_dDecayTimeScalar = 1.0 - dScale;
                    calculateDecayTime();
            }
    }

    // --- sustain pedal
    if(m_uModSourceSustainOverride != DEST_NONE)
    {
            double dSustain = m_pModulationMatrix->m_dDestinations
                                            [m_uModSourceSustainOverride];
            if(dSustain == 0)
                    setSustainOverride(false);
            else
                    setSustainOverride(true);
    }
}
```

Take a minute to look at the calculation functions so you can see how the times are scaled. You can see that when the scalar value is 0, the attack or decay time is 0 (fastest) and when the value is 1.0, the attack or decay time is the normal value set in the GUI. This is where you could alter this scaling if desired.

The good news is that the modulation matrix makes it easy to add these new routings. Once again, there are two steps: first add the new *modMatrixRows* (there are six new row pairs in Table 8.4, so there will be six corresponding rows in the matrix) and then set up the objects with new source and destination index values. When you add the new rows to the matrix, the order doesn't really matter. Notice also that the velocity to attack and note number to decay modulations are disabled by default.

```
<< ** Code Listing 8.4: Mod Matrix Routings II ** >>

// VELOCITY -> DCA VEL
pRow = createModMatrixRow(SOURCE_VELOCITY,
                          DEST_DCA_VELOCITY,
                          &m_dDefaultModIntensity,
                          &m_dDefaultModRange,
                          TRANSFORM_NONE,
                          true);
m_GlobalModMatrix.addModMatrixRow(pRow);
```

```
// PITCHBEND -> PITCHBEND
pRow = createModMatrixRow(SOURCE_PITCHBEND,
                          DEST_ALL_OSC_FO,
                          &m_dDefaultModIntensity,
                          &m_dOscFoPitchBendModRange,
                          TRANSFORM_NONE,
                          true);
m_GlobalModMatrix.addModMatrixRow(pRow);

// MIDI Volume CC07
pRow = createModMatrixRow(SOURCE_MIDI_VOLUME_CC07,
                          DEST_DCA_AMP,
                          &m_dDefaultModIntensity,
                          &m_dAmpModRange,
                          TRANSFORM_INVERT_MIDI_NORMALIZE,
                          true);
m_GlobalModMatrix.addModMatrixRow(pRow);

// MIDI Pan CC10
pRow = createModMatrixRow(SOURCE_MIDI_PAN_CC10,
                          DEST_DCA_PAN,
                          &m_dDefaultModIntensity,
                          &m_dDefaultModRange,
                          TRANSFORM_MIDI_TO_PAN,
                          true);
m_GlobalModMatrix.addModMatrixRow(pRow);

// MIDI Sustain Pedal
pRow = createModMatrixRow(SOURCE_SUSTAIN_PEDAL,
                                      DEST_ALL_EG_SUSTAIN_OVERRIDE,
                                      &m_dDefaultModIntensity,
                                      &m_dDefaultModRange,
                                      TRANSFORM_MIDI_SWITCH,
                                      true);
m_GlobalModMatrix.addModMatrixRow(pRow);

// VELOCITY -> EG ATTACK SOURCE_VELOCITY
// 0 velocity -> scalar = 1, normal attack time
// 128 velocity -> scalar = 0, fastest (0) attack time;
// We use TRANSFORM_MIDI_NORMALIZE and the inversion takes
// place in the EG update()
pRow = createModMatrixRow(SOURCE_VELOCITY,
                          DEST_ALL_EG_ATTACK_SCALING,
                          &m_dDefaultModIntensity,
                          &m_dDefaultModRange,
                          TRANSFORM_MIDI_NORMALIZE,
                          false); /* DISABLED BY DEFAULT */
m_GlobalModMatrix.addModMatrixRow(pRow);

// NOTE NUMBER -> EG DECAY SCALING
// note#0 -> scalar = 1, normal decay time
```

```
// note#128 -> scalar = 0, fastest (0) decay time
// We use TRANSFORM_MIDI_NORMALIZE and the inversion takes
// place in the EG update()
pRow = createModMatrixRow(SOURCE_MIDI_NOTE_NUM,
                          DEST_ALL_EG_DECAY_SCALING,
                          &m_dDefaultModIntensity,
                          &m_dDefaultModRange,
                          TRANSFORM_MIDI_NORMALIZE,
                          false); /* DISABLED BY DEFAULT */
m_GlobalModMatrix.addModMatrixRow(pRow);
<< END ** Code Listing 8.4: Mod Matrix Routings II ** END >>
```

The EG and DCA need to have their modulation index values changed. You did this in the constructor, so you will need to modify that chunk of code too.

```
<< ** Code Listing 8.5: Mod Matrix Connections II ** >>
// --- EG Setup:
m_EG1.m_pModulationMatrix = &m_GlobalModMatrix;
m_EG1.m_uModDestEGOutput = SOURCE_EG1;
m_EG1.m_uModDestBiasedEGOutput = SOURCE_BIASED_EG1;
m_EG1.m_uModSourceEGAttackScaling = DEST_EG1_ATTACK_SCALING;
m_EG1.m_uModSourceEGDecayScaling = DEST_EG1_DECAY_SCALING;
m_EG1.m_uModSourceSustainOverride = DEST_EG1_SUSTAIN_OVERRIDE;

// --- DCA Setup:
m_DCA.m_pModulationMatrix = &m_ModulationMatrix;
m_DCA.m_uModSourceEG = DEST_DCA_EG;
m_DCA.m_uModSourceAmp_dB = DEST_NONE; // not connected
m_DCA.m_uModSourceVelocity = DEST_DCA_VELOCITY;
m_DCA.m_uModSourcePan = DEST_DCA_PAN;

<< END ** Code Listing 8.5: Mod Matrix Connections II ** END >>
```

Finally, the synth *update()* function needs code for enabling/disabling the new routings, just like the filter key-tracking.

```
<< ** Code Listing 8.6: Mod Matrix Update I ** >>

if(m_uVelocityToAttackScaling == 1)
       m_GlobalModMatrix.enableModMatrixRow(SOURCE_VELOCITY,
                                            DEST_ALL_EG_ATTACK_SCALING,
                                            true);
else
       m_GlobalModMatrix.enableModMatrixRow(SOURCE_VELOCITY,
                                            DEST_ALL_EG_ATTACK_SCALING,
                                            false);

if(m_uNoteNumberToDecayScaling == 1)
       m_GlobalModMatrix.enableModMatrixRow(SOURCE_MIDI_NOTE_NUM,
```

Table 8.5: GUI parameter table for the new modulation routings.

NanoSynth Enumerated String Parameters (UINT)			
Control Name	**Variable Name**	**enum String**	**VST3/AU Index**
Vel->Att Scale	m_uVelocityToAttackScaling	OFF,ON	VELOCITY_TO_ATTACK
Note->Dcy Scale	m_uNoteNumberToDecayScaling	OFF,ON	NOTE_NUM_TO_DECAY

```
                                                DEST_ALL_EG_DECAY_SCALING,
                                                true);
else
          m_GlobalModMatrix.enableModMatrixRow(SOURCE_MIDI_NOTE_NUM,
                                                DEST_ALL_EG_DECAY_SCALING,
                                                false);
<< END ** Code Listing 8.6: Mod Matrix Update I ** END >>
```

You will also need to make some modifications to the MIDI message handling since these modulations all come from MIDI; these are platform specific, so we will address them individually. All platforms will need to add the following GUI controls using the normal methods in Chapter 2. Table 8.5 lists the new parameters—these are just on/off controls for the new modulation routings.

8.8 NanoSynth MM Part Two: RackAFX

Add the GUI controls for the new modulation routings in Table 8.5; we placed these controls inside the RackAFX LCD, but you can also use the radio buttons or sliders. Next, declare a couple of new modulation range variables in the project's *.h* file:

NanoSynth.h

Add the range variable declarations:

```
class CNanoSynth : public CPlugIn
{
public:
      <SNIP SNIP SNIP>

      double m_dFilterModRange;     //
      double m_dOscFoPitchBendModRange;
      double m_dAmpModRange;

      void update();

      etc...
```

NanoSynth.cpp

In the constructor:

- initialize the new range variables
- add the new mod sources to the EG for velocity and note number scaling and sustain pedal
- add the new volume and pan mod sources to the DCA
- create and add the new modulation matrix rows

```
CNanoSynth::CNanoSynth()
{
     <SNIP SNIP SNIP>

     // --- initialize mod ranges
     m_dOscFoModRange = OSC_FO_MOD_RANGE;
     m_dFilterModRange = FILTER_FC_MOD_RANGE;
     m_dOscFoPitchBendModRange = OSC_PITCHBEND_MOD_RANGE;
     m_dAmpModRange = AMP_MOD_RANGE;

     <SNIP SNIP SNIP>

     // NOTE NUMBER -> FILTER Fc CONTROL
     pRow = createModMatrixRow(SOURCE_MIDI_NOTE_NUM,
                               DEST_ALL_FILTER_KEYTRACK,
                               &m_dFilterKeyTrackIntensity,
                               &m_dDefaultModRange,
                               TRANSFORM_NOTE_NUMBER_TO_FREQUENCY,
                               true);
     m_GlobalModMatrix.addModMatrixRow(pRow);

     << INSERT ** Code Listing 8.4: Mod Matrix Routings II ** HERE >>

     m_LFO1.m_uModDestOutput1 = SOURCE_LFO1;
     m_LFO1.m_uModDestOutput2 = SOURCE_LFO1Q;

     << INSERT ** Code Listing 8.5: Mod Matrix Connections II ** HERE >>

} // end of constructor
```

An issue with the MIDI volume and pan controls is that they need to be initialized at startup so that the volume is turned all the way up and the pan is in the center. When the synth loads, it can't request MIDI messages for these values, so we need to make a default setting. This is easily done in *prepareForPlay()* by simply forcing values into the matrix *Sources* array:

```
bool __stdcall CNanoSynth::prepareForPlay()
{
     <SNIP SNIP SNIP>

     update();

     // --- default turn on volume and center the pan
     m_GlobalModMatrix.m_dSources[SOURCE_MIDI_VOLUME_CC07] = 127;
     m_GlobalModMatrix.m_dSources[SOURCE_MIDI_PAN_CC10] = 64;

     return true;
}
```

Now we need to add code to the MIDI functions to trap and add the MIDI messages to the matrix Sources array. The list breaks down as follows:

midiNoteOn()

- Velocity
- (already have MIDI note number from previous project)

midiPitchBend()

- Pitch Bend

midiMessages()

- Volume (CC 7)
- Pan (CC 10)
- Sustain Pedal

So, alter the functions to transmit the information to the matrix:

```
bool __stdcall CNanoSynth::midiNoteOn(UINT uChannel, UINT uMIDINote,
                                      UINT uVelocity)
{
      // test channel/ignore
      if(m_uMidiRxChannel != MIDI_CH_ALL && uChannel != m_uMidiRxChannel)
              return false;

      <SNIP SNIP SNIP>

      // --- set the note number in the mod matrix for filter key track
      m_ModulationMatrix.m_dSources[SOURCE_MIDI_NOTE_NUM] = uMIDINote;

      // --- velocity routing
      m_GlobalModMatrix.m_dSources[SOURCE_VELOCITY] = uVelocity;

      return true;
}

bool __stdcall CNanoSynth::midiPitchBend(UINT uChannel,
                                         int nActualPitchBendValue,
                                         float fNormalizedPitchBendValue)
{
      <SNIP SNIP SNIP>

      // --- send to matrix
      m_GlobalModMatrix.m_dSources[SOURCE_PITCHBEND] =
                                              fNormalizedPitchBendValue;
      return true;
}

bool __stdcall CNanoSynth::midiMessage(unsigned char cChannel,
                                       unsigned char cStatus,
                                       unsigned char cData1,
                                       unsigned char cData2)
{
      <SNIP SNIP SNIP>

      switch(cStatus)
      {
              <SNIP SNIP SNIP>
```

```
            case CONTROL_CHANGE:
            {
                switch(cData1)
                {
                    case VOLUME_CC07:
                    {
                        // MIDI LOGGING HERE
                        // --- send to matrix
                        m_GlobalModMatrix.m_dSources
                            [SOURCE_MIDI_VOLUME_CC07] = (UINT)cData2;

                        break;
                    }
                    case PAN_CC10:
                    {
                        // MIDI LOGGING HERE
                        // --- send to matrix
                        m_GlobalModMatrix.m_dSources
                            [SOURCE_MIDI_PAN_CC10] = (UINT)cData2;

                        break;
                    }
                    case EXPRESSION_CC11:
                    {
                        // not implemented yet
                        break;
                    }
                    case SUSTAIN_PEDAL:
                    {
                        // MIDI LOGGING HERE
                        // --- send to matrix
                        m_GlobalModMatrix.m_dSources
                            [SOURCE_SUSTAIN_PEDAL] = (UINT)cData2;

                        break;
                    }
```

Lastly, add the code to enable and disable the routing, much like you did for filter key-track in the *update()* function.

```
void CNanoSynth::update()
{
    <SNIP SNIP SNIP>

    // --- mod matrix stuff
    if(m_uFilterKeyTrack == 1)
        m_GlobalModMatrix.enableModMatrixRow(SOURCE_MIDI_NOTE_NUM,
                                  DEST_ALL_FILTER_KEYTRACK, true);
    else
        m_GlobalModMatrix.enableModMatrixRow(SOURCE_MIDI_NOTE_NUM,
                                  DEST_ALL_FILTER_KEYTRACK, false);
```

```
<< INSERT ** Code Listing 8.6: Mod Matrix Update I ** HERE >>

etc...
```

Set your controller to transmit volume and pan, build and test the synth. It will react to volume, pan, and pitch bend. Enable and disable the velocity to attack and note to decay modulations to verify these work properly.

8.9 NanoSynth MM Part Two: VST3

Add the GUI controls for the new modulation routings in Table 8.5. Next, you need to declare a couple of new modulation range variables in the project's *.h* file:

VSTSynthProcessor.h

Add the range variable declarations:

```
class Processor : public AudioEffect
{
public:
      <SNIP SNIP SNIP>

      // NS MM2
      UINT m_uVelocityToAttackScaling;
      UINT m_uNoteNumberToDecayScaling;
      double m_dOscFoPitchBendModRange;
      double m_dAmpModRange;

      etc...
```

VSTSynthProcessor.cpp

In the constructor, initialize the new range variables

```
Processor::Processor()
{
      <SNIP SNIP SNIP>

      // --- initialize mod ranges
      m_dOscFoModRange = OSC_FO_MOD_RANGE;
      m_dFilterModRange = FILTER_FC_MOD_RANGE;
      m_dOscFoPitchBendModRange = OSC_PITCHBEND_MOD_RANGE;
      m_dAmpModRange = AMP_MOD_RANGE;

      <SNIP SNIP SNIP>

      etc...
```

In *setActive()* add the new rows for the modulation matrix from Code Listing 8.5 when the object is activated. An issue with the MIDI volume and pan controls is that they need to be initialized at startup so that the volume is turned all the way up and the pan is in the center. When the synth loads, it can't request MIDI messages for these values, so we need to make a default setting. So, you need to:

- add the new mod sources to the EG for velocity and note number scaling and sustain pedal
- force the MIDI volume and pan to take their default values, otherwise the note may not sound or may be panned incorrectly until the user moves a control

- add the new attack and decay mod sources to the EG
- add the new volume and pan mod sources to the DCA

```
tresult PLUGIN_API Processor::setActive(TBool state)
{
      if(state)
      {
            <SNIP SNIP SNIP>

            update();

            // --- default turn on volume and center the pan
            m_GlobalModMatrix.m_dSources[SOURCE_MIDI_VOLUME_CC07] = 127;
            m_GlobalModMatrix.m_dSources[SOURCE_MIDI_PAN_CC10] = 64;

            <SNIP SNIP SNIP>

            // NOTE NUMBER -> FILTER Fc CONTROL
            pRow = createModMatrixRow(SOURCE_MIDI_NOTE_NUM,
                                      DEST_ALL_FILTER_KEYTRACK,
                                      &m_dFilterKeyTrackIntensity,
                                      &m_dDefaultModRange,
                                      TRANSFORM_NOTE_NUMBER_TO_FREQUENCY,
                                      false); /* DISABLED BY DEFAULT */
            m_GlobalModMatrix.addModMatrixRow(pRow);

            << INSERT ** Code Listing 8.4: Mod Matrix Routings II ** HERE >>

            <SNIP SNIP SNIP>

            m_LFO1.m_uModDestOutput1 = SOURCE_LFO1;
            m_LFO1.m_uModDestOutput2 = SOURCE_LFO1Q;

            << INSERT ** Code Listing 8.5: Mod Matrix Connections II ** HERE
            >>
```

Next you add code to the MIDI functions to trap and add the MIDI messages to the matrix *Sources* array. The list breaks down as follows:

doProcessEvent() - Note On:

- Velocity
- (already have MIDI note number from previous project)

The note message is trapped in *doProcessEvent()*, and you need to add the velocity routing:

```
bool Processor::doProcessEvent(Event& vstEvent)
{
      <SNIP SNIP SNIP>

            // --- NOTE ON
            case Event::kNoteOnEvent:
```

```
            {
                    <SNIP SNIP SNIP>

                    // --- note number in the mod matrix for filter key track
                    m_GlobalModMatrix.m_dSources[SOURCE_MIDI_NOTE_NUM] =
                                                    uMIDINote;
                    // --- for Vel->Att scaling
                    m_GlobalModMatrix.m_dSources[SOURCE_VELOCITY] =
                                             uMIDIVelocity;

                    break;
            }

            etc...
```

Next, we have all the other MIDI messages:

doControlUpdate()

- Pitch Bend
- Volume (CC 7)
- Pan (CC 10)
- Sustain Pedal

Alter the function to send the messages to the modulation matrix:

```
bool Processor::doControlUpdate(ProcessData& data)
{

      <SNIP SNIP SNIP Indents Removed>

      // --- MIDI messages
      case MIDI_PITCHBEND: // want -1 to +1
      {
              // LOG MIDI
              // --- send to matrix
              m_dMIDIPitchBend = unipolarToBipolar(value);
              m_GlobalModMatrix.m_dSources[SOURCE_PITCHBEND] =
                                                  m_dMIDIPitchBend;

              break;
      }

      case MIDI_VOLUME_CC7: // want 0 to 127
      {
              // LOG MIDI
              // --- send to matrix
              m_uMIDIVolumeCC7 = unipolarToMIDI(value);
              m_GlobalModMatrix.m_dSources[SOURCE_MIDI_VOLUME_CC07] =
                                                     m_uMIDIVolumeCC7;

              break;
      }

      case MIDI_PAN_CC10: // want 0 to 127
      {
              // LOG MIDI
```

```
            // --- send to matrix
            m_uMIDIPanCC10 = unipolarToMIDI(value);
            m_GlobalModMatrix.m_dSources[SOURCE_MIDI_PAN_CC10] =
                                                  m_uMIDIPanCC10;
            break;
        }

        case MIDI_SUSTAIN_PEDAL: // want 0 to 1
        {
            // LOG MIDI
            // --- send to matrix
            m_GlobalModMatrix.m_dSources[SOURCE_SUSTAIN_PEDAL] =
                                             unipolarToMIDI(value);
            break;
        }
```

Lastly, add the code to enable and disable the routing, much like you did for filter key-track in the *update()* function.

```
void Processor::update()
{
    <SNIP SNIP SNIP>

    // --- mod matrix stuff
    if(m_uFilterKeyTrack == 1)
        m_GlobalModMatrix.enableModMatrixRow(SOURCE_MIDI_NOTE_NUM,
                                  DEST_ALL_FILTER_KEYTRACK, true);
    else
        m_GlobalModMatrix.enableModMatrixRow(SOURCE_MIDI_NOTE_NUM,
                                  DEST_ALL_FILTER_KEYTRACK, false);

    << INSERT ** Code Listing 8.6: Mod Matrix Update I ** HERE >>

    etc...
```

Set your controller to transmit volume and pan and build and test the synth. It will react to volume, pan, and pitch bend. Enable and disable the velocity to attack and note to decay modulations to verify these work properly.

8.10 NanoSynth MM Part Two: AU

Add the GUI controls for the new modulation routings in Table 8.5. Next, you need to declare a couple of new modulation range variables in the project's *.h* file:

```
AUSynth.h
Add the range variable declarations:

class AUSynth : public AUInstrumentBase
{
public:
    <SNIP SNIP SNIP>

    double m_dFilterModRange;    //
```

```
    double m_dOscFoPitchBendModRange;
    double m_dAmpModRange;

    etc...
```

AUSynth.cpp

In the constructor:

- initialize the new range variables
- add the new mod sources to the EG for velocity and note number scaling and sustain pedal
- add the new volume and pan mod sources to the DCA
- create and add the new modulation matrix rows

```
AUSynth::AU Synth()
{
    <SNIP SNIP SNIP>

    // --- initialize mod ranges
    m_dOscFoModRange = OSC_FO_MOD_RANGE;
    m_dFilterModRange = FILTER_FC_MOD_RANGE;
    m_dOscFoPitchBendModRange = OSC_PITCHBEND_MOD_RANGE;
    m_dAmpModRange = AMP_MOD_RANGE;

    <SNIP SNIP SNIP>

    // NOTE NUMBER -> FILTER Fc CONTROL
    pRow = createModMatrixRow(SOURCE_MIDI_NOTE_NUM,
                              DEST_ALL_FILTER_KEYTRACK,
                              &m_dFilterKeyTrackIntensity,
                              &m_dDefaultModRange,
                              TRANSFORM_NOTE_NUMBER_TO_FREQUENCY,
                              true);
    m_GlobalModMatrix.addModMatrixRow(pRow);

    << INSERT ** Code Listing 8.4: Mod Matrix Routings II ** HERE >>

    <SNIP SNIP SNIP>

    m_LFO1.m_uModDestOutput1 = SOURCE_LFO1;
    m_LFO1.m_uModDestOutput2 = SOURCE_LFO1Q;

    << INSERT ** Code Listing 8.5: Mod Matrix Connections II ** HERE >>

} // end of constructor
```

An issue with the MIDI volume and pan controls is that they need to be initialized at startup so that the volume is turned all the way up and the pan is in the center. When the synth loads, it can't request MIDI messages for these items, so we need to make a default setting. This is easily done in *Initialize()* by simply forcing values into the matrix *Sources* array:

```
ComponentResult AUSynth::Initialize()
{
    <SNIP SNIP SNIP>
```

```
        update();

        // --- default turn on volume and center the pan
        m_GlobalModMatrix.m_dSources[SOURCE_MIDI_VOLUME_CC07] = 127;
        m_GlobalModMatrix.m_dSources[SOURCE_MIDI_PAN_CC10] = 64;

        return noErr;
    }
```

Now you add code to the MIDI functions to trap and add the MIDI messages to the matrix *Sources* array. The list breaks down as follows:

StartNote()

- Velocity
- (already have MIDI note number from previous project)

HandlePitchWheel()

- Pitch Bend

HandleControlChange()

- Volume (CC 7)
- Pan (CC 10)
- Sustain Pedal

So, alter the functions to transmit the information to the matrix:

```
OSStatus AUSynth::StartNote(MusicDeviceInstrumentID inInstrument,
                            MusicDeviceGroupID inGroupID,
                            NoteInstanceID *outNoteInstanceID,
                            UInt32 inOffsetSampleFrame,
                            const MusicDeviceNoteParams &inParams)
{

    <SNIP SNIP SNIP>

    // --- set the note number in the mod matrix for filter key track
    m_GlobalModMatrix.m_dSources[SOURCE_MIDI_NOTE_NUM] = uMIDINote;

    // --- for Vel->Att scaling
    m_GlobalModMatrix.m_dSources[SOURCE_VELOCITY] = uVelocity;

    return noErr;
}

// -- Pitch Bend handler
OSStatus AUSynth::HandlePitchWheel(UInt8 inChannel,
                                   UInt8 inPitch1,
                                   UInt8 inPitch2,
                                   UInt32 inStartFrame)
{
    <SNIP SNIP SNIP>
```

```
    // LOG MIDI
    // --- send to matrix
    m_GlobalModMatrix.m_dSources[SOURCE_PITCHBEND] =
                                          fNormalizedPitchBendValue;

    return noErr;
}

OSStatus AUSynth::HandleControlChange(UInt8 inChannel,
                                      UInt8 inController,
                                      UInt8 inValue,
                                      UInt32 inStartFrame)
{
    <SNIP SNIP SNIP Indents Removed>

    case VOLUME_CC07:
    {
        // LOG MIDI
        // --- send to matrix
        m_GlobalModMatrix.m_dSources[SOURCE_MIDI_VOLUME_CC07] = inValue;
        break;
    }
    case PAN_CC10:
    {
        // LOG MIDI
        // --- send to matrix
        m_GlobalModMatrix.m_dSources[SOURCE_MIDI_PAN_CC10] = inValue;
        break;
    }
    case SUSTAIN_PEDAL:
    {
        // LOG MIDI
        // --- send to matrix (note - need actual MIDI here)
        m_GlobalModMatrix.m_dSources[SOURCE_SUSTAIN_PEDAL] = inValue;
        break;
    }

    etc...
```

Lastly, add the code to enable and disable the routing, much like you did for filter key-track in the *update()* function.

```
void AUSynth::update()
{
    <SNIP SNIP SNIP>

    // --- mod matrix stuff
    // --- mod matrix stuff
    if(Globals()->GetParameter(FILTER_KEYTRACK))
        m_GlobalModMatrix.enableModMatrixRow(SOURCE_MIDI_NOTE_NUM,
        DEST_ALL_FILTER_KEYTRACK, true);
    else
```

```
        m_GlobalModMatrix.enableModMatrixRow(SOURCE_MIDI_NOTE_NUM,
                          DEST_ALL_FILTER_KEYTRACK, false);

    if(Globals()->GetParameter(VELOCITY_TO_ATTACK))
        m_GlobalModMatrix.enableModMatrixRow(SOURCE_VELOCITY,
                          DEST_ALL_EG_ATTACK_SCALING, true);
    else
        m_GlobalModMatrix.enableModMatrixRow(SOURCE_VELOCITY,
                          DEST_ALL_EG_ATTACK_SCALING, false);

    if(Globals()->GetParameter(NOTE_NUM_TO_DECAY))
        m_GlobalModMatrix.enableModMatrixRow(SOURCE_MIDI_NOTE_NUM,
                          DEST_ALL_EG_DECAY_SCALING, true);
    else
        m_GlobalModMatrix.enableModMatrixRow(SOURCE_MIDI_NOTE_NUM,
                          DEST_ALL_EG_DECAY_SCALING, false);
}
```

Set your controller to transmit volume and pan and build and test the synth. It will react to volume, pan, and pitch bend. Enable and disable the velocity to attack and note to decay modulations to verify these work properly.

8.11 User Controlled Modulation Routings

In this section, we will allow the user some control over the modulation routing. The more flexible you make your modulation routings, the more patches the user can create. This in turn creates a larger palette of sounds your synth can generate. In this section, we will modify NanoSynth and allow the user to choose the destination for LFO1. Currently, it is hard-wired to the oscillator to produce a vibrato effect. We will add another control to the GUI that lets the user select the destination as either Osc (oscillator pitch) or Filter (filter f_c). This is shown in Figure 8.10.

Table 8.6 shows the attributes for this new parameter. Add this control to your project and GUI. Table 8.7 shows the new modulation matrix row entry. This modification is refreshingly easy to add, thanks to the modulation matrix.

The modulation routing in Table 8.7 results in the addition of a new matrix row shown in Code Listing 8.7.

```
<< ** Code Listing 8.7: Mod Matrix Routings III ** >>

// LFO1 -> FILTER1 FC
pRow = createModMatrixRow(SOURCE_LFO1,
                          DEST_ALL_FILTER_FC,
                          &m_dDefaultModIntensity,
```

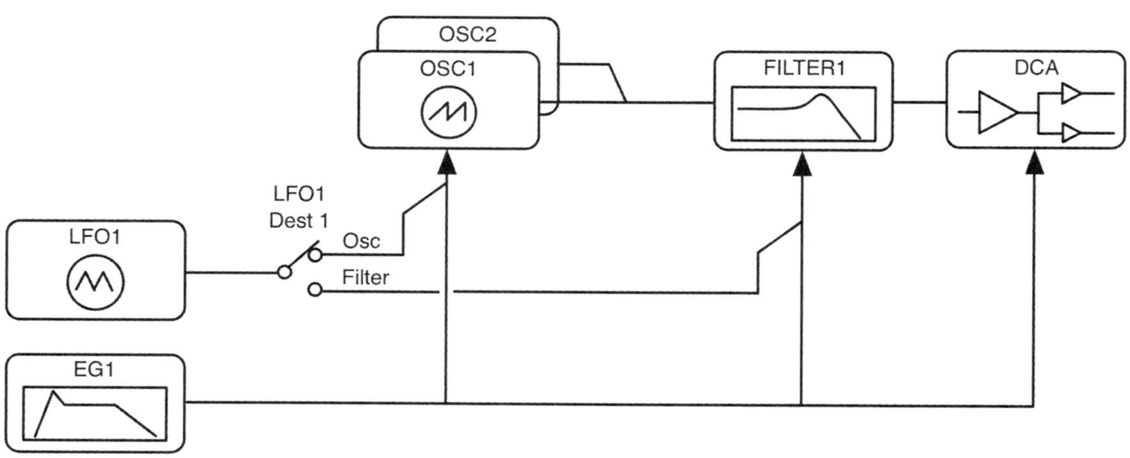

Figure 8.10: NanoSynth gets an upgrade with the addition of the LFO1 Destination 1 switch.

Table 8.6: GUI parameter table for the LFO1 Destination routing.

NanoSynth Enumerated String Parameters (UINT)			
Control Name	**Variable Name**	**enum String**	**VST3/AU Index**
LFO1 Dest 1	m_uLFO1Destination	Osc,Filter	LFO1_DESTINATION

Table 8.7: The modulation matrix row for the new routing.

NanoSynth Modulation Matrix			
Source	**Destination/Intensity**	**Transform/Range**	**enabled**
SOURCE_LFO1	DEST_ALL_FILTER_FC	TRANSFORM_NONE	FALSE
	m_dDefaultModIntensity	m_dFilterModRange	

```
                                &m_dFilterModRange,
                                TRANSFORM_NONE,
                                false); /* DISABLED BY DEFAULT */
    m_GlobalModMatrix.addModMatrixRow(pRow);

    << END ** Code Listing 8.7: Mod Matrix Routings III END ** >>
```

Since we've added a new destination for the user, you need to modify the *update()* function to switch the destinations—notice the logic here: you can add as many destination options as you like, including combinations (osc, filter, both).

```
    << ** Code Listing 8.8: Mod Matrix Update II ** >>

    // --- LFO routing
    if(m_uLFO1Destination == Osc)
    // VST3 if(m_uLFO1Destination == 0)
    {
        // --- enable/disable
        m_GlobalModMatrix.enableModMatrixRow(SOURCE_LFO1,
                                              DEST_ALL_OSC_FO,
                                              true); /* enable */
        m_GlobalModMatrix.enableModMatrixRow(SOURCE_LFO1,
                                              DEST_ALL_FILTER_FC,
                                              false); /* disable */
    }
    else if(m_uLFO1Destination == Filter)
    // VST3 if(m_uLFO1Destination == 1)
    {
        // --- disable/enable
        m_GlobalModMatrix.enableModMatrixRow(SOURCE_LFO1,
                                              DEST_ALL_OSC_FO,
                                              false);/* disable */
        m_GlobalModMatrix.enableModMatrixRow(SOURCE_LFO1,
                                              DEST_ALL_FILTER_FC,
                                              true); /* enable */
    }

    << END ** Code Listirg 8.8: Mod Matrix Update II END ** >>
```

8.12 NanoSynth MM Part Three: RackAFX

Add the GUI control for the LFO1 Destination routing in Table 8.6. All the rest of the work is done in *NanoSynth.cpp*.

NanoSynth.cpp

Add the new *modMatrixRow* using Table 8.6 and the source and destination enumerations in *synthfunctions.h*. Make sure to set the *bEnable* flag to *false* so that it is disabled by default. Add this code at the end of the constructor:

```
CNanoSynth::CNanoSynth()
{
      <SNIP SNIP SNIP>

      << INSERT ** Code Listing 8.7: Mod Matrix Routings III ** HERE >>
}
```

Next, add code to the *update()* function (this is the simplest option, but you could also declare your own sub-function for this). This code simply toggles the *bEnable* flag on and off for the various combinations.

```
void CNanoSynth::update()
{
      <SNIP SNIP SNIP>

      if(m_uFilterKeyTrack == 1)
              m_GlobalModMatrix.enableModMatrixRow(SOURCE_MIDI_NOTE_NUM,
                                                   DEST_ALL_FILTER_KEYTRACK,
                                                   true);
      else
      m_GlobalModMatrix.enableModMatrixRow(SOURCE_MIDI_NOTE_NUM,
                                           DEST_ALL_FILTER_KEYTRACK,
                                           false);

      << INSERT ** Code Listing 8.8: Mod Matrix Update II ** HERE >>
}
```

8.13 NanoSynth MM Part Three: VST3

Add the GUI controls for the new modulation routings in Table 8.6. You need to add the new matrix row to the *setActive()* function and enable/disable the rows in *update()*. Notice that in update() you will need to use the alternate version of the if statements:

```
if(m_uLFO1Destination == 0) rather than if(m_uLFO1Destination == Osc)
```

unless you wish to declare enumerations for them.

```
tresult PLUGIN_API Processor::setActive(TBool state)
{
      if(state)
      {
              <SNIP SNIP SNIP>

              pRow = createModMatrixRow(SOURCE_MIDI_NOTE_NUM,
                                        DEST_ALL_EG_DECAY_SCALING,
                                        &m_dDefaultModIntensity,
                                        &m_dDefaultModRange,
```

```
                                    TRANSFORM_MIDI_NORMALIZE,
                                    false); /* DISABLED BY DEFAULT */
        m_GlobalModMatrix.addModMatrixRow(pRow);

        << INSERT ** Code Listing 8.7: Mod Matrix Routings III ** HERE >>

        etc...

void Processor::update()
{
    <SNIP SNIP SNIP>

    if(m_uNoteNumberToDecayScaling == 1)
        m_GlobalModMatrix.enableModMatrixRow(SOURCE_MIDI_NOTE_NUM,
                                              DEST_ALL_EG_DECAY_SCALING,
                                              true);
    else
        m_GlobalModMatrix.enableModMatrixRow(SOURCE_MIDI_NOTE_NUM,
                                              DEST_ALL_EG_DECAY_SCALING,
                                              false);

    << INSERT ** Code Listing 8.8: Mod Matrix Update II ** HERE >>
    etc...
```

8.14 NanoSynth MM Part Three: AU

Add the GUI controls for the new modulation routings in Table 8.6. You need to add the new matrix row in the Constructor and enable/disable the rows in *update()*. Notice that in *update()* you will need to use the alternate version of the code listing that uses the global parameter container.

```
AUSynth::AUSynth(AudioUnit inComponentInstance)
       : AUInstrumentBase(inComponentInstance, 0, 1)
{
    <SNIP SNIP SNIP>

    pRow = createModMatrixRow(SOURCE_MIDI_NOTE_NUM,
                              DEST_ALL_EG_DECAY_SCALING,
                              &m_dDefaultModIntensity,
                              &m_dDefaultModRange,
                              TRANSFORM_MIDI_NORMALIZE,
                              false); /* DISABLED BY DEFAULT */
        m_GlobalModMatrix.addModMatrixRow(pRow);

        << INSERT ** Code Listing 8.7: Mod Matrix Routings III ** HERE >>

        etc...

void AUSynth::update()
{
    <SNIP SNIP SNIP>
```

```
	if(Globals()->GetParameter(NOTE_NUM_TO_DECAY))
		m_GlobalModMatrix.enableModMatrixRow(SOURCE_MIDI_NOTE_NUM,
						DEST_ALL_EG_DECAY_SCALING, true);
	else
		m_GlobalModMatrix.enableModMatrixRow(SOURCE_MIDI_NOTE_NUM,
						DEST_ALL_EG_DECAY_SCALING, false);

	// --- LFO routing
	if(Globals()->GetParameter(LFO1_DESTINATION) == 0)
	{
		// --- enable/disable
		m_GlobalModMatrix.enableModMatrixRow(SOURCE_LFO1,
						DEST_ALL_OSC_FO, true); /* enable */
		m_GlobalModMatrix.enableModMatrixRow(SOURCE_LFO1,
						DEST_ALL_FILTER_FC, false); /* disable */
	}
	else if(Globals()->GetParameter(LFO1_DESTINATION) == 1)
	{
		// --- disable/enable
		m_GlobalModMatrix.enableModMatrixRow(SOURCE_LFO1,
						DEST_ALL_OSC_FO, false); /* disable */
		m_GlobalModMatrix.enableModMatrixRow(SOURCE_LFO1,
						DEST_ALL_FILTER_FC, true); /* enable */
	}
}
```

That's it! Build and test the synth; turn up the LFO amplitude and listen to the effect change from vibrato to wah-wah when you alter the routing.

8.15 Polyphony Part One

NanoSynth is coming along nicely with its new modulation matrix and the ability to extend its articulation capabilities. In this section, we will modify NanoSynth to become polyphonic with the capability of playing two notes at once. In the next chapter, we will extend the polyphony to 16 notes in MiniSynth. Limiting NanoSynth to just two notes will make it easier to test things like Reset-To-Zero mode. In this section our goal is to add the polyphony with as little code as required. You are going to find that the plug-in code is becoming more complex and that the plug-in object is growing. The plug-in object knows too much about the underlying synth, but that's OK for now because the coding is easier. In the next chapter, we will take a step back and figure out how to streamline operations.

NanoSynth's core contains a set of objects that make a single synth voice:

- *QBLimitedOscillators* 1 and 2
- *CEnvelopeGenerator*
- *CMoogLadderFilter*
- *CLFO*
- *CDCA*
- *CModulationMatrix* (each must have its own velocity, note number, etc.)

In this book, the term "voice" means a collection of synth components. Their exact wiring would constitute a patch. One voice could have its components connected to form many different patches.

> In some synthesizers, polyphony is defined in terms of oscillators; some patches might use more oscillators than others and reduce polyphony. For our synths, polyphony is defined as the maximum number of voices that can play at once; some synths have voices that use less resources and can achieve greater maximum polyphony.

There are different approaches to implementing polyphony, but since we are dealing with C/C++, one option would be to take the synth core objects and put them in a synth voice structure:

```
// --- one complete voice
struct nanoSynthVoice
{
     CQBLimitedOscillator m_Osc1;
     CQBLimitedOscillator m_Osc2;
     CLFO m_LFO1;
     CEnvelopeGenerator m_EG1;
     CMoogLadderFilter m_Filter1;
     CDCA m_DCA;
     CModulationMatrix m_ModulationMatrix;
};
```

A *#define* statement makes it easy to change the voice limit, so we could add this:

```
#define MAX_VOICES 2
```

Then, in the plug-in's *.h* file, we could remove the fixed static declarations of the components and replace them with an array of *nanoSynthVoice* structures:

```
nanoSynthVoice m_Voices[MAX_VOICES];
```

Now, we have two copies of the same voice structure, each with its own set of objects. What you are going to see is that the polyphonic version is nearly identical, except we update and process an array of voices rather than dealing with a single set of objects.

Sharing the Global Modulation Matrix Core

You saw how the monophonic NanoSynth simply shared its one and only modulation matrix in the plug-in so that the plug-in could make changes to the matrix core when new MIDI events occurred or when the user wanted to reconfigure it. With polyphony, each NanoSynth voice will need its own modulation matrix because the voice's sources and destinations are different from all others; each voice needs its own source and destination array. However, the modulation matrix core is the same set of rows for all voices. When the user wants to reconfigure the matrix, we don't want to update each voice's matrix.

So, the voice modulation matrices need to share the same core as the plug-in—in other words, there is one and only one core. One way of handling this is with a singleton object, which in theory can be constructed only once and is useful as a shared resource. In iOS programming, it is a common paradigm. However, there is much debate over the utility of the singleton. For our purposes, a singleton actually increases the complexity somewhat, so we are going to stick with a single global modulation matrix that the plug-in owns, initialize it the same way as before, and then provide a mechanism to share the core with the voices. This is simple enough since the object has *getModMatrixCore()* and *setModMatrixCore()* methods. Figure 8.11 shows the concept of sharing the matrix core among multiple voices.

Another thing we will need to deal with is voice-stealing. If the user plays three notes in succession, but we can only render two at a time, we will need to drop one of the currently playing voices and steal it to play the new note. This will also let us test the shutdown mode of the EG. In order to make this as simple as possible, we need arrays that hold the newly stolen note number and note velocity while the EG goes through its shutdown operation. We will discuss the details later, but for now you need to add this array into the plug-in object:

```
int m_nPendingMIDINote[MAX_VOICES];       // if -1, no pending note
int m_nPendingMIDIVelocity[MAX_VOICES];   // if -1 no pending velocity
```

We share the single mod matrix core with each voice in the array. This is done with a *for()* loop on the array. Notice the last statement in the loop, which sets the pending note to −1, effectively clearing the array. Also, if you compare the code to the last version of NanoSynth, you can see it is identical, except that the objects now belong to the *m_Voices* array instead of standing alone. You can see that polyphony with multiple structures (or C++ objects) means replicating the same initialization over and over. This looping-through-voices will be a common paradigm, though we will try to get more clever as the synths progress.

```
<< ** Code Listing 8.9: Global Parameter Init I ** >>

for(int i=0; i<MAX_VOICES; i++)
```

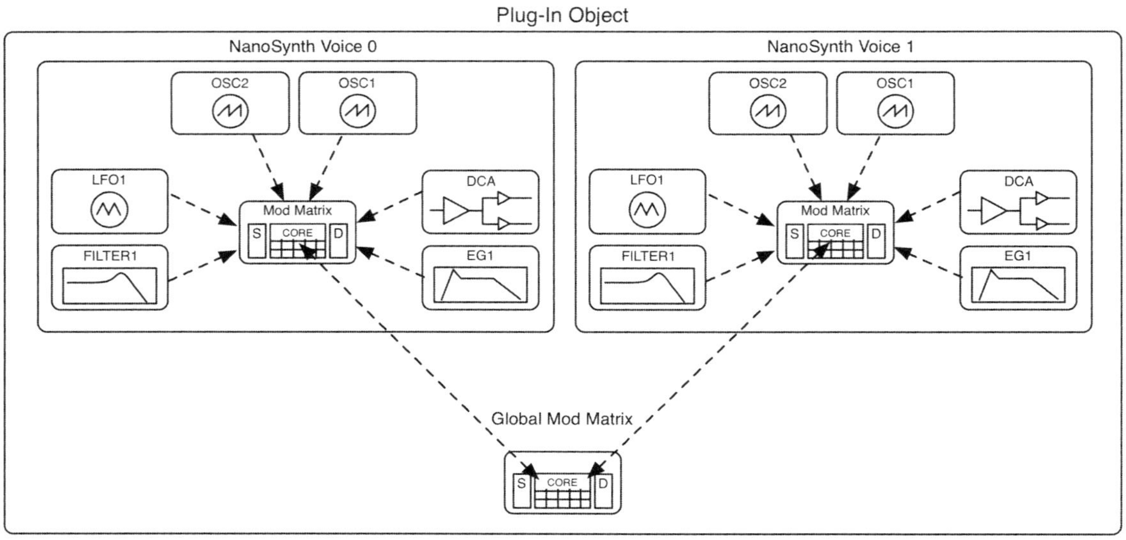

Figure 8.11: The plug-in shares the Global Mod Matrix core with the synth voices' modulation matrices; only the core is shared and not the source and destination arrays.

```
{
        // --- NOTE: sub objects of a single voice share a modulation
        //          matrix
        m_Voices[i].m_ModulationMatrix.setModMatrixCore
                                 (m_GlobalModMatrix.getModMatrixCore());

        // --- this sets up the DEFAULT CONNECTIONS!
        m_Voices[i].m_Osc1.m_pModulationMatrix = &m_Voices[i]
                                                   m_ModulationMatrix;

        // --- NOTE: Oscillator Source is a Destination of a modulator
        m_Voices[i].m_Osc1.m_uModSourceFo = DEST_OSC1_FO;
        m_Voices[i].m_Osc1.m_uModSourceAmp = DEST_OSC1_OUTPUT_AMP;

        // --- do same for Osc2
        m_Voices[i].m_Osc2.m_pModulationMatrix = &m_Voices[i]
                                                   .m_ModulationMatrix;
        m_Voices[i].m_Osc2.m_uModSourceFo = DEST_OSC2_FO;
        m_Voices[i].m_Osc2.m_uModSourceAmp = DEST_OSC2_OUTPUT_AMP;

        m_Voices[i].m_Filter1.m_pModulationMatrix = &m_Voices[i]
                                                      .m_ModulationMatrix;
        m_Voices[i].m_Filter1.m_uModSourceFc = DEST_FILTER1_FC;
        m_Voices[i].m_Filter1.m_uSourceFcControl =
                                          DEST_ALL_FILTER_KEYTRACK;

        // --- these are modulators: they write their outputs into what
        //     will be a Source for something else
        m_Voices[i].m_LFO1.m_pModulationMatrix =
                                    &m_Voices[i].m_ModulationMatrix;

        m_Voices[i].m_LFO1.m_uModDestOutput1 = SOURCE_LFO1;
        m_Voices[i].m_LFO1.m_uModDestOutput2 = SOURCE_LFO1Q;
```

```
        m_Voices[i].m_EG1.m_pModulationMatrix =
                                   &m_Voices[i].m_ModulationMatrix;
        m_Voices[i].m_EG1.m_uModDestEGOutput = SOURCE_EG1;
        m_Voices[i].m_EG1.m_uModDestBiasedEGOutput = SOURCE_BIASED_EG1;
        m_Voices[i].m_EG1.m_uModSourceEGAttackScaling =
                          DEST_EG1_ATTACK_SCALING;
        m_Voices[i].m_EG1.m_uModSourceEGDecayScaling =
                          DEST_EG1_DECAY_SCALING;
        m_Voices[i].m_EG1.m_uModSourceSustainOverride =
                          DEST_EG1_SUSTAIN_OVERRIDE;

        // --- DCA Setup:
        m_Voices[i].m_DCA.m_pModulationMatrix = &m_Voices[i].
                                           m_ModulationMatrix;
        m_Voices[i].m_DCA.m_uModSourceEG = DEST_DCA_EG;
        m_Voices[i].m_DCA.m_uModSourceAmp_dB = DEST_DCA_AMP;
        m_Voices[i].m_DCA.m_uModSourceVelocity = DEST_DCA_VELOCITY;
m_Voices[i].m_DCA.m_uModSourcePan = DEST_DCA_PAN;

        // --- for voice stealing
        m_nPendingMIDINote[i] = -1;
        m_nPendingMIDIVelocity[i] = -1;
}

<< END ** Code Listing 8.9: Global Parameter Init I ** END >>
```

Likewise, in the one-time-initialization function, we need to setup an array of voices rather than a single set (and once again "clear" the pending note array with −1 values). This is the same code as before but now applied to an array of structures.

VST3:

Replace (double)m_nSampleRate with
(double)processSetup.sampleRate

AU:

Replace (double)m_nSampleRate with
(double)getOutput(0)->GetStreamFormat().mSampleRate

```
<< ** Code Listing 8.10: Global Parameter Init II ** >>

for(int i=0; i<MAX_VOICES; i++)
{
        m_Voices[i].m_Osc1.setSampleRate((double)m_nSampleRate);
        m_Voices[i].m_Osc2.setSampleRate((double)m_nSampleRate);
        m_Voices[i].m_Osc2.m_nCents = 2.5; // +2.5 cents detuned

        m_Voices[i].m_LFO1.setSampleRate((double)m_nSampleRate);
        m_Voices[i].m_EG1.setSampleRate((double)m_nSampleRate);
        m_Voices[i].m_EG1.m_bOutputEG = true;
        m_Voices[i].m_Filter1.setSampleRate((double)m_nSampleRate);

        // --- for voice stealing
        m_nPendingMIDINote[i] = -1;
        m_nPendingMIDIVelocity[i] = -1;
```

```
        // --- default turn on volume and center the pan
        m_Voices[i].m_ModulationMatrix.m_dSources
                                        [SOURCE_MIDI_VOLUME_CC07] = 127;
        m_Voices[i].m_ModulationMatrix.m_dSources
                                        [SOURCE_MIDI_PAN_CC10] = 64;
}

<< END ** Code Listing 8.10: Global Parameter Init II ** END >>
```

And, in the *update()* function, we need to update each voice structure using the same *for()* loop concept. Notice this is just a looped duplication of the original code from the last NanoSynth. You don't need to modify the global mod matrix code, however, since the plug-in only applies changes to the shared matrix core.

```
<< ** Code Listing 8.11: Global Parameter Update I ** >>

for(int i=0; i<MAX_VOICES; i++)
{
        // --- set public attributes on objects
        //
        // --- Oscillators
        m_Voices[i].m_Osc1.m_uWaveform = m_uOscWaveform;
        m_Voices[i].m_Osc2.m_uWaveform = m_uOscWaveform;

        // --- Filter
        m_Voices[i].m_Filter1.m_dFcControl = m_dFcControl;
        m_Voices[i].m_Filter1.m_dQControl = m_dQControl;

        // --- LFO
        m_Voices[i].m_LFO1.m_uWaveform = m_uLFO1Waveform;
        m_Voices[i].m_LFO1.m_dAmplitude = m_dLFO1Amplitude;
        m_Voices[i].m_LFO1.m_dOscFo = m_dLFO1Rate;
        m_Voices[i].m_LFO1.m_uLFOMode = m_uLFO1Mode;

        // ---EG1
        m_Voices[i].m_EG1.setAttackTime_mSec(m_dAttackTime_mSec);
        m_Voices[i].m_EG1.setDecayTime_mSec(m_dDecayTime_mSec);
        m_Voices[i].m_EG1.setSustainLevel(m_dSustainLevel);
        m_Voices[i].m_EG1.setReleaseTime_mSec(m_dReleaseTime_mSec);
        m_Voices[i].m_EG1.m_bResetToZero = (bool)m_uResetToZero;
        m_Voices[i].m_EG1.m_bLegatoMode = (bool)m_uLegatoMode;

        // --- DCA
        m_Voices[i].m_DCA.setPanControl(m_dPanControl);
        m_Voices[i].m_DCA.setAmplitude_dB(m_dVolume_dB);
}

<< END ** Code Listing 8.11: Global Parameter Update I ** END >>

// --- mod matrix stuff (same as before)
if(m_uFilterKeyTrack == 1)
```

```
        m_GlobalModMatrix.enableModMatrixRow(SOURCE_MIDI_NOTE_NUM,
                                             DEST_ALL_FILTER_KEYTRACK, true);
else
        m_GlobalModMatrix.enableModMatrixRow(SOURCE_MIDI_NOTE_NUM,
                                             DEST_ALL_FILTER_KEYTRACK, false);
```

Finally, in *process()*, we do the same kind of looping code duplication. We need to accumulate (or mix) the voices together, however, before writing to the outputs, so we declare accumulator variables as well as the normal voice output variables. The two oscillators are mixed with scalar values of 0.5 to try to minimize clipping. We will discuss the code that deals with note stealing and turning off the oscillators in the next section so ignore it for now.

```
<< ** Code Listing 8.12: Mod Matrix Render II ** >>

for(int i=0; i<MAX_VOICES; i++)
{
     // --- clear for loop
     dOutL = 0.0;
     dOutR = 0.0;

     if(m_Voices[i].m_Osc1.m_bNoteOn)
     {
          // --- ARTICULATION BLOCK --- //
          // --- layer 0 modulators: velocity->attack
          //                                    note number->decay
          m_Voices[i].m_ModulationMatrix.doModulationMatrix(0);

          // --- update layer 1 modulators
          m_Voices[i].m_EG1.update();
          m_Voices[i].m_LFO1.update();

          // --- layer 1 modulators
          m_Voices[i].m_EG1.doEnvelope();
          m_Voices[i].m_LFO1.doOscillate();

          // --- modulation matrix Layer 1
          m_Voices[i].m_ModulationMatrix.doModulationMatrix(1);

          // --- update DCA and Filter
          m_Voices[i].m_DCA.updateDCA();
          m_Voices[i].m_Filter1.updateFilter();

          // --- update oscillators
          m_Voices[i].m_Osc1.updateOscillator();
          m_Voices[i].m_Osc2.updateOscillator();

          // --- DIGITAL AUDIO ENGINE BLOCK --- //
          // (OSC1 + OSC2) --> FILTER --> DCA
          double dOscOut = 0.5*m_Voices[i].m_Osc1.doOscillate() +
                           0.5*m_Voices[i].m_Osc2.doOscillate();

          double dFilterOut = m_Voices[i].m_Filter1.
                                            doFilter(dOscOut);
```

```
            m_Voices[i].m_DCA.doDCA(dFilterOut, dFilterOut,
                                    dOutL, dOutR);

            // --- accumulate notes
            dAccumOutL += dOutL;
            dAccumOutR += dOutR;

            // now check for note off
            //      if note is ON but EG is shut OFF, note is finished
            if(m_Voices[i].m_EG1.getState() == 0) // off
            {
                  // --- is voice being stolen?
                  if(m_nPendingMIDINote[i] >= 0)
                  {
                        // --- set new note numbers and update
                        m_Voices[i].m_Osc1.m_uMIDINoteNumber = m_nPendingMIDINote[i];
                        m_Voices[i].m_Osc1.m_dOscFo =
                                    midiFreqTable[m_nPendingMIDINote[i]];

                        m_Voices[i].m_Osc2.m_uMIDINoteNumber =
                                    m_nPendingMIDINote[i];
                        m_Voices[i].m_Osc2.m_dOscFo =
                                    midiFreqTable[m_nPendingMIDINote[i]];

                        m_Voices[i].m_Osc1.updateOscillator();
                        m_Voices[i].m_Osc2.updateOscillator();

                        // --- crank the EG up again
                        m_Voices[i].m_EG1.startEG();

                        // --- set the note # and velocity of newest note
                        m_Voices[i].m_ModulationMatrix.m_dSources
                              [SOURCE_MIDI_NOTE_NUM] = m_nPendingMIDINote[i];
                        m_Voices[i].m_ModulationMatrix.m_dSources
                              [SOURCE_VELOCITY] = m_nPendingMIDIVelocity[i];

                        // --- reset
                        m_nPendingMIDINote[i] = -1;
                        m_nPendingMIDIVelocity[i] = -1;
                  }
                  else
                  {
                        m_Voices[i].m_Osc1.stopOscillator();
                        m_Voices[i].m_Osc2.stopOscillator();
                        m_Voices[i].m_LFO1.stopOscillator();
                        m_Voices[i].m_EG1.stopEG();
                  }
            }
      }
}

      << END ** Code Listing 8.12: Mod Matrix Render II ** END >>
```

8.16 Dynamic Voice Allocation

Voice stealing (also called voice allocation or dynamic voice allocation) is a by-product of polyphony, and it can be tricky and complicated. If the user triggers a new note but the supply of voices is exhausted, you need a way to shut one voice off and steal it for the new note. Deciding on which voice to terminate is up to you, the synth designer. A heuristic is used to decide on the fate of the stolen note. Heuristics involve trade-offs to make a decision about an outcome that may or may not be optimal. In the case of voice-stealing, there is no perfect mechanism; all have their strengths and weaknesses. Some options are:

- steal the oldest note
- steal the oldest note that isn't the lowest pitched note
- steal the note with the lowest velocity
- steal the first note that has already been released
- steal notes that are inside of chord voicings
- steal notes that are outside of chord voicings
- steal notes that are not part of a melody line
- MIDI channel priority based

The list goes on—see Limberis and Bryan (1993) for an interesting paper on dynamic voice allocation for pure software synthesizers. The last item in the list comes from the MMA DLS specification, in which multi-timbral voices are distributed across the 16 MIDI channels. The channels are prioritized according to number, with channel 1 as the highest priority and 16 as the lowest. Since our synths are mono-timbral, we will use note-based heuristics.

For this version of NanoSynth, the heuristic is to steal the note that isn't the lowest pitched note:

- first try to steal a note with the same note number that happens if the user releases and then quickly re-strikes the same note
- if the higher note is not already being stolen, steal it
- if the new note is lower than the others, steal the lower of the two currently playing
- if both notes are being stolen, arbitrarily steal the second note

To facilitate polyphony and note stealing, we need a couple of helper functions declared in the plug-in's *.h* file:

```
void startNote(int nIndex, UINT uMIDINote, UINT uMIDIVelocity);
void stealNote(int nIndex, UINT uPendingMIDINote, UINT uPendingVelocity);
```

The implementations are in the *.cpp* file (RackAFX shown here). For the start note event, it's the same as the monophonic version, except we choose a voice from the array. The modulation matrix code got moved from the note on handler since it is now voice-specific information.

```
void CNanoSynth::startNote(int nIndex, UINT uMIDINote, UINT uMIDIVelocity)
{
    << ** Code Listing 8.13: Start Note ** >>

    if(nIndex > MAX_VOICES-1)
            return;

    // --- set pitches
    m_Voices[nIndex].m_Osc1.m_uMIDINoteNumber = uMIDINote;
    m_Voices[nIndex].m_Osc1.m_dOscFo = midiFreqTable[uMIDINote];

    m_Voices[nIndex].m_Osc2.m_uMIDINoteNumber = uMIDINote;
    m_Voices[nIndex].m_Osc2.m_dOscFo = midiFreqTable[uMIDINote];

    // --- start the modulators FIRST
    m_Voices[nIndex].m_LFO1.startOscillator();
    m_Voices[nIndex].m_EG1.startEG();
```

```
        // --- not playing, reset and do updateOscillator()
        m_Voices[nIndex].m_Osc1.startOscillator();
        m_Voices[nIndex].m_Osc2.startOscillator();

        // --- set the note number in the mod matrix
        m_Voices[nIndex].m_ModulationMatrix.m_dSources[SOURCE_MIDI_NOTE_NUM] =
                         uMIDINote;

        // --- velocity modulation
        m_Voices[nIndex].m_ModulationMatrix.m_dSources[SOURCE_VELOCITY] =
                         uMIDIVelocity;

        << END ** Code Listing 8.13: Start Note ** END >>
}
```

For the steal note event, it's fairly simple—you just put the EG into shutdown mode. The EG object will handle legato and return to zero conditions for you. You might also add a TRACE statement so you can watch the steal occur.

```
void CNanoSynth::stealNote(int nIndex, UINT uPendingMIDINote,
UINT uPendingVelocity)
{
        << ** Code Listing 8.14: Steal Note ** >>

        if(nIndex > MAX_VOICES-1)
                return;

        // --- shutdown the EG with fast linear taper
        m_Voices[nIndex].m_EG1.shutDown();

        // --- save the pending note and velocity
        m_nPendingMIDINote[nIndex] = uPendingMIDINote;
        m_nPendingMIDIVelocity[nIndex] = uPendingVelocity;

        << END ** Code Listing 8.14: Steal Note ** END >>

        etc...

}
```

The note on and note off handlers are the last thing to be changed. In the note on handler, you first test to see if there is an available note—if so, trigger with a call to *startNote()*. If not, make the note stealing decision and then call the *stealNote()* function accordingly. Make sure you can follow the heuristic—it's very basic but preserves the lowest note at all times.

```
bool __stdcall CNanoSynth::midiNoteOn(UINT uChannel, UINT uMIDINote,
                                      UINT uVelocity)
{
        // test channel/ignore
        if(m_uMidiRxChannel != MIDI_CH_ALL && uChannel != m_uMidiRxChannel)
```

```
            return false;

    #ifdef LOG_MIDI
            TRACE("-- Note On Ch:%d Note:%d Vel:%d \n", uChannel,
                  uMIDINote, uVelocity);
    #endif

    << ** Code Listing 8.15: Note On ** >>

    // --- call the helper function
    if(!m_Voices[0].m_Osc1.m_bNoteOn)
            startNote(0, uMIDINote, uVelocity);
    else if(!m_Voices[1].m_Osc1.m_bNoteOn)
            startNote(1, uMIDINote, uVelocity);
    else
    {
            // voice steal; NanoSynth heuristic is
            // --- if new note is lower than both, steal the lower of the two
            //     otherwise steal the higher one
            //
            // --- test note
            UINT uNote0 = m_Voices[0].m_Osc1.m_uMIDINoteNumber;
            UINT uNote1 = m_Voices[1].m_Osc1.m_uMIDINoteNumber;

            // --- if new note is lower than both, steal the lower of the two
            if(uMIDINote < uNote0 && uMIDINote < uNote1)
            {
                    if(uNote0 < uNote1)
                            stealNote(0, uMIDINote, uVelocity);
                    else
                            stealNote(1, uMIDINote, uVelocity);
            }
            else // --- steal the higher one
            {
                    if(uNote0 > uNote1)
                            stealNote(0, uMIDINote, uVelocity);
                    else
                            stealNote(1, uMIDINote, uVelocity);
            }
    }

    << ** END Code Listing 8.15: Note On ** END >>

    etc...
}
```

The note off handler is simple. In this case you just find the note with the matching MIDI note number and send the *noteOff()* message to the EG, placing it in shutdown mode.

```
bool __stdcall CNanoSynth::midiNoteOff(UINT uChannel, UINT uMIDINote,
UINT uVelocity, bool bAllNotesOff)
{
	<SNIP SNIP SNIP>

	// --- turn off IF this is the proper note (last note played)
	if(bAllNotesOff)
	{
		m_Voices[0].m_EG1.noteOff();
		m_Voices[1].m_EG1.noteOff();
		return true;
	}

	<< ** Code Listing 8.16: Note Off ** >>

	// --- test by MIDI Note number
	if(uMIDINote == m_Voices[0].m_Osc1.m_uMIDINoteNumber)
		m_Voices[0].m_EG1.noteOff();
	if(uMIDINote == m_Voices[1].m_Osc1.m_uMIDINoteNumber)
		m_Voices[1].m_EG1.noteOff();

	<< ** END Code Listing 8.16: Note Off ** END >>

	etc...
}
```

Pitch bend, volume and panning need MIDI message handlers that are platform dependent, so we will look at those handlers on a per-platform basis.

Now, go back and examine the remaining chunk of code near the end of the process function where we rendered the audio. After checking the envelope generator to see if the note is finished, we then check the pending MIDI note array; if the value there is 0 or greater, then the note is being stolen (this array is doing double duty in that respect).

If stolen:

- set the new MIDI note number and frequency information on the oscillators
- re-start the EG
- update the MIDI values in the modulation matrix
- reset the pending arrays with −1 to clear them

If the note is not stolen, we just use the same code as before to stop the note, but this time applied to the individual voice.

```
		// now check for note off
		//	if note is ON but EG is shut OFF, note is finished
		if(m_Voices[i].m_EG1.getState() == 0) // off
		{
			// --- is voice being stolen?
			if(m_nPendingMIDINote[i] >= 0)
			{
				// --- set new note numbers and update
				m_Voices[i].m_Osc1.m_uMIDINoteNumber = m_nPendingMIDINote[i];
				m_Voices[i].m_Osc1.m_dOscFo =
					midiFreqTable[m_nPendingMIDINote[i]];
```

```
                m_Voices[i].m_Osc2.m_uMIDINoteNumber =
                            m_nPendingMIDINote[i];
                m_Voices[i].m_Osc2.m_dOscFo =
                            midiFreqTable[m_nPendingMIDINote[i]];

                m_Voices[i].m_Osc1.updateOscillator();
                m_Voices[i].m_Osc2.updateOscillator();

                // --- crank the EG up again
                m_Voices[i].m_EG1.startEG();

                // --- set the note # and velocity of newest note
                m_Voices[i]. m_ModulationMatrix.m_dSources
                      [SOURCE_MIDI_NOTE_NUM] = m_nPendingMIDINote[i];
                m_Voices[i].m_ModulationMatrix.m_dSources
                      [SOURCE_VELOCITY] = m_nPendingMIDIVelocity[i];

                // --- reset
                m_nPendingMIDINote[i] = -1;
                m_nPendingMIDIVelocity[i] = -1;
        }
        else
        {
                m_Voices[i].m_Osc1.stopOscillator();
                m_Voices[i].m_Osc2.stopOscillator();
                m_Voices[i].m_LFO1.stopOscillator();
                m_Voices[i].m_EG1.stopEG();
        }
```

That takes care of our first attempt at polyphony. Now, start your compilers and add the functionality for Poly NanoSynth.

8.17 Poly NanoSynth: RackAFX

There are no added GUI controls, so we can go directly to the *NanoSynth.h* file and add the new declarations.

NanoSynth.h

Outside of the object declaration, add the new voice structure and MAX_VOICES definitions and, inside the object, declare the arrays and helper functions. Remove the previous object declarations as well.

```
// --- one complete voice
struct nanoSynthVoice
{
      CQBLimitedOscillator m_Osc1;
      CQBLimitedOscillator m_Osc2;
      CLFO m_LFO1;
      CEnvelopeGenerator m_EG1;
      CMoogLadderFilter m_Filter1;
      CDCA m_DCA;
      CModulationMatrix m_ModulationMatrix;
};
```

```
#define MAX_VOICES 2

class CNanoSynth : public CPlugIn
{
     <SNIP SNIP SNIP>

     // Add your code here: ----------------------------------------- //
     // --- the Modulation Matrix
     CModulationMatrix m_GlobalModMatrix;

     nanoSynthVoice m_Voices[MAX_VOICES];
     int m_nPendingMIDINote[MAX_VOICES];  // if -1 no pending note
     int m_nPendingMIDIVelocity[MAX_VOICES];     // if -1 no pending velocity

     void startNote(int nIndex, UINT uMIDINote, UINT uMIDIVelocity);
     void stealNote(int nIndex, UINT uPendingMIDINote,
                    UINT uPendingVelocity);

     etc...
}
```

NanoSynth.cpp

We need to alter all the functions we discussed so far, plus a few MIDI-specific ones. Most of the code is just cut-and-paste from the listings.

Constructor

Remove the original code and replace with polyphonic version; notice this occurs after the global mod matrix has been initialized and the range/intensity variables have been set:

```
CNanoSynth::CNanoSynth()
{
     <SNIP SNIP SNIP>

     m_dOscFoPitchBendModRange = OSC_PITCHBEND_MOD_RANGE;
     m_dAmpModRange = AMP_MOD_RANGE;

     << INSERT ** Code Listing 8.9: Global Parameter Init I ** HERE >>
}
```

Destructor

Just delete our master modulation matrix core:

```
CNanoSynth::~CNanoSynth(void)
{
     // --- delete on master ONLY
     m_GlobalModMatrix.deleteModMatrix();
}
```

prepareForPlay()

Likewise, remove the old code and replace with the polyphonic version:

```
bool __stdcall CNanoSynth::prepareForPlay()
{
      << INSERT ** Code Listing 8.10: Global Parameter Init II ** HERE >>

      update();

      return true;
}
```

update()

Here, we polyphone-ize again by setting all the voice parameters on all voices at once; only replace the synth update and not the modulation matrix code.

```
void CNanoSynth::update()
{
      << INSERT ** Code Listing 8.11: Global Parameter Update I ** HERE >>

      // --- mod matrix stuff
      if(m_uFilterKeyTrack == 1)

      etc...
}
```

processAudioFrame()

Remove the old code and add the new accumulating code with the voice-steal code intact. Note that the outputs are now taken from the new accumulator variables.

```
bool __stdcall CNanoSynth::processAudioFrame(float* pInputBuffer,
                                             float* pOutputBuffer,
                                             UINT uNumInputChannels,
                                             UINT uNumOutputChannels)
{
      double dOutL = 0.0;
      double dOutR = 0.0;
      double dAccumOutL = 0.0;
      double dAccumOutR = 0.0;

      << INSERT ** Code Listing 8.12: Mod Matrix Render II ** HERE >>

      pOutputBuffer[0] = dAccumOutL;

      // Mono-In, Stereo-Out (AUX Effect)
      if(uNumInputChannels == 1 && uNumOutputChannels == 2)
             pOutputBuffer[1] = dAccumOutL;

      // Stereo-In, Stereo-Out (INSERT Effect)
      if(uNumInputChannels == 2 && uNumOutputChannels == 2)
            pOutputBuffer[1] = dAccumOutR;
```

```
    return true;
}
```

startNote() *and* stealNote()

Implement the *startNote()* and *stealNote()* functions using the code listings.

```
void CNanoSynth::startNote(int nIndex, UINT uMIDINote, UINT uMIDIVelocity)
{
    << INSERT ** Code Listing 8.13: Start Note ** HERE >>
}

void CNanoSynth::stealNote(int nIndex, UINT uPendingMIDINote,
                           UINT uPendingVelocity)
{
    << INSERT ** Code Listing 8.14: Steal Note ** HERE >>
}
```

midiNoteOn() *and* midiNoteOff()

Remove the old code and implement the functions using the code listings.

```
bool __stdcall CNanoSynth::midiNoteOn(UINT uChannel, UINT uMIDINote,
                                      UINT uVelocity)
{
    // test channel/ignore
    if(m_uMidiRxChannel != MIDI_CH_ALL && uChannel != m_uMidiRxChannel)
        return false;

    << INSERT ** Code Listing 8.15: Note On ** HERE >>

    return true;
}

bool __stdcall CNanoSynth::midiNoteOff(UINT uChannel, UINT uMIDINote,
                                       UINT uVelocity, bool bAllNotesOff)
{
    // test channel/ignore
    if(m_uMidiRxChannel != MIDI_CH_ALL && uChannel != m_uMidiRxChannel)
        return false;

    // --- all notes off!
    if(bAllNotesOff)
    {
        m_Voices[0].m_EG1.noteOff();
        m_Voices[1].m_EG1.noteOff();
        return true;
    }

    << INSERT ** Code Listing 8.16: Note Off ** HERE >>

    return true;
}
```

midiPitchBend()

Remove the old code and insert the code to send these messages to all voices.

```
bool __stdcall CNanoSynth::midiPitchBend(UINT uChannel,
                                        int nActualPitchBendValue,
                                        float fNormalizedPitchBendValue)
{
    // test channel/ignore
    if(m_uMidiRxChannel != MIDI_CH_ALL && uChannel != m_uMidiRxChannel)
        return false;

    #ifdef LOG_MIDI
        TRACE("-- Pitch Bend Ch:%d int:%d float:%f \n", uChannel,
            nActualPitchBendValue, fNormalizedPitchBendValue);
    #endif

    for(int i=0; i<MAX_VOICES; i++)
    {
        // --- send to matrix
    m_Voices[i].m_ModulationMatrix.m_dSources[SOURCE_PITCHBEND] =
            fNormalizedPitchBendValue;
    }

    return true;
}
```

midiMessages()

Remove the old code and insert the code to send volume and pan messages to all voices.

```
bool __stdcall CNanoSynth::midiMessage(unsigned char cChannel,
                                      unsigned char cStatus,
                                      unsigned char cData1,
                                      unsigned char cData2)
{
    // test channel/ignore
    if(m_uMidiRxChannel != MIDI_CH_ALL && (UINT)cChannel !=
      m_uMidiRxChannel)
        return false;

    switch(cStatus)
    {
        <SNIP SNIP SNIP>

        case CONTROL_CHANGE:
        {
            switch(cData1)
            {
                case VOLUME_CC07:
```

```
            {
                // --- send to matrix
                for(int i=0; i<MAX_VOICES; i++)
                {
                        m_Voices[i].m_ModulationMatrix.m_dSources
                         [SOURCE_MIDI_VOLUME_CC07] = (UINT)cData2;
                }

                break;
            }
            case PAN_CC10:
            {
                // --- send to matrix
                                                      for(int i=0; i<MAX_VOICES;
                i++)
                {
                                m_Voices[i].m_ModulationMatrix.m_dSources
                                  [SOURCE_MIDI_PAN_CC10] = (UINT)cData2;
                }

                break;
            }

            etc...

            case SUSTAIN_PEDAL:
            {

    // indents removed for readability
    for(int i=0; i<MAX_VOICES; i++)
    {
            // ---send to matrix
            m_pVoiceArray[i]-> m_ModulationMatrix.m_dSources
                        [SOURCE_SUSTAIN_PEDAL] = (UINT)cData2;
    }

            break;
```

8.18 Poly NanoSynth: VST3

There are no added GUI controls, so we can go directly to *VSTSynthProcessor.h* file and add the new declarations.

VSTSynthProcessor.h

Outside of the object declaration, add the new voice structure and MAX_VOICES definitions and, inside the object, declare the arrays and helper functions. Remove the previous object declarations.

```
// --- one complete voice
struct nanoSynthVoice
{
```

```
    CQBLimitedOscillator m_Osc1;
    CQBLimitedOscillator m_Osc2;
    CLFO m_LFO1;
    CEnvelopeGenerator m_EG1;
    CMoogLadderFilter m_Filter1;
    CDCA m_DCA;
    CModulationMatrix m_ModulationMatrix;
};

#define MAX_VOICES 2

class Processor : public AudioEffect
{
    <SNIP SNIP SNIP>

    // Add your code here: ------------------------------------------- //
    // --- the Modulation Matrix
    CModulationMatrix m_GlobalModMatrix;

    nanoSynthVoice m_Voices[MAX_VOICES];
    int m_nPendingMIDINote[MAX_VOICES];  // if -1 no pending note
    int m_nPendingMIDIVelocity[MAX_VOICES];     // if -1 no pending velocity

    void startNote(int nIndex, UINT uMIDINote, UINT uMIDIVelocity);
    void stealNote(int nIndex, UINT uPendingMIDINote,
                   UINT uPendingVelocity);
    etc...
}
```

VSTSynthProcessor.cpp

setActive()

Remove the old code and replace with the polyphonic version in the activation section. The code listing order is 8.10 and then 8.9 since the operation is in a different order from RackAFX and AU.

```
tresult PLUGIN_API Processor::setActive(TBool state)
{
    if(state)
    {
        << INSERT ** Code Listing 8.10: Global Parameter Init II ** HERE
        >>

        update();

        // clear
        m_dLastNoteFrequency = -1.0;

        // --- for individual rows
        modMatrixRow* pRow = NULL;
```

```
<SNIP SNIP SNIP>

// LFO1 -> FILTER1 FC
pRow = createModMatrixRow(SOURCE_LFO1,
                          DEST_ALL_FILTER_FC,
                          &m_dDefaultModIntensity,
                          &m_dFilterModRange,
                          TRANSFORM_NONE,
                          false); /* DISABLED BY DEFAULT */
m_GlobalModMatrix.addModMatrixRow(pRow);

<< INSERT ** Code Listing 8.9: Global Parameter Init I ** HERE >>

etc...
```

update()

Here, we polyphone-ize again by setting all the voice parameters on all voices at once; only replace the synth update and not the modulation matrix code.

```
void Processor::update()
{
    << INSERT ** Code Listing 8.11: Global Parameter Update I ** HERE >>

    // --- mod matrix stuff
    if(m_uFilterKeyTrack == 1)

    etc...
}
```

process()

Remove the old code and add the new accumulating code with the voice steal code intact. Note that the outputs are now taken from the accumulators.

```
tresult PLUGIN_API Processor::process(ProcessData& data)
{
            <SNIP SNIP SNIP>
            // --- output "accumulator"
            double dOutL = 0.0;
            double dOutR = 0.0;
            double dAccumOutL = 0.0;
            double dAccumOutR = 0.0;

            for(int32 j=0; j<samplesToProcess; j++)
            {
                    // --- clear accumulators
                    dAccumOutL = 0.0;
                    dAccumOutR = 0.0;

                    << INSERT ** Code Listing 8.12: Mod Matrix Render II ** HERE >>
```

```
            // write out to buffer
            buffers[0][j] = dAccumOutL;  // left
            buffers[1][j] = dAccumOutR; // right
        }

        // --- update the counter
        for(int i = 0; i < OUTPUT_CHANNELS; i++)
            buffers[i] += samplesToProcess;
        etc...
```

startNote() *and* stealNote()

Implement the *startNote()* and *stealNote()* functions using the code listings.

```
void Processor::startNote(int nIndex, UINT uMIDINote, UINT uMIDIVelocity)
{
    << INSERT ** Code Listing 8.13: Start Note ** HERE >>
}

void Processor::stealNote(int nIndex, UINT uPendingMIDINote,
                          UINT uPendingVelocity)
{
    << INSERT ** Code Listing 8.14: Steal Note ** HERE >>
}
```

doProcessEvent()

Remove the code for the note on and note off handing and replace it with the new polyphonic version.

```
bool Processor::doProcessEvent(Event& vstEvent)
{
    bool noteEvent = false;

    // --- process Note On or Note Off messages here
    switch(vstEvent.type)
    {
        // --- NOTE ON
        case Event::kNoteOnEvent:
        {
            <SNIP SNIP SNIP>
            // place after logging the MIDI
            // message

            << INSERT ** Code Listing 8.15: Note On ** HERE >>

            break;
        }

        // --- NOTE OFF
        case Event::kNoteOffEvent:
```

```
            {
                    <SNIP SNIP SNIP>
                    // place after logging the MIDI
                    // message

                    << INSERT ** Code Listing 8.16: Note Off ** HERE >>

                    break;
            }

            etc...
```

doControlChange()

Remove the code for MIDI message handling for pitch bend, volume, panning, all notes off and sustain pedal and replace with the polyphonic version, which loops through the voices and sets the modulation matrix source values.

```
bool Processor::doControlUpdate(ProcessData& data)
{
        <SNIP SNIP SNIP Indents Removed>

        // --- MIDI messages
        case MIDI_PITCHBEND: // want -1 to +1
        {
                m_dMIDIPitchBend = unipolarToBipolar(value);

                // LOG MIDI
                // --- send to matrix poly
                for(int i=0; i<MAX_VOICES; i++)
                {
                        m_Voices[i].m_ModulationMatrix.m_dSources
                                        [SOURCE_PITCHBEND] = m_dMIDIPitchBend;
                }
                break;
        }
        case MIDI_VOLUME_CC7: // want 0 to 127
        {
                m_uMIDIVolumeCC7 = unipolarToMIDI(value);

                // LOG MIDI
                // --- send to matrix poly
                for(int i=0; i<MAX_VOICES; i++)
                {
                        m_Voices[i].m_ModulationMatrix.m_dSources
                                        [SOURCE_MIDI_VOLUME_CC07] = m_uMIDIVolumeCC7;
                }

                break;
        }
        case MIDI_PAN_CC10: // want 0 to 127
```

```
{
        m_uMIDIPanCC10 = unipolarToMIDI(value);

        // LOG MIDI
        // --- send to matrix poly
        for(int i=0; i<MAX_VOICES; i++)
        {
                m_Voices[i].m_ModulationMatrix.m_dSources
                                [SOURCE_MIDI_PAN_CC10] = m_uMIDIPanCC10;
        }

        break;
}
case MIDI_ALL_NOTES_OFF:
{
        for(int i=0; i<MAX_VOICES; i++)
                m_Voices[i].m_EG1.noteOff();

        break;
}
case MIDI_SUSTAIN_PEDAL: // want 0 to 1
{
        bool bSus = value > 0.5 ? true : false;

        // LOG MIDI
        // --- send to matrix poly
        UINT uMIDI = unipolarToMIDI(value);
        for(int i=0; i<MAX_VOICES; i++)
        {
                m_Voices[i].m_ModulationMatrix.m_dSources
                                [SOURCE_SUSTAIN_PEDAL] = uMIDI;
        }

        break;
}
```

8.19 Poly NanoSynth: AU

There are no added GUI controls, so we can go directly to *NanoSynth.h* file and add the new declarations.

AUSynth.h

Outside of the object declaration, add the new voice structure and MAX_VOICES definitions and, inside the object, declare the arrays and helper functions. Remove the previous object declarations as well.

```
// --- one complete voice
struct nanoSynthVoice
{
     CQBLimitedOscillator m_Osc1;
     CQBLimitedOscillator m_Osc2;
```

```
      CLFO m_LFO1;
      CEnvelopeGenerator m_EG1;
      CMoogLadderFilter m_Filter1;
      CDCA m_DCA;
      CModulationMatrix m_ModulationMatrix;
};

#define MAX_VOICES 2

class AUSynth : public AUInstrumentBase
{
      <SNIP SNIP SNIP>

      // Add your code here: --------------------------------------------- //
      // --- the Modulation Matrix
      CModulationMatrix m_GlobalModMatrix;

      nanoSynthVoice m_Voices[MAX_VOICES];
      int m_nPendingMIDINote[MAX_VOICES];          // if -1 no pending note
      int m_nPendingMIDIVelocity[MAX_VOICES];      // if -1 no pending velocity

      void startNote(int nIndex, UINT uMIDINote, UINT uMIDIVelocity);
      void stealNote(int nIndex, UINT uPendingMIDINote,
                     UINT uPendingVelocity);

      etc...
}
```

AUSynth.cpp

We need to alter all the functions we discussed so far, plus a few MIDI-specific ones. Most of the code is just cut-and-paste from the listings.

Constructor

Remove the original code and replace with polyphonic version; notice this occurs after the global mod matrix has been initialized and the range/intensity variables have been set:

```
AUSynth::AUSynth()
{
      <SNIP SNIP SNIP>

      m_dOscFoPitchBendModRange = OSC_PITCHBEND_MOD_RANGE;
      m_dAmpModRange = AMP_MOD_RANGE;

      << INSERT ** Code Listing 8.9: Global Parameter Init I ** HERE >>
}
```

Destructor

Just delete our master modulation matrix core.

```
AUSynth::~AUSynth(void)
{
    // --- delete on master ONLY
    m_GlobalModMatrix.deleteModMatrix();
}
```

Initialize()

Likewise, remove the old code and replace with the polyphonic version:

```
ComponentResult AUSynth::Initialize()
{
    AUInstrumentBase::Initialize();

    << INSERT ** Code Listing 8.10: Global Parameter Init II ** HERE >>

    update();

    etc...
}
```

update()

Here, we polyphone-ize again by setting all the voice parameters on all voices at once; only replace the synth update and not the modulation matrix code.

```
void AUSynth::update()
{
    for(int i=0; i<MAX_VOICES; i++)
    {
        // --- set public attributes on objects
        //
        // --- Oscillators
        m_Voices[i].m_Osc1.m_uWaveform = Globals()-> GetParameter(OSC_WAVEFORM);
        m_Voices[i].m_Osc2.m_uWaveform = Globals()-> GetParameter(OSC_WAVEFORM);

        // --- Filter
        m_Voices[i].m_Filter1.m_dFcControl = Globals()-> GetParameter(FILTER_FC);
        m_Voices[i].m_Filter1.m_dQControl = Globals()-> GetParameter(FILTER_Q);

        // --- LFO
        m_Voices[i].m_LFO1.m_uWaveform = Globals()-> GetParameter(LFO1_WAVEFORM);
        m_Voices[i].m_LFO1.m_dAmplitude = Globals()-> GetParameter(LFO1_AMPLITUDE);
        m_Voices[i].m_LFO1.m_dOscFo = Globals()->GetParameter(LFO1_RATE);
        m_Voices[i].m_LFO1.m_uLFOMode = Globals()->GetParameter(LFO1_MODE);

        // ---EG1
        m_Voices[i].m_EG1.setAttackTime_mSec(Globals()-> GetParameter(EG1_ATTACK_MSEC));
        m_Voices[i].m_EG1.setDecayTime_mSec(Globals()-> GetParameter(EG1_DECAY_MSEC));
        m_Voices[i].m_EG1.setSustainLevel(Globals()-> GetParameter(EG1_SUSTAIN_LEVEL));
        m_Voices[i].m_EG1.setReleaseTime_mSec(Globals()-> GetParameter(EG1_RELEASE_MSEC));
```

```
            m_Voices[i].m_EG1.m_bResetToZero = Globals()-> GetParameter(RESET_TO_ZERO);
            m_Voices[i].m_EG1.m_bLegatoMode = Globals()-> GetParameter(LEGATO_MODE);

            // --- DCA
            m_Voices[i].m_DCA.setPanControl(Globals()->GetParameter(OUTPUT_PAN));
            m_Voices[i].m_DCA.setAmplitude_dB(Globals()-> GetParameter(OUTPUT_AMPLITUDE_DB));
        }

        // --- mod matrix stuff
        if(m_uFilterKeyTrack == 1)

        etc...

    }
```

Render()

Remove the old code and add the new accumulating code with the voice steal code intact. Note that the outputs are now taken from the new accumulator variables.

```
OSStatus AUSynth::Render(AudioUnitRenderActionFlags& ioActionFlags,
                         const AudioTimeStamp& inTimeStamp,
                         UInt32 inNumberFrames)
{

            <SNIP SNIP SNIP>
    float* right = numChans == 2 ? (float*)bufferList.mBuffers[1].mData : NULL;

    // --- output "accumulators"
    double dOutL = 0.0;
    double dOutR = 0.0;
    double dAccumOutL = 0.0;
    double dAccumOutR = 0.0;

    // --- the frame processing loop
    for(UInt32 frame=0; frame<inNumberFrames; ++frame)
    {
            // --- clear accumulators
            dAccumOutL = 0.0;
            dAccumOutR = 0.0;

            << INSERT ** Code Listing 8.12: Mod Matrix Render II ** HERE >>

            // write out to buffer
            // --- mono
            left[frame] = dAccumOutL;

            // --- stereo
            if(right) right[frame] = dAccumOutL;
            }
    }
```

```
        return noErr;
    }
```

startNote() *and* stealNote()

Implement the *startNote()* and *stealNote()* functions using the code listings.

```
void AUSynth::startNote(int nIndex, UINT uMIDINote, UINT uMIDIVelocity)
{
        << INSERT ** Code Listing 8.13: Start Note ** HERE >>
}

void AUSynth::stealNote(int nIndex, UINT uPendingMIDINote,
                        UINT uPendingVelocity)
{
        << INSERT ** Code Listing 8.14: Steal Note ** HERE >>
}
```

StartNote() *and* StopNote()

Remove the old code and implement the functions using the code listings; the code is inserted after the MIDI logging statements and just before the end brackets.

```
OSStatus AUSynth::StartNote(MusicDeviceInstrumentID inInstrument,
                            MusicDeviceGroupID inGroupID,
                            NoteInstanceID *outNoteInstanceID,
                            UInt32 inOffsetSampleFrame,
                            const MusicDeviceNoteParams &inParams)
{
        <SNIP SNIP SNIP>
        // LOG MIDI

        << INSERT ** Code Listing 8.15: Note On ** HERE >>


        return noErr;
}

// --- Note Off handler
OSStatus AUSynth::StopNote(MusicDeviceGroupID inGroupID,
                           NoteInstanceID inNoteInstanceID,
                           UInt32 inOffsetSampleFrame)
{
        <SNIP SNIP SNIP>
        // LOG MIDI

        << INSERT ** Code Listing 8.16: Note Off ** HERE >>


        return noErr;
}
```

HandlePitchWheel()

Remove the old code and insert the code to send this message to all voices.

```
OSStatus AUSynth::HandlePitchWheel(UInt8 inChannel,
                                   UInt8 inPitch1,
                                   UInt8 inPitch2,
                                   UInt32 inStartFrame)
{

    <SNIP SNIP SNIP>
    // LOG MIDI

    // --- send to matrix poly
    for(int i=0; i<MAX_VOICES; i++)
    {
        m_Voices[i].m_ModulationMatrix.m_dSources[SOURCE_PITCHBEND] =
                                            fNormalizedPitchBendValue;
    }

    return noErr;
}
```

HandleControlChange()

Remove the old code and insert the code to send volume and pan messages to all voices.

```
OSStatus AUSynth::HandleControlChange(UInt8 inChannel,
                                      UInt8 inController,
                                      UInt8 inValue,
                                      UInt32 inStartFrame)
{
    switch(inController)
    {
        case VOLUME_CC07:
        {
            // LOG MIDI

            // --- send to matrix poly
            for(int i=0; i<MAX_VOICES; i++)
            {
                m_Voices[i].m_ModulationMatrix.
                    m_dSources[SOURCE_MIDI_VOLUME_CC07] = inValue;
            }

            break;
        }
        case PAN_CC10:
        {
            // LOG MIDI
```

```
            // --- send to matrix poly
            for(int i=0; i<MAX_VOICES; i++)
            {
                    m_Voices[i].m_ModulationMatrix.
                            m_dSources[SOURCE_MIDI_PAN_CC10] = inValue;
                    }

            break;
            }
    case SUSTAIN_PEDAL:
    {
            // LOG MIDI
            // --- send to matrix poly
            for(int i=0; i<MAX_VOICES; i++)
            {
                    m_Voices[i].m_ModulationMatrix.
                            m_dSources[SOURCE_SUSTAIN_PEDAL] = inValue;
            }

            break;
    }
    case ALL_NOTES_OFF:
    {
            // LOG MIDI
            // --- send to matrix poly
            for(int i=0; i<MAX_VOICES; i++)
                    m_Voices[i].m_EG1.noteOff();

            break;
    }
    etc...
```

Build and test the new polyphonic NanoSynth; make sure to test the note stealing and reset-to-zero mode, which becomes more important with polyphony. You may be able to trick our simple heuristic by re-triggering the same pairs of note or alternating trills—don't spend much time on it, as we are going to be using a different and more robust logic in the subsequent synths.

8.20 Global Parameterization

Handling polyphony by replicating structures (or objects) is fairly straightforward; you saw the use of the *for()* loop to iterate through the voices and deal with them. We have a shared modulation matrix core, so when the user changes or enables/disable routings, we only need to change the matrix core once. But if you look at the *update()* function for the Poly NanoSynth plug-in, you will see some wasted code. We are looping through the objects and repeatedly setting the same variable on each one. And, we are setting variables on voices that might not even be active. Imagine a synth with 16 voices of polyphony and 40-50 GUI controls, as we will have in the rest of the projects. Updating all the voices at once would result in lots of wasted function calls. Since the voice's objects all share the same GUI controls (i.e. changing the filter cutoff control changes the cutoff in all the voices), why not have a way to share common or global parameters? Figure 8.12 shows the global parameterization concept.

You've already seen how the modulation matrix and polyphony have bloated the code some. Making our synth parameters global isn't going to reduce the amount of code, but it will make the synth more efficient—we will only update one set of global variables and the objects will use them instead of their own local variables when they are updated. If you have the MMA DLS Level II specification, you will see that they specify using the modulation matrix to hold global parameters. The downside, however, is that global variables are updated on every sample period, even if no GUI control has moved. We separate the global parameters into their own data structures to avoid this processing, but merging global parameters into the modulation matrix is certainly something you can experiment with. The extent of this global parameter bookkeeping and data structuring code may be a turn-off, but it's required. And, in the next chapter,

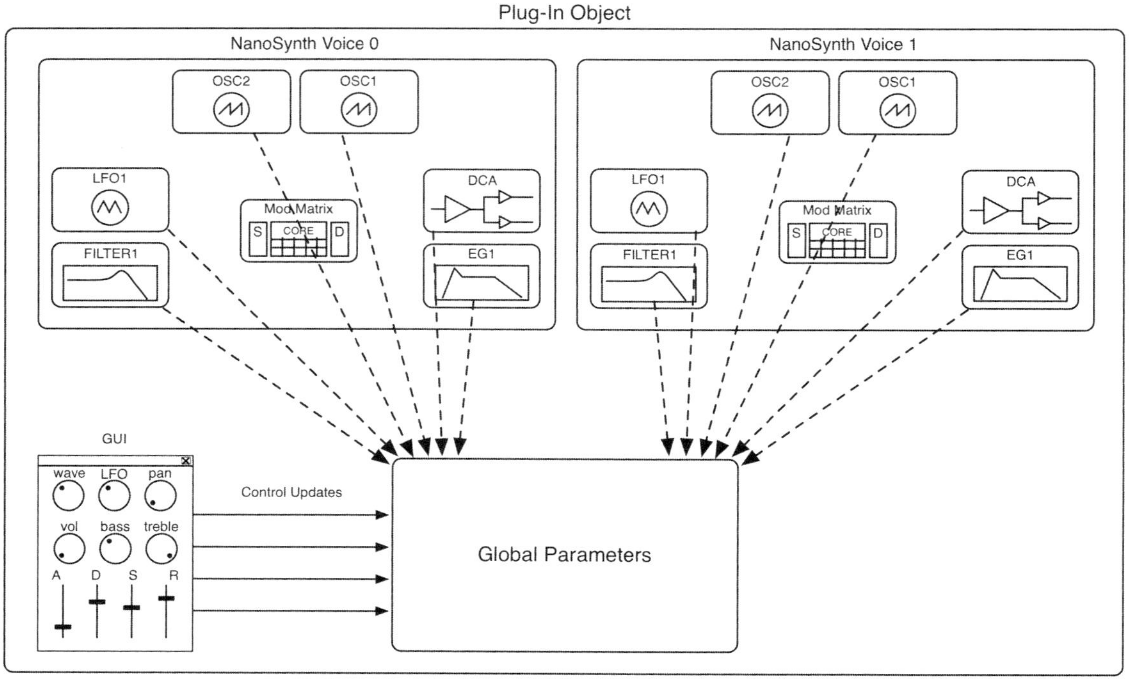

Figure 8.12: GUI controls that are common to all voice components can be globalized and stored/set only once (the shared mod matrix core connections are not shown).

we will take steps to minimize the amount of it we need to do by creating a voice base class that is common to all synths and does much of the work that we discussed in this chapter.

In our synth projects, the global parameters are packaged in structures. There is a separate structure for each component: oscillator, filter, EG and DCA, as well as a container structure for the voice. If you look at each of our C++ component objects, you can see the variables that the user can potentially control. The *synthfunctions.h* file declares all the structures for all our objects and synths in the book. In fact, all but NanoSynth will use the exact same voice global parameter structure. Take a look at the structures for the various synth objects (note—some of the variables might not make sense to you yet, as they relate to future synth projects). Remember that these structures only contain variables that the user is allowed to adjust. The *globalOscillatorParams* struct contains the oscillator's GUI parameters. We will get to the Loop mode in Chapter 10.

```
struct globalOscillatorParams
{
    // --- common
    double dOscFo;
    double dFoRatio;
    double dAmplitude;
    double dPulseWidthControl;
    int nOctave;                // octave tweak
    int nSemitones;             // semitones tweak
    int nCents;                 // cents tweak
    UINT uWaveform;             // to store type

    // --- LFOs
    UINT uLFOMode;

    // --- CSampleOscillators
    UINT uLoopMode;
};
```

Now look at the filter, EG and DCA global parameter structures. All of these parameters should look familiar. In fact, they are all named identically to their object counterparts, except they are missing the *m_* found on the object variable names.

```
struct globalFilterParams
{
      double dFcControl;
      double dQControl;
      double dAuxControl;
      double dSaturation;
      UINT uFilterType;
      UINT uNLP;
};

struct globalEGParams
{
      double dAttackTime_mSec;
      double dDecayTime_mSec;
      double dReleaseTime_mSec;
      double dSustainLevel;
      double dShutdownTime_mSec;
      bool bResetToZero;
      bool bLegatoMode;
};

struct globalDCAParams
{
      double dAmplitude_dB;
      double dPanControl;
};
```

The total global parameter structure for a NanoSynth voice is another structure that contains instances of these structures as members. There is one structure for each component.

```
struct globalNanoSynthParams
{
      globalOscillatorParams   osc1Params;
      globalOscillatorParams   osc2Params;
      globalOscillatorParams   lfo1Params;
      globalFilterParams       filter1Params;
      globalEGParams           eg1Params;
      globalDCAParams          dcaParams;
};
```

When we introduced the modulation matrix, we had to edit each synth object and add some code to allow the synth to use the modulation matrix if it is being used. The objects may still operate in a stand-alone manner because we left the other code intact. We will use the same strategy again for the global parameters; we will augment rather than replace code. The modulation matrix and global parameters are optional, though we will use them for the rest of the book. This allows you to use the objects in other projects and plug-ins outside the scope of our synth projects.

Each of our synth objects requires the same modification for global parameters:

- declare a global parameter structure pointer; when NULL, global parameters are not used
- implement a *initGlobalParameters()* function in which you save your new global parameter pointer (thus enabling the functionality), and then initialize your structure's variables

- use the global parameters in your *update()* function, where the object's parameters are updated based (in part) on GUI control values
- remember to NULL the global pointer in the constructor to disable it by default

Lets go through each object and make the modifications—they are all simple and straightforward.

Oscillator.h

Add the new global parameter variable:

```
class COscillator
{
public:
      COscillator(void);
      virtual ~COscillator(void);
      <SNIP SNIP SNIP>

      // --- destinations that we write to
      //        indexes in m_pModulationMatrix->Destinations[]
      UINT m_uModDestOutput1;
      UINT m_uModDestOutput2;
      // ----------------------------------------

      // --- Global Parameters -------------------
      //
      globalOscillatorParams* m_pGlobalOscParams;
      // ----------------------------------------

      etc...
```

Next, add the initialization function where you:

- save the global parameter pointer
- initialize elements with your own variables
- for the oscillator, you always initialize the *dOscFo* variable to –1, which means "not set," because this variable is automatically set to the MIDI note frequency for pitched oscillators; this variable is only used for LFOs

```
      // --- init the global params
      inline void initGlobalParameters(globalOscillatorParams*
                                       pGlobalOscParams)
      {
              // --- save the pointer
              m_pGlobalOscParams = pGlobalOscParams;

              // --- init
              m_pGlobalOscParams->dOscFo = -1.0;    // NOTE OFF
              m_pGlobalOscParams->dFoRatio = m_dFoRatio;
              m_pGlobalOscParams->dAmplitude = m_dAmplitude;
              m_pGlobalOscParams->dPulseWidthControl = m_dPulseWidthControl;
              m_pGlobalOscParams->nOctave = m_nOctave;
              m_pGlobalOscParams->nSemitones = m_nSemitones;
              m_pGlobalOscParams->nCents = m_nCents;
              m_pGlobalOscParams->uWaveform = m_uWaveform;
              m_pGlobalOscParams->uLFOMode = m_uLFOMode;
      }
```

```
// --- update the frequency, amp mod and PWM
inline virtual void update()

etc...
```

Then, use the global parameters, if any, in the *update()* function. Notice that you first check for a non-negative oscillator value before applying it since this base class function is common to both pitched oscillators and LFOs.

```
inline virtual void update()
{
// --- Global Parameters
if(m_pGlobalOscParams)
{
        if(m_pGlobalOscParams->dOscFo >= 0)
                m_dOscFo = m_pGlobalOscParams->dOscFo;

        m_dFoRatio = m_pGlobalOscParams->dFoRatio;
        m_dAmplitude = m_pGlobalOscParams->dAmplitude;
        m_dPulseWidthControl = m_pGlobalOscParams->dPulseWidthControl;
        m_nOctave = m_pGlobalOscParams->nOctave;
        m_nSemitones = m_pGlobalOscParams->nSemitones;
        m_nCents = m_pGlobalOscParams->nCents;
        m_uWaveform = m_pGlobalOscParams->uWaveform;
        m_uLFOMode =
                m_pGlobalOscParams->uLFOMode;
}

// --- ignore LFO mode for noise sources
if(m_uWaveform == rsh || m_uWaveform == qrsh)
   m_uLFOMode = free;

// --- Modulation Matrix
//
// --- get from matrix Sources
if(m_pModulationMatrix)
{
        // --- zero is norm for these
        m_dFoMod = m_pModulationMatrix->
                m_dDestinations[m_uModSourceFo];

        etc...
```

Oscillator.cpp

All you need to do is NULL the global parameter pointer to disable it.

```
COscillator::COscillator(void)
{
     <SNIP SNIP SNIP>

     m_uModDestOutput2 = SOURCE_NONE;
     m_uModSourceAmp = DEST_NONE;
```

```
        // --- default is NO Global Params
        m_pGlobalOscParams = NULL;
}
```

Filter.h

The process is the same for the rest of the objects, so you declare, initialize then use the globals as follows:

```
class CFilter
{
        <SNIP SNIP SNIP>

        // --- Global Parameters --------------------
        //
        globalFilterParams* m_pGlobalFilterParams;
        // -----------------------------------------

        <SNIP SNIP SNIP>

        // --- init the global params
        inline virtual void initGlobalParameters(globalFilterParams* pGlobalFilterParams)
        {
                // --- save pointer
                m_pGlobalFilterParams = pGlobalFilterParams;

                // --- init
                m_pGlobalFilterParams->dAuxControl = m_dAuxControl;
                m_pGlobalFilterParams->dFcControl = m_dFcControl;
                m_pGlobalFilterParams->dQControl = m_dQControl;
                m_pGlobalFilterParams->dSaturation = m_dSaturation;
                m_pGlobalFilterParams->uFilterType = m_uFilterType;
                m_pGlobalFilterParams->uNLP = m_uNLP;
        }

        // --- recalculate the Fc (called after modulations)
        inline virtual void update()
        {
                // --- Global Parameters
                if(m_pGlobalFilterParams)
                {
                        m_dAuxControl = m_pGlobalFilterParams->dAuxControl;
                        m_dFcControl = m_pGlobalFilterParams->dFcControl;
                        m_dQControl = m_pGlobalFilterParams->dQControl;
                        m_dSaturation = m_pGlobalFilterParams->dSaturation;
                        m_uFilterType = m_pGlobalFilterParams->uFilterType;
                        m_uNLP = m_pGlobalFilterParams->uNLP;
                }

                // --- Modulation Matrix
                //

                etc...
```

Filter.cpp

Just NULL out the pointer in the constructor:

```
CFilter::CFilter(void)
{
      <SNIP SNIP SNIP>

      // --- default is NO Global Params
      m_pGlobalFilterParams = NULL;
}
```

EnvelopeGenerator.h

Follow the same pattern as the previous two objects; however, the functions that calculate the attack, decay and release times require a trigonometric function call, so we first check to see if they have changed before updating them. The other variables are simply stored for the update.

```
class CEnvelopeGenerator
{
      <SNIP SNIP SNIP>

      // --- Global Parameters --------------------
      //
      globalEGParams* m_pGlobalEGParams;
      // ----------------------------------------

      <SNIP SNIP SNIP>

      // --- init the global params
      inline void virtual initGlobalParameters( globalEGParams* pGlobalEGParams)
      {
            // --- save
            m_pGlobalEGParams = pGlobalEGParams;

            // --- init
            m_pGlobalEGParams->dAttackTime_mSec = m_dAttackTime_mSec;
            m_pGlobalEGParams->dDecayTime_mSec = m_dDecayTime_mSec;
            m_pGlobalEGParams->dReleaseTime_mSec = m_dReleaseTime_mSec;
            m_pGlobalEGParams->dSustainLevel = m_dSustainLevel;
            m_pGlobalEGParams->dShutdownTime_mSec = m_dShutdownTime_mSec;
            m_pGlobalEGParams->bResetToZero = m_bResetToZero;
            m_pGlobalEGParams->bLegatoMode = m_bLegatoMode;
      }

      // --- update params
      inline void update()
      {
            // --- Global Parameters
            if(m_pGlobalEGParams)
```

```
{
        // --- only update if changed
        if(m_dAttackTime_mSec !=
        m_pGlobalEGParams->dAttackTime_mSec)
        setAttackTime_mSec(m_pGlobalEGParams->dAttackTime_mSec);

        if(m_dDecayTime_mSec != m_pGlobalEGParams->dDecayTime_mSec)
        setDecayTime_mSec(m_pGlobalEGParams->dDecayTime_mSec);

        if(m_dReleaseTime_mSec !=
        m_pGlobalEGParams->dReleaseTime_mSec)
        setReleaseTime_mSec(m_pGlobalEGParams->dReleaseTime_mSec);

        if(m_dSustainLevel != m_pGlobalEGParams->dSustainLevel)
                setSustainLevel(m_pGlobalEGParams->dSustainLevel);

        m_dShutdownTime_mSec = m_pGlobalEGParams->dShutdownTime_mSec;

        // --- just store
        m_bResetToZero = m_pGlobalEGParams->bResetToZero;
        m_bLegatoMode =  m_pGlobalEGParams->bLegatoMode;
}

// --- Modulation Matrix
//
etc...
```

EnvelopeGenerator.cpp

Again, remember to NULL the pointer in the constructor:

```
CEnvelopeGenerator::CEnvelopeGenerator(void)
{
        <SNIP SNIP SNIP>

        // --- default is NO Global Params
        m_pGlobalEGParams = NULL;
}
```

DCA.h

You know the drill by now: declare, init and use the global parameter structure:

```
class CDCA
{
        <SNIP SNIP SNIP>

        // --- Global Parameters -------------------
        //
        globalDCAParams* m_pGlobalDCAParams;
        // ----------------------------------------
```

```
<SNIP SNIP SNIP>

// --- init the global params
inline virtual void initGlobalParameters(globalDCAParams* pGlobalDCAParams)
{
        // --- save
        m_pGlobalDCAParams = pGlobalDCAParams;

        // --- init
        pGlobalDCAParams->dAmplitude_dB = m_dAmplitude_dB;
        pGlobalDCAParams->dPanControl = m_dPanControl;
}

// --- DCA operation functions
// --- recalculate gain values
inline void update()
{
        // --- Global Parameters
        if(m_pGlobalDCAParams)
        {
                setAmplitude_dB(m_pGlobalDCAParams->dAmplitude_dB);
                m_dPanControl = m_pGlobalDCAParams->dPanControl;
        }

        // --- Modulation Matrix
        //
        etc...
```

DCA.cpp

NULL out the pointer one more time—this is the last object to modify!

```
CDCA::CDCA(void)
{
      <SNIP SNIP SNIP>

      // --- default is NO Global Params
      m_pGlobalDCAParams = NULL;
}
```

Let's finish off NanoSynth by implementing the global parameter changes. Your final NanoSynth is actually quite remarkable; it's polyphonic, uses a voice-stealing heuristic, and implements its interconnections with a modulation matrix. Global parameters make the synth updates more efficient. Believe it or not, adding this finishing touch to NanoSynth is refreshingly easy and consists of four steps; most of the work is done in the synth objects during the initialization and update functions.

- modify the oscillator, filter, envelope generator and DCA base classes as shown previously (or download them from my website)
- add a global parameter declaration to the plug-in's *.h* file
- call the global parameter initialization functions on each voice sub-component
- remove the *for()* loop in the plug-in's *update()* function and replace the loop with a single set of global parameter adjustments

Initializing the sub-components is done in the constructor in the same loop where you set the matrix cores and routing information on the voice components. In this code, the variable *m_GlobalSynthParams* is the plug-in object's global parameter structure .

```
for(int i=0; i<MAX_VOICES; i++)
{
        << ** Code Listing 8.17: Global Parameter Init III ** >>

        // --- setup the global param struct pointers to enable them m_Voices[i].m_Osc1.init-
        GlobalParameters
        (&m_GlobalSynthParams.osc1Params);
        m_Voices[i].m_Osc2.initGlobalParameters
                                        (&m_GlobalSynthParams.osc2Params);
        m_Voices[i].m_Filter1.initGlobalParameters
                                        (&m_GlobalSynthParams.filter1Params);
        m_Voices[i].m_EG1.initGlobalPaameters
                                        (&m_GlobalSynthParams.eg1Params);
        m_Voices[i].m_LFO1.initGlobalParameters
                                        (&m_GlobalSynthParams.lfo1Params);
        m_Voices[i].m_DCA.initGlobalParameters
                                        (&m_GlobalSynthParams.dcaParams);
        // ----------------------------------------------------------

        << ** END Code Listing 8.17: Global Parameter Init III ** END >>
```

Updating the global parameters is easy once you decode the structure-within-structure format of the code. You have to match up your GUI controls with each of the voice's components.

```
<< ** Code Listing 8.18: Global Parameter Update II ** >>

// --- set the global parameters
//
// --- oscillators
m_GlobalSynthParams.osc1Params.uWaveform = m_uOscWaveform;
m_GlobalSynthParams.osc2Params.uWaveform = m_uOscWaveform;

// --- filter
m_GlobalSynthParams.filter1Params.dFcControl = m_dFcControl;
m_GlobalSynthParams.filter1Params.dQControl = m_dQControl;

// --- LFO1
m_GlobalSynthParams.lfo1Params.uWaveform = m_uLFO1Waveform;
m_GlobalSynthParams.lfo1Params.dAmplitude = m_dLFO1Amplitude;
m_GlobalSynthParams.lfo1Params.uLFOMode = m_uLFO1Mode;
m_GlobalSynthParams.lfo1Params.dOscFo = m_dLFO1Rate;

// --- EG1
m_GlobalSynthParams.eg1Params.dAttackTime_mSec = m_dAttackTime_mSec;
m_GlobalSynthParams.eg1Params.dDecayTime_mSec = m_dDecayTime_mSec;
m_GlobalSynthParams.eg1Params.dSustainLevel = m_dSustainLevel;
m_GlobalSynthParams.eg1Params.dReleaseTime_mSec = m_dReleaseTime_mSec;
m_GlobalSynthParams.eg1Params.bResetToZero = (bool)m_uResetToZero;
m_GlobalSynthParams.eg1Params.bLegatoMode = (bool)m_uLegatoMode;
```

```
// --- DCA
m_GlobalSynthParams.dcaParams.dPanControl = m_dPanControl;
m_GlobalSynthParams.dcaParams.dAmplitude_dB = m_dVolume_dB;

<< ** END Code Listing 8.18: Global Parameter Update II ** END >>
```

In *prepareForPlay(), setActive()* or *initialize()*, there is one detail to deal with. Oscillator number 2 is detuned by 2.5 cents, however this is now a global parameter. So, we need to replace the voice initialization with a global parameter initialization so that:

```
m_Voices[i].m_Osc2.m_nCents = 2.5;
```

becomes

```
m_GlobalSynthParams.osc2Params.nCents = 2.5;
```

and since it is a global variable, you only need to set it once.

8.21 Final NanoSynth: RackAFX

NanoSynth.h

The final NanoSynth starts with the plug-in's *.h* file for the global parameter declaration.

```
class CNanoSynth : public CPlugIn
{
	<SNIP SNIP SNIP>

	// --- the Modulation Matrix
	CModulationMatrix m_GlobalModMatrix;

	// --- global params
	globalNanoSynthParams m_GlobalSynthParams;

	etc...
```

NanoSynth.cpp

Modify the voice setup in the constructor.

```
CNanoSynth::CNanoSynth()
{
	<SNIP SNIP SNIP>

	for(int i=0; i<MAX_VOICES; i++)
	{
		<< INSERT ** Code Listing 8.17: Global Parameter Init III ** HERE
		>>

		// --- NOTE: sub objects of a single voice share a modulation
		// matrix
		m_Voices[i].m_ModulationMatrix.
			setModMatrixCore(m_GlobalModMatrix.getModMatrixCore());

		etc...

}
```

prepareForPlay()

In *prepareForPlay()* replace the old initialization code with the slightly altered version that places the detuning in a global parameter.

```
bool __stdcall CNanoSynth::prepareForPlay()
{
      <SNIP SNIP SNIP>

      // --- anything global here: detune
      m_GlobalSynthParams.osc2Params.nCents = 2.5;

      // --- mass update
      update();

      return true;
}
```

update()

Finally, knock out the *update()* function and replace the *for()* loop. Make sure to leave the modulation matrix code alone.

```
void CNanoSynth::update()
{
      << INSERT ** Code Listing 8.18: Global Parameter Update II ** HERE >>

      // --- enable/disable mod matrix stuff
      if(m_uLFO1Destination == Osc)
      {
      m_GlobalModMatrix.enableModMatrixRow(SOURCE_LFO1,
                                    DEST_ALL_OSC_FO, true); // enable
            etc...
```

8.22 Final NanoSynth: VST3

VSTSynthProcessor.h

The final NanoSynth starts with the plug-in's *.h* file for the global parameter declaration.

```
class Processor : public AudioEffect
{
      <SNIP SNIP SNIP>

      // --- the Modulation Matrix
      CModulationMatrix m_GlobalModMatrix;

      // --- global params
      globalNanoSynthParams m_GlobalSynthParams;

      etc...
```

VSTSynthProcessor.cpp

setActive()

In *setActive()* add the global initialization function calls to the voice objects inside the same *for()* loop where you setup the sample rates, and at the same time, move the detuning outside the loop and into the global parameter.

```
tresult PLUGIN_API Processor::setActive(TBool state)
{
      if(state)
      {
              for(int i=0; i<MAX_VOICES; i++)
              {
                      << INSERT ** Code Listing 8.17: Global Parameter Init III
                      ** HERE >>

                      m_Voices[i].m_Osc1.setSampleRate(
                                          (double)processSetup.sampleRate);
                      etc...
              }

              // --- anything global here: detune
              m_GlobalSynthParams.osc2Params.nCents = 2.5;

              // --- mass update
              update();
```

update()

Finally, knock out the *update()* function and replace the *for()* loop. Make sure to leave the modulation matrix code alone.

```
void Processor::update()
{
      << INSERT ** Code Listing 8.18: Global Parameter Update II ** HERE >>

      // --- enable/disable mod matrix stuff
      if(m_uLFO1Destination == Osc)
      {
      m_GlobalModMatrix.enableModMatrixRow(SOURCE_LFO1,
                                   DEST_ALL_OSC_FO, true); // enable
              etc...
```

8.23 *Final NanoSynth: AU*

AUSynth.h

The final NanoSynth starts with the plug-in's *.h* file for the global parameter declaration.

```
class AUSynth : public AUInstrumentBase
{
      <SNIP SNIP SNIP>

      // --- the Modulation Matrix
      CModulationMatrix m_GlobalModMatrix;
```

```
// --- global params
globalNanoSynthParams m_GlobalSynthParams;

etc...
```

AUSynth.cpp

Constructor

In the Constructor add the global initialization function calls to the voice objects inside the same *for()* loop where you setup the sample rates.

```
AUSynth::AUSynth(AudioUnit inComponentInstance)
        : AUInstrumentBase(inComponentInstance, 0, 1)
{
    for(int i=0; i<MAX_VOICES; i++)
        {
                << INSERT ** Code Listing 8.17: Global Parameter Init III ** HERE >>

                // --- NOTE: sub objects share a modulation matrix
                m_Voices[i].m_ModulationMatrix.setModMatrixCore
                                    (m_GlobalModMatrix.getModMatrixCore());

        etc...
```

Initialize()

In the *Initialize()* function, just move the oscillator detuning outside the loop and into the global parameter.

```
ComponentResult AUSynth::Initialize()
{
    // --- init the base class
    AUInstrumentBase::Initialize();

    <SNIP SNIP SNIP>

    // --- anything global here: detune
    m_GlobalSynthParams.osc2Params.nCents = 2.5;

    // --- do the global update
    update();
```

update()

Finally, knock out the *update()* function and replace the *for()* loop with the fixed global code. Make sure to leave the modulation matrix code alone.

```
void AUSynth::update()
{
    // --- set the global parameters
    //
    // --- oscillators
```

```
m_GlobalSynthParams.osc1Params.uWaveform = Globals()->
                                          GetParameter(OSC_WAVEFORM);
m_GlobalSynthParams.osc2Params.uWaveform = Globals()->
                                          GetParameter(OSC_WAVEFORM);

// --- filter
m_GlobalSynthParams.filter1Params.dFcControl = Globals()->
                                             GetParameter(FILTER_FC);
m_GlobalSynthParams.filter1Params.dQControl = Globals()->
                                             GetParameter(FILTER_Q);

// --- LFO1
m_GlobalSynthParams.lfo1Params.uWaveform = Globals()->
                                          GetParameter(LFO1_WAVEFORM);
m_GlobalSynthParams.lfo1Params.dAmplitude = Globals()->
                                          GetParameter(LFO1_AMPLITUDE);
m_GlobalSynthParams.lfo1Params.uLFOMode = Globals()->
                                          GetParameter(LFO1_RATE);
m_GlobalSynthParams.lfo1Params.dOscFo = Globals()->
                                          GetParameter(LFO1_MODE);

// --- EG1
m_GlobalSynthParams.eg1Params.dAttackTime_mSec = Globals()->
                                     GetParameter(EG1_ATTACK_MSEC);
m_GlobalSynthParams.eg1Params.dDecayTime_mSec = Globals()->
                                     GetParameter(EG1_DECAY_MSEC);
m_GlobalSynthParams.eg1Params.dSustainLevel = Globals()->
                                     GetParameter(EG1_SUSTAIN_LEVEL);
m_GlobalSynthParams.eg1Params.dReleaseTime_mSec = Globals()->
                                     GetParameter(EG1_RELEASE_MSEC);
m_GlobalSynthParams.eg1Params.bResetToZero = Globals()->
                                     GetParameter(RESET_TO_ZERO);
m_GlobalSynthParams.eg1Params.bLegatoMode = Globals()->
                                     GetParameter(LEGATO_MODE);

// --- DCA
m_GlobalSynthParams.dcaParams.dPanControl = Globals()->
                                     GetParameter(OUTPUT_PAN);
m_GlobalSynthParams.dcaParams.dAmplitude_dB = Globals()->
                                     GetParameter(OUTPUT_AMPLITUDE_DB);

// --- mod matrix stuff
if(Globals()->GetParameter(FILTER_KEYTRACK))

etc...
```

Build and test your final NanoSynth. In the next chapter, we will start a new synth called MiniSynth that will build on everything you've learned so far. We won't have the room to print every line of code for the rest of the projects when it comes to the modulation matrix and global parameters since so much of it will be the same or nearly the same as what you've done so far. You may want to bookmark this chapter for future reference.

Bibliography

Limberis, Alex and Bryan, Joe. 1993. "An Architecture for a Multiple Digital Signal Processor Based Music Synthesizer with Dynamic Voice Allocation." Presented at the 95th Audio Engineering Society Convention. New York.

MIDI Manufacturers Association. 1999. *Downloadable Sounds Level 2,* vol. 1.0.

MIDI Manufacturers Association. 2004. *Downloadable Sounds Level 1,* vol 1.1b.

MIDI Manufacturers Association. 2006. *Downloadable Sounds Level 2,* Amendment 2.

CHAPTER 9

MiniSynth: Analog Modeling Synthesizer

MiniSynth is based on the architectures of the Korg Volca Keys and Moog MiniMoog synths. MiniSynth features the same MIDI implementation as NanoSynth and uses a modulation matrix to simplify programming and increase flexibility. You can spin off many variations of MiniSynth for your own projects. In this chapter, we will replace the NanoSynth voice structure with a new voice object called *CMiniSynthVoice*. This object is derived from the base class *CVoice*. The *CVoice* object is going to handle much of the core functionality that the rest of the synths will use, and each new synth in this chapter will introduce a new derived voice class based on the specific needs of each synth design. *CVoice* does so much of the work that creating new voice architectures and synth designs is greatly simplified.

> This chapter is a turning point in the book. The underlying synth object code is now set and will not change. You have seen an example of wiring the components in code using intermediate variables and function calls to implement modulation. You have also seen the implementation with the modulation matrix. In the following chapters, we derive new synth voice objects from the *CVoice* base class; there is one new voice object per synth. The synths all use the modulation matrix for connections. Polyphony is implemented in a more advanced way than NanoSynth.
>
> However, this is a point where you may easily deviate from the book code and design your own voice objects. You might decide not to use the modulation matrix or to implement polyphony differently. Go for it! This also makes an excellent programming assignment. The synth voices, modulation matrix connections and GUI parameter lists follow the same pattern, so you are free to implement the code as you wish. You might also decide to use the book code first, then go back and refine it in a way that best suits your programming style.

Figure 9.1 shows the simplified block diagram for MiniSynth. You can see that is very similar indeed to NanoSynth; additions include more oscillators and voice modes (oscillator combinations), a sub-oscillator and noise generator. The LFO can also modulate panning in the DCA. Before we look at the complete block diagram, let's look at the *CVoice* object.

9.1 Voice Architectures and CVoice

The MiniSynth voice architecture consists of:

- four oscillators
- one filter
- one DCA
- one LFO
- one EG

You can see that it is nearly the same as NanoSynth, but with a few more modulation routings and oscillators. The *CVoice* object is designed to encapsulate the functionality of a generic synth voice. But what is a generic voice? Let's look at a few commercial synthesizers and study their voice architectures. Figures 9.2–9.6 show the simplified voice architectures for the Korg Polysix, Korg MS-20, Yamaha EX-5, Sequential Circuits Prophet VS, and Korg Triton/Karma.

You can see many similarities and differences in the voice architectures, but they are all a combination of oscillators, filters, EGs and DCAs. The Korg H.I. architecture might win the prize for most number of sub-components. The *CVoice* Object consists of the following sub-components shown in Figure 9.7.

- four oscillators
- two filters
- two LFOs
- four EGs
- one DCA
- one Modulation Matrix
- one Global Voice Parameter Structure
- one Global Synth Parameter Structure

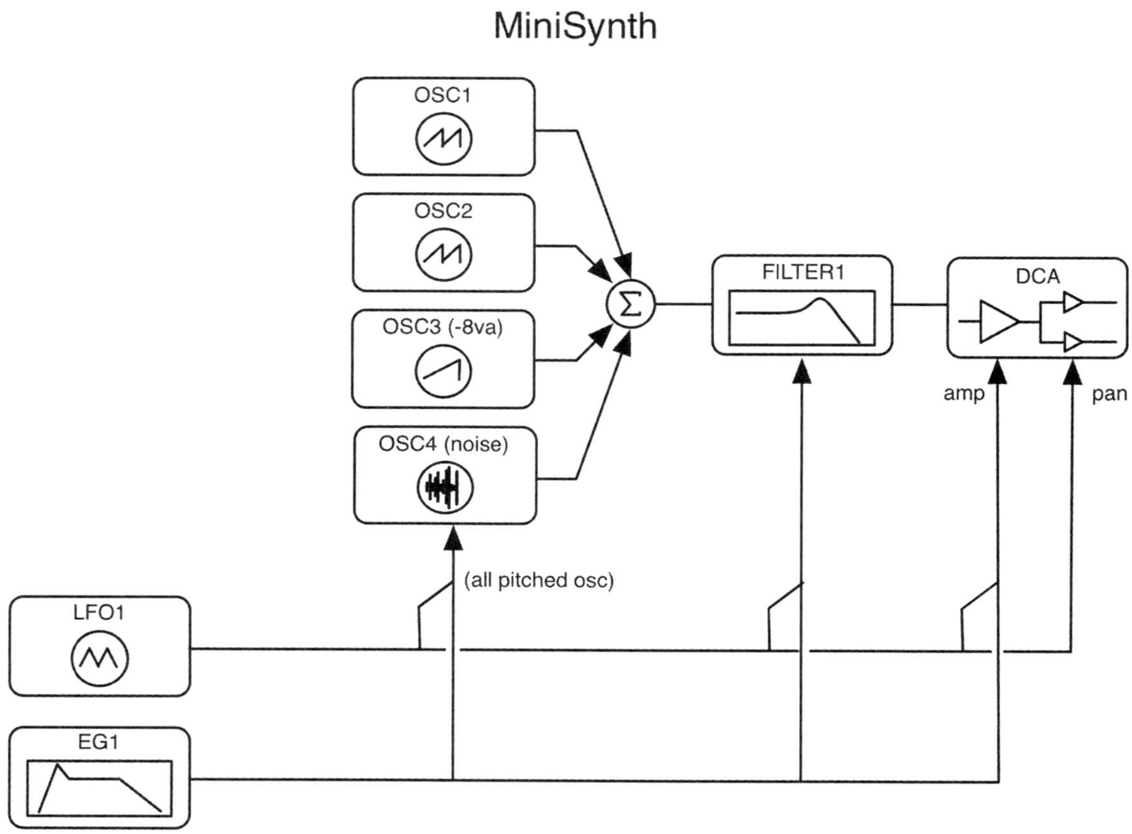

Figure 9.1: MiniSynth simplified block diagram.

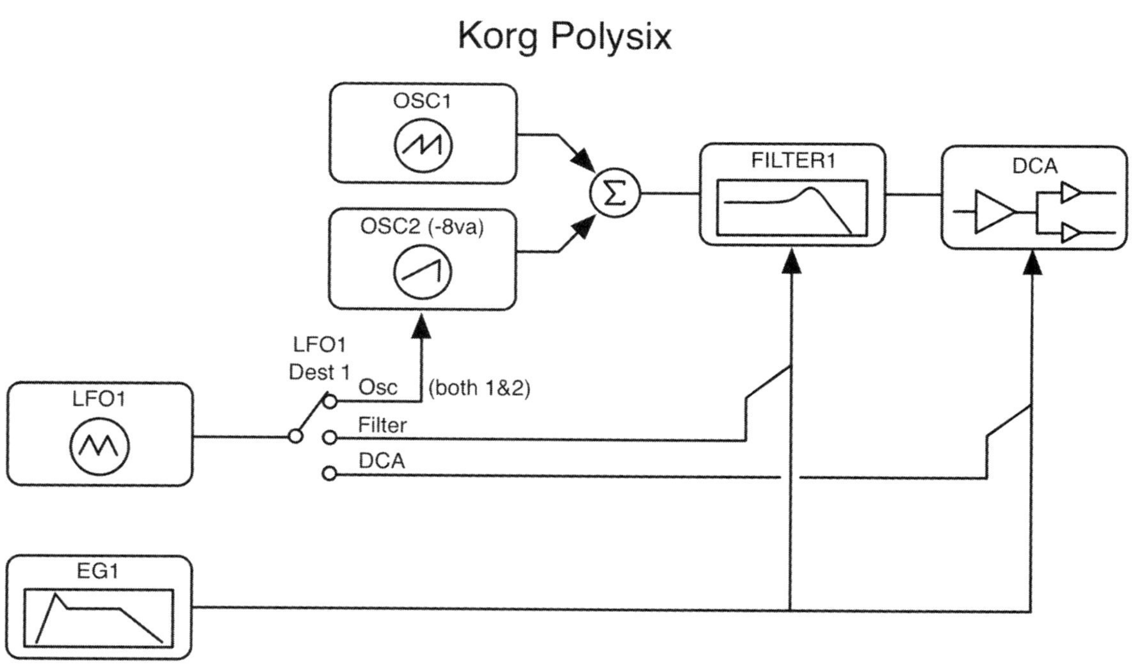

Figure 9.2: The Korg Polysix voice architecture.

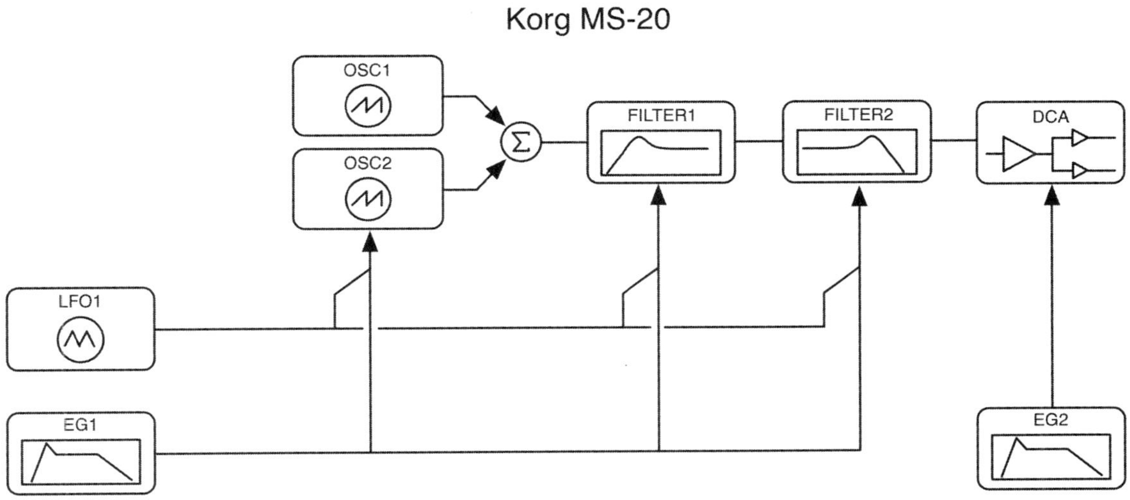

Figure 9.3: The Korg MS-20 voice architecture (patch-bay connections not shown).

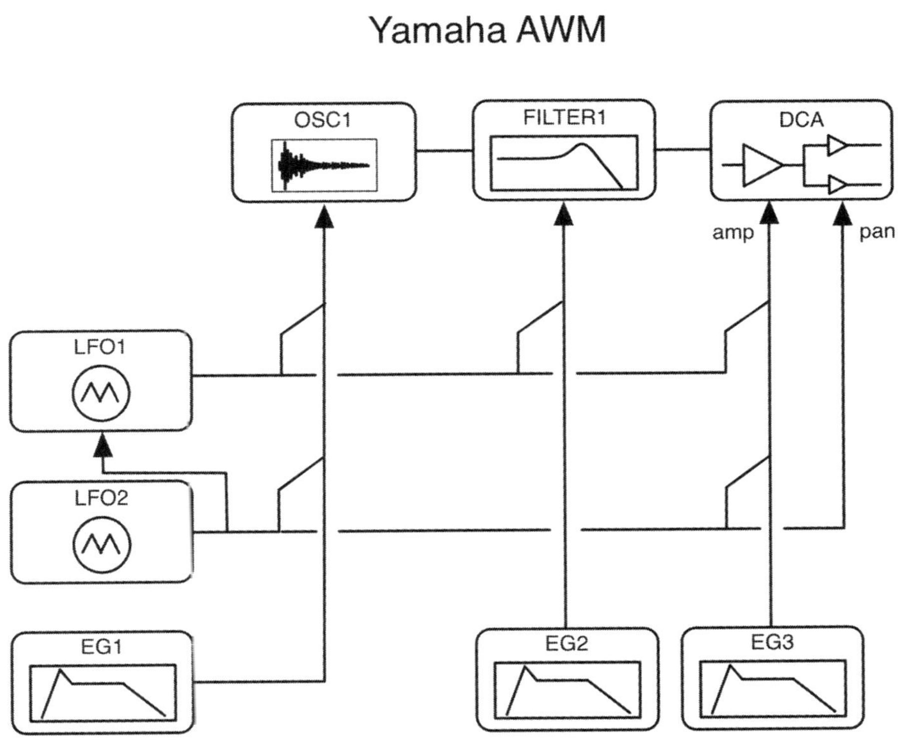

Figure 9.4: The Yamaha AWM voice architecture from the EX-5.

CVoice uses global parameterization only—it cannot operate in a stand-alone manner unless you add member functions to set the component values (e.g. *setLFO1Rate()*, *setEG2AttackTime()*, etc.) We will discuss the global synth and global voice parameters shortly. You are also free to add or remove components. By default, all the components are disconnected. Patches are programmed via the modulation matrix.

In *CVoice*, we want to be able to use any oscillator and any filter combination we like. The pitched oscillators and filters are all derived from the *COscillator* and *CFilter* base classes. We only have one kind of LFO, EG and DCA object (though of course you are free to derive new objects from them). *CVoice* is designed as a base class, and we will use it that way although it is not pure abstract. The oscillator and filter member objects are declared as pointers, while the rest of the core synth objects are statically defined. The two global parameter structures are defined as pointers. The very top of the class declaration is:

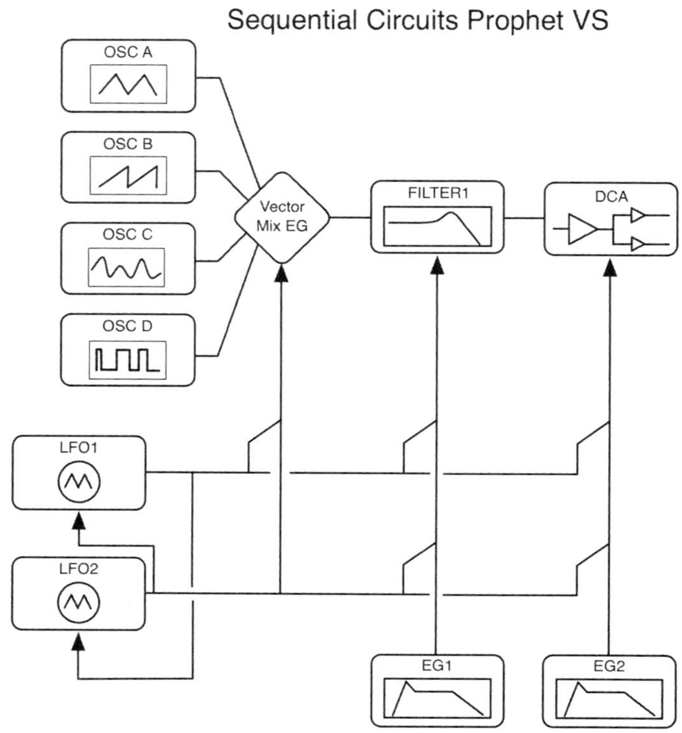

Figure 9.5: The Sequential Circuits Prophet VS voice architecture—this is the basis for Chapter 11's VectorSynth, where we will discuss its unique Vector Mix Envelope Generator.

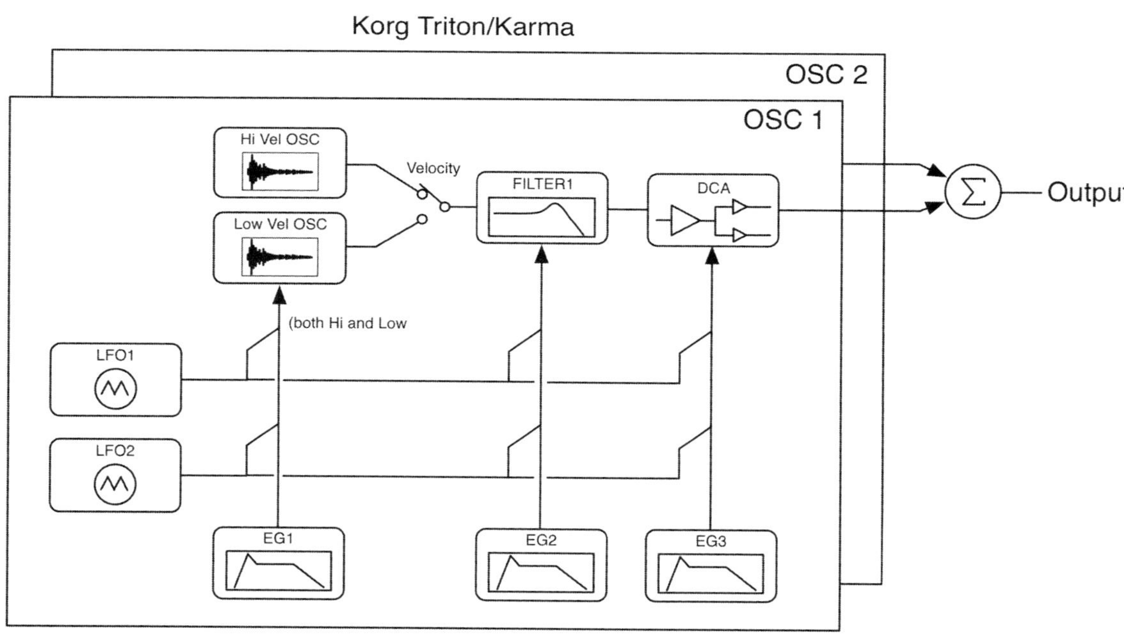

Figure 9.6: The Korg H.I. voice architecture from the Triton and Karma; here Korg calls a sub-voice an "OSC," which consists of oscillators, filter, LFOs, EGs, and DCA—two OSCs make up a single voice.

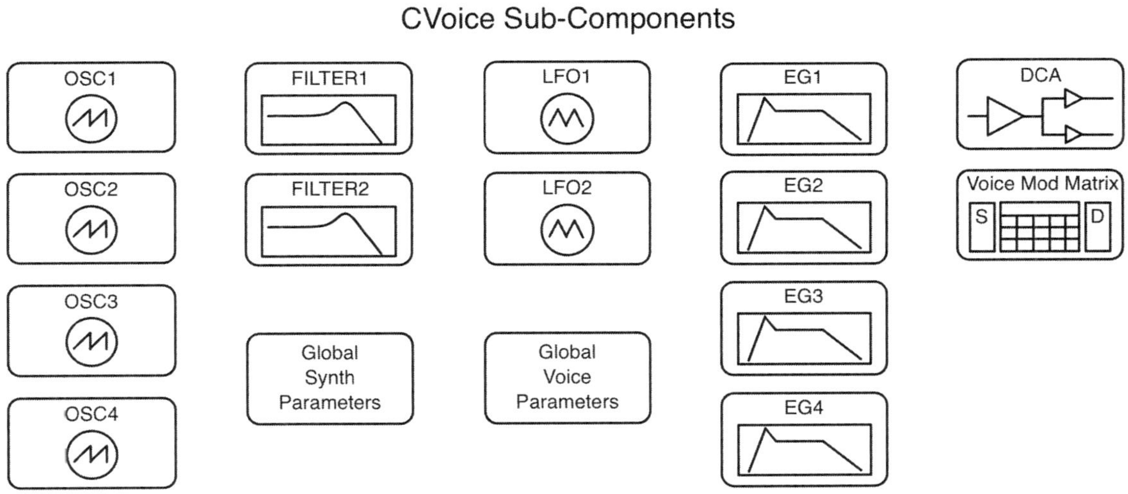

Figure 9.7: ***CVoice*** **is a collection of synth objects that you connect to make a voice; patch programming is done via the modulation matrix, and the object uses global parameters for adjusting component attributes.**

```
class CVoice
{
public:
	CVoice(void);
	virtual ~CVoice(void);

	// NOTE: public; this is shared by sources and destinations
	CModulationMatrix m_ModulationMatrix;

protected:
	// --- 4 oscillators
	COscillator* m_pOsc1;
	COscillator* m_pOsc2;
	COscillator* m_pOsc3;
	COscillator* m_pOsc4;

	// --- 2 filters; 2 mono or 1 stereo
	CFilter* m_pFilter1;
	CFilter* m_pFilter2;

	// --- 4 EGs
	CEnvelopeGenerator m_EG1;
	CEnvelopeGenerator m_EG2;
	CEnvelopeGenerator m_EG3;
	CEnvelopeGenerator m_EG4;

	// --- 2 LFOs
	CLFO m_LFO1;
	CLFO m_LFO2;

	// --- 1 DCA (can be mono or stereo)
	CDCA m_DCA;
```

```
    // --- global parameters
    globalVoiceParams* m_pGlobalVoiceParams;
    globalSynthParams* m_pGlobalSynthParams;
```

The LFOs, EGs and DCA are simply static declarations since they don't vary. In the Constructor, all pointers (oscillators, filters and global parameters) are nulled out, which disables them. Deriving new classes and setting up their components is easy. You declare the oscillators and filters that are specific to the new voice and initialize the pointers in the derived class Constructor. Since MiniSynth is an analog modeling synth, we use the following components:

Oscillators: Quasi bandlimited (*CQBLimitedOscillator*)
Filter: Moog ladder filter in fourth order LPF configuration (*CMoodLadderFilter*)

Therefore, the declaration for the *CMiniSynthVoice* object looks like this:

```
class CMiniSynthVoice : public CVoice
{
public:
    CMiniSynthVoice(void);
    ~CMiniSynthVoice(void);

protected:
    // --- Four oscillators
    CQBLimitedOscillator m_Osc1;
    CQBLimitedOscillator m_Osc2;
    CQBLimitedOscillator m_Osc3; // sub-osc
    CQBLimitedOscillator m_Osc4; // noise

    // --- 1 filter
    CMoogLadderFilter m_MoogLadderFilter;
```

The objects are connected to the pointers in the constructor:

```
CMiniSynthVoice::CMiniSynthVoice(void)
{
    // --- oscillators
    m_pOsc1 = &m_Osc1;
    m_pOsc2 = &m_Osc2;
    m_pOsc3 = &m_Osc3;
    m_pOsc4 = &m_Osc4;

    // --- filters
    m_pFilter1 = &m_MoogLadderFilter;
    m_pFilter2 = NULL;
```

The *CVoice* object will test the oscillator and filter pointers before using them, so setting the second filter pointer to NULL effectively disables it. If you decided later to change the oscillators to *CWaveTable* and the filter to the *CDiodeLadderFilter*, you just change the declarations in the *.h* file and everything else is done automatically. Notice that the filter is named *m_MoogLadderFilter* as a reminder of its type; however, you might choose *m_Filter1* or the like to make switching objects easier in your own designs. The *CVoice* object contains all the necessary member variables and functions for basic voice operation. Table 9.1 lists the member variables and functions. Don't be intimidated by the number of variables—the derived classes, where you do most of the coding, are simple in comparison. Notice that the *CVoice* base class is set up for hard sync operation with the addition of a single parameter *m_dHSRatio*—this was a Challenge from Chapter 5. If you are experimenting with hard sync, you can use this built-in variable; it is not used in the MiniSynth project.

Table 9.1: *CVoice* member variables and functions.

CVoice **Member Variables**		
Type	**Variable Name**	**Description**
COscillator*	m_pOsc1, m_pOsc2, m_pOsc3, m_pOsc4	assignable oscillators
CFilter*	m_pFilter1, m_pFilter2	assignable filters
CEnvelopeGenerator	m_EG1, m_EG2, m_EG3, M_EG4	fixed EGs
CLFO	m_LFO1, m_LFO2	fixed LFOs
CDCA	m_DCA	fixed DCA
CModulatior Matrix	m_ModulationMatrix	shared mod matrix for synth components
globalVoiceParams*	m_pGlobalVoiceParams	global parameters for voice
globalSynthParams*	m_pGlobalSynthParams	global parameters for synth
double	m_dSampleRate	sample rate fs
double	m_dHSRatio	hard sync ratio (if using hard sync)
double	m_dOscPitch	MIDI pitch of the voice's oscillators
double	m_dOscPitchPending	pitch of the pending note (for voice stealing)
double	m_dPortamentoTime_mSec	portamento glide time
double	m_dPortamentoStart	portamento start pitch
double	m_dPortamentoModulo	portamento modulo counter
double	m_dPortamentoInc	portamento modulo counter increment
double	m_dPortamentoSemitones	number of semitones between portamento start and end pitches
double	m_dDefaultModIntensity	mod intensity variable (always 1.0)
double	m_dDefaultModRange	mod range variable (always 1.0)
UINT	m_uVoiceMode	synth-specific voice mode
UINT	m_uTimeStamp	timestamp counter for voice steal
UINT	m_uLegatoMode	legato mode switch for the EGs
UINT	m_uMIDINoteNumber	MIDI note number of currently playing note
UINT	m_uMIDIVelocity	velocity of currently playing note
UINT	m_uMIDINoteNumberPending	MIDI note number of pending note (for voice stealing)
UINT	m_uMIDIVelocityPending	velocity of pending note (for voice stealing)
bool	m_bNotePending	flag for pending note (for voice stealing)
bool	m_bNoteOn	note on state flag
enum	mono,legato	enum for legato mode
enum	off,attack,decay,sustain,release,shutdown	enum for EG state (for queries)
enum	sine,usaw,dsaw,tri,square, expo,rsh,qrsh	LFO waveforms
enum	SINE,SAW1,SAW2,SAW3, TRI,SQUARE,NOISE, PNOISE	pitched oscillator waveforms
enum	ON,OFF	on/off switch states
enum	analog, digital	EG modes

CVoice **Member Functions**	
Function Name	**Description**
initGlobalParameters	sets up all sub-components with their global parameter structures
setModMatrixCore	sets the matrix core pointer
initializeModMatrix	sets all common voice modulation routings
isActiveVoice	returns true if note is currently playing and EGs are active
canNoteOff	returns true if the voice can be turned off

CVoice Member Functions	
Function Name	**Description**
clearDestinations	clears the mod matrix destination array
isVoiceDone	returns true if output EGs are all in the off state
inLegatoMode	returns true if output EGs are all in legato mode
setSampleRate	distributes sample rate to all sub-components
prepareForPlay	one-time initialization; occurs after sub-component pointers have been set (i.e. post construction of derived classes)
enableModMatrixRow	enables or disables an existing row for flexible routing
update	update new voice parameters
reset	reset all sub-components
noteOn	performs basic note on operations
note off	performs basic note off operations
doVoice	performs basic note rendering, including portamento and voice steal operations

Many of the variables and functions should be familiar to you, having worked your way through the chapters. You can see duplications of *enums* for the sub-components and some initialization functions that are self-explanatory. The *CVoice* object stores a pointer to the global synth parameter, which is a generalized version of the *globalNanoSynthParams* that you saw in the last chapter. You can see that it has sub-structures for each of its own sub-components. If you add new components to *CVoice*, you need to modify this structure accordingly. This structure is declared in *synthfunctions.h*.

```
struct globalSynthParams
{
      globalVoiceParams       voiceParams;
      globalOscillatorParams  osc1Params;
      globalOscillatorParams  osc2Params;
      globalOscillatorParams  osc3Params;
      globalOscillatorParams  osc4Params;
      globalOscillatorParams  lfo1Params;
      globalOscillatorParams  lfo2Params;
      globalFilterParams      filter1Params;
      globalFilterParams      filter2Params;
      globalEGParams          eg1Params;
      globalEGParams          eg2Params;
      globalEGParams          eg3Params;
      globalEGParams          eg4Params;
      globalDCAParams         dcaParams;
};
```

The first sub-structure you see is for the voice's global parameters—all the stuff that is common to the voice level of operation. These global parameters include every kind of intensity and range variable for modulation of the sources to the destinations. The intensity and mod ranges are familiar and self-explanatory by their names (e.g., *dLFO1Filter2ModIntensity* is the modulation intensity from LFO2 to Filter2), so I won't describe each in detail. We will discuss the vector and DX synth parameters in later chapters. Table 9.2 lists the global voice parameters.

There are also new variables for portamento and voice stealing, and new functions that involve testing the state of one or more sub-component. The *noteOn()*, *noteOff()* and *doVoice()* functions all contain code from various sections of NanoSynth that is common to all note and voice operations.

Table 9.2: The member variables for *globalVoiceParams*.

struct *globalVoiceParams*	
// --- common UINT uVoiceMode; double dHSRatio; double dPortamentoTime_mSec; // --- ranges double dOscFoPitchBendModRange; double dFilterModRange; double dAmpModRange; double dOscFoModRange; double dOscHardSyncModRange; // --- intensities double dFilterKeyTrackIntensity; double dLFO1OscModIntensity; double dLFO1Filter1ModIntensity; double dLFO1Filter2ModIntensity; double dLFO1DCAAmpModIntensity; double dLFO1DCAPanModIntensity; double dLFO2OscModIntensity; double dLFO2Filter1ModIntensity; double dLFO2Filter2ModIntensity; double dLFO2DCAAmpModIntensity; double dLFO2DCAPanModIntensity; // --- DX synth double dOp1Feedback; double dOp2Feedback; double dOp3Feedback; double dOp4Feedback;	double dEG1OscModIntensity; double dEG1Filter1ModIntensity; double dEG1Filter2ModIntensity; double dEG1DCAAmpModIntensity; double dEG2OscModIntensity; double dEG2Filter1ModIntensity; double dEG2Filter2ModIntensity; double dEG2DCAAmpModIntensity; double dEG3OscModIntensity; double dEG3Filter1ModIntensity; double dEG3Filter2ModIntensity; double dEG3DCAAmpModIntensity; double dEG4OscModIntensity; double dEG4Filter1ModIntensity; double dEG4Filter2ModIntensity; double dEG4DCAAmpModIntensity; // --- vector synth double dOrbitXAmp; double dOrbitYAmp; double dAmplitude_A; double dAmplitude_B; double dAmplitude_C; double dAmplitude_D; double dAmplitude_ACmix; double dAmplitude_BDmix; UINT uVectorPathMode;

9.2 CVoice Initialization

NanoSynth was fairly straightforward to put together, but it has some C++ issues that *CVoice* is going to clean up. For example, the plug-in had to create and initialize the modulation matrix rows, set the modulation source and destinations on the voice objects, handle voice stealing, and wire the audio engine together. It really shouldn't have to do any of these things, nor should it need to know these details. The *CVoice* object is going to greatly simplify the plug-in coding such that all the synths will have nearly identical code for everything except GUI controls. The plug-in object will still hold the master modulation matrix and global parameters since all the voices will share them. (Note: you could actually remove this dependency by creating a *CSynth* object, but we chose to stop with the voice level object.)

Open the *Voice.h* and *Voice.cpp* files and examine the contents. Let's start with the basic parts and then move to the more complicated code.

Constructor

In the *.cpp* file, you can see that the constructor just initializes the member variables and nulls out all pointers. Notice the familiar setup on the default intensity and range variables. The oscillator defaults are declared in *oscillator.h*.

```
CVoice::CVoice(void)
{
      m_dPortamentoTime_mSec = 0.0;
      m_bNoteOn = false;
      m_uTimeStamp = 0;
      m_bNotePending = false;
      m_dSampleRate = 44100;
      m_uVoiceMode = 0;  // this will vary in meaning depending on synth
      m_dHSRatio = 1.0;
```

```
    m_dOscPitch = OSC_FO_DEFAULT;
    m_dOscPitchPending = OSC_FO_DEFAULT;
    m_dPortamentoStart = OSC_FO_DEFAULT;
    m_dModuloPortamento = 0.0;
    m_dPortamentoInc = 0.0;
    m_dPortamentoSemitones = 0.0;
    m_uLegatoMode = legato; // legato
    m_dDefaultModIntensity = 1.0;
    m_dDefaultModRange = 1.0;

    m_pOsc1 = NULL;
    m_pOsc2 = NULL;
    m_pOsc3 = NULL;
    m_pOsc4 = NULL;
    m_pFilter1 = NULL;
    m_pFilter2 = NULL;
    m_pGlobalSynthParams = NULL;
    m_pGlobalVoiceParams = NULL;
}
```

initializeModMatrix()

In *initializeModMatrix()* you create and add the rows of all common modulation routings for all synths; most rows are enabled by default. The common modulation routings are:

- velocity to DCA amplitude
- pitch bend to Osc frequency
- MIDI volume to DCA volume
- MIDI pan to DCA pan
- MIDI sustain pedal to all EG sustain overrides
- note number to filter f_c (for key track, disabled by default)
- velocity to attack scaling (disabled by default)
- note number to decay scaling (disabled by default)

You saw all these modulation row setups in NanoSynth, so this is simply a repeat and re-shuffling of responsibilities; it moves the mod matrix initialization out of the plug-in object and into the voice object where it belongs.

```
void CVoice::initializeModMatrix(CModulationMatrix* pMatrix)
{
    // --- The Mod matrix "wiring" for DEFAULTS for all synths
    // --- create a row for each source/destination pair
    modMatrixRow* pRow = NULL;

    // VELOCITY -> DCA VEL
    pRow = createModMatrixRow(SOURCE_VELOCITY,
                              DEST_DCA_VELOCITY,
                              &m_dDefaultModIntensity,
                              &m_dDefaultModRange,
                              TRANSFORM_NONE,
                              true);
    pMatrix->addModMatrixRow(pRow);

    etc. . . - you've seen this before!
```

setSampleRate()

The *setSampleRate()* function stores the sample rate and then sets it on the sub-components. Notice the pointers are checked before use.

```
void CVoice::setSampleRate(double dSampleRate)
{
	m_dSampleRate = dSampleRate;

	if(m_pOsc1)m_pOsc1->setSampleRate(dSampleRate);
	if(m_pOsc2)m_pOsc2->setSampleRate(dSampleRate);
	if(m_pOsc3)m_pOsc3->setSampleRate(dSampleRate);
	if(m_pOsc4)m_pOsc4->setSampleRate(dSampleRate);

	if(m_pFilter1)m_pFilter1->setSampleRate(dSampleRate);
	if(m_pFilter2)m_pFilter2->setSampleRate(dSampleRate);

	m_EG1.setSampleRate(dSampleRate);
	m_EG2.setSampleRate(dSampleRate);
	m_EG3.setSampleRate(dSampleRate);
	m_EG4.setSampleRate(dSampleRate);

	m_LFO1.setSampleRate(dSampleRate);
	m_LFO2.setSampleRate(dSampleRate);
}
```

prepareForPlay()

The *prepareForPlay()* function is where you initialize the modulation matrix source and destinations for all sub-components. This contains all the default wiring used in NanoSynth, as well as every possible sub-component default routing. It also initializes the MIDI volume and pan values at power-on time. Notice in particular the part of the DCA setup in bold; the default EG connection MUST be done in the derived class. This is because not every synth (or everyone) will use EG1 for the DCA output EG. And, in the FM synth called DXSynth, there are a variable number of output EGs ranging from 1 to 4 in number. This is the function where you can change the default modulation routings if you wish.

```
// power on defaults, one time init
void CVoice::prepareForPlay()
{
	// --- clear source array
	m_ModulationMatrix.clearSources();

	// --- power on defaults
	m_ModulationMatrix.m_dSources[SOURCE_MIDI_VOLUME_CC07] = 127;
	m_ModulationMatrix.m_dSources[SOURCE_MIDI_PAN_CC10] = 64;

	// --- setup the mod matrix for defaults
	m_LFO1.m_pModulationMatrix = &m_ModulationMatrix;
	m_LFO1.m_uModDestOutput1 = SOURCE_LFO1;
	m_LFO1.m_uModDestOutput2 = SOURCE_LFO1Q;

	m_LFO2.m_pModulationMatrix = &m_ModulationMatrix;
	m_LFO2.m_uModDestOutput1 = SOURCE_LFO2;
	m_LFO2.m_uModDestOutput2 = SOURCE_LFO2Q;
```

```
    m_EG1.m_pModulationMatrix = &m_ModulationMatrix;
    m_EG1.m_uModDestEGOutput = SOURCE_EG1;
    m_EG1.m_uModDestBiasedEGOutput = SOURCE_BIASED_EG1;
    m_EG1.m_uModSourceEGAttackScaling = DEST_EG1_ATTACK_SCALING;
    m_EG1.m_uModSourceEGDecayScaling = DEST_EG1_DECAY_SCALING;
    m_EG1.m_uModSourceSustainOverride = DEST_EG1_SUSTAIN_OVERRIDE;

    <SNIP SNIP SNIP>

    // --- DCA
    m_DCA.m_pModulationMatrix = &m_ModulationMatrix;
    // this must be connected on derived class, if used normally EG1
    // m_DCA.m_uModSourceEG = DEST_NONE;
    m_DCA.m_uModSourceAmp_dB = DEST_DCA_AMP;
    m_DCA.m_uModSourceVelocity = DEST_DCA_VELOCITY;
    m_DCA.m_uModSourcePan = DEST_DCA_PAN;

    // --- oscillators
    if(m_pOsc1)
    {
        m_pOsc1->m_pModulationMatrix = &m_ModulationMatrix;
        m_pOsc1->m_uModSourceFo = DEST_OSC1_FO;
        m_pOsc1->m_uModSourcePulseWidth = DEST_OSC1_PULSEWIDTH;
        m_pOsc1->m_uModSourceAmp = DEST_OSC1_OUTPUT_AMP;
    }

    <SNIP SNIP SNIP>

    // --- filters
    if(m_pFilter1)
    {
        m_pFilter1->m_pModulationMatrix = &m_ModulationMatrix;
        m_pFilter1->m_uModSourceFc = DEST_FILTER1_FC;
        m_pFilter1->m_uSourceFcControl = DEST_ALL_FILTER_KEYTRACK;
    }

    etc. . .
```

update()

In the *update()* function you apply changes made to the global parameters. This function is called once per sample period. It stores the voice mode and calculates a new portamento increment value if the portamento has changed (we will get to portamento shortly). The hard sync ratio is stored, but not used in the book projects. Notice that these variables are contained in the *globalVoiceParams* structure.

```
void CVoice::update()
{
    // --- voice mode
    m_uVoiceMode = m_pGlobalVoiceParams->uVoiceMode;

    // --- update only if changed
    if(m_dPortamentoTime_mSec != m_pGlobalVoiceParams
                                          ->dPortamentoTime_mSec)
```

```
        {
                m_dPortamentoTime_mSec = m_pGlobalVoiceParams
                                                  ->dPortamentoTime_mSec;

                if(m_dPortamentoTime_mSec == 0.0)
                      m_dPortamentoInc = 0.0;
                else
                      m_dPortamentoInc = 1000.0/m_dPortamentoTime_mSec/
                                                         m_dSampleRate;
        }

        // --- hard sync ratio
        m_dHSRatio = m_pGlobalVoiceParams->dHSRatio;
}
```

reset()

The *reset()* function simply forwards the reset call to the sub-objects:

```
void CVoice::reset()
{
     if(m_pOsc1)m_pOsc1->reset();
     if(m_pOsc2)m_pOsc2->reset();
     if(m_pOsc3)m_pOsc3->reset();
     if(m_pOsc4)m_pOsc4->reset();

     if(m_pFilter1)m_pFilter1->reset();
     if(m_pFilter2)m_pFilter2->reset();

     m_EG1.reset();
     m_EG2.reset();
     m_EG3.reset();
     m_EG4.reset();

     m_LFO1.reset();
     m_LFO2.reset();

     m_DCA.reset();
}
```

In the *Voice.h* file, you can find the remaining initialization and state functions.

initGlobalParameters() and *setModMatrixCore()*

You initialize the voice-level and sub-component global parameters in this single function. Most of the work is done in the sub-component initialization functions that you saw in the last chapter. In *setModMatrixCore()* you just forward the function call to the mod matrix. Remember the voice will hold the mod matrix that is common to its sub-components, and each voice has its own modulation matrix.

```
inline virtual void initGlobalParameters(globalSynthParams* pGlobalParams)
{
     // --- save Global Param Ptr
     m_pGlobalSynthParams = pGlobalParams;
```

```
        // --- Voice params
        m_pGlobalVoiceParams = &pGlobalParams->voiceParams;
        m_pGlobalVoiceParams->uVoiceMode = m_uVoiceMode;
        m_pGlobalVoiceParams->dHSRatio = m_dHSRatio;
        m_pGlobalVoiceParams->dPortamentoTime_mSec =
                                        m_dPortamentoTime_mSec;

        // --- Range Variables
        m_pGlobalVoiceParams->dOscFoPitchBendModRange
                                        = OSC_PITCHBEND_MOD_RANGE;
        m_pGlobalVoiceParams->dOscFoModRange = OSC_FO_MOD_RANGE;
        m_pGlobalVoiceParams->dOscHardSyncModRange = OSC_HARD_SYNC_RATIO_RANGE;
        m_pGlobalVoiceParams->dFilterModRange = FILTER_FC_MOD_RANGE;
        m_pGlobalVoiceParams->dAmpModRange = AMP_MOD_RANGE;

        // --- Intensity variables
        m_pGlobalVoiceParams->dFilterKeyTrackIntensity = 1.0;

        // --- init sub-components
        if(m_pOsc1)m_pOsc1->initGlobalParameters(&m_pGlobalSynthParams
                                                    ->osc1Params);
        if(m_pOsc2)m_pOsc2->initGlobalParameters(&m_pGlobalSynthParams
                                                    ->osc2Params);
        if(m_pOsc3)m_pOsc3->initGlobalParameters(&m_pGlobalSynthParams
                                                    ->osc3Params);
        if(m_pOsc4)m_pOsc4->initGlobalParameters(&m_pGlobalSynthParams
                                                    ->osc4Params);

        etc. . .

void setModMatrixCore(modMatrixRow** pModMatrix)
{
        m_ModulationMatrix.setModMatrixCore(pModMatrix);
}
```

State Functions

There are four state functions that you may need to override. All of our synths except the DXSynth use EG1 as the output EG by default. These four functions are used to query the voice during note on and note off operations. Refer to the *EnvelopeGenerator.h* file if you need to; the EG is "active" if it is in any state except *release*, *off* or *releasePending*, and it *canNoteOff()* if in any state except *release*, *off*, *shutdown* or *releasePending*. The voice is "done" when the output EG is in the off state.

```
inline virtual bool isActiveVoice()
{
        if(m_bNoteOn && m_EG1.isActive())
              return true;

        return false;
}

inline virtual bool canNoteOff()
```

```
{
    if(m_bNoteOn && m_EG1.canNoteOff())
        return true;

    return false;
}

inline virtual bool isVoiceDone()
{
    if(m_EG1.getState() == off)
        return true;

    return false;
}

inline virtual bool inLegatoMode()
{
    return m_EG1.m_bLegatoMode;
}
```

Before looking at the remaining three functions (*noteOn*, *noteOff* and *doVoice*), let's discuss portamento.

9.3 Portamento

Many synths offer a portamento or glide feature. With this effect engaged, successively triggered notes will not start at the MIDI note pitch, but will glide smoothly up or down from the previously triggered note. The user controls the glide time. The pitch moves in an exponential manner as it does during normal pitch modulation. The effect is identical to someone using the pitch bend wheel or joystick—as they move the control linearly, the pitch changes exponentially in a continuous or gliding manner. All the synths in this book will have portamento built-in. The *CVoice* object is going to handle every bit of that functionality, so you won't have to re-code anything.

During the portamento operation, you calculate the number of semitones between the start and end pitches. The plug-in keeps track of the last MIDI note frequency since it receives the MIDI messages. The portamento modulo counter increment value is calculated in the *update()* function we just saw. The equation is the same as the modulo counter we use in the LFO and Quasi Bandlimited oscillators.

$$inc = \frac{1000T}{PoratmentoTime\ \ (\text{mSec})} \qquad T = \frac{1}{f_s} \tag{9.1}$$

A non-zero increment value is the flag that portamento is engaged (i.e., the user entered a non-zero portamento time). The portamento modulo counter can then be used to calculate the instantaneous glide pitch; it moves from 0 to 1.0 as the pitch moves from start to end using the *pitchShiftMultiplier()* function.

$$pitch = (\text{start pitch})^{*}\ \text{pitchShiftMultiplier}(\text{modulo}^{*}\ \text{portamentoSemitones}) \tag{9.2}$$

Note On Logic

The note on logic is based on what we used in NanoSynth, plus the portamento. The logic also handles voice stealing. Figure 9.8 shows the flowchart. A note is considered to be available if no note is playing and no note is pending. In this case you set the event information, calculate starting pitch (if using portamento), and start up the oscillators, EGs and LFOs. If the voice is being stolen, you first store all the pending note information and set the pending note flag. An issue arises if the voice being stolen is currently in the middle of a portamento glide. In this case, the portamento increment value is calculated from the semitones between the current oscillator pitch and the target pitch, rather than the last note pitch. Lastly, you shut down the EGs for the steal event. This function may or may not be overridden, depending on the synth requirements. None of our synths will require an override, but you might come up with an architecture that does.

noteOn()

The *noteOn()* function follows the flowchart in Figure 9.8. Notice that all components are started, even if not all are used in the voice algorithm. Starting an EG or LFO that is not being used is benign. Notice that the timestamp is set to 0 if the note is available and

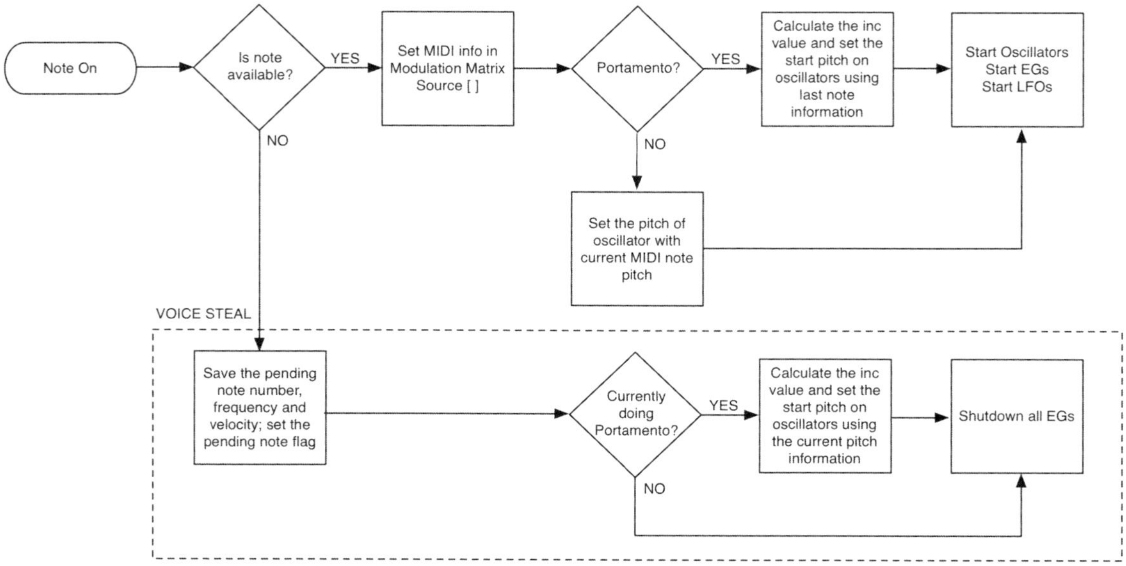

Figure 9.8: The *CVoice* Note on logic.

playing; we will discuss the timestamp shortly. Examine the code for the portamento carefully and make sure you understand how it works—it sets up the starting pitch based on the last note frequency and calculates a semitone-per-sample increment value. During the note event, the pitch will move to the target frequency that is stored as *m_dOscPitch* on the voice object. There is also some room for optimization here involving the oscillators; if you hard code the oscillator members, you don't have to check their pointers, but the object will not be as flexible.

```
inline void noteOn(UINT uMIDINote, UINT uMIDIVelocity, double dFrequency,
                   double dLastNoteFrequency)
{
     // --- save note pitch
     m_dOscPitch = dFrequency;

     // --- is our voice available?
     if(!m_bNoteOn && !m_bNotePending)
     {
            // --- save the note number (for voice steal later)
            m_uMIDINoteNumber = uMIDINote;

            // --- save the velocity (alternate voice steal heuristic)
            m_uMIDIVelocity = uMIDIVelocity;

            // --- set the velocity info in mod matrix
            m_ModulationMatrix.m_dSources[SOURCE_VELOCITY] =
                                        (double)m_uMIDIVelocity;

            // --- set note number in mod matrix
            m_ModulationMatrix.m_dSources[SOURCE_MIDI_NOTE_NUM] =
            (double)uMIDINote;

            // --- set portamento
            if(m_dPortamentoInc > 0.0 && dLastNoteFrequency >= 0)
                   {
                   // --- reset
```

```
        m_dModuloPortamento = 0.0;

        // --- calc semitones in glide
        m_dPortamentoSemitones = semitonesBetweenFrequencies
        (dLastNoteFrequency, dFrequency);

        // --- save start frequency
        m_dPortamentoStart = dLastNoteFrequency;

        // --- set osc start pitch
        if(m_pOsc1)m_pOsc1->m_dOscFo = m_dPortamentoStart;
        if(m_pOsc2)m_pOsc2->m_dOscFo = m_dPortamentoStart;
        if(m_pOsc3)m_pOsc3->m_dOscFo = m_dPortamentoStart;
        if(m_pOsc4)m_pOsc4->m_dOscFo = m_dPortamentoStart;
}
else
{
        // --- no portamento; set final pitch
        if(m_pOsc1)m_pOsc1->m_dOscFo = m_dOscPitch;
        if(m_pOsc2)m_pOsc2->m_dOscFo = m_dOscPitch;
        if(m_pOsc3)m_pOsc3->m_dOscFo = m_dOscPitch;
        if(m_pOsc4)m_pOsc4->m_dOscFo = m_dOscPitch;
}

// --- set MIDI note number (needed for Sample based osc)
if(m_pOsc1)m_pOsc1->m_uMIDINoteNumber = m_uMIDINoteNumber;
if(m_pOsc2)m_pOsc2->m_uMIDINoteNumber = m_uMIDINoteNumber;
if(m_pOsc3)m_pOsc3->m_uMIDINoteNumber = m_uMIDINoteNumber;
if(m_pOsc4)m_pOsc4->m_uMIDINoteNumber = m_uMIDINoteNumber;

// --- start; NOTE this will reset but NOT update()
if(m_pOsc1)m_pOsc1->startOscillator();
if(m_pOsc2)m_pOsc2->startOscillator();
if(m_pOsc3)m_pOsc3->startOscillator();
if(m_pOsc4)m_pOsc4->startOscillator();

//--- start EGs
m_EG1.startEG();
m_EG2.startEG();
m_EG3.startEG();
m_EG4.startEG();

// --- start LFOs
m_LFO1.startOscillator();
m_LFO2.startOscillator();

// --- we are rendering!
m_bNoteOn = true;

// --- voice stealing
m_uTimeStamp = 0;
```

```
            return;
        }

        // --- IF we get here, we are playing a note and need to steal it
        //
        // --- already stealing this voice? (rapid retrigger)
        if(m_bNotePending && m_uMIDINoteNumberPending == uMIDINote)
            return;

        // --- Save PENDING note number and velocity and pitch
        m_uMIDINoteNumberPending = uMIDINote;
        m_uMIDIVelocityPending = uMIDIVelocity;
        m_dOscPitchPending = dFrequency;

        // --- set the flag that we have a note pending
        m_bNotePending = true;

        // --- set portamento stuff
        if(m_dPortamentoInc > 0.0 && dLastNoteFrequency > 0)
        {
            if(m_dModuloPortamento > 0.0)
            {
                double dPortamentoPitchMult = pitchShiftMultiplier
                        (m_dModuloPortamento*m_dPortamentoSemitones);
                m_dPortamentoStart =
                        m_dPortamentoStart*dPortamentoPitchMult;
            }
            else
            {
                m_dPortamentoStart = dLastNoteFrequency;
            }

            // --- reset counter
            m_dModuloPortamento = 0.0;

            // --- calc num semitones in glide
            m_dPortamentoSemitones = semitonesBetweenFrequencies
                    (m_dPortamentoStart, dFrequency);
        }

        // ---  shutdown the EGs
        m_EG1.shutDown();
        m_EG2.shutDown();
        m_EG3.shutDown();
        m_EG4.shutDown();
    }
```

Note Off Logic

The note off logic is much simpler than the note on logic. The flowchart is shown in Figure 9.9. The EGs can only be turned off if:

- the note is ON and the output EGs are in a non-note off state
- the note number is the same as the playing note

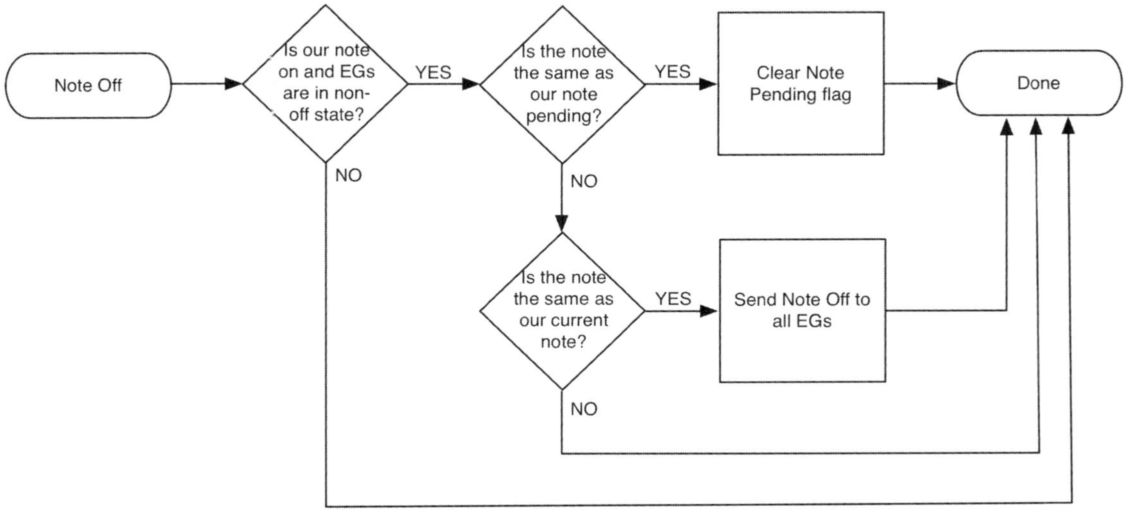

Figure 9.9: The *CVoice* note off logic.

If the note off event is for a note that is pending but not yet playing, just clear the pending flag and let the note continue.

noteOff()

The *noteOff()* function follows the flowchart. Notice that the function *canNoteOff()* is used in the logic. The *canNoteOff()* function is overridden when a synth voice uses other EG(s) than EG1 for the output EG. This happens in DXSynth. All other synths use EG1 as the output EG (Note: if you use a different EG, you will need to modify the *canNoteOff()* function too.)

```
inline virtual void noteOff(UINT uMIDINoteNumber)
{
      // --- if no note on, ignore
      if(m_bNoteOn && canNoteOff())
      {
            // --- if note pending is this note, clear flag
            if(m_bNotePending && (uMIDINoteNumber ==
                                    m_uMIDINoteNumberPending))
            {
                  m_bNotePending = false;
                  return;
            }

            // --- only shut off our note
            if(uMIDINoteNumber != m_uMIDINoteNumber)
                  return;

            // --- else, do the note off event
            m_EG1.noteOff();
            m_EG2.noteOff();
            m_EG3.noteOff();
            m_EG4.noteOff();
      }
}
```

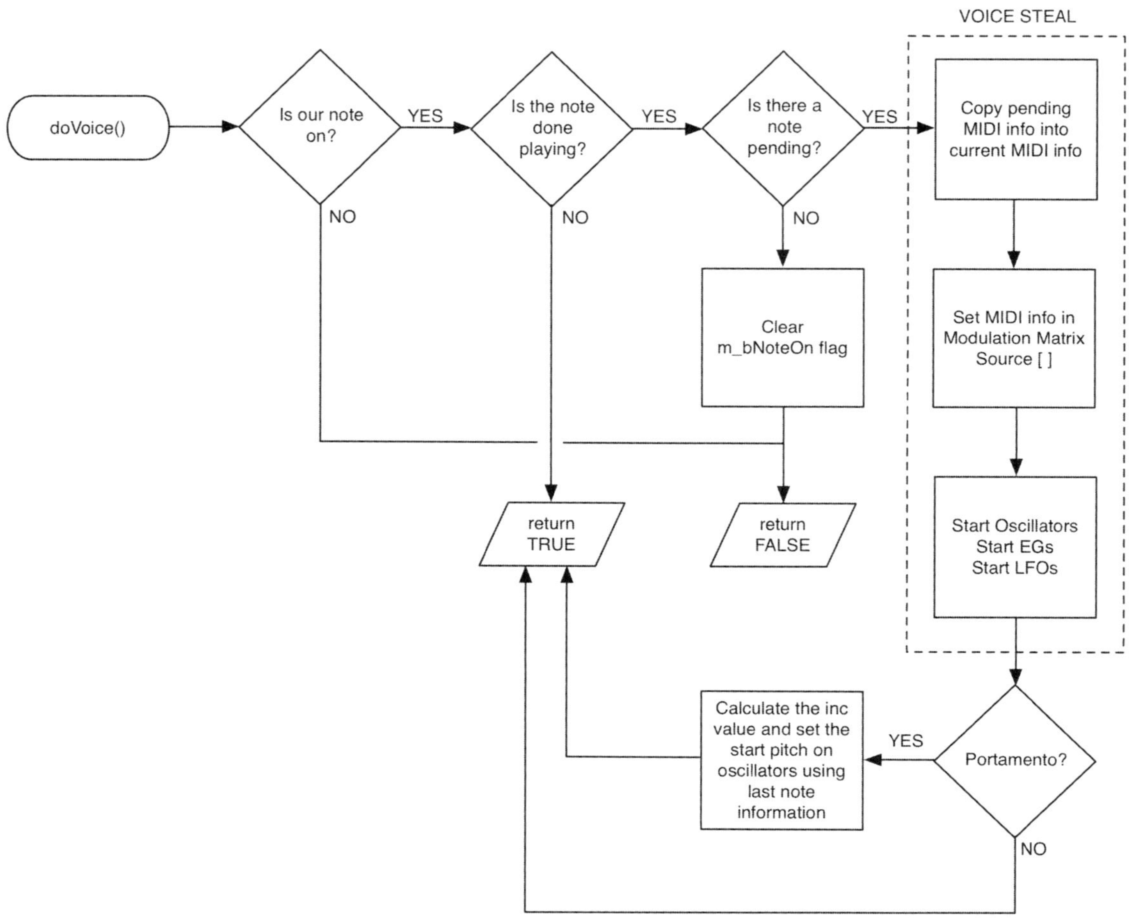

Figure 9.10: The *CVoice doVoice()* flowchart.

doVoice() Logic

The *CVoice* class handles the low level rendering operations common to all synths. You will always override this function in your derived synth voice objects, and you will always call this base class function first; if it returns *false*, then there is no note event to render, which can happen if the note has just ended. The flowchart for the *doVoice()* function is shown in Figure 9.10. Notice that it only returns *true* if a note is currently playing or we just stole a voice.

Compare the code to the flowchart to make sure you understand the implementation. Notice the way the portamento works. If portamento is enabled when a pending note is transferred, the portamento start pitch is the current portamento pitch value. If the function makes it to the code marked Portamento Block, then a note is currently playing. It may have just been stolen. The portamento block examines the portamento modulo counter; if it has expired, then the portamento event is done and the pitch has now reached the target. If not, it calculates the new pitch for the current sample period. Your derived class will call this function first, then add voice-specific articulation and audio engine implementations.

```
// returns true if voice is ON
inline virtual bool doVoice(double& dLeftOutput, double& dRightOutput)
{
      // clear destinations
      dLeftOutput = 0.0;
      dRightOutput = 0.0;

      // bail if no note
      if(!m_bNoteOn)
              return false;
```

```
// did EG finish? - its the flag for us as a voice
if(isVoiceDone() || m_bNotePending)
{
        // did EG finish with NO note pending?
        if(isVoiceDone() && !m_bNotePending)
        {
                // --- shut off and reset everything
                if(m_pOsc1)m_pOsc1->stopOscillator();
                if(m_pOsc2)m_pOsc2->stopOscillator();
                if(m_pOsc3)m_pOsc3->stopOscillator();
                if(m_pOsc4)m_pOsc4->stopOscillator();

                // need this in case of steal mode
                if(m_pOsc1)m_pOsc1->reset();
                if(m_pOsc2)m_pOsc2->reset();
                if(m_pOsc3)m_pOsc3->reset();
                if(m_pOsc4)m_pOsc4->reset();

                // stop the LFOs
                m_LFO1.stopOscillator();
                m_LFO2.stopOscillator();

                // stop the EGs
                m_EG1.reset();
                m_EG2.reset();
                m_EG3.reset();
                m_EG4.reset();

                // --- no more note
                m_bNoteOn = false;

                // --- done
                return false;
        }
        // --- note is pending, turn on
        else if(m_bNotePending && (isVoiceDone() || inLegatoMode()))
        {
                // transfer information from PENDING values
                m_uMIDINoteNumber = m_uMIDINoteNumberPending;
                m_uMIDIVelocity =     m_uMIDIVelocityPending;
                m_dOscPitch = m_dOscPitchPending;

                m_uTimeStamp = 0; // reset

                // set note number
                m_ModulationMatrix.m_dSources[SOURCE_MIDI_NOTE_NUM] =
                                                  (double)m_uMIDINoteNumber;

                if(!inLegatoMode())
                      // new velocity value
```

```
                    m_ModulationMatrix.m_dSources[SOURCE_VELOCITY] =
                                            (double)m_uMIDIVelocity;

                // portamento on? use start pitch
                double dPitch = m_dPortamentoInc > 0.0 ?
                                m_dPortamentoStart : m_dOscPitch;

                if(m_pOsc1)m_pOsc1->m_dOscFo = dPitch;
                if(m_pOsc2)m_pOsc2->m_dOscFo = dPitch;
                if(m_pOsc3)m_pOsc3->m_dOscFo = dPitch;
                if(m_pOsc4)m_pOsc4->m_dOscFo = dPitch;

                // MIDI note number
                if(m_pOsc1)m_pOsc1->m_uMIDINoteNumber = m_uMIDINoteNumber;
                if(m_pOsc2)m_pOsc2->m_uMIDINoteNumber = m_uMIDINoteNumber;
                if(m_pOsc3)m_pOsc3->m_uMIDINoteNumber = m_uMIDINoteNumber;
                if(m_pOsc4)m_pOsc4->m_uMIDINoteNumber = m_uMIDINoteNumber;

                // go to shutdown mode if enabled
                if(!m_uLegatoMode)
                {
                    if(m_pOsc1)m_pOsc1->reset();
                if(m_pOsc2)m_pOsc2->reset();
                    if(m_pOsc3)m_pOsc3->reset();
                    if(m_pOsc4)m_pOsc4->reset();
                }

                // --- crank the EGs back up
                m_EG1.startEG();
                m_EG2.startEG();
                m_EG3.startEG();
                m_EG4.startEG();

                // --- start LFOs
                m_LFO1.startOscillator();
                m_LFO2.startOscillator();

                // --- clear flag
                m_bNotePending = false;
            }
    }

    // --- PORTAMENTO BLOCK --- //
    if(m_dPortamentoInc > 0.0 && m_pOsc1->m_dOscFo != m_dOscPitch)
    {
        // --- if modulo wrapped, portamento is done
        if(m_dModuloPortamento >= 1.0)
        {
                // --- reset
                m_dModuloPortamento = 0.0;
```

```
                // --- target pitch has now been hit
                if(m_pOsc1) m_pOsc1->m_dOscFo = m_dOscPitch;
                if(m_pOsc2) m_pOsc2->m_dOscFo = m_dOscPitch;
                if(m_pOsc3) m_pOsc3->m_dOscFo = m_dOscPitch;
                if(m_pOsc4) m_pOsc4->m_dOscFo = m_dOscPitch;
            }
            else
            {
                // --- calculate current glide pitch
                double dPortamentoPitch =
                        m_dPortamentoStart*pitchShiftMultiplier
                         (m_dModuloPortamento*m_dPortamentoSemitones);

                // --- set in oscillators
                if(m_pOsc1) m_pOsc1->m_dOscFo = dPortamentoPitch;
                if(m_pOsc2) m_pOsc2->m_dOscFo = dPortamentoPitch;
                if(m_pOsc3) m_pOsc3->m_dOscFo = dPortamentoPitch;
                if(m_pOsc4) m_pOsc4->m_dOscFo = dPortamentoPitch;

                // --- inc the portamento modulo
                m_dModuloPortamento += m_dPortamentoInc;
            }
        }

        // --- if we make it here, we are rendering
        return true;
}
```

9.4 MiniSynth Specifications

The *CMiniSynthVoice* derived class won't make much sense until you understand the deeper specifications for MiniSynth. Specifically, we need to address the voice modes of MiniSynth. You will remember from the block diagram in Figure 9.1 that there are four oscillators. One oscillator always plays the sub-octave note (OSC 3) while another is a noise oscillator (OSC4). However, there are multiple waveform modes of operation. This idea was taken from the Korg Volca Keys; it cleverly saves UI controls by presenting the user with a pre-set list of waveform combinations. The MiniSynth's voice modes also determine the type of LFO modulation that is applied to the oscillators. Sawtooth and triangle waves have their pitch modulated. Square waves have their pulse width modulated. For voice modes that are combinations of square and others, both pitch and pulse-width are modulated. These combinations yield an interesting and wide sonic palette. *Saw2Sqr* is quite interesting; with the square wave at 50% duty cycle, the sub-oscillator component is canceled. Moving the pulse width in either direction causes the sub-oscillator to come back. Modulating the pulse-width produces interesting effects as the sub-octave component mixes in and out. Detuning slightly creates a thicker sound. Table 9.3 shows the MiniSynth voice modes and abbreviations used in the enumeration. Figure 9.13 shows the detailed connection diagram; compare it with NanoSynth.

Table 9.3: MiniSynth Voice Modes are combinations of oscillators and modulations.

Voice Mode enum	Details	LFO -> Osc Mod
Saw3	Three sawtooth oscillators	pitch
Sqr3	Three square wave oscillators	pulse width
Saw2Sqr	Two sawtooth and one square wave oscillator	pitch and pulse width
Tri2Saw	Two triangle and one sawtooth oscillator	pitch
Tri2Sqr	Two triangle and one square wave oscillator	pitch and pulse width

MiniSynth also features modulation intensity controls for most routings. Table 9.4 shows the modulation matrix for MiniSynth, while Table 9.5 shows the GUI control list. Note that the modulation matrix does not list the common modulations we set up in the *CVoice* base class—the common MIDI modulations (volume, pan, sustain pedal, etc.) that all synths feature and that we discussed in the last Chapter. The intensity and range variables are global parameters. Figures 9.11 and 9.12 show the GUIs for RackAFX and VST3/AU respectively.

Table 9.4: The Modulation Matrix for MiniSynth.

***MiniSynth* Modulation Matrix**			
Source	**Destination/Intensity**	**Transform/Range**	**enabled**
SOURCE_LFO1	DEST_ALL_OSC_FO	TRANSFORM_NONE	TRUE
	dLFO1OscModIntensity	dOscFoModRange	
SOURCE_BIASED_EG1	DEST_ALL_FILTER_FC	TRANSFORM_NONE	TRUE
	dEG1Filter1ModIntensity	dFilterModRange	
SOURCE_EG1	DEST_DCA_EG	TRANSFORM_NONE	TRUE
	dEG1DCAAmpModIntensity	m_dDefaultModRange	
SOURCE_BIASED_EG1	DEST_ALL_OSC_FO	TRANSFORM_NONE	TRUE
	dEG1OscModIntensity	dOscFoModRange	
SOURCE_LFO1	DEST_ALL_FILTER_FC	TRANSFORM_NONE	TRUE
	dLFO1Filter1ModIntensity	dFilterModRange	
SOURCE_LFO1	DEST_ALL_OSC_PULSEWIDTH	TRANSFORM_NONE	TRUE
	m_dDefaultModIntensity	m_dDefaultModRange	
SOURCE_LFO1	DEST_DCA_AMP	TRANSFORM_BIPO- LAR_TO_UNIPOLAR	TRUE
	dLFO1DCAAmpModIntensity	dAmpModRange	
SOURCE_LFO1	DEST_DCA_PAN	TRANSFORM_NONE	TRUE
	dLFO1DCAPanModIntensity	m_dDefaultModRange	

Table 9.5: MiniSynth GUI Control List.

***MiniSynth* Continuous Parameters**				
Control Name (units)	**Type**	**Variable Name (VST3, RAFX)**	**Low/Hi/Default ***	**VST3/AU Index**
Noise Osc (dB)	double	m_dNoiseOsc_dB	-96 / 0 / 0	NOISE_OSC_AMP_DB
Sub Osc (dB)	double	m_dSubOsc_dB	-96 / 0 / 0	SUB_OSC_AMP_DB
Pulse Width (%)	double	m_dPulseWidth_Pct	1 / 99 / 50	PULSE_WIDTH_PCT
Osc EG Int	double	m_dEG1OscIntensity	-1 / 0 / 1	EG1_TO_OSC_INTENSITY
Filter fc (Hz) volt/octave	double	m_dFcControl	80 / 18000 / 10000	FILTER_FC
Filter Q	double	m_dQControl	1 / 10 / 1	FILTER_Q
Filter EG Int	double	m_dEG1FilterIntensity	-1 / 0 / 1	EG1_TO_FILTER_INTENSITY
Key Track Int	double	m_dFilterKeyTrackIntensity	0.5 / 10 / 1	FILTER_KEYTRACK_INTENSITY
Attack (mS)	double	m_dAttackTime_mSec	0 / 5000 / 100	EG1_ATTACK_MSEC
Decay/ Release (mS)	double	m_dDecayReleaseTime_mSec	0 / 10000 / 1000	EG1_DECAY_RELEASE_MSEC
Sustain	double	m_dSustainLevel	0 / 1 / 0.707	EG1_SUSTAIN_LEVEL
LFO Rate	double	m_dLFO1Rate	0.02 / 20 / 0.5	LFO1_RATE
LFO Depth	double	m_dLFO1Amplitude	0 / 1 / 0	LFO1_AMPLITUDE
LFO Cutoff Int	double	m_dLFO1FilterFcIntensity	-1 / 1 / 0	LFO1_TO_FILTER_INTENSITY
LFO Pitch Int	double	m_dLFO1OscPitchIntensity	-1 / 1 / 0	LFO1_TO_OSC_INTENSITY
LFO Amp Int	double	m_dLFO1AmpIntensity	0 / 1 / 0	LFO1_TO_DCA_INTENSITY

MiniSynth **Continuous Parameters**				
Control Name (units)	**Type**	**Variable Name (VST3, RAFX)**	**Low/Hi/Default ***	**VST3/AU Index**
LFO Pan Int	double	m_dLFO1PanIntensity	0 / 1 / 0	LFO1_TO_PAN_INTENSITY
Volume	double	m_dVolume_dB	-96 / 20 / 0	OUTPUT_AMPLITUDE_DB
DCA EG Int	double	m_dEG1DCAIntensity	-1 / 1 / 1	EG1_TO_DCA_INTENSITY
Detune	double	m_dDetune_cents	-100 / 100 / 0	DETUNE_CENTS
Portamento (mS)	double	m_dPortamentoTime_mSec	0 / 5000 / 0	PORTAMENTO_TIME_MSEC
Octave	int	m_nOctave	-4 / 4 / 0	OCTAVE
PBendRange (semi)	int	m_nPitchBendRange	0 / 12 / 1	PITCHBEND_RANGE

* low, high and default values are #defined for VST3 and AU in ***SynthParamLimits.h*** for each project

MiniSynth **Enumerated String Parameters (UINT)**			
Control Name	**Variable Name**	**enum String**	**VST3/AU Index**
LFO Waveform	m_uLFO1Waveform	sine,usaw,dsaw,tri, square,expo,rsh,qrsh	LFO1_WAVEFORM
Voice Mode	m_uVoiceMode	Saw3,Sqr3,Saw2Sqr, Tri2Saw,Tri2Sqr	VOICE_MODE
Vel->Att Scale	m_uVelocityToAttackScaling	OFF,ON	VELOCITY_TO_ATTACK
Note->Dcy Scale	m_uNoteNumberToDecayScaling	OFF,ON	NOTE_NUM_TO_DECAY
Reset to Zero	m_uResetToZero	OFF,ON	RESET_TO_ZERO
Filter KeyTrack	m_uFilterKeyTrack	OFF,ON	FILTER_KEYTRACK
Legato Mode	m_uLegatoMode	OFF,ON	LEGATO_MODE

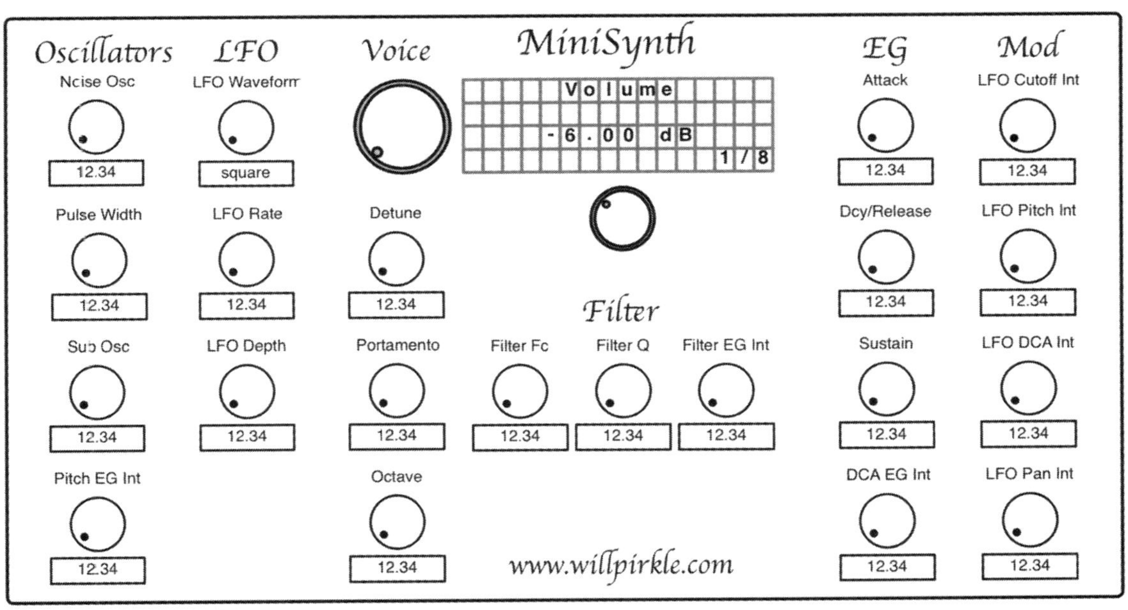

Figure 9.11: One possible MiniSynth GUI in RackAFX; notice that several controls are embedded in the LCD control.

RackAFX: in the MiniSynth sample project, the following controls are located inside the RackAFX LCD Control in this order:

- Volume
- Legato Mode
- Reset To Zero
- PBend Range

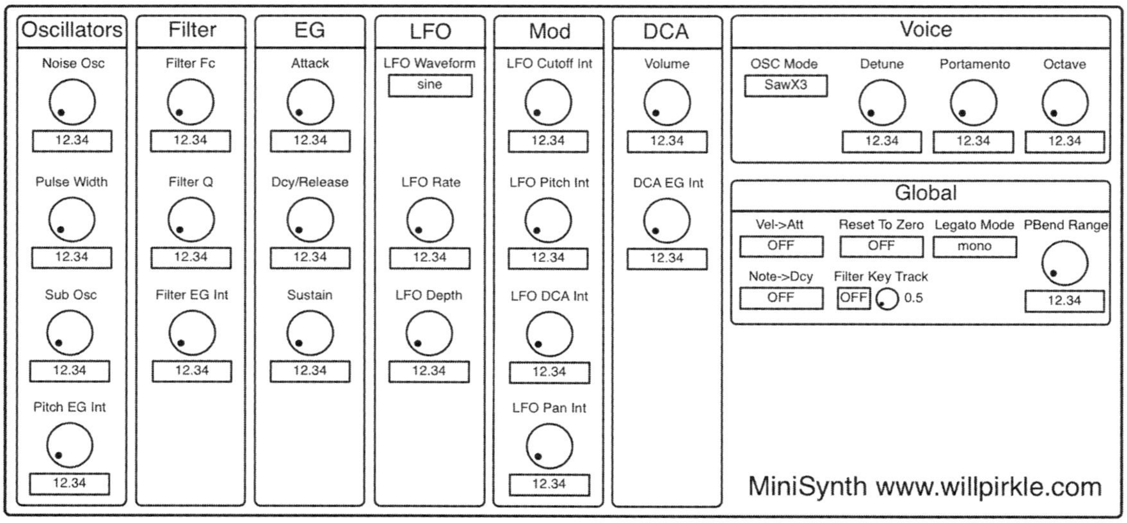

Figure 9.12: The MiniSynth GUI for the VST3 and AU projects.

- Filter KeyTrack
- KeyTrack Int
- Vel->Att Scale
- Note->Dcy Scale

VST3/AU: the limits and defaults are *#defined* in *SynthParamLimits.h* for each project; the VST3/AU Index values are enumerated in the same file. For AU, the order doesn't matter. For VST3, however, the order must match the tags in VSTGUI—if you add your own controls, be sure not to disturb the present indexing; add new index values after the last entry in the enumeration, but before the total-synth-parameters value.

9.5 CMiniSynthVoice Object

Now that you've seen the *CVoice* base class, the modulation matrix, and voice modes, let's look at the derived class for our MiniSynth Project. Hopefully you will be delighted with its simplicity; the base class handles most of the low level chores. Open *MiniSynthVoice.h* and *.cpp*, and we will go through the variables and functions. The oscillators and filter are declared first. Notice the enumeration for voice mode is repeated from the GUI for ease of coding.

Constructor

The constructor performs the following initializations, some of which you may modify:

- connects oscillators to member pointers
- connects the filter to member pointer
- turns off NLP on filter (optional)
- sets the *m_dAuxControl* on the filter to 0.75 for passband compensation (more bass)
- initialize oscillators to voice mode 0 (optional)
- set EG mode to analog (optional)
- set EG1 output flag
- set the DCA EG mod source for EG1 (important—must always be done in derived class constructor!)

```
CMiniSynthVoice::CMiniSynthVoice(void)
{
    // 1) --- declare your oscillators and filters
    // --- oscillators
    m_pOsc1 = &m_Osc1;
    m_pOsc2 = &m_Osc2;
    m_pOsc3 = &m_Osc3;
    m_pOsc4 = &m_Osc4;
```

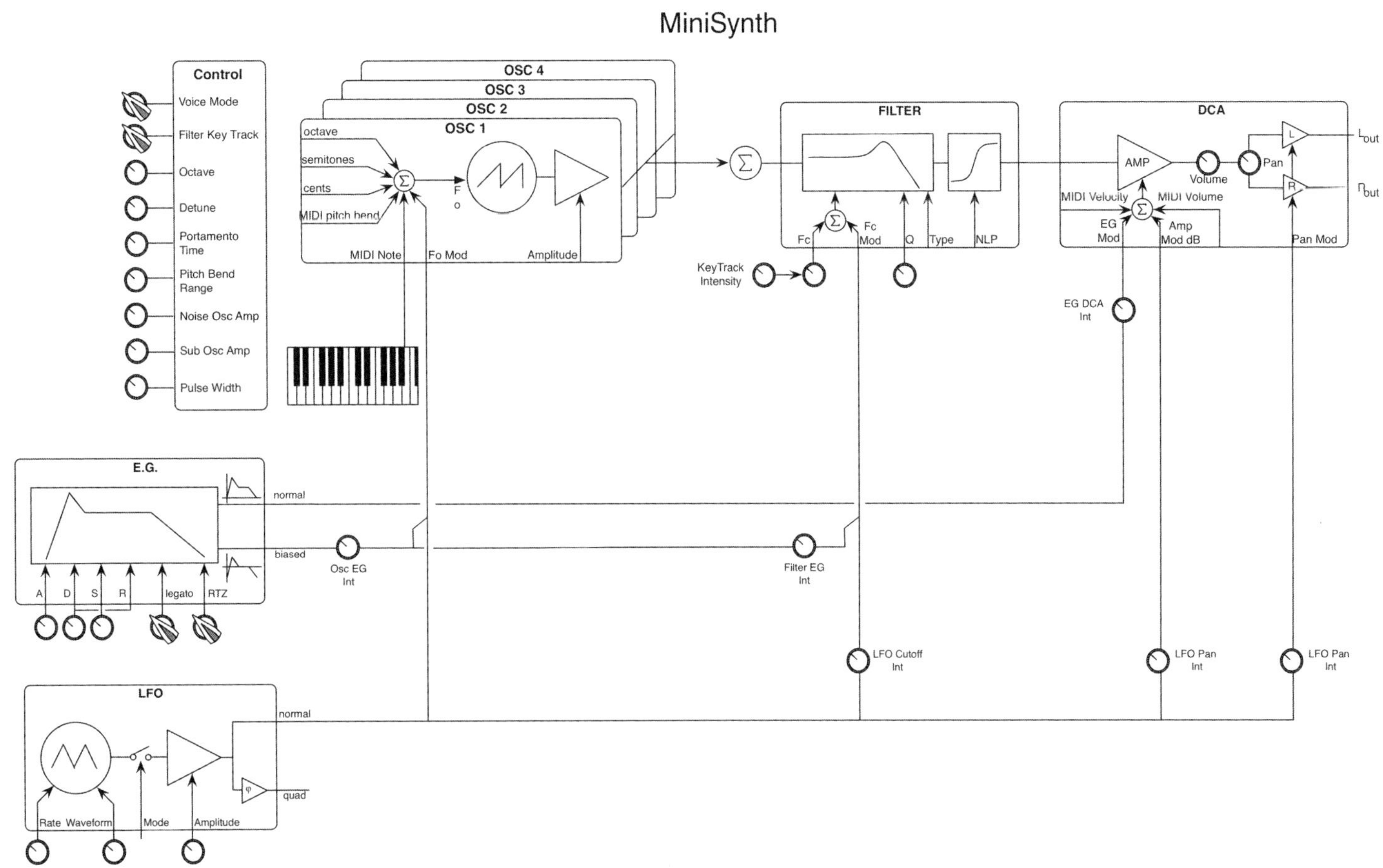

Figure 9.13: MiniSynth detailed connection diagram.

Table 9.6: *CMiniSynthVoice* member variables and functions.

***CMiniSynthVoice* Member Variables**		
Type	**Variable Name**	**Description**
CQBLimitedOscillator	m_Osc1	Oscillator 1
CQBLimitedOscillator	m_Osc2	Oscillator 2
CQBLimitedOscillator	m_Osc3	Oscillator 3 (sub)
CQBLimitedOscillator	m_Osc4	Oscillator 4 (noise)
CMoogLadderFilter	m_MoogLadderFilter	Low Pass Filter
UINT	m_uSourceFoRatio	hard sync ratio index in mod matrix
enum	Saw3,Sqr3,Saw2Sqr,Tri2Saw,Tri2Sqr	voice mode strings repeated here for easier coding

***CMiniSynthVoice* Member Functions**	
Function Name	**Description**
initGlobalParameters	sets up all sub-components with their global parameter structures
initializeModMatrix	sets all common voice modulation routings
setSampleRate	distributes sample rate to all sub-components
prepareForPlay	one-time initialization; occurs after sub-component pointers have been set (i.e. post construction of derived classes)
update	update new voice parameters
reset	reset all sub-components
doVoice	performs MiniSynth specific rendering

```
        // --- filters
        m_pFilter1 = &m_MoogLadderFilter;
        m_pFilter2 = NULL;

        // --- experiment with NLP
        m_MoogLadderFilter.m_uNLP = OFF;
        // --- for passband gain comp in MOOG; can make user adjustable
        m_MoogLadderFilter.m_dAuxControl = 0.75;

        // --- voice mode 0
        m_Osc1.m_uWaveform = SAW1;
        m_Osc2.m_uWaveform = SAW1;
        m_Osc3.m_uWaveform = SAW1;
        m_Osc4.m_uWaveform = NOISE;

        // 2) --- set any component specific stuff
        m_EG1.setEGMode(analog);
        m_EG1.m_bOutputEG = true; // our DCA EG

        // --- DCA Setup: set the source EG here
        m_DCA.m_uModSourceEG = DEST_DCA_EG;
}
```

initGlobalParameters()

This function first calls the base class and then sets the default values for the intensity controls. Notice that they default to 1.0 in case the user has no controls on the GUI. You may want to alter this behavior in your synth, especially if you remove the intensity controls to make room for others.

```
inline virtual void initGlobalParameters(globalSynthParams* pGlobalParams)
{
    // --- always call base class first
    CVoice::initGlobalParameters(pGlobalParams);

    // --- add any CThisVoice specific variables here
    //     (you need to add them to the global param struct first)
    // these default to 1.0 in case user doesn't have GUI controls for them
    //
    // NOTE: we only set the intensities we use in THIS VOICE
    m_pGlobalVoiceParams->dLFO1OscModIntensity = 1.0;
    m_pGlobalVoiceParams->dLFO1Filter1ModIntensity = 1.0;
    m_pGlobalVoiceParams->dLFO1Filter2ModIntensity = 1.0;
    m_pGlobalVoiceParams->dLFO1DCAPanModIntensity = 1.0;
    m_pGlobalVoiceParams->dLFO1DCAAmpModIntensity = 1.0;
    m_pGlobalVoiceParams->dEG1OscModIntensity = 1.0;
    m_pGlobalVoiceParams->dEG1Filter1ModIntensity = 1.0;
    m_pGlobalVoiceParams->dEG1Filter2ModIntensity = 1.0;
    m_pGlobalVoiceParams->dEG1DCAAmpModIntensity = 1.0;
}
```

initializeModMatrix()

In this function, you program the modulation matrix using Table 9.4 to create the rows. Notice how you always call the base class function first.

```
void CMiniSynthVoice::initializeModMatrix(CModulationMatrix* pMatrix)
{
    // --- always first: call base class to create core and
    //     init with basic routings
    CVoice::initializeModMatrix(pMatrix);

    if(!pMatrix->getModMatrixCore()) return;

    // --- MiniSynth Specific Routings
    // --- create a row for each source/destination pair
    modMatrixRow* pRow = NULL;

    // LFO1 -> ALL OSC1 FC
    pRow = createModMatrixRow(SOURCE_LFO1,
                              DEST_ALL_OSC_FO,
                              &m_pGlobalVoiceParams->dLFO1OscModIntensity,
                              &m_pGlobalVoiceParams->dOscFoModRange,
                              TRANSFORM_NONE,
                              true);
    pMatrix->addModMatrixRow(pRow);
    etc. . .
```

setSampleRate()

Just call the base class implementation here.

```
void CMiniSynthVoice::setSampleRate(double dSampleRate)
{
      CVoice::setSampleRate(dSampleRate);
}
```

prepareForPlay()

In *prepareForPlay()* you just call the base class then *reset()*.

```
void CMiniSynthVoice::prepareForPlay()
{
      CVoice::prepareForPlay();
      reset();
}
```

update()

The *update()* function is important for MiniSynth because this is where you configure the oscillators based on the voice mode. Notice the voice mode is saved prior to calling the base class function that will overwrite it (this is the only time that happens in any of the voice objects). If the voice mode has changed, you reconfigure the oscillator types. After configuring, you call *reset()* on the oscillators; remember that we need to preserve the phase relationship between different waveforms, and that is done in *reset()*. Notice how you use the global parameters to update the oscillator waveforms.

```
void CMiniSynthVoice::update()
{
      // --- voice specific updates
      if(!m_pGlobalVoiceParams) return;

      // --- save, base class overwrites
      UINT uCurrentVoiceMode = m_uVoiceMode;

      // --- always call base class first
      CVoice::update();

      // --- Voice Mode
      // --- only update if needed
      if(m_uVoiceMode != uCurrentVoiceMode)
      {
            m_uVoiceMode = m_pGlobalVoiceParams->uVoiceMode;

            // --- osc3 is sub osc
            m_Osc3.m_nOctave = -1.0;

            // osc4 is always noise
            m_pGlobalSynthParams->osc4Params.uWaveform = NOISE;

            switch(m_uVoiceMode)
            {
```

```
            case Saw3:
                  m_pGlobalSynthParams->osc1Params.uWaveform = SAW1;
                  m_pGlobalSynthParams->osc2Params.uWaveform = SAW1;
                  m_pGlobalSynthParams->osc3Params.uWaveform = SAW1;
                  break;

            case Sqr3:
                  m_pGlobalSynthParams->osc1Params.uWaveform = SQUARE;
                  m_pGlobalSynthParams->osc2Params.uWaveform = SQUARE;
                  m_pGlobalSynthParams->osc3Params.uWaveform = SQUARE;
                  break;

            case Saw2Sqr:
                  m_pGlobalSynthParams->osc1Params.uWaveform = SAW1;
                  m_pGlobalSynthParams->osc2Params.uWaveform = SQUARE;
                  m_pGlobalSynthParams->osc3Params.uWaveform = SAW1;
                  break;

            case Tri2Saw:
                  m_pGlobalSynthParams->osc1Params.uWaveform = TRI;
                  m_pGlobalSynthParams->osc2Params.uWaveform = SAW1;
                  m_pGlobalSynthParams->osc3Params.uWaveform = TRI;
                  break;

            case Tri2Sqr:
                  m_pGlobalSynthParams->osc1Params.uWaveform = TRI;
                  m_pGlobalSynthParams->osc2Params.uWaveform = SQUARE;
                  m_pGlobalSynthParams->osc3Params.uWaveform = TRI;
                  break;

            default:
                  m_pGlobalSynthParams->osc1Params.uWaveform = SAW1;
                  m_pGlobalSynthParams->osc2Params.uWaveform = SAW1;
                  m_pGlobalSynthParams->osc3Params.uWaveform = SAW1;
                  break;
      }

      m_Osc1.reset();
      m_Osc2.reset();
      m_Osc3.reset();
      // don't need to reset Osc4 since it is noise
   }
}
```

reset()

In *reset()* you just call the base class first, then configure the oscillator types and zero the portamento time.

```
void CMiniSynthVoice::reset()
{
      CVoice::reset();

      m_dPortamentoInc = 0.0;
      m_Osc1.m_uWaveform = SAW1;
      m_Osc2.m_uWaveform = SAW1;
      m_Osc3.m_uWaveform = SAW1;
      m_Osc4.m_uWaveform = NOISE;
}
```

doVoice()

This is the most important function of all since it implements the rendering, and it is nearly identical to NanoSynth's rendering code. The modulation layers are the same, the only difference is in the wiring of the audio engine. Notice the call to the base class and the scale-before-summing on the pitched oscillators in the audio engine. The articulation block is nearly identical to NanoSynth because the programming is done in the modulation matrix. The only difference is the call to the voice object's *update()* function after modulation Layer 1, but before updating the rest of the components.

```
inline virtual bool doVoice(double& dLeftOutput, double& dRightOutput)
{

      // this does basic on/off work zero impact on speed
      if(!CVoice::doVoice(dLeftOutput, dRightOutput))
             return false;

      // --- ARTICULATION BLOCK --- //
      // --- layer 0 modulators: velocity->attack
      //                               note number->decay
      m_ModulationMatrix.doModulationMatrix(0);

      // --- update layer 1 modulators
      m_EG1.update();
      m_LFO1.update();

      // --- do layer 1 modulators
      m_EG1.doEnvelope();
      m_LFO1.doOscillate();

      // --- modulation matrix Layer 1
      m_ModulationMatrix.doModulationMatrix(1);

      // --- update Voice, DCA and Filter
      this->update();
      m_DCA.update();
      m_MoogLadderFilter.update();

      // --- update oscillators
      m_Osc1.update();
      m_Osc2.update();
      m_Osc3.update();
      m_Osc4.update();
```

```
        // --- DIGITAL AUDIO ENGINE BLOCK --- //
        double dOscMix = 0.333*m_Osc1.doOscillate() +
                         0.333*m_Osc2.doOscillate() +
                         0.333*m_Osc3.doOscillate() +
                              m_Osc4.doOscillate();

        // --- apply the filter
        double dLPFOut = m_MoogLadderFilter.doFilter(dOscMix);

        // --- apply the DCA
        m_DCA.doDCA(dLPFOut, dLPFOut, dLeftOutput, dRightOutput);

        return true;
    }
```

Notice how the *MiniSynthVoice* object does most of the work that had previously been done in the plug-in object. Next, we will deal with polyphony and setup a scheme that will make the code nearly identical on all three of our platforms.

9.6 Polyphony Part Two

NanoSynth used a simple and easy to fool voice stealing heuristic on just two voices that were implemented as structures. MiniSynth uses a different heuristic and uses the C++ *CMiniSynthVoice* object instead. To set up any of the plug-in APIs for polyphony, we will switch to storing an array of voice object pointers. The voice objects are created dynamically at startup and destroyed during shutdown. There are three functions that are the same for all synths in a given API that involve searching the array for voices that meet certain criteria. MiniSynth uses a voice stealing heuristic called "steal the oldest note," which means that it needs a way to keep track of the order of the note events. We need a timestamp variable to know which voice is playing the oldest note. The other heuristics listed in Chapter 8 involve information we already have in the form of note number or velocity. The timestamp variable *m_uTimeStamp* was added to the *CVoice* object to handle keeping track of the note order. We don't really care about the absolute time that the notes arrived, just the order of them. So, the time stamping works as follows:

- when a note is turned on, the voice object sets *m_uTimeStamp* to zero
- then, the plug-in increments the value of the timestamp variable on all voices, including the one that was just turned on
- the voice with the highest timestamp is playing the oldest note
- the *m_bNoteOn* flag is used to identify if the note is on, so there is no need to clear the timestamp until the note is re-triggered

In the plug-in object's *.h* file, you will declare the array of voices and the three helper functions. The *update()* function works the same way as NanoSynth, and all future synths will use it. You also need to declare the last-note-frequency variable for portamento and MIDI receive channel, as will all future synths.

```
  << ** Code Listing 9.1: Declarations ** >>

        CMiniSynthVoice* m_pVoiceArray[MAX_VOICES];

        // -- MmM
        CModulationMatrix m_GlobalModMatrix;

        // --- global params
        globalSynthParams m_GlobalSynthParams;

        // --- helper functions for note on/off/voice steal
        void incrementVoiceTimestamps();
        CMiniSynthVoice* getOldestVoice();
        CMiniSynthVoice* getOldestVoiceWithNote(UINT uMIDINote);
```

```
    // updates all voices at once
    void update();

    // for portamento
    double m_dLastNoteFrequency;

    // our receive channel
    UINT m_uMidiRxChannel;

    << END ** Code Listing 9.1: Declarations ** END >>
```

The implementation of the three helper functions is the same for all synths, except the type of voice pointer in the array. These functions are all simple and self-explanatory. They either increment the time stamp or check and compare the time stamp and MIDI note number.

```
// --- increment the timestamp for new note events
void CMiniSynth::incrementVoiceTimestamps()    // RAFX
void Processor::incrementVoiceTimestamps()     // VST3
void AUSynth::incrementVoiceTimestamps()       // AU
{
    for(int i=0; i<MAX_VOICES; i++)
    {
        CMiniSynthVoice* pVoice = m_pVoiceArray[i];

        // -- if on, increment
        if(pVoice->m_bNoteOn)
            pVoice->m_uTimeStamp++;
    }
}

// --- get oldest note
void CMiniSynth::getOldestVoice()  // RAFX
void Processor::getOldestVoice()   // VST3
void AUSynth::getOldestVoice()     // AU
{
    int nTimeStamp = -1;
    CMiniSynthVoice* pFoundVoice = NULL;
    for(int i=0; i<MAX_VOICES; i++)
    {
        CMiniSynthVoice* pVoice = m_pVoiceArray[i];

        // --- if on and older, save
        //     highest timestamp is oldest
        if(pVoice->m_bNoteOn && (int)pVoice->m_uTimeStamp > nTimeStamp)
        {
            pFoundVoice = pVoice;
            nTimeStamp = (int)pVoice->m_uTimeStamp;
        }
    }
    return pFoundVoice;
}
```

```
// --- get oldest voice with a MIDI note also
void CMiniSynth::getOldestVoiceWithNote(UINT uMIDINote) // RAFX
void Processor::getOldestVoiceWithNote(UINT uMIDINote)  // VST3
void AUSynth::getOldestVoiceWithNote(UINT uMIDINote)    // AU
{
      int nTimeStamp = -1;
      CMiniSynthVoice* pFoundVoice = NULL;
      for(int i=0; i<MAX_VOICES; i++)
      {
            CMiniSynthVoice* pVoice = m_pVoiceArray[i];

            // if on and older and same MIDI note, save
            // lowest timestamp is oldest
            if(pVoice->canNoteOff() && (int)pVoice->m_uTimeStamp > nTimeStamp
               && pVoice->m_uMIDINoteNumber == uMIDINote)
            {
                  pFoundVoice = pVoice;
                  nTimeStamp = (int)pVoice->m_uTimeStamp;
            }
      }
      return pFoundVoice;
}
```

Initializing and Setting up Voices

The initialization is done in the constructor in RackAFX and AU, and in *setActive()* in VST3. The code is nearly identical for every synth project and consists of:

- initializing the last note and MIDI receive variables
- in a *for()* loop, create each voice and add to the array, then initialize global parameters
- next, use the first voice in the array to initialize the global modulation matrix
- in a *for()* loop, set each voice's modulation matrix core to the global modulation matrix core using the *set()* function

```
<< ** Code Listing 9.2: Init Voices ** >>

// Finish initializations here
m_dLastNoteFrequency = -1.0;

// receive on all channels
m_uMidiRxChannel = MIDI_CH_ALL;

// load up voices
for(int i=0; i<MAX_VOICES; i++)
{
      // --- create voice
      m_pVoiceArray[i] = new CMiniSynthVoice;

      // --- should never happen
      if(!m_pVoiceArray[i]) return;

      // --- global params (MUST BE DONE before setting up mod matrix!)
      m_pVoiceArray[i]->initGlobalParameters(&m_GlobalSynthParams);
}
```

```
// --- use the first voice to setup the MmM
m_pVoiceArray[0]->initializeModMatrix(&m_GlobalModMatrix);

// --- then set the mod matrix cores on the rest of the voices
for(int i=0; i<MAX_VOICES; i++)
{
        // --- all matrices share a common core array of matrix rows
        m_pVoiceArray[i]->setModMatrixCore
                      (m_GlobalModMatrix.getModMatrixCore());
}

<< END ** Code Listing 9.2: Init Voices ** END >>
```

Destruction

Destruction is done in the destructor in RackAFX and AU, and in *setActive()* in VST3. The code is nearly identical for every synth project; you delete the global modulation matrix, then delete the voices.

```
<< ** Code Listing 9.3: Destruction ** >>

// --- delete on master ONLY
m_GlobalModMatrix.deleteModMatrix();

// --- delete voices
for(int i=0; i<MAX_VOICES; i++)
{
        delete m_pVoiceArray[i];
}

<< END ** Code Listing 9.3: Destruction ** END >>
```

One Time Plug-in Initialization

The one-time initialization is done in:

- RackAFX: prepareForPlay()
- VST3: setActive()
- AU: Initialize()

This code is the same for all projects except the type of voice pointer in the array. You set the sample rate and then call *prepareForPlay()* on each voice. This is followed by the mass *update()* call for global parameters.

VST3:

Replace (double)m_nSampleRate with
(double)processSetup.sampleRate

AU:

Replace (double)m_nSampleRate with
(double)getOutput(0)->GetStreamFormat().mSampleRate

```
<< ** Code Listing 9.4: One Time Init ** >>

for(int i=0; i<MAX_VOICES; i++)
{
```

```
        CMiniSynthVoice* pVoice = m_pVoiceArray[i];
        pVoice->setSampleRate((double)m_nSampleRate);
        pVoice->prepareForPlay();
    }

    // mass update
    update();

    // clear
    m_dLastNoteFrequency = -1.0;

    << END ** Code Listing 9.4: One Time Init ** END >>
```

Global Parameter Updates

The global parameters are updated in the familiar *update()* function on the plug-in object.

```
void CMiniSynth::update()   // RAFX
void Processor::update()    // VST3
{
    // --- update global parameters
    //
    // --- Voice:
    m_GlobalSynthParams.voiceParams.uVoiceMode = m_uVoiceMode;
    m_GlobalSynthParams.voiceParams.dPortamentoTime_mSec =
                                    m_dPortamentoTime_mSec;

    // --- ranges
    m_GlobalSynthParams.voiceParams.dOscFoPitchBendModRange =
                                    m_nPitchBendRange;

    // --- intensities
    m_GlobalSynthParams.voiceParams.dFilterKeyTrackIntensity =
                                    m_dFilterKeyTrackIntensity;
    m_GlobalSynthParams.voiceParams.dLFO1Filter1ModIntensity =
                                    m_dLFO1FilterFcIntensity;
    m_GlobalSynthParams.voiceParams.dLFO1OscModIntensity =
                                    m_dLFO1OscPitchIntensity;
    m_GlobalSynthParams.voiceParams.dLFO1DCAAmpModIntensity =
                                    m_dLFO1AmpIntensity;
    m_GlobalSynthParams.voiceParams.dLFO1DCAPanModIntensity =
                                    m_dLFO1PanIntensity;

    m_GlobalSynthParams.voiceParams.dEG1OscModIntensity =
                                    m_dEG1OscIntensity;
    m_GlobalSynthParams.voiceParams.dEG1Filter1ModIntensity =
                                    m_dEG1FilterIntensity;
    m_GlobalSynthParams.voiceParams.dEG1DCAAmpModIntensity =
                                    m_dEG1DCAIntensity;
```

```
// --- Oscillators:
double dNoiseAmplitude = m_dNoiseOsc_dB == -96.0 ? 0.0 :
                         pow(10.0, m_dNoiseOsc_dB/20.0);

double dSubAmplitude = m_dSubOc_dB == -96.0 ? 0.0 :
                       pow(10.0, m_dSubOsc_dB/20.0);

// --- OSC3 is Sub Osc
m_GlobalSynthParams.osc3Params.dAmplitude = dSubAmplitude;

// --- OSC4 is Noise Osc
m_GlobalSynthParams.osc4Params.dAmplitude = dNoiseAmplitude;

// --- pulse width
m_GlobalSynthParams.osc1Params.dPulseWidthControl = m_dPulseWidth_Pct;
m_GlobalSynthParams.osc2Params.dPulseWidthControl = m_dPulseWidth_Pct;
m_GlobalSynthParams.osc3Params.dPulseWidthControl = m_dPulseWidth_Pct;

// --- octave
m_GlobalSynthParams.osc1Params.nOctave = m_nOctave;
m_GlobalSynthParams.osc2Params.nOctave = m_nOctave;
m_GlobalSynthParams.osc3Params.nOctave = m_nOctave - 1; // sub-osc

// --- detuning for MiniSynth
m_GlobalSynthParams.osc1Params.nCents = m_dDetune_cents;
m_GlobalSynthParams.osc2Params.nCents = -m_dDetune_cents;
// no detune on 3rd oscillator

// --- Filter:
m_GlobalSynthParams.filter1Params.dFcControl = m_dFcControl;
m_GlobalSynthParams.filter1Params.dQControl = m_dQControl;

// --- LFO1:
m_GlobalSynthParams.lfo1Params.uWaveform = m_uLFO1Waveform;
m_GlobalSynthParams.lfo1Params.dAmplitude = m_dLFO1Amplitude;
m_GlobalSynthParams.lfo1Params.dOscFo = m_dLFO1Rate;

// --- EG1:
m_GlobalSynthParams.eg1Params.dAttackTime_mSec = m_dAttackTime_mSec;
m_GlobalSynthParams.eg1Params.dDecayTime_mSec =
                                        m_dDecayReleaseTime_mSec;
m_GlobalSynthParams.eg1Params.dSustainLevel = m_dSustainLevel;
m_GlobalSynthParams.eg1Params.dReleaseTime_mSec =
                                          m_dDecayReleaseTime_mSec;
m_GlobalSynthParams.eg1Params.bResetToZero = (bool)m_uResetToZero;
m_GlobalSynthParams.eg1Params.bLegatoMode = (bool)m_uLegatoMode;

// --- DCA:
m_GlobalSynthParams.dcaParams.dAmplitude_dB = m_dVolume_dB;
```

```
    // --- enable/disable mod matrix stuff
    if(m_uVelocityToAttackScaling == 1)
    m_GlobalModMatrix.enableModMatrixRow(SOURCE_VELOCITY,
                    DEST_ALL_EG_ATTACK_SCALING, true); // enable
    else
    m_GlobalModMatrix.enableModMatrixRow(SOURCE_VELOCITY,
            DEST_ALL_EG_ATTACK_SCALING, false);

    if(m_uNoteNumberToDecayScaling == 1)
    m_GlobalModMatrix.enableModMatrixRow(SOURCE_MIDI_NOTE_NUM,
                    DEST_ALL_EG_DECAY_SCALING, true); // enable
    else
    m_GlobalModMatrix.enableModMatrixRow(SOURCE_MIDI_NOTE_NUM,
                    DEST_ALL_EG_DECAY_SCALING, false);

    if(m_uFilterKeyTrack == 1)
    m_GlobalModMatrix.enableModMatrixRow(SOURCE_MIDI_NOTE_NUM,
                    DEST_ALL_FILTER_KEYTRACK, true); // enable
    else
    m_GlobalModMatrix.enableModMatrixRow(SOURCE_MIDI_NOTE_NUM,
                    DEST_ALL_FILTER_KEYTRACK, false);
}

void AUSynth::update()
{
    // --- Voice:
    m_GlobalSynthParams.voiceParams.uVoiceMode =
                            Globals()->GetParameter(VOICE_MODE);
    m_GlobalSynthParams.voiceParams.dPortamentoTime_mSec =
                    Globals()->GetParameter(PORTAMENTO_TIME_MSEC);

    // --- ranges
    m_GlobalSynthParams.voiceParams.dOscFoPitchBendModRange =
                    Globals()->GetParameter(PITCHBEND_RANGE);

    // --- intensities
    m_GlobalSynthParams.voiceParams.dFilterKeyTrackIntensity =
                    Globals()->GetParameter(FILTER_KEYTRACK_INTENSITY);
    m_GlobalSynthParams.voiceParams.dLFO1Filter1ModIntensity =
                    Globals()->GetParameter(LFO1_TO_FILTER_INTENSITY);
    m_GlobalSynthParams.voiceParams.dLFO1OscModIntensity =
                    Globals()->GetParameter(LFO1_TO_OSC_INTENSITY);
    m_GlobalSynthParams.voiceParams.dLFO1DCAAmpModIntensity =
                    Globals()->GetParameter(LFO1_TO_DCA_INTENSITY);
    m_GlobalSynthParams.voiceParams.dLFO1DCAPanModIntensity =
                    Globals()->GetParameter(LFO1_TO_PAN_INTENSITY);

    m_GlobalSynthParams.voiceParams.dEG1OscModIntensity =
                    Globals()->GetParameter(EG1_TO_OSC_INTENSITY);
```

```
m_GlobalSynthParams.voiceParams.dEG1Filter1ModIntensity =
                   Globals()->GetParameter(EG1_TO_FILTER_INTENSITY);
m_GlobalSynthParams.voiceParams.dEG1DCAAmpModIntensity =
                   Globals()->GetParameter(EG1_TO_DCA_INTENSITY);

// --- Oscillators:
double dNoiseAmplitude = Globals()->GetParameter(NOISE_OSC_AMP_DB) ==
-96.0 ? 0.0 : w(10.0, Globals()->GetParameter(NOISE_OSC_AMP_DB)/
                20.0);

double dSubAmplitude = Globals()->GetParameter(SUB_OSC_AMP_DB) ==
-96.0 ? 0.0 : pow(10.0, Globals()->GetParameter(SUB_OSC_AMP_DB)/
                  20.0);

// --- OSC3 is Sub Osc
m_GlobalSynthParams.osc3Params.dAmplitude = dSubAmplitude;

// --- OSC4 is Noise Osc
m_GlobalSynthParams.osc4Params.dAmplitude = dNoiseAmplitude;

// --- pulse width
m_GlobalSynthParams.osc1Params.dPulseWidthControl =
                  Globals()->GetParameter(PULSE_WIDTH_PCT);
m_GlobalSynthParams.osc2Params.dPulseWidthControl =
                  Globals()->GetParameter(PULSE_WIDTH_PCT);
m_GlobalSynthParams.osc3Params.dPulseWidthControl =
                  Globals()->GetParameter(PULSE_WIDTH_PCT);

// --- octave
m_GlobalSynthParams.osc1Params.nOctave =
                  Globals()->GetParameter(OCTAVE);
m_GlobalSynthParams.osc2Params.nOctave =
                  Globals()->GetParameter(OCTAVE);
m_GlobalSynthParams.osc3Params.nOctave =
                  Globals()->GetParameter(OCTAVE) - 1; // sub osc

// --- detuning for MiniSynth
m_GlobalSynthParams.osc1Params.nCents =
                  Globals()->GetParameter(DETUNE_CENTS);
m_GlobalSynthParams.osc2Params.nCents =
                  -Globals()->GetParameter(DETUNE_CENTS);
// no detune on 3rd oscillator

// --- Filter:
m_GlobalSynthParams.filter1Params.dFcControl =
                  Globals()->GetParameter(FILTER_FC);
m_GlobalSynthParams.filter1Params.dQControl =
                  Globals()->GetParameter(FILTER_Q);

// --- LFO1:
m_GlobalSynthParams.lfo1Params.uWaveform =
                  Globals()->GetParameter(LFO1_WAVEFORM);
```

```
m_GlobalSynthParams.lfo1Params.dAmplitude =
                        Globals()->GetParameter(LFO1_AMPLITUDE);
m_GlobalSynthParams.lfo1Params.dOscFo =
                        Globals()->GetParameter(LFO1_RATE);

// --- EG1:
m_GlobalSynthParams.eg1Params.dAttackTime_mSec =
                                Globals()->GetParameter(EG1_ATTACK_MSEC);
m_GlobalSynthParams.eg1Params.dDecayTime_mSec =
                        Globals()->GetParameter(EG1_DECAY_RELEASE_MSEC);
m_GlobalSynthParams.eg1Params.dSustainLevel =
                        Globals()->GetParameter(EG1_SUSTAIN_LEVEL);
m_GlobalSynthParams.eg1Params.dReleaseTime_mSec =
                        Globals()->GetParameter(EG1_DECAY_RELEASE_MSEC);
m_GlobalSynthParams.eg1Params.bResetToZero =
                        (bool)Globals()->GetParameter(RESET_TO_ZERO);
m_GlobalSynthParams.eg1Params.bLegatoMode =
                        (bool)Globals()->GetParameter(LEGATO_MODE);

// --- DCA:
m_GlobalSynthParams.dcaParams.dAmplitude_dB =
                        Globals()->GetParameter(OUTPUT_AMPLITUDE_DB);

// --- enable/disable mod matrix stuff
if((bool)Globals()->GetParameter(VELOCITY_TO_ATTACK) == 1)
        m_GlobalModMatrix.enableModMatrixRow(SOURCE_VELOCITY,
                        DEST_ALL_EG_ATTACK_SCALING, true); // enable
else
m_GlobalModMatrix.enableModMatrixRow(SOURCE_VELOCITY,
                DEST_ALL_EG_ATTACK_SCALING, false);

if((bool)Globals()->GetParameter(NOTE_NUM_TO_DECAY) == 1)
        m_GlobalModMatrix.enableModMatrixRow(SOURCE_MIDI_NOTE_NUM,
                        DEST_ALL_EG_DECAY_SCALING, true); // enable
else
m_GlobalModMatrix.enableModMatrixRow(SOURCE_MIDI_NOTE_NUM,
                DEST_ALL_EG_DECAY_SCALING, false);

if((bool)Globals()->GetParameter(FILTER_KEYTRACK) == 1)
        m_GlobalModMatrix.enableModMatrixRow(SOURCE_MIDI_NOTE_NUM,
                        DEST_ALL_FILTER_KEYTRACK, true); // enable
else
m_GlobalModMatrix.enableModMatrixRow(SOURCE_MIDI_NOTE_NUM,
                DEST_ALL_FILTER_KEYTRACK, false);
}
```

Rendering Audio

The voice objects make it easy to render the audio. The plug-in doesn't know or care how the audio is synthesized, and the code is the same for all synths. You loop over the voices and accumulate all notes that are turned on. The voice outputs are scaled by 0.25 in MiniSynth to give 12 dB of headroom for summing a potentially large number of voices together. Note that there are other ways of handling the headroom issue including dynamic range compression. We choose this method as a simple and reasonably effective way of dealing with potential overflow and as usual you are encouraged to experiment with other methods.

```
<< ** Code Listing 9.5: Rendering ** >>

double dLeftAccum = 0.0;
double dRightAccum = 0.0;

// --- 12dB headroom
float fMix = 0.25;
double dLeft = 0.0;
double dRight = 0.0;

// --- loop and accumulate voices
for(int i=0; i<MAX_VOICES; i++)
{
        // --- render synth
        m_pVoiceArray[i]->doVoice(dLeft, dRight);

        // --- accumulate and scale
        dLeftAccum += fMix*dLeft;
        dRightAccum += fMix*dRight;
}

<< END ** Code Listing 9.5: Rendering ** END >>
```

MIDI Note On

During the note on event, you first try to find a free voice; if a free voice can be found, you increment the timestamps then call the voice's *noteOn()* function. If no free voices are found, you set the *bStealNote* flag for the next *if()* statement. You use the helper function to find the proper note to steal, then follow the same procedure; you increment the timestamps then call the voice's *noteOn()* function. The MIDI logging is optional. Notice how the note is saved as *m_dLastNoteFrequency* and used in the voice's *noteOn()* call for portamento.

```
<< ** Code Listing 9.6: Note On ** >>

bool bStealNote = true;
for(int i=0; i<MAX_VOICES; i++)
{
     // --- loop and find free voice
     CMiniSynthVoice* pVoice = m_pVoiceArray[i];

     // -- if we have a free voice, turn on
     if(!pVoice->m_bNoteOn)
     {
             // --- do this first
             incrementVoiceTimestamps();

             // --- then note on
             pVoice->noteOn(uMIDINote, uVelocity, midiFreqTable[uMIDINote],
                            m_dLastNoteFrequency);

             // LOG MIDI EVENT

             // --- save
             m_dLastNoteFrequency = midiFreqTable[uMIDINote];
```

```
                bStealNote = false;
                break;
        }
}

// --- need to steal
if(bStealNote)
{
        // --- steal oldest note
        CMiniSynthVoice* pVoice = getOldestVoice();
        if(pVoice)
        {
                // --- do this first
                incrementVoiceTimestamps();

                // --- then note on
                pVoice->noteOn(uMIDINote, uVelocity, midiFreqTable[uMIDINote],
                                m_dLastNoteFrequency);

                // LOG MIDI EVENT
        }

        // --- save
        m_dLastNoteFrequency = midiFreqTable[uMIDINote];
}

<< END ** Code Listing 9.6: Note On ** END >>
```

MIDI Note Off/All Notes Off

The note off events are easy to handle. For the all notes off event, you just loop through the voices and force each one off by using its own MIDI note number in the *noteOff()* argument. For the single note off event, you use the helper function to find the oldest note with a matching note number so that notes are turned off in succession.

```
<< ** Code Listing 9.7: All Notes Off ** >>

// force all off
for(int i=0; i<MAX_VOICES; i++)
{
        m_pVoiceArray[i]->noteOff(m_pVoiceArray[i]->m_uMIDINoteNumber);
}

<< END ** Code Listing 9.7: All Notes Off ** END >>


<< ** Code Listing 9.8: Note Off ** >>

// find and turn off
// may have multiple notes sustaining; this ensures the oldest
// note gets the event by starting at top of stack
for(int i=0; i<MAX_VOICES; i++)
{
```

```
        CMiniSynthVoice* pVoice = getOldestVoiceWithNote(uMIDINote);

        if(pVoice)
        {
                pVoice->noteOff(uMIDINote);
                // LOG MIDI
                break;
        }
    }
    << END ** Code Listing 9.8: Note Off ** END >>
```

All Other MIDI events

The rest of the MIDI events that we support are simple to implement. You just loop through the voices and set the sources on each modulation matrix. Globalization of MIDI messages is left as a Chapter Challenge for you. Since these are slightly different for each API, they are shown below in the full implementation.

9.7 MiniSynth Files

MiniSynth uses the following files that you will need to add into your compiler's project in the usual manner. You may also download the complete project code from http://www.willpirkle.com/synthbook/. The MiniSynth core files consist of:

DCA.h DCA.cpp EnvelopeGenerator.h EnvelopeGenerator.cpp Filter.h Filter.cpp LFO.h LFO.cpp MiniSynthVoice.h MiniSynthVoice.cpp ModulationMatrix.h ModulationMatrix.cpp	MoogLadderFilter.h MoogLadderFilter.cpp Oscillator.h Oscillator.cpp QBLimitedOscillator.h QBLimitedOscillator.cpp synthfunctions.h VAOnePoleFilter.h VAOnePoleFilter.cpp Voice.h Voice.cpp

For VST3 and AU, you also need to add the file *SynthParamLimits.h*, which is in the MiniSynth sample code—remember that this file is slightly different for each synth because it contains the GUI control index enumeration.

9.8 MiniSynth: RackAFX

Create a new project named MiniSynth and setup the GUI using Table 9.5.

MiniSynth.h

Add the declarations for the voice array, helper functions and last-note and MIDI receive variables:

```
class CMiniSynth : public CPlugIn
{
public:
     <SNIP SNIP SNIP>
```

```
    // Add your code here: ------------------------------------------ //

    << INSERT ** Code Listing 9.1: Declarations ** HERE >>

    etc
```

MiniSynth.cpp

Constructor

- create and initialize voices
- synchronize all mod matrix cores

```
CMiniSynth::CMiniSynth()
{
    <SNIP SNIP SNIP>

    m_bOutputOnlyPlugIn = true;

    // set flag for all messages
    m_bWantAllMIDIMessages = true;

    << INSERT ** Code Listing 9.2: Init Voices ** HERE >>
}
```

Destructor

- destroy global mod matrix
- destroy voices

```
CMiniSynth::~CMiniSynth(void)
{
    << INSERT ** Code Listing 9.3: Destruction ** HERE >>
}
```

prepareForPlay()

- set sample rate and call *prepareForPlay()* on voices
- mass update
- init last note frequency

```
bool __stdcall CMiniSynth::prepareForPlay()
{
    << INSERT ** Code Listing 9.4: One Time Init ** HERE >>

    return true;
}
```

update()

Insert this function, which is listed in its entirety above.

processAudioFrame()

- insert the rendering code to do the render loop
- write out the accumulated values.

```
bool __stdcall CMiniSynth::processAudioFrame(args. . .)
{
      << INSERT ** Code Listing 9.5: Rendering ** HERE >>

      pOutputBuffer[0] = dLeftAccum;

      // Mono-In, Stereo-Out (AUX Effect)
      if(uNumInputChannels == 1 && uNumOutputChannels == 2)
            pOutputBuffer[1] = dLeftAccum;

      // Stereo-In, Stereo-Out (INSERT Effect)
      if(uNumInputChannels == 2 && uNumOutputChannels == 2)
            pOutputBuffer[1] = dRightAccum;

      return true;
}
```

incrementVoiceTimestamps();
getOldestVoice();
getOldestVoiceWithNote();

These functions are listed in their entirety above; just insert them into the *.cpp* file wherever you like.

midiNoteOn()

- Use the note on code to complete the function
- Note: this function will be identical for the rest of the synth projects, with the exception of the type of pointer in the voice array, and so it will not be shown again

```
bool __stdcall CMiniSynth::midiNoteOn(args. . .)
{
      // --- test channel/ignore
      if(m_uMidiRxChannel != MIDI_CH_ALL && uChannel != m_uMidiRxChannel)
            return false;

      << INSERT ** Code Listing 9.6: Note On ** HERE >>

      return true;
}
```

midiNoteOff()

- Use the note off code to complete the function
- Note: this function will be identical for the rest of the synth projects, with the exception of the type of pointer in the voice array, and so it will not be shown again

```
bool __stdcall CMiniSynth::midiNoteOff(args. . .)
{
      // test channel/ignore
      if(m_uMidiRxChannel != MIDI_CH_ALL && uChannel != m_uMidiRxChannel)
      {
            return false;
      }
```

```
        if(bAllNotesOff)
        {
                << INSERT ** Code Listing 9.7: All Notes Off ** HERE >>
                return true;
        }

        << INSERT ** Code Listing 9.8: Note Off ** HERE >>

        return true;
}
```

midiModWheel()
midiPitchBend()

- loop through voices and set appropriate source value in mod matrix
- Note: these functions will be identical for the rest of the synth projects, and so they will not be shown again

```
bool __stdcall CMiniSynth::midiModWheel(args. . .)
{
        // test channel/ignore
        if(m_uMidiRxChannel != MIDI_CH_ALL && uChannel != m_uMidiRxChannel)
                return false;

        for(int i=0; i<MAX_VOICES; i++)
        {
                 m_pVoiceArray[i]->m_ModulationMatrix.m_dSources[SOURCE_MODWHEEL] = uModValue;
        }

        return true;
}

bool __stdcall CMiniSynth::midiPitchBend(args. . .)
{
        // test channel/ignore
        if(m_uMidiRxChannel != MIDI_CH_ALL && uChannel != m_uMidiRxChannel)
                return false;

        for(int i=0; i<MAX_VOICES; i++)
        {
                // --- send to matrix
                 m_pVoiceArray[i]->m_ModulationMatrix.
                        m_dSources[SOURCE_PITCHBEND] = fNormalizedPitchBendValue;
        }

        return true;
}
```

midiMessage()

- decode the message
- loop through voices and set appropriate source value in mod matrix for:
    - Volume
    - Pan
    - Expression

Sustain Pedal

- Note: this function will be identical for the rest of the synth projects, and so it will not be shown again

```
bool __stdcall CMiniSynth::midiMessage(args. . .)
{
    // test channel/ignore
    if(m_uMidiRxChannel != MIDI_CH_ALL && (UINT)cChannel !=
       m_uMidiRxChannel)
            return false;

    switch(cStatus)
    {
            <SNIP SNIP SNIP>

            case CONTROL_CHANGE:
            {
                    switch(cData1)
                    {
                          case VOLUME_CC07:
                          {
                                // --- send to matrix
                                for(int i=0; i<MAX_VOICES; i++)
                                {
                                        m_pVoiceArray[i]
                                             ->m_ModulationMatrix.m_dSources
                                                  [SOURCE_MIDI_VOLUME_CC07] =
                                                  (UINT)cData2;
                                }

                                break;
                          }
                          case PAN_CC10:
                          {
                                // --- send to matrix
                                for(int i=0; i<MAX_VOICES; i++)
                                {
                                 m_pVoiceArray[i]
                                            ->m_ModulationMatrix.m_dSources
                                                  [SOURCE_MIDI_PAN_CC10] =
                                                  (UINT)cData2;
                                }

                                break; SOURCE_MIDI_EXPRESSION_CC11
                          }
                          case EXPRESSION_CC11:
                          {
                                // --- send to matrix
                                for(int i=0; i<MAX_VOICES; i++)
                                {
```

```
                    m_pVoiceArray[i]
                        ->m_ModulationMatrix.m_dSources [SOURCE_MIDI_EXPRES-
                        SION_CC11] = (UINT)cData2;
                }
                break;
            }

            case SUSTAIN_PEDAL:
            {
                for(int i=0; i<MAX_VOICES; i++)
                {
                    m_pVoiceArray[i]
                        ->m_ModulationMatrix.m_dSources
                        [SOURCE_SUSTAIN_PEDAL] =
                        (UINT)cData2;
                }

                break;
            }

            etc. . .
```

9.9 MiniSynth: VST3

Create a new project with the namespace MiniSynth and setup the GUI using Table 9.5.

VSTSynthProcessor.h

Add the declarations for the voice array, helper functions and last-note and MIDI receive variables:

```
class Processor : public AudioEffect
{
public:
    <SNIF SNIP SNIP>

    // Add your code here: --------------------------------------------- //

    << INSERT ** Code Listing 9.1: Declarations ** HERE >>

    etc. . .
```

VSTSynthProcessor.cpp

Constructor

- initialize all variables you declared for the GUI controls; the defaults are in *SynthParamLimits.h* for this project

```
Processor::Processor()
{
    // --- we are a Processor
    setControllerClass(Controller::cid);
```

```
    // --- our inits
    m_dNoiseOsc_dB = DEFAULT_NOISE_OSC_AMP_DB;
    m_dPulseWidth_Pct = DEFAULT_PULSE_WIDTH_PCT;
    m_dHSRatio = DEFAULT_HARD_SYNC_RATIO;
    m_dEG1OscIntensity = DEFAULT_BIPOLAR;

    <SNIP SNIP SNIP>

    // VST3 specific
    m_dMIDIPitchBend = DEFAULT_MIDI_PITCHBEND;// -1 to +1
    m_uMIDIModWheel = DEFAULT_MIDI_MODWHEEL;
    m_uMIDIVolumeCC7 = DEFAULT_MIDI_VOLUME;      // note defaults to 127
    m_uMIDIPanCC10 = DEFAULT_MIDI_PAN;           // 64 = center pan
    m_uMIDIExpressionCC11 = DEFAULT_MIDI_EXPRESSION;

    // Finish initializations here
    m_dLastNoteFrequency = -1.0;

    // receive on all channels
    m_uMidiRxChannel = MIDI_CH_ALL;

    // this is created/destroyed in SetActive()
    m_pFilterLogParam = NULL;
}
```

setActive()

- for activated state:
    - create and initialize voices
    - synchronize all mod matrix cores
    - set sample rate and call *prepareForPlay()* on voices
    - mass update

- for de-activated state:
    - destroy global mod matrix
    - destroy voices

Note: feel free to consolidate the *for()* loops for the voice setup (listing 9.2 and 9.4); these are separated in RackAFX and AU and are kept separate here only for consistency.

```
tresult PLUGIN_API Processor::setActive(TBool state)
{
    if(state)
    {

        << INSERT ** Code Listing 9.2: Init Voices ** HERE >>

        << INSERT ** Code Listing 9.4: One Time Init ** HERE >>

        // mass update
        update();

        // helper
        m_pFilterLogParam = newLogScaleParameter<ParamValue>
                            (USTRING("Filter fc"),FILTER_FC,
```

```
                                        filterLogScale2, (USTRING("Hz")));
        }
        else
        {
                << INSERT ** Code Listing 9.3: Destruction ** HERE >>
        }

        // base class method call is last
        return AudioEffect::setActive (state);
    }
```

update()

Insert this function, which is listed in its entirety above.

process()

- insert the rendering code to do the render loop
- write out the accumulated values.

```
    tresult PLUGIN_API Processor::process(ProcessData& data)
    {
        <SNIP SNIP SNIP>

        float fMix = 0.25; // 12dB headroom
        double dLeft = 0.0;
        double dRight = 0.0;
        double dLeftAccum = 0.0;
        double dRightAccum = 0.0;

        for(int32 j=0; j<samplesToProcess; j++)
        {
                    // --- clear accumulators
            dLeftAccum = 0.0;
            dRightAccum = 0.0;

            for(int i=0; i<MAX_VOICES; i++)
            {

                    // --- render left and right
                    m_pVoiceArray[i]->doVoice(dLeft, dRight);

                    // --- accumulate notes
                    dLeftAccum += fMix*dLeft;
                    dRightAccum += fMix*dRight;
            }

            // write out to buffer
            buffers[0][j] = dLeftAccum;  // left
            buffers[1][j] = dRightAccum; // right
        }

        etc. . .
```

incrementVoiceTimestamps();
getOldestVoice();
getOldestVoiceWithNote();

These functions are listed in their entirety above; just insert them into the *.cpp* file wherever you like.

doProcessEvent()

- Use the note on code to complete the function for the note on event
- Use the note off code to complete the function for the note off event
- Note: this function will be identical for the rest of the synth projects, with the exception of the type of pointer in the voice array, and so it will not be shown again

```
bool Processor::doProcessEvent(Event& vstEvent)
{
     bool noteEvent = false;

     switch(vstEvent.type)
     {
          // --- NOTE ON
          case Event::kNoteOnEvent:
          {
               // --- get the channel/note/vel
               UINT uMIDIChannel = (UINT)vstEvent.noteOn.channel;
               UINT uMIDINote = (UINT)vstEvent.noteOn.pitch;
               UINT uVelocity = (UINT)(127.0*vstEvent.noteOn.velocity);

               // --- test channel/ignore
               if(m_uMidiRxChannel != MIDI_CH_ALL && uMIDIChannel !=
               m_uMidiRxChannel)
                    return false;

               // --- event occurred
               noteEvent = true;

               // --- fix noteID as per SDK
               if(vstEvent.noteOn.noteId == -1)
                    vstEvent.noteOn.noteId = uMIDINote;

                    << INSERT ** Code Listing 9.6: Note On ** HERE >>

               break;
          }

          // --- NOTE OFF
          case Event::kNoteOffEvent:
          {
               // --- get the channel/note/vel
               UINT uMIDIChannel = (UINT)vstEvent.noteOff.channel;
               UINT uMIDINote = (UINT)vstEvent.noteOff.pitch;
               UINT uVelocity =
                         (UINT)(127.0*vstEvent.noteOff.velocity);
```

```
            // --- test channel/ignore
            if(m_uMidiRxChannel != MIDI_CH_ALL && uMIDIChannel !=
            m_uMidiRxChannel)
                  return false;

            // --- event occurred
            noteEvent = true;

            // --- fix noteID as per SDK
            if(vstEvent.noteOff.noteId == -1)
                  vstEvent.noteOff.noteId = uMIDINote;

            << INSERT ** Code Listing 9.8: Note Off ** HERE >>
            break;
      }

      etc. . .
```

doControlChange()

- loop through voices and set appropriate source value in mod matrix for:
    - Mod Wheel
    - Pitch Bend
    - Volume
    - Pan
    - Expression
    - All Notes Off
    - Sustain Pedal
- Note: this part of the function will be identical for the rest of the synth projects, and so it will not be shown again

```
bool Processor::doControlUpdate(ProcessData& data)
{
      bool paramChange = false;

      <SNIP SNIP SNIP>

      switch(pid) // same as RAFX uControlID
      {

            <SNIP SNIP SNIP Indents Removed>

            // --- MIDI messages
            case MIDI_PITCHBEND: // want -1 to +1
            {
                  m_dMIDIPitchBend = unipolarToBipolar(value);
                  for(int i=0; i<MAX_VOICES; i++)
                  {
                        // --- send to matrix
                        m_pVoiceArray[i]->m_ModulationMatrix.
                        m_dSources[SOURCE_PITCHBEND] = m_dMIDIPitchBend;
                  }
                  break;
            }
```

```
case MIDI_MODWHEEL: // want 0 to 127
{
        m_uMIDIModWheel = unipolarToMIDI(value);
        for(int i=0; i<MAX_VOICES; i++)
        {
              m_pVoiceArray[i]->m_ModulationMatrix.
              m_dSources[SOURCE_MODWHEEL] = m_uMIDIModWheel;
        }
        break;
}
case MIDI_VOLUME_CC7: // want 0 to 127
{
        m_uMIDIVolumeCC7 = unipolarToMIDI(value);
        for(int i=0; i<MAX_VOICES; i++)
        {
              m_pVoiceArray[i]->m_ModulationMatrix.
              m_dSources[SOURCE_MIDI_VOLUME_CC07] =
                                              m_uMIDIVolumeCC7;
        }
        break;
}
case MIDI_PAN_CC10: // want 0 to 127
{
        m_uMIDIPanCC10 = unipolarToMIDI(value);
        for(int i=0; i<MAX_VOICES; i++)
        {
              m_pVoiceArray[i]->m_ModulationMatrix.
              m_dSources[SOURCE_MIDI_PAN_CC10] = m_uMIDIPanCC10;
        }
        break;
}
case MIDI_EXPRESSION_CC11: // want 0 to 127
{
        m_uMIDIExpressionCC11 = unipolarToMIDI(value);
        for(int i=0; i<MAX_VOICES; i++)
        {
              m_pVoiceArray[i]->m_ModulationMatrix.
              m_dSources[SOURCE_MIDI_EXPRESSION_CC11] =
                                        m_uMIDIExpressionCC11;
        }
        break;
}
case MIDI_SUSTAIN_PEDAL: // want 0 to 1
{
        UINT uMIDI = value > 0.5 ? 127 : 0;
        for(int i=0; i<MAX_VOICES; i++)
        {
              m_pVoiceArray[i]->m_ModulationMatrix.
              m_dSources[SOURCE_SUSTAIN_PEDAL] = uMIDI;
        }
```

```
                break;
            }
            case MIDI_ALL_NOTES_OFF:
            {
                // force all off
                for(int i=0; i<MAX_VOICES; i++)
                {
                    m_pVoiceArray[i]->noteOff(m_pVoiceArray[i] ->m_uMIDINoteNumber);
                }
                break;
            }
            etc. . .
```

9.10 MiniSynth: AU

Create a new project named MiniSynth and setup the GUI using Table 9.5.

AUSynth.h

Add the declarations for the voice array, helper functions and last-note and MIDI receive variables:

```
class AUSynth : public AUInstrumentBase
{
public:
    <SNIP SNIP SNIP>

    // Add your code here: ------------------------------------------- //

    << INSERT ** Code Listing 9.1: Declarations ** HERE >>

    etc. . .
```

AUSynth.cpp
Constructor

- initialize all variables you declared for the GUI controls; the defaults are in *SynthParamLimits.h* for this project
- create and initialize voices
- synchronize all mod matrix cores

```
AUSynth::AUSynth(AudioUnit inComponentInstance)
    : AUInstrumentBase(inComponentInstance, 0, 1)
{
    // --- create input, output ports, groups and parts
    CreateElements();

    // --- setup default factory preset (as example)
    factoryPreset[NOISE_OSC_AMP_DB] = -12.0;
    factoryPreset[PULSE_WIDTH_PCT] = 25;

    <SNIP SNIP SNIP>

    // --- define number of params (controls)
    Globals()->UseIndexedParameters(NUMBER_OF_SYNTH_PARAMETERS);
```

```
    // --- initialize the controls here!
    // --- these are defined in SynthParamLimits.h
    //
    Globals()->SetParameter(NOISE_OSC_AMP_DB, DEFAULT_NOISE_OSC_AMP_DB);
    Globals()->SetParameter(PULSE_WIDTH_PCT, DEFAULT_PULSE_WIDTH_PCT);

    <SNIP SNIP SNIP>

    << INSERT ** Code Listing 9.2: Init Voices ** HERE >>
}
```

Destructor

- destroy global mod matrix
- destroy voices

```
AUSynth::~AUSynth(void)
{
    << INSERT ** Code Listing 9.3: Destruction ** HERE >>
}
```

Reset()

Initialize()

- these functions are identically coded; call the base class first, then:
- set sample rate and call *prepareForPlay()* on voices
- mass update
- init last note frequency

```
ComponentResult AUSynth::Reset(args. . .)
{
    // --- reset the base class
    AUBase::Reset(inScope, inElement);

    << INSERT ** Code Listing 9.4: One Time Init ** HERE >>

    return noErr;
}

ComponentResult AUSynth::Initialize()
{
    // --- init the base class
    AUInstrumentBase::Initialize();

    << INSERT ** Code Listing 9.4: One Time Init ** HERE >>

    return noErr;
}
```

update()

Insert this function, which is listed in its entirety above.

Render()

- insert the rendering code to do the render loop
- write out the accumulated values.

```
OSStatus AUSynth::Render(args. . .)
{
     // --- broadcast MIDI events
     PerformEvents(inTimeStamp);

     // --- do the mass update for this frame
     update();

     // --- get the number of channels
     AudioBufferList& bufferList = GetOutput(0)->GetBufferList();
     UInt32 numChans = bufferList.mNumberBuffers;


     <SNIP SNIP SNIP>

     float fMix = 0.25; // -12dB HR per note
     double dLeft = 0.0;
     double dRight = 0.0;
     double dLeftAccum = 0.0;
     double dRightAccum = 0.0;

     // --- the frame processing loop
     for(UInt32 frame=0; frame<inNumberFrames; ++frame)
     {
            // --- zero out for each trip through loop
            dLeftAccum = 0.0;
            dRightAccum = 0.0;

            // --- synthesize and accumulate each note's sample
            for(int i=0; i<MAX_VOICES; i++)
            {
                   // --- render
                   m_pVoiceArray[i]->doVoice(dLeft, dRight);

                   // --- accumulate and scale
                   dLeftAccum += fMix*(float)dLeft;
                   dRightAccum += fMix*(float)dRight;
            }

            // --- accumulate in output buffers
            // --- mono
            left[frame] = dLeftAccum;

            // --- stereo
            if(right) right[frame] = dRightAccum;
     }

     return noErr;
}
```

incrementVoiceTimestamps();
getOldestVoice();
getOldestVoiceWithNote();

These functions are listed in their entirety above; just insert them into the *.cpp* file wherever you like.

StartNote()

- Use the note on code to complete the function
- Note: this function will be identical for the rest of the synth projects, with the exception of the type of pointer in the voice array, and so it will not be shown again

```
OSStatus AUSynth::StartNote(args. . .)
{
        UINT uMIDINote = (UINT)inParams.mPitch;
        UINT uVelocity = (UINT)inParams.mVelocity;
        UINT uChannel = (UINT)inGroupID;

        // --- test channel/ignore
        if(m_uMidiRxChannel != MIDI_CH_ALL && uChannel != m_uMidiRxChannel)
                return false;

        << INSERT ** Code Listing 9.6: Note On ** HERE >>

        return noErr;
}
```

StopNote()

- Use the note off code to complete the function
- Note: this function will be identical for the rest of the synth projects, with the exception of the type of pointer in the voice array, and so it will not be shown again

```
OSStatus AUSynth::StopNote(args. . .)
{
        UINT uMIDINote = (UINT)inNoteInstanceID;
        UINT uChannel = (UINT)inGroupID;

        // --- test channel/ignore
        if(m_uMidiRxChannel != MIDI_CH_ALL && uChannel != m_uMidiRxChannel)
                return false;

        << INSERT ** Code Listing 9.6: Note On ** HERE >>

        return true;
}
```

HandlePitchWheel()

- loop through voices and set appropriate source value in mod matrix
- Note: these functions will be identical for the rest of the synth projects, and so it will not be shown again

```
OSStatus AUSynth::HandlePitchWheel(args. . .)
{
        UINT uChannel = (UINT)inChannel;
```

```
    // --- test channel/ignore
    if(m_uMidiRxChannel != MIDI_CH_ALL && uChannel != m_uMidiRxChannel)
        return noErr;

    // --- convert 14-bit concatentaion of inPitch1, inPitch2
    int nActualPitchBendValue = (int) ((inPitch1 & 0x7F) | ((inPitch2 & 0x7F)
                                << 7));
    float fNormalizedPitchBendValue = (float)(nActualPitchBendValue -
                                    0x2000)/(float)(0x2000);

#ifdef LOG_MIDI
    printf("-- Pitch Bend Ch:%d int:%d float:%f \n", uChannel,
                nActualPitchBendValue, fNormalizedPitchBendValue);
#endif

    // --- set in voices
    for(int i=0; i<MAX_VOICES; i++)
    {
        // --- send to matrix
        m_pVoiceArray[i]->m_ModulationMatrix.m_dSources[SOURCE_PITCHBEND] =
                                            fNormalizedPitchBendValue;
    }
    return noErr;
}
```

HandleControlChange()

- decode the message
- loop through voices and set appropriate source value in mod matrix for:
    - Mod Wheel
    - Volume
    - Pan
    - Expression
    - All Notes Off
    - Sustain Pedal

- Note: this function will be identical for the rest of the synth projects, and so it will not be shown again

```
OSStatus AJSynth::HandleControlChange(args. . .)
{
    // --- Handle other MIDI messages we are interested in
    UINT uChannel = (UINT)inChannel;

    // --- test channel/ignore
    if(m_uMidiRxChannel != MIDI_CH_ALL && uChannel != m_uMidiRxChannel)
        return noErr;

    CMiniSynthVoice* pVoice = NULL;
    switch(inController)
    {
        case VOLUME_CC07:
        {
```

```
                // --- NOTE: LOGIC 9 CAPTURES VOLUME FOR ITSELF ---
                for(int i=0; i<MAX_VOICES; i++)
                {
                      m_pVoiceArray[i]->m_ModulationMatrix.m_dSources
                            [SOURCE_MIDI_VOLUME_CC07] = (UINT)inValue;
                }
                break;
          }
          case PAN_CC10:
          {
                // --- NOTE: LOGIC 9 CAPTURES PAN FOR ITSELF ---

                for(int i=0; i<MAX_VOICES; i++)
                {
                      m_pVoiceArray[i]->m_ModulationMatrix.m_dSources
                            [SOURCE_MIDI_PAN_CC10] = (UINT)inValue;
                }
                break;
          }
          case EXPRESSION_CC11:
          {
                for(int i=0; i<MAX_VOICES; i++)
                {
                      m_pVoiceArray[i]->m_ModulationMatrix.m_dSources
                             [SOURCE_MIDI_EXPRESSION_CC11] = (UINT)inValue;
                }
                break;
          }
          case MOD_WHEEL:
          {
                for(int i=0; i<MAX_VOICES; i++)
                {
                      m_pVoiceArray[i]->m_ModulationMatrix.m_dSources
                            [SOURCE_MODWHEEL] = (UINT)inValue;
          }
          break;
    }
    case SUSTAIN_PEDAL:
    {
          for(int i=0; i<MAX_VOICES; i++)
          {
                m_pVoiceArray[i]->m_ModulationMatrix.m_dSources [SOURCE_SUSTAIN_PEDAL] =
                                                                 (UINT)inValue;
                }
          }

          break;
          }
          case ALL_NOTES_OFF:
```

```
{
        // --- NOTE: some clients may trap this
        for(int i=0; i<MAX_VOICES; i++)
        {
              m_pVoiceArray[i]->noteOff(m_pVoiceArray[i]
                     ->m_uMIDINoteNumber);
        }
        break;
}

etc. . .
```

Build and test MiniSynth; try the different voice modes and really exercise the modulation routings.

9.11 Challenges

Bronze

Modify the EG GUI controls and split the shared decay/release control into two controls so that you have the full set of attack, decay, sustain and release controls.

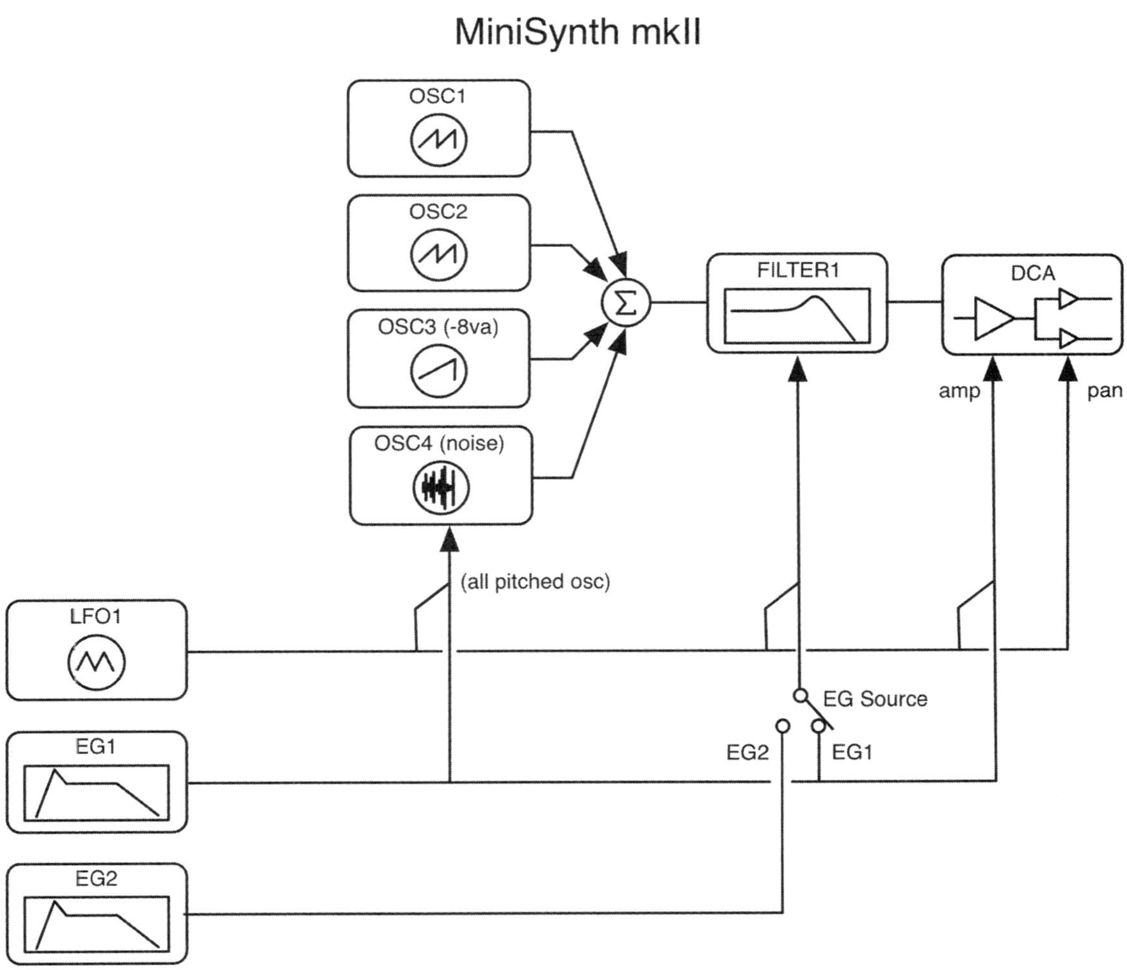

Figure 9.14: MiniSynth mkII features a second EG and switch.

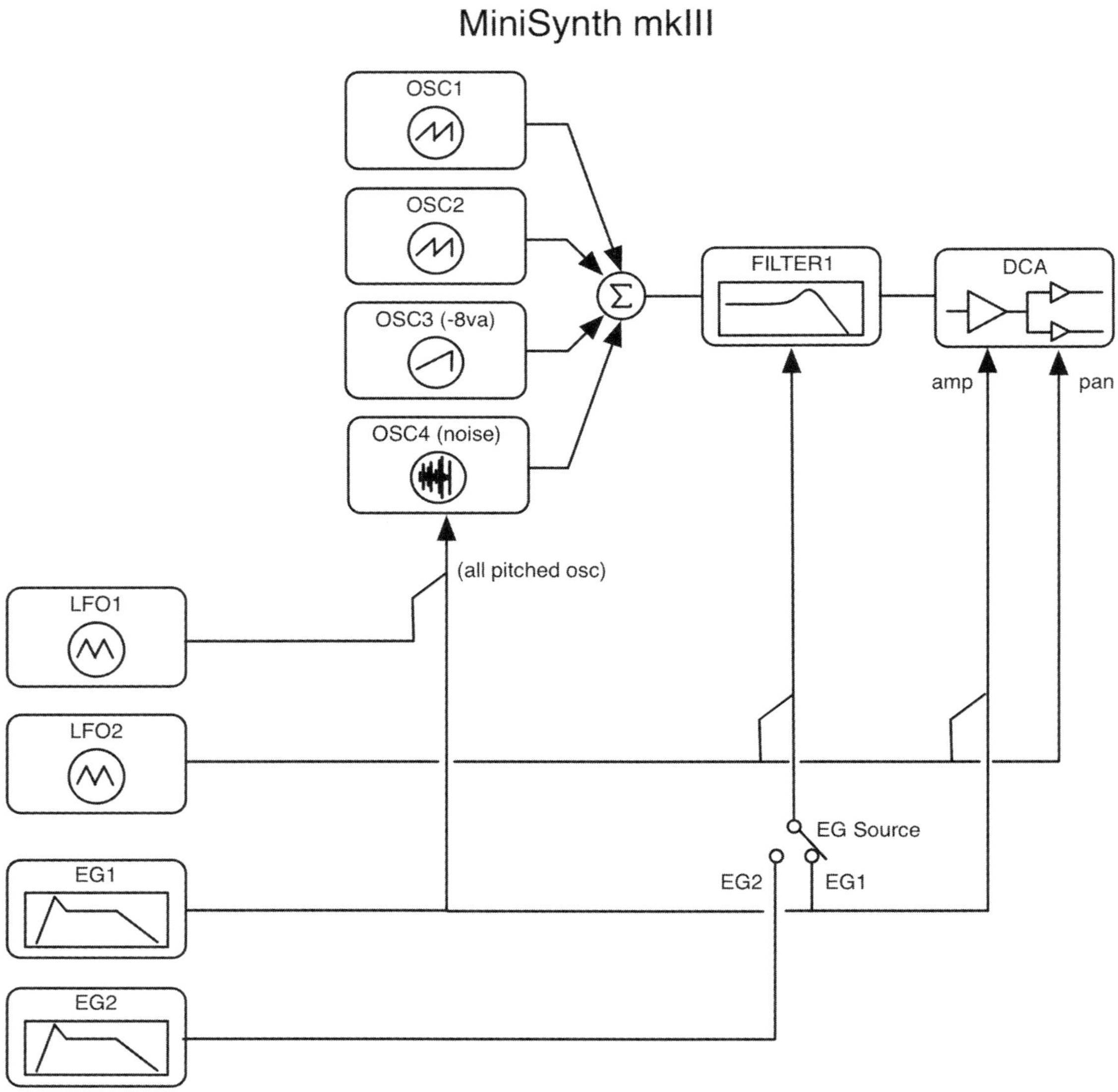

Figure 9.15: MiniSynth mkIII adds another LFO.

Silver

Upgrade the filter to a multi-filter object that allows the user to select any of the filters from Chapter 7. This will likely require subclassing *CFilter* and using pointers to select and manipulate the various filters. If you implemented the Moog half ladder filter, you will have a total of 16 different filters in the synth.

Gold

Implement MiniSynth mkII shown in Figure 9.14. This version adds a second EG connected to the filter, allowing it to have a completely different contour. Allow the user to choose between EG1 (classic mode) and EG2 for the filter EG.

Platinum

Implement MiniSynth mkIII shown in Figure 9.15. This version adds a second LFO in a stereotypical connection; LFO1 is reserved for vibrato only (sometimes called a "vibrato LFO"), while LFO2 is a general purpose "modulation LFO."

Diamond

If you have implemented hard sync from Chapter 5's Platinum Challenge, use the second LFO to modulate the hard sync ratio parameter.

Bibliography

Junglieb, Stanley. 1986. *Prophet VS Digital Vector Synthesizer*. San Jose: Sequential Circuits, Inc.
Junglieb, Stanley. 1990. *Wavestation Player's Guide*. Tokyo: Korg, Inc.
Korg, Inc. 1978. *MS-20 User's Manual*. Tokyo: Korg, Inc.
Korg, Inc. 1981. *Polysix Service Manual*. Tokyo: Korg, Inc.
Korg, Inc. 1997. *Karma Music Workstation Parameter Guide*. Tokyo: Korg, Inc.
Korg, Inc. 1997. *Triton Music Workstation Basic Guide*. Tokyo: Korg, Inc.
Phillips, Dan. 1991. *Wavestation SR Reference Guide*. Tokyo: Korg, Inc.
Yamaha, Inc. 1998. *EX5/EX7 User's Manual*. Tokyo: Yamaha, Inc.

CHAPTER 10

DigiSynth: Sample Playback Synthesizer

By the late 1980s, synthesizer companies had switched paradigms from using analog circuits to using audio samples. A sample is a recorded sound. It could be an acoustic instrument, a sound of nature, or even a recording of another synthesizer. In the early days of sample-based synthesis, solid-state memory was expensive, so the samples were typically very short. Even with today's cheap memory prices, sampling still has issues where sample length is concerned. For example, how long would a sample of a concert grand piano's lowest note (A1) last if the note was played fortissimo (*fff*) in a large concert hall? You would need to sample the note until it decayed below the digital noise floor (−96 dB for 16-bit audio). In addition, there are many instruments whose envelopes do not decay, such as the pipe organ—these note events last as long as the keys are held down. The early pioneers came up with an interesting way to get the most from their short samples, and we still use this method today. DigiSynth is a sample playback synthesizer that will incorporate the traditional transient-then-loop method of handing samples in addition to playing loops or one-shot samples. It uses a C++ object we created called *CWaveData* that handles the task of opening a .wav file and extracting its entire audio contents into a 32-bit floating point buffer. DigiSynth can playback either single samples or arrays of samples known as multi-samples.

10.1 Audio Samples

Let's consider a sample of a typical musical event such as an acoustic instrument's output. Musical note events often consist of a noisy transient attack followed by a quasi-periodic steady state section that may or may not decay away; for instance, a plucked string decays fairly quickly, while a bowed string can be made to sustain for as long as the musician wishes. Figure 10.1 shows what a typical sample might look like zoomed all the way out so that the transient and steady state sections are discernible.

Zooming in on the quasi-periodic steady state section of an actual sample reveals something like what you see in Figure 10.2; these are both from samples used in DigiSynth.

The idea is to truncate the audio sample so that it contains the transient attack portion and a piece of the steady-state section that is loop-able. By choosing the loop points carefully, the quasi-periodic nature of this section can be made to sustain forever. This transient-loop technique is shown in Figure 10.3.

Applying an envelope to the steady state section can mimic the natural decay and release of the original event. Sometimes, the AHDSR (attack-hold-decay-sustain-release) EG is employed with either no attack or a very short one followed by a hold period when the transient plays. In some cases, there is no sustain section of the envelope, and it moves from decay (or hold) directly to release.

There are three basic ways to play an audio sample:

- one-shot—the sample plays once from beginning to end and stops
- loop—the sample loops from beginning to end
- transient-loop—the sample plays the transient section and then goes into the looped section forever with the envelope applied

A fourth playback option also exists called loop-and-release. In this version shown in Figure 10.4, the normal transient-loop method is implemented until the note off event occurs, at which time the audio plays from wherever it is in the loop straight through to the end of the sample, with or without a release envelope applied. This may be used to preserve the original release portion of the sample. DigiSynth's sample based oscillators are designed for the three most common modes of playback operation; loop-and-release is a Chapter Challenge.

Samples typically come in four versions:

- pitch-less
- single cycle
- loop
- sustain loop

Pitch-less samples include sound effects or other alert noises. Single cycle samples are the equivalent of a wavetable and are treated the same way. Looping samples might include drum or musical lines that loop indefinitely. We will be focusing on the sustain loop variety for this chapter and part of the next. We will use the single-cycle samples in the AniSynth. The oscillators in DigiSynth can play any of these four types of samples.

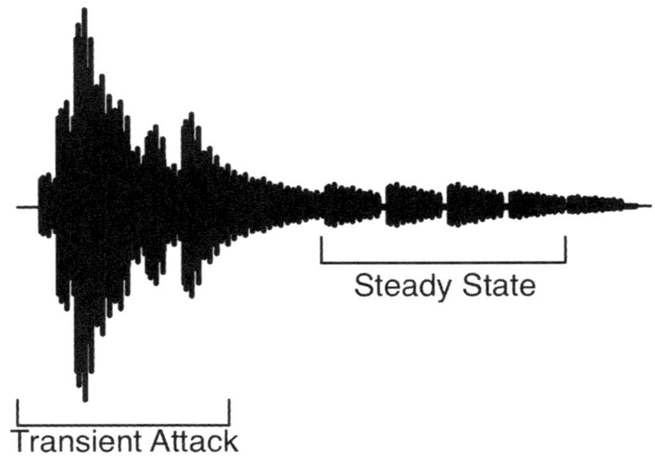

Figure 10.1: A typical note event consists of a transient attack followed by a steady state section.

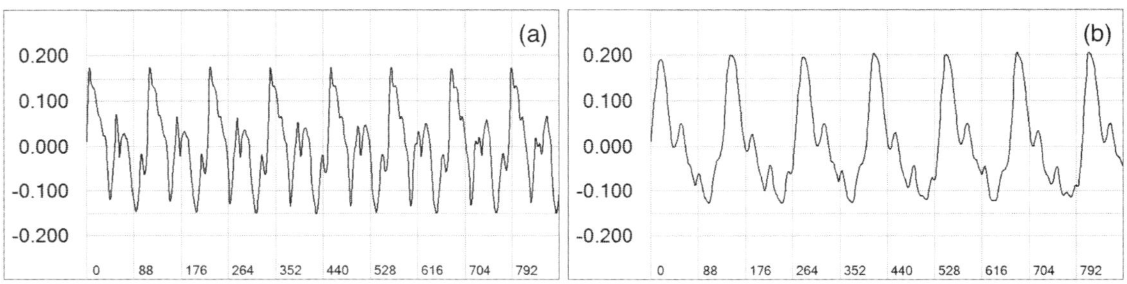

Figure 10.2: The quasi-periodic, steady state sections of two audio samples.

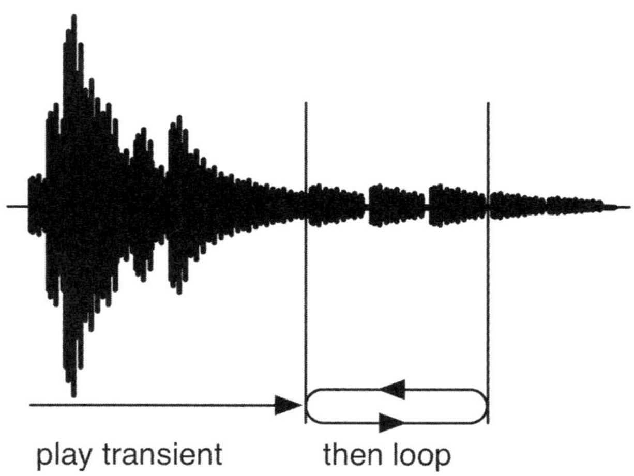

Figure 10.3: Transient and loop method of sustaining a sample indefinitely.

The *CSampleOscillator* is new for this chapter. It opens and loads the contents of *.wav* files into buffers. Then, it treats these buffers nearly the same as a wave table, reading and interpolating samples (with linear interpolation again). An increment value is used to update a read index that ultimately controls the pitch of the sample.

10.2 .wav Files

The *.wav* file format is very popular for delivering audio samples. It was designed to hold pertinent information that we need in order to play the samples at proper pitches. These .wav files are sometimes called "wave files." In addition to the audio data itself, *.wav* files also encode the:

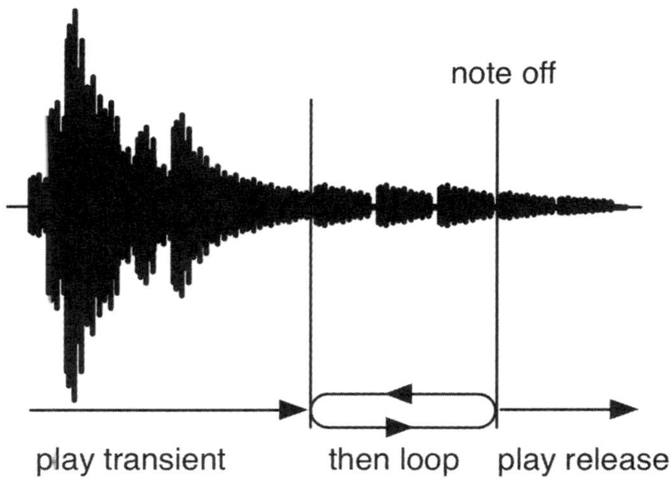

Figure 10.4: In loop-and-release mode, a note off event while looping triggers the oscillator to play to the end of the sample.

- manufacturer name
- product name
- sample period ($1/f_s$)
- MIDI Unity Note
- MIDI Pitch Fraction
- SMPTE time code information
- loop points

The MIDI Unity Note is the MIDI note number of the pitch that was originally sampled. You need this to set the pitch of your playback notes. The MIDI Pitch Fraction is a fine-tuning tweak—our samples are tuned properly, so we will ignore this for simplification; it is left as a Chapter Challenge for you. We will also ignore the SMPTE time code information. These files can contain any number of loop start and stop points, which are coded as absolute sample locations within the audio data. The *CWaveData* object reads most of this extra data, including the SMPTE time code and MIDI Pitch Fraction, if you want to experiment. The object only reads and saves the first set of loop points it finds, though you could easily modify it to collect all the loop points.

Playback Ratio

There are a couple of different ways to calculate the read increment value, also called the playback ratio. The first method requires a power-of-two operation, and the two MIDI note numbers; the number of the note that was played (M) and the MIDI Unity Note number (U) from the *.wav* file.

$$ratio = 2^{\frac{M-U}{12}} \tag{10.1}$$

$$\text{M} = \text{the MIDI note number of desired pitch}$$

$$\text{U} = \text{the MIDI unity note number}$$

If the MIDI note played was 60 and the Unity note was 54, the ratio would be 20.5 or 1.414, so the increment value would be 1.414, which makes sense. Given that the original note in the sample is lower than the target note, we would expect the increment value to be greater than 1.0. Notice that this equation works because subtracting MIDI note numbers gives you their difference in semitones. In our *CSampleOscillator*, we use a different calculation that avoids the power of two and lets us re-use the modulo counter and increment value that all oscillators share and that is used in the update function when modulating frequency, octaves, semitones, cents, etc. Remember from Chapter 5 that the oscillator's modulo *inc* value is:

$$inc_{(\text{modulo})} = \frac{f_o}{f_s} \tag{10.2}$$

and that the wavetable increment value is:

$$\begin{aligned} inc_{(\text{wavetable})} &= L\frac{f_o}{f_s} \\ &= (L)inc_{(\text{modulo})} \end{aligned} \tag{10.3}$$

where L is the length of the wavetable. A wavetable contains only one cycle of the waveform, so L is the length of only one cycle. We can determine this equivalent length easily as:

$$L_{equiv} = \frac{f_s}{f_{unity}}$$
$$f_{unity} = \text{frequency of MIDI Unity Note}$$
$$\text{thus} \tag{10.4}$$
$$inc_{(\text{sample})} = \frac{f_s}{f_{unity}} inc_{(\text{modulo})}$$

Note: if you are not using a modulo counter/increment timebase you could reduce the equation slightly as:

$$inc_{(\text{sample})} = \frac{f_o}{f_{unity}} \tag{10.5}$$

For a single-cycle sample, we can find the equivalent f_{unity} as:

$$f_{unity} = \frac{C}{N} f_s \tag{10.6}$$
$$C = \text{channel count}$$
$$N = \text{sample count}$$

For pitch-less samples, the table increment value is simply 1.0.

> Beware of *.wav* files that do not have the MIDI Unity Note encoded in them. We see these on occasion, sometimes from reputable loop companies. In these cases, the unity pitch is often coded in the file name, such as *piano_A1.wav*. You may use these kinds of files, but you will need to manually code the unity note number. Alternatively you can invest in audio software that will let you modify the embedded information and correct these incomplete files.

10.3 Multi-Samples

Sampling traditional musical instruments was common in the early days of sample based synthesis; this was a time when there was much focus on making synthesizers sound exactly like other instruments. The desire to mimic traditional instruments was also a prime motivator for the development of FM synthesis. A fundamental problem with sampling any type of pitched instrument, including another synthesizer, is that the formant ratios are not preserved when the playback ratio changes from unity. This gives the "chipmunk effect," which is unnatural and generally unwanted at high playback ratios. For very low playback ratios, the transient becomes smeared out in time, and the sample can sound grainy or noisy. Additionally, many musical instruments produce a variety of timbres such that the same note can sound vastly different when played loudly versus softly. The solution to this problem is to use brute force and capture many samples of sounds at a variety of pitches and a variety of amplitudes. This yields a set of samples known as multi-samples.

For sampling different pitches, you might decide to sample every single MIDI note (or as many as the instrument's range dictates). We used wavetables sampled in octaves for the non-sinusoidal waveforms in Chapter 5. A common strategy is to sample in minor thirds, typically *C*, *Eb*, *F#* and *A* across every octave in the instrument's range. Since aliasing is possible when the playback ratio is greater than 1.0, we can use another tactic of always shifting downward when possible. Figure 10.5 depicts this scheme; the *C* sample is used to playback the *Bb* and *B* below it. The *A* sample would be used for *Ab* and *G*, while *F#* would be used for *F* and *E*, etc. In this way, only two notes are ever pitch shifted versions. Another variation is to shift up on one side and down on the other side of the sampled note.

With a set of pitches established, you could then sample each note at multiple amplitudes, which would map to velocities in the synth. When sampling musical instruments, you need a talented musician capable of striking notes with the same force. This might result in

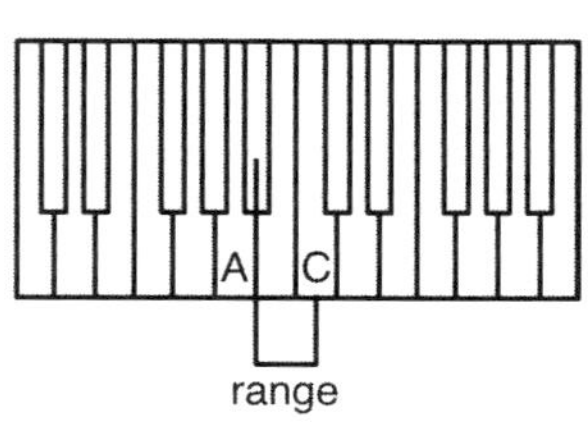

Figure 10.5: The *C* note is used to play the three notes; *Bb*, *B* and *C*.

a map of notes and velocities as shown in Figure 10.6, where the samples are taken every octave. Depending on the type of sound, you might use more or less samples over different velocity levels. If all the samples are pre-loaded into buffers, the logic is simple to select a sample given a target pitch and velocity.

10.4 Splits, Layers, and Note Regions

You can see the velocity layers depicted in Figure 10.6 clearly, and the range of each sample is one octave. Dividing the keyboard up like this allows for another option—splits and layers. These are often performed at the patch level but can also be employed at the sample (oscillator) level. Remember from the last chapter that the Korg H.I. synthesis voice uses two sets of samples labeled “High Velocity” and “Low Velocity”. A split refers to an arrangement where the keyboard is split into two or more sections at some note boundaries. The split point determines which patch is played. A layer is an area that two velocity levels define, which maps to a specific patch. A note region describes the note range of a split and velocity range of a layer simultaneously. Note regions may overlap in both split points and velocities. Figure 10.7 shows the keyboard divided into four different note regions corresponding to four different samples (or patches). You can see that they overlap in some places; overlapping note regions produce a mix of samples.

In DigiSynth, we use two stereo *CSampleOscillators*; each loads it buffers from a folder of multi-samples. Each *CSampleOscillator* has a note region that defines its boundaries. There are four voice modes:

- Osc 1
- Osc 2
- split
- layer

In Osc 2 and Osc 2 modes, only one multi-sample is played across the keyboard. The note number determines which sample is played and how much pitch shift is applied. The split and layer modes use the note regions to determine which sample is played and if multiple samples need to be mixed due to overlapping ranges. This give you a nice starting point for your own designs.

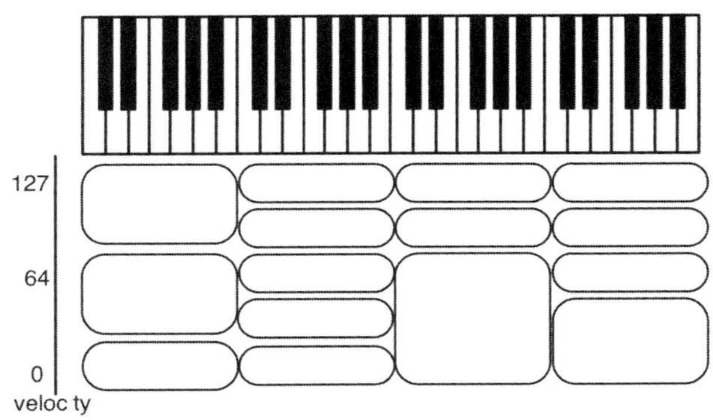

Figure 10.6: Each rounded box represents a single sample that covers a pitch range of one octave and a velocity range determined by the height.

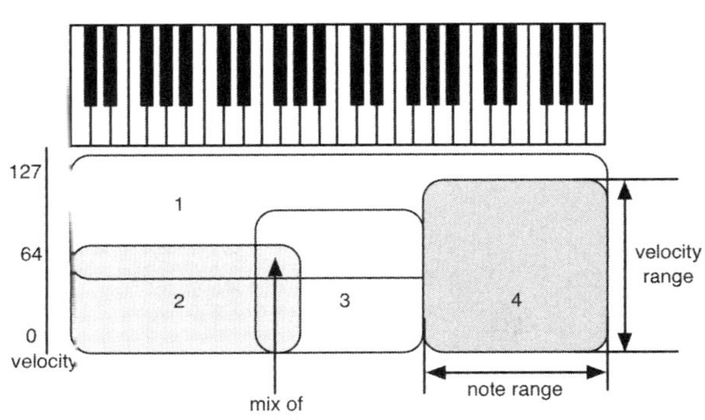

Figure 10.7: Four note regions; regions 2 and 4 are shaded for easier viewing.

10.5 The CWaveData Object

Let's have a look at the *CWaveData* object. Remember that its job is to crack open a *.wav* file and extract the audio into a floating point buffer. The object can handle files with any number of channels, though it is up to you to decode the interleaved samples. For stereo *.wav* files, the channels are coded L,R,L,R,L,R etc. *CWaveData* can open and read the following *.wav* file types on both Windows and MacOS:

- 16-bit signed integer
- 24-bit signed integer packed in three or four bytes
- 32-bit signed integer
- 32-bit floating point
- 64-bit double floating point

It does not read 8-bit files (though you could add that yourself fairly easily), and will only read PCM or uncompressed files. The industry standard for sample files has been 24-bit integer for a while, though that may change. The sample files for the synth are all 24-bit integer. You initialize the *CWaveData* object with a string that is the path for the *.wav* file. It opens the file and extracts the audio guts into a newly created floating point buffer. Once successful, you can access its member variables to get information about the sample, such as its MIDI Unity Note, MIDI Pitch Fraction, length, channel count, and so on. The object can be re-used to open multiple files, but the buffers will be destroyed and recreated with the new contents. We are going to use one object per *.wav* file in the oscillator object. You can find this object declaration in the *pluginconstants.h* file and the implementation in *pluginobjects.cpp*. If you are a seasoned RackAFX user, this object has been there all along, albeit undocumented. Table 10.1 shows the *CWaveData* member variable and functions.

SMPTE Format

0 no SMPTE offset
24 24 frames per second
25 25 frames per second
29 30 frames per second with frame dropping (30 drop)
30 30 frames per second

SMPTE Offset

"The SMPTE Offset value specifies the time offset to be used for the synchronization/calibration to the first sample in the waveform. This value uses a format of 0xhhmmssff where hh is a signed value that specifies the number of hours (−23 to 23), mm is an unsigned

Table 10.1: *CWaveData's* member variables give you all the information you need about the *.wav* file.

***CWaveData* Member Variables**		
Type	**Variable Name**	**Description**
float*	m_pWaveBufer	the buffer of audio data extracted from the *.wav* file
bool	m_bWaveLoaded	true if the object successfully opened and parsed the audio data
HANDLE	m_hFile	handle to the file (Windows only)—you can safely ignore it
UINT	m_uNumChannels	channel count
UINT	m_uSampleRate	sample rate of file
UINT	m_uSampleCount	total number of samples in file
UINT	m_uLoopCount	number of loops in file
UINT	m_uLoopStartIndex	start index of first loop
UINT	m_uLoopEndIndex	end index of first loop
UINT	m_uLoopType	Value Loop Type 0 Loop forward (normal) 1 Alternating loop (bckfrth) 2 Loop backward (reverse) 3-31 Reserved 32 Manufacturer Specific
UINT	m_uMIDINote	MIDI Unity Note number
UINT	m_uMIDIPitchFraction	MIDI pitch fraction
UINT	m_uSMPTEFormat	SMPTE format
UINT	m_uSMPTEOffset	SMPTE Offset

value that specifies the number of minutes (0 to 59), ss is an unsigned value that specifies the number of seconds (0 to 59) and ff is an unsigned value that specifies the number of frames (0 to −1)" (sonicspot.com, n.d.).

The *CWaveData* object only has two member functions and both involve the extraction of audio data. The Constructor is:

```
CWaveData(char* pFilePath = NULL);
```

If you pass a valid file path during construction, it will be used to locate and initialize the object all at once. If you pass a NULL pointer, the object is constructed, but the audio data array is not allocated.

```
bool initWithUserWAVFile(char* pInitDir = NULL);
```

The *initWithUserWAVEFile()* function is only available in the Windows version. When you call this function, a Windows File Open dialog appears, and you let the user browse to find the *.wav* file; you can suggest an initial directory as the argument or leave it blank to default to the current directory. We won't use this function in our synths, but you might come up with an interesting way to use it.

Using this object could not be simpler. Just construct it and pass the file path as the argument, then check the *m_bWaveLoaded* flag for success or failure.

```
// create the new object
m_pWaveSample = new CWaveData(pSamplePath);

// did we find the sample?
if(!m_pWaveSample->m_bWaveLoaded)
{
        // ERROR! FILE NOT LOADED
}
```

Iterating through the audio buffer requires that you check the channel count first; multi-channel files are interleaved.

10.6 The CSampleOscillator Object

This oscillator is used in the next three synth designs, so you need to understand it well. Since it is derived from *COscillator*, it features all the same functionality and function names for resetting, updating, rendering etc. The big difference, however, is in the way the object is initialized since it needs audio files to operate. This object was designed to operate in two modes: single-sample and multi-sample. In single-sample mode, you load only one *.wav* file, which is played across the range of notes. This is useful for pitch-less samples like sound effects and drums where you don't intend on shifting pitch, or loops that are likewise pitch-less. We will use multi-sample mode for DigiSynth and VectorSynth and single-sample mode for AniSynth.

> The multi-sample sets we use and that you receive with the book projects were distributed as royalty-free samples in a CD-ROM from *Computer Music* magazine Number 171 and designed by *Cyclick*. These are all stereo samples with the correct MIDI Unity Note information. As a free distribution, the sample designers give you three octaves of samples on minor third boundaries. These are all designed to work well in a bass synth application. Future Music Publishing grants full rights for commercial or non-commercial use, providing the samples are not sold as part of a sample library. If you like them, you might wish to contact *Cyclick* and purchase the rest of the samples in the sets.
> In all sample-based synths in this book, the quality of the synthesis ultimately depends on the quality of the samples. No amount of math or signal processing will fix poorly recorded or looped samples. I urge you to find your own suppliers and find the best sounding samples for the synth at hand. Many sample and loop suppliers will give you free samples if you sign up for a newsletter. Also, check magazines like *Future Music* that deliver gigabytes of royalty free samples and loops every month.

CSampleOscillator is initialized with a single file path in single sample-mode or a folder path in multi-sample mode. When using a folder to initialize multi-samples, *CSampleOscillator* finds every *.wav* file and opens it regardless of file name. *CSampleOscillator* stores its samples in two different manners corresponding to the two modes.

Single-Sample Mode

In this mode, the *.wav* file is opened and its contents are stored in the member variable:

```
CWaveData* m_pWaveSample;
```

You access its internal buffer simply:

```
m_pWaveSample->m_pWaveBuffer
```

Since this variable is a pointer, it is possible for multiple *CSampleOscillators* to share the same *CWaveData* object.

Multi-Sample Mode

In this mode, a set of *CWaveData* objects are constructed and pointers to each are stored in an array capable of holding 128 pointers:

```
CWaveData*  m_WaveSamplePtrArray[128];
```

The array index values correspond to MIDI note numbers, so you can theoretically populate the array with 128 samples taken on semitone boundaries. When playing back notes, the index value is used to extract the proper sample. Most likely you'll have far less than 128 samples, which would leave gaps in the array. To simplify using the array, we comb through it and replicate pointers in groups based on the idea in Figure 10.8. The samples we use are sampled on minor third boundaries *C*, *Eb*, *F#* and *A*. For example, for MIDI note 60 (middle *C*), the array would have the *CWaveData* pointer for the middle *C* file in slots 60, 59 and 58 corresponding to *C*, *Bb* and *B*. This is shown in Figure 10.8, which depicts a piece of the array. This makes selecting a wave data object easy—the MIDI note number is the index of the *CWaveData* object pointer in the array. Like the single sample operation, you can set up multiple *CSampleOscillators* to share a common array of wave objects via a pointer-to-a-pointer. We will use this option in VectorSynth and AniSynth. The very first and very last wave object pointers are copied into the extremes of the array; if the lowest note is 32, it will be used for all notes below it, down to MIDI note 0, while the highest note pointer will be used for all notes above it, up to MIDI note 127.

Table 10.2 lists the *CSampleOscillator's* member variables, and Table 10.3 lists the member functions and descriptions.

After first pass on folder

Note	Index	
F#	54	0x1234ABCD
G	55	0x00000000
Ab	56	0x00000000
A	57	0x1234AAAA
Bb	58	0x00000000
B	59	0x00000000
C	60	0x1234BBBB
Db	61	0x00000000
D	62	0x00000000
Eb	63	0x1234CCCC

After comb through

Note	Index	
F#	54	0x1234ABCD
G	55	0x1234AAAA
Ab	56	0x1234AAAA
A	57	0x1234AAAA
Bb	58	0x1234BBBB
B	59	0x1234BBBB
C	60	0x1234BBBB
Db	61	0x1234CCCC
D	62	0x1234CCCC
Eb	63	0x1234CCCC

Figure 10.8: After reading the multi-sample files, some slots in the array may be empty (NULL); the comb-through process replicates pointers for the groups of notes that share them.

Table 10.2: *CSampleOscillator* Member Variables.

***CSampleOscillator* Member Variables**		
Type	**Variable Name**	**Description**
CWaveData*	m_pWaveSample	wave sample object for single samples
CWaveData*	m_WaveSamplePtrArray[128]	wave sample object array for multi-samples
CWaveData**	m_ppWaveSamplePtrArray	a pointer to an array of *shared* wave sample objects (defaults to point to object's own array first)
bool	m_bSharedWaveSample	true if we are sharing a wave object with other *CSampleOscillators*
bool	m_bSharedWaveSamplePtrArray	true if we are sharing an array of wave objects with other *CSampleOscillators*
bool	m_bSingleCycleSample	set this before the file is loaded; true for single-cycle samples
bool	m_PitchlessSample	set this before the file is loaded; true for pitch-less samples
UINT	m_uLoopMode	looping mode
enum	sustain, loop, oneShot	enum for loop mode
double	m_dReadIndex	current read location; it is a double because we will most likely have fractional increment values
double	m_dLeftOutputSample	the current left output sample
double	m_dRightOutputSample	the current right output sample

Table 10.3: *CSampleOscillator* Member Functions.

***CSampleOscillator* Member Functions**	
Function Name	**Description**
initGlobalParameters	initialize the global parameters
update	update oscillator
reset	reset all variables
startOscillator	start the oscillator
stopOscillator	stop the oscillator
clearDestinations	clears the mod matrix destination array
addWaveSample	add a new multi-sample to the array
getNumChannels	returns number of *.wav* file channels
getSampleMIDINote	returns the MIDI Unity Note number from .wav file
sampleIsLoaded	true if sample is loaded
initWithFilePath	initialize a single sample with a *.wav* file path
initWithFolderPath	initialize a multi-sample with all *.wav* files in a folder
setWaveDataPtr	set the shared single sample data pointer
setWaveSamplePtrArray	set the shared multi sample data array pointer
readSampleBuffer	helper function to read a buffer with a given index and increment value
doOscillate	the audio render function

Let's look at the object's functions in more detail. Refer to the *CSampleOscillator.h* and *.cpp* files for the complete function definitions.

Constructor

The constructor nulls out all the wave data pointers and clears the pointer array, then it sets the default values for the object. Notice that the default loop mode is *sustain*, which is the normal transient-loop operation of audio samples.

```
CSampleOscillator::CSampleOscillator(void)
{
      // --- NULL
      m_pWaveSample = NULL;
```

```
        // --- clear the array
        memset(&m_WaveSamplePtrArray[0], 0, sizeof(CWaveData*)*128);

        // --- this is to allow the array to be shared
        m_ppWaveSamplePtrArray = &m_WaveSamplePtrArray[0];

        // --- clear outputs
        m_dLeftOutputSample = 0.0;
        m_dRightOutputSample = 0.0;

        // --- reset read index to top of buffer (address 0)
        m_dReadIndex = 0.0;

        // --- set defaults
        m_bSingleCycleSample = false;
        m_bPitchlessSample = false;
        m_bSharedWaveSample = false;
        m_bSharedWaveSamplePtrArray = false;
        m_uLoopMode = sustain; // default loop mode
}
```

initGlobalParameters()

This is the usual global parameter initialization function where you first call the base class then initialize any object-specific globals. There is a new global parameter for oscillators called *uLoopMode* that establishes our looping mechanism.

update()

This function calculates the new read index increment value, depending on the oscillator's pitch after first checking to make sure there is either a single sample or multi-samples. Notice the logic there—it is used repeatedly in the rest of the object:

```
void CSampleOscillator::update()
{
        // --- this calculates the modulated pitch
        COscillator::update();

        // --- Global Parameters
        if(m_pGlobalOscParams)
        {
                m_uLoopMode = m_pGlobalOscParams->uLoopMode;
        }

        // --- check sample
        CWaveData* pSample = m_pWaveSample;
        if(!pSample)
                pSample = m_pWaveSamplePtrArray[m_uMIDINoteNumber];

        if(!pSample) return;

        // --- pitch-less is simple
        if(m_bPitchlessSample)
```

```
        {
                m_dInc = 1.0;
                return;
        }

        // --- get unity note frequency
        double dUnityFrequency = m_bSingleCycleSample ?
        (m_cSampleRate/(pSample->m_uSampleCount/pSample->m_uNumChannels)) :
        midiFreqTable[pSample->m_uMIDINote];

        // equivalent length
        double dLength = m_dSampleRate/dUnityFrequency;

        // calculate increment
        // inc = L(fo/fs) = L(inc)
        m_dInc *= dLength;
}
```

reset()

This function simply clears the output variables and resets the read index to 0 (top of buffer).

```
void CSampleOscillator::reset()
{
        // --- base class first
        COscillator::reset();

        // --- clear outputs
        m_dLeftOutputSample = 0.0;
        m_dRightOutputSample = 0.0;

        // --- reset read index to top of buffer (address 0)
        m_dReadIndex = 0.0;

        //---  update
        update();
}
```

startOscillator() and *stopOscillator()*

These are identical to all other oscillators—just set/clear the note on flag and *reset()* if needed.

addWaveSample()

This is a helper function that simplifies coding when looping through files; it simply creates the object with the supplied file path and adds the pointer to the array. If the *nMIDINoteNumber* argument is −1, then there is no MIDI Unity Note information.

```
bool CSampleOscillator::addWaveSample(char* pSamplePath, int nMIDINoteNumber)
{
        // --- create the new object
        CWaveData* pSample = new CWaveData(pSamplePath);
```

```
        // --- has MIDI Note number?
        if(pSample && nMIDINoteNumber < 0)
                nMIDINoteNumber = pSample->m_uMIDINote;

        // --- add to wave table list
        m_pWaveSamplePtrArray[nMIDINoteNumber] = pSample;

        return true;
}
```

getNumChannels() and *getMIDISampleNote()* and *sampleIsLoaded()*

These are self-explanatory; the new *CDigiSynthVoice* object will use them for queries.

initWithFilePath()

This function initializes the *m_pWaveSample* pointer with a freshly created *CWaveData* object. It also clears the shared data flag.

```
bool CSampleOscillator::initWithFilePath(char* pSamplePath)
{
        // --- destroy if existing
        if(m_pWaveSample)
                delete m_pWaveSample;

        // --- create the new object
        m_pWaveSample = new CWaveData(pSamplePath);

        // --- did we find the sample?
        if(!m_pWaveSample->m_bWaveLoaded)
        {
                delete m_pWaveSample;
                m_pWaveSample = NULL;
                return false;
        }

        // --- not sharing if we just created it
        m_bSharedWaveSample = false;

        return true;
}
```

initWithFolderPath()

This function initializes the array of wave data objects with a folder full of *.wav* files and implements the comb-through procedure to set up the array for use. The details of locating the files are OS specific and are removed for easier reading here. Notice that we store the pointer to our array in case another object wants to share it.

```
bool CSampleOscillator::initWithFolderPath(char* pSampleFolderPath)
{
```

```
	// clear out
	if(!m_bSharedWaveSamplePtrArray)
	{
		CWaveData* pSample = NULL;
		CWaveData* pDeletedSample = NULL;
		for(int i=0; i<127; i++)
		{
			if(m_WaveSamplePtrArray[i])
			{
				pSample = m_WaveSamplePtrArray[i];
				if(pSample != pDeletedSample)
				{
					pDeletedSample = pSample;
					delete pSample;
				}
				m_WaveSamplePtrArray[i] = NULL;
			}
		}
	}

	// --- iterate through the .wav files in the folder
	for()…
	{
		// call sub-function to add the files
		if(success) addWaveSample(path);

		// delete path
		delete [] path;
	}

	// --- now comb the array and replicate pointers

	<SNIP SNIP SNIP>

	// --- this is to allow the array to be shared
	m_pWaveSamplePtrArray = &m_WaveSamplePtrArray[0];

	// --- can't be sharing anyone else's
	m_bSharedWaveSamplePtrArray = false;

	return true;
}
```

setWaveDataPtr()

This function sets up sharing for single samples—it copies the new data pointer and sets the sharing flag to true.

```
bool CSampleOscillator::setWaveDataPtr(CWaveData* pWaveData)
{
     // --- have sample?
     if(!pWaveData)
            return false;

     // --- just copy the pointer
     m_pWaveSample = pWaveData;

     // --- we are sharing so set flag
     m_bSharedWaveSample = true;

     return true;
}
```

setWaveSamplePtrArray()

This function sets up sharing for multi-samples—it copies the new data pointer and sets the sharing flag to true.

```
bool CSampleOscillator::setWaveSamplePtrArray(CWaveData**
                                              ppWaveSamplePtrArray)
{
     // --- test
     if(!ppWaveSamplePtrArray)
            return false;

     // --- just copy it
     m_pWaveSamplePtrArray = ppWaveSamplePtrArray;

     // --- flag so we don't delete
     m_bSharedWaveSamplePtrArray = true;

     return true;
}
```

readSampleBuffer()

This function reads and interpolates samples from a wave data buffer. It handles both mono and stereo file buffers and uses the same technique you saw in the *CWaveTable* object. It is nearly identical in core operation. If mono, it writes the left channel to the right output. You will see that this function mainly deals with indexing and bookkeeping and treats the buffer like a wave table.

```
void CSampleOscillator::readSampleBuffer(CWaveData* pWaveSample,
                                         double& dReadIndex, double dInc,
                                         double& dLeftSample,
                                         double& dRightSample)
{
     // --- wavetable reads; starting with left channel
     int nReadIndex = (int)dReadIndex;

     // --- get FRAC part
     float fFrac = dReadIndex - nReadIndex;
```

```
    // --- mono or stereo file? CURRENTLY ONLY SUPPORTING THESE 2
    if(pWaveSample->m_uNumChannels == 1)
    {
            // setup second index for interpolation;
            // wrap the buffer if needed
            int nReadIndexNext = nReadIndex + 1 >
                   pWaveSample->m_uSampleCount-1 ? 0 :  nReadIndex + 1;

            // interpolate between the two
            dLeftSample = dLinTerp(0, 1, pWaveSample->
                        m_pWaveBuffer[nReadIndex], pWaveSample->
                        m_pWaveBuffer[nReadIndexNext], fFrac);
            dRightSample = dLeftSample;

            // inc for next time
            dReadIndex += dInc;
    }
    else if(pWaveSample->m_uNumChannels == 2)
    {
            // --- interpolate across interleaved buffer!
            int nReadIndexLeft = (int)dReadIndex * 2;

            // --- setup second index for interpolation;
            //      wrap the buffer if needed, we know last sample is Right
            //      channel so reset to top (the 0 after ?)
            int nReadIndexNextLeft = nReadIndexLeft + 2 >
                  pWaveSample->m_uSampleCount-1 ? 0 :  nReadIndexLeft + 2;

            // --- interpolate between the two
            dLeftSample = dLinTerp(0, 1, pWaveSample->
                        m_pWaveBuffer[nReadIndexLeft],
                        pWaveSample->m_pWaveBuffer[nReadIndexNextLeft],
                        fFrac);

            // --- do the right channel
            int nReadIndexRight = nReadIndexLeft + 1;

            // --- find the next one, skipping over,
            //      note wrap goes to index 1 ---> 1
            int nReadIndexNextRight = nReadIndexRight + 2 >
                  pWaveSample->m_uSampleCount-1 ? 1 :  nReadIndexRight + 2;

            // --- interpolate between the two
            dRightSample = dLinTerp(0, 1, pWaveSample->
                    m_pWaveBuffer[nReadIndexRight], pWaveSample->
                    m_pWaveBuffer[nReadIndexNextRight], fFrac);

            // --- inc for next time
            dReadIndex += dInc;
    }
}
```

doOscillate()

The render function makes use of the helper function above, which handles the details of reading and interpolating the audio data. The *doOscillate()* function primarily handles wrapping and looping of the read index value. It uses the start and end loop values for the sustain loop mode. For one-shot mode, once the sample plays through a single time, the read index is set to −1; this is the flag to exit the function and return the 0.0 samples we cleared. If the file has no loops, sustain mode is treated like one-shot.

In loop mode, the wrapping code works just like the *CWaveTable* object. In sustain mode, the read index is calculated using the loop start and end points, and a wrap is occurring when you move outside the end-loop sample, so the logic is:

```
if(m_dReadIndex > (double)(pSample->m_uLoopEndIndex)/dChannels)
```

For a wrap event, the new read index is calculated with:

$$\text{readIndex} = \text{readIndex} - \frac{\text{endLoopPoint}}{C} + \frac{\text{startLoopPoint}}{C} \qquad (10.8)$$
$$C = \text{number of channels in file data}$$

```
double CSampleOscillator::doOscillate(double* pAuxOutput)
{
      // --- clear in case of no sample
      m_dLeftOutputSample = 0.0;
      m_dRightOutputSample = 0.0;
      if(pAuxOutput) *pAuxOutput = 0.0;

      // --- get the sample pointer
      CWaveData* pSample = m_pWaveSample;
      if(!pSample)
             pSample = m_pWaveSamplePtrArray[m_uMIDINoteNumber];

      // --- check and bail if no sample loaded
      if(!pSample || !m_bNoteOn)
             return 0.0;

      // --- one-shot sample
      if(m_dReadIndex < 0)
             return 0.0;

      // --- do the buffer read operation
      readSampleBuffer(pSample, m_dReadIndex, m_dInc,
                       m_dLeftOutputSample, m_dRightOutputSample);

      // --- channel count
      double dChannels = (double)pSample->m_uNumChannels;

      // --- check for wrap
      if(pSample->m_uLoopCount > 0)
      {
             // --- use loop points for looping
             if(m_uLoopMode == sustain)
```

```
        {
                if(m_dReadIndex > (double)(pSample->m_uLoopEndIndex)/
                   dChannels)
                        m_dReadIndex = m_dReadIndex -
                               (double)(pSample->m_uLoopEndIndex)/dChannels +
                               (double)(pSample->m_uLoopStartIndex)/dChannels;
        }
        else if(m_uLoopMode == loop) // use end->start samples
        {
                if(m_dReadIndex > (double)(pSample->m_uSampleCount -
                   dChannels - 1)/dChannels)
                       m_dReadIndex = 0.0;
        }
        else if(m_uLoopMode == oneShot) // read index = -1 flag
        {
                if(m_dReadIndex > (double)(pSample->m_uSampleCount -
                   dChannels - 1)/dChannels)
                      m_dReadIndex = -1;
        }
}

// --- if no loop count, treat sustain like one-shot
if(pSample->m_uLoopCount == 0)
{
        if(m_uLoopMode == oneShot || m_uLoopMode == sustain)
        {
                if(m_dReadIndex > (double)(pSample->m_uSampleCount -
                   dChannels - 1)/dChannels)
                       m_dReadIndex = -1;
        }
        else if(m_uLoopMode == loop) // use end->start samples
        {
                if(m_dReadIndex > (double)(pSample->m_uSampleCount -
                   dChannels - 1)/dChannels)
                       m_dReadIndex = 0.0;
        }
}

// --- write to outputs
if(m_pModulationMatrix)
{
        // --- write our outputs into their destinations
        m_pModulationMatrix->m_dSources[m_uModDestOutput1] =
                          m_dLeftOutputSample*m_dAmplitude*m_dAmpMod;

        // --- CSampleOscillator is stereo!
        m_pModulationMatrix->m_dSources[m_uModDestOutput2] =
                          m_dRightOutputSample*m_dAmplitude*m_dAmpMod;
}
```

```
    // --- aux is right
    if(pAuxOutput)
            *pAuxOutput = m_dRightOutputSample*m_dAmplitude*m_dAmpMod;

    // --- for stand alone use
    return m_dLeftOutputSample*m_dAmplitude*m_dAmpMod;
}
```

10.7 Audio File Location

Our sample-based synths are going to require either single samples or folders of samples, and the plug-in will need to know where these files are located. Some options include hardcoding the location, using an installer to write the location in a secret file or the registry, or using some other method of letting the DLL know the sample file/folder location. An easy way to simplify this problem without the need for reading the registry or secret files is to place the files/folders in the same directory as the DLL (or component if AU), or in a preset sub-directory of this folder. The reason is that in both Windows and MacOS, you can query the OS to get the location of the DLL/component, regardless of the location of the application that is using it.

> All sample-based synths in this book will use the DLL or component folder to store samples. The samples themselves will be in sub-directories of two central folders called /Samples and /MultiSamples.

Finding the DLL/Component folder is easy, so place your audio samples in this folder now:

RackAFX: open the software and use *PlugIn->Open PlugIns Folder* to find the ..\PlugIns folder
VST3: this is the same as the VST folder you setup in your VST3 client
AU: ~/Library/Audio/Plug-Ins/Components

At run-time, you use various functions to locate the DLL or component's folder.

RackAFX:
CPlugIn::getMyDLLDirectory(), found in *PlugIn.cpp*

VST3:
VSTSynthProcessor::getMyDLLDirectory(), found in *VSTSynthProcessor.h*

AU:
getMyComponentDirectory(), globally declared at the top of *AUSynth.h*

Single-Sample Example

Here is an example of initializing a *CSampleOscillator* with a single-sample called *FuzzVibeA1.wav* in each plug-in API. Individual samples are in a directory called \Samples.

RackAFX

Notice the use of the *addStrings()* helper; this is the same one you learned about in Chapter 3 when we logged MIDI events with the status window. You must always delete the string that *addStrings()* returns.

```
// --- get path
char* pPath = addStrings(getMyDLLDirectory(),"\\Samples\\FuzzVibeA1.wav");
```

VST3

In VST3, the function requires that you pass it the name of the plug-in's DLL file, then you use *addStrings()* like RackAFX. You must always delete the string that *addStrings()* returns.

```
// --- get path
char* pDLLPath = getMyDLLDirectory(USTRING("DigiSynth.vst3"));
char* pPath = addStrings(pDLLPath,"\\Samples\\FuzzVibeA1.wav");
```

AU

In AU, the function requires that you pass it the bundle ID that you set up for each project, then you use *addStrings()* like RackAFX. You must always delete the string that *addStrings()* returns.

```
// --- get path
char* componentFolder = getMyComponentDirectory(
                        CFSTR("developer.audiounit.yourname.digisynth"));

char* pPath = addStrings(componentFolder,"/Samples/FuzzVibeA1.wav");
```

With the path established, the code is identical in each API to initialize the oscillators:

```
// --- init
pSampleOsc->initWithFilePath(pPath);

// --- delete path
delete [] pPath;
```

Multi-Sample Example

Here is an example of initializing a *CSampleOscillator* with a multi-sample from a folder named *OldFlatty*, which is located in the \MultiSamples folder.

RackAFX

```
// --- get path
char* pPath = addStrings(getMyDLLDirectory(),"\\MultiSamples\\OldFlatty");
```

VST3

```
// --- get path
char* pDLLPath = getMyDLLDirectory(USTRING("DigiSynth.vst3"));
char* pPath = addStrings(pDLLPath,"\\MultiSamples\\OldFlatty");
```

AU

```
// --- get path
char* componentFolder = getMyComponentDirectory(
                        CFSTR("developer.audiounit.yourname.digisynth"));

char* pPath = addStrings(componentFolder,"/MultiSamples/OldFlatty");
```

With the path established, the code is identical in each API to initialize the oscillators:

```
// --- init
pSampleOsc->initWithFolderPath(pPath);

// --- delete path
delete [] pPath;
```

10.8 DigiSynth Specifications

The architecture for DigiSynth is nearly identical to that of MiniSynth, making it easy for you to re-use your GUI and other coding. The only differences are that DigiSynth uses two oscillators instead of four, each oscillator has an amplitude control, there is no pulse width control, it uses split and layer voice modes and it has a loop mode you can play with. The loop mode allows you to experiment with different looping files. Figure 10.9 shows the simplified block diagram and Figure 10.10 shows the detailed connection graph. One thing that is apparent in both is that the oscillators are stereo and require two filters, one for each channel. The oscillators and filters chosen for the design are:

Oscillators: two *CSampleOscillators*
Filters: two *CSEMFilters*, one for left and another for right, NLP engaged (ON)

noteRegion

The *noteRegion* structure contains the note and velocity range information for a note region. DigiSynth needs a note region structure for each oscillator. The default range settings are shown in Figure 10.1. Notice that they overlap in both velocity and note ranges.

```
struct noteRegion
{
      // --- note range of the Region
      UINT uMIDINoteLow;
      UINT uMIDINoteHigh;

      // --- velocity range of the Region
      UINT uMIDIVelocityLow;
      UINT uMIDIVelocityHigh;
};
```

Voice Mode

In DigiSynth the *m_uVoiceMode* variable has four choices, shown in Table 10.4. Figure 10.12 shows the arrangement for split and layer modes. In split mode, some notes overlap, while in layer mode, some velocities overlap. In these cases, both oscillators are mixed.

Table 10.5 shows the DigiSynth modulation matrix, and Table 10.6 shows the GUI control list. The modulation matrix is the same as MiniSynth, but without the LFO to pulse width modulation routing. The default modulation connections that are handled in the *CVoice* base class are not listed.

Figures 10.13 and 10.14 show the GUIs for the RackAFX and VST3/AU projects.

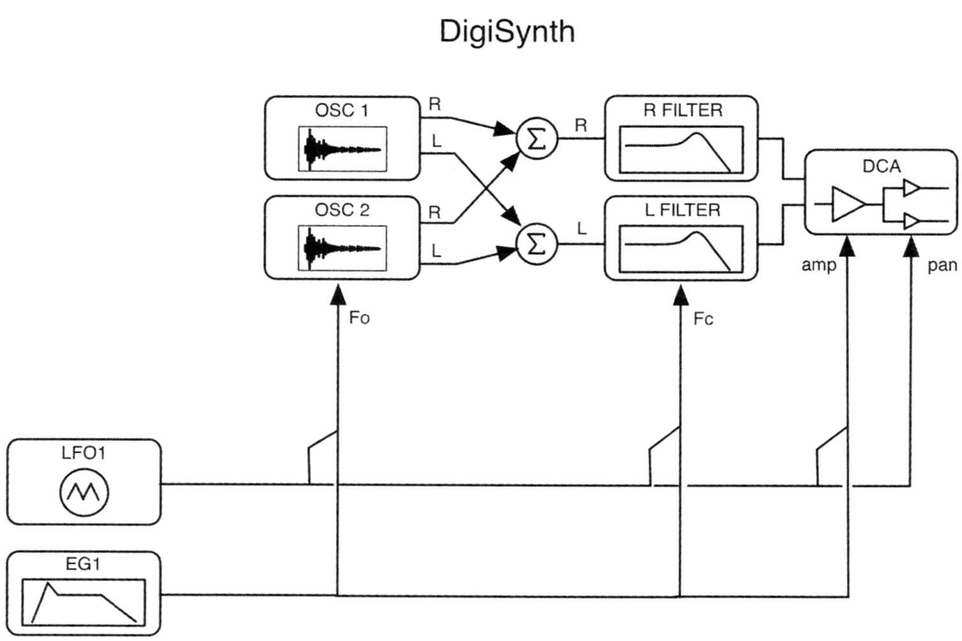

Figure 10.9: DigiSynth simplified block diagram.

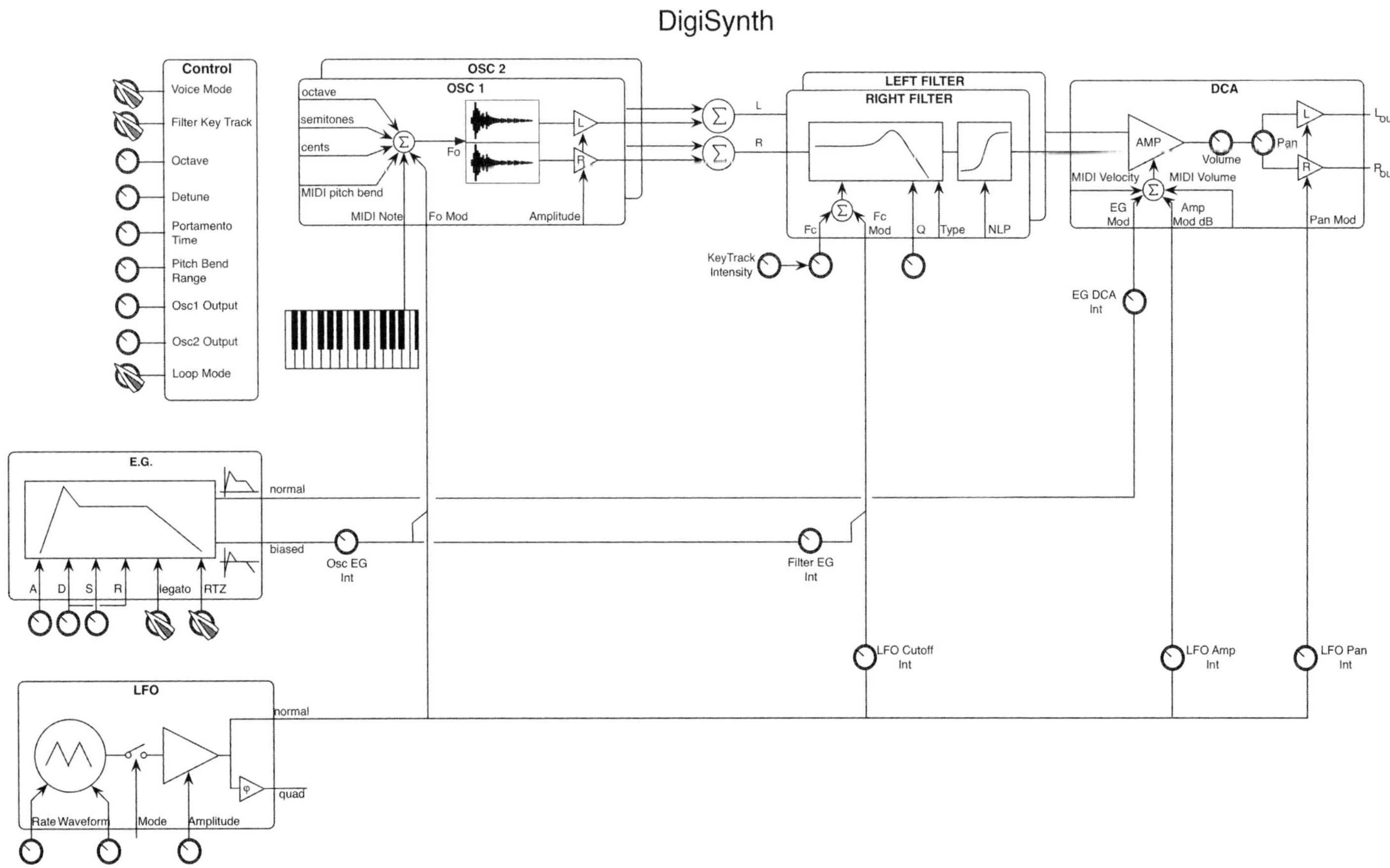

Figure 10.10: DigiSynth detailed connection graph.

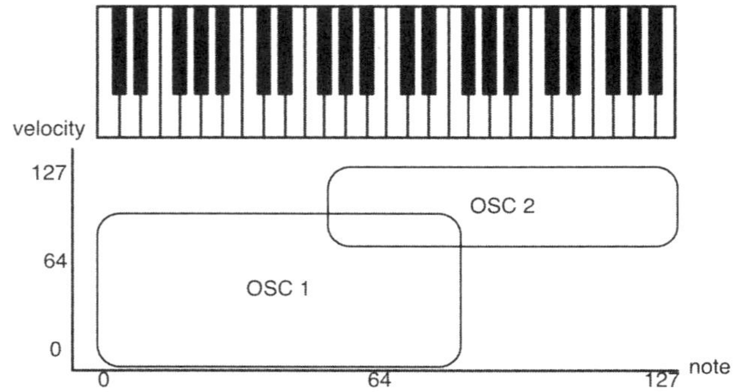

Figure 10.11: Note regions for the two oscillators in DigiSynth.

Table 10.4: Voice Modes for DigiSynth.

Voice Mode	Description
Osc 1	Osc 1 plays over the full range of the keyboard
Osc 2	Osc 2 plays over the full range of the keyboard
Split	Osc 1 plays from note 0 to note 70, all velocities Osc 2 plays from note 60 to 127, all velocities In the overlap region between notes 60 and 70, both oscillators play
Layer	Osc 1 plays from velocity 0 to 100, all notes Osc 2 plays from velocity 70 to 127, all notes In the overlap region between velocity 70 and 100, both oscillators play

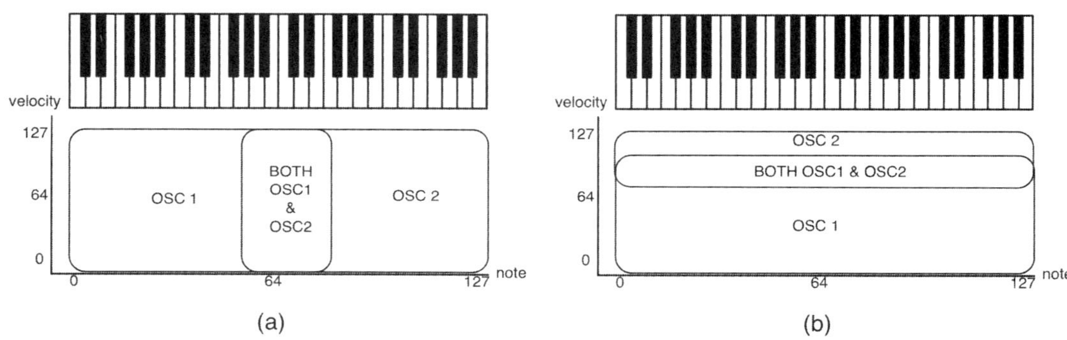

Figure 10.12: DigiSynth's (a) split and (b) layer modes.

Table 10.5: The modulation matrix for DigiSynth is nearly identical to MiniSynth.

***DigiSynth* Modulation Matrix**			
Source	**Destination/Intensity**	**Transform/Range**	**enabled**
SOURCE_LFO1	DEST_ALL_OSC_FO	TRANSFORM_NONE	TRUE
	dLFO1OscModIntensity	dOscFoModRange	
SOURCE_BIASED_EG1	DEST_ALL_FILTER_FC	TRANSFORM_NONE	TRUE
	dEG1Filter1ModIntensity	dFilterModRange	
SOURCE_EG1	DEST_DCA_EG	TRANSFORM_NONE	TRUE
	dEG1DCAAmpModIntensity	m_dDefaultModRange	
SOURCE_BIASED_EG1	DEST_ALL_OSC_FO	TRANSFORM_NONE	TRUE
	dEG1OscModIntensity	dOscFoModRange	
SOURCE_LFO1	DEST_ALL_FILTER_FC	TRANSFORM_NONE	TRUE
	dLFO1Filter1ModIntensity	dFilterModRange	
SOURCE_LFO1	DEST_DCA_AMP	TRANSFORM_BIPOLAR_TO_UNIPOLAR	TRUE
	dLFO1DCAAmpModIntensity	dAmpModRange	
SOURCE_LFO1	DEST_DCA_PAN	TRANSFORM_NONE	TRUE
	dLFO1DCAPanModIntensity	m_dDefaultModRange	

Table 10.6: DigiSynth GUI Control List.

***DigiSynth* Continuous Parameters**				
Control Name (units)	**Type**	**Variable Name (VST3, RAFX)**	**Low/Hi/Default ***	**VST3/AU Index**
Noise Osc (dB)	double	m_dNoiseOsc_dB	-96 / 0 / 0	NOISE_OSC_AMP_DB
Osc EG Int	double	m_dEG1OscIntensity	-1 / 0 / 1	EG1_TO_OSC_INTENSITY
Filter fc (Hz) volt/octave	double	m_dFcControl	80 / 18000 / 10000	FILTER_FC
Filter Q	double	m_dQControl	1 / 10 / 1	FILTER_Q
Filter EG Int	double	m_dEG1FilterIntensity	-1 / 0 / 1	EG1_TO_FILTER_INTENSITY
Key Track Int	double	m_dFilterKeyTrackIntensity	0.5 / 10 / 1	FILTER_KEYTRACK_INTENSITY
Attack (mS)	double	m_dAttackTime_mSec	0 / 5000 / 100	EG1_ATTACK_MSEC
Decay/Release (mS)	double	m_dDecayReleaseTime_mSec	0 / 10000 / 1000	EG1_DECAY_RELEASE_MSEC
Sustain	double	m_dSustainLevel	0 / 1 / 0.707	EG1_SUSTAIN_LEVEL
LFO Rate	double	m_dLFO1Rate	0.02 / 20 / 0.5	LFO1_RATE
LFO Depth	double	m_dLFO1Amplitude	0 / 1 / 0	LFO1_AMPLITUDE
LFO Cutoff Int	double	m_dLFO1FilterFcIntensity	-1 / 1 / 0	LFO1_TO_FILTER_INTENSITY
LFO Pitch Int	double	m_dLFO1OscPitchIntensity	-1 / 1 / 0	LFO1_TO_OSC_INTENSITY
LFO Amp Int	double	m_dLFO1AmpIntensity	0 / 1 / 0	LFO1_TO_DCA_INTENSITY
LFO Pan Int	double	m_dLFO1PanIntensity	0 / 1 / 0	LFO1_TO_PAN_INTENSITY
Volume	double	m_dVolume_dB	-96 / 20 / 0	OUTPUT_AMPLITUDE_DB
DCA EG Int	double	m_dEG1DCAIntensity	-1 / 1 / 1	EG1_TO_DCA_INTENSITY
Detune	double	m_dDetune_cents	-100 / 100 / 0	DETUNE_CENTS
Portamento (mS)	double	m_dPortamentoTime_mSec	0 / 5000 / 0	PORTAMENTO_TIME_MSEC
Osc 1 Output	double	m_dOsc1Amplitude_dB	-96 / 24 / 0	OSC1_AMPLITUDE_DB
Osc2 Output	double	m_dOsc2Amplitude_dB	-96 / 24 / 0	OSC2_AMPLITUDE_DB
Octave	int	m_nOctave	-4 / 4 / 0	OCTAVE
PBendRange (semi)	int	m_nPitchBendRange	0 / 12 / 1	PITCHBEND_RANGE
* low, high and default values are #defined for VST3 and AU in *SynthParamLimits.h* for each project				

***DigiSynth* Enumerated String Parameters (UINT)**			
Control Name	**Variable Name**	**enum String**	**VST3/AU Index**
LFO Waveform	m_uLFO1Waveform	sine,usaw,dsaw,tri, square,expo,rsh,qrsh	LFO1_WAVEFORM
Voice Mode	m_uVoiceMode	Osc1,Osc2,split,layer	VOICE_MODE
Loop Mode	m_uLoopMode	sustain,loop,oneShot	LOOP_MODE
Vel->Att Scale	m_uVelocityToAttackScaling	OFF,ON	VELOCITY_TO_ATTACK
Note->Dcy Scale	m_uNoteNumberToDecayScaling	OFF,ON	NOTE_NUM_TO_DECAY
Reset to Zero	m_uResetToZero	OFF,ON	RESET_TO_ZERO
Filter KeyTrack	m_uFilterKeyTrack	OFF,ON	FILTER_KEYTRACK
Legato Mode	m_uLegatoMode	OFF,ON	LEGATO_MODE

RackAFX: in the DigiSynth sample project, the following controls are located inside the RackAFX LCD Control in this order:

- Volume
- Legato Mode
- Reset To Zero
- PBend Range
- Filter KeyTrack
- KeyTrack Int
- Vel->Att Scale
- Note->Dcy Scale

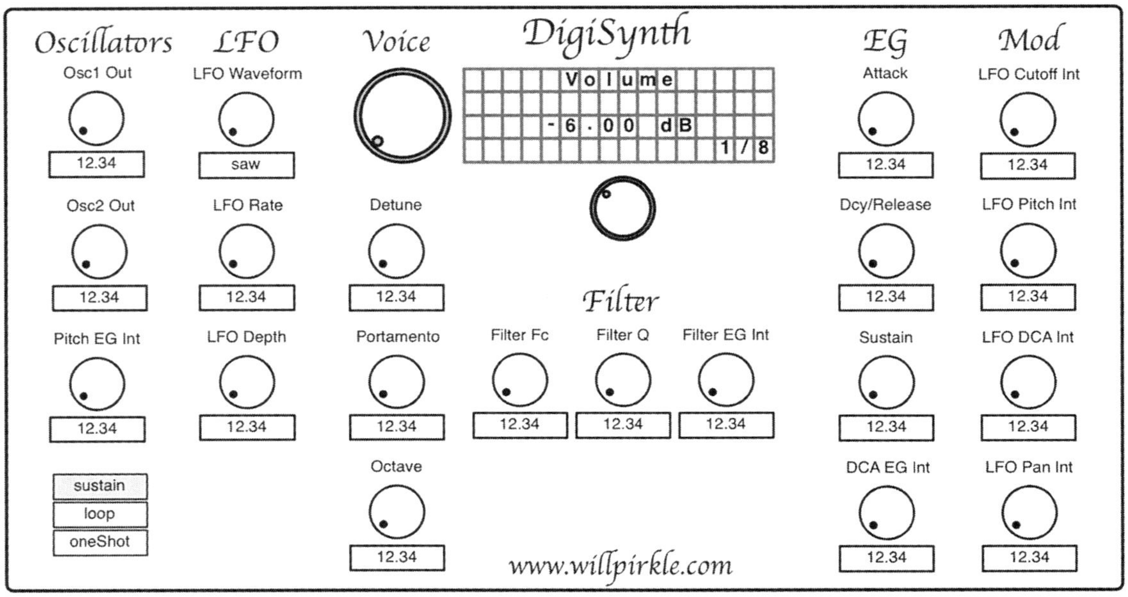

Figure 10.13: One possible DigiSynth GUI in RackAFX; notice that several controls are embedded in the LCD control.

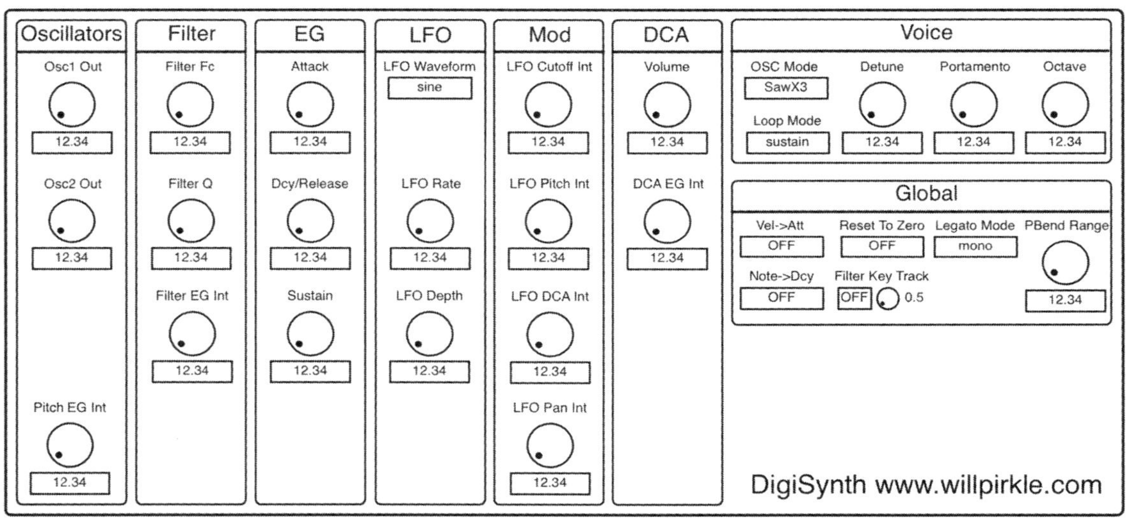

Figure 10.14: The DigiSynth GUI for the VST3 and AU projects.

VST3/AU: the limits and defaults are *#defined* in *SynthParamLimits.h* for each project; the VST3/AU index values are enumerated in the same file. For AU, the order doesn't matter. For VST3, however, the order must match the Tags in VSTGUI—if you add your own controls, be sure not to disturb the present indexing; add new index values after the last entry in the enumeration, but before the total-synth-parameters value.

10.9 The CDigiSynthVoice Object

The *CDigiSynthVoice* object implements the audio rendering; however, much of the object is devoted to initializing the oscillators either directly with files or folders or via sample and array sharing. The voice object provides both *get* and *set* access to the sample and array pointers. The *CDigiSynthVoice* object is set up to access all four oscillators, though we only use two in this design. We will use all four of them in VectorSynth and AniSynth. Table 10.7 lists the member variables, and Table 10.8 lists the member functions. By now, these should look familiar.

Table 10.7: *CDigiSynthVoice* member variables.

***CDigiSynthVoice* Member Variables**		
Type	**Variable Name**	**Description**
CSampleOscillator	m_Osc1, m_Osc2	the two oscillators
CSEMFilter	m_LeftSEMFilter, m_RightSEMFilter	filters for left and right channels
noteRegion	m_Osc1NoteRegion, m_Osc2NoteRegion	note region structures for the two oscillators
enum	Osc1,Osc2,split,layer	enum for Voice Mode decoding

Table 10.8: *CDigiSynthVoice* member functions.

***CDigiSynthVoice* Member Functions**	
Function Name	**Description**
initGlobalParameters	initialize the globals
initializeModMatrix	initialize the modulation matrix
setSampleRate	set sample rate on sub-components
prepareForPlay	prepareForPlay on sub-components, one time init
update	update voice variables
reset	reset voice variables
inOscSplitRange	given an oscillator index (0,1,2,3), determine if our MIDI note is in its split range
inOscVelocityRange	given an oscillator index (0,1,2,3), determine if our MIDI velocity is in its velocity range
isOscSingleCycle	given an oscillator index (0,1,2,3), returns true if the oscillator has a single-cycle sample loaded
getOscWaveData	given an oscillator index (0,1,2,3), returns the pointer to that oscillator's *m_pWaveSample* object
getOscWaveSamplePtrArray	given an oscillator index (0,1,2,3), returns the pointer to that oscillator's *m_WaveSamplePtrArray* object
initOscWithFilePath	initialize a *CSampleOscillator* with a single file
initOscWithFolderPath	initialize a *CSampleOscillator* with a multi-sample set from a folder
initAllOscWithDigiSynthVoice	shares all oscillator wave data pointers with a given *CDigiSynthVoice* object
doVoice	render the audio

The voice object's member variables are self-explanatory, so lets focus on the member functions, some of which are nearly identical to the *CMiniSynthVoice* object from the last chapter.

Constructor

The constructor performs the following initializations, some of which you may modify:

- connects oscillators to member pointers
- connects the filters to member pointers
- turns on NLP on filters (optional)
- set EG mode to analog (optional)
- set EG1 output flag
- set the DCA EG mod source for EG1 (important—must always be done in derived class constructor!)

```
CDigiSynthVoice::CDigiSynthVoice(void)
{
      // --- declare your oscillators and filters
      m_pOsc1 = &m_Osc1;
      m_pOsc2 = &m_Osc2;
      m_pOsc3 = NULL;
      m_pOsc4 = NULL;

      m_pFilter1 = &m_LeftSEMFilter;
      m_pFilter2 = &m_RightSEMFilter;
```

```
        // --- set note regions for oscillators
        m_Osc1NoteRegion.uMIDINoteLow = 0;
        m_Osc1NoteRegion.uMIDINoteHigh = 72;
        m_Osc1NoteRegion.uMIDIVelocityLow = 0;
        m_Osc1NoteRegion.uMIDIVelocityHigh = 100;

        m_Osc2NoteRegion.uMIDINoteLow = 60;
        m_Osc2NoteRegion.uMIDINoteHigh = 127;
        m_Osc2NoteRegion.uMIDIVelocityLow = 70;
        m_Osc2NoteRegion.uMIDIVelocityHigh = 127;

        // --- setup filters
        m_LeftSEMFilter.m_uNLP = ON;
        m_RightSEMFilter.m_uNLP = ON;

        // --- set EG
        m_EG1.setEGMode(analog);
        m_EG1.m_bOutputEG = true; // our DCA EG

        // --- DCA Setup: set the source EG here
        m_DCA.m_uModSourceEG = DEST_DCA_EG;
    }
```

initGlobalParameters()

This function is nearly identical to the one in *CMiniSynthVoice*; the operation is the same—call the base class, and then initialize the sub-components (oscillators and filters) and intensity values (these are same as MiniSynth).

```
    inline virtual void initGlobalParameters(globalSynthParams* pGlobalParams)
    {
        // --- always call base class first
        CVoice::initGlobalParameters(pGlobalParams);

        // --- add any CThisVoice specific variables here
        if(m_pOsc1)((CSampleOscillator*)m_pOsc1)->initGlobalParameters
                                        (&pGlobalParams->osc1Params);
        if(m_pOsc2)((CSampleOscillator*)m_pOsc2)->initGlobalParameters
                                        (&pGlobalParams->osc2Params);

        <SNIP SNIP SNIP>

        if(m_pFilter1)((CSEMFilter*)m_pFilter1)->initGlobalParameters
                                (&pGlobalParams->filter1Params);
        if(m_pFilter2)((CSEMFilter*)m_pFilter2)->initGlobalParameters
                                (&pGlobalParams->filter2Params);

        // NOTE: we only set the intensities we use in THIS VOICE
        m_pGlobalVoiceParams->dLFO1OscModIntensity = 1.0;

        etc…
```

initializeModMatrix()

This function creates and sets up the modulation matrix rows using Table 10.5; it is identical to MiniSynth, except it lacks the LFO to pulse width routing.

```
void CDigiSynthVoice::initializeModMatrix(CModulationMatrix* pMatrix)
{
     // --- always first: call base class to create core and
     //     init with basic routings
     CVoice::initializeModMatrix(pMatrix);

     if(!pMatrix->getModMatrixCore()) return;

     // --- MiniSynth Specific Routings
     // --- create a row for each source/destination pair
     modMatrixRow* pRow = NULL;

     // LFO1 -> ALL OSC1 FC
     pRow = createModMatrixRow(SOURCE_LFO1,
                               DEST_ALL_OSC_FO,
                               &m_pGlobalVoiceParams->dLFO1OscModIntensity,
                               &m_pGlobalVoiceParams->dOscFoModRange,
                               TRANSFORM_NONE,
                               true);
     pMatrix->addModMatrixRow(pRow);

     etc…
```

setSampleRate()

Here you only need to call the base class.

```
void CDigiSynthVoice::setSampleRate(double dSampleRate)
{
     CVoice::setSampleRate(dSampleRate);
}
```

prepareForPlay()

In *prepareForPlay()* you just call the base class then *reset()*.

```
void CDigiSynthVoice::prepareForPlay()
{
     CVoice::prepareForPlay();
     reset();
}
```

update()

The *update()* function is simple in *DigiSynthVoice*—just call the base class first, then do any voice specific initializations; there are none to do here, but we leave the verification of global parameters in case you want to modify the object.

```
void CDigiSynthVoice::update()
{
	// --- always call base class first
	CVoice::update();

	// --- voice specific updates
	if(!m_pGlobalVoiceParams) return;

	// --- add any new stuff here
}
```

reset()

In *reset()* you just call the base class first, then zero the portamento time.

```
void CDigiSynthVoice::reset()
{
	CVoice::reset();
	m_dPortamentoInc = 0.0;
}
```

inOscSplitRange()
inOscVelocityRange()
isOscSingleCycle()

These first two functions check the current MIDI note number and MIDI velocity values against the limits defined in the *noteRegion* structures for each oscillator and return true or false depending on the result. The third function simply queries the oscillator for the result.

In these and subsequent functions, the oscillators are indexed with a zero-based index value; 0 is Osc1, 1 is Osc2, etc.

```
// --- test to see if in Osc Split Range
inline bool inOscSplitRange(int nOscIndex)
{
	if(nOscIndex == 0)
	{
		if(m_uMIDINoteNumber >= m_Osc1NoteRegion.uMIDINoteLow &&
			m_uMIDINoteNumber <= m_Osc1NoteRegion.uMIDINoteHigh)
			return true;
	}
	else if(nOscIndex == 1)
	{
		if(m_uMIDINoteNumber >= m_Osc2NoteRegion.uMIDINoteLow &&
			m_uMIDINoteNumber <= m_Osc2NoteRegion.uMIDINoteHigh)
			return true;
	}

	return false;
}

// --- test to see if in Osc Velocity Range
inline bool inOscVelocityRange(int nOscIndex)
{
	if(nOscIndex == 0)
```

```
	{
		if(m_uMIDIVelocity >= m_Osc1NoteRegion.uMIDIVelocityLow &&
			m_uMIDIVelocity <= m_Osc1NoteRegion.uMIDIVelocityHigh)
			return true;
	}
	else if(nOscIndex == 1)
	{
		if(m_uMIDIVelocity >= m_Osc2NoteRegion.uMIDIVelocityLow &&
			m_uMIDIVelocity <= m_Osc2NoteRegion.uMIDIVelocityHigh)
			return true;
	}
	return false;
}

inline bool isOscSingleCycleSample(UINT uOsc)
{
	// < Decode Oscillator Index >
	CSampleOscillator* pOsc = NULL;
	switch(uOsc)
	{
		case 0:
			pOsc = (CSampleOscillator*)m_pOsc1; break;
		case 1:
			pOsc = (CSampleOscillator*)m_pOsc2; break;
		case 2:
			pOsc = (CSampleOscillator*)m_pOsc3; break;
		case 3:
			pOsc = (CSampleOscillator*)m_pOsc4; break;
		default:
			break;
	}

	// --- return the flag
	if(pOsc)
		return pOsc->m_bSingleCycleSample;

	return false;
}
```

getOscWaveData()
getOscWaveSamplePtrArray()
initOscWithFilePath()
initOscWithFolderPath()

These functions all decode the oscillator index the same way you just saw in *isOscSingleCycleSample()*, then simply call member functions or get member variables directly.

```
inline CWaveData* getOscWaveData(UINT uOsc)
{
	< Decode Oscillator Index >
```

```
    // --- return the pointer from object
    if(pOsc)
        return pOsc->getWaveData();

    return NULL;
}

inline CWaveData** getOscWaveSamplePtrArray(UINT uOsc)
{
    < Decode Oscillator Index >

    // --- return the pointer to array
    if(pOsc)
        return pOsc->getWaveSamplePtrArray();

    return NULL;
}

// --- for single samples
inline bool initOscWithFilePath(UINT uOsc, char* pPath,
                                bool bSingleCycleSample,
                                bool bPitchlessSample)
{
    < Decode Oscillator Index >

    // --- call the initializer function
    if(pOsc)
    {
        ((CSampleOscillator*)pOsc)->m_bSingleCycleSample =
                                        bSingleCycleSample;
        ((CSampleOscillator*)pOsc)->m_bPitchlessSample =
                                        bPitchlessSample;
        return pOsc->initWithFilePath(pPath);
    }

    return false;
}

// --- for multi-samples
inline bool initOscWithFolderPath(UINT uOsc, char* pPath,
                                  bool bSingleCycleSample,
                                  bool bPitchlessSample)
{
    < Decode Oscillator Index >

    // --- call the initializer function
    if(pOsc)
    {
        ((CSampleOscillator*)pOsc)->m_bSingleCycleSample =
                                        bSingleCycleSample;
```

```
            ((CSampleOscillator*)pOsc)->m_bPitchlessSample =
                                              bPitchlessSample;
            return ((CSampleOscillator*)pOsc)->initWithFolderPath(pPath);
        }

        return false;
    }
```

initAllOscWithDigiSynthVoice()

This function clones the wave data guts from one *CDigiSynthVoice* object into the current object. You copy all pointers and flags in a brute force manner.

```
    inline bool initAllOscWithDigiSynthVoice(CDigiSynthVoice* pVoice,
                                             bool bSingleCycleSample,
                                             bool bPitchlessSample)
    {
        if(pVoice->getOscWaveData(0))
            ((CSampleOscillator*)m_pOsc1)->setWaveDataPtr(
                                        pVoice->getOscWaveData(0));
        if(pVoice->getOscWaveSamplePtrArray(0))
            ((CSampleOscillator*)m_pOsc1)->setWaveSamplePtrArray(
                                        pVoice->getOscWaveSamplePtrArray(0));

        <SNIP SNIP SNIP - same for other oscillators>

        if(m_pOsc1)
        {
            ((CSampleOscillator*)m_pOsc1)->m_bSingleCycleSample =
                                                  bSingleCycleSample;
            ((CSampleOscillator*)m_pOsc1)->m_bPitchlessSample =
                                                  bPitchlessSample;
        }

        <SNIP SNIP SNIP - same for other oscillators>

        return true;
    }
```

doVoice()

This is the most important function of all since it does the rendering, and it is nearly identical to MiniSynth. The modulation layers are the same; the only difference is in the wiring of the audio engine since there are two filters. We need to decode the Voice Mode to determine which oscillators are sounding and if oscillator outputs need to be mixed. Notice the call to the base class first. The differences from MiniSynth are shown in **bold.**

```
    inline virtual bool doVoice(double& dLeftOutput, double& dRightOutput)
    {
        // this does basic on/off work
        if(!CVoice::doVoice(dLeftOutput, dRightOutput))
            return false;
```

```
// --- ARTICULATION BLOCK --- //
// --- layer 0 modulators: velocity->attack
//                                         note number->decay
m_ModulationMatrix.doModulationMatrix(0);

// --- update layer 1 modulators
m_EG1.update();
m_LFO1.update();

// --- do layer 1 modulators
m_EG1.doEnvelope();
m_LFO1.doOscillate();

// --- modulation matrix Layer 1
m_ModulationMatrix.doModulationMatrix(1);

// --- update Voice, DCA and Filter
this->update();
m_DCA.update();
m_LeftSEMFilter.update();
m_RightSEMFilter.update();

// --- update oscillators
m_Osc1.update();
m_Osc2.update();

// --- DIGITAL AUDIO ENGINE BLOCK --- //
double dLeftAccum = 0.0;
double dRightAccum = 0.0;
double dLeft1 = 0.0;
double dRight1 = 0.0;
double dLeft2 = 0.0 ;
double dRight2 = 0.0;

// --- check for velocity and split location
if(m_pGlobalVoiceParams->uVoiceMode == Osc1)
        dLeftAccum = m_Osc1.doOscillate(&dRightAccum);
else if(m_pGlobalVoiceParams->uVoiceMode == Osc2)
        dLeftAccum = m_Osc2.doOscillate(&dRightAccum);
else if(m_pGlobalVoiceParams->uVoiceMode == split)
{
        bool Osc1On = inOscSplitRange(0);
        bool Osc2On = inOscSplitRange(1);

        dLeft1 = m_Osc1.doOscillate(&dRight1);
        dLeft2 = m_Osc2.doOscillate(&dRight2);

        if(Osc1On && Osc2On)
```

```
        {
            dLeftAccum = 0.5*dLeft1 + 0.5*dLeft2;
            dRightAccum = 0.5*dRight1 + 0.5*dRight2;
        }
        else if(Osc1On)
        {
            dLeftAccum = dLeft1;
            dRightAccum = dRight1;
        }
        else if(Osc2On)
        {
            dLeftAccum = dLeft2;
            dRightAccum = dRight2;
        }
    }
    else if(m_pGlobalVoiceParams->uVoiceMode == layer)
    {
        bool Osc1On = inOscVelocityRange(0);
        bool Osc2On = inOscVelocityRange(1);

        dLeft1 = m_Osc1.doOscillate(&dRight1);
        dLeft2 = m_Osc2.doOscillate(&dRight2);

        if(Osc1On && Osc2On)
        {
            dLeftAccum = 0.5*dLeft1 + 0.5*dLeft2;
            dRightAccum = 0.5*dRight1 + 0.5*dRight2;
        }
        else if(Osc1On)
        {
            dLeftAccum = dLeft1;
            dRightAccum = dRight1;
        }
        else if(Osc2On)
        {
            dLeftAccum = dLeft2;
            dRightAccum = dRight2;
        }
    }

    // --- apply the filters
    dLeftOutput = m_LeftSEMFilter.doFilter(dLeftAccum);
    dRightOutput = m_RightSEMFilter.doFilter(dRightAccum);

    // --- apply the DCA
    m_DCA.doDCA(dLeftOutput, dRightOutput, dLeftOutput, dRightOutput);

    return true;
}
```

10.10 DigiSynth Files

DigiSynth uses the following files, which you will need to add into your compiler's project in the usual manner. Also, don't forget to copy the folders of samples and multi-samples to your proper DLL or component folder.

DCA.h	SEMFilter.h
DCA.cpp	SEMFilter.cpp
EnvelopeGenerator.h	Oscillator.h
EnvelopeGenerator.cpp	Oscillator.cpp
Filter.h	SampleOscillator.h
Filter.cpp	SampleOscillator.cpp
LFO.h	synthfunctions.h
LFO.cpp	VAOnePoleFilter.h
DigiSynthVoice.h	VAOnePoleFilter.cpp
DigiSynthVoice.cpp	Voice.h
ModulationMatrix.h	Voice.cpp
ModulationMatrix.cpp	

For VST3 and AU, you also need to add the file *SynthParamLimits.h*, which is in the DigiSynth sample code—remember that this file is slightly different for each synth because it contains the GUI control index enumeration.

DigiSynth uses nearly identical code in the majority of plug-in object functions as MiniSynth; the only difference is the type of voice pointer stored in the voice array. There is no need to repeatedly print that code for each synth project. There are also differences in the GUI control setup and initialization. By using the *CVoice* base class, we are able to reuse the same core code over and over.

For the plug-in's *.h* file declarations:

- *#include "DigiSynthVoice.h"* at the top of the file
- copy the same code as MiniSynth, but with different voice pointers (the differences are shown in **bold**)
- add the *loadSamples()* function

```
<< ** Code Listing 10.1: Declarations ** >>

// --- our array of voices
CDigiSynthVoice* m_pVoiceArray[MAX_VOICES];

// --- MmM
CModulationMatrix m_GlobalModMatrix;

// --- global params
globalSynthParams m_GlobalSynthParams;

// --- helper functions for note on/off/voice steal
void incrementVoiceTimestamps();
CDigiSynthVoice* getOldestVoice();
CDigiSynthVoice* getOldestVoiceWithNote(UINT uMIDINote);

// --- load sample sets
bool loadSamples();

// updates all voices at once
void update();
```

```
    // for portamento
    double m_dLastNoteFrequency;

    // our recieve channel
    UINT m_uMidiRxChannel;

    << END ** Code Listing 10.1: Declarations ** END >>
```

Loading Samples

The code for loading the samples is nearly identical across the three APIs; only the path setup is different. For this synth, we chose the *Heaver* and *OldFlatty* multi-sample folders, but you are free to replace them with your own folders of properly looped samples. Sample loading is done in a separate function *loadSamples()*, declared in the *.h* file.

```
<< ** Code Listing 10.2: Load Samples ** >>

bool CDigiSynth::loadSamples()     //RAFX
bool Processor::loadSamples()      //VST3
bool AUSynth::loadSamples()        //AU
{
    // --- RackAFX ---------------------------------------------
    char* pPath0 = addStrings(getMyDLLDirectory(),"\\MultiSamples
                              \\Heaver");
    char* pPath1 = addStrings(getMyDLLDirectory(),"\\MultiSamples
                              \\OldFlatty");
    // ---------------------------------------------------------
    // --- VST3 ------------------------------------------------
    char* pDLLPath = getMyDLLDirectory(USTRING("DigiSynth.vst3"));

    char* pPath0 = addStrings(pDLLPath,"\\MultiSamples\\Heaver");
    char* pPath1 = addStrings(pDLLPath,"\\MultiSamples\\OldFlatty");
    // ---------------------------------------------------------
    // --- AU --------------------------------------------------
    char* componentFolder = getMyComponentDirectory(
                  CFSTR("developer.audiounit.yourname.digisynth"));

    char* pPath0 = addStrings(componentFolder,"/MultiSamples/Heaver");
    char* pPath1 = addStrings(componentFolder,"/MultiSamples/OldFlatty");
    // ---------------------------------------------------------

    // to speed up sample loading, init the first voice here
    // --- init false, false = NOT single-sample, NOT pitchless sample
    if(!m_pVoiceArray[0]->initOscWithFolderPath(0, pPath0, false, false))
        return false;
    if(!m_pVoiceArray[0]->initOscWithFolderPath(1, pPath1, false, false))
        return false;

    // then use the other function to copy the sample pointerrs
    // so they share pointers to same buffers of data
    for(int i=1; i<MAX_VOICES; i++)
    {
```

```
            // --- init false, false = NOT single-sample,
            //     NOT pitchless sample
            m_pVoiceArray[i]->initAllOscWithDigiSynthVoice(m_pVoiceArray[0], false, false);
        }

        // always delete what comes back from addStrings()
        delete [] pPath0;
        delete [] pPath1;

        // --- VST3 only
        delete [] pDLLPath;

        // --- AU only
        delete [] componentFolder;

        return true;
    }
        << END ** Code Listing 10.2: Load Samples ** END >>
```

10.11 DigiSynth: RackAFX

Create a new project named DigiSynth and setup the GUI using Table 10.6. Alternatively you may also download the complete project from http://www.willpirkle.com/synthbook/.

DigiSynth.h

At the top of the file, add the *#include* statement for *DigiSynthVoice.h* and then setup the array of voices and all helper member functions. Add the *loadSamples()* function as well.

```
class CDigiSynth : public CPlugIn
{
public:
        <SNIP SNIP SNIP>

        // Add your code here: ------------------------------------------- //

        << INSERT ** Code Listing 10.1: Declarations ** HERE >>

        etc...
```

DigiSynth.cpp

The following functions are identical to MiniSynth (and the rest of the book projects), with the exception of the type of voice pointers created and stored in the voice array.

- constructor
- destructor
- *prepareForPlay()*
- *processAudioFrame()*
- *midiNoteOn()*
- *midiNoteOff()*
- *midiModWheel()*
- *midiPitchBend()*
- *midiMessage()*

loadSamples()

Insert Code Listing 10.2 anywhere you wish inside the *.cpp* file.

initialize()

This is a RackAFX function you have not used yet; *initialize()* is called after the constructor. This is the function where we load the samples.

```
bool __stdcall CDigiSynth::initialize()
{
      // --- load samples
      return loadSamples();
}
```

update()

The other difference is in the *update()* function, which is only slightly different, as a few controls have been deleted and others added. Also, there are now two filters to handle. This function shows only the newly added code in **bold**.

Removed from MiniSynth:

- pulse width
- all references to Oscillator 3 (sub osc) and Oscillator 4 (noise)

Added new:

- Osc1 Output (dB)
- Osc2 Output (dB)
- Loop Mode

```
void CDigiSynth::update()   // RAFX
{
      // --- update global parameters
      //
      // --- Oscillators:
      double dOscAmplitude = m_dOsc1Amplitude_dB == -96.0 ? 0.0 :
                              pow(10.0, m_dOsc1Amplitude_dB/20.0);
      m_GlobalSynthParams.osc1Params.dAmplitude = dOscAmplitude;

      dOscAmplitude = m_dOsc2Amplitude_dB == -96.0 ? 0.0 :
                              pow(10.0, m_dOsc2Amplitude_dB/20.0);
      m_GlobalSynthParams.osc2Params.dAmplitude = dOscAmplitude;

      // --- loop mode
      m_GlobalSynthParams.osc1Params.uLoopMode = m_uLoopMode;
      m_GlobalSynthParams.osc2Params.uLoopMode = m_uLoopMode;

      // --- Filter:
      m_GlobalSynthParams.filter1Params.dFcControl = m_dFcControl;
      m_GlobalSynthParams.filter1Params.dQControl = m_dQControl;
      m_GlobalSynthParams.filter2Params.dFcControl = m_dFcControl;
      m_GlobalSynthParams.filter2Params.dQControl = m_dQControl;

      etc...
}
```

10.12 DigiSynth: VST3

Create a new project named DigiSynth and setup the GUI using Table 10.6. Alternatively you may also download the complete project from http://www.willpirkle.com/synthbook/.

Processor.h

At the top of the file, add the *#include* statement for *DigiSynthVoice.h*, and then setup the array of voices and all helper member functions. Add the l*oadSamples()* function as well. Don't forget to add all the variables you need from the GUI table.

```
class Processor : public AudioEffect
{
public:
      <SNIP SNIP SNIP>

      // Add your code here: ------------------------------------------- //

      << INSERT ** Code Listing 10.1: Declarations ** HERE >>

      etc…
```

Processor.cpp

The following functions are identical to MiniSynth (and the rest of the book projects), with the exception of the type of voice pointers created and stored in the voice array.

- destructor
- *process()*
- *doProcessEvent()*

Constructor

Initialize all the GUI variables from Table 10.6; the rest is identical to MiniSynth.

```
Processor::Processor()
{
      // --- define our controller FUID
      setControllerClass(Controller::cid);

      // --- our inits
      m_dOsc1Amplitude_dB = DEFAULT_OUTPUT_AMPLITUDE_DB;
      m_dOsc2Amplitude_dB = DEFAULT_OUTPUT_AMPLITUDE_DB;
      m_dEG1OscIntensity = DEFAULT_BIPOLAR;

      etc… rest is same as MiniSynth
```

loadSamples()

Insert Code Listing 10.2 anywhere you wish inside the *.cpp* file.

setActive()

This is where you will perform the normal initializations as in MiniSynth, but you will also load the samples.

```
tresult PLUGIN_API Processor::setActive(TBool state)
{
     if(state)
     {
            <SNIP SNIP SNIP>

            // --- keeping separate because they are separate in RAFX/AU
            for(int i=0; i<MAX_VOICES; i++)
            {
                   CDigiSynthVoice* pVoice = m_pVoiceArray[i];
                   pVoice->setSampleRate((double)processSetup.sampleRate);
                   pVoice->prepareForPlay();
            }
            // --- now load samples
            loadSamples();

            // --- mass update
            update();

            etc...
```

update()

The other difference is in the *update()* function, which is only slightly different, as a few controls have been deleted and others added. Also, there are now two filters to handle. This function shows the newly added code in **bold**.

Removed from MiniSynth:

- pulse width
- all references to Oscillator 3 (sub osc) and Oscillator 4 (noise)

Added new:

- Osc1 Output (dB)
- Osc2 Output (dB)
- Loop Mode

```
void Processor::update()
{
     // --- update global parameters
     //
     // --- Oscillators:
     double dOscAmplitude = m_dOsc1Amplitude_dB == -96.0 ? 0.0 :
                            pow(10.0, m_dOsc1Amplitude_dB/20.0);
     m_GlobalSynthParams.osc1Params.dAmplitude = dOscAmplitude;

     dOscAmplitude = m_dOsc2Amplitude_dB == -96.0 ? 0.0 :
                     pow(10.0, m_dOsc2Amplitude_dB/20.0);
     m_GlobalSynthParams.osc2Params.dAmplitude = dOscAmplitude;

     // --- loop mode
     m_GlobalSynthParams.osc1Params.uLoopMode = m_uLoopMode;
     m_GlobalSynthParams.osc2Params.uLoopMode = m_uLoopMode;
```

```
        // --- Filter:
        m_GlobalSynthParams.filter1Params.dFcControl = m_dFcControl;
        m_GlobalSynthParams.filter1Params.dQControl = m_dQControl;
        m_GlobalSynthParams.filter2Params.dFcControl = m_dFcControl;
        m_GlobalSynthParams.filter2Params.dQControl = m_dQControl;

        etc...
    }
```

doControlUpdate()

The *doControlUpdate()* function must be altered from MiniSynth to match the new variables additions/removals listed above. In the switch/case statement, delete the case statements for the removed variables and add case statements for the new ones, shown here in **bold**.

```
    bool Processor::doControlUpdate(ProcessData& data)
    {
        <SNIP SNIP SNIP Indents Removed>

    switch (pid)
    {
        // cookVSTGUIVariable(min, max, currentValue) <- cooks raw data into
        // meaningful info for us
        case OSC1_AMPLITUDE_DB:
        {
               m_dOsc1Amplitude_dB = cookVSTGUIVariable(MIN_OUTPUT_AMPLITUDE_DB,
                                                        MAX_OUTPUT_AMPLITUDE_DB,
                                                        value);
               break;
        }

        case OSC2_AMPLITUDE_DB:
        {
               m_dOsc2Amplitude_dB = cookVSTGUIVariable(MIN_OUTPUT_AMPLITUDE_DB,
                                                        MAX_OUTPUT_AMPLITUDE_DB,
                                                        value);
               break;
        }

        case LOOP_MODE:
        {
               m_uLoopMode = (UINT)cookVSTGUIVariable(MIN_LOOP_MODE,
                                                      MAX_LOOP_MODE, value);
               break;
        }
```

10.13 DigiSynth: AU

Create a new project named DigiSynth and setup the GUI using Table 10.6. Alternatively you may also download the complete project from http://www.willpirkle.com/synthbook/.

AUSynth.h

At the top of the file, add the *#include* statement for *DigiSynthVoice.h* and then setup the array of voices and all helper member functions. Add the *loadSamples()* function as well.

```
class AUSynth : public AUInstrumentBase
{
public:
      <SNIP SNIP SNIP>

      // Add your code here: ------------------------------------------ //

      << INSERT ** Code Listing 10.1: Declarations ** HERE >>

      etc..
```

AUSynth.cpp

The following functions are identical to MiniSynth (and the rest of the book projects), with the exception of the type of voice pointers created and stored in the voice array.

- destructor
- *Reset()*
- *Render()*
- *StartNote()*
- *StopNote()*
- *HandlePitchWheel()*
- *HandleControlChange()*

Constructor

Initialize the factory preset (optional) and all the GUI variables from Table 10.6; the rest is identical to MiniSynth.

```
AUSynth::AUSynth(AudioUnit inComponentInstance)
      : AUInstrumentBase(inComponentInstance, 0, 1)
{
      // --- create input, output ports, groups and parts
      CreateElements();

      // --- setup default factory preset (as example)
      factoryPreset[OSC1_AMPLITUDE_DB] = 0.0;
      factoryPreset[OSC2_AMPLITUDE_DB] = 0.0;

      <SNIP SNIP SNIP>

      // --- define number of params (controls)
      Globals()->UseIndexedParameters(NUMBER_OF_SYNTH_PARAMETERS);

      // --- initialize the controls here!
      // --- these are defined in SynthParamLimits.h
      //
      Globals()->SetParameter(OSC1_AMPLITUDE_DB,
                              DEFAULT_OUTPUT_AMPLITUDE_DB);
```

```
        Globals()->SetParameter(OSC2_AMPLITUDE_DB,
                                DEFAULT_OUTPUT_AMPLITUDE_DB);
        Globals()->SetParameter(LOOP_MODE, DEFAULT_LOOP_MODE);

        etc…
```

loadSamples()

Insert Code Listing 10.2 anywhere you wish inside the *.cpp* file.

Initialize()

Initialize() only differs from MiniSynth with the addition of the call to *loadSamples()*.

```
ComponentResult AUSynth::Initialize()
{
     // --- init the base class
     AUInstrumentBase::Initialize();

     // clear
     m_dLastNoteFrequency = -1.0;

     // --- NOTE: very important to set the sample rate and call
     //   prepareForPlay()!
     for(int i=0; i<MAX_VOICES; i++)
     {
          CDigiSynthVoice* pVoice = m_pVoiceArray[i];
          pVoice->setSampleRate(GetOutput(0)->
                              GetStreamFormat().mSampleRate);
          pVoice->prepareForPlay();
     }

     // --- now load samples
     loadSamples();

     // --- update the synth
     update();

     return noErr;
}
```

update()

The other difference is in the *update()* function, which is only slightly different, as a few controls have been deleted and others added. Also, there are now two filters to handle. This function shows ONLY the newly added code in **bold**.

Removed from MiniSynth:

- pulse width
- all references to Oscillator 3 (sub osc) and Oscillator 4 (noise)

Added new:

- Osc1 Output (dB)
- Osc2 Output (dB)
- Loop Mode

```
void AUSynth::update()
{
    // --- update global parameters
    //
    // --- Oscillators:
    // --- Oscillators:
    double dOscAmplitude = Globals()->GetParameter(OSC1_AMPLITUDE_DB) ==
                           -96.0 ? 0.0 : pow(10.0, Globals()->
                           GetParameter(OSC1_AMPLITUDE_DB)/20.0);
    m_GlobalSynthParams.osc1Params.dAmplitude = dOscAmplitude;

    dOscAmplitude = Globals()->GetParameter(OSC2_AMPLITUDE_DB) ==
                            -96.0 ? 0.0 : pow(10.0, Globals()->
                            GetParameter(OSC2_AMPLITUDE_DB)/20.0);
    m_GlobalSynthParams.osc2Params.dAmplitude = dOscAmplitude;

    // --- loop mode
    m_GlobalSynthParams.osc1Params.uLoopMode =
                           Globals()->GetParameter(LOOP_MODE);
    m_GlobalSynthParams.osc2Params.uLoopMode =
                           Globals()->GetParameter(LOOP_MODE);

    // --- Filter:
    m_GlobalSynthParams.filter1Params.dFcControl =
                          Globals()->GetParameter(FILTER_FC);
    m_GlobalSynthParams.filter1Params.dQControl =
                          Globals()->GetParameter(FILTER_Q);
    m_GlobalSynthParams.filter2Params.dFcControl =
                          Globals()->GetParameter(FILTER_FC);
    m_GlobalSynthParams.filter1Params.dQControl =
                          Globals()->GetParameter(FILTER_Q);

    etc…
}
```

Build and test DigiSynth on your platform of choice. You should enjoy the fact that so much of the core synth code is identical to MiniSynth. Try many other sample sets, loops and one-shot files.

10.14 Challenges

Bronze

Change the way the multi-sample pitch shifting works so that each sampled note produces one note above and one note below it. So, the sample of note *C* is shifted down for *Bb* and up for *C#*, rather than the current scheme that shifts down only.

Silver

Set all note regions to have note ranges and velocity ranges from 0 to 127 and place the synth in "layer" mode permanently; then add another LFO that modulates the mix of the oscillators by modulating the output amplitude variable in the oscillator object shown in Figure 10.15. This small change can really make a big difference in the synthesized sound.

Gold

Implement "loop and release" mode in *CSampleOscillator*. Then, implement the MIDI Pitch Fraction tuning. From the .wav file spec:

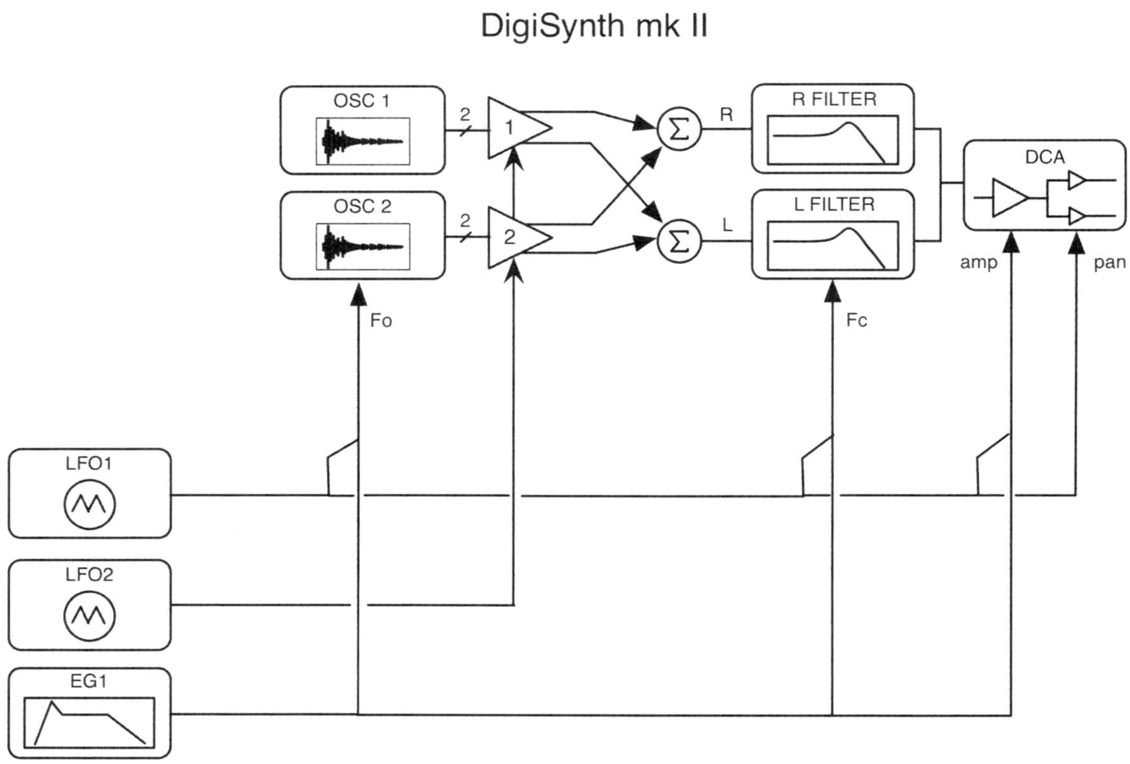

Figure 10.15: DigiSynth mkII features a second LFO to crossfade the mix of the two oscillators.

"The MIDI pitch fraction specifies the fraction of a semitone up from the specified MIDI unity note field. A value of 0x80000000 means 1/2 semitone (50 cents) and a value of 0x00000000 means no fine tuning between semitones" (sonicspot.com, n.d.).

Platinum

Create a synth that loads many sets of multi-samples into memory, but only plays two of them at a time in a combination you call a Patch. Then, let the user select from a list of these Patches. Next, allow the user to choose from the many different filter modes of the SEM filter; it has HPF, BPF and BSF outputs. Connect another LFO to the BSF "Aux Control" variable to modulate its asymmetry during note events. This new modulation can create some fantastic and dramatic sweeps, especially when used at the same rate as the cutoff modulation.

Diamond

You will notice in VST3 and RackAFX that there is a significant time-hit up front when you load all the samples into buffers (this doesn't seem to be an issue for AU); subclass the *CWaveData* object and modify it to read out chunks of audio rather than the whole file at once. Then, build the buffers in real-time as needed.

Bibliography

Braut, Christian. 1994. *The Musician's Guide to MIDI*, Chap. 5–7. Alameda: SYBEX.
MIDI Manufacturers Association. 1999. *Downloadable Sounds Level 2, v1.0.*
MIDI Manufacturers Association. 2006. *Downloadable Sounds Level 2, Amendment 2.*
sonicspot.com. n.d. "Wave File Format." Accessed June 2014, http://www.sonicspot.com/guide/wavefiles.html

CHAPTER 11

VectorSynth and AniSynth: Vector Synthesizers

Dave Smith and his company Sequential Circuits, Inc. invented Vector Synthesis (VS) and introduced the ProphetVS in 1986. Not long after, Yamaha acquired Sequential Circuits and incorporated vector synthesis in the SY22/SY35/TG33 synths. Dave Smith and some of the original VS team members then moved to Korg Research and Development to design the Wavestation family of synthesizers, which were all vector synths. A fundamental goal in synthesis is creating sounds that evolve in both time and frequency. Traditionally, you use envelope generators and filters to manipulate amplitude and timbre during note events. MiniSynth and DigiSynth use EGs to manipulate both the filter and DCA to create this kind of evolution, but it follows the same pattern for each note event and the pattern is relatively short-lived; the EGs only have four segments. Vector synthesis takes a different approach that is actually ingeniously simple: you dynamically crossfade (mix) the outputs of multiple sound sources. This crossfading naturally introduces shifts in amplitude and frequency based on the original amplitude and frequency content of the sound sources. The Wavestation could generate complex, lush, evolving sounds by holding only one key. In the ProphetVS, the crossfading could take place on sounds that were previously made with the same mixing engine so that stacks of mixed sounds could be mixed and re-mixed again and again with each other. With the correct programming, long evolving pad sounds could be made that did not appear to really loop, and some patches did not use an EG on the filter. This made it ideal for creating long pads and movie soundtrack beds. The Wavestation introduced Wave Sequencing, which crossfades individual waveforms in a time sequence creating rhythmic patches, though we will not be using that form of vector synthesis in this chapter's VectorSynth. Vector synthesis faded in popularity in the 1990s but has reappeared in the award-winning Moog AniMoog iPad app, which is the basis for the second project in this chapter: AniSynth. Korg recently re-introduced the WavestationSR as a software plug-in. Other forms of vector synthesis have appeared in current synth designs including Alchemy, which uses vector mixing on modulation variables as well as pitched sounds, and the John Bowen Synth Design Solaris. John was an original member of the VS teams at both Sequential and Korg, so vector synthesis is an integral component in Solaris. Figure 11.1 shows a simplified block diagram of the ProphetVS. The "vector mix EG" actually generates four separate envelopes that are applied to the four wavetable oscillators labeled A, B, C, and D, so you can think of it as four EGs in one.

In the ProphetVS, the four wavetable oscillators could be loaded with any of 96 on-board "waves," which mainly consisted of mathematically generated waveforms and some short slices of audio samples. Although it shares many similarities with the ProphetVS, the Korg Wavestation voice architecture is very different as shown in Figure 11.2. Each "oscillator" is actually a complete voice unto itself; there are separate filters, DCAs, amp EGs, two assignable LFOs, and one assignable EG for each one. The filters are non-resonant, although the new WavestationSR plug-in features resonant filters. The oscillator waves could be individual wave samples or wave sequences. The WavestationSR featured 484 on-board waves consisting of single cycles, multiple cycles, transient blasts, transient+loops, mathematically created waveforms, drums, and clips of samples of acoustic instruments. While the ProphetVS was a hybrid digital/analog design, the Wavestation was pure digital.

11.1 The Vector Joystick

The heart of the original vector synths is a joystick that is used to mix the outputs of four sound sources labeled A, B, C, and D. The joystick operates over a "mixture plane" or "vector plane." The joystick axes are labeled A-C (x-axis) and B-D (y-axis), as shown in Figure 11.3. If you've used a joystick for surround mixing or an arcade game, you may have used one that rotates in a circle. The Prophet and Wavestation joysticks also move in a circle, but only the central diamond (a square turned on its side) is the active region of operation; the remaining area is a keep-out zone.

There are a few properties of this joystick that are important:

- linear motion of the joystick produces exponential mix envelopes that create proper sounding crossfading for our ears
- the mix values for the four sources will always add up to 1.0; with the joystick in the center, the mix values are: A:0.25 B:0.25 C:0.25 D:0.25, as shown in Figure 11.3
- the range of joystick coordinates is $x = [-1..+1]$ and $y = [-1..+1]$ with (0,0) at the origin

Figure 11.4 shows the exponential nature of the mix values; here the joystick moves along the x-axis towards the A vertex. As it moves, you can see the value for the C mix-component drops off quickly, while the A component ramps up quickly—they are moving in an exponential manner. Since the distance from the joystick to the B and D vertices is always the same, their mix values are the same, but they also drop off exponentially. When the joystick is at $(x,y) = (-1,0)$, the mix value is 100% A and 0% for everything else. Notice also that the sum of all the mix values is 1.0 (or 100%) at any given time.

Moving the joystick around the perimeter of the diamond crossfades one source into the next in sequence as shown in Figure 11.5:

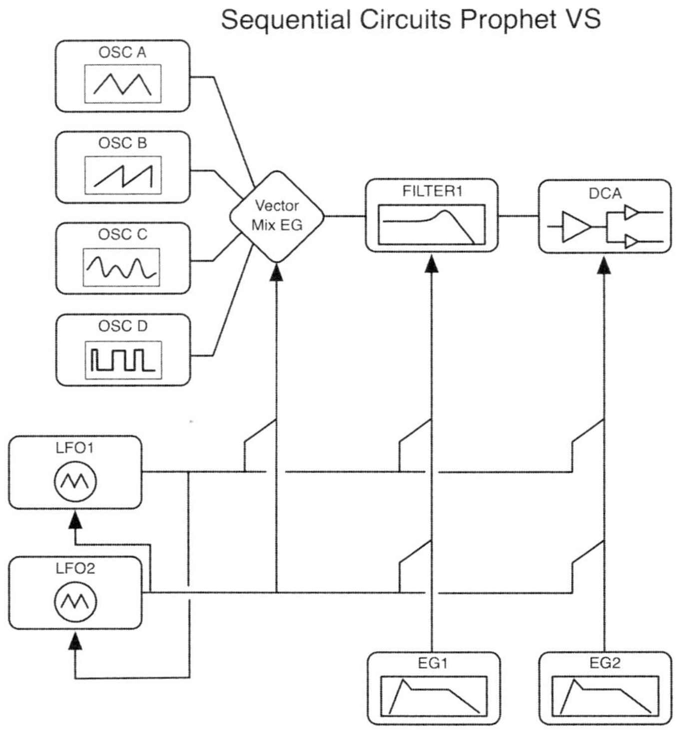

Figure 11.1: Simplified block diagram of the ProphetVS.

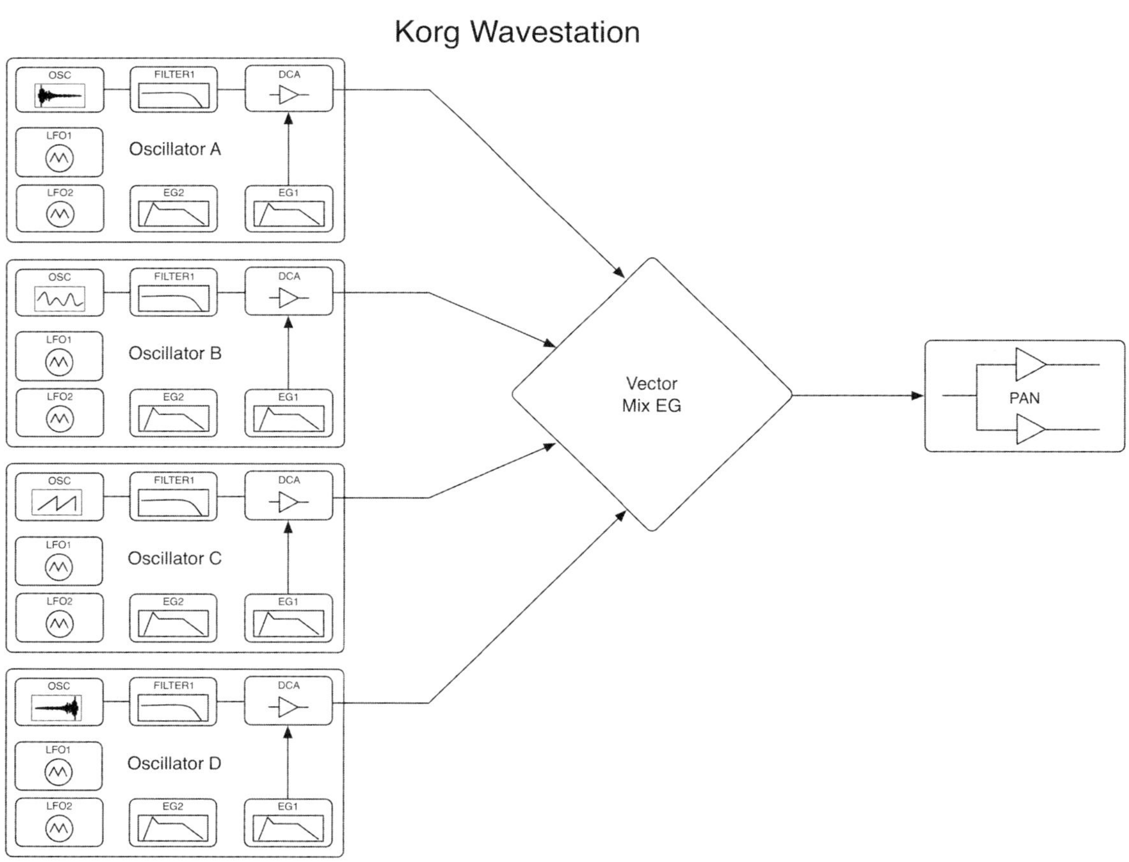

Figure 11.2: The voice architecture of the Wavestation family.

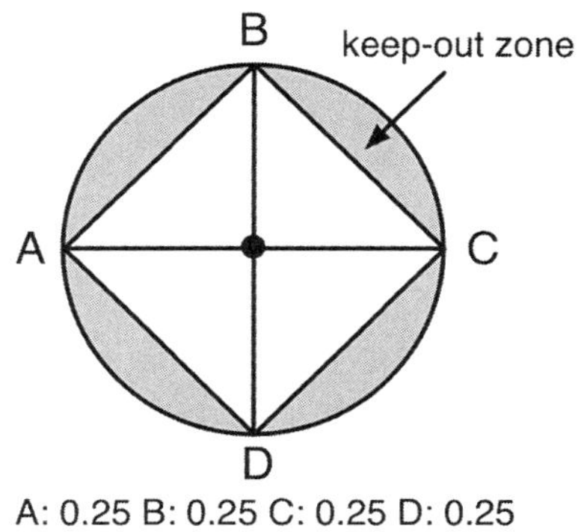

Figure 11.3: The vector joystick with diamond shaped active area and surrounding keep-out zone; with the joystick in the center position, there is an equal vector mix of the four sources.

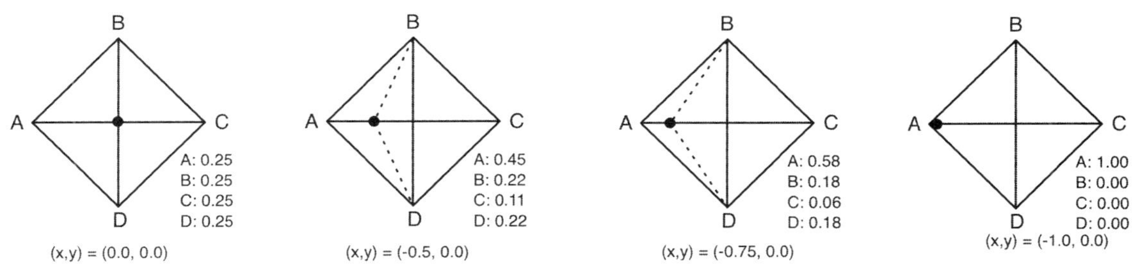

Figure 11.4: The vector mix values move exponentially as the joystick moves linearly.

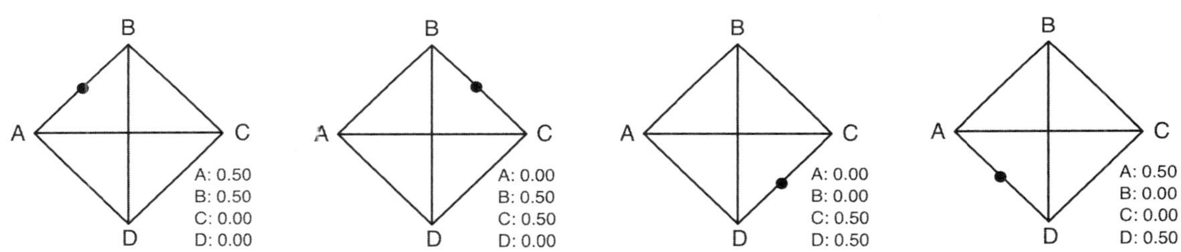

Figure 11.5: The 50/50 mix ratios between adjacent vertices is found midway between them on the outer diamond edge.

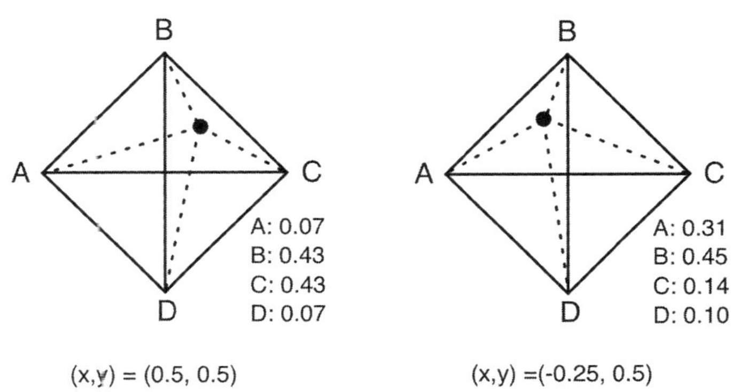

Figure 11.6: A few more sample joystick-position-to-mix ratios show the exponential mapping.

Figure 11.6 shows a few more positions of the joystick and the non-linear mapping from the (x,y) joystick coordinates to the mixing variables.

Vector Mix Calculation

Korg kindly shares the vector mix calculation for software developers. It is available at Dan Phillips' website, which is also full of Wavestation resources. See the Bibliography for the link. The user does not see the coordinates, only the mix ratios. If we use the

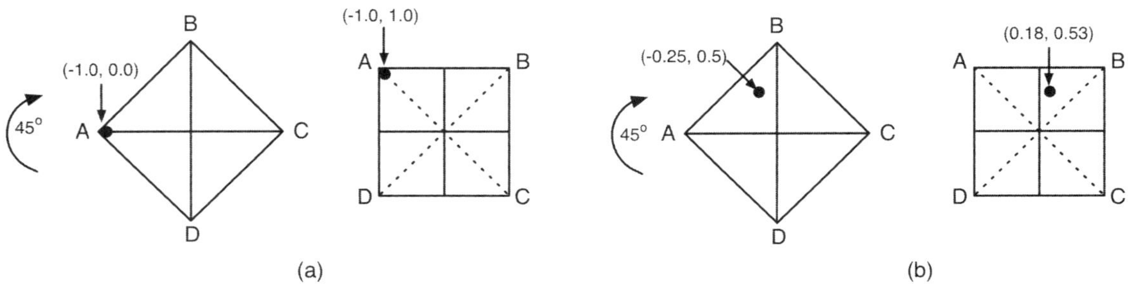

Figure 11.7: Rotation of the joystick plane results in (a) the original joystick coordinate point (−1.0, 0.0) is mapped to (−1.0, 1.0) (b) joystick coordinates (−0.25, 0.5) is mapped to (0.18, 0.53).

literal joystick coordinate system, where the coordinates of the *A* vertex are (−1, 0), the *B* vertex coordinates are (0, 1), and so on, the calculation first involves rotating the diamond shape by −45 degrees (i.e. clockwise) to produce a proper square shape. Figure 11.7 shows how this re-maps the literal vector joystick coordinates.

> In this book and in all the projects, the term *joystick coordinates* refers to the literal coordinates in the ProphetVS/Wavestation mix plane prior to rotation for the calculation.

After rotation, the mix is calculated using the Sequential/Korg equations that generate MIDI values. The coordinates are normalized to +/−127 prior to the calculation. The full calculation can be found in *calculateVectorMixValues()* in *synthfunctions.h*; here is the heart of the calculation, where *dPointX* and *dPointY* are the rotated and normalized coordinates of the joystick location and *dAmag, dBmag, dCmag,* and *dDmag* are the mix values; notice the values are calculated as percentages, so we convert back to scalar values after the calculation, and that the mixes will always add up to 100% (or 1.0).

```
// the Korg/Sequential Circuits VS Equations
dBmag = dPointX*dPointY/645;                /* Calculate individual wave % */
dCmag = dPointX*(255 - dPointY)/645;        /* 645=(255^2/100)*127/128 */
dDmag = (255-dPointX)*(255-dPointY)/645;
dAmag = 100.0 - dBmag - dCmag - dDmag;

// convert from percent
dAmag /= 100.0;
dBmag /= 100.0;
dCmag /= 100.0;
dDmag /= 100.0;
```

AC and BD Mix Outputs

At any given time, the vector joystick generates not only the four mix ratios, but also two more output values that are the reflections on the joystick's *x* and *y* axes. For our projects these values are unipolar over a range of [0..+1] and shown in Figure 11.8. (Note: this

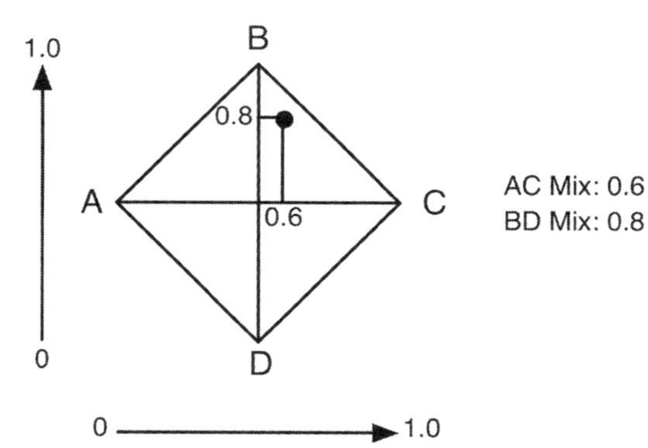

Figure 11.8: The vector joystick also transmits AC and BD mix values in a unipolar format.

is different from both the ProphetVS and Wavestation, where the values are bipolar over the range [−127..+127].) These outputs may be ignored or used for other modulation. For example, you could modulate the DCA's pan value with the AC mix, and the filter cutoff frequency with the BD mix; joystick motion would then not only change the sound's amplitude and mix, but also the pan and timbre as well. This opens up a new dimension of modulation possibilities. The *calculateVectorMixValues()* function also generates the AC and BD mix values, which are easily calculated by converting the bipolar coordinates to unipolar.

11.2 Vector Paths

One way to use the joystick is to simply move it around in real-time while you hold a note or multiple notes. The output is a mix of the sources. As you move the joystick, the sound evolves as the mix ratios change, always totaling 1.0 so that no clipping occurs. As you move the joystick, the vector EG generates a separate EG amplitude value for each source. It's a neat performance trick, but you use up a playing-hand to move the joystick. A more interesting and useful feature of vector synths is the ability to program the joystick to move in a path. Each time you trigger a new note, the joystick moves along the path you've assigned. The path consists of a set of vertices and timing values between each one as shown in Figure 11.9. Each pair of vertices forms a segment. In this case, the path starts at vertex 0 and makes its way to vertex 1 in 1 second, then on to vertex 2 in 0.75 seconds, and so on, until it stops at vertex 4. Therefore, segment 1 lasts 1 second and segment 2 is 0.75 seconds.

As Stanley Jungleib (1986) notes in the ProphetVS manual, setting short durations in the segment times tends to induce quicker playing in the musician, while long settings invite the musician to play sustaining pads. The author also notes that a vector is defined as something that has both a magnitude and a direction. The vector path dictates the direction of the joystick, which controls the instantaneous mix. It should be noted that in all these synths, the programed joystick does not physically move (it would need to move separately for each note event!) and may still be used even when the programmed vector path is in motion. In Figure 11.10, the joystick is sitting in the center of the mix surface at (0,0), shown as a small black puck. Moving the joystick shifts the center of the path as shown in Figure 11.10. Notice how the path is bound to the diamond shape—it is not allowed in the keep-out zone. Figure 11.10

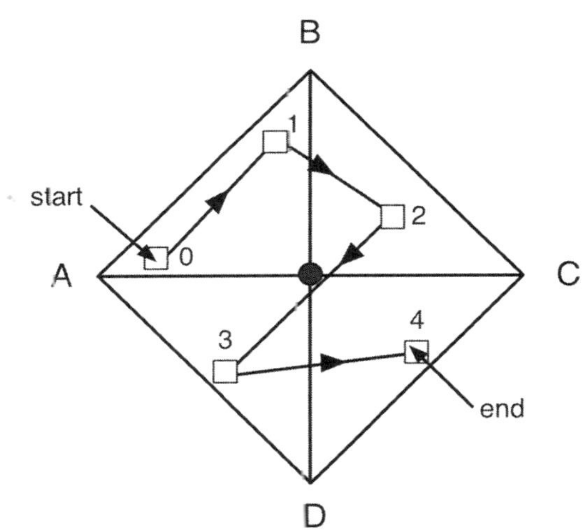

vertex number	time to next vertex (mSec)
0	1000
1	750
2	2500
3	50
4	-----

Figure 11.9: Example of a programmed vector path and timing values.

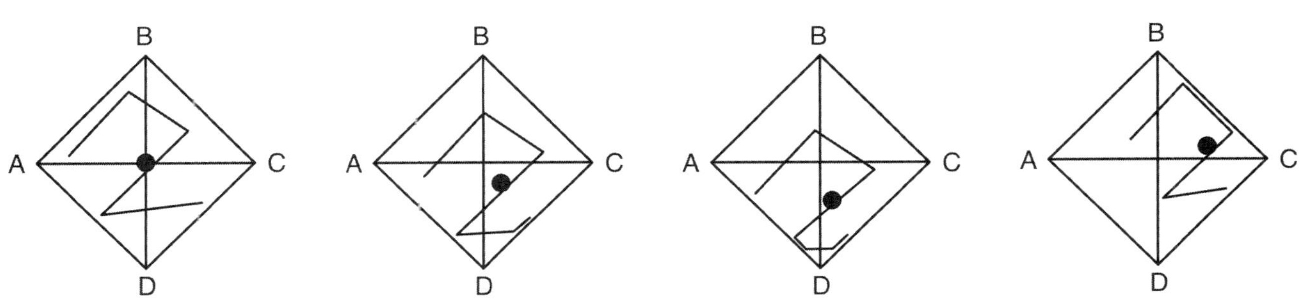

Figure 11.10: Moving the joystick shifts the center point of the path; notice how the path is clamped and does not move outside the diamond.

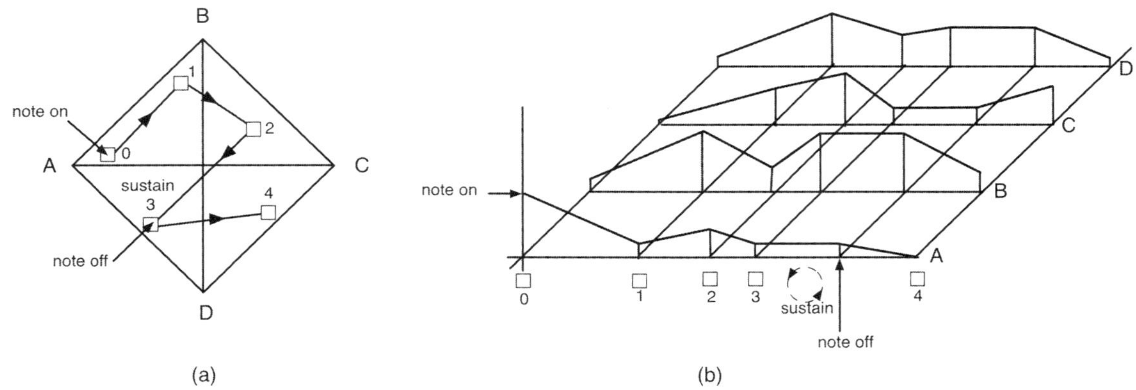

Figure 11.11: (a) The vector path shown in the mix surface and (b) the individual envelopes that evolve over the path lifecycle; notice that the path stops at vertex 3 until the note is released; notice also that the envelopes may not necessarily end at zero.

is also somewhat simplified. If you move the joystick while a note/program is playing—for example, if you move the joystick after the first segment has played though—only the future segments will actually be moved since the previous one has already expired. This effectively stretches the path out in the direction of joystick motion.

The ProphetVS and Wavestation allow you to program a path consisting of four segments that correspond to the traditional attack, decay, sustain and release components of an EG. RackAFX's built-in path programmer allows up to 15 segments, and the optional vector path generator object (available for all APIs) gives you an unlimited number of segments.

The programmed path in Figure 11.11(a) is only one type. In this simplest case, the vector mix starts at vertex 0 during the note on event, travels through the path terminating at vertex 4, and stays there until the note is released. If the note is released before the path is finished, it simply stops. This is one of the path modes in our VectorSynth. But the ProphetVS and Wavestation did not feature this path mode; instead their paradigm is to move though the first three segments as usual then stop on vertex 3 and stay there until note off, at which time the path moves into the last segment, as shown in Figure 11.11(b) (adapted from the WavestationSR Player's Guide).

Both VectorSynth and AniSynth feature this mode of operation, called sustain mode, and the second-to-last vertex in the joystick program is used as the sustain point. In addition to the normal sustain mode, the ProphetVS and Wavestation offer looping options. For example, instead of moving through the path to vertex 3 and sitting on it during the sustain portion, you could move to vertex 3 and then loop back over some or all of the previous segments, such as: 0->1->2->3->2->3->2->3..., where you are looping back and forth between vertex 2 and 3 during the sustain portion.

11.3 Rotors and Orbits

You can modulate the (x,y) coordinates of the vector joystick with LFOs, envelope generators, MIDI note numbers or other modulation sources. Both the ProphetVS and Wavestation allow you to modulate the x and y coordinates independently. For example, you might modulate the x coordinate with an LFO and leave the y coordinate alone. This would shift the joystick location from left to right as shown in Figure 11.12 (the joystick could be located anywhere; it is located at (0,0) in this example). The LFO amplitude sets the modulation depth and the, LFO frequency sets the rate at which the joystick coordinates move. In Figure 11.12(b) the sound fluctuates between 100% A and 100% C at the extremes.

A particularly interesting way to modulate the vector mix is to apply an LFO to the coordinates using the normal output to modulate one axis and the quad phase output to modulate the other axis. This produces a motion that varies from elliptical to perfectly circular, depending on the amplitude of the two modulation components, as shown in Figure 11.13. You might remember using a phasor (a rotating point in space) to generate sine and cosine functions in your math or physics classes. This is the opposite idea—here, the sine and cosine functions are used to generate the rotating point.

This kind of modulation creates a rotor—a term that Klaus Piehl coined in 1998 when he created the "Rotor Module" for the Scope DSP Library. According to John Bowen, Piehl got the idea for the term rotor from the Wankel rotary engine. It creates a modulated sound with a defined cyclical nature. Moog calls this modulation an orbit in the AniMoog vector synth app. We will use the two terms interchangeably; our projects will have a rotor that allows you to adjust the orbit-X and orbit-Y depths. If you modify your LFO to allow an adjustable phase relationship between the two outputs, you can then create any kind of angled ellipse, such as Lissagous patterns. If you modulated the output amplitudes of the LFO with another LFO, you could create an orbit that varies from each ellipse extreme to circular, as shown in Figure 11.14.

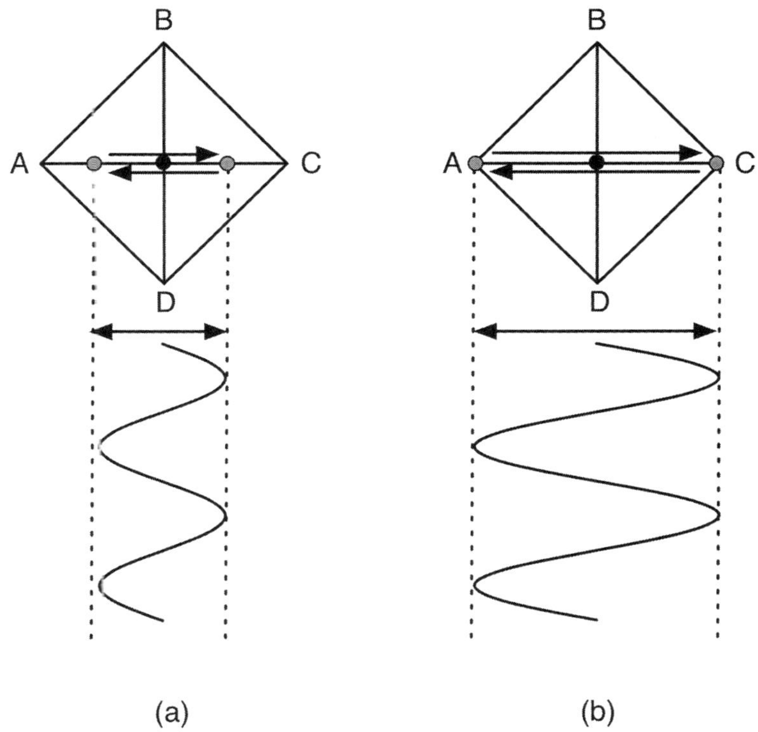

Figure 11.12: A LFO modulates the x coordinate of the joystick at (a) 50% depth and (b) 100% depth.

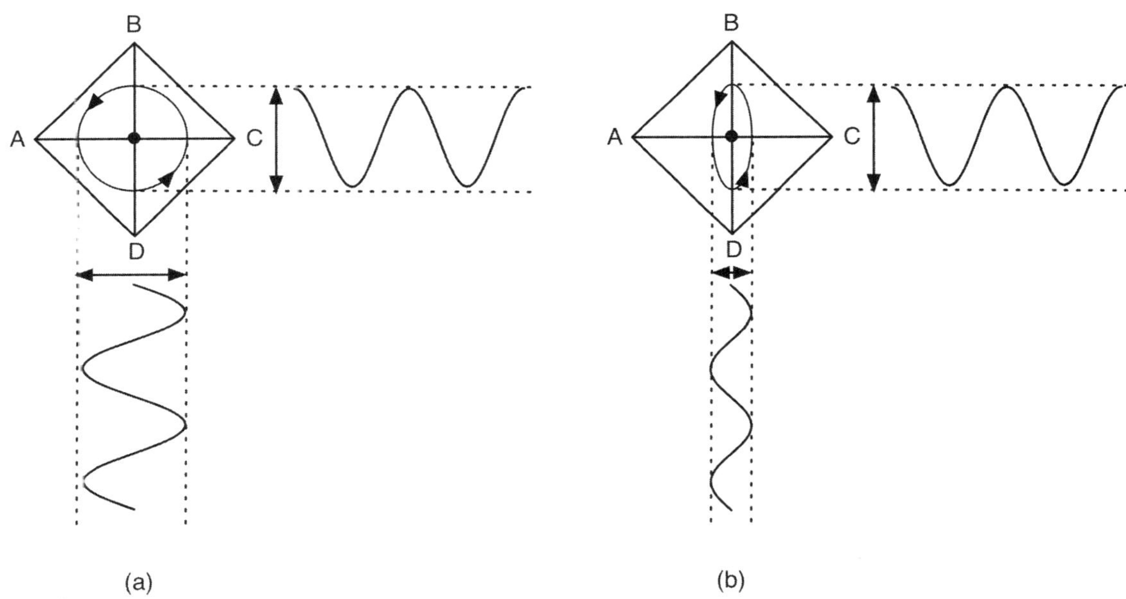

Figure 11.13: Modulating the coordinates with normal and quad phase outputs of a single LFO creates (a) a circular orbit when the two output amplitudes are identical and (b) an elliptical orbit when one amplitude is different from the other.

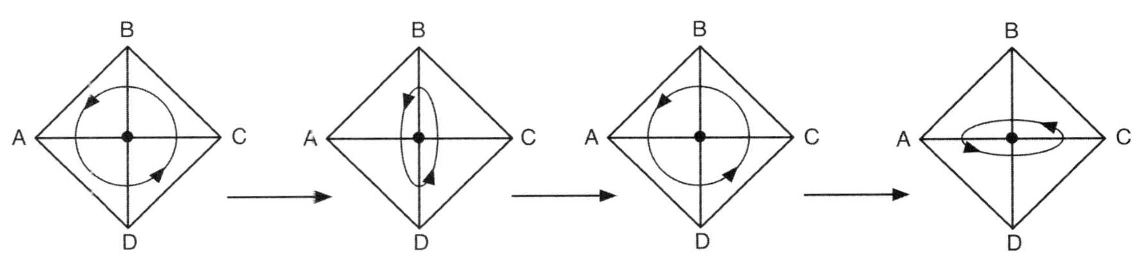

Figure 11.14: Modulating the LFO output amplitudes with another LFO results in a rotor whose shape varies from each ellipse extreme to circular and back.

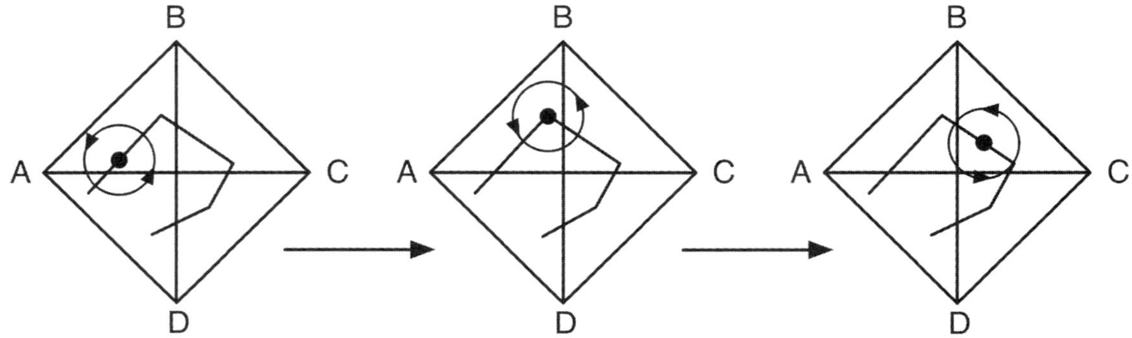

Figure 11.15: Combining a rotor with a path results in complex modulation.

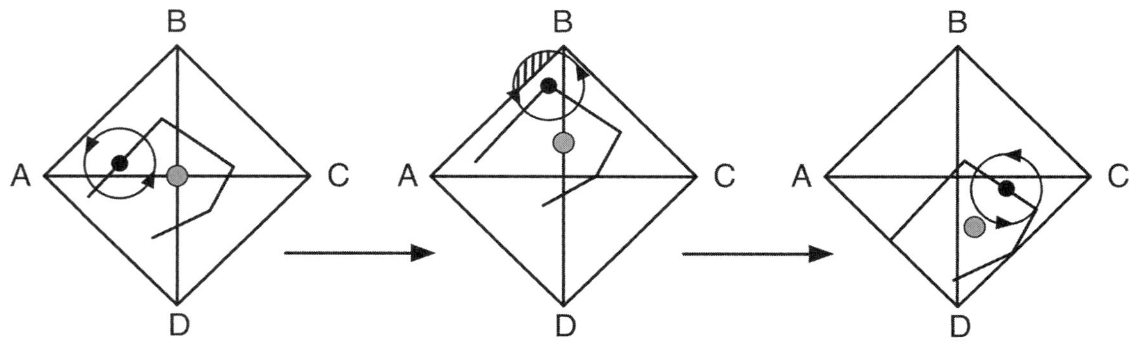

Figure 11.16: Moving the joystick (shown as the grey-filled circle) while a path/orbit is moving causes the entire path and orbit to shift; the keep-out rules apply, as shown in the center diagram (hatched area in orbit).

11.4 Combining Paths and Orbits

You can combine paths and orbits together to create complex sounds that seem to evolve and mutate almost forever. In this case, the rotor spirals around the path creating an orbiting set of (x,y) coordinates that are used to calculate the vector mix as shown in Figure 11.15. And, the same bounding rule applies—if the rotor takes the vector mix point outside the diamond, it is clamped to the boundary.

In the same manner, you can move the joystick around while the notes are playing to shift the overall center of operation as shown in Figure 11.16.

11.5 The Moog AniMoog Anisotropic Synthesizer

In 2011, Moog re-introduced vector synthesis to the world with its AniMoog iOS app. The app has won multiple awards in both musical and technical categories. Like its predecessors, it excels at producing lush evolving patches as well as searing, quickly modulated lead sounds. Moog names their brand of vector synthesis anisotropic synthesis. Merriam-Webster defines anisotropic as "exhibiting properties with different values when measured in different directions" which, like the word vector, emphasizes direction as well as magnitude. The control surface consists of a rectangular grid of 128 wavetables comprising eight rows and 16 columns, as shown in Figure 11.17. There is no vector joystick, as the grid and touch surface replace it.

The rows are called timbres. Each row consists of 16 wavetables that are musically or sonically related. Each wavetable in a row is a sample of a sound with a slight variation in amplitude, timbre, noise or some other attribute from the timbres in the same row. For example, one row might feature a synth bass sound. Moving across the row from left to right reveals that each successive wavetable is slightly brighter in timbre than the previous, as if it were sampled with the filter knob in a slightly different but increasing position. The wavetables might get more or less resonant, noisy, bass-y, midrange-y, transient, etc., as you move from left to right. Each row is a complete set of sounds. When you assign the rows, you may assign similar or different sounding timbres. You might populate the upper rows with harsh metallic sounds and the lower rows with soft mellow ones, or interleave them. The timbres themselves are named in a way that is reminiscent of the ProphetVS, such as "Distorted Primes" and "Saw Octave Drift." In other words, they are not named "Slap Bass" or "Liquid Lead"—rather, they are named after the waveform clips they contain.

AniMoog allows you to create a vector path consisting of up to 14 segments using 15 vertices by tapping on the iOS device screen. This results in a familiar vector path as shown in Figure 11.18—the obvious difference is that the path is stretched across a rectangle of 128

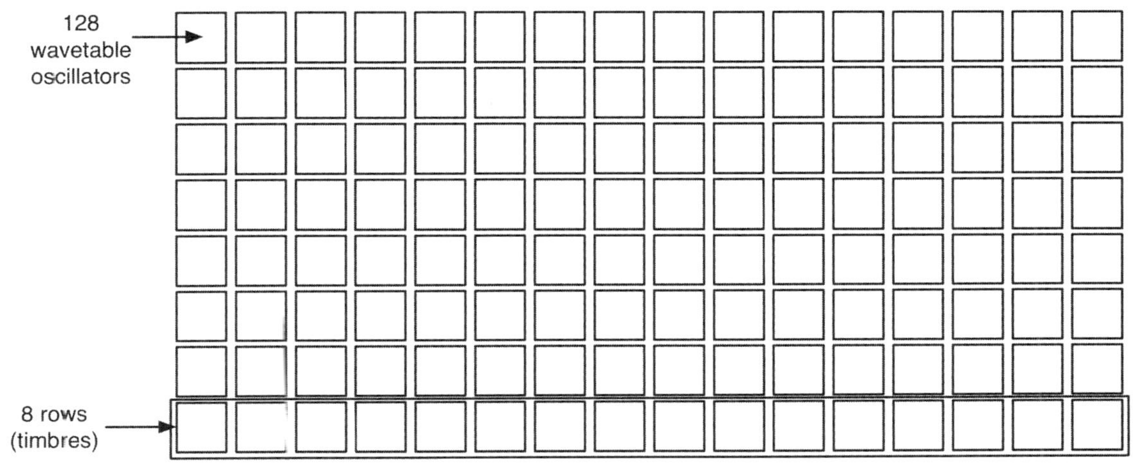

Figure 11.17: The mix surface of AniMoog consists of eight rows called timbres, each consisting of 16 wavetables.

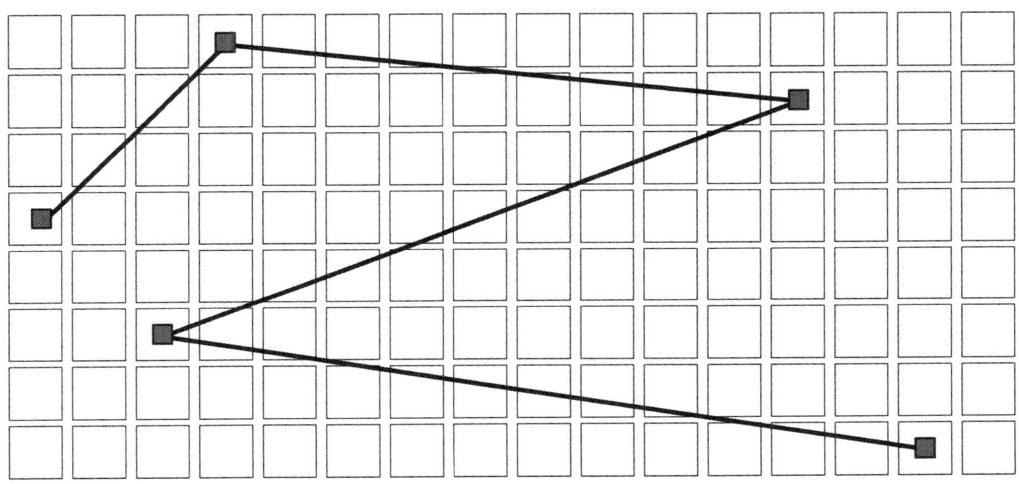

Figure 11.18: The AniMoog mix surface with five vertices and four segments.

sounds rather than a diamond of only four. Likewise, you can hear the wavetables smoothly crossfading into one another as you move along the path. You are not allowed to program the time between each segment, as in the ProphetVS and Wavestation; instead you control a single rate value that controls the overall time from the beginning vertex to the end vertex. Thus, longer segments will have a longer time from beginning to end, and shorter segments will have a shorter time. You can also program the path mode as once, loop, or back-and-forth. There are not as many looping options compared with the original vector synths, but you can set up many more segments.

A simplified block diagram is shown in Figure 11.19. You can see that there is one LFO hardwired as a rotor, with its normal and quad phase outputs connected to the vector mix generator. There are controls for rate, *x*-amplitude and *y*-amplitude. The rate is the LFO oscillator frequency, and the *x* and *y* values are the amplitudes of the normal and quad phase LFO outputs. In addition to the hardwired amp EG and filter EG, you also have a general purpose EG and LFO to use as modulation sources. The modulation matrix consists of four programmable rows, each with a source, control and destination.

With the slick touchscreen interface, the AniMoog takes the path/rotor concept up a notch by showing you the orbits of each note you trigger in different colors. The orbits chase each other around the path, looking rather like electrons orbiting nuclei that are constantly moving. For slow orbit rates, this produces a corkscrew trace; as you increase the orbit rate, the circular orbit becomes dodecahedral, then octagonal, and so on until it resembles a multi-pointed star. These visual clues aren't just there because they look cool—they let you know when the rate becomes so fast that wavetables are being skipped as the (*x*,*y*) position moves quickly. The orbits are also bound just as in the previous synths, but in this case, the keep-out zone is the outer rectangle that contains the grid. Figure 11.20 shows a slow orbiting rotor. We'll discuss more of the details when we get to the AniSynth project in a few sections. As with the other vector synths, you can shift the entire path and its orbits around by tapping on it and moving it, and likewise the same keep-out rules apply.

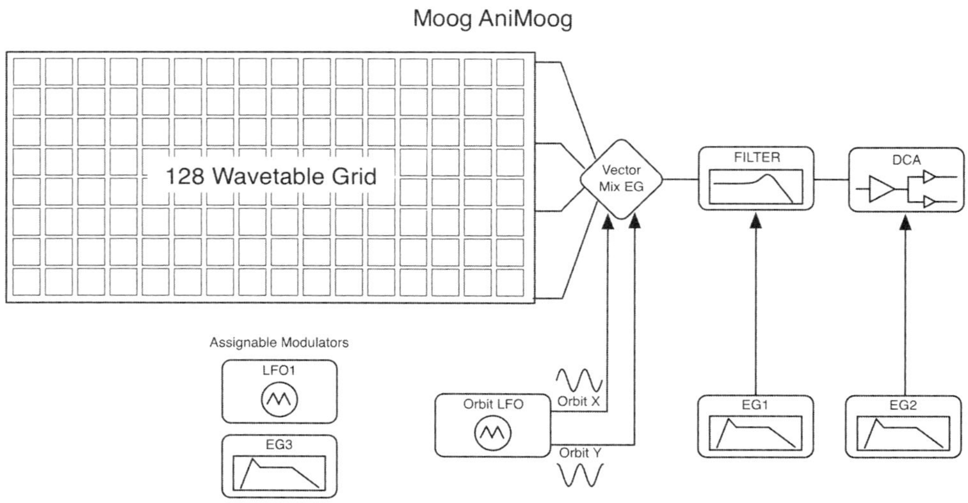

Figure 11.19: Simplified block diagram of the Moog AniMoog.

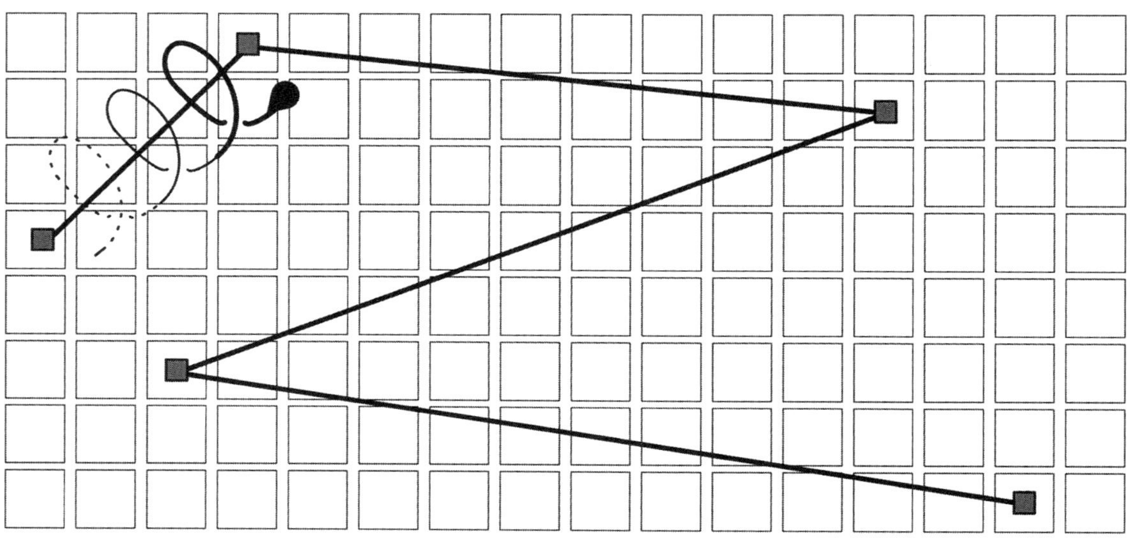

Figure 11.20: In AniMoog, the orbit is a visual animation that orbits around the path and shows you the range of wavetables in use; the orbit leaves trails as it rotates around the path.

11.6 VectorSynth and AniSynth Path Modes

The joystick programmer is different between RackAFX and VST3/AU—part of the programmer is built-in to the RackAFX client. RackAFX uses a C++ object *CJoystickProgram* that stores and executes the vector path generation. VST3 and AU use an almost identical object called *CVectorPathGenerator* that you may also use with RackAFX if you wish. However, both objects feature the same vector path modes, which are a mix of the path modes found in the ProphetVS and the AniMoog. Figure 11.21 shows the different modes. In both objects, the mix ratios morph linearly through the segments over the desired segment time.

once

In *once* mode, the joystick moves along the vector path from beginning to end without pausing. When it reaches the end vertex it sits on it until the note event is over. If the note is released mid-track, it simply follows along the path until it hits the last vertex or the note event is over. This mode is taken from the AniMoog and is not available on the ProphetVS/Wavestation.

loop

In *loop* mode, the joystick moves from the starting vertex to the ending vertex and then loops back again to the beginning over a pre-defined time. Thus this mode contains a hidden segment—the segment from end to start, as shown in Figure 11.21. In *loop* mode the program never pauses. This mode is taken from the AniMoog and is not available on the ProphetVS/Wavestation.

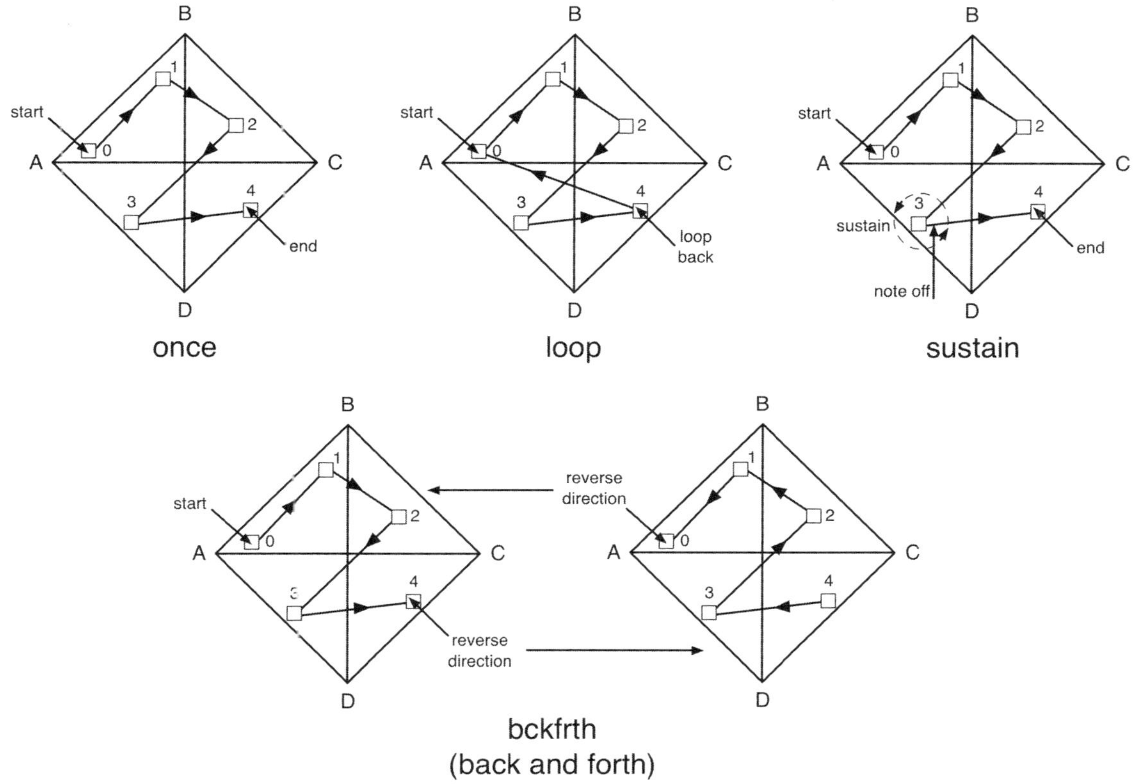

Figure 11.21: The path modes for VectorSynth and AniSynth are *once, loop, sustain* and *bckfrth*.

sustain

In *sustain* mode, the vector path will start from the beginning and move along until it reaches the second-to-last vertex in the program. It will pause the program and sit on this vertex until a note off event resumes the program operation, at which point it will move along the final segment. This mode is taken from the ProphetVS/Wavestation and is not available on AniMoog.

bckfrth (back and forth)

In the *bckfrth* mode, the vector path starts at vertex 0 and travels uninterrupted to the final vertex, where it turns around and moves backwards to the starting vertex 0, then reverses direction again and moves towards the last vertex. This operation repeats and the program never pauses. This mode is taken from the AniMoog and is not available on the ProphetVS/Wavestation.

11.7 The Vector Joystick and JS Program in RackAFX

RackAFX includes a vector joystick control in the classic ProphetVS/Wavestation orientation, a square turned on it side and shaped like a diamond as shown in Figure 11.22. The *x*-axis is labeled A-C and the y-axis is B-D. The *<Joystick>* button shows the control and the *<Program>* button is used for path programming. There is also set of four drop down list boxes that you may optionally populate with values and receive messages when the user selects an item. The idea is to show the user what kind of oscillator, waveform or sound source is attached to each of the four apexes A, B, C, and D, and to allow the user to change that sound source. For VectorSynth and AniSynth, populating these boxes is optional and since these synths have fixed sources, they won't mean much. You can, however, add more multi-samples to the project and eventually populate the controls with multiple choices to allow the user to map many different sounds to the apexes of the mix surface. To set these boxes up, you click on the down-arrow to the right, and an item appears that says "Select to Setup." Select this item from the list, and the familiar enumerated UINT dialog opens—the same as for the radio buttons. You enter a variable name like *m_uVSApexAList*, and then an enumerated list, like "saw, sine, triangle, square." When the user selects an item, the underlying variable is set with the zero-based index of the item in the list, and *userInterfaceChange()* is called. The *ControlID* values for the four boxes are 60, 61, 62, and 63 for the A, B, C, and D controls, respectively.

For our projects the more important controls are the vector joystick itself and the joystick program. Unlike most of the RackAFX controls, the joystick does not map to an underlying variable in your plug-in and does not call *userInterfaceChange()*. Instead, it calls an exclusive message handler named *joystickControlChange()*.

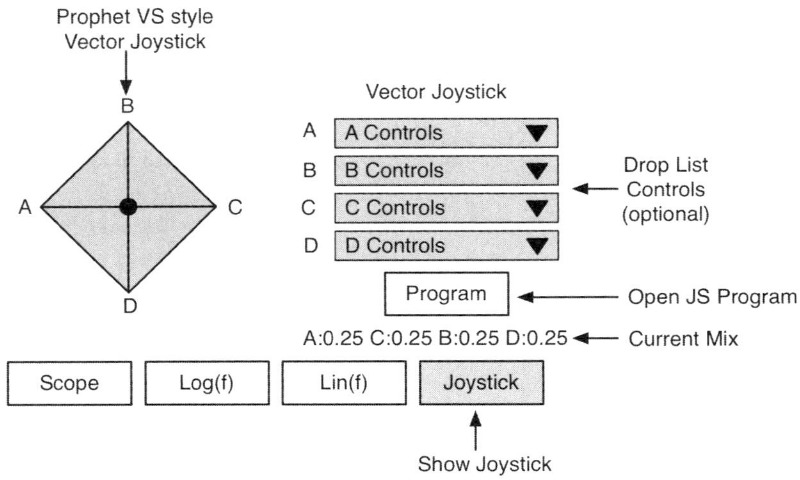

Figure 11.22: The vector joystick in RackAFX uses the classic ProphetVS orientation.

```
joystickControlChange(float fControlA, /* Vector Mix A */
                      float fControlB, /* Vector Mix B */
                      float fControlC, /* Vector Mix C */
                      float fControlD, /* Vector Mix D */
                      float fACMix,    /* A-C Projection */
                      float fBDMix)    /* B-D Projection */
```

There is a comment chunk above the function to remind you what the arguments are.

```
Indicates the user moved the joystick point the variables are the relative mixes of each axis; the
values will add up to 1.0

          B
          |
    A -   x    - C
          |
          D

The point in the very center (x) would be:
fControlA = 0.25
fControlB = 0.25
fControlC = 0.25
fControlD = 0.25

AC Mix = projection on X Axis (0 -> 1)
BD Mix = projection on Y Axis (0 -> 1)
```

This function is called when the user moves the joystick by one pixel on the screen, so it may be called in rapid fire succession; make sure you don't place time consuming code in this message handler. Typically, we just copy the new joystick mix values into the plug-in variables; here we are using global parameters:

```
bool __stdcall CVectorSynth::joystickControlChange(args...)
{
     // --- update globals
     m_GlobalSynthParams.voiceParams.dAmplitude_A = fControlA;
     m_GlobalSynthParams.voiceParams.dAmplitude_B = fControlB;
     m_GlobalSynthParams.voiceParams.dAmplitude_C = fControlC;
     m_GlobalSynthParams.voiceParams.dAmplitude_D = fControlD;
```

Table 11.1: A multi-dimensional array stores the joystick program as a set of rows.

Vertex	A	B	C	D	time (mSec)	AC	BD
0	0.25	0.25	0.25	0.25	2500	0.5	0.5
1	1.00	0.0	0.0	0.0	750	0.0	0.5
2	0.0	0.0	1.0	0.0	3000	1.0	0.5

```
    m_GlobalSynthParams.voiceParams.dAmplitude_ACmix = fACMix;
    m_GlobalSynthParams.voiceParams.dAmplitude_BDmix = fBDMix;

    return true;
}
```

RackAFX includes a built-in object named *CJoystickProgram* that encapsulates a vector joystick program with up to 15 segments. The object is programmed with a simple interface. The declaration is in *pluginconstants.h*, and the implementation is in *pluginobjects.cpp*. For VST3 and AU users, we have created a similar object named *CVectorPathGenerator* that you may also use in RackAFX. You program this object with code, but the function names are identical to *CJoystickProgram*, so it is simple to switch between them. *CVectorPathGenerator* can have an unlimited number of segments. If you are interested in using it, read the following sections for VST3 and AU.

CJoystickProgram does almost all of the work for you, and you don't need to know most of the gory details unless you want to try one of the Challenges; visit the website for a detailed description of the object. At the heart of the object is a multi-dimensional array that holds information about each vertex in the path in its rows. Table 11.1 shows a typical program that has three vertices or two segments. The array is zero-indexed, where each row is a vertex in the path. Here, the path starts at vertex 0 with the joystick centered and all mix ratios at 0.25 (25%). The duration to the next vertex is 2.5 seconds (2,500 mSec). The AC and BD mixes are pre-calculated from the A, B, C, and D mix values, and stored in the table when it is programmed to save time later. The vector mix will morph into the next row over a period of 2.5 seconds, at which point the mix is now 100% A and 0% everything else. The time to the next segment is 750 mSec. If the program is using sustain mode, the program would stop and sit on vertex 1 until a note off event resumes the program execution to the next row. The final row shows that the vector mix will end at 100% C and 0% everything else. Notice the time-to-next-segment is 3,000 mSec in this example. If the program is in *loop* mode, this is the time it takes to loop back to vertex 0.

Multidimensional arrays can be tricky in C/C++ when you need to pass a pointer to the array as a function argument. Therefore *CJoystickProgram* uses a classic programming trick where you flatten out the array as a single one-dimensional chunk of memory, arranged as concatenated table rows (this is how the compiler usually does it too). A macro is defined that allows you to easily find cells in the array. The macro is called JS_PROG_INDEX:

```
#define JS_PROG_INDEX(x,y) ((x)+(MAX_JS_PROGRAM_STEPS*(y)))
```

For example, if the array is named *m_pJSProgramTable*, you would find the cell at row 2, column 5 as:

```
fAC_Mix = m_pJSProgramTable[JS_PROG_INDEX(2,5)];
```

You don't have to worry about this unless you want to modify the object.

The *CJoystickProgram* object requires that you create the blank, flattened table prior to instantiating the object, and that you pass a pointer to this object as an argument in the default constructor. Fortunately, this has already been done in the *CPlugIn* base class constructor. All RackAFX plug-ins have a built-in member variable named *m_pVectorJSProgram,* which is created and cleared at construction time. It is also automatically destroyed for you at destruction. The reason for using a dynamically declared flattened table is that in RackAFX, you can change the program anytime you wish, even after the plug-in has been compiled (this is a RackAFX exclusive, and not available for VST3/AU unless you add some GUI controls and code). In RackAFX, you can create a default joystick program that is compiled into the object or leave it blank. In the others, you are forced to declare a default program or else there will be no program to execute. Table 11.2 shows a selected set of member functions you will need to use the object. It's actually very simple to set up.

Programming the CJoystickProgram *Object*

RackAFX makes it simple to program the object. It uses a method similar to that in the ProphetVS/Wavestation. In those synths, you open the program panel and move the joystick to the desired location, usually while auditioning that mix. As you move the joystick, you see the mix ratios changing. When satisfied, you enter this mix as the first vertex. Then, you would move the joystick to the second vertex position, enter it, and enter the time for the segment. This continues until all vertex points and times are defined.

In RackAFX, when you hit the <*Program*> button, a dialog appears like the one shown in Figure 11.23.

Table 11.2: The *CJoystickProgram* functions you will be using.

***CJoystickProgram* Selected Member Functions**	
Function Name	**Description**
CJoystickProgram	Constructor
setSampleRate	set the sample rate for timing the program operation
startProgram	start the program at note on time
resumeProgram	resume the program at note off time if in *sustain* mode
incTimer	increment the program timer by one sample interval
getVectorMixValues	returns the A, B, C, D, AC-mix and BD-mix values
getVectorABCDMixes	returns only the AC-mix and BD-mix values

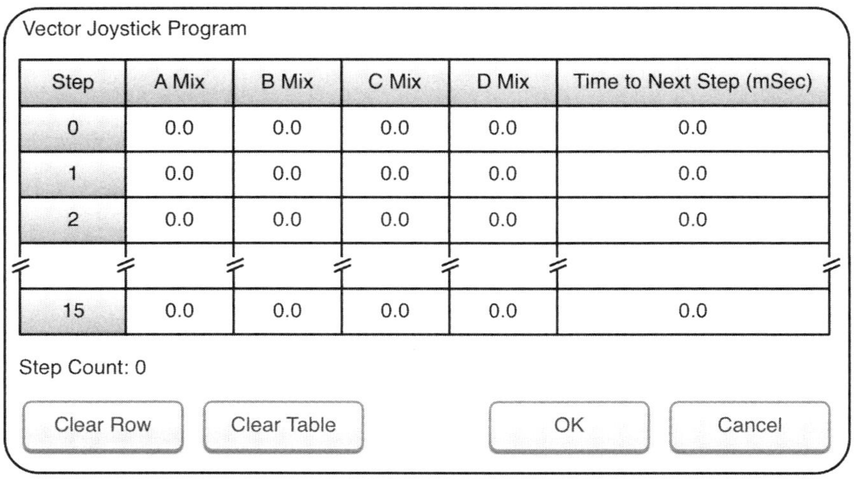

Figure 11.23: A blank RackAFX Vector joystick program dialog awaiting programming.

You then follow a similar sequence as outlined in Figure 11.24 to program the rows:

1. select the first row by clicking on it
2. move the joystick to the location for vertex 0; you will see the mix values update in real time as you move the joystick
3. when satisfied with the location, click on the Time to Next Step cell and enter the duration in mSec for the first segment, then hit <*Return*>
4. this advances the selected row to the next one down (you can always click on a row to select it too)
5. move the joystick to the next vertex and repeat from step 3
6. continue until you are done entering rows (you are not allowed to skip rows); on the last row, the Time to Next Step, you enter will only be valid in *loop* mode, where the last vertex advances to the first in a hidden segment

You can use the <*Clear Row*> and <*Clear Table*> buttons to make mass edits to the rows.

You can program the joystick at development time to create a preset, and you can also reprogram it at run time while auditioning notes. This <*Joystick Program*> button and dialog are also available when you use the *Make VST2 Compatible* function and create a custom GUI—there is a drag-and-drop joystick control on the GUI Designer page, so you can still use the VS programmer in your VST2 synths.

Using the CJoystickProgram *Object*

Once you've got a program set up in development mode, you need to create and implement the object. In our synth projects, we will declare an enumerated UINT *m_uVectorPathMode*, with the enum string {*once, loop, sustain, bckfrth*}.

Construction

When you construct the object, you need to pass it the flattened table and the default mode of operation like this:

```
m_pVoiceArray[i]->m_pJSProgram = new CJoystickProgram(m_pVectorJSProgram,
                                                       m_uVectorPathMode);
```

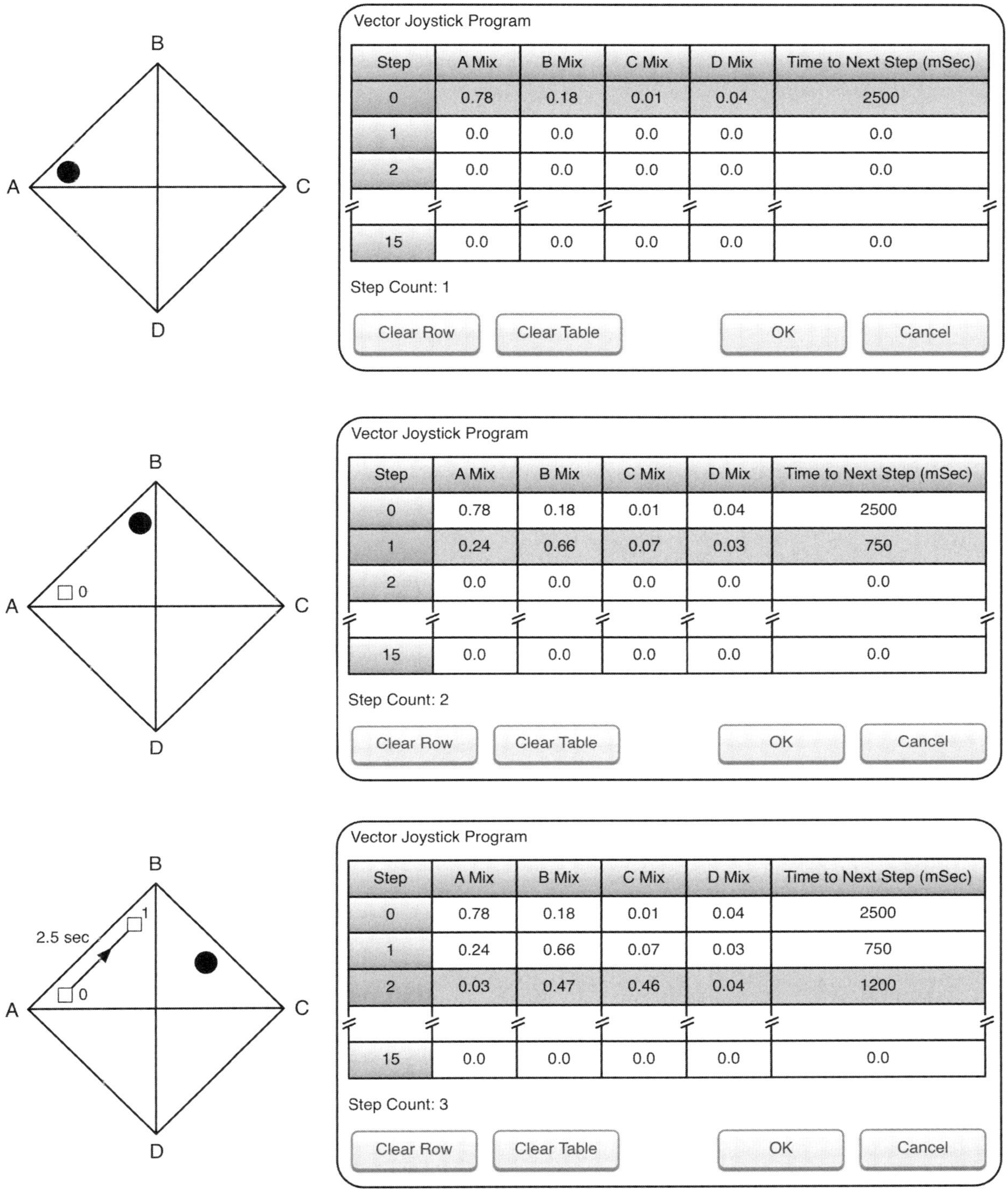

Figure 11.24: Programming the vector joystick in RackAFX is easy; select a row, move the joystick and enter the segment time.

Our *CVectorSynthVoice* and *CAniSynthVoice* objects each include a pointer to a *CJoystickProgram* for use with RackAFX. Here the arguments are:

`m_pVectorJSProgram`: the built-in, pre-made flattened table available at construction time

`m_uVectorPathMode`: the mode variable on the plug-in which defaults to *once*

Starting/Stopping

You start the program during a note on event with *startProgram()*. If the joystick program is in *sustain* mode, it will pause itself once the sustain vertex is hit (remember, it's the second to last one in the program list). When the note off event occurs, you resume operation with *resumeProgram()*, which takes the path through the last segment. If the program is not in *sustain* mode, there is nothing else to do there.

Incrementing the Program

You have to increment the program on each sample interval to update the new vector mix. After incrementing the program, you can query it for the new vector mix. These two steps always go together.

```
// --- some variables to hold the mix values
float fA, fB, fC, fD, fAC, fBD;
m_pJSProgram->incTimer();

// --- uses pass-by-reference to set our vars with values
m_pJSProgram->getVectorMixValues(fA, fB, fC, fD);
m_pJSProgram->getVectorACBDMixes(fAC, fBD);
```

That's all there is to programming the joystick path in RackAFX. The program is deleted for you when the plug-in is destroyed.

11.8 The Vector Joystick in VST3

So far, all of the controls we've used in the VST3 projects have been limited to knobs and option menu groups. These controls automatically connect to a control index value (tag), and they generate a single value per control. The joystick presents a bit of a problem because we need to generate two signals, one for the *x*-coordinate and another for the *y*-coordinate. These two signals will automatically control two *Parameter* objects you create to hold the *x* and *y* coordinates of the joystick. As usual, this requires index values that we place in the control enumeration in *SynthParamLimits.h*:

```
VECTORJOYSTICK_X
VECTORJOYSTICK_Y
```

You declare and create these controls in *Controller::initialize()*, along with the other usual controls.

VTSGUI has a built-in C++ object for the GUI control called *CXYPad,* a two dimensional track-pad style control—in effect, a vector joystick rotated by 45 degrees. In order to get two values out of the control, you need to use the VSTGUI sub-controller feature. A sub-controller is a C++ object that you can connect to a VTGUI object for finer control over its operation or appearance. VSTGUI comes with a few built-in C++ objects for some of the more common controls; you can also write your own. VSTGUI provides you with an object called *PadController*. Its functionality is coded in *vst3padcontroller.h* and *vst3padcontroller.cpp,* though you don't need to edit any of it. You connect the C++ pad controller object to the *CXYPad* GUI control and then pass it pointers to the *Parameter* objects you created during initialization. Setting up this new custom joystick control is a two-part process.

Part One: Controller

In the Controller object, you need to add a new function to allow the use of the sub-controller. It is an override of a function in the *VST3EditorDelegate* object, so your Controller object must inherit from this new object. Step one is to change the class definition and add the overridden function *createSubController()* (you can safely ignore the VSTGUI_OVERRIDE_VMETHOD macro at the end of the function):

```
class Controller: public EditController, public IMidiMapping,
                  public VST3EditorDelegate

      <SNIP SNIP SNIP>

      // --- VST3EditorDelegate overrides (for the joystick controller)
      //
      IController* createSubController(UTF8StringPtr name,
                                       IUIDescription* description,
                                       VST3Editor* editor)
                                       VSTGUI_OVERRIDE_VMETHOD;
```

In the *VSTSynthController.cpp* file, you implement this function. This function is a catch-all function for all the sub-controllers in your GUI, so if you add more of them, you will alter this function accordingly. The sub-controllers are identified by a simple string value. We chose the string "VectorJoystick" as the identifier for the vector joystick, though you can rename it if you wish. The GUI will query this function for any sub-controllers that are tagged in the GUI design editor. The function is reasonably simple enough:

- decode the sub-controller name looking for VectorJoystick
- get the joystick X and Y parameters
- create the new *PadController* object and connect it to the joystick X and Y parameters

```
IController* Controller::createSubController (UTF8StringPtr _name,
                                              IUIDescription* description,
                                              VST3Editor* editor)
{
    // --- get the name string to test
    ConstString name (_name);

    // --- check the sub-controller name
    if(name == "VectorJoystick")
    {
        // --- get the X and Y parameter objects from our list
        Parameter* jsX = getParameterObject(VECTORJOYSTICK_X);
        Parameter* jsY = getParameterObject(VECTORJOYSTICK_Y);

        // --- create the pad controller and pass it the X and Y
        //     parameter pointers
        PadController* padController = new PadController(editor, this,
                                                          jsX, jsY);

        // --- return the newly created object
        return padController;
    }

    return NULL;
}
```

This is the only code you need to write—everything else is handled in VSTGUI and the *PadController* object.

Part Two: GUI

Now you can open the VSTGUI editor in your VST3 client and add the new joystick control, or use the sample code with the control already added. The steps are:

- select the outer view container to hold the control
- drag an instance of *CXYPad* into the container and position/size it as you wish
- go to the upper right of the editor to the Attributes section where you normally set the x,y coordinates, size and control-tag; in this case, instead of connecting the control to a control-tag, you connect it to a sub-controller that is at the bottom of the list; you simply type in the sub-controller name string "VectorJoystick" as shown in Figure 11.25

That's all there is to creating the control; it will automatically update our X and Y parameters as the user moves the puck around the pad. We have also added some static text objects A, B, C, and D to the GUI, placing them at the four vertices of the square. In addition, we added an image file that shows a radial gradient. The joystick control in VectorSynth looks like what you see in Figure 11.26.

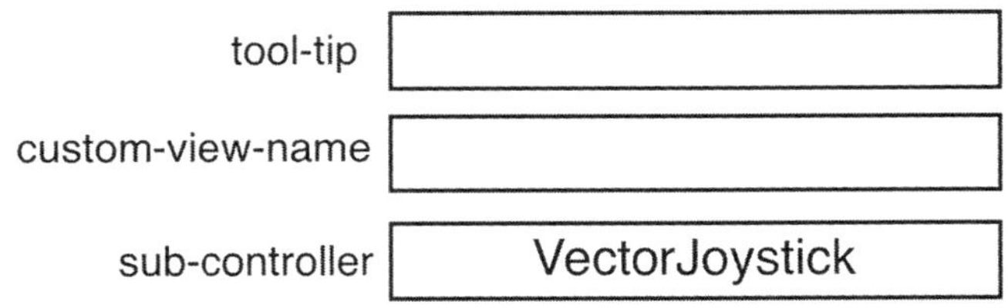

Figure 11.25: Connecting the *CXYPad* to the *PadController* object is easy—just supply the ID string of the sub-controller we created in the *createSubController()* function.

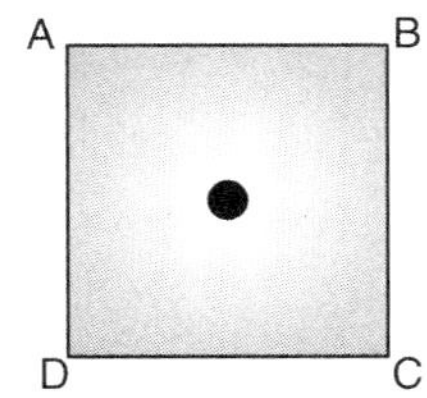

Figure 11.26: The vector joystick in VST3 is just a rotated version of the classic diamond shape, with an optional gradient background image.

11.9 The Vector Joystick in AU

For the AU synths, we created another custom control subclassed from *NSControl* named *WPTrackPad*. The interface and implementation are in *WPTrackPad.h* and *WPTrackPad.cpp*. You don't need to really know anything about the operation since it's fully encapsulated and works in a similar manner to the other custom objects you are already accustomed to using. The object is actually very simple—when you click in the object's frame, it tracks the location of the mouse and converts the mouse screen coordinates to (x,y) coordinates on the range [−1..+1]. Like the VST3 control, it is not diamond shaped but is the result of rotating the diamond by 45 degrees—a square. The location of the joystick is shown using the similar puck plus lines drawn form the vertices drawn from the four corners.

The declaration for *WPTrackPad* is shown below. There is only one member method called *getControlCoordsX:Y:*, which returns the (x,y) coordinates on the range [−1..+1]. The other variables are for maintaining the mouse positions for button down and button up events. The *knobScale* variable is reserved for future use.

```
@interface WPTrackPad : NSControl
{
    // --- these are raw positions -1 to +1 ordinarily
    CGSize currentPosition;  // current position
    CGSize mouseDownPosition; // position of knob when mousedown

    // --- mouse down location
    CGSize mouseDownLocation;

    // --- mouse point location
    NSPoint mousePoint;

    // --- default is 1.0
    float knobScale;
}
// --- get the XY coordinates of mouse
-(void)getControlCoordsX:(float*)x Y:(float*)y;
```

Adding the joystick control to your plug-in is a three part process. Remember that. because of the flat namespace in Cocoa, you need to rename the control and its custom cell for each new synth project, but you should be used to this by now.

Part One: Declare the Controls

As usual, this requires index values that we place in the control enumeration in *SynthParamLimits.h*:

```
VECTORJOYSTICK_X
VECTORJOYSTICK_Y
```

You declare and create these controls in *AUSynth::GetParameterInfo()* along with the other usual controls as if they were just two more continuous controls. You also need to initialize them in the constructor as usual. They are available as global parameters in your plug-in.

Part Two: View Object

In the view object, *#include* the proper files and add an *IBOutlet* for the new object; here the view is *VectorSynthView*. You also need to declare a message handler for the control named *WPTrackPadChanged* (my choice, you are free to name the function whatever you wish).

```
#import "WPTrackPad.h"

@interface VectorSynthView : NSView
{
      // --- rotary knob groups
      //
      // --- column 1
      IBOutlet WPRotaryKnob* wpRotaryKnob_0;
      IBOutlet WPRotaryKnob* wpRotaryKnob_1;

      <SNIP SNIP SNIP>

      // --- the custom NSControl for vector joystick
      IBOutlet WPTrackPad* vectorJoystick;

      // --- array for controls
      NSMutableArray* controlArray;

      <SNIP SNIP SNIP>
}

- (id)getControlWithIndex:(int)index;

#pragma mark ____ PUBLIC FUNCTIONS ____
- (void)setAU:(AudioUnit)inAU;

#pragma mark ____ INTERFACE ACTIONS ____

- (IBAction)WPRotaryKnobChanged:(id)sender;
- (IBAction)WPOptionMenuItemChanged:(id)sender;
- (IBAction)WPTrackPadChanged:(id)sender;

etc...
```

Next, you implement the message handler in the *.m* file in the usual way that you implement the knob and option menu handlers, only this control issues two values instead of one. You also need to convert the bipolar coordinates to unipolar values since VectorSynth and AniSynth use the unipolar version.

```
- (IBAction)WPTrackPadChanged:(id)sender
{
    // --- the WPTrackPad generates bi-polar x,y values on the ranges
    //     x:[-1..+1] and y:[-1..+1]
    float x,y;
    [sender getControlCoordsX:&x
                            Y:&y];

    // --- BUT the vector joystick in the Synth is unipolar
    //     so convert here first
    x = 0.5*x + 0.5;
    y = 0.5*y + 0.5;

    // --- make an AudioUnitParameter set in our AU buddy
    AudioUnitParameter paramX = {buddyAU, VECTORJOYSTICK_X,
                                 kAudioUnitScope_Global, 0 };

    // --- set the AU Parameter; this calls SetParameter() in the au
    AUParameterSet(AUEventListener, sender, &paramX, (Float32)x, 0);

    // --- make an AudioUnitParameter set in our AU buddy
    AudioUnitParameter paramY = {buddyAU, VECTORJOYSTICK_Y,
                                 kAudioUnitScope_Global, 0 };

    // --- set the AU Parameter; this calls SetParameter() in the au
    AUParameterSet(AUEventListener, sender, &paramY, (Float32)y, 0);
}
```

Part Three: Interface Builder

In Interface Builder (IB), you edit the *CocoaView.nib* file to add the new control:

- drag and drop an instance of the *CustomView* object into the GUI
- in the inspector, set its Custom Class to *WPTrackPad*
- set the object's Referencing Outlet to connect to the *IBOutlet* variable you previously declared, vectorJoystick
- connect the object's Sent Actions to the handler *WPTrackPadChanged*

With the global parameters declared in the *AUSynth* object and the GUI controls connected, there is nothing left to do but pick up the (*x,y*) values and use them during processing. Figure 11.27 shows the AU version of the vector joystick control.

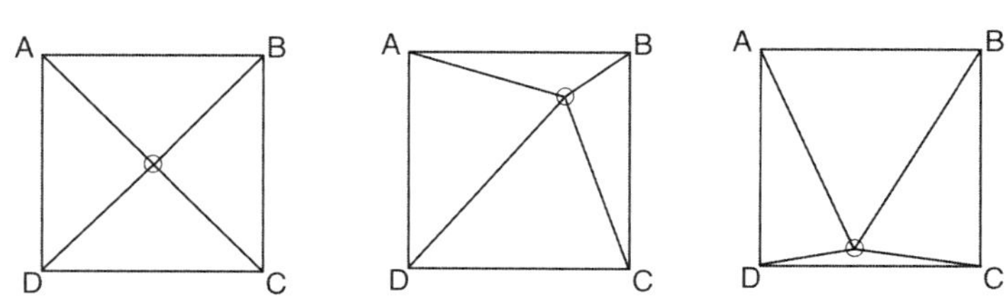

Figure 11.27: The AU version of the vector joystick.

11.10 Programming a Vector Path: VST3 and AU

RackAFX already features a built-in joystick programming interface, and RackAFX plug-ins use an existing object called *CJoystickProgram* to store the program, and run it to generate a path. VST3 and AU use an object that is virtually identical to *CJoystickProgram* called *CVectorPathGenerator.*

CVectorPathGenerator does almost all of the work for you, and you don't need to know most of the gory details unless you want to try one of the Challenges; visit the website for a detailed description of the object. At the heart of the object is a multi-dimensional array that holds information about each vertex in the path in its rows. Table 11.3 shows a typical program that has three vertices or two segments. The array is zero-indexed, and each row is a vertex in the path. Here, the path starts at vertex 0 with the joystick centered and all mix ratios at 0.25. The duration to the next vertex is 2.5 seconds (2500 mSec). The AC and BD mixes are pre-calculated from the A, B, C, and D mix values, and stored in the table when it is programmed to save time later. The vector mix will morph into the next row over a period of 2.5 seconds, at which point the mix is now 100% A and 0% everything else. The time to the next segment is 750 mSec. If the program is using *sustain* mode, the program would stop and sit on vertex 1 until a note off event resumes the program execution to the next row. The final row shows that the vector mix will end at 100% C and 0% everything else. Notice the time-to-next-segment is 3000 mSec in this example. If the program is in *loop* mode, this is the time it takes to loop back to vertex 0.

Multidimensional arrays can be tricky in C/C++ when you want to pass a pointer to the array as a function argument. Therefore *CVectorPathGenerator* uses a classic programming trick where you flatten out the array as a single one-dimensional chunk of memory, arranged as concatenated table rows (this is how the compiler usually does it too). A macro is defined that allows you to easily find cells in the array. The macro is called JS_PROG_INDEX:

```
#define JS_PROG_INDEX(x,y) ((x)+(MAX_JS_PROGRAM_STEPS*(y)))
```

For example, if the array is named *m_pVPGProgramTable*, you would find the cell at row 2, column 5 as:

```
fAC_Mix = m_pVPGProgramTable[JS_PROG_INDEX(2,5)];
```

You don't have to worry about this unless you want to modify the object.

Table 11.4 shows a selected set of member functions you will need to use the object. It's actually very simple to set up.

Programming the CVectorPathGenerator *Object*

Unlike RackAFX's *CJoystickProgram*, the vector path generator must be programmed in code unless you want to create a programming dialog/panel as suggested in the Challenges, and you must set this one and only default program at construction time. The reason for the difference is that the GUI panel that is used for programming and updating the RackAFX path generator is built into the client, not

Table 11.3: A multi-dimensional array stores the joystick program as a set of rows.

Vertex	A	B	C	D	time (mSec)	AC	BD
0	0.25	0.25	0.25	0.25	2500	0.5	0.5
1	1.00	0.0	0.0	0.0	750	0.0	0.5
2	0.0	0.0	1.0	0.0	3000	1.0	0.5

Table 11.4: The *CVectorPathGenerator* functions you will be using.

***CVectorPathGenerator* Selected Member Functions**	
Function Name	**Description**
CVectorPathGenerator	Constructor
setProgramStep	adds a new row to the array
setSampleRate	set the sample rate for timing the program operation
startProgram	start the program at note on time
resumeProgram	resume the program at note off time if in *sustain* mode
incTimer	increment the program timer by one sample interval
getVectorMixValues	returns the A, B, C, D, AC-mix and BD-mix values
getVectorABCDMixes	returns only the AC-mix and BD-mix values

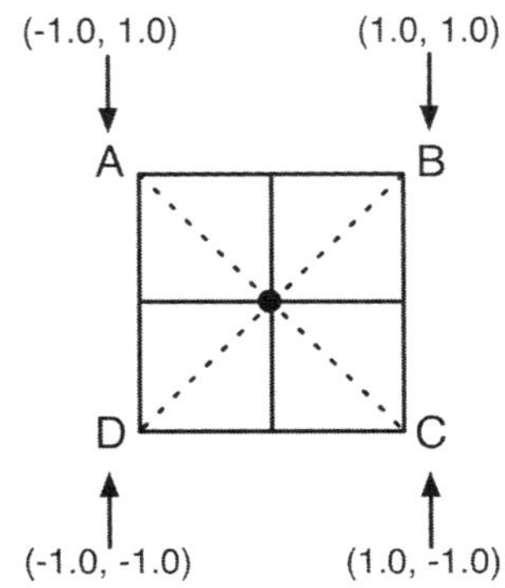

Figure 11.28: The *CVectorPathGenerator* object uses the rotated coordinates to identify locations in the mix plane, though you can also program it with the traditional literal joystick coordinates.

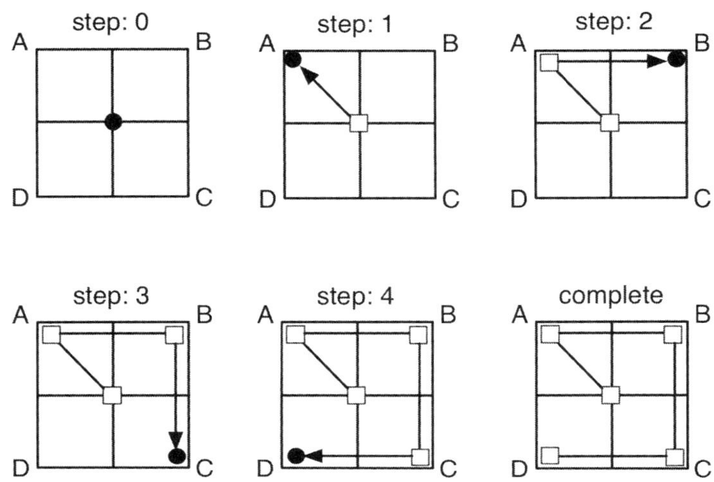

Figure 11.29: An example path for programming.

the plug-in. If you are talented with Windows dialog boxes or MacOS windows, then you can make your own interface. That design is beyond the scope of this book.

When working with the *CVectorPathGenerator* object, the main thing to remember is that the joystick control has already been rotated by 45 degrees, so the diamond is lying on its side like a square. Figure 11.28 shows the coordinates for the A, B, C, and D vertices. The center is still (0,0) as usual.

When programming *CVectorPathGenerator* object, you have the choice of using *joystick coordinates*, the literal coordinate system from the ProphetVS/Wavestation and what RackAFX uses, or you can program with the rotated coordinates; since the vertices are at easy-to-remember locations, this is actually fairly simple and your choice. The sample code shows how to use the rotated coordinates.

Programming

Both vector synths in this chapter use the now familiar *CVoice* derived objects to handle the voice chores. Both declare a static member variable of type *CVectorPathGenerator* named *m_VPG*. Programming it requires a set of function calls to only one function named *setProgramStep()*.

```
void CVectorPathGenerator::setProgramStep(int nIndex, float fX, float fY,
                                          float fTimeToNextStep_mSec,
                                          bool bJoystickCoords)
```

The arguments are:

- nIndex: the zero-based index of the step (path vertex) you are adding
- *fX* and *fY*: the *(x,y)* coordinate of the new vertex
- *fTimeToNextStep_mSec*: the segment transition time to the next vertex
- *bJoystickCoords*: true if you are using the literal joystick coordinates, false if you are using the rotated version

For example, let's program the following path in non-joystick coordinates shown in Figure 11.29. This path starts at the c enter then moves through all four vertices so that the sound starts at an equal mix then morphs between 100% versions of each sound source.

The coordinates for each step are:

0: (0.0, 0.0) = 25% A, 25% B, 25% C, 25% D
1: (−1.0, 1.0) = 100% A
2: (1.0, 1.0) = 100% B
3: (1.0, −1.0) = 100% C
4: (−1.0, −1.0) = 100% D

For simplicity let's make the segment times 2 seconds each. The programming is then simply:

```
m_VPG.setProgramStep(0, 0.0, 0.0, 2000, false);
m_VPG.setProgramStep(1, -1.0, 1.0, 2000, false);
m_VPG.setProgramStep(2, 1.0, 1.0, 2000, false);
m_VPG.setProgramStep(3, 1.0, -1.0, 2000, false);
m_VPG.setProgramStep(4, -1.0, -1.0, 2000, false);
```

Notice the last argument, which is the joystick coordinate flag—it is *false* here because we are using rotated coordinates.

Starting/Stopping

You start the program during a note on event with *startProgram()*. If the joystick program is in *sustain* mode, it will pause itself once the sustain vertex is hit (remember, it's the second to last one in the program). When the note off event occurs, you resume operation with *resumeProgram()*, which takes the path through the last segment. If the program is not in *sustain* mode, there is nothing else to do here.

Incrementing the Program

You have to increment the program on each sample interval to update the new vector mix. After incrementing the program, you can query it for the new vector mix values. These two steps always go together.

```
// --- some variables to hold the mix values
float fA, fB, fC, fD, fAC, fBD;
m_VPG.incTimer();

// --- uses pass-by-reference to set our vars with values
m_VPG.getVectorMixValues(fA, fB, fC, fD);
m_VPG.getVectorACBDMixes(fAC, fBD);
```

11.11 VectorSynth Specifications

Figure 11.30 shows VectorSynth's simplified block diagram, while Figure 11.31 shows the detailed connection graph. You can see that it is another evolutionary step from DigiSynth and adds the second Rotor LFO with controls for Rate, Waveform, Orbit X (normal) and Orbit Y (quad phase) Amplitudes, and changes Loop Mode to Vector Path Mode. DigiSynth's Osc1 Output and Osc2 Output controls have now changed to A-C Output and B-D Output, allowing you to fine tune the vector mix even more.

Oscillators

- four *CSampleOscillators* with four sets of stereo multi-samples

Filters

- two *CKThreeFiveFilters* (one for left, one for right), LPF mode, NLP engaged

LFOs

- two *CLFOs*, one general purpose and one for the rotor

Voice Mode

- *manual:* you use the vector joystick to mix your oscillators in realtime
- *program:* you run a vector path program

Vector Path Mode

- *once:* one time through path
- *loop:* loop over complete path
- *sustain:* stop at second to last vertex during sustain, resume after note off
- *bckfrth:* move back and forth over complete path

You already understand the details of the *CSampleOscillator* for loading multi-samples, so we don't need to go over that again.

Table 11.5 shows the VectorSynth modulation matrix, and Table 11.6 shows the GUI control list. The modulation matrix is the same as DigiSynth but with the addition of the rotor LFO2; notice the use of the quad output (LFO2Q) and how they modulate the AC and BD axes.

VST3 and AU

These clients do not have a built-in vector joystick control, so you will need to add two more parameters (and two more variables for VST3) so we can connect the new custom joystick controls to the plug-in. These two additional control parameters are at the end of the continuous control list.

Other than the VST3 and AU additions, you will see that the controls are about 98% the same as DigiSynth, so you can re-use a lot of the code you've previously written.

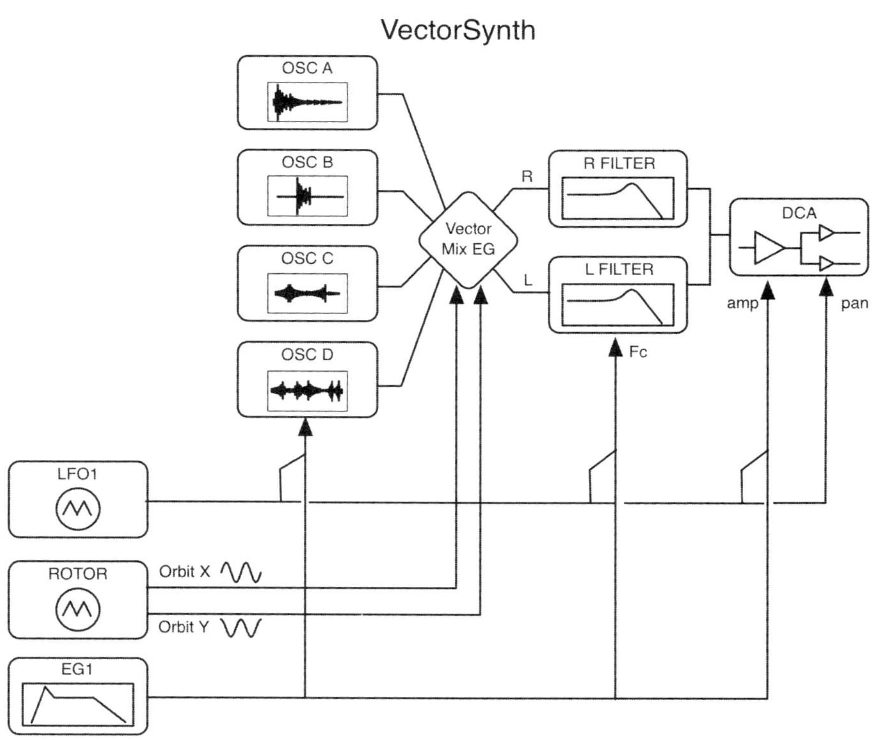

Figure 11.30: VectorSynth simplified block diagram.

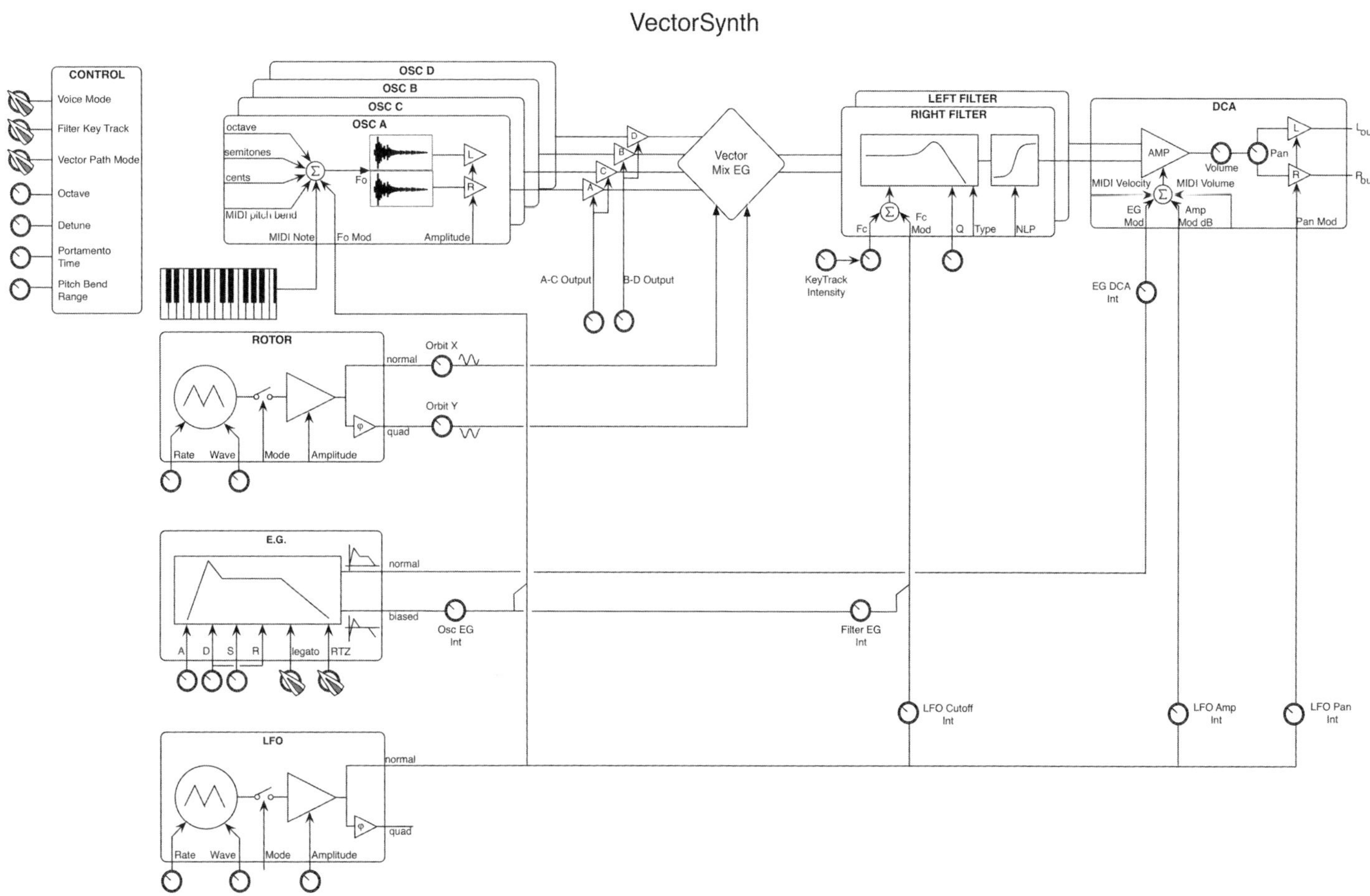

Figure 11.31: VectorSynth detailed connection graph.

Table 11.5: The modulation matrix for VectorSynth is nearly identical to DigiSynth; the new additions show LFO2 a the rotor oscillator.

VectorSynth Modulation Matrix			
Source	**Destination/Intensity**	**Transform/Range**	**enabled**
SOURCE_LFO1	DEST_ALL_OSC_FO	TRANSFORM_NONE	TRUE
	dLFO1OscModIntensity	dOscFoModRange	
SOURCE_BIASED_EG1	DEST_ALL_FILTER_FC	TRANSFORM_NONE	TRUE
	dEG1Filter1ModIntensity	dFilterModRange	
SOURCE_EG1	DEST_DCA_EG	TRANSFORM_NONE	TRUE
	dEG1DCAAmpModIntensity	m_dDefaultModRange	
SOURCE_BIASED_EG1	DEST_ALL_OSC_FO	TRANSFORM_NONE	TRUE
	dEG1OscModIntensity	dOscFoModRange	
SOURCE_LFO1	DEST_ALL_FILTER_FC	TRANSFORM_NONE	TRUE
	dLFO1Filter1ModIntensity	dFilterModRange	
SOURCE_LFO1	DEST_DCA_AMP	TRANSFORM_BIPOLAR_TO_UNIPOLAR	TRUE
	dLFO1DCAAmpModIntensity	dAmpModRange	
SOURCE_LFO1	DEST_DCA_PAN	TRANSFORM_NONE	TRUE
	dLFO1DCAPanModIntensity	m_dDefaultModRange	
SOURCE_LFO2	DEST_VS_AC_AXIS	TRANSFORM_NONE	TRUE
	m_dDefaultModIntensity	m_dDefaultModRange	
SOURCE_LFO2Q	DEST_VS_BD_AXIS	TRANSFORM_NONE	TRUE
	m_dDefaultModIntensity	m_dDefaultModRange	

Table 11.6: VectorSynth GUI Control List.

VectorSynth Continuous Parameters				
Control Name (units)	**Type**	**Variable Name (VST3, RAFX)**	**Low/Hi/Default***	**VST3/AU Index**
Osc EG Int	double	m_dEG1OscIntensity	-1 / 0 / 1	EG1_TO_OSC_INTENSITY
Filter fc (Hz) volt/octave	double	m_dFcControl	80 / 18000 / 10000	FILTER_FC
Filter Q	double	m_dQControl	1 / 10 / 1	FILTER_Q
Filter EG Int	double	m_dEG1FilterIntensity	-1 / 0 / 1	EG1_TO_FILTER_INTENSITY
Key Track Int	double	m_dFilterKeyTrackIntensity	0.5 / 10 / 1	FILTER_KEYTRACK_INTENSITY
Attack (mS)	double	m_dAttackTime_mSec	0 / 5000 / 100	EG1_ATTACK_MSEC
Decay/Release (mS)	double	m_dDecayReleaseTime_mSec	0 / 10000 / 1000	EG1_DECAY_RELEASE_MSEC
Sustain	double	m_dSustainLevel	0 / 1 / 0.707	EG1_SUSTAIN_LEVEL
LFO Rate	double	m_dLFO1Rate	0.02 / 20 / 0.5	LFO1_RATE
LFO Depth	double	m_dLFO1Amplitude	0 / 1 / 0	LFO1_AMPLITUDE
LFO Cutoff Int	double	m_dLFO1FilterFcIntensity	-1 / 1 / 0	LFO1_TO_FILTER_INTENSITY
LFO Pitch Int	double	m_dLFO1OscPitchIntensity	-1 / 1 / 0	LFO1_TO_OSC_INTENSITY
LFO Amp Int	double	m_dLFO1AmpIntensity	0 / 1 / 0	LFO1_TO_DCA_INTENSITY
LFO Pan Int	double	m_dLFO1PanIntensity	0 / 1 / 0	LFO1_TO_PAN_INTENSITY
Volume	double	m_dVolume_dB	-96 / 20 / 0	OUTPUT_AMPLITUDE_DB
DCA EG Int	double	m_dEG1DCAIntensity	-1 / 1 / 1	EG1_TO_DCA_INTENSITY
Detune	double	m_dDetune_cents	-100 / 100 / 0	DETUNE_CENTS

VectorSynth Continuous Parameters				
Control Name (units)	**Type**	**Variable Name (VST3, RAFX)**	**Low/Hi/Default***	**VST3/AU Index**
Portamento (mS)	double	m_dPortamentoTime_mSec	0 / 5000 / 0	PORTAMENTO_TIME_MSEC
A-C Output	double	m_dOsc1Amplitude_dB	−96 / 24 / 0	OSC1_AMPLITUDE_DB
B-D Output	double	m_dOsc2Amplitude_dB	−96 / 24 / 0	OSC2_AMPLITUDE_DB
Rotor Rate	double	m_dRotorRate	0.01 / 2 / 0.5	ROTOR_RATE
Orbit X	double	m_dOrbitX	0 / 1 / 0	ORBIT_X
Orbit Y	double	m_dOrbitY	0 / 1 / 0	ORBIT_Y
Octave	int	m_nOctave	−4 / 4 / 0	OCTAVE
PBendRange (semi)	int	m_nPitchBendRange	0 / 12 / 1	PITCHBEND_RANGE
Vector Joystick X **	double	m_dJoystickX	0 / 1 / 0	VECTORJOYSTICK_X
Vector Joystick Y **	double	m_dJoystickY	0 / 1 / 0	VECTORJOYSTICK_Y
* low, high and default values are #defined for VST3 and AU in *SynthParamLimits.h* for each project ** VST3 and AU ONLY (since the client does not have a built-in joystick control)				

VectorSynth Enumerated String Parameters (UINT)			
Control Name	**Variable Name**	**enum String**	**VST3/AU Index**
LFO Waveform	m_uLFO1Waveform	sine,usaw,dsaw,tri, square,expo,rsh,qrsh	LFO1_WAVEFORM
Rotor Waveform	m_uRotorWaveform	sine,usaw,dsaw,tri, square,expo,rsh,qrsh	ROTOR_WAVEFORM
Voice Mode	m_uVoiceMode	manual,program	VOICE_MODE
Path Mode	m_uVectorPathMode	once,loop,sustain,bckfrth	PATH_MODE
Vel->Att Scale	m_uVelocityToAttackScaling	OFF,ON	VELOCITY_TO_ATTACK
Note->Dcy Scale	m_uNoteNumberToDecayScaling	OFF,ON	NOTE_NUM_TO_DECAY
Reset to Zero	m_uResetToZero	OFF,ON	RESET_TO_ZERO
Filter KeyTrack	m_uFilterKeyTrack	OFF,ON	FILTER_KEYTRACK
Legato Mode	m_uLegatoMode	OFF,ON	LEGATO_MODE

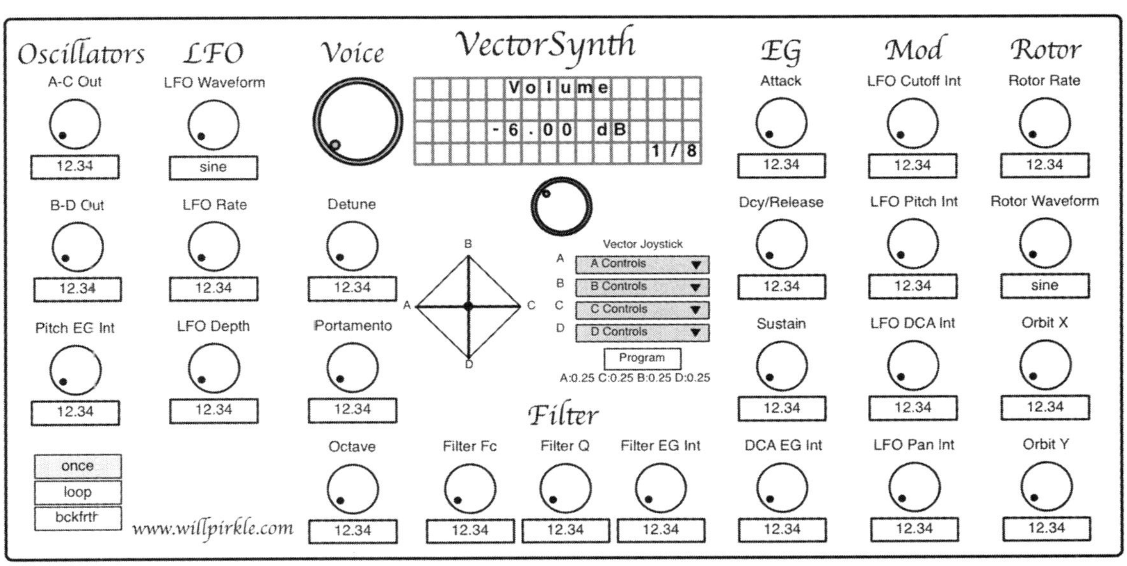

Figure 11.32: One possible VectorSynth GUI in RackAFX; notice that several controls are embedded in the LCD control.

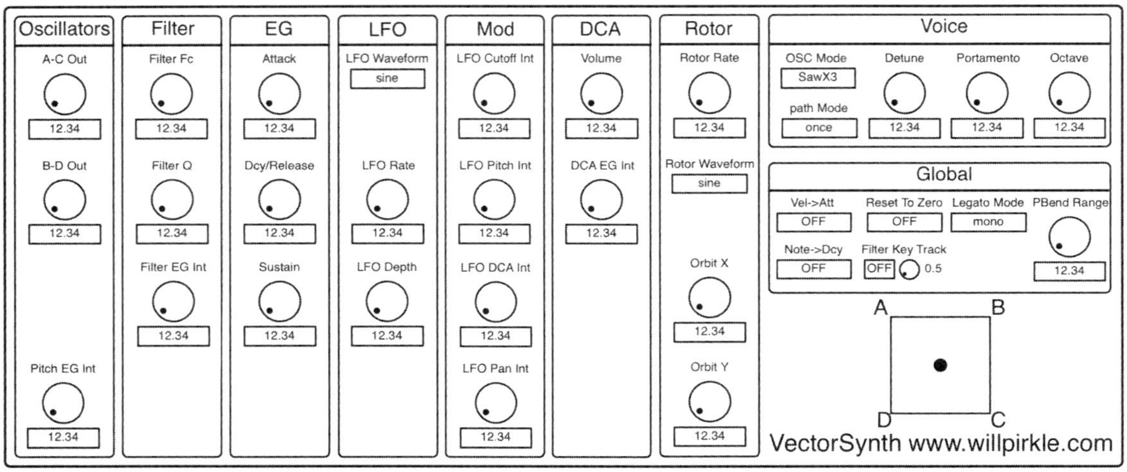

Figure 11.33: The VectorSynth GUI for the VST3 and AU projects.
Figures 11.32 and 11.33 show the GUIs for RackAFX and VST3/AU respectively.

11.12 The CVectorSynthVoice Object

The *CVectorSynthVoice* object is derived from *CDigiSynthVoice*, so it inherits all of the sample oscillator loading functionality. It adds new variables required for the vector joystick and a few simple helper functions. It overrides the standard *CVoice* functions just like all previous synths. Table 11.7 lists the member variables, and Table 11.8 lists the member functions. By now, these should look familiar.

Voice Global Parameters

We need to use a few more of the default global parameters for the new *CVectorSynthVoice* object. These include the following (see struct *globalVoiceParams* in *synthfunctions.h*).

```
// --- vector synth
double dOrbitXAmp;
double dOrbitYAmp;
double dAmplitude_A;
double dAmplitude_B;
double dAmplitude_C;
double dAmplitude_D;
double dAmplitude_ACmix;
double dAmplitude_BDmix;
UINT uVectorPathMode;
```

The voice object's member variables are self-explanatory, so lets focus on the member functions, some of which are nearly identical to the CMiniSynthVoice object from the last Chapter.

Constructor

The constructor performs the following initializations, some of which you may modify:

- connects oscillators to member pointers
- connects the filters to member pointers
- turns on NLP on filters (optional)
- set EG mode to analog (optional)
- set EG1 output flag
- set the DCA EG mod source for EG1 (important—must always be done in derived class constructor)
- initializes new vector synth variables
- initializes the vector path generator (notice the #define _RAFX)

Table 11.7: *CVectorSynthVoice* member variables.

CVectorSynthVoice Member Variables		
Type	**Variable Name**	**Description**
CSampleOscillator	m_OscA, m_OscB, m_OscC, m_OscD	the four oscillators
CKThreeFiveFilter	m_LeftK35Filter, m_RightK35Filter	filters for left and right channels
double	m_dAmplitude_A, m_dAmplitude_B, m_dAmplitude_C, m_dAmplitude_D, m_dAmplitude_ACmix, m_dAmplitude_BDmix	variables for storing the current vector mix amplitudes; these are updated every sample period
double	m_dVectorCenterX, m_dVectorCenterY, m_dOrbitXAmp, m_dOrbitYAmp	variables for dealing with the rotor and the ability to shift the entire center of path operation via the joystick control
CJoystickProgram*	m_pJSProgram	the RackAFX joystick program
CVectorPathGenerator	m_VPG	vector path object for all APIs
bool	m_bEnableVPG	for RackAFX only—allows you to choose joystick program or vector path generator
UINT	m_uVectorPathMode	the path mode for path programs
enum	once, loop, sustain, bckfrth	enum for path mode
enum	manual, program	enum for voice mode

Table 11.8: *CVectorSynthVoice* member functions.

CVectorSynthVoice Member Functions	
Function Name	**Description**
initGlobalParameters	initialize the global parameters
initializeModMatrix	initialize the modulation matrix
setSampleRate	set sample rate on sub-components
prepareForPlay	prepareForPlay on sub-components, one time init
update	update voice variables
reset	reset voice variables
noteOn	override of base class method; need to start the vector joystick program (if used) during note on event
noteOff	override of base class method; need to resume the vector joystick program (if used and in *sustain* mode) during note off event
doVoice	render the audio

The constructor also contains a simple vector path program as an example; for RackAFX it is disabled, so you can use the built-in joystick program but feel free to override this by setting *m_bEnableVPG = true* and experiment with this object instead.

```
CVectorSynthVoice::CVectorSynthVoice(void)
{
    // --- declare your oscillators and filters
    m_pOsc1 = &m_OscA;
    m_pOsc2 = &m_OscB;
    m_pOsc3 = &m_OscC;
    m_pOsc4 = &m_OscD;

    m_pFilter1 = &m_LeftK35Filter;
    m_pFilter2 = &m_RightK35Filter;
```

```
    // --- for voice stealing
    m_EG1.m_bResetToZero = true;

    // --- experiment with NLP
    m_LeftK35Filter.m_uNLP = ON;
    m_RightK35Filter.m_uNLP = ON;

    m_EG1.setEGMode(analog);
    m_EG1.m_bOutputEG = true;

    // --- VS Specific
    m_dAmplitude_A = 0.25;
    m_dAmplitude_B = 0.25;
    m_dAmplitude_C = 0.25;
    m_dAmplitude_D = 0.25;
    m_dAmplitude_ACmix = 0.5;
    m_dAmplitude_BDmix = 0.5;
    m_dVectorCenterX = 0.0;
    m_dVectorCenterY = 0.0;
    m_dOrbitXAmp = 0.0;
    m_dOrbitYAmp = 0.0;

    // --- plug-in must set this RAFX only!!
    m_pJSProgram = NULL;
    m_uVoiceMode = manual;

    // example of programmatically creating a vector path
    // without RAFX program generator
    //
    // -- Setup vector path generator; this just moves around from
    //    one apex to the next.
    // start at 100% A morph to next step in 2 sec
    // start at 100% B morph to next step in 2 sec
    // start at 100% C morph to next step in 2 sec
    // start at 100% D morph to BEGINNING in 2 sec (if LOOP mode)
    //
#ifdef _RAFX
    // -- the true argument means use the Korg/RAFX coordinates
    m_VPG.setProgramStep(0, -1.0, 0.0, 2000, true);
    m_VPG.setProgramStep(1, 0.0, 1.0, 2000, true);
    m_VPG.setProgramStep(2, 1.0, 0.0, 2000, true);
    m_VPG.setProgramStep(3, 0.0, -1.0, 2000, true);

    // --- RAFX version, VPG is disabled so you can use the easy to
    //     program JoystickProgram in RAFX (hit the Program button)
    m_bEnableVPG = false;
    // m_bEnableVPG = true; //<-- uncomment to use VPG instead of JSProgram
#else
    // -- the false argument means use the rotated coordinates
    m_VPG.setProgramStep(0, -1.0, 1.0, 2000, false);
```

```
        m_VPG.setProgramStep(1, 1.0, 1.0, 2000, false);
        m_VPG.setProgramStep(2, 1.0, -1.0, 2000, false);
        m_VPG.setProgramStep(3, -1.0, -1.0, 2000, false);

        // --- for VST3/AU, there is no built-in program generator, so do it by
        //     hand here
        m_bEnableVPG = true;
#endif
}
```

initGlobalParameters()

This function is nearly identical to the one in *CDigiSynthVoice*; the operation is the same—call the base class (notice that is *CDigiSynthVoice* now) and then initialize the new voice params.

```
inline virtual void initGlobalParameters(globalSynthParams* pGlobalParams)
{
        // --- always call base class first
        CDigiSynthVoice::initGlobalParameters(pGlobalParams);

        // --- add any CThisVoice specific variables here
        //     (you need to add them to the global param struct first)
        m_pGlobalVoiceParams->dOrbitXAmp = m_dOrbitXAmp;
        m_pGlobalVoiceParams->dOrbitYAmp = m_dOrbitYAmp;
        m_pGlobalVoiceParams->uVectorPathMode = m_uVectorPathMode;

        m_pGlobalVoiceParams->dAmplitude_A = m_dAmplitude_A;
        m_pGlobalVoiceParams->dAmplitude_B = m_dAmplitude_B;
        m_pGlobalVoiceParams->dAmplitude_C = m_dAmplitude_C;
        m_pGlobalVoiceParams->dAmplitude_D = m_dAmplitude_D;

        m_pGlobalVoiceParams->dAmplitude_ACmix = m_dAmplitude_ACmix;
        m_pGlobalVoiceParams->dAmplitude_BDmix = m_dAmplitude_BDmix;
}
```

initializeModMatrix()

This function creates and sets up the modulation matrix rows using Table 11.5; it is identical to DigiSynth, except it adds the new Rotor LFO2 routings.

```
void CVectorSynthVoice::initializeModMatrix(CModulationMatrix* pMatrix)
{
        // --- always first: call base class to create core and init
        //     with basic routings
        CDigiSynthVoice::initializeModMatrix(pMatrix);

        if(!pMatrix->getModMatrixCore()) return;

        modMatrixRow* pRow = NULL;

        // --- VS uses LFO2 as "Rotor"
        //
        // LFO2 -> VS AC Axis Mod
```

```
        pRow = createModMatrixRow(SOURCE_LFO2,
                                  DEST_VS_AC_AXIS,
                                  &m_dDefaultModIntensity,
                                  &m_dDefaultModRange,
                                  TRANSFORM_NONE,
                                  true);
        pMatrix->addModMatrixRow(pRow);

        // LFO2Quad -> VS BD Axis Mod
        pRow = createModMatrixRow(SOURCE_LFO2Q,
                                  DEST_VS_BD_AXIS,
                                  &m_dDefaultModIntensity,
                                  &m_dDefaultModRange,
                                  TRANSFORM_NONE,
                                  true);
        pMatrix->addModMatrixRow(pRow);
}
```

setSampleRate()

Here you need to call the base class and then set the sample rate on the vector path generator objects; they need the sample rate since they generate events in time.

```
void CVectorSynthVoice::setSampleRate(double dSampleRate)
{
        CDigiSynthVoice::setSampleRate(dSampleRate);

        // --- all APIs have access to m_VPG
        m_VPG.setSampleRate((float)dSampleRate);

        // --- RackAFX only
        if(m_pJSProgram)
              m_pJSProgram->setSampleRate((int)dSampleRate);
}
```

prepareForPlay()

In *prepareForPlay()* you just call the base class function.

```
void CVectorSynthVoice::prepareForPlay()
{
        CDigiSynthVoice::prepareForPlay();
}
```

update()

The *update()* function is similar to *DigiSynthVoice*—just call the base class first, then do any voice specific initializations. You need to update the new global parameter variables here, where you simply parse the variables off your global parameter structure.

```
void CVectorSynthVoice::update()
{
        // --- voice specific updates
        if(!m_pGlobalVoiceParams) return;
```

```
    // --- call base class first
    CDigiSynthVoice::update();

    // --- VS Specific
    //
    // --- path mode
    m_uVectorPathMode = m_pGlobalVoiceParams->uVectorPathMode;

    // --- for RAFX
    if(m_pJSProgram)
        m_pJSProgram->setJSMode(m_uVectorPathMode);

    // --- for everyone else (or RAFX)
    m_VPG.setVPGPathMode(m_uVectorPathMode);

    // --- vector joystick params
    m_dAmplitude_A = m_pGlobalVoiceParams->dAmplitude_A;
    m_dAmplitude_B = m_pGlobalVoiceParams->dAmplitude_B;
    m_dAmplitude_C = m_pGlobalVoiceParams->dAmplitude_C;
    m_dAmplitude_D = m_pGlobalVoiceParams->dAmplitude_D;
    m_dAmplitude_ACmix = m_pGlobalVoiceParams->dAmplitude_ACmix;
    m_dAmplitude_BDmix = m_pGlobalVoiceParams->dAmplitude_BDmix;
    m_dVectorCenterX = unipolarToBipolar(m_dAmplitude_ACmix);
    m_dVectorCenterY = unipolarToBipolar(m_dAmplitude_BDmix);
    m_dOrbitXAmp = m_pGlobalVoiceParams->dOrbitXAmp;
    m_dOrbitYAmp = m_pGlobalVoiceParams->dOrbitYAmp;
}
```

reset()

In *reset()* you just call the base class function.

```
void CVectorSynthVoice::reset()
{
    CDigiSynthVoice::reset();
}
```

noteOn()

In *noteOn()* you need to add a call to start up the vector path generator or RackAFX joystick program; the path is executed for each note that is played. This is done after calling the base class implementation. Notice the use of the *m_bEnableVPG* flag and checking of the *JSProgram* pointer prior to calling the *startProgram()* function.

```
inline virtual void noteOn(args...)
{
    CVoice::noteOn(uMIDINote, uMIDIVelocity, dFrequency,
                   dLastNoteFrequency);

    if(m_uVoiceMode == program)
    {
        if(m_bEnableVPG)
            m_VPG.startProgram();
```

```
            else if(m_pJSProgram)
                    m_pJSProgram->startProgram();
        }
    }
```

noteOff()

In *noteOff()* you need to add a call to resume the vector path generator or RackAFX joystick program if in *sustain* mode since these objects will halt their programs at the second-to-last vertex during the sustain portion of the event.

```
inline virtual void noteOff(UINT uMIDINoteNumber)
{
    CVoice::noteOff(uMIDINoteNumber);

    if(m_uVoiceMode == program && m_uVectorPathMode == sustain)
    {
        // need to restart the JSProgram;
        // it will pause itself during the sustain portion
        if(m_bEnableVPG)
            m_VPG.resumeProgram();
        else if(m_pJSProgram)
            m_pJSProgram->resumeProgram();
    }
}
```

doVoice()

This is the most important function of all since it does the rendering, and it is nearly identical to DigiSynth. The modulation layers are the same, however you need to deal with the vector mix component and the new Rotor LFO2. The differences from DigiSynth are shown in **bold.**

The vector synth implementation requires a call to the function calculateVectorMixValues(), which takes into account all possible modulations—the path, rotor and joystick-center-of-operation—and produces the vector mix components for the current sample period.

```
void calculateVectorMixValues(double dOriginX, double dOriginY,
                              double dPointX, double dPointY,
                              double& dAmag, double& dBmag,
                              double& dCmag, double& dDmag,
                              double& dACMix, double& dBDMix,
                              int nCellsPerSide, bool bJoystickCoords = true)
```

The arguments are:

- *dOriginX, dOriginY:* the current center of operation, based on location of joystick
- *dPointX, dPointY:* the X and Y offsets, which are the rotor X and rotor Y values from the LFO scaled by the orbit amplitudes
- *dAmag, dBmag, dCmag, dDmag:* the four vector mix outputs (pass by reference)
- *dACMix, dBDMix:* AC and BD mix based on the path, rotor, and center of operation (pass by reference)—these are not used in the default implementation, but you may use them in the Challenge section
- *nCellsPerSide:* for VectorSynth, we have only one cell with four vertices (this will change for AniSynth in the following section)
- *bJoystickCoords:* flag for letting the function know if it needs to rotate the coordinates first (if flag is *true*) for RackAFX plug-ins

Finally, notice that if the user has both the RackAFX joystick program and the vector path generator (VPG) enabled, the logic defaults to the VPG.

```
inline virtual bool doVoice(double& dLeftOutput, double& dRightOutput)
{
```

```
// this does basic on/off work
if(!CVoice::doVoice(dLeftOutput, dRightOutput))
      return false;

// --- ARTICULATION BLOCK --- //
// --- layer 0 modulators: velocity->attack
//                                    note number->decay
m_ModulationMatrix.doModulationMatrix(0);

// --- update layer 1 modulators
m_EG1.update();
m_LFO1.update();
m_LFO2.update();  // rotor

// --- do layer 1 modulators
m_EG1.doEnvelope();
m_LFO1.doOscillate();
m_LFO2.doOscillate(); // rotor

// --- mod matrix Layer 1
m_ModulationMatrix.doModulationMatrix(1);

// --- update Voice, DCA and Filter
this->update();
m_DCA.update();
m_LeftK35Filter.update();
m_RightK35Filter.update();

// --- update oscillators
m_OscA.update();
m_OscB.update();
m_OscC.update();
m_OscD.update();

// --- do the voice
double dLeftA,dRightA;
double dLeftB,dRightB;
double dLeftC,dRightC;
double dLeftD,dRightD;

// --- if in program mode, run the JS or VPG
if(m_uVoiceMode == program)
{
      // --- nudge timer; VPG "wins" if both present
      if(m_bEnableVPG)
      {
            m_VPG.incTimer();

            // --- uses pass-by-reference to set our amps with values
```

```
            m_VPG.getVectorMixValues(m_dAmplitude_A, m_dAmplitude_B,
                                     m_dAmplitude_C, m_dAmplitude_D);
            m_VPG.getVectorACBDMixes(m_dAmplitude_ACmix,
                                     m_dAmplitude_BDmix);
        }
        else if(m_pJSProgram)
        {
            // --- JS Program is older and uses floats
            //     since these are pass-by-reference need
            //     to declare and set here
            float fA, fB, fC, fD, fAC, fBD;
            m_pJSProgram->incTimer();

            // --- uses pass-by-reference to set our amps with values
            m_pJSProgram->getVectorMixValues(fA, fB, fC, fD);
            m_pJSProgram->getVectorACBDMixes(fAC, fBD);

            //--- set on our variables
            m_dAmplitude_A = fA;
            m_dAmplitude_B = fB;
            m_dAmplitude_C = fC;
            m_dAmplitude_D = fD;
            m_dAmplitude_ACmix = fAC;
            m_dAmplitude_BDmix = fBD;
        }

        // --- find the current center location
        m_dVectorCenterX = unipolarToBipolar(m_dAmplitude_ACmix);
        m_dVectorCenterY = unipolarToBipolar(m_dAmplitude_BDmix);
    }

    double dRotorACMix, dRotorBDMix = 0.0;

    // --- these are from LFO2
    double dRotorX = m_ModulationMatrix.m_dDestinations[DEST_VS_AC_AXIS];
    double dRotorY = m_ModulationMatrix.m_dDestinations[DEST_VS_BD_AXIS];

    // --- for RAFX, use the Korg joystick coordinates
    bool bJoystickCoords = true;

#ifndef _RAFX
        bJoystickCoords = false;
#endif

    // --- calculate the final vector mix values based on path and rotor
    //     and joystick location
    calculateVectorMixValues(m_dVectorCenterX, m_dVectorCenterY,
                             dRotorX*m_dOrbitXAmp, dRotorY*m_dOrbitYAmp,
                             m_dAmplitude_A, m_dAmplitude_B,
```

```
                                m_dAmplitude_C, m_dAmplitude_D,
                                dRotorACMix, dRotorBDMix, 1,
                                bJoystickCoords);

        // --- get our 4 osc outputs
        dLeftA = m_pOsc1->doOscillate(&dRightA);
        dLeftB = m_pOsc2->doOscillate(&dRightB);
        dLeftC = m_pOsc3->doOscillate(&dRightC);
        dLeftD = m_pOsc4->doOscillate(&dRightD);

        // --- do the massive mix
        double dLeftVectorMix = m_dAmplitude_A*dLeftA + m_dAmplitude_B*dLeftB +
                               m_dAmplitude_C*dLeftC + m_dAmplitude_D*dLeftD;
        double dRightVectorMix = m_dAmplitude_A*dRightA +
                                m_dAmplitude_B*dRightB +
                                m_dAmplitude_C*dRightC +
                                m_dAmplitude_D*dRightD;

        // --- Challenge: apply AC and BD mix to left and right filter cutoffs!
        dLeftOutput = m_LeftK35Filter.doFilter(dLeftVectorMix);
        dRightOutput = m_RightK35Filter.doFilter(dRightVectorMix);

        // --- apply the DCA
        m_DCA.doDCA(dLeftOutput, dRightOutput, dLeftOutput, dRightOutput);

        return true;
}
```

11.13 VectorSynth Files

VectorSynth uses the following files, which you will need to add into your compiler's project in the usual manner.

> For VST3 and AU, you also need to add the file *SynthParamLimits.h*, which is in the VectorSynth sample code—remember that this file is slightly different for each synth because it contains the GUI control index enumeration.

DCA.h	Oscillator.h
DCA.cpp	Oscillator.cpp
EnvelopeGenerator.h	SEMFilter.h
EnvelopeGenerator.cpp	SEMFilter.cpp
Filter.h	SampleOscillator.h
Filter.cpp	SampleOscillator.cpp
LFO.h	synthfunctions.h
LFO.cpp	VAOnePoleFilter.h
DigiSynthVoice.h	VAOnePoleFilter.cpp
DigiSynthVoice.cpp	VectorSynthVoice.h
ModulationMatrix.h	VectorSynthVoice.cpp
ModulationMatrix.cpp	VectorPathGenerator.h
KThreeFiveFilter.h	VectorPathGenerator.cpp
KThreeFiveFilter.cpp	Voice.h
	Voice.cpp

VectorSynth uses identical code in the majority of plug-in object functions as MiniSynth and DigiSynth; the main difference is the type of voice pointer stored in the voice array. There is no need to repeatedly print that code for each synth project. There are also differences in the GUI control setup and initialization. By using the *CVoice* base class, we are able to reuse the same core code over and over.

For the plug-in's *.h* file declarations:

- *#include "VectorSynthVoice.h"* at the top of the file
- copy the same code as DigiSynth, but with different voice pointers (the only difference is shown in **bold**)
- the *loadSamples()* function is a carryover from DigiSynth

```
<< ** Code Listing 11.1: Declarations ** >>

// --- our array of voices
CVectorSynthVoice* m_pVoiceArray[MAX_VOICES];

// --- MmM
CModulationMatrix m_GlobalModMatrix;

// --- global params
globalSynthParams m_GlobalSynthParams;

// --- helper functions for note on/off/voice steal
void incrementVoiceTimestamps();
CVectorSynthVoice* getOldestVoice();
CVectorSynthVoice* getOldestVoiceWithNote(UINT uMIDINote);

// --- load sample sets
bool loadSamples();

// updates all voices at once
void update();

// for portamento
double m_dLastNoteFrequency;

// our recieve channel
UINT m_uMidiRxChannel;

<< END ** Code Listing 11.1: Declarations ** END >>
```

Loading Samples

The code for loading the samples is slightly different from DigiSynth, only because there are now four oscillators rather than two. These use the same royalty-free sample sets as DigiSynth.

Osc A: Heaver
Osc B: OldFlatty
Osc C: Divider
Osc D: FuzzVibe

```
<< ** Code Listing 11.2: Load Samples ** >>

bool CVectorSynth::loadSamples()    //RAFX
bool Processor::loadSamples()       //VST3
```

```
bool AUSynth::loadSamples()        //AU
{
      // --- load 4 sets of multis
      // ------- FOR MULTI SAMPLES ------- //

      // --- RackAFX -----------------------------------------------
      char* pPath0 = addStrings(getMyDLLDirectory(),"\\MultiSamples
                                 \\Heaver");
      char* pPath1 = addStrings(getMyDLLDirectory(),"\\MultiSamples
                                 \\OldFlatty");
      char* pPath2 = addStrings(getMyDLLDirectory(),"\\MultiSamples
                                 \\Divider");
      char* pPath3 = addStrings(getMyDLLDirectory(),"\\MultiSamples
                                 \\FuzzVibe");
      // -----------------------------------------------------------

      // --- VST3 --------------------------------------------------
      char* pDLLPath = getMyDLLDirectory(USTRING("VectorSynth.vst3"));
      char* pPath0 = addStrings(pDLLPath,"\\MultiSamples\\Heaver");
      char* pPath1 = addStrings(pDLLPath,"\\MultiSamples\\OldFlatty");
      char* pPath2 = addStrings(pDLLPath,"\\MultiSamples\\Divider");
      char* pPath3 = addStrings(pDLLPath,"\\MultiSamples\\FuzzVibe");
      // -----------------------------------------------------------

      // --- AU ----------------------------------------------------
      char* componentFolder = getMyComponentDirectory(
                        CFSTR("developer.audiounit.yourname.vectorsynth"));

      char* pPath0 = addStrings(componentFolder,"/MultiSamples/Heaver");
      char* pPath1 = addStrings(componentFolder,"/MultiSamples/OldFlatty");
      char* pPath2 = addStrings(componentFolder,"/MultiSamples/Divider");
      char* pPath3 = addStrings(componentFolder,"/MultiSamples/FuzzVibe");
      // -----------------------------------------------------------

      // --- to speed up sample loading, init the first voice here
      //     init(...false, false) = NOT single-sample, NOT pitchless sample
      if(!m_pVoiceArray[0]->initOscWithFolderPath(0, pPath0, false, false))
            return false;
      if(!m_pVoiceArray[0]->initOscWithFolderPath(1, pPath1, false, false))
            return false;
      if(!m_pVoiceArray[0]->initOscWithFolderPath(2, pPath2, false, false))
            return false;
      if(!m_pVoiceArray[0]->initOscWithFolderPath(3, pPath3, false, false))
            return false;

      // --- then use the other function to copy the sample pointerrs
      //     so they share pointers to same buffers of data
      for(int i=1; i<MAX_VOICES; i++)
      {
```

```
            // --- init false, false = NOT single-sample,
            //     NOT pitchless sample
            m_pVoiceArray[i]->initAllOscWithDigiSynthVoice(m_pVoiceArray[0],
                                                            false, false);
        }

        // always delete what comes back from addStrings()
        delete [] pPath0;
        delete [] pPath1;
        delete [] pPath2;
        delete [] pPath3;

        // --- VST3 only
        delete [] pDLLPath;

        // --- AU only
        delete [] componentFolder;
    }

        << END ** Code Listing 11.2: Load Samples ** END >>
```

11.14 VectorSynth: RackAFX

Create a new project named *VectorSynth* and setup the GUI using Table 11.6.

VectorSynth.h

At the top of the file, add the *#include* statement for *VectorSynthVoice.h*, and then setup the array of voices and all helper member functions. Add the *loadSamples()* function as well.

```
class CVectorSynth : public CPlugIn
{
public:
        <SNIP SNIP SNIP>

        // Add your code here: ---------------------------------------------- //

        << INSERT ** Code Listing 11.1: Declarations ** HERE >>

        etc...
```

VectorSynth.cpp

The following functions are identical to MiniSynth/DigiSynth (and the rest of the book projects), with the exception of the type of voice pointers created and stored in the voice array.

- destructor
- *prepareForPlay()*
- *processAudioFrame()*
- *midiNoteOn()*
- *midiNoteOff()*
- *midiModWheel()*
- *midiPitchBend()*
- *midiMessage()*

Constructor

The constructor is identical to DigiSynth (with the exception of the type of voice pointers created and stored in the voice array), but you also need to create and set the *CJoystickProgram* objects on the voice objects. This can be done in the same loop as the voice creation.

```
CVectorSynth::CVectorSynth()
{
      <SNIP SNIP SNIP>

      // load up voices
      for(int i=0; i<MAX_VOICES; i++)
      {
            // --- create voice
            m_pVoiceArray[i] = new CVectorSynthVoice;

            // --- global params (MUST BE DONE before setting up mod matrix!
            m_pVoiceArray[i]->initGlobalParameters(&m_GlobalSynthParams);

            // --- VectorSynth addition RAFX ONLY
            //
            // CJoystickProgram(m_pVectorJSProgram, m_uVectorPathMode)
            // m_pVectorJSProgram = pointer to our JS Program Array
            //                        (programmed in RAFX, no code)
            // m_uVectorPathMode = initial path mode
            m_pVoiceArray[i]->m_pJSProgram = new
                  CJoystickProgram(m_pVectorJSProgram, m_uVectorPathMode);
      }

      etc...
}
```

loadSamples()

Insert Code Listing 11.2 anywhere you wish inside the *.cpp* file.

initialize()

This is the function where we load the samples.

```
bool __stdcall CVectorSynth::initialize()
{
      // --- load samples
      return loadSamples();
}
```

update()

The *update()* function is slightly different, as a few controls have been deleted and others added. This function shows only the newly added code in **bold**.

Removed from DigiSynth:

- loop mode
- Osc1, Osc2 Output Amplitude

Added new:

- path mode
- orbit X and Y amounts
- rotor rate
- rotor waveform
- AC, BD Output Amplitude

```
void CVectorSynth::update() // RAFX

{
      // --- update global parameters
      //

      etc...
      // --- AC/BD Mix values:
      double dOscAmplitude = m_dOsc1Amplitude_dB == -96.0 ? 0.0 :
                                    pow(10.0, m_dOsc1Amplitude_dB/20.0);
      m_GlobalSynthParams.osc1Params.dAmplitude = dOscAmplitude;
      m_GlobalSynthParams.osc2Params.dAmplitude = dOscAmplitude;

      dOscAmplitude = m_dOsc2Amplitude_dB == -96.0 ? 0.0 :
                              pow(10.0, m_dOsc2Amplitude_dB/20.0);
      m_GlobalSynthParams.osc3Params.dAmplitude = dOscAmplitude;
      m_GlobalSynthParams.osc4Params.dAmplitude = dOscAmplitude;

      // --- VS Specific
      m_GlobalSynthParams.voiceParams.uVectorPathMode = m_uVectorPathMode;
      m_GlobalSynthParams.voiceParams.dOrbitXAmp = m_dOrbitX;
      m_GlobalSynthParams.voiceParams.dOrbitYAmp = m_dOrbitY;

      // --- LFO2:
      m_GlobalSynthParams.lfo2Params.uWaveform = m_uRotorWaveform;
      m_GlobalSynthParams.lfo2Params.dOscFo = m_dRotorRate;

      etc...
}
```

11.15 VectorSynth: VST3

Create a new project named VectorSynth and set up the GUI using Table 11.6. Add the new custom vector joystick control as described in Section 11.x.

Processor.h

At the top of the file, add the *#include* statement for *VectorSynthVoice.h* and then setup the array of voices and all helper member functions. Add the *loadSamples()* function as well. Don't forget to add all the variables you need from the GUI table.

```
class Processor : public AudioEffect
{
public:
      <SNIP SNIP SNIP>

      // Add your code here: --------------------------------------------- //
```

```
<< INSERT ** Code Listing 11.1: Declarations ** HERE >>

etc...
```

Processor.cpp

The following functions are identical to DigiSynth, with the exception of the type of voice pointers created and stored in the voice array.

- Destructor
- *setActive()*
- *process()*
- *doProcessEvent()*

Constructor

Initialize all the GUI variables from Table 11.6; the rest is identical to DigiSynth.

```
Processor::Processor ()
{
	// --- we are a Processor
	setControllerClass(Controller::cid);

	// --- our inits
	m_dOsc1Amplitude_dB = DEFAULT_OUTPUT_AMPLITUDE_DB;
	m_dOsc2Amplitude_dB = DEFAULT_OUTPUT_AMPLITUDE_DB;

	// vector joystick
	m_dJoystickX = DEFAULT_UNIPOLAR_HALF; // NOTE these are 0->1
	m_dJoystickY = DEFAULT_UNIPOLAR_HALF; // ditto
	m_uVectorPathMode = DEFAULT_PATH_MODE;
	m_dOrbitX = DEFAULT_BIPOLAR;
	m_dOrbitY = DEFAULT_BIPOLAR;
	m_dRotorRate = DEFAULT_SLOW_LFO_RATE;
	m_uRotorWaveform = DEFAULT_LFO_WAVEFORM;

	etc… rest is same as DigiSynth
```

loadSamples()

Insert Code Listing 11.2 anywhere you wish inside the *.cpp* file.

update()

The *update()* function is slightly different, as a few controls have been deleted and others added. This function shows the newly added code in **bold**. For VST3 and AU, you also need to calculate the vector mix values from the joystick control (in RackAFX, the client does this for you). Notice that this function uses pass-by-reference, so we can calculate the values directly into the global parameters.

Removed from DigiSynth:

- loop mode
- Osc1, Osc2 Output Amplitude

Added new:

- path mode
- orbit X and Y amounts
- rotor rate
- rotor waveform

- AC, BD Output Amplitude
- Loop Mode

```
void Processor::update()
{
      // --- update global parameters
      //

      etc…

      // --- VS Specific
      m_GlobalSynthParams.voiceParams.uVectorPathMode = m_uVectorPathMode;
      m_GlobalSynthParams.voiceParams.dOrbitXAmp = m_dOrbitX;
      m_GlobalSynthParams.voiceParams.dOrbitYAmp = m_dOrbitY;

      // --- VST3/AU ONLY ---
      // --- calculate the vector joystick mix values based on x,y location
      //     (x,y are 0->1)
      calculateVectorJoystickValues(m_dJoystickX, m_dJoystickY,
                         m_GlobalSynthParams.voiceParams.dAmplitude_A,
                         m_GlobalSynthParams.voiceParams.dAmplitude_B,
                         m_GlobalSynthParams.voiceParams.dAmplitude_C,
                         m_GlobalSynthParams.voiceParams.dAmplitude_D,
                         m_GlobalSynthParams.voiceParams.dAmplitude_ACmix,
                         m_GlobalSynthParams.voiceParams.dAmplitude_BDmix);

      // --- LFO2:
      m_GlobalSynthParams.lfo2Params.uWaveform = m_uRotorWaveform;
      m_GlobalSynthParams.lfo2Params.dOscFo = m_dRotorRate;

      etc...
}
```

doControlUpdate()

The *doControlUpdate()* function must be altered from DigiSynth to match the new variable *additions/removals listed above. In the switch/case statement, delete the case statements for* the removed variables and add case statements for the new ones, shown here in **bold**. These are the same additions/removals you implemented in the *update()* function. Notice also that you pick up the vector joystick position here; it comes from the new joystick control.

```
bool Processor::doControlUpdate(ProcessData& data)
{
      <SNIP SNIP SNIP Indents Removed>

switch (pid)
{
      // cookVSTGUIVariable(min, max, currentValue) <- cooks raw data into
      // meaningful info for us

      case VECTORJOYSTICK_X:
      {
            m_dJoystickX = value;
            break;
      }
```

```
case VECTORJOYSTICK_Y:
{
      m_dJoystickY = value;
      break;
}
case PATH_MODE:
{
      m_uVectorPathMode = (UINT)cookVSTGUIVariable(MIN_PATH_MODE,
                                MAX_PATH_MODE, value);
      break;
}
case ORBIT_X:
{
      m_dOrbitX = value;
      break;
}
case ORBIT_Y:
{
      m_dOrbitY = value;
      break;
}
case ROTOR_RATE:
{
      m_dRotorRate = cookVSTGUIVariable(MIN_SLOW_LFO_RATE,
                                          MAX_SLOW_LFO_RATE, value);
      break;
}
case ROTOR_WAVEFORM:
{
      m_uRotorWaveform = (UINT)cookVSTGUIVariable(MIN_LFO_WAVEFORM,
                                                  MAX_LFO_WAVEFORM,
                                                  value);
      break;
}

// --- MIDI messages
case MIDI_PITCHBEND: // want -1 to +1

etc...
```

11.16 VectorSynth: AU

Create a new project named VectorSynth and setup the GUI using Table 11.6. Add the new custom vector joystick control as described in Section 11.9.

AUSynth.h

At the top of the file, add the *#include* statement for *VectorSynthVoice.h* and then setup the array of voices and all helper member functions. Add the *loadSamples()* function as well.

```
class AUSynth : public AUInstrumentBase
{
```

```
public:
      <SNIP SNIP SNIP>

      // Add your code here: ------------------------------------------ //

      << INSERT ** Code Listing 11.1: Declarations ** HERE >>

      etc...
```

AUSynth.cpp

The following functions are identical to DigiSynth, with the exception of the type of voice pointers created and stored in the array.

- destructor
- *Initialize()*
- *Reset()*
- *Render()*
- *StartNote()*
- *StopNote()*
- *HandlePitchWheel()*
- *HandleControlChange()*

Constructor

Initialize the factory preset (optional) and all the GUI variables from Table 11.6; the rest is identical to MiniSynth.

```
AUSynth::AUSynth(AudioUnit inComponentInstance)
      : AUInstrumentBase(inComponentInstance, 0, 1)
{
      // --- create input, output ports, groups and parts
      CreateElements();

      // --- setup default factory preset (as example)
      factoryPreset[OSC1_AMPLITUDE_DB] = 0.0;
      factoryPreset[OSC2_AMPLITUDE_DB] = 0.0;

      <SNIP SNIP SNIP>

      // --- define number of params (controls)
      Globals()->UseIndexedParameters(NUMBER_OF_SYNTH_PARAMETERS);

      // --- initialize the controls here!
      // --- these are defined in SynthParamLimits.h

      <SNIP SNIP SNIP>

      // -- VS specific
      Globals()->SetParameter(VECTORJOYSTICK_X, DEFAULT_UNIPOLAR_HALF);
      Globals()->SetParameter(VECTORJOYSTICK_Y, DEFAULT_UNIPOLAR_HALF);
      Globals()->SetParameter(PATH_MODE, DEFAULT_PATH_MODE);
      Globals()->SetParameter(ORBIT_X, DEFAULT_UNIPOLAR);
      Globals()->SetParameter(ORBIT_Y, DEFAULT_UNIPOLAR);
```

```
Globals()->SetParameter(ROTOR_RATE, DEFAULT_SLOW_LFO_RATE);
Globals()->SetParameter(ROTOR_WAVEFORM, DEFAULT_LFO_WAVEFORM);

etc...
```

loadSamples()

Insert Code Listing 11.2 anywhere you wish inside the *.cpp* file.

update()

The other difference is in the *update()* function, which is only slightly different, as a few controls have been deleted and others added. Also, there are now two filters to handle. This function shows the newly added code in **bold**. For VST3 and AU, you also need to calculate the vector mix values from the joystick control (in RackAFX, the client does this for you). Notice that this function uses pass-by-reference, so we can calculate the values directly into the global parameters.

Removed from *DigiSynth:*

- loop mode
- Osc1, Osc2 Output Amplitude

Added new:

- path mode
- orbit X and Y amounts
- rotor rate
- rotor waveform
- AC, BD Output Amplitude

```
void AUSynth::update()
{
      // --- update global parameters
      //

      etc...

      // --- VS Specific
      m_GlobalSynthParams.voiceParams.uVectorPathMode =
                                   Globals()->GetParameter(PATH_MODE);
      m_GlobalSynthParams.voiceParams.dOrbitXAmp =
                                   Globals()->GetParameter(ORBIT_X);
      m_GlobalSynthParams.voiceParams.dOrbitYAmp =
                                   Globals()->GetParameter(ORBIT_Y);

      // --- VST3/AU ONLY ---
      // --- calculate the vector joystick mix values based on x,y
      //     location (x,y are 0->1)
      calculateVectorJoystickValues(
                       Globals()->GetParameter(VECTORJOYSTICK_X),
                       Globals()->GetParameter(VECTORJOYSTICK_Y),
                       m_GlobalSynthParams.voiceParams.dAmplitude_A,
                       m_GlobalSynthParams.voiceParams.dAmplitude_B,
                       m_GlobalSynthParams.voiceParams.dAmplitude_C,
                       m_GlobalSynthParams.voiceParams.dAmplitude_D,
```

```
                    m_GlobalSynthParams.voiceParams.dAmplitude_ACmix,
                    m_GlobalSynthParams.voiceParams.dAmplitude_BDmix);

    etc…

    // --- LFO2:
    m_GlobalSynthParams.lfo2Params.uWaveform =
                    Globals()->GetParameter(ROTOR_WAVEFORM);
    m_GlobalSynthParams.lfo2Params.dOscFo =
                    Globals()->GetParameter(ROTOR_RATE);

}
```

11.17 AniSynth

> AniSynth is our interpretation of the Moog AniMoog Anisotropic Synth app. Since Moog has not released their algorithm or vector mix equations, we do not represent the following algorithm and code as "the Moog Anisotropic Synth Engine."

The AniMoog app uses a grid of 128 wavetables as the basis for its oscillators and vector synthesis arranged in a rectangular manner. It features the same vector path and rotor/orbit as the earlier vector synths. At the vector mix level, it would appear that the only thing different is the sheer number of timbres that the mix morphs though as the vector mix point moves along the path. After some observations, however, we can make a few hypotheses about its operation. Notice that we use the terms wavetable, oscillator and timbre interchangeably in these bullet points.

- making a vector mix surface with 128 oscillators and 128 vector mix values would be difficult and inefficient; at any given time, most of the mix values would be zero or close to it for samples far away from the mix point
- running 128 oscillators per note event would be cumbersome on the iPad, if not impossible
- if all 128 oscillators were mixed at non-zero mix ratios when the mix point was between wavetables, you would have a big mess of noise
- when auditioning notes on the device, you hear a mix of the oscillators that are nearby the mix point, and none of the far-away timbres
- the sounds morph into one another smoothly without discontinuities unless the rotor rate and orbit amplitudes are very high, when you can hear that wavetables are being skipped over
- the vector mix equations work great and are simple to implement—why reinvent the wheel?

AniSynth treats the grid of wavetable oscillators as a set of smaller vector mix surfaces. That is, each group of four adjacent wavetables comprises one ordinary vector mix surface. The name for a group of four adjacent oscillators is a cell. The mix surface is a set of these cells.

> At any given time, the output of the synth voice is a combination of the four oscillators in the cell that contains the mix point, calculated with the standard Sequential/Korg equations. This cell is called the active cell.

Figure 11.34 shows a few cells in the AniMoog's rectangular array of wavetables. Notice that any pair of adjacent cells will share two wavetables in common.

In order to make the calculations simpler, and to re-use equations and the joystick control, AniSynth uses a square grid of wavetables instead of the rectangular one. If you modified the joystick control to be rectangular, you could replicate the Moog mix surface exactly. In addition, it is easier to see the way AniSynth works by using the non-joystick coordinate system, where the mix diamond is laying on its side as a square. In AniSynth, you must first decide on the number of cells per side of the square mix surface. Not only does it dictate the number of wavetables, but it is also used as part of the calculation process. The equation that relates the number of cells per side to the total number of wavetables is:

$$\text{num samples} = (C + 1)^2$$
$$C = \text{number of cells per side}$$

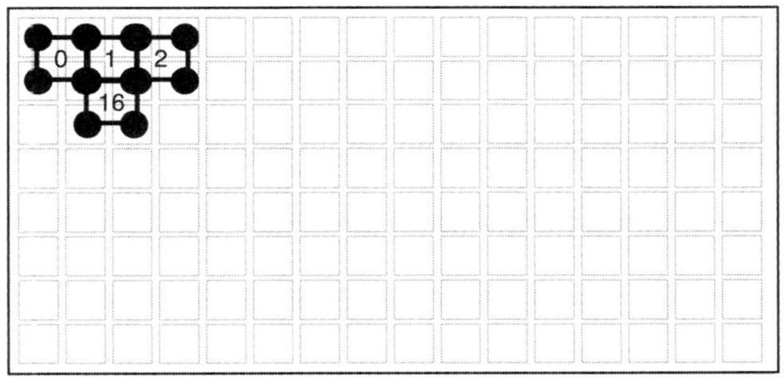

Figure 11.34: A few cells in the AniMoog mix surface.

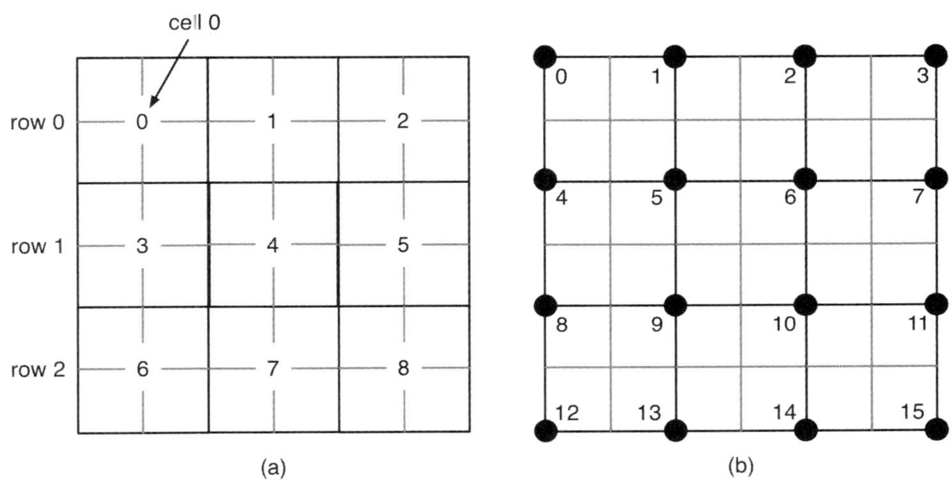

Figure 11.35: With C = 3 there are (a) nine total cells with three rows and three columns and (b) 16 total wavetables shown as pucks and numbered 0 to 15.

AniSynth uses C = 5, which requires 35 wavetables. We will discuss the criteria for these tables shortly. To show how AniSynth cleanly morphs mixes across the vast mix surface, it is easier to diagram with a smaller surface of C = 3 or 16 wavetables. The cell structure and wavetables are shown in Figure 11.35. Notice that the number of cells per side is also the number of rows of cells. The row index value is needed for the calculation later. In this case, C = 3 is used to make the diagram less complicated.

When the mix point is inside one of the cells, the cell becomes activated and its vertices are treated as the A, B, C, and D vertices of the normal VS mix surface. As the mix point moves around due to the path/rotor, the active cell switches around. Since each adjacent cell shares a common pair of vertices, it is just a matter of mapping the proper four wavetables into the voice object. The *CAniSynthVoice* object is similar to the *CVectorSynthVoice* object in that it still has four oscillators, each reading from a sample file. The trick with AniSynth is keeping track of the active cell and slotting its four wavetables into the voice's current set. Figure 11.36(a) shows a mix point in the first cell, moving towards the cell below it. Notice the way the vertices are indexed. Cell 1 consists of vertices 0, 1, 4 and 5, which are mapped to oscillators A, B, D, and C respectively. In Figure 11.36(b) the mix point has just touched the D-C boundary, where its mix ratios happen to be 50% C, 50% D and zero of everything else.

Now suppose the mix point crosses over the D-C boundary into the cell below (cell 3) as shown in Figure 11.37. When this occurs, the voice object must switch out the current four wavetables for the next cell. However, two are shared—the wavetables 4 and 5 (D and C) become the A and B tables in the next cell. At the boundary, the D and C wavetables are re-named A and B because of their location relative to the local cell. Notice the mix ratios are now 50% A, 50% B and zero of everything else, but since the wavetables are shared, the cell switch occurs without a glitch or discontinuity. If the path goes directly through a vertex, then that mix value will be at 100%, the wavetables will be re-distributed, and it will continue into the next cell at the 100% level.

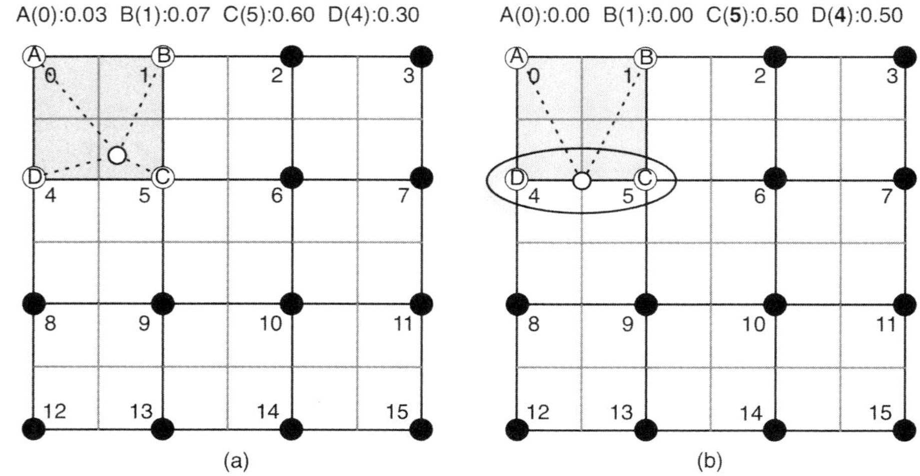

Figure 11.36: (a) A mix point in cell 0 uses the cells vertices to calculate the current local mix (b) the mix point has moved to the edge of the cell between vertices D and C.

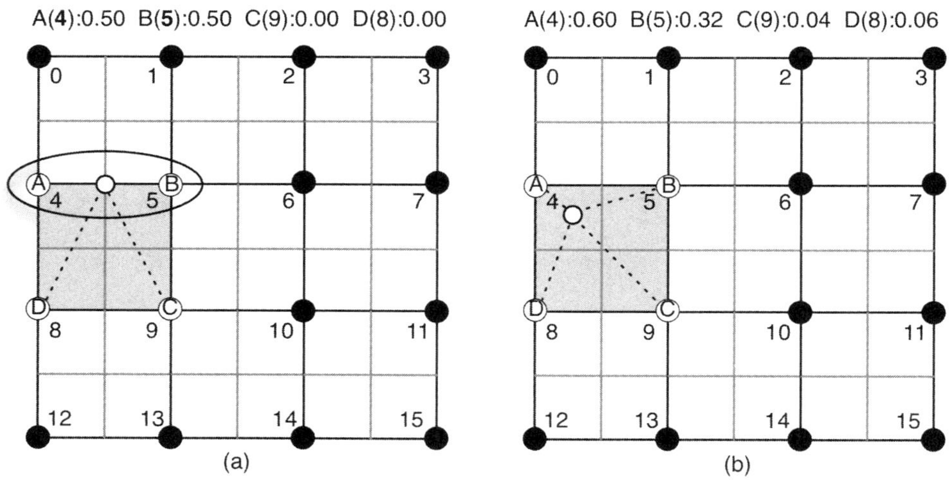

Figure 11.37: (a) The mix point crosses into the next cell where the oscillator names are shuffled, but the edge wavetables remain the same, so there is no audible click when the mix point crosses into the new cell (b) the mix point continues to move along a vector path in cell 3.

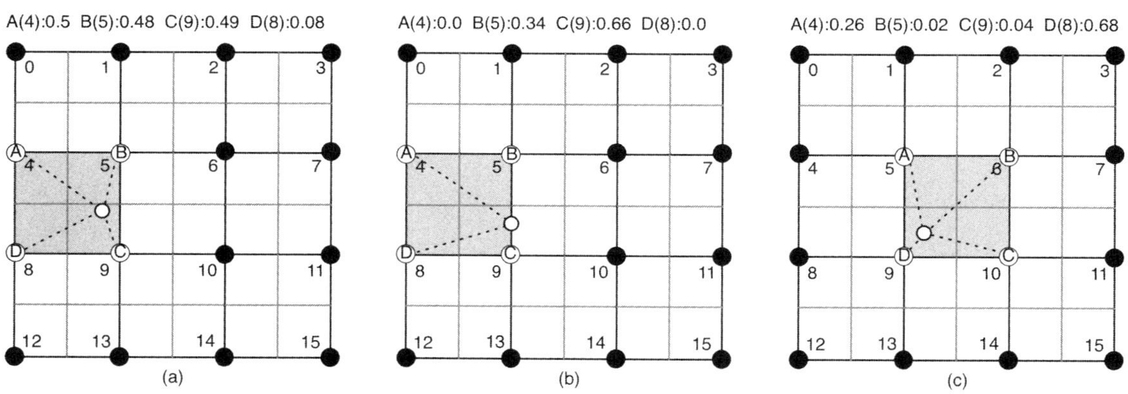

Figure 11.38: (a) The mix point approaches the B-C boundary (b) the mix point touches the B-C boundary, crossing into the next cell where (c) the local oscillator pointers swap to A and D.

Figure 11.38 shows the mix point as it continues to move along its path, now to the right entering the next cell (cell 4). As it crosses over the B-C boundary, the table pointers are swapped to become the A-D boundary, and the mix morphs smoothly and without discontinuities.

As Figure 11.39 shows, the concepts of paths and orbits stay the same, it's just applied to a larger square surface.

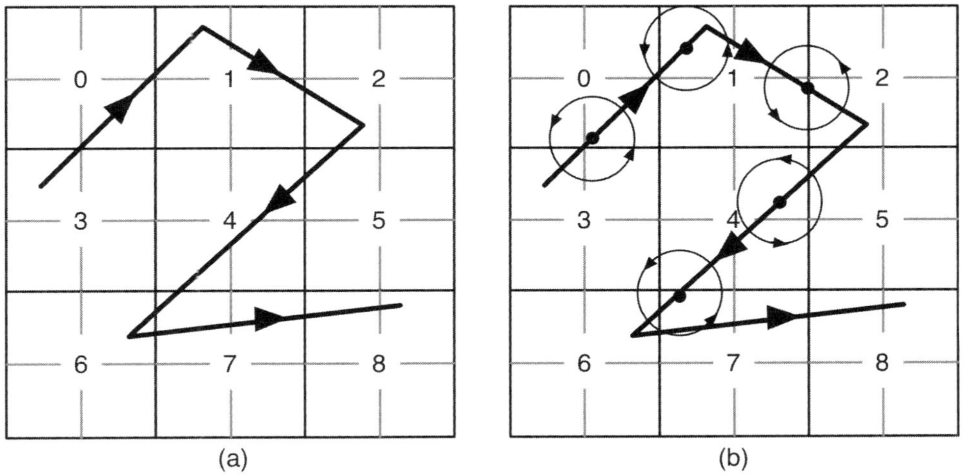

Figure 11.39: (a) A vector path and (b) path plus rotor now move over a larger mix surface, but they are treated as local vector mixes inside each cell.

11.18 AniSynth Specifications

Figure 11.40 shows AniSynth's simplified block diagram. It is identical to VectorSynth, except that the matrix of wavetables feeds the four oscillators A, B, C, and D.

Figure 11.41 shows how the 36 wavetables are mapped to the joystick control. When you move the joystick, the mix surface is now much more dense, with eight times as many wavetables.

The wavetables are indexed starting with 0 and advance through consecutive rows as shown in Figure 11.40. AniSynth really only differs from VectorSynth in the rendering and *loadSamples()* functions. The GUI and modulation matrix are identical, so you can either modify VectorSynth or use it as a basis for AniSynth. To demonstrate another filter, we use the diode ladder filter in this synth project.

Oscillators:

- four *CSampleOscillators*, which each play back one of 36 different wavetables; each wavetable is extracted from a .wav file

Filter:

- two *CDiodeLadderFilters* (one for left, one for right)

LFOs

- two *CLFOs*, one general purpose and one for the rotor

AniSynth does not pre-define any *CSampleOscillators* the way VectorSynth does. Instead, it operates off of an array of *CSampleOscillator* objects. It keeps track of the current active cell. The *CAniSynthVoice* object switches out the four oscillator pointers as different cells become active. This is shown in Figure 11.42. This version of AniSynth uses single-samples and not multi-samples.

Wavetables

There are some important restrictions on the wavetables. The *CAniSynthVoice* swaps out table pointers as the active cell changes. The oscillator's index values are not altered during the swap. Therefore it is imperative that the wavetables adhere to the following rules (note: you can use single-samples or multi-samples).

- all tables must be the same length in samples
- all tables should hold one cycle of a waveform and must hold the same number of cycles per table
- if the number of cycles per table is more than one, you need to alter the tuning equation
- the quality of the synthesis is directly related to the quality of the wavetables
- arrangement of the table rows (aka AniMoog's timbres) is also an important consideration

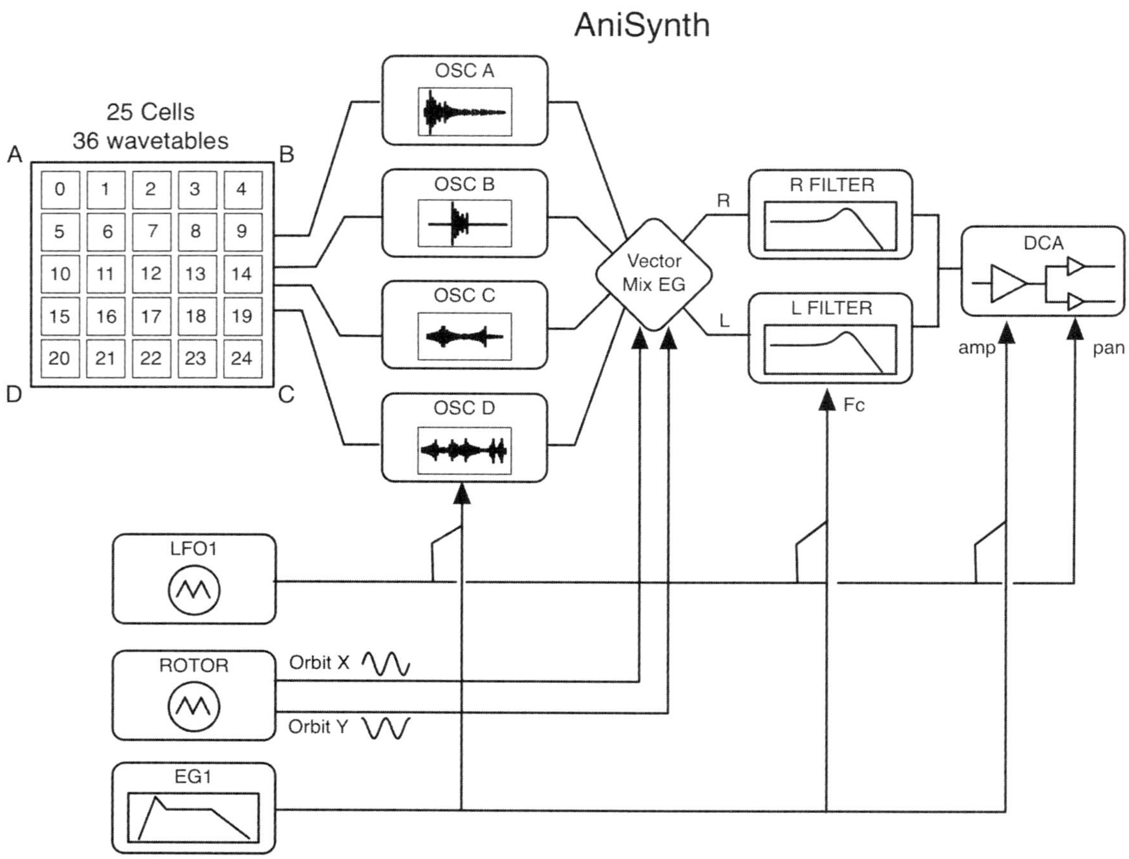

Figure 11.40: AniSynth simplified block diagram.

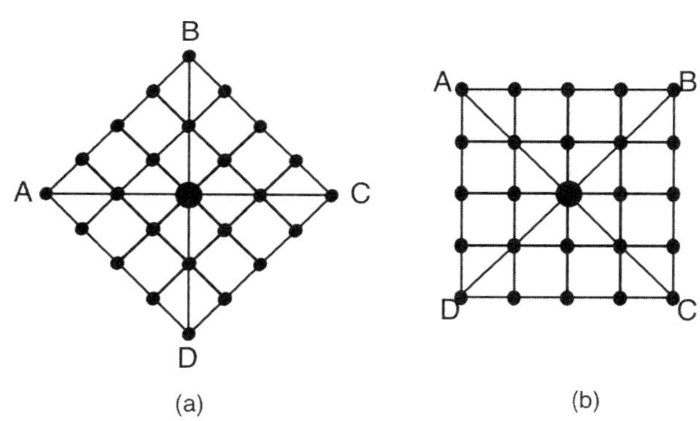

Figure 11.41: Mapping the 36 wavetables to the joystick control in (a) RackAFX and (b) VST3 and AU.

For AniSynth we use a library of 4,300 single-cycle wavetables as a basis for choosing the 36 required wavetables. The library is called *Adventure Kid Wave Forms* (AKWF) and is free from www.adventurekid.se/akrt/waveforms/adventure-kid-waveforms/, or my website. The collection includes 4,300 single-cycle wavetables culled from synthesizers, computers, nature, and acoustic instruments like the cello, clarinet and flute. There are also FM, primitive (saw, sine, square), and human voice wavetables. These wavetables are all monophonic, and are all 600 samples in length.

The wavetables are loaded in the *loadTables()* function. The *CAniSynthVoice* object stores an array of pointers to dynamically created *CSampleOscillator* objects initialized from the .wav files. These *CSampleOscillator* objects are effectively wavetables. The pointers populate the array in the same sequence as the samples are loaded. You can see the pattern of how the pointers are arranged into cells in Figure 11.43.

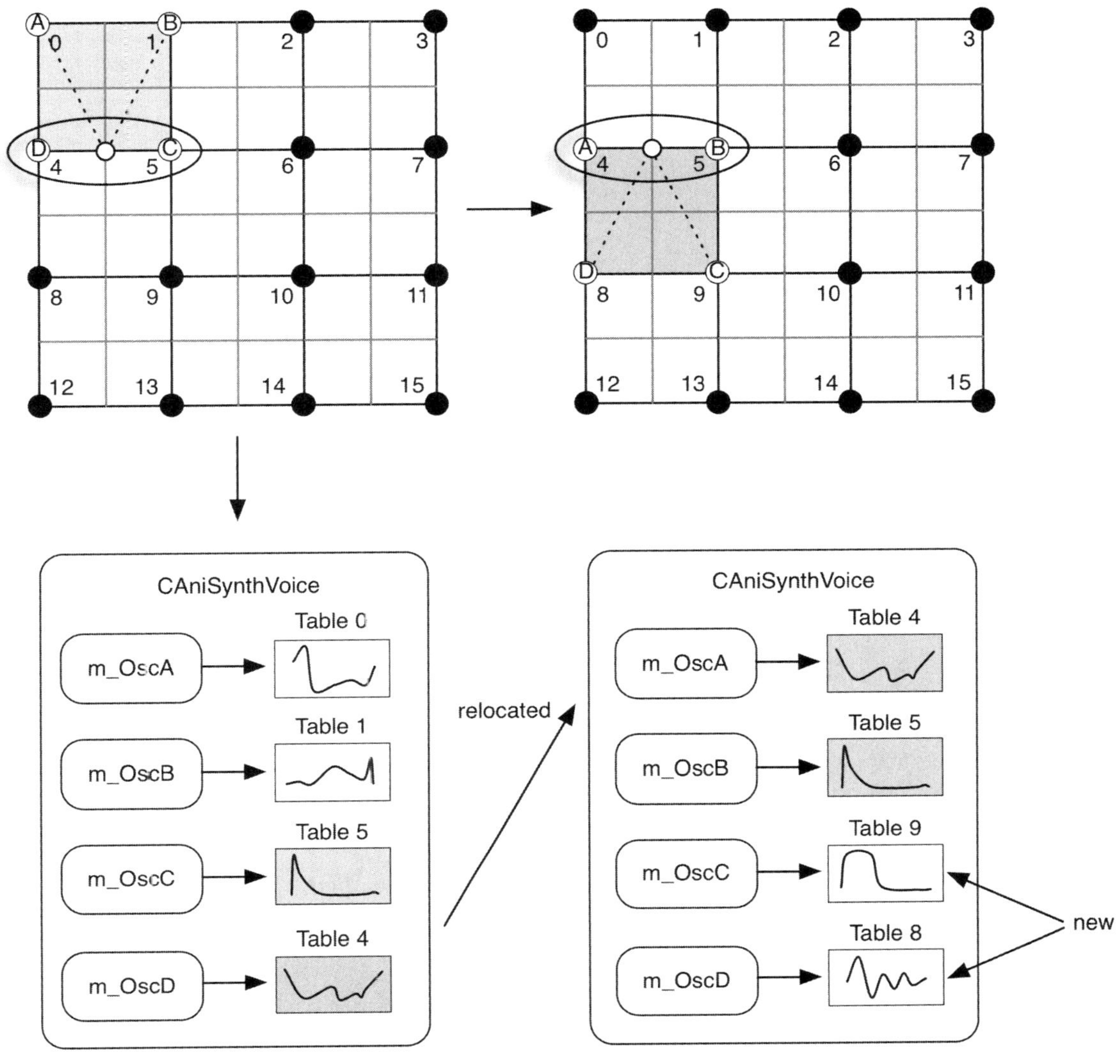

Figure 11.42: AniSynth swaps out the oscillator table pointers when the active cell changes; notice how Table 5 and Table 4 move from OscC and OscD to OscB and OscA, respectively, according to the local mix cell; two new tables are added while the other two are discarded.

> **Some of the AKWF wavetables are sonically pleasing while others clearly alias.** However, the library is enormous and free. You are strongly encouraged to find your own supply of high quality single-cycle wavetables for this project. Stereo wavetables are preferred, as they sound better/fuller. You should also experiment with using rows of similar-sounding samples. This is easy with the AKWF samples, which are grouped into sets of files based on the origin or sound of the wavetables.

The logic for selecting a set of buffer pointers based on cell location is as follows:

```
nCell = cell index
m_nCellsPerSide = number of cells per side of the joystick control (5 here)
m_nCells = total number of cells (25 here)

nTargetRow = nCell/m_nCellsPerSide;
nSkip = m_nCellsPerSide - 1;

nIndex_A = nCell+nTargetRow;
nIndex_B = nCell+nTargetRow+1;
```

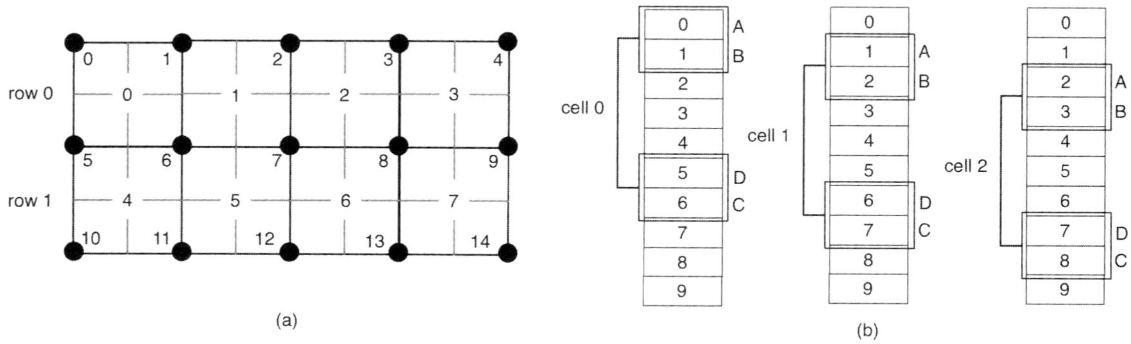

Figure 11.43: (a) The first two rows of zero-indexed wavetables and (b) the corresponding pattern of cells in the array of pointers to the *CSampleOscillator* objects.

```
nIndex_C = nCell+nTargetRow+nSkip+3;
nIndex_D = nCell+nTargetRow+nSkip+2;
```

11.19 The CAniSynthVoice Object

CAniSynthVoice is derived from *CVectorSynthVoice*, and so it inherits all of the vector synth member variables and functions. The only real difference is in the *doVoice()* function, and the fact that *CAniSynthVoice* needs to maintain the array of wavetable buffer pointers. The voice object creates a set of uninitialized *CSampleOscillator* objects depending on the number of cells per side you choose. You then initialize each oscillator with a separate .wav file or a folder of files. The *setActiveCell()* implements the lookup logic for swapping the oscillator pointers around.

Table 11.9 lists the member variables, and Table 11.10 lists the member functions. By now, these should look familiar.

The CAniSynthVoice member variables are self-explanatory, so let's step through the member functions.

Constructor

In the constructor, you initialize the variables. Since this is a derived class, the constructor will be called last in the sequence (*CVoice->CDigiSynthVoice->CVectorSynthVoice->CAniSynthVoice*). The majority of work here is in setting up the filters; the diode ladder filter has a severe cut in passband response as Q is increased, so we add a little compensation here—as always, feel free to experiment with this.

```
CAniSynthVoice::CAniSynthVoice(void)
{
      m_ppOscArray = NULL;
      m_nCellsPerSide = 0;
      m_nCells = 0;
      m_nCurrentCell = -1;

      // --- connect our filters
      m_pFilter1 = &m_LeftDiodeFilter;
      m_pFilter2 = &m_RightDiodeFilter;

      // --- experiment with NLP
      m_LeftDiodeFilter.m_uNLP = OFF;
      m_RightDiodeFilter.m_uNLP = OFF;

      // --- for passband gain comp in DIODE; can make user adjustable
      m_LeftDiodeFilter.m_dAuxControl = 0.5;
      m_RightDiodeFilter.m_dAuxControl = 0.5;
}
```

Table 11.9: *CAniSynthVoice* member variables.

CAniSynthVoice Member Variables		
Type	**Variable Name**	**Description**
CDiodeLadderFilter	m_LeftDiodeFilter, m_RightDiodeFilter	filters for left and right channels
CSampleOscillator**	m_ppOscArray;	array of pointers to CSampleOscillator objects
int	m_nCellsPerSide	number of cells per side of joystick control/mix surface
int	m_nCells	total number of cells
int	m_nCurrentCell	the current (active) cell

Table 11.10: *CAniSynthVoice* member functions.

CAniSynthVoice Member Functions	
Function Name	**Description**
initGlobalParameters	initialize the global parameters
initializeModMatrix	initialize the modulation matrix
prepareForPlay	prepareForPlay on sub-components, one time init
createOscArray	create the master array of *CSampleOscillator* objects
initOscWithFilePath	initialize a *CSampleOscillator* with a WAV file (single-sample); the oscillator is zero-indexed in the master array
initOscWithFolderPath	initialize a *CSampleOscillator* with a folder of WAV files (multi-sample); the oscillator is zero-indexed in the master array
setActiveCell	swap out the oscillator pointers depending on the active cell
doVoice	render the audio

initializeGlobalParameters()

There is nothing else to initialize here, so this function simply calls the base class; the global parameters are identical to VectorSynth.

```
inline virtual void initGlobalParameters(globalSynthParams* pGlobalParams)
{
      // --- always call base class first
      CVectorSynthVoice::initGlobalParameters(pGlobalParams);
}
```

initializeModMatrix

There is nothing else to initialize here, so this function simply calls the base class; the modulation matrix is identical to *VectorSynth* and is initialized in the base classes.

```
void CAniSynthVoice::initializeModMatrix(CModulationMatrix* pMatrix)
{
      // --- always first: call base class to create core and
      //     init with basic routings
      CVectorSynthVoice::initializeModMatrix(pMatrix);
}
```

prepareForPlay()

In *prepareForPlay()* you call the base class function first, then set the active cell to be the center cell found at *(m_nCells – 1)/2.0.*

```
void CAniSynthVoice::prepareForPlay()
{
      // --- always call base class first
      CVectorSynthVoice::prepareForPlay();
```

```
        // --- find center cell
        if(m_nCells != 0)
              setActiveCell((m_nCells - 1)/2.0);
}
```

createOscArray()

In *createOscArray()* you create the array and load it with freshly created oscillator pointers. Notice this may be called more than once since it first deletes the original array; this means you can extend the plug-in to load new sets of wavetables without re-compiling.

```
bool CAniSynthVoice::createOscArray(int nCellsPerSide)
{
        // --- delete if existing
        if(m_ppOscArray)
        {
              // --- size
              int nArraySize = pow(m_nCellsPerSide + 1.0, 2.0);

              for(int i=0; i<nArraySize; i++)
              delete m_ppOscArray[i];
              delete [] m_ppOscArray;
        }

        // --- size   (use argument)
        int nArraySize = pow(nCellsPerSide + 1.0, 2.0);

        // --- create new array of pointers
        m_ppOscArray = new CSampleOscillator*[nArraySize];

        // --- validate
        if(!m_ppOscArray)return false;

        // --- load up with new oscillator pointers
        for(int i=0; i<nArraySize; i++)
              m_ppOscArray[i] = new CSampleOscillator;

        // --- store for later
        m_nCellsPerSide = nCellsPerSide;
        m_nCells = pow(m_nCellsPerSide, 2.0);

        return true;
}
```

initOscWithFilePath()
initOscWithFolderPath()

These two functions initialize a zero-indexed oscillator from the master array with a file or folder. It simply finds the oscillator in the array and calls its initialization function.

```
inline bool initOscWithFilePath(int nOscIndex, char* pPath,
                                bool bSingleCycleSample,
                                bool bPitchlessSample)
```

```
{
    if(!m_ppOscArray) return false;

    ((CSampleOscillator*)m_ppOscArray[nOscIndex])->m_bSingleCycleSample =
                                                  bSingleCycleSample;
    ((CSampleOscillator*)m_ppOscArray[nOscIndex])->m_bPitchlessSample =
                                                  bSingleCycleSample;

    return m_ppOscArray[nOscIndex]->initWithFilePath(pPath);
}
inline bool initOscWithFolderPath(int nOscIndex, char* pPath,
                                  bool bSingleCycleSample,
                                  bool bPitchlessSample)
{
    if(!m_ppOscArray) return false;

    ((CSampleOscillator*)m_ppOscArray[nOscIndex])->m_bSingleCycleSample =
                                                  bSingleCycleSample;
    ((CSampleOscillator*)m_ppOscArray[nOscIndex])->m_bPitchlessSample =
                                                  bSingleCycleSample;

    return m_ppOscArray[nOscIndex]->initWithFolderPath(pPath);
}
```

setActiveCell()

This function implements the lookup logic for setting the four oscillator pointers based on the cell index.

```
inline void setActiveCell(int nCell)
{
    int nTargetRow = nCell/m_nCellsPerSide;
    int nSkip = m_nCellsPerSide - 1;

    // A nTargetRow
    ((CSampleOscillator*)m_pOsc1)->setWaveDataPtr(
                   m_ppOscArray[nCell+nTargetRow]->getWaveData());

    // B nTargetRow+1
    ((CSampleOscillator*)m_pOsc2)->setWaveDataPtr(
                   m_ppOscArray[nCell+nTargetRow+1]->getWaveData());

    // C nTargetRow+3 (yes, 3)
    ((CSampleOscillator*)m_pOsc3)->setWaveDataPtr(
              m_ppOscArray[nCell+nTargetRow+nSkip+3]->getWaveData());

    // D nTargetRow+2
    ((CSampleOscillator*)m_pOsc4)->setWaveDataPtr(
              m_ppOscArray[nCell+nTargetRow+nSkip+2]->getWaveData());
}
```

doVoice()

The *doVoice()* function is nearly identical to the implementation in *CVectorSynthVoice()*, so we will only discuss the new part. The fundamental difference is that after running the joystick program and finding the current joystick mix point, you need to find the cell in which the point lies. This is done with a function called *translateRotorPointToGridCell()* in *synthfunctions.h*. It is simply a mathematical mapping from the coordinates to a cell. If the cell has changed since the last sample period, the *setActiveCell()* function is called to swap out the oscillator pointers. The cell is treated as a local mix-surface, and the rest of the function is the same as in *CVectorSynthVoice*.

```
inline virtual bool doVoice(double& dLeftOutput, double& dRightOutput)
{
      // this does basic on/off work
      if(!CVoice::doVoice(dLeftOutput, dRightOutput))
            return false;

      <SNIP SNIP SNIP>

      // --- this is the different chunk for AniSynth
      // --- making copies here because translateRotorPointToGridCell
      //     will alter the arguments (for other manifestations not in the
      //     book)
      double dJSX = m_dVectorCenterX;
      double dJSY = m_dVectorCenterY;

      // --- calc the rotor x,y
      double dRotorX = m_dRotorX*m_dOrbitXAmp;
      double dRotorY = m_dRotorY*m_dOrbitYAmp;

      // --- find the cell for this x,y location
      int cell = translateRotorPointToGridCell(dJSX, dJSY, dRotorX, dRotorY,
                                               m_nCellsPerSide, true);

      // --- set active cell; changes pointers to samples
      if(m_nCurrentCell != cell)
      {
            m_nCurrentCell = cell;
            setActiveCell(m_nCurrentCell);
      }

      // --- AniSynth uses rotated coordinates
      bool bJoystickCoords = false;

      // --- calculate the final vector mix values based on path and rotor
      calculateVectorMixValues(0.0, 0.0, dRotorX, dRotorY,
                               m_dAmplitude_A, m_dAmplitude_B,
                               m_dAmplitude_C, m_dAmplitude_D,
                               dRotorACMix, dRotorBDMix, m_nCellsPerSide,
                               bJoystickCoords);

      // --- get our 4 osc outputs
      dLeftA = m_pOsc1->doOscillate(&dRightA);
      dLeftB = m_pOsc2->doOscillate(&dRightB);
```

```
        dLeftC = m_pOsc3->doOscillate(&dRightC);
        dLeftD = m_pOsc4->doOscillate(&dRightD);

        // --- do the massive mix - same as vector synth
        etc...
```

The *loadSamples()* function is nearly the same for each platform and similar to VectorSynth. The function initializes every oscillator with a separate .wav file; the file names are preserved, and so the function is prohibitively long to repeat in its entirety here. Please download the sample code for the complete listing. The RackAFX version is shown here; the only real difference between the platforms is generating the path from the DLL location.

```
bool CAniSynth::loadSamples()
{
        for(int i=0; i<MAX_VOICES; i++)
        {
                CAniSynthVoice* pVoice = m_pVoiceArray[i];

                // --- create the array
                pVoice->createOscArray(5); // (N+1)^2 = 36 samples

                // --- initialize the oscillators
                int nIndex = 0;

                // --- make the first path
                char* pPath = addStrings(getMyDLLDirectory(),"\\Samples
                                         \\AKWF_0001\\AKWF_0001.wav");
                // --- init
                pVoice->initOscWithFilePath(nIndex++, pPath, true, false);
                delete [] pPath;

                // --- next path...
                pPath = addStrings(getMyDLLDirectory(),"\\Samples\\AKWF_0001
                                         \\AKWF_0002.wav");

                // --- init next osc...
                pVoice->initOscWithFilePath(nIndex++, pPath, true, false);
                delete [] pPath;

                etc...
```

11.20 AniSynth Files

AniSynth uses the following files, which you will need to add into your compiler's project in the usual manner.

For VST3 and AU, you also need to add the file *SynthParamLimits.h*, which is in the AniSynth sample code—remember that this file is slightly different for each synth because it contains the GUI control index enumeration.

AniSynth is identical to VectorSynth, except the *CAniSynthVoice* is used instead of *CVectorSynthVoice,* and the *loadSamples()* function is different. The modulation matrix and GUI controls are all identical. You have the choice of copying and modifying your existing *VectorSynth* project or starting a new one.

AniSynthVoice.h	Oscillator.h
AniSynthVoice.cpp	Oscillator.cpp
DCA.h	SEMFilter.h
DCA.cpp	SEMFilter.cpp
DiodeLadderFilter.h	SampleOscillator.h
DiodeLadderFilter.cpp	SampleOscillator.cpp
EnvelopeGenerator.h	synthfunctions.h
EnvelopeGenerator.cpp	VAOnePoleFilter.h
Filter.h	VAOnePoleFilter.cpp
Filter.cpp	VectorSynthVoice.h
LFO.h	VectorSynthVoice.cpp
LFO.cpp	VectorPathGenerator.h
DigiSynthVoice.h	VectorPathGenerator.cpp
DigiSynthVoice.cpp	Voice.h
ModulationMatrix.h	Voice.cpp
ModulationMatrix.cpp	
KThreeFiveFilter.h	
KThreeFiveFilter.cpp	

For the plug-in's *.h* file declarations:

- *#include "AniSynthVoice.h"* at the top of the file
- use the code listing below—notice the only difference is the type of voice object pointer stored in the array

```
<< ** Code Listing 11.3: Declarations ** >>

// --- our array of voices
CVectorSynthVoice* m_pVoiceArray[MAX_VOICES];

// --- MmM
CModulationMatrix m_GlobalModMatrix;

// --- global params
globalSynthParams m_GlobalSynthParams;

// --- helper functions for note on/off/voice steal
void incrementVoiceTimestamps();
CVectorSynthVoice* getOldestVoice();
CVectorSynthVoice* getOldestVoiceWithNote(UINT uMIDINote);

// --- load sample sets
bool loadSamples();

// updates all voices at once
void update();

// for portamento
double m_dLastNoteFrequency;

// our recieve channel
UINT m_uMidiRxChannel;

<< END ** Code Listing 11.1: Declarations ** END >>
```

11.21 AniSynth: RackAFX, VST3, and AU

Create the AniSynth project using *VectorSynth* as a starting point—the GUI controls are identical. Substitute the new *loadSamples()* function for the original function and change all references to *CVectorSynthVoice* to *CAniSynthVoice* in the plug-in object. Do not delete or modify *CVectorSynthVoice* since *CAniSynthVoice* is derived from it. This synth looks and behaves identically to VectorSynth, except the mix surface has 36 sound sources instead of four. The paths, rotors and programming are all identical. If you decide to use your own wavetable files, make sure you adhere to the restrictions.

11.22 Challenges

Bronze

Use the AC and BD mix values to modulate other synth parameters, such as the left and right filter cutoffs, LFO rates, etc.

Silver

A cool trick with vector synths involves detuning one or more of the four oscillators with musical intervals in semitones. A perfect fifth is seven semitones, while a major third is four semitones. With some of the oscillators detuned this way, the evolution of sound contains musical intervals that come and go. For example, if you detuned oscillators B, C and D with four, seven, and ten semitone offsets with the joystick in the center position, you would hear a four note dominant 7th chord. As the vector mix changes, the intervals move in and out. Add the ability to detune the oscillators against each other.

Gold

Allow the user to choose from a variety of both samples and traditional waveforms for the four oscillators. For example, they might use digital samples for oscillators A and B, and quasi bandlimited sawtooth and square for oscillators B and D. Add the objects and controls for this new feature. Allow the AC and BD mix to modulate parameters like pulse width or sawtooth waveshaping saturation.

Platinum

AU/VST users: create a joystick programming interface that the voice object can use to program the vector path generator.

Diamond

AniSynth has an issue when the mix point is moving so fast that it moves to a non-adjacent cell, causing a possible glitch—find a way to smooth over the discontinuity that may arise in this case.

Bibliography

danphillips.com. "Wavestation Vector Mix Calculation." Accessed June 2014, http://www.danphillips.com/wavestation/SYSEX/WSDevDoc.zip

Junglieb, Stanley. 1986. *Prophet VS Digital Vector Synthesizer*. San Jose: Sequential Circuits, Inc.

Junglieb, Stanley. 1990. *Wavestation Player's Guide*. Tokyo: Korg, Inc.

musictech.net. "Vector Synthesis Tutorial." Accessed June 2014, http://www.musictech.net/2012/06/10mm-no207-vector-synthesis/

Phillips, Dan. 1991. *Wavestation SR Reference Guide*. Tokyo: Korg, Inc.

Roads, Curtis. 1996. *The Computer Music Tutorial*, Chap. 5. Cambridge: MIT Press.

CHAPTER 12

DXSynth: FM Synthesizer

In 1973, John Chowning published "The Synthesis of Complex Audio Spectra by Means of Frequency Modulation" in the *Journal of the Audio Engineering Society*. It described a method of synthesizing sounds with potentially dense spectra from just a few sinusoidal oscillators and envelope generators. Frequency Modulation (FM) produces multiple harmonics from just two sinusoids. The ability to alter the spectrum in realtime is so powerful that filtering is not required. This synthesis technique is one of the filter-less varieties, along with additive synthesis in which spectral components were directly synthesized and modified. For stable operation, the oscillators need to be digital so that their outputs are exactly repeatable, and they need to operate in forward time (positive frequencies) or reverse time (negative frequencies). A decade after Chowning's original publication, the technology caught up with the theory to the point that a reasonably priced synthesizer could be produced. After licensing the synthesis method, Yamaha produced and marketed the first commercially available FM synthesizer, called the DX7, in 1983. It became the second bestselling synthesizer of all time, at about 160,000 units sold, behind the Korg M1, at about 250,000 units. Yamaha spun off the product into multiple DX synths, all marketed as FM synths. The manuals refer to the technology as "digital FM tone generation."

However, neither the DX7 nor any of the DX variants were FM synths. They were all Phase Modulation (PM) synthesizers. Some speculate that the term "FM" was already in use and well known to the public from FM radio, whereas PM was not. Also, at that time FM was synonymous with "high quality" since its fidelity was so much better than AM radio. In any event, phase modulation is virtually identical to frequency modulation, so that much of the theory is interchangeable. It's also relatively simple to implement. Both the wavetable and quasi bandlimited oscillators are already designed to run forward or backward. For this chapter's DXSynth project, you will only need sinusoidal oscillators and envelope generators. In addition, there are no filters, so DXSynth is capable of high polyphony counts.

FM/PM synthesis is capable of producing a vast range of timbres, from searing, paint-peeling lead sounds, to muted piano sounds, to the most convincing bell and gong sounds you will probably ever synthesize without using samples. But, if you want to understand the theory, there is a little math to deal with. Fortunately, it is well known and reasonably easy.

12.1 FM and PM Theory

Both frequency modulation and phase modulation were well understood in the engineering community at the time Chowning published his paper in 1973. Both are covered in any engineering textbook on communication systems and theory. Chowning applied what was normally reserved for high frequency applications to very low frequency audio. In this section, we will look at the way FM generates spectral components from two sinusoids. The sinusoids are named carrier and modulator. Both FM and PM are forms of angle modulation. We typically fashion the sinusoidal functions (*sin* and *cos*) in a generalized form:

$$
\begin{aligned}
&f(t) = A\sin(\omega t + \phi)\\
&g(t) = A\cos(\omega t + \phi)\\
&or\\
&f(t) = A\sin(\theta(t))\\
&g(t) = B\cos(\theta(t))\\
&\theta(t) = \omega t + \phi
\end{aligned}
\tag{12.1}
$$

$\theta(t)$ is the argument of the trig functions and is called the angle. It is broken into two parts: frequency and phase. The frequency of oscillation is ω, the angular velocity of a rotating phasor and the phase component is φ. Ordinarily the frequency is fixed and not time-varying. Likewise the phase component is static; it is usually a phase offset, and often we set it to 0.0 for convenience. It represents the phasor's initial starting point. If the frequency and phase are not fixed, however, but rather vary in time, how do you quantify frequency and phase? The answer is with the instantaneous frequency and phase relationship. The instantaneous frequency ω_i and phase θ_i are related as:

$$
\begin{aligned}
&\omega_i(t) = \frac{d\theta_i}{dt}\\
&\theta_i(t) = \int_0^t \omega_i(\tau)dt
\end{aligned}
\tag{12.2}
$$

This makes sense—ω_i is the angular velocity or the rate of change of the phase angle in time—the time derivative. In both FM and PM, you replace the oscillator frequency with a new instantaneous frequency ω_i. In frequency modulation, you vary the instantaneous frequency and keep the phase constant. In Phase modulation, you vary the instantaneous phase and keep the frequency constant, however the altered phase also changes the instantaneous frequency. In both cases the frequency of oscillation ω_c is called the carrier frequency.

In FM, the instantaneous frequency is the sum of the carrier frequency and some function *f(t)*, scaled by the frequency deviation $\Delta\omega$. Typically, we set the phase offset φ_0 to 0.0 and ignore it. In PM, the carrier frequency remains constant, and its instantaneous phase is altered by some function *f(t)*, scaled by the phase deviation $\Delta\theta$.

$$\begin{aligned} FM\ \ f(t) &= \sin(\omega_i t + \phi_0) \\ \text{Let } \phi_0 &= 0.0 \\ \omega_i &= \omega_c + \Delta\omega f(t) \\ \theta_i(t) &= \omega_c + \Delta\omega \int f(t) \end{aligned}$$

$$\begin{aligned} PM\ \ f(t) &= \sin(\omega_c t + \Delta\theta f(t)) \\ \theta(\mathrm{t}) &= \omega_c t + \Delta\theta f(t) \end{aligned} \quad (12.3)$$

The function that alters the frequency or phase is either *sin*(ω_m t) or *cos*(ω_mt), where ω_m is the modulation frequency. This sets up four possible combinations of *sin/cos* as carrier/modulator. Suppose we choose *sin*(ω_ct) as the carrier and *cos*(ω_mt) as the modulator. You can choose any combination of *sin/cos* as carrier/modulator pairs—the spectra of the resulting signals are the same.

$$\begin{aligned} FM\ \ f(t) &= \sin\left[\omega_c t + \Delta\omega \int \cos(\omega_m t)\right] \\ &= \sin\left[\omega_c t + \frac{\Delta\omega}{\omega_m}\sin(\omega_m t)\right] \end{aligned} \quad (12.4)$$

The *cos()* function outputs values that fluctuate between −1 and +1, so if the carrier frequency is 500 Hz and the frequency deviation Δf is 250 Hz, the instantaneous frequency will vary between 250 Hz and 750 Hz, or $f_c \pm \Delta f$.

$$PM\ \ f(t) = \sin(\omega_c t + \Delta\theta\cos(\omega_m t)) \quad (12.5)$$

Likewise in PM, if you set the phase deviation to 3.1415 (i.e., π), then the instantaneous phase will vary between −π and +π radians. In both cases the strength or depth of modulation is controlled with the term in front of the modulator component. This term is called the modulation index, or index of modulation, and is found as:

Index of Modulation

$$PM: \quad I = \Delta\theta \qquad\qquad FM: \quad I = \frac{\Delta\omega}{\omega_m} \quad (12.6)$$

So, you can see that in FM, the index of modulation is dependent on the modulation frequency, whereas in PM it is not—this is the first desirable attribute we will exploit later. When you alter the instantaneous phase of the oscillator, it in turn alters the instantaneous frequency and creates a peak frequency deviation of:

$$\Delta\omega = \Delta\theta\omega_m \quad (12.7)$$

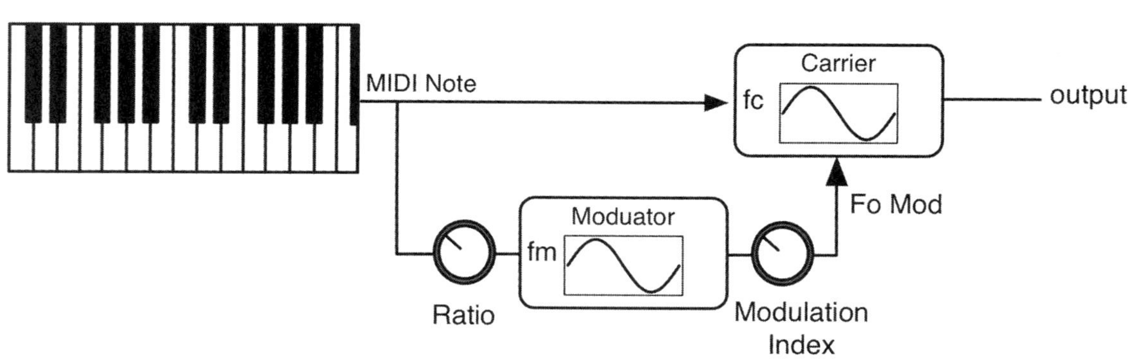

Figure 12.1: A simple FM synth patch; the carrier frequency f_c is the MIDI note frequency, and the modulator frequency is set as some ratio of f_c.

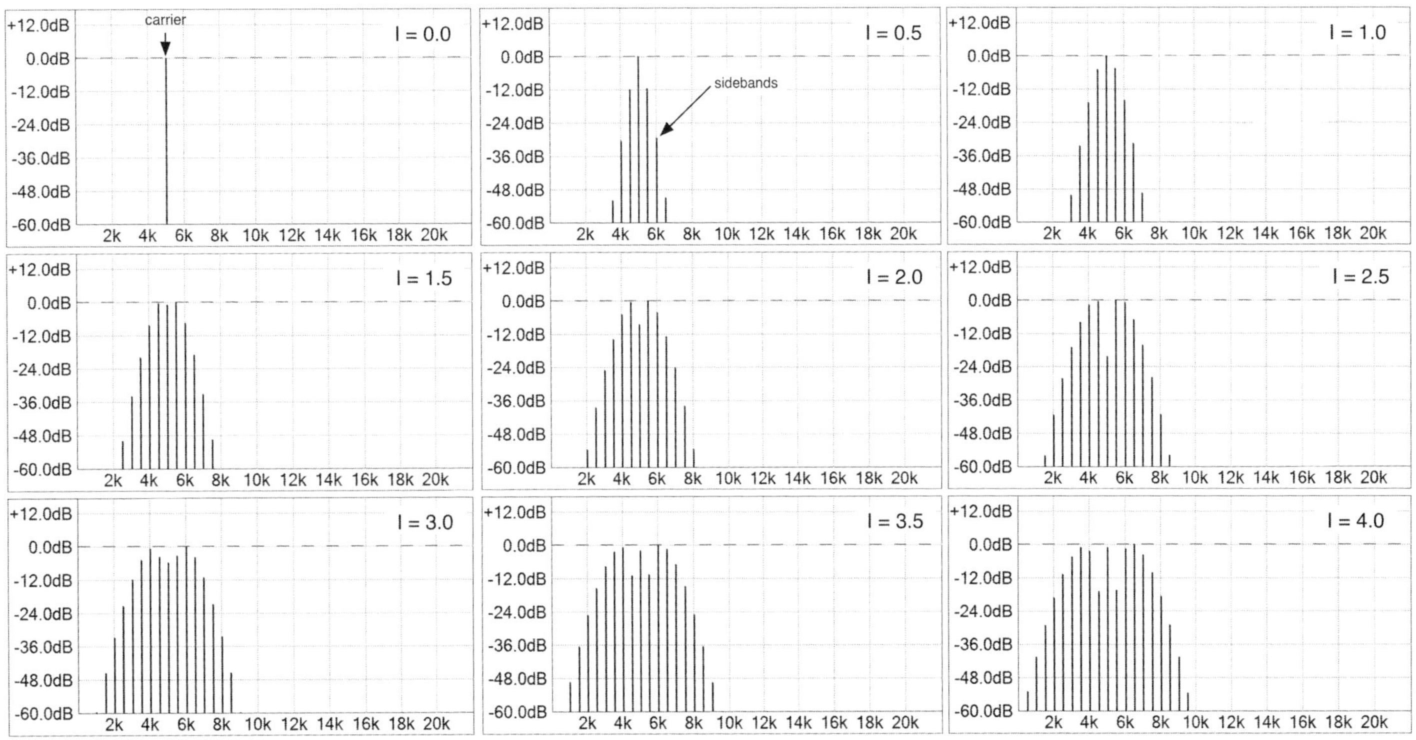

Figure 12.2: The normalized spectra of the simple FM patch in Figure 12.1, with the index of modulation varied between 0.0 and 4.0, shows how the bandwidth widens as the number of effective sidebands increases.

This is the link that lets us use the FM theory to describe the PM operation. In both cases, the index of modulation is adjustable from zero (no modulation, pure sinusoid output) to some maximum value called I_{MAX}. In both PM and FM, the modulation index is proportional to the deviation (phase or frequency). Figure 12.1 shows a simple FM oscillator patch as applied to synthesis. The frequency of the MIDI note sets the carrier's oscillator frequency f_c. The modulator frequency f_m is usually set as a ratio of the carrier; for the Yamaha DX series, the ratio is selected from a list of interesting values from 0.5 to 25.95. The ratio of the two frequencies, along with the index of modulation, determines the resulting spectrum and sets rules about the signal's characteristics and musical qualities. These two sinusoidal oscillators and the two controls (ratio and modulation index) can create a vast number of complex and harmonically interesting signals.

The spectrum of an FM signal consists of the carrier frequency plus other mathematically related harmonics in sidebands. The harmonics appear both above and below the carrier frequency. The carrier and harmonics are scaled depending on the index of modulation. In some cases, the carrier may disappear altogether. Figure 12.2 shows the progression of harmonics for the following FM setup (note that the plots are normalized to the highest peak; without normalization, you would see the sidebands get lower in amplitude as the index increases—the total energy is conserved):

- fc = 5000 Hz
- fm = 500 Hz (or 0.1 fc)
- modulation index: varies from 0 to 4

Let's make some observations before looking at any more math. You can see how increasing the index of modulation adds more sidebands and that they form around the carrier. If you observe any individual frequency component including the carrier, you can see that as the index of modulation increases or decreases, the amplitudes of the harmonic components undulate. The carrier and the harmonic components bob up and down. Unlike typical spectra, where the fundamental frequency is the lowest component (often with the highest amplitude) and the harmonics taper off as they increase, FM produces a different kind of spectrum. In fact, where is the fundamental frequency in any of the plots in Figure 12.2?

A difficult aspect of FM synthesis is in creating a patch. It is not intuitively obvious how the index changes the harmonic components that make up the spectrum. When you turn the cutoff frequency knob of a lowpass filter, it is obvious how the position of the knob affects the spectrum. In FM synthesis, the relationship of the index value to the spectrum is not as simple. You will notice in Figure 12.2 that we stopped the experiment at I = 4.0, just before the lower sidebands hit the 0 Hz wall. What happens if we lower the carrier or increase the index so that harmonics appear below 0 Hz? The answer is that these harmonics are reflected back into the positive frequency domain as shown in Figure 12.3.

When the harmonics reflect across the 0 Hz line, they may or may not line up with harmonics in the positive half. Figure 12.3 shows a situation where they do not line up and instead fill in the spaces between harmonics. This will have a certain audible effect on the spectrum. So, we observed that all the frequency components including the carrier will move up and down in amplitude as the index changes. We also observed that sidebands below 0 Hz are reflected as positive frequencies. Math confirms these observations.

12.2 FM Spectra

Taking the Fourier transform of Equation 12.4 reveals an interesting solution, and it explains our observations. The first thing the transform tells us is that there will be an infinite number of sidebands, and their harmonic frequencies are going to occur at multiples of the carrier +/- the harmonics of the modulator, that is:

$$f_c \pm nf_m\big|_{n=1 \text{ to } \infty} \tag{12.8}$$

So if f_c = 1000 Hz and f_m = 400 Hz, FM would produce components at the carrier plus those listed in Table 12.1; the negative components would reflect back into the positive frequency domain.

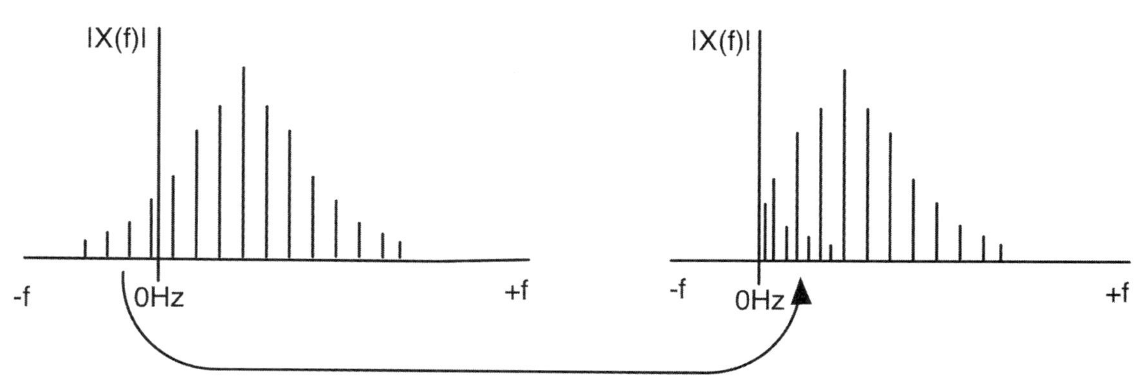

Figure 12.3: Negative frequency sidebands are reflected back across the 0 Hz line as positive frequencies.

Table 12.1: The first few pairs of sidebands for the f_c = 1000 Hz and f_m = 400 Hz.

n	$f_c - nf_m$	$f_c + nf_m$
1	600 Hz	1400 Hz
2	200 Hz	1800 Hz
3	-200 Hz	2200 Hz
4	-600 Hz	2600 Hz

Table 12.2: The carrier amplitude is $J_0(I)$ and the sideband amplitudes are shown next to each frequency component.

$$J_0(I)fc$$

Amp	$f_{sideband(-)}$	Amp	$f_{sideband(+)}$
$-J_1(I)$	$f_c - f_m$	$J_1(I)$	$f_c + f_m$
$-J_2(I)$	$f_c - 2f_m$	$J_2(I)$	$f_c + 2f_m$
$-J_3(I)$	$f_c - 3f_m$	$J_3(I)$	$f_c + 3f_m$
$-J_4(I)$	$f_c - 4f_m$	$J_4(I)$	$f_c + 4f_m$

The next thing the transform tells us is that these harmonics have amplitudes that vary as Bessel functions of the first kind and depending on the index of modulation. The Bessel functions are part of the solution to the Fourier transform of the FM signal. This family of functions are all damped sinusoids; they undulate up and down. Since the sideband amplitudes are related to these functions, it explains why they move up and down as the index of modulation changes. The Bessel functions of the first kind are labeled J and indexed from 0 to infinity, producing a set *{J0, J1, J2, …}*. Their argument here is the index of modulation *I*, producing a new set *{J0 (I), J1(I), J2(I), …}*. The set of harmonic components making up the FM spectrum is called *φFM(t)*, and the amplitudes are:

$$\phi_{FM}(t) = A\sum_{n=-\infty}^{+\infty} J_n(I)\cos(\omega_c + n\omega_m)t \tag{12.9}$$

Expanding the summation:

$$\begin{aligned}\phi_{FM}(t) = \{&J_0(I)\sin(\omega_c t)\\ &+J_1(I)\sin(\omega_c+\omega_m)t - J_1(I)\sin(\omega_c-\omega_m)t\\ &+J_2(I)\sin(\omega_c+2\omega_m)t + J_2(I)\sin(\omega_c-2\omega_m)t\\ &+J_3(I)\sin(\omega_c+3\omega_m)t - J_3(I)\sin(\omega_c-3\omega_m)t\\ &+J_4(I)\sin(\omega_c+4\omega_m)t + J_4(I)\sin(\omega_c-4\omega_m)t\\ &+\ldots\}\end{aligned} \tag{12.10}$$

The first term represents the carrier alone, and the rest are the pairs of sidebands. Notice that the signs in front of the Bessel terms alternate for the frequencies that sit below the carrier frequency. This sign shows you the phase of the harmonic component. So, the amplitudes of the harmonics are $J_n(I)$, and the phase of every other component is negative. This is summed up in Table 12.2, which may be easier to interpret than Equation 12 10.

The easiest way to understand how this works is by doing a simple example. Figure 12.4 shows the first six Bessel functions of the first kind. Let's find the amplitude of the carrier and a few sidebands using the plots for the values:

- fc = 200 Hz
- fm = 200 Hz (ratio = 1)
- modulation index: 5

First, locate the index of modulation (5) on the *x*-axis and find where it intersects the curve. For $I = 5$, we get the following values (these are actual computed values):

$J_0(5) = -0.1776$
$J_1(5) = -0.3267$
$J_2(5) = 0.0466$
$J_3(5) = 0.3648$
$J_4(5) = 0.3912$
$J_5(5) = 0.2611$

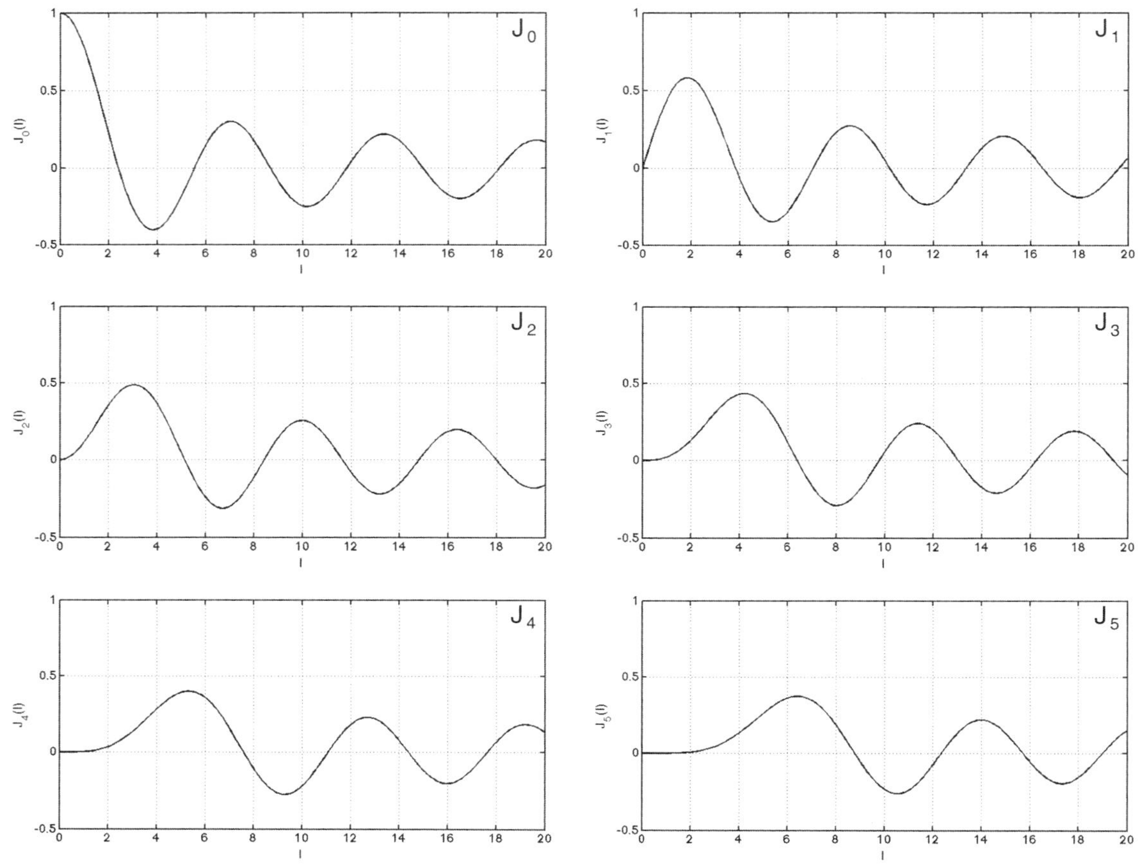

Figure 12.4: The first six Bessel functions of the first kind J_0 to J_5.

Table 12.3: The first few sidebands and their amplitudes.

Lower Sideband	Amplitude	Upper Sideband	Amplitude
$f_c - f_m$ = 0 Hz	$-J_1(5)$ = 0.3276	$f_c + f_m$ = 400 Hz	$J_1(5)$ = −0.3276
$f_c - 2f_m$ = −200 Hz	$J_2(5)$ = 0.0466	$f_c + 2f_m$ = 600 Hz	$J_2(5)$ = 0.0466
$f_c - 3f_m$ = −400 Hz	$-J_3(5)$ = −0.3648	$f_c + 3f_m$ = 800 Hz	$J_3(5)$ = 0.3648
$f_c - 4f_m$ = −600 Hz	$J_4(5)$ = 0.3912	$f_c + 4f_m$ = 1000 Hz	$J_4(5)$ = 0.3912
$f_c - 5f_m$ = −800 Hz	$-J_5(5)$ = −0.2611	$f_c + 5f_m$ = 1200 Hz	$J_5(5)$ = 0.2611

This set of values scales each of the harmonic components; the carrier amplitude is $J_0(5) = -0.1776$. The sidebands are listed in Table 12.3. The sign determines the phase (+ is in phase, – is 180 degrees out of phase) of the component, as shown in Figure 12.5 where the sidebands are plotted. Notice that as the sidebands reflect across the 0 Hz axis, they are inverted. In this choice of carrier and modulator frequency, the reflected components line up exactly with other positive frequency sidebands, so they will add or subtract depending on the phase (sign). The final magnitude plot in Figure 12.5(d) reveals a fairly sizable DC offset. This is going to be an important issue later on that will ultimately seal the fate of using FM in musical synthesis.

Now imagine moving a control that changed the index of modulation. The harmonic amplitudes of each component would move to a new location on the Bessel function curves, reflection across the 0 Hz axis would alter the spectrum in the positive half, and the timbre would change; the harmonic components would undulate up and down along with the motion of the Bessel Functions. Figure 12.6

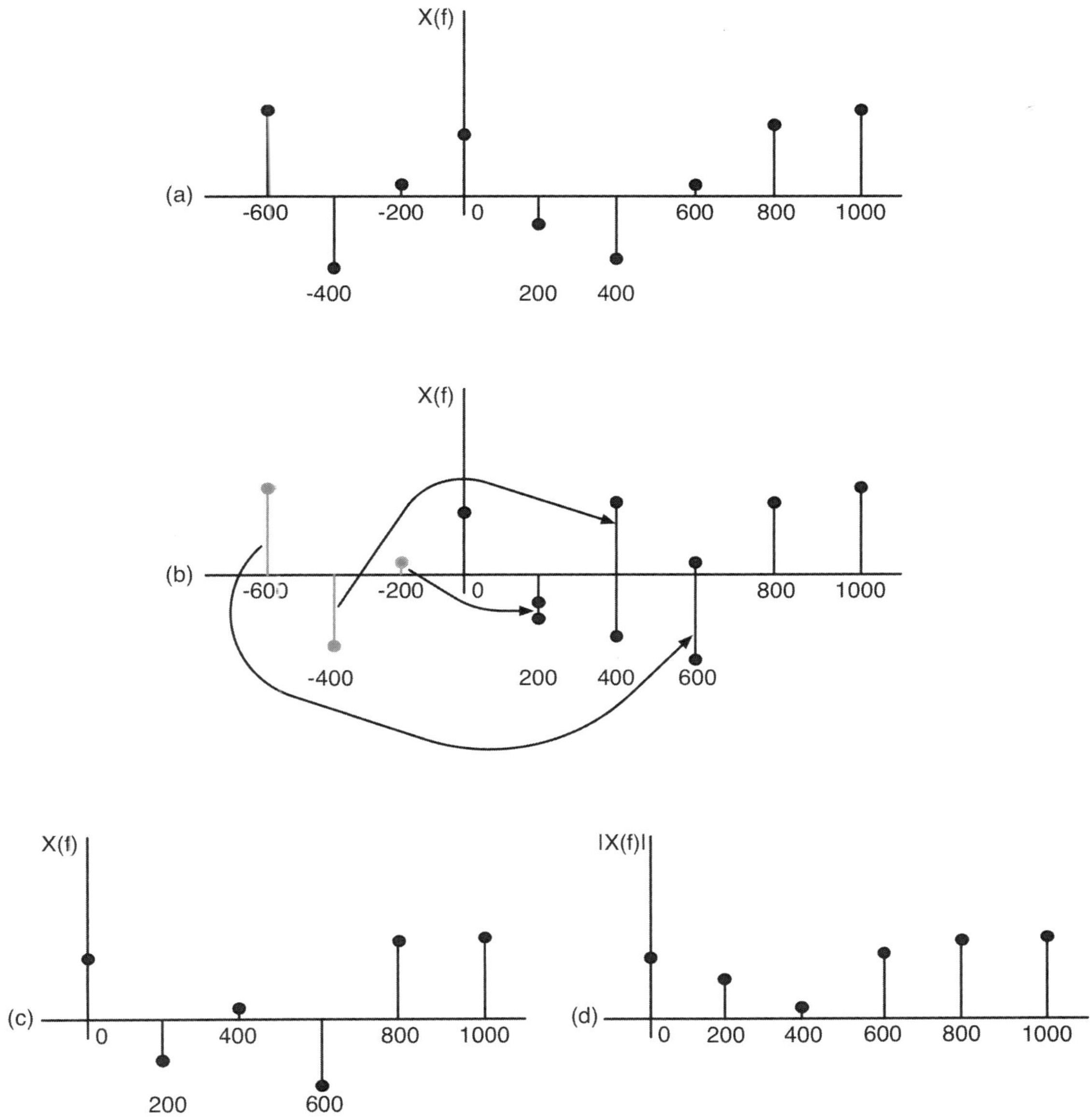

Figure 12.5: (a) The sidebands scaled by the Bessel functions (b) reflection across the 0 Hz axis inverts the phase of the sidebands, positive becomes negative and vice versa (c) the resulting spectrum after adding or subtracting the components and (d) the final magnitude plot; notice the DC offset present at 0 Hz.

shows a progression of spectra as the carrier frequency is reduced; you can see how the reflected components build and turn the shape into a asymmetrical one.

Next, consider a doubly-modulated FM "stack," shown in the block diagram of Figure 12.7. In this case the two modulators form a carrier-modulator pair. That is, on a local basis, Modulator 2 is behaving like the carrier of Modulator 1. Assume the index of modulation between them is the same as our example, 5.

Since the two modulators are operating under the same conditions as our previous analysis, the output of Modulator 2 is the same signal we calculated and contains the same sizable DC offset. How is this constant offset going to affect the carrier? It will add a tuning offset. Since the DC offset happens to be positive in this case (+0.3276), it will cause the carrier's pitch to go sharp. This means the patch will play out of tune. And, if you alter the index of modulation, the DC offset will change, and the tuning of the note will be unstable. This is clearly unacceptable for a musical instrument.

Phase modulation fixes the tuning problem. The theory of operation and development of PM sidebands is the same as FM, but in phase modulation, the DC component disappears—it represents a constant phase offset and DC has no phase. From now on, the term "FM Synth" really means "PM Synth."

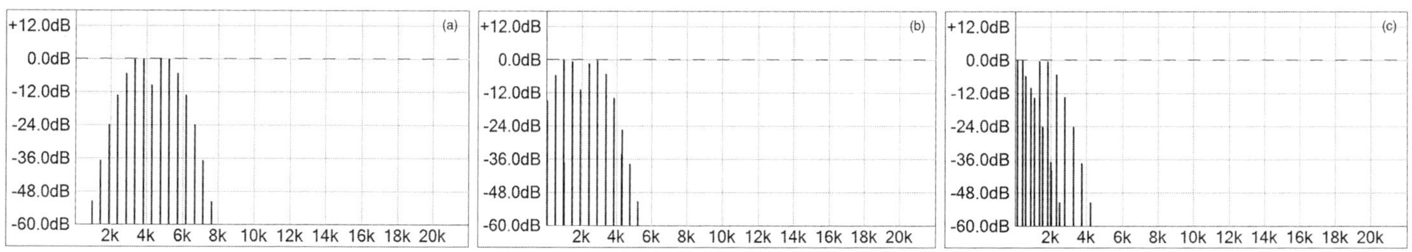

Figure 12.6: As the carrier frequency is reduced, the reflected components fold over and change the shape and density of harmonics.

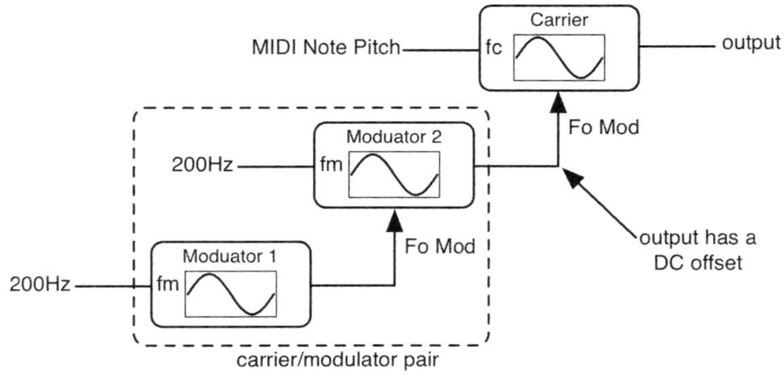

Figure 12.7: A doubly modulated patch; a modulator modulates another modulator that modulates the carrier; notice that locally, the two modulators form their own carrier/modulator pair relationship.

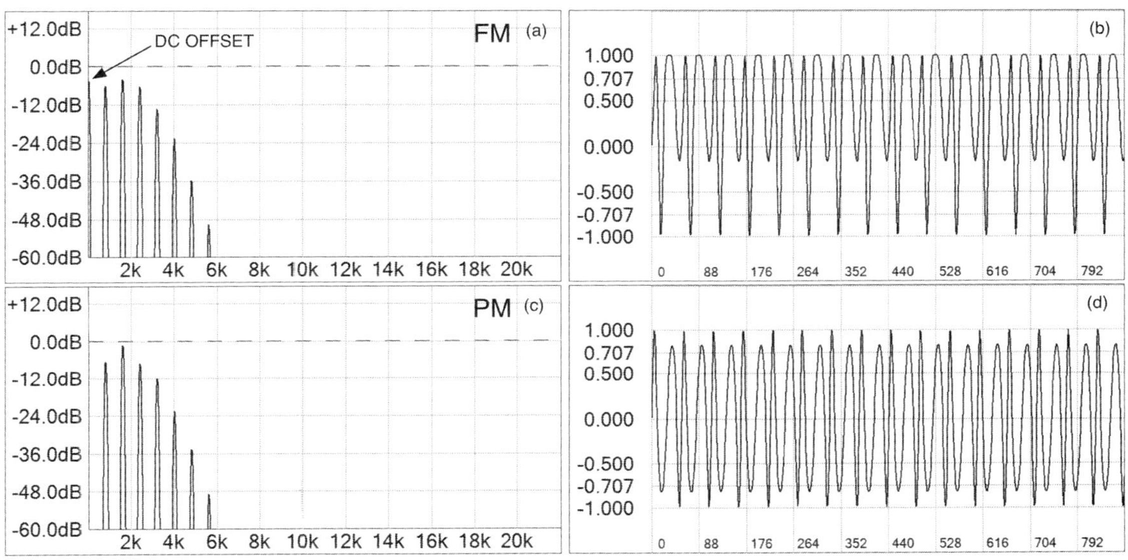

Figure 12.8: (a) The FM spectrum has a DC offset that is clearly visible in both the frequency and (b) the time domain plot, while the PM spectrum (c) and waveform (d) lack the DC offset, but the PM spectrum has virtually the same frequency component amplitudes as the FM spectrum.

To illustrate this, consider Figure 12.8. This shows both FM and PM for the following patch setup. The oscillator frequencies are chosen at 800 Hz to spread out the spectral components for easier viewing.

FM and PM:

- fc = 800 Hz
- fm = 800 Hz (ratio = 1)

PM:

- index of modulation = 0.37 = phase deviation (in DXSynth, the index of modulation is given as a multiple of 2π)

FM:

- index of modulation = $(2\pi)(0.37) = 2.32$

You can see the DC offset in both the spectrum and time domain waveform in the FM case while the PM version lacks this problem, evidenced in both spectrum and waveform. So, PM is the angle modulation of choice for musical applications. As a bonus, it's also easier to implement. The spectra are virtually identical to the point that they are sonically the same. The frequency deviations are the same:

$$\begin{aligned}&PM\\&\Delta f = \Delta\theta f_m = (0.37)(2\pi)(800) = 5.027\ kHz\\&FM\\&\Delta f = I(f_m) = 2.32(800) = 5.027\ kHz\end{aligned} \tag{12.11}$$

The plots show the last significant sideband at about 6 kHz (800 Hz + 5027 Hz).

12.3 FM/PM Rules

So far, we have only discussed the effect of the index of modulation on the FM and PM spectra. As the index increases, so do the sidebands. However, the ratio of the carrier and modulator play an equally important role in the timbre of the sound. Here are the rules. They are based on the ratio of the carrier to modulator. You first want to fashion the ratio as follows:

$$\frac{f_c}{f_m} = \frac{N_1}{N_2} \tag{12.12}$$

Where N_1 and N_2 are integers with no common divisors.

Rule One: Fundamental Frequency

The fundamental frequency of the resulting patch is:

$$f_o = \frac{f_c}{N_1} = \frac{f_m}{N_2} \tag{12.13}$$

For example:

$$\begin{aligned}&f_c = 200\ Hz\\&f_m = 1200\ Hz\\&\frac{N_1}{N_2} = \frac{200}{1200} = \frac{1}{6}\\&f_o = \frac{f_c}{N_1} = \frac{f_m}{N_2} = 200\ Hz\end{aligned} \tag{12.14}$$

Or:

$$\begin{aligned}&f_c = 100\ Hz\\&f_m = 133.333\ Hz\\&\frac{N_1}{N_2} = \frac{3}{4}\\&f_o = \frac{f_c}{N_1} = \frac{f_m}{N_2} = 33.333\ Hz\end{aligned} \tag{12.15}$$

Notice in this second example that the resulting fundamental frequency is neither the carrier nor the modulator frequency!

Rule Two: Spectral Purity

The value of N_2 affects the purity of the spectrum (whether it contains all harmonics or has gaps in the spectrum):

$$\begin{aligned}&N_2 = 1 && \text{spectrum contains all harmonic multiples}\\&N_2 \geq 2 && \text{spectrum is missing every } N_2\text{th harmonic}\end{aligned} \tag{12.16}$$

Rule Three: Reflected Frequencies

The value of N_2 also governs the way negative frequency components are reflected across the 0 Hz axis:

$$\begin{array}{ll} N_2 = 1 \text{ or } N_2 = 2 & \text{all}(-) \text{ harmonics line up perfectly with } (+) \text{ harmonics} \\ N_2 > 2 & \text{none of the } (-) \text{ harmonics line up with any } (+) \text{ harmonics} \end{array} \tag{12.17}$$

Rule Four: Inharmonicity

The value of the N_1/N_2 ratio predicts the inharmonicity.

$$\begin{array}{ll} \frac{N_1}{N_2} \geq 5 & f_o \text{ is low in amplitude; difficult to locate pitch, sounds somewhat inharmonic} \\ N_1, N_2 \neq \text{integers} & f_o \text{ does not exist; completely inharmonic} \end{array} \tag{12.18}$$

When the ratio is non-integer based (and especially when irrational), the sound is inharmonic—there is technically no fundamental. However, this makes fantastic bell/gong and percussion sounds, which are difficult to synthesize with subtractive synthesis. The bell sounds are so good that many FM synth patches automatically include them as a matter of practice.

12.4 Dynamic Spectra

In previous synths, we primarily used dynamic filtering to shape the timbre in time: we used EGs and LFOs to shift the filter cutoff frequency during the note events. For the vector synthesizers, crossfading between sounds with different timbres adds even more sonic evolution. In FM synthesis, the index of modulation ultimately controls the bandwidth of the output. If you vary this index in time, it will vary the bandwidth of the spectrum, and it can be made to sound very much like lowpass filter sweeps without the filter. The idea is to place an envelope generator on the output of each oscillator. For the carrier, this EG affects the time domain amplitude envelope in the same way we used an EG to control the DCA. For the modulator, the EG controls the depth of modulation of its carrier oscillator. For our PM synth, this means that it controls the phase deviation. By varying the deviation in time, we vary the spectrum. Figure 12.9 shows the simple FM synth with the addition of EGs—one per oscillator.

In Figure 12.9, notice that the structures inside the dotted line boxes are identical; the only difference is in naming the oscillators (Carrier or Modulator). Also note that the EGs control the output amplifiers within the oscillators themselves and not a DCA. This simple patch is made of two of these building blocks. Chowning named these structures FM operators, or just operators, and they are the basis for the architecture of the DX synths, as well as the DXSynth in this chapter. The fundamental quality of an FM patch (searing, mellow, muted, sharp, bell-like, etc.) is a result of the arrangement of multiple operators. Chowning drew his signal flow diagrams from top to bottom, so the oscillator outputs point downwards. Figure 12.10 shows the Chowning abbreviation. Notice that the details about the EG and oscillator frequency controls are omitted. Each operator always includes an accompanying EG, the carrier oscillators are always set to the MIDI note pitch, and the modulator oscillators always use some ratio of the MIDI note pitch; each modulator oscillator can be tuned to a different ratio.

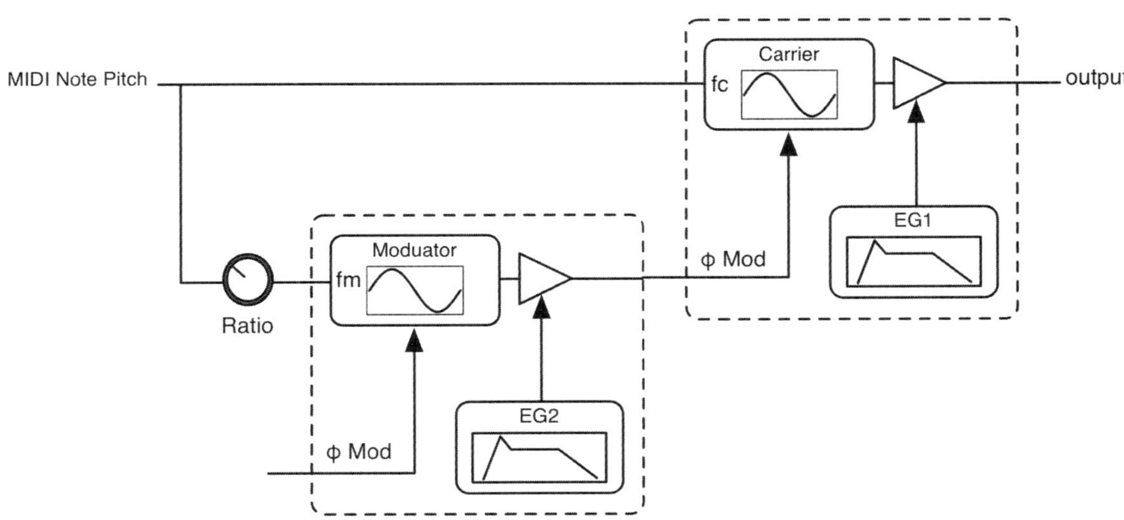

Figure 12.9: Block diagram of a simple FM patch with one carrier and one modulator.

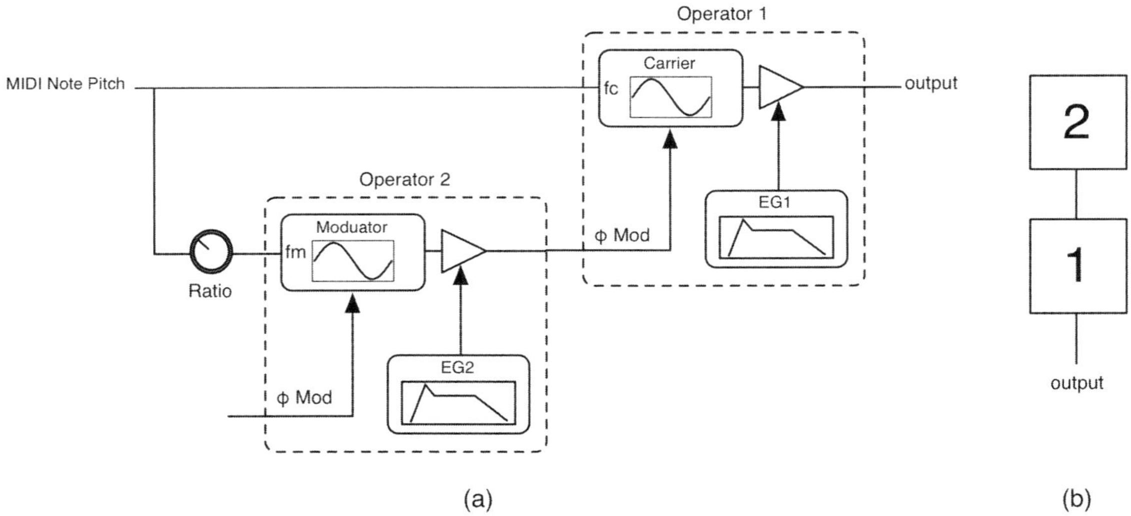

Figure 12.10: (a) A simple two operator FM patch (b) Chowning's version.

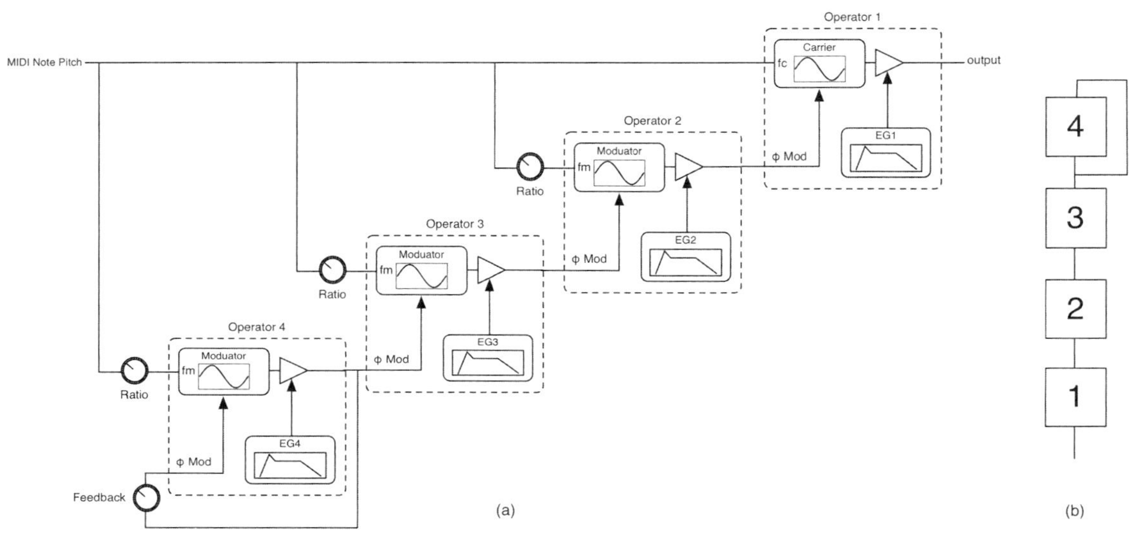

Figure 12.11: (a) A four operator FM patch with details and (b) the Chowning abbreviation.

In addition to stacking multiple modulators upon modulators, an FM operator can also self-modulate, as in the stacked set of four operators in Figure 12.11. The last operator in the chain (number 4) is self-modulating.

The DX7 features six FM operators arranged in 32 different combinations. The DX100 has four FM operators arranged in eight different combinations. Chowning called the combinations algorithms, and the DX synthesizers were branded "Digital Programmable Algorithm Synthesizers"—in fact, "FM" appears nowhere on the synth enclosures. Operators can be placed in series or parallel, and there can be more than one carrier. Figure 12.12 shows two more of these algorithms and the implied summers that are involved. The DXSynth in this chapter is a close replica of the DX100 using four operators in the same algorithm combinations. These eight algorithms are shown in Figure 12.13. From left to right, they tend to move from bright, distorted, intense (left) to mellower (center) to organ and bell-like (right).

12.5 DXSynth Specifications

Since DXSynth is based on the DX100, its voice object will need four oscillators and four envelope generators. There are no filters. There is a DCA, but it is used for panning and volume control; there is no EG connected to the DCA. Instead, the envelopes of the carriers dictate the final time domain envelope. As in the DX100, there is one LFO, which may be used to modulate pitch vibrato or operator output amplitude (Amplitude Modulation or AM) independently for each operator. Figure 12.14 shows the simplified block diagram, while Figure 12.15 shows the detailed connection diagram. Don't let the simplicity of this synth fool you—it can synthesize a much wider variety of sounds than the other synths in the book with little CPU overhead.

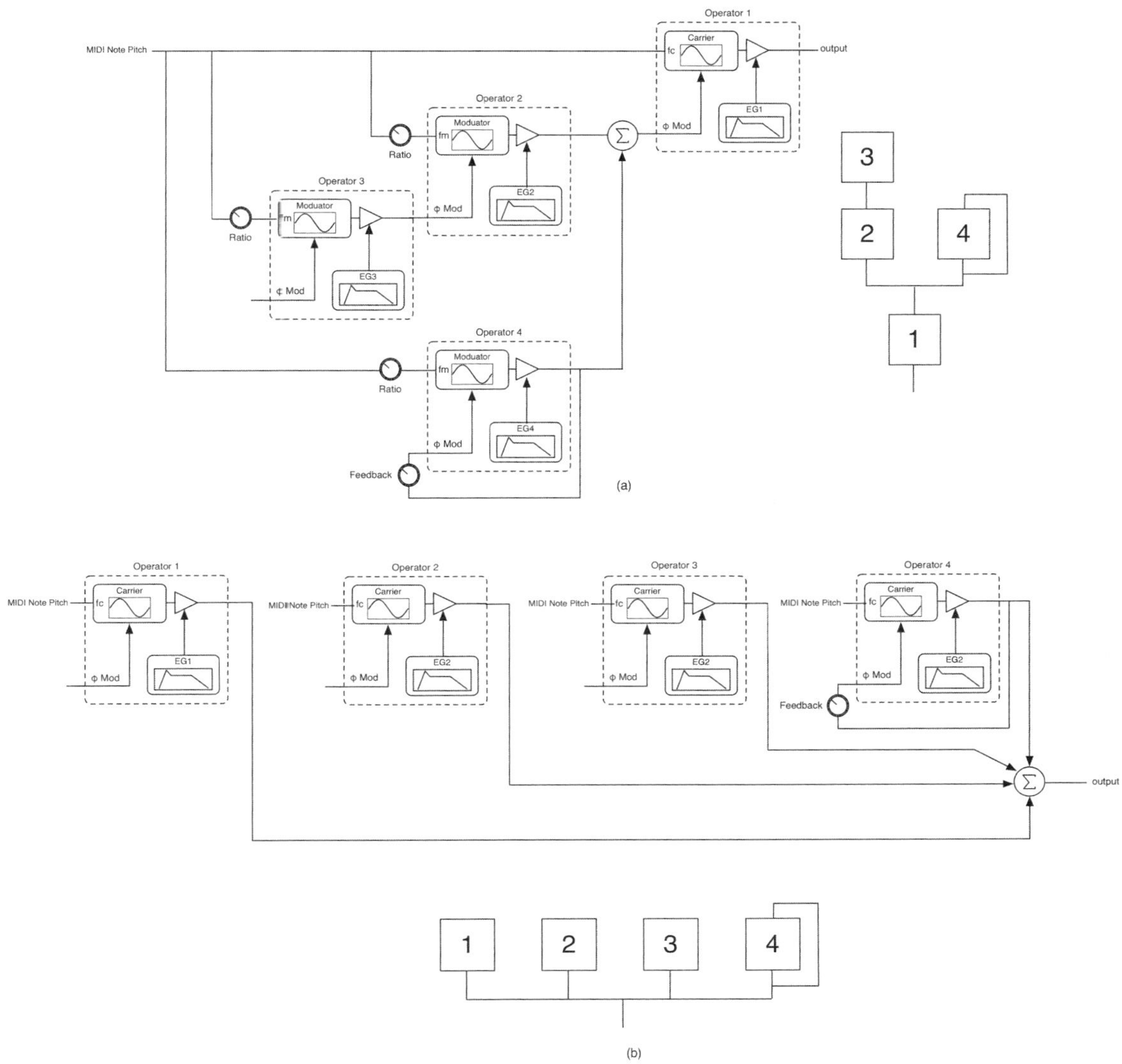

Figure 12.12: (a) A four operator patch with multiple modulator outputs summed in parallel combining to modulate the carrier (b) four carriers in parallel; their outputs are summed to form the final output.

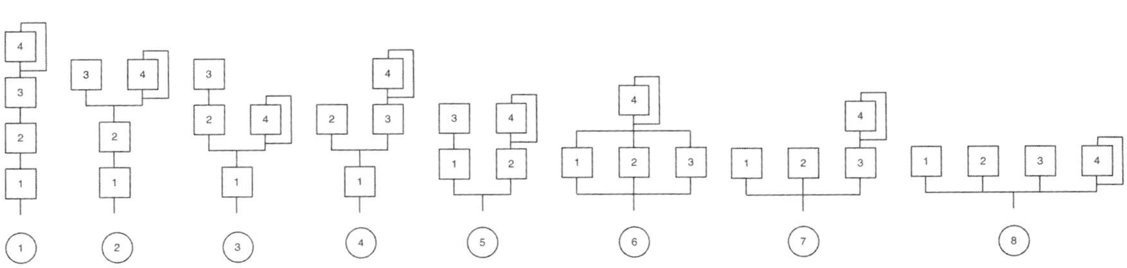

Figure 12.13: The eight algorithms in the DX100 and DXSynth.

Table 12.4 shows the modulation matrix for DXSynth consisting of eight rows. These route the LFO output to separate destinations (AM or vibrato) on each operator. Table 12.5 shows the GUI controls. These are mostly repeated sets of operator controls. Figures 12.16 and 12.17 show the GUI designs for RackAFX and VST3/AU respectively. VST3 and AU synths get a bonus—a graphic of the eight DX algorithms is included.

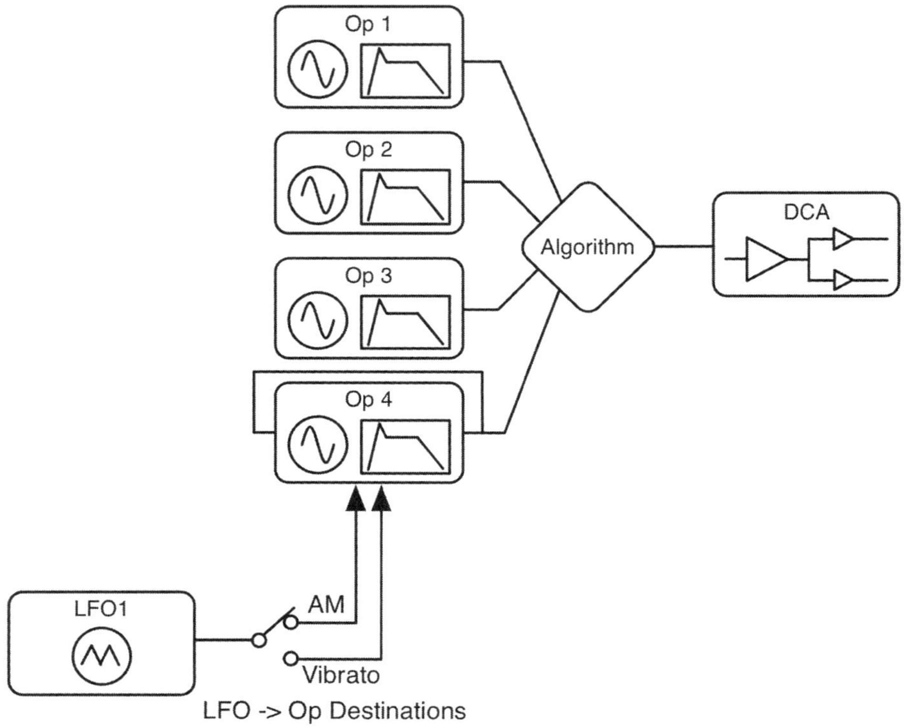

Figure 12.14: DXSynth simplified block diagram.

Table 12.4: The modulation matrix for DXSynth contains disconnected routings for the LFO to feed destinations on each operator.

***DXSynth* Modulation Matrix**			
Source	**Destination/Intensity**	**Transform/Range**	**enabled**
SOURCE_LFO1	DEST_OSC1_OUTPUT_AMP	TRANSFORM_BIPOLAR_TO_UNIPOLAR	FALSE
	dLFO1OscModIntensity	m_dDefaultModRange	
SOURCE_LFO1	DEST_OSC1_FO	TRANSFORM_NONE	FALSE
	dLFO1OscModIntensity	dOscFoModRange	
SOURCE_LFO1	DEST_OSC2_OUTPUT_AMP	TRANSFORM_BIPOLAR_TO_UNIPOLAR	FALSE
	dLFO1OscModIntensity	m_dDefaultModRange	
SOURCE_LFO1	DEST_OSC2_FO	TRANSFORM_NONE	FALSE
	dLFO1OscModIntensity	dOscFoModRange	
SOURCE_LFO1	DEST_OSC3_OUTPUT_AMP	TRANSFORM_BIPOLAR_TO_UNIPOLAR	FALSE
	dLFO1OscModIntensity	m_dDefaultModRange	
SOURCE_LFO1	DEST_OSC3_FO	TRANSFORM_NONE	FALSE
	dLFO1OscModIntensity	dOscFoModRange	
SOURCE_LFO1	DEST_OSC4_OUTPUT_AMP	TRANSFORM_BIPOLAR_TO_UNIPOLAR	FALSE
	dLFO1OscModIntensity	m_dDefaultModRange	
SOURCE_LFO1	DEST_OSC4_FO	TRANSFORM_NONE	FALSE
	dLFO1OscModIntensity	dOscFoModRange	

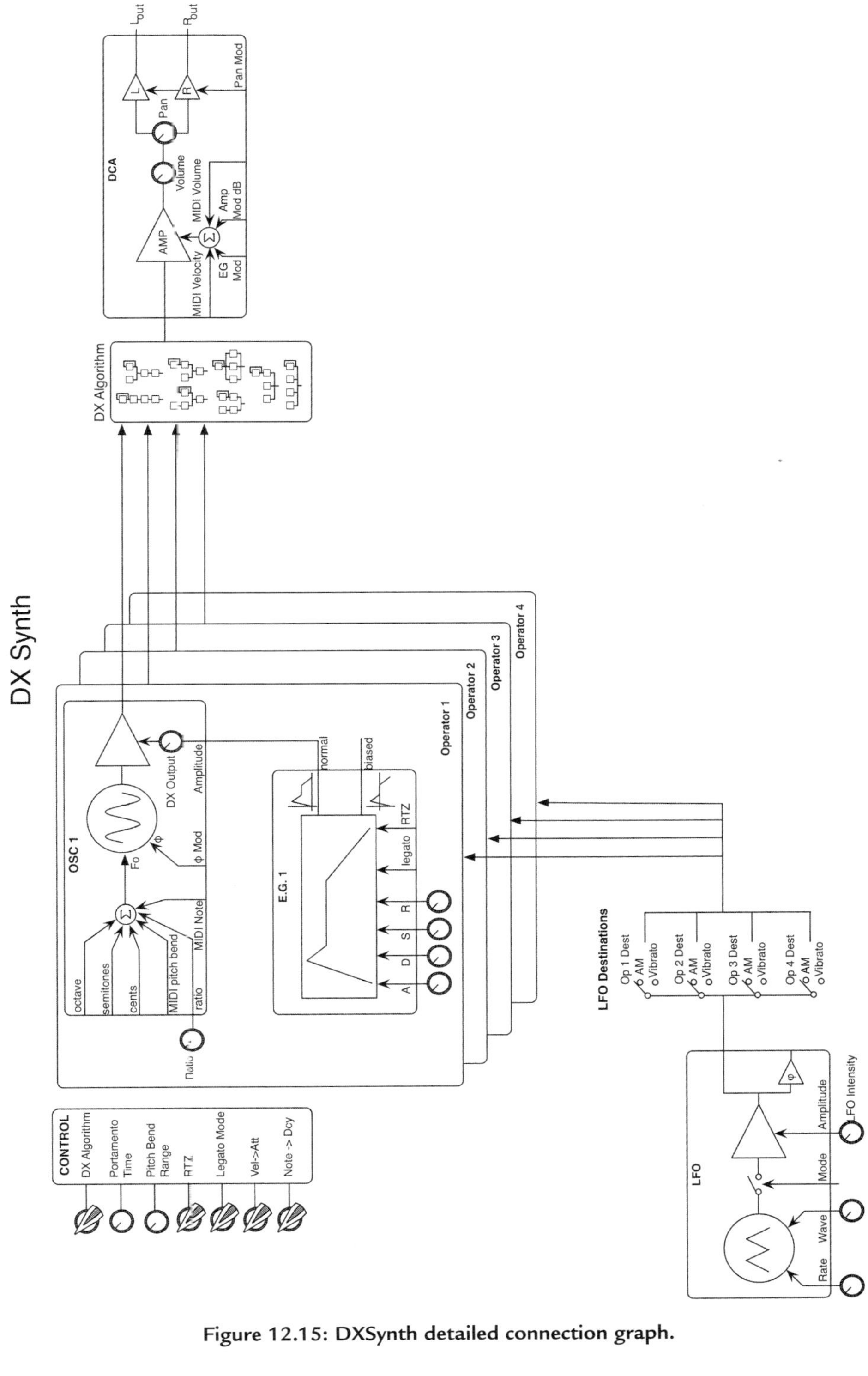

Figure 12.15: DXSynth detailed connection graph.

Table 12.5: DXSynth GUI Control List.

DXSynth Continuous Parameters				
Control Name (units)	**Type**	**Variable Name (VST3, RAFX)**	**Low/Hi/Default ***	**VST3/AU Index**
Volume	double	m_dVolume_dB	−96 / 20 / 0	OUTPUT_AM-PLITUDE_DB
Portamento Time (mS)	double	m_dPortamentoTime_mSec	0 / 5000 / 0	PORTAMEN-TO_TIME_MSEC
LFO Depth	double	m_dLFO1Intensity	0 / 1 / 0	LFO1_AMPLITUDE
LFO Rate	double	m_dLFO1Rate	0.02 / 20 / 0.5	LFO1_RATE
Op1 Ratio	double	m_dOp1Ratio	0.01 / 10 / 1	OP1_RATIO
EG1 Att (mS)	double	m_dEG1Attack_mSec	0 / 5000 / 100	EG1_ATTACK_MSEC
EG1 Dcy (mS)	double	m_dEG1Decay_mSec	0 / 5000 / 100	EG1_DECAY_MSEC
EG1 Stn	double	m_dEG1SustainLevel	0 / 1/ 0.707	EG1_SUSTAIN_LEVEL
EG1 Rel (mS)	double	m_dEG1Release_mSec	0 / 10000 / 2000	EG1_RELEASE_MSEC
Op1 Out	double	m_dOp1OutputLevel	0 / 99 / 75	OP1_OUTPUT_LEVEL
Op2 Ratio	double	m_dOp2Ratio	0.01 / 10 / 1	OP2_RATIO
EG2 Att (mS)	double	m_dEG2Attack_mSec	0 / 5000 / 100	EG2_ATTACK_MSEC
EG2 Dcy (mS)	double	m_dEG2Decay_mSec	0 / 5000 / 100	EG2_DECAY_MSEC
EG2 Stn	double	m_dEG2SustainLevel	0 / 1/ 0.707	EG2_SUSTAIN_LEVEL
EG2 Rel (mS)	double	m_dEG2Release_mSec	0 / 10000 / 2000	EG2_RELEASE_MSEC
Op2 Out	double	m_dOp2OutputLevel	0 / 99 / 75	OP2_OUTPUT_LEVEL
Op3 Ratio	double	m_dOp3Ratio	0.01 / 10 / 1	OP3_RATIO
EG3 Att (mS)	double	m_dEG3Attack_mSec	0 / 5000 / 100	EG3_ATTACK_MSEC
EG3 Dcy (mS)	double	m_dEG3Decay_mSec	0 / 5000 / 100	EG3_DECAY_MSEC
EG3 Stn	double	m_dEG3SustainLevel	0 / 1/ 0.707	EG3_SUSTAIN_LEVEL
EG3 Rel (mS)	double	m_dEG4Release_mSec	0 / 10000 / 2000	EG3_RELEASE_MSEC
Op3 Out	double	m_dOp4OutputLevel	0 / 99 / 75	OP3_OUTPUT_LEVEL
Op4 Ratio	double	m_dOp4Ratio	0.01 / 10 / 1	OP4_RATIO
EG4 Att (mS)	double	m_dEG4Attack_mSec	0 / 5000 / 100	EG4_ATTACK_MSEC
EG4 Dcy (mS)	double	m_dEG4Decay_mSec	0 / 5000 / 100	EG4_DECAY_MSEC
EG4 Stn	double	m_dEG4SustainLevel	0 / 1/ 0.707	EG4_SUSTAIN_LEVEL
EG4 Rel (mS)	double	m_dEG4Release_mSec	0 / 10000 / 2000	EG4_RELEASE_MSEC

DXSynth Continuous Parameters				
Control Name (units)	**Type**	**Variable Name (VST3, RAFX)**	**Low/Hi/Default ***	**VST3/AU Index**
Volume	double	m_dVolume_dB	-96 / 20 / 0	OUTPUT_AM-PLITUDE_DB
Portamento Time (mS)	double	m_dPortamentoTime_mSec	0 / 5000 / 0	PORTAMEN-TO_TIME_MSEC
Op4 Out	double	m_dOp4OutputLevel	0 / 99 / 75	OP4_OUTPUT_LEVEL
Op4 Feedback (%)	double	m_dOp4Feedback	0 / 70 / 0	OP4_FEEDBACK
PBendRange (semi)	int	m_nPitchBendRange	0 / 12 / 1	PITCHBEND_RANGE
* low, high and default values are #defined for VST3 and AU in *SynthParamLimits.h* for each project				

DXSynth Enumerated String Parameters (UINT)			
Control Name	Variable Name	enum String	VST3/AU Index
Algorithm	m_uVoic-eMode	DX1,DX2,DX3,DX4, DX5,DX6,DX7,DX8	VOICE_MODE
LFO Waveform	m_uLFO-1Waveform	sine,usaw,dsaw,tri, square,expo,rsh,qrsh	LFO1_WAVEFORM
Vel->Att Scale	m_uVeloc-ityToAt-tackScaling	OFF,ON	VELOCITY_TO_ATTACK
Note->Dcy Scale	m_uNote-NumberTo-DecayScaling	OFF,ON	NOTE_NUM_ TO_DECAY
Reset to Zero	m_uReset-ToZero	OFF,ON	RESET_TO_ZERO
Legato Mode	m_uLega-toMode	OFF,ON	LEGATO_MODE
Op1 LFO Dest	m_uLFO-1ModDest1	None,AmpMod,Vibrato	LFO1_DESTINA-TION_OP1
Op2 LFO Dest	m_uLFO-1ModDest2	None,AmpMod,Vibrato	LFO1_DESTINA-TION_OP2
Op3 LFO Dest	m_uLFO-1ModDest3	None,AmpMod,Vibrato	LFO1_DESTINA-TION_OP3
Op4 LFO Dest	m_uLFO-1ModDest4	None,AmpMod,Vibrato	LFO1_DESTINA-TION_OP4

Notice that the four operator output controls labeled *Op1 Out, Op2 Out, Op3* Out and *Op4* Out have ranges from 0 to 99 with a default of 75. This is a special kind of output calculation unique to this project. The DX series of synths have output controls with a 0 to 99 range. They produce nearly logarithmic volume changes across that range. Using empirical data collected from a DX100, the function *calculateDXAmplitude()* found in *synthfunctions*.h replicates the behavior and calculates an amplitude scalar with an input from 0 to 99. This will let you compare your own versions of DX algorithms with the real product.

Another issue that is specific to DXSynth involves the output EGs. You can see from looking at the algorithm diagram that in some cases, there is more than one carrier. The carrier EGs are actually output EGs that control the time envelope for each carrier. This lets you create some interesting patches because you are in control of the way separate sets of harmonics fade away during the release portion. Some harmonics might fade away faster, so they have a faster release time. In all the previous synths, we used EG1 as the output EG by default. In DXSynth the EGs that are targeted as output EGs will depend on the algorithm. Therefore, we need to override a few base class functions that involve targeting output EGs.

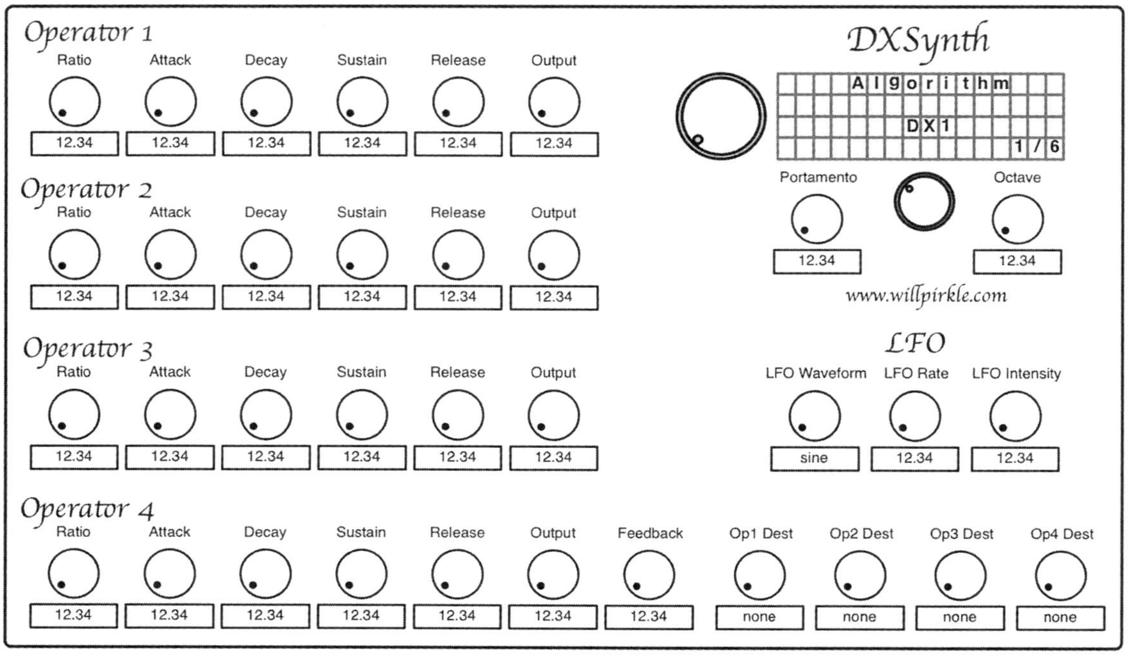

Figure 12.16: One possible DXSynth GUI in RackAFX; notice that several controls are embedded in the LCD control.

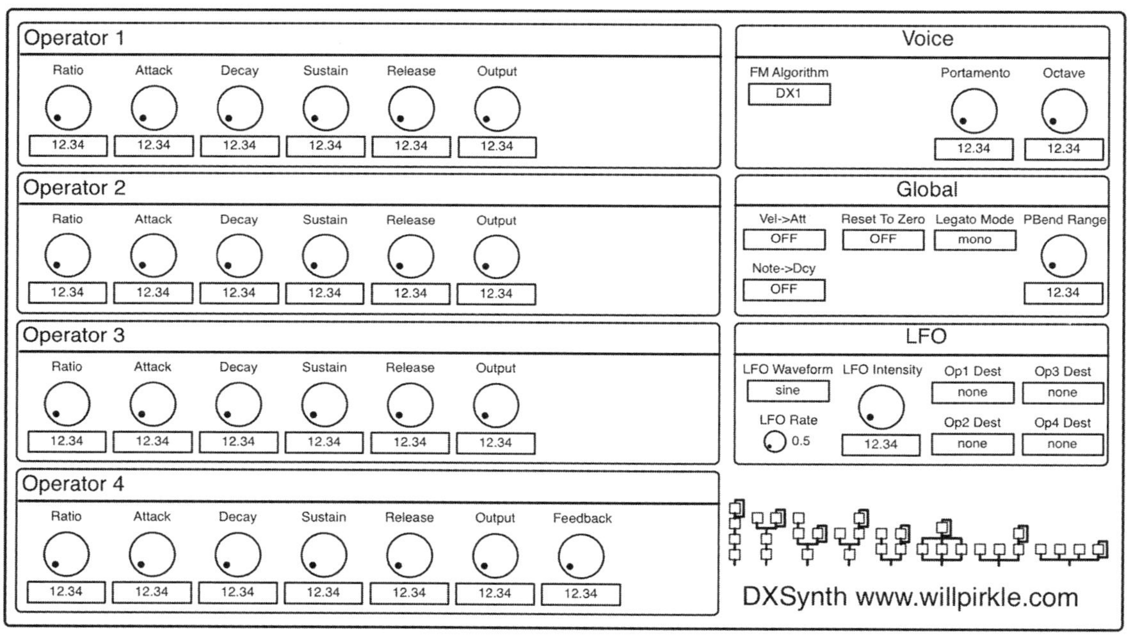

Figure 12.17: The DXSynth GUI for the VST3 and AU projects.

> For a DX algorithm, the note event is only considered finished when all EGs on carrier operators have expired. In addition, legato mode and reset to zero are only applied to output EGs and not EGs belonging to modulators, though you may experiment with this as well.

We will be using the stock EGs that we have used in all the previous projects for DXSynth, but if you want to get as realistic as possible, consider implementing an EG that more closely matches the DX EG shown in Figure 12.18; not only does this EG have five segments and different programming paradigms, the curve for the attack portion is different than any other states. See the Chapter Challenges for sources on the exact operation of the EG.

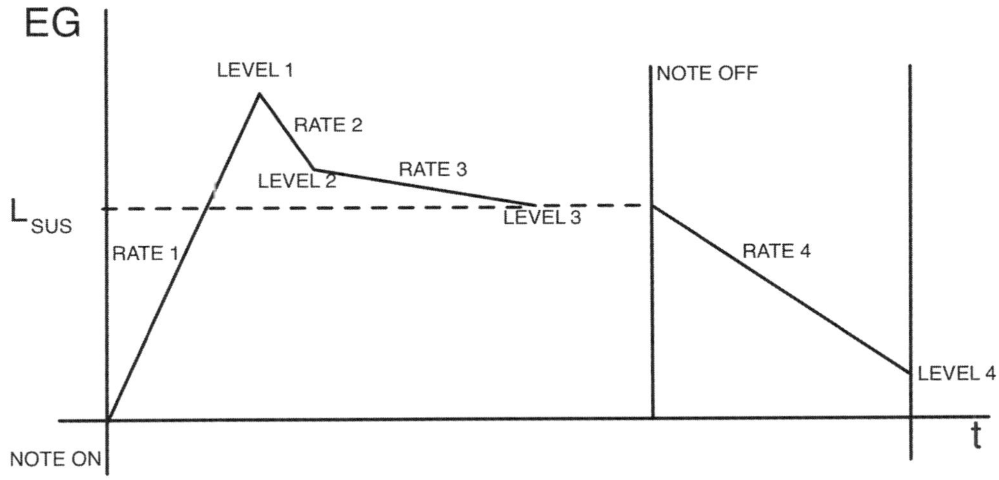

Figure 12.18: Yamaha DX Envelope Generators have an additional segment and use LEVEL and RATE values for programming.

12.6 FM and PM in Oscillator Objects

The two pitched oscillator objects *CWTOscillator* and *CQBLimitedOscillator* are already designed and coded for FM and PM operation. First, both allow for positive or negative frequencies, as we discussed in Chapter 5. Next, both allow the instantaneous frequency or phase to change. We skipped over that code previously, so let's take a look at it now.

FM

Both oscillators inherit from *COscillator*, so both use the same *update()* function. This is where FM is calculated (yes, we are ultimately designing a PM synth, but you can still experiment with FM this way). The frequency modulation is calculated as an offset to the note frequency prior to the *inc* calculation—we are literally changing the instantaneous frequency on each sample interval.

$$\omega_{MOD} = \frac{\Delta\omega}{\omega_m}\sin(\omega_m t)$$
$$\theta_{FM} = (\omega_c + \omega_{MOD})t \tag{12.19}$$

This code is inside the *update()* function:

```
// --- do the  complete frequency mod
m_dFo = m_dOscFo*m_dFoRatio*pitchShiftMultiplier(m_dFoMod +
                                                  m_dPitchBendMod +
                                                  m_nOctave*12.0 +
                                                  m_nSemitones +
                                                  m_nCents/100.0);
// --- apply linear FM (not used in book projects)
m_dFo += m_dFoModLin;

// --- calculate inc, etc...
```

You use the function *setFoModLin()* to set the linear frequency offset. To use this in a plug-in, you would multiply the output of the modulator by the frequency deviation value, which would scale the modulator to some positive and negative frequency offset.

```
// --- output of Op2*EG2 value
dOut2 = dEG2*m_Op2.doOscillate();

// --- calculate frequency deviation DF = I(fm)
dFreqDev = IMAX*m_Op1.m_dOscFo;
```

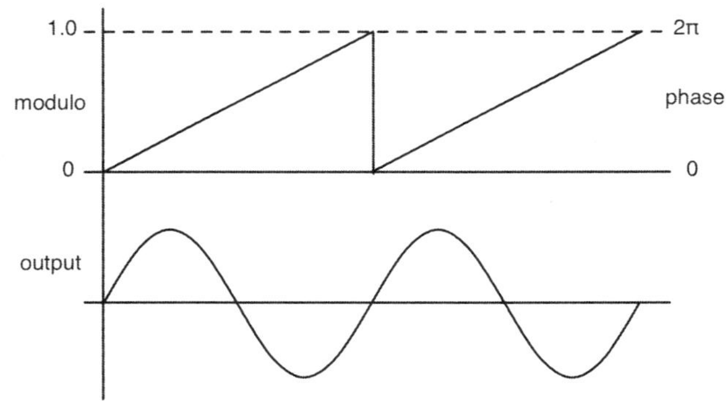

Figure 12.19: The modulo counter is also a phase increment counter; as it swings between 0.0 and 1.0, the oscillator's instantaneous phase moves from 0 to 2ϖ radians.

```
// --- set FM Lin Modulation
m_Op1.setFoModLin(dFreqDev*dOut2);

// --- update new oscillator fo
m_Op1.update();
```

PM

Phase modulation is implemented slightly differently between the two oscillator objects. In the *CQBLimitedOscillator* we use the modulo counter and increment it not only as the timebase but also to fashion the output waveform. The modulo counter goes from 0.0 to 1.0 during one cycle of the waveform, therefore the current modulo output represents a phase value of 0 to 2π radians. This is shown in Figure 12.19.

Therefore, we can alter the instantaneous phase of the oscillator by offsetting the current value of the modulo counter.

> In DXSynth, the index of phase modulation, which is also the phase deviation, is given as a multiple of 2π radians. Experimenting with a DX100 revealed the maximum phase deviation to be 8.0π radians. In DXSynth the phase deviation is given as a value from 0.0 to 4.0, which corresponds to Chowning's I_{MAX} range of 0 to 4. When applied to a bipolar sinusoidal modulator, it produces a phase deviation from -8.0π to $+8.0\pi$ radians. Thus a phase deviation of +1.0 means a shift equal to one complete waveform or $+2\pi$ radians.

So, if we add a value of 1.0 to the current modulo count value, we are shifting the phase forward by 2π radians. If we subtract 1.0, we are shifting backwards by 2π radians. The *COscillator* object already has a phase modulation variable and a *set()* function for it. So, phase modulation is implemented as an offset to the modulo counter. Because the offset can be greater than 1, we have to wrap the increment value multiple times until it falls inside the modulo interval of [0..1]. This code is *CQBLimitedOscillator's doOscillate()* method.

```
virtual inline double doOscillate(double* pAuxOutput = NULL)
{
      if(!m_bNoteOn)
            return 0.0;

      double dOut = 0.0;

      // always first
      bool bWrap = checkWrapModulo();

      // added for PHASE MODULATION
      double dCalcModulo = m_dModulo + m_dPhaseMod;
            checkWrapIndex(dCalcModulo);
```

```
switch(m_uWaveform)
{
        case SINE:
        {

        etc...
```

The function *checkWrapIndex()* is found in *synthfunctions.h*, and it simply wraps the value repeatedly until it is inside the range.

```
inline void checkWrapIndex(double& dIndex)
{
      while(dIndex < 0.0)
            dIndex += 1.0;

      while(dIndex >= 1.0)
            dIndex -= 1.0;
}
```

In the wavetable oscillator, we have nearly the same situation—the modulo counter still keeps track of the time for one cycle, but we use an index value to move through the table. Since the increment value is:

$$inc = L\frac{f_o}{f_s} \tag{12.20}$$

A phase deviation of 1.0 (which represents 2π radians) means that we need to alter the current read index value by the length of one complete cycle, which is the length of the wavetable itself. Thus, inside of its *doWavetable()* function, we alter the read index value for use in the lookup by multiplying it by the table length. So you can see both PM calculations are nearly the same and very easy to implement.

```
double CWTOscillator::doWaveTable(double& dReadIndex, double dWT_inc)
{
      double dOut = 0;

      // apply phase modulation, if any
      double dModReadIndex = dReadIndex + m_dPhaseMod*WT_LENGTH;

      // check for multi-wrapping on new read index
      checkWrapIndex(dModReadIndex);

      // get INT part
      int nReadIndex = abs((int)dModReadIndex);

      etc...
```

12.7 Yamaha DX100 vs. DXSynth

The basic architecture of DXSynth matches closely with the original DX100. When designing the DXSynth, an actual DX100 was used for comparison and tweaking. The DX output amplitude modeling facilitated testing so that patches could be quickly evaluated. Figures 12.20–12.23 show the time domain output of the DX100 versus the DXSynth for the a few different settings.

Figures 12.24–12.25 show the spectra of the DX100 versus the DXSynth for a few patches. The analog noise floor is evident in both sets of plots. We also noticed that tiny changes in the DX output amplitude created vast changes in the spectral components. For example, in Figure 12.24, changing the DXSynth Op3 Output from 75.0 to 75.2 resulted in very different spectra. This results in the differences you see in the spectra.

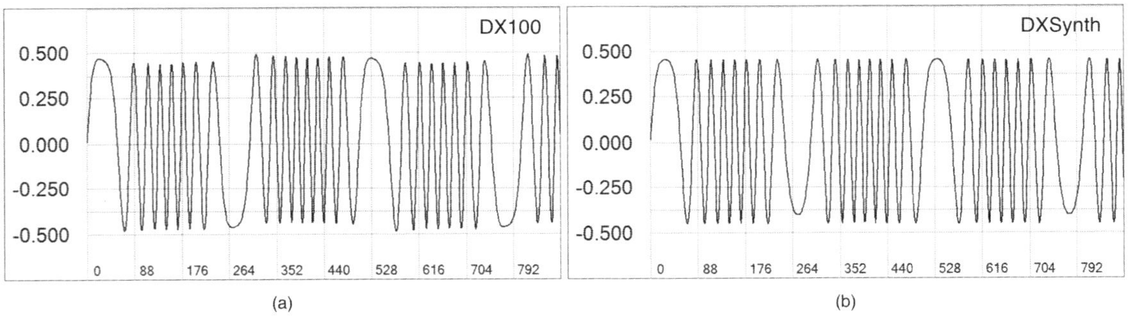

Figure 12.20: (a) Actual DX100 and (b) DXSynth output for a basic two-operator patch: Algorithm: DX1, Op1 Output: 99, Op2 Output: 99, Op3 Output: 0, Op4 Output: 0, Note: F2.

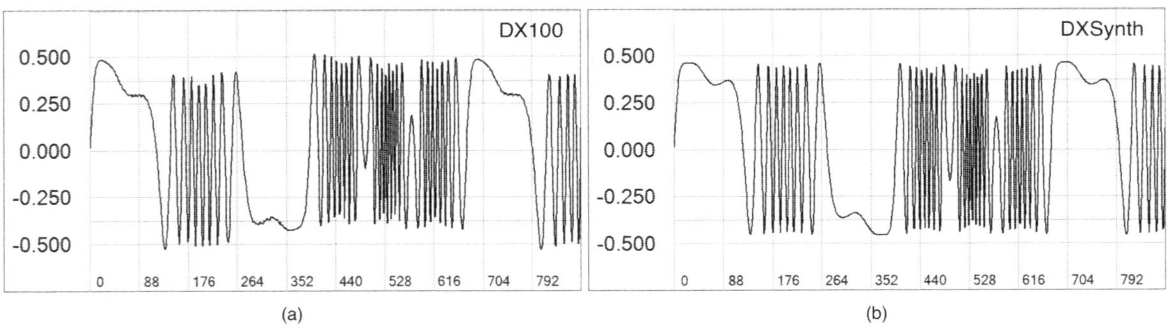

Figure 12.21: (a) Actual DX100 and (b) DXSynth output for a basic three-operator patch: Algorithm: DX1, Op1 Output: 99, Op2 Output: 99, Op3 Output: 75, Op4 Output: 0, Note: F2.

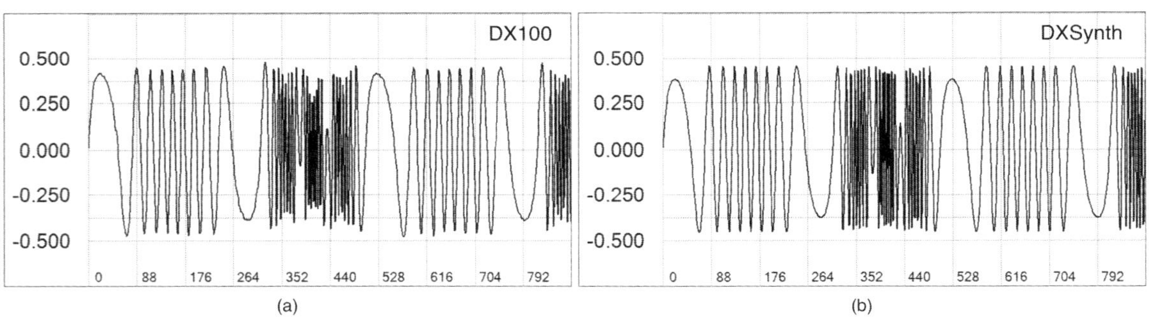

Figure 12.22: (a) Actual DX100 and (b) DXSynth output for a basic four-operator patch: Algorithm: DX1, Op1 Output: 99, Op2 Output: 99, Op3 Output: 75, Op4 Output: 50, Note: F2.

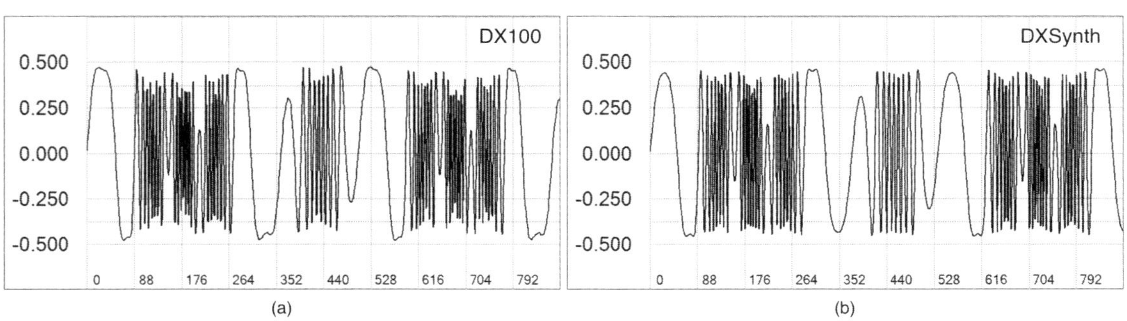

Figure 12.23: (a) Actual DX100 and (b) DXSynth output for a basic four-operator patch: Algorithm: DX2, Op1 Output: 99, Op2 Output: 99, Op3 Output: 75, Op4 Output: 50, Note: E2.

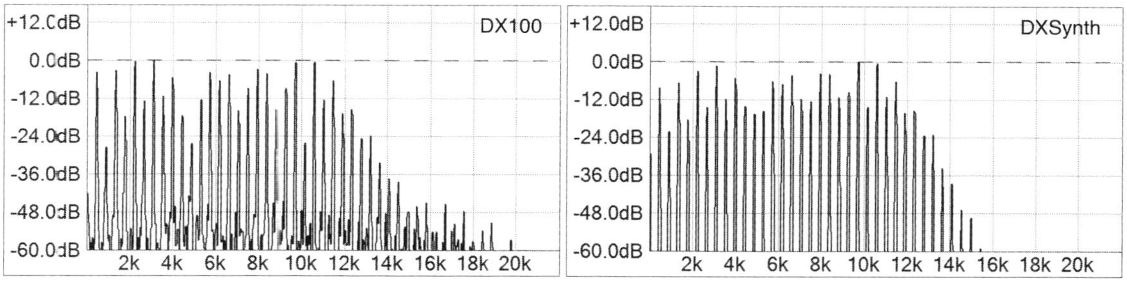

(a) (b)

Figure 12.24: (a) Actual DX100 and (b) DXSynth spectra for a basic two-operator patch: Algorithm: DX1, Op1 Output: 99, Op2 Output: 99, Op3 Output: 0, Op4 Output: 0, Note: A4.

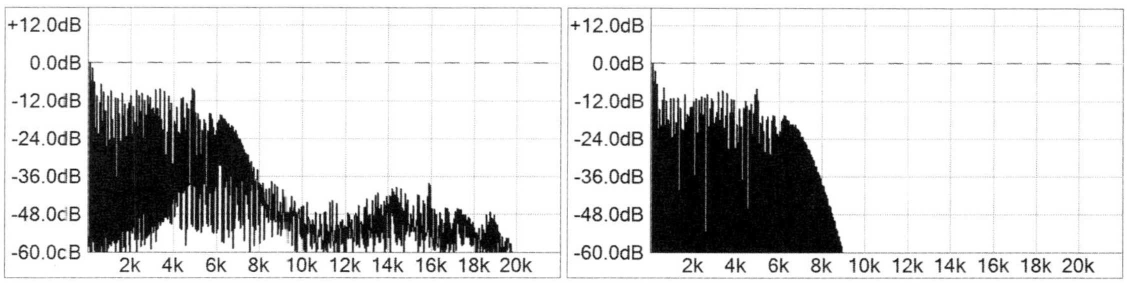

(a) (b)

Figure 12.25: (a) Actual DX100 and (b) DXSynth spectra for a basic three-operator patch: Algorithm: DX1, Op1 Output: 99, Op2 Output: 99, Op3 Output: 75, Op4 Output: 0, Note: C2 (the information above 12 kHz is analog noise).

Table 12.6: CDXSynthVoice member variables.

CDXSynthVoice **Member Variables**		
Type	**Variable Name**	**Description**
CWTOscillator	m_Op1, m_Op2, m_Op3, m_Op4	four oscillators for operators
double	m_dOp1Feedback, m_dOp2Feedback, m_dOp3Feedback, m_dOp4Feedback	four possible feedback values for operators; only Op 4 includes feedback in DXSynth
enum	None,AmpMod,Vibrato	enum for LFO Destinations

New Global Parameters

With DXSynth we add the last of our global voice parameters. There are only four new variables, one for the feedback value of each operator.

```
struct globalVoiceParams
{
	// --- common
	UINT uVoiceMode;

	<SNIP SNIP SNIP>

	// --- DX synth
	double dOp1Feedback;
	double dOp2Feedback;
	double dOp3Feedback;
	double dOp4Feedback;
};
```

Table 12.7: *CDXSynthVoice* member functions.

CDXSynthVoice Member Functions	
Function Name	**Description**
initGlobalParameters	initialize the global parameters
initializeModMatrix	initialize the modulation matrix
setSampleRate	set sample rate on sub-components
prepareForPlay	prepareForPlay on sub-components, one time init
update	update voice variables
reset	reset voice variables
setLFO1Destination	sets the destination from LFO to any of the Operator Amp Mod or Vibrato Mod inputs
canNoteOff	override; returns true when all carrier EGs canNoteOff()
isVoiceDone	override; returns true when all carrier EGs have expired
setOutputEGs	sets the output EG flag on the carrier EGs (for legato, return to zero and any other output EG specific operation)
doVoice	render the audio

12.8 The CDXSynthVoice Object

DXSynth is similar to the rest of the synth projects; the majority of the plug-in object code operates the same way as the others. The *CDXSynthVoice* object handles the rendering and few other chores specific to DXSynth. Table 12.6 shows the member variables, and Table 12.7 shows the member functions. Most of the member functions are familiar by now; notice the overrides involving the output EG.

Constructor

The constructor just initializes the oscillator pointers to our four wavetable or quasi bandlimited oscillators and clears the four feedback variables (remember that we only use one of them in this synth).

```
CDXSynthVoice::CDXSynthVoice(void)
{
    // --- declare your oscillators and filters
    m_pOsc1 = &m_Op1;
    m_pOsc2 = &m_Op2;
    m_pOsc3 = &m_Op3;
    m_pOsc4 = &m_Op4;

    // --- clear our new variables
    m_dOp1Feedback = 0.0;
    m_dOp2Feedback = 0.0;
    m_dOp3Feedback = 0.0;
    m_dOp4Feedback = 0.0;
}
```

initGlobalParameters()

This function is nearly identical to the rest of the synthesizers; call the base class then initialize any global parameters; we have the four new feedback values. The LFO intensity is forced to 1.0 in case there is no GUI control.

```
inline virtual void initGlobalParameters(globalSynthParams* pGlobalParams)
```

```
{
    // --- always call base class first
    CVoice::initGlobalParameters(pGlobalParams);

    // --- add any CThisVoice specific variables here
    //
    // NOTE: we only set the intensities we use in THIS VOICE
    m_pGlobalVoiceParams->dOp1Feedback = m_dOp1Feedback;
    m_pGlobalVoiceParams->dOp2Feedback = m_dOp2Feedback;
    m_pGlobalVoiceParams->dOp3Feedback = m_dOp3Feedback;
    m_pGlobalVoiceParams->dOp4Feedback = m_dOp4Feedback;

    // --- set to 1.0 in case user has no GUI control
    m_pGlobalVoiceParams->dLFO1OscModIntensity = 1.0;
}
```

initializeModMatrix()

This function creates and sets up the modulation matrix rows using Table 12.4—these are all for routing the LFO to either the amp modulation or vibrato for each oscillator, and they are all disconnected by default. See the code for the complete listing. When the LFO is used to modulate the oscillator amplitude, we apply it to the destination DEST_OSC_OUTPUT_AMP, which is a linear attenuator on each oscillator. This is amplitude modulation (AM) that is linear and not in dB, although you could modify it to do so. When the LFO is used for vibrato, it modulates the same destination as usual: DEST_OSC1_FO, DEST_OSC2_FO, etc.

```
void CDXSynthVoice::initializeModMatrix(CModulationMatrix* pMatrix)
{
    // --- always first: call base class to create core and
    //     init with basic routings
    CVoice::initializeModMatrix(pMatrix);

    if(!pMatrix->getModMatrixCore()) return;

    // --- DX SYNTH SPECIFIC MOD MATRIX - different from the others
    //     because only uses a singe LFO Intensity control for all LFO
    //     mod routings
    // --- these are also OFF by default but you can easily allow the user
    //     to enable/disable
    modMatrixRow* pRow = NULL;

    // LFO1 -> DEST_OSC1_OUTPUT_AMP (Amplitude Modulation)
    pRow = createModMatrixRow(SOURCE_LFO1,
                              DEST_OSC1_OUTPUT_AMP,
                              &m_pGlobalVoiceParams->dLFO1OscModIntensity,
                              &m_dDefaultModRange, // this is used for AM
  TRANSFORM_BIPOLAR_TO_UNIPOLAR,
                                        false); /* DISABLED BY DEFAULT */
    pMatrix->addModMatrixRow(pRow);

    etc... add next rows here
```

setSampleRate()

Here you only need to call the base class.

prepareForPlay()

In *prepareForPlay()* you call the base class then *reset()* as with the previous synths.

reset()

In *reset()* you call the base class first, then zero the portamento time as with the previous synths.

update()

The *update()* function is simple in *DXSynthVoice*—just call the base class first, then do any voice specific initializations; we only need to set the four new global parameters on the objects.

```
void CDXSynthVoice::update()
{
    // --- voice specific updates
    if(!m_pGlobalVoiceParams) return;

    // --- always call base class first
    CVoice::update();

    // --- new DX additions
    m_dOp1Feedback = m_pGlobalVoiceParams->dOp1Feedback;
    m_dOp2Feedback = m_pGlobalVoiceParams->dOp2Feedback;
    m_dOp3Feedback = m_pGlobalVoiceParams->dOp3Feedback;
    m_dOp4Feedback = m_pGlobalVoiceParams->dOp4Feedback;
}
```

setLFO1Destination()

In *setLFODestination()* you decode the index of the operator and then manipulate its modulation matrix source values. You set the *m_uModSourceAmp* and/or *m_uModSourceFo* to the appropriate LFO output destination in a giant switch/case statement. If the user selects *none*, then you set both to DEST_NONE. This is done on each operator independently (DEST_OSC1_OUTPUT_AMP and DEST_OSC1_FO go with Operator 1, while DEST_OSC2_OUTPUT_AMP and DEST_OSC2_FO go with Operator 2, etc.)

```
inline void setLFO1Destination(UINT uOperator, UINT uDestination)
{
    switch(uOperator)
    {
        case 0:
        {
            if(uDestination == AmpMod && m_Op1.m_uModSourceAmp !=
               DEST_OSC1_OUTPUT_AMP)
            {
                m_Op1.m_uModSourceAmp = DEST_OSC1_OUTPUT_AMP;
                m_Op1.m_uModSourceFo = DEST_NONE;
            }
            else if(uDestination == Vibrato && m_Op1.m_uModSourceFo !=
```

```
                    DEST_OSC1_FO)
            {
                m_Op1.m_uModSourceFo = DEST_OSC1_FO;
                m_Op1.m_uModSourceAmp = DEST_NONE;
            }
            else if(uDestination == None && (m_Op1.m_uModSourceAmp !=
                    DEST_NONE || m_Op1.m_uModSourceFo != DEST_NONE))
            {
                m_Op1.m_uModSourceAmp = DEST_NONE;
                m_Op1.m_uModSourceFo = DEST_NONE;
            }
            break;
        }

        case 1:
        {
            if(uDestination == AmpMod && m_Op2.m_uModSourceAmp !=
              DEST_OSC2_OUTPUT_AMP)
            {
                m_Op2.m_uModSourceAmp = DEST_OSC2_OUTPUT_AMP;
                m_Op2.m_uModSourceFo = DEST_NONE;
            }

            etc...
```

canNoteOff()

This is the first time we need to override this function. Ordinarily, it forwards the call to the default output EG (EG1). The EG returns *true* if it can go to a note off state, which means it is not in the *release, releasePending, shutdown* or *off* states. For the DXVoice, we need to return *true* when all of the EGs are connected to a carrier that can go to a note off state. This involves checking the algorithm and checking all carrier EGs. Notice the offset in the algorithm index; this is only done to match the numbers given on the DX graphic (available for AU and VST3 users). Thus algorithm 1 is really voice mode 0. The switch/case statement is broken into sections depending on the number of carrier oscillators.

```
inline virtual bool canNoteOff()
{
     bool bRet = false;
     if(!m_bNoteOn)
          return bRet;
     else
     {
          switch(m_uVoiceMode+1)
          {
               case 1:
               case 2:
               case 3:
               case 4:
               {
                    if(m_EG1.canNoteOff())
                         bRet = true;
```

```
                    break;
                }

                case 5:
                {
                    if(m_EG1.canNoteOff() && m_EG2.canNoteOff())
                        bRet = true;
                    break;
                }

                case 6:
                case 7:
                {
                    if(m_EG1.canNoteOff() && m_EG2.canNoteOff() &&
                       m_EG3.canNoteOff())
                        bRet = true;
                    break;
                }

                case 8:
                {
                    if(m_EG1.canNoteOff() && m_EG2.canNoteOff() &&
                       m_EG3.canNoteOff() && m_EG4.canNoteOff())
                        bRet = true;
                    break;
                }
            }

        }
        return bRet;
    }
```

isVoiceDVone()

The next DX-specific override *isVoiceDone()*, which checks the carrier EGs in the same fashion as *canNoteOff()*.

```
inline virtual bool isVoiceDone()
{
    bool bRet = false;
    switch(m_uVoiceMode+1)
    {
        case 1:
        case 2:
        case 3:
        case 4:
        {
            if(m_EG1.getState() == off)
                bRet = true;
            break;
        }
```

```
        case 5:
        {
                if(m_EG1.getState() == off && m_EG2.getState() == off)
                        bRet = true;
                break;
        }

        etc...
```

setOutputEGs()

In *setOutputEGs()* you follow the same pattern as the previous two functions—identify the output EGs (the EGs connected to carriers) and set the flag on them.

```
inline void setOutputEGs()
{
     m_EG1.m_bOutputEG = false;
     m_EG2.m_bOutputEG = false;
     m_EG3.m_bOutputEG = false;
     m_EG4.m_bOutputEG = false;

     switch(m_uVoiceMode+1)
     {
           case 1:
           case 2:
           case 3:
           case 4:
           {
               m_EG1.m_bOutputEG = true;
               break;
     }

           case 5:
           {
               m_EG1.m_bOutputEG = true;
               m_EG2.m_bOutputEG = true;
               break;
           }

           etc...
```

doVoice()

The audio rendering in *doVoice()* is slightly different from the rest of the synths, in part because there is no filter. This is the only rendering function that does not use the modulation matrix to connect EGs to oscillators. It certainly could be done that way, but it makes for somewhat complicated modulation matrix re-programming since changes to the algorithm index would re-wire the modulator and signal flow. Instead, the modulation matrix is only used for the LFO modulation routings and the MIDI velocity-to-attack and note-to-decay modulations. The algorithm blocks are wired together the old fashioned way, as we did in the early versions of NanoSynth. This makes the code easy to read and easy to modify for your own experiments.

After calling the base class, you do the two modulation matrix layers. The first operates on the EGs if the modulations are enabled, and the second layer is for the LFO->Oscillator modulations. After updating the voice, oscillators, and DCA, you move to the final switch/case statement that implements the algorithms shown in Figure 12.13.

```
inline virtual bool doVoice(double& dLeftOutput, double& dRightOutput)
{
      // this does basic on/off work
      if(!CVoice::doVoice(dLeftOutput, dRightOutput))
            return false;

      double dOut1, dOut2, dOut3, dOut4 = 0.0;
      double dEG1, dEG2, dEG3, dEG4 = 0.0;
      double dOut = 0.0;

      // --- user could change algo on the fly
      setOutputEGs();

      // --- Layer 0 modulations include Vel->Att and Note->Dcy
      //     But those are not standard in the DX Synth
      m_ModulationMatrix.doModulationMatrix(0);

      // --- update
      m_EG1.update();
      m_EG2.update();
      m_EG3.update();
      m_EG4.update();

      // --- all algos use the same EG code; get EG outputs
      dEG1 = m_EG1.doEnvelope();
      dEG2 = m_EG2.doEnvelope();
      dEG3 = m_EG3.doEnvelope();
      dEG4 = m_EG4.doEnvelope();

      // --- LFO is MOD source
      m_LFO1.update();
      m_LFO1.doOscillate();

      // --- Layer 1 modulations (LFO->AM or LFO->Vibrato)
      m_ModulationMatrix.doModulationMatrix(1);

      // --- apply modulations
      this->update();
      m_Op1.update();
      m_Op2.update();
      m_Op3.update();
      m_Op4.update();

      // --- DCA
      m_DCA.update();
```

```
        // --- now decode algorithm (m_uVoiceMode+1) and implement
        //     NOTE: using the mod matrix for this could get messy
        switch(m_uVoiceMode+1)
        {
                // -- below -- //
        }

        // --- do the DCA: we have a mono signal so repeating dOut, dOut as L/R
        m_DCA.doDCA(dOut, dOut, dLeftOutput, dRightOutput);

        return true;
}
```

Algorithm DX1

The first algorithm produces everything from mellow, muted sinusoids to screeching, torturous howls. It is able to produce the most intense sounds because it is a stack of four operators with each modulator operating in series. You can easily cause the synth to alias with high output settings on each operator (this is also true of the hardware version). Figure 12.26 shows the connection diagram and algorithm; greyed boxes represent carriers.

When you implement the algorithm, work from top to bottom in the Chowning abbreviated diagram. Here we start with operator four, which modulates itself (for the next sample period). The output is applied to operator three's phase modulation input, and operator three is then updated. Operator three's output is applied to operator two, whose output is applied to the carrier operator one. Notice that all oscillators are scaled by *IMAX*, which is *#defined* as 4.0 at the top of the *.h* file (feel free to experiment with this). This includes the carrier operators as well. Removing the scaling by *IMAX* changes the output amplitude.

```
case 1:
{
        // --- modulator level 3
        dOut4 = IMAX*dEG4*m_Op4.doOscillate();

        // --- self modulate
        m_Op4.setPhaseMod(dOut4*m_dOp4Feedback);
```

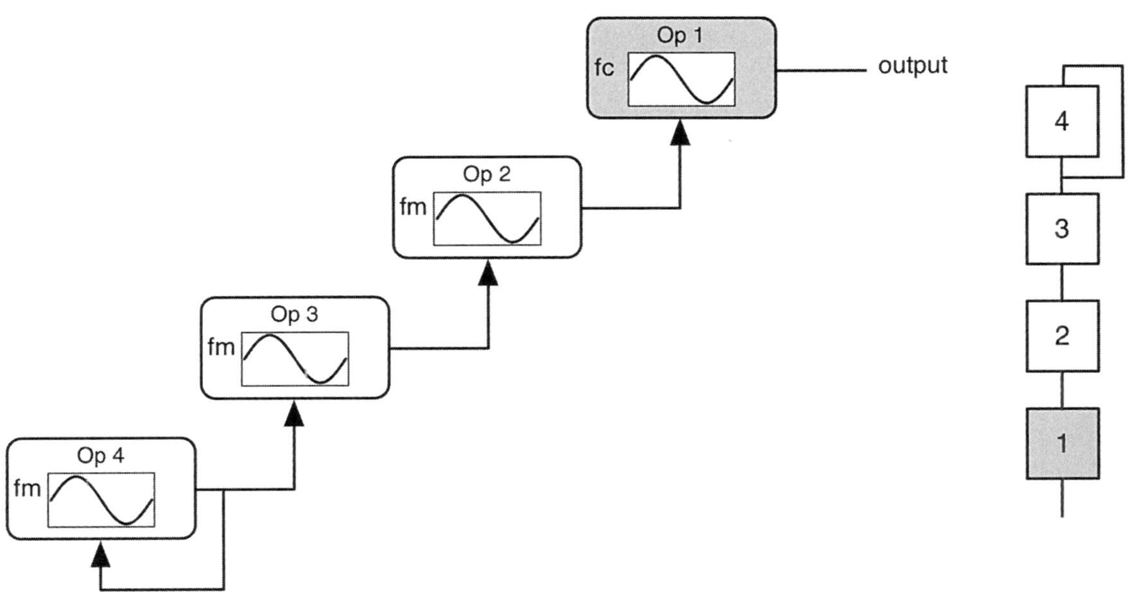

Figure 12.26: The DX1 algorithm.

```
        m_Op4.update();

        // --- modulator level 2
        m_Op3.setPhaseMod(dOut4);
        m_Op3.update();

        // --- form Op3 Output
        dOut3 = IMAX*dEG3*m_Op3.doOscillate();

        // --- modulator level 1
        m_Op2.setPhaseMod(dOut3);
        m_Op2.update();

        // --- form Op2 Output
        dOut2 = IMAX*dEG2*m_Op2.doOscillate();

        // --- carrier level 1
        m_Op1.setPhaseMod(dOut2);
        m_Op1.update();

        // --- form Op1 Output
        dOut1 = IMAX*dEG1*m_Op1.doOscillate();

        // --- single carrier is Op1
        dOut = dOut1;

        break;
    }
```

Algorithm DX2

The second algorithm produces nearly the same range of sounds as the first, but with a different timbre. It can also produce mellow to screeching sounds. Figure 12.27 shows algorithm two. This version is one of several that involve summing modulators before applying them.

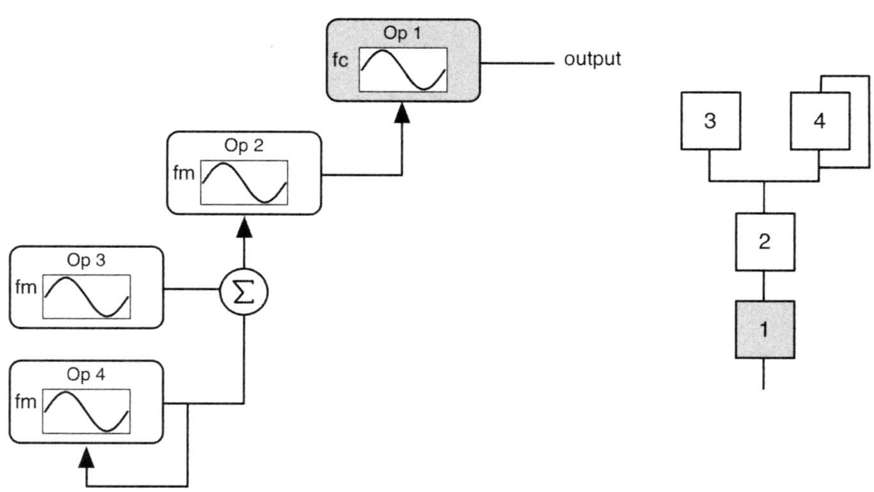

Figure 12.27: The DX2 algorithm.

```
case 2:
{
     // --- modulator level 2
     dOut4 = IMAX*dEG4*m_Op4.doOscillate();

     // --- self modulate
     m_Op4.setPhaseMod(dOut4*m_dOp4Feedback);
     m_Op4.update();

     // --- form Op3 output
     dOut3 = IMAX*dEG3*m_Op3.doOscillate();

     // --- modulator level 1
     m_Op2.setPhaseMod(dOut3 + dOut4);
     m_Op2.update();

     // --- form Op2 output
     dOut2 = IMAX*dEG2*m_Op2.doOscillate();

     // --- carrier level 1
     m_Op1.setPhaseMod(dOut2);
     m_Op1.update();

     // --- form Op1 output
     dOut1 = IMAX*dEG1*m_Op1.doOscillate();

     // --- single carrier
     dOut = dOut1;

     break;
}
```

Algorithm DX3

Similar to the DX2 algorithm, this version produces a different timbre as well, and is shown in Figure 12.28. Likewise it has a similar range of timbres, but is generally more soft and mellow in nature.

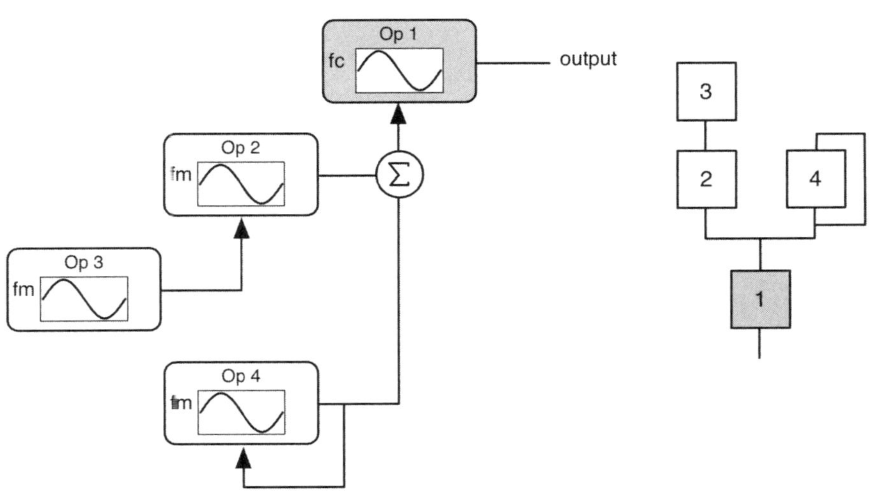

Figure 12.28: The DX3 algorithm.

```
case 3:
{
     // --- modulator level 2
     dOut4 = IMAX*dEG4*m_Op4.doOscillate();

     // --- self modulate
     m_Op4.setPhaseMod(dOut4*m_dOp4Feedback);
     m_Op4.update();

     // --- form Op3 Output
     dOut3 = IMAX*dEG3*m_Op3.doOscillate();

     // --- modulator level 1
     m_Op2.setPhaseMod(dOut3);
     m_Op2.update();

     // --- form Op2 Output
     dOut2 = IMAX*dEG2*m_Op2.doOscillate();

     // --- carrier level 1
     m_Op1.setPhaseMod(dOut2 + dOut4);
     m_Op1.update();

     // --- form Op1 Output
     dOut1 = IMAX*dEG1*m_Op1.doOscillate();

     // --- single carrier
     dOut = dOut1;

     break;
}
```

Algorithm DX4

The DX4 algorithm is shown in Figure 12.29. Comparisons with the previous two reveal similar features, so you expect them to have similar sounds. This algorithm can be used to create sounds with a vocal or nasal quality and is generally less aggressive-sounding than the previous algorithms.

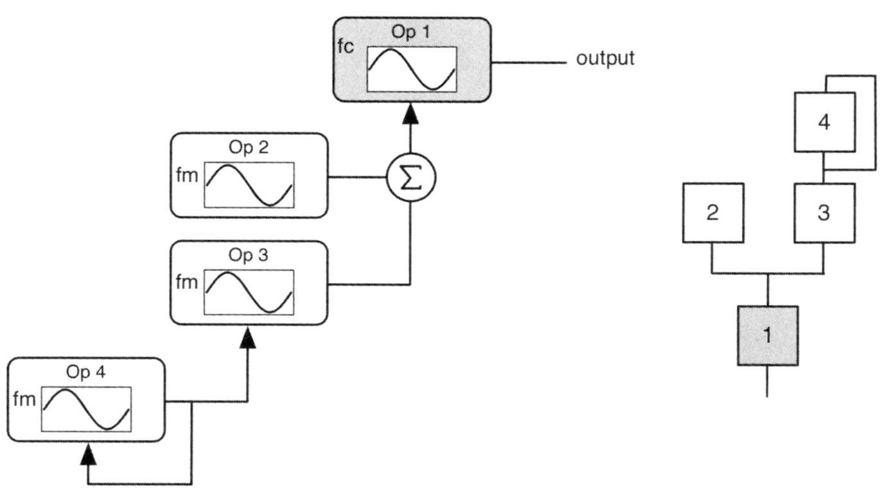

Figure 12.29: The DX4 algorithm.

```
case 4:
{
    // --- modulator level 2
    dOut4 = IMAX*dEG4*m_Op4.doOscillate();

    // --- self modulate
    m_Op4.setPhaseMod(dOut4*m_dOp4Feedback);
    m_Op4.update();

    // --- set Op3
    m_Op3.setPhaseMod(dOut4);
    m_Op3.update();

    // --- form Op3 output
    dOut3 = IMAX*dEG3*m_Op3.doOscillate();

    // --- modulator level 1
    dOut2 = IMAX*dEG2*m_Op2.doOscillate();

    // --- carrier level 1
    m_Op1.setPhaseMod(dOut2 + dOut3);
    m_Op1.update();

    // --- form Op1 Output
    dOut1 = IMAX*dEG1*m_Op1.doOscillate();

    // --- single carrier
    dOut = dOut1;

    break;
}
```

Algorithm DX5

The DX5 algorithm is shown in Figure 12.30. It takes a departure from the others as the first with multiple carriers. This has a drastic effect on the timbres it produces. It is generally less intense-sounding. This algorithm can produce cello and piano sounds.

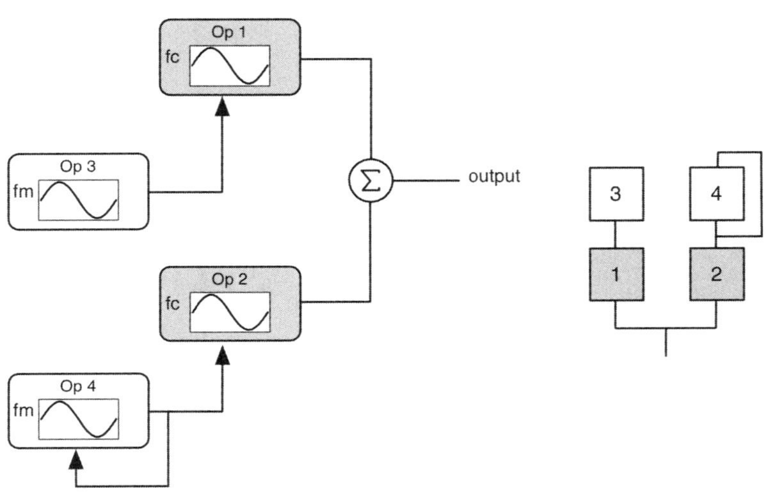

Figure 12.30: The DX5 algorithm.

```
case 5:
{
    // --- modulator level 3
    dOut4 = IMAX*dEG4*m_Op4.doOscillate();

    // --- self modulate
    m_Op4.setPhaseMod(dOut4*m_dOp4Feedback);
    m_Op4.update();

    // --- modulator level 2
    dOut3 = IMAX*dEG3*m_Op3.doOscillate();

    // --- modulator level 1
    m_Op2.setPhaseMod(dOut4);
    m_Op2.update();

    // --- carrier level 1
    dOut2 = IMAX*dEG2*m_Op2.doOscillate();

    // --- carrier level 1
    m_Op1.setPhaseMod(dOut3);
    m_Op1.update();

    // --- form final output
    dOut1 = IMAX*dEG1*m_Op1.doOscillate();

    // --- double carrier
    dOut = 0.5*dOut1 + 0.5*dOut2;

    break;
}
```

Algorithm DX6

The DX6 algorithm, along with the remaining two, produce a different set of sounds; these are additive or bell-like. When you set the ratio of operator four to non-integer values, you get into the bell and gong sounds. This algorithm is shown in Figure 12.31.

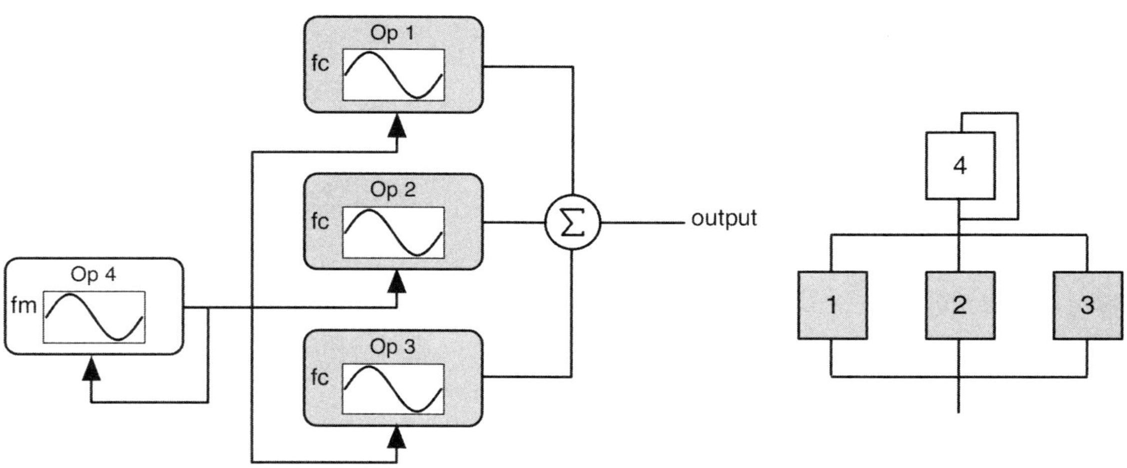

Figure 12.31: The DX6 algorithm.

```
case 6:
{
    // --- modulator level 3
    dOut4 = IMAX*dEG4*m_Op4.doOscillate();

    // --- self modulate
    m_Op4.setPhaseMod(dOut4*m_dOp4Feedback);
    m_Op4.update();

    // --- modulator level 2
    m_Op3.setPhaseMod(dOut4);
    m_Op3.update();

    // --- form Op3 Output
    dOut3 = IMAX*dEG3*m_Op3.doOscillate();

    // --- modulator level 1
    m_Op2.setPhaseMod(dOut4);
    m_Op2.update();

    // --- form Op3 Output
    dOut2 = IMAX*dEG2*m_Op2.doOscillate();

    // -- carrier level 1
    m_Op1.setPhaseMod(dOut4);
    m_Op1.update();

    // --- form Op1 Output
    dOut1 = IMAX*dEG1*m_Op1.doOscillate();

    // --- triple carrier
    dOut = 0.33*dOut1 + 0.33*dOut2 + 0.33*dOut3;

    break;
}
```

Algorithm DX7

The DX7 algorithm shown in Figure 12.32 is the first to include carriers that are not modulated. This makes another drastic change in the kinds of sounds you can get—much mellower and less intense than the stacked modulation algorithms. It continues with more organ and bell-like sounds. This patch is not named after the DX7 synth, it is simply the seventh of the DX algorithms.

```
case 7:
{
    // --- modulator level 3
    dOut4 = IMAX*dEG4*m_Op4.doOscillate();

    // --- self modulate
    m_Op4.setPhaseMod(dOut4*m_dOp4Feedback);
    m_Op4.update();
```

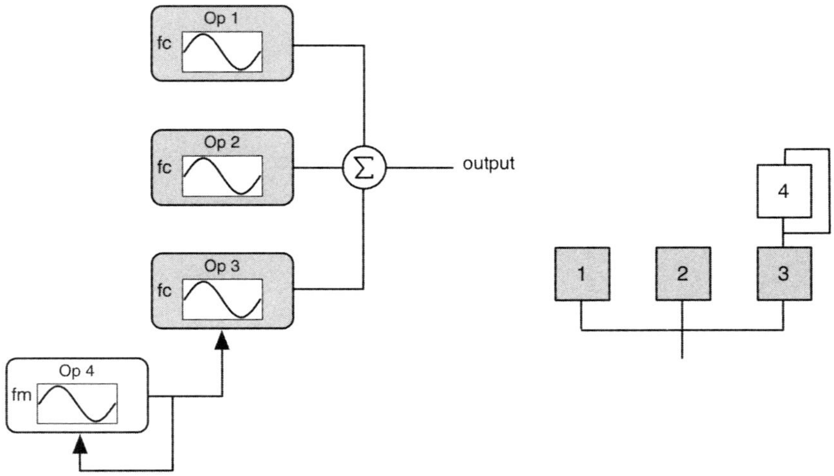

Figure 12.32: The DX7 algorithm.

```
        // --- modulator level 2
        m_Op3.setPhaseMod(dOut4);
        m_Op3.update();

        // --- form Op3 output
        dOut3 = IMAX*dEG3*m_Op3.doOscillate();

        // --- modulator level 1
        dOut2 = IMAX*dEG2*m_Op2.doOscillate();

        // --- carrier level 1
        dOut1 = IMAX*dEG1*m_Op1.doOscillate();

        // --- triple carrier
        dOut = 0.33*dOut1 + 0.33*dOut2 + 0.33*dOut3;

        break;
    }
```

Algorithm DX8

The last DX8 algorithm in Figure 12.33 produces the most realistic bells and gongs, as well as organ and other additive sounds. It has the least amount of modulation of any algorithm and produces the softest and least intense sounds of any of the algorithms. You can also synthesize wood block or other muted percussion sounds with this algorithm.

```
    case 8:
    {
        // --- carrier and modulator level 3
        dOut4 = IMAX*dEG4*m_Op4.doOscillate();

        // --- self modulate
        m_Op4.setPhaseMod(dOut4*m_dOp4Feedback);
        m_Op4.update();
```

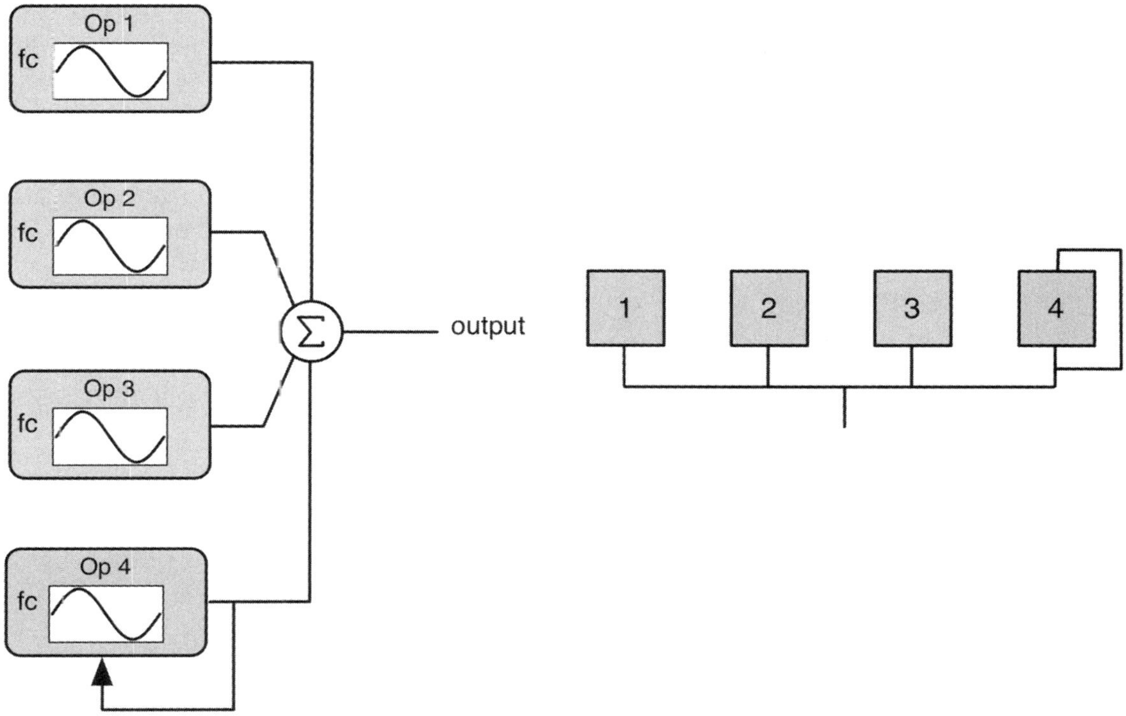

Figure 12.33: The DX8 algorithm.

```
        // --- carrier 3
        dOut3 = IMAX*dEG3*m_Op3.doOscillate();

        // --- carrier 2
        dOut2 = IMAX*dEG2*m_Op2.doOscillate();

        // --- carrier 1
        dOut1 = IMAX*dEG1*m_Op1.doOscillate();

        // --- quadruple carrier
        dOut = 0.25*dOut1 + 0.25*dOut2 + 0.25*dOut3 + 0.25*dOut4;

        break;
    }
```

Programming

See the website for more information and videos on programming this kind of synthesizer. It can be very challenging since all of the algorithms are capable of producing absolutely horrible sounds (unless that's your thing), and the way the controls adjust the overall timbre for a given algorithm takes a lot of practice to understand. Even Chowning was aware of this when he wrote, "The presence of reflected side frequencies in the dynamic spectrum enormously complicates the evolution of individual components to the extent that it is difficult to visualize the amplitude functions with any precision" (Chowning, 1973).

The easiest thing to do is to start with algorithm DX1 and get an interesting sound. Then, change the algorithm without changing anything else. You will notice subtle changes for the algorithms that are similar and very drastic changes for the later algorithms. Play with the controls in each algorithm to get a feel for the types of sounds you can get. Then go back and concentrate on them one at a time.

Ratios

The ratios have an extreme effect on the timbres. Start with algorithm DX1 and set the EGs and outputs all the same, as in the default. Then, adjust the ratio values by typing them in. First, try perfect values like 2.0 and 3.0—these will introduce octave shifts up in the sound components. Perfect ratios below 1.0 will likewise drop the octave; 0.5 shifts the output down an octave. Next, try making the ratios very close to integers, like 1.99 and 0.99; this often produces a nice beating effect like detuned analog synth oscillators. Interestingly, once you go below a certain point, say 1.90 or 0.90 the detuning can blow up, and the whole sound falls apart. Setting the values to irrational numbers like the square root of 2 (1.414214) produces inharmonic sounds. For the lower numbered algorithms, it generally makes noise. For the higher numbered algorithms, it contributes to creating the bell and gong-like sounds.

A key difference between the Yamaha DX synths and the DXSynth here is that we allow the ratio to be any number on a range of 0.1 to 10. The DX series does not offer such control; instead the user must select a ratio from a list of "carefully chosen" values. They are:

0.5	0.71	0.78	0.87	1.00	1.41
1.57	1.73	2.00	2.82	3.00	3.14
3.46	4.00	4.24	4.71	5.00	5.19
5.65	6.00	6.28	6.92	7.00	7.07
7.85	8.00	8.48	8.65	9.00	9.42
9.89	10.00	10.38	10.99	11.00	11.30
12.00	12.11	12.56	12.72	13.00	13.84
14.00	14.10	14.13	15.00	15.55	15.57
15.70	16.96	17.27	17.30	18.37	18.84
19.03	19.78	20.41	20.76	21.20	21.98
22.49	23.53	24.22	25.95		

EGs

Each operator has its own EG, giving you the ability to dynamically control the spectrum of each one. You can set very different attack and release times so that you can hear each set of sidebands fade in or out. The stacked operator algorithms behave differently from the parallel algorithms, so you definitely want to experiment with those. For percussion sounds, try setting the sustain and release to 0.0, then use the attack and decay to shape the fast envelope portions. After some practice, it will get easier to imagine how the EGs affect the timbral components. In many cases, you can clearly hear the layers of sidebands moving in and out.

Outputs

The output controls for each operator work on the oscillator itself. For the stacked operators, tiny changes in the upstream modulators (operator three and four) can have big consequences on the overall sound. Also watch out for operator four's feedback—you can add a subtle noisy transient to smooth bass sounds, or create parrot-squawking patches. For the parallel algorithms, the outputs blend the different frequency components. You can make toy xylophone sounds easily turn chaotic by blending in carriers at non-integer tuning ratios.

12.9 DXSynth Files

DXSynth uses the following files, which you will need to add into your compiler's project in the usual manner.

DCA.h	Oscillator.h
DCA.cpp	Oscillator.cpp
EnvelopeGenerator.h	WTOscillator.h
EnvelopeGenerator.cpp	WTOscillator.cpp
Filter.h	synthfunctions.h
Filter.cpp	Voice.h
LFO.h	Voice.cpp
LFO.cpp	*Optional:*
ModulationMatrix.h	QBLimitedOscillator.h
ModulationMatrix.cpp	QBLimitedOscillator.cpp

DXSynth uses identical code in the majority of plug-in object functions as the rest of the synthesizers; the only difference is the type of voice pointer stored in the voice array.

Voice Declaration

For the plug-in's *.h* file declarations:

- #include *"DXSynthVoice.h"* at the top of the file
- copy the same code as the other synths, but with different voice pointers (the only difference is shown in **bold**)

```
<< ** Code Listing 12.1: Declarations ** >>

// --- our array of voices
CDXSynthVoice* m_pVoiceArray[MAX_VOICES];

// --- MmM
CModulationMatrix m_GlobalModMatrix;

// --- global params
globalSynthParams m_GlobalSynthParams;

// --- helper functions for note on/off/voice steal
void incrementVoiceTimestamps();
CDXSynthVoice* getOldestVoice();
CDXSynthVoice* getOldestVoiceWithNote(UINT uMIDINote);

// updates all voices at once
void update();

// for portamento
double m_dLastNoteFrequency;

// our recieve channel
UINT m_uMidiRxChannel;

<< END ** Code Listing 12.1: Declarations ** END >>
```

Updating the Voice

The DX update function is massive—longer than any previous update. The synth has more controls and parameters to adjust and a very flexible modulation routing for LFO1. These combine to make for a long list of variables to update. There is so much repetitive code that it is impractical to print it all here. Please see the full sample code for all updates.

```
<< ** Code Listing 12.2: Update ** >>

// --- update global parameters
//
// --- Voice:
// for FM synth, Voice Mode = FM Algorithm
m_GlobalSynthParams.voiceParams.uVoiceMode = m_uVoiceMode;
m_GlobalSynthParams.voiceParams.dOp4Feedback = m_dOp4Feedback/100.0;
m_GlobalSynthParams.voiceParams.dPortamentoTime_mSec =
     m_dPortamentoTime_mSec;
```

```
// --- ranges
m_GlobalSynthParams.voiceParams.dOscFoPitchBendModRange = m_nPitchBendRange;

// --- intensities
m_GlobalSynthParams.voiceParams.dLFO1OscModIntensity = m_dLFO1Intensity;

// --- Oscillators:
m_GlobalSynthParams.osc1Params.dAmplitude =
                                calculateDXAmplitude(m_dOp1OutputLevel);
m_GlobalSynthParams.osc2Params.dAmplitude =
                                calculateDXAmplitude(m_dOp2OutputLevel);
m_GlobalSynthParams.osc3Params.dAmplitude =
                                calculateDXAmplitude(m_dOp3OutputLevel);
m_GlobalSynthParams.osc4Params.dAmplitude =
                                calculateDXAmplitude(m_dOp4OutputLevel);

m_GlobalSynthParams.osc1Params.dFoRatio = m_dOp1Ratio;
m_GlobalSynthParams.osc2Params.dFoRatio = m_dOp2Ratio;
m_GlobalSynthParams.osc3Params.dFoRatio = m_dOp3Ratio;
m_GlobalSynthParams.osc4Params.dFoRatio = m_dOp4Ratio;

// --- EG1:
m_GlobalSynthParams.eg1Params.dAttackTime_mSec = m_dEG1Attack_mSec;
m_GlobalSynthParams.eg1Params.dDecayTime_mSec = m_dEG1Decay_mSec;
m_GlobalSynthParams.eg1Params.dSustainLevel = m_dEG1SustainLevel;
m_GlobalSynthParams.eg1Params.dReleaseTime_mSec = m_dEG1Release_mSec;
m_GlobalSynthParams.eg1Params.bResetToZero = (bool)m_uResetToZero;
m_GlobalSynthParams.eg1Params.bLegatoMode = (bool)m_uLegatoMode;

// --- EG2:
<SNIP SNIP SNIP - essentially same as above>

// --- EG3:
<SNIP SNIP SNIP - essentially same as above>

// --- EG4:
<SNIP SNIP SNIP - essentially same as above>

// --- LFO1:
m_GlobalSynthParams.lfo1Params.uWaveform = m_uLFO1Waveform;
m_GlobalSynthParams.lfo1Params.dOscFo = m_dLFO1Rate;

// --- DCA:
m_GlobalSynthParams.dcaParams.dAmplitude_dB = m_dVolume_dB;

// --- LFO1 Destination 1
if(m_uLFO1ModDest1 == None)
{
```

```
        m_GlobalModMatrix.enableModMatrixRow(SOURCE_LFO1, DEST_OSC1_OUTPUT_AMP,
                                                                false);
        m_GlobalModMatrix.enableModMatrixRow(SOURCE_LFO1, DEST_OSC1_FO, false);
    }
    else if(m_uLFO1ModDest1 == AmpMod)
    {
        m_GlobalModMatrix.enableModMatrixRow(SOURCE_LFO1, DEST_OSC1_OUTPUT_AMP,
                                                                true);
        m_GlobalModMatrix.enableModMatrixRow(SOURCE_LFO1, DEST_OSC1_FO, false);
    }
    else // vibrato
    {
        m_GlobalModMatrix.enableModMatrixRow(SOURCE_LFO1, DEST_OSC1_OUTPUT_AMP,
                                                                false);
        m_GlobalModMatrix.enableModMatrixRow(SOURCE_LFO1, DEST_OSC1_FO, true);
    }

    // --- LFO1 Destination 2
    <SNIP SNIP SNIP - essentially same as above>

    // --- LFO1 Destination 3
    <SNIP SNIP SNIP - essentially same as above>

    // --- LFO1 Destination 4
    <SNIP SNIP SNIP - essentially same as above>

        << END ** Code Listing 12.2: Updates ** END >>
```

12.10 DXSynth: RackAFX

Create a new project named DXSynth and setup the GUI using Table 12.5

DXSynth.h

At the top of the file, add the *#include* statement for *DXSynthVoice.h* and then setup the array of voices and all helper member functions.

```
    class CDXSynth : public CPlugIn
    {
    public:
        <SNIP SNIP SNIP>

        // Add your code here: --------------------------------------------- //

        << INSERT ** Code Listing 12.1: Declarations ** HERE >>

        etc...
```

DXSynth.cpp

The following functions are identical to MiniSynth/DigiSynth (and the rest of the book projects), with the exception of the type of voice pointers created and stored in the voice array.

- *destructor*
- *prepareForPlay()*
- *processAudioFrame()*
- *midiNoteOn()*
- *midiNoteOff()*
- *midiModWheel()*
- *midiPitchBend()*
- *midiMessage()*

Constructor

The constructor is identical to MiniSynth (with the exception of the type of voice pointers created and stored in the voice array).

```
CDXSynth::CDXSynth()
{
     <SNIP SNIP SNIP>

     // receive on all channels
     m_uMidiRxChannel = MIDI_CH_ALL;

     // load up voices
     for(int i=0; i<MAX_VOICES; i++)
     {
            // --- create voice
            m_pVoiceArray[i] = new CDXSynthVoice;

            // --- should never happen
            if(!m_pVoiceArray[i]) return;

            // --- global params (MUST BE DONE before setting up mod matrix!
            m_pVoiceArray[i]->initGlobalParameters(&m_GlobalSynthParams);
     }

     // --- use the first voice to setup the MmM
     m_pVoiceArray[0]->initializeModMatrix(&m_GlobalModMatrix);

     // --- then set the mod
     for(int i=0; i<MAX_VOICES; i++)
     {
            // --- mod matrix
            m_pVoiceArray[i]->setModMatrixCore
                           (m_GlobalModMatrix.getModMatrixCore());
     }
}
```

update()

Add the *update()* function with the code listing above.

```
void CDXSynth::update()
{
    << INSERT ** Code Listing 12.2: Updates ** HERE >>
}
```

processAudioFrame()

The process function is identical to all the others synths.

```
bool __stdcall CDXSynth::processAudioFrame(args...)
{
    double dLeftAccum = 0.0;
    double dRightAccum = 0.0;

    // --- 12dB HR
    float fMix = 0.25;
    double dLeft = 0.0;
    double dRight = 0.0;

    // --- loop and accumulate voices
    for(int i=0; i<MAX_VOICES; i++)
    {
        // --- render synth
        m_pVoiceArray[i]->doVoice(dLeft, dRight);

        // --- accumulate and scale
        dLeftAccum += fMix*dLeft;
        dRightAccum += fMix*dRight;
    }

    // outputs
    pOutputBuffer[0] = dLeftAccum;

    // Mono-In, Stereo-Out (AUX Effect)
    if(uNumInputChannels == 1 && uNumOutputChannels == 2)
        pOutputBuffer[1] = dLeftAccum;

    // Stereo-In, Stereo-Out (INSERT Effect)
    if(uNumInputChannels == 2 && uNumOutputChannels == 2)
        pOutputBuffer[1] = dRightAccum;

    return true;
}
```

12.11 DXSynth: VST3

Create a new project named *DXSynth* and setup the GUI using Table 12.5.

Processor.h

At the top of the file, add the *#include* statement for *DXSynthVoice.h* and then setup the array of voices and all helper member functions.

```
class Processor : public AudioEffect
{
public:
     <SNIP SNIP SNIP>

     // Add your code here: ------------------------------------------- //

     << INSERT ** Code Listing 12.1: Declarations ** HERE >>

     etc...
```

Processor.cpp

The following functions are identical to the previous synths, with the exception of the type of voice pointers created and stored in the voice array.

- destructor
- *setActive()*
- *process()*
- *doProcessEvent()*

Constructor

Initialize all the GUI variables from Table 12.5; the default values are found in *SynthParamLimts.h*.

```
Processor::Processor ()
{
     // --- define our Controller Class FUID
     setControllerClass(Controller::cid);

     // our inits
     m_uVoiceMode = DEFAULT_VOICE_MODE;

     m_uLFO1Waveform = DEFAULT_LFO_WAVEFORM;
     m_dLFO1Intensity = DEFAULT_UNIPOLAR;
     m_dLFO1Rate = DEFAULT_LFO_RATE;

     m_uLFO1ModDest1 = DEFAULT_DX_LFO_DESTINATION;
     m_uLFO1ModDest2 = DEFAULT_DX_LFO_DESTINATION;
     m_uLFO1ModDest3 = DEFAULT_DX_LFO_DESTINATION;
     m_uLFO1ModDest4 = DEFAULT_DX_LFO_DESTINATION;

     m_dOp1Ratio = DEFAULT_OP_RATIO;
     m_dEG1Attack_mSec = DEFAULT_EG_ATTACK_TIME;
     m_dEG1Decay_mSec = DEFAULT_EG_DECAY_TIME;
     m_dEG1SustainLevel = DEFAULT_EG_SUSTAIN_LEVEL;
     m_dEG1Release_mSec = DEFAULT_EG_RELEASE_TIME;
     m_dOp1OutputLevel = DEFAULT_DX_OUTPUT_LEVEL;

     <SNIP SNIP SNIP --- essentially same for other operators>
```

```
        m_dPortamentoTime_mSec = DEFAULT_PORTAMENTO_TIME_MSEC;
        m_dVolume_dB = DEFAULT_OUTPUT_AMPLITUDE_DB;
        m_uLegatoMode = DEFAULT_LEGATO_MODE;
        m_uResetToZero = DEFAULT_RESET_TO_ZERO;
        m_nPitchBendRange = DEFAULT_PITCHBEND_RANGE;
        m_uVelocityToAttackScaling = DEFAULT_VELOCITY_TO_ATTACK;
        m_uNoteNumberToDecayScaling = DEFAULT_NOTE_TO_DECAY;

        // VST3 specific
        m_dMIDIPitchBend = DEFAULT_MIDI_PITCHBEND; // -1 to +1
        m_uMIDIModWheel = DEFAULT_MIDI_MODWHEEL;
        m_uMIDIVolumeCC7 = DEFAULT_MIDI_VOLUME;  // note defaults to 127
        m_uMIDIPanCC10 = DEFAULT_MIDI_PAN;      // 64 = center pan
        m_uMIDIExpressionCC11 = DEFAULT_MIDI_EXPRESSION;

        // Finish initializations here
        m_dLastNoteFrequency = -1.0;

        // receive on all channels
        m_uMidiRxChannel = MIDI_CH_ALL;
}
```

update()

Add the *update()* function with the code listing above.

```
void Processor::update()
{
        << INSERT ** Code Listing 12.2: Updates ** HERE >>
}
```

doControlUpdate()

The *doControlUpdate()* will need to parse through the control queue and set any new variables. See the sample code for the complete function; it follows the same strategy and coding as all the rest of the synth projects.

```
bool Processor::doControlUpdate(ProcessData& data)
{
        bool paramChange = false;

        <SNIP SNIP SNIP and Indents Removed>

        switch (pid) // same as RAFX uControlID
        {
                case VOICE_MODE:
                {
                        // cookVSTGUIVariable(min, max, currentValue)
                        m_uVoiceMode = (UINT)cookVSTGUIVariable(MIN_VOICE_MODE,
                                        MAX_VOICE_MODE, value);
                        break;
```

```
        }

        case LFO1_WAVEFORM:
        {
                m_uLFO1Waveform = (UINT)cookVSTGUIVariable
                                (MIN_LFO_WAVEFORM, MAX_LFO_WAVEFORM, value);
                break;
        }

        case LFO1_AMPLITUDE:
        {
                m_dLFO1Intensity = value; // don't need to cook, unipolar
                break;
        }

        case LFO1_RATE:
        {
                m_dLFO1Rate = cookVSTGUIVariable(MIN_LFO_RATE,
                                                        MAX_LFO_RATE, value);
                break;
        }

        case LFO1_DESTINATION_OP1:
        {
                m_uLFO1ModDest1 = (UINT)cookVSTGUIVariable
                (MIN_DX_LFO_DESTINATION, MAX_DX_LFO_DESTINATION, value);
                break;
        }

        case LFO1_DESTINATION_OP2:
        {
                m_uLFO1ModDest2 = (UINT)cookVSTGUIVariable
                (MIN_DX_LFO_DESTINATION, MAX_DX_LFO_DESTINATION, value);
                break;
        }

        etc...
```

12.12 DXSynth: AU

Create a new project named DXSynth and setup the GUI using Table 12.5.

AUSynth.h

At the top of the file, add the *#include* statement for *DXSynthVoice.h* and then setup the array of voices and all helper member functions.

```
class AUSynth : public AUInstrumentBase
{
public:
```

```
<SNIP SNIP SNIP>

// Add your code here: -------------------------------------------- //

<< INSERT ** Code Listing 12.1: Declarations ** HERE >>

etc...
```

AUSynth.cpp

The following functions are identical to MiniSynth (and the rest of the book projects), with the exception of the type of voice pointers created and stored in the array.

- destructor
- *Reset()*
- *Render()*
- *StartNote()*
- *StopNote()*
- *HandlePitchWheel()*
- *HandleControlChange()*

Constructor

Initialize the factory preset (optional) and all the GUI variables from Table 12.5; the rest is identical to MiniSynth.

```
AUSynth::AUSynth(AudioUnit inComponentInstance)
     : AUInstrumentBase(inComponentInstance, 0, 1)
{
     // --- create input, output ports, groups and parts
     CreateElements();

     // --- setup default factory preset (as example)
      factoryPreset[VOICE_MODE] = 3;
      factoryPreset[OP1_RATIO] = 1.00;
      factoryPreset[EG1_ATTACK_MSEC] = 100.0;

     <SNIP SNIP SNIP>

     // --- define number of params (controls)
     Globals()->UseIndexedParameters(NUMBER_OF_SYNTH_PARAMETERS);

     // --- initialize the controls here!
     // --- these are defined in SynthParamLimits.h
     //
     Globals()->SetParameter(VOICE_MODE, DEFAULT_VOICE_MODE);
     Globals()->SetParameter(OP1_RATIO, DEFAULT_OP_RATIO);
     Globals()->SetParameter(EG1_ATTACK_MSEC, DEFAULT_EG_ATTACK_TIME);
     Globals()->SetParameter(EG1_DECAY_MSEC, DEFAULT_EG_DECAY_TIME);

     etc...
```

Initialize()

Initialize() is identical to the rest of the synths that do not load samples.

```
ComponentResult AUSynth::Initialize()
{
    // --- init the base class
     AUInstrumentBase::Initialize();

     // clear
     m_dLastNoteFrequency = -1.0;

     // --- inits
     CDXSynthVoice* pVoice;
     for(int i=0; i<MAX_VOICES; i++)
     {
             pVoice = m_pVoiceArray[i];
             pVoice->setSampleRate(GetOutput(0)->GetStreamFormat
                                        ().mSampleRate);
             pVoice->prepareForPlay();
             pVoice->update();
     }

     // --- update the synth
     update();

     return noErr;
}
```

update()

The *update()* function works the same as all the others; you retrieve parameters from the global container and apply them to the various global parameters in the structure. The LFO modulation routing section is the same as the other synths.

```
void AUSynth::update()
{
     // --- update global parameters
     //
     // for FM synth, Voice Mode = FM Algorithm
     m_GlobalSynthParams.voiceParams.uVoiceMode =
                              Globals()->GetParameter(VOICE_MODE);
     m_GlobalSynthParams.voiceParams.dOp4Feedback =
                              Globals()->GetParameter(OP4_FEEDBACK)/100.0;
     m_GlobalSynthParams.voiceParams.dPortamentoTime_mSec =
                              Globals()->GetParameter(PORTAMENTO_TIME_MSEC);

     <SNIP SNIP SNIP>

     // --- DCA:
     m_GlobalSynthParams.dcaParams.dAmplitude_dB =
```

```
                                   Globals()->GetParameter(OUTPUT_AMPLITUDE_DB);

        // --- LFO1 Destination 1
        if(Globals()->GetParameter(LFO1_DESTINATION_OP1) == None)
        {
                m_GlobalModMatrix.enableModMatrixRow(SOURCE_LFO1,
                                                       DEST_OSC1_OUTPUT_AMP,
                                                       false);
                m_GlobalModMatrix.enableModMatrixRow(SOURCE_LFO1, DEST_OSC1_FO,
                                                       false);
        }
        else if(Globals()->GetParameter(LFO1_DESTINATION_OP1) == AmpMod)
        {
                m_GlobalModMatrix.enableModMatrixRow(SOURCE_LFO1,
                                                       DEST_OSC1_OUTPUT_AMP, true);
                m_GlobalModMatrix.enableModMatrixRow(SOURCE_LFO1, DEST_OSC1_FO,
                                                       false);
        }
        else // vibrato
        {
                m_GlobalModMatrix.enableModMatrixRow(SOURCE_LFO1,
                                                       DEST_OSC1_OUTPUT_AMP,
                                                       false);
                m_GlobalModMatrix.enableModMatrixRow(SOURCE_LFO1, DEST_OSC1_FO,
                                                       true);
        }

        // rest of LFO is same as other synths
```

12.13 Challenges

Bronze

Really nail the analog noisy nature of the DX100 by adding a filtered noise oscillator and blending it in with the notes. Then, add feedback to every operator (like Native Instruments' FM8).

Silver

Allow the four oscillators to be any of the pitched waveforms (like Native Instruments' FM8); saw, square, triangle and sine. The theory regarding the sideband amplitudes and locations is especially complicated. You cannot simply use superposition to apply the same sideband calculations to all of the harmonics in a non-sinusoid signal. Implementing it is simple, however: allow the user to choose the oscillator waveforms. Beware of aliasing or screeching/interesting noises that you can produce. The DX line allowed the oscillators to be detuned by about +/−3 cents; next, add the detuning controls and code to the project

Gold

See the website at https://code.google.com/p/music-synthesizer-for-android/wiki/Dx7Envelope, which has a detailed description and analysis of the DX EGs; use this to create a realistic replica of the DX EG for your plug-in. Note that this Challenge was also in Chapter 6.

Platinum

The DX7 had six operators in 32 algorithms; add two more operators and find these 32 algorithm block diagrams to implement your version of a DX7.

Diamond

You may recall from the last chapter that Yamaha briefly consulted with Dave Smith and some of the original vector synthesizer engineers and designers. The TG33 and SY35 were the result. These were hybrid synthesizers that combined FM/PM, sample playback, and vector synthesis into one product. FM/PM and sample playback oscillators are mixed with a vector joystick and program. Create your own version of this synth by combining the technology from the last three chapters into one design.

Bibliography

Boulanger, Richard (Ed.). 2000. *The CSound Book, Perspectives in Software Synthesis, Sound Design, Signal Processing, and Programming*, pp. 266–269. Cambridge: MIT Press.

Chowning, John. 1973. "The Synthesis of Complex Audio Spectra by Means of Frequency Modulation." *Journal of the Audio Engineering Society*, vol. 21, no. 7, pp. 526–534. New York.

code.google.com. "DX7 Envelope." Accessed June 2014, https://code.google.com/p/music-synthesizer-for-android/wiki/Dx7Envelope

Dodge, Charles and Jerse, Thomas. 1985. *Computer Music Synthesis, Composition and Performance*, pp. 115–139. New York: Schirmer.

Roads, Curtis. 1996. *The Computer Music Tutorial*, pp. 221–250. Cambridge: MIT Press.

Stremier, Ferrel. 1982. *Introduction to Communication Systems*, 2nd Ed., Chapter 6. Meno Park: Addison-Wesley.

Yamaha, Inc. 1983. *DX100 Owners Manual*. Tokyo: Yamaha, Inc.

CHAPTER 13

Delay Effects

A deep discussion of audio effect signal processing is beyond the scope of this book; you can find many algorithms and theoretical discussions in *Designing Audio Effects Plug-Ins in C++*. Audio effects, however, are now standard in most synthesizers. The more popular synth effects (FX) are delay, reverb, chorus/flanger, and vocoder. If you have played a professionally programmed patch on just about any commercial synth, you have most likely heard at least one audio effect operating on the synthesized signal. There is something that audio effects bring out in the patches that can't be done with oscillators, EGs and filters. Rather than try to give a brief rundown on several effects, let's focus on the most versatile and powerful family—delay effects.

Just about every one of my favorite synth sounds has at least the stereo delay effect on it. The addition of a simple delay effect makes a surprising difference in the final synth sound—fuller, deeper and wider. MiniSynth is reborn again with the addition of delay effects; simple one-note lines can turn into a frenzy of patterns or long swells. You will be amazed at what the addition of this chapter's delay-based effects will do for your synth patches, especially if you use samples that already have effects added to them. In this chapter, we will add not one but four very interesting and often used types of delay effects: stereo delay, two multi-tap delays and a ping-pong delay.

Audio effects come in two flavors in music synthesizers: insert and master effects. The master effects are sometimes called "Aux Bus" or "Aux" effects. An insert effect is inline with the voice block of the synth. It is often placed before or after the DCA and may be mono or stereo, depending on placement and voice type. These effects typically include equalizers, dynamics processors and distortion effects. Master effects operate on the final (or master) stereo output of the synthesizer on all voices that are sounding. These effects include delay, reverb, chorus/flanger, and anything else that needs to be mixed in with the original dry signal with some wet/dry ratio. This is a good rule of thumb—if it has a wet/dry mix control, it is probably a master effect. Our delay is a master effect, operating on the final output. Therefore, we only need one global delay unit rather than one for each voice. That said, many synths will allow you to use an effect in either way—a delay effect might be applied to a single voice as an insert or as a master effect. Figure 13.1 shows MiniSynth fitted with an insert effect (compressor) and a master effect (stereo delay with wet/dry mix). It also reveals something unique to synth effects—they are usually designed so that their parameters may be modulated along with the other synth parameters. In this case, the modulation sources are from a MIDI controller, however there are some synths that will allow you to use voice modulators as well. For example, the Korg Wavestation allows you to use the combined value of all currently playing amplitude envelopes as an effect modulation source. The ability to synchronously modulate effect parameters with the same modulators that are applied to synth components opens up a new world of sounds and sound control. Notice that the delay effect sits outside the voices since it is a master effect.

13.1 Circular Buffers

Delay effects exploit a DSP programming concept called circular buffering. A buffer is really just an array of values. When you use an index to step through the array, you can move in the forward (positive) or reverse (negative) direction by incrementing the index up or down. But when you get to a boundary of the array at the top or bottom and you increment or decrement the index, you move outside the array, often ending with a crash. In a circular buffer, movement over a boundary loops back into the array. When you try to move past the end of the array, the circular buffer automatically wraps the index around to the starting point. In the opposite direction, the same thing applies but in reverse. This is shown in Figure 13.2, where we are using a pointer and index offset to access a circular buffer. The index offset is +5, so the pointer moves in steps of five buffer locations, skipping through the array. When it skips over the end boundary, it wraps back to the top and offsets the same number of buffer locations.

Suppose we have been using the pointer to write audio samples into this buffer and that this has been going on for some time so that the pointer has wrapped back around the top a few times. If we freeze time during a write-event and think about the contents of the buffer, we can see how the samples line up in time. Let's assume we have been using an index value called *m_nWrite* to keep track of the writing location in the buffer, incrementing it by one each sample period. We are going to use another index value *m_nRead* to read values from the array. In Figure 13.3(a) you can see that the oldest sample in the buffer is the one we are writing over. The youngest sample is one location before the write location. The other delayed values are between the oldest and youngest. If we want to delay the input signal by 100 samples, we offset the read index 100 samples before the write index; this might mean that the index would wrap around the top of the buffer. Thus as Figure 13.3(b) shows, the distance between the read and write index determines the delay time in samples.

So, by implementing a circular buffer and reading/writing audio samples from/to it, we can create a basic delay. But this delay time is set in samples, not seconds or milliseconds. And as it turns out, we need more precision than the sample period has to offer. For example,

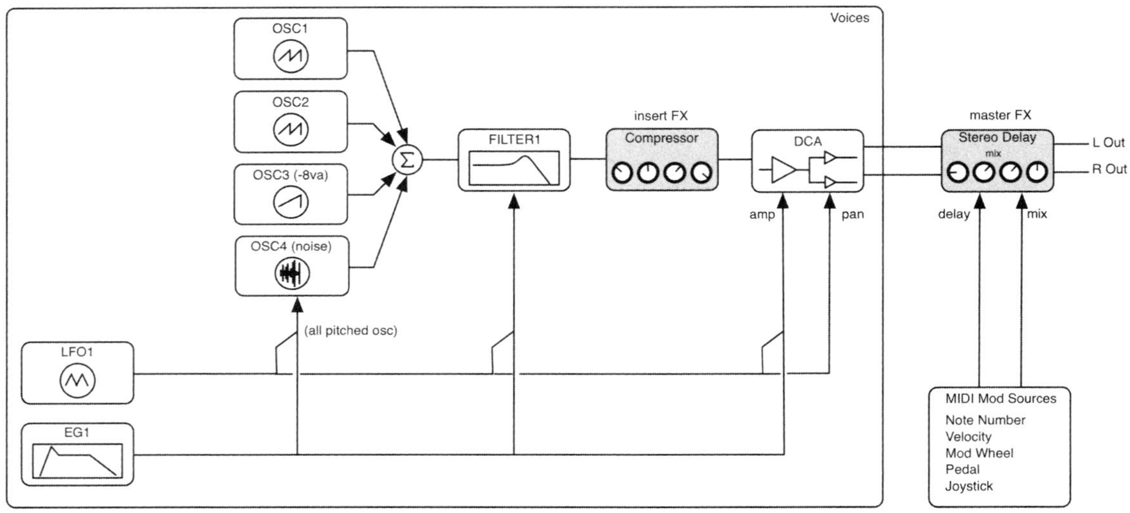

Figure 13.1: MiniSynth with an effects upgrade adds an insert effect (compressor) and master effect (delay)—notice that the delay effect allows you to modulate some of its parameters with MIDI; in this chapter we will design the delay effect, while the FX modulation is left as a Chapter Challenge.

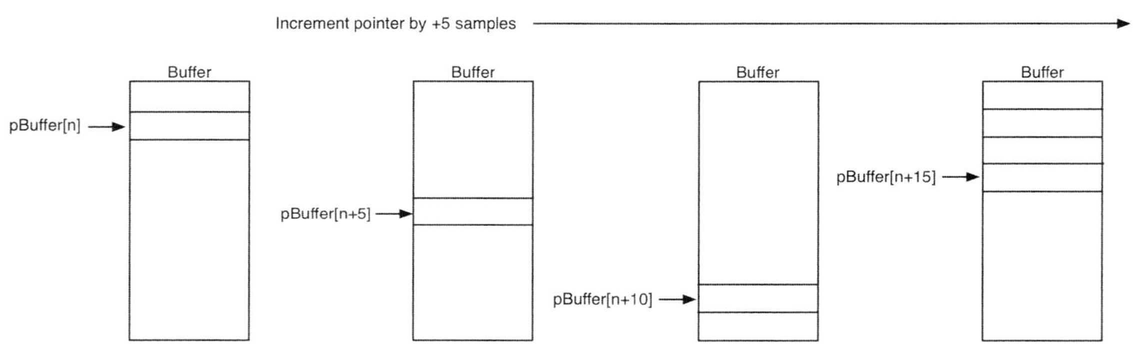

Figure 13.2: The circular buffer access operation: as the pointer moves across the end boundary, it wraps back to the top.

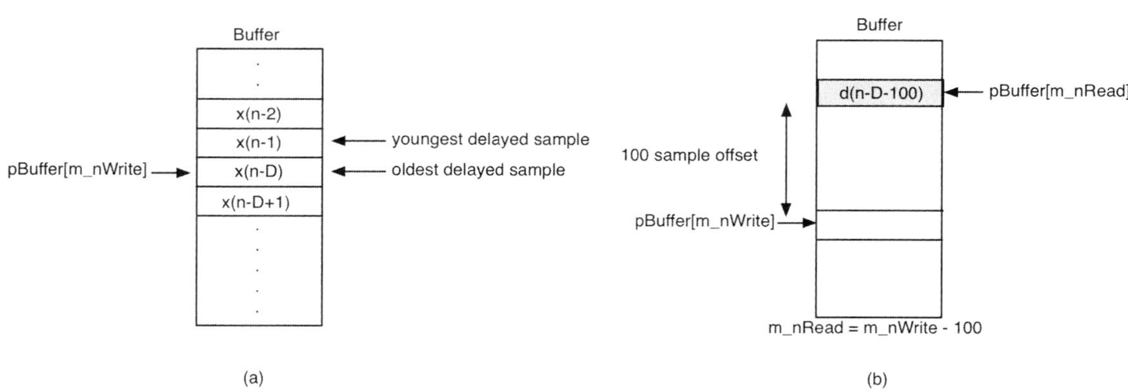

Figure 13.3: (a) The oldest sample in the buffer is the one we are going to write over. (b) The offset between the read and write pointers determines the delay time in samples.

at 44.1 kHz, the sample period is about 23μSec. That might seem like a small value, but if that is the resolution of our delay effect, we will have problems if the user tries to synchronize the delay time to the beats per minute (BPM) of the song. If the delays do not fall precisely on the required intervals, the delay will drift over time. It might take a while, but during a long song, the delay could drift significantly. Therefore we need to be able to specify—and implement—a fractional delay time with the delay value in milliseconds. This means we need to be able to read out values that are technically between two actual values; the delay is a fraction of the distance of one sample period. A simple way to do this is with interpolation. While interpolators are inherently lowpass filters, the convenience and ease of implementation makes them attractive. See the Bibliography for more information on fractional delays with and without filtering.

Since linear interpolation is the simplest form, let's look at that operation. There are several ways to implement linear interpolation, but the easiest method is to treat it like a DSP filter rather than $y = mx + b$. You can also view interpolation as a weighted sum operation. For example, if the interpolation point is 0.5 between samples 1 and 2, then the interpolated value is made up of 50% of sample 1 plus 50% of sample 2. Suppose we want a fractional delay of 23.7186 samples. The interpolated distance is 0.7183 between samples 23 and 24. We call the fractional component *frac* and the integer part *int*. The scheme is shown in Figure 13.4. We can re-map the samples 23 and 24 to index values 0 and 1, then just interpolate the frac distance between them. We can then write the interpolated output as:

```
interp_output = (frac)(Sample 24) + (1-frac)(Sample 23)

interp_output = (0.7183)(Sample 24) + (0.2187)(Sample 23)
```

Here is a linear interpolation function you can use; it is already declared in your *pluginconstants.h* file:

```
float dLinTerp (float x1, float x2, float y1, float y2, float x);
```

You give it a pair of data points, (*x1*,*y1*) and (*x2*,*y2*) plus a distance between them on the *x*-axis (*x*) and it returns the interpolated value using the weighted sum method.

Interestingly, this interpolator can be viewed as a kind of filter—a first order feed-forward variety as shown in Figure 13.5.

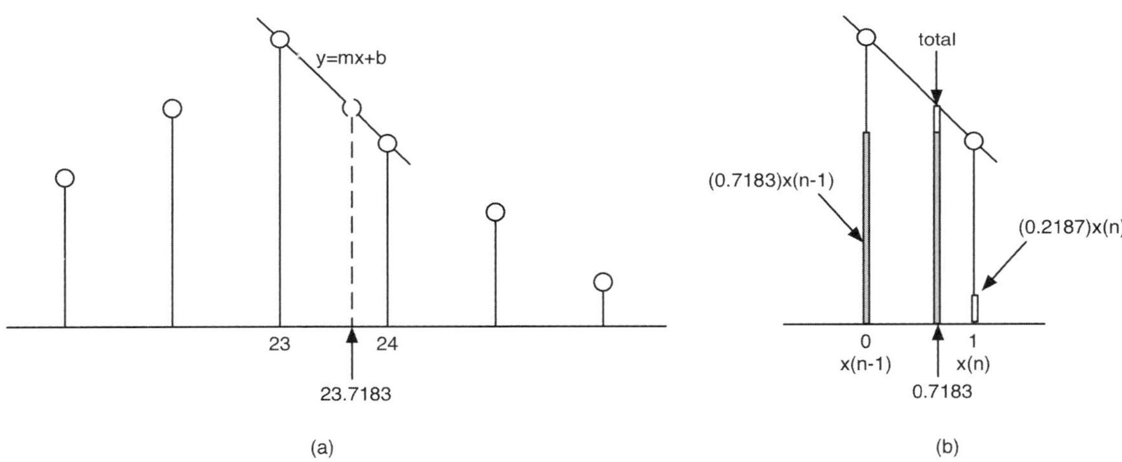

Figure 13.4: (a) A fractional delay value of 23.7183 samples is desired and can be seen as (b) a weighted sum of the two known values using the coefficients (*1-frac*) and (*frac*) and operating on an inter-sample basis, allowing us to re-index the *x*-axis and *frac* amount.

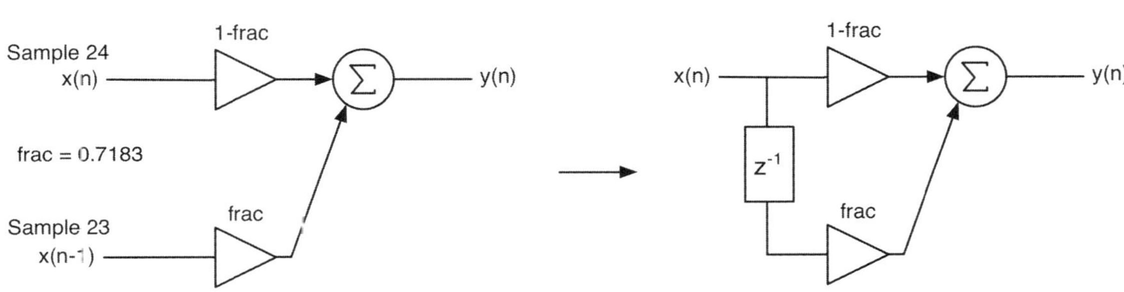

Figure 13.5: A linear interpolator viewed as a feed forward filter.

13.2 Delay Effect Topologies

Our delay effect includes two separate structures, one for the left channel and one for the right. These are basic delay lines with feedback. A single delay line with feedback is shown in Figure 13.6. The delay implements z^{-D} or D samples of delay, and it is a circular buffer. Notice that the value written into the delay line is a sum of the input $x(n)$ and the current output $y(n)$, scaled by a feedback value. This leads to the paradigm "read before write," which we use on all delay effects. It means that we read out the feedback value first, then write the input + feedback value into the delay line. The user can adjust the delay amount from zero to some maximum that we choose (2 seconds). When the user changes the delay time, they are really changing the distance between the read and write index values.

In order for the delay to be interesting, we need to add the dry unprocessed signal to the delayed output. In our plug-in, the delay object will handle this wet/dry mixing. In some systems, the wet/dry mix is part of the main voice or plug-in object. Our delay object is fully self-contained. Figure 13.7 shows the basic stereo delay with feedback and wet/dry mix components.

We can spin off useful variations on the basic delay, giving our synths a delay effect with four different algorithms. The first is the simple stereo delay. We'll allow the user to adjust the delay times between left and right as a ratio. The second is the ping-pong delay shown in Figure 13.8. The ping-pong delay crosses both the input and feedback paths to the opposite channel. It produces a circular kind of delay sound that starts in the center, then moves to one side, then the other, then back to the center where it starts all over. A key ingredient is the ability to set the left and right delays as ratios of one another. When the ratios are perfect (1:2, 3:5, 8:7, etc.), the effects become even more rhythmic in nature. So, we can re-use the ratio control in the ping-pong delay.

A multi-tap delay has multiple outputs from the delay line. Ours will have two taps—the main delayed output and a second delay with a shorter value for each channel. This will produce two slightly different variations, as shown in Figure 13.9: in the *tap1* version, the

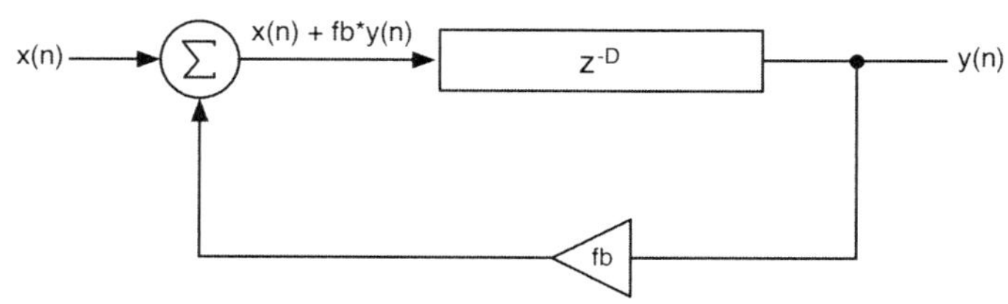

Figure 13.6: The basic delay with feedback structure.

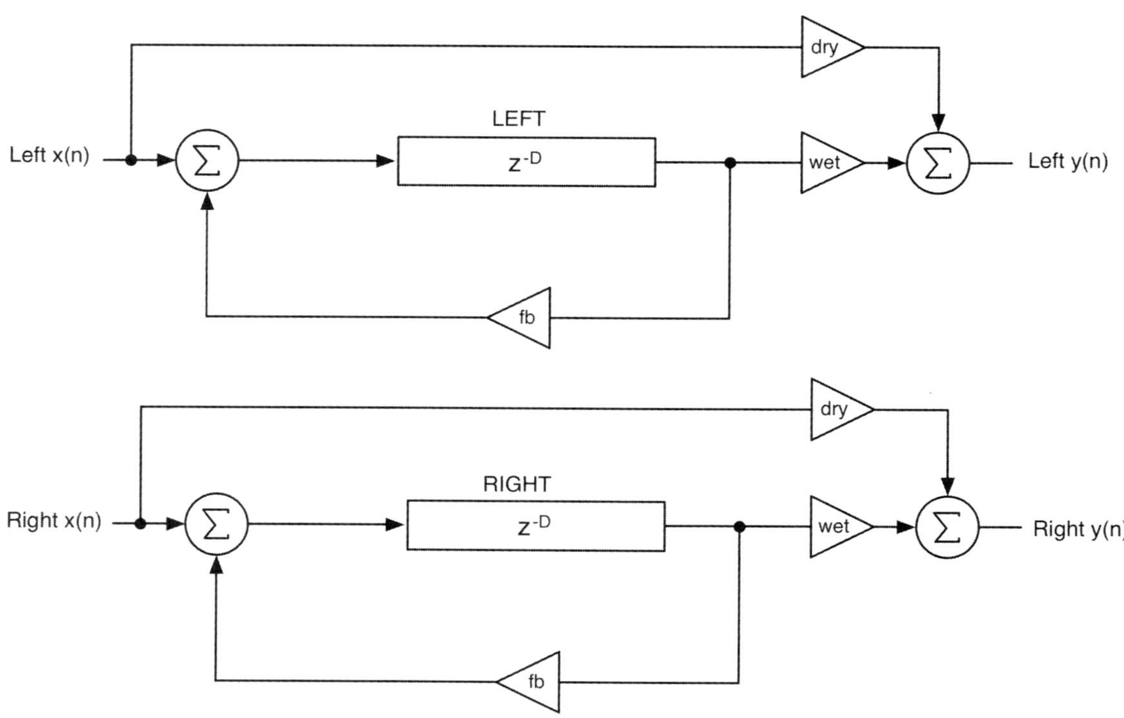

Figure 13.7: The basic stereo delay with feedback and wet/dry mix controls.

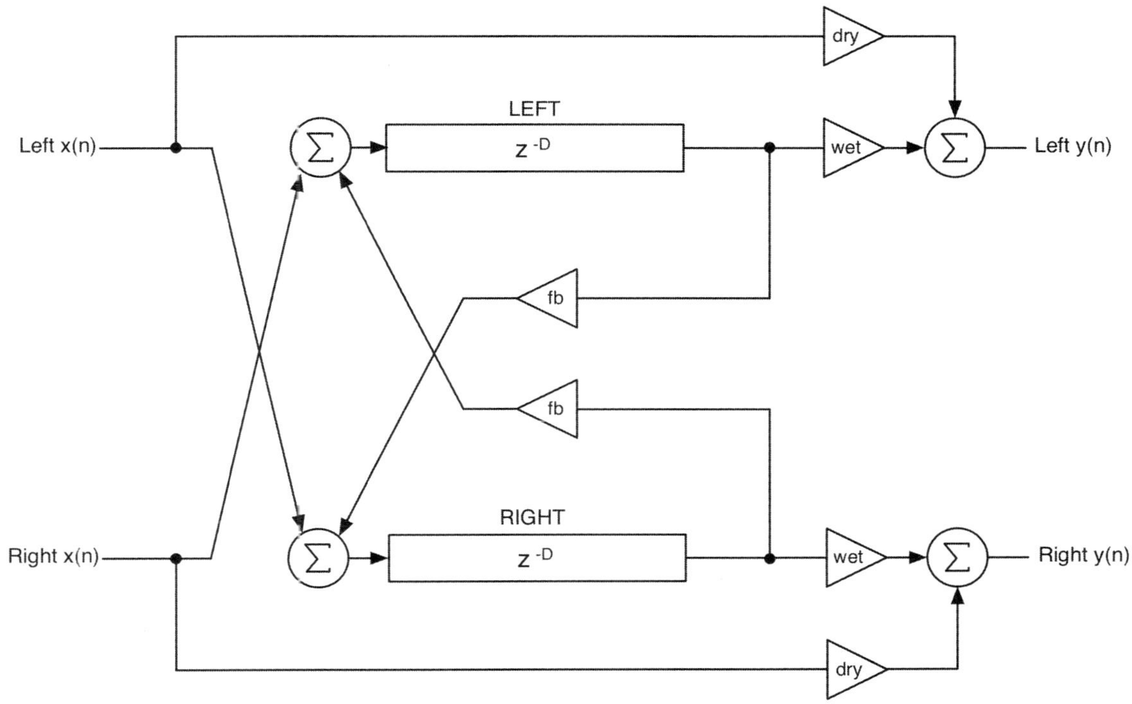

Figure 13.8: The ping-pong delay crosses inputs and feedback for a recirculating effect.

feedback is taken only from the main delay output. In *tap2,* the feedback is a mix of the normal and second tap outputs. You will notice quite a difference in sound between the two modes; *tap1* will sound more rhythmic and less dense while *tap2* is thicker and fuller. Also, both work well with short delay times, long feedback, and low ratio values—they will ping and ring at various frequencies as the delay times get short and they become more like filters than delays.

In the multi-tap versions, we will not use two separate circular buffers for each channel as the figure implies; instead, we will use one buffer and two read index values—the normal output and a secondary output. The *tap1* topology could be redrawn as in Figure 13.10, showing how one delay line produces both outputs. It also shows the nature of the delay ratio control; for these two effects, the ratio controls the length of the secondary tap compared to the main tap.

In all four effects, a single wet/dry mix control will operate on both left and right channels. Since all of our delay effects are based on the same pair of delay structures, let's focus on these for now. What we need is a C++ object that encapsulates a single delay.

13.3 The CDelayLine Object

The *CDelayLine* object handles the low level operation of a single delay with no feedback and no wet/dry path. It is only the delay line core. You can use this object (or many of them) to create complex delay effects. We will use two of these objects as members of another C++ object called *CStereoDelayFX*, which you can use as the basis for a large and robust suite of delay effects if you are so inclined. Table 13.1 shows the *CDelayLine* member variables and Table 13.2 shows the member functions.

The variables consist of all the attributes of the single delay line. The read and write index values are crucial to operation.

Constructor

Initialize the variables and reset. The destructor (not shown) will delete the buffer.

```
CDelayLine::CDelayLine(void)
{
        // --- zero everything
        m_pBuffer = NULL;
        m_dDelay_ms = 0.0;
        m_dDelayInSamples = 0.0;
```

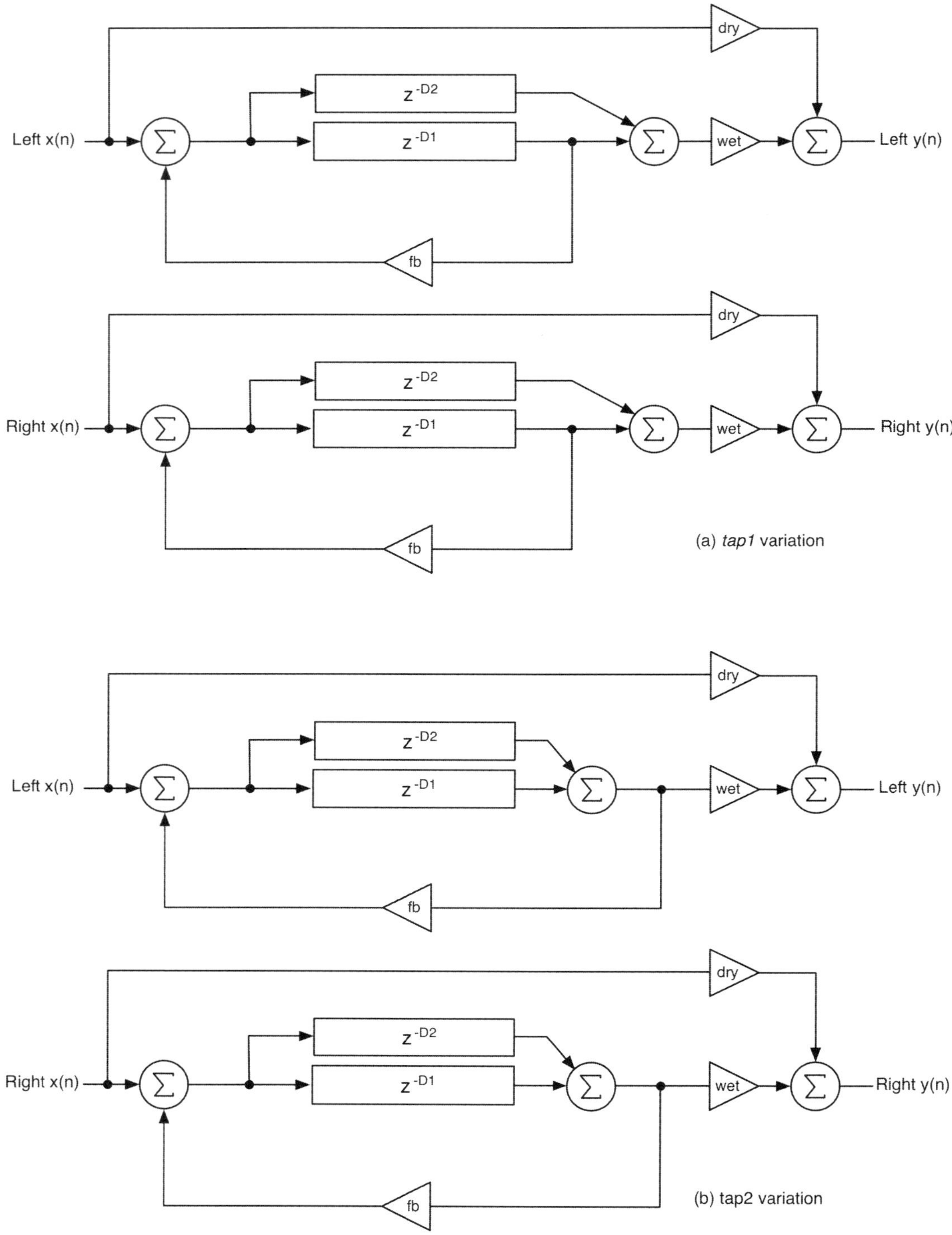

Figure 13.9: (a) The *tap1* topology feeds back only the main delay, while the (b) *tap2* variation mixes the main and secondary outputs for the feedback signal.

```
    m_nSampleRate = 0;

    // --- reset
    resetDelay();
}
```

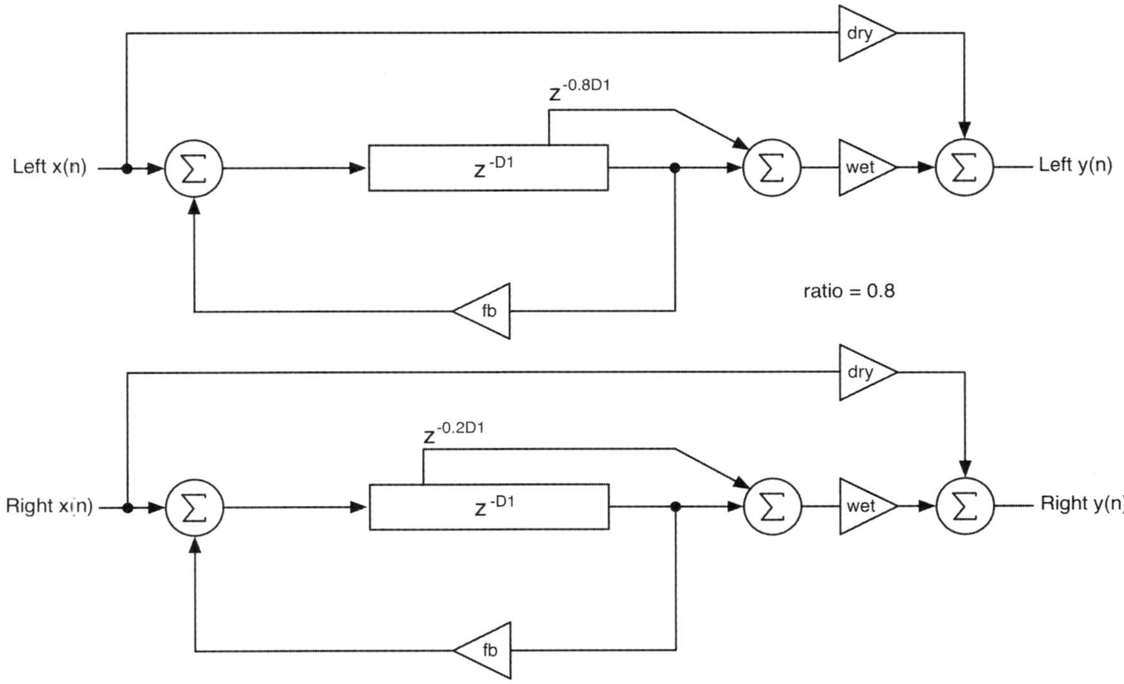

Figure 13.10: An alternate version of the multi-tap delay (*tap1* variation), showing the second tap taken from inside the main delay line; here the ratio control is +0.8, which gives a secondary tap time of 80% of the total length in the left channel and 20% of the total length in the right channel.

Table 13.1: *CDelayLine* member variables.

***CDelayLine* Member Variables**		
Type	**Variable Name**	**Description**
double*	m_pBuffer	pointer to the circular buffer that implements the delay
double	m_dDelay_ms	user controlled delay time in mSec
double	m_dDelayInSamples	delay time in fractional samples
Int	m_nReadIndex	index of current read location in buffer
Int	m_nWriteIndex	index of current write location in buffer
Int	m_nBufferSize	length of buffer in samples
Int	m_nSampleRate	sample rate

Table 13.2: *CDelayLine* member functions.

***CDelayLine* Member Functions**	
Function Name	**Description**
init	allocate the buffer; length is given in samples
resetDelay	clear the delay line, reset the index values to 0
setSampleRate	set sample rate
setDelay_mSec	set the delay time in mSec
cookVariables	convert the user settings into index values for read/write operation (used internally, not normally called from outside object)
readDelay	read the current user-assigned delay output
readDelayAt	read the delay at an arbitrary time in mSec for multi-tapped effects (optional)
writeDelayAndInc	write a value into the delay line and increment the index values (optional)
processAudio	take an input and process it into an output

init()

Accepts the length in samples as the argument and dynamically declares then clears the buffer.

```
void CDelayLine::init(int nDelayLength)
{
	// --- save for later
	m_nBufferSize = nDelayLength;

	// --- delete if existing
	if(m_pBuffer)
		delete m_pBuffer;

	// --- create
	m_pBuffer = new double[m_nBufferSize];

	// --- flush buffer
	memset(m_pBuffer, 0, m_nBufferSize*sizeof(double));
}
```

resetDelay()

Flushes old data from delay line and resets the index values to top; then it cooks variables in case anything has changed since last run.

```
void CDelayLine::resetDelay()
{
	// --- flush buffer
	if(m_pBuffer)
		memset(m_pBuffer, 0, m_nBufferSize*sizeof(double));

	// --- init read/write indices
	m_nWriteIndex = 0;
	m_nReadIndex = 0;

	// --- cook
	cookVariables();
}
```

setSampleRate()

Set the sample rate variable. This is important since the object calculates delay time based upon it.

```
void setSampleRate(int nFs){m_nSampleRate = nFs;};
```

setDelay_mSec()

Set the delay time in milliseconds, then cook the variables to convert the delay time into an offset between read and write index values.

```
void CDelayLine::setDelay_mSec(double dmSec)
{
	// --- save
	m_dDelay_ms = dmSec;
```

```
        // --- cook
        cookVariables();
}
```

cookVariables()

Convert the delay time to an offset between read and write index values. Remember that the read index is behind the write index, so the index is subtracted. We need to check to see, however, if we have gone past the beginning of the array and wrap around to the other end if needed.

```
void CDelayLine::cookVariables()
{
        // --- calculate fractional delay
        m_dDelayInSamples = m_dDelay_ms*((double)m_nSampleRate/1000.0);

        // --- subtract to make read index
        m_nReadIndex = m_nWriteIndex - (int)m_dDelayInSamples;

        // --- the check and wrap BACKWARDS if the index is negative
        if(m_nReadIndex < 0)
                m_nReadIndex += m_nBufferSize;// amount of wrap is Read + Length
}
```

readDelay()

This function finds the two samples that surround the interpolated value we desire based on the fractional delay time in samples. Then, the two samples are fetched and the interpolation is applied following Figure 13.4. Notice how the fractional component is extracted from the total delay value by subtracting off the integer part.

```
double CDelayLine::readDelay()
{
        // --- Read the output of the delay at m_nReadIndex
        double yn = m_pBuffer[m_nReadIndex];

        // --- Read the location ONE BEHIND yn at y(n-1)
        int nReadIndex_1 = m_nReadIndex - 1;
        if(nReadIndex_1 < 0)
                nReadIndex_1 = m_nBufferSize-1;

        // --- get y(n-1)
        double yn_1 = m_pBuffer[nReadIndex_1];

        // --- get fractional component
        double dFracDelay = m_dDelayInSamples - (int)m_dDelayInSamples;

        // --- interpolate: (0, yn) and (1, yn_1) by fracDelay
        return dLinTerp(0, 1, yn, yn_1, dFracDelay);
}
```

readDelayAt()

Similar to *readDelay()*, but reads from any arbitrary location in the buffer. It must calculate its own read index values so as to not disturb the object variables. Otherwise, it does the same operation of interpolating the data.

```
double CDelayLine::readDelayAt(double dmSec)
{
      // --- local variables
      double dDelayInSamples = dmSec*((float)m_nSampleRate)/1000.0;

      // --- subtract to make read index
      int nReadIndex = m_nWriteIndex - (int)dDelayInSamples;

      // --- wrap if needed
      if (nReadIndex < 0)
            nReadIndex += m_nBufferSize;  // amount of wrap is Read + Length

      //---  Read the output of the delay at m_nReadIndex
      double yn = m_pBuffer[nReadIndex];

      // --- Read the location ONE BEHIND yn at y(n-1)
      int nReadIndex_1 = nReadIndex - 1;
      if(nReadIndex_1 < 0)
            nReadIndex_1 = m_nBufferSize-1;

      // -- get y(n-1)
      double yn_1 = m_pBuffer[nReadIndex_1];

      // --- get the fractional component
      double dFracDelay = dDelayInSamples - (int)dDelayInSamples;

      // --- interpolate: (0, yn) and (1, yn_1) by the amount fracDelay
      return dLinTerp(0, 1, yn, yn_1, dFracDelay);
}
```

writeDelayAndInc()

Writes a value into the current write location, then increments both the read and write indexes and checks for wrap.

```
void CDelayLine::writeDelayAndInc(double dDelayInput)
{
      // --- write to the delay line
      m_pBuffer[m_nWriteIndex] = dDelayInput; // external feedback sample

      // --- increment the pointers and wrap if necessary
      m_nWriteIndex++;
      if(m_nWriteIndex >= m_nBufferSize)
            m_nWriteIndex = 0;

      m_nReadIndex++;
      if(m_nReadIndex >= m_nBufferSize)
            m_nReadIndex = 0;
}
```

processAudio()

This function reads the delay at the current location using *readDelay()* then writes the incoming value into it using *writeDelayAndInc()*.

```
bool CDelayLine::processAudio(double* pInput, double* pOutput)
{
	// --- read delayed output
	*pOutput = m_dDelayInSamples == 0 ? *pInput : readDelay();

	// --- write to the delay line
	writeDelayAndInc(*pInput);

	return true; // all OK
}
```

13.4 The CStereoDelayFX Object

The *CStereoDelayFX* object combines two of the *CDelayLine* objects into the four algorithms:

- *norm:* normal stereo delay
- *tap1:* multi-tap delay variation 1
- *tap2:* multi-tap delay variation 2
- *pingpong:* ping-pong delay

The object is responsible for initializing and maintaining the underlying delay line member objects. It also implements methods that the GUI uses to update these underlying objects. Finally, it implements the four different modes of operation. Table 13.3 shows the *CStereoDelayFX* member variables, and Table 13.4 shows the member functions. The object is fairly straightforward.

The delay ratio control is interesting. This control allows you to set the left and right delay times as ratios like the Korg Wavestation's delays. In those products, the user selects from a list of pre-defined ratios to set up the scaling of the delay time. One channel always gets the full delay time, while the other gets a fraction of it. The delay ratio controls this fraction. Rather then implement and decode a table of ratios, we implement a continuous control adjustable from −0.9 to +0.9 as follows for the normal and ping-pong delays:

If ratio is negative:

- left delay is abs(ratio)*(total delay time)
- right delay is total delay time

If ratio is positive:

- left delay is total delay time
- right delay is ratio*(total delay time)

If ratio is zero:

- ratio is 1:1, so left and right delays are both the total delay time (identical)

For the multi-tap variations, the control behaves slightly differently, adjusting the time of the secondary tap as a ratio of the primary tap.

If ratio is negative:

- left delay secondary tap is abs(ratio)*(total delay time)
- right delay secondary tap is total delay time (1.0 − abs(ratio))*(total delay time)

If ratio is positive:

- left delay secondary tap is total delay time (1.0 − abs(ratio))*(total delay time)
- right secondary tap is abs(ratio)*(total delay time)

If ratio is zero:

- left delay secondary tap = 0 mSec
- right delay secondary tap = 0 mSec

Table 13.3: *CStereoDelayFX* member variables.

CStereoDelayFX Member Variables		
Type	**Variable Name**	**Description**
CDelayLine	m_LeftDelay, m_RightDelay	the left and right delay line objects
double	m_dDelayTime_mSec	user controlled delay time in mSec
double	m_dFeedback_Pct	user controlled feedback in %
double	m_dDelayRatio	the ratio of delay times between left and right channels
double	m_dWetMix	the wet (delayed) mix amount from 0 to 1.0; 0.5 = 50/50 mix
UINT	m_uMode	the mode of operation (currently have three of them in enum below)
enum	norm,tap1,tap2,pingpong	enum for mode of operation

Table 13.4: *CStereoDelayFX* member functions.

CStereoDelayFX Member Functions	
Function Name	**Description**
setMode	sets the mode variable
setDelayTime_mSec	sets the delay time variable
setFeedback_Pct	sets the feedback variable
setDelayRatio	sets the ratio variable
setWetMix	sets the wet mix variable
prepareForPlay	one time initialization function
reset	flushes and resets the two delay lines
update	decodes the mode variable and sets the two delay times on the two delay line objects
processAudio	performs the delay effect

Like the *CDelayLine* object, *CStereoDelayFX* is also a short and simple object. You can add more modes of operation, more delay lines, or even add filters and other processing components to the object. The plug-in will need to expose five new controls to go along with the object: delay time, feedback, delay ratio, wet/dry mix, and delay mode. These controls call the five *set()* functions you see in Table 13.4. The other functions are as follows:

Constructor

Initialize the member variables.

```
CStereoDelayFX::CStereoDelayFX(void)
{
      // --- zero everything
      m_dDelayTime_mSec = 0.0;
      m_dFeedback_Pct = 0.0;
      m_dDelayRatio = 0.0; // 1:1
      m_dWetMix = 0.5;  // 50%
}
```

reset()

The *reset()* function simply calls the *resetDelay()* function on the two member objects.

```
void CStereoDelayFX::reset()
{
      // --- flush buffers and reset index values
```

```
        m_LeftDelay.resetDelay();
        m_RightDelay.resetDelay();
}
```

prepareForPlay()

This is the one-time-initialization function for the object. The plug-in calls it during its own one-time-initialization function and passes the current sample rate. This function passes that sample rate to the member objects and then calls the *init()* function to request the allocation of two seconds worth of buffers.

```
// --- one time init
void CStereoDelayFX::prepareForPlay(double dSampleRate)
{
        // --- set sample rate first
        m_LeftDelay.setSampleRate((int)dSampleRate);
        m_RightDelay.setSampleRate((int)dSampleRate);

        // --- initialize to 2 sec max delay
        m_LeftDelay.init(2.0*dSampleRate);
        m_RightDelay.init(2.0*dSampleRate);

        // --- do the flush
        reset();
}
```

update()

The *update()* function takes the delay ratio and calculates the individual delay times on the left and right delay lines using the logic at the beginning of the section. For negative ratios, notice the negation operation, which is the equivalent of calling an absolute value function here.

```
void CStereoDelayFX::update()
{
        if(m_uMode == tap1 || m_uMode == tap2)
        {
                //      if (-) bias to left
                //      if (+) bias to right
                //      if 0.0 ratio is 1:1
                if(m_dDelayRatio < 0)
                {
                        // --- note negation of ratio!
                        m_dTap2LDelayTime_mSec = -m_dDelayRatio*m_dDelayTime_mSec;
                        m_dTap2RDelayTime_mSec = (1.0 + m_dDelayRatio)
                                                                *m_dDelayTime_mSec;
                }
                else if(m_dDelayRatio > 0)
                {
                        m_dTap2LDelayTime_mSec = (1.0 - m_dDelayRatio)
                                                                *m_dDelayTime_mSec;
                        m_dTap2RDelayTime_mSec = m_dDelayRatio*m_dDelayTime_mSec;
                }
```

```
            else
            {
                  m_dTap2LDelayTime_mSec = 0.0;
                  m_dTap2RDelayTime_mSec = 0.0;
            }

            // normal times here
            m_LeftDelay.setDelay_mSec(m_dDelayTime_mSec);
            m_RightDelay.setDelay_mSec(m_dDelayTime_mSec);

            return;
      }

      // else
      m_dTap2LDelayTime_mSec = 0.0;
      m_dTap2RDelayTime_mSec = 0.0;

      // --- set the delay times based on the ratio control
      //     if (-) bias to left
      //     if (+) bias to right
      //     if 0.0 ratio is 1:1
      if(m_dDelayRatio < 0)
      {
            // --- note negation of ratio!
            m_LeftDelay.setDelay_mSec(-m_dDelayRatio*m_dDelayTime_mSec);
            m_RightDelay.setDelay_mSec(m_dDelayTime_mSec);
      }
      else if(m_dDelayRatio > 0)
      {
            m_LeftDelay.setDelay_mSec(m_dDelayTime_mSec);
            m_RightDelay.setDelay_mSec(m_dDelayRatio*m_dDelayTime_mSec);
      }
      else
      {
            m_LeftDelay.setDelay_mSec(m_dDelayTime_mSec);
            m_RightDelay.setDelay_mSec(m_dDelayTime_mSec);
      }
}
```

processAudio()

This is the main function that implements the stereo delay effect. It follows the basic delay logic:

- get the left and right delay outputs
- form the input to the delay; this is based on the mode of operation
- call the *processAudio()* functions to process the delay inputs
- mix the dry inputs with the wet outputs according to user control

```
bool CStereoDelayFX::processAudio(double* pInputL, double* pInputR,
                                  double* pOutputL,double* pOutputR)
```

```
{
    // --- do the delays
    //     common components:
    double dLeftDelayOut = m_LeftDelay.readDelay();
    double dRightDelayOut = m_RightDelay.readDelay();

    // --- inputs to delays;default is norm
    double dLeftDelayIn = *pInputL + dLeftDelayOut*(m_dFeedback_Pct/100.0);
    double dRightDelayIn = *pInputR + dRightDelayOut*(m_dFeedback_Pct/
                                                                  100.0);

    double dLeftTap2Out = 0.0;
    double dRightTap2Out = 0.0;

    // --- do the other modes:
    switch(m_uMode)
    {
        // --- NOTE: cross mode sounds identical to ping-pong if
        //     the input is mono (same signal applied to both)
        case tap1: // tap1 not fed back
        {
            dLeftTap2Out = m_LeftDelay.readDelayAt
                                        (m_dTap2LDelayTime_mSec);
            dRightTap2Out = m_RightDelay.readDelayAt
                                        (m_dTap2RDelayTime_mSec);
            break;
        }
        case tap2: // adds feedback
        {
            // Left Input -> Left Delay; Left Feedback -> Right Delay
            // Right Input -> Right Delay; Right Feedback -> Left Delay
            dLeftTap2Out = m_LeftDelay.readDelayAt
                                        (m_dTap2LDelayTime_mSec);
            dRightTap2Out = m_RightDelay.readDelayAt
                                        (m_dTap2RDelayTime_mSec);

            dLeftDelayIn = *pInputL + (0.5*dLeftDelayOut +
            0.5*dLeftTap2Out)*(m_dFeedback_Pct/100.0);
            dRightDelayIn = *pInputR + (0.5*dRightDelayOut +
            0.5*dRightTap2Out)*(m_dFeedback_Pct/100.0);
            break;
        }
        case pong:
        {
         // Left Input -> Right Delay; Left Feedback -> Right Delay
         // Right Input -> Left Delay; Right Feedback -> Left Delay
         dLeftDelayIn = *pInputR + dRightDelayOut*(m_dFeedback_Pct/
                                                          100.0);
```

```
            dRightDelayIn = *pInputL + dLeftDelayOut*(m_dFeedback_Pct/
                                                            100.0);
            break;
          }
      }

      // --- intermediate variables
      double dLeftOut = 0.0;
      double dRightOut = 0.0;

      // --- do the delay lines
      m_LeftDelay.processAudio(&dLeftDelayIn, &dLeftOut);
      m_RightDelay.processAudio(&dRightDelayIn, &dRightOut);

      // --- form outputs
      *pOutputL = *pInputL*(1.0 - m_dWetMix) + m_dWetMix*(dLeftOut +
                                                   dLeftTap2Out);
      *pOutputR = *pInputR*(1.0 - m_dWetMix) + m_dWetMix*(dRightOut +
                                                   dRightTap2Out);

      // --- return All OK
      return true;
  }
```

13.5 Using the CStereoDelayFX Object in Your Plug-ins

Using the *CStereoDelayFX* object is refreshingly easy. Of course you will need to set up your GUI controls for interfacing, but after that there are only a few function calls required for operation. This delay object is not a member of any voice—as a master effect, it lies outside the stack of voices. For ease of implementation, we are going to make the delay object a member of the plug-in object. The plug-in object will form the current sample period output then process it through the delay plug-in before writing to its output

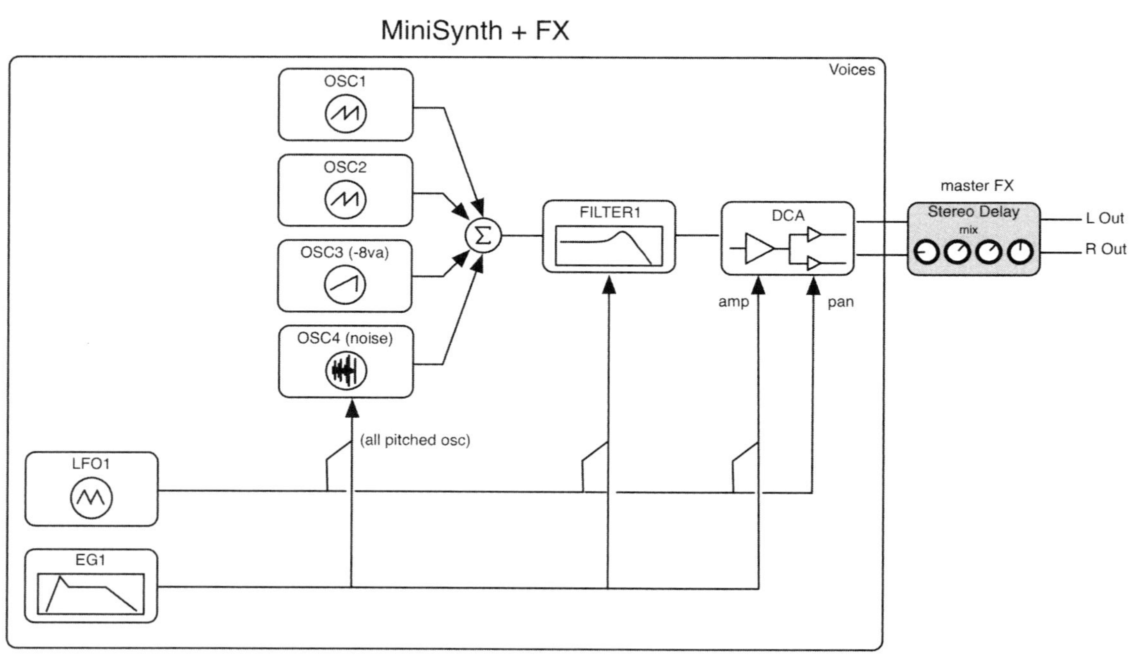

Figure 13.11: The new and improved MiniSynth + FX.

locations. Remember that this happens on a per-sample-period basis and not a per-voice-render basis. Figure 13.11 shows the new *MiniSynth* with the delay added after the DCA. We won't be adding the modulation routings but that is offered as a Chapter Challenge. Remember that the plug-in object shares its modulation matrix core with the voices and that it receives the main MIDI control inputs, so it can apply them to the FX section if desired. Table 13.5 lists the new GUI controls you need to add to your plug-in for interfacing with the delay object. Figures 13.12 and 13.13 show the GUIs for RackAFX and VST3/AU respectively.

DelayLine.h
DelayLine.cpp
StereoDelayFX.h
StereoDelayFX.cpp

To use the delay object, you need to implement the following chunks of code:

Declaration

In the plug-in's *.h* file, add the *#include* statement and add a member variable for the delay.

```
CStereoDelayFX m_DelayFX;
```

Initialization

Initialize the object in your one-time init function where the sample rate is known. This is one line of code to add before the main update function.

Table 13.5: *CStereoDelayFX* GUI Control List.

CStereoDelayFX Continuous Parameters				
Control Name (units)	**Type**	**Variable Name (VST3, RAFX)**	**Low/Hi/Default ***	**VST3/AU Index**
Delay Time (mS)	double	m_dDelayTime_mSec	0 / 2000 / 0	DELAY_TIME_MSEC
Feedback (%)	double	m_dFeedback_Pct	−100 / 100 / 0	DELAY_FEEDBACK_PCT
Delay Ratio	double	m_dDelayRatio	−0.9 / 0 / 0.9	DELAY_RATIO
Delay Mix	double	m_dWetMix	0 / 1 / 0	DELAY_MIX
* low, high and default values are #defined for VST3 and AU in *SynthParamLimits.h* for each project				
***CStereoDelayFX* Enumerated String Parameters (UINT)**				
Control Name	**Variable Name**	**enum String**		**VST3/AU Index**
Delay Mode	m_uDelayMode	norm,tap1,tap2,pingpong		DELAY_FX_MODE

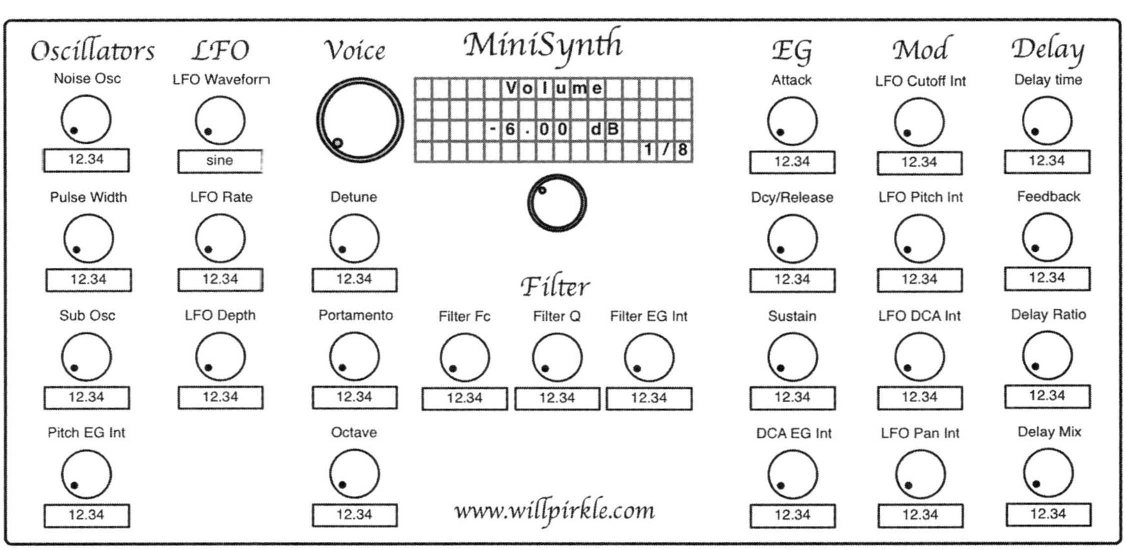

Figure 13.12: One possible MiniSynth + FX GUI in RackAFX; notice that several controls are embedded in the LCD control.

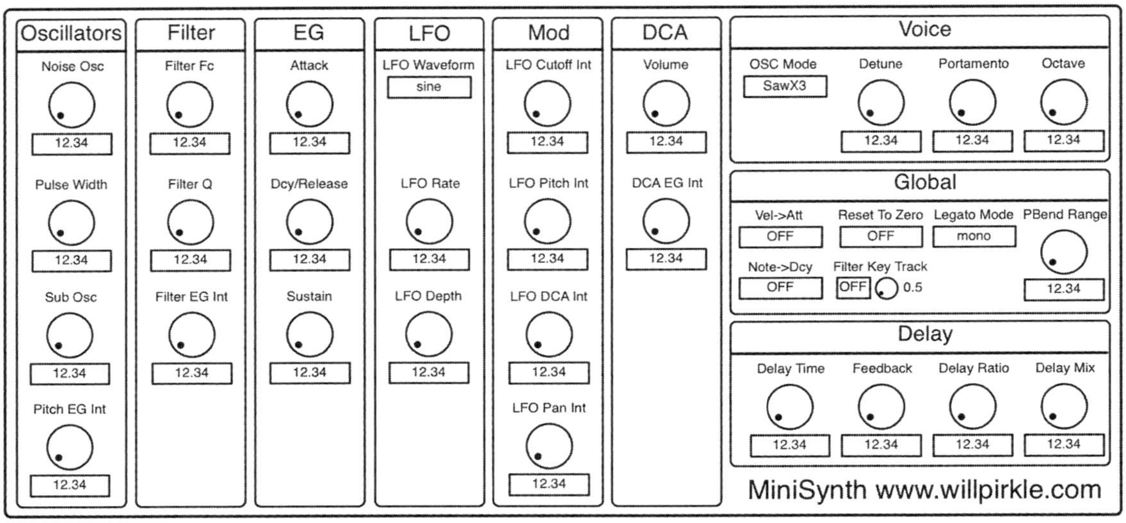

Figure 13.13: The MiniSynth + FX GUI for the VST3 and AU projects.

RackAFX: prepareForPlay()
VST3: *setActive()*
AU: Initialize()

The RackAFX version is here:

```
bool __stdcall CMiniSynth::prepareForPlay()
{
      // Add your code here:
      for(int i=0; i<MAX_VOICES; i++)
      {
            CMiniSynthVoice* pVoice = m_pVoiceArray[i];
            pVoice->setSampleRate((double)m_nSampleRate);
            pVoice->prepareForPlay();
      }

      // --- pFP creates and flushes the delay
      m_DelayFX.prepareForPlay((double)m_nSampleRate);

      etc...
}
```

Updating

Update the object in your user control change function. The updating code can come before or after the global parameter updates. You update the plug-in with your control values:

RackAFX and VST3:

```
      m_DelayFX.setDelayTime_mSec(m_dDelayTime_mSec);
      m_DelayFX.setFeedback_Pct(m_dFeedback_Pct);
      m_DelayFX.setDelayRatio(m_dDelayRatio);
      m_DelayFX.setWetMix(m_dWetMix);
      m_DelayFX.setMode(m_uDelayMode);
      m_DelayFX.update();
```

AU:

```
m_DelayFX.setDelayTime_mSec(Globals()->GetParameter(DELAY_TIME));
m_DelayFX.setFeedback_Pct(Globals()->GetParameter(DELAY_FEEDBACK));
m_DelayFX.setDelayRatio(Globals()->GetParameter(DELAY_RATIO));
m_DelayFX.setWetMix(Globals()->GetParameter(DELAY_WET_MIX));
m_DelayFX.setMode(Globals()->GetParameter(DELAY_MODE));
m_DelayFX.update();
```

Processing

Process the synthesized output before it is applied to the output buffers. This happens outside the voice *for()* loop and before writing to the output. The only trick here is to process the samples in-place so that the same variable is used for the input as the output. This is acceptable since we don't need the unprocessed values later.

```
// --- add master FX
//     note: processing in place to save variables
m_DelayFX.processAudio(&dLeftAccum, &dRightAccum,  // input values
                       &dLeftAccum, &dRightAccum); // output values
```

13.6 MiniSynth + FX: RackAFX

Open the MiniSynth project and add the new files. Add the GUI controls in Table 13.5.

MiniSynth.h

At the top of the file, add the *#include* statement for *StereoDelayFX.h* and declare a member variable *m_DelayFX*.

```
class CMiniSynthSynth : public CPlugIn
{
public:
      <SNIP SNIP SNIP>

      // Add your code here: ------------------------------------------- //
      // --- NEW  DELAY FX
      CStereoDelayFX m_DelayFX;

      etc...
}
```

MiniSynth.cpp

Modify the functions using the previous instructions:

prepareForPlay ()

Add the single line to call *prepareForPlay()* on the delay object.

```
bool __stdcall CMiniSynth::prepareForPlay()
{
      // Add your code here:
      for(int i=0; i<MAX_VOICES; i++)
      {
            CMiniSynthVoice* pVoice = m_pVoiceArray[i];
            pVoice->setSampleRate((double)m_nSampleRate);
```

```
            pVoice->prepareForPlay();
        }

        // --- pFP creates and flushes the delay
        m_DelayFX.prepareForPlay((double)m_nSampleRate);

        // mass update
        update();

        // clear
        m_dLastNoteFrequency = -1.0;

        return true;
    }
```

update()

Add the updating code to the update function; here we add it after the global variables are set.

```
    void CMiniSynth::update()
    {
        <SNIP SNIP SNIP>

        // --- update master FX delay
        m_DelayFX.setDelayTime_mSec(m_dDelayTime_mSec);
        m_DelayFX.setFeedback_Pct(m_dFeedback_Pct);
        m_DelayFX.setDelayRatio(m_dDelayRatio);
        m_DelayFX.setWetMix(m_dWetMix);
        m_DelayFX.setMode(m_uDelayMode);
        m_DelayFX.update();
    }
```

processAudioFrame()

Add the processing code outside the voice loop.

```
    bool __stdcall CMiniSynth::processAudioFrame(args...)
    {
        double dLeftAccum = 0.0;
        double dRightAccum = 0.0;

        // --- 12dB headroom
        float fMix = 0.25;
        double dLeft = 0.0;
        double dRight = 0.0;

        // --- loop and accumulate voices
        for(int i=0; i<MAX_VOICES; i++)
        {
            // --- render synth
            m_pVoiceArray[i]->doVoice(dLeft, dRight);
```

```
            // --- accumulate and scale
            dLeftAccum += fMix*dLeft;
            dRightAccum += fMix*dRight;
        }

        // --- add master FX
        //     note: processing in place to save variables
        m_DelayFX.processAudio(&dLeftAccum, &dRightAccum,  // input values
                               &dLeftAccum, &dRightAccum); // output values

        pOutputBuffer[0] = dLeftAccum;

        // Mono-In, Stereo-Out (AUX Effect)
        if(uNumInputChannels == 1 && uNumOutputChannels == 2)
            pOutputBuffer[1] = dLeftAccum;

        // Stereo-In, Stereo-Out (INSERT Effect)
        if(uNumInputChannels == 2 && uNumOutputChannels == 2)
            pOutputBuffer[1] = dRightAccum;

        return true;
    }
```

13.7 MiniSynth + FX: VST3

Open the MiniSynth project and add the new files. Add the GUI controls in Table 13.5.

VSTSynthProcessor.h

At the top of the file, add the *#include* statement for *StereoDelayFX.h* and declare a member variable *m_DelayFX*. You will also declare your GUI variables from Table 13.5 in the *.h* file.

```
class Processor : public AudioEffect
{
public:
    <SNIP SNIP SNIP>

    // --- NEW  DELAY FX
    CStereoDelayFX m_DelayFX;

    etc...
```

VSTSynthProcessor.cpp

Modify the functions using the previous instructions:

Constructor

Initialize the new GUI control variables as usual.

```
Processor::Processor()
{
```

```
        // --- we are a Processor
        setControllerClass(Controller::cid);

        <SNIP SNIP SNIP>

        // --- delay FX
        m_dDelayTime_mSec = DEFAULT_DELAY_TIME;
        m_dFeedback_Pct = DEFAULT_DELAY_FEEDBACK;
        m_dDelayRatio = DEFAULT_DELAY_RATIO;
        m_dWetMix = DEFAULT_DELAY_WET_MIX;
        m_uDelayMode = DEFAULT_DELAY_MODE;

        // VST3 specific
        m_dMIDIPitchBend = DEFAULT_MIDI_PITCHBEND; // -1 to +1
        m_uMIDIModWheel = DEFAULT_MIDI_MODWHEEL;
        m_uMIDIVolumeCC7 = DEFAULT_MIDI_VOLUME;  // note defaults to 127

        etc...
}
```

setState()
getState()

First, revise the synth version number at the top of the *Processor.cpp* file. You need this for backwards compatibility when loading presets from or into an earlier version, otherwise a crash may occur.

```
// --- for versioning in serialization
static uint64 MiniSynthVersion = 1; // v1 adds the stereo delay
```

In both functions, add code to the versioning block for version = 1. We are serializing the file in the same order, adding each new revision's block of read/write functionality. For the file-writing function getState(), there is no check for versioning—we always write the full set of variables for any revision; it is up to the reading functions to decode it.

```
tresult PLUGIN_API Processor::setState(IBStream* fileStream)
{
        IBStreamer s(fileStream, kLittleEndian);
        uint64 version = 0;

        // --- needed to convert to our UINT reads
        uint32 udata = 0;
        int32 data = 0;

        // read the version
        if(!s.readInt64u(version)) return kResultFalse;

        if(!s.readDouble(m_dNoiseOsc_dB)) return kResultFalse;
        if(!s.readDouble(m_dPulseWidth_Pct)) return kResultFalse;

        <SNIP SNIP SNIP>

        // --- do next version...
        if (version >= 1)
```

```
	{
		// --- delay FX stuff
		if(!s.readDouble(m_dDelayTime_mSec)) return kResultFalse;
		if(!s.readDouble(m_dFeedback_Pct)) return kResultFalse;
		if(!s.readDouble(m_dDelayRatio)) return kResultFalse;
		if(!s.readDouble(m_dWetMix)) return kResultFalse;
		if(!s.readInt32u(udata)) return kResultFalse;
		else m_uDelayMode = udata;
	}

	// --- do next version...
	if (version >= 2)
	{
		// add v2 stuff here
	}

	return kResultTrue;
}

tresult PLUGIN_API Processor::getState(IBStream* fileStream)
{
	// get a stream I/F
	IBStreamer s(fileStream, kLittleEndian);

	// --- MiniSynthVersion - place this at top so versioning can be used
	//     during the READ operation
	if(!s.writeInt64u(MiniSynthVersion)) return kResultFalse;

	// --- these follow the same order as the enum for the
	//     index values (they don't nec have to)
	if(!s.writeDouble(m_dNoiseOsc_dB)) return kResultFalse;
	if(!s.writeDouble(m_dPulseWidth_Pct)) return kResultFalse;

	<SNIP SNIP SNIP>

	// --- v1
	// --- delay FX stuff
	if(!s.writeDouble(m_dDelayTime_mSec)) return kResultFalse;
	if(!s.writeDouble(m_dFeedback_Pct)) return kResultFalse;
	if(!s.writeDouble(m_dDelayRatio)) return kResultFalse;
	if(!s.writeDouble(m_dWetMix)) return kResultFalse;
	if(!s.writeInt32u(m_uDelayMode)) return kResultFalse;

	return kResultTrue;
}
```

setActive()

Add one line of code to call *prepareForPlay()* on the new delay FX object. We need to do this here because we want to re-initialize it each time the plug-in is turned on, as the sample rate may have been changed.

```
tresult PLUGIN_API Processor::setActive(TBool state)
{
      if(state)
      {
            // Finish initializations here
            m_dLastNoteFrequency = -1.0;

            // receive on all channels
            m_uMidiRxChannel = MIDI_CH_ALL;

            // --- pFP creates and flushes the delay
            m_DelayFX.prepareForPlay((double)processSetup.sampleRate);

            // load up voices
            for(int i=0; i<MAX_VOICES; i++)
            {
                  // --- create voice
                  m_pVoiceArray[i] = new CMiniSynthVoice;

                  etc...
```

update()

Add the updating code to the update function; here we add it after the global variables are set.

```
void Processor::update()    // VST3
{
      // --- update global parameters

      <SNIP SNIP SNIP>

      // --- update master FX delay
      m_DelayFX.setDelayTime_mSec(m_dDelayTime_mSec);
      m_DelayFX.setFeedback_Pct(m_dFeedback_Pct);
      m_DelayFX.setDelayRatio(m_dDelayRatio);
      m_DelayFX.setWetMix(m_dWetMix);
      m_DelayFX.setMode(m_uDelayMode);
      m_DelayFX.update();
}
```

doControlUpdate()

Add the new logic for decoding your new delay variables. There will be five new case statements, one for each new variable.

```
bool Processor::doControlUpdate(ProcessData& data)
{
      bool paramChange = false;

      <SNIP SNIP SNIP and Indents Removed)

      switch(pid) // same as RAFX uControlID
```

```
{
    // -- delay FX
    case DELAY_TIME:
    {
        m_dDelayTime_mSec = cookVSTGUIVariable(MIN_DELAY_TIME,
                                               MAX_DELAY_TIME,
                                               value);
        break;
    }
    case DELAY_FEEDBACK:
    {
        m_dFeedback_Pct = cookVSTGUIVariable(MIN_DELAY_FEEDBACK,
                                             MAX_DELAY_FEEDBACK,
                                             value);
        break;
    }
    case DELAY_RATIO:
    {
        m_dDelayRatio = cookVSTGUIVariable(MIN_DELAY_RATIO,
                                           MAX_DELAY_RATIO,
                                           value);
        break;
    }
    case DELAY_WET_MIX:
    {
        m_dWetMix = cookVSTGUIVariable(MIN_DELAY_WET_MIX,
                                       MAX_DELAY_WET_MIX, value);
        break;
    }
    case DELAY_MODE:
    {
        m_uDelayMode = (UINT)cookVSTGUIVariable(MIN_DELAY_MODE,
                                                MAX_DELAY_MODE,
                                                value);
        break;
    }

    etc...
```

Process()

Add the processing code outside the voice loop.

```
tresult PLUGIN_API Processor::process(ProcessData& data)
{
    // --- check for conrol chages and update synth if needed
    doControlUpdate(data);

    <SNIP SNIP SNIP and Indents Removed>
```

```
for(int32 j=0; j<samplesToProcess; j++)
{
      // --- clear accumulators
      dLeftAccum = 0.0;
      dRightAccum = 0.0;

      for(int i=0; i<MAX_VOICES; i++)
      {
            // --- render left and right
            m_pVoiceArray[i]->doVoice(dLeft, dRight);

            // --- accumulate notes
            dLeftAccum += fMix*dLeft;
            dRightAccum += fMix*dRight;
      }
      // --- add master FX
      //     note: processing in place to save variables
      m_DelayFX.processAudio(&dLeftAccum, &dRightAccum,  // input
                             &dLeftAccum, &dRightAccum); // output

      // write out to buffer
      buffers[0][j] = dLeftAccum;  // left
      buffers[1][j] = dRightAccum; // right
}
```

VSTSynthController.cpp

In addition to adding the GUI controls to the *initialize()* function, remember to add code to *setComponentState()* to read the GUI controls from presets. You have been doing this through all the other synth projects by default; however, this function is also slightly different in the same manner as *getComponentState()*, where you need to decode the version number and add the delay control initializations in the appropriate location. As usual, these follow the same ordering as the *getState()* and *setState()* functions.

```
tresult PLUGIN_API Controller::setComponentState(IBStream* fileStream)
{
      // --- make a streamer interface using the
      //     IBStream* fileStream; this is for PC so
      //     data is LittleEndian
      IBStreamer s(fileStream, kLittleEndian);

      // --- variables for reading
      uint64 version = 0;
      double dDoubleParam = 0;

      // --- needed to convert to our UINT reads
      uint32 udata = 0;
      int32 data = 0;

      // --- read the version
      if(!s.readInt64u(version)) return kResultFalse;
```

```
        <SNIP SNIP SNIP>

        if(version >= 1)
        {
              if(!s.readDouble(dDoubleParam)) return kResultFalse;
              else
                    setParamNormalizedFromFile(DELAY_TIME, dDoubleParam);

              if(!s.readDouble(dDoubleParam)) return kResultFalse;
              else
                    setParamNormalizedFromFile(DELAY_FEEDBACK, dDoubleParam);

              if(!s.readDouble(dDoubleParam)) return kResultFalse;
              else
                    setParamNormalizedFromFile(DELAY_RATIO, dDoubleParam);

              if(!s.readDouble(dDoubleParam)) return kResultFalse;
              else
                    setParamNormalizedFromFile(DELAY_WET_MIX, dDoubleParam);

              if(!s.readInt32u(udata)) return kResultFalse;
              else
                    setParamNormalizedFromFile(DELAY_MODE, (ParamValue)udata);
        }

        // --- do next version...
        if(version >= 2)
        {
              // add v2 stuff here

        }

        return kResultTrue;
  }
```

Now you can open the new MiniSynth in your VST3 client and use the VSTGUI4 editor to add the new controls to the UI.

13.8 MiniSynth + FX: AU

Open the MiniSynth project and add the new files. Add the GUI controls in Table 13.5.

AUSynth.h

At the top of the file, add the *#include* statement for *StereoDelayFX.h* and declare a member variable *m_DelayFX*. You will also declare your GUI variables from Table 13.5 in the *.h* file.

```
  class AUSynth : public AUInstrumentBase
  {
  public:
        <SNIP SNIP SNIP>

  private:
        // --- NEW  DELAY FX
```

```
CStereoDelayFX m_DelayFX;

etc...
```

AUSynth.cpp

Modify the functions using the previous instructions:

Constructor

Initialize the factory preset (optional) and all the GUI variables from Table 13.5.

```
AUSynth::AUSynth(AudioUnit inComponentInstance)
      : AUInstrumentBase(inComponentInstance, 0, 1)
{
      // --- create input, output ports, groups and parts
      CreateElements();

      // --- setup default factory preset (as example)
      <SNIP SNIP SNIP>

      factoryPreset[DELAY_TIME] = 125.0;
      factoryPreset[DELAY_FEEDBACK] = 20;
      factoryPreset[DELAY_RATIO] = 0.5;
      factoryPreset[DELAY_WET_MIX] = 0.5;
      factoryPreset[DELAY_MODE] = 3;

      // --- define number of params (controls)
      Globals()->UseIndexedParameters(NUMBER_OF_SYNTH_PARAMETERS);

      <SNIP SNIP SNIP>

      // Delay FX stuff
      Globals()->SetParameter(DELAY_TIME, DEFAULT_DELAY_TIME);
      Globals()->SetParameter(DELAY_FEEDBACK, DEFAULT_DELAY_FEEDBACK);
      Globals()->SetParameter(DELAY_RATIO, DEFAULT_DELAY_RATIO);
      Globals()->SetParameter(DELAY_WET_MIX, DEFAULT_DELAY_WET_MIX);
      Globals()->SetParameter(DELAY_MODE, DEFAULT_DELAY_MODE);

      // Finish initializations here
      m_dLastNoteFrequency = -1.0;

      etc...
```

Reset()

Initialize()

Call *prepareForPlay()* on the delay FX object in both functions for detecting sample rate changes.

```
ComponentResult AUSynth::Reset(AudioUnitScope inScope,
                               AudioUnitElement inElement)
```

```
{
    // --- reset the base class
    AUBase::Reset(inScope, inElement);

    // --- pFP creates and flushes the delay
    m_DelayFX.prepareForPlay(GetOutput(0)->GetStreamFormat().mSampleRate);

    for(int i=0; i<MAX_VOICES; i++)
    {
        CMiniSynthVoice* pVoice = m_pVoiceArray[i];
        pVoice->setSampleRate(GetOutput(0)->GetStreamFormat().mSampleRate);
        pVoice->prepareForPlay();
    }

    // mass update
    update();

    // clear
     m_dLastNoteFrequency = -1.0;

    return noErr;
}

ComponentResult AUSynth::Initialize()
{
    // --- init the base class
     AUInstrumentBase::Initialize();

    // --- pFP creates and flushes the delay
    m_DelayFX.prepareForPlay(GetOutput(0)->GetStreamFormat().mSampleRate);

    for(int i=0; i<MAX_VOICES; i++)
    {
        CMiniSynthVoice* pVoice = m_pVoiceArray[i];
        pVoice->setSampleRate(GetOutput(0)->GetStreamFormat().mSampleRate);
        pVoice->prepareForPlay();
    }

    // mass update
    update();

    // clear
     m_dLastNoteFrequency = -1.0;

     return noErr;
}
```

update()

Add the updating code to the update function; here we add it after the global variables are set.

```
void AUSynth::update()
{
      // --- update global parameters
      <SNIP SNIP SNIP>

      // --- update master FX delay
      m_DelayFX.setDelayTime_mSec(Globals()->GetParameter(DELAY_TIME));
      m_DelayFX.setFeedback_Pct(Globals()->GetParameter(DELAY_FEEDBACK));
      m_DelayFX.setDelayRatio(Globals()->GetParameter(DELAY_RATIO));
      m_DelayFX.setWetMix(Globals()->GetParameter(DELAY_WET_MIX));
      m_DelayFX.setMode(Globals()->GetParameter(DELAY_MODE));
      m_DelayFX.update();
}
```

Render()

Add the processing code outside the voice loop.

```
OSStatus AUSynth::Render(args...)
{
      // --- broadcast MIDI events
      PerformEvents(inTimeStamp);

      <SNIP SNIP SNIP>
      // --- the frame processing loop
      for(UInt32 frame=0; frame<inNumberFrames; ++frame)
      {
            // --- zero out for each trip through loop
            dLeftAccum = 0.0;
            dRightAccum = 0.0;

            // --- synthesize and accumulate each note's sample
            for(int i=0; i<MAX_VOICES; i++)
            {
                  // --- render
                  m_pVoiceArray[i]->doVoice(dLeft, dRight);

                  // --- accumulate and scale
                  dLeftAccum += fMix*(float)dLeft;
                  dRightAccum += fMix*(float)dRight;
            }

        // --- add master FX
        //     note: processing in place to save variables
        m_DelayFX.processAudio(&dLeftAccum, &dRightAccum,  // input values
                               &dLeftAccum, &dRightAccum); // output values

        // --- accumulate in output buffers
        // --- mono
        left[frame] = dLeftAccum;
```

```
            // --- stereo
            if(right) right[frame] = dRightAccum;
        }

        return noErr;
    }
```

Finally, modify the Cocoa view files to add the new GUI controls as usual.

That's it—test your code and listen to the cool delay effects, especially with the ping-pong delay at exact ratios. Make sure to set the delay ratio to a non-zero value to hear the ping and pong (try starting at 0.9 and then work down from there to hear the difference).

13.9 Challenges

Bronze

Add the new Delay Effect block to all the rest of the synth projects; like the new MiniSynth, the others will sound much more professional with this addition.

Silver

Download the Korg Triton Parameter Guide at http://www.tritonhaven.com/downloads/docs/ParameterGuide.zip—this guide has all the effects in the Triton as block diagrams with parameter limits and defaults. It also lists the modulate-able effect parameters. Pick a few of the delay effects and implement those in the *CStereoDelayFX* object to allow for even more delay modes.

Gold

Download the Korg Triton Parameter Guide at http://www.tritonhaven.com/downloads/docs/ParameterGuide.zip and implement the "Reverse" effect. (Hint: use two circular buffers in a double-buffering scheme.)

Platinum

Figure out a way to modulate the Delay FX parameters with incoming MIDI controllers, note numbers, velocities, etc. For example, let the current MIDI note number scale the delay time; the higher the note number, the more delay is added.

Diamond

Use any of the effects from *Designing Audio Effects Plug-Ins in C++* as both insert and master effects. If you have worked through the projects in that book, you can add compressors, EQs, reverb, chorus/flanger/vibrato, tremolo, ring modulation, phaser, and more to your synth plug-ins.

Bibliography

Dattorro, Jon. 1997. "Effect Design Part 2: Delay Line Modulation and Chorus." *Journal of the Audio Engineering Society*, Vol. 45, No. 10.

Pirkle, Will. 2012. *Designing Audio Effects Plug-Ins in C++*, Chap. 8. Burlington: Focal Press.

Appendix A

A.1 Converting the VST3 TemplateSynth (Nine Steps)

Example: Converting the TemplateSynth to NewSynth (where NewSynth is the name of your new project)—you will need a simple text editor to edit the *.sln*, *.vcproj* and *.vcxproj* files

1. copy the TemplateSynth directory and change the name of the new directory to NewSynth
2. open that directory and change all file names from TemplateSynth.xxx to NewSynth.xxx
3. open the *.sln* file (for VS2008) or the *_vc10.sln* file (for VS2010 and higher) with a text editor, and Replace All TemplateSynth with NewSynth and save
4. open the *.vcproj* file with a text editor, and Replace All TemplateSynth with NewSynth and save
5. open the *.vcxproj* file with a text editor, and Replace All TemplateSynth with NewSynth and save
6. open the *.sln* file (for VS2008) or the *_vc10.sln* file (for VS2010 and higher)in Visual Studio (everything else is done in VS), and do a Replace in Current Project to replace all instances of TemplateSynth with NewSynth
7. important: use *guidgen.exe* to make new GUIDs for the following:

```
FUID Controller::cid (0xB561D747, 0xBA004597, 0xA3BF911A, 0x5DA2AFA4);
FUID Processor::cid (0x91F037DC, 0xA35343AB, 0x852C37B1, 0x3774DC90);
```

   Guidgen.exe and FUIDs are explained in Chapter 2. Replace the existing FUIDs at the top of the *VSTSynthProcessor.cpp* and *VSTSynthController.cpp* files with your newly generated and properly formatted FUIDs
8. set your Output Directories: open the Project Properties for your NewSynth and on the General panel, browse for your Output Directory and Intermediate Directory; this is where your final *.vst3* will be delivered. Then, do the same thing for the base_vc project. Make sure to use the same directories as in the NewSynth project
9. set your debugger's VST3 host: open the Project Properties and open the Debugging panel; in the Command field, browse to find your VST3 host executable file, for example *Cubase LE AI Elements 7.exe*, and then set the Attach field to YES. If you forget the Attach part, the debugger will never launch

A.2 Converting the AU TemplateSynth (Ten Steps)

Example: Converting the TemplateSynth to NewSynth (where NewSynth is the name of your new project)

1. copy the TemplateSynth directory and change the name of the new directory to NewSynth
2. open the *.xcodeproj* file (you don't need to rename it): at upper left of Xcode, double click on the TemplateSynth project (it says "Two Targets" below it), and change the name to NewSynth; when prompted to Rename Project Items, answer YES
3. use Find/Replace to do a brute force replacement of TemplateSynth with NewSynth
4. close and re-open Xcode—click on the project in the upper left (now renamed NewSynth), and you will see two targets, Info, Build Settings, and Build Phases. In the Info settings:
   - open the AudioComponents array, then open the Item 0 dictionary (See Chapter 2 for more information about this) and change:
     - manufacturer: your 4 character company code (mine is WILL)
     - subtype: your 4 character plug-in code (for MiniSynth mine is MS00)
     - name: concatenation of your Company Name: plug-in title (mine is Will Pirkle: MiniSynth)
5. open the AUSynth.r file and change the following to match (for backwards compatibility with Logic 9)
   - COMP_MANUF: <your four digit company code> (mine is WILL)
   - COMP_SUBTYPE: <your four digit plug-in code> (for MiniSynth mine is MS00)
   - NAME: concatenation of your Company Name : plug-in title (mine is Will Pirkle: MiniSynth)

7. change the names of:
   TemplateSynthView.h
   TemplateSynthView.cpp

TemplateSynthViewFactory.h
TemplateSynthViewFactory.cpp
to
NewSynthView.h
NewSynthView.cpp
NewSynthViewFactory.h
NewSynthViewFactory.cpp

8. in XCode, do a brute force Find and Replace to replace:
   - WPEditBoxTS with WPEditBoxNS (NS = NewSynth)
   - WPRotaryKnobTS with WPRotaryKnobNS
   - WPPopUpButtonCellTS with WPPopUpButtonCellNS
   - WPOptionMenuGroupTS with WPOptionMenuGroupNS
9. click on the *CocoaSynthView.nib* file to open it in Interface Builder and:
   - set the File's Owner to *NewSynthViewFactory*
   - set the View (the NSView laying in the center of the window you see) to *NewSynthView*
10. set up the debugger by clicking on the Scheme and choose Edit Scheme
    - click on Run (left) and then choose Development from the drop-down list
    - click on the Executable box and browse to find your AU host (e.g. Logic 9, Ableton, etc.), and you are ready to debug

Validate your plug-in by opening Terminal and using the AU validation:

```
auval -v aumu <PLUG> <COMP)
```

Where <PLUG> is your four-character plug-in code and <COMP> is your four character company name, for my MiniSynth that would be:

```
auval -v aumu MS00 WILL
```

If your validation does not succeed, go back and check your conversion. Once it does succeed, you are ready to code the rest of the synth.

For debugging, edit the Scheme for your project. Go to the Run panel and choose the Executable drop-down. Browse to find your AU client's executable file.

Index

H

I

J

K

L

M

N

O

Taylor & Francis eBooks

eBooks
from Taylor & Francis

Helping you to choose the right eBooks for your Library

Add to your library's digital collection today with Taylor & Francis eBooks. We have over 50,000 eBooks in the Humanities, Social Sciences, Behavioural Sciences, Built Environment and Law, from leading imprints, including Routledge, Focal Press and Psychology Press.

ORDER YOUR FREE INSTITUTIONAL TRIAL TODAY

Free Trials Available

We offer free trials to qualifying academic, corporate and government customers.

Choose from a range of subject packages or create your own!

Benefits for you

- Free MARC records
- COUNTER-compliant usage statistics
- Flexible purchase and pricing options
- 70% approx of our eBooks are now DRM-free.

Benefits for your user

- Off-site, anytime access via Athens or referring URL
- Print or copy pages or chapters
- Full content search
- Bookmark, highlight and annotate text
- Access to thousands of pages of quality research at the click of a button.

eCollections

Choose from 20 different subject eCollections, including:

- Asian Studies
- Economics
- Health Studies
- Law
- Middle East Studies

eFocus

We have 16 cutting-edge interdisciplinary collections, including:

- Development Studies
- The Environment
- Islam
- Korea
- Urban Studies

For more information, pricing enquiries or to order a free trial, please contact your local sales team:

UK/Rest of World: **online.sales@tandf.co.uk**
USA/Canada/Latin America: **e-reference@taylorandfrancis.com**
East/Southeast Asia: **martin.jack@tandf.com.sg**
India: **journalsales@tandfindia.com**

www.tandfebooks.com